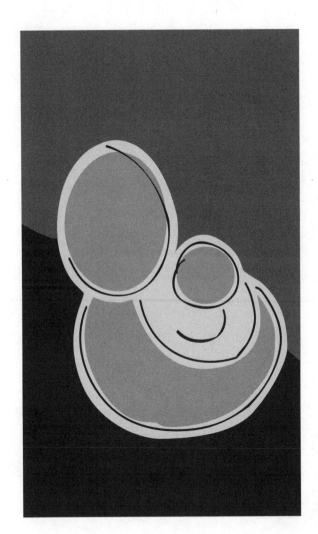

Children
with
Disabilities

Children with Disabilities
Fourth Edition

edited by

Mark L. Batshaw, M.D.
Children's Seashore House
Children's Hospital of Philadelphia
University of Pennsylvania School of Medicine
Philadelphia

·P A U L·H·
BROOKES
PUBLISHING C⁰

Baltimore • London • Toronto • Sydney

Paul H. Brookes Publishing Co.
Post Office Box 10624
Baltimore, Maryland 21285-0624

Appendix C, Commonly Used Medications, which appears on pages 835–850, provides information about numerous drugs frequently used to treat children with disabilities. This appendix is in no way meant to substitute for a physician's advice or expert opinion; readers should consult a medical practitioner if they are interested in more information.

Typeset by Brushwood Graphics, Inc., Baltimore, Maryland.
Manufactured in the United States of America by
The Maple Press Co., York, Pennsylvania.

Library of Congress Cataloging-in-Publicaton Data

Children with disabilities / edited by Mark L. Batshaw. — 4th ed.
    p.   cm.
    Third ed. published in 1994 with subtitle: A medical primer.
    Includes bibliographical references and index.
    ISBN 1-55766-293-2
    1. Child development deviations.   2. Child development deviations—Etiology.
3. Developmentally disabled children—Care.   4. Handicapped children—Care.
I. Batshaw, Mark L., 1945–
RJ135.B38   1997
618.92—dc21
                                         97-6941
                                           CIP

British Library Cataloguing in Publication data are available from the British Library.

Contents

About the Editor...xv
Contributors..xvii
A Personal Note to the Reader...xxi
Preface..xxiii
Acknowledgments..xxvii
Letters from *Andrew Batshaw*...xxviii

I   As Life Begins

1   Understanding Your Chromosomes
    Mark L. Batshaw...3
    The Cell
    Chromosomes
    Cell Division
    What Can Go Wrong?

2   Heredity: A Toss of the Dice
    Mark L. Batshaw...17
    The Genetic Principles of Mendel
    Genes
    Mendelian Disorders
    Revising Mendelian Genetics
    Mitochondrial Inheritance
    Multifactorial Inheritance

3   Birth Defects, Prenatal Diagnosis, and Fetal Therapy
    Mark L. Batshaw and Nancy C. Rose...................................35
    Population Screening: Maternal Serum Screening
    Real Time Ultrasound
    Chorionic Villus Sampling
    Amniocentesis
    Percutaneous Umbilical Blood Sampling
    Preimplantation Diagnosis and Circulating Fetal Cell Diagnosis
    Carrier Detection for Genetic Diseases
    Fetal Therapy
    Anne

4   Growth Before Birth
    Ernest M. Graham and Mark A. Morgan.............................53
    Fertilization
    Embryogenesis
    Fetal Development
    Maternal Nutrition
    Malformations
    Deformations

5   Having a Baby: The Birth Process
Iraj Forouzan, Mark A. Morgan, and Mark L. Batshaw 71
Maternal Factors
Fetal Factors
Antenatal Fetal Surveillance
Cesarean Delivery

6   The First Weeks of Life
Jacquelyn R. Evans 93
The Apgar Score
Physiological Changes at Birth
Causes of Illness and Death in Newborns

7   Born Too Soon, Born Too Small
Judy C. Bernbaum and Mark L. Batshaw 115
Definitions
Incidence of Low Birth Weight Infants
Prematurity
Small for Gestational Age Infants
Medical Care of the Low Birth Weight Infant
Survival and Outcome of Low Birth Weight Infants
Care in the Home
Early Intervention Programs
Rosa

II   **The Developing Child**
8   Substance Abuse: A Preventable Threat to Development
Mark L. Batshaw and Charles J. Conlon...................................... 143
Alcohol
Nicotine
Cocaine
Opiates
Phencyclidine
Marijuana
Intervention Strategies for Infants of Drug-Dependent Mothers
Prevention Strategies
Billy: A Child with Fetal Alcohol Syndrome
Jon: A Baby Prenatally Exposed to Cocaine

9   HIV and AIDS: From Mother to Child
Richard M. Rutstein, Charles J. Conlon, and Mark L. Batshaw 163
The Biological Basis of HIV Infection
The Epidemiology of HIV Infection in Adults
The Epidemiology of HIV Infection in Children
Transmission of HIV in Adults
Transmission of HIV in Infants and Children
Risk of Transmission in the Home and School
Natural History of Pediatric HIV Infection
Neurodevelopmental Effects of HIV Infection
Detecting HIV Infection

Interdisciplinary Management
Prevention
Manuel: A Child with HIV Infection

10   Nutrition: Good and Bad
     Abigail F. Farber, Colleen Comonitski Yanni, and Mark L. Batshaw 183
     Typical Growth During Childhood
     Infant Nutrition
     Malnutrition
     Obesity
     Nutrients and Their Deficiencies
     Nontraditional Alternative Diets
     Nutritional Assessment
     Interventions for Nutritional Problems
     Hazardous Ingestions

11   Vision: Our Window to the World
     Sheryl J. Menacker and Mark L. Batshaw 211
     Structure of the Eye
     Development of the Eye
     Development of Visual Skills
     Function and Diseases of the Eye
     Refractive Errors in Children
     Vision Tests
     Blindness

12   Hearing: Sounds and Silences
     Annie G. Steinberg and Carol A. Knightly 241
     Defining Sound
     The Hearing System
     Embryological Development of the Hearing Apparatus
     Hearing Loss
     Hearing Screening
     Degrees of Hearing Loss
     Treatment of Middle-Ear Disease
     Treatment of Hearing Loss
     Amy: A Child Who Is Deaf
     Prognosis

13   Language: A Code for Communicating
     Paul P. Wang and Marleen Ann Baron 275
     Language and Speech: Two Sides of a Coin
     Language Development: A Commonplace Miracle
     The Biological Basis of Language: Ear to Brain to Lips
     Speech Disorders and Their Causes
     Language Disorders and Their Causes
     Who Should See a Speech-Language Therapist?
     Speech-Language Assessment
     Speech-Language Therapy
     Alternative Modes of Communication

Doug: A Boy with an Expressive Language Disorder
Prognosis

14   The Brain and Nervous System: Our Computer
     David R. Lynch and Mark L. Batshaw 293
     Development of the Central Nervous System
     The Mature Central Nervous System: Brain and Spinal Cord
     The Peripheral Nervous System
     The Cerebrospinal Fluid and Hydrocephalus
     Imaging the Brain

15   Muscles, Bones, and Nerves: The Body's Framework
     John P. Dormans and Mark L. Batshaw 315
     The Musculoskeletal System
     The Neuromuscular System

III   Developmental Disabilities

16   Mental Retardation
     Mark L. Batshaw and Bruce K. Shapiro 335
     Early Development
     Piaget's Theory of Intellectual Development
     Developmental Delay
     Early Identification
     Early Intervention Services
     Mental Retardation
     Prognosis

17   Down Syndrome
     Nancy J. Roizen 361
     Chromosomal Abnormalities
     Prevalence
     Etiology
     Early Identification
     Medical Complications in Down Syndrome
     Neurodevelopmental and Behavior Impairments
     Evaluation and Treatment
     Early Intervention
     Prognosis
     Jason

18   Fragile X Syndrome
     Mark L. Batshaw 377
     Prevalence
     The Genetics of Fragile X Syndrome
     Clinical Findings in Affected Males
     Clinical Findings in Affected Females
     Origins of Abnormalities
     Diagnosing Fragile X Syndrome
     Intervention Strategies
     Outcome
     Tony

19 PKU and Other Inborn Errors of Metabolism
    Mark L. Batshaw 389
    Types of Inborn Errors of Metabolism
    Clinical Manifestations
    Mechanism of Brain Damage
    Associated Disabilities
    Diagnostic Testing
    Newborn Screening
    Therapeutic Approaches
    Outcome
    Lisa
    Darnel

20 Dual Diagnosis: Mental Retardation and Psychiatric Disorders
    Mark Reber and Breck G. Borcherding 405
    A Historical Perspective
    Prevalence and Causes of Psychiatric Disorders
    Diagnosis
    Affective Disorders
    Anxiety Disorders
    Psychosis
    Disorders of Social Communication (Pervasive Developmental Disorders)
    Attention-Deficit/Hyperactivity Disorder
    Adjustment Disorders
    Posttraumatic Stress Disorder
    Conduct Disorders
    Substance Abuse Disorders
    Maladaptive Behavior Disorders
    Associated Medical Problems
    Genetic Syndromes and Behavioral Phenotypes
    Evaluation
    Treatment
    John

21 Autism: And Other Pervasive Developmental Disorders
    Joyce Elizabeth Mauk, Mark Reber, and Mark L. Batshaw 425
    A Historical Perspective
    Defining Pervasive Developmental Disorder
    Prevalence and Origin of PDD
    Distinguishing Autism from Other Disabilities
    Early Identification of Autism
    Evaluation
    Treatment
    Ian: A Child with Autism
    Julio: A Child with Asperger Syndrome
    Prognosis

22 Attention-Deficit/Hyperactivity Disorder
    Nathan J. Blum and Marianne Mercugliano 449
    Characteristics of Attention-Deficit/Hyperactivity Disorder

Causes of Attention-Deficit/Hyperactivity Disorder
Diagnosing Attention-Deficit/Hyperactivity Disorder
Management of Attention-Deficit/Hyperactivity Disorder
Matthew
ADHD in Young Adults

23 Learning Disabilities
    Robin P. Church, M.E.B. Lewis, and Mark L. Batshaw 471
    Defining Learning Disabilities
    Subtypes of Learning Disabilities
    Prevalence
    Genetics of Learning Disabilities
    The Causes of Specific Reading Disability
    Neuroanatomy of Specific Reading Disability
    Associated Impairments
    Early Identification
    School Problems Simulating Learning Disabilities
    Assessment Procedures
    Intervention Strategies
    Other Intervention Issues
    David: A Child with Dyslexia
    Maria: A Child with Dysgraphia and Dyscalculia
    Outcome

24 Cerebral Palsy
    Louis Pellegrino 499
    Causes of Cerebral Palsy
    Types of Cerebral Palsy
    Early Diagnosis of Cerebral Palsy
    Associated Impairments in Cerebral Palsy
    Habilitation
    Preventing Impairment: Managing the Musculoskeletal Complications of
        Cerebral Palsy
    Preventing Disability: Promoting Optimal Function
    Tommy
    Tina
    Prognosis

25 Neural Tube Defects
    Gregory S. Liptak 529
    Prevalence of Neural Tube Defects
    The Origin of Neural Tube Defects
    Prevention Using Folic Acid Supplementation
    Prenatal Diagnosis
    Treatment in the Newborn Period
    Primary Neurological Impairments in Children with Meningomyelocele
    Associated Impairments and Medical Complications
    Educational Programs
    Psychosocial Issues for the Child
    Multidisciplinary Management

Jessica
Prognosis

26   Seizure Disorders
     Lawrence W. Brown 553
     What Is a Seizure?
     Precipitants of Seizures
     Types of Seizures
     Epileptic Syndromes
     Self-Limited and Epileptic-Like Disorders
     Status Epilepticus
     Diagnosing Epilepsy
     Treatment of Seizure Disorders
     What to Do in the Event of a Seizure
     Multidisciplinary Intervention
     Tiffany
     Juanita
     Yoshi
     Prognosis

27   Traumatic Brain Injury
     Linda Michaud, Ann-Christine Duhaime, and Mary F. Lazar 595
     Incidence of Head Injuries
     Causes of Traumatic Brain Injury
     Types of Brain Injuries
     Detecting Significant Brain Injury
     Severity of Brain Injury
     Treatment Approaches
     Functional Impairments
     Prevention
     Carmen
     Ethan
     Prognosis

IV   Interventions, Families, and Outcomes

28   Feeding
     Peggy S. Eicher 621
     The Feeding Process
     Influence of Medical Conditions
     Influence of Development
     Feeding Problems in Children with Disabilities
     Evaluation
     Managing Feeding Problems
     Hector

29   Dental Care: Beyond Brushing and Flossing
     Mark L. Helpin and Howard M. Rosenberg 643
     Formation and Emergence of Teeth
     Problems Affecting the Development of Teeth
     Oral Diseases

Malocclusion
Dental Trauma
Dental Care and Treatment
Dental Care for Children with Developmental Disabilities

30   Behavior Management: Promoting Adaptive Behavior
      John M. Parrish 657
      Origin of Behavior Problems
      Definitions
      Fundamental Principles and Procedures of Applied Behavior Analysis
      Selected Instructional Procedures
      Punishment
      Behavioral Diagnosis and Treatment

31   Technological Assistance: Innovations for Independence
      Susan E. Levy and Maureen O'Rourke 687
      Definition and Incidence of Medical Technology Assistance
      Disorders Associated with Medical Technology Assistance
      Types of Medical Technology Assistance
      Effects of Medical Technology Assistance on the Child and Family
      Funding Medical Technology Assistance
      Preparing for Home Care
      Outcome
      Ray

32   Rehabilitation Interventions: Physical Therapy and Occupational Therapy
      Lisa A. Kurtz and Susan E. Harryman 709
      Frames of Reference Guiding Physical and Occupational Therapy
      Selected Interventions
      Outcomes Measurement
      Kia: A School-Age Child with Cerebral Palsy and Assistive Technology Needs
      George: A Preshool-Age Child with PDD

33   Ethical Choices: Questions of Care
      Mark L. Batshaw and Mildred K. Cho 727
      Ethical Choices in Health Care
      Withholding Treatment
      Organ Donation
      Research Involving Children with Disabilities
      Sexual and Reproductive Rights
      Genetic Testing and Screening Programs
      Prenatal Diagnosis, Therapeutic Abortion, and Fetal Therapy
      George: A Newborn with Trisomy 18
      Emily: A Young Adult with Down Syndrome

34   Caring and Coping: The Family of a Child with Disabilities
      Symme Wilson Trachtenberg and Mark L. Batshaw 743
      The Life Cycle of the Family
      Family Reactions and Adaptations to Having a Child with a Disability
      The Effect of the Disability on Family Members, Friends, and the Child
      The Role of the Professional

The Role of Society and Community
Olay and His Family

35   Adulthood: What the Future Holds
     Adadot Hayes, Lisa J. Bain, and Mark L. Batshaw 757
     Childhood Activities as Foundations for Transition to Adulthood
     Transition from Dependence to Independence
     Transition from Home to Community Living
     Transition from School to Work
     Transition from Pediatric to Adult Health Care
     Recreation, Leisure, and Socialization
     Issues of Sexuality
     Planning for the Transition
     Life Span and Aging
     Competency as an Adult
     Estate Planning
     Kelvin

36   Providing Health Care in the 21st Century
     Angelo P. Giardino and Lowell Ives Arye 773
     The Changing Health Care Environment
     Managed Care
     Paying for Health Care Services for Children with Disabilities
     Looking Toward the Future
     Providing a Medical Home
     Health Care Use by Children with Disabilities
     Principles to Guide Care Management
     Danielle

Appendix A: Glossary 789

Appendix B: Syndromes and Inborn Errors of Metabolism 813

Appendix C: Commonly Used Medications 835

Appendix D: Resources for Children with Disabilities 851

Index 881

About the Editor

Mark Levitt Batshaw, M.D., is Physician-in-Chief of Children's Seashore House, a regional children's hospital for specialized care and rehabilitation. He is also Chief of the Division of Child Development and Rehabilitation Medicine at the Children's Hospital of Philadelphia and the W.T. Grant Professor of Pediatrics and Professor of Neurology and Rehabilitation Medicine at the University of Pennsylvania School of Medicine in Philadelphia.

Dr. Batshaw's experience includes 25 years of treating children with developmental disabilities. While on the faculty at The Johns Hopkins University, Dr. Batshaw was the recipient of the Alexander Schaffer Teaching Award in Pediatrics. A course he taught, "Medical and Physical Aspects of the Disabled Child," led him to develop the first edition of this book in 1981, then titled *Children with Handicaps: A Medical Primer.*

A Joseph P. Kennedy, Jr., Scholar and recipient of major grants from the March of Dimes Birth Defects Foundation and the National Institutes of Health (NIH), Dr. Batshaw is Director of the NIH-funded Mental Retardation and Developmental Disabilities (MRDD) Research Center at the University of Pennsylvania and serves as president of the national group of MRDD directors. He is also principal investigator of a program project grant developing gene therapy for the treatment of ornithine transcarbamylase deficiency, an inborn error of metabolism causing developmental disabilities.

Recognized as an international authority on inborn errors of metabolism, Dr. Batshaw has published more than 70 articles in such highly respected journals as the *New England Journal of Medicine, Science, Lancet,* and the *Journal of Clinical Investigation.* He serves as Editor-in-Chief of the journal *Mental Retardation and Developmental Disabilities Research Reviews.* Dr. Batshaw is a fellow of the American Academy of Pediatrics and a member of the American Pediatric Society, the Society of Pediatric Research, the Society for Inherited Metabolic Disorders, and the Society for Developmental Pediatrics.

Dr. Batshaw is also the author of *Your Child Has a Disability: A Complete Sourcebook of Daily and Medical Care* (Little, Brown, 1991). With colleagues at Children's Seashore House, he edited the *Handbook of Developmental Disabilities: Resources for Interdisciplinary Care* (Kurtz, Dowrick, Levy, & Batshaw; Aspen Publishers, 1996). Dr. Batshaw lives in Philadelphia with his wife, who is a social worker. They have three grown children.

Contributors

Lowell Ives Arye, M.S.S.A.
Associate Director
Center for Child Health Policy
Center for Health Care Policy
Leonard Davis Institute of Health Economics
University of Pennsylvania
3641 Locust Walk
Philadelphia, PA 19104

Lisa J. Bain, M.A.
181 Stoneway Lane
Bala Cynwyd, PA 19004

Marleen Ann Baron, M.A., CCC/SLP
Director
Speech-Language Pathology
Children's Seashore House
3405 Civic Center Boulevard
Philadelphia, PA 19104

Judy C. Bernbaum, M.D.
Associate Professor of Pediatrics
University of Pennsylvania School of Medicine
Director
Neonatal Follow-Up Program
Children's Hospital of Philadelphia
34th Street and Civic Center Boulevard
Philadelphia, PA 19104

Nathan J. Blum, M.D.
Assistant Professor of Pediatrics
University of Pennsylvania School of Medicine
Children's Seashore House
3405 Civic Center Boulevard
Philadelphia, PA 19104

Breck G. Borcherding, M.D.
Frederick Psychiatric Resources
10 North Jefferson Street
Frederick, MD 21701

Lawrence W. Brown, M.D.
Assistant Professor of Neurology and Pediatrics
Division of Neurology
Children's Hospital of Philadelphia
34th Street and Civic Center Boulevard
Philadelphia, PA 19104

Mildred K. Cho, Ph.D.
Assistant Professor
Center for Bioethics
University of Pennsylvania
3401 Market Street
Suite 320
Philadelphia, PA 19104

Robin P. Church, Ed.D.
Assistant Vice President for Educational Programs
Kennedy Krieger Institute
1750 East Fairmount Avenue
Baltimore, MD 21201

Charles J. Conlon, M.D.
Head
Early Intervention Service Team
Assistant Professor of Pediatrics and Developmental
    Medicine
Section Head
Uniformed Services
University of Health Sciences
Bethesda, MD 20889

John P. Dormans, M.D.
Chief
Division of Orthopedic Surgery
Children's Hospital of Philadelphia
34th Street and Civic Center Boulevard
Wood Building, 2nd floor
Philadelphia, PA 19104

Ann-Christine Duhaime, M.D.
Associate Neurosurgeon
Children's Hospital of Philadelphia
34th Street and Civic Center Boulevard
Philadelphia, PA 19104

Peggy S. Eicher, M.D.
Co-director
Pediatric Center for Dysphagia and Feeding
    Management
Children's Seashore House
3405 Civic Center Boulevard
Philadelphia, PA 19104

Jacquelyn R. Evans, M.D.
Associate Clinical Professor
University of Pennsylvania Medical Center
34th Street and Civic Center Boulevard
Philadelphia, PA 19104

Abigail F. Farber, M.D.
Medical Director
Inpatient Services
Children's Seashore House
3405 Civic Center Boulevard
Philadelphia, PA 19104

Iraj Forouzan, M.D.
Assistant Professor
Department of Obstetrics and Gynecology
University of Pennsylvania School of Medicine
3400 Spruce Street
2000 Courtyard
Philadelphia, PA 19104

Angelo P. Giardino, M.D., M.S.Ed.
Vice President
Clinical Operations
Assistant Physician-in-Chief
Children's Seashore House
3405 Civic Center Boulevard
Philadelphia, PA 19104

Ernest M. Graham, M.D.
Assistant Professor of Obstetrics and Gynecology
Allegheny University of the Health Sciences
3300 Henry Avenue
Philadelphia, PA 19129

Susan E. Harryman, M.S., P.T.
Director of Physical Therapy
Instructor of Pediatrics
School of Medicine
The Johns Hopkins University
Kennedy Krieger Institute
707 North Broadway
Baltimore, MD 21205

Adadot Hayes, M.D.
Medical Director
Tennessee Department of Mental Retardation
266 Lake Terrace Drive
Hendersonville, TN 37075

Mark L. Helpin, D.M.D.
Chairman and Associate Professor of Pediatric
    Dentistry
Chief
Dental Division
University of Pennsylvania
School of Medicine
4001 Spruce Street
Children's Hospital of Philadelphia
34th Street and Civic Center Boulevard
Philadelphia, PA 19104

Carol A. Knightly, M.A., CCC-A
Director of Audiology Services
Children's Seashore House
3405 Civic Center Boulevard
Philadelphia, PA 19104

Lisa A. Kurtz, M.Ed., OTR/L, BCP
Assistant Clinical Professor of Occupational Therapy
Thomas Jefferson University
Director of Occupational Therapy
Associate Director of Interdisciplinary Training
University Affiliated Program/LEND
Children's Seashore House
3405 Civic Center Boulevard
Philadelphia, PA 19104

Mary F. Lazar, Psy.D.
Pediatric Neuropsychologist
Children's Seashore House
3405 Civic Center Boulevard
Philadelphia, PA 19104

Susan E. Levy, M.D.
Clinical Associate Professor
University of Pennsylvania
Children's Seashore House
3405 Civic Center Boulevard
Philadelphia, PA 19104

M.E.B. Lewis, Ed.D.
Principal
Lower School
Kennedy Krieger Institute
1750 East Fairmount Avenue
Baltimore, MD 21201

Gregory S. Liptak, M.D., M.P.H.
Associate Professor of Pediatrics
University of Rochester Medical Center
601 Elmwood Avenue
Rochester, NY 14642

David R. Lynch, M.D., Ph.D.
Assistant Professor of Neurology and Pediatrics
University of Pennsylvania
502 Abramson
Children's Hospital of Philadelphia
34th Street and Civic Center Boulevard
Philadelphia, PA 19104

Joyce Elizabeth Mauk, M.D.
Assistant Professor of Pediatrics
University of Pennsylvania School of Medicine
Children's Seashore House
3405 Civic Center Boulevard
Philadelphia, PA 19104

Sheryl J. Menacker, M.D.
Pediatric Ophthalmologist
Division of Ophthalmology
Children's Hospital of Pennsylvania
Clinical Associate
Division of Ophthalmology
University of Pennsylvania
34th Street and Civic Center Boulevard
Philadelphia, PA 19104

Marianne Mercugliano, M.D.
Assistant Professor of Pediatrics
University of Pennsylvania School of Medicine
Children's Seashore House
3405 Civic Center Boulevard
Philadelphia, PA 19104

Gretchen Meyer, M.D.
Fellow
Neurodevelopmental Disabilities
Children's Seashore House
3405 Civic Center Boulevard
Philadelphia, PA 19104

Linda Michaud, M.D., M.Ed.
Director of Pediatric Rehabilitation
Children's Hospital Medical Center
Associate Professor
Departments of Physical Medicine and
    Rehabilitation and Pediatrics
University of Cincinnati Medical Center
3333 Burnet Avenue
Cincinnati, OH 45229

Mark A. Morgan, M.D.
Associate Professor
Director of Obstetrics and Maternal–Fetal Medicine
Department of Obstetrics and Gynecology
University of Pennsylvania School of Medicine
3400 Spruce Street
2000 Courtyard
Philadelphia, PA 19104

Maureen O'Rourke, M.D.
Assistant Professor of Pediatrics
University of Pennsylvania School of Medicine
Children's Hospital of Philadelphia
34th Street and Civic Center Boulevard
Philadelphia, PA 19104

John M. Parrish, Ph.D.
Associate Professor of Psychology in Pediatrics and
    Psychiatry
University of Pennsylvania School of Medicine
Children's Seashore House
3405 Civic Center Boulevard
Philadelphia, PA 19104

Louis Pellegrino, M.D.
Assistant Professor of Pediatrics
University of Pennsylvania School of Medicine
Children's Seashore House
3405 Civic Center Boulevard
Philadelphia, PA 19104

Mark Reber, M.D.
Clinical Associate in Psychiatry
University of Pennsylvania School of Medicine
3405 Civic Center Boulevard
Philadelphia, PA 19104

Nancy J. Roizen, M.D.
Associate Professor of Pediatrics and Psychiatry
University of Chicago Pritzker School of Medicine
5841 South Maryland Avenue
MC 0900
Chicago, IL 60637

Margaret Rose
Children's Seashore House
3405 Civic Center Boulevard
Philadelphia, PA 19104

Nancy C. Rose, M.D.
Assistant Professor
Department of Obstetrics and Gynecology
University of Pennsylvania Medical Center
3400 Spruce Street
Philadelphia, PA 19104

Howard M. Rosenberg, D.D.S., M.Ed.
Assistant Professor of Pediatric Dentistry
University of Pennsylvania School of Dental
    Medicine
4001 Spruce Street
Philadelphia, PA 19104

Richard M. Rutstein, M.D.
Department of General Pediatrics
Children's Hospital of Philadelphia
34th Street and Civic Center Boulevard
Philadelphia, PA 19104

Bruce K. Shapiro, M.D.
Associate Professor of Pediatrics
The Johns Hopkins University School
    of Medicine
707 North Broadway
Baltimore, MD 21205

Annie G. Steinberg, M.D.
Director of Psychiatry
Children's Seashore House
3405 Civic Center Boulevard
Philadelphia, PA 19104

**Symme Wilson Trachtenberg, M.S.W., A.C.S.W.,
    L.S.W.**
Director of Social Work, Community, and
    Government
Clinical Associate in Pediatrics
University of Pennsylvania Medical Liaison School
3405 Civic Center Boulevard
Philadelphia, PA 19104

Paul P. Wang, M.D.
Assistant Professor of Pediatrics
University of Pennsylvania School of Medicine
Children's Seashore House
3405 Civic Center Boulevard
Philadelphia, PA 19104

Colleen Comonitski Yanni, M.S., R.D.
Chief Clinical Dietician
Children's Seashore House
3405 Civic Center Boulevard
Philadelphia, PA 19104

A Personal Note to the Reader

As it enters its fourth edition, *Children with Disabilities* has changed in ways that mirror changes in my own life. The first edition evolved from lectures I developed for a special education course I taught at The Johns Hopkins University in Baltimore. The book contained 450 pages in 23 chapters, and I authored or co-authored all of them. When I started writing the book, I was 33 years old and 3 years out of my developmental pediatrics fellowship training program, and I knew everything there was to know about developmental disabilities! I was also an expert in my own children's development, having just welcomed into our family our third child, Andrew.

As I prepared this fourth edition, I have turned 50. The book is 944 pages long, with 36 chapters, and the original subtitle, *A Medical Primer*, has been dropped to more accurately reflect the book's comprehensive nature. I have authored or co-authored only half of the chapters, an acknowledgment of the fact that I no longer have the expertise I once thought I had. Our son Andrew, who was diagnosed as having ADHD in elementary school, is now a computer science major at Vassar. He wrote a letter for the third edition and has written an update for this edition; my wife and I are very proud of him.

It has been both personally and professionally rewarding to develop this book over nearly 20 years. Many of those rewards have come from the students, parents, and colleagues who have shared with me their thoughts and advice about the book. It is my hope that *Children with Disabilities* will continue to fill the needs of its diverse users for many years and many editions to come.

Mark L. Batshaw

Preface

One of the first questions asked about a subsequent edition of a book is "What's new?" The challenge of determining what to revise, what to add, and, in some cases, what to delete is always significant in preparing a new edition in a field changing as rapidly as developmental disabilities. Since the publication of the third edition in 1994, the fields of neuroscience and genetics have been revolutionized, greatly enhancing our understanding of the brain and inheritance and bringing forth the possibilities of treatments previously not thought possible for children with developmental disabilities. The human genome is being dissected, the brain probed by functional imaging techniques, the potential of gene therapy explored. The need to examine and explain these enormous advances and their significance for children with disabilities has necessitated a 50% increase in the length of the book. Yet, while the book is now more expansive and an edited text, I have worked hard to ensure that it retains its clarity and cohesion. Its mission continues to be to provide the individual working with and caring for children with disabilities the necessary background to understand different disabilities and their treatments, thereby enabling affected children to reach their full potential.

THE AUDIENCE

Since it was originally published, *Children with Disabilities* has been used as a medical textbook for students in a wide range of disciplines, addressing the impact of disabilities on child development and function. It has also served as a professional reference to special educators, general educators, physical therapists, occupational therapists, speech-language pathologists, psychologists, child life specialists, social workers, nurses, physicians, advocates, and others providing care for children with disabilities. Finally, as a family resource, parents, grandparents, siblings, and other family members and friends have found useful information on medical and (re)habilitative aspects of care for the child with developmental disabilities.

FEATURES FOR THE READER

I have been told that the strengths of previous editions of this book have been the accessible writing style, the clear illustrations, and the up-to-date information and references. We have dedicated our efforts to retaining these strengths. Some of the features you will find include the following:

- Teaching goals—Each chapter begins with learning objectives to orient you to the content of that particular chapter.
- Situational examples—Most chapters include one or more stories, or case studies, to help bring alive the conditions and issues discussed in the chapter.
- Key terms—As medical terms are introduced in the text, they appear in bold type at their first use; definitions for these terms appear in the Glossary (Appendix A).
- Illustrations—More than 200 drawings, photographs, X-rays, and tables reinforce the points of the text and provide ways for you to more easily understand and remember the material you are reading.

- Summary—Each chapter closes with a final section that reviews its key elements and provides you with an abstract of the covered material.
- References—The reference list accompanying each chapter is more than just a list of the literature cited in the chapter. You will find citations for review articles and other key references that can help direct you to additional information on topics you may want to research further.
- Appendices—In addition to the Glossary, there are three other helpful appendices: "Syndromes and Inborn Errors of Metabolism," a mini reference of pertinent information on more than 150 inherited disorders causing disabilities; "Commonly Used Medications," to describe indications and side effects of medications often prescribed for children with disabilities; and "Resources for Children with Disabilities," a directory of a wide range of national organizations, specialized hospitals, protection and advocacy programs, and university affiliated programs that can provide assistance to families and professionals.

CONTENT

In developing this fourth edition, I have aimed for a balance between consistency with the text that many of you have come to know so well in its previous editions and innovation in exploring the new topics that demand our attention as we move into the 21st century. All of the chapters from the third edition have been rewritten to include discussions of new (re)habilitative and educational interventions as well as to provide information discovered through medical and scientific advances since 1992. In addition, six new chapters have been added: "HIV and AIDS: From Mother to Child"; "Down Syndrome"; "Fragile X Syndrome"; "Rehabilitation Interventions: Physical Therapy and Occupational Therapy"; "Adulthood: What the Future Holds"; and "Providing Health Care in the 21st Century."

Each new chapter reflects either refocused emphasis or new discoveries. For example, HIV infection is now moving from being a universally fatal illness to becoming a chronic disease, associated with unique developmental disabilities. Down syndrome and fragile X syndrome make up such a large percentage of inherited developmental disabilities that they warrant individual chapters, especially with recent advances in understanding their biological origins and long-term consequences. The rehabilitation intervention chapter focuses on the use of physical and occupational therapy in treating disabilities and addresses the issue of outcomes assessment that is so important in a managed care environment. The revolution in health care delivery and its potential effects, both good and bad, on children with disabilities is further discussed in another new chapter. Finally, the recognition that children with disabilities become adults with disabilities is the focus of the chapter on transition to adulthood.

To accommodate all this new information, the book contains more than 330 additional pages than the third edition; to increase figure size and for ease of reading, the page size has been increased 25%. The book is also now in hardcover, accommodating both its substantial size and the need for endurance from the use it is likely to receive from its owners (and friends).

The chapters are now grouped in sections and reorganized to help guide readers through the breadth of content. The book starts with a section entitled **As Life Begins,** which addresses what happens before, during, or shortly after birth to cause a child at risk to have a developmental disability. The concepts and consequences of genetics, embryology and fetal development, the birth process, and prematurity are explained. The next section of the book, **The Developing Child,** covers environmental causes of developmental disabilities and examines the various organ systems—how they develop and work and what can go wrong. Substance abuse, HIV infection, nutrition, vision, hearing, language, and the brain and musculoskeletal systems are discussed in individual chapters. As its title implies,

Section III provides comprehensive descriptions of various **Developmental Disabilities** and genetic syndromes causing disabilities and includes chapters on mental retardation, Down syndrome, fragile X syndrome, inborn errors of metabolism, psychiatric disorders in developmental disabilities, autism, attention-deficit/hyperactivity disorder, learning disabilities, cerebral palsy, neural tube defects, seizure disorders, and traumatic brain injury. The final section focuses on **Interventions, Families, and Outcomes** with chapters that discuss various interventions including feeding, dental care, behavior management, technology assistance, and physical and occupational therapy. This section also concentrates on the ethical, emotional, and transition-to-adulthood issues that are common to most families of children with disabilities and to professionals who work with them. The book closes with a discussion of the prospects for providing health care in the next century.

THE AUTHORS AND EDITORS

I have chosen physicians and other health care professionals, who are experts in the areas they write about, as authors of *Children with Disabilities*. Most are my colleagues from Children's Seashore House, Children's Hospital of Philadelphia, and the Kennedy Krieger Institute in Baltimore. Each chapter in the book has undergone extensive editing by a senior medical writer, Lisa Bain; a production editor at Brookes Publishing Co., Lisa Pilcher; and myself to ensure consistency in style and accessibility in content. Once completed, each chapter was sent for peer review and revision by two or three major clinical and academic leaders in the field.

A FEW NOTES ABOUT TERMINOLOGY AND STYLE

As is the case with any book of this scope, the editor or author faces decisions about the use of particular words or the presentation style of information. I'd like to share with you some of the decisions we have made for this book.

- Reference style—In general, the citation style of the American Psychological Association has been followed, with one particular exception. To conserve space, given the number of co-authors so often listed on primary source material, we have elected to use the "et al." format for all references with three or more names.
- Categories of mental retardation—In accordance with the guidelines established by the American Association on Mental Retardation (1992), we have replaced references to degrees of mental retardation (i.e., mild, moderate, severe, profound) with references to supports these individuals need to lead fulfilling lives in the community (e.g., requiring limited, intermittent, extensive, or pervasive support).
- "Typical" and "normal"—Recognizing diversity and the fact that no one type of person or lifestyle is inherently "normal," we have chosen to refer to the general population of children as "typical" or "typically developing," meaning that they follow the natural continuum of development.
- Person-first language—We have tried to preserve the dignity and personhood of all individuals with disabilities by consistently using person-first language, speaking, for example, of "a boy with autism," instead of "an autistic boy." In this way, we are able to emphasize the person, not the condition with which he or she lives.

As you read this fourth edition of *Children with Disabilities,* I hope you will find that the text continues to address the frequently asked question "Why this child?" and to provide the medical background you will need, as parents and professionals, to care for children with developmental disabilities.

Acknowledgments

A book such as *Children with Disabilities* is best understood with illustrations that help to explain medical concepts. A medical illustrator is indispensable in this effort, and two of the best, Lynn Reynolds and Elaine Kasmer, have contributed to this endeavor. They were given the ideas that needed illustration and produced the more than 125 beautiful images that fill this book. I gratefully acknowledge their important contribution. Lynn Reynolds contributed the following figures: 1.4, 1.5, 1.6, 1.8, 1.10, 1.11, 1.12, 2.2, 2.3, 2.5, 2.6, 2.8, 2.9, 2.10, 2.11, 2.12, 3.2, 3.3b, 3.4, 3.6, 3.7, 3.8, 3.9, 5.1a, 5.3, 5.4, 6.1, 6.2, 6.3, 6.4, 7.6, 8.1, 8.2, 9.1, 9.2, 11.8, 12.3a, 12.5, 12.6, 12.9, 12.10, 12.11, 13.2, 15.2a, 15.2b, 17.1, 17.2, 17.3, 18.1, 19.1, 19.2, 19.3, 19.5, 19.6, 24.1, 24.2, 24.4, 24.8, 24.9, 24.11, 24.14, 25.1, 25.2, 25.3, 25.4, 25.6, 25.7, 25.9, 26.11, 27.1, 28.1, 28.2, 28.3, 28.4, 28.5, 28.9, 28.10, 29.1, 29.3, 29.4, 30.1, 31.1, 31.2, 31.4, 31.5, 32.1, and 32.2. Elaine Kasmer contributed the following figures: 1.1, 1.2, 1.9, 2.1, 2.7, 3.5, 4.1, 4.3, 5.2a, 6.5, 7.3, 7.5, 11.1, 11.2, 11.3, 11.4, 11.5, 11.7, 11.9, 11.10, 12.1, 12.2, 12.3b, 12.4, 13.3, 14.1, 14.2, 14.3, 14.4, 14.5, 14.6, 14.7, 14.8, 14.9, 14.10, 14.11, 15.1, 15.2b, 15.3, 15.5, 15.7, 24.3, 24.5, 24.7, 24.10, 24.12, 26.2, 26.3, 26.4, 26.5, 26.6, 26.7, and 29.2.

I also acknowledge my assistant, Margaret Rose, who helped to copyedit the manuscript, obtained consents, revised the resource section, and kept me and my colleagues on schedule throughout the production of this fourth edition. She is a wonderful person who is irreplaceable. I also wish to acknowledge Lisa Bain, a senior medical writer who did the developmental editing of this book, ensuring its concise and clear writing style. I also thank my production editor at Brookes Publishing Co., Lisa Pilcher, who enhanced the book with her careful and expert editing. I wish to recognize Yvonne Perret, who was involved in writing the first and second editions of the book.

Finally, many friends and colleagues at Children's Seashore House, Children's Hospital of Philadelphia, and elsewhere reviewed and edited the manuscript for content and accuracy. I would like to acknowledge their efforts: Joy Accamma, Marilee Allen, Michael Aman, Forrest C. Bennett, Marie Bristol, Allen C. Crocker, Richard Depp, John J. Downes, Peter Dowrick, John C. Fletcher, John M. Freeman, Nicole Gabriel, Randi Hagerman, Benjamin Handen, Bernadette Kappen, William L. Kissick, Ruth Landsman, G. Reid Lyon, Maureen Marcenko, Donna M. McDonald-McGinn, Donald Morgan, Michael Msall, Donna Mueller, Catherine Nebe, Arthur Nowak, Frederick Palmer, Brian Rogers, Lee Segal, Harry Shaw, David Shurtleff, Ann P. Streissguth, Jocelyn Trachtenberg, Eileen P.G. Vining, Renee Wachtel, Lana Warren, Mark Wolraich, and Elaine Zackai.

Preceding book production, Brookes Publishing Co. shared early versions of the manuscript with professionals who specialize in various associated fields. I extend my thanks to all of the reviewers, both those who chose to remain anonymous and those who are listed here: Pasquale J. Accardo, Carolyn Seval Brooks, Mary Jane Brotherson, Philippa H. Campbell, Edward Carr, Thomas O. Crawford, Juliann Woods Cripe, Allen Crocker, Christopher Duggan, Elizabeth Dykens, Kristina English, Marci J. Hanson, Chris P. Johnson, Jeanne M. Johnson, Timothy R.B. Johnson, Katherine J. Inge, Richard I. Kelley, Stephen L. Kinsman, Janette Klingner, Libby Kumin, Katlyne Luban, Bobbie Lubker, Williams F. Martin, III, Nancy Miller, Michael Msall, Laura Nathanson, James Riviello, Jr., Richard Ruth, Sharon Zeil Sacks, Ellin Siegel-Causey, Harold Smith, Rosella D. Smith, Dick Sobsey, and David E. Yoder.

MLB

Why me?
Why me?
Why do I have to do so much more than others?
Why am I so forgetful?
Why am I so hyperactive?
And why can't I spell?
Why me? O'why me?

I remember when I almost failed first grade because I couldn't read. I would cry hour after hour because my mother would try to make me read. Now I love to read. I couldn't write in cursive but my mother helped me and now I can. I don't have as bad a learning disability as others. At lest I can go to a normal school. I am trying as hard as I can (I just hope it is enough). My worst nightmare is to go to a special school because I don't want to be treated differently.

I am getting to like working. I guess since my dad is so successful and has a learning disability, it helps make me not want to give up. Many people say that I am smart, but sometimes I doubt it. I am very good at math, but sometimes I read a number like 169 as 196, so that messes things up. I also hear things incorrectly, for instants entrepreneur as horse manure (that really happened). I guess the reason why a lot of people don't like me is because I say the wrong answer a lot of times.

I had to take medication, but then I got off the medication and did well. Then in 7th grade I wasn't doing well but I didn't tell my parents because I thought they would just scream at me. My dad talked to the guidance counselor and found out. It wasn't till a week ago that I started on the medication again; I have been doing fine since than. As I have been getting more organized, I have had more free time. I guess I feel good when I succeed in things that take hard work.

This is my true story. . . Andrew Batshaw, 1989

Andrew Batshaw

In applying to colleges during my senior year of high school, I found that most had as an essay topic, "Tell us something about yourself." I decided to write about my ADHD and learning disability as it is a big part of who I am. I wrote "I have found that while a disability inherently leaves you with a weakness, adapting to that disability can provide rewards. I feel that from coping with my disability, I have gained pride, determination, and a strength that will be with me all of my life." I guess Vassar College agreed; they admitted me.

When it came time for high school graduation, we had a problem. My sister was graduating from the University of Chicago on the same day that I graduated from high school in Philadelphia. The only solution was for one parent to attend my graduation while the other one was with my sister in Chicago. The decision as to who would go to which graduation was easy. My mother insisted that she attend my graduation because it was a product of her hard work as well as my own. I remember she said to me that day, "When I think of the boy who cried himself to sleep because he could not remember how to spell the word 'who,' it makes me so happy to see you now."

My parents expressed themselves in different ways about my leaving for college. My mother and I found ourselves getting into many arguments over simple things (the old severing of the umbilical cord; I am the baby of the family). My father, however, made sure to remind me to start my stimulant medication 2 weeks before classes began!

The first semester I took four courses: Poetry, Linear Algebra, Computer Science, and Music Theory. As the semester continued, I developed an increasing interest in computer science, until finally I decided to become a computer science major. I was very flattered, however, when during a meeting with my English professor, she asked if I planned to be an English major. To think that someone who could not read until the end of second grade would become a member of the Vassar English department seemed almost unbelievable. Well, I might have been proud but not that proud. I stuck with computer science.

On the whole, I would say that my freshman year was a good one. I learned a great deal, both inside and outside of classes, about myself and others. What will I do after college? What will I end up doing with my life? These are questions that continually run through my mind. I have no clear answers, but there is one thing of which I am sure: My disability will not keep me from doing anything. I will not let it.

Andrew Batshaw

Andrew Batshaw
June, 1996

To Manny Batshaw, social worker, champion of children's rights, my father

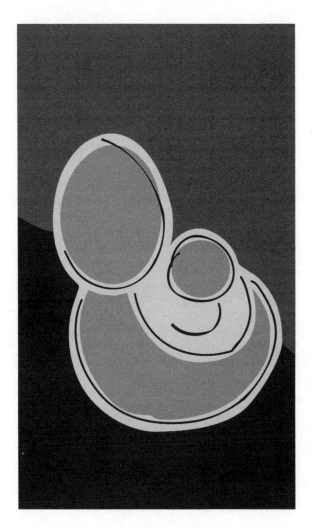

Children
with
Disabilities

As Life Begins

1 Understanding Your Chromosomes

Mark L. Batshaw

Upon completion of this chapter, the reader will:

- know the components of the cell and their functions
- understand the functions of chromosomes
- be familiar with various aspects of mitosis and meiosis
- be able to explain errors in mitosis and meiosis, including nondisjunction, translocation, and deletion

A child is born, and the preceding 9 months have witnessed a marvelous process. So complex and numerous are the steps involved from the fertilization of an egg to the birth of an infant that the chances for errors in that process seem limitless. The surprise, then, is not that so many children are born with birth defects, but that so few are. Tracing the path of human development, beginning with the fertilized egg, quickly points out the opportunities that exist for mistakes to occur.

As an introduction to the discussion in the chapters that follow, this chapter describes the human cell, explains what chromosomes are, reviews the processes of **mitosis** and **meiosis,** and provides some illustrations of the errors that can occur in these processes. As you progress through this book, bear in mind that the purpose of this discussion is to focus on the abnormalities that can, but seldom do, occur in human development; few infants are actually affected by the disorders that result from these abnormalities.

THE CELL

Our bodies are composed of approximately 100 trillion cells. There are many cell types, including nerve cells, muscle cells, white blood cells, and skin cells, to name a few. Each cell is divided into two compartments: 1) a central, enclosed core—the nucleus; and 2) an outer area—the **cytoplasm** (Figure 1.1), except for the red blood cell, which does not have a nucleus. The nucleus houses chromosomes (Greek for "colored bodies"), structures that contain the genetic code (DNA [**deoxyribonucleic acid**]) for our physical and biochemical properties.

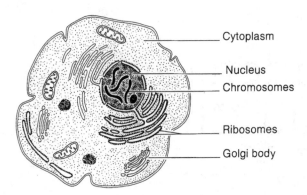

Figure 1.1.   An idealized cell. The genes within chromosomes direct the creation of a product on the ribosome. The product is then packaged in the Golgi body and released from the cell.

Hundreds of these units of heredity, commonly termed **genes,** are located on each chromosome. The cytoplasm, under the direction of the nucleus, generates the products that are needed for the growth and functioning of the organism, including waste disposal and the release of energy. The nucleus, then, contains the blueprint for an individual's development, and the cytoplasm provides the products needed to complete the task (Gore, 1976).

CHROMOSOMES

Each organism has a fixed number of chromosomes that direct the cell's activities. In humans, there are 46 chromosomes in each cell. These 46 (termed the **diploid** number) chromosomes are organized into 23 (termed the **haploid** number) pairs of complementary chromosomes. In every pair, one chromosome comes from the mother and one from the father. Egg and sperm cells, however, each contain only 23 chromosomes, one from each pair. During conception, these **germ cells** fuse to produce a fertilized egg with the full complement of 46 chromosomes.

Among the 23 pairs of chromosomes, 22 contain twin chromosomes, termed **autosomes**. Only the pair of **sex chromosomes,** commonly known as X and Y, look quite different from each other. The Y chromosome, which determines "maleness," is one third to one half as long as the X chromosome and has a different shape. In determining the sex of a fetus, two X chromosomes mean the child is female, and an X and a Y chromosome mean the child is male.

CELL DIVISION

Cells have the ability to divide into daughter cells that contain the same genetic information. In fact, the prenatal development of a human being, a complex process that takes about 280 days, is primarily accomplished through cell division. There are two kinds of cell division: mitosis and meiosis. In mitosis, or nonreductive division, two daughter cells, each containing 46 chromosomes, are created from one parent cell. In meiosis, or reductive division, four daughter cells, each containing only 23 chromosomes, are created from one parent cell. While mitosis occurs in all cells, meiosis takes place only in the germ cells and creates sperm and eggs (Jorde, Carey, & White, 1995). The ability of cells to continue to divide throughout the life span is essential for the proper functioning of the organism. All cells divide at different rates, however, ranging from once every 10 hours in skin cells to once a year in liver cells. This is why a skin abrasion heals in a few days, but it may take a year for the liver to recover from hepatitis. Some cells, including muscle and nerve cells, appear to have a greatly decreased ability to divide by adulthood. This limits the capacity to recover after a stroke or other acquired brain injury.

Mitosis

Mitosis occurs in four steps: **prophase, metaphase, anaphase,** and **telophase** (Figure 1.2). This cycle, once begun, takes only 1–2 hours to complete. Therefore, cells, even rapidly dividing skin cells, spend most of their lives in **interphase,** which is the "rest" period between cycles of mitosis. However, during interphase, the cell is actually preparing for mitosis; some genes in the cell continue to carry out their functions, while others are replicating. During this stage, the DNA and associated proteins form a complex referred to as **chromatin,** which resembles loosely packaged yarn. Late in interphase, the DNA replicates to form two identical copies (called **sister chromatids**) of the 46 chromosomes, which are essential to the first stage of mitosis.

During prophase, actual cell division begins. The chromosomes thicken and shorten, and the sister chromatids lie together, attached at the center by a **centromere** (Figure 1.2). The membrane surrounding the nucleus disappears, and spindle fibers form at the two poles of the cell. In prometaphase, the spindle fibers become attached to the centromere of each chromosome.

In metaphase, these fibers start to pull the two sister chromatids toward opposite poles of the cell. If division is arrested in metaphase, the chromosomes appear under a microscope as separate and distinct bodies that can be counted and divided into groups according to size, shape, and **banding pattern.** This process, called **karyotyping,** is used to determine an individual's chromosomal pattern. Figure 1.3 shows a karyotype of a typically developing girl.

During the next stage of cell division, anaphase, the spindles pull the chromatids to opposite poles of the two daughter cells (Figure 1.2). In the final phase, telophase, new nuclear membranes appear in the two daughter cells, the spindle fibers disappear, and the chromosomes begin to decondense. The two daughter cells, each containing 46 chromosomes, then separate and enter interphase.

Meiosis

Because meiosis is a much more complicated process than mitosis, it is more often associated with abnormalities (Levitan, 1988; Nora, 1994). Unlike mitosis, meiosis involves two cell divisions instead of one: The first division is reductive, and the second replicative. Each division has analogous stages of prophase, metaphase, anaphase, and telophase. It takes a sperm cell but a few hours to undergo meiosis, while the process can take decades in an egg cell.

One of the primary differences between mitosis and meiosis can be seen during the first meiotic division (termed meiosis I). During prophase I, the corresponding chromosomes line up beside each other in pairs (e.g., the two #1 chromosomes line up together). However, unlike mitosis, these chromatids intertwine and may **cross over,** exchanging genetic material (Figure 1.4). Although this crossing over (or recombination) of the chromosomes may result in disorders, it also allows for the mutual transfer of genetic information, enabling us to be similar to, but not exactly like, our **siblings.** Some of the variability among siblings can also be attributed to the random assortment of maternal and paternal chromosomes in meiosis I.

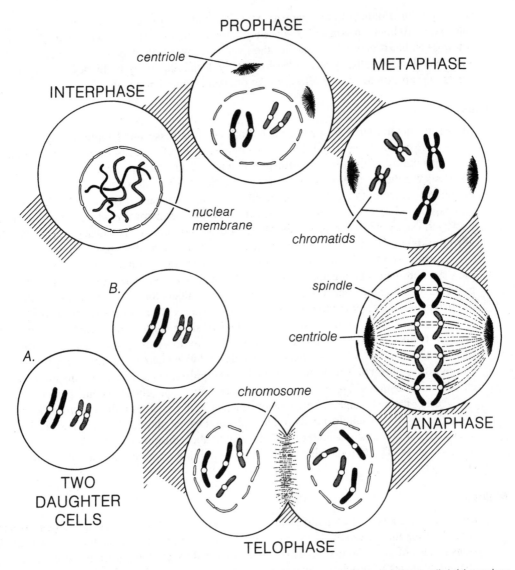

Figure 1.2.   Mitosis. This process produces two daughter cells, each containing a diploid number (46) of chromosomes.

In metaphase I, each chromosome doubles, becoming two chromatids, and the spindle is formed and attached to the centromere (Figure 1.5), again, much like mitosis. In anaphase I of meiosis, however, both chromatids of one #1 chromosome move toward one daughter cell and both chromatids of the other #1 chromosome move toward the other daughter cell, instead of doubled #1 chromatids moving toward each of the two daughter cells. In telophase I, the daughter cells form and separate, with each of the two daughter cells containing 23 double-stranded chromatids instead of 46 single-stranded chromosomes as in mitosis.

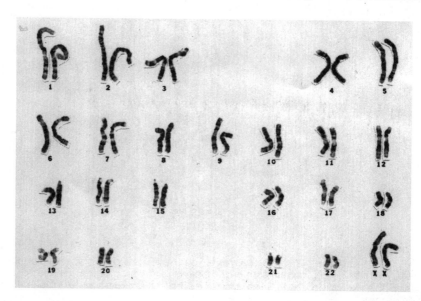

Figure 1.3. Illustration of the karyotype of a typical female (46, XX). To produce this karyotype, a teaspoon of blood was obtained, and a chemical was added to start mitosis of the white blood cells. Subsequently, another chemical was inserted to arrest the division in metaphase. The cell was then photographed under a microscope and a print was made. The chromosomes were cut out; matched in pairs; and numbered according to size, shape, position of the centromere, and banding pattern. (Courtesy of Dr. Beverly Emanuel, The Children's Hospital of Philadelphia.)

In the second meiotic division (meiosis II), the 23 chromosomes, each with double-stranded chromatids, line up in the center of each daughter cell (prophase II) and undergo division. In metaphase II and anaphase II, the doubled chromatids separate and move to the opposite poles of the cell (Figure 1.5). Thus, the two daughter cells that formed after the first meiotic division split into two more cells, each containing 23 chromosomes.

Throughout the life span of the male, meiosis of the immature sperm continually produces four spermatocytes with 23 chromosomes each. These cells will lose most of their cytoplasm, sprout tails, and become mature sperm. In the female, meiosis forms four oocytes, three of which will become **polar bodies:** small, nonfunctional cells that eventually break down. The one remaining daughter cell will receive virtually all of the cytoplasm and will ultimately become a mature egg. By the time a girl is born, her body has produced all of the 2 million eggs she will ever produce and has suspended them in prophase I. Meiosis I will proceed in individual eggs upon ovulation, and the second meiotic division will begin only once the egg is fertilized by a sperm.

WHAT CAN GO WRONG?

A number of events that subsequently affect a child's development can occur during cell division. Often when chromosomes or chromatids divide unequally, a process known as **nondisjunction,** the cells do not survive. However, on occasion they do survive and can cause chromosomal abnormalities. For example, sometimes during mitosis, a pair of chromatids does not split

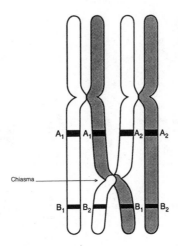

Figure 1.4.   The process of crossing over or recombination at a chiasma permits exchange of genetic material among chromosomes and accounts for much of the genetic variability of human traits. In this illustration, there is an exchange on the banding area labeled B between two chromosomes.

during anaphase, resulting in one daughter cell that contains 47 chromosomes (a **trisomy**) and the other daughter cell that contains 45 chromosomes (a **monosomy**). If no split occurs in any of the pairs of chromatids, one daughter cell will not have any chromosomes while the other will have 92, a condition called **tetraploidy.**

Most abnormalities, however, occur during meiosis (Hassold, Hunt, & Sherman, 1993). The loss or addition of part of a chromosome or an entire chromosome can result in the deletion or addition of hundreds of genes, which can lead to severe consequences. Among those who survive these genetic mishaps, mental retardation, unusual facial appearances, and various congenital malformations are common. In the general population, chromosomal aberrations occur in 0.6%–0.9% of all live births. In children who have mental retardation and multiple malformations, however, the incidence doubles (Nielsen, Hansen, Sillesen, et al., 1981).

Nondisjunction of Autosomes

The most frequent chromosomal abnormality is nondisjunction of autosomes, and the most common clinical consequence is trisomy 21, or Down syndrome (see Chapter 17). Nondisjunction can occur during either mitosis or meiosis but is more common in meiosis (Figure 1.6). When nondisjunction occurs during the first meiotic division, both #21 chromosomes end up in one cell. Instead of an equal distribution (23 each) among cells, one daughter cell receives 24 chromosomes while the other receives only 22. The cell containing 22 chromosomes is unable to survive. However, the egg (or sperm) with 24 chromosomes occasionally can survive. After fertilization with a sperm (or egg) containing 23 chromosomes, the resulting embryo contains three #21 chromosomes, or trisomy 21. The child will be born with Down syndrome (Figure 1.7).

A majority of individuals with Down syndrome (approximately 90%) acquire it as a result of a nondisjunction during meiosis of the egg; only 5% of individuals acquire Down syndrome from nondisjunction of the sperm (Antonarakis, 1991; McIntosh, Olshan, & Baird, 1995). An-

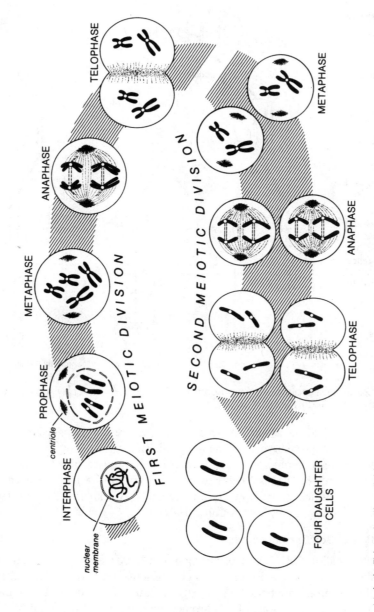

Figure 1.5. Meiosis. This reductive division occurs only in the germ cells. The result is egg and sperm cells containing a haploid number (23) of chromosomes.

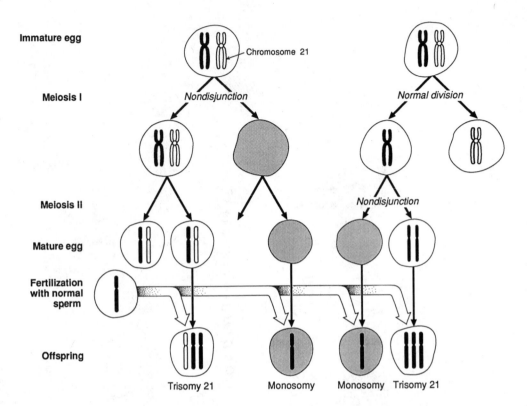

Figure 1.6.   Nondisjunction of chromosome #21 in meiosis. Unequal division during meiosis I or meiosis II can result in trisomy or monosomy.

other 5% of individuals acquire Down syndrome as a result of nondisjunction or translocation during mitosis of the embryo, resulting in **mosaicism.**

Other non-sex chromosomes that seem particularly susceptible to nondisjunction are chromosomes 13 and 18. The resulting trisomy 13 and trisomy 18 are associated with more severe cognitive impairments than Down syndrome (Baty, Blackburn, & Carey, 1994; Baty, Jorde, Blackburn, & Carey, 1994; Root & Carey, 1994).

Nondisjunction of Sex Chromosomes

Klinefelter syndrome (47, XXY), occurring in 1 in 1,000 male births, is the most common disorder arising from nondisjunction of the sex chromosomes (Paulsen & Plymate, 1992). Males with Klinefelter syndrome are born with an extra X chromosome (derived from the mother 60% of the time), giving them a total of 47 chromosomes, instead of the usual 46. As a result, these males produce inadequate **testosterone** and do not develop many of the typical secondary male sexual characteristics. They grow to be tall, slender men with disproportionately long arms and legs, underdeveloped testes, and small genitalia. They generally have IQ scores in the low-average range.

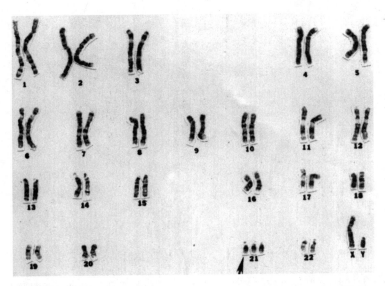

Figure 1.7.   Karyotype of a boy with Down syndrome (47, XY). Note that the child has 47 chromosomes; the extra one is a #21.

Other sex chromosome abnormalities resulting from nondisjunction do exist, although they are extremely rare: 47, XXX (the only one of these disorders producing a female); 47, XYY; 48, XXXY; 48, XXYY; and 49, XXXYY syndromes (Linden, Bender, & Robinson, 1995). Abnormal physical, sexual, and cognitive development characterize these syndromes, and the severity of intellectual impairment increases with the number of extra X chromosomes.

Chromosomal Loss

Turner syndrome (45, X), which affects girls, is the only disorder in which an individual can survive despite the loss of a complete chromosome. Even so, more than 99% of the 45, X conceptions are estimated to be spontaneously aborted (Hall, 1992). Females (1 in every 5,000 live births) with Turner syndrome have only a single X chromosome and no second X or Y chromosome, for a total of 45, rather than 46, chromosomes. In contrast to Down syndrome, 80% of individuals with **monosomy X** conditions are affected by meiotic errors in their fathers; these children usually receive an X chromosome from their mothers but no sex chromosome from their fathers.

Girls with Turner syndrome are very short and have a webbed neck, a broad shield-like chest, and nonfunctional ovaries (Figure 1.8). Twenty percent have obstruction of the left side of the heart, most commonly caused by a **coarctation** of the aorta. Unlike children with Down syndrome, most girls with Turner syndrome have typical intelligence. However, they do have visual-perceptual impairments that predispose them to develop learning disabilities (Money, 1993; Ross, Stefanatos, Roeltgen, et al., 1995; Temple & Carney, 1993). Human growth hormone injections have been effective in increasing their height, and estrogen has led to the emergence of secondary sexual characteristics; however, they remain sterile (Naeraa, Nielsen, & Kastrup, 1994).

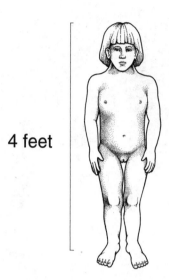

4 feet

Figure 1.8.   Girls with Turner syndrome have only one X chromosome. They are short in stature and have webbed necks, shield-shaped chests with widely spaced nipples, and nonfunctional ovaries.

About 50% of females with Turner syndrome have a 45, X karyotype in all of their cells; 30%–40% have mosaicism (see following section). The remainder have structural X chromosome abnormalities involving a deletion of some or all of the short arm of the X chromosome, or an **isochromosome.**

Mosaicism

In mosaicism, different cells have different genetic makeup (Colman, Rasmussen, Ho, et al., 1996; Saito, Ikeya, Kondo, et al., 1995). The chromosomal patterns of affected children are "mosaics" of some normal cells and some abnormal cells. For example, a child may have trisomy 21 in blood cells but not in skin cells or in some, but not all, brain cells. Children with mosaicism often appear as if they have the condition (in this case Down syndrome), although the physical features and cognitive impairments may be less obvious. Usually mosaicism occurs when some cells in a trisomy conception lose the extra chromosome via nondisjunction during mitosis. Mosaicism also can occur if some cells lose a chromosome after a normal conception, as in Turner syndrome (some cells lose an X chromosome). Mosaicism is rare and accounts for only 5%–10% of all children with chromosomal abnormalities (Gravholt, Friedrich, & Nielsen, 1991).

Translocations and Deletions

Two other relatively common dysfunctions in cell division can lead to structural abnormalities of chromosomes and result in birth defects: **Translocations** and **deletions** occur during mitosis and meiosis when the chromosomes break and lose or exchange parts with other chromosomes.

Translocation involves the transfer of a portion of one chromosome to a completely different chromosome. For example, a portion of chromosome #21 might attach itself to chromosome #14 (Figure 1.9). If this occurs during meiosis, one daughter cell will then have 23 chromosomes but with both a #21 and a #14/21 translocation chromosome. Fertilization of this egg or sperm

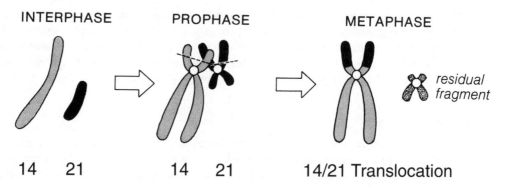

INTERPHASE   **PROPHASE**   **METAPHASE**

14   21   14   21   14/21 Translocation

residual
fragment

Figure 1.9.   Translocation. During prophase of meiosis in a parent, there may be a transfer of a portion of one chromosome to another. In this figure, the long arm of #21 is translocated to chromosome #14, and the residual fragments are lost.

with a cell containing the normal complement of 23 chromosomes will result in a child with 46 chromosomes, including two #21 chromosomes, one #14/21 chromosome, and one #14 chromosome. This child will have Down syndrome because of the partial trisomy 21 caused by the translocation.

Chromosomal deletions occur in two forms, visible deletions and **microdeletions.** Those that are large enough to be seen through karyotyping are called visible deletions. Those that are so small that they can be detected only by technicians using special chromosomal banding techniques are called microdeletions. The **cri-du-chat ("cat cry") syndrome** is an example of a visible chromosomal deletion in which a portion of the short arm of chromosome #5 is lost (Figure 1.10). Cri-du-chat syndrome affects 1 in 50,000 children, causing microcephaly, an unusual facial appearance, a high-pitched cry, and mental retardation requiring extensive supports. An example of a microdeletion syndrome is velocardiofacial (VCF) syndrome, which is associated

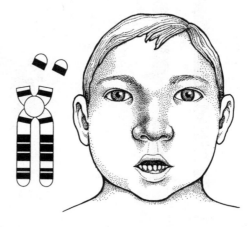

Figure 1.10.   Children with cri-du-chat syndrome have an unusual facial appearance with microcephaly, a round face, widely spaced eyes, epicanthal folds, and low-set ears. The chromosomal abnormality is a partial deletion of the short arm of the #5 chromosome.

with a deletion in the long arm of chromosome #22 (McLean, Saal, Spinner, et al., 1993). Children with VCF syndrome have cleft palates, congenital heart defects, a characteristic facial appearance, and learning disabilities. Microdeletion syndromes are also called **contiguous gene syndromes** because they involve the deletion of a series of adjacent genes. As a general rule, microdeletion disorders result in less severe developmental disabilities than do visible deletion syndromes.

Chromosome Breakage

Chromosome breakage during meiosis or mitosis can yield rare structural abnormalities, including **ring chromosomes, inversions,** and isochromosomes (Jorde et al., 1995). A ring chromosome forms when deletions occur at both tips of a chromosome, with subsequent fusion of the two "sticky" ends (Figure 1.11). The deleted segments usually cause clinical abnormalities (Kosztolany, Mehes, & Hook, 1991). In ring chromosome #6, affected children have short stature, mental retardation, microcephaly, and eye abnormalities (Teyssier, Charrin, Corgiolu Theuil, et al., 1992). Inversions result when a chromosome breaks in two places and is then reconnected in reverse order. Because the affected individual still maintains the normal complement of genes, he or she is not affected by the inversion. However, as a parent, this individual can pass on the inversion to offspring, leading to chromosomal deletions or duplications (Delicado, Escribano, Lopez-Pajares, et al., 1991). An isochromosome has two copies of one arm of a chromosome and no copies of the other (Figure 1.12). As noted previously, some cases of Turner syndrome result from an isochromosome X.

In total, about 25% of eggs and 3%–4% of sperm have an extra or missing chromosome, and an additional 1% and 5%, respectively, have a structural chromosomal abnormality (Martin, Ko, & Rademaker, 1991). As a result, 10%–15% of all conceptions have a chromosomal abnormality. Somewhat more than half of these abnormalities are trisomies, 20% are monosomies, and 15% are **triploids** (69 chromosomes). The remainder are structural abnormalities and tetraploids. It may seem surprising then that more children are not born with chromosomal ab-

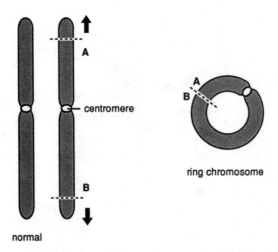

Figure 1.11. The formation of a ring chromosome requires deletion at both tips of the chromosome with subsequent fusing of the ends.

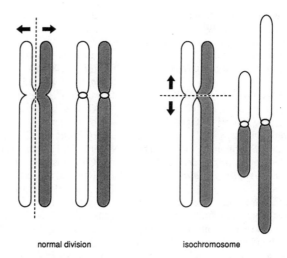

normal division   isochromosome

Figure 1.12.   An isochromosome has two copies of one arm of a chromosome and no copies of the other.

normalities (Jacobs, Browne, Gregson, et al., 1992), but more than 95% of fetuses with chromosomal abnormalities do not survive to term. In fact, fetuses with certain abnormalities never survive; for example, trisomy 16 is the most common trisomy at conception but has never been reported in a live birth (Jorde et al., 1995).

SUMMARY

Each human cell contains a full complement of genetic information encoded in 46 chromosomes. Not only does this genetic code determine our physical appearance and biochemical makeup, but it is also the legacy we pass on to our children. The unequal division of the reproductive cells or the deletion or translocation of a chromosome can have significant consequences, such as Down syndrome or cri-du-chat syndrome. Yet, despite these and other potential problems that can occur during the development of the embryo and fetus, about 95% of infants are born with no significant birth defects.

REFERENCES

Antonarakis, S.E. (1991). Parental origin of the extra chromosome in trisomy 21 as indicated by analysis of DNA polymorphisms. *New England Journal of Medicine, 324,* 872–876.

Baty, B.J., Blackburn, B.L., & Carey, J.C. (1994). Natural history of trisomy 18 and trisomy 13: I. Growth, physical assessment, medical histories, survival and recurrence risk. *American Journal of Medical Genetics, 49,* 175–188.

Baty, B.J., Jorde, L.B., & Blackburn, B.L. (1994). Natural history of trisomy 18 and trisomy 13: II. Psy-

chomotor development. *American Journal of Medical Genetics, 49,* 189–194.

Colman, S.D., Rasmussen, S.A., Ho, V.T., et al. (1996). Somatic mosaicism in a patient with neurofibromatosis type I. *American Journal of Human Genetics, 58,* 484–490.

Delicado, A., Escribano, E., Lopez-Pajares, I., et al. (1991). A malformed child with a recombinant chromosome 7, rec(7) dup p, derived from a maternal pericentric inversion inv(7)(p15q36). *Journal of Medical Genetics, 28,* 126–127.

Gore, R. (1976). The awesome worlds within a cell. *National Geographic, 150,* 354–395.

Gravholt, C.H., Friedrich, U., & Nielsen, J. (1991). Chromosomal mosaicism: A follow-up study of 39 unselected children found at birth. *Human Genetics, 88,* 49–52.

Hall, J.C. (1992). Turner syndrome. In R.A. King, J.I. Rotter, & A.G. Motulsky (Eds.), *The genetic basis of common disease* (pp. 895–914). Oxford, England: Oxford University Press.

Hassold, T., Hunt, P.A., & Sherman, S. (1993). Trisomy in humans: Incidence, origin, and etiology. *Current Opinion in Genetic Development, 3,* 398–403.

Jacobs, P.A., Browne, C., Gregson, N., et al. (1992). Estimates of the frequency of chromosome abnormalities detectable in unselected newborns using moderate levels of banding. *Journal of Medical Genetics, 29,* 103–108.

Jorde, L.B., Carey, J.C., & White, R.W. (1995). *Medical genetics.* St. Louis: C.V. Mosby.

Kosztolany, G., Mehes, K., & Hook, E.B. (1991). Inherited ring chromosomes: An analysis of published cases. *Human Genetics, 87,* 320–324.

Levitan, M. (1988). *Textbook of human genetics* (3rd ed.). New York: Oxford University Press.

Linden, M.G., Bender, B.G., & Robinson, A. (1995). Sex chromosome tetrasomy and pentasomy. *Pediatrics, 96,* 672–682.

Martin, R.H., Ko, E., & Rademaker, A. (1991). Distribution of aneuploidy in human genetics: Comparison between human sperm and oocytes. *American Journal of Medical Genetics, 39,* 321–331.

McIntosh, G.C., Olshan, A.F., & Baird, P.A. (1995). Paternal age and the risk of birth defects in offspring. *Epidemiology, 6,* 282–288.

McLean, S.D., Saal, H.M., Spinner, N.B., et al. (1993). Velo cardio facial syndrome: Intrafamilial variability of the phenotype. *American Journal of Diseases of Children, 147,* 1212–1216.

Money, J. (1993). Specific neuro-cognitive impairments associated with Turner (45,X) and Klinefelter (47, XXY) syndromes: A review. *Social Biology, 40,* 147–151.

Naeraa, R.W., Nielsen, J., & Kastrup, K.W. (1994). Growth hormone and 17 beta-oestradiol treatment of Turner girls: 2-year results. *European Journal of Pediatrics, 153,* 72–77.

Nielsen, J., Hansen, K.B., Sillesen, I., et al. (1981). Chromosome abnormalities in newborn children: Physical aspects. *Human Genetics, 59,* 194–200.

Nora, J.J. (1994). *Medical genetics: Principles and practice* (4th ed.). Philadelphia: Lea & Febiger.

Paulsen, C.A., & Plymate, S.R. (1992). Klinefelter's syndrome. In R.A. King, J.I. Root, & J.C. Carey (Eds.), Survival in trisomy 18. *American Journal of Medical Genetics, 49,* 170–174.

Root, S., & Carey, J.C. (1994). Survival in trisomy 18. *American Journal of Medical Genetics, 49,* 170–174.

Ross, J.L., Stefanatos, G., Roeltgen, D., et al. (1995). Ullrich-Turner syndrome: Neurodevelopmental changes from childhood through adolescence. *American Journal of Medical Genetics, 58,* 74–82.

Saito, K., Ikeya, K., Kondo, E., et al. (1995). Somatic mosaicism for a DMD gene deletion. *American Journal of Medical Genetics, 56,* 80–86.

Temple, C.M., & Carney, R.A. (1993). Intellectual functioning of children with Turner syndrome: A comparison of behavioural phenotypes. *Developmental Medicine and Child Neurology, 35,* 691–698.

Teyssier, M., Charrin, C., Corgiolu Theuil, G., et al. (1992). Ring chromosome 17: Case report and review of the literature. *Annales de Genetique, 35,* 75–78.

2 Heredity

A Toss of the Dice

Mark L. Batshaw

Upon completion of this chapter, the reader will:

- be aware of the role genes and mutations play in hereditary disorders
- know the differences and similarities among autosomal recessive, autosomal dominant, and sex-linked genetic disorders
- be able to describe some of the major chromosomal abnormalities
- understand the concepts of genomic imprinting and anticipation
- understand mitochondrial inheritance
- understand the ways in which environment and heredity contribute to the development of multifactorial disorders

Whether we have brown or blue eyes is determined by genes passed to us by our parents. Other traits, such as height and weight, are affected by genes and by our environments both before and after birth. In a similar manner, genes alone or in combination with environmental factors can lead to many disorders, including birth defects. The spectrum of disorders ranges from purely genetic disorders, such as **muscular dystrophy,** which results from a single-gene defect; to purely environmental diseases, including infectious diseases such as meningitis; to multifactorial disorders, which are influenced by both genetics and environment, such as **meningomyelocele.** This chapter describes the ways in which genetically determined birth defects are passed from one generation to another.

THE GENETIC PRINCIPLES OF MENDEL

Gregor Mendel (1822–1884), an Austrian monk who enjoyed gardening, pioneered our understanding of genetics. He was the first to recognize the existence of genetic traits, that is, characteristics in organisms that show variability. While cultivating pea plants, he noted that when he bred two differently colored plants—yellow and green—the hybrid offspring all were green, rather than mixed in color. Mendel concluded that the green trait was **dominant,** while the yellow trait was **recessive** (from the Latin "hidden"), sometimes appearing in subsequent generations. Later, scientists determined that many human traits, including some birth defects, are also inherited from single genes. These traits, which also may be dominant or recessive, are referred to as **Mendelian traits** (King, Rotter, & Motulsky, 1992).

GENES

The human **genome** contains about 100,000 genes. Genes are responsible for producing specific products (e.g., hormones, enzymes, blood type) as well as regulating the development and function of the body. As of 1997, more than 16,000 genes have been mapped to specific chromosome locations; by the year 2005, the remaining sites are likely to be identified. An error, or **mutation,** in a gene can lead to a genetic disorder. Genetics has already been shown to play a primary role in about 7,000 disorders (McKusick, 1994).

The particular genes that a person possesses determine that person's **genotype,** while the manner in which those genes are expressed is called the **phenotype.** For some clinical syndromes, the same genotype can produce quite different phenotypes, depending on environmental influences. For example, a child with the inborn error of metabolism **phenylketonuria (PKU)** will develop mental retardation requiring extensive supports if the PKU is not treated early but will have typical development if it is treated from infancy (see Chapter 19). Conversely, very different genotypes can produce the same phenotype. For example, two different enzyme deficiencies, caused by gene defects on two different chromosomes, can lead to the elevated phenylalanine levels that cause brain damage in PKU. Thus, a person's genetic makeup may not always predict what will be observed physically; the converse is also true.

Genes provide the cells with instructions for producing the specific proteins needed for body functions, such as insulin for the metabolism of glucose. These instructions are encoded by deoxyribonucleic acid, or DNA, which is formed as a double **helix,** a structure that resembles a twisted ladder. The sides of the ladder are composed of sugar and phosphate, while the "rungs" are made up of four chemicals called **nucleotide bases:** cytosine (C), adenine (A), thymine (T), and guanine (G) (Figure 2.1). Pairs of nucleotides interlock to form each rung: Adenine bonds with thymine, and cytosine with guanine. The sequence of nucleotide bases (spelled out by the 4-letter alphabet, G, C, A, T) on a segment of DNA make up one's genetic code. Genes range in size, containing from 1,500 to more than 2 million nucleotide base pairs.

The production of a specific protein begins when the DNA for that gene unwinds, and the two strands, or sides of the ladder, unzip to expose the code (Jorde, Carey, & White, 1995). The exposed DNA sequence then serves as a template for the formation, or **transcription,** of a similar nucleotide sequence called **messenger ribonucleic acid (mRNA)** (Figure 2.2). As might be expected, errors or mutations may occur during transcription; however, a proofreading enzyme generally catches and corrects these errors. If not corrected, the transcription error can lead to the production of a disordered protein and a disease state.

Once transcribed, the single-stranded mRNA detaches, and the double-stranded DNA zips back together. The mRNA then moves out of the nucleus into the cytoplasm, where it serves as a template for the production of a protein (Figure 2.2), a process termed **translation.** Once in the cytoplasm, the mRNA attaches itself to a **ribosome** (Figure 2.3). The ribosome moves along the mRNA strand, reading the message like a videocassette recorder in three-letter "words" or

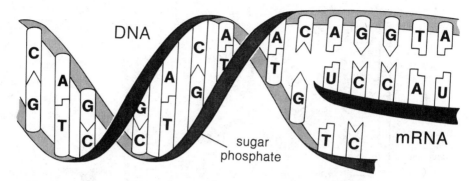

Figure 2.1.   DNA. Four nucleotides (G = guanine, C = cytosine, A = adenine, and T = thymine) form the genetic code. On the mRNA molecule, U (uracil) substitutes for thymine. The DNA unzips to transcribe its message as mRNA.

codons, such as GCU, CUA, and UAG. Most of these triplets code for a specific **amino acid,** the building blocks of proteins. As these triplets are read, another type of RNA, transfer RNA (tRNA), carries the requisite amino acids to the ribosome, where they are linked to form a polypeptide chain. Certain triplets, termed *stop codons,* instruct the ribosome to terminate the sequence. The stop codon indicates that all of the correct amino acids are in place to form the complete protein.

Once the protein is complete, the mRNA, ribosome, and protein separate, and the protein is released into the cytoplasm. The protein is either used by the cytoplasm or prepared for secretion into the bloodstream. If the protein is to be secreted, it is transferred to the Golgi body (Figure 1.1), which packages it in a form that can be released through the cell membrane and carried throughout the body.

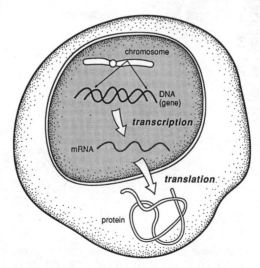

Figure 2.2.   A summary of the steps leading from gene to protein formation. Transcription of the DNA (gene) onto mRNA occurs in the cell nucleus. The mRNA is then transported to the cytoplasm, where translation into protein occurs.

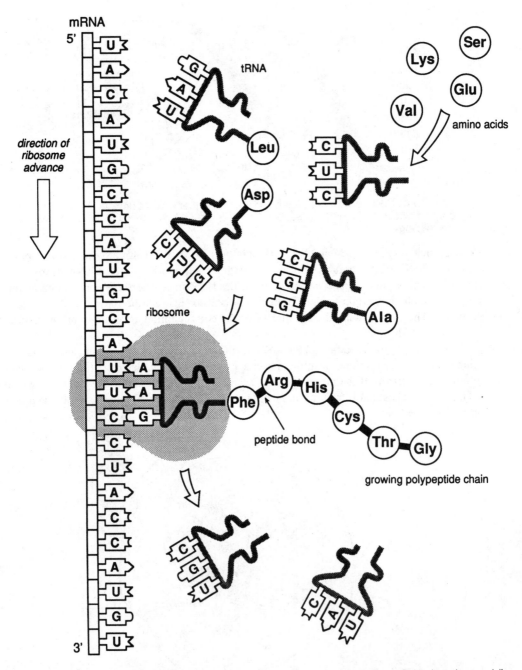

Figure 2.3.   Translation of mRNA to protein. The ribosome moves along the mRNA strand assembling a growing polypeptide chain using tRNA–amino acid complexes . In this example, it has already assembled six amino acids (phenylalanine [Phe], arginine [Arg], histidine [His], cystine [Cys], threonine [Thr], and glycine [Gly]) into a polypeptide chain.

Mutations

An abnormality at any step in this process can cause the body to produce a structurally abnormal protein, reduced amounts of a novel protein, or no protein at all. When the error occurs in the gene itself, thus disrupting the subsequent steps, that mistake is called a *mutation.* The likelihood of a mutation occurring increases with the size of the gene. In egg and sperm cells, the mutation rate also increases with age, especially in males (Figure 2.4) (Risch, Reich, Wishnick, et al., 1987). Although most mutations occur spontaneously, they can also be induced by ionizing and nonionizing radiation, chemicals, and viruses. Once they occur, mutations can become part of a person's genetic code and can be passed down from one generation to another.

The most common type of mutation is a single base pair substitution (Cooper & Krawczak, 1990), also called a *point mutation.* Because there is a lot of redundancy in our DNA, many of these mutations have no adverse effects. However, depending on where in the gene they occur, point mutations are capable of causing a **missense mutation** or a **nonsense mutation** (Figure 2.5). A missense mutation results in a change in the triplet code that substitutes a different amino acid in the protein chain. For example, in sickle cell anemia, a single base substitution results in

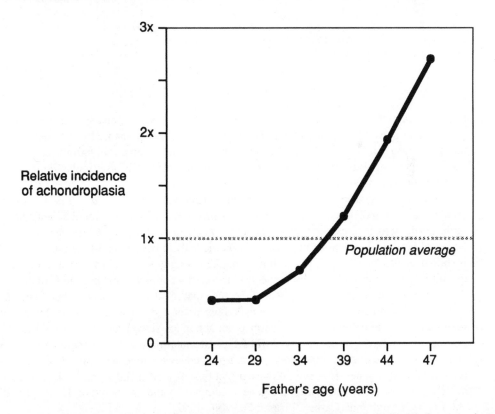

Figure 2.4.   The risk of producing a child with the single-gene autosomal dominant disease achondroplasia (Y-axis) increases with the father's age (X-axis). (From Vogel, F., & Rathenberg, R. [1975]. Spontaneous mutation in man. *Advances in Human Genetics, 5,* 267; reprinted by permission of Plenum.)

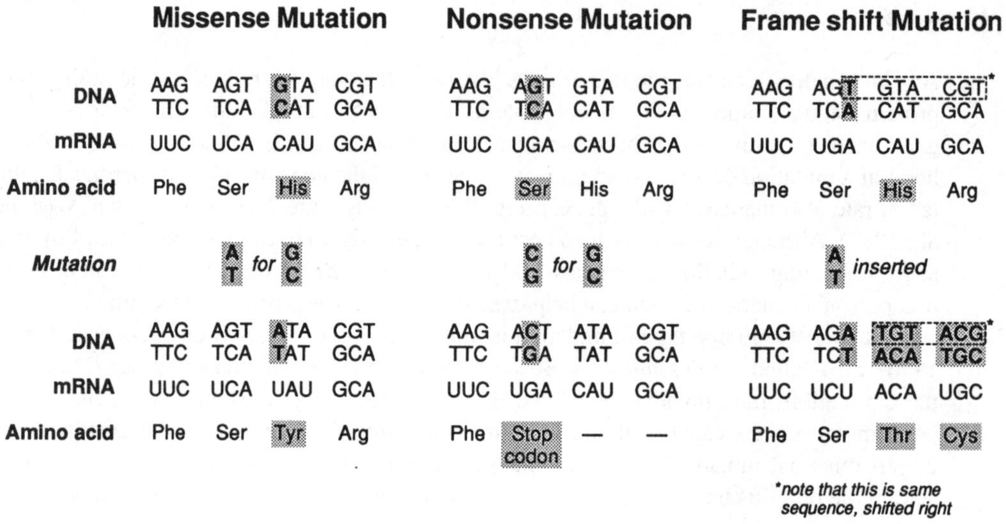

Missense Mutation   Nonsense Mutation   Frame shift Mutation

	Missense Mutation	Nonsense Mutation	Frame shift Mutation
DNA	AAG AGT **G**TA CGT TTC TCA **C**AT GCA	AAG A**G**T GTA CGT TTC T**C**A CAT GCA	AAG AG**T GTA CGT*** TTC TC**A CAT GCA
mRNA	UUC UCA CAU GCA	UUC UGA CAU GCA	UUC UGA CAU GCA
Amino acid	Phe Ser **His** Arg	Phe **Ser** His Arg	Phe Ser **His** Arg

Mutation	**A**/T for **G**/C	**C**/G for **G**/C	**A**/T inserted

DNA	AAG AGT **A**TA CGT TTC TCA **T**AT GCA	AAG A**C**T ATA CGT TTC T**G**A TAT GCA	AAG AG**A TGT ACG*** TTC TC**T ACA TGC
mRNA	UUC UCA UAU GCA	UUC UGA CAU GCA	UUC UCU ACA UGC
Amino acid	Phe Ser **Tyr** Arg	Phe **Stop codon** — —	Phe Ser **Thr** **Cys**

*note that this is same
sequence, shifted right

Figure 2.5.   Examples of single gene mutations: Missense mutation, nonsense mutation, and frame shift mutation. The shaded areas mark the point of mutation.

the production of the amino acid valine instead of glutamic acid at one spot on the hemoglobin protein. This substitution causes the red cells to assume a sickle shape. In a nonsense mutation, the single base pair substitution produces a stop codon that prematurely terminates the polypeptide. In this case, no useful protein is formed. Another blood disease, thalassemia, can result from this type of mutation.

Mutations may also result in the insertion or deletion of one or more bases. The most common mutation in individuals with cystic fibrosis involves a 3-base deletion that leads to a defect in the cystic fibrosis transmembrane conductive regulator (CFTR) gene, the cause of the illness. Base additions or subtractions may lead to a **frame shift** in which the 3-base pair reading frame is shifted, as occurs when one places fingers on the wrong typewriter keys. As a result, all subsequent triplets are misread, leading to the production of a nonfunctional protein (Figure 2.5).

Other mutations can affect regions of the gene that regulate transcription but do not actually code for an amino acid. These areas are called promoter and enhancer regions. Mutations here may result in a normal protein being formed but at a much slower rate than usual, leading to an enzyme or other protein deficiency. A final type of mutation involves a **triplet repeat expansion.** For reasons not fully understood, some triplet codes are repeated multiple times in certain regions of normal genes. However, if these triplet repeats are expanded markedly, usually during defective meiosis, they can disrupt the gene, leading to conditions including Huntington disease and fragile X syndrome (Caskey, Pizzuti, Fu, et al., 1992).

The incidence of a genetic disease in a population depends on the difference between the rate of mutation production and that of mutation removal. Typically, genetic diseases are introduced into populations by mutation errors. Natural selection, the process by which individuals with a selective advantage survive and pass on their genes, works to remove these errors. For instance, because individuals with sickle cell anemia, an autosomal recessively inherited blood disorder, typically have a decreased life span, the gene that causes the disorder would be expected to be gradually removed from the gene pool. However, sometimes natural selection favors the individual who carries one copy of a mutated recessive gene. In the case of sickle cell anemia, unaffected carriers who appear clinically normal actually have minor differences in their hemoglobin that make it resistant to a malarial parasite. In Africa, where malaria is endemic, this gives the carriers a selective advantage. This selection has maintained the sickle cell trait among Africans. Northern Europeans, for whom malaria is not an issue, do not carry the sickle cell gene at all; this mutation has died out via natural selection. Likewise, the absence of malaria in the United States eliminates the selective advantage that has allowed sickle cell anemia to survive in Africa (Jorde et al., 1995). The result is that African Americans have a lower incidence of sickle cell anemia than Africans.

Geneticists generally believe that everyone carries a number of mutations that can pass to offspring. Some of these mutations are helpful to the process of natural evolution. For example, a mutation leading to increased height might confer a selective advantage. Other mutations are harmful and predispose one to various diseases, including diabetes and cancer. Most have no observable effect and do not pose a serious threat to our well-being.

MENDELIAN DISORDERS

Approximately 1% of the population has a Mendelian, or single-gene, disorder (Table 2.1). These disorders may be transmitted to offspring on the autosomes (the non-sex chromosomes, numbered 1–22) or on the female (X) chromosome. Mendelian traits may be either dominant or recessive. Thus, Mendelian disorders are characterized as being autosomal recessive, autosomal dominant, or X-linked.

Autosomal Recessive Disorders

Among the Mendelian disorders, approximately 1,700 are inherited as autosomal recessive traits. For a child to inherit a disorder that is autosomal recessive, he or she must receive an abnormal gene from both the mother and father.

Tay-Sachs disease is an example of an autosomal recessive, progressive neurological disorder caused by the absence of an enzyme, hexosaminidase A, that usually converts a toxin of nerve cell metabolism into a nontoxic product (Kaback, Lim-Steele, Dabholkar, et al., 1993). In individuals with Tay-Sachs disease, this toxin cannot be broken down and accumulates in the brain, leading to brain damage and early death. Children with Tay-Sachs disease initially develop typically. At about 6 months of age, however, the child's health begins to deteriorate, and he or she can no longer sit or babble. The disease progresses rapidly, causing blindness, mental retardation, and early death.

Alternate forms of the gene for hexosaminidase A are known to exist. These different forms, called **alleles,** include the normal gene, symbolized by a capital "A," and the mutated Tay-Sachs disease-carrying allele, symbolized by the lowercase "a" (Figure 2.6). After fertilization, the embryo has two genes for hexosaminidase A, one from the father and one from the mother. The following combinations of alleles could theoretically occur: the **homozygous** combinations, AA and aa; and the heterozygous combinations, aA and Aa. Because Tay-Sachs dis-

Table 2.1.   Prevalence of genetic disorders

Disease	Approximate prevalence
Chromosomal disorders	
Down syndrome	1/700–1/1,000
Klinefelter syndrome	1/1,000 males
Trisomy 13	1/10,000
Trisomy 18	1/6,000
Turner syndrome	1/2,500–1/10,000
Single-gene disorders	
Duchenne muscular dystrophy	1/3,500 males
Fragile X syndrome	1/1,500 males; 1/2,500 females
Neurofibromatosis	1/3,000–1/3,500
Phenylketonuria	1/14,000
Tay-Sachs disease	1/3,000 in Ashkenazic Jews
Multifactorial inheritance	
Cleft lip/palate	1/500–1/1,000
Neural tube defects	1/1,000
Club foot	1/1,000
Pyloric stenosis	3/1,000
Mitochondrial inheritance	
Leber optic neuropathy	Rare
Mitochondrial encephalopathy	Rare
MELAS and MERFF	Rare

From Jorde et al. (1995). *Medical genetics.* St. Louis: C.V. Mosby; adapted by permission.

ease is a recessive disorder, two abnormal recessive or "a" genes are needed to produce a child who has the disease. Therefore, a child with "aa" would have Tay-Sachs disease, a child with "aA" or "Aa" would be a healthy carrier of Tay-Sachs disease, and a child with AA would be a healthy noncarrier.

If two carriers were to mate (aA x Aa), the following combinations could occur: AA, aA or Aa, and aa (Figure 2.6). According to the law of probability, one fourth of the children would be noncarriers (AA), one half would be carriers (aA or Aa), and one fourth would have Tay-Sachs disease (aa). If a carrier mates with a noncarrier (aA x AA), half of the children would be carriers (aA, Aa) and half would be noncarriers (AA); none of the children would have Tay-Sachs disease (Figure 2.6). The significance is that siblings of affected children, even if they are carriers, are unlikely to have affected children of their own unless they mate with another carrier (an unlikely occurrence in these rare diseases).

Remember that the 25% risk of having an affected child when two carriers mate is a probability risk. This does not mean that if a family has one affected child, the next three will be unaffected. Each new pregnancy carries the same 25% risk; the parents could by chance have three affected children in a row or five unaffected ones. In the case of Tay-Sachs disease, carrier

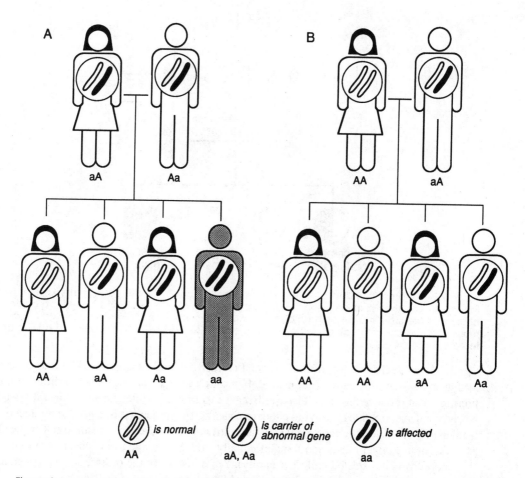

Figure 2.6.   Inheritance of autosomal recessive disorders. Two copies of the abnormal gene (aa) must be present to produce the disease state. A) Two carriers mating will result, on average, in 25% of the children being unaffected, 50% being carriers, and 25% being affected. B) A carrier and a noncarrier mate, resulting in 50% normal children and 50% carriers. No children are affected.

screening and prenatal diagnosis are available, which permit the choice of having nonaffected children (see Chapter 3).

Because it is unlikely for a carrier of an unusual disease to mate with another carrier of the same disease, these types of disorders are quite rare, ranging from 1 in 2,000 to 1 in 200,000 births (McKusick, 1994). However, when intermarriage within an extended family or among ethnically, religiously, or geographically isolated populations occurs, the incidence of these disorders increases markedly, which probably underlies the biblical proscription against marrying one's immediate relatives (Figure 2.7). For example, Tay-Sachs disease tends to strike Jewish children. The origin of the principal mutation leading to Tay-Sachs disease has been traced to Jewish families living in eastern Europe in the early 1800s. Prior to this time, Tay-Sachs disease probably did not occur.

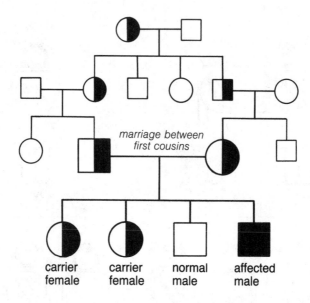

Figure 2.7.   A family tree illustrating the effect of consanguinity (in this case, a marriage between first cousins) on the risk of inheriting an autosomal recessive disorder. If one parent is a carrier, the chance of the other parent being a carrier is usually less than 1 in 300. However, when first cousins marry, the chance of the other parent being a carrier rises to 1 in 8. The risk, then, of having an affected child increases almost 40-fold.

Like Tay-Sachs disease, most autosomal recessive disorders are caused by mutations that lead to an enzyme deficiency of some kind. In most cases, there are a number of different mutations that can produce the same disease. Because these enzyme deficiencies generally lead to biochemical abnormalities involving either the insufficient production of a needed product or the buildup of toxic materials, developmental disabilities or early death may result (see Chapter 19). These disorders affect males and females equally, and there tends to be clustering in families (i.e., more than one affected child per family). Yet, a history of the disease in past generations rarely exists unless blood relatives have married (**consanguinity**).

Autosomal Dominant Disorders

Approximately 4,500 autosomal dominant disorders have been identified, the most common ones having a frequency of 1 in 500 (McKusick, 1994). Autosomal dominant disorders are quite different from autosomal recessive disorders in mechanism, incidence, and clinical characteristics. Because they are caused by a single abnormal allele, individuals with the genotypes AA, Aa, and aA are all affected.

To better understand this, consider achondroplasia, a form of short-limbed dwarfism. Suppose "a" represents the normal recessive gene and "A" indicates the abnormal dominant gene for achondroplasia. If a person with achondroplasia, aA, mates with an unaffected individual, aa, half of the children, statistically speaking, will have the disorder (aA), and half will be unaffected (aa) (Figure 2.8). The unaffected children will not carry the abnormal allele and, therefore, cannot pass it to their children. However, if two affected parents (aA x aA) mate, statistics predict that one half of their offspring would have achondroplasia (aA or Aa), one fourth would

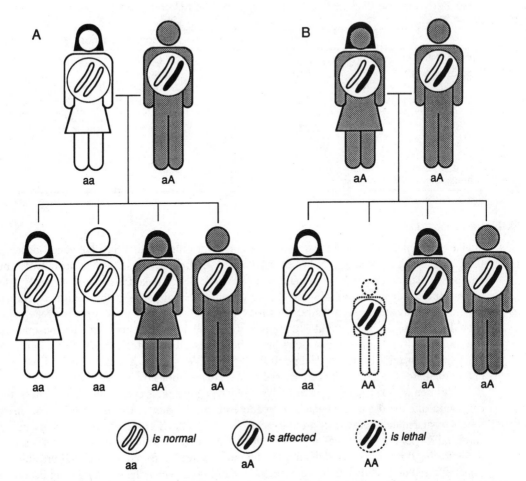

Figure 2.8.   Inheritance of autosomal dominant disorders. Only one copy of the abnormal gene (A) must be present to produce the disease state. A) An affected person marries an unaffected person. Statistically, 50% of the children will be affected and 50% will be unaffected. B) If two affected people marry, 25% of the children will be unaffected, 50% will be affected, and 25% will have an often fatal double dose of the abnormal gene.

be unaffected (aa), and one fourth of the children would have a severe form of dwarfism (AA). This double dose of the achondroplasia allele is usually fatal (Figure 2.8).

Autosomal dominant disorders affect men and women with equal frequency (Table 2.2). They tend to involve structural (physical) abnormalities, rather than enzymatic abnormalities. In affected individuals, there is often a family history of the disease; but about half of affected individuals represent a new mutation. Although individuals with a new mutation will risk passing the mutated gene to their offspring, with rare exceptions, their parents are unaffected and at no greater risk than the general population of having a second affected child.

Table 2.2.   Comparison of autosomal recessive, autosomal dominant, and X-linked inheritance patterns

	Autosomal recessive	Autosomal dominant	X-linked
Number of identified disorders[a]	1,730	4,458	412
Type of disorder	Enzyme deficiency	Structural abnormalities	Mixed
Examples of disorder	Tay-Sachs	Achondroplasia	Fragile X syndrome
	PKU	Neurofibromatosis	Muscular dystrophy
Carrier expresses disorder	No	Yes	Sometimes
Increased risk in other family members from consanguinity	Yes	No	No

[a]Source: McKusick (1994).

X-Linked Disorders

Unlike autosomal recessive and autosomal dominant disorders, which involve genes located on the 22 non-sex chromosomes, X-linked (also called sex-linked) recessive disorders involve mutant genes located on the X, or female, sex chromosome. X-linked disorders primarily affect males. Because males have only one X chromosome, a single dose of the abnormal recessive gene can still cause disease. As females have two X chromosomes, a single recessive allele should not cause disease, provided there is a normal allele on the second X chromosome. Approximately 400 X-linked disorders have been described (McKusick, 1994), including Duchenne muscular dystrophy, hemophilia (Figure 2.9), fragile X syndrome, and red-green color blindness. These disorders are passed between generations by carrier mothers.

Children with Duchenne muscular dystrophy develop a progressive muscle weakness, typically requiring the use of a wheelchair by adolescence (Worton & Brooke, 1995). The disease results from a mutation in the dystrophin gene, located on the X chromosome, which usually ensures stability of the muscle cell membrane. Because the disease affects all of the muscles, eventually the heart muscle and the diaphragmatic muscles needed for circulation and breathing are impaired, leading to early death. Hemophilia is a disease in which the blood-clotting Factor VIII is missing (Jones & Ratnoff, 1991). As a result, a minor injury or accident can lead to uncontrolled bleeding. Injecting a concentrate of the missing clotting factor is needed to stop the bleeding.

Besides causing physical disabilities, some X-linked disorders are associated with cognitive impairments. Approximately 25% of males with mental retardation and 10% of females with learning disabilities are affected by X-linked syndromes (Feng, Lakkis, Devys, et al., 1995). The most common of these is fragile X syndrome (see Chapter 18). Fortunately, not all sex-linked disorders carry these serious consequences (e.g., red-green color blindness).

The mechanism for passing an X-linked trait to the next generation is as follows: Women who have a recessive mutation (Xa) on one of their X chromosomes are designated carriers. Although usually clinically unaffected, they can pass the abnormal gene to their children. Assuming the father is unaffected, the female children born to a carrier mother have a 50% chance of being carriers themselves (i.e., inheriting the mutant X from their mothers and the normal X allele from their fathers) (Figure 2.9). The male children (who have only one X chromosome), however, have a 50% chance of actually having the disorder, if they inherit the X chromosome

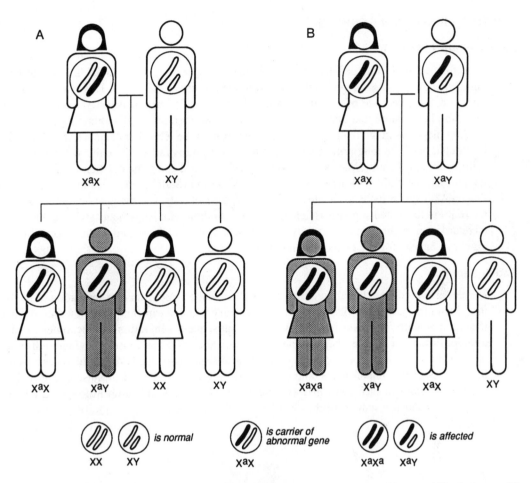

Figure 2.9. Inheritance of sex-linked disorders: A carrier woman mates with an unaffected man. Of the male children, statistically speaking, 50% will be affected and 50% will be unaffected. Of the female children, 50% will be carriers and 50% will be affected.

containing the mutation (X^aY) instead of the normal X chromosome (XY). A family tree frequently reveals that maternal uncles and male siblings have the disease.

Occasionally, females may be affected by X-linked diseases. This is attributable to a phenomenon termed **lyonization,** named after the geneticist Mary Lyon, who questioned why women have the same amount of X-chromosome–derived gene product as men instead of twice as much, as their genetic makeup would suggest. Dr. Lyon postulated that early in embryogenesis, one of the two X chromosomes in each female's cell was inactivated, making every female fetus a mosaic, with some cells containing an active X chromosome derived from her father and others containing an active X derived from her mother. This hypothesis was later proved correct. In most instances, the cells in a woman's body have a fairly equal division between maternally and paternally derived active X chromosomes. However, in a minority of women, the distribution will be very unequal. If the normal X chromosome is inactivated preferentially in cells of a carrier of an X-linked disorder, the woman may manifest the disease.

REVISING MENDELIAN GENETICS

Genomic Imprinting

According to Mendelian genetics, the phenotype, or appearance, of an individual should be the same whether the given gene is inherited from the mother or the father. This is not always the case, however, because of a phenomenon called **genomic imprinting** (Driscoll, 1994). Researchers have found that genes inherited from the mother, although containing the identical DNA sequence as in the father, differ in their imprint on the fetus. For example, if a child inherits a deletion of the long arm of chromosome #15 from his father, the child will have Prader-Willi syndrome (Knoll, Wagstaff, & Lalande, 1993), but if the same deletion is inherited from the mother, the child will develop Angelman syndrome (Saitoh, Harada, Jinno, et al., 1994). Prader-Willi syndrome is associated with short stature, obesity, and mental retardation requiring intermittent to limited supports (Nicholls, 1993); children with Angelman syndrome have mental retardation requiring more extensive supports, as well as epilepsy and a gait abnormality. The exact mechanism for this phenomenon remains unclear.

Anticipation

Mendel also predicted that an inherited trait will look the same from one generation to the next in a given family. In a few disorders associated with expanded triplet repeats, however, the manifestation actually increases in severity in each subsequent generation—a phenomenon called **anticipation.** For example, the expanded triplet repeat (CAG) that causes Huntington disease—an autosomal dominant, progressive neurological disease associated with a movement disorder (chorea), cognitive impairments, and behavior disturbances (La Spada, Paulson, & Fischbeck, 1994)—increases in each generation (Figure 2.10). The greater the number of repeats, the more severe are the manifestations of the disorder.

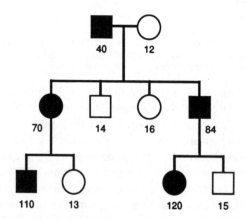

Figure 2.10. Triplet repeat expansion (anticipation) in a Huntington disease kindred. This disorder is inherited as an autosomal dominant trait. Numbers indicate the number of CAG triplet repeats. Normal range is 11–34 and affected 37–121. In subsequent generations, the number of triplet repeats increases in affected individuals. Shaded areas indicate affected individuals. Squares represent males; circles, females.

MITOCHONDRIAL INHERITANCE

Each cell contains several hundred mitochondria in its cytoplasm (Figure 1.1). Mitochondria produce the energy needed for cellular function through a complex process termed **oxidative-phosphorylation.** Some scientists believe that mitochondria were originally independent micro-organisms that invaded our bodies during the process of human evolution and then developed a symbiotic relationship with the cells in the human body. They are unique among cellular organelles in that they possess their own DNA, which is circular and contains genes different from those found in nuclear DNA (Figure 2.11). A mutation in a mitochondrial gene can result in defective energy production and severe diseases (Shoffner & Wallace, 1992), an example being MELAS (mitochondrial encephalomyelopathy, lactic acidosis, and stroke-like episodes), a progressive neurological disorder marked by episodes of stroke and dementia (Tulinius, Holme, Kristiansson, et al., 1991). Other mitochondrial disorders lead to blindness, deafness, and muscle weakness (DeVries, Went, Bruyn, et al., 1996; Gold & Rapin, 1994; Harding, 1991; Hu, Qui, Wu, et al., 1991).

Because only eggs, not sperm, contain cytoplasm, all mitochondria are inherited from one's mother. Mitochondrial disorders are passed from generally unaffected mothers to virtually all of their children, both male and female. As expected, men affected with mitochondrial disorders cannot pass the trait to their children (Figure 2.12).

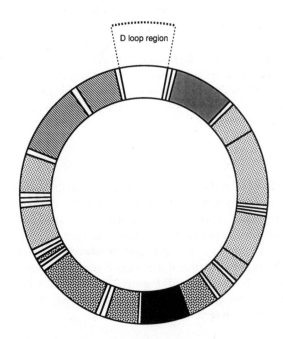

Figure 2.11.   Mitochondrial DNA genome. The genes code for various enzyme complexes involved in energy production in the cell. (Key: ▨ Complex I genes [NADH dehydrogenase]; ■ Complex III genes [ubiquinol: cytochrome c oxidoreductase]; □ Transfer RNA genes; ▨ Complex IV genes [cytochrome c oxidase]; ■ Complex V genes [ATP synthase]; ▨ Ribosomal RNA genes.)

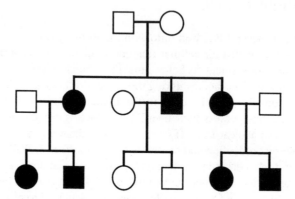

Figure 2.12.   Mitochondrial inheritance. As mitochondria are inherited exclusively from the mother, defects in mitochondrial disease will be passed on from the mother to her children, as illustrated in this pedigree. Shaded areas are affected. Squares are males, circles females.

MULTIFACTORIAL INHERITANCE

Although bright parents have a greater chance of having bright children, and obese parents more often have obese children, the interaction of genetics with the prenatal and postnatal environments (**multifactorial inheritance**) allows for many possible outcomes in certain traits and disorders. Height, blood pressure, and diabetes are also inherited in this manner, as are spina bifida, cleft palate, and pyloric stenosis (Bishop, 1990).

Pyloric stenosis, a malformation of the stomach muscle that leads to a blockage in the passage of food from the stomach to the small intestine, is thought to occur when an intrauterine viral infection, male gender, and certain genetic factors are all present. A viral infection alone, for example, will not produce the defect. However, the combination of the three factors increases the risk of pyloric stenosis from 3 in 1,000 births to 1 in 20 in a family with a previously affected child (Mitchell & Risch, 1993).

SUMMARY

Genes, composed of DNA and located in chromosomes in the nucleus of cells, are the blueprint for the construction and functioning of our bodies. When mutations or mistakes occur in genes, disorders frequently occur. A number of developmental disabilities result from single-gene defects, which are inherited as autosomal dominant, autosomal recessive, or X-linked. Variations in this classic pattern have led to new concepts of inheritance, termed *imprinting* and *anticipation*. In addition, it has been discovered that mitochondria have separate DNA from that found in the nucleus and carry their own risk of disease. Multifactorial inheritance, which takes into account the interaction between heredity and environment, has also been identified as a cause of developmental disabilities in recent years.

REFERENCES

Bishop, D.T. (1990). Multifactorial inheritance. In A.E.H. Emery & D.L. Rimoin (Eds.), *Principles and practice of medical genetics* (2nd ed., Vol. 1). New York: Churchill Livingstone.

Caskey, C.T., Pizzuti, A., Fu, Y., et al. (1992).Triplet repeat mutations in human disease. *Science, 256,* 784–789.

Cooper, D.N., & Krawczak, M. (1990). The mutational spectrum of single base-pair substitutions causing human genetic disease: Patterns and predictions. *Human Genetics, 85,* 55–74.

DeVries, D.D., Went, L.N., Bruyn, G.W., et al. (1996). Genetic and biochemical impairment of mitochondrial complex I activity in a family with Leber hereditary optic neuropathy and hereditary spastic dystonia. *American Journal of Human Genetics, 58,* 703–711.

Driscoll, D.J. (1994). Genomic imprinting in humans. In T. Friedmann (Ed.), *Molecular genetic medicine* (Vol. 4, pp. 37–77). Orlando, FL: Academic Press.

Feng, Y., Lakkis, L., Devys, D., et al. (1995). Quantitative comparison of FMRI gene expression in normal and premutation alleles. *American Journal of Human Genetics, 56,* 106–113.

Gold, M., & Rapin, I. (1994). Non-Mendelian mitochondrial inheritance as a cause of progressive genetic sensorineural hearing loss. *International Journal of Pediatric Otorhinolaryngology, 30,* 91–104.

Harding, A.E. (1991). Neurological disease and mitochondrial genes. *Trends in Neurosciences, 14,* 279–284.

Hu, D.N., Qui, W.Q., Wu, B.T., et al. (1991). Genetic aspects of antibiotic induced deafness: Mitochondrial inheritance. *Journal of Medical Genetics, 28,* 79–83.

Jones, P.K., & Ratnoff, O.D. (1991). The changing prognosis of classic hemophilia. *Annals of Internal Medicine, 114,* 641–648.

Jorde, L.B., Carey, J.C., & White, R.W. (1995). *Medical genetics.* St. Louis: C.V. Mosby.

Kaback, M., Lim-Steele, J., Dabholkar, D., et al. (1993). Tay-Sachs disease-carrier screening, prenatal diagnosis and the molecular era: An international perspective, 1970 to 1993. *Journal of the American Medical Association, 270,* 2307–2315.

King, R.A., Rotter, J.I., & Motulsky, A.G. (Eds.). (1992). *The genetic basis of common diseases.* New York: Oxford University Press.

Knoll, J.H., Wagstaff, J., & Lalande, M. (1993). Cytogenetic and molecular studies in the Prader-Willi and Angelman syndromes: An overview. *American Journal of Medical Genetics, 46,* 2–6.

La Spada, A.R., Paulson, H.L., & Fischbeck, K.H. (1994). Trinucleotide repeat expansion in neurological disease. *Annals of Neurology, 36,* 814–822.

McKusick, V.A. (1994). *Mendelian inheritance in man: Catalogs of autosomal dominant, autosomal recessive, and X-linked phenotypes* (11th ed.). Baltimore: Johns Hopkins University Press.

Mitchell, L.E., & Risch, N. (1993). The genetics of infantile hypertrophic pyloric stenosis. A reanalysis. *American Journal of Diseases of Children, 147,* 1203–1211.

Nicholls, R.D. (1993). Genomic imprinting and candidate genes in the Prader-Willi and Angelman syndromes. *Current Opinion in Genetic Development, 3,* 445–456.

Risch, N., Reich, E.W., Wishnick, M.M., et al. (1987). Spontaneous mutation and parental age in humans. *American Journal of Human Genetics, 41,* 218–248.

Saitoh, S., Harada, N., Jinno, Y., et al. (1994). Molecular and clinical study of 61 Angelman syndrome patients. *American Journal of Medical Genetics, 52,* 158–163.

Shoffner, J.M., & Wallace, D.C. (1992). Mitochondrial genetics: Principles and practice. *American Journal of Human Genetics, 51,* 1179–1186.

Tulinius, M.H., Holme, E., Kristiansson, B., et al. (1991). Mitochondrial encephalomyopathies in childhood: II. Clinical manifestations and syndromes. *Journal of Pediatrics, 119,* 251–259.

Vogel, F., & Rathenberg, R. (1975). Spontaneous mutation in man. *Advances in Human Genetics, 5,* 223–318.

Worton, R.G., & Brooke, M.H. (1995). The X-linked muscular dystrophies. In C.R. Scriver, A.L. Beaudet, W.S. Sly, & D. Valle (Eds.), *The metabolic and molecular bases of inherited disease* (7th ed., Vol. 3, pp. 4195–4266). New York: McGraw-Hill.

Birth Defects, Prenatal Diagnosis, and Fetal Therapy

3

Mark L. Batshaw
Nancy C. Rose

Upon completion of this chapter, the reader will:

- be aware of the maternal serum screening tests used for identifying birth defects
- understand the use of ultrasound in fetal assessment
- be knowledgeable about the risks and benefits of chorionic villus sampling, amniocentesis, and percutaneous umbilical blood sampling
- be aware of experimental prenatal diagnostic procedures, including preimplantation diagnosis and the extraction of fetal cells from maternal circulation
- know the potential uses of carrier detection for genetic disease
- be informed about the prospects for fetal therapy

Although the vast majority of pregnancies do not require and, in fact, will not benefit from prenatal diagnostic techniques, there are those families for whom the option of prenatal diagnosis is very important. For families at risk, these techniques can provide reassurance that the fetus is unlikely to be affected. Even when prenatal diagnostic testing reveals an affected fetus, this early detection can provide the opportunity for the mother to weigh her reproductive options. If a family chooses to carry an affected fetus to term, prenatal diagnosis allows them to prepare both psychologically and practically for the baby's birth and allows the physician to plan the delivery, management, and special care needed in the newborn period.

Before suggesting that a pregnant woman undergo a prenatal diagnostic procedure, the obstetrician often refers her for genetic counseling services. During the initial visit, the geneticist or genetic counselor will determine by taking a medical history whether the fetus is at significant risk for a specific disorder and whether the disorder is diagnosable prenatally. Perhaps not surprising is that the most common indicator for prenatal testing is advanced maternal age (Table 3.1). In women who are 45 years old, the risk of bearing a fetus with Down syndrome or another chromosomal abnormality is about 1 in 20 live births, compared with a risk of 1 in 1,500 for women between 20 and 25 years old (Figure 3.1). At age 35, the risk of trisomy 21 and other

Table 3.1.   Common indications for amniocentesis/CVS

- Mother 35 years old or older
- Previous offspring with a chromosomal abnormality
- Increased risk of a genetic disorder (e.g., previously affected child, positive carrier screening, family history)
- Increased risk based on MSAFP or triple marker screening
- Anatomical abnormality on ultrasound

chromosomal abnormalities (1 in 270) is considered sufficiently high to warrant genetic counseling and the offering of a prenatal diagnostic procedure (Hook, 1981). For younger women who have already had one child with a chromosomal disorder, prenatal diagnosis is offered in subsequent pregnancies (Terje Lie, Wilcox, & Skjerven, 1994).

If a non-Mendelian birth defect is identified in a previous child, the family runs an 8-fold increased risk of having another child with that defect in a subsequent pregnancy (Terje Lie et al., 1994). Thus, if they have had one child with meningomyelocele (spina bifida), a risk of 1 in 1,000 in the general population, the chance of having a second affected child increases to about 1 in 125. If they have had a child with a Mendelian birth defect, the recurrence risk ranges from 0% to 50%, depending on the inheritance pattern (see Chapter 2).

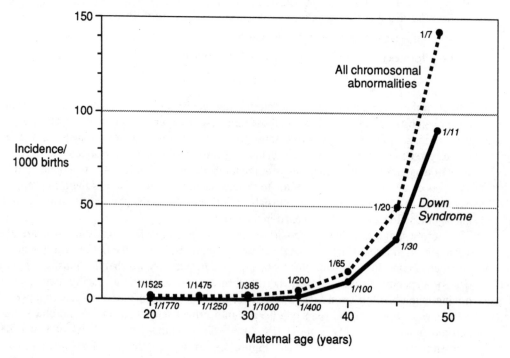

Figure 3.1.   Risk of trisomy 21 and all chromosomal abnormalities in pregnant women of various ages. The risk increases markedly after 35 years of age (Hook, 1981).

It is important to emphasize that prenatal diagnosis does not ensure a healthy baby; it serves only to detect the presence or absence of a specific disorder for which a test can be performed. It should be noted that, despite these potential risks, 98% of all prenatal diagnostic tests performed will indicate an unaffected fetus.

There are several prenatal diagnostic tools used to identify a serious medical problem in a fetus, including **real time ultrasound, chorionic villus sampling (CVS), amniocentesis,** and **percutaneous umbilical blood sampling,** that reveal many birth defects caused by chromosomal disorders (e.g., Down syndrome); congenital anomalies (e.g., meningomyelocele); and **inborn errors of metabolism** (e.g., phenylketonuria [PKU]). These techniques can be divided into those that visualize the fetus and those that analyze fetal cells or fluids (D'Alton & DeCherney, 1993; Garmel & D'Alton, 1994). Two thirds of pregnant women now undergo ultrasound, and approximately half of all pregnant women 35 years or older undergo amniocentesis or CVS.

This chapter examines population screening tests for birth defects and the benefits and risks of prenatal diagnostic techniques available to detect specific disorders associated with developmental disabilities. Also discussed are some experimental techniques, including preimplantation diagnosis and circulating fetal cell analysis. In addition, methods for carrier detection to determine the risk couples have of conceiving a child with a specific genetic disease are explained. The chapter concludes with a discussion of the prospects for fetal therapy.

POPULATION SCREENING: MATERNAL SERUM TESTING

Population screening tests are meant to evaluate a large group of individuals who are at low risk for a particular problem. Once identified by the screen as being at increased risk for the disorder, a specific diagnostic test is performed. A common example of population screening is cholesterol blood testing to detect an increased risk for heart disease. In pregnant women, population screening involves a serum test at 16–18 weeks' gestation to screen fetuses for an increased risk of having meningomyelocele, Down syndrome, and trisomy 18 (Figure 3.2) (Rose & Mennuti, 1993a). The test measures three substances in the mother's blood that, in combination, suggest an increased risk of the fetus being affected by one of these disorders. A venous blood specimen is obtained in the obstetrician's office and sent for biochemical testing. Results are available in a few days. A positive result, however, is not diagnostic; rather, a thorough evaluation, including genetic counseling, ultrasound examination, and/or amniocentesis, is needed to confirm a diagnosis.

Screening for Neural Tube Defects

Alpha-fetoprotein (AFP) is an albumin-like substance usually produced solely by the fetus. Its function is unknown. In a typical pregnancy, some AFP may be found in the mother's circulation; however, when the fetus has an open abdominal wall (**gastroschisis** or **omphalocele**), a neural tube defect (NTD)(meningomyelocele or anencephaly), or certain other disorders such as congenital nephrosis (kidney disease) or significant antenatal bleeding, excess AFP leaks from the fetal defect into the amniotic fluid and from there enters the maternal bloodstream. Five to seven percent of pregnant women have a positive screen using maternal serum alpha-fetoprotein (MSAFP), placing them at an increased risk for carrying a fetus with an NTD.

If a woman has an elevated MSAFP level, the test is generally repeated, provided she is not at more than 20 weeks' gestation or does not have an extremely elevated result. (In these instances,

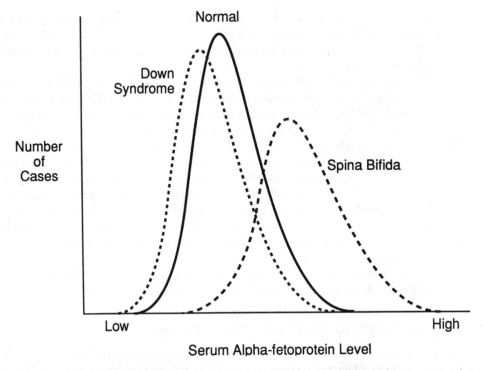

Figure 3.2.   Distribution of MSAFP levels from women in the second trimester of pregnancy who are carrying: a fetus with Down syndrome, an unaffected fetus, and a fetus with an open NTD (spina bifida). In general, women carrying a fetus with Down syndrome have lower MSAFP levels than normal, and women carrying children with neural tube defects have higher than normal levels.

prenatal diagnostic tests are immediately performed if desired.) If the repeat specimen is normal, the pregnancy does not need to be further evaluated. If, however, her MSAFP level appears to be increasing, an ultrasound is performed to confirm gestational age and viability and to look for congenital anomalies. At this point, genetic counseling is used to discuss the risks and benefits of performing an amniocentesis, which measures amniotic fluid levels of AFP and the enzyme acetylcholinesterase to diagnose an open NTD (Wald, Cuckle, & Nanchahal, 1989). Although there are a significant number of false positive results, MSAFP screening detects approximately 75% of open abdominal wall defects and about 85% of open meningomyeloceles (Elias, 1992).

Screening for Down Syndrome and Trisomy 18

Although the risk of carrying a fetus with Down syndrome increases with maternal age, 80% of all children with Down syndrome are born to mothers under 35 years of age (Elias, 1992). This seeming paradox can be explained by the higher rate of pregnancies in younger women and the fact that there are fewer prenatal diagnostic options available to them. Until the mid-1980s, there was no way of screening for chromosomal abnormalities in these young women. Since then, a second trimester population screening test has been made available that measures three substances in the mother's serum: AFP, human chorionic gonadotrophin (hCG), and unconjugated estriol (Haddow, Palomaki, Knight, et al., 1992) (Figure 3.2). A significantly *low* MSAFP level can detect about 20% of fetal Down syndrome in women under 35 years of age; when combined with serum testing for hCG and unconjugated estriol, the detection rate reaches 60% (Aitken, Wallace, Crossley, et al., 1996; Rose & Mennuti, 1993a). This increases to 90% in women more than 35 years of age.

As with screening for NTDs, once a woman has a positive screening test, she is first offered genetic counseling and ultrasound to confirm the gestational age and viability of the fetus and to rule out fetal physical anomalies. Here again, there is a high false positive rate. She is then offered an amniocentesis for chromosome studies (Ashwood, Cheng, & Luthy, 1987). For women who are more than 35 years of age, it is standard care to offer prenatal diagnosis for chromosomal anomalies. However, some of these women will use the maternal serum screening test to revise their risk before deciding whether to undergo amniocentesis. In addition to detecting trisomy 21, the three markers together detect about 60% of trisomy 18 in families at high risk (Haddow et al., 1992).

REAL TIME ULTRASOUND

Approximately two thirds of pregnant women undergo real time ultrasonography (ultrasound) during pregnancy (Garmel & D'Alton, 1994). First trimester (less than 12 weeks' gestation) ultrasound can be performed to determine gestational age, fetal viability, and the location of the pregnancy. It is generally not possible to visualize a birth defect so early in pregnancy unless it is extremely severe. In the second trimester, after 16–18 weeks, ultrasound can be performed to evaluate the fetus for large birth defects as well as to establish placental location and amniotic fluid volume.

Ultrasonography utilizes sound waves to produce a moving image of the fetus. The sound waves penetrate the body and are reflected back as "echoes" when they reach structures of varying densities. This allows visualization of the placenta, individual fetal body parts, and fetal movement. The improved resolution of ultrasound equipment has permitted an increasingly detailed evaluation of the fetus. It can diagnose many major malformations, including meningomyelocele, anencephaly, microcephaly, hydrocephalus, heart defects, and limb abnormalities (Platt, Feuchtbaum, Filly, et al., 1992). For example, in meningomyelocele, the abnormally shaped vertebral bodies can be seen in 90% of cases (Platt et al., 1992) (Figure 3.3). In major malformation syndromes such as trisomies 13, 18, and 21, ultrasound can detect heart defects, brain cysts, and abnormal limbs (Table 3.2) (Nicolaides, Snijders, Gosden, et al., 1992; Norton, 1994). In addition, by comparing the gestational age of the fetus with his or her body size, the physician can determine whether the fetus is growing appropriately. Movement and breathing also can be used to assess fetal well-being (Sanders, Chin, Parness, et al., 1985).

CHORIONIC VILLUS SAMPLING

CVS obtains minute biopsies of the **chorion**, the outermost membrane surrounding the embryo, to diagnose birth defects. Because the fetal cells of the chorion are rapidly dividing, they can be analyzed directly and relatively quickly (i.e., a few days) (Blakemore, 1988). CVS is performed during the first trimester, before the mother is noticeably pregnant and before she feels fetal movement.

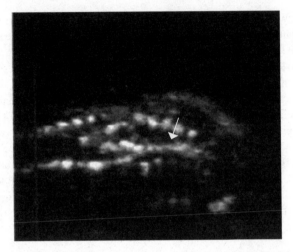

Figure 3.3a.   Ultrasound showing a fetus with meningomyelocele at 20 weeks' gestation. The open spine is indicated with an arrow (From Rose, N.C., & Mennuti, M.T. [1994]. Alpha-fetoprotein and neural tube defects. In J.J. Sciarra & P.V. Dilts, Jr. [Eds.], *Gynecology and obstetrics* [Rev. ed., p. 4]. Philadelphia: J.B. Lippincott; reprinted by permission.)

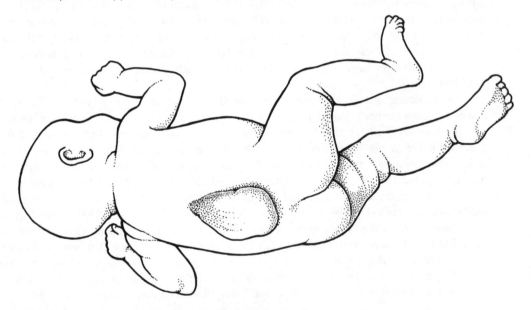

Figure 3.3b.   Illustration of a baby with meningomyelocele.

Chorionic villi can be obtained under ultrasound guidance by aspiration through a transcervical catheter (Figure 3.4) or a transabdominal needle (Jackson, Zachary, Fowler, et al., 1992). Both methods seem equally effective and have similar complication rates. Obstetricians usually choose a method based on their experience and the location of the placenta. Physicians using the transcervical method insert a tube into the vagina, passing it through the cervix into the uterus, where it uses suction to remove a tiny amount of chorionic tissue. In the transabdominal tech-

Table 3.2.   Ultrasound findings in certain chromosomal abnormalities

---

Trisomy 21
Abnormal gastrointestinal tract
Congenital heart defect
Excess neck skin

Trisomy 18
Growth retardation
Excessive amniotic fluid
Clenched hands with overlapping fingers
Rocker-bottom feet
Congenital heart defect

Trisomy 13
Midline facial defect
Cleft lip and palate
Congenital heart defect
Extra finger or toe
Cystic kidneys

Adapted from D'Alton & DeCherney (1993).

nique, a needle is directed, under ultrasound guidance, through the abdominal and uterine walls into the placenta and directly aspirates tissues from the chorion.

CVS increases the risk of a first trimester spontaneous pregnancy loss by 1% (Goldberg, Porter, & Golbus, 1990). In addition, CVS is associated, on rare occasions (in fewer than 1 of every 1,000 cases), with limb reduction defects (short, abnormal limbs) (Burton, Schultz, & Burd, 1992; Firth, Boyd, Chamberlain, et al., 1994),which may be a consequence of the placental bleeding or hypoxia that follows the procedure. (If this bleeding disrupts the blood flow to the placenta and reduces blood pressure to the farthest embryonic structures [the limbs], abnormalities may result.) These abnormalities seem to occur more commonly when the CVS is performed before 10 weeks' gestation and by a less experienced operator. As a result, CVS is now generally performed between 10 and 12 weeks' gestation.

Another difficulty with CVS is that the chromosomal analysis from the chorion may be different from that found in the fetus. This is the result of the chorion being a separate fetal organ, derived from the first cell of the pregnancy. It may, on occasion, have a different chromosomal constitution from the fetus. For example, 1% of CVS procedures detect chromosomal mosaicism, a mixture of cells with different numbers of chromosomes (Ledbetter, Martin, Verlinsky, et al., 1990). This requires genetic counseling, followed by amniocentesis, to determine the fetal karyotype. In these cases, even if the fetal karyotype turns out to be normal, the fetus is still at increased risk for intrauterine growth retardation and needs to be monitored carefully.

AMNIOCENTESIS

Usually performed between 14 and 18 weeks after the last menstrual period, amniocentesis involves inserting a needle through the maternal abdominal wall into the amniotic sac and withdrawing 1–2 ounces of fluid (Figure 3.5). Ultrasound monitoring is usually performed prior to the procedure to screen for significant birth defects and during the procedure to help guide the

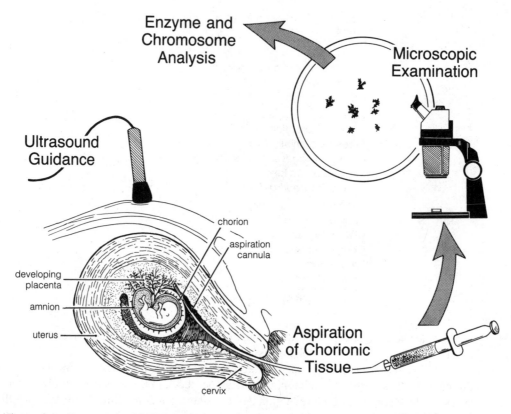

Enzyme and
Chromosome
Analysis

Microscopic
Examination

Ultrasound
Guidance

chorion

aspiration
cannula

developing
placenta

amnion

uterus

Aspiration
of Chorionic
Tissue

cervix

Figure 3.4.   Transcervical CVS is performed between 9 and 11 weeks' gestation. A hollow instrument is inserted through the vagina and passed into the uterus, guided by ultrasound. A small amount of chorionic tissue is removed by suction. The tissue is then examined under a microscope to make sure it is sufficient. Karyotype, enzyme, and DNA analyses can be performed without first growing the cells. Results are available in a few days.

needle away from the fetus. Testing of the amniotic fluid AFP level takes only a few days; results of the karyotyping tests are generally available in 10–14 days.

The risks of amniocentesis to the fetus and mother are quite low. The risk of miscarriage is considered to be 0.5%–1% above the spontaneous miscarriage rate (Canadian Collaborative CVS-Amniocentesis Clinical Trial Group, 1989; Tabor, Madsen, & Obel, 1986). There is also a very small risk of fetal morbidity (i.e., infants born prematurely or with lung or orthopedic deformities resulting from chronic leakage of amniotic fluid). With newer techniques, amniocentesis can now be done as early as 12 weeks' gestation. Early amniocentesis carries about a 1% increased risk of miscarriage for the fetus.

CVS and amniocentesis are simply techniques for obtaining fetally derived tissue and fluid. Depending on the disorder being investigated, any of a number of tests are conducted after collection. Following CVS, testing can be performed immediately. Following amniocentesis, however, the fetal-derived cells must be separated and placed into a culture medium to grow for about a week until there are enough cells for the testing. Tests include karyotype (chromosome) analysis, enzyme determination, and DNA studies. In fact, because chromosomal abnormalities

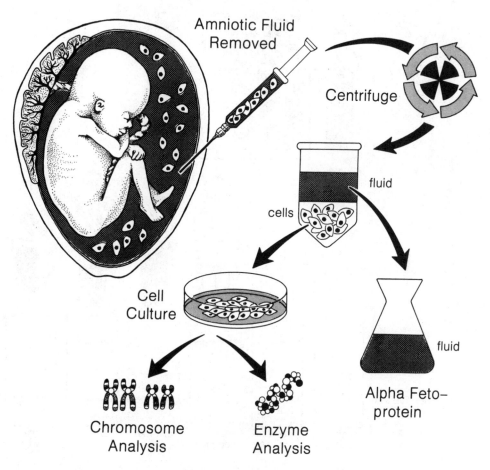

Figure 3.5. Amniocentesis. Approximately 1–2 ounces of amniotic fluid are removed at 14–18 weeks' gestation. The fluid is spun in a centrifuge to separate the fluid from the fetal cells. The fluid is used to test for a NTD. The cells are grown for a week, and then karyotype, enzyme, or DNA analyses can be performed. Results are usually available in about 10–14 days.

are the most common form of birth defect that can be identified prenatally, karyotype analysis is performed routinely, even when a chromosomal disorder is not the primary reason for the prenatal diagnostic procedure. In order to diagnose an inborn error of metabolism, the fetal cells are used to measure a specific enzyme or to analyze the DNA pattern of the cells for a mutation (Figure 3.6). DNA studies also can be used to detect mutations associated with a number of other genetic disorders, including fragile X syndrome, muscular dystrophy, and neurofibromatosis (Sutherland, Gedeon, Kornman, et al., 1991).

PERCUTANEOUS UMBILICAL BLOOD SAMPLING

Percutaneous umbilical blood sampling (PUBS or cordocentesis) is generally performed after the 18th week of gestation. Under ultrasound guidance, a needle is inserted through the abdomi-

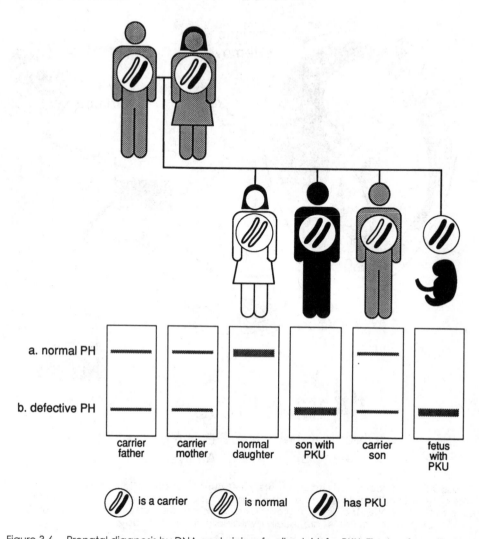

Figure 3.6.   Prenatal diagnosis by DNA analysis in a family at risk for PKU. The top figure illustrates the members of the family. One of their sons has already been diagnosed as having PKU. They have two other children who are unaffected. As this is an autosomal recessively inherited disorder, both parents must be carriers (i.e., each has one normal and one defective gene for phenylalanine hydroxylase [PH], the enzyme deficient in PKU). The mother is now pregnant with her fourth child and has undergone CVS to determine whether her fetus is also affected. The other members of the family were also tested using blood specimens. The bottom figure shows the results of this testing. A procedure was done in which the DNA containing the gene for PH was broken into segments of different lengths depending on whether the enzyme was unaffected or defective. The segments appear as bands on a special gel. In this case, the upper band (a) is associated with the gene for the normal PH while the (b) band is associated with the defective PH gene. As expected, both the father and mother were shown to be carriers, each with one normal PH (a) band and one defective PH (b) band. Their daughter was shown to be normal with a double (a) band. Their first son is known to have PKU; as expected, he had a double defective PH (b) band. Their next son was found to be a carrier like his parents with one (a) band and one (b) band. Finally, the fetus was found to be affected, with two (b) bands. This infant will be treated from birth with a low-phenylalanine diet.

nal and uterine walls and into the umbilical vein to sample fetal blood (Figure 3.7). Initially developed to detect intrauterine infections, PUBS is now used to evaluate fetal anemias and blood type in rhesus (Rh)-sensitized pregnancies as well (see Chapter 5) (Hickok & Mills, 1992). It carries about a 1% increased risk of miscarriage for the fetus.

PREIMPLANTATION DIAGNOSIS AND CIRCULATING FETAL CELL DIAGNOSIS

In the 1990s, a number of innovative prenatal diagnostic tools are being tested. Preimplantation diagnosis is used, on occasion, in conjunction with in vitro fertilization (the fertilization of an egg in a "test tube") to detect a birth defect in the fertilized egg before implantation (Handyside,

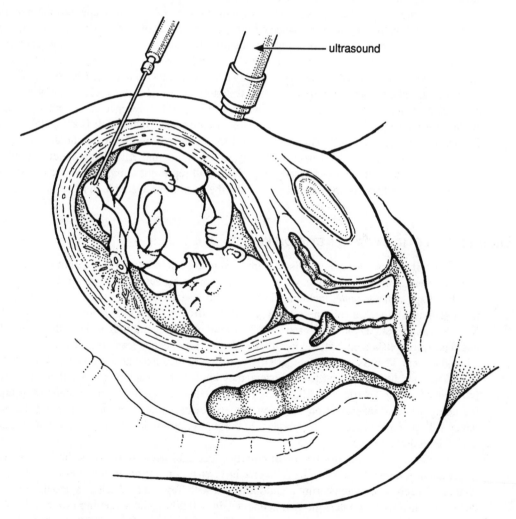

Figure 3.7.   Percutaneous umbilical blood sampling (PUBS). Using ultrasound guidance, the needle is inserted through the abdominal and uterine walls and into the umbilical vein to obtain fetal blood.

Lesko, Tarin, et al., 1992). Two methods are available, embryo biopsy and polar body biopsy, both of which are expensive and technologically difficult. In embryo biopsy, a single cell is removed from an 8- or 16-cell embryo that has resulted from in vitro fertilization (Figure 3.8). The removal of one cell does not appear to harm the embryo. This cell can then be tested, using DNA methodology, for very specific birth defects in which the mutation is known. If found to be unaffected, the embryo is implanted into the mother's uterus. Polar body biopsy, a variation of embryo biopsy, examines the polar body that is released and removed from the mother at the same time as the egg (see Chapter 1) for the suspected mutation (Monk, 1993). If the polar body is found not to carry the suspected mutation, the egg is assumed to be unaffected and may be fertilized and implanted. Because polar body diagnosis examines the DNA of the egg prior to fertilization, only X-linked disorders can be diagnosed.

Circulating fetal cell diagnosis involves capturing fetal cells that escape into the maternal circulation and testing them for a suspected birth defect (Bianchi, 1994; Simpson, 1993). This technique uses a sophisticated cell-sorting machine that separates fetal red blood cells from those of the mother during the late first or early second trimester. This is possible because red blood cells in the fetus have nuclei, whereas those in the mother do not (see Chapter 1). The nucleated fetal red cells are separated and then tested using a molecular biology method termed fluorescent in situ hybridization, or FISH, which can detect the presence and number of copies of chromosomes #21, #13, #18, X, and Y (Geifman-Holtzman, Blatman, & Bianci, 1994; Ward, Gersen, Carelli, et al., 1993). This can be used to diagnose a number of disorders, including Down syndrome, trisomy 13, trisomy 18, Turner syndrome, and Klinefelter syndrome. If this method proves accurate and technically feasible, it will represent a major advance for prenatal diagnosis because there is no risk to the fetus and the results are available in a few days.

CARRIER DETECTION FOR GENETIC DISEASES

Carrier detection tests for genetic disease are used to complement prenatal diagnostic measures and are often applied to a number of severe, life-shortening autosomal recessive disorders for which therapy is inadequate, including Tay-Sachs disease, cystic fibrosis (CF), various types of thalassemias, and sickle cell anemia (Brock, 1994; Brown, Houck, Jeziorowska, et al., 1993; Kaback, Lim-Steele, Dabholkar, et al., 1993). In the past, prenatal diagnosis of these disorders could be accomplished only after a family had already produced at least one affected child. Now, a blood test can identify carriers of these diseases before they have an affected child. If a couple is screened and both are found to be carriers, they know that in each pregnancy there is a one in four risk of having an affected child. They then can consider a number of reproductive options, including artificial insemination with donor sperm or egg, adoption, or monitoring the pregnancy with prenatal diagnostic techniques. In the future, preimplantation diagnosis may also be available to these couples.

Tay-Sachs screening has been particularly successful because it can be limited to a relatively small number of people, the Ashkenazic Jewish population (Kaback et al., 1993). The chance of a Jewish couple bearing a child affected with Tay-Sachs disease is about 1 in 2,500. (Among non-Jewish couples, the risk is about 1 in 360,000.) The screening program has been well accepted and has proven to be extremely successful in identifying couples at risk. As a result, very few Jewish infants are being born with this rapidly fatal disease.

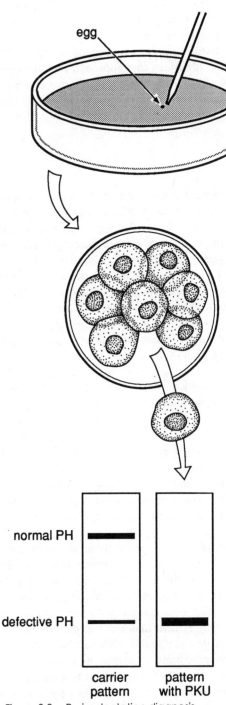

egg

A woman's egg is fertilized in a Petri dish.

When the resulting embryo reaches the eight-cell stage, one cell is removed for testing.

normal PH

defective PH

carrier pattern

pattern with PKU

DNA from this cell is analyzed to determine if it contains the genetic defect in question (*e.g.*, phenylalanine hydroxylase [PH]). If the defect is present, the embryo will not be implanted.

Figure 3.8. Preimplantation diagnosis.

A more complicated situation has been encountered in developing genetic screening for CF (Brock, 1994). CF is the most common inborn error of metabolism in the Caucasian population, with an incidence of 1 in 2,000 and a carrier frequency of 1 in 25. Affected individuals can develop a severe, progressive multi-organ system disease, and survival beyond young adulthood is rare. Although there is great hope for gene therapy trials, this approach remains unproven (Knowles, Hohneker, Zhou, et al., 1995). Unlike Tay-Sachs disease, there are a number of genetic mutations that can cause CF, so the screening test is more complex and will identify only about 85% of carriers. Therefore, CF screening during pregnancy is offered only when a close relative is affected.

FETAL THERAPY

The ultimate goal of prenatal diagnosis and carrier detection is to prevent severe disabilities by identifying affected fetuses and treating them before birth (Adzick & Harrison, 1994). As of 1997, this approach has been successful in only a few instances. The first disease to be treated in a fetus was an inborn error of metabolism, multiple carboxylase deficiency (see Chapter 19), which is responsive to the vitamin biotin. A mother who had previously given birth to one affected child was found by prenatal diagnosis to be carrying a second affected child. The mother received oral biotin therapy from 23 weeks' gestation onward, and the child continued to receive this therapy after birth (Evans & Schulman, 1991). This child has done well, as has a child with vitamin B_{12}-responsive methylmalonic acidemia (van der Meer, Spaapen, Fowler, et al., 1990). Unfortunately, most inborn errors of metabolism are not vitamin responsive. However, advances in enzyme replacement and gene therapy offer the promise of improved treatment in the future.

In 1996, the first *in utero* transplantation for enzyme replacement was performed. Bone marrow from the father was transplanted into a 16-week-old fetus who had been found by prenatal molecular diagnosis to have severe combined immunodeficiency ("Bubble Baby" syndrome). His brother, also affected by this X-linked disorder, had died previously of a severe infection at 7 months of age. The bone marrow transplant "took" and produced the missing enzyme; and the child, age 11 months at the time of the report, is doing well without additional therapy (Flake, Roncarolo, Puck, et al., 1996). The fetus is particularly well suited to transplantation and gene therapy as it is immunologically tolerant and therefore less likely to reject a **viral vector** or a foreign organ. Ultimately, it may even be possible to provide therapy to the preimplantation embryo (less than 14 days from fertilization) obtained through in vitro fertilization (Edwards & Hollands, 1988).

The first success in fetal surgery involved shunting blockages of the fetal urinary tract (Figure 3.9) (Crombleholme, 1994; Manning, Harrison, Rodeck, et al., 1986). If untreated, these malformations obstruct the passage of fetal urine, resulting in bladder enlargement and kidney damage. In addition, because urine is the primary constituent of amniotic fluid, decreased production of urine leads to underdeveloped lungs, which are squeezed by the shrunken uterine cavity. To treat this disorder, a shunt is placed in the fetal bladder to drain urine directly into the amniotic sac and decompress the fetal bladder. There is about a 50% survival rate with this procedure, which is a significant improvement over the almost universal mortality that results if this obstruction is not treated prenatally (Manning et al., 1986). Fetuses who are candidates for this shunt are carefully screened by ultrasound to ensure that there are no other serious fetal de-

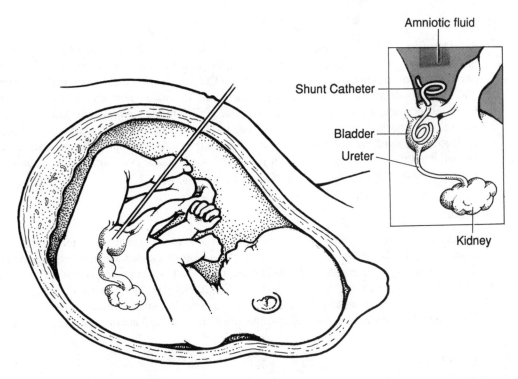

Figure 3.9. Fetal therapy. This fetus was found by ultrasound to have an obstruction of the bladder outlet. Swelling of the entire urinary tract can be seen in the large illustration that was done at the time of the surgical procedure at 20 weeks' gestation. The insert shows the results of the placement of the catheter, shunting the urine from the fetal bladder into the amniotic fluid. One week after the shunt placement, the urinary tract has been effectively decompressed so that it looks nearly normal.

fects; they also receive an amniocentesis for karyotyping and a fetal urine evaluation to determine if the kidney damage is too severe for the surgery to be successful.

Other more complex fetoscopic surgical procedures are being tested in experimental animals. These procedures take advantage of the unique wound-healing properties of the fetus. Endoscopic techniques (microsurgery using a fiberoptic device) have been used experimentally to repair cleft palates and to place skin grafts over open NTDs in sheep (Estes, Whitley, Lorenz, et al., 1992; Meuli, Meuli-Simmen, Hutchins, et al., 1995). The repair of the cleft palate was accomplished without scarring, and the protection of the open spinal cord from the inflammatory effects of amniotic fluid led to improved neurological outcomes in the sheep.

Although the prospects for fetal therapy are exciting, there are a number of complications that must be addressed before these procedures are used on a regular basis. One significant risk is premature delivery following surgery. The procedure requires cutting into the uterine wall, which often precipitates contractions. Even when these contractions are suppressed, the median interval from fetal surgery to delivery is only 5 weeks (Harrison, 1993).

ANNE

After her first child was born with meningomyelocele, Anne's physician recommended she begin oral folic acid supplementation several months prior to conceiving her second child to reduce the risk of having another affected child (see Chapter 25) (Rose & Mennuti, 1994). Anne is now in the fourth month of this second pregnancy. At 15 weeks' gestation, she had an MSAFP blood test performed to screen for the presence of a NTD in her unborn child. Although the test was mildly abnormal, an ultrasound study suggested that her fetus was unaffected. To further evaluate the pregnancy, she underwent an amniocentesis. As a result of this procedure, Anne learned that this fetus, a boy, does not have a NTD or any diagnosable chromosomal abnormalities revealed by amniocentesis. Many of her fears are allayed.

SUMMARY

Currently, the various methods of prenatal diagnosis can identify many inherited disorders. Additional progress will come as more disorders are not only diagnosed, but also become amenable to treatment before birth. Although prenatal diagnosis leads some parents to choose to abort an affected fetus, it helps others to have additional children. Although prenatal diagnosis can tell prospective parents about a specific abnormality, it does not ensure anyone a well-born child. Unfortunately, many causes of developmental disabilities are still not diagnosable prenatally.

REFERENCES

Adzick, N.S., & Harrison, M.R. (1994). Fetal surgical therapy. *Lancet, 343,* 897–902.

Aitken, D.A., Wallace, E.M., Crossley, J.A., et al. (1996). Dimeric inhibin A as a marker for Down's syndrome in early pregnancy. *New England Journal of Medicine, 334,* 1231–1236.

Ashwood, E.R., Cheng, E., & Luthy, D.A. (1987). Maternal serum alpha-fetoprotein and fetal trisomy-21 in women 35 years and older: Implications for alpha-fetoprotein screening programs. *American Journal of Medical Genetics, 26,* 531–539.

Bianchi, D.W. (1995). Prenatal diagnosis by analysis of fetal cells in maternal blood. *Journal of Pediatrics, 127,* 847–856.

Blakemore, K.J. (1988). Prenatal diagnosis by chorionic villus sampling. *Obstetrics and Gynecology Clinics of North America, 15*(2), 179–213.

Brock, D.J.H. (1994). Carrier screening for cystic fibrosis. *Prenatal Diagnosis, 14,* 1243–1252.

Brown, W.T., Houck, G.E., Jr., Jeziorowska, A., et al. (1993). Rapid fragile X carrier screening and prenatal diagnosis using a nonradioactive PCR test. *Journal of the American Medical Association, 270,* 1569–1575.

Burton, B.K., Schultz, C.J., & Burd, L.I. (1992). Limb abnormalities associated with chorionic villus sampling. *Obstetrics and Gynecology, 79,* 726–730.

Canadian Collaborative CVS-Amniocentesis Clinical Trial Group. (1989). Multicenter randomized clinical trial of chorion villus sampling and amniocentesis: First report. *Lancet, 1,* 1–6.

Crombleholme, T.M. (1994) Invasive fetal therapy: Current status and future directions. *Seminars in Perinatology, 18,* 385–397.

Czeizel, A.E., & Dudas, I. (1992). Prevention of the first occurrence of neural tube defects by periconceptional vitamin supplementation. *New England Journal of Medicine, 327*(26), 1832–1835.

D'Alton, M.E., & DeCherney, A.H. (1993). Prenatal diagnosis. *New England Journal of Medicine, 328,* 114–119.

Edwards, R.G., & Hollands, P. (1988). New advances in human embryology: Implications of the preimplantation diagnosis of genetic disease. *Human Reproduction, 3*(4), 549–556.

Elias, S. (1992). *Maternal serum screening for fetal genetic disorders.* Edinburgh, Scotland: Churchill Livingstone.

Estes, J.M., Whitley, D.J., Lorenz, H.P., et al. (1992). Endoscopic creation and repair of fetal cleft lip. *Plastic and Reconstructive Surgery, 90,* 743–749.

Evans, M.I., & Schulman, J.D. (1991). In utero treatment of fetal metabolic disorders. *Clinics in Obstetrics and Gynecology, 34,* 268–276.

Ewigman, B.G., Crane J.P., Frigoleeto, F.D., et al. (1993). Effect of prenatal ultrasound screening on perinatal outcome. *New England Journal of Medicine, 329,* 821–827.

Firth, H.V., Boyd, P.A., Chamberlain, P.F., et al. (1994). Analysis of limb reduction defects in babies exposed to chorionic villus sampling. *Lancet, 343,* 1069–1071.

Flake, A.W., Roncarolo, M-G., Puck, J.M., et al. (1996). Treatment of X-linked severe combined immunodeficiency by in utero transplantation of paternal bone marrow. *New England Journal of Medicine, X,* 1806–1810.

Garmel, S.H., & D'Alton, M.E. (1994). Diagnostic ultrasound in pregnancy: An overview. *Seminars in Perinatology, 18,* 117–132.

Geifman-Holtzman, O., Blatman, R.N., & Bianci, D.W. (1994). Prenatal genetic diagnosis by isolation and analysis of fetal cells circulating in maternal blood. *Seminars in Perinatology, 18,* 366–375.

Goldberg, J.D., Porter, A.E., & Golbus, M.S. (1990). Current assessment of fetal losses as a direct consequence of chorionic villus sampling. *American Journal of Medical Genetics, 35*(2), 174–177.

Haddow, J.E., Palomaki, G.E., Knight, G.J., et al. (1992). Prenatal screening for Down's Syndrome with use of maternal serum markers. *New England Journal of Medicine, 327,* 588–593.

Handyside, A.H., Lesko, J.G., Tarin, J.J., et al. (1992). Birth of a normal girl after in vitro fertilization and preimplantation diagnostic testing for cystic fibrosis. *New England Journal of Medicine, 327,* 905–909.

Harrison, M.R. (1993). Fetal surgery. *The Western Journal of Medicine, 159,* 341–349.

Hickok, D.E., & Mills, M. (1992). Percutaneous umbilical blood sampling: Results from a multicenter collaborative registry: The Western Collaborative Perinatal Group. *American Journal of Obstetrics and Gynecology, 166,* 1614–1617.

Hook, E.B. (1981). Rates of chromosome abnormalities at different maternal ages. *Obstetrics and Gynecology, 58,* 282–285.

Jackson, L.G., Zachary, J.M., Fowler, S.E., et al. (1992). A randomized comparison of transcervical and transabdominal chorionic-villus sampling. *New England Journal of Medicine, 327,* 594–598.

Kaback, M., Lim-Steele, J., Dabholkar, D., et al. (1993). Tay-Sachs disease-carrier screening, prenatal diagnosis and the molecular era: An international perspective, 1970 to 1993. *Journal of the American Medical Association, 270,* 2307–2315.

Knowles, M.R., Hohneker, K.W., Zhou, Z., et al. (1995). A controlled study of adenoviral-vector-mediated gene transfer in the nasal epithelium of patients with cystic fibrosis. *New England Journal of Medicine, 333,* 823–831.

Ledbetter, D.H., Martin, A.O., Verlinsky, Y., et al. (1990). Cytogenetic results of chorionic villus sampling: High success rate and diagnostic accuracy in the United States collaborative study. *American Journal of Obstetrics and Gynecology, 162,* 495–501.

Manning, F.A., Harrison, M.R., Rodeck, C., et al. (1986). Catheter shunts for fetal hydronephrosis and hydrocephalus. *New England Journal of Medicine, 315*(5), 336–340.

Meuli, M., Meuli-Simmen, C., Hutchins, G.M., et al. (1995). In utero surgery rescues neurological function at birth in sheep with spina bifida. *Nature Medicine, 4,* 342–347.

Monk, M. (1993). Preimplantation diagnosis of genetic disease. *Annals of Medicine, 25,* 463–466.

Nicolaides, K.H., Snijders, R.J., Gosden, C.M., et al. (1992). Ultrasonographic detectable markers of fetal chromosomal abnormalities. *Lancet, 340,* 704–707.

Norton, M.E. (1994). Biochemical and ultrasound screening for chromosomal abnormalities. *Seminars in Perinatology, 18,* 256–265.

Platt, L.D., Feuchtbaum, L., Filly, R., et al. (1992). The California maternal serum alpha fetoprotein screening program: The role of ultrasonography in the detection of spina bifida. *American Journal of Obstetrics and Gynecology, 166,* 1328–1329.

Rose, N.C., & Mennuti, M.T. (1993a). Alpha-fetoprotein and neural tube defects. In J.J. Sciano (Ed.), *Gynecology and obstetrics* (pp. 1–14). Philadelphia: Harper & Row.

Rose, N.C., & Mennuti, M.T. (1993b). Maternal serum screening for neural tube defects and fetal chromosome abnormalities. *The Western Journal of Medicine, 159,* 312–317.

Rose, N.C., & Mennuti, M.T. (1994). Periconceptional folate supplementation and neural tube defects. *Clinical Obstetrics and Gynecology, 37,* 605–620.

Sanders, S.P., Chin, A.J., Parness, I.A., et al. (1985). Prenatal diagnosis of congenital heart defects in thoracoabdominally conjoined twins. *New England Journal of Medicine, 313,* 370–374.

Simpson, J.L. (1993). Isolating fetal cells from maternal blood: Advances in prenatal diagnosis through molecular technology: 1993. *Journal of the American Medical Association, 270,* 2357–2361.

Sutherland, G.R., Gedeon, A., Kornman, L., et al. (1991). Prenatal diagnosis of fragile X syndrome by direct detection of the unstable DNA sequence. *New England Journal of Medicine, 325,* 1720–1722.

Tabor, A., Madsen, M., & Obel, E.B. (1986). Randomised controlled trial of genetic amniocentesis in 4606 low-risk women. *Lancet, 2,* 1287–1293.

Terje Lie, R., Wilcox, A.J., & Skjerven, R. (1994). A population-based study of the risk of recurrence of birth defects. *New England Journal of Medicine, 331,* 1–4.

van der Meer, S.B., Spaapen, L.J.M., Fowler, B., et al. (1990). Prenatal treatment of a patient with vitamin B_{12}–responsive methylmalonic acidemia. *Journal of Pediatrics, 117,* 923–926.

Wald, N., Cuckle, H., & Nanchahal, K. (1989). Amniotic fluid acetylcholinesterase measurement in the prenatal diagnosis of open neural tube defects: Second report of the Collaborative Acetylcholinesterase Study. *Prenatal Diagnosis, 9*(12), 813–829.

Ward, B.E., Gersen, S.L., Carelli, M.P., et al. (1993). Rapid prenatal diagnosis of chromosomal aneuploidies by fluorescence in situ hybridization: Clinical experience with 4,500 specimens. *American Journal of Human Genetics, 52,* 854–865.

4 Growth Before Birth

Ernest M. Graham
Mark A. Morgan

Upon completion of this chapter, the reader will:

- understand the fertilization and implantation process
- be aware of the various stages of prenatal development
- be able to discuss the effects of maternal nutrition on fetal development
- know the various causes of malformations, including the major teratogens
- be able to identify some of the causes of deformities
- be acquainted with some of the methods available to detect malformations in utero

Many factors, both environmental and genetic, influence the formation of a human being from fertilization to birth. In terms of the environment, maternal health and nutrition greatly affect fetal growth. Other factors, such as radiation, drugs, and infections during pregnancy, can contribute to a harmful fetal environment that causes malformations. Genetically transmitted disorders can have equally devastating results. This chapter outlines prenatal development and describes how environmental and genetic factors can lead to the birth of a child with developmental disabilities.

FERTILIZATION

An infant girl is born with 2 million oocytes, or immature ova. During her lifetime, only about 500 of these will mature into fully developed eggs; by 45–55 years of age, all the remaining oocytes will have disappeared. During a woman's reproductive years, one mature ovum will ripen each month, be extruded from the ovary, and picked up by the fallopian tube (Figure 4.1). Fertilization occurs about one third of the way down the fallopian tube. If fertilization does not occur, the **menses** washes away the egg and the lining of the uterine wall. The cycle repeats itself unless conception takes place.

Unlike females who are born with all the reproductive cells they will ever possess, males continue to produce sperm throughout their lives. With each ejaculation, hundreds of millions of

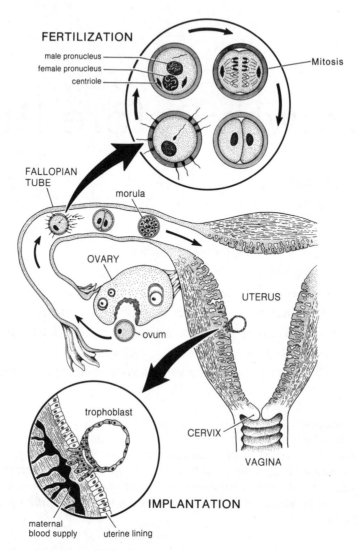

Figure 4.1.   Fertilization and implantation. The ovum or egg is dropped from the ovary into the fallopian tube where it is fertilized by a sperm. The fertilized egg regains its diploid number of chromosomes and starts dividing as it travels toward the uterus. It reaches the uterus after 7 days, and implantation of the embryo (trophoblast) then takes place.

sperm are released into the vagina, where they begin to swim toward the cervix. Most of them die en route. Midway through the woman's menstrual cycle, however, the **mucosal** secretions of the vagina and cervix are thinned and easier to penetrate. If intercourse occurs at this time, the sperm have a better chance of reaching and fertilizing the egg. Once the sperm have pushed through the cervix and into the uterus, a few thousand of them find their way to the correct fallopian tube. The journey is difficult, as they are swimming against the current created by the fallopian tube's **cilia**, the tiny, hairlike protrusions that help push the ova downward.

After the few hundred surviving sperm reach the egg, they poke and push at the outer layer until one breaks through (Figure 4.1). Why one sperm succeeds where another has failed is unclear. Once one sperm fertilizes the egg, however, another sperm cannot penetrate it. These unsuccessful sperm die within 24 hours.

Once inside the egg, the sperm nucleus quickly detaches from its **flagellum,** or tail, and edges toward the ovum's nucleus. The two nuclei join, restoring to the fertilized egg the diploid number of 46 chromosomes (Figure 4.1). Because the egg always contains an X chromosome, if the sperm nucleus also contains an X chromosome, a female (XX) will result. If the sperm carries a Y chromosome, a male (XY) will be produced. Thus, it is the sperm that determines the sex of the fetus.

On rare occasions, two eggs are released simultaneously from the ovary. When they are both fertilized within a few days of each other, fraternal twins result. Although they share the same environment at the same time, they are as genetically different as any two siblings. The incidence of fraternal twins is greatly influenced by race, heredity, maternal age, parity, and, especially, fertility drugs. When a single fertilized egg divides by chance into two separate organisms, identical twins result. They share the same environment and the same genetic inheritance. Yet, even they may differ because of external influences during pregnancy. For example, one may be better nourished and larger at birth than the other. The incidence of identical twins is 1 set per 250 births and is largely attributed to chance rather than to any specific factors (e.g., race, heredity) (MacGillivray, 1986).

EMBRYOGENESIS

After fertilization, the egg quickly begins to divide, first into two, then four, then eight cells. At this stage, the solid mass of multiplying cells is called the **morula.** Just 5 days after conception, the mass contains more than 50 cells. It develops a hollow cavity and is now called the **blastocyst.** Although all the cells start out as primitive, unspecialized units, they soon develop into three distinct layers: 1) the ectoderm, which evolves into the skin, the spinal cord, and the teeth; 2) the mesoderm, which becomes the blood vessels, the muscles, and the bone; and 3) the endoderm, which turns into the digestive system, the lungs, and the urinary tract (Oppenheimer, 1989).

Seven days after conception, the blastocyst reaches the uterus. Only about half of all fertilized eggs survive to this point. When one does survive, it attaches itself to the wall of the uterus, beginning a process called **implantation** (Figure 4.1). To ensure success, the embryo produces a hormone, **chorionic gonadotrophin,** which prevents the mother from menstruating and sweeping away the microscopic embryo. The spongy layers of the uterine wall, rich in blood supply, allow the embryo to push its minute roots, or villi, alongside the maternal blood vessels that will feed it.

By the third week, a primitive placenta has formed, providing an improved means of supplying nutrition. Now oval-shaped, the embryo is beginning to round up at one end to form the brain (Figure 4.2). The pattern of development is from head to tail, or **cephalocaudal.** Surrounding the embryo is a layer that will form the amniotic sac. Fluid will gradually fill this sac to protect the embryo and keep it from drying out.

At the fourth week, the embryo is less than half a centimeter long. Yet, its central nervous system (CNS) is starting to form with the **neural tube** folding over to form the spinal cord. The

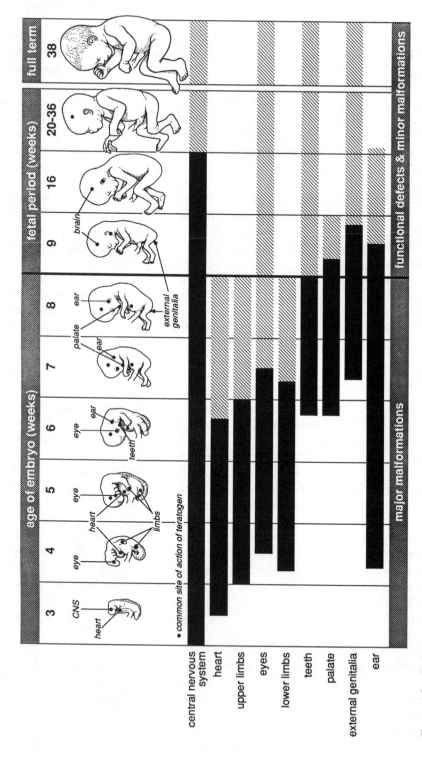

Figure 4.2. Embryogenesis and fetal development. The changes that take place during embryogenesis, between 3 and 8 weeks after fertilization, are enormous. All body systems are formed, and the embryo takes on a human form. Length increases 20-fold during this time. The fetal period lasts from 9 weeks to birth. Teratogens cause malformations by acting during the time a specific organ or group of organs are being formed. Damage to an organ during the time represented by a solid bar will lead to a major malformation, and damage during the time represented by the hatched bar will lead to functional defects or minor morphological abnormalities. (From Moore, K.L. & Persaud, T.V.N. [1993]. *Before we are born: Essentials of embryology and birth defects* [inside back cover]. Philadelphia: W.B. Saunders; adapted by permission.)

facial structure is also taking shape; six **pharyngeal** arches will join in the center to form lips, palate, and **mandible** or jaw.

Because the rapidly growing embryo needs an efficient method of acquiring nutrients and disposing of waste products, the cardiovascular system is the first system to function in the embryo, and blood begins to circulate by the end of the third week. The heart starts out as a U-shaped tube that fuses into a single tube and becomes partitioned into four chambers between the fourth and seventh weeks. Other organs are also experiencing swift changes. During the fourth week, the limb buds become evident (Figure 4.2). And, in only 35 days, the embryo has grown from 1 cell to more than 10,000.

Soon, the embryo begins to take on a more human form. During the second month, the system of blood vessels expands. The brain grows rapidly. Optic swellings at the side of the **forebrain** become eyes and move toward the center of the face. Eyebrows and the **retina** are evident. The primitive sexual organs begin to undergo meiotic division and produce primitive eggs and sperm. The embryo is now about 1½ inches long.

During this period of development, the changes are so precise and predictable that geneticists can tell when certain congenital (birth) defects took place. For example, they know that if a child is born with a cleft palate, the defect occurred between the seventh and eighth weeks, when the **palatal** arches usually close (Figure 4.2).

FETAL DEVELOPMENT

By the end of these 2 months, the embryo has become a fetus. The next 7 months of fetal development are devoted to the refining and enlarging of the organs and body parts that formed during embryogenesis (Figure 4.2). In the third month, the fetus, although weighing only about an ounce, is active, kicking, and turning. The fetal heart rate can be heard with an instrument called a Doppler stethoscope. The amniotic fluid, being produced in greater quantities now, measures approximately 8 ounces. This fluid is constantly recirculated, being swallowed by the fetus and then excreted as urine. During the fourth month, the fetus, weighing about 6 ounces and measuring about 10 inches in length, kicks with authority. This is when the mother usually begins to feel movement, called **quickening.**

As growth continues, the placenta assumes more and more importance to the fetus. It acts as a barrier against the penetration of harmful substances, a remover of waste materials, and a source of nutrition from the maternal circulation. It functions as lungs, kidneys, intestine, and liver for the fetus. Hormones, some produced by the placenta, aid in the continuation of the pregnancy.

During the fifth and sixth months, fingernails form, and the skin becomes thicker. Muscle control improves, and movements become more purposeful. The fetus startles at loud noises, stretches, and moves about. By the end of the sixth month, the infant weighs about 2 pounds and is roughly 14 inches long. Most infants born at this time survive.

The final 3 months are primarily associated with weight and height gain. During this time, the infant usually grows from 2 pounds to around 7 pounds and increases in length from 14 to 19 inches. The baby is so large now that he or she assumes a fetal position, usually head down, awaiting the end of the pregnancy. Total reliance on the mother's body for food and protection will soon end.

MATERNAL NUTRITION

During intrauterine development, the fetus gets all its nutrition from the mother. Adequate supplies of carbohydrates, proteins, fats, vitamins, minerals, and water are needed for growth, metabolic maintenance, and differentiation of new organ systems. The fetus, like a parasite, absorbs these substances from the mother.

Maternal malnutrition affects the fetus differently, depending on when it occurs during pregnancy. Severe malnutrition very early in pregnancy is associated with an increased risk of miscarriage as well as an increased incidence of neural tube defects (NTDs), hydrocephalus, and prematurity (DeLong, 1993). If the mother is malnourished later in pregnancy, the fetus will typically have a low birth weight (Metcoff, 1994). For example, in Holland, in 1944, the Dutch organized a transportation strike against the occupying Nazi forces. This limited the shipment of food from the countryside to the cities. Pregnant women were placed on rations that provided only half their nutritional requirements during the latter part of pregnancy. Although their infants were small, they were otherwise well (Lumey, 1992). Twenty years later, follow-up studies showed the intellectual functioning of these children to be unaffected (Stein & Susser, 1975).

MALFORMATIONS

Congenital malformations are defined as physical abnormalities of prenatal origin that are present at birth and interfere with the child's development. The formation of the major body organs occurs between 18 and 60 days after conception, placing the embryo at risk to develop malformations (Figure 4.2). Overall, they occur in approximately 3% of all births. These defects can result from genetic problems as well as from maternal infections, drugs, and other environmental **teratogens.** Approximately 25% of malformations can be attributed to genetic causes and 10% to environmental causes, including drugs and infections; the remaining 65% are of unknown origin (Beckman & Brent, 1986).

Genetic Abnormalities

Genetic abnormalities are present from the stage of the fertilized egg and affect the formation of the fetus or the production of a specific enzyme. The two principal types of genetic abnormalities are chromosomal abnormalities (see Chapter 1) and single gene defects (see Chapter 2). Abnormalities in the number or structure of the chromosomes can cause defects in the developing embryo. In many cases, these are incompatible with survival (Fretts, Schmittdiel, McLean, et al., 1995). Yet, approximately 1 in 500 infants is born with a chromosomal abnormality. Most of the affected children have mental retardation, short stature, and an unusual appearance. Some have extra or lost fingers or toes; others have congenital heart defects. At least one disorder has been associated with each of the 23 pairs of chromosomes.

Abnormalities resulting from single gene defects arise when a mistake in decoding the DNA message of a single gene leads to the production of a defective protein or the impaired regulation of a developmental process (see Chapter 2). As a result, single gene defects may adversely affect the process of morphogenesis and differentiation. For example, Hox, or homeobox, genes are master regulatory switches that specify the position and orientation of groups of differentiating cells along an axis. Abnormalities in Hox gene structure and expression are likely to be implicated in specific human congenital malformation syndromes involving the CNS, vertebrae (NTDs), face, heart, limbs, genitourinary system, gastrointestinal tract, and lung (Botas, 1993; Redline, Neish, Holmes, et al., 1992). Pax, or paired box, genes also play an important role in the developing nervous system (Noll, 1993). At least two human syndromes have been associated with Pax gene mutations: type I Waardenburg syndrome (a combination of facial, eye, and ear malformations) and aniridia (lack of the iris of the eye).

Teratogens

A teratogen is any agent that causes a defect in the developing embryo/fetus. Teratogens include radiation, drugs, infections, and chronic illnesses (Pacifici & Nottoli, 1995). Susceptibility to a teratogen depends both on the degree and timing of the exposure (Figure 4.2). For environmental toxins, exposure in the first days after conception generally has an all or none effect; the embryo either dies or survives unaffected. Environmental influences at a later date do not affect organ formation but rather the size of the fetus, producing microcephaly or a low birth weight infant. The magnitude of the malformation is also affected by the dosage of the teratogen; the higher the dose, the more severe the defect. Below a certain threshold, however, a teratogen may not cause a malformation. Finally, there is individual variation. Some children will be more susceptible to a particular teratogen because of their individual genetic makeup.

Radiation

Radiation was the first agent shown to cause birth defects, initially in animals and later in survivors of the atomic bombings of Hiroshima and Nagasaki. Research studies found a direct relationship between the distance a pregnant woman was from the focal point of the atomic bomb explosion in Hiroshima and the amount of damage her fetus suffered. Many pregnant women who survived the explosion despite being only a ½ mile away had miscarriages. Women who were about 1¼ miles from the focal point had a very high incidence of children with microcephaly (Wood, Johnson, & Omori, 1967). Farther away, the children were healthy at birth but were shown to have an increased risk of leukemia later in life (Miller, 1968).

Malformations have also been seen in fetuses of women receiving large doses of medical radiation. Dekaban (1968) reported on 22 infants exposed to an average of 250 **rads** of medical radiation between the 3rd and 20th weeks of gestation, while their mothers were being treated for various tumors or diseases of the abdominal and pelvic regions. The fetuses exhibited one or more of the following abnormalities: growth retardation; mental retardation; microcephaly; and eye (small eyes, cataracts, and retinal pigmentary abnormalities), genital, and skeletal malformations.

Radiation's effect on the fetus depends not only on the amount but also on the time in gestation when exposure occurred. For the first weeks after conception, the embryo is insensitive to the teratogenic and growth-retarding effects of radiation but is very sensitive to its lethal effects. Thus, the embryo either dies or is unaffected. During the second and third month of pregnancy, the embryo is very sensitive to the teratogenic, growth-retarding, and lethal effects of radiation. During the fourth and fifth months, the fetus has diminished sensitivity to the teratogenic effects of radiation but retains CNS sensitivity; microcephaly and eye abnormalities are frequent sequelae.

Although researchers are not certain how much radiation is safe for an expectant woman, exposure to less than 5 rads has not been observed to cause congenital malformations or growth retardation (Table 4.1). This suggests that medically indicated diagnostic X rays are safe for

Table 4.1. Dose to the uterus for common radiological procedures of concern in obstetrics

Study	Dose/study (rads)
Skull	Less than .0001
Chest	Less than .0001
Mammogram	Less than .02
Spine	Less than .4
Abdomen	Less than .3
Intravenous pyelogram	0.5–1.4

Adapted from Cunningham et al. (1993).

pregnant women and that there is no medical justification for terminating a pregnancy in women exposed to 5 rads or less. Other diagnostic studies, however, should be used when they can provide the same information as X rays (e.g., using ultrasound to measure fetal size).

Ultrasound and Microwave

Ultrasound and microwave are two forms of energy that, unlike X rays, do not produce the tissue ionization thought to underlie radiation-induced teratogenicity. Ultrasound has been shown to be safe for the fetus (Garmel & D'Alton, 1994) and is widely used to diagnose abnormalities of the fetus. Exposure to microwaves; magnetic fields (e.g., MRI scans); radar; shortwave; radio waves; and emissions from computer screens also poses no known risk to the fetus.

Drugs

Drugs, both medically indicated and illicit, can cause malformations. Although only a few are highly teratogenic, a larger number may carry some increased risk of malformation. Many also cause other problems of prenatal development, such as low birth weight. Most teratogenic effects are noted at birth, but, in a few instances, the problems appear only in later childhood. Most doctors advise pregnant women to refrain, if possible, from taking any medications about which teratogenic effects are known, including thalidomide, antiepileptic drugs, chemotherapeutic agents, sex hormones, vitamin A, tetracycline, and aspirin. Drugs of abuse should also be avoided. The potential teratogenic effects of marijuana, alcohol, and cocaine are discussed further in Chapter 8.

Thalidomide   The use of thalidomide for nausea during the first trimester of pregnancy was a common practice in Europe in the late 1950s. The drug was never released in the United States because the Food and Drug Administration has stricter regulations about testing for teratogenic effects. Europeans, however, found thalidomide to have few obvious side effects, and it sold well to expectant mothers. A few years later, in 1961, a number of reports began appearing describing a previously rarely reported fetal malformation, **phocomelia.** Affected children had shortened or missing arms and legs. An epidemiological study found that all the women with affected children had received thalidomide during their first trimester (Taussig, 1962). The type of malformation appeared related to the time at which the drug was ingested. Taken between 21 and 35 days after conception, thalidomide resulted in infants born with shortened or missing arms or legs. After the 35th day, no defects occurred. Apparently, thalidomide prevented the normal formation of arm and leg buds between days 21 and 35 (Newman, 1985). However, if the limb buds had already formed, no defects occurred.

Antiepileptic Drugs Most drugs used to treat seizure disorders have been found to have teratogenic effects (Chiriboga, 1993; Koch, Losche, Jager-Roman, et al., 1992). Although researchers have long known that infants born to mothers with seizure disorders have a high incidence of cleft lip and palate, they initially hypothesized that the maternal seizures themselves were responsible for fetal malformations (Yerby, 1994; Yerby & Devinsky, 1994). Perhaps the lack of oxygen or vigorous contractions during tonic-clonic seizures caused malformations. Subsequent research, focusing on the antiepileptic drug phenytoin (Dilantin), however, found that about 10% of the children born to mothers receiving this medication had an unusual facial appearance, cleft lip and palate, congenital heart disease, microcephaly, and abnormalities of the nails and fingers. Children born to epileptic mothers who were not receiving medication did not have these malformations (Van Dyke, Hodge, Heide, et al., 1988).

As studies were done with other antiepileptic drugs, each was shown to have teratogenic effects. Similar to phenytoin, carbamazepine (Tegretol) has been shown to cause craniofacial defects, fingernail abnormalities, and developmental delays in 10%–20% of those children whose mothers took the drug during early pregnancy (Gladstone, Bologa, Maguire, et al., 1992). Diazepam (Valium) and its derivatives have been associated with growth retardation and CNS abnormalities similar to those seen in children with fetal alcohol syndrome (see Chapter 8) (Bergman, Rosa, Baum, et al., 1992; Laegreid, Hagberg, & Lundberg, 1992). Phenobarbital and primidone (Mysoline) have been associated with fetal growth retardation and decreased head circumference (Daval, DeVasconcelos, & Lartaud, 1988). Trimethadione (Tridione) causes developmental delays and abnormalities of the face, ears, teeth, and cardiovascular system (Beckman & Brent, 1986). Valproate (Depakene/Depakote) has been associated with an increased risk of NTDs and craniofacial and digital abnormalities (Christianson, Chesler, & Kromberg, 1994).

These malformations do not occur in all children born to women receiving antiepileptic drugs. Only about 10%–20% of these children are affected, and the effects appear to be dose related. Work is being done to determine whether there are enzymatic markers in the amniotic fluid that indicate an increased risk in a particular pregnancy (Buehler, Rao, & Finnell, 1994). Furthermore, ultrasound studies of the fetus may reveal malformations, giving parents the opportunity to terminate the pregnancy if malformations are evident.

Ideally, to avoid malformations, antiepileptic drug use should be stopped before conception. This is possible in women who have been seizure free for 2 years or more (see Chapter 26) (Delgado-Escueta & Janz, 1992). Unfortunately, discontinuing the medications in a woman with frequent seizures puts her at risk for convulsions that may harm both her and her fetus. In this case, the antiepileptic drug dosage should be kept in the low therapeutic range, especially during the first trimester when the most harm to the developing embryo would occur.

Chemotherapeutic Agents Chemotherapeutic agents, or anticancer drugs, aim to injure or kill the most rapidly dividing cells in the body, usually cancer cells if a tumor is present. In a pregnant woman, however, the most rapidly dividing cells are those within the developing embryo. Because many anticancer drugs can cross the placenta, they may lead to a higher incidence of malformations and miscarriages. As an example, cyclophosphamide (used in treating breast cancer and leukemia) carries an increased risk of fetal growth retardation and finger and cardiovascular malformations. Because of the increased risk of fetal malformations with chemotherapeutic agents, therapeutic abortion is often discussed if anticancer therapy is needed during the first trimester of pregnancy.

Sex Hormones   Many women who do not yet know they are pregnant continue to take estrogen and progestin combination drugs as oral contraceptives. Although sex hormones are not conclusively linked to congenital anomalies, they may present certain risks to the developing fetus. For those progestins that have high androgen activity, an increased risk exists for masculinization of the developing fetal female genitalia. Male fetuses exposed to progestin during development of the penis may have an increased incidence of **hypospadias** (abnormal urethral opening). Finally, diethylstilbestrol (DES), an estrogen used primarily in the early 1950s to prevent miscarriages, has been shown to increase the risk of structural defects of the genital tract in females, thus leading to reproductive problems and vaginal cancer some 20 years later (Palmlund, Apfel, Buitendijk, et al., 1993). It is now used only as a "morning after" pill to prevent implantation of an embryo.

Vitamin A   Studies have found that isotretinoin (Accutane), a vitamin A preparation used to treat severe acne, results in fetal cranial and facial malformations; its use should be avoided during early pregnancy. Other vitamin A preparations should also be avoided. Supplementation with 5,000 IU of vitamin A per day should be considered the maximum intake prior to and during pregnancy (Rothman, Moore, Singer, et al., 1995). This is well below the probable minimum human teratogenic dose of 50,000 IU. Use of beta-carotene, the precursor of vitamin A, which is found in fruits and vegetables, has not been shown to produce toxicity (American College of Obstetrics and Gynecology, 1995). The skin metabolizes most of vitamin A when applied as a cream with no apparent absorption, and systemic concentrations are undetectable; because there has been little human experience, however, its use is not recommended during pregnancy.

Tetracycline   Tetracycline, an antibiotic often used to treat acne, can also affect the fetus by staining the developing fetal teeth. Although both primary and permanent teeth do not emerge until much later in life, they are formed before birth. During gestation, the tetracycline mixes with calcium to stain the teeth that are subsequently at high risk for developing cavities. Because many other safe antibiotics are available, pregnant women can easily avoid taking tetracycline.

Aspirin   Aspirin is the most frequently ingested drug during pregnancy; however, its use should be avoided. Aspirin can affect maternal and newborn blood clotting and lead to an increased risk of bleeding. Low-dose aspirin (80 milligrams per day) may be beneficial in some pregnancies complicated by hypertension, but high doses are associated with decreased amniotic fluid, fetal growth restriction, and premature closure of the **ductus arteriosus** in the fetus (Briggs, Freeman, & Sumner, 1994).

Although the previously mentioned drugs have been linked to problems in prenatal development, a number of commonly used drugs, so far, appear to be harmless. These include penicillin, acetaminophen (Tylenol), and diphenhydramine (Benadryl) (Kacew, 1994). Also, studies have not found an association between caffeine consumption and birth defects (Nehlig & Debry, 1994). However, it is probably wise to avoid taking any medication, unless clearly needed, during the first trimester of pregnancy.

Infections

Although the placenta acts as a barrier to some harmful substances, it does not always prevent the passing of drugs or infectious organisms from the mother to the embryo. Intrauterine infections can cause fetal malformations, the most common of these carrying the acronym STORCH, which includes **syphilis (S), toxoplasmosis (T), varicella** and other congenital infections (O), **rubella (R), cytomegalovirus (C),** and **herpes simplex virus (H).**

Syphilis   Syphilis in the mother can cross the placenta and infect the fetus in utero; fortunately, the fetal infection can be treated by administering penicillin to the mother. Unless syphilis is adequately treated with penicillin during pregnancy, however, the child can be born with congenital syphilis. Affected infants have skin rashes, sniffles, an enlarged liver and spleen, edema, and meningitis.

Toxoplasmosis   Toxoplasmosis is a rare illness that causes birth defects, including microcephaly or hydrocephalus, blindness, deafness, and mental retardation in 40% of children born to infected mothers. Damage can be assessed by performing an ultrasound in the latter half of the pregnancy to detect calcified areas in the fetal brain. (Cerebral calcifications are caused by other intrauterine viral infections as well.) Evidence of severe brain damage may be helpful in the decision as to whether to continue the pregnancy. Fetal toxoplasmosis is diagnosed by observing an increase in maternal **immunoglobin G (IgG)** followed by the presence of toxoplasma-specific IgM or by parasite isolation from amniotic fluid or fetal blood. Combination maternal therapy with spiramycin, pyrimethamine, sulfadiazine, and folinic acid has been shown to improve long-term fetal outcome if begun early enough (Matsui, 1994). Studies have also shown that routine neonatal screening for toxoplasmosis can identify subclinical congenital infections and early treatment may reduce the severe long-term sequelae (Guerina, Hsu, Meissner, et al., 1994).

Varicella and Other Congenital Infections   Varicella, or chickenpox, a common and extremely contagious disease, has also been associated with malformations. The abnormalities it causes, however, are both less severe and less common than most other intrauterine infections. There is a 25% chance that varicella will spread from mother to fetus but only a 2% risk that the fetus will develop varicella embryopathy, which results in limb, facial, skeletal, and neurological abnormalities (Jones, Johnson, & Chambers, 1994). A vaccine for this virus is now available.

Certain congenital infections result in an increased risk of miscarriage but have not been shown to result in fetal malformations. These include parvovirus, enterovirus, influenza, mononucleosis, and malaria. There is controversy as to whether human immunodeficiency virus (HIV), the infectious agent of acquired immunodeficiency syndrome (AIDS), causes malformations (see Chapter 9).

Rubella   Rubella, or German measles, was first identified as a cause of birth defects in 1942. Before 1969, when a vaccine was developed, rubella epidemics occurred about every 8 years. The disease itself was innocuous. Women would develop a salmon-colored rash and a low-grade fever, both of which went away in a few days. Serious complications in the adults rarely followed. Unfortunately, the harm was relegated to the embryo. Scores of infants were born with congenital heart defects, severe vision and hearing loss, microcephaly, mental retardation, and cerebral palsy (Griffith & Booss, 1994). Furthermore, because the virus is shed by the infected infant for up to 2 years after birth, female nurses and other health care workers, who might themselves be pregnant, were at high risk of contracting rubella.

As with exposure to thalidomide, the timing of the infection is crucial. The risk of congenital rubella syndrome with a primary maternal infection ranges from 50% in the first month of pregnancy to 10% in the third month of pregnancy. Infection after 16 weeks' gestation is associated with infants who are asymptomatic at birth; however, up to one third of these individuals will develop an "extended rubella syndrome," with symptoms of a progressive panencephalitis and diabetes, appearing in the second or third decade of life (American College of Obstetrics and Gynecology, 1988).

Since the development of the rubella vaccine, which is given to all children between the ages of 12 and 15 months, the congenital rubella syndrome has substantially decreased. In the United States, fewer than 100 children are born with congenital rubella each year (Miller, Tookey, Morgan-Capner, et al., 1994). Women who have not received the vaccine as children should be tested for immunity. If they are not immune, they should receive the rubella vaccine before becoming pregnant. This vaccination is not given to pregnant women because it is made with the weakened live rubella virus that, in theory, could cause fetal infection. After they are vaccinated, women should avoid becoming pregnant for 3 months (Gibbs & Sweet, 1994).

If a woman is not immune and contracts rubella during the first trimester of her pregnancy, attempts can be made to diagnose the affected fetus (Hwa, Shyu, Lee, et al., 1994). Beginning at 16–20 weeks' gestation, fetal blood can be obtained from the umbilical vein. The fetal blood can be tested for the presence of IgM, an antibody that the fetus produces to fight the rubella virus. If this substance is present in the fetal blood, the fetus is presumed to have been infected. There are, however, serious limitations to this test, including a significant risk of false positive and false negative results (i.e., the absence of clinical congenital rubella syndrome even when IgM is present in fetal blood [false positive] and the presence of a fetal infection by the rubella virus in the absence of an IgM response [false negative]). Innovative techniques, including a test for viral DNA in fetal blood samples, may offer improved diagnostic possibilities (Gibbs & Sweet, 1994).

Cytomegalovirus Cytomegalovirus (CMV), a virus from the herpes family, is the most common cause of intrauterine infection, occurring in 5–25 per 1,000 births. About half of all pregnant women have antibodies against this type of infection, indicating prior exposure. However, most infections are asymptomatic. As with other herpes viruses, maternal exposure to CMV does not prevent recurrence, nor unfortunately does it prevent congenital infection. CMV infections that occur in the first or second trimester are more likely to lead to an infected fetus. Approximately 10% of fetuses infected during the first trimester are born with CMV and have significant neurological sequelae (Bale & Murph, 1992). Of the asymptomatic infants, about 5%–15% will develop late sequelae such as hearing loss, below-average intelligence, or behavior problems (Stagno, Pass, Dworsky, et al., 1983). When CMV occurs late in pregnancy, the primary effect is on hearing (Williamson, Percy, Yow, et al., 1990). Postnatal CMV infections are not associated with any developmental disabilities. As of 1997, there is no effective treatment for maternal or fetal CMV infection, and there is no practical method to determine the presence of fetal infection. The incidence of CMV is sufficiently high that scientists are now working on developing a vaccine with the hope that it will be as effective as the rubella vaccine.

Herpes Simplex Virus Herpes simplex virus can also infect the fetus and newborn. Of all infants born with a herpes infection, 85% acquired the virus during birth, 10% after birth, and 5% *in utero* (Connelly & Stanberry, 1995). The clinical findings in newborn infants with congenital (*in utero*) herpes virus infection include growth delay, skin lesions, retinal abnormalities, and microcephaly. For infants acquiring the virus during birth, skin lesions are often the presenting sign. If untreated, 75% of these infants progress to disseminated disease or encephalitis with a mortality rate of more than 70% (Overall, 1994). Two antiviral agents, vidarabine and acyclovir, can be used to treat the mother and baby. Yet, even with treatment, disseminated neonatal infection is associated with a mortality rate of at least 60%. The attack rate of perinatal herpes depends on the type of maternal genital infection at the time of birth. A first maternal infection results in an attack rate of 50%, a symptomatic recurrent infection has an attack rate of 5%–10%, and an asymptomatic recurrent infection has an attack rate of less than 1%. If active maternal herpes lesions are present over the genital area at the time of labor or rupture of membranes, these infants are delivered by cesarean section to decrease the risk of transmission to the fetus.

Maternal Chronic Illness

The most common chronic maternal illness associated with an increased risk of malformations is diabetes mellitus. Fetuses of insulin-dependent diabetics have a 10% risk of malformations of the spine, cardiovascular system, and legs (Martinez-Frias, 1994). However, one study has shown that effective control of diabetes from before conception can reduce the risk of malformation to levels near those observed in the nondiabetic population (Kitzmiller, Gavin, Gin, et al., 1991). Because high levels of glucose may act as a teratogen to the developing embryo, diabetics who are considering pregnancy are strongly encouraged to have preconceptional counseling. Diabetic individuals should be aware that they will be required to maintain much more stringent glucose control during pregnancy.

Thyroid disease itself does not injure the fetus, but the treatment may (Perelman & Clemons, 1992). Nonpregnant women who have hyperthyroidism are often treated with radioactive iodine, and those with iodine-deficient goiter will receive iodine supplements. Iodine crosses the placenta and can interfere with normal thyroid gland formation in the fetus, causing the infant to be born with hypothyroidism. If this is not caught early, cretinism, with growth delay and mental retardation, will result (Becks & Burrow, 1991). The expectant mother with hypothyroidism should be treated with supplements of thyroid hormone, and the mother with hyperthyroidism should be given propylthiouracil (PTU), which decreases the excess thyroid function. Although PTU readily crosses the placenta and is capable of inducing fetal hypothyroidism and goiter, this rarely occurs.

Individuals with other chronic medical illnesses, such as lupus erythematosus and chronic hypertension, as well as transplant recipients are at increased risk for adverse pregnancy outcomes and benefit from preconceptual counseling. Individuals with rheumatological disorders including lupus and rheumatoid arthritis are at increased risk for spontaneous abortion and intrauterine growth retardation. Disease activity should be in remission for at least 6 months before conception. These women may have a better pregnancy outcome when treated with aspirin, heparin, or prednisone. Methotrexate, however, should be avoided as it is a known teratogen.

Hypertensive women should be counseled about their increased risk for preeclampsia, preterm delivery, and intrauterine growth retardation. The underlying cause of their hypertension should be sought. Moderate to severe kidney dysfunction, especially if associated with hypertension, markedly decreases the chance of a successful pregnancy outcome. Approximately 2% of renal transplant recipients of childbearing age become pregnant. These individuals should postpone pregnancy for at least 2 years after the transplant. A successful pregnancy is more likely if these women do not have hypertension or protein in their urine (Dacus, Meyer, & Sibai, 1995).

DEFORMATIONS

Deformations refer to fetal abnormalities produced by uterine constraints during the third trimester (Figure 4.3). Unlike malformations, deformations are often reversible and are not usually genetically inherited. Deformities are isolated defects usually unassociated with developmental disabilities.

A number of deformities result from the fetus simply not having enough room to move in the amniotic sac. This can be of maternal or fetal origin. With twinning, crowding is more likely, and deformities can occur. The human uterus was only intended to carry one fetus. It may not be able to expand to the point of permitting free movement and kicking of two (or more) fetuses. The consequence might be a twisted or deformed foot (club foot) or a misshapen head that has been caught in one position. If the fetus does not have normal kidney function (e.g., Potter syndrome), very little amniotic fluid (most of which is composed of fetal urine) will be produced. Without the buffering capacity of the amniotic fluid, there is little "padding," and deformities of the chest or long bones can occur.

Certain deformities such as bowed legs usually correct themselves when the child learns to walk. Orthopedic surgery or the placing of a cast can correct other bony deformities.

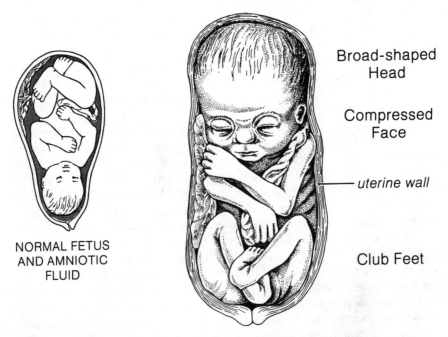

Broad-shaped
Head

Compressed
Face

— *uterine wall*

Club Feet

NORMAL FETUS
AND AMNIOTIC
FLUID

Figure 4.3.   Deformations. During the third trimester, insufficient amniotic fluid or a lack of fetal movement caused by inadequate room within the uterus may lead to bony deformities (shown).

SUMMARY

A multitude of malformations and deformations exist that can create long-standing difficulties for a child. Of these, deformations are easier to correct. Treatment of malformations is rather limited, and prevention seems to be the key. The best protection against the teratogenic effects of drugs and radiation is the limitation of all but essential medications, absence of substance abuse, abstinence from alcohol and smoking (see Chapter 8), and avoidance of excessive radiation exposure, especially during the early months of pregnancy. To prevent congenital rubella infection, women may be tested for past rubella infection by checking their antibody level. If unprotected, nonpregnant women can be given a vaccine to immunize themselves against a future rubella infection. Although treatment is limited for many of these conditions, it is important to realize that in the 1970s most of the reasons for these malformations were unknown. If the causes of malformations can be identified, then strategies for prevention or treatment can be developed.

REFERENCES

American College of Obstetrics and Gynecology. (1988, March). *Perinatal viral and parasitic infections* (Technical Bulletin No. 114). Washington, DC: Author.

American College of Obstetrics and Gynecology. (1995, September). *Vitamin A supplementation during pregnancy* (Committee Opinion No. 157). Washington, DC: Author.

Bale, J.F., Jr., & Murph, M.R. (1992). Congenital infections and the nervous system. *Pediatric Clinics of North America, 39,* 669–690.

Beckman, A.A., & Brent, R.L. (1986). Mechanism of known environmental teratogens: Drugs and chemicals. *Clinics in Perinatology, 13,* 649–687.

Becks, G.P., & Burrow, G.N. (1991). Thyroid disease and pregnancy. *Medical Clinics of North America, 75,* 121–150.

Bergman, U., Rosa, F.W., Baum, C., et al. (1992). Effects of exposure to benzodiazepine during fetal life. *Lancet, 340,* 694–696.

Botas, J. (1993). Control of morphogenesis and differentiation by HOM/Hox genes. *Current Opinion in Cell Biology, 5,* 1015–1022.

Briggs, G.G., Freeman, R.K., & Sumner, J.Y. (Eds.). (1994). *Drugs in pregnancy and lactation.* Baltimore: Williams & Wilkins.

Buehler, B.A., Rao, V., & Finnell, R.H. (1994). Biochemical and molecular teratology of fetal hydantoin syndrome. *Neurologic Clinics, 12,* 741–748.

Chiriboga, C.A. (1993). Fetal effects. *Neurologic Clinics, 11,* 707–728.

Christianson, A.L., Chesler, M., & Kromberg, J.G. (1994). Fetal valproate syndrome: Clinical and neuro-developmental features in two sibling pairs. *Developmental Medicine and Child Neurology, 36,* 361–369.

Connelly, B.L., & Stanberry, L.R. (1995). Herpes simplex virus infections in children. *Current Opinion in Pediatrics, 7,* 19–23.

Cornelius, M.D., Taylor, P.M., Geva, D., et al. (1995). Prenatal tobacco and marijuana use among adolescents: Effects on offspring gestational age, growth, and morphology. *Pediatrics, 95,* 738–743.

Cunningham, F.G., MacDonald, P.C., Levano, K.J., et al. (1993). *Williams obstetrics* (19th ed.). Norwalk, CT: Appleton & Lange.

Dacus, J.V., Meyer, N.L., & Sibai, B.M. (1995, June). How preconception counseling improves pregnancy outcome. *Contemporary Ob/Gyn, 40,* 111–126.

Daval, J.L., DeVasconcelos, A.P., & Lartaud, I. (1988). Morphological and neurochemical effects of diazepam and phenobarbital on selective culture of neurons from fetal rat brain. *Journal of Neurochemistry, 50,* 665–672.

Dekaban, A.S. (1968). Abnormalities in children exposed to x-irradiation during various stages of gestation: Tentative timetable of radiation injury to the human fetus. *Journal of Nuclear Medicine, 9,* 471–477.

Delgado-Escueta, A.V., & Janz, D. (1992). Consensus guidelines: Preconception counseling, management, and care of the pregnant woman with epilepsy. *Neurology, 42*(4 Suppl. 5), 149–160.

DeLong, G.R. (1993). Effects of nutrition on brain development in humans. *American Journal of Clinical Nutrition, 57,* 286S–290S.

Fretts, R.C., Schmittdiel, M.A., McLean, F.H., et al. (1995). Increased maternal age and the risk of fetal death. *New England Journal of Medicine, 333,* 953–957.

Garmel, S.H., & D'Alton, M.E. (1994). Diagnostic ultrasound in pregnancy: An overview. *Seminars in Perinatology, 18,* 117–132.

Gibbs, R.S., & Sweet, R.L. (1994). Maternal and fetal infections, clinical disorders. In R.K. Creasy & R. Resnik (Eds.), *Maternal-fetal medicine: Principles and practice* (pp. 639–703). Philadelphia: W.B. Saunders.

Gladstone, D.J., Bologa, M., Maguire, C., et al. (1992). Course of pregnancy and fetal outcome following maternal exposure to carbamazepine and phenytoin: A prospective study. *Reproductive Toxicology, 6,* 257–261.

Griffith, B.P., & Booss, J. (1994). Neurologic infections of the fetus and newborn. *Neurologic Clinics, 12,* 541–564.

Guerina, N.G., Hsu, H., Meissner, H.C., et al. (1994). Neonatal serologic screening and early treatment for congenital toxoplasma gondii infection. *New England Journal of Medicine, 330,* 1858–1863.

Hwa, H.L., Shyu, M.K., Lee, C.N., et al. (1994). Prenatal diagnosis of congenital rubella infection from maternal rubella in Taiwan. *Obstetrics and Gynecology, 84,* 415–419.

Jones, K.L., Johnson, K.A., & Chambers, C.D. (1994). Offspring of women infected with varicella during pregnancy: A prospective study. *Teratology, 49,* 29–32.

Kacew, S. (1994). Fetal consequences and risks attributed to the use of prescribed and over-the-counter (OTC) preparations during pregnancy. *International Journal of Clinical Pharmacology and Therapeutics, 32,* 335–343.

Kitzmiller, J.L., Gavin, L.A., Gin, G.D., et al. (1991). Preconception care of diabetes: Glycemic control prevents congenital anomalies. *Journal of the American Medical Association, 265,* 731–736.

Koch, S., Losche, G., Jager-Roman, E., et al. (1992). Major and minor birth malformations and antiepileptic drugs. *Neurology, 42*(Suppl. 5), 83–88.

Laegreid, L., Hagberg, G., & Lundberg, A. (1992). The effect of benzodiazepines on the fetus and the newborn. *Neuropediatrics, 23,* 18–23.

Lumey, L.H. (1992). Decreased birthweights in infants after maternal in utero exposure to the Dutch famine of 1944–45. *Paediatric and Perinatal Epidemiology, 6,* 240–253.

MacGillivray, I. (1986). Epidemiology of twin pregnancy. *Semin Perinatol, 10,* 4.

Martinez-Frias, M.L. (1994). Epidemiological analysis of outcomes of pregnancy in diabetic mothers: Identification of the most characteristic and most frequent congenital anomalies. *American Journal of Medical Genetics, 51,* 108–113.

Matsui, D. (1994). Prevention, diagnosis, and treatment of fetal toxoplasmosis. *Clinics in Perinatology, 21,* 675–689.

Metcoff, J. (1994). Clinical assessment of nutritional status at birth: Fetal malnutrition and SGA are not synonymous. *Pediatric Clinics of North America, 41,* 875–891.

Miller, E., Tookey, P., Morgan-Capner, P., et al. (1994). Rubella surveillance to June 1994: Third joint report from the PHLS and the National Congenital Rubella Surveillance Programme: Communicable disease report. *CDR Review, 4,* 146–152.

Miller, R.W. (1968). Effects of ionizing radiation from the atomic bomb on Japanese children. *Pediatrics, 41,* 257–270.

Moore, K.L., & Persaud, T.V.N. (1993). *Before we are born: Essentials of embryology and birth defects.* Philadelphia: W.B. Saunders.

Nehlig, A., & Debry, G. (1994). Potential teratogenic and neurodevelopmental consequences of coffee and caffeine exposure: A review of human and animal data. *Neurotoxicology and Teratology, 16,* 531–543.

Newman, C.G. (1985). Teratogen update: Clinical aspects of thalidomide embryopathy: A continuing preoccupation. *Teratology, 32,* 133–144.

Noll, M. (1993). Evolution and role of Pax genes. *Current Opinion in Genetics and Development, 3,* 595–605.

Olds, D.L., Henderson, C.R., & Tatelbaum, R. (1994). Intellectual impairment in children of women who smoke cigarettes during pregnancy. *Pediatrics, 93,* 221–227.

Oppenheimer, S.B. (1989). *Introduction to embryonic development* (3rd ed.). Needham, MA: Allyn & Bacon.

Overall, J.C., Jr. (1994). Herpes simplex virus infection of the fetus and newborn. *Pediatric Annals, 23,* 131–136.

Pacifici, G.M., & Nottoli, R. (1995). Placental transfer of drugs administered to the mother. *Clinical Pharmacokinetics, 28,* 235–269.

Palmlund, I., Apfel, R., Buitendijk, S., et al. (1993). Effects of diethylstilbestrol (DES) medication during pregnancy: Report from a symposium at the 10th international congress of ISPOG. *Journal of Psychosomatic Obstetrics and Gynaecology, 14,* 71–89.

Perelman, A.H., & Clemons, R.D. (1992). The fetus in maternal hyperthyroidism. *Thyroid, 2,* 225–228.

Redline, R.W., Neish, A., Holmes, L.B., et al. (1992). Biology of disease: Homeobox genes and congenital malformations. *Laboratory Investigation, 66,* 659–668.

Rothman, K.J., Moore, L.L., Singer, M.R., et al. (1995). Teratogenicity of high vitamin A intake. *New England Journal of Medicine, 333,* 1369–1373.

Spinillo, A., Capuzzo, E., Nicola, S.E., et al. (1994). Factors potentiating the smoking-related risk of fetal growth retardation. *British Journal of Obstetrics and Gynaecology, 101,* 954–958.

Stagno, S., Pass, R.F., Dworsky, M.E., et al. (1983). Congenital and perinatal cytomegalovirus infection. *Semin Perinatol, 7,* 302.

Stein, Z., & Susser, M. (1975). The Dutch famine, 1944–45, and the reproductive process: I. Effects or six indices at birth. *Pediatric Research, 9,* 70–76.

Taussig, H.B. (1962). Thalidomide: A lesson in remote effects of drugs. *American Journal of Diseases of Children, 104,* 111–113.

Van Dyke, D.C., Hodge, S.E., Heide, F., et al. (1988). Family studies in fetal phenytoin exposure. *Journal of Pediatrics, 113,* 301–306.

Williamson, W.D., Percy, A.K., Yow, M.D., et al. (1990). Asymptomatic congenital cytomegalovirus infection: Audiologic, neuroradiologic, and neurodevelopmental abnormalities during the first year. *American Journal of Diseases of Children, 144,* 1365–1368.

Wood, J.W., Johnson, K.G., & Omori, Y. (1967). In utero exposure to the Hiroshima atomic bomb: An evaluation of head size and mental retardation: Twenty years later. *Pediatrics, 39,* 385–392.

Yerby, M.S. (1994). Pregnancy, teratogenesis, and epilepsy. *Neurologic Clinics, 12,* 749–771.

Yerby, M.S., & Devinsky, O. (1994). Epilepsy and pregnancy. *Advances in Neurology, 64,* 45–63.

5 Having a Baby

The Birth Process

Iraj Forouzan
Mark A. Morgan
Mark L. Batshaw

Upon completion of this chapter, the reader will:

- be able to identify and characterize the maternal factors that cause problems during the later stages of pregnancy
- know the stages of labor
- be aware of the fetal factors that cause problems during labor and delivery
- know the antenatal fetal surveillance methods that have improved the outcome of high-risk pregnancies

The duration of a typical pregnancy is 266 days from conception or 40 weeks from first day of the last normal menstrual period. The due date, also called the **estimated date of confinement (EDC),** is calculated by counting back 3 months from the first day of the last menstrual period and adding 7 days. Approximately 85% of women deliver within 14 days of this date. Another 10% deliver before completing 37 weeks' gestation (**preterm birth**) and 5% deliver after 42 weeks (**prolonged pregnancy**).

The mechanism that triggers labor is not fully understood. Some mild and irregular uterine contractions occur throughout pregnancy without causing cervical changes or fetal descent into the mother's pelvis. True labor begins when uterine contractions are of sufficient frequency, intensity, and duration to produce effacement (thinning) and dilation of the cervix. This first stage of labor, which may last 12–30 hours, is considered complete when the cervix has dilated 10 centimeters. At this point, the second stage of labor begins; and usually within 2 hours, the infant is delivered. The third stage of labor begins immediately after delivery of the infant and usually lasts only minutes, ending with the delivery of the placenta (Cunningham, MacDonald, Gant, et al., 1993). In the majority of cases, labor begins with a healthy fetus and progresses to the delivery of a healthy newborn.

Fetal and neonatal deaths may arise from difficulties originating prenatally, during labor (intrapartum), or at birth. Yet perinatal mortality, the prevalence of stillbirths (deaths occurring after 20 weeks' gestation but prior to the birth of the infant) plus neonatal deaths (deaths in the first 28 days of life), has been falling steadily since the 1970s (Table 5.1). In 1995, the stillbirth rate in the United States was 7.5 per 1,000 births, the lowest ever recorded (Guyer, Strobino, Ventura, et al., 1996). The prevalence of neonatal deaths also declined. Perinatal mortality in high-risk pregnancies has also been reduced 4-fold since 1984 (Creasy & Resnik, 1994). Improvements in quality of care during pregnancy and labor have contributed to the decline in stillbirth rate, and improved intensive care of newborns has resulted in the decline in neonatal deaths.

Problems occurring with either the mother or the fetus can affect the late stages of pregnancy as well as labor and delivery. Two thirds of the cases involving perinatal mortality and morbidity are attributable to problems in late pregnancy, the remaining one third to problems with labor and delivery. The most common cause of neonatal death is low birth weight, usually as a result of preterm delivery. The second most common cause is congenital malformations. These two are also the primary causes of infant mortality, defined as death occurring between 28 days and 1 year of age (National Center for Health Statistics, 1991).

MATERNAL FACTORS

Maternal factors that may contribute to a poor perinatal outcome can be subgrouped under chronic maternal diseases, acute maternal illnesses, harmful behaviors, and obstetric complications.

Table 5.1.   Infant mortality rates for selected causes per 100,000 births

Cause	Death rate[a]
Congenital anomalies	171
Perinatal conditions not listed separately	194
Sudden infant death syndrome	105
Preterm birth and low birth weight	97
Respiratory distress syndrome	40
Accidents and adverse affects	25
Intrauterine hypoxia–birth asphyxia	14
Birth trauma	6
Physical abuse	8
Infections	11
Gastrointestinal disease	7
Other	114
Total	**792**

Source: Guyer, Strobino, Ventura, et al. (1996).
[a]Provisional data, estimated from 10% sample of deaths.

Chronic Maternal Diseases

Chronic maternal diseases that affect pregnancies include most commonly endocrine disorders (e.g., diabetes); rheumatological disorders (e.g., lupus); cardiovascular disorders (e.g., hypertension); and anemia. They predispose the infant to preterm delivery and intrauterine growth retardation (IUGR). Uncontrolled diabetes leads to a high incidence of preeclampsia, fetal malformations, preterm births, and fetal deaths (Hunter, Burrows, Mohide, et al., 1993). Fetuses of diabetic mothers develop **hyperglycemia** because maternal blood glucose easily crosses the placenta. In fact, the sugar itself is thought to cause many of the fetal problems, although the mechanism is not entirely clear. In an attempt to combat the hyperglycemia, the fetal pancreas produces excessive insulin, which places the infant at high risk for developing **hypoglycemia** soon after birth when less insulin is required. Because scrupulous control of the mother's blood glucose level during pregnancy markedly decreases the risks of malformations, preterm births, and postnatal hypoglycemia (Thompson, Dansereau, Creed, et al., 1994), women with diabetes should seek maternal and fetal health counseling prior to conception. Other endocrine abnormalities such as thyroid and adrenal diseases also can adversely affect maternal and fetal well-being.

Hypertensive diseases complicate about 7% of pregnancies. Preeclampsia/eclampsia syndrome accounts for approximately 5%, and the remaining 2% are preexisting (chronic) hypertension. Chronic hypertension can have detrimental effects on the fetus, including IUGR and fetal death. Individuals with chronic hypertension who conceive while on medication may continue on their medication except for angiotensin-converting enzyme inhibitors. Diuretics should not be initiated during pregnancy. Prospective mothers with hypertension should be monitored for possible development of IUGR and superimposed preeclampsia/eclampsia.

Pregnancy in systemic lupus erythematosus can be dangerous for the mother by accentuating hypertension and kidney failure. It also can cause miscarriage, late pregnancy loss, and heart block or other cardiac defects in the newborn. Therefore, individuals with lupus should be carefully monitored for fetal and maternal well-being. Medications controlling the disease may have to be adjusted as pregnancy advances.

Anemia may also complicate a pregnancy. The most frequent causes of anemia during pregnancy are iron deficiency, folic acid deficiency, and hemoglobinopathies (e.g., sickle cell anemia, thalassemias). Anemia of pregnancy is defined by the Centers for Disease Control (1989) as **hemoglobin** less than 11 grams per 100 milliliters or **hematocrit** less than 33% during the first and third trimesters, and hemoglobin less than 10.5 grams per 100 milliliters or hematocrit less than 32% in the second trimester.

Iron deficiency anemia complicates up to 30% of pregnancies, increasing the risk of preterm delivery and IUGR (Scholl, Hediger, Fischer, et al., 1992). During pregnancy, the demand on the body's iron stores is increased, predisposing the woman to iron deficiency. The presence of inadequate nutrition, a chronic disease, or bleeding further increases this risk. Diagnosing iron deficiency anemia during pregnancy is difficult because most affected women do not exhibit clinical symptoms, although the ingestion of excessive ice may be a subtle sign of iron deficiency. Measurement of serum ferritin level will aid in the diagnosis of anemia. To avoid problems related to iron deficiency anemia, obstetricians have traditionally prescribed prophylactic iron supplementation to all pregnant women during their third trimester. During the first and second trimesters, pregnant women receive this treatment only if their ferritin levels are less than 20 micrograms per liter (Institute of Medicine, 1993).

Folic acid deficiency also causes anemia in the mother and carries an increased risk for neural tube defects in the fetus (see Chapter 25). Folic acid intake of 0.4 milligrams per day is recommended for all women contemplating pregnancy (Centers for Disease Control, 1991, 1992).

Hemoglobinopathies are conditions caused by abnormal hemoglobin structure or production. More than 325 different structural abnormalities of the hemoglobin molecule have been identified. The most common disorder is sickle cell disease, a recessively inherited disorder, which occurs in 1 in 625 African Americans and places affected individuals at an increased risk for preterm labor and IUGR (Brown, Sleeper, Pegelow, et al., 1994). The second most common hemoglobinopathy is thalassemia. This condition occurs when there is a defect in the production of normal hemoglobin chains. It is also inherited as an autosomal recessive disorder. There is an increased risk of preterm births and stillbirths in mothers who have the severe form of this disease. Maintaining good control of the disease during pregnancy, however, improves the chance of a healthy full-term delivery (Koshy, Chisum, Burd, et al., 1991).

Acute Maternal Illnesses

Chapter 4 described some of the fetal malformations caused by intrauterine infections in the first and second trimesters. During the third trimester of pregnancy and at the time of labor and delivery, viral and bacterial infections can no longer cause malformations in the fetus (except in the brain), but they can be transmitted from the mother to the relatively immune-deficient newborn, sometimes with fatal results.

Viral Infections

In the United States, cytomegalovirus (CMV) is the most common cause of late congenital viral infection. About 1% of all live-born infants contract CMV perinatally, 10% of whom will show clinical symptoms (Consten, Brummelkamp, & Henny, 1993; Fowler, Stagno, Pass, et al., 1992). Fetal infection can be diagnosed by ultrasound, amniotic fluid culture, and fetal blood analysis. Although a vaccine is under development, as of 1997 it is not possible to prevent congenital CMV infection (see Chapter 4).

Another common maternal viral infection is genital herpes, characterized by blisters and oozing lesions (Prober, Corey, Brown, et al., 1992). Infants delivered vaginally to women with their first episodes of infection have a 40%–60% risk for developing herpes infections themselves. Neonatal herpes infection can be localized to the central nervous system, eyes, skin, or mucosa, or the infection can be disseminated throughout the body. For systemic infections, the mortality rate can be as high as 60%, even with antiviral therapy using acyclovir (see Chapter 6)(Whitley, Arvin, Prober, et al., 1991). Mothers with recurrent genital herpes infection carry less than an 8% risk of passing on the infection to their infants (Brown, Vonter, Benedetti, et al., 1987). Women with a history of genital herpes infection should have a careful gynecological examination at the time of labor. If a lesion is found, cesarean delivery should be performed. If no lesion is present, the risk of transmission to the neonate is extremely low, and vaginal delivery is recommended.

Varicella (chickenpox) is a highly contagious viral illness with an incubation period of 11–21 days followed by a rash lasting for 7–10 days. Although it is uncommon, pregnant mothers with varicella are at significant risk for developing pneumonia (Zambrano, Martinez, Minguez, et al., 1995). In order to reduce the severity of infection, some obstetricians recommend that passive immunization with VZIG (varicella-zoster immune globulin) be given within 96 hours of exposure. However, 80% of individuals with no known history of varicella already have protective antibodies from an unrecognized exposure and thus do not need VZIG (McGregor, Mark, Crawford, et al., 1987). If the mother has the infectious rash between 5 days before and 2 days after delivery, her infant is likely to develop a clinical infection. These newborns should receive passive immunization with VZIG to reduce the risk of their developing pneumonia (Centers for Disease Control, 1984). If varicella pneumonia develops, it can be treated with acyclovir (Smego & Asperilla, 1991). A varicella vaccine is now available for children older than 18 months (Dennely, 1995).

Human B_{19} parvovirus causes erythema infectiosum or fifth disease (Kirchner, 1994), which is characterized by a bright red flat rash affecting the face and giving a "slapped cheek" appearance. About half of pregnant women are immune to this virus. Maternal infection with this virus at any time during pregnancy carries a 5%–10% risk of adverse pregnancy outcome, including spontaneous abortion, hydrops fetalis (massive fetal edema, which can be diagnosed by ultrasound), and fetal death. If hydrops fetalis develops, intrauterine blood transfusion is often used to rescue the fetus (Peters & Nicolaides, 1990; Sahakian, Weiner, Naides, et al., 1991).

Maternally derived HIV infection has a more insidious effect on the fetus. It does not lead to illness in the first few months of life but usually results in death during childhood (see Chapter 8) (Braddick, Kreiss, Embree, et al., 1990; Hutto, Parks, Lai, et al., 1991). In the United States, there are approximately 7,000 children born to HIV-infected mothers each year (Centers for Disease Control, 1994). The rate of vertical transmission of HIV infection can be reduced from 25% to less than 10% by treatment of infected mothers with zidovudine (AZT) during pregnancy and labor, followed by AZT treatment of the newborn infants (Connor, Sperling, Gelber, et al., 1994).

Bacterial Infections

While viral infections are usually contracted prior to or during delivery, most bacterial infections develop after birth, with the exception of Group B streptococcal (GBS) infections. In the United States, approximately 12,000 proven cases of maternally transmitted GBS infections occur yearly. Although maternal GBS infections are fairly benign, neonatal GBS infections carry a high risk of morbidity and mortality (see Chapter 6). Therefore, penicillin G is recommended for women colonized with GBS or those at high risk (Allen, Navas, & King, 1993; American College of Obstetrics and Gynecology, 1996). Maternal GBS colonization is diagnosed by lower vaginal or rectal culture. The American College of Obstetrics and Gynecology concurs with recommendations of the Centers for Disease Control and Prevention to culture all pregnant women at 35–37 weeks or to adopt a strategy for selective culturing based on clinical risk factors.

Harmful Behaviors

Women who abuse drugs are also more likely to have high-risk pregnancies and should be considered to have a chronic illness. Illicit drug use is associated with a high incidence of maternal infectious diseases, malnutrition, and inadequate prenatal care. This topic is discussed in Chapter 8.

Obstetric Complications

Obstetric complications include preeclampsia and eclampsia, IUGR, abnormal placental localization, premature rupture of the membranes, and preterm delivery.

Preeclampsia and Eclampsia

When hypertension is combined with edema (the accumulation of fluid in tissue) and protein in the urine, it is called preeclampsia. This syndrome occurs most commonly after 20 weeks' gestation in teenage and older women, about 10% of whom are affected. Bedrest is often helpful in stabilizing the blood pressure, but the problem will only resolve with delivery. Thus, careful surveillance of the mother and fetus is essential. If symptoms worsen, the obstetrician may induce labor to avoid life-threatening maternal and fetal complications (Friedman, Schiff, Kao, et al., 1995). Symptoms of severe preeclampsia include headache, decreased urine output, visual disturbances, abdominal pain, markedly elevated blood pressure, and liver dysfunction. In rare cases, preeclampsia progresses to eclampsia, and the mother develops tonic-clonic seizures that can be life threatening to both mother and child (Hernandez & Cunningham, 1990). The etiology of preeclampsia/eclampsia remains unknown, but many of the clinical changes seem to be the result of an imbalance between prostacyclin (a potent blood vessel dilator) and thromboxane (a potent blood vessel constrictor) (Satoh, Seki, & Sakamoto, 1991). Both the prevention and treatment of eclampsia involve infusing intravenous magnesium sulfate. It has been found that VLBW infants whose mothers received magnesium sulfate have a significantly decreased risk of developing cerebral palsy or mental retardation (Schendel, Berg, Yeargin-Allsopp, et al., 1996).

Intrauterine Growth Retardation

When a fetus grows at a rate below the 10th percentile of normal intrauterine growth, it has a condition termed IUGR. Typically IUGR is caused by an intrinsic fetal abnormality or an abnormality of the uterus or placenta. Uteroplacental insufficiency results in the inadequate exchange of nutrients, oxygen, and waste products from the mother to the fetus. A number of conditions, including substance abuse, chronic maternal illness, and preeclampsia, can cause uteroplacental insufficiency. Affected fetuses are more likely to be born prematurely; to have hyperbilirubinemia, hypoglycemia, and/or polycythemia; and to manifest developmental disabilities later in childhood. Detection relies on the antenatal fetal surveillance techniques discussed on pages 82–87. Treatment often includes early delivery.

Placenta Previa, Placenta Accreta, and Abruptio Placenta

Usually, the placenta is attached to the upper third of the uterus. One in every 200 pregnancies is complicated by placenta previa, in which the placenta is implanted low in the uterus and lies over the cervical opening (Figure 5.1). The more extensive the overlay, the greater the risk of bleeding when the cervix dilates during labor (Mabie, 1992). Even before labor begins, the effacement of the cervix or uterine contractions can cause bleeding. If the amount of bleeding is extensive, both the mother and fetus may be at risk (Crane, Chun, & Acker, 1993).

Placenta previa can be detected by obstetric ultrasound. With improvements in obstetric care, including the performance of cesarean delivery and blood transfusions, maternal mortality is rare. However, perinatal mortality remains a concern, primarily as a result of preterm birth. Placenta previa is more common in women who are older than 35 years of age or who have had

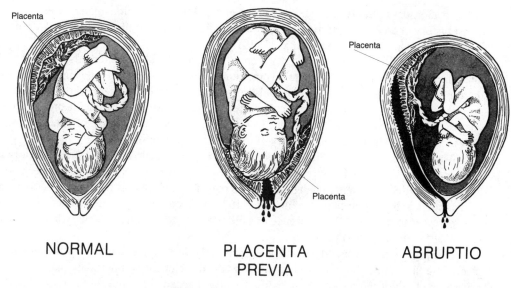

NORMAL

PLACENTA
PREVIA

ABRUPTIO

Figure 5.1a.   A normal placenta is located in the upper third of the uterus. In placenta previa, the placenta is abnormally placed so that it lies over the cervical opening. During labor, as the cervix dilates, the placenta may tear and bleeding occurs. In abruptio placenta, a normally placed placenta becomes partially separated from the uterine wall in the second or third trimester, and bleeding results.

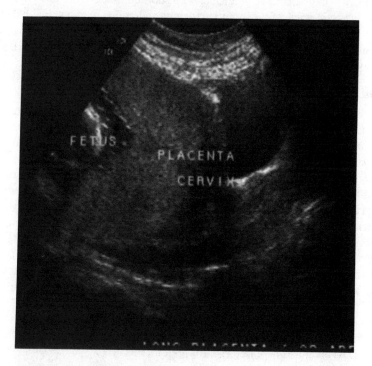

Figure 5.1b.   Ultrasound showing placenta previa.

multiple abortions (Parazzini, Dindelli, Luchini, et al., 1994). In addition, maternal smoking and a past history of a cesarean section are risk factors for developing placenta previa (Monica & Lilja, 1995; Taylor, Kramer, Vaughan, et al., 1994).

A related condition termed placenta accreta, in which the placenta directly attaches to the muscular layer of the uterus called the myometrium, is usually associated with significant bleeding immediately after delivery. Individuals without prior uterine surgery who have placenta previa are at a 4% risk for having placenta accreta. Patients with placenta previa and one previous cesarean delivery have a 25% risk of having placenta accreta. The risk of placenta accreta rises to 50%–60% when there is a history of multiple cesarean births.

Women with placenta previa are advised to get plenty of bedrest so that they can carry the fetus as long as possible. A cesarean delivery is frequently performed once it is has been determined that the fetus is mature enough to survive outside the uterus. At the time of cesarean delivery, individuals with placenta previa have a 10% likelihood of requiring a hysterectomy; this risk increases to 66% with the presence of both placenta previa and accreta (Chattopadhyay, Kharif, & Sherbeeni, 1993).

While placenta previa and accreta are conditions involving the abnormal placement of the placenta in the uterus, abruptio placenta involves the detachment of a normally placed placenta prior to the birth of the fetus (Figure 5.1a). This can happen either during the second or third trimester. Abruptio placenta occurs in about 1 of every 100 pregnancies, and the fetal mortality rate is close to 30% (Lowe & Cunningham, 1990). An increased risk for an abruption has been linked to cigarette smoking, prolonged preterm rupture of membranes, maternal hypertension, grandmultiparity (more than five pregnancies), a short umbilical cord, and physical trauma (e.g., a car accident). Symptoms of an abruption include abdominal pain, vaginal bleeding, fetal heart rate (FHR) changes, and increased uterine contractions. The presence of an abnormal FHR often requires immediate cesarean delivery. A delay in delivery may result in fetal death. The mother also may suffer from shock and require multiple blood transfusions.

Premature Rupture of Membranes

Usually fetal membranes rupture after the onset of labor. When the membranes rupture before labor begins, it is called premature rupture of membranes (PROM) and carries the risk of intra-amniotic infection. Most cases of PROM occur at term, for which most obstetricians advocate induction of labor after a short period of observation. However, some cases occur before 37 weeks' gestation and are called preterm PROM. Regardless of the duration of the pregnancy, when intra-amniotic infection is present, the fetus should be delivered, and both mother and infant should be placed on intravenous antibiotics (Nordenvall & Sandstedt, 1990).

Preterm PROM may be caused by inflammatory weakening of the amniotic membranes, hydramnios (excessive amniotic fluid), an incompetent cervix, abruptio placenta, or amniocentesis. However, the majority of cases are due to unknown causes (Kelly, 1995). Preterm PROM occurs in 10% of pregnancies and can have a number of adverse consequences for the mother and infant. It can precipitate preterm labor and delivery; lead to infection, requiring early delivery; and if prolonged, cause fetal deformities such as club foot (Veille, 1988). It is the single most common diagnosis leading to newborn intensive care nursery admission (Maxwell, 1993). Indigent individuals, teenagers, single mothers, smokers, and those with sexually transmitted diseases (STDs) all are at increased risk for preterm PROM.

Preterm Labor and Delivery

Many factors increase the risk of preterm delivery. A history of a prior preterm delivery is the most important. Other factors include an overdistended uterus (e.g., from twins); uterine abnormalities (e.g., bicornuate [two-horned] uterus); poor prenatal care; low socioeconomic status; STDs; intrauterine infections; and substance abuse. About half of the individuals who develop preterm labor, however, have no identifiable risk factor. The measurement of fibronectin in vaginal secretions has been proposed as a predictor of preterm delivery in this low-risk group (Lockwood, Senyei, Dische, et al., 1991). Preterm delivery is an extreme risk factor for the fetus. Three quarters of all neonatal deaths not associated with congenital anomalies are attributable to complications of preterm birth (see Chapter 7).

Labor and Delivery Factors

The term dystocia is used to describe a difficult labor or childbirth. There are three stages of labor. The first stage, the interval between the onset of labor and full cervical dilation, is subdivided into latent and active phases. Prolongation of the latent phase of labor (more than 20 hours in nulliparous [first] pregnancies and more than 14 hours in multiparous individuals) has little direct effect on infant mortality and morbidity and is usually treated with bedrest. The active phase has been subdivided into 1) an acceleration phase, when the frequency of contractions increases and the cervix dilates to 4 centimeters; 2) a phase of maximum slope, when cervical dilation is even faster; and 3) a deceleration phase, when cervical dilation slows. Abnormalities include protraction disorders (slower than normal uterine contractions) and arrest disorders (complete cessation of contractions). They are often treated with an oxytocin infusion, which stimulates contractions. At times, labor is halted when the descent of the fetus is hindered by fetopelvic disproportion (i.e., a disproportionately large fetal head or a small maternal pelvis). This can be diagnosed utilizing a combination of ultrasound and maternal X-ray pelvimetry, and delivery can be safely performed by cesarean (Morgan & Thurnau, 1988).

Abnormalities of the second stage of labor (the interval between full cervical dilation and delivery of the infant) involve either protraction or arrest of descent, both of which are usually due to dysfunctional uterine contractions or fetopelvic disproportion. Evaluation of the maternal pelvis and observation of the fetal heart rate (FHR) help the physician decide when to employ oxytocin infusion, vaginal delivery, or cesarean birth (Gabbe, Niebyl, & Simpson, 1996). In 0.2%–2% of the population, abnormalities at the second stage result from shoulder dystocia (arrest of the delivery of the fetal body after the head has been delivered) (Baskett & Allen, 1995; Benedetti, 1995). Shoulder dystocia cannot always be predicted prior to delivery or prevented by cesarean birth. Risk factors include prior large infants, maternal obesity, maternal diabetes, increased maternal age, and postmaturity.

When the second stage of labor is complicated by shoulder dystocia, the infant may experience physical injury. The most common injury, occurring in 0.5–1 per 1,000 newborns, involves the brachial plexus, the nerve tract running behind the collar bone (Alfonso, Papazian, Reyes, et al., 1995). This injury results in weakness or total paralysis of the arm and/or hand on the affected side. Two types of brachial plexus injuries have been recognized, those involving the upper nerve roots, called Erb's palsy, and those involving the lower nerve roots, called Klumpke's palsy. The infant with Erb's palsy has very little movement of the affected arm and sometimes weakness at the wrist. An infant with Klumpke's palsy has paralysis of the muscles of the hand and wrist. If the entire brachial plexus is damaged, there is complete paralysis of the arm, wrist, and hand. More than 90% of infants recover completely with therapy. Marked improvement usually occurs within the first 2 weeks; but for some children, recovery can continue for up to 18 months. Permanent injuries are accompanied by muscle atrophy, contractures, and impaired limb growth. In the 1990s, physicians have discovered that neurosurgical correction improves function in the majority of infants with permanent injuries (Laurent & Lee, 1994).

FETAL FACTORS

The most common fetal factors adversely affecting the later stages of pregnancy, labor, and delivery are abnormal presentations, birth defects, multifetal pregnancies, and prolapsed cord.

Abnormal Presentations

In breech delivery, the infant is born buttocks or lower extremities first instead of head first (vertex presentation). When an infant is delivered vertex, the head is gradually molded during labor to fit through the maternal pelvis. In a breech birth, the presenting buttocks or lower extremities can be delivered without difficulty, but the infant's head may get stuck, which can compromise the fetus's oxygen supply (Gifford, Morton, Fiske, et al., 1995). Only 3% of children present in this manner (Eller & VanDorsten, 1993), most of whom are delivered by cesarean section (Eller & VanDorsten, 1995). Breech presentation is often associated with preterm labor, abnormal placement of the placenta, or weakness and decreased movement of the fetus.

Other abnormal presentations occur with even less frequency. For example, 1 in 600 infants are born with a face presentation, in which the head is so hyperextended that the chin is the presenting part (Cruikshank & White, 1973). Face presentations are confirmed by a vaginal examination. Cesarean delivery is frequently preferred, although successful vaginal delivery can be performed in some cases. A contracted pelvis, a large fetus, multiparity with a pendulous abdomen, and fetal anomalies (rarely) are associated with face presentation. When an extremity prolapses alongside the presenting part, it is called compound presentation; this occurs in about 1 of 2,200 pregnancies. Delivery is usually accomplished by cesarean section, although a prolapsed arm can sometimes be pushed upward to convert the situation to a vertex presentation. Brow presentation, the management of which is much the same as for face presentation, is even rarer with an incidence of 1 in 4,400.

Birth Defects

Certain abnormalities intrinsic to the fetus can lead to problems with labor and delivery. For example, an infant who has osteogenesis imperfecta, a birth defect causing brittle bones, may sustain multiple fractures or even die of complications of a skull fracture during the birth process. Or a child with congenital hydrocephalus may have an enlarged head, making vaginal delivery difficult or impossible. In both cases, diagnosis can be made by ultrasound and cesarean delivery is recommended (McCurdy & Seeds, 1993). A number of other birth defects are associated with an increased risk of stillbirths, even in the absence of an abnormal labor. Five percent of stillborn infants have been found to have a major chromosomal abnormality (Valdes-Dapena & Arey, 1970). These infants may have malformations of the heart, lungs, and brain that are incompatible with survival outside the womb.

Multifetal Pregnancies

Human beings, as is true of other two-breasted mammals, are designed to produce a single off-spring from a pregnancy. When a woman is carrying more than one fetus, the uterine space is crowded, and problems often develop. Twins account for about 1% of all births. The major complications associated with twins are preterm delivery, preeclampsia, and difficult deliveries (de Veciana, Major, & Morgan, 1995). In about one quarter of the cases, the second twin is in a breech position at the time of delivery (Lantz & Johnson, 1993) (Figure 5.2). The first twin is generally delivered rapidly and without incident. When the second twin is in the breech presentation, however, he or she may be difficult to deliver. To avoid this problem, the obstetrician may attempt to turn the second twin so that he or she is vertex, or a cesarean delivery may be performed.

Prolapsed Cord

An umbilical cord prolapse occurs when the umbilical cord is below the fetus, preceding it down the birth canal. At times, this arrangement may block blood flow through the cord, which can lead to fetal death. The likelihood of a prolapsed umbilical cord increases with twins and breech

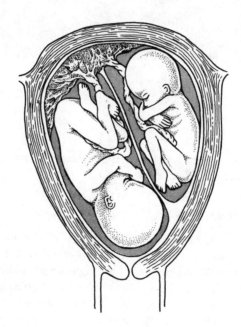

TWIN
PREGNANCY

Figure 5.2a.   Twin pregnancy. The second twin to be born is often smaller than the first and is in a breech position.

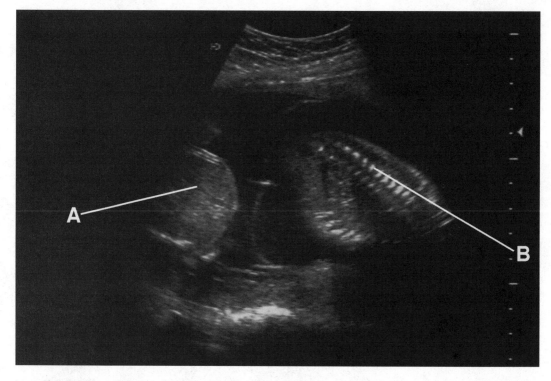

Figure 5.2b.   Ultrasound of a pregnant woman carrying twins. This is a cross-section view through the maternal abdomen. The head of one fetus (A) and the spinal column of the second fetus (B) can be seen.

presentations. A prolapsed cord is considered an emergency and requires immediate cesarean delivery (Critchlow, Leet, Benedetti, et al., 1994).

ANTENATAL FETAL SURVEILLANCE

As described in this chapter, the period of late pregnancy, labor, and delivery can be risky and at times unpredictable. Fortunately, the majority of pregnancies proceed smoothly. In addition, a number of antenatal surveillance measures have significantly reduced the risk of stillbirth and poor perinatal outcome in high-risk pregnancies (American College of Obstetrics and Gynecology, 1994). These procedures, which are not part of routine prenatal care, determine fetal well-being and include ultrasound, fetal movement monitoring, nonstress test, biophysical profile, contraction stress test, Doppler blood flow analysis, amniotic fluid assessment, amniocentesis, and uterine contractions and FHR monitoring. Multiple tests are often used to obtain a comprehensive view of fetal function in the third trimester (Allen, 1993).

Because fetal surveillance testing has a high false positive rate, multiple tests are also necessary to obtain an accurate assessment (Nelson, Dambrosia, Ting, et al., 1996). Fortunately, these tests have a very low false negative rate. Therefore, when the results of the test are reassuring, the risk of fetal death is extremely low.

Fetal Movement Monitoring

Movement marks the well-being of a fetus and can be detected by ultrasound as early as the seventh week of gestation. By the 10th week, these movements have assumed specific patterns. As the fetus matures, the movements become more complex and coordinated. By 16 weeks, they can be perceived by the mother; and at 20 weeks the movements become forceful, frequent, and easily recognizable (Rayburn, 1995). From that point, pregnant women can discern between one third and two thirds of all fetal movements.

Fetal movements vary with the time of day, especially in the third trimester. There are few movements in the morning and many in the evening, especially between 9 P.M. and 1 A.M. The periodic fetal quiet sleep typically lasts from 20 to 80 minutes; during this time, fetal movements diminish. Conversely, in active sleep stages, fetal movements increase. These quiet–active cycles can vary in duration and timing and are affected by such maternal factors as illness or drug use. Nicotine from smoking, sedatives, and narcotics decrease fetal activity; caffeine does not seem to affect fetal movements. Maternal illness also can affect fetal movements, either increasing or decreasing them. In addition to external factors, endogenous factors can influence fetal activity; for example, fetuses with congenital malformations tend to have decreased fetal movements.

Fetal movements can be monitored subjectively by the mother or objectively using real-time ultrasound. There are various methods for obtaining fetal movement counts. One approach is a 12-hour count by the mother; less than 10 movements in this time period is defined as abnormal (Pearson & Weaver, 1976). Once a day, 1 hour counting is another method (Rayburn, 1995); less than four movements during the hour for 2 consecutive days is considered abnormal. A third method is to record the time required to achieve 10 fetal movements during evening hours (7 P.M.–11 P.M.); a time interval of greater than 2 hours is considered abnormal (Moore & Piacquadio, 1989). However, the ideal number of kicks or ideal time interval between movements has not been established; these are merely screening tests.

Nonstress Test

Because fetal body movement is typically accompanied by FHR acceleration, a nonstress test (NST) can be used to assess the integrity of fetal autonomic function (Paul & Miller, 1995). For this test, the physician can either wait for a spontaneous movement to occur or fetal movement may be induced by applying a vibratory acoustic stimulus, such as an artificial larynx, to the mother's abdomen. FHR is monitored using a transducer that continually transmits and receives an ultrasound signal (Jackson, Forouzan, & Cohen, 1991). The normal baseline FHR is 120–160 beats per minute. Usually, there will be two or more FHR accelerations within 20 minutes, which should peak at least 15 beats per minute above the baseline FHR and last 15 seconds from baseline to baseline. When there are insufficient FHR accelerations in 40 minutes, it is called a nonreactive test. Nonreactive NSTs have been associated with fetuses who have IUGR, acidosis, or are destined to be stillborn. There is a high rate of false positive results, however, so the NST can only be used as a screening procedure and not as a diagnostic test. Although the false positive rate for the NST is quite high, the false negative rate is very low. Only 1–2 in 1,000 fetuses who demonstrate a reassuring NST will subsequently be stillborn.

Biophysical Profile

In those fetuses who have a nonreactive NST, a biophysical profile (BPP) and/or contraction stress test will be performed. Some obstetricians use a BPP as their first-line test as it is much more specific than the NST. It has five parts and a 10-point scale and takes 30 minutes to perform (Manning, 1990). The first part uses real-time ultrasound to monitor fetal breathing patterns. The second part requires identifying at least three gross fetal movements during a ½ hour. The third measure is of muscle tone, denoted by active limb extension and flexion. The fourth measure detects acceleration of the fetal heart beat, which occurs together with movement. Finally, the fifth part assesses volume of amniotic fluid; decreased volume is seen in postmature infants and sometimes in those with uteroplacental insufficiency. Two points are given for each measure so that a perfect score is 10 (Table 5.2). Scores of 6 or less indicate an increased risk of stillbirth and later newborn mortality. If a low score is obtained, the test is either prolonged to 120 minutes or repeated 24 hours later. A repeated low score would lead the obstetrician to consider delivering the infant early, either by inducing labor or by performing a cesarean delivery. In high-risk pregnancies, even with a normal BPP score, the profile is usually repeated weekly during the third trimester. BPPs have a low false negative rate (0.6 per 1,000 fetuses) (Nageotte, Towers, Asrat, et al., 1994).

Contraction Stress Test

Uterine contractions cause pressure increases in both the amniotic cavity and the uterine wall, resulting in brief periods of oxygen deprivation to the fetus. A healthy fetus tolerates uterine contractions without difficulty. However, in the presence of uteroplacental insufficiency, there

Table 5.2.   Biophysical profile scoring: Technique and interpretation

Biophysical variable	Normal (score = 2)	Abnormal (score = 0)
Fetal breathing movements (FBM)	At least one episode of FBM of at least 30 seconds' duration in a 30-minute observation	Absent FBM or no episode of more than 30 seconds in 30 minutes
Gross body movement	At least three discrete body/limb movements in 30 minutes (episodes of active continuous movements considered as single movement)	Two or fewer episodes of body limb/movements in 30 minutes
Fetal tone	At least one episode of active extension with return to flexion of fetal limb(s) or trunk	Either slow extension with return to partial flexion or movement of limb in full extension
	Opening and closing of hand considered normal tone	Absent fetal movement
Reactive fetal heart rate (FHR)	At least two episodes of FHR acceleration of more than 15 beats per minute and of at least 15 seconds' duration associated with fetal movement in 30 minutes	Less than two episodes of acceleration of FHR or acceleration of more than 15 beats per minute in 30 minutes
Qualitative amniotic fluid (AF) volume	At least one pocket of AF that measures at least 2 centimeters in two perpendicular planes	Either no AF pockets or a pocket less than 2 centimeters in two perpendicular planes

From Manning, F.A. (1995). Dynamic ultrasound-based fetal assessment: The fetal biophysical profile score. *Clinical Obstetrics and Gynecology, 38*(1), 28; Copyright © 1995 by J.B. Lippincott Company, Medical Department, 227 East Washington Square, Philadelphia, PA 19106; reprinted by permission.

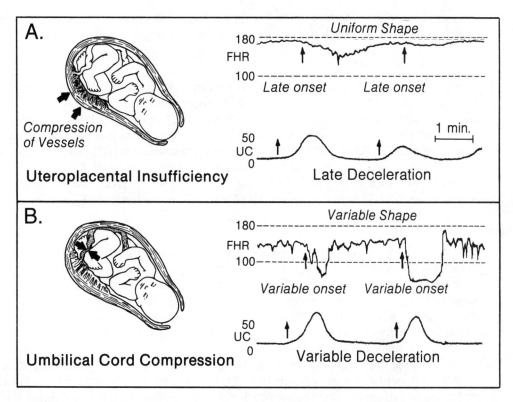

Figure 5.3.   Fetal monitoring. A) In uteroplacental insufficiency, late deceleration of fetal heart rate (FHR) occurs if the placental blood vessels are abnormally pressed together during the end of the uterine contraction (UC, see arrows). B) In umbilical cord compression, there is variable deceleration of the FHR. This abnormal finding of early, mid, and late deceleration suggests compression and obstruction of the umbilical cord circulation during labor. (Redrawn with permission from Hon, E. [1968]. *An atlas of fetal heart rate patterns.* New Haven, CT: Harty.)

may be repetitive late decelerations of the FHR, which necessitate a contraction stress test (CST). An intravenous infusion of oxytocin is given to induce uterine contractions after a typical FHR has been established. Following this challenge at least three contractions lasting 40 seconds or more should occur within 10 minutes. The test indicates a possible problem if half of the contractions are associated with a late deceleration of the FHR (Lagrew, 1995), in which decreases in FHR begin at or after the peak of the uterine contraction and return to normal only after the contraction has ended (Figure 5.3). CST cannot be used if oxytocin is likely to induce preterm labor, in the presence of placenta previa, in multiple pregnancies, following ruptured membranes, or when cesarean delivery is planned. The false negative rate for CST is 0.4 per 1,000 fetuses (Freeman, Anderson, & Dorchester, 1982).

Doppler Blood Flow Analysis

Doppler ultrasound may also be used to measure the movement of red blood cells through blood vessels (Alfirevic & Neilson, 1995). With placental insufficiency, flow through the umbilical artery can be markedly decreased (Maulik, Yarlagadda, & Downing, 1990). When blood flow velocity is absent in the umbilical artery, the risk of perinatal mortality is high (Forouzan, 1995).

Amniotic Fluid Assessment

Because a relationship exists among fetal health, maturity, and the amount and content of amniotic fluid, an amniotic fluid assessment is often part of the biophysical profile (Williams, 1993). For example, oligohydramnios (too little amniotic fluid) can result from abnormalities in the fetal kidneys. The decreased buffering capacity associated with oligohydramnios can lead to fetal deformities ranging from club foot to skull abnormalities and compressed lungs. Decreased amniotic fluid volume also occurs in infants who are either postmature or have IUGR. Here, decreasing amounts of amniotic fluid have been correlated with fetal death. Finally, with premature rupture of membranes, decreased amniotic fluid volume has been associated with a high risk of infection.

Amniocentesis

Amniotic fluid is most commonly obtained by amniocentesis in the third trimester in order to assess fetal lung maturity, especially if early delivery is required. Fetal lung maturity is assessed either by measuring the ratio of two chemicals present in amniotic fluid, lecithin (L) and sphingomyelin (S), or by detecting phosphatidylglycerol (PG) in the fluid (Amenta & Silverman, 1983). Lecithin is necessary to produce surfactant, which keeps the newborn infant's lungs expanded and functioning properly (see Chapter 7). Researchers have found that the ratio of concentration of lecithin and sphingomyelin (called the L/S ratio) changes as the fetus approaches maturity; more lecithin is produced although the sphingomyelin level remains unchanged. As a result, the L/S ratio increases to greater than 2:1. Lower ratios indicate immature lungs and a greater risk for respiratory distress syndrome in the preterm infant (Figure 5.4). Delivery is generally delayed until a ratio of at least 2:1 is achieved. The measurement of PG is helpful in predicting the risk of respiratory distress syndrome especially in infants of mothers with diabetes, those with Rh sensitization, and those with severe infections. The presence of PG suggests that the infant will not develop respiratory distress syndrome. A kit for measuring "foam stability" of amniotic fluid, another marker for surfactant production, is also available. Amniotic fluid and ethanol are combined and shaken; a foamy layer indicates the presence of surfactant and suggests a low risk of respiratory distress syndrome.

The amniotic fluid also can be sampled to assess its cellular and biochemical constitution. In terms of cellular content, the presence of white blood cells and the culturing of bacteria from amniotic fluid following premature rupture of membranes confirms chorioamnionitis (infection of the fetal membranes) and the requirement for early delivery.

Uterine Contractions and Fetal Heart Rate Monitoring

Once labor begins, uterine contractions and FHR can be monitored (Vintzileos, Nochimson, Guzman, et al., 1995). With each uterine contraction, physiological changes occur in the fetus. Periodic decelerations in the FHR during sequential contractions suggest the possibility of a number of problems that may place the fetus at risk, including uteroplacental insufficiency and cord prolapse or compression (Figure 5.3). The risk to the fetus is commonly determined by assessing fluctuation in the baseline FHR between contractions. By recognizing problems early, the obstetrician can better determine the need for a cesarean delivery.

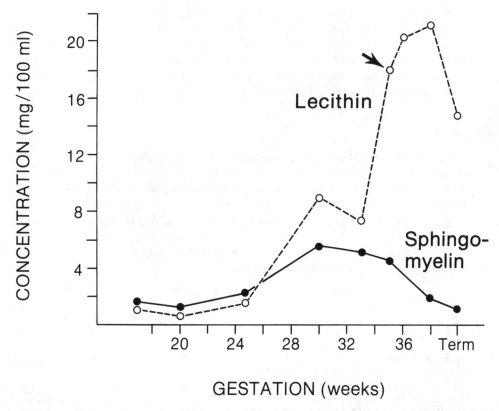

Figure 5.4. Concentration of lecithin (L) and sphingomyelin (S) in the amniotic fluid. Note that before 33 weeks, the L/S ratio is less than 2:1, indicating that inadequate surfactant is being produced. Respiratory distress syndrome (RDS) is more likely to develop at this stage. Delivery is delayed until after the L/S ratio is more than 2:1 in the hope of avoiding RDS. (From Gluck, L., Kulovich, M.V., Borer, R.C., et al. [1971]. Diagnosis of the respiratory distress syndrome by amniocentesis. *American Journal of Obstetrics and Gynecology, 109,* 440; reprinted by permission.)

When a woman is in the first or second stage of labor and her membranes have ruptured, FHR can be monitored directly with a fetal scalp electrode. An abnormal FHR pattern can be further evaluated by measuring acidity in fetal scalp blood, which is obtained using a lancet. If the infant's blood is acidotic, delivery must be hastened by forceps or cesarean delivery.

CESAREAN DELIVERY

A cesarean delivery involves making an incision through the abdominal and uterine walls and extracting the infant. This procedure is usually done while the mother is awake, under epidural or spinal anesthesia, and the infant can be removed within minutes. Although this method of delivery can serve as a means of saving the fetus when problems arise, it is a surgical procedure with potential risks to both fetus and mother. Therefore, it should be used only when indicated for medical reasons, not just for convenience (Elferink-Stinkens, Brand, & Van Hemel, 1995). Problems for the mother include the risk of anesthesia, infection, and bleeding. Although the maternal mortality rate is very low (2 per 10,000 births), it is still five times higher than for vaginal delivery (Lilford, Van Coeverden De Groot, Moore, et al., 1990). The greatest risk to the fetus is preterm delivery as a result of incorrect assessment of gestational age. Infants delivered by cesarean are also more likely to have "wet lungs" and transient respiratory distress. This is because the fetus does not undergo the second stage of labor during which the uterine contractions and passage through the birth canal squeeze most of the fluid from the fetal lungs.

SUMMARY

The period of late pregnancy, labor, and delivery is a critical one for the normal development of the infant. Complications can result from such divergent sources as chronic maternal diseases, acute maternal illnesses, preeclampsia and hypertension, placenta previa, premature rupture of membranes, preterm labor and delivery, breech presentation, birth defects, or the presence of twins. The impact of such complications can be severe and long-lasting. Although antenatal surveillance techniques aid in decreasing the risk of birth injuries, additional public health measures, including improved prenatal care of teenage and indigent women, are needed to ensure the health of pregnant women and their infants.

REFERENCES

Alfirevic, Z., & Neilson, J.P. (1995). Doppler ultrasonography in high-risk pregnancies: Systematic review with meta-analysis. *American Journal of Obstetrics and Gynecology, 172,* 1379–1387.

Alfonso, I., Papazian, O., Reyes, M., et al. (1995). Obstetric brachial plexus injury. *International Pediatrics, 10,* 208–213.

Allen, M.C. (1993). The limit of viability: Neonatal outcome of infants born at 22 to 25 weeks' gestation. *New England Journal of Medicine, 329,* 1597–1601.

Allen, U.D., Navas, L., & King, S.M. (1993). Effectiveness of intrapartum penicillin prophylaxis in preventing early-onset group B streptococcal infection: Results of a meta-analysis. *Canadian Medical Association Journal, 149,* 1659–1665.

Amenta, J.S., & Silverman, J.A. (1983). Amniotic fluid lecithin, phosphatidylglycerol, L/S ratio, and foam stability test in predicting respiratory distress in the newborn. *American Journal of Clinical Pathology, 79,* 52–64.

American Academy of Pediatrics Committee on Infectious Diseases and Committee on Fetus and Newborn. (1992). Guidelines for prevention of group B streptococcal (GBS) infection by chemoprophylaxis. *Pediatrics, 90,* 775–778.

American College of Obstetrics and Gynecology. (1990). *Diagnosis and management of postpartum bleeding* (Technical Bulletin No. 143). Washington, DC: Author.

American College of Obstetrics and Gynecology. (1994). Antepartum fetal surveillance (Technical Bulletin No. 188). *International Journal of Gynaecology and Obstetrics, 44,* 289–294.

American College of Obstetrics and Gynecology. (1996, June). *Prevention of early-onset group B streptococcal disease in newborns* (Committee Opinion No. 173). Washington, DC: Author.

Baskett, T.F., & Allen, A.C. (1995). Perinatal implications of shoulder dystocia. *Obstetrics and Gynecology, 86,* 14–17.

Benedetti, T.J. (1995). Shoulder dystocia. *Contemporary OB/GYN, 40,* 39–43.

Braddick, M.R., Kreiss, J.K., Embree, J.B., et al. (1990). Impact of maternal HIV infection on obstetrical and early neonatal outcome. *AIDS, 4,* 1001–1005.

Brown, A.K., Sleeper, L.A., Pegelow, C.H., et al. (1994). The influence of infant and maternal sickle cell disease on birth outcome and neonatal course. *Archives of Pediatrics and Adolescent Medicine, 148,* 1156–1162.

Brown, Z.A., Vonter, L.A., Benedetti, J., et al. (1987). Effects on infants of a first episode genital herpes during pregnancy. *New England Journal of Medicine, 317,* 1246–1251.

Centers for Disease Control. (1984). Varicella-zoster immune globulin for the prevention of chickenpox. *Morbidity and Mortality Weekly Report, 111,* 592–595.

Centers for Disease Control. (1989). CDC criteria for anemia in children and childbearing age women. *Morbidity and Mortality Weekly Report, 38,* 400–404.

Centers for Disease Control. (1991). Use of folic acid for prevention of spina bifida and other neural tube defects. *Morbidity and Mortality Weekly Report, 40,* 513.

Centers for Disease Control. (1992). Recommendation for the use of folic acid to reduce the number of cases of spina bifida and other neural tube defects. *Morbidity and Mortality Weekly Report, 41*(RR14), 1–7.

Centers for Disease Control. (1994). Zidovudine for prevention of HIV transmission from mother to infant. *Morbidity and Mortality Weekly Report, 43,* 285–287.

Centers for Disease Control. (1996). Prevention of perinatal group B streptococcus disease: A public health perspective. *Morbidity and Mortality Weekly Report, 45,* 1–24.

Chattopadhyay, S.K., Kharif, H., & Sherbeeni, M.M. (1993). Placenta previa and accreta after previous caesarean section. *European Journal of Obstetrics, Gynecology, and Reproductive Biology, 52,* 151–156.

Connor, E.M., Sperling, R.S., Gelber, R., et al. (1994). Reduction of maternal–infant transmission of human immunodeficiency virus type 1 with zidovudine treatment. *New England Journal of Medicine, 331,* 1173–1180.

Consten, E.C., Brummelkamp, W.H., & Henny, C.P. (1993). Cytomegalovirus infection in the pregnant women. *European Journal of Obstetrics, Gynecology, and Reproductive Biology, 52,* 139–142.

Crane, S., Chun, B., & Acker, D. (1993). Treatment of obstetrical hemorrhagic emergencies. *Current Opinion in Obstetrics and Gynecology, 5,* 675–682.

Creasy, R.K., & Resnik, R. (1994). *Maternal–fetal medicine: Principles and practice* (3rd ed.). Philadelphia: W.B. Saunders.

Critchlow, C.W., Leet, T.L., Benedetti, T.J., et al. (1994). Risk factors and infant outcomes associated with umbilical cord prolapse: A population-based case-control study among births in Washington State. *American Journal of Obstetrics and Gynecology, 170,* 613–618.

Cruikshank, D.P., & White, C.A. (1973). Obstetric malpresentations: Twenty years' experience. *American Journal of Obstetrics and Gynecology, 116,* 1097–1104.

Cunningham, F.G., MacDonald, P.C., Gant, N.F., et al. (1993). *Williams obstetrics* (19th ed.). Norwalk, CT: Appleton & Lange.

David, R.J., & Siegel, E. (1983). Decline in neonatal mortality, 1968–1977: Better babies or better care? *Pediatrics, 71,* 531–540.

Dennely, P.H. (1995). Varicella vaccine for prevention of chickenpox. *Rhode Island Medicine, 78,* 14–16.

de Veciana, M., Major, C., & Morgan, M.A. (1995). Labor and delivery management of the multiple gestation. *Obstetrics and Gynecology Clinics of North America, 22,* 235–246.

Elferink-Stinkens, P.M., Brand, R., & Van Hemel, O.J. (1995). Trends in caesarean section rates among high- and medium-risk pregnancies in The Netherlands 1983–1992. *European Journal of Obstetrics, Gynecology, and Reproductive Biology, 59,* 159–167.

Eller, D.P., & VanDorsten, J.P. (1993). Breech presentation. *Current Opinion in Obstetrics and Gynecology, 5,* 664–668.

Eller, D.P., & VanDorsten, J.P. (1995). Route of delivery for the breech presentation: A conundrum. *American Journal of Obstetrics and Gynecology, 173,* 393–398.

Forouzan, I. (1995). Absence of end-diastolic flow velocity in the umbilical artery: A review. *Obstetrical and Gynecological Survey, 50,* 219–227.

Fowler, K.B., Stagno, S., Pass, R.F., et al. (1992). The outcome of congenital cytomegalovirus infection in relation to maternal antibody status. *New England Journal of Medicine, 326,* 663.

Freeman, R.K., Anderson, G., & Dorchester, W. (1982). A prospective multi-institutional study of antepartum FHR monitoring: II. Contraction stress test versus nonstress test for primary surveillance. *American Journal of Obstetrics and Gynecology, 143,* 778–781.

Friedman, S.A., Schiff, E., Kao, L., et al. (1995). Neonatal outcome after preterm delivery for preeclampsia. *American Journal of Obstetrics and Gynecology, 176,* 1785–1788.

Gabbe, S.G., Niebyl, J.R., & Simpson, J.L. (1991). *Obstetrics in normal and problem pregnancies* (2nd ed.). New York: Churchill Livingstone.

Gifford, D.S., Morton, S.C., Fiske, M., et al. (1995). A meta-analysis of infant outcomes after breech delivery. *Obstetrics and Gynecology, 85,* 1047–1054.

Gluck, L., Kulovich, M.V., Borer, R.C., et al. (1971). Diagnosis of the respiratory distress syndrome by amniocentesis. *American Journal of Obstetrics and Gynecology, 109,* 440–445.

Guyer, B., Strobino, D.M., Ventura, S.J., et al. (1996). Annual summary of vital statistics: 1995. *Pediatrics, 98,* 1007–1019.

Hernandez, C., & Cunningham, F.G. (1990). Eclampsia. *Clinical Obstetrics and Gynecology, 33,* 460–466.

Hon, E. (1968). *An atlas of fetal heart rate patterns.* New Haven, CT: Harty.

Hunter, D.J., Burrows, R.F., Mohide, P.T., et al. (1993). Influence of maternal insulin-dependent diabetes mellitus on neonatal morbidity. *Canadian Medical Association Journal, 149,* 47–52.

Hutto, C., Parks, W.P., Lai, S.H., et al. (1991). A hospital-based prospective study of perinatal infection with human immunodeficiency virus type 1. *Journal of Pediatrics, 118,* 347–353.

Institute of Medicine. (1993). *Iron deficiency anemia: Recommended guidelines for prevention, detection, and management among U.S. children and women of childbearing age.* Washington, DC: National Academy Press.

Jackson, G.M., Forouzan, I., & Cohen, A.W. (1991). Fetal well-being: Nonimaging assessment and the biophysical profile. *Seminars in Roentgenology, 26,* 21–31.

Johenning, A., & Lindheimer, M.D. (1993). Hypertension in pregnancy. *Current Opinion in Nephrology and Hypertension, 2,* 307–313.

Kelly, T. (1995). The pathophysiology of premature rupture of the membranes. *Current Opinion in Obstetrics and Gynecology, 7,* 140–145.

Kirchner, J.T. (1994). Erythema infectiosum and other parvovirus B19 infections. *American Family Physician, 50,* 335–341.

Koshy, M., Chisum, D., Burd, L., et al. (1991). Management of sickle cell anemia and pregnancy. *Journal of Clinical Apheresis, 6,* 230–233.

Lagrew, D.C., Jr. (1995). The contraction stress test. *Clinical Obstetrics and Gynecology, 38,* 11–25.

Lantz, M.E., & Johnson, T.R. (1993). Multiple pregnancy. *Current Opinion in Obstetrics and Gynecology, 5,* 657–663.

Laurent, J.P., & Lee, R.T. (1994). Birth-related upper brachial plexus injuries in infants: Operative and non-operative approaches. *Journal of Child Neurology, 9,* 111–117.

Lilford, R.J., Van Coeverden De Groot, H.A., Moore, P.J., et al. (1990). The relative risk of caesarean section (intrapartum and elective) and vaginal delivery: A detailed analysis to exclude the effects of medical disorders and other acute physiological disturbances. *British Journal of Obstetrics and Gynaecology, 97,* 883–892.

Lockwood, C.J., Senyei, A.E., Dische, M.R., et al. (1991). Fetal fibronectin in cervical and vaginal secretions as a predictor of preterm delivery. *New England Journal of Medicine, 325,* 669–674.

Lowe, T.W., & Cunningham, F.G. (1990). Placental abruption. *Clinical Obstetrics and Gynecology, 33,* 406–413.

Mabie, W.C. (1992). Placenta previa. *Clinics in Perinatology, 19,* 425–435.

Manning, F.A. (1990). The fetal biophysical profile score: Current status. *Obstetrics and Gynecology Clinics of North America, 17,* 147–162.

Manning, F.A. (1995). Dynamic ultrasound-based fetal assessment: The fetal biophysical profile score. *Clinical Obstetrics and Gynecology, 38(1),* 26–44.

Maulik, D., Yarlagadda, P., & Downing, G. (1990). Doppler velocimetry in obstetrics. *Obstetrics and Gynecology Clinics of North America, 17,* 163–186.

Maxwell, G.L. (1993). Preterm premature rupture of membranes. *Obstetrical and Gynecological Survey, 48,* 576–583.

McCurdy, C.M., Jr., & Seeds, J.W. (1993). Route of delivery of infants with congenital anomalies. *Clinics in Perinatology, 20,* 81–106.

McGregor, J.A., Mark, S., Crawford, G.P., et al. (1987). Varicella zoster antibody testing in the care of pregnant women exposed to varicella. *American Journal of Obstetrics and Gynecology, 157,* 281–284.

Monica, G., & Lilja, C. (1995). Placenta previa, maternal smoking and recurrence risk. *Acta Obstetricia et Gynecologica Scandinavica, 74,* 341–345.

Moore, T.R., & Piacquadio, K. (1989). A prospective evaluation of fetal movement screening can reduce the incidence of antepartum fetal death. *American Journal of Obstetrics and Gynecology, 160,* 1075–1080.

Morgan, M.A., & Thurnau, G.R. (1988). Efficacy of the fetal-pelvic index in patients requiring labor inductions. *American Journal of Obstetrics and Gynecology, 159,* 621.

Naeye, R.L., & Tafari, N. (1983). *Risk factors in pregnancy and diseases of the fetus and newborn.* Baltimore: Williams & Wilkins.

Nageotte, M.P., Towers, C.V., Asrat, T., et al. (1994). Perinatal outcome with the modified biophysical profile. *American Journal of Obstetrics and Gynecology, 170,* 1672–1676.

National Center for Health Statistics. (1991). Births, marriages, divorces, and deaths for May 1991. *Monthly Vital Statistics Report, 40,* 5.

Nelson, K.B., Dambrosia, J.M., Ting, T.Y., et al. (1996). Uncertain value of electronic fetal monitoring in predicting cerebral palsy. *New England Journal of Medicine, 334,* 613–618.

Nelson, K.B., & Ellenberg, J.H. (1995). Childhood neurological disorders in twins. *Paediatric Perinatal Epidemiology, 9,* 135–145.

Nordenvall, M., & Sandstedt, B. (1990). Chorioamnionitis in relation to gestational outcome in a Swedish population. *European Journal of Obstetrics, Gynecology, and Reproductive Biology, 36,* 59–67.

Parazzini, F., Dindelli, M., Luchini, L., et al. (1994). *Placenta, 15,* 321–326.

Paul, R.H., & Miller, D.A. (1995). Nonstress test. *Clinical Obstetrics and Gynecology, 38,* 3–10.

Pearson, J.F., & Weaver, J.B. (1976) Fetal activity and fetal well-being: An evaluation. *British Medical Journal, 1,* 1305–1307.

Peters, M.T., & Nicolaides, K.H. (1990). Cordocentesis for the diagnosis and treatment of human parvovirus infection. *Obstetrics and Gynecology, 75,* 501.

Prober, C.G., Corey, L., Brown, Z.A., et al. (1992). The management of pregnancies complicated by genital infections with herpes simplex virus. *Clinical Infectious Diseases, 15,* 1031–1038.

Rayburn, W.F. (1995). Fetal movement monitoring. *Clinical Obstetrics and Gynecology, 38,* 59–67.

Sahakian, V., Weiner, C.P., Naides, S.J., et al. (1991). Intrauterine transfusion treatment of nonimmune hydrops fetalis secondary to human parvovirus B19 infection. *American Journal of Obstetrics and Gynecology, 164,* 1090–1091.

Satoh, K., Seki, H., & Sakamoto, H. (1991). Role of prostaglandins in pregnancy-induced hypertension. *American Journal of Kidney Disease, 17,* 133–138.

Schendel, D.E., Berg, C.J., Yeargin-Allsopp, M., et al. (1996). Prenatal magnesium sulfate exposure and the risk for cerebral palsy or mental retardation among very low-birth-weight children aged 3 to 5 years. *Journal of the American Medical Association, 276*(22), 1805–1843.

Scholl, T.O., Hediger, M.L., Fischer, R.L., et al. (1992). Anemia versus iron deficiency: Increased risk of preterm delivery in a prospective study. *American Journal of Clinical Nutrition, 55,* 985–988.

Smego, R.A., Jr., & Asperilla, M.O. (1991). Use of acyclovir for varicella pneumonia during pregnancy. *Obstetrics and Gynecology, 78,* 1112–1116.

Taylor, V.M., Kramer, M.D., Vaughan, T.L., et al. (1994). Placenta previa and prior cesarean delivery: How strong is the association? *Obstetrics and Gynecology, 84,* 55–57.

Thompson, D.M., Dansereau, J., Creed, M., et al. (1994). Tight glucose control results in normal perinatal outcome in 150 patients with gestational diabetes. *Obstetrics and Gynecology, 83,* 262–266.

Valdes-Dapena, M.A., & Arey, J.B. (1970). The causes of neonatal mortality: An analysis of 501 autopsies on newborn infants. *Journal of Pediatrics, 77,* 366–375.

Veille, J.C. (1988). Management of preterm premature rupture of membranes. *Clinics in Perinatology, 15,* 851–862.

Vintzileos, A.M., Nochimson, D.J., Guzman, E.R., et al. (1995). Intrapartum electronic fetal heart rate monitoring versus intermittent auscultation: A meta-analysis. *Obstetrics and Gynecology, 85,* 149–155.

Whitley, R., Arvin, A., Prober, C., et al. (1991). National Institute of Allergy and Infectious Diseases Collaborative Antiviral Study Group: A controlled trial comparing vidarabine with acyclovir in neonatal herpes simplex virus infection. *New England Journal of Medicine, 324,* 444–449.

Williams, K. (1993). Amniotic fluid assessment. *Obstetrical and Gynecological Survey, 48,* 795–800.

Zambrano, M.A., Martinez, A., Minguez, J.A., et al. (1995). Varicella pneumonia complicating pregnancy. *Acta Obstetricia et Gynecologica Scandinavica, 74,* 318–320.

6 The First Weeks of Life

Jacquelyn R. Evans

Upon completion of this chapter, the reader will:

- be familiar with the significance and limitations of the Apgar score
- know the physiological changes that take place immediately after birth
- have a basic understanding of asphyxia and hypoxic-ischemic encephalopathy
- be aware of the various kinds of intracranial hemorrhages newborns experience and the significance of each
- understand the basic components of the body's immune system and the more common infections seen in the newborn period
- know why jaundice occurs and when it can be dangerous for the newborn
- be familiar with the reasons hypoglycemia occurs and the possible consequences for a newborn
- understand the significance of seizures in the first week of life

Jessica has given the last push, and Michael's torso emerges from the birth canal. Life outside the womb has begun. On examination at 1 minute, the obstetrician notes that Michael has a heart rate of 120 beats per minute and good respiratory effort. He has some flexion of his extremities, but no active movement. His cry is vigorous. While his body is pink, his arms and legs are blue. The Apgar score at 1 minute is 8 (Table 6.1). The baby is fine. By 5 minutes, Michael has continued to make good progress. He is actively moving about, and his entire body has become pink. The 5-minute Apgar score is 10. Jessica, relieved and pleased, smiles contentedly.

Maria, however, is having difficulty delivering her son, David. She has just undergone an emergency cesarean section because of an abruptio placenta. She has lost a great deal of blood and has needed several blood transfusions. David is delivered quickly, but, at birth, he is limp and pale with no heartbeat or respiratory effort. The Apgar score is 0. Immediately, the pediatrician places a tube down David's trachea, and he is artificially ventilated. Another tube is inserted into one of the blood vessels in his umbilical cord, and his heart is stimulated with intravenous bicarbonate and adrenalin. After several minutes, David's color has begun to improve, his heart rate is 110, and irregular breathing has started. He is still limp. The 5-minute Apgar score is 5. By 10 minutes after birth, David is breathing regularly, his lips are pink, and his tone improved. The Apgar score is now 7 (Table 6.1). The doctors breathe a sigh of relief, although they know that as a result of this episode David could develop disabilities that may not be apparent for several months. Years ago, David would have been stillborn or would have survived with severe disabilities.

THE APGAR SCORE

Michael and David have both survived. Their risk of having a developmental disability, however, is different. Their Apgar scores may reflect this difference. This scoring system, developed by Dr. Virginia Apgar in the early 1950s, measures the effect of various complications of labor and delivery on the newborn infant and helps indicate the need for resuscitation at birth. There are five measures comprising the Apgar score: heart rate, respiratory effort, muscle tone, gag reflex, and body color (Table 6.1). Each component of the score is assigned a value of 0, 1, or 2 depending on the newborn's condition. The total score is between 0 and 10 and is taken at 1 minute, 5 minutes, and if there are complications, 10 and 15 minutes after birth. The Apgar score has also been widely used as a predictor of long-term disability, although it does have significant limitations in this regard. The Apgar score was not designed for premature infants, who often have low scores more as a result of their prematurity than of asphyxia in labor. In addition, the Apgar score was designed before more accurate markers for asphyxia were developed. In the 1990s, information such as neurological status after birth, evidence of other organ effects of asphyxia, neuroimaging, and electroencephalograms (EEGs) provide much more insight into the likelihood of long-term disability from asphyxia. However, the Apgar remains a universally available, simple scoring system that is deeply ingrained in the practice of newborn care.

A normal Apgar score is highly predictive of normal neurodevelopment; outcome after a low Apgar score, however, is less predictable. One study reported that of 99 children who had 5-minute Apgar scores below 4, 12% (four times the usual occurrence) later developed disabilities including cerebral palsy, mental retardation, and seizures. In addition, 27% of children diagnosed as having cerebral palsy during childhood were found retrospectively to have 5-minute Apgar scores below 6 (Nelson, 1989). Of those infants who had Apgar scores below 4 at 15 minutes, 50% developed disabilities (Jain, Ferre, Vidyasagar, et al., 1991). Although a low Apgar score beyond 5 minutes after birth carries an increased statistical risk for disability, the majority of children with low Apgar scores still develop typically. Yet, although the predictive value of the Apgar score is limited, it is safe to say that David is more likely than Michael to have developmental problems and will need close follow up.

PHYSIOLOGICAL CHANGES AT BIRTH

As the Apgar score illustrates, many changes take place in the first few moments after birth. The most important ones involve the respiratory and circulatory systems. Other changes include the infant's ability to regulate temperature and to absorb nutrients (Fanaroff & Martin, 1996).

For the infant, the first breath is the most difficult because the lungs are collapsed and waterlogged. An extremely strong force must be exerted to open the air pockets, or **alveoli,** to permit the adequate exchange of oxygen. The first cry increases the pressure enough to open the

Table 6.1. The Apgar scoring system

	Points			Score			
				1 minute		5 minutes	
	0	1	2	Michael	David	Michael	David
Heart rate	Absent	Less than 100	More than 100	2	0	2	1
Respiratory effort	Absent	Slow, irregular	Normal respiration; crying	2	0	2	1
Muscle tone	Limp	Some flexion	Active motion	1	0	2	1
Gag reflex	No response	Grimace	Sneeze; cough	2	0	2	1
Color	Blue all over; pale	Blue extremities	Pink all over	1	0	2	1
			Totals	8	0	10	5

alveoli. Once open, they do not collapse completely, even when air is expelled, because of the presence of surfactant (see Chapter 5). It is a lack of surfactant that causes some premature infants to develop respiratory distress syndrome (see Chapter 7).

Equally important are the changes in the circulatory system. During fetal life, the lungs and liver are bypassed because the placenta takes care of oxygenation and detoxification. At birth, these bypasses must cease so the infant can function independently from the mother. The three most important bypasses are the foramen ovale, the ductus arteriosus, and the ductus venosus (Figure 6.1). The first two take blood around the unexpanded lungs, while the third transports blood around the fetal liver.

To understand how the first two bypasses work, it is important to know something about the usual flow of postnatal circulation (Figure 6.1). The heart has four chambers: the right and left atria, or upper chambers, and the right and left ventricles, or lower chambers. Typically, the blood brought to the heart by the vena cava, one of the body's main veins, flows from the right atrium to the right ventricle. It is then carried by the pulmonary artery to the lungs, where it is oxygenated. The pulmonary veins return the oxygenated blood to the left atrium. The blood then

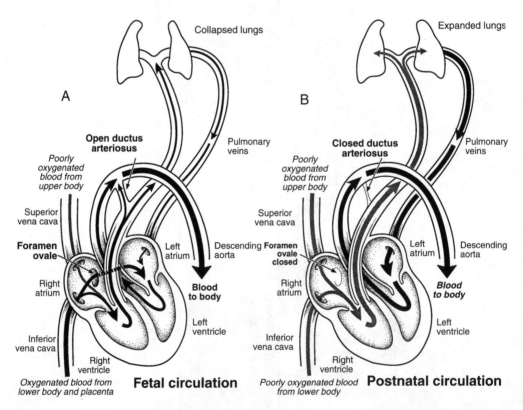

Figure 6.1.   A) Fetal circulation showing the foramen ovale and patent (open) ductus arteriosus that allow the blood flow to bypass the unexpanded lungs. B) Postnatal circulation. The fetal bypasses close off with expansion of the lungs.

passes to the left ventricle and out to the body via the aorta, the body's primary artery, thus completing the cycle.

In the fetus, an opening called the foramen ovale permits much of the blood to flow directly from the right to the left atrium, bypassing the right ventricle and the lungs (Figure 6.1). The blood that does not pass through the foramen ovale flows to the right ventricle and pulmonary artery. However, this blood also bypasses the collapsed lungs by entering the ductus arteriosus, which diverts the blood flow from the pulmonary artery directly into the aorta.

With the first breaths, a series of muscle contractions closes the ductus arteriosus. In addition, a flap folds over and covers the foramen ovale. The closure of these two bypasses must take place for proper oxygenation of the blood to occur. Usually, these bypasses have closed completely by the time the infant is a few days old, and the postnatal adult circulatory pattern has been established. These closures often occur more slowly in the premature or sick term infants and can lead to respiratory and circulatory problems (see Chapter 7). In a small number of newborns, an incomplete transition from the fetal circulation, called persistent pulmonary hypertension of the newborn (PPHN), may be life threatening and may require special types of mechanical ventilation, drugs, or, in the most severe cases, a type of heart-lung bypass treatment called extracorporeal membrane oxygenation (ECMO) for survival (Glass, Wagner, Papero, et al., 1995).

The third fetal bypass involves the umbilical circulation. Typically, the liver serves as a processor of wastes in our bodies. In the fetus, however, the umbilical vessels bypass the liver, and the placenta acts as the purifier of toxic products. A small channel, the ductus venosus, accomplishes this detour around the liver (Figure 6.2). After birth, the umbilical cord is clamped, and the placenta is thereby removed from the circulation. The ductus venosus, the umbilical vein, and two umbilical arteries all close. Venous blood then passes through the liver to be cleansed on its way back to the heart.

In addition to the closing of these three bypasses, the newborn infant must quickly begin to establish temperature regulation. This is very difficult because the newborn has a large surface area, is born soaking wet, and has little fatty tissue to protect against temperature loss. These factors explain the necessity of drying and warmly swaddling of the newborn. Sick or premature infants often need to be placed in incubators or under radiant warmers.

A final change after birth relates to the mode of nourishment. Because placental circulation is no longer available, the infant must obtain nutrition independently. The newborn must develop a strong root and suck and coordinated swallow response to seek and obtain nourishment, either from the mother's breast or the bottle. These responses, too, are less well developed in the premature infant. Alternate means of nutrition (e.g., by intravenous fluids or nasogastric tube feedings) are often necessary until these responses are better developed (see Chapter 10).

CAUSES OF ILLNESS AND DEATH IN NEWBORNS

After an infant has successfully navigated the hazards of labor and delivery, the incidence of severe illness occurring during the first month of life is about 1 in 100, and the incidence of death in the first month is about 1 in 200 (Guyer, Strobino, Ventura, et al., 1996) (Figure 6.3). Severe illnesses include hypoxic-ischemic encephalopathy, intracranial hemorrhage, infection, hyperbilirubinemia, hypoglycemia, inborn errors of metabolism, maternal substance abuse, neonatal seizures, and congenital anomalies (Table 6.2). The clinical presentation of these disorders may

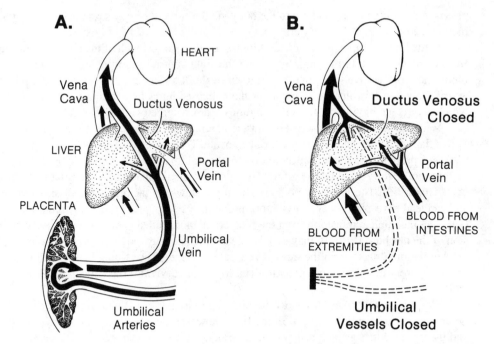

Figure 6.2.   A) Fetal circulation. The blood from the umbilical vein bypasses the liver through the ductus venosus. B) Postnatal circulation. The umbilical vein ceases to function and the ductus venosus closes. Now blood from the body passes through the liver where it is cleansed.

be similar because newborns have relatively few ways of indicating severe illness. They may have feeding or breathing difficulties or become irritable, lethargic, and floppy. This may progress to seizures, coma, and death. Early appropriate treatment may help to avoid severe developmental disabilities in these infants.

Hypoxic-Ischemic Encephalopathy

The most common severe problem immediately following birth is asphyxia. In asphyxia, the brain is subjected not only to hypoxia (i.e., lack of oxygen) but also to ischemia (i.e., lack of circulation) and acidosis. An asphyxiated infant has a very low Apgar score and urgently needs resuscitation. Severely affected infants will develop a neurological condition called hypoxic-ischemic encephalopathy that affects approximately 1–2 of 1,000 term infants (Hull & Dodd, 1992). The causes of asphyxia include placenta previa, abruptio placenta, prolapsed cord, cephalopelvic disproportion (CPD), and prolonged labor (see Chapter 5). Emergency treatment involves establishing gas exchange in the lungs, supporting the heart and blood pressure, and correcting metabolic acidosis. Some experimental evidence suggests that the use of calcium antagonists (e.g., verapamil [used in angina]); excitatory amino acid antagonists (e.g., dextromethorphan [the active ingredient in Robitussin cough syrup]); and free-radical scavengers (e.g., allopurinol [used in gout]) also may hold some benefit (Espinoza & Parer, 1991; Gunn, Williams, Mallard, et al., 1994; Lipton & Rosenberg, 1994). Even better is prevention of in-

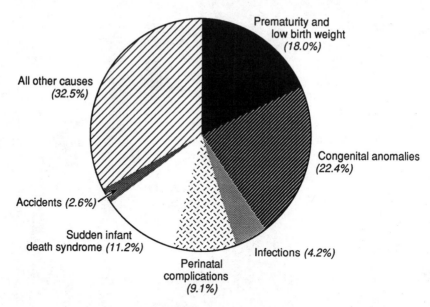

Figure 6.3.   Causes of death in the first year of life. In the United States, the infant mortality is around 8 in 1,000. Two thirds of all children who die in the first year have their problems originating in the fetal or perinatal period. (From Guyer, B., Strobino, D.M., Ventura, S.J., et al. [1996]. Annual summary of vital statistics: 1995. *Pediatrics, 98,* 1017; adapted by permission.)

trauterine asphyxia by fetal monitoring and early delivery when the fetus appears to be in trouble (see Chapter 5).

Hypoxic-ischemic damage often can be visualized using neuroimaging techniques such as ultrasound, computed tomography (CT) scan, or magnetic resonance imaging (MRI), which may show signs of cysts or loss of brain tissue. The specific patterns of abnormalities have different terms associated with them. Watershed infarcts result from a generalized reduction in cerebral blood flow in the full-term infant. Damage occurs in the border regions between two major blood vessels, areas that are the least well supplied with oxygen and nutrients (Figure 6.4a). In severe cases, the result is spastic quadriplegia and mental retardation; with subtle damage, the result may be attention-deficit/hyperactivity disorder (ADHD) or learning disabilities. Focal infarcts (strokes) occur when a major cerebral artery is blocked (Figure 6.4b). Hemiplegia usually results. A prolonged hypoxic state leads to diffuse hypodense areas on neuroimaging that

Table 6.2.   Medical disorders in newborns

Hypoxic-ischemic encephalopathy
Intracranial hemorrhage
Sepsis
Hyperbilirubinemia
Hypoglycemia
Inborn errors of metabolism
Maternal substance abuse
Seizures

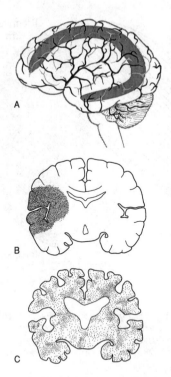

Figure 6.4. Types of hypoxic-ischemic brain injury. A) A watershed infarct (solid) occurs in the bor-der zone between two major arterial circulation supplies. B) A focal infarct (stippled) occurs due to complete disruption of flow of a major artery. C) Diffuse hypodense areas (stippled) and general-ized brain atrophy usually occur due to prolonged lack of oxygen.

may eventually develop into multiple cysts or generalized atrophy (Figure 6.4c). This usually represents widespread brain damage and manifests as quadriplegia, mental retardation, and a seizure disorder. A related condition, status marmoratus, involves a pattern of damage resulting from hypoxia to the basal ganglia and leads to dyskinetic cerebral palsy (Hill & Volpe, 1989). In premature infants, a different pattern often results from generalized ischemia called periventric-ular leukomalacia (PVL) (see Chapter 7). The brain surrounding the ventricles develops areas of focal damage, eventually forming cysts (Figure 7.6). This area controls movement of the lower limbs, and damage leads to spastic diplegia or, if more extensive, to quadriplegic cerebral palsy (see Chapter 24) (Rogers, Msall, Owens, et al., 1994).

Prognosis after hypoxia-ischemia is correlated with the severity of the clinical symptoms in the neonatal period. Virtually all infants with a mild neonatal syndrome will survive neurologi-cally intact. In contrast, approximately 75% of infants with a severe neonatal syndrome, includ-ing seizures and coma, will die. The survivors will almost all have significant neurological se-quelae, primarily mental retardation and cerebral palsy (Robertson & Finer, 1993). It is important to recognize, however, that asphyxia is but one of many causes of neurological impair-ments and is thought to be the origin of less than 10% of all cases of cerebral palsy (Nelson, 1989). Even this may be an overestimation, as it includes children who have a preexisting con-genital abnormality that may have predisposed them to asphyxia.

Intracranial Hemorrhage

After birth, about 2.5% of all infants have a large swelling on the back or side of the head, a cephalohematoma (Figure 6.5). This collection of blood under the outer layer of the skull results from trauma to the blood vessels in the scalp during delivery. Although occasionally associated with an underlying skull fracture, brain injury is rare, and the prognosis excellent (Thacker, Lim, & Drew, 1987). No treatment is necessary and the swelling usually disappears within a few weeks. While cephalohematomas are usually inconsequential, intracranial hemorrhages can be much more serious. There are many causes of intracranial hemorrhage, but both hypoxia-ischemia and direct trauma are known to be important. For example, hypoxia-ischemia can cause brain damage not only by directly injuring cortical tissue, but also by disrupting blood vessels. Blood vessels also can be disrupted by injury during a difficult delivery.

There are a number of types of intracranial hemorrhages: subdural, subarachnoid, and periventricular-intraventricular. If the bleeding occurs from blood vessels beneath the outer covering of the brain, the dura mater, it is called a subdural hematoma. If the bleeding occurs beneath the middle covering of the brain, the arachnoid mater, it is called a subarachnoid hemorrhage (Figure 6.5). If the bleeding occurs in the capillary vessels surrounding the ventricles of the brain, it is called a periventricular-intraventricular hemorrhage (Volpe, 1995).

Subdural hemorrhages are uncommon and tend to occur in full-term infants who have experienced a traumatic delivery, such as may occur with cephalopelvic disproportion or a difficult breech delivery. This type of hemorrhage may result in seizures, coma, hydrocephalus, and, in severe cases, death. Neurosurgery may be necessary to remove the collection of blood. If hydro-

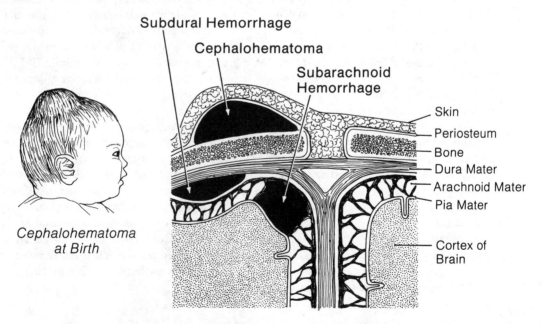

Figure 6.5.   Types of hemorrhages in the newborn. Cephalohematoma is frequent, and the child with this problem has a good prognosis. Subdural and subarachnoid hemorrhages carry more guarded prognoses.

cephalus results, a shunt from the subdural space to the abdominal cavity may be needed to relieve the increased intracranial pressure.

Subarachnoid hemorrhages may result from trauma or asphyxia. These hemorrhages are generally less severe than subdural hemorrhages and are most common in premature infants. Unlike the subdural hemorrhage, which involves arterial bleeding under high pressure, the subarachnoid hemorrhage is venous bleeding under low pressure. Sometimes an infant with this type of hemorrhage has no symptoms; at other times, the infant will experience seizures. The outcome is generally good after traumatic injury but more uncertain if there has been asphyxia as well.

Periventricular-intraventricular hemorrhages are also most frequent in premature infants whose developmentally immature capillary blood vessels are particularly sensitive to lack of oxygen or altered blood pressure. Although the incidence has decreased since the 1980s, up to 20% of premature infants still have some hemorrhaging from capillary beds surrounding the ventricles (Volpe, 1995). The risk of bleeding decreases as gestational age increases. By the ninth month, the support for these capillary vessels improves, making this complication rare in full-term infants. Bleeding starts in the capillary vessels surrounding the ventricles (the germinal matrix) but there is usually leakage into the ventricle and sometimes bleeding spreads to the surrounding brain tissue. If the bleeding is severe, the blood count, or hematocrit, may drop; the soft spot of the head may bulge; the head circumference may increase; and seizures may develop. More commonly, symptoms are subtle or nonspecific. Because of the common lack of specific symptoms and the frequency of these hemorrhages, many pediatricians routinely screen very premature infants (birth weight less than 1,000 grams) by head ultrasound (Figure 6.6). This procedure visualizes the ventricular and periventricular areas well and is easily performed at the bedside. CT (Figure 6.7) or MRI scans are usually performed only after head ultrasound has detected abnormalities or to detect damage in areas that are not well imaged with ultrasound.

Until the mid-1990s, there was no specific treatment for periventricular-intraventricular hemorrhage, other than attempting to prevent preterm delivery. Now there is some evidence that prophylactic use of indomethacin (Ment, Oh, Ehrenkranz, et al., 1994) and vitamin E (Fish, Cohen, Franzek, et al., 1990) can reduce the risk and severity of hemorrhage in very premature infants. Studies have also suggested the potential value of giving the mother steroids and phenobarbital during preterm labor to protect against hemorrhage in the fetus (Volpe, 1995).

The prognosis after periventricular-intraventricular hemorrhages correlates with the extent of the bleeding. Small hemorrhages (Grades I–II) are common in premature infants and generally have little adverse effect. Larger hemorrhages that involve enlargement of the ventricles (Grade III; Figure 6.6) or bleeding into brain tissue (Grade IV; Figure 6.7), however, can result in long-term problems. A large amount of bleeding into the ventricle can obstruct the flow of cerebrospinal fluid, causing hydrocephalus. If the bleeding occurs within the substance of the brain, it can destroy tissue and result in a porencephalic cyst, a cavity in the brain substance that communicates with the ventricle. This carries an increased risk of cerebral palsy and mental retardation (Krishnamoorthy, Kuban, Leviton, et al., 1990). When periventricular-intraventricular hemorrhages are found in conjunction with periventricular leukomalacia, there is a much higher incidence of brain damage (see Chapter 7).

Infections

When an infant develops symptoms of lethargy, poor feeding, and temperature instability, the pediatrician's first concern is the possibility of **sepsis.** Although bacterial sepsis is the most common type of systemic infection that requires urgent intervention, other types, particularly viral infections, also can be devastating to a newborn or fetus. In newborn infants, the organisms causing infections are often different from organisms that cause infections in older children and adults. Some of the organisms that attack newborns are the same ones that harmlessly exist as part of the vaginal, skin, or gastrointestinal flora of the mother. Infections can be contracted through the placenta (HIV), the maternal vagina (herpes simplex), or the amniotic fluid (beta streptococcus) or transmitted from other infants or hospital staff in the nursery (staphylococcus). To understand why these infections occur and can be so dangerous to the developing fetus or infant, a basic knowledge of the immune system is necessary.

The defenses against infection include the skin, mucous secretions, B and T lymphocytes, phagocytes, and the complement system. Newborn infants, however, do not have the fully developed defense or immune system that older children and adults do.

The skin is the body's first line of defense against infection. Skin provides a protective covering and prevents the entrance of bacteria or viruses into the bloodstream. The infant's skin covering, though thinner than an older child's, is usually adequate. However, if this covering is removed, for example by trauma or burns, or disrupted by invasive procedures or indwelling foreign bodies (e.g., intravenous catheters), the likelihood of sepsis greatly increases.

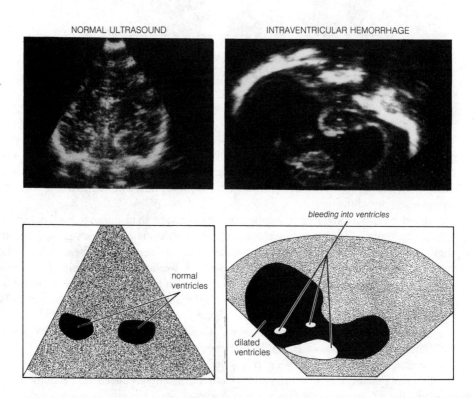

Figure 6.6.   Intraventricular hemorrhage as shown on an ultrasound. (Courtesy of Dr. Roger Sanders, Department of Radiology, The Johns Hopkins Hospital, Baltimore.)

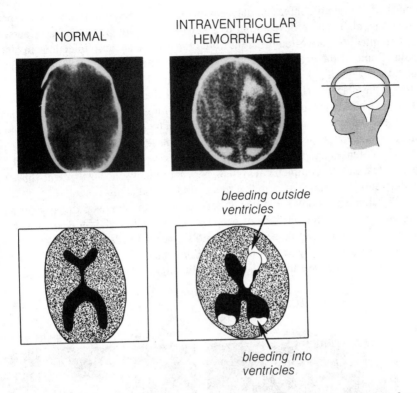

NORMAL

INTRAVENTRICULAR HEMORRHAGE

bleeding outside ventricles

bleeding into ventricles

Figure 6.7.   Intraventricular hemorrhage as shown on a CT scan. (Courtesy of Dr. Roger Sanders, Department of Radiology, The Johns Hopkins Hospital, Baltimore.)

The next line of defense is the mucous secretions. Saliva and the secretions of the trachea prevent bacteria from stagnating and growing in the inviting warmth and moistness of the body. Also, these secretions contain antibodies that attack the bacteria before they can reach the bloodstream. The secretions in the newborn may not contain sufficient antibodies to protect against certain respiratory infections.

B and T cells are involved in another step in immunity. In response to bacterial infections, B cells (a type of lymphocyte or white blood cell) produce the major antibody groups, immunoglobulins called IgG, IgA, and IgM. These antibodies attach themselves to bacteria to form complexes that can be engulfed by phagocytes that are bacteria-swallowing white cells. Newborns do not produce enough of these antibodies to effectively combat bacteria. Until they are about 6 months of age, infants must primarily rely on the immunoglobulins transmitted from their mothers during fetal life and the small amounts of immunoglobulin A contained in breast milk.

Whereas B cells primarily fight bacteria, T cells combat viral infections. In fact, many of the clinical manifestations of HIV infection result from damage inflicted on the T cells by the virus. Because the newborn also is deficient in T cells, viral infections (e.g., herpes) can cause life-threatening illnesses. Increasing amounts of T cells are produced after the first few months of life, so the risk to the infant diminishes over time.

The final armament in the body's immune defense mechanism is the complement system. This system consists of a cascade of chemicals produced in the body that, among other things, attract phagocytes to the area of infection. These chemicals act like a ZIP code, directing the immune responses of the body. Both these chemicals and phagocytes are inadequate in the newborn.

Bacterial Infections

Because the newborn is deficient in so many components of the body's immune system, it is understandable that infection in the neonate can be dangerous. Bacterial infections occur in about 1 in 500 full-term infants and in a higher proportion of premature infants (Ferrieri, 1990). Infections can be contracted from the mother's bloodstream via the placenta, from bacterial flora that live in the maternal vagina, or from infections of the amniotic fluid, usually after prolonged rupture of fetal membranes. After birth, infections can be transmitted from other infants or hospital staff in the nursery. Factors predisposing an infant to sepsis include prolonged rupture of fetal membranes prior to delivery and maternal infection such as chorioamnionitis or urinary tract infection. Before antibiotics were available, more than 90% of newborn infants with sepsis died; now mortality ranges from less than 10% to 50%, depending on the organism and how soon it is detected and treated (Ferrieri, 1990). Although treatment has improved, the frequency of such infections has increased because more very low birth weight infants are surviving. These infants are both more susceptible to infection than are full-term infants and are more likely to undergo invasive procedures that bypass normal immune protective mechanisms.

Because of the ease with which newborns are infected, infants whose mothers have had infections or prolonged rupture of the membranes are carefully observed for signs of infection. Early diagnosis and treatment with intravenous antibiotics is essential; if untreated, infection can spread rapidly throughout the infant's body. If a blood culture grows bacteria, antibiotics specific for the offending organism will be continued for a period of 1–3 weeks, depending on the severity of the infection. At present, the most common organism causing sepsis in the newborn period is the bacteria Group B *streptococcus,* and the second most common organism is *E. coli.*

With appropriate treatment, clinical improvement generally occurs within 2–3 days. Most infants with systemic bacterial infections will recover without significant complications. If the infection spreads to the coverings of the brain, causing meningitis, however, the mortality rate rises to 20%–25%, and about half of the survivors are left with severe neurological impairments (Remington & Klein, 1995).

As a result of the continuing high mortality and morbidity of bacterial sepsis, despite antibiotic therapy, a number of adjunctive and preventive therapies are being investigated. Adjunctive therapies include giving affected newborns hyperimmune serum that contains antibodies against a specific organism and giving white blood cell transfusions. Preventive therapies include immunizing the mother against specific organisms and giving factors that stimulate the infant to produce more white cells and macrophages (Remington & Klein, 1995).

Viral and Other Nonbacterial Infections

Antibiotics only destroy bacteria; they have no effect on viruses. Thus, different approaches must be used to fight severe viral infections. Viral infections that are often not serious for an adult or older child may cause life-threatening illnesses in the newborn (e.g., herpes) or severe damage to the developing fetus (e.g., rubella, cytomegalovirus, syphilis).

Herpes is the most common life-threatening viral infection of the newborn, occurring in about 1 in 2,000–5,000 births (Remington & Klein, 1995). It most often results from contact with infected genital secretions during delivery. The infection may either be limited to the skin and mucous membranes or become systemic, spreading to other body organs including the brain by 1–2 weeks of life. Rarely, infection is contracted in utero, and symptoms are present at birth (Brown, Vontver, & Benedetti, 1987). Symptoms mimic bacterial sepsis but also may include a rash with blisters.

Only since the 1970s have antiviral drugs been developed that interfere with viral replication and thereby limit their spread. Without therapy, the mortality rate of systemic herpes is about 90%. Using acyclovir, provided the infection is localized to the skin, eyes, and mouth, survival is universal and developmental outcome usually good. (Retinal damage and neurological impairment still occur in a small percentage of children.) If the infection spreads to the brain, however, there is a 14% mortality rate, and two thirds of survivors sustain severe disabilities including blindness, mental retardation, and/or cerebral palsy. If the infection is disseminated throughout the body, more than half the infants die, and about half of the survivors have developmental disabilities (Whitley, Arvin, Prober, et al., 1991).

Cytomegalovirus is a very common infection in pregnant women, and it is estimated that 1% of all newborns have congenital cytomegalovirus infection. Usually mothers present with only a mild flu-like illness. However, 10% of congenitally infected newborns have a severe disease at birth, resulting in death or neurological sequelae. An additional 25% of infected newborns appear asymptomatic at birth but subsequently manifest sequelae including hearing loss, eye damage, mental retardation, and neuromuscular impairments (Remington & Klein, 1995). Although in the past there has been no treatment available for this disease, the antiviral drug ganciclovir has shown promise in reducing mortality and morbidity in congenitally infected infants (Nigro, Scholz, & Bartmann, 1994).

An infectious disease that has markedly increased in incidence in infants since the mid-1980s is human immunodeficiency virus (HIV) infection (see Chapter 9). Information suggests that approximately one quarter of infants born to untreated mothers who are infected with HIV will develop an HIV infection. The provision of antiviral therapy (AZT) to HIV-infected women during pregnancy and to their infants after birth, however, has been shown to markedly reduce transmission of the virus to the infant (Connor & Mofenson, 1995).

Hyperbilirubinemia

Jaundice, the yellow discoloration of the body and eyes due to an excessive accumulation of bilirubin (hyperbilirubinemia), is a common problem in the newborn period. Jaundice results from the following course of events: When red blood cells die (usually after a life span of about 90 days in infants), hemoglobin, the oxygen-carrying blood protein, is broken down, and one of the components released is bilirubin. The circulatory system then carries the bilirubin to the liver where it is metabolized in a process called conjugation and excreted into the intestines. Bilirubin can accumulate when too many red blood cells break down, when there is inadequate activity of the conjugation process, or when there is a blockage to excretion.

Although jaundice is a sign of severe liver disease in the adult, it is often quite innocuous in a newborn infant. Usually, jaundice in infants results from an increased rate of breakdown of red blood cells in the first days after birth and an immaturity of the system necessary for conjugation of bilirubin. The infant becomes yellow-tinged at 2–3 days of age but ordinarily returns to a normal color by 1 week of age without therapy. The bilirubin level is usually below 10–15 milligrams per 100 milliliters in a full-term infant. This is called physiological jaundice. If the bilirubin level becomes too high, placement of the baby under special phototherapy lights or wrapping in a phototherapy blanket will usually lead to a drop in the bilirubin level. Phototherapy acts by changing bilirubin to a more easily excretable compound. Phototherapy has been shown to be quite safe (Scheidt, Graubard, Nelson, et al., 1991), the most common side effects being loose stools, rash, and dehydration.

A modest elevation in the bilirubin level has little effect on the developing infant, but a marked increase may pose a serious threat. The most severe cause of hyperbilirubinemia is Rh incompatibility, in which a massive breakdown of red blood cells leads to jaundice. The Rh factor is a minor blood group attached to the four major blood types: A, B, AB, and O. Thus, a person may be ORh$^-$ or ORh$^+$, ARh$^-$ or ARh$^+$, and so on.

Incompatibility of the Rh blood groups between mother and fetus may have disastrous consequences for the fetus. Problems develop in the following sequence: 1) Although the fetal and maternal circulatory systems are separate, an occasional fetal blood cell gets into the maternal circulation; 2) the mother's immune system then recognizes the baby's red cells as being foreign and forms antibodies that cross the placenta to the fetus and begin to destroy the fetus's red blood cells; 3) the fetus may become severely anemic; and 4) although jaundice is not a problem in utero because the maternal liver rapidly metabolizes fetal bilirubin, once born the infant often rapidly develops severe hyperbilirubinemia.

In the past, many affected fetuses died in utero from severe anemia. Those who survived often developed severe hyperbilirubinemia after birth and a resultant condition called kernicterus. This syndrome includes mental retardation, cerebral palsy, high-frequency hearing loss, paralysis of the upward gaze, and discoloration of the teeth (Connolly & Volpe, 1990).

Over the years, treatment of Rh incompatibility has made great progress and moved from palliation to prevention. In the 1950s, intrauterine blood transfusions were given to save severely affected fetuses. Beginning in the second trimester, a needle was inserted through the uterus into the fetal abdominal cavity, and a transfusion of red blood cells was given. The red blood cells were absorbed into the fetal circulation and improved the anemia. More recently, transfusions have been performed by directly inserting a needle through the abdominal wall of the mother into the umbilical vein of the fetus. Even with these maneuvers during pregnancy, the infant often needs multiple exchange blood transfusions in the newborn period to lower the bilirubin level.

Problems with Rh incompatibility have become much less common in the 1980s and 1990s as a result of the development of Rh immunoglobulin (RhoGAM). This is a gamma globulin or type of blocking antibody given by injection to Rh$^-$ women during the last trimester of pregnancy and after delivery or miscarriage of all Rh$^+$ infants. Rh immunoglobulin works by blocking the formation of antibodies in the mother's circulation. As a result, subsequent Rh$^+$ infants will be born without anemia and will not develop severe hyperbilirubinemia.

Incompatibility of the major blood groups (A, B, AB, and O) and a variety of other conditions also may cause jaundice, but usually the problem is far less severe than with Rh incompatibility and generally resolves with phototherapy. Bilirubin levels of up to 20 milligrams per 100 milliliters do not appear to be dangerous to otherwise healthy full-term infants. The long-term effects of bilirubin levels above 20–25 milligrams per 100 milliliters in full-term infants are unclear (Bryla, 1991; Newman & Maisels, 1990; Scheidt et al., 1991). There may be a delay in motor development and a modest hearing impairment in some infants. New approaches to assessing damage include the use of auditory brainstem response (ABR) (see Chapter 12) and taking an MRI of the brain. The ABR can demonstrate subtle functional auditory abnormalities in the brain stem that accompany bilirubin damage, and an MRI can demonstrate bilirubin staining of certain areas of the brain.

Hyperbilirubinemia is more of a problem for the premature than the full-term infant. The severe neurological damage seen in kernicterus can occur at lower levels of bilirubin than in the full-term infant (van de Bor, Ens-Dokkum, Schreuder, et al., 1992). Although much remains unknown regarding the various factors involved in the development of kernicterus, the combination of monitoring of serum bilirubin levels, administration of phototherapy, and performance of exchange transfusion, when necessary, has resulted in a marked decrease in bilirubin neurotoxicity in premature infants since the 1980s (Watchko & Oski, 1992).

Hypoglycemia

At birth, infants are suddenly faced with the need to supply their own energy requirements for maintenance of body temperature, breathing, feeding, muscle activity, and other metabolic needs. This can be accomplished only if the infant receives sufficient oxygen and nutrients, particularly glucose. Hypoglycemia or low blood sugar levels result when too much glucose is used or not enough is produced. The hypoglycemic infant appears lethargic and jittery and may have intermittent breathing (apnea), temperature instability, and/or seizures (Ogata, 1986).

Hypoglycemia most commonly occurs in infants who have been asphyxiated, are premature, are poorly nourished, or whose mothers had diabetes during pregnancy (Sann, 1990). The mechanism of the hypoglycemia varies. In asphyxia, the infant is forced to use **anaerobic** metabolism to produce energy. This is a very wasteful form of metabolism that rapidly depletes glycogen, the storage form of glucose. Because the ability to produce sugar is developmentally deficient in the newborn, the blood glucose level can drop precipitously. In premature infants, the problem is amplified as they usually have decreased quantities of glycogen to begin with. Poorly nourished infants often have a combination of decreased glycogen stores and a decreased ability to produce glucose. Full-term, well-nourished infants, however, have adequate glycogen stores and can utilize them to produce glucose. Yet, they too can become hypoglycemic under circumstances of increased metabolic need related to severe illness. These include sepsis, pneumonia, congenital heart disease, brain hemorrhage, and drug withdrawal.

The mechanism of hypoglycemia in the infant of a mother with diabetes is different. Here, hypoglycemia occurs because the fetal pancreas has been overproducing insulin to compensate for the mother's lack of insulin production. Insulin takes care of two functions: 1) lowering of blood sugar and 2) laying down of fatty tissue. Because of the overproduction of insulin, infants of mothers with diabetes appear obese and have enlarged body organs containing increased body fat. After birth, the pancreas continues to overproduce insulin. This results in a rapid fall in the blood sugar level that is often difficult to control. The insulin production falls off within a few days to 2 weeks, and the infant should do well if given supplemental glucose during this period.

Prognosis after hypoglycemia is unclear as there have been few long-term outcome studies. Asymptomatic hypoglycemia would appear to have a better prognosis than symptomatic hypoglycemia, particularly if there have been seizures. However, persistent asymptomatic hypoglycemia may be associated with significant neurodevelopmental consequences (Lucas, Morley,

& Cole, 1988). If the hypoglycemia is detected and treated promptly, the primary determinant of prognosis is the condition predisposing to hypoglycemia rather than the hypoglycemia itself.

Mineral imbalances can lead to symptoms that simulate hypoglycemia. Most common are deficiencies in calcium and magnesium (Salle, Delvin, Glorieux, et al., 1990). These tend to occur in low birth weight infants and often accompany hypoxic-ischemic encephalopathy. As with hypoglycemia, if these disorders are diagnosed early, they can usually be corrected with an intravenous feeding of the deficient mineral.

Inborn Errors of Metabolism

A number of congenital enzyme deficiencies occur with episodes of vomiting, lethargy, and coma in the first week of life (see Chapter 19). Examples of these rare disorders include maple syrup urine disease, inborn errors of the urea cycle, and organic acidemias. Prior to birth, the mother's placenta removes toxins that are produced as a result of these enzyme deficiencies. However, after birth the toxins accumulate, usually derived from the protein in the formula or breast milk that the child ingests. In contrast to infants with asphyxia, infants with a severe enzyme deficiency have an uncomplicated birth history and normal Apgar scores. They generally look well for the first 24–48 hours of life but then develop severe symptoms over the next few days. If the disorder is unrecognized, most of these children will die in the first weeks of life. If diagnosis is delayed and the child remains in a coma for many days, he or she may survive but is likely to have severe developmental disabilities. Thus, early identification and treatment are essential.

Maternal Substance Abuse

A problem of increasing concern is drug withdrawal of the infant during the first week of life. The pattern of withdrawal symptoms varies depending on the abused drug, the size of the dose, the duration of the maternal drug use, and when the drug was last taken by the mother. Withdrawal from barbiturates often leads to seizures on the second or third day of life. Heroin and methadone withdrawal generally leads to a persistent and high-pitched cry, hyperactivity, sneezing, vomiting, respiratory distress, and diarrhea beginning by the fourth day. Symptoms of methadone withdrawal can continue for 3–6 weeks.

Caring for the infant in a quiet darkened environment seems to improve symptoms. When severe symptoms occur, treatment with barbiturates or other sedatives can help to lessen the withdrawal symptoms. Long-term effects of intrauterine exposure to cocaine, heroin, and methadone are difficult to assess because of problems with follow-up in this group of individuals and the strong interplay of other socioeconomic factors (see Chapter 8).

Neonatal Seizures

Seizures are not rare in the newborn period. The clinical manifestations are quite different from those occurring in an older child. Although generalized tonic-clonic seizures are the most common form observed in older children, seizures in the newborn tend to be subtle and focal. Neonatal seizures are not generalized because the newborn's immature cortex has a sparse network of neurons (Figure 6.8). Because the spread of the seizure relies on the recruitment of nearby cells, the fewer cells surrounding the abnormal area, the more localized the seizure.

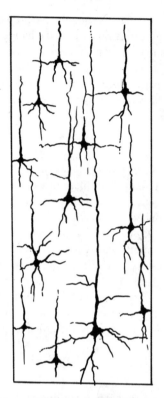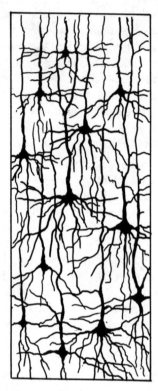

Figure 6.8.   Progressive development of neurons during fetal life and the first year of life. On the left is a drawing of a section of brain from a newborn infant. The illustration on the right shows a section of brain from a 6-year-old child. Because of the few interconnections, the newborn rarely has a full-fledged generalized tonic-clonic seizure; it may well involve only one or two limbs. By 1 year, the increased interconnections lead to a typical tonic-clonic seizure in a susceptible child. (From *Your child has a disability: A complete sourcebook of daily and medical care* by Mark Batshaw [p. 48]. Copyright © 1991 by M.L. Batshaw; illustrations copyright © 1991 by Lynn Reynolds. Boston: Little, Brown; reprinted by permission.)

Newborn seizures can be divided into four types based on their appearance and cause: subtle, clonic, myoclonic, and tonic (Volpe, 1995). Subtle seizures have manifestations that may be overlooked. They may consist of only deviation of the eyes, staring, blinking, sucking motions, tonic posturing of a limb, or apnea. There may be unusual movements of the arms resembling boxing or of the legs resembling peddling. These seizures are most common in premature infants. The second type, clonic seizures, manifest as slow rhythmic movements and can be focal or multifocal. Focal clonic seizures commonly involve the face or a limb on one side of the body and often occur after cerebral infarction (stroke), hypoglycemia, hypocalcemia, and other metabolic disorders. Multifocal clonic seizures start in one limb and then progress to a second limb; they are most common in full-term infants who have sustained asphyxia.

Myoclonic seizures involve episodes of multiple jerking of upper and/or lower limbs. This type of seizure has been linked to intracranial infections and developmental brain malformations. The fourth type, the tonic seizure, manifests as extensions of all extremities and, unlike the other types, frequently is not associated with electrical seizure activity on the EEG (Volpe,

1995). This clinical seizure type occurs most commonly in premature infants with severe intracerebral hemorrhages.

Prognosis after newborn seizures is variable and dependent on cause. Mortality has improved since the 1950s and 1960s, dropping from around 40% to 20%, likely as a result of improved obstetrical and neonatal care. However, neurological sequelae (mental retardation, cerebral palsy, seizures) have not changed substantially during this time period, remaining at about 25%–35% (Volpe, 1995). Some evidence suggests that neonatal seizures themselves may have adverse effects on the developing brain. However, the prognosis depends most on the precipitant of the seizure. The best prognosis is associated with seizures precipitated by drug withdrawal and uncomplicated hypocalcemia. Infants who have seizures related to hypoglycemia, hypoxic-ischemic encephalopathy, or intracranial infection have a 50% risk of manifesting neurodevelopmental sequelae, and those with brain malformations almost uniformly have developmental disabilities. Sequelae after seizures caused by intracranial hemorrhage are dependent on the type of hemorrhage. Newborns with subarachnoid hemorrhage have less than a 10% risk of sequelae, while those with severe intraventricular hemorrhage have more than a 90% risk (Volpe, 1995).

Treatment with antiepileptic drugs, most commonly phenobarbital and sometimes phenytoin or lorazepam, is usually effective in controlling the seizures. In some instances, the seizures do not return, and antiepileptic medication can be stopped during the neonatal period. In about 30% of individuals, however, the seizures are a harbinger for the future development of a seizure disorder. Here, antiepileptic therapy may need to be continued on a long-term basis (see Chapter 26).

Congenital Anomalies

Developmental anomalies of the brain (see Chapter 14) and other body organs are the other major cause of morbidity and mortality in the newborn period. Examples include holoprosencephaly, anencephaly, hypoplastic left heart syndrome, and Potter syndrome. Although many of these congenital defects are incompatible with survival outside the womb, infants with these defects who do survive have an increased susceptibility to various problems in the newborn period, including intracranial hemorrhage, apnea, hypoglycemia, and infection. After the neonatal period, these children are at greatly increased risk for seizures, cerebral palsy, mental retardation, and other developmental disabilities as a result of both the underlying congenital anomaly and the perinatal complications. Although for many of these individuals, treatment has little effect on the outcome, it is important that they be identified early so that they can receive early intervention services to prevent superimposed impairments and so that their families can receive assistance in obtaining appropriate care and psychosocial support.

SUMMARY

The first month of life is a critical period in the infant's development. Birth itself can be a hazardous event. After birth, many metabolic and anatomical changes must take place for the infant to cope with the new environment outside the protection of the womb. Because these changes are so momentous and rapid, many abnormalities can occur. Some complications, such as hypoglycemia, are readily correctable if identified early. Others, such as asphyxia, can best be handled prophylactically, with fetal monitoring and early delivery. Advances in obstetric and neonatal care since the 1960s have led to a dramatic improvement in the prevention and management of common medical problems that occur around the time of birth. Other abnormalities, such as most birth defects, have no effective prevention or treatment but require intervention to avoid additional problems from occurring. For infants who have experienced brain damage in the fetal or neonatal period, the extent of their impairments may not be known for months or even years. It must be emphasized, however, that more than 99% of all newborns survive the first month of life, and the vast majority will grow up healthy and with typical development.

REFERENCES

Batshaw, M.L. (1991). *Your child has a disability: A complete source book of daily and medical care.* Boston: Little, Brown.

Brown, Z.A., Vontver, L.A., & Benedetti, J. (1987). Effects on infants of a first episode of genital herpes during pregnancy. *New England Journal of Medicine, 317,* 1246–1251.

Bryla, D.A. (1991). Intelligence at six years in relation to neonatal bilirubin levels: Follow-up of the National Institute for Child and Human Development clinical trial of phototherapy. *Pediatrics, 87,* 797–805.

Connolly, A.M., & Volpe, J.J. (1990). Clinical features of bilirubin encephalopathy. *Clinics in Perinatology, 17,* 371–379.

Connor, E.M., & Mofenson, L.M. (1995). Zidovudine for the reduction of perinatal human immunodeficiency virus transmission: Pediatric AIDS Clinical Trials Group Protocol 076: Results and treatment recommendations. *Pediatric Infectious Disease Journal, 14,* 536–541.

Espinoza, M.I., & Parer, J.T. (1991). Mechanisms of asphyxial brain damage, and possible pharmacologic interventions, in the fetus. *American Journal of Obstetrics and Gynecology, 164,* 1582–1589.

Fanaroff, A.A., & Martin, R.J. (1996). *Neonatal-perinatal medicine: Diseases of the fetus and infant* (6th ed.). St. Louis: C.V. Mosby.

Ferrieri, P. (1990). Neonatal susceptibility and immunity to major bacterial pathogens. *Reviews of Infectious Diseases, 12,* 394–400.

Fish, W.H., Cohen, M., Franzek, D., et al. (1990). Effect of intramuscular vitamin E on mortality and intracranial hemorrhage in neonates of 1000 grams or less. *Pediatrics, 85,* 578–584.

Glass, P., Wagner, A.E., Papero, P.H., et al. (1995). Neurodevelopmental status at age five years of neonates treated with extracorporeal membrane oxygenation. *Journal of Pediatrics, 127,* 447–457.

Gunn, A.J., Williams, C.E., Mallard, C., et al. (1994). Flunarizine, a calcium channel antagonist is partially neuroprotective in hypoxic-ischemic encephalopathy in fetal sheep. *Pediatric Research, 35,* 657–663.

Guyer, B., Strobino, D.M., Ventura, S.J., et al. (1996). Annual summary of vital statistics: 1995. *Pediatrics, 98,* 1007–1019.

Hill, A., & Volpe, J.J. (1989). Perinatal asphyxia: Clinical aspects. *Clinics in Perinatology, 16,* 435–457.

Hull, J., & Dodd, K.L. (1992). Falling incidence of hypoxic-ischemic encephalopathy in term infants. *British Journal of Obstetrics and Gynecology, 99,* 386–391.

Jain, L., Ferre, C., Vidyasagar, D., et al. (1991). Cardiopulmonary resuscitation of apparently stillborn infants: Survival and long-term outcome. *Journal of Pediatrics, 118,* 778–782.

Krishnamoorthy, K.S., Kuban, K.C., Leviton, A., et al. (1990). Periventricular-intraventricular hemorrhage, sonographic localization, phenobarbital, and motor abnormalities in low birth weight infants. *Pediatrics, 85,* 1027–1033.

Lipton, S.A., & Rosenberg, P.A. (1994). Excitatory amino acids as a final common pathway for neurologic disorders. *New England Journal of Medicine, 330,* 613–622.

Lucas, A., Morley, R., & Cole, T.J. (1988). Adverse neurodevelopmental outcome of moderate neonatal hypoglycemia. *British Medical Journal, 297,* 1304–1308.

Ment, L.R., Oh, W., Ehrenkranz, R.A., et al. (1994). Low-dose indomethacin and prevention of intraventricular hemorrhage: A multicenter randomized trial. *Pediatrics, 93,* 543–550.

Nelson, K.B. (1989). Relationship of intrapartum and delivery room events to long-term neurologic outcome. *Clinics in Perinatology, 16,* 995–1007.

Nigro, G., Scholz, H., & Bartmann, U. (1994). Ganciclovir therapy for symptomatic congenital cytomegalovirus infection in infants: A 2-regimen experience. *Journal of Pediatrics, 124,* 318–322.

Newman, T.B., & Maisels, M.J. (1990). Does hyperbilirubinemia damage the brain of healthy full-term infants? *Clinics in Perinatology, 17,* 331–358.

Ogata, E.S. (1986). Carbohydrate metabolism in the fetus and neonate and altered neonatal glucoregulation. *Pediatric Clinics of North America, 33,* 25–45.

Remington, J.S., & Klein, J.O. (1995). *Infectious diseases of the fetus and newborn infant* (4th ed.). Philadelphia: W.B. Saunders.

Robertson, C., & Finer, N. (1993). Long-term follow up of term neonates with perinatal asphyxia. *Clinics in Perinatology, 20,* 483–499.

Rogers, B., Msall, M., Owens, T., et al. (1994). Cystic periventricular leukomalacia and type of cerebral palsy in preterm infants. *Journal of Pediatrics, 125,* S1–S8.

Salle, B.L., Delvin, E., Glorieux, F., et al. (1990). Human neonatal hypocalcemia. *Biology of the Neonate, 58*(Suppl. 1), 22–31.

Sann, L. (1990). Neonatal hypoglycemia. *Biology of the Neonate, 58*(Suppl. 1), 16–21.

Scheidt, P.C., Graubard, B.I., Nelson, K.B., et al. (1991). Intelligence at six years in relation to neonatal bilirubin levels: Follow-up of the National Institute of Child Health and Human Development clinical trial of phototherapy. *Pediatrics, 87,* 797–805.

Thacker, K.E., Lim, T., & Drew, J.H. (1987). Cephalhaematoma: A 10–year review. *Australian and New Zealand Journal of Obstetrics and Gynaecology, 27,* 210–212.

van de Bor, M., Ens-Dokkum, M., Schreuder, A.M., et al. (1992). Hyperbilirubinemia in low birth weight infants and outcome at 5 years of age. *Pediatrics, 89,* 359–364.

Vannucci, R.C. (1990). Current and potentially new management strategies for perinatal hypoxic-ischemic encephalopathy. *Pediatrics, 85,* 961–968.

Volpe, J.J. (1995). *Neurology of the newborn* (3rd ed.). Philadelphia: W.B. Saunders.

Volpe, J.J. (1997). Brain injury in the premature infant: Neuropathology, clinical aspects, and pathogenesis. *Mental Retardation and Developmental Disabilities Research Reviews, 3,* 3–12.

Watchko, J.F., & Oski, F.A. (1992). Kernicterus in preterm newborns: Past, present, and future. *Pediatrics, 90,* 707–715.

Whitley, R., Arvin, A., Prober, C., et al. (1991). A controlled trial comparing vidarabine with acyclovir in neonatal herpes simplex virus infection. *New England Journal of Medicine, 324,* 444–449.

7 Born Too Soon, Born Too Small

Judy C. Bernbaum
Mark L. Batshaw

Upon completion of this chapter, the reader will:

- be able to distinguish between the premature infant and the small for gestational age infant
- recognize some of the causes of prematurity and intrauterine growth retardation
- be able to identify distinguishing physical characteristics of the premature infant
- understand the complications and illnesses associated with prematurity
- be aware of the methods used to care for low birth weight infants
- know the results of outcome studies and the value of early intervention programs

Infants born too soon or too small are at risk for a number of complications during the newborn period and early infancy, some related to the immaturity of the lungs and central nervous system (CNS), others to environmental stressors. These problems place the low birth weight (LBW) infant at increased risk for developmental disabilities. This chapter addresses the problems of LBW infants and discusses some new forms of medical management that have improved their outcomes.

DEFINITIONS

When a child is born weighing less than 2,500 grams, he or she is classified as an LBW infant. Infants who weigh less than 1,500 grams at birth are considered very low birth weight (VLBW) infants, those weighing less than 1,000 grams are termed extremely low birth weight infants, and those weighing less than 800 grams are classified as micropremies. These infants may be premature and/or small for gestational age (SGA). A premature infant is defined as one born at or before the 36th week of gestation, 1 month before the estimated due date. Infants born before 28 weeks' gestation have extreme prematurity. An SGA infant refers to a newborn whose weight is below the 10th percentile for gestational age; SGA infants are sometimes also called dysmature, light for dates, or small-for-dates. SGA infants can be full term or premature.

As an example, at 40 weeks' gestational age, the 10th percentile for weight is 5½ pounds, or 2,500 grams (Figure 7.1). Therefore, an infant born at 35 weeks' gestation who weighs 5 pounds, or 2,250 grams, is considered premature but appropriate in size for the gestational age (AGA) (25th percentile), but an infant born at term weighing the same 5 pounds is considered SGA (less than 10th percentile). Both premature and SGA infants have higher rates of neonatal complications and death than full-term AGA infants.

INCIDENCE OF LOW BIRTH WEIGHT INFANTS

Each year, approximately 350,000 LBW infants are born in the United States (Guyer, Strobino, Ventura, et al., 1995). In 1994, LBW infants accounted for 7.2% of all births and VLBW infants an additional 1.3% (Guyer et al., 1995). LBW infants are born to African American women twice as often as to Caucasian and Hispanic women. Of LBW infants, 70% are premature (both AGA and SGA) while 30% are full-term SGA infants. This contrasts with developing countries, where approximately 70% of LBW infants are SGA, largely as a result of maternal malnutrition or disease (National Center for Chronic Disease Prevention and Health Promotion, Division of

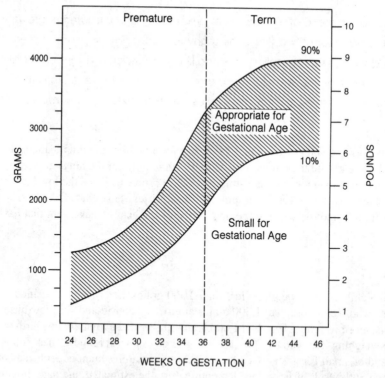

Figure 7.1.   Newborn weight chart by gestational age. The shaded area between the 10th and 90th percentiles represents infants who are appropriate for gestational age. Weight below the 10th percentile makes an infant small for gestational age. Prematurity is defined as an infant born before 36 weeks' gestation. (From Lubchenco, L.O. [1976]. *The high risk infant.* Philadelphia: W.B. Saunders; reprinted by permission.)

Nutrition; National Center for Health Statistics, Division of Vital Statistics; and Centers for Disease Control, 1994).

PREMATURITY

A number of maternal factors increase the likelihood of a preterm delivery (Table 7.1). The largest single factor is maternal age. Adolescent mothers account for 20% of all premature births, although less than 5% of all pregnancies occur in adolescents (Cooper, Leland, & Alexander, 1995). The mechanism for this is not entirely clear, but there is evidence that the immature uterus of the adolescent is more susceptible to early contractions than that of a woman in her early 20s. In addition, poor nutrition, inadequate prenatal care, illicit drug use, and toxemia play a role. Other factors that lead to an increased risk for preterm births include many previous pregnancies, weak cervical muscles, and multiple births. In addition, infections during the third trimester, premature rupture of membranes, and chronic maternal illnesses make premature deliveries more likely to occur (see Chapter 5). Finally, certain congenital malformations or injuries to the fetus may lead to a premature birth. Although these are the most common known causes of prematurity, the precipitating cause for the majority of prematurely born infants remains unknown.

Physical and Developmental Characteristics of Premature Infants

Several physical and neurodevelopmental characteristics distinguish the premature infant from the full-term infant. Dubowitz, Dubowitz, and Goldberg (1970) developed a scoring system that takes into account these findings and enables physicians to confirm the mother's dates or to arrive at the gestational age when the mother's dates are unknown. Ballard, Khoury, Wedig, et al. (1991) have updated this system (Figure 7.2).

The main characteristics that distinguish a premature infant are the presence of body hair; a reddish skin color; and the absence of skin creases, ear cartilage, and breast buds. Premature infants have fine hair, or **lanugo,** over the entire body; this is lost by 38 weeks' gestation. Also, the

Table 7.1.   Known causes of prematurity

Amniotic fluid/membrane infection
  (chorioamnionitis)
Drug /alcohol abuse
Fetal distress
Maternal age (adolescent or older mother)
Maternal chronic illnesses
Maternal bacterial vaginosis
Maternal pyelonephritis (kidney infection)
Multiple gestation
Placental bleeding (abruptio, previa)
Polyhydramnios (excessive amniotic fluid)
Poor prenatal care
Premature rupture of the membranes
Preeclampsia
Uterine abnormalities / incompetent cervix

Neuromuscular Maturity

	-1	0	1	2	3	4	5
Posture							
Square Window (wrist)	>90°	90°	60°	45°	30°	0°	
Arm Recoil		180°	140°-180°	110°-140°	90-110°	<90°	
Popliteal Angle	180°	160°	140°	120°	100°	90°	<90°
Scarf Sign							
Heel to Ear							

Physical Maturity

Skin	sticky friable transparent	gelatinous red, translucent	smooth pink, visible veins	superficial peeling &/or rash. few veins	cracking pale areas rare veins	parchment deep cracking no vessels	leathery cracked wrinkled
Lanugo	none	sparse	abundant	thinning	bald areas	mostly bald	
Plantar Surface	heel-toe 40-50mm:-1 <40mm:-2	>50mm no crease	faint red marks	anterior transverse crease only	creases ant. 2/3	creases over entire sole	
Breast	imperceptible	barely perceptible	flat areola no bud	stippled areola 1-2mm bud	raised areola 3-4mm bud	full areola 5-10mm bud	
Eye/Ear	lids fused loosely:-1 tightly:-2	lids open pinna flat stays folded	sl. curved pinna; soft; slow recoil	well-curved pinna; soft but ready recoil	formed &firm instant recoil	thick cartilage ear stiff	
Genitals male	scrotum flat, smooth	scrotum empty faint rugae	testes in upper canal rare rugae	testes descending few rugae	testes down good rugae	testes pendulous deep rugae	
Genitals female	clitoris prominent labia flat	prominent clitoris small labia minora	prominent clitoris enlarging minora	majora & minora equally prominent	majora large minora small	majora cover clitoris & minora	

Maturity Rating

score	weeks
-10	20
-5	22
0	24
5	26
10	28
15	30
20	32
25	34
30	36
35	38
40	40
45	42
50	44

Figure 7.2.   Scoring system to assess newborn infants. The score for each of the neuromuscular and physical signs is added together to obtain a score called the total maturity score. Gestational age is determined from this score. (From Ballard, J.L., Khoury, J.C., Wedig, K., et al. [1991]. New Ballard score, expanded to include extremely premature infants. *Journal of Pediatrics, 119,* 418; reprinted by permission.)

extremely premature infant lacks skin creases on the soles of the feet; these develop after 32 weeks. Skin color is ruddier because the blood vessels are closer to the surface, and the skin appears translucent. Finally, breast buds and cartilage in the ear lobe do not appear until around the 34th week of gestation (Figure 7.3).

In addition to physical characteristics, differences in neurological and behavioral development also are evident in the premature infant. In the third trimester, neurological maturation principally involves an increase in muscle tone and changes in reflex activity and joint mobility (Amiel-Tison, 1968; Constantine, Kraemer, Kendall-Tackett, et al., 1987). An infant born before 28 weeks' gestation is very floppy. After that time, flexor tone gradually improves, starting with the legs and moving up to the arms by 32 weeks. Thus, while the premature infant lies in an extended, rag-doll position, the full-term infant rests in a semi-flexed position. Associated with increased tone is reduced flexibility of the joints. Premature infants are "double-jointed," while full-term infants are not. Finally, although certain primitive reflexes, such as the asymmetric tonic neck reflex (see Figure 24.3), can be seen in rudimentary form as early as 25 weeks' gestation, they are not expressed as a more complete form until 30–32 weeks' gestation (Allen & Capute, 1986; Mandrich, Simons, Ritchie, et al., 1994). As a result, extremely premature infants may not have well-developed primitive reflexes at birth. In terms of behavior, premature infants appear apathetic as compared with full-term infants. They mostly sleep and require vigorous stimulation to remain alert. They also appear behaviorally disorganized.

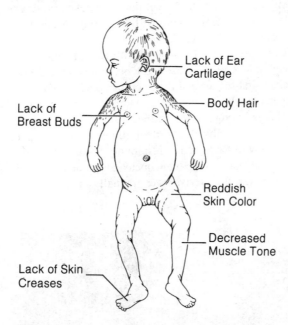

Figure 7.3. Typical physical features of a premature infant.

Complications of Prematurity

In addition to having distinctive physical, neurological, and behavioral features, premature infants are more susceptible to medical complications in the newborn period than full-term infants. Among these complications are respiratory distress syndrome (RDS), **bronchopulmonary dysplasia (BPD),** intracerebral insults, patent ductus arteriosus, apnea and **bradycardia,** sudden infant death syndrome, necrotizing enterocolitis and gastroesophgeal reflux, retinopathy of prematurity, infections, and other physiological abnormalities.

Respiratory Distress Syndrome

Approximately 20% of all premature infants develop RDS during their first or second day of life. The degree of prematurity affects the prevalence of this disorder. For example, less than 10% of the infants born between 34 and 36 weeks' gestation develop RDS, while more than 60% of infants born at 32 weeks' gestation or less do (Verma, 1995).

In the extremely preterm infant (less than 28 weeks), the primary cause of RDS is the physical immaturity of the lung and breathing apparatus. In the more mature preterm infant, RDS is caused by a lack of a chemical called **surfactant** in the alveoli, or air pockets, of the lungs. Surfactant is a soapy-like substance that allows the alveoli to expand easily and prevents their collapse after each breath. In the absence of sufficient amounts of surfactant, each breath requires a tremendous amount of energy in order to re-inflate the stiff alveoli. Infants with RDS appear to have normal breathing patterns at birth but within hours have grunting respirations, as they begin to use their abdominal muscles to help with breathing. A chest X ray can easily confirm RDS. If a newborn has normal lung expansion, the chest is filled with translucent air that appears black on the X ray; the lungs of a neonate with RDS, however, have a "ground glass" appearance, as the collapsed alveoli are dense and look white on the X ray (Figure 7.4).

In 1970, physicians first recognized the importance of keeping the alveoli open while providing adequate oxygen (Avery, Fletcher, & MacDonald, 1994). Before this time enough oxygen was supplied to the lungs by ventilators but because the alveoli remained collapsed, the exchange of oxygen between the alveoli and the pulmonary blood vessels was inadequate, and more than half of infants with RDS died of respiratory failure (Figure 7.5). Once constant pressure was delivered to the alveoli to keep them open and promote an efficient exchange of oxygen and carbon dioxide, however, the survival rate gradually increased to the current level of 90% (Scanlon, 1994).

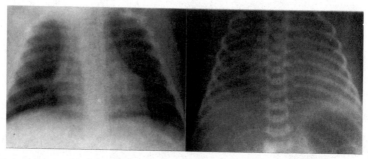

Figure 7.4.   Chest X rays of a normal newborn (left) and of a premature infant with RDS (right).

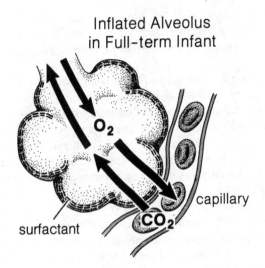
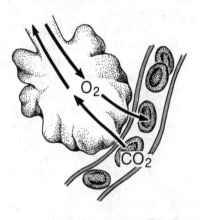

Inflated Alveolus in Full-term Infant

O₂

surfactant

capillary

CO₂

Collapsed Alveolus in Premature with RDS

O₂

CO₂

Figure 7.5.   Schematic drawing of alveoli in a normal newborn and in a premature infant with RDS. Note that the inflated alveolus is kept open by surfactant. Oxygen moves from the alveolus to the red blood cells in the pulmonary capillary. Carbon dioxide moves in the opposite direction. This exchange is much less efficient when the alveolus is collapsed. The result is hypoxia.

In mildly affected infants, supplemental oxygen alone or in combination with continuous positive airway pressure (CPAP) may be sufficient to keep the alveoli open. With CPAP, a mixture of oxygen and air is provided under continuous pressure through short two-pronged tubes placed in the nostrils, which prevents the alveoli from collapsing between breaths. More severely affected infants require **intubation** and the delivery of a mixture of oxygen and air by a ventilator under positive end expiration pressure (PEEP). The concept of PEEP is similar to CPAP, but there is more direct access to the lungs and improved control of respiratory efforts. There are various adaptations of PEEP using high-frequency jet or oscillatory ventilators and other devices that further enhance gas exchange (Raphael, Atkinson, & Bexton, 1995) as well as the use of perfluorocarbon liquid or partial liquid ventilation (Leach, Greenspan, Rubenstein, et al., 1996).

Another advance that holds great promise for the treatment of RDS in VLBW infants is surfactant replacement therapy (Long, 1993; Patel & Klein, 1995). Both synthetic and bovine (cow) surfactant can be administered directly into the lungs of the premature infant via an endotracheal tube. Research has shown that if surfactant is given before the development of RDS, the illness is less severe and the likelihood of mortality and morbidity is significantly reduced (Horbar, Wright, & Onstad, 1993; Kattwinkel, Bloom, Delmore, et al., 1993). Less oxygen is required, and artificial ventilation is needed for a shorter period of time. The risk of chronic lung disease (see following section on BPD) and neurodevelopmental impairments also may be decreased (Gerdes, Gerdes, Beaumont, et al., 1995; Gong, Anday, Boros, et al., 1995).

A related approach that has helped reduce the incidence of RDS involves stimulating surfactant production. There is some evidence that the steroid medication dexamethasone administered to the mother 24–36 hours before delivery stimulates maturation of the lungs and production of surfactant (especially in males), thus lessening the likelihood of RDS or decreasing its severity (Crowley, 1992; Kari, Hallman, Eronen, et al., 1994; Moya & Gross, 1993). Antenatal treatment with thyroid-releasing hormone may also help to decrease the risk of RDS (Australian Collaborative Trial, 1995). Both of these treatments are still considered experimental and are not in routine use.

Occasionally, preterm infants with severe RDS develop a further complication, a narrowing of the blood vessels in the damaged lung. This leads to high resistance to blood flow from the heart into the pulmonary (lung) circulation, a condition called **pulmonary hypertension.** This, in turn, interferes with oxygen getting into the red blood cells at the level of the alveoli (Figure 7.5). Treatment involves using high-frequency ventilators (Majewski, Telmanik, & Arrington, 1994). Because these ventilators cycle rapidly, they can use less pressure to obtain adequate gas exchange in the lungs. This decreases the pulmonary vascular pressure and reduces the strain on the heart. Inhaled nitric oxide also reverses pulmonary vasoconstriction and may improve pulmonary hypertension (Frostell, Bolmqvist, Hedenstierna, et al., 1993).

The outcome for infants who develop RDS has clearly improved with the availability of new technology. Although the prognosis varies with the gestational age and weight of the infant, the risk for severe developmental disability is less than 15%, only slightly greater than for premature infants who do not experience RDS (Scanlon, 1994). Yet, there remains a risk for two significant long-term complications: BPD and intracerebral insults.

Bronchopulmonary Dysplasia

With proper treatment, most infants with RDS can be weaned off oxygen or the ventilator within 1–2 weeks. Some infants, however, particularly those who are extremely premature, will require ventilation for months and develop a chronic lung disease termed BPD (Vanhatalo, Ekblad, Kero, et al., 1994). BPD can result from **barotrauma,** infection, **meconium aspiration,** or asphyxia.

With BPD, the walls of the immature lungs thicken, making the exchange of oxygen and carbon dioxide more difficult. In addition, the mucous lining of the lungs is often swollen as a result of chronic inflammation. This leads to a reduced airway diameter, and the infant has to work much harder than usual to obtain sufficient oxygen to survive.

Fortunately, the proportion of infants who survive RDS but then develop BPD has dropped from three quarters to one third since the early 1990s when early surfactant treatment became commonplace (Fujiwara, Konishi, Chida, et al., 1990; Long, Corbet, Cotton, et al., 1991). If BPD develops, the child may require many months or even years of artificial ventilation. During this time, bronchodilators and diuretics (water pills) are also used to help keep the airways open and the lungs "dry" (see Chapter 31) (Abman & Groothius, 1994).

Even with this treatment, BPD has significant consequences. First, children with BPD have a limited tolerance for physical exercise. Second, because they are using so much excess energy to breathe, they have an increased caloric requirement. Finally, they have an increased risk of developmental disabilities as compared with matched children who only have acute RDS (Laudry, Fletcher, Denson, et al., 1993; Valleur-Masson, Vodovar, Zeller, et al., 1993). Thus, in addition to respiratory therapy, infants with BPD need to be placed in early intervention programs that will focus on physical and developmental skills, and they often need nutritional supplements or concentrated formulas to establish adequate growth.

Intracerebral Insults

Premature infants have a fragile network of blood vessels that supply the brain. These vessels are particularly sensitive to the changes in oxygen and blood pressure that are caused by such complications of prematurity as perinatal asphyxia, RDS, sepsis, apnea, and patent ductus arteriosus. Children who develop these complications are at an increased risk for intracerebral insults, most prominently, periventricular leukomalacia (PVL) and periventricular hemorrhagic infarction (Volpe, 1994, 1997).

Periventricular Leukomalacia   In approximately 15% of premature infants, the poor oxygenation and decreased blood flow associated with RDS and other neonatal complications leads to **necrosis** of the white matter surrounding the brain ventricles, a condition termed PVL (Figure 7.6). Because of the symmetry and characteristic evolution of this lesion, PVL can be readily di-

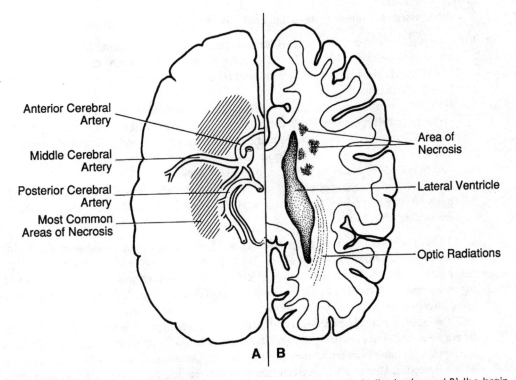

Figure 7.6.   Periventricular leukomalacia. A) The blood vessel supply to the brain, and B) the brain structures. The area of the white matter surrounding the lateral ventricle (particularly the top part) is especially susceptible to hypoxic-ischemic damage because it is not well supplied by blood vessels. It lies in a watershed area between the anterior, middle, and posterior cerebral arteries. In premature infants, poor oxygenation and decreased blood flow associated with respiratory distress syndrome may lead to necrosis of this brain tissue, a condition termed periventricular leukomalacia. When the posterior portion is affected, the optic radiations may be damaged resulting in cortical blindness.

agnosed on ultrasound. Initially, an infant at risk for PVL can be seen to have multiple **echodensities** that may totally resolve if the decreased oxygenation or hypoxia is transient. Infants should have two or three follow-up ultrasounds to ensure that the echodensity is indeed gone and the apparent normalcy is not just a temporary stage of transition to PVL. If the insult is more sustained, brain tissue can be destroyed and a cyst can remain. When the hypoxia is longer standing and the resultant damage severe, multiple cysts may develop in the echodensity area, surrounding the ventricles in the next few weeks, giving it a "Swiss cheese" appearance. After 1–3 months the cysts disappear, leaving enlarged ventricles resulting from loss of white matter tissue. At this point, the infant has full-blown PVL.

Eighty to ninety percent of infants with residual cysts greater than 3 millimeters in diameter will develop a type of cerebral palsy called spastic diplegia, involving spasticity of both legs (see Chapter 24) (Graziani, Pasto, & Stanley, 1986). This occurs because the descending fibers from the motor cortex that control lower-extremity movement run close to the lateral ventricles and are at risk for being disrupted by PVL. In addition to the physical disability, mild to moderate cognitive impairments are also present.

PVL-associated injury to the white matter is caused by three interrelated factors:

1. The periventricular region is a **watershed zone** that is very vulnerable to a fall in cerebral blood flow pressure (Figure 7.6). The more premature the infant, the more immature the blood vessels and the greater the avascular border zone and resultant risk of decreased blood flow and **ischemia.**

2. Because premature infants lack the autoregulatory mechanism that stabilizes cerebral blood pressure in full-term newborns, their pressure fluctuates with systemic blood pressure. As the sick premature newborn has great lability of systemic blood pressure, the brain is subjected to marked variations in blood flow and pressure. (This is particularly true in RDS, during periods of apnea and bradycardia, and in sepsis.)

3. The actively developing glial cells, which produce the white matter, have increased vulnerability to ischemic injury. Other factors, such as free radicals, also may increase the risk of developing PVL (Volpe, 1995).

PVL is best prevented by the maintenance of normal systemic blood pressure during the first weeks of the premature infant's life. This requires stable oxygenation, control of biochemical abnormalities, and rapid treatment of infections. Near-infrared spectroscopy, a novel technology, may enable physicians to detect cerebral blood flow abnormalities early enough to permit more effective intervention (Volpe, 1995).

Periventricular Hemorrhagic Infarction   Periventricular hemorrhagic infarction is a stroke-like condition caused by the unilateral hemorrhagic destruction of periventricular white matter. Acute clinical symptoms may include lethargy, hypotonia, abnormal eye movements, and apneic episodes. Unlike PVL, periventricular hemorrhagic infarction is marked by a single lesion (identifiable on ultrasound) that evolves over a week into a permanent cyst. Periventricular hemorrhagic infarction leads to a type of cerebral palsy called spastic hemiplegia, or spasticity of one side of the body (see Chapter 24). In addition to the physical disability, there is usually significant cognitive impairment.

Periventricular hemorrhage is caused by severe bleeding in the germinal matrix, a network of blood vessels in the roof of the ventricles that, in the premature infant, is extremely fragile. Although ultrasound can identify some intraventricular blood in more then half of premature infants younger than 34 weeks' gestation, most of these hemorrhages are limited to the ventricular space. These Grade I and II hemorrhages have not been conclusively shown to cause subsequent neurological impairment. About one fifth of these hemorrhages, however, are severe enough to invade the cerebrum (termed Grades III and IV hemorrhages) and can cause periventricular hemorrhagic infarction (Volpe, 1992).

Damage from a severe intraventricular bleed can be further complicated by poor absorption of the blood from within the ventricles. The clotted blood may interfere with the egress of cerebrospinal fluid from the ventricles, sometimes resulting in hydrocephalus. If a blockage develops, it may be treated acutely with diuretics to decrease the production of cerebrospinal fluid or serial lumbar punctures to decrease the intracranial pressure in the hope that the clotted blood will eventually resorb. If these methods are ineffective, a ventriculo-peritoneal (VP) shunt may be placed surgically to divert the blocked fluid from the ventricle to the peritoneal space in the abdomen.

Intraventricular hemorrhage is prevented by avoiding periods of hypoxia-ischemia (Wells & Ment, 1995). This requires effective newborn resuscitation, adequate ventilation, prevention of major hemodynamic disturbances, and correction of abnormalities of coagulation. Stabilization of cerebral blood flow requires gentle handling (and tracheal suctioning) and may require the use of muscle paralysis agents during ventilation (Volpe, 1995). Protection against intraventricular hemorrhage using vitamin E, vitamin K, and/or indomethacin is under experimental study (Greer, 1995; Ment, Oh, Ehrenkranz, et al., 1994). It has been suggested that antenatal treatment with phenobarbital, vitamin K, and dexamethasone also may decrease the risk of intraventricular hemorrhage in the premature infant (Leviton, Kuban, Bagano, et al., 1993; Shankaran, Cepeda, Muran, et al., 1996; Thorp, Ferrette-Smith, Gaston, et al., 1995).

Patent Ductus Arteriosus

Certain vascular changes occur in the first days after birth (see Chapter 6). For example, the ductus arteriosus, which connects the pulmonary artery and the aorta during fetal life (Figure 6.1), closes. In about 30% of premature infants, however, this closure does not take place immediately after birth, causing a condition called **patent ductus arteriosus (PDA).** Usually, the constriction of muscle fibers that leads to closure of the ductus is stimulated by oxygen intake following birth. In the premature infant with RDS, however, the oxygen level in the blood simply does not become high enough to stimulate muscle contraction in the ductus. Thus, besides poor ventilation, the infant must cope with a patent, or open, ductus arteriosus, which leads to heart failure in about half of affected infants (Scanlon, 1994). If symptoms of heart failure develop, treatment involves the use of the medication **indomethacin,** which stimulates contraction of the muscular walls of the ductus, closing it in most cases (Couser, Ferrara, Wright, et al., 1996). In a small percentage of infants, closure does not occur even with medication and a surgical procedure, a PDA ligation, must be performed (Mavroudis, Backer, & Gevitz, 1994).

Apnea and Bradycardia

The CNS control of respiratory effort is immature in many premature infants. Not only do premature newborns have difficulty moving air into the lungs, but they often "forget" to breathe for periods of 20 seconds or more. These periods are called apneic episodes and occur most commonly during sleep. If apnea is associated with a significant slowing of the heart rate (bradycardia), close monitoring and treatment are indicated (Marchal, Bairam, & Vert, 1987). About 10% of LBW infants have apnea and bradycardia, while more than 40% of VLBW infants have these episodes (Scanlon, 1994).

When apnea and bradycardia occur together, the precipitating cause needs to be identified and treated. Acutely, apnea and bradycardia may be symptoms heralding an underlying medical problem such as anemia, a severe infection, hypoglycemia, hypocalcemia, intraventricular hemorrhage, seizures, or a cardiac abnormality. Prolonged apnea and bradycardia may indicate that the child has sustained brain damage. In cases in which there is no clear precipitant, the infant is presumed to have "apnea of prematurity" and is treated with caffeine or theophylline, which stimulates the respiratory center in the brainstem (Larsen, Brendstrup, Skov, et al., 1995). Apneic episodes decline as the infant approaches full-term gestational age.

Sudden Infant Death Syndrome

Sudden infant death syndrome (SIDS), also called crib death, occurs more than twice as frequently in premature infants as in full-term infants. With SIDS, a previously healthy infant is found lifeless in the crib, usually between 2 and 5 months of life. Contrary to earlier beliefs, apnea of prematurity is not considered a major predisposing factor for SIDS (Goyco & Beckerman, 1990). Because of the increased risk of SIDS, however, VLBW premature infants may be sent home attached to cardiorespiratory (CR) monitors that sound alarms if the infants stop breathing (Keens & Ward, 1993). Although these monitors have not been shown conclusively to improve a child's chance for survival, they do reassure parents and physicians about the status of the infant, especially when asleep and out of view (Silvestri, Weese-Mayer, Kenny, et al., 1994). Parents should be trained to give cardiopulmonary resuscitation (CPR) in the event the monitor signals an arrest. (Unlike in adults, virtually all arrests in infants and children are of respiratory, rather than cardiac, origin.)

In order to prevent SIDS, the American Academy of Pediatrics (1992) recommends that full-term infants be placed in the supine (back-lying) sleeping position. This position, however, is not recommended for preterm infants, many of whom experience gastroesophageal reflux (GER), placing them at an increased risk for vomiting and aspiration after feedings. The safest sleeping position for preterm infants is the sidelying position.

Necrotizing Enterocolitis and Gastroesophageal Reflux

The gastrointestinal tract may be affected in premature infants. During the first 2 weeks of life, about 2%–5% of VLBW infants will develop a life-threatening condition called necrotizing enterocolitis (NEC). These infants will initially present with abdominal distension, lethargy, and vomiting and may progress to gastrointestinal bleeding or bowel wall perforation. Abdominal X rays will show air in the bowel wall of the ileum (the last portion of the small intestine) or the colon (the large intestine). The mortality rate of infants with NEC is 20% (Caplan & MacKendrick, 1993).

NEC is thought to arise from the interaction of three factors: ischemic injury to the intestinal wall, bacteria, and too early (within the first few days of life) formula feedings (Vasan & Gotoff, 1994). Normal intestinal bacteria acting on milk-based formula are thought to produce hydrogen gas that causes distension and ultimate rupture of an intestinal wall already weakened by lack of blood flow. Breast milk feeding has a somewhat protective effect against the development of NEC (Vasan & Gotoff, 1994). Prophylactic treatment with the oral antibiotic gentamicin and/or with immunoglobulin also has been suggested in infants at high risk for NEC (Scanlon, 1994).

Medical management of NEC involves providing nasogastric suction to decompress the bowel, antibiotics, and intravenous fluids and nutrition in lieu of formula feedings. Despite this therapy, about half of the infants will require surgery to remove the diseased section of bowel. In about 10% of cases, surgery will lead to a "short gut syndrome," which can cause chronic diarrhea and malabsorption, leading to nutritional deficiencies and impaired growth. If this occurs, the child may require prolonged intravenous hyperalimentation using a high-caloric solution.

Some premature infants, because of the immaturity of their muscular control, will present with GER, a syndrome in which the contents of the stomach are regurgitated back into the esophagus (Marino, Assing, Carbone, et al., 1995). The reflux causes vomiting and, in some cases, aspiration of formula into the lungs. This may be worsened by bolus feedings through a nasogastric tube. Additional signs and symptoms include refusal of oral feedings, episodes of apnea, and back arching. Treatment involves special positioning techniques to decrease the likelihood of reflux and antireflux medications (see Chapter 28).

Retinopathy of Prematurity

Premature infants also are at risk for retinopathy of prematurity (ROP), previously referred to as retrolental fibroplasia, an eye problem resulting from the abnormal growth of blood vessels in the retina during the first 2 months of life (Bossi & Koerner, 1995; Keith & Doyle, 1995). ROP can lead to detachment of the retina and blindness. Although this problem was once ascribed solely to excessive concentrations of oxygen that were used to treat RDS, subsequent reduction of the use of high-concentration oxygen has decreased but not eliminated the prevalence and severity of ROP (Phelps, 1995). Therefore, other factors must be involved. One of these factors may be oxygen **free radicals.** Free radicals are molecules with extra electrons in their outer ring. They have been found to be toxic to a number of human tissues, including the retina. Treatment trials with the antioxidant vitamin E suggest that it may decrease the risk of ROP in susceptible infants (Johnson, Quinn, Abbasi, et al., 1995). For early detection of ROP, the infant's eyes should be checked repeatedly by an ophthalmologist during the first months of life. If an ROP-related retinal tear is found, it can be treated with cryotherapy or laser therapy to prevent a permanent retinal detachment.

Infections

The immune system in premature infants is not fully functional. As a result, infants are at increased risk for bacterial, viral, and fungal infections (Avery et al., 1994). In addition, local infections, for example from an indwelling catheter, can become generalized if not treated aggressively with intravenous antibiotics. A generalized infection, or sepsis, occurs in about one fifth of preterm infants and can be life threatening. The infection or its treatment also can lead to complications and adversely affect neurodevelopmental outcome. Hearing loss is one significant concern, and all premature infants should receive an ABR hearing test during their hospitalization (see Chapter 12). VLBW infants who remain in the hospital for prolonged periods should receive the usual immunizations including DPT and *Haemophilis* influenza b (HIB) conjugate vaccines.

Physiological Abnormalities

Premature infants have an increased susceptibility to the transient physiological abnormalities that affect full-term infants during the newborn period, including jaundice, hypoglycemia, hypocalcemia, and hypothermia (see Chapter 6). In addition, they are at risk for some abnormalities specific to prematurity, such as anemia and hypothyroidism.

Jaundice, caused by hyperbilirubinemia, occurs more commonly in premature neonates than in full-term infants because their bilirubin conjugating mechanism in the liver is immature. In addition, the blood–brain barrier in the premature infant may be weakened by RDS-associated acidosis and hypoxia permitting more toxic bilirubin to enter their brains. This combination leads to an increased risk of bilirubin-induced brain damage, a condition called **kernicterus.** Thus, premature infants must be treated earlier than full-term infants for an elevated bilirubin level (Watchko & Claassen, 1994).

Hypoglycemia, **hypocalcemia**, and **hypothermia** also are more common among premature infants who have smaller reserves of glucose, calcium, and fatty tissues than their full-term counterparts. Symptoms of these metabolic disturbances include lethargy, vomiting, and seizures. Hypoglycemia is avoided by providing adequate nutrition, administering intravenous glucose, and monitoring blood glucose levels. Hypocalcemia can be corrected with calcium supplementation. And, loss of heat, the cause of hypothermia, can be prevented by the use of radiant heaters and incubators.

Among those transient physiological abnormalities specific to prematurity, anemia is the most prominent. Infants with anemia have insufficient red blood cells, which are needed to carry oxygen to the lungs. Blood transfusions can correct anemia. And in severe cases, the hormone erythropoietin may stimulate red blood cell production in the bone marrow (Obladen & Maier, 1995; Yu & Bacsain, 1994). Often, premature infants have a transient deficiency in their thyroid hormone production. In severe cases, treatment with thyroid hormone may be indicated to prevent neurodevelopmental impairments (Reuss, Paneth, Pinto-Martin, et al., 1996).

SMALL FOR GESTATIONAL AGE INFANTS

At birth, the SGA infant is not only small but typically appears malnourished and wasted, usually as a result of intrauterine growth retardation (IUGR) (see Chapter 5). About half of SGA infants experience growth retardation as a result of maternal illness or malnutrition. These infants tend to be underweight but have normal length and growth potential; they have the best outcomes. The other half of SGA infants are both short and small and have a poorer prognosis. Twenty percent of SGA infants have congenital defects attributable to intrauterine exposure to smoking, alcohol, other drugs of abuse, or infections (e.g., cytomegalovirus) (Crouse & Cassady, 1994) while another 10%–20% have chromosomal and other genetic disorders. In the remaining 60%, the origin of the SGA remains unclear (Leger & Czernichow, 1994). Improved prenatal care to detect maternal illness, enhance nutrition, and counsel against smoking and drugs of abuse has been found to decrease the incidence of environmentally induced SGA (Joffe, Symonds, Alverson, et al., 1995).

SGA infants (both full term or premature) have many of the same complications as premature infants. However, they have a greater morbidity and neonatal mortality than gestationally age-matched AGA infants. They are at increased risk for perinatal asphyxia, meconium aspiration, hypothermia, and hypoglycemia. SGA infants often do not develop RDS. It seems that the same prenatal stresses that interfere with normal intrauterine growth induce steroid production and stimulate surfactant production (Tyson, Kennedy, Broyles, et al., 1995).

Another difference between SGA and AGA infants is their growth and development. Unlike AGA premature infants, who by 2 years of age have generally achieved normal height and weight, about one third of SGA infants (both premature and full term) remain short in stature and underweight throughout their lives (Hokken-Koelega, De Ridder, Lemmen, et al., 1995). In these children, treatment with growth hormone has been shown to increase the height potential (Job, Chaussain, Job, et al., 1996). The incidence of developmental disabilities is also higher in SGA infants than in gestationally age-matched AGA infants (Sung, Vohr, & Oh, 1993). Full-term SGA infants are more likely to have learning disabilities, behavior problems, and ADHD, and premature SGA infants are at an increased risk for mental retardation and cerebral palsy (Paz, Gale, Laor, et al., 1995).

MEDICAL CARE OF THE LOW BIRTH WEIGHT INFANT

The best treatment for LBW infants (both preterm and SGA) is prevention, including early identification of women at high risk for premature delivery (e.g., adolescents, women with substance abuse or chronic illness); providing these women with education, comprehensive health care, and early detection of preterm labor; and arresting premature labor using tocolytic agents (Collaborative Low-Dose Aspirin Study in Pregnancy, 1994; Joffe et al., 1995).

It is best to deliver the children of women who are at high risk of having LBW infants at a hospital with a neonatal intensive care unit (NICU), even if this requires moving a woman in labor. The outcome for premature infants born at hospitals with NICUs is much better than for infants transported emergently after birth from outlying hospitals (Volpe, 1995), possibly because transportation itself places additional stress on the infant. About half of premature infants are delivered by cesarean section, to protect the fragile baby from the trauma of labor, to permit a controlled delivery in a hospital with a NICU, and to decrease the risk of intracerebral hemorrhage (Anderson, Bada, & Shaver, 1992).

Once born, these infants are immediately placed under a radiant heater to stabilize body temperature, and respirations and heart rate are monitored. If body temperature is not controlled, the child is likely to develop apnea, hypoglycemia, and acidosis, all of which can be life threatening. About half of VLBW infants require some respiratory support in the delivery room: oxygen, intubation, and/or mechanical ventilation (Scanlon, 1994).

Most VLBW newborns are unable to feed from a nipple. Although they can suck and swallow quite early in gestation, they do not coordinate these actions well until after 32 weeks' gestation. Thus, for the first few weeks of life, these infants need to receive sustenance by nasogastric feeding tubes. They also require special formula or breast milk supplemented with a human milk fortifier (Canadian Paediatric Society, Nutrition Committee, 1995; Chan, Borschel, & Jacobs, 1994; Karlberg & Albertsson-Wikland, 1995). These feedings are high in calories and contain trace elements, such as zinc and copper, and increased amounts of certain amino acids, including arginine, taurine, and cystine, that are essential for the premature infant. As noted previously, it has been found that preterm infant formulas and breast milk are less likely to precipitate necrotizing enterocolitis; breast milk also reduces the risk of infections (Gale & Martyn, 1996; Oski, 1994). If the gastrointestinal tract is too immature to tolerate formula or breast milk, intravenous alimentation may be used. Over time the infant gradually will be able to accept oral feedings. However, the feedings may be lengthy and difficult and may need to be repeated at 2- to 3-hour intervals throughout the day and night. This produces additional strain on the family following hospital discharge.

As metabolic disorders are more likely to occur in the premature newborn than in the full-term infant, blood samples are routinely taken during the first weeks of life to test for glucose, calcium, bilirubin, acid-base balance, and electrolyte levels. Intravenous fluids are given to compensate for biochemical imbalances. An infant with hyperbilirubinemia is given phototherapy (i.e., placed under special fluorescent ["bili"] lights) or wrapped in a "bili-blanket" or "Wal-abee"). In rare instances when the bilirubin level rises rapidly, partial exchange blood transfu-sions may be required to prevent this rise from injuring the brain.

LBW infants also may have a generalized blood infection or sepsis. A major predisposing cause of sepsis is an indwelling catheter such as an intravenous line. Signs of a serious infection include lethargy, hypothermia, and poor feeding. If these symptoms occur, blood cultures are ob-tained and intravenous antibiotics are started. Like their full-term counterparts, preterm infants can also develop viral illnesses, which are difficult to differentiate from episodes of bacterial sepsis.

In addition to providing for the physical needs of the infant and tending to the medical complications, individualized developmental care is also important (Fleisher, VandenBerg, Con-stantinou, et al., 1995). Once the child has stabilized, an "infant team," consisting of a physical therapist, occupational therapist, speech-language therapist, and developmental pediatrician, should start working with the child. The focus of care may include positioning for feeding, pas-sive range of motion, splinting, and the developmental stimulation that is a precursor for early intervention programs.

SURVIVAL AND OUTCOME OF LOW BIRTH WEIGHT INFANTS

Since the 1960s, progress in neonatology has been phenomenal. Immediate transfer to a NICU, support of respiration and nutrition, and rapid treatment of complications have led to a marked decrease in both mortality and morbidity of LBW neonates (both preterm and SGA) (Lee, Kim, Khoshnood, et al., 1995). In 1960, the survival rate for infants weighing 1,500–2,500 grams (3.5–5.5 pounds) was approximately 50%, and for infants weighing 1,000–1,500, it was less than 30%; in the 1990s, more than 90% of these infants survive (McCormick, Gortmaker, & Sobol, 1990; Veen, Ens-Dokkum, Schreuder, et al., 1991). Only 10% of infants weighing less than 1,000 grams survived the newborn period in 1960. Today, two thirds to three quarters of these extremely LBW infants, weighing 750–1,000 grams, survive, and one third of micro-premies, weighing 500–750 grams, live (Hack, Friedman, & Fanaroff, 1996; La Pine, Jackson, & Bennett, 1995; Robertson, Hrynchshyn, Etches, et al., l992). It should be noted, however, that although these VLBW infants account for only about 1% of the newborn population, they still account for more than 80% of all deaths in the newborn period (Scanlon, 1994).

The neurodevelopmental outcomes for LBW infants have also improved significantly. In 1960 among infants surviving with a birth weight less than 1,500 grams, less than 10% survived with no disability (Budetti, Barrand, McManus, et al., 1981). In the 1980s, the overall incidence of developmental disability in LBW infants was less than 20% (Table 7.2). In these studies there was a significant correlation between birth weight and outcome. Although only 7% of infants weighing 1,500–2,500 grams at birth had severe disabilities, 20% of infants between 500 and 1,500 grams were adversely affected (Hack, Klein, & Taylor, l995; Roth, Baudin, Pezzani-Goldsmith, et al., 1994). Infants who were both premature and small for gestational age fared the worst.

Although neurodevelopmental outcome has improved markedly in LBW infants, it contin-ues to lag behind full-term AGA infants. Severe disability is approximately six times more likely to occur in the extremely low birth weight infant than in the full-term infant, while borderline normal intelligence (19% versus 9%) and learning disabilities and ADHD (45% versus 15%)

Table 7.2.   Outcome at 8 years of age in infants with birth weight less than 1,000 grams

Disability	Percentage affected
Cerebral palsy	9
Mental retardation	7
Visual impairment	12
Hearing loss	6
Seizure disorder	2

Source: Victorian Infant Collaborative Study Group (1991).

are 3-fold increased in former VLBW infants (Hille, den Ouden, Bauer, et al., 1994; Lou, 1996; McCarton, Wallace, Divon, et al., 1996; McCormick, Workman-Daniels, & Brooks-Gunn, 1996; Victorian Infant Collaborative Study Group, 1991). Overall about 61% of premature infants have some developmental disability, versus 23% in the full-term population (Teplin, Burchinal, Johnson-Martin, et al., 1991). Accordingly, a higher proportion of these children fail in school or are enrolled in special education programs (Hack et al., 1995).

Head circumference is a useful tool in predicting which infants are more likely to have neurodevelopmental impairments. Microcephaly (head circumference below the 3rd percentile) has been found in 10% of VLBW infants, three times that found in the full-term population (Hack, Breslau, Weissman, et al., 1991). At school age, these children score lower on IQ tests and have decreased language and visual-motor skills. Academic performance in reading, math, and spelling also are lower than in the control group.

In addition to being at increased risk for cognitive impairments, premature infants are also more likely to have physical disabilities, most commonly spastic cerebral palsy (Aziz, Vickar, Sauve, et al., 1995). The incidence and permanence of cerebral palsy, however, is somewhat controversial. When a premature infant is diagnosed with PVL, especially with residual cyst formation, one can, with greater certainty, predict that he or she will develop spastic diplegia or quadriplegia (Bennett, Silver, Levy, et al., 1990). Yet it has been suggested that one quarter to one half will "grow out" of cerebral palsy, especially spastic diplegia and hemiplegia (Nelson & Ellenberg, 1982), although the motor impairments, though less obvious, are not completely gone by school age in most of these children (Teplin et al., 1991). There remain abnormalities in tone, reflexes, immaturities of speech patterns, poor balance, and strabismus.

Neurodevelopmental outcome is also a function of the type of neonatal complications sustained by the preterm infant. Certain complications are compatible with a good outcome, including RDS, hyperbilirubinemia, hypoglycemia, and hypocalcemia. Others are associated with a poorer prognosis including intracerebral hemorrhage, sepsis, prolonged requirement for ventilation, and persistent episodes of apnea and bradycardia. Environmental factors are also important in determining outcome. If the infant has been transported from an outlying hospital or born to a mother of low socioeconomic status, the child is more likely to have a poor prognosis than a matched infant who was born at a hospital with a NICU and to a mother who has good economic resources (Roth, Resnick, Ariet, et al., 1995).

In predicting outcome, one of the major issues has been how to correct for prematurity in developmental testing. The classic approach has been to completely correct for gestational age until the child reaches 2 years of age, by which time he or she is presumed to have "caught up." Thus, a 9-month-old who was born at 32 weeks (i.e., 2 months early) would be expected to function as a 7-month-old; and when this child becomes 20 months old, he or she would be considered as an 18-month-old child. Using this approach, especially in the extremely premature infants, allows more accurate comparisons with their full-term equivalents. However, for more gestationally mature infants, complete correction in the second year leads to an overestimation of the child's eventual IQ score (Den Ouden, Rijken, Brand, et al., 1991).

Using complete correction and comparing 2-year assessments to 8-year follow-up, about one quarter of infants have their abilities overestimated and about 10% underestimated (Victorian Infant Collaborative Study Group, 1991). Comparing 5-year and 8-year assessments, the correlation (81%) was much improved. The most common causes of overestimation were missed vision and hearing and language impairments, while underestimation was often due to initial muscle tone abnormalities that interfered with the acquisition of early motor skills but improved over time. It is now more common to completely correct for only 12 months.

A more difficult issue is how much to correct for a premature infant who has experienced an intracerebral insult. In this case, correction may actually mask a significant developmental impairment and contribute to a delay in diagnosis and treatment. Thus, some investigators suggest that assessing the rate of development rather than the absolute mental or motor age is more useful in infants at high risk. In other words, if a premature infant is tested at 4 months of age and found to be functioning at 2 months but when retested at 7 months is at a 5-month developmental level (a gain of 3 months skills in the past 3 months), there would be less concern about the developmental delay compared with the infant who had only gained 1 month of skills in 3 months.

CARE IN THE HOME

Usually, a premature infant's condition stabilizes within 2–3 weeks of birth. By then, adequate nutrition is possible and weight gain begins. The RDS subsides and the child no longer needs assisted ventilation. The jaundice abates, the baby starts maintaining a normal temperature, and biochemical levels normalize. The child is then transferred from the NICU to an intermediate care unit, to feed and grow (often euphemistically called "the pasture"). The baby is ready for discharge when he or she is able to take in sufficient nutrition to establish weight gain (from a nipple, the breast, or tube feedings); maintain temperature control outside the isolette; and tolerate sitting in an infant or car seat without developing hypoxia (Bass & Mehta, 1995; Bull & Stroup, 1985). Usually, the baby weighs between 1,800 and 2,500 grams (4–5.5 pounds) when ready for discharge from the hospital. The usual hospital stay for a 1,000- to 1,500-gram baby is 2–3 months (Scanlon, 1994).

Once the child comes home and the excitement of the new arrival subsides, the difficulty of caring for this very needy infant becomes rapidly apparent. This places major stresses on any family and is a particular challenge to the single young mother. Premature infants tend to be irritable, crying much of the time. They also have poor sleep–wake cycles, typically sleeping only for short periods of time throughout the day and night. This can lead to sleep deprivation in the parent(s). In addition, their sucking pattern is immature, and they need to be fed frequently. Furthermore, their formulas may be nonstandard (and expensive), or if breast fed, the breast milk may need to be expressed and fortified to provide more calories and nutrients. The infant also may have GER such that he or she will vomit after feedings. This may prevent adequate weight gain and place the infant at high risk for aspiration pneumonia. There may be medications to give for respiratory problems or to control reflux. Parents may have difficulty getting the infant to take the medications without vomiting and worry that the baby will get sick because of inadequate medication. Alternately, in trying to compensate for lost medication from vomiting, they may accidentally overdose the child.

The prolonged hospitalization may also have interfered with usual maternal–infant bonding; the mother may actually be afraid of her baby, worried that she may do something wrong and the baby will be injured or die. This is more frequently the case if the infant has experienced apneic episodes and is sent home on a cardiorespiratory monitor, which may increase the parents' anxiety level about SIDS.

It is important that the preterm infant return to a home that is free of smoke and any other potential respiratory irritants such as kerosene heaters, fresh paint, and people with respiratory-related viral illnesses, all of which play a crucial role in causing intercurrent respiratory illnesses or exacerbating underlying lung disease. In addition, passive exposure to tobacco smoke is thought to increase the risk of SIDS (Klonoff-Cohen, Edelstein, Lefkowitz, et al., 1995).

Because of all these stressors, it is important to provide an adequate support system to the family. This should include close medical supervision in a follow-up clinic for infants at high risk (Bernbaum & Hoffman-Williamson, 1991). Visits should focus on respiratory monitoring and treatment, medication and nutrition, vision and hearing testing, and so on. The clinic may also help supervise a range of home care services, including a visiting nurse, a home care company to supply oxygen and other technical needs, and a social worker to advocate for financial resources and provide emotional support to the family. In addition, parents should be encouraged to enroll their infants in early intervention programs that will provide for support and training of parent and child.

EARLY INTERVENTION PROGRAMS

Studies suggest that early intervention programs can enhance the neurodevelopmental outcome of premature infants (Blair, Ramey, & Hardin, 1995; Brooks-Gunn, McCarton, Casey, et al., 1994; Guralnick, 1996). The program should start at discharge from the hospital and continue until 36 months corrected age. The intervention strategy incorporates parent group meetings, home visits, and attendance at a multidisciplinary child development center with a low teacher-to-infant ratio (1:3–1:4). In a collaborative study, infants enrolled in the early intervention program had mean IQ scores that were significantly higher than the control group at 5-year follow-up (Brooks-Gunn et al., 1994; McCarton, Wallace, & Bennett, 1995; Ramey, Bryant, Wasik, et al., 1992). This was especially true for those infants with mild delays and low socioeconomic status. In the under–1,500-gram group, however, children with IQ scores of less than 70 did not demonstrate significant benefits from early intervention. This suggests that environmentally induced impairments are more amenable to correction than biological abnormalities (Levy-Shiff, Einat, Mogilner, et al., 1994). It is also important to recognize that once these children complete the early intervention program, they may remain in need of special services, including speech therapy, occupational therapy, special education, behavior therapy, and treatment of emotional problems (Ross, Lipper, & Auld, 1990). If they do not receive these services, it is likely that the benefits of early intervention will be lost.

ROSA

Rosa was born to her 16-year-old single mother at 32 weeks' gestation weighing 1,800 grams (appropriate for gestational age). Within 4 hours of birth, Rosa began to breathe rapidly, and her chest X ray showed evidence of RDS. She was intubated and placed on a ventilator. Because she was too weak to suck properly, Rosa received a special premature formula through a nasogastric tube. When she was 7 days old, an X ray showed that the RDS was resolving and she was extubated.

Episodes of apnea and bradycardia, however, developed. Every 5 or 10 minutes, Rosa would cease breathing for about 20 seconds and her heart rate would fall. Touching her with a finger usually made her gulp a breath of air; she would begin to breathe again, and her heart rate would increase. She was placed on caffeine and, within a few days, the episodes of apnea and bradycardia became less frequent.

Rosa was then transferred out of the intensive care unit to the intermediate care unit to establish growth. She started to take formula through a nipple and, by 6 weeks of age, weighed 2,200 grams and was ready to go home. At the time of her discharge, Rosa followed objects visually, was alert to the sound of a bell, and appeared to be an active and healthy baby. Rosa's mother received training on how to care for her and to use a cardiorespiratory monitor, and Rosa was entered in a home-based early intervention program. Her prognosis is good, although she is at increased risk for developing learning problems by school age.

SUMMARY

For LBW infants, different complications lead to different prognoses. Complications consistent with a good developmental outcome include RDS, hyperbilirubinemia, hypoglycemia, and hypocalcemia. Those associated with a poorer prognosis include intracerebral insults, sepsis, and persistent apnea and bradycardia. Even though an increased risk of developmental disabilities exists with these complications, many of these children still fare well. With improved prenatal care and an increased number of neonatal intensive care units, the prognosis for LBW infants should continue to improve.

REFERENCES

Abman, S.H., & Groothius, J.R. (1994). Pathophysiology and treatment of bronchopulmonary dysplasia: Current issues. *Pediatric Clinics of North America, 41,* 277–315.

Allen, M.C., & Capute, A.J. (1986). The evolution of primitive reflexes in extremely premature infants. *Pediatric Research, 20,* 1284–1289.

American Academy of Pediatrics Task Force on Infant Positioning and SIDS. (1992). Infant positioning and SIDS. *Pediatrics, 89,* 1120–1126.

Amiel-Tison, C. (1968). Neurological evaluation of the maturity of newborn infants. *Archives of Disease in Childhood, 43,* 89–93.

Anderson, G.D., Bada, H.S., & Shaver, D.C. (1992). The effect of cesarean section on intraventricular hemorrhage in the preterm infant. *American Journal of Obstetrics and Gynecology, 166,* 1091–1101.

Australian collaborative trial of antenatal thyrotropin-releasing hormone (ACTOBAT) for prevention of neonatal respiratory disease. (1995). *Lancet, 345,* 877–882.

Avery, G.B., Fletcher M.A., & MacDonald, M.G. (1994). *Neonatology, pathophysiology, and management of the newborn* (4th ed.). Philadelphia: J.B. Lippincott.

Aziz, K., Vickar, D.B., Sauve, R.S., et al. (1995). Province-based study of neurologic disability of children weighing 500 through 1249 grams at birth in relation to neonatal cerebral ultrasound findings. *Pediatrics, 95,* 837–844.

Ballard, J.L., Khoury, J.C., Wedig, K., et al. (1991). New Ballard score, expanded to include extremely premature infants. *Journal of Pediatrics, 119,* 417–423.

Bass, J.L., & Mehta, K.A. (1995). Oxygen desaturation of selected term infants in car seats. *Pediatrics, 96,* 288–290.

Bennett, F.C., Silver, G., Levy, E.J., et al. (1990). Periventricular echodensities detected by cranial ultrasonography: Usefulness in predicting neurodevelopmental outcome in LBW, preterm infants. *Pediatrics, 85,* 400–404.

Bernbaum, J.C., & Hoffman-Williamson, M. (1991). *Primary care of the preterm infant.* St. Louis: C.V. Mosby.

Blair, C., Ramey, C.T., & Hardin, J.M. (1995). Early intervention for low birthweight, premature infants: Participation and intellectual development. *American Journal of Mental Retardation, 99,* 542–554.

Bossi, E., & Koerner, F. (1995). Retinopathy of prematurity. *Intensive Care Medicine, 21,* 241–246.

Brooks-Gunn, J., McCarton, C.M., Casey, P.H., et al. (1994). Early intervention in low-birth-weight premature infants: Results through age 5 years from the Infant Health and Development Program. *Journal of the American Medical Association, 272,* 1257–1262.

Budetti, P., Barrand, N., McManus, P., et al. (1981). *The costs and effectiveness of neonatal intensive care.* Washington, DC: U.S. Government Printing Office, Office of Technology Assessment.

Bull, M.J., & Stroup, K.B. (1985). Premature infants in car seats. *Pediatrics, 75,* 336–339.

Canadian Paediatric Society, Nutrition Committee. (1995). Nutrient needs and feeding of premature infants. *Canadian Medical Association Journal, 152,* 1765–1785.

Caplan, M.S., & MacKendrick, W. (1993). Necrotizing enterocolitis: A review of pathogenetic mechanisms and implications for prevention. *Pediatric Pathology, 13,* 357–369.

Chan, G.M., Borschel, M.W., & Jacobs, J.R. (1994). Effects of human milk or formula feeding on the growth, behavior, and protein status of preterm infants discharged from the newborn intensive care unit. *American Journal of Clinical Nutrition, 60,* 710–716.

Collaborative Low-Dose Aspirin Study in Pregnancy (CLASP). (1994). CLASP: A randomised trial of low-dose aspirin for the "prevention" and treatment of pre-eclampsia among 9364 pregnant women. *Lancet, 343,* 619–629.

Constantine, N.A., Kraemer, H.C., Kendall-Tackett, K.A., et al. (1987). Use of physical and neurologic observations in assessment of gestational age in low-birth-weight infants. *Journal of Pediatrics, 110,* 921–928.

Cooper, L.G., Leland, N.L., & Alexander, G. (1995). Effect of maternal age on birth outcomes among young adolescents. *Social Biology, 42,* 22–35.

Couser, R.J., Ferrara ,T.B., Wright, G.B., et al. (1996). Prophylactic indomethacin therapy in the first twenty-four hours of life for the prevention of patent ductus arteriosus in preterm infants treated prophylactically with surfactant in the delivery room. *Journal of Pediatrics, 128,* 631–637.

Crouse, D.T., & Cassady, G. (1994). The small-for-gestational-age infant. In G.B. Avery, M.A. Fletcher, & M.G. MacDonald (Eds.), *Neonatology: Pathophysiology and management in the newborn* (4th ed., pp. 369–398). Philadelphia: J.B. Lippincott.

Crowley, P. (1992). Corticosteroids after preterm premature rupture of membranes. *Obstetrics and Gynecology Clinics of North America, 19,* 317–326.

Den Ouden, L., Rijken, M., Brand, R., et al. (1991). Is it correct to correct? Developmental milestones in 555 "normal" preterm infants compared with term infants. *Journal of Pediatrics, 118,* 399–404.

Dubowitz, L.M., Dubowitz, V., & Goldberg, C. (1970). Clinical assessment of gestational age in the newborn infant. *Journal of Pediatrics, 77,* 1–10.

Fleisher, B.E., VandenBerg, K., Constantinou, J., et al. (1995). Individualized developmental care for very-low-birth-weight premature infants. *Clinical Pediatrics, 34,* 523–529.

Frostell, C.G., Bolmqvist, H., Hedenstierna, G., et al. (1993). Inhaled nitric oxide selectively reverses human hypoxic pulmonary vasoconstriction without causing systemic vasodilation. *Anesthesiology, 78,* 427–435.

Fujiwara, T., Konishi, M., Chida, S., et al. (1990). Surfactant replacement therapy with a single postventilatory dose of a reconstituted bovine surfactant in preterm neonates with respiratory distress syndrome: Final analysis of a multicenter, double-blind, randomized trial and comparison with similar trials: The Surfactant-TA Group. *Pediatrics, 86,* 753–764.

Gale, C.R., & Martyn, C.N. (1996). Breastfeeding, dummy use, and adult intelligence. *Lancet, 20,* 1072–1075.

Gerdes, J., Gerdes, M., Beaumont, E., et al. (1995). Health and neurodevelopmental outcome at 1–year adjusted age in 508 infants weighing 700 to 1100 grams who received prophylaxis with one versus three doses of synthetic surfactant: American Exosurf Neonatal Study Groups I and II. *Journal of Pediatrics, 126,* S26–S32.

Gong, A., Anday, E., Boros, S., et al. (1995). One-year follow-up evaluation of 260 premature infants with respiratory distress syndrome and birth weights of 700 to 1350 grams randomized to two rescue doses of synthetic surfactant or air placebo: American Exosurf Neonatal Study Group I. *Journal of Pediatrics, 126,* S68–S74.

Goyco, P.G., & Beckerman, R.C. (1990). Sudden infant death syndrome. *Current Problems in Pediatrics, 20,* 297–346.

Graziani, L.J., Pasto, M., Stanley, C., et al. (1986). Neonatal neurosonography correlation of cerebral palsy in preterm infants. *Pediatrics, 78,* 88–95.

Greer, F.R. (1995). Vitamin K deficiency and hemorrhage in infancy. *Clinics in Perinatology, 22,* 759–777.

Guralnick, M.J. (Ed.). (1996). *The effectiveness of early intervention.* Baltimore: Paul H. Brookes Publishing Co.

Guyer, B., Strobino, D.M., Ventura, S.J., et al. (1995). Annual Summary of Vital Statistics: 1994. *Pediatrics, 96,* 1029–1039.

Hack, M., Breslau, N., Weissman, B., et al. (1991). Effect of very low birth weight and subnormal head size on cognitive abilities at school age. *New England Journal of Medicine, 325,* 231–237.

Hack, M., Friedman, H., & Fanaroff, A.A. (1996). Outcomes of extremely low birth weight infants. *Pediatrics, 98,* 931–937.

Hack, M., Klein, N.K., & Taylor, H.G. (1995). Long-term developmental outcomes of low birth weight infants. *The Future of Children, 5,* 176–196.

Hille, E.T., den Ouden, A.L., Bauer, L., et al. (1994). School performance at nine years of age in very premature and very low birth weight infants: Perinatal risk factors and predictors at five years of age: Collaborative Project on Preterm and Small for Gestational Age (POPS) Infants in The Netherlands. *Journal of Pediatrics, 125,* 426–434.

Hillier, S.L., Nugent, R.P., Eschenbach, D.A., et al. (1995). Association between bacterial vaginosis and preterm delivery of a low-birth-weight infant. *New England Journal of Medicine, 333,* 1737–1742.

Hokken-Koelega, A.C., De Ridder, M.A., Lemmen, R.J., et al. (1995). Children born small for gestational age: Do they catch up? *Pediatric Research, 38,* 267–271.

Horbar, J.D., Wright, E.C., & Onstad, L. (1993). Decreasing mortality associated with the introduction of surfactant therapy: An observational study of neonates weighing 601 to 1300 grams at birth. The members of the National Institute of Child Health and Human Development Neonatal Research Network, Department of Pediatrics, University of Vermont College of Medicine. *Pediatrics, 92(2),* 191–196.

Job, J.C., Chaussain, J.L., Job, B., et al. (1996). Follow-up of three years of treatment with growth hormone and of one post-treatment year, in children with severe growth retardation of intrauterine onset. *Pediatric Research, 39,* 354–359.

Joffe, G.M., Symonds, R., Alverson, D., et al. (1995). The effect of a comprehensive prematurity prevention program on the number of admissions to the neonatal intensive care unit. *Journal of Perinatology, 15,* 305–309.

Johnson, L., Quinn, G.E., Abbasi, S., et al. (1995). Severe retinopathy of prematurity in infants with birth weights less than 1250 grams: Incidence and outcome of treatment with pharmacologic serum levels of vitamin E in addition to cryotherapy from 1985–1991. *Journal of Pediatrics, 127,* 632–639.

Kari, M.A., Hallman, M., Eronen, M., et al. (1994). Prenatal dexamethasone treatment in conjunction with rescue therapy of human surfactant: A randomized placebo-controlled multicenter study. *Pediatrics, 93,* 730–736.

Karlberg, J., & Albertsson-Wikland, K. (1995). Growth in full-term small-for-gestational-age infants: From birth to final height. *Pediatric Research, 38,* 733–739.

Kattwinkel, J., Bloom, B.T., Delmore, P., et al. (1993). Prophylactic administration of calf ling surfactant extract is more effective than early treatment of respiratory distress syndrome in neonates of 29 through 32 weeks' gestation. *Pediatrics, 92(1),* 90–98.

Keens, T.G., & Ward, S.L. (1993). Apnea spells, sudden death, and the role of the apnea monitor. *Pediatric Clinics of North America, 40,* 897–911.

Keith, C.G., & Doyle, L.W. (1995). Retinopathy of prematurity in extremely low birth weight infants. *Pediatrics, 95,* 42–45.

Klonoff-Cohen, H.S., Edelstein, S.L., Lefkowitz, E.S., et al. (1995). The effect of "passive" smoking and tobacco exposure through breast milk on sudden infant death syndrome. *Journal of the American Medical Association, 273,* 795–798.

La Pine, T.R., Jackson, J.C., & Bennett, F.C. (1995). Outcome of infants weighing less than 800 grams at birth: 15 years' experience. *Pediatrics, 96,* 479–482.

Larsen, P.B., Brendstrup, L., Skov, L., et al. (1995). Aminophylline versus caffeine citrate for apnea and bradycardia prophylaxis in premature neonates. *Acta Paediatrica, 84,* 360–364.

Laudry, S.H., Fletcher, J.M., Denson, S.E., et al. (1993). Longitudinal outcome for low birth weight infants: Effects of intraventricular hemorrhage and bronchopulmonary dysplasia. *Journal of Clinical Experimental Neuropsychology, 15,* 205–218.

Leach, C.L., Greenspan, J.S., Rubenstein, S.D., et al. (1996). Partial liquid ventilation with perflybron in premature infants with severe respiratory distress syndrome. *New England Journal of Medicine, 335,* 761–767.

Lee, K.S., Kim, B.I., Khoshnood, B., et al. (1995). Outcome of very low birth weight infants in industrialized countries: 1947–1987. *American Journal of Epidemiology, 141,* 1188–1193.

Leger, J., & Czernichow, P. (1994). Retardation of intrauterine growth: Prognosis and therapeutic perspectives [Editorial]. *Presse Med, 23,* 969–971.

Leviton, A., Kuban, K., Bagano, M., et al. (1993). Antenatal corticosteroids appear to reduce the risk of postnatal germinal matrix hemorrhage in intubated low birthweight newborns. *Pediatrics, 81,* 1083–1088.

Levy-Shiff, R., Einat, G., Mogilner, M.B., et al. (1994). Biological and environmental correlates of developmental outcome of prematurely born infants in early adolescence. *Journal of Pediatric Psychology, 19,* 63–78.

Long, W. (1993). Synthetic surfactant. *Seminars in Perinatology, 17,* 275–284.

Long, W., Corbet, A., Cotton, R., et al. (1991). A controlled trial of synthetic surfactant in infants weighing 1250 grams or more with respiratory distress syndrome. *New England Journal of Medicine, 325,* 1696–1703.

Lou, H.C. (1996). Etiology and pathogenesis of attention-deficit hyperactivity disorder (ADHD): Significance of prematurity and perinatal hypoxic-haemodynamic encephalophathy. *Acta Paediatrica, 85,* 1266–1271.

Lubchenco, L.O. (1976). *The high risk infant.* Philadelphia: W.B. Saunders.

Majewski, A., Telmanik, S., & Arrington, V. (1994). High frequency oscillatory ventilation. *Virginia Medical Quarterly, 121,* 230–232.

Mandrich, M., Simons, C.J., Ritchie, S., et al. (1994). Motor development, infantile reactions and postural responses of preterm, at-risk infants. *Developmental Medicine and Child Neurology, 36,* 397–405.

Marchal, F., Bairam, A., & Vert, P. (1987). Neonatal apnea and apneic syndromes. *Clinics in Perinatology, 14,* 509–529.

Marino, A.J., Assing, E., Carbone, M.T., et al. (1995). The incidence of gastroesophageal reflux in preterm infants. *Journal of Perinatology, 15,* 369–371.

Mavroudis, C., Backer, C.L., & Gevitz, M. (1994). Forty-six years of patent ductus arteriosus division at Children's Memorial Hospital of Chicago: Standards for comparison. *Annals of Surgery, 220,* 402–409.

McCarton, C.M., Wallace, I.F., & Bennett, F.C. (1995). Preventive interventions with low birth weight premature infants: An evaluation of their success. *Seminars in Perinatology, 19,* 330–340.

McCarton, C.M., Wallace, I.F., Divon, M., et al. (1996). Cognitive and neurologic development of the premature, small for gestational age infant through age 6: Comparison by birth weight and gestational age. *Pediatrics, 98*(6), 1167–1169.

McCormick, M.C., Gortmaker, S.L., & Sobol, A.M. (1990). Very low birth weight children: Behavior problems and school difficulty in a national sample. *Journal of Pediatrics, 117,* 687–693.

McCormick, M.C., Workman-Daniels, K., & Brooks-Gunn, J. (1996). The behavioral and emotional well-being of school-age children with different birth weights. *Pediatrics, 97,* 18–25.

Ment, L.R., Oh, W., Ehrenkranz, R.A., et al. (1994). Low dose indomethacin and prevention of intraventricular hemorrhage: A multicenter randomized trial. *Pediatrics, 93,* 543–550.

Moya, F.R., & Gross, I. (1993). Combined hormonal therapy for the prevention of respiratory distress syndrome and its consequences. *Seminars in Perinatology, 17,* 267–274.

National Center for Chronic Disease Prevention and Health Promotion, Division of Nutrition; National Center for Health Statistics, Division of Vital Statistics; and Centers for Disease Control. (1994). Increasing incidence of LBW: United States, 1981–1991. *Morbidity and Mortality Weekly Report, 43,* 335.

Nelson, K.B., & Ellenberg, J.H. (1982). Children who outgrew cerebral palsy. *Pediatrics, 69,* 529–536.

Obladen, M., & Maier, R.F. (1995). Recombinant erythropoietin for "prevention" of anemia in preterm infants. *Journal of Perinatal Medicine, 23,* 119–126.

Oski, F.A. (1994). Infant nutrition, physical growth, breastfeeding, and general nutrition. *Current Opinion in Pediatrics, 6,* 361–364.

Patel, C.A., & Klein, J.M. (1995). Outcome of infants with birth weights less than 1000 g with respiratory distress syndrome treated with high-frequency ventilation and surfactant replacement therapy. *Archives of Pediatrics and Adolescent Medicine, 149,* 317–321.

Paz, I., Gale, R., Laor, A., et al. (1995). The cognitive outcome of full-term small for gestational age infants at late adolescence.*Obstetrics and Gynecology, 85,* 452–456.

Phelps, D.L. (1995). Retinopathy of prematurity. *Pediatrics in Review, 16,* 50–56.

Ramey, C.T., Bryant, D.M., Wasik, B.H., et al. (1992). Infant Health and Development Program for low birth weight, premature infants: Program elements, family participation, and child intelligence. *Pediatrics, 89,* 454–465.

Raphael, J.H., Atkinson, I., & Bexton, M.D. (1995). A combined high frequency oscillator and intermittent positive pressure ventilator. *Anaesthesia, 50,* 611–613.

Reuss, M.L., Paneth, N., Pinto-Martin, J.A., et al. (1996). The relation of transient hypothyroxinemia in preterm infants to neurologic development at two years of age. *New England Journal of Medicine, 334,* 821–827.

Robertson, C.M.T., Hrynchshyn, G.J., Etches, P.C., et al. (1992). Population-based study of the incidence, complexity, and severity of neurologic outcome among survivors weighing 500 through 1250 grams at birth: A comparison of two birth cohorts. *Pediatrics, 90,* 750–755.

Ross, G., Lipper, E.G., & Auld, P. (1990). Social competence and behavior problems in premature children at school age. *Pediatrics, 86,* 391–397.

Roth, S.C., Baudin, J., Pezzani-Goldsmith, M., et al. (1994). Relation between neurodevelopmental status of very preterm infants at one and eight years. *Developmental Medicine and Child Neurology, 36,* 1049–1062.

Roth, J., Resnick, M.B., Ariet, M., et al. (1995). Changes in survival patterns of very low birth-weight infants from 1980 to 1993. *Archives of Pediatrics and Adolescent Medicine, 149,* 1311–1317.

Scanlon, J.W. (1994). The very-low-birth-weight infant. In G.B. Avery, M.A. Fletcher, & M.G. MacDonald (Eds.), *Neonatology: Pathophysiology and management in the newborn* (4th ed., pp. 399–416). Philadelphia: J.B. Lippincott.

Shankaran, S., Cepeda, E., Muran, G., et al. (1996). Antenatal phenobarbital therapy and neonatal outcome: I. Effect on intracranial hemorrhage. *Pediatrics, 97,* 644–648.

Silvestri, J.M., Weese-Mayer, D.E., Kenny, A.S., et al. (1994). Prolonged cardiorespiratory monitoring of children more than twelve months of age: Characterization of events and approach to discontinuation. *Journal of Pediatrics, 125,* 51–56.

Sung, I.K., Vohr, B., & Oh, W. (1993). Growth and neurodevelopmental outcome of very low birth weight infants with intrauterine growth retardation: Comparison with control subjects matched by birth weight and gestational age. *Journal of Pediatrics, 123,* 618–624.

Teberg, A.J., Walther, F.J., & Pena, I.C. (1988). Mortality, morbidity, and outcome of the small-for-gestational age infant. *Seminars in Perinatology, 12,* 84–94.

Teplin, S.W., Burchinal, M., Johnson-Martin, N., et al. (1991). Neurodevelopmental, health, and growth status at age 6 years of children with birth weights less than 1001 grams. *Journal of Pediatrics, 118,* 768–777.

Thorp, J.A., Ferrette-Smith, D., Gaston, L.A., et al. (1995). Combined antenatal vitamin K and phenobarbital therapy for preventing intracranial hemorrhage in newborns less than 34 weeks gestation. *Obstetrics and Gynecology, 86,* 1–8.

Tyson, J.E., Kennedy, K., Broyles, S., et al. (1995). The small for gestational age infant: Accelerated or delayed pulmonary maturation? Increased or decreased survival? *Pediatrics, 95,* 534–538.

Valleur-Masson, D., Vodovar, M., Zeller, J., et al. (1993). Bronchopulmonary dysplasia: Course over 3 years in 88 children born between 1984 and 1988. *Archives of Pediatrics, 50,* 553–559.

Vanhatalo, A.M., Ekblad, H., Kero, P., et al. (1994). Incidence of bronchopulmonary dysplasia during an 11-year period in infants weighing less than 1500 g at birth. *Annales Chirurgiae et Gynaecologiae, 208*(Suppl.), 113–116.

Vasan, U., & Gotoff, S.P. (1994). Prevention of neonatal necrotizing enterocolitis. *Clinics in Perinatology, 21,* 425–435.

Veen, S., Ens-Dokkum, M.H., Schreuder, A.M., et al. (1991). Impairments, disabilities and handicaps of very preterm and very-low-birth-weight infants of five years of age. *Lancet, 338,* 33–36.

Verma, R.P. (1995). Respiratory distress syndrome of the newborn infant. *Obstetrical and Gynecological Survey, 50,* 542–555.

Victorian Infant Collaborative Study Group. (1991). Eight-year outcome in infants with birth weight of 500 to 999 grams: Continuing regional study of

1979 and 1980 births. *Journal of Pediatrics, 118,* 761–767.

Volpe, J.J. (1992). Brain injury in the premature infant: Current concepts of pathogenesis and prevention. *Biology of the Neonate, 62,* 231–242.

Volpe, J.J. (1994). Brain injury in the premature infant: Current concepts. *Preventive Medicine, 23,* 638–645.

Volpe, J.J. (1995). *Neurology of the newborn: Pathophysiology and management of the newborn* (3rd ed.). Philadelphia: W.B. Saunders.

Volpe, J.J. (1997). Brain injury in the premature infant: Neuropathology, clinical aspects, and pathogene-

sis. *Mental Retardation and Developmental Disabilties Research, 3,* 3–12.

Watchko, J.F., & Claassen, D. (1994). Kernicterus in premature infants: Current prevalence and relationship to NICHD Phototherapy Study exchange criteria. *Pediatrics, 93,* 996–999.

Wells, J.T., & Ment, L.R. (1995). Prevention of intraventricular hemorrhage in preterm infants. *Early Human Development, 42,* 209–233.

Yu, V.Y., & Bacsain, M.B. (1994). Avoidance of red blood cell transfusion in an extremely preterm infant given recombinant human erythropoietin therapy. *Journal of Paediatrics & Child Health, 30,* 360–362.

The Developing Child

8 Substance Abuse
A Preventable Threat to Development

Mark L. Batshaw
Charles J. Conlon

Upon completion of this chapter, the reader will:

- understand the impact of substance abuse during pregnancy
- be able to describe the effects of prenatal exposure to alcohol, nicotine, and illicit drugs of abuse on the newborn
- be aware of the neurodevelopmental alterations in infancy associated with *in utero* exposure to drugs of abuse, including cocaine, opiates, marijuana, and phencyclidine
- be familiar with common intervention strategies for the child and family
- be knowledgeable about approaches to prevention
- be aware of the interaction among genetics, demographics, and environment in determining outcome

Thus far, the principal focus of this book has been on genetic risks to the development of the fetus and child. However, equally important are environmental risks, especially substance abuse. Among pregnant women, 5%–10% abuse alcohol, 20% smoke cigarettes, 10% use marijuana, about 1% use cocaine, and 0.5% use opiates (Center on Addiction and Substance Abuse, 1996). Each year, about 11% of newborns are born to mothers who use illicit drugs, and an additional 25%–30% are born to mothers who are heavy users of alcohol or nicotine (Wheeler, 1993). The highest rates of maternal drug abuse are among 18- to 25-year-olds, African Americans, and urban dwellers; but substance abuse is common in all races and socioeconomic statuses, and the prevalence is not decreasing.

It should be emphasized that three quarters of individuals who abuse one substance are likely to abuse others as well (Center on Addiction and Substance Abuse, 1996). Thus, cocaine abuse and alcohol abuse often occur together and may be associated with the use of nicotine, phencyclidine (PCP), marijuana, and/or heroin. Polydrug use makes it difficult to discriminate the specific effect on the fetus of each substance. Other confounding maternal factors are undernutrition, sexually transmitted diseases (STDs), and inadequate prenatal care. As a result, the following discussions must be read with the understanding that these are shared effects.

ALCOHOL

Though seemingly a modern problem, maternal alcohol ingestion is one of the oldest known causes of developmental disabilities (Abel, 1984). The Bible contains a proscription against alcohol consumption during pregnancy in reference to the conception of Samson: "Behold now, thou art barren, and barest not; but thou shalt conceive, and bear a son. Now therefore beware, I pray thee, and drink not wine nor strong drink" (Judges 13:3–4, Authorized [King James] Version). Aristotle, in his tract "Problemata," written in the 4th century B.C., was the first to associate alcohol with fetal abnormalities (Hett, 1936). The first epidemic of what is now called fetal alcohol syndrome (FAS) appears to have occurred in 18th century England, following the removal of restrictions on the distillation of spirits. The so-called "gin epidemic" that followed was reported to cause "weak, feebled and distemper'd children" (Warner & Rosset, 1975, p. 1396). Yet, if the linkage was once known, it was subsequently forgotten until the 1973 article by Jones, Smith, Ulleland, and colleagues that set forth the group of physical findings that define FAS.

Characteristics of Alcohol-Related Birth Defects

Alcohol ingestion during pregnancy has been associated with a spectrum of physical and neurodevelopmental effects on the fetus (Astley & Clarren, 1996; Streissguth, Landesman-Dwyer, Martin, et al., 1980). These range from physical malformations and mental retardation (collectively termed FAS) to typical appearance and milder cognitive impairments usually accompanied by learning and behavior problems (termed fetal alcohol effects [FAE] or alcohol-related neurodevelopmental disorder [ARND]) to no overt signs or symptoms. When there are abnormal findings, these syndromes are referred to as alcohol-related birth defects (ARBD) (Sokol & Clarren, 1989; Spohr & Steinhausen, 1996).

The criteria for the diagnosis of FAS include prenatal and postnatal growth retardation, central nervous system (CNS) abnormalities, and craniofacial malformations (Lewis & Woods, 1994) (Table 8.1). Although children with FAS are typically born at term, about 80% have low birth weights (LBWs; weight and length below the 10th percentile) (Committee on Substance Abuse and Committee on Children with Disabilities, 1993). During infancy, about 70% of these children have severe feeding problems, often leading to failure to thrive. They tend to remain thin and short in childhood but by late adolescence may have attained normal height and weight.

Combined with LBW and neurobehavioral impairments, characteristic physical features can help identify those young children with full-blown FAS (Autti-Rämö, Gaily, & Granström, 1992; Clarren & Smith, 1978; Jones et al., 1973). These children frequently have microcephaly, with head circumferences below the 5th percentile. Their eyes are widely spaced with short eye slits. Their noses are short and upturned, the upper lips thin, and the groove in the midline of the lips (philtrum) flattened (Figure 8.1). Although the craniofacial characteristics diminish with time, the microcephaly remains (Spohr, Willms, & Steinhausen, 1993). In addition, 20%–50% of children with FAS have cardiac anomalies (most commonly ventricular septal defect), hemangiomas, genito-urinary malformations, and minor joint and limb abnormalities (Bratton, 1995). During childhood, vision complications including strabismus, nystagmus, astigmatism,

Table 8.1.   Criteria for the diagnosis of FAS

Category 1: Prenatal and postnatal growth retardation	Category 2: CNS abnormalities	Category 3: Craniofacial abnormalities
• Prenatal growth retardation (less than 10th percentile) or postnatal growth retardation (less than 10th percentile)	• Mental retardation • Irritability in infancy • Hyperactivity and attention impairments in childhood • Developmental delays • Hypotonia and motor problems • Microcephaly • Seizures	• Microphthalmia and/or short palpebral fissure • Thin upper lip, poorly developed philtrum, flat maxillae

Source: Streissguth et al. (1980).

and myopia may become evident (see Chapter 11). Malformations of the middle ear result in an increased risk of recurrent otitis media and conductive hearing loss (see Chapter 12).

In the first 2 years of life, developmental delays become evident, particularly in the area of speech and language (Jacobson, Jacobson, Sokol, et al., 1993). There is also hypotonia and associated motor delays. By school age, however, there is only subtle motor impairment, manifested as fine-motor incoordination and clumsiness. At school entry, children with FAS exhibit a wide range of IQ scores, classifying them as having anything from mental retardation to low-average intelligence. On average, children with FAS exhibit mental retardation requiring intermittent supports, and IQ scores tend to remain stable into adolescence (Janzen, Nanson, & Block, 1995; Streissguth, Herman, & Smith, 1978; Streissguth, Randels, & Smith, 1991).

In addition to the physical and cognitive abnormalities, about two thirds of children and adolescents with FAS manifest significant behavior and/or emotional disturbances. These problems include poor judgment, oppositional and defiant behavior, lying, stealing, inappropriate response to social cues, absence of reciprocal friendships, social withdrawal, mood lability, bullying, and anxiety (Committee on Substance Abuse and Committee on Children with Disabilities, 1993). These maladaptive behaviors may be profound, pervasive, and persistent; they may, in fact, be the principal factors that determine prognosis (Steinhausen, Willms, & Spohr, 1993, 1994). Although these complications may be the result of teratogenic effects of alcohol, they are equally likely to reflect a genetic inheritance from their alcoholic parent(s). For example, alcoholism has been found to originate from "self-medication" in some individuals with genetically determined mood disorders. In sum, it is likely that the behavioral and psychiatric symptoms in children with FAS are the result of cognitive impairment superimposed on genetic and environmental influences (Wilson, 1977).

Children who have milder intellectual and behavioral impairments than those typically associated with FAS and who do not have craniofacial malformations are said to have FAE (Bratton, 1995). These children tend to have intellectual functioning in the borderline-average range and behavior problems. They often demonstrate subtle impairments in memory, language, and fine motor skills. In school, they have particular problems with reading and math (Streissguth, Barr, Olsen, et al., 1994).

In mothers who have been drinking in the days immediately preceding birth, the amniotic fluid will smell of alcohol, and the newborn infant may have a mild withdrawal syndrome. This

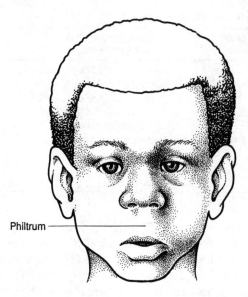

Philtrum —

Figure 8.1.   Facial appearance of a child with FAS. These children tend to have microcephaly; widely spaced eyes with narrow eyelids; a short, upturned nose; large philtrums; large low-set ears; and underdeveloped jaws with malocclusion.

includes jitteriness (especially in reaction to loud noises), tremors, irritability, and, infrequently, seizures during the first days of life. The infant's muscle tone may be low, sleep patterns abnormal, and suck weak.

Prevalence of Alcohol-Related Birth Defects

The prevalence of ARBD worldwide is estimated to be around 1 in 200 births (consisting of 1–2 in 1,000 for FAS and 3–5 in 1,000 for FAE). ARBDs account for about 5% of all congenital anomalies and 10%–20% of all cases of mental retardation requiring intermittent supports (Spohr et al., 1993), which surpasses the number of cases attributable to Down syndrome and fragile X syndrome, making ABRD the leading cause of mental retardation. The incidence varies among populations; Native Americans are at particular risk (Abel, 1995). Low socio-economic status, smoking, poor nutrition, poor maternal health, and polydrug use all are risk factors for ARBD.

The average amount of alcohol consumed per person varies from one country to another, and as expected, the incidence of ARBD parallels the level of general alcohol use. France, second in alcohol intake in the world, with a per capita average of four drinks per day, was actually the first country to report FAS (Lemoine, Haronsseau, Borteyu, et al., 1968). Portugal ranks first, and the United States is 15th in alcohol consumption. In the United States, approximately 80% of women indicate that they have used alcohol sometimes during their lives, and 60% have at least one drink weekly. Forty-five percent report drinking alcohol during the 3 months before learning they were pregnant, and 20% drank after learning they were pregnant (Centers for Disease Control and Prevention, 1995a). Overall, 5%–10% of pregnant women are thought to drink at levels sufficient to place their fetuses at significant risk for ARBD (Coles, 1993). Chronic alcoholics have a 30%–40% chance of bearing a child with ARBD (Coles, 1993). Once a woman has had one child with ARBD, she has a 75% risk of having a second affected child (Abel & Sokol, 1987). The risk of bearing a child with ARBD also increases with maternal age, although the reason for this is unclear.

Relationship of Alcohol Intake to Fetal Effects

Alcohol is considered a weak teratogen; in animal models, large amounts need to be ingested over prolonged periods of time to cause fetal malformations. Because it is a small molecule, alcohol rapidly traverses the placental membrane and the fetal blood–brain barrier. As a result, a high maternal blood level can lead to significant fetal exposure. Alcohol and its metabolite, acetaldehyde, have been shown to decrease protein synthesis, impair cellular growth and migration, cause neuronal cell death, decrease production of neurotransmitters, increase free radical formation, and inhibit myelination of axons (West, Chen, & Pantazis, 1994). Alcohol also can cause adverse effects indirectly by leading to fetal hypoxia. In addition, the poor nutritional status of many woman who drink heavily may lead to deficiencies of vitamins and minerals in the fetus (e.g., B_6, folate, zinc), which may increase the teratogenic potential of alcohol. Together, these biochemical abnormalities are thought to be sufficient to explain the malformations, growth retardation, and cognitive impairments that mark children with ARBD.

In discussing alcohol intake, it is useful to have a common definition. A standard "drink" contains approximately 0.6 ounces of absolute alcohol. This is equivalent to 12 ounces of beer, 5 ounces of wine, or 1.5 ounces of 80-proof distilled spirits. One set of guidelines offered by Lewis and Woods (1994) suggested that if a woman admits to ingesting up to one and a half drinks per day she is considered a moderate drinker, and a woman who reports ingesting more than two drinks per day is considered a heavy drinker (alcoholic). (It is important to remember, though, that alcoholism is a very complex disease with many features, a minimum of which need to be present to constitute a diagnosis of alcoholism.) The interpretation of data in studying these issues is complicated by the frequent inaccuracy of maternal intake histories and by disagreement among researchers about how many drinks constitute heavy use. Studies of alcohol use during early pregnancy have shown that even lower alcohol intakes can cause developmental impairments; consumption of two drinks per week is associated with a decrease in birth weight, and three drinks per week has been reported to decrease IQ scores by 5–7 points (Autti-Ramo, Gaily, et al., 1992; Olsen, 1994). Although some studies suggest that more modest alcohol intake does not affect the fetus, other studies indicate subtle impairments in learning and attention with intakes of less than one drink per week. As of 1997, no safe level of alcohol intake during pregnancy has been identified (Jacobson & Jacobson, 1994).

If a high intake of alcohol occurs during the first trimester of pregnancy, it may lead to miscarriage or to full-blown FAS (Abel, 1984). If it occurs only in the second to third trimester, it may lead to LBW and cognitive and behavioral abnormalities but not malformations (i.e., it produces FAE) (Abel, 1984). In many cases, the fetus is exposed to alcohol throughout the pregnancy. Although maternal alcohol intake appears to be the predominant influence on the occurrence of FAS, there is some evidence that the father's alcohol intake at the time of conception may have some teratogenic potential (West et al., 1994).

In addition to the amount and duration of alcohol intake, there are other factors that influence the effect of alcohol on the fetus, including binge drinking, genetics, and polydrug use (Abel & Hannigan, 1995). Binge drinking has a more adverse effect on the fetus than does steady drinking of the same volume of alcohol. Maternal factors, such as the level of activity of the enzyme alcohol dehydrogenase, also may play a role in causing fetal malformations. Native Americans appear to have a genetically determined decrease in activity of this enzyme. As a result, they metabolize alcohol more slowly and generate higher and more prolonged blood alcohol concentration levels than is typical following alcohol ingestion. This leads to an increased risk for the fetus. Finally, there may be a synergism among various drugs of abuse. It is common for an individual who abuses alcohol to also use cocaine and possibly smoke tobacco or use heroin. The effect of each of these compounds on the fetus may be more than additive.

Outcome of ARBD

Only about 30% of children with FAS are in the care of their mothers through adolescence (Spohr et al., 1993; Spohr, Willms, & Steinhausen, 1994). For children who remained at home in one study, 86% of the mothers have been cited for neglect and 52% for child abuse (Streissguth, Aase, Clarren, et al., 1991). Approximately two thirds of mothers of children with FAS die from alcohol-related causes (e.g., cirrhosis, car accident, suicide, overdose) during the early years of the child's life (Abel & Sokol, 1987). However, out-of-home placement of these children is often difficult because of their extreme hyperactive and noncompliant behavior combined with poor intellectual and language skills. Adoption may be further complicated by the preponderance of ethnic minorities among these children (Abel, 1984).

Some children with FAS have been assessed through adulthood, and the preliminary results are not encouraging (Streissguth, Aase, et al., 1991). Few adults with FAS are living independently, and alcohol abuse is quite frequent among them (Blum, Noble, Sheridan, et al., 1990). Studies of prognosis in adulthood for individuals with FAE are less available. The outcome is likely to be better than for FAS because of the milder cognitive and behavior impairments (Streissguth, Aase, et al., 1991).

Although, in the past, the prognosis for these children has seemed bleak, it is likely that outcome can be significantly improved using a comprehensive intervention approach beginning in infancy (Streissguth, 1997). The ideal plan is to get the alcoholic mother into treatment and provide the social, financial, and medical supports so that she can remain healthy and capable of caring for her child. If this is not possible, the child should be placed in a foster home that has received training in caring for children with special needs. The infant should receive early intervention services, especially focusing on language. In preschool, the emphasis should be on social skills and behavior training. Education during school age will need to address academic impairments while providing behavioral supports. In adolescence, vocational training and counseling services should be provided. By young adulthood, the individual should have a supportive employment placement and independent living opportunity. As more of these life span programs are developed, it is likely that future outcome studies will show a significantly improved prognosis.

NICOTINE

The percentage of women smoking tobacco during pregnancy (as well as at other times) has significantly declined in the 1990s as a result of increased knowledge about the many health complications resulting from long-term use. Still, one third of women with low socioeconomic status smoke during pregnancy, about twice the rate observed in the upper socioeconomic strata (Chiriboga, 1993). The adverse effects of smoking on the fetus include an increased risk of miscarriage and LBW; however, there is no teratogenic effect. Intrauterine growth retardation results from the accumulation of carbon monoxide from the tar in cigarettes and decreased placental blood flow of nutrients due to the vasoconstrictor action of nicotine (Wheeler, 1993). The effect on fetal growth is dose related; there is a 3-fold increased risk of LBW with a one pack per day habit and a 6-fold increase with two packs per day intake (Fried, 1993). When smoking and a high caffeine intake are combined, the effect is doubled; and when cigarettes and alcohol are used together, the effect on birth weight is quadrupled (Chiriboga, 1993). Conversely, cessation of smoking during pregnancy increases birth weight. In the newborn period, there may be subtle neurobehavioral abnormalities as a consequence of recent maternal nicotine intake. These symptoms are similar to those seen with marijuana and represent a mild withdrawal reaction. It is controversial as to whether there is any long-term impairment in language and cognitive development resulting from cigarette smoking during pregnancy (Cornelius, Taylor, Geva, et al., 1995).

COCAINE

Cocaine is both one of the most powerfully addictive and most commonly used illicit drugs. Fetal exposure to cocaine occurs in about 1% of all pregnant women (Sumner, Mandoki, & Matthews-Ferrari, 1993). It has been associated with an increased risk of prematurity, abruption, LBW, and infantile neurobehavioral abnormalities. As cocaine is rarely used alone, it has been difficult to discriminate its long-term effects from those of other concurrently used drugs of abuse (Hawley, 1994). Like alcohol, there are also confounding prenatal, genetic, and environmental variables.

Cocaine is derived from the leaves of the erythroxylon coca plant, which is indigenous to Bolivia, Ecuador, and Peru. These leaves were chewed by the Incas for thousands of years. It was considered a "heavenly plant," the use of which was restricted to the highest socioeconomic strata of the culture (Rosenak, Diamant, Yaffe, et al., 1990). Coca leaves were brought to Europe in the 16th century by Spanish explorers of the New World. Until the late 19th century, however, these leaves were used only in limited amounts, most often in the coal mines to permit long days of strenuous work. In the mid-1800s, cocaine was first extracted from coca leaves and became available for medicinal use. Sigmund Freud (1974) wrote a classic paper in 1884 on its use as a local anesthetic and stimulant. He used cocaine himself and ultimately became addicted to it, as did, in literature, Sherlock Holmes (Myer, 1974). Until 1903, cocaine was a constituent of the "pick me up" drink Coca Cola; it was subsequently replaced by caffeine (Snodgrass, 1994). The first modern reports of addiction to cocaine were recorded in the early part of the 20th century. However, cocaine addiction reached epidemic proportions only in the 1980s when inexpensive and accessible "crack" became readily available (Abelson & Miller, 1985).

Prevalence of Cocaine Abuse

Up to 60 tons of cocaine, worth $55 billion, enter the United States each year. More than 20 million citizens have tried it at least once, and 4 million use it regularly (Glanz & Woods, 1993). Approximately 5% of all infants born in suburban hospitals have the cocaine metabolite benzoylecgonine in their meconium, suggesting maternal ingestion in the week preceding delivery (Wheeler, 1993). The percentage of affected infants in urban hospitals is 2- to 3-fold higher. Even this may be an underestimate as about half of positive cocaine screens during pregnancy come from women who deny cocaine use (Volpe, 1992).

Metabolism of Action of Cocaine

Cocaine is a potent, short-acting, CNS stimulant that heightens the body's natural response to pleasure, creating feelings of euphoria. Cocaine (methylbenzoylecgonine) is available in two forms: a cocaine hydrochloride salt (the usual street preparation) and a purified alkaloidal base known as "crack" cocaine. Cocaine hydrochloride is soluble in water and is therefore readily absorbed when administered orally, intranasally, or intravenously (Farrar & Kearns, 1989). Conversely, crack is almost insoluble in water and is heat stable. It vaporizes at low temperatures, and smoking is the preferred route of administration (Farrar & Kearns, 1989). It is called "crack" because of the popping sound it makes when heated and "rock" because of its appearance. Other street names for cocaine include "snow," "coke," "gold dust," and "lady."

Cocaine affects brain chemistry principally by blocking the reuptake and thus increasing the levels of three neurotransmitters: norepinephrine, dopamine, and serotonin (Gonzales & Campbell, 1994) (Figure 8.2). Acute increases in norepinephrine result in constriction of blood vessels, leading to rapid heart rate and elevated blood pressure. Norepinephrine is also the likely source of the euphoria experienced following cocaine intake. Alterations in serotonin levels decrease appetite and the need for sleep. Dopamine stimulation results in hyperactivity and sexual arousal. Yet long-term cocaine exposure ultimately leads to depletion of dopamine and the reverse effects (Hurt, Brodsky, Betancourt, et al., 1995). The effects of cocaine as a local anesthetic are related to its blockage of peripheral nerve conduction.

Cocaine is often used with other drugs of abuse; in one study, 47% of cocaine users also were heavy alcohol users, while 14% used opiates (Davis, Fennoy, Laraque, et al., 1992). When used together, alcohol and cocaine produce a unique metabolite, cocaethylene, which is a more potent constrictor of blood vessels than cocaine alone (Snodgrass, 1994). In infants exposed *in utero* to both drugs, especially premature infants, there is an increased risk of intracerebral hemorrhage and a stroke-like syndrome.

Cocaine Addiction

Cocaine is not physically addictive like alcohol and heroin, but it causes a rapid "psychological addiction." An initial intense euphoria ("rush") begins 5–10 minutes after smoking "crack" and lasts 45–60 minutes. During this state, cocaine enhances energy, self-esteem, and the pleasure experienced in most types of activities. It also decreases anxiety and social inhibitions. These feelings, however, are rapidly followed by a prolonged period of anxiety, lethargy, and dysphoria. Attempts at cushioning the withdrawal "crash" often involve the use of other drugs, particularly alcohol, marijuana, opiates, barbiturates, and diazepam (Valium). The biphasic effect results in a compulsion to reexperience the "high," and users are unable to predict or control the extent to which they will crave the drug. Long-term use can lead to severe depression, insomnia, fatigue, irritability, memory problems, impotence, paranoia, anorexia, and even stroke (Scherling, 1994).

An acute overdose of cocaine leads to sweating, tremors, cardiac arrhythmias, and seizures. Other complications relate to the route of administration. Swallowing the drug may result in intestinal obstruction; sniffing it may result in perforation of the nasal septum; and smoking it may cause lung damage. Finally, the sharing of syringes for intravenous administration increases the risk of viral hepatitis and human immunodeficiency virus (HIV) infection.

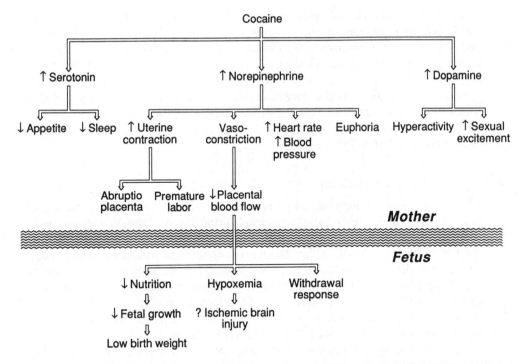

Figure 8.2.   Mechanism of action of cocaine on mother and fetus. Cocaine blocks the reuptake of three neurotransmitters: norepinephrine, dopamine, and serotonin. The resultant increase in serotonin supresses the appetite and the need for sleep in the mother, while the dopamine stimulation results in hyperactivity and sexual arousal. Increases in norepinephrine result in increased uterine contractions, predisposing the mother to abruption and premature labor. Norepinephrine also leads to a sense of euphoria and constricts blood vessels, leading to rapid heart rate and elevated blood pressure. Increased norepinephrine also results in decreased placental blood flow, predisposing the infant to intrauterine growth retardation, ischemic brain injury, and a withdrawal reaction following birth.

Effects of Fetal Cocaine Exposure

Rodent models have been used to study the effects of fetal cocaine exposure during gestation. Pregnant mice or rats are fed cocaine at various times during gestation, and the progeny are examined from a behavioral and neuropathological perspective. Cocaine has been found to rapidly cross the placenta and to be associated with transient **vasoconstriction, tachycardia, hypertension,** and decreased uterine artery blood flow. This results in decreased blood and oxygen reaching the fetus (Gonzales & Campbell, 1994; Plessinger & Woods, 1993). However, vasoconstriction does help to limit the amount of cocaine reaching the fetus (Woods, Plessinger, & Clark, 1987). The clearest effect of fetal cocaine exposure is stunted growth resulting from chronic vasoconstriction of the placental blood vessels. The vasoconstriction also has been associated with stroke in mice.

Animal studies do not support a direct teratogenic effect of cocaine at levels similar to those ingested by humans. However, at higher doses, cocaine can alter neuronal migration and brain development. At levels similar to those found in humans, cocaine exposure early in gestation in the mouse does lead to abnormalities of the heart, limbs, and genito-urinary tract. These are thought to result from vasoconstriction and hypoxic-ischemic damage to the developing body organs. There is controversy as to whether cocaine can cause similar abnormalities in children. Mice exposed to high doses of cocaine later in gestation have decreased brain size (Kosofsky, Wilkins, Gressens, et al., 1994). This is compatible with the finding of decreased head circumference in infants exposed to cocaine *in utero*. Late-gestation cocaine ingestion also leads to increased uterine contractility. This is consistent with the finding of an increased risk of placental abruptions, miscarriages, premature deliveries, and stillbirths in human fetuses exposed to cocaine (Levy & Koren, 1990) (Table 8.2).

Effects of Cocaine During Infancy

Neonatal withdrawal symptoms can occur in newborn infants exposed to cocaine (Doberczak, Shanzer, Senie, et al., 1988). Symptoms include irritability, restlessness, lethargy, poor feeding, abnormal sleep pattern, tremors, increased muscle tone, vomiting, and a high-pitched cry. The onset of symptoms is usually within 24–48 hours of birth and withdrawal lasts 2–3 days. In addition to withdrawal, the newborn may show toxic symptoms if there is direct exposure to cocaine from contaminated breast milk, rubbing cocaine to shrink swollen gums, or inhalation (Bateman & Heagarty, 1989). Toxic symptoms include vomiting, diarrhea, irritability, and seizures, while physical findings involve dilated pupils, increased heart rate, increased blood pressure, and irregular breathing (Chaney, Franke, & Wadlington, 1988).

Although acute withdrawal and toxic symptoms are short lived, infants exposed to cocaine *in utero* may demonstrate neurobehavioral abnormalities related to mood and sleep state, feeding, attention, and interactive response that may persist for up to 6 months (Tronick, Frank, Cabral, et al., 1996; Tsay, Partridge, Villarreal, et al., 1996). There is a low threshold to overstimulation, and these infants tend to be irritable, cry inconsolably, have abnormal sleep patterns, and feed poorly (Hawley, 1994; Singer, Yamashita, Hawkins, et al., 1994). They often show other signs of distress, including rapid respiration and disorganized motor activity.

Prolonged behavioral alterations of this type can interfere with the typical bonding of the mother and child and place an already fragile mother at risk for neglecting or abusing her diffi-

Table 8.2.   Selected perinatal outcomes, according to whether the mother used cocaine

Outcome	Cocaine users (%)	Nonusers (%)	Adjusted relative risk
Birth weight less than 2,500 grams	28	6	2.8
Gestational age below 37 weeks	29	9	2.4
Small for gestational age	29	9	3.4 for smokers, 2.1 for nonsmokers
Decreased head circumference	16	6	2.1 for smokers, 1.1 for nonsmokers
Abruptio placenta	4	1	4.5
Perinatal death	4	1	2.1

Adapted from Volpe, J.J. (1992). Effect of cocaine use on the fetus. *New England Journal of Medicine, 327*, 400; copyright © 1992. Massachusetts Medical Society. All rights reserved.

cult and unresponsive infant (Dixon, Bresnahan, & Zuckerman, 1990). Those caring for the infant must consider the infant's need for a quiet, nurturing environment. This can be achieved by swaddling, rocking, and providing a pacifier. Because these infants are easily overstimulated, using only one sensory modality at a time is most effective. For example, if the caregiver is singing to the infant, the lights should be kept low and the infant swaddled in the crib. In addition, these infants may need frequent "time outs" from stimulation (Chasnoff, Griffith, MacGregor, et al., 1989).

In addition to these behavior problems, the infant exposed to cocaine may have differences in growth and motor development. At birth, approximately 20% of these infants have weight, length, and head circumference below the 5th percentile (Volpe, 1992). These children also may exhibit abnormalities in muscle tone and movement (Chiriboga, Vibbert, Malouf, et al., 1995; Fetters & Tronick, 1996). If this persists, the age at which the child sits and walks may be significantly delayed. Even when these neuromotor signs are transient, they are often markers for future development of learning disabilities, or attention and behavior problems (VanDyke & Fox, 1990). Although there was initial concern that "crack" infants had a significantly increased risk of sudden infant death syndrome (SIDS), this has not proven to be the case (Hawley, 1994).

In sum, the proven risks of *in utero* cocaine exposure include abruption, prematurity, LBW, and decreased head size. It is suggested that these problems, together with the neurobehavioral abnormalities in infancy, may increase the risk of subsequent impairments in language and motor skills, attention span, organizational strategies, and interpersonal relationships. This association, however, has not yet been proven (Azuma & Chasnoff, 1993; Jacobsen, Jacobsen, Sokol, et al., 1996; Mayes, Granger, Bornstein, et al., 1992; Neuspiel, 1994).

Effects of Cocaine on the Family

Cocaine use affects every aspect of family life (Lewis & Bendersky, 1995). The addictive nature of cocaine leads the parent(s) to focus on acquiring and using the drug rather than on caring for the child. They may engage in illegal activities such as drug dealing or prostitution as a means of earning money to support their habit. The money is then spent on drugs rather than on food, clothing, or housing; as a result, the family is likely to be indigent and homeless. Furthermore, the cocaine abuse may be associated with or lead to depression or a personality disorder in the parent(s). Finally, more than half of cocaine-dependent women will suffer physical abuse, STDs, and/or separation from their child by incarceration (Richardson & Day, 1994).

When mothers inject cocaine intravenously, their infants face approximately a 6-fold increased risk of HIV infection (Volpe, 1992). In urban areas, more than 90% of caregivers reported for child abuse are active substance abusers, and 75% of child abuse fatalities involve drug abuse (Scherling, 1994). At least 30% of the children of cocaine-dependent mothers end up in foster homes (Richardson & Day, 1994). In the late 1980s and early 1990s, the number of cocaine-exposed children requiring foster care escalated so rapidly that many child welfare agencies became overwhelmed. Adding to this problem, cocaine-exposed infants may be difficult to place because of the developmental and behavioral effects of this drug. The irritable, stiff, and difficult to calm infant may undergo frequent changes in placement as a result of foster parent "burnout." This disruption puts such children at further risk for developmental and behavior problems.

Prognosis in Fetal Cocaine Exposure

Although children who are exposed prenatally to cocaine are both biologically and environmentally at risk for subsequent disabilities, the severity of these impairments may have been overstated in the past. Although there is considerable variability, studies suggest that the majority of children exposed to cocaine *in utero* will have typical cognitive functioning and will not have significant physical problems by school entry (van Baar, Soepatmi, Gunning, et al., 1994).

However, there may be behavioral and emotional impairments including attention deficits, problems with attachment and separation, and poor social skills. They also may have poor organizational skills and learning impairments, most prominently in reading and mathematics.

In one follow-up study of infants who had been exposed to cocaine prenatally, evaluation at 2 years of age showed catch-up growth in weight and height and typical intellectual functioning in the vast majority (Chasnoff, Griffith, & Freier, 1992). In another study, however, 30%–40% of preschool children prenatally exposed to cocaine showed some neurodevelopmental impairments, most commonly in language (Singer et al., 1994). Cognitive functioning appears to be influenced by the postnatal environment. One study showed that when mothers continued to ingest cocaine after the child's birth, 40% of their infants had verbal IQ scores more than 1 standard deviation below the mean; while among the children of mothers who no longer use drugs, only 15% had significantly lower IQ scores (Scherling, 1994).

OPIATES

Opium is a mixture of alkaloids derived from the seeds of the poppy *Papaver somniferum*. Morphine comprises 10% of these alkaloids and can be converted chemically to heroin. Heroin was first manufactured in 1874 but only became popular as a drug of abuse in the United States in the 1960s. It can be ingested, injected, or absorbed through mucous membranes. Most users administer heroin intravenously so there is immediate onset of action. Its effects, which last about 2 hours, range from analgesia and sedation to feelings of well-being and euphoria. Continued use leads to the phenomenon of tolerance, in which increasingly higher doses are required to produce the desired effect. This leads to physical dependence.

A high incidence of heroin abuse occurred among service men during the Vietnam War. They brought back their addiction to the United States and often shared it with their partners. In response to the need for treatment of heroin addiction, methadone was developed as an oral substitute. It binds to opiate receptors and produces milder effects. Even when on a methadone maintenance program, however, 50%–90% of individuals will abuse other drugs, and most fail to kick the habit (Glanz & Woods, 1993).

Heroin places women at significant risk for hepatitis, subacute bacterial endocarditis, and/or HIV infection from shared needles; syphilis and other STDs from prostitution; malnutrition from inadequate food intake; pulmonary edema; overdoses; and withdrawal reactions. Twelve to 30% of heroin addicts have been exposed to the hepatitis B virus, 13%–25% to syphilis, and 3%–9% per year convert to HIV positive (Glanz & Woods, 1993).

Although the prevalence of heroin addiction has declined in the 1990s, about 0.5% of infants born each year are exposed *in utero* to it or to methadone (Glanz & Woods, 1993). The principal direct effect of both heroin and methadone on the fetus is growth retardation. Forty-five percent of infants born to mothers who abuse heroin have LBW versus 25% of infants exposed to methadone and 15% of infants whose mothers were drug free (Glanz & Woods, 1993). There is also a 2-fold increased risk of prematurity and a 4-fold increased risk of stillbirth. Heroin itself is not a teratogen, but some fetuses will be infected by syphilis, which can cause malformations. The most serious risk to the fetus relates to the sharing of needles, which carries a significant chance of vertical transmission of hepatitis and HIV infection from the mother. Infants born to mothers using heroin should receive hepatitis immune globulin to decrease the risk of developing hepatitis, and AZT if the mother is HIV positive (see Chapter 9).

For a heroin-exposed newborn, the major concern is a severe withdrawal response. Sixty to 95% of infants of mothers using heroin or methadone have withdrawal symptoms and may need pharmacological intervention (van Baar et al., 1994). Onset is usually at 24–72 hours of age and the reaction lasts 7–10 days. Symptoms include irritability, tremors, sweating, stuffy nose, uncoordinated suck, diarrhea, vomiting, sleep disturbances, hypertonicity, and occasionally seizures (Wheeler, 1993). If symptoms are severe, they may require treatment with phenobarbitol or paregoric. Methadone withdrawal is more delayed and also can be more severe. For some months after recovery, heroin- and methadone-exposed infants may show neurobehavioral abnormalities, similar to "crack" infants, that include a deranged sleep pattern, decreased interactive behavior, resistance to cuddling, and decreased orientation to auditory and visual stimuli (van Baar & de Graaff, 1994).

Long-term effects of fetal opiate exposure remain unclear. There have been reports of decreased head growth, but this is controversial. IQ scores generally are in the low-average range, although there is an increased risk of learning problems. Behavior dysfunction and inattention have also been reported in school-age children (Wheeler, 1993).

PHENCYCLIDINE

PCP was first used in the 1950s as a general anesthetic. As a result of frequent toxic reactions that included hallucinations and delusions, however, it was soon removed from the market. It remains in use as a veterinary anesthetic for large animals. In the 1970s, PCP became popular as a recreational drug, with street names such as "angel dust," "crystal," "hog," "horse tranquilizer," and "peace pill." PCP is easily synthesized and inexpensive. When smoked or ingested, it gives a "high" that lasts 4–6 hours, with feelings of intoxication, euphoria, and unreality. There may also be unusual sensory perceptions, emotional lability, and "religious experiences." At very high doses, however, there can be delusions, hallucinations, and episodes of violent aggression. The psychoactive effects of PCP are thought to be modulated through dopamine and norepinephrine, in a manner similar to cocaine. Because of its side effects, the popularity of PCP fell in the 1980s. In 1988, only 3% of high school graduates reported using PCP, compared with 13% of high school seniors who reported using PCP at least once in 1979 (Glanz & Woods, 1993). Its usage, however, has started to climb again. Although it is not physically addictive, PCP leads to a psychological craving. The few studies of its use in pregnancy suggest that it has no teratogenic effect. Its effects on the fetus and infant are likely to be similar to cocaine.

MARIJUANA

Although cocaine use during pregnancy is more common in women of poverty, marijuana use is more prevalent in the middle class. Approximately half of all women 18–25 years of age have used marijuana at least once, 21% have used it during the past year, and 9% in the past month. Approximately 10% of women smoke marijuana during their pregnancy, more in the first trimester than the third (Richardson, Day, & McGauhey, 1993).

Marijuana is smoked as a "joint" or ingested. It causes a mild euphoria and sleepiness and is not thought to be addictive. Adverse effects include impaired short-term memory, increased risk-taking behavior, decreased motivation, and altered interpersonal relations. Chronic usage can lead to decreased coordination and visual tracking and respiratory problems (Wheeler, 1993).

There is little information concerning the effects of marijuana on the fetus. What data exist suggest that there are no differences in miscarriage rate, Apgar scores, or fetal malformations in infants of mothers who have smoked marijuana consistently during pregnancy (Wheeler, 1993). However, marijuana use is associated with reduced gestational age and may decrease birth weight (Chiriboga, 1993). This may be a consequence of the accumulation of carbon monoxide while smoking a "joint"; levels are five times higher than those found during cigarette smoking. As a result, the fetus may have less oxygen capacity than usual and this could affect growth.

If the mother has smoked marijuana in the hours prior to labor, the newborn may demonstrate a mild withdrawal response with tremor and an exaggerated startle response (Cornelius et al., 1995). This does not require treatment and subsides in a few days. Prenatal marijuana exposure does not seem to have an important impact on postnatal growth or development (Chasnoff, Griffith, Freier, et al., 1992; Day, Richardson, Geva, et al., 1994; Richardson, Day, & Goldschmidt, 1995). When used during pregnancy in combination with cocaine, however, it has been reported to be associated with subsequent impairment in abstract and visual reasoning (Griffith, Azuma, & Chasnoff, 1994).

INTERVENTION STRATEGIES FOR INFANTS OF DRUG-DEPENDENT MOTHERS

Ideally intervention should start with prevention strategies; women who use illicit drugs should stop prior to conception. This ideal is rarely followed, so the pregnant woman with drug dependence should receive prenatal care in a clinic for women at high risk. Nutritional management is particularly important, and many women may require caloric supplements.

Once the mother has given birth, she must deal with her own addiction. She may also be coping with feelings of guilt for having exposed her baby to the drug(s). The mother should be reassured that her infant's lack of responsiveness and excessive crying are not evidence of the infant rejecting her, but a side effect of the drug exposure. She should be taught parenting skills and referred to a treatment program (Howard, Beckwith, Espinosa, et al., 1995). The situation must be monitored closely so that referral to child welfare can be made at early signs of neglect or abuse. Because most mothers with drug dependence have few financial and emotional resources or family support systems, a team approach by health care professionals is essential (Bays, 1992). A multidisciplinary clinic offers substance abuse counseling, family planning services, parenting classes for the mother, and developmental and behavioral assessments and pediatric care for the child.

As infants, many of these children qualify for early intervention services and as preschoolers, for a Head Start program. The program should strive to create a home and school partnership by providing home visits, maintaining frequent telephone contacts, and encouraging parents or guardians to visit and perform volunteer work at the program. The long-term effects of this intervention are still unclear, but the short-term benefits have been encouraging in terms of gains in language acquisition and socialization skills (Dixon et al., 1990).

In elementary school, the academic needs of the children are a function of both their cognitive abilities and behavioral/emotional symptoms. The Salvin Special Education Center in Los Angeles is an example of an excellent school program that deals effectively with these issues. In order to provide stability, each child has the same teacher for 2 years and the same support team for at least 1 year. Class size is restricted to eight pupils, seat assignments and time schedules are fixed, overstimulation is minimized, and hands-on activities with frequent positive reinforcement are emphasized.

PREVENTION STRATEGIES

The developmental and behavioral risks imposed by maternal use of illicit drugs are preventable. This requires education of school-age children and their parents, teachers, and health care professionals (American Academy of Pediatrics, Committee on Substance Abuse, 1990). Schools have instituted teaching modules about substance abuse beginning in elementary school. Alcoholic beverage containers now display a warning label about the harmful effects of drinking during pregnancy. And many cities have ordinances that require warnings to be posted wherever alcohol is sold or served.

Prenatal intervention programs that offer prevention education have been shown to reduce the intake of alcohol during pregnancy by two thirds in the general population. However, teaching women with alcoholism to decrease their intake during pregnancy has been much less successful. In fact, the reported incidence of FAS actually increased between 1979 and 1993 (Centers for Disease Control and Prevention, 1995b). Health care providers should advocate for improved social support, health care, and drug treatment for drug-dependent women and their children.

BILLY: A CHILD WITH FETAL ALCOHOL SYNDROME

Billy is the fourth child born to Mary, a 36-year-old Native American living on a Navaho reservation. Mary, who had problems with alcoholism during her pregnancy, has two other children with FAS. Born at term, Billy weighed only 4 pounds. He displayed the typical features of FAS—a small head, widely spaced eyes, upturned nose, large ears, and a small chin. He was also found to have a ventricular septal heart defect.

Billy did not stay with his mother long because she continued to have alcoholic binges and was eventually hospitalized for treatment of cirrhosis of the liver, from which she died 2 years later. Billy was placed in a series of foster homes because hyperactivity and oppositional defiant behavior made him difficult to manage. When tested at age 4, he was found to have mental retardation requiring intermittent supports. Now 7 years of age, Billy attends a self-contained special education class with behavior support services and is gaining academic and social skills. He has been in his current foster home for 2 years, and they are considering adoption. Overall, his behavior is under better control and he seems happier and more interactive with his peers.

JON: A BABY PRENATALLY EXPOSED TO COCAINE

Jon was born at term to a 24-year-old who was a crack-cocaine user up to the time of delivery. Jon weighed only 4½ pounds, and his head circumference was small. In the first days of life, he was irritable and ate poorly. He often regurgitated formula, cried inconsolably, and did not like to be held. He did best when swaddled in a blanket and rocked. Even then, he slept fitfully. The nurses were concerned that his mother would have difficulty coping with him, but this became a moot point, as she abandoned him on his third day of life.

Since discharge from the hospital, Jon has been placed in a stable foster home. His development has been somewhat slow, but psychological testing shows that his intelligence is within the average range. Now, at 5 years of age, he is in kindergarten, where he shows some signs of attention deficit and hyperactivity. He has recently been placed on a stimulant medication, Dexedrine, which has improved these symptoms.

SUMMARY

Substance abuse is a serious and preventable cause of developmental disabilities. The teratogenic, cognitive, and behavioral effects of alcohol abuse on the fetus have been proved. Many women who are heavy drinkers ingest other drugs as well, most commonly cocaine, marijuana, heroin, and tobacco. It has been difficult to discriminate the individual effects or to determine if there is a synergy among these drugs. In isolation, the most convincing evidence for fetal effects of cocaine, opiates, marijuana, and nicotine is intrauterine growth retardation (Table 8.3). Significant differences in IQ scores at school age have not been documented following exposure to these drugs (Streissguth, Barr, Sampson, et al., 1989). It is unclear whether neonatal withdrawal reactions to opiates and cocaine affect subsequent development. However, these infants tend to be difficult to manage. There appear to be increased behavioral and emotional difficulties among children of drug-dependent women. These complications, however, are potentially preventable or treatable, and these children should not be considered "doomed" (Zuckerman & Frank, 1992). Early intervention and family support services can have a positive impact on outcome.

Table 8.3. Comparison of effects on growth and development of children exposed in utero to various drugs of abuse

Drug	Withdrawal response	Teratogenic effect	Prenatal/ postnatal growth retardation	Developmental disabilities
Alcohol	++	++	++	+++
Cocaine	+	±	+	+
Heroin	+++	−	±	+
PCP	−	−	−	±
Marijuana	+	−	±	±
Nicotine	−	−	+	±

Key: − = not present; + = mild; ++ = moderate; +++ = severe; ± = uncertain.

REFERENCES

Abel, E.L. (1984). *Fetal alcohol syndrome and fetal alcohol effects.* New York: Plenum.

Abel, E.L. (1995). An update on incidence of FAS: FAS is not an equal opportunity birth defect. *Neurotoxicology and Teratology, 17,* 437–443.

Abel, E.L., & Hannigan, J.H. (1995). Maternal risk factors in fetal alcohol syndrome: Provocative and permissive influences. *Neurotoxicology and Teratology, 17,* 445–462.

Abel, E.L., & Sokol, R.J. (1987). Incidence of fetal alcohol syndrome and economic impact of FAS-related anomalies. *Drug and Alcohol Dependence, 19,* 51–70.

Abelson, H., & Miller, J. (1985). A decade of trends in cocaine use in the household population. *National Institute of Drug Abuse Research Monograph Series,* No. 61, 35–49.

American Academy of Pediatrics, Committee on Substance Abuse. (1990). Drug-exposed infants. *Pediatrics, 86,* 639–642.

Astley, S.J., & Clarren, S.K. (1996). A case definition and photographic screening tool for the facial phenotype of fetal alcohol syndrome. *Journal of Pediatrics, 129,* 33–41.

Autti-Rämö, I., Gaily, E., & Granström, M-L. (1992). Dysmorphic features in offspring of alcoholic mothers. *Archives of Disabled Children, 67,* 712–716.

Autti-Rämö, I., Korkman, M., Hilakivi-Clarke, L., et al. (1992). Mental development of 2-year-old children exposed to alcohol in utero. *Journal of Pediatrics, 120,* 740–746.

Azuma, S.D., & Chasnoff, I.J. (1993). Outcome of children prenatally exposed to cocaine and other drugs: A path analysis of three-year data. *Pediatrics, 92,* 396–402.

Bateman, D.A., & Heagarty, M.C. (1989). Passive freebase cocaine ("crack") inhalation by infants and toddlers. *American Journal of Diseases of Children, 143,* 25–27.

Bays, J. (1992). The care of alcohol- and drug-affected infants. *Pediatric Annals, 21,* 485–495.

Blum, K., Noble, E.P., Sheridan, P.J., et al. (1990). Allelic association of human dopamine D2 receptor gene in alcoholism. *Journal of the American Medical Association, 263,* 2055–2060.

Bratton, R.L. (1995). Fetal alcohol syndrome: How you can help prevent it: Postgraduate medicine. *Fetal Alcohol Syndrome, 98,* 197–200.

Center on Addiction and Substance Abuse. (1996). *Substance abuse and the American woman.* New York: Columbia University.

Centers for Disease Control and Prevention. (1995a). Sociodemographic and behavioral characteristics associated with alcohol consumption during pregnancy: United States, 1988. *Journal of the American Medical Association, 273,* 1406.

Centers for Disease Control and Prevention. (1995b). Update: Trends in fetal alcohol syndrome: United States, 1979–1993. *Journal of the American Medical Association, 273,* 1406.

Chaney, N.E., Franke, J., & Wadlington, W.B. (1988). Cocaine convulsions in a breast-feeding baby. *Journal of Pediatrics, 112,* 134–135.

Chasnoff, I.J., Burns, K.A., & Burns, W.J. (1987). Cocaine use in pregnancy: Perinatal morbidity and mortality. *Neurotoxicology and Teratology, 9,* 291–293.

Chasnoff, I.J., Griffith, D.R., Freier, C., et al. (1992). Cocaine/polydrug use in pregnancy: Two year follow-up. *Pediatrics, 89,* 284–289.

Chasnoff, I.J., Griffith, D.R., MacGregor, S., et al. (1989). Temporal patterns of cocaine use in pregnancy: Perinatal outcome. *Journal of American Medical Association, 261,* 1741–1744.

Chiriboga, C.A. (1993). Fetal effects. *Neurologic Clinics, 11,* 707–728.

Chiriboga, C.A., Vibbert, M., Malouf, R., et al. (1995). Neurological correlates of fetal cocaine exposure: Transient hypertonia of infancy and early childhood. *Pediatrics, 96,* 1070–1077.

Clarren, S.K., & Smith, D.W. (1978). The fetal alcohol syndrome. *New England Journal of Medicine, 298,* 1063–1067.

Coles, C.D. (1993). Impact of prenatal alcohol exposure on the newborn and the child. *Clinical Obstetrics and Gynecology, 36,* 255–266.

Committee on Substance Abuse and Committee on Children with Disabilities. (1993). Fetal alcohol syndrome and fetal alcohol effects. *Pediatrics, 91,* 1004–1006.

Cornelius, M.D., Taylor, P.M., Geva, D., et al. (1995). Prenatal tobacco and marijuana use among adolescents: Effects on offspring gestational age, growth, and morphology. *Pediatrics, 95,* 738–743.

Davis, E., Fennoy, I., Laraque, D., et al. (1992). Autism and developmental abnormalities in children with perinatal cocaine exposure. *Journal of the National Medical Association, 84,* 315–319.

Day, N.L., Richardson, G.A., Geva, D., et al. (1994). Alcohol, marijuana, and tobacco: Effects of prenatal exposure on offspring growth and morphology at age six. *Alcoholism: Clinical and Experimental Research, 18,* 786–794.

Dixon, S.D., Bresnahan, K., & Zuckerman, B. (1990). Cocaine babies: Meeting the challenge of management. *Contemporary Pediatrics, 7*(6), 70–92.

Doberczak, T.M., Shanzer, S., Senie, R.T., et al. (1988). Neonatal neurologic and electroencephalographic effects of intrauterine cocaine exposure. *Journal of Pediatrics, 113,* 354–358.

Farrar, H.C., & Kearns, G.L. (1989). Cocaine: Clinical pharmacology and toxicology. *Journal of Pediatrics, 115,* 665–675.

Fetters, L., & Tronick, E.Z. (1996). Neuromotor development of cocaine-exposed and control infants from birth through 15 months: Poor and poorer performance. *Pediatrics, 98,* 938–943.

Freud, S. (1974). *Cocaine papers.* New York: Stonehill Press.

Fried, P.A. (1993). Prenatal exposure to tobacco and marijuana: Effects during pregnancy, infancy, and early childhood. *Clinical Obstetrics and Gynecology, 36,* 319–337.

Glanz, J.C., & Woods, J.R., Jr. (1993). Cocaine, heroin, and phencyclidine: Obstetric perspectives. *Clinical Obstetrics and Gynecology, 36,* 279–301.

Gonzalez, N.M., & Campbell, M. (1994). Cocaine babies: Does prenatal exposure to cocaine affect development? *Journal of the American Academy of Child and Adolescent Psychiatry, 33,* 16–19.

Griffith, D.R., Azuma, S.D., & Chasnoff, I.J. (1994). Three-year outcome of children exposed prenatally to drugs. *Journal of the American Academy of Child and Adolescent Psychiatry, 33,* 20–27.

Hawley, T.L. (1994). The development of cocaine-exposed children. *Current Problems in Pediatrics, 24,* 259–266.

Hett, W.S. (1936). *Aristotle's problemata.* Cambridge, MA: Harvard University Press.

Howard, J., Beckwith, L., Espinosa, M., et al. (1995). Development of infants born to cocaine-abusing women: Biologic/maternal influences. *Neurotoxicology and Teratology, 17,* 403–411.

Hurt, H., Brodsky, N.L., Betancourt, L., et al. (1995). Cocaine-exposed children: Follow-up through 30 months. *Journal of Developmental and Behavioral Pediatrics, 16,* 29–35.

Jacobson, J.L., & Jacobson, S.W. (1994). Prenatal alcohol exposure and neurobehavioral development: Where is the threshold? *Alcohol Health and Research World, 18,* 30–36.

Jacobson, J.L., Jacobson, S.W., Sokol, J.J., et al. (1993). Teratogenic effects of alcohol on infant development. *Alcoholism: Clinical and Experimental Research, 17,* 174–183.

Jacobson, S.W., Jacobson, J.L., Sokol, R.J., et al. (1996). New evidence for neurobehavioral effects of in utero cocaine exposure. *Journal of Pediatrics, 129,* 581–590.

Janzen, L.A., Nanson, J.L., & Block, G.W. (1995). Neuropsychological evaluation of preschoolers with fetal alcohol syndrome. *Neurotoxicology and Teratology, 17,* 273–279.

Jones, K.L., Smith, D.W., Ulleland, C.N., et al. (1973). Pattern of malformation in offspring of chronic alcoholic mothers. *Lancet, 1,* 1267–1271.

Judges 13:3–4. (1982). *Authorized (King James) Version* (p. 362). New York: Harper & Row.

Kosofsky, B.E., Wilkins, A.S., Gressens, P., et al. (1994). Transplacental cocaine exposure: A mouse model demonstrating neuroanatomic and behavioral abnormalities. *Journal of Child Neurology, 9,* 234–241.

Lemoine, P., Haronsseau, H., Borteyu, J-P., et al. (1968). Les enfants de parents alcoholiques: Anomalies observees a oriois de 127 cas. *L'ouest Medical, 67,* 1154–1160.

Levy, M., & Koren, G. (1990). Obstetric and neonatal effects of drugs of abuse. *Emergency Medicine Clinics of North America, 8,* 633–652.

Lewis, D.D., & Woods, S.E. (1994). Fetal alcohol syndrome. *American Family Physician, 50,* 1025–1032.

Lewis, M., & Bendersky, M. (Eds.). (1995). *Mothers, babies, and cocaine: The role of toxins in development.* Hillsdale, NJ: Lawrence Erlbaum Associates.

Mayes, L.C., Granger, R.H., Bornstein, M.H., et al. (1992). The problem of prenatal cocaine exposure, a rush to judgment. *Journal of the American Medical Association, 267,* 406–408.

Myer, D. (1974). *The seven percent solution.* New York: E.P. Dutton.

Neuspiel, D.R. (1994). Behavior in cocaine-exposed infants and children: Association versus causality. *Drug and Alcohol Dependence, 36,* 101–107.

Olsen, J. (1994). Effects of moderate alcohol consumption during pregnancy on child development at 18 and 42 months. *Alcoholism: Clinical and Experimental Research, 18,* 1109–1113.

Plessinger, M.A., & Woods, J.R. (1993). Maternal, placental, and fetal pathophysiology of cocaine exposure during pregnancy. *Clinical Obstetrics and Gynecology, 36,* 267–278.

Richardson, G.A., & Day, N.J. (1994). Detrimental effects of prenatal cocaine exposure: Illusion or reality? *Journal of the American Academy of Child and Adolescent Psychiatry, 33,* 28–34.

Richardson, G.A., Day, N.L., & Goldschmidt, L. (1995). Prenatal alcohol, marijuana, and tobacco use: Infant mental and motor development. *Neurotoxicology and Teratology, 17,* 479–487.

Richardson, G.A., Day, N.L., & McGauhey, P.J. (1993). The impact of prenatal marijuana and cocaine use on the infant and child. *Clinical Obstetrics and Gynecology, 36,* 302–318.

Rosenak, D., Diamant, Y.Z., Yaffe, H., et al. (1990). Cocaine: Maternal use during pregnancy and its effect on the mother, the fetus, and the infant. *Obstetrical and Gynecological Survey, 45,* 348–359.

Scherling, D. (1994). Prenatal cocaine exposure and childhood psychopathology: A developmental analysis. *American Journal of Orthopsychiatry, 64,* 9–19.

Singer, L., Arendt, R., & Minnes, S. (1993). Neurodevelopmental effects of cocaine. *Clinics in Perinatology, 20,* 245–262.

Singer, L.T., Yamashita, T.S., Hawkins, S., et al. (1994). Increased incidence of intraventricular hemorrhage and developmental delay in cocaine-exposed, very low birth weight infants. *Journal of Pediatrics, 124,* 765–771.

Snodgrass, S.R. (1994). Cocaine babies: A result of multiple teratogenic influences. *Journal of Child Neurology, 9,* 227–233.

Sokol, R.J., & Clarren, S.K. (1989). Guidelines for use of terminology describing the impact of prenatal alcohol on the offspring. *Alcoholism: Clinical and Experimental Research, 13,* 597–598.

Spohr, H-L., & Steinhausen, H-C. (1996). *Alcohol, pregnancy and the developing child.* New York: Cambridge University Press.

Spohr, H-L., Willms, J., & Steinhausen, H-C. (1993). Prenatal alcohol exposure and long-term developmental consequences. *Lancet, 341,* 907–910.

Spohr, H-L., Willms, J., & Steinhausen, H-C. (1994). Fetal alcohol syndrome in adolescence. *Acta Paediatrica, 404*(Suppl.), 19–26.

Steinhausen, H-C., Willms, J., & Spohr, H-L. (1993). Long-term psychopathological and cognitive outcome of children with fetal alcohol syndrome. *Journal of American Academy of Child and Adolescent Psychiatry, 32,* 990–994.

Steinhausen, H-C., Willms, J., & Spohr, H-L. (1994). Correlates of psychopathology and intelligence in children with fetal alcohol syndrome. *Journal of Child Psychology and Psychiatry, 35,* 323–331.

Streissguth, A. (1997). *Fetal alcohol syndrome: A guide for families and communities.* Baltimore: Paul H. Brookes Publishing Co.

Streissguth, A.P., Aase, J.M., Clarren, S.K., et al. (1991). Fetal alcohol syndrome in adolescents and adults. *Journal of the American Medical Association, 265,* 1961–1967.

Streissguth, A.P., Barr, H.M., Olsen, H.C., et al. (1994). Drinking during pregnancy decreases word attack and arithmetic scores on standardized tests: Adolescent data from a population-based prospective study. *Alcoholism: Clinical and Experimental Research, 18,* 248–254.

Streissguth, A.P., Barr, H.M., Sampson, P.D., et al. (1989). IQ at age 4 in relation to maternal alcohol use and smoking during pregnancy. *Developmental Psychology, 25,* 3–11.

Streissguth, A.P., Herman, C.S., & Smith, D.W. (1978). Stability of intelligence in the fetal alcohol syndrome: A preliminary report. *Alcoholism: Clinical and Experimental Research, 2,* 165–170.

Streissguth, A.P., Landesman-Dwyer, S., Martin, J.C., et al. (1980). Teratogenic effects of alcohol in humans and laboratory animals. *Science, 209,* 353–361.

Streissguth, A.P., Randels, S.P., & Smith, D.F. (1991). A test-retest study of intelligence in patients with fetal alcohol syndrome: Implications for care. *Journal of the American Academy of Child and Adolescent Psychiatry, 30,* 584–587.

Streissguth, A.P., Sampson, P.D., & Olson, H.C. (1994). Maternal drinking during pregnancy: Attention and short-term memory in 14-year-old offspring: A longitudinal prospective study. *Alcoholism: Clinical and Experimental Research, 18,* 202–218.

Sumner, G.S., Mandoki, M.W., & Matthews-Ferrari, K. (1993). A psychiatric population of prenatally cocaine-exposed children. *Journal of the American Academy of Child and Adolescent Psychiatry, 32,* 1003–1006.

Tronick, E.Z., Frank, D.A., Cabral, H., et al. (1996). Late dose-response effects of prenatal cocaine exposure on newborn neurobehavioral performance. *Pediatrics, 98,* 76–83.

Tsay, C.H., Partridge, J.C., Villarreal, S.F., et al. (1996). Neurologic and ophthalmologic findings in children exposed to cocaine in utero. *Journal of Child Neurology, 11,* 25–30.

U.S. Department of Agriculture/U.S. Department of Health and Human Services. (1990). *Nutrition and your health: Dietary guidelines for Americans* (3rd ed.). Washington, DC: Author.

van Baar, A., & de Graaff, B.M.T. (1994). Cognitive development at preschool-age of infants of drug-dependent mothers. *Developmental Medicine and Child Neurology, 36,* 1063–1075.

van Baar, A.L., Soepatmi, S., Gunning, W.B., et al. (1994). Development after prenatal exposure to cocaine, heroin and methadone. *Acta Paediatrica, 404*(Suppl.), 40–46.

VanDyke, D.C., & Fox, A.A. (1990). Fetal drug exposure and its possible implications for learning in the preschool and school-age population. *Journal of Learning Disabilities, 23,* 160–163.

Volpe, J.J. (1992). Effect of cocaine use on the fetus. *New England Journal of Medicine, 327,* 399–407.

Warner, R., & Rosset, H.L. (1975). The effects of drinking on offspring: A historical survey of the American and British literature. *Journal of Studies on Alcoholism, 36,* 1395–1420.

West, J.R., Chen, W.J.A., & Pantazis, N.J. (1994). Fetal alcohol syndrome: The vulnerability of the developing brain and possible mechanisms of damage. *Metabolic Brain Disease, 9,* 291–322.

Wheeler, S.F. (1993). Substance abuse during pregnancy. *Primary Care Clinics in Office Practice, 20,* 191–207.

Wilson, J.G. (1977). Teratogenic effects of environmental chemicals. *Federation Proceedings, 36,* 1698–1703.

Woods, J.R., Jr., Plessinger, M.A., & Clark, K. (1987). Effect of cocaine on uterine blood flow and fetal oxygenation. *Journal of the American Medical Association, 257,* 957–961.

Zuckerman, B., & Frank, D.A. (1992). "Crack kids": Not broken. *Pediatrics, 89,* 337–339.

9 HIV and AIDS

From Mother to Child

Richard M. Rutstein
Charles J. Conlon
Mark L. Batshaw

Upon completion of this chapter, the reader will:

- understand the biology, immunology, mode of transmission, and presentation of HIV infection
- be aware of the developmental and neurological problems associated with pediatric HIV infection
- be knowledgeable about approaches to treatment
- understand the natural history of the disease

Acquired immunodeficiency syndrome (AIDS) was first described in the early 1980s, although it was known by other names for several years. In its short existence, this disease, caused by the human immunodeficiency virus (HIV), has become pandemic. In the United States, it initially appeared to affect primarily gay men; however, it is now known to occur worldwide, among all populations, with an increasing incidence among women and, secondarily, their newborns. Although the 1990s have witnessed major advances in treatment, HIV infection remains an ultimately fatal disorder. Among children, it is also often associated with developmental disabilities. This chapter describes pediatric HIV infection, including the pathophysiology of the disease, its presentation, treatment options, and prevention.

THE BIOLOGICAL BASIS OF HIV INFECTION

AIDS develops as the end result of long-term infection with one of two closely related viruses, HIV-1 and the less common HIV-2. The two viruses are very similar structurally and cause identical clinical manifestations. They are both single-stranded RNA retroviruses, so named because they can transcribe their viral RNA into DNA (Krasinski, 1994). For HIV infection to occur, the virus must first be absorbed into the bloodstream. Then surface protein on the virus outer wall, or envelope, bind to receptors on the outer surface of CD4+ cells, including T-lymphocytes (Figure 9.1). After attachment, the viral RNA enters the host cell and is transcribed by a viral reverse transcriptase enzyme into double-stranded DNA. This viral-encoded DNA is transported into the cell nucleus, where it is incorporated into the host-cell DNA. The viral DNA then directs the host cell to produce HIV-specific proteins. These proteins must be cut, or cleaved, by another viral protein, called a protease, into segments. The segments are then assembled into infectious viruses, which either bud off from the host cell or are released on cell death. The mechanism of viral replication is important to understand because approaches to treatment are based on the viral life cycle.

HIV infection inflicts damage to the host immune system through the progressive loss of CD4+ T-lymphocytes. These lymphocytes, termed helper/suppressor cells, are critical in modulating the normal immune response. At first, the body's immune response keeps up with the active viral replication (up to 1 billion viral particles are produced each day, even in asymptomatic HIV-infected individuals) by replacing the lost CD4+ cells. Over time, however, the body's ability to replace the lost CD4+ T-lymphocytes wanes, and progressive immunodeficiency results. This leaves the host susceptible to a range of unusual infections (referred to as opportunistic infections) and cancers, which collectively represent the clinical disorder termed AIDS.

THE EPIDEMIOLOGY OF HIV INFECTION IN ADULTS

HIV infection was first identified in the United States in 1981 (Siegel, Lopez, Hammer, et al., 1981), occurring principally in gay men, individuals with hemophilia, and Haitian immigrants. It is now clear that HIV infection occurs worldwide among all socioeconomic and ethnic groups. Since 1988, the rates of infection among women and their children in particular have been rapidly increasing. In the United States, AIDS is now the fourth leading cause of death among women 25–44 years of age, exceeded only by cancer, injuries, and suicide/homicide (Centers for Disease Control and Prevention, 1995a). The overall prevalence of HIV infection is estimated at 3–4 per 1,000 adults in the United States (Karon, Rosenberg, McQuillan, et al., 1996). It is predominantly a disease of low-income, inner-city citizens. More than 75% of cases are reported among women of color, and 75% of infected adults reside in large cities on the East Coast (New York, Newark, Miami) or in Puerto Rico (Rogers, Caldwell, Gwinn, et al., 1994). In homeless and adolescent runaway populations, HIV **seropositivity** has been found to be 5%, and among intravenous (IV) drug users it has been reported to be greater than 50% (Annunziato & Frenkel, 1993; Simonds & Rogers, 1992).

The vast majority of individuals with HIV infection, however, are not in the United States, but rather in the developing countries of sub-Saharan Africa, Asia, and South America. In these areas, the prime mode of spread of HIV infection is by heterosexual contact, and equal numbers of men and women are infected. The incidence of HIV infection in many of these areas is staggering. In Botswana, the prevalence of HIV infection in urban areas has been measured at 18% (Stoneburner, Sato, Burton, et al., 1994). Prenatal clinics in several areas of Africa report that 20%–30% of pregnant women are HIV infected (contrasted to rates of 3%–4% in the highest prevalence urban areas in the United States). In some areas of Africa, 80% of hospital beds are occupied by individuals with AIDS who are being treated for severe infections such as tuberculosis, pneumocystis pneumonia, and meningitis. India has emerged as one of the countries with

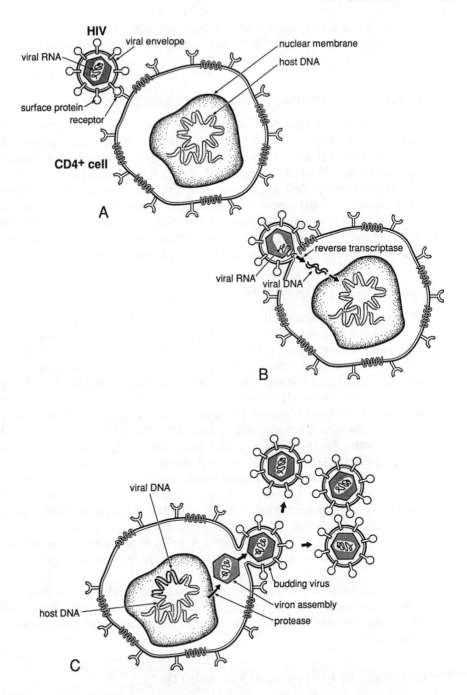

Figure 9.1.   The HIV life cycle and destruction of T4 (CD4+) cells by HIV. The CD4 T lymphocyte is critical to immune defense and its destruction is the major cause of the progressive immunodeficiency disorder that is the hallmark of HIV infection. One mechanism of destruction involves the HIV virus entering and replicating in the CD4 cell, and then budding from and damaging the cell membrane.

the largest number of people with HIV infection, with over 3 million believed infected. The World Health Organization (WHO, 1996) estimated that 22 million people were infected with HIV worldwide in 1996, with 8,500 new infections occurring each day.

THE EPIDEMIOLOGY OF HIV INFECTION IN CHILDREN

The first cases of HIV infection in children were reported in 1982 (Rubinstein, Sicklick, Gupta, et al., 1983). By 1993, 15,000 children had been identified as having been born with HIV infection in the United States; 5,330 of these children have subsequently developed AIDS, and 2,680 have died (Davis, Byers, Lindegren, et al., 1995). It is estimated that each year approximately 7,000 infants born in the United States are at risk for developing HIV infection, and each year 1,000 new cases of AIDS are reported in children younger than 13 years of age (Centers for Disease Control and Prevention, 1995b). In New York City, the prevalence of HIV infection in newborns is 6 per 1,000 births (Annunziato & Frenkel, 1993). In 1994, HIV infection was the seventh leading cause of death in children 1–4 years of age (Rogers & Jaffe, 1994).

TRANSMISSION OF HIV IN ADULTS

HIV is transmitted primarily through contact with blood, semen, or cervical secretions of an infected person. In adults, HIV most commonly enters the body after being deposited on mucus membranes during unprotected sexual intercourse (especially during anal intercourse because there may be bleeding) or through needle puncture from intravenous drug use (through sharing of paraphernalia contaminated with infected blood). Risk factors for HIV infection (as reported by adults at the time of AIDS diagnosis) include homosexual or bisexual contact (42% of cases diagnosed in the United States in 1995), intravenous drug use and/or sexual contact with an IV drug user (29%), and heterosexual contact (11% of all U.S. adult cases, but 38% of female cases) (Centers for Disease Control and Prevention, 1995a). There is also an association between other sexually transmitted diseases (STDs) and HIV infection, as the genital ulcers caused by many STDs permit more efficient transmission of HIV during sexual contact. It has been reported that female prostitutes in sub-Saharan Africa have a 50%–80% HIV prevalence rate, and individuals at clinics for STDs have a 50% rate (Stoneburner et al., 1994). Although heterosexual transmission is bidirectional, male to female transmission appears more efficient than female to male, by a ratio of 3:2 (Simonds & Rogers, 1992). In urban areas, nonintravenous cocaine use (crack) is also associated with HIV infection, by virtue of the lifestyles that may accompany heavy crack use.

In an infected individual, HIV can be cultured from blood, genital secretions, and breast milk. However, the virus rarely can be isolated from other body fluids, such as tears and saliva; thus, these secretions are not thought to represent significant sources for transmission (Fauci, 1988).

TRANSMISSION OF HIV IN INFANTS AND CHILDREN

Until 1985, the most common route of transmission to children between the ages of 1 and 12 years was through contaminated blood products. This was a particular threat to boys with hemophilia, who require frequent transfusions of blood products. In the mid-1980s, as many as 60% of those individuals became infected with HIV through transfusions of tainted blood products. Since 1985, however, the blood supply in the United States has been screened for HIV antibodies, thereby greatly reducing the risk of exposure through contaminated blood and blood products. The rate of HIV transmission through screened blood is estimated to be between 1 per 60,000 and 1 per 250,000 transfused units (Busch, Eble, Khayam-Bashi, et al., 1991).

Although a small number of children still contract the virus from contaminated blood products, sexual abuse, or accidental contact with contaminated needles, or as adolescents from sexual partners or intravenous drug use, more than 90% of children newly diagnosed with HIV infection in 1997 have acquired the virus vertically (i.e., from their mothers) during gestation or birth or postnatally. The transmission to the newborn occurs in one of three ways: either *in utero,* with the virus crossing the placenta; during the birth process via exposure to infected genital fluid; or through breast feeding (Figure 9.2). It is estimated that *in utero* infection accounts for one third to one half of vertical transmission, with most occurring during the birth

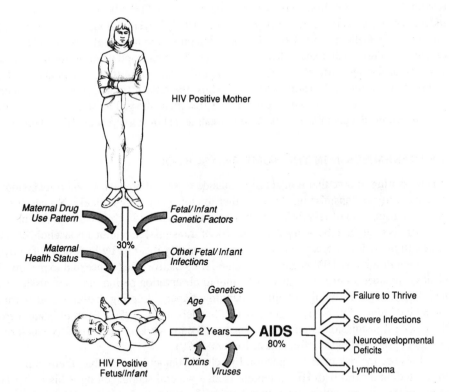

Figure 9.2.   The natural history of AIDS in children. A mother who is HIV positive passes the virus to her fetus. Not all fetuses are infected. Infection depends on multiple factors, including the maternal drug use pattern, maternal health status, and other genetic and infectious factors. The age at which the infant who is HIV positive develops AIDS depends on other genetic and infectious factors, some known, some unknown. The disease itself manifests as recurrent and severe infections and an increased risk of lymphoma.

process (Caldwell & Rogers, 1991; Cutting, 1994; Davis et al., 1995; Mofenson, 1995). Cesarean section is not proven to prevent transmission and is not routinely recommended at this time.

Although vertical transmission accounts for the vast majority of new pediatric cases, most infants born to infected women are not infected themselves. Worldwide, vertical transmission rates range from 13% in Europe, to 20%–30% in the United States, and 40% in Africa (Oxtoby, 1994). The reasons behind these differences in the rate of transmission are unclear and the subject of intense study. Women with symptomatic HIV infection, an AIDS diagnosis, or with a low CD4 count have an increased risk of having an infected child. In addition, women with untreated STDs or uterine infections at the time of birth also have an increased risk of vertical transmission. And finally, premature birth and prolonged rupture of membranes prior to birth are associated with an increased risk of transmission of HIV to the newborn.

A number of therapeutic interventions have been proposed to decrease the risk of transmission during labor and delivery. These include administering antiretroviral therapy to mother and child, maintaining placental integrity by treating STDs, providing passive anti-HIV antibodies, and enhancing anti-HIV antibody immunity by an HIV-specific vaccine (European Collaborative Study, 1994a). Of these approaches, zidovudine (AZT) has been found to most significantly reduce the risk of vertical transmission (Bayer, 1994; Boyer, Dillon, Navaie, et al., 1994; Connor, Sperling, Gelber, et al., 1994; Sperling, Shapiro, Coombs, et al., 1996). When mothers received AZT during labor and delivery and the newborn received the drug for 6 weeks after birth, only 8% of the newborns were infected. The infection rate in the mothers and infants who received placebo (control group) was 26%. Thus, the risk of transmission was reduced by two thirds. Mothers and infants who received AZT treatment showed no significant side effects other than mild transient anemia. This is the first treatment shown to prevent HIV infection.

RISK OF TRANSMISSION IN THE HOME AND SCHOOL

It is reassuring to note that transmission outside of sexual contact, blood transfusions, IV drug use, and vertical transmission (from mother to child) is highly unlikely. No case of person-to-person transmission of HIV infection has been documented in child care centers or schools; the risk there is thought to be negligible. The risk of transmission within a household also is thought to be extremely low. Researchers have tried to quantify this risk by looking for family members who, though initially HIV negative, became HIV positive after nonsexual exposure to an HIV-positive member. In one study over a 15-month observation period, no transmission was identified despite regular kissing, hugging, changing diapers, drooling, bathing, and sharing beds in the 89 individuals followed (Rogers, White, Sanders, et al., 1990). Even in health care settings, the risk of transmission is only 0.4% for health care workers inadvertently stuck by a needle containing infected blood (Simonds & Rogers, 1992).

Because the risk of HIV infection by school contact is negligible, there is no justification for excluding a child with HIV infection from a general school setting if his or her health permits. No special precautions other than handwashing are needed in handling body fluids such as urine, stool, oral or nasal secretions, sweat, tears, or vomitus (when no visible blood is present). Though a source of concern to parents and educators, there has never been a documented case of HIV transmission in childhood secondary to a bite. Precautions, however, should be taken if there is an injury that results in bleeding or if the child has a weeping skin lesion. The blood should be washed off with soap and water, and surgical gloves should be worn when tending to wounds. Blood spills should be cleaned with disinfectants, such as household bleach at dilutions of 1:10 to 1:100. For maximum effectiveness, the disinfectant solution should be prepared daily (Task Force in Pediatric AIDS, 1988). Using these few precautions, there is virtually no risk of transmission in caring for a child with HIV infection. In fact, these "universal precautions" should be used with *all* blood spills in *any* school because not all HIV-infected children will have been identified and because other blood-borne diseases may be present.

The major concern in a child care center or school, in fact, is the risk to the child with HIV infection, who has a limited ability to fight infection. Even the common illnesses of childhood can be life threatening to these children. Parents and physicians must weigh the risks and benefits of placing the young child with HIV infection in the school environment. Risks may be minimized by identifying outbreaks of infectious diseases early so that treatment can be instituted. For example, during an outbreak of chickenpox or measles in a school setting, a child with HIV infection may require additional treatment (i.e., hyperimmune globulin). Overall, most experts feel that the benefits of social contact outweigh the risks of infection and that children with HIV infection should remain in school as much as possible (Spiegel & Mayers, 1991).

Many parents of HIV-infected children are concerned about the risk of disclosure of the child's, or their, HIV status when enrolling the child in school. Most states now protect the family's right to confidentiality regarding HIV-related information. In many states, physicians cannot release HIV-related information on school health appraisal forms without specific parental consent. Most states also proscribe teachers or other educators from disseminating information about HIV infection if they acquire the information in an informal manner. In some school systems, there may still be personnel who would attempt to obstruct an HIV-infected child's enrollment. In general, the courts have protected the right of the HIV-infected child to attend general classes.

NATURAL HISTORY OF PEDIATRIC HIV INFECTION

In children with vertically acquired HIV infection, survival statistics indicate a bimodal distribution, in that the disease follows one of two patterns of progression. One quarter of the children will manifest serious symptoms related to the infection by 12 months of age (slowed growth, delayed developmental milestones, or opportunistic infections) and will succumb to the disease by 3–5 years of age (Abrams, Matheson, Thomas, et al., 1995). These children probably represent those who acquire the infection *in utero* before the immune system is functional and, therefore, cannot mount a response to the virus. The larger group of infected children, those who acquire the infection at birth, usually remain asymptomatic in the first 5 years of life and have a median survival of more than 9 years (Figure 9.3) (Barnhart, Caldwell, Thomas, et al., 1996). Many perinatally infected children are now living into their teens.

There are certain harbingers of a poor prognosis. The occurrence of an opportunistic infection is associated with survival of less than 12–18 months (Sanders-Laufer, DeBruin, & Edelson, 1991). Those children who develop progressive neurological disease, heart disease, or kidney disease also tend to succumb within 12–24 months. The rate of disease progression in children also appears to vary with the severity of disease in the mother at the time of delivery and the CD4+ blood count in the child (Blanche, Mayaux, Rouzioux, et al., 1994; Tardieu, Mayaux, Siebel, et al., 1995).

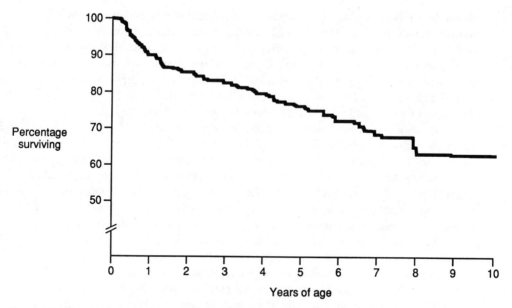

Figure 9.3. Survival curve of a cohort of 624 children infected perinatally with HIV. As of 1996, the 10-year survival rate was 67% (Barnhart, Caldwell, Thomas, et al., 1996).

When first diagnosed, children with clinical HIV infection or AIDS may exhibit a variety of medical problems. The most common physical findings are generalized enlargement of lymph nodes, liver, and spleen (Belman, Ultmann, Horoupian, et al., 1985). The tonsils and adenoids also may be markedly enlarged (Church, 1993). The child may appear to be chronically ill with symptoms of fatigue, recurrent diarrhea, failure to thrive, and/or acute weight loss. There may be associated plateauing or loss of developmental milestones.

These children are predisposed to develop severe bacterial infections, including sepsis, meningitis, pneumonia, internal organ abscesses, and osteomyelitis (Hauger & Powell, 1990). Additional less severe but still important bacterial infections occur in more than a third of individuals and include chronic sinusitis, middle ear infections (which can result in hearing loss), dental caries, and periodontitis (European Collaborative Study, 1994b). Common bacterial organisms include *Streptococcus* pneumonia, *Haemophilus* influenza, and *Salmonella* (European Collaborative Study, 1994b). Affected children also are at risk for life-threatening illness from common childhood viral illnesses such as measles and chickenpox (Burroughs & Edelson, 1991). Other viral infections include cytomegalovirus (CMV) of the eye (which can lead to visual impairment) and recurrent episodes of herpes skin infections and cold sores (which can interfere with eating). The most common opportunistic infection is pneumonia secondary to *Pneumocystis carinii*. Esophagitis caused by a fungal infection (candida) and disseminated infection secondary to *Mycobacterium avium* are late-stage manifestations in severely immunocompromised children. As a consequence of the immune system failure, these children also have an increased risk of developing malignancies, most commonly lymphoma. Additional body organs may be affected by direct HIV infection, resulting in heart disease with congestive heart failure, chronic lung disease (lymphoid interstitial pneumonia or LIP), anemia, and/or kidney disease or failure.

NEURODEVELOPMENTAL EFFECTS OF HIV INFECTION

Early retrospective studies of children with HIV infection were very pessimistic about neurodevelopmental outcome, reporting significant abnormalities in 75%–90% of affected children (Belman, Diamond, Dickson, et al., 1988). Many children with HIV infection, however, exhibit near-normal neurodevelopmental functioning until late in the course of the illness. There appear to be two main patterns of neurodevelopmental outcome relative to HIV infection. The first pattern is a devastating progressive encephalopathy. This affects 10%–20% of HIV-infected infants, with the onset of symptoms between 6 and 24 months of age. In this situation, an infant will suddenly lose previously acquired developmental milestones. In addition, this decline in developmental level may be associated with the appearance of neurological abnormalities including hyperreflexia, toe walking, tremors, weakness, abnormal tone, and progressive motor dysfunction (Msellati, Lepage, & Hitimana, 1993). Careful monitoring will reveal a lack of growth in the head circumference. Cortical atrophy and calcification in the basal ganglia and frontal lobes can be detected on neuroimaging (Belman, Lantos, Horoupian, et al., 1986). Many of these children will manifest a rapidly progressive neurological deterioration, resulting in a spastic quadriplegia (Belman, 1992; Brouwers, Belman, & Epstein, 1994; Diamond & Cohen, 1992; Gay, Armstrong, Cohen, et al., 1995). Death follows within 1–2 years of onset of the neurodevelopmental decline.

In the second pattern, an initial period of deterioration will be followed by a "plateau" phase, with neither loss nor gain of milestones. After a variable interval, some children will begin to acquire new skills, while others will deteriorate further. Early antiretroviral therapy may prevent the occurrence of a progressive encephalopathy in some children and may improve neurological status in others.

In infected infants without evidence of a progressive encephalopathy, there are frequently subtle signs of a static encephalopathy (Aylward, Butz, Hutton, et al., 1992; Nozyce, Hittleman, Munez, et al., 1994; Wachtel, Tepper, Houch, et al., 1993). Development in the first 2 years of life is slower than in noninfected children born of infected mothers, even when controlling for maternal drug use, illness, and poverty (Fowler, 1994; Gay et al., 1995). Mean scores on developmental testing for children with HIV infection at 1 year, 2 years, and 4 years of age are all in the low-average range. For many children, these lower than usual scores probably represent the subtle effects of HIV infection on cognition and development. The cognitive scores may remain stable over several years, indicating that for the vast majority of children, the infection causes subtle, but not necessarily progressive or catastrophic, effects (Italian Register for HIV Infection in Children, 1994). In a cohort of perinatally infected children followed at one center since birth and now more than 6 years of age, 75% are in the appropriate grade for age (R. Rutstein, personal communication, November, 1996). Many of these older survivors, however, require special school services. There is an increased incidence of attention-deficit/hyperactivity disorder, as well as learning disabilities, in this population (Grubman, Gross, Lerner-Weiss, et al., 1995). Specific problems with expressive language skills are also common in school-age infected children (Brouwers et al., 1994). For the older infected child, regular monitoring of school performance and appropriate use of school resources is critical for optimizing educational outcomes.

DETECTING HIV INFECTION

Traditionally, HIV infection was diagnosed by detection of antibodies to the virus. In adults, antibodies usually appear within 6–12 weeks of infection, although a few people may not develop antibodies for up to 18 months (Steckelberg & Cockerill, 1988). In infants and young children, the diagnosis is complicated by the presence of maternal antibodies to HIV that can cross the placenta from mother to fetus. These maternal antibodies are indistinguishable from those produced by the infant and, thus, may be present even when the child is not infected. On average, children lose these maternal antibodies by 10 months of age, but, in some cases, maternal antibodies can persist for 15–18 months. Thus, the diagnosis of HIV infection in infants cannot be made on the sole basis of antibodies but requires culturing the virus or using the molecular biological techniques of polymerase chain reaction (PCR) to detect viral DNA (Bremer, Lew, Cooper, et al., 1996). Using these approaches, detection of HIV infection can be made in the first week of life in one third to one half of infected infants and after 1 month of age in most of the remaining cases (Lambert, 1993).

INTERDISCIPLINARY MANAGEMENT

Management of pediatric HIV infection must be truly interdisciplinary to be effective. Comprehensive management should include well-child care, anticipatory guidance for treatment of common childhood illnesses, modification of the immunization schedule, nutritional support, and provision of early intervention services and psychosocial support when needed. Assessment and treatment is best carried out in a child-centered, family-focused, culturally sensitive program that is usually part of a special immunology clinic in a children's hospital (Mok & Newell, 1995; Woodruff, Driscoll, & Sterzin, 1992). Services should include medical care, psychological testing, social services, educational planning, speech-language therapy, nutritional counseling, advocacy, and service coordination.

Medical Management of Pediatric HIV Infection

Although the range of medical complications of HIV infection is daunting, evidence suggests that survival can be prolonged by early identification and treatment. Major medical advances have included the use of antiretroviral therapy to inhibit viral replication, prophylactic antibiotic therapy to guard against *Pneumocystis carinii* pneumonia, and immunotherapy with IVIG (intravenous immunoglobulin) to reduce the frequency of febrile illnesses and sepsis.

Antiretroviral therapy is directed at interrupting the life cycle of HIV. AZT and dideoxyinosine (ddI, Videx) are the principal antiretroviral agents used in the management of pediatric HIV infection. Both AZT and ddI block HIV replication by inhibiting DNA polymerase and reverse transcriptase. The principal side effect of AZT, occurring in one quarter of individuals, is bone marrow suppression and resultant anemia (Cvetkovich & Frenkel, 1993). DdI can result in inflammation of the pancreas or a painful peripheral neuropathy. DdI is now considered the standard of single-drug therapy or is used in combination with AZT (Butler, Husson, Balis, et al., 1991; Pizzo & Wilfert, 1994).

Antiretroviral therapy is recommended treatment for all children who have symptomatic HIV infection and for asymptomatic HIV-infected children who have evidence of significant immunodeficiency based on a low CD4+ T-lymphocyte count (Pizzo & Wilfert, 1994). In these children, AZT and ddI have been shown to decrease viremia, and increase immune competence. Resultant clinical improvement includes weight gain, decreased hepatosplenomegaly, lymphadenopathy, and improved neurodevelopmental status (Husson, Mueller, Farley, et al., 1994). Researchers are trying to determine whether asymptomatic HIV-infected children with normal T-lymphocyte counts also can benefit from early initiation of antiretroviral treatment.

Long-term effects of antiretroviral drugs in children are not known. It is clear, however, that drug resistance can occur and interfere with drug treatment (Dimitrov, Hollinger, Baker, et al., 1993). Thus, the quest for additional antiretroviral medications continues. Several drugs that interfere with viral reverse transcriptase are undergoing clinical trials including d4T (stavudine, Zerit); ddC (dideoxycytidine, Zalcitabin); and 3TC (lamuvidine, Epivir) (Katlama, Ingrand, Loveday, et al., 1996).

A promising new category of drugs is the so-called protease inhibitors that prevent the viral protease from cleaving viral protein into active forms (Kline, Dunkle, Church, et al., 1995). Several drugs in this class are already on the market, and more are undergoing clinical trials. Studies indicate that these antiretroviral agents are the most potent thus far. When used in combination with other antiretroviral agents, they have been found to bring the amount of HIV virus in the blood down to undetectable levels, with sustained activity for more than 1 year (Kline, Fletcher, Federici, et al., 1996). For the first time, it appears that long-term suppression of HIV infection may be possible.

Another major advance in treatment has been the use of prophylactic antibiotics (e.g., trimethoprim-sulfamethoxazole [TMP-SMX, Bactrim, Septra]; pentamidine aerosols) to protect against a life-threatening pneumonia caused by the organism *Pneumocystis carinii* (Simonds, Lindegren, Thomas, et al., 1995). Additional regimens are available, or under active study, to prevent or delay the occurrence of disease secondary to CMV infection (Spector, McKinley, Lalezari, et al., 1996).

Finally, a national multicenter study has confirmed the effectiveness of using infusions of IVIG to support the immune system. This treatment has been shown to reduce the incidence of fever, sepsis, and hospitalizations. This effect was primarily seen in children who were not receiving trimethoprim-sulfamethoxazole for prophylaxis against PCP. Unfortunately, overall survival did not improve when using IVIG (National Institute of Child Health and Human Development, Intravenous Immunoglobulin Study Group, 1991; Spector, Gelber, McGrath, et al., 1994).

Developing an effective HIV vaccine is a major research goal. It is hoped that eventually a vaccine will protect adults from HIV infection and prevent infected pregnant women from transmitting the infection to their newborns. In addition, an effective vaccine could boost an infected individual's immune response against HIV and help prolong the clinical latency period. As of 1997, the majority of tested vaccines use portions of the HIV envelope as a viral target. Several of these candidate vaccines are presently undergoing testing in large clinical trials in Africa, sponsored by the WHO (Hoff, McNamara, Flower, et al., 1994). So far, it appears that these vaccines will not be completely protective against infection. The information learned from these trials, however, will tell us a lot about our ability to manipulate the human immune system to combat HIV. On the horizon is a new vaccine technology based on the use of a novel DNA-based vaccine. Very preliminary data suggest that these vaccines may induce a more effective immune response to HIV.

Children with HIV infection should receive immunizations against the common childhood illnesses. There is a theoretical risk that vaccines (which use inactivated or live antigens to activate the immune system), however, will lead to increased HIV viral replication. This could accelerate the immune depression associated with HIV infection. There seems to be, however, only a brief and clinically unimportant upregulation of viral replication. A second risk is that a live virus vaccine may induce the illness being vaccinated against (e.g., measles) in an immunocompromised host.

All children with HIV infection should receive the standard inactivated vaccines (DPT or DaPT, HIB, hepatitis b) as well as yearly influenza A/B vaccine, and the pneumococcal vaccine at 2 years of age. The inactivated injectable polio vaccine (Salk, IPV) should replace the administered live (Sabin) oral polio vaccine (Mueller & Pizzo, 1992). It should also be noted that when there is an HIV-infected family member, all members of that family should receive the IPV (killed polio vaccine) in lieu of the OPV (live vaccine). This is because of the theoretical risk of polio infection in immunocompromised household contacts of OP recipients. Although the use of the live measles, mumps, rubella (MMR) vaccine is controversial, most physicians believe that the risk to the child of measles, which can be fatal in HIV-infected children, outweighs the risk of the vaccine. It should not be given, however, to children with severe immune dysfunction (as measured by low age-adjusted CD4 counts). Though the MMR is also a live virus vaccine, there has been no intra-family spread documented following this vaccine. For that reason, the MMR can be safely given to siblings and family contacts of HIV-infected individuals. As of 1997, the new varicella (chickenpox) vaccine was not being recommended for children with HIV infection, although there is a national trial under the auspices of the NIH to study its effectiveness and safety in this population. There is contradictory data related to this vaccine. There have been a few isolated cases of family contacts developing varicella following vaccination of household members. However, there is a greater risk of immunocompromised individuals acquiring varicella from children who become infected with varicella at school and bring the disease home. Therefore, it is probably safer to administer the varicella vaccine to uninfected children.

It is important to realize that despite immunization, many children with HIV infection remain at risk for vaccine-preventable illnesses, as their immune system is unable to mount a competent response to the vaccine. In fact, only 50%–90% of these children will have demonstrable antibody titers (indicating a satisfactory response) to the childhood immunizations. Therefore, in addition to this active immunization, passive vaccines should be given when a child is exposed to certain viral illnesses. Hyperimmune globulin against hepatitis B, measles, or varicella/zoster (chickenpox) virus (VZIG) should be administered within 72 hours of exposure (Mueller & Pizzo, 1992). If the child contracts varicella or systemic herpes, the antiviral agent acyclovir should be used (Fletcher, 1992); ganciclovir may be effective against CMV infections (Spector, Busch, Follansbee, et al., 1995).

Developmental Assessment and Early Intervention Services

The development of children with HIV infection may be affected not only by the virus but also by other confounding environmental and biological factors, such as *in utero* exposure to drugs of abuse, prematurity, LBW, and failure to thrive (Johnson, 1993). Long-term hospitalizations, chaotic family environments, and neglect also may add to the effects of HIV infection. Finally, parental illness or death, often accompanied by foster care placement, can affect the child's development (Butler et al., 1991). One study showed that only 38% of HIV-positive children live long term with their biological parent as compared with 80% of children with other developmental disabilities (Papola, Alvarez, & Cohen, 1994).

To identify neurodevelopmental delays as early as possible, children with HIV infection need developmental assessments at regular intervals. In general, infants who are HIV positive should be evaluated by 2 months of age and then at least every 6 months for the first 2 years of life if they remain asymptomatic. After 2 years of age, these children should have a neurodevelopmental assessment at least yearly (Butler et al., 1991). If clinical symptoms develop, assessments should be more frequent, especially if a developmental delay, "plateauing," or a decline in skills is identified. In older children, neurodevelopmental assessment should include tests of cognition, communication, motor development, social-emotional and adaptive functioning, and academic abilities (Schmitt, Seeger, Kreuz, et al., 1991).

Children with HIV infection who are younger than 3 years of age and have associated developmental disabilities should be enrolled in an early intervention program (Rosen & Granger, 1992). Children ages 3–5 years should be referred to their county school committee for preschool special education placement if they have a developmental delay or to Head Start if developing typically. Habilitative services (e.g., occupational therapy, physical therapy, speech-language therapy) also should be provided to children who have these neurodevelopmental impairments. School-age children may need special education services (Pizzo & Wilfert, 1994).

Psychosocial Aspects of HIV Infection

The psychological and social aspects of pediatric HIV infection are complex and require an interdisciplinary team approach, with care delivered in a nonjudgmental, culturally sensitive manner. Pediatric HIV infection is a family disease, with one or both parents and frequently several children infected. Many of these families are already severely stressed, with their family life buffeted by poor finances, substandard housing, crime, intrafamily physical abuse, and substance abuse. As with any chronic illness, the diagnosis of HIV infection may at first be met with denial, disbelief, and anger. In addition, it is still a socially stigmatizing illness. Infected adults may fear disclosure of their status and are afraid of losing their jobs, homes, health insurance, and the support of their families and friends.

Within most communities there exists a network of social agencies to assist families with many issues relating to HIV infection. Individual counseling, support groups, and case management or service coordination may help the families through the crisis surrounding the initial diagnosis. Access to state-of-the-art medical care and new treatment protocols is also an important part of caring for children with HIV infection and their families.

An important issue that each family faces involves disclosure of the diagnosis to the infected child. Many parents are reluctant to discuss the infection with their children, out of fear that they will indiscriminately disclose their status to friends, teachers, and extended family members. In addition, parental guilt over having passed on the illness to their children may hinder disclosure. There is no set best time to discuss HIV status with a child; it is a process and must fit the developmental level of the child and the needs of the parents. Again, nonjudgmental support from the treatment team will help families through these difficult decisions.

With new treatment modalities, many children infected perinatally with HIV will survive well into their teenage years. As adolescents, they will face multiple issues, in addition to reactions to disclosure of their illness, including sexual activity, personal responsibility, and group identity. These issues, especially sexual activity, take on added importance and complexity when the adolescent is HIV-infected and need to be addressed in a nonjudgmental but directive and persistent manner. Support groups of/for infected teenagers can be a valuable resource for helping them to deal with these issues in a responsible way.

Children with HIV infection may exhibit multiple mental health problems, including depression, anxiety, and adjustment reactions. These can be secondary to neurological aspects of the illness itself or be related to the child's reaction to the fatigue and pain of a chronic illness. In addition, many of the medications prescribed for infected children can lead to a general feeling of malaise, through frequent gastrointestinal side effects. Lack of parental attention and supervision, secondary to the parent's own illness, can also play a role in a child's behavioral problems. Older children may require antidepressant medication and psychotherapy to help them understand and adjust to the diagnosis and prognosis of HIV infection (Speigel & Mayers, 1991).

PREVENTION

With further improvements in medical care and, ultimately, with the development of an HIV vaccine, it is hoped that HIV infection will be converted from a universally fatal disease to a chronic illness and, like smallpox, will eventually be eradicated. Until that time, however, the best treatment is avoiding the infection. Every teacher and health care professional must be involved in educating individuals about HIV infection and the required behavior changes necessary to reduce the risk of exposure. This includes teaching adolescents and adults about safe sex, providing intravenous drug users with clean needles, and improving the availability of HIV testing and perinatal therapies to all pregnant women to reduce vertical transmission. Only through a coordinated, global effort will the spread of this deadly disease be slowed.

MANUEL: A CHILD WITH HIV INFECTION

Manuel was born at term to a 26-year-old mother and a 28-year-old father who was a cocaine and heroin user. At 4 months of age, Manuel was taken to the emergency room of the local hospital because of failure to thrive. He had a history of diarrhea and poor feeding. His mother, who also appeared chronically ill and debilitated, agreed to be tested for HIV infection and was found to be positive for HIV antibodies.

The PCR DNA test for HIV was positive in Manuel, and he was started on long-term treatment with ddI, AZT, Bactrim, and IVIG. He was kept in the hospital 1 month until the diarrhea stopped and he started to gain weight. By this time, his mother was so sick that she could no longer care for him. She had a relentless downhill course with her final illness, which was meningitis; she died within 12 months of her diagnosis. Manuel was placed in a medical foster home. His foster mother had previously taken a special course on caring for children with HIV infection. Manuel was examined monthly in a special immunology clinic that uses a multidisciplinary approach to treatment. Now 2 years old, he attends an early intervention program. He continues to show a mild developmental delay, functioning at an 18-month level, but has not plateaued in skills. He has had a few infections to this point, none life threatening.

SUMMARY

HIV infection represents a threat to the development and survival of children across the world. Millions of adults and children have been infected, children typically from their mothers late in pregnancy or during labor and delivery. Women commonly contract the infection as a result of IV drug use or unprotected sex with an infected man. STDs also contribute to the mother's risk of contracting and transmitting the HIV infection. AZT treatment during late pregnancy and the neonatal period appears to significantly decrease the rate of vertical transmission.

In both children and adults, there is a latency period of months to years between HIV infection and clinical disease. During this time, the individual appears clinically healthy, even though the virus is actively replicating. Eventually, the HIV kills sufficient CD4+ T-lymphocytes to produce a profound immunodeficiency that places the infected individual at risk for life-threatening viral and bacterial infections. This marks the onset of clinical AIDS. Over time, progressive motor, communication, and cognitive impairments may become evident.

Medical treatment focuses on antiretroviral therapy using ddI or combined therapy (ddI, AZT, and protease inhibitors), prophylaxis against bacterial infections, and active and passive immunization against viral infections. This approach has markedly increased survival time such that many perinatally infected children are living into adolescence. The prolonged survival also emphasizes the importance of an interdisciplinary approach to management which includes, in addition to medical care, the provision of early intervention and special education services, psychosocial counseling, and advocacy for the family.

REFERENCES

Abrams, E.J., Matheson, P.B., Thomas, P.A., et al. (1995). Neonatal predictors of infection status and early death among 332 infants at risk of HIV-1 infection monitored prospectively from birth. *Pediatrics, 96,* 451–458.

Annunziato, P.W., & Frenkel, L.M. (1993). The epidemiology of pediatric HIV-1 infection. *Pediatric Annals, 22,* 401–405.

Arpadi, S.M., Markowitz, L.E., Baughman, A.L., et al. (1996). Measles antibody in vaccinated human immunodeficiency virus type 1–infected children. *Pediatrics, 97,* 653–657.

Aylward, E.H., Butz, A.M., Hutton, N., et al. (1992). Cognitive and motor development in infants at risk for human immunodeficiency virus. *American Journal of Diseases of Children, 146,* 218–222.

Barnhart, H.X., Caldwell, M.B., Thomas, P., et al. (1996). Natural history of human immunodeficiency virus disease in perinatally infected children: An analysis from the pediatric spectrum of disease project. *Pediatrics, 97,* 710–716.

Bayer, R. (1994). Reducing the risk of maternal infant transmission of HIV: A door is opened. *New England Journal of Medicine, 331,* 1222–1225.

Belman, A.L. (1992). Acquired immunodeficiency syndrome and the child's central nervous system. *Pediatric Clinics of North America, 39,* 691–714.

Belman, A.L., Diamond, G., Dickson, D., et al. (1988). Pediatric acquired immunodeficiency syndrome: Neurological syndromes. *American Journal of Diseases of Children, 142,* 29–35.

Belman, A.L., Lantos, G., Horoupian, D., et al. (1986). AIDS: Calcification of the basal ganglia in infants and children. *Neurology, 36,* 1192–1199.

Belman, A.L., Muenz, L.R., Marcus, J.C., et al. (1996). Neurologic status of human immunodeficiency virus 1-infected infants and their controls: A prospective study from birth to 2 years. *Pediatrics, 98*(6), 1109–1118.

Belman, A.L., Ultmann, M.H., Horoupian, D., et al. (1985). Neurological complications in infants and children with acquired immune deficiency syndrome. *Annals of Neurology, 18,* 560–566.

Blanche, S., Mayaux, M., Rouzioux, C., et al. (1994). Relation of the course of HIV infection in children to the severity of the disease in their mothers at delivery. *New England Journal of Medicine, 330,* 308–312.

Boulos, R., Ruff, A.J., Nahmias, A., et al. (1992). Herpes simplex virus type 2 infection, syphilis, and hepatitis B virus infection in Haitian women with human immunodeficiency virus type 1 and human T lymphotropic virus type 1 infection. *Journal of Infectious Diseases, 166,* 418–420.

Boyer, P.J., Dillon, M., Navaie, M., et al. (1994). Factors predictive of maternal–fetal transmission of HIV-1. *Journal of the American Medical Association, 271,* 1925–1930.

Boyer, P.J. (1993). HIV infection in pregnancy. *Pediatric Annals, 22,* 406–412.

Bremer, J.W., Lew, J.F., Cooper, E., et al. (1996). Diagnosis of infection with human immunodeficiency virus type 1 by a DNA polymerase chain reaction assay among infants enrolled in the Women and Infants' Transmission Study. *Journal of Pediatrics, 129,* 198–207.

Brouwers, P., Belman, A.L., & Epstein, L. (1994). Central nervous system involvement: Manifestation, evaluation, and pathogenesis. In P.A. Pizzo & C.M. Wilfert (Eds.), *Pediatric AIDS: The challenge of HIV infection in infants, children, and adolescents* (2nd ed., pp. 433–455). Baltimore: Williams & Wilkins.

Burns, D.N., Landesman, S., Muenz, L.R., et al. (1994). Cigarette smoking, premature rupture of membranes, and vertical transmission of HIV-1 among women with low CD4+ levels. *Journal of Acquired Immune Deficiency Syndromes, 7,* 718–726.

Burroughs, M.H., & Edelson, P.J. (1991). Medical care of the HIV-infected child. *Pediatric Clinics of North America, 38,* 45–67.

Busch, M.P., Eble, B.E., Khayam-Bashi, H., et al. (1991). Evaluation of screened blood donations for human immunodeficiency virus type 1 infection by culture and DNA amplification of pooled cells. *New England Journal of Medicine, 325,* 1–5.

Butler, K.M., Husson, R.N., Balis, F.M., et al. (1991). Dideoxyinosine in children with symptomatic human immunodeficiency virus. *New England Journal of Medicine, 324,* 137–144.

Caldwell, M.B., & Rogers, M.F. (1991). Epidemiology of pediatric HIV infection. *Pediatric Clinics of North America, 38*(1), 1–16.

Centers for Disease Control and Prevention. (1995a). First 500,000 AIDS cases: United States, 1995. *Morbidity and Mortality Weekly Report, 44,* 849–853.

Centers for Disease Control and Prevention. (1995b). *HIV/AIDS Surveillance Report, 7,* 1–38.

Church, J.A. (1993). Clinical aspects of HIV infection in children. *Pediatric Annals, 22,* 417–427.

Connor, E.M., Sperling, R.S., Gelber, R., et al. (1994). Reduction of maternal–infant transmission of human immunodeficiency virus type 1 with zidovudine treatment. *New England Journal of Medicine, 331,* 1173–1180.

Cutting, W.A. (1994) Breast feeding and HIV: A balance of risks. *Journal of Tropical Pediatrics, 40,* 6–11.

Cvetkovich, T.A., & Frenkel, M. (1993). Current management of HIV infection in children. *Pediatric Annals, 22,* 428–435.

Danner, S.A., Carr, A., Leonard, J.M., et al. (1995). A short-term study of the safety, pharmacokinetics and efficacy of ritonavir, an inhibitor of HIV-1 protease. *New England Journal of Medicine, 333,* 1528–1533.

Davis, S.F., Byers, R.H., Lindegren, M.L., et al. (1995). Prevalence and incidence of vertically acquired HIV infection in the United States. *Journal of the American Medical Association, 247,* 952–955.

Diamond, G.W., & Cohen, H.J. (1992). Developmental disabilities in children with HIV infection. In A.C. Crocker, H.J. Cohen, & T.A. Kastner (Eds.), *HIV infection and developmental disabilities: A resource for service providers* (pp. 33–42). Baltimore: Paul H. Brookes Publishing Co.

Dimitrov, D.H., Hollinger, F.B., Baker, C.J., et al. (1993). Study of human immunodeficiency virus resistance 2′, 3′-dideoxyinosine and zidovudine in sequential isolates from pediatric patients on long-term therapy. *Journal of Infectious Diseases, 167,* 818–823.

European Collaborative Study. (1992). Risk factors for mother to child transmission of HIV-1. *Lancet, 339,* 1007–1012.

European Collaborative Study. (1994a). Caesarean section and risk of vertical transmission of HIV-1 infection. *Lancet, 343,* 1464–1467.

European Collaborative Study. (1994b). Natural history of vertically acquired human immunodeficiency virus-1 infection. *Pediatrics, 94,* 815–819.

Fauci, A.S. (1988). The human immunodeficiency virus: Infectivity and mechanisms of pathogenesis. *Science, 239,* 617–622.

Feng, Y., Broder, C.C., Kennedy, P.E., et al. (1996). HIV-1 entry cofactor: Functional cDNA cloning of a seven-transmembrane, G protein-coupled receptor. *Science, 272,* 872–877.

Fletcher, C.V. (1992). Treatment of herpes virus infections in HIV-infected individuals. *Annals of Pharmacotherapy, 26,* 955–962.

Fowler, M.G. (1994). Pediatric HIV infection: Neurological and neuropsychologic findings. *Acta Paediatrics, 400*(Suppl.), 59–62.

Gay, C.L., Armstrong, F.D., Cohen, D., et al. (1995). The effects of HIV on cognitive and motor development in children born to HIV-seropositive women with no reported drug use: Birth to 24 months. *Pediatrics, 96,* 1078–1082.

Gellert, G.A., Durfee, M.J., & Berkowitz, C.D. (1990). Developing guidelines for HIV antibody testing among victims of pediatric sexual abuse. *Child Abuse and Neglect, 14,* 9–17.

Grosz, J., & Hopkins, K. (1992). Family circumstances affecting caregivers and brothers and sisters. In A.C. Crocker, H.J. Cohen, & T.A. Kastner (Eds.), *HIV infection and developmental disabilities: A resource for service providers* (pp. 43–51). Baltimore: Paul H. Brookes Publishing Co.

Grubman, S., Gross, E., Lerner-Weiss, X., et al. (1995). Older children and adolescents living with perinatally acquired human immunodeficiency virus infection. *Pediatrics, 95,* 657–663.

Hauger, S.B., & Powell, K.R. (1990). Infectious complications in children with HIV infection. *Pediatric Annals, 19,* 421–436.

Hoff, R., McNamara, J., Flower, M.G., et al. (1994). HIV vaccine development and clinical trials. *Acta Paediatrics, 400*(Suppl.), 73–77.

Husson, R.N., Mueller, B.U., Farley, M., et al. (1994). Zidovudine and didanosine combination therapy in children with human immunodeficiency virus infection. *Pediatrics, 93,* 316–322.

Italian Register for HIV Infection in Children. (1994). Features of children perinatally infected with HIV-1 surviving longer than 5 years. *Lancet, 343,* 191–195.

Johnson, C.B. (1993). Developmental issues: Children infected with the human immunodeficiency virus. *Journal of Infants and Young Children, 6,* 1–10.

Karon, J.M., Rosenberg, P.S., McQuillan, G., et al. (1996). Prevalence of HIV infection in the United States, 1984 to 1992. *Journal of the American Medical Association, 276,* 126–131.

Katlama, C., Ingrand, D., Loveday, C., et al. (1996). Safety and efficacy of lamivudine-zidovudine combination therapy in antiretroviral-naive patients: A randomized controlled comparison with zidovudine monotherapy. *Journal of the American Medical Association, 276,* 118–125.

Kline, M.W., Dunkle, L.M., Church, J.A., et al. (1995). A phase I/II evaluation of stavudine (d4t) in children with human immunodeficiency virus infection. *Pediatrics, 96,* 247–252.

Kline, M.W., Fletcher, C.V., Federici, M.E., et al. (1996). Combination therapy with stavudine and didanosine in children with advanced human immunodeficiency virus infection: Pharmacokinetic properties, safety, and immunologic and virologic effects. *Pediatrics, 97,* 886–890.

Krasinski, K. (1994). Antiretroviral therapy for children. *Acta Paediatrics, 400*(Suppl.), 63–69.

Lambert, J.S. (1993). Maternal–fetal transmission of HIV-1 infection. *Pediatric Annals, 22,* 413–416.

Landesman, S.H., Kalish, L.A., Burns, D.N., et al. (1996). Obstetrical factors and the transmission of human immunodeficiency virus type I from mother to child. *New England Journal of Medicine, 334,* 1617–1623.

Markowitz, M., Saag, M., Powderly, W.G., et al. (1995). A preliminary study of ritonavir, an inhibitor of HIV-1 protease, to treat HIV-1 infections. *New England Journal of Medicine, 333,* 1534–1539.

Meandzija, B., O'Connor, P.G., Fitzgerald, B., et al. (1994). HIV infection and cocaine use in methadone maintained and untreated intravenous drug users. *Drug and Alcohol Dependence, 36,* 109–113.

Mofenson, L. (1995). A critical review of studies evaluating the relationship of mode of delivery to perinatal transmission of human immunodeficiency virus. *Pediatrics Infectious Disease Control, 14,* 169–177.

Mok, J., & Newell, M.L. (Eds.). (1995). *HIV infection in children: A guide to practical management.* New York: Cambridge University Press.

Molla, A., Korneyeva, M., Gao, Q., et al. (1996). Ordered accumulation of mutations in HIV protease confers resistance to ritonavir. *Nature Medicine, 2,* 760–766.

Msellati, P., Lepage, P., & Hitimana, D-G. (1993). Neurodevelopmental testing of children born to human immunodeficiency virus type 1 seropositive and seronegative mothers: A prospective cohort study in Kigali, Rwanda. *Pediatrics, 92,* 843–848.

Mueller, B.U., & Pizzo, P.A. (1992). Medical treatment of children with HIV infection. In A.C. Crocker, H.J. Cohen, & T.A. Kastner (Eds.), *HIV infection and developmental disabilities: A resource for service providers* (pp. 63–73). Baltimore: Paul H. Brookes Publishing Co.

National Institute of Child Health and Human Development, Intravenous Immunoglobulin Study Group. (1991). Intravenous immune globulin for the prevention of bacterial infections in children with symptomatic human immunodeficiency virus infection. *New England Journal of Medicine, 325,* 73–80.

Newel, M-L., & Peckham, C. (1994). Vertical transmission of HIV infection. *Acta Paediatrics, 400* (Suppl.), 43–45.

Nozyce, M., Hittleman, J., Muenz, L., et al. (1994). Effect of perinatally acquired human immunodeficiency virus infection on neurodevelopment in children during the first two years of life. *Pediatrics, 94,* 883–891.

Oxtoby, M. (1994). Vertically acquired HIV infection in the United States. In P. Pizzo & C.M. Wilfert (Eds.), *Pediatric AIDS: The challenge of HIV infection in infants, children, and adolescents* (2nd ed., pp. 1–20). Baltimore: Williams & Wilkins.

Papola, P., Alvarez, M., & Cohen, H.J. (1994). Developmental and service needs of school-age children with human immunodeficiency virus infection: A descriptive study. *Pediatrics, 94,* 914–918.

Pizzo, P.A., & Wilfert, C. (1994). Antiretroviral treatment for children with HIV infection. In P. Pizzo & C.M. Wilfert (Eds.), *Pediatric AIDS: The challenge of HIV infection in infants, children, and adolescents* (2nd ed., pp. 651–687). Baltimore: Williams & Wilkins.

Quinn, T.C., Ruff, A., & Halsey, N. (1994). Special considerations for developing nations. In P. Pizzo & C.M. Wilfert (Eds.), *Pediatric AIDS: The challenge of HIV infection in infants, children, and adolescents* (2nd ed., pp. 31–49). Baltimore: Williams & Wilkins.

Rogers, M.F., Caldwell, M.B., Gwinn, M.L., et al. (1994). Epidemiology of pediatric human immunodeficiency virus infection in the United States. *Acta Paediatrics, 400*(Suppl.), 5–7.

Rogers, M.F., & Jaffe, H.W. (1994). Reducing the risk of maternal-infant transmission of HIV: A door is opened. *New England Journal of Medicine, 331,* 1222–1223.

Rogers, M.F., White, C.R., Sanders, R., et al. (1990). Lack of transmission of human immunodeficiency virus from infected children to their household contacts. *Pediatrics, 85,* 210–214.

Rosen, S., & Granger, M. (1992). Early intervention and school programs. In A.C. Crocker, H.J. Cohen, & T.A. Kastner (Eds.), *HIV infection and developmental disabilities: A resource for service providers* (pp. 75–84). Baltimore: Paul H. Brookes Publishing Co.

Rubinstein, A., Sicklick, M., Gupta, A., et al. (1983). Acquired immunodeficiency with reversed T4/T8 ratio in infants born to promiscuous and drug-addicted mothers. *Journal of the American Medical Association, 249,* 2350–2356.

Sanders-Laufer, D., DeBruin, W., & Edelson, P.J. (1991). Pneumocystis carinii infections in HIV-infected children. *Pediatric Clinics of North America, 38,* 69–88.

Schmitt, B., Seeger, J., Kreuz, W., et al. (1991). Central nervous system involvement of children with HIV infection. *Developmental Medicine and Child Neurology, 33,* 535–540.

Sherwen, L.N., & Boland, M. (1994). Overview of psychosocial research concerning pediatric human immunodeficiency virus infection. *Journal of Developmental and Behavioral Pediatrics, 15,* S5–S11.

Siegel, F.P., Lopez, C., Hammer, G.S., et al. (1981). Severe acquired immunodeficiency in male homosexuals, manifested by chronic perianal ulcerative herpes simplex lesions. *New England Journal of Medicine, 305,* 1439–1444.

Simonds, R.J., Lindegren, M.L., Thomas, P., et al. (1995). Prophylaxis against Pneumocystis carinii pneumonia among children with perinatally acquired human immunodeficiency virus infection in the United States: Pneumocystic carinii pneumonia prophylaxis evaluation working group. *New England Journal of Medicine, 332,* 786–790.

Simonds, R.J., & Rogers, M.F. (1992). Epidemiology of HIV infection in children and other populations. In A.C. Crocker, H.J. Cohen, & T.A. Kastner (Eds.), *HIV infection and developmental disabilities: A resource for service providers* (pp. 3–13). Baltimore: Paul H. Brookes Publishing Co.

Spector, S.A., Busch, D.F., Follansbee, S., et al. (1995). Pharmacokinetic, safety, and antiviral profiles of oral ganciclovir in persons infected with human immunodeficiency virus: A phase I/II study: AIDS Clinical Trials group and Cytomegaolvirus Cooperative Study group. *Journal of Infectious Diseases, 171,* 1431–1437.

Spector, S.A., Gelber, R.D., McGrath, N., et al. (1994). A controlled trial of intravenous immune globulin for the prevention of serious bacterial infections in children receiving zidovudine for advanced human immunodeficiency virus infection. *New England Journal of Medicine, 331,* 1181–1187.

Spector, S.A., McKinley, G.F., Lalezari, J.P., et al. (1996). Oral gangiclovir for the prevention of cytomegalovirus disease in persons with AIDS. *New England Journal of Medicine, 334,* 1491–1497.

Sperling, R.S., Shapiro, D.E., Coombs, R.W., et al. (1996). Maternal viral load, zidovudine treatment, and the risk of transmission of human immunodeficiency virus type-1 from mother to infant. *New England Journal of Medicine, 335,* 1621–1629.

Spiegel, H., & Mayers, A. (1991). Psychosocial aspects of AIDS in children and adolescents. *Pediatric Clinics of North America, 38,* 153–167.

Steckelberg, J.M., & Cockerill, F.R., III. (1988). Serologic testing for human immunodeficiency virus antibodies. *Mayo Clinic Proceedings, 63,* 373–380.

Stoneburner, R.L., Sato, P., Burton, A., et al. (1994). The global HIV pandemic. *Acta Paediatrics, 400*(Suppl), 1–4.

Tardieu, M., Mayaux, M-J., Siebel, N., et al. (1995). Cognitive assessment of school-age children infected with maternally transmitted human immunodeficiency virus type 1. *Pediatrics, 126,* 375–438.

Task Force in Pediatric AIDS. (1988). Pediatric guidelines for infection control of human immunodeficiency virus (acquired immunodeficiency virus) in hospitals, medical offices, schools, and other settings. *Pediatrics, 82,* 801–807.

Temmerman, M., Nyong'o, A.O., Bwayo, J., et al. (1995). Risk factors for mother-to-child transmission of human immunodeficiency virus-1 infection. *American Journal of Obstetrics and Gynecology, 172,* 700–705.

Van de Perre, P., Simonon, A., Msellati, P., et al. (1991). Postnatal transmission of human immunodeficiency virus type 1 from mother to infant: A prospective cohort study in Kigali, Rwanda. *New England Journal of Medicine, 325,* 593–598.

Wachtel, R.C., Tepper, V.J., Houch, D.L., et al. (1993). Neurodevelopment in pediatric HIV-1 infection: A prospective study. *Pediatric AIDS and HIV Infection, 4,* 198–203.

Woodruff, G., Driscoll, P., & Sterzin, E.D. (1992). Providing comprehensive and coordinated services to children with HIV infection and their families: A transagency model. In A.C. Crocker, H.J. Cohen, & T.A. Kastner (Eds.), *HIV infection and developmental disabilities: A resource for service providers* (pp. 105–112). Baltimore: Paul H. Brookes Publishing Co.

World Health Organization (WHO). (1996). AIDS global data. *Weekly Epidemiology Record, 70,* 353–355.

10 Nutrition

Good and Bad

Abigail F. Farber
Colleen Comonitski Yanni
Mark L. Batshaw

Upon completion of this chapter, the reader will:

- know the principles of good nutrition
- be aware of the effects of malnutrition on the developing brain
- recognize the unique nutritional issues of children with developmental disabilities
- understand the techniques of nutritional rehabilitation
- be aware of currently accepted and controversial nutritional treatments

Optimal nutrition is the foundation for normal growth and development. This chapter reviews the fundamental principles of good nutrition, nutritional assessment, and treatment. It also addresses the unique growth patterns and nutritional needs and risks of children with developmental disabilities. The developmental consequences of malnutrition during the prenatal period and early childhood are also reviewed. This chapter concludes with a discussion of current controversies in nutrition and the therapeutic effects of nutritional interventions in selected developmental disabilities.

TYPICAL GROWTH DURING CHILDHOOD

After an initial weight loss in the first week of life, a newborn gains 20–30 grams (about an ounce) each day for several months. By 4–6 months of age, the birth weight has doubled; and by 12 months, it has tripled. After this period of rapid weight gain, growth slows to about 5 pounds per year until approximately 9–10 years of age when the adolescent growth spurt begins (Guo, Roche, Fomon, et al., 1991). Height moves at a slower pace than weight, increasing by 50% during the first year of life, doubling by 4 years of age, and tripling by 13 years of age (Smith, 1977). Head circumference increases by 1–2 centimeters a month during the first year of life, and brain weight doubles by 2 years of age, by which time the number of neurons has reached the adult range (Karlberg, Engstrom, Lichtenstein, et al., 1968). Further growth mainly takes place in the form of increased cell size and intercellular connections (see Chapter 14). Because children with developmental disabilities often have decreased growth potential, it is especially important to monitor their weight, height, and head circumference. Typical growth curves for height and weight are included at the end of this chapter (Hamill, Drizd, Johnson, et al., 1977).

INFANT NUTRITION

For infants, breast milk is the best nourishment. It contains an ideal ratio of carbohydrates, fats (including long chain–polyunsaturated fatty acids), and protein; and it supplies needed calories, vitamins, and minerals. In addition, breast milk is more digestible than commercial infant formulas because of its different protein quality and higher carbohydrate content (Winikoff, Myers, Laukaran, et al., 1987). It also provides immunological protection to the infant. Breast-feeding is inadvisable only when an infection (e.g., HIV) or toxic drug (e.g., alcohol, cocaine) can be transmitted from mother to child. In general, solely breast-fed infants need supplementation with vitamin D and fluoride (if the water is not fluoridated). An iron supplement also is advisable if the introduction of solid foods is to be delayed beyond 4–6 months of age.

In developing countries, breast-feeding often is continued until another baby is born, at which time the weanling becomes at risk for developing severe malnutrition. In the United States, however, although 50% of women breast-feed during their baby's first weeks of life, fewer than 25% nurse after their infant reaches 5 months of age (Winikoff, 1990), often because of employment outside the home. When breast-feeding cannot be continued, commercial formulas are an appropriate substitute, especially those containing long chain–polyunsaturated fatty acids. The most commonly used infant formulas are composed of reconstituted skim milk (containing lactose as the carbohydrate) and a mixture of corn and other oils, which provide fat. Lactose-free formulas that contain sucrose or corn syrup as the carbohydrate can be used in children who are intolerant of lactose, usually manifested as diarrhea or vomiting (Klish, 1990).

An average infant in the United States is exclusively fed breast milk or formula until 4–6 months of age when solids are gradually introduced. By 1–2 years of age, the child has made the transition to solid table foods and whole milk (American Academy of Pediatrics, Committee on Nutrition Staff, 1993).

MALNUTRITION

Undernutrition implies the underconsumption of energy or nutrients. Severe undernutrition leads to a condition termed **malnutrition,** which is manifest as severe failure to thrive. This can be of prenatal or postnatal origin. In general, the earlier in development undernutrition or malnutrition occurs, the more severe the neurodevelopmental consequences.

Prenatal Growth Retardation

Intrauterine growth retardation (IUGR) is defined as a birth weight equal to or less than the 10th percentile for gestational age. The term applies both to full-term and preterm infants. Of those infants with IUGR, 60% have proportional growth impairments, meaning that head and brain growth also have been affected, and 40% have disproportionate growth impairment, in which the brain is relatively spared.

In the majority of children with proportional growth impairment, the problem originates early in gestation during embryogenesis. These infants often have a genetic disorder (e.g., trisomy 18); a malformation syndrome (e.g., Cornelia de Lange syndrome); an early intrauterine infection (e.g., cytomegalovirus); exposure to a toxin (e.g., alcohol); or access to specific maternal nutrient excess (e.g., vitamin A) or deficiency (e.g., folic acid). These children tend to remain small and have microcephaly and cognitive impairments as part of an underlying neurological maldevelopment (Table 10.1).

In infants with disproportionate IUGR, the growth retardation generally occurs in the last trimester and is usually the result of maternal illness, undernutrition, or uteroplacental insufficiency. At birth, these infants are at increased risk for hypoglycemia and **hyperviscosity,** which can lead to seizures and stroke, respectively. Although infants with disproportionate IUGR may be more unstable at birth than infants with proportional IUGR, they usually have better neurodevelopmental outcomes. Studies of the effects of the famine in The Netherlands during World War II suggested that, although the birth weight of newborns was decreased, head circumference and intellectual functioning were not adversely affected (Stein & Susser, 1975). More recent studies have shown that 85% of children with disproportionate IUGR, whether preterm or term, manifest catch-up growth by 2 years of age and have typical intellectual development (Hokken-Koelega, De Ridder, Lemmen, et al., 1995). They may, however, be at higher risk for cardiovascular disease and the development of diabetes later in life (Warshaw, 1994).

Table 10.1.   Effect of selected prenatal nutrients on fetal development

Deficiency/Excess states	Effects on development
Deficiency states	
Folic acid	Neural tube defects, craniofacial abnormalities
Thiamin	Hypomyelination
Iodine	Cretinism, affects neuron and dendritic growth after 14th week, replacement by third trimester is no longer effective
Zinc (independently or as zinc-nutrient interaction)	Abortions, prematurity, intrauterine growth retardation, congenital malformations, hydrocephalus
Iron	Low birth weight, prematurity
Protein-calorie malnutrition	Intrauterine growth retardation, prematurity
Essential fatty acids	Intrauterine growth retardation, prematurity
Excess states	
Mercury	Cerebral palsy, congenital malformations, mental retardation
Aluminum	Progressive encephalopathy
Vitamin A	Malformations of bone, urinary tract, and central nervous system

Postnatal Growth Failure

To grow normally after birth, an infant must have an adequate nutritional intake. Early signs of undernutrition include poor weight gain and a decrease in muscle and fatty tissue. **Failure to thrive** is the clinical term applied to an infant or young child who is failing to meet the standards for age, both in growth and development. Inadequate intake affects development not only directly (by causing deficits in nutrition to the brain), but also indirectly by causing diminished physical energy for exploring and learning. Traditionally, failure to thrive was thought to be of either nonorganic (i.e., psychosocial) or organic (i.e., biological) origin. It is now understood that both factors are usually intertwined. Although more common among the impoverished, the failure to thrive syndrome can occur in all socioeconomic strata. A child may have nonorganic failure to thrive because he or she is offered an inadequate diet due to lack of food availability or lack of parental knowledge or involvement. Alternatively, the food may be presented in an erratic, poorly balanced, or developmentally inappropriate manner. When failure to thrive results in severe postnatal proportional growth retardation associated with bizarre and sometimes excessive eating and drinking behaviors, sleep and emotional disorders, and developmental and cognitive impairments, it is termed psychosocial-deprivation dwarfism. Although this disorder is of "nonorganic" origin, it has been suggested that chronic stress-induced neurotransmitter regulatory changes may be part of the etiology (Vargas & Tenore, 1993).

From an organic perspective, the child with a developmental disability may have multiple factors contributing to the risk of undernutrition, including 1) difficulty with ingestion or digestion (e.g., dysphagia, anorexia, food refusal, selectivity, rumination); 2) unrecognized gastrointestinal dysmotility (e.g., reflux, delayed gastric emptying); 3) a metabolic abnormality affecting nutritional requirements (e.g., phenylketonuria); or 4) medication that alters appetite (e.g., methylphenidate). The first two factors are common in cerebral palsy, the third in inborn errors of metabolism, and the fourth in attention-deficit/hyperactivity disorder (ADHD). Undernutrition ultimately may be both the cause and the result of neurodevelopmental impairments.

If undernutrition progresses, it can become malnutrition in which there is usually a reduced rate of growth in length and head circumference as well as in weight. Malnutrition is the leading cause of infant illness and death in the developing world. Although much less common in developed countries, it is a potential problem among individuals who do not have access to a balanced diet, have restriction of their food choices, or have chronic diseases or developmental disabilities.

Malnutrition can severely affect the neurodevelopment of the young child (Brown & Pollitt, 1996; Suskind & Lewind-Suskind, 1993). In fact, it has been shown that infantile malnutrition can reduce brain cell count by as much as 20% (Crosby, 1991; Winick, 1979). It is surprising, therefore, that the brain is quite resilient to malnutrition and that psychoeducational rehabilitation can reduce the impact on cognitive development (DeLong, 1993). In one study, Korean War orphans who had experienced malnutrition in early childhood were followed neurodevelopmentally after placement in adoptive families in the United States. By school entry, the physical and intellectual development of these children fell within normal limits. It was noted, however, that the infants who were well nourished during the first 6 months of life had significantly higher IQ scores than those who had been malnourished in early infancy (Winick, 1979). More recent adoption studies have confirmed that nutritional rehabilitation of malnourished infants combined with a psychosocially enriched environment can result in children who achieve average IQ scores

(Colombo, dela Parra, & Lopez, 1992). This contrasts with control groups, raised in institutions or with their impoverished biological families, who have significant cognitive impairments.

In addition to the environment, the content of early supplementary feedings is important in determining outcome in children who have experienced malnutrition. In general, infants who received diets with a high protein and caloric content had better neurodevelopmental outcomes than those who received low protein/calorie supplements. Premature infants receiving too high a protein intake, however, actually had a worse neurodevelopmental outcome (Pollitt, Gorman, Engle, et al., 1995).

OBESITY

While undernutrition results in failure to thrive, excessive intake of food relative to the metabolic needs of the individual leads to obesity. Obesity is a disorder of energy balance, in which there is a chronic disequilibrium between energy intake and expenditure. Obesity has a prevalence in the general population of 5%–25% depending on age, sex, and socioeconomic status; in school-age children, it is around 10%. Obesity tends to follow children into adulthood, and there is a genetic predisposition. Eighty percent of children of obese parents also become obese (Thorp, Peirce, & Deedwania, 1987).

A mouse *ob* (obese) gene and its human counterpart have been cloned (Zhang, Proenca, Maffel, et al., 1994). The *ob* gene product, leptin, is expressed only in fat tissue and appears to be a signaling factor that regulates body weight and energy balance. Treatment of obese mice with leptin has been shown to both reduce appetite and increase energy expenditure (Halaas, Gajiwala, Maffel, et al., 1995). These animals lost 40% of their body weight during 1 month of daily injections of leptin and maintained their weight loss. This raises the hope for a more specific form of weight loss therapy in the future.

Obesity occurs more commonly in individuals with developmental disabilities than in the general population. Children with Down syndrome, for example, have a lower metabolic rate than average, placing them at increased risk for obesity (Luke, Roizen, Sutton, et al., 1994). In addition, unrecognized hypothyroidism in these children may result in excessive weight gain. Prader-Willi syndrome, as another example, is associated with compulsive eating and often with food stealing. In children with physical disabilities such as muscular dystrophy and meningomyelocele, activity restriction may lead to obesity (Atencio-LaFollette, Ekvall, Oppenheimer, et al., 1992; Shepherd, Roberts, Golding, et al., 1991). When present, obesity further restricts the activity and mobility of children with disabilities. It also places them at increased risk for such medical complications as diabetes and sleep apnea.

NUTRIENTS AND THEIR DEFICIENCIES

A healthy diet supplies all the essential nutrients and calories for normal growth and development during childhood. It should provide choices from each of the six major food groups, with variety, balance, and moderation. The food guide pyramid (Figure 10.1) illustrates the different food groups and the suggested number of daily servings from each group. A child's diet is balanced over several days, not necessarily with every meal. Decisions about food choices have been made easier by the availability of food labeling information, mandated by the Nutrition La-

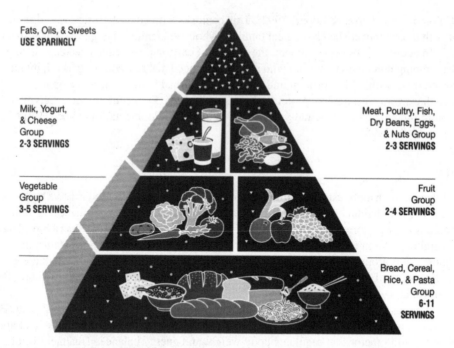

Figure 10.1.   The food guide pyramid (from the Dietary Guidelines for Americans) (Key: ○ = fat [naturally occurring and added]; ◇ = sugars [added]. These symbols show fat and added sugars in foods.)

beling and Education Act Amendments of 1993, PL 103-80. This provides consumer-friendly listings of all ingredients in descending order by weight. The following discussion focuses on the various nutrients that comprise a good diet and the adverse effects of deficiencies.

Water

Water is second only to oxygen as essential for life. Water transports nutrients to and waste products from cells, helps regulate body temperature, and is involved in metabolic reactions. Our requirements for water are related to caloric consumption and average about 1 milliliter (⅕ of a teaspoon) of water per 1 calorie consumed in people of all ages. Thus, an infant needs to consume far larger amounts of water for weight than an older child. In young infants, the average intake of fluid should be about 90–150 milliliters per kilogram of weight each day or 1.5–2.5 ounces per pound of weight each day (American Academy of Pediatrics, Committee on Nutrition Staff, 1993). In older infants and children, eating solid foods provides additional water. Water is lost through the skin and respiratory tract and by elimination in the feces and urine. Water is also an important adjunct in the prevention of constipation. Although it is not necessary for a child to ingest all the recommended calories needed each day, the child must receive adequate fluid each day to prevent dehydration.

Protein

In children and adolescents, protein should constitute about 10%–15% of the total calories ingested (Queen & Lang, 1993). High-protein foods include milk, cheese, meat, eggs, and fish.

Following ingestion, protein is broken down into its constituted amino acids and nitrogen. Amino acids are involved in the synthesis of new tissue, hormones, enzymes, and antibodies; nitrogen is needed to keep existing tissue healthy. There are eight essential amino acids (valine, leucine, isoleucine, phenylalanine, tryptophan, threonine, methionine, and lysine) that must be supplied in the diet. The other 12 can be synthesized in the body. The quality of a specific protein depends on whether it contains all eight essential amino acids. In general, animal protein contains essential amino acids in greater amounts and better balance than plant protein. For example, milk protein or casein is a complete protein; it contains all of the essential amino acids. Grains, beans, and seeds, however, contain some, but not all of the essential amino acids and are thus considered incomplete proteins. The relative requirements for various essential amino acids decrease with age and the overall requirement for protein also declines. A lack of protein in the diet can lead to a reduction in growth rate as well as a failure to develop normal secondary sexual characteristics, such as pubic hair and breast tissue. An increased incidence of infections and poor digestion, due to deficiencies of certain enzymes, also may result (Shils, Olson, & Shike, 1994; Suskind & Lewind-Suskind, 1993).

Lipids

While proteins are involved primarily in body growth and tissue maintenance, fats mainly produce energy (Hardy & Kleinman, 1994). In addition, two long chain fatty acids, linoleic and arachidonic acids, are essential because they cannot be synthesized in the body and are necessary for the formation of cell membranes. Because cow's milk fat (butter) contains much less of the essential fatty acids than does human milk, infant formulas are made with skim milk and supplemented with vegetable oils to provide the essential fats. In one study, adequately nourished 4-month-old full-term infants fed formulas fortified with long chain–polyunsaturated fatty acids had better neurodevelopmental outcomes at 4 years of age compared with infants fed standard nonfortified formulas (Agostoni, Trojan, Bellu, et al., 1995; Hack, Breslau, Weissman, et al., 1991).

Fatty acid deficiency is rare except in certain chronic diseases, such as cystic fibrosis and celiac disease, in which there is impaired fatty acid absorption. A deficiency state increases susceptibility to infection and bleeding. Treatment may involve the use of formulas, which are supplemented with medium and long chain fatty acids.

Fats in food consist primarily of triglycerides, which are either saturated or unsaturated. Saturated fats come principally from animal sources (meats, milk, butter, eggs), while polyunsaturated fats come from vegetable sources (corn oil, margarine, olive oil). Animal fats also contain cholesterol. Fats yield 9 calories per gram, whereas carbohydrates and protein yield only 4 calories per gram. Foods high in fats include ice cream, nuts, and potato chips. Fats produce energy, give food its taste, and make us feel full. This is one reason that dieting on low-fat foods tends to leave one feeling hungry.

In children older than 2 years of age, fats should provide 30%–35% of the total caloric intake (Queen & Lang, 1993). Infants have a much greater growth rate and require a higher percentage of calories from fat. Breast milk and infant formulas contain 40%–50% of energy from fat; poor growth has been associated with a lower fat intake. It is generally recommended that infants switch from breast milk or commercial formula to whole cow's milk around 1 year of age and continue the use of whole milk in the diet until 2 years of age (American Academy of Pediatrics, Committee on Nutrition Staff, 1993). At this time, the fat content of the diet can come from more varied sources. For the underweight child, fat can provide supplemental calories; for the overweight child, the intake of fat needs to be carefully monitored and regulated. Unfortunately, labeling of foods for children under 2 years of age currently does not carry detailed information about fat content.

Studies in adult populations suggest that diets low in total fats, saturated fats, and cholesterol reduce the risk of coronary artery disease. Whether these recommendations are also appropriate for young children is controversial. Several professional organizations, however, promote a generally balanced diet for all children older than the age of 2, recommending also that no more than 30% of one's total calories should be derived from fat, less than 10% of energy from saturated fat, and less than 300 milligrams of dietary cholesterol per day (National Cholesterol Education Program, 1990).

Carbohydrates

At least 50% of all calories should come from carbohydrates (Queen & Lang, 1993). Similar to fatty foods, high carbohydrate foods are used as fuel and provide energy, as glucose, for brain metabolism. Carbohydrates also can be stored in muscle as glycogen and released as needed for energy (American Academy of Pediatrics, Committee on Nutrition Staff, 1993). There are two classes of carbohydrates: simple sugars and complex carbohydrates. Lactose, the sugar in milk, and sucrose (table sugar) are examples of simple sugars. They are rapidly absorbed and readily available for use as energy. Polysaccharides, or complex carbohydrates, are present in cereals, grains, potatoes, and corn. These starches are broken down slowly into simple sugars and fibers.

Fiber

Dietary fiber is that part of food that is not degraded in the digestive tract. Plants, including whole grains, fruits, and vegetables, are the primary sources of fiber in our diet. One portion each of high-fiber cereal, bread, fresh fruit, and raw vegetables is recommended daily. Specifically, children older than 2 years should consume fiber equaling their age plus 5 grams per day (i.e., a 5-year-old should ingest 10 grams of fiber per day) (Williams, Bollella, & Wynder, 1995). Fiber induces water intake in the stool; promotes softer, more frequent, and bulkier stool; and helps prevent constipation (see Chapter 28). A more controversial claim about fiber is that it may decrease the risk for colon cancer, cardiovascular disease, and adult-onset diabetes. Excessive fiber, however, can delay gastric emptying, take up room in the small stomach of a child, and interfere with the absorption of certain nutrients.

Vitamins

Although children need large quantities of fats, proteins, and carbohydrates for normal growth, they require only minute amounts of vitamins. Vitamins are used primarily as cofactors in metabolic reactions; they stimulate, or **catalyze,** the reactions without being used up themselves. Although fresh foods contain them naturally, most processed foods in the United States are supplemented with vitamins. For example, whole milk is fortified with vitamin D, skim milk with vitamins A and D, and infant formulas are supplemented with various essential vitamins. The published Recommended Dietary Allowances (RDA) (National Academy of Sciences, National Research Council, 1989) are a guideline for the amount of vitamins (and minerals) a healthy person needs. As long as the child eats a well-balanced and appropriately prepared diet, there should be no need for vitamin or mineral supplements. Children who have special nutritional stresses (e.g., premature infants, children who receive vegetarian or therapeutic restricted diets and certain antiepileptic drugs), however, do require vitamin supplementation. The body can store fat-soluble vitamins so that a deficiency does not become evident until weeks or months after the undernutrition state has developed. Vitamin supplements are available in liquid form, and vitamin and mineral combinations are available in chewable tablets and pills. Chewable tablets can be crushed and added to food, which may be useful for the child who needs dosing beyond infancy but cannot chew or swallow pills. Table 10.2 lists functions of selected vitamins, their food sources, and manifestations of states of deficiency and excess.

Carnitine

Carnitine is essential for transport of fats into the mitochondria of cells, where they can be oxidized to release energy. Although we can manufacture some carnitine from amino acids, most is obtained from milk and dairy products. Typically, children receive adequate carnitine in their diets and do not require supplements. However, children with certain inborn errors of metabolism, such as the organic acidemias and fatty acid oxidation defects, may benefit from carnitine supplements. Certain antiepileptic drugs, including valproic acid, carbamazepine, phenobarbital, and phenytoin, also have been associated with increased carnitine loss (Opala, Winter, Vance, et al., 1991; Winter, Szabo-Aczel, Curry, et al., 1987). A mild carnitine deficiency is usually asymptomatic, while severe carnitine deficiency can be associated with low blood sugar, hyperammonemia, liver dysfunction, and even coma. Supplemental carnitine should be administered under medical supervision as it can lead to diarrhea.

Minerals

Children and adults need various minerals to ensure appropriate body functioning. Some minerals are required in substantial amounts (e.g., calcium, magnesium, phosphorus). They comprise 98% of all the mineral content of the body and are required for the formation of bones and teeth and for normal muscle contraction (American Academy of Pediatrics, Committee on Nutrition Staff, 1993). A deficiency in any of these minerals can lead to brittle bones, rickets, poor muscle tone, and poor linear growth. Decreased use of bones due to paralysis or immobilization causes these minerals to come out of the bones.

Minerals needed in smaller amounts include potassium, chloride, and sodium. These "electrolytes" maintain the body's fluid balance. An imbalance can result in nausea, muscle weakness, states of confusion, and seizures.

Still other minerals are required only in minute amounts. These "trace" minerals include zinc, copper, fluoride, selenium, manganese, iodine, and iron. Most are essential for the activation of certain enzymes. Except for iron, trace mineral deficiency states are rare. However, they can occur with malnutrition; in premature infants on restricted diets; or in children with ongoing medical conditions who have malabsorption, are fed intravenously, or require dialysis. Zinc deficiency results in growth failure, skin rashes, and impaired immunity against infections. Copper deficiency has been linked to anemia and weakened bones. Fluoride deficiency affects tooth integrity and bone strength. Iodine deficiency leads to hypothyroidism. Selenium deficiency has been associated with heart failure and neurological impairments.

The most common trace mineral problem by far, however, is iron deficiency (Moffatt, Longstaffe, Besant, et al., 1994). Iron is an important constituent of hemoglobin, and its deficiency leads to anemia. Infants under 1 year of age may become anemic as a result of iron defi-

Table 10.2. Food sources for selected minerals and vitamins: Their functions, deficiencies, and excess states

Mineral/vitamin	Sources	Functions	Deficiency (excess) states
Calcium	Dairy products, sardines, salmon, calcium-precipitated tofu, broccoli, cooked dried bean and peas, dark green leafy vegetables	• Development and maintenance of healthy bones and teeth • Blood clotting that begins the wound healing process • Nerve transmission and muscle contractions	Seizures, rickets, tetany (found in Williams syndrome)
Phosphorus	Meats, especially organ meat (e.g., liver, fish, poultry, eggs); cheese; milk; peanut butter; soybeans	• Component of bone • Conversion of dietary carbohydrate, protein, and fat into energy • Component of cell membranes • Helps maintain pH balance in blood	Rickets (calcium deficiency)
Magnesium	Nuts, dried beans, peas, whole grain breads and cereals, soybeans, dark green leafy vegetables	• Conversion of carbohydrate, protein, and fat into energy • Muscle contraction and relaxation and nerve transmission • Synthesis of bone and teeth	Seizures
Iron	Organ meats, lean meats, dried apricots, raisins, molasses, dried beans and peas, spinach	• Component of hemoglobin	Cognitive deficits, immunological deficits (precipitates vitamin E deficiency in preterm infants)
Sodium	Salt, monosodium glutamate, soy sauce, baking powder, cheese, milk, shellfish	• Regulates water and acid-base balance	Dehydration, malnutrition (stroke)
Potassium	Legumes, dried fruits, bananas, cantaloupe, apricots, citrus fruits, dark green leafy vegetables, meats	• Maintenance of water balance • Formation of muscle tissue • Activates enzyme reaction	Muscle weakness (heart arrhythmia)
Zinc	Meats, poultry, fish and organ meats, whole grain breads and cereals	• Induces mineralization • Production of protein • Wound healing • Maintenance of immune system	Acrodermatitis enteropathica (growth retardation, copper deficiency)
Vitamin A	Liver, carrots, sweet potatoes, spinach, apricots, winter squash, cantaloupe, broccoli, dark green and yellow vegetables	• Essential for normal eyesight • Normal body growth and formation of bones and soft tissue • Fights infection • Enhances activity of immune system	Impaired growth, immune deficiency (increased intracranial pressure, anorexia)

Vitamin	Sources	Function	Deficiency
Vitamin D	Milk fortified with vitamin D, canned sardines, fresh salmon, fresh herring	• Regulates absorption and use of calcium and phosphorous	Rickets
Vitamin C	Citrus fruits and juices, brussel sprouts, strawberries, broccoli, collard greens, cantaloupe, tomato juice	• Formation and maintenance of collagen • Antioxidant • Enhances absorption of iron • Conversion of folic acid to its active form	Scurvy (interferes with B_{12} absorption)
Folic acid	Beef liver, beans, green leafy vegetables, orange juice	• Formation of DNA and certain amino acids • Formation of blood cells	Anemia, teratogenic effect on fetus
Thiamin Riboflavin Niacin	Whole grain or enriched breads and cereal, dark green leafy vegetables, dairy products, eggs, fish, liver, poultry, beef, veal, lamb, pork, organ meats, brewer's yeast, peanut butter	• Functioning of the heart and nervous system • Converts carbohydrate into energy • Healthy skin • Assists in hormone synthesis	Beriberi, ataxia (corneal vascularization, poor growth, pellagra)
Pyridoxine	Meats, wheatgerm, poultry, fish, soybeans, brewer's yeast, peanuts	• Conversion of carbohydrates, fats, and protein into energy • Aids in the conversion of one amino acid to another	Seizures (neuropathy)
Vitamin B_{12}	Lean meats, poultry, fish, shellfish, milk, organ meats, cheese and eggs	• Normal processing of carbohydrate, protein, and fat • Formation of myelin sheath • Essential for the replacement and maintenance of all cells	Megaloblastic anemia, ataxia
Vitamin E	Vegetable oil, seeds, wheatgerm, nuts	• Antioxidant	Hemolytic disease in premature infant (interferes with vitamin K metabolism)
Vitamin K	Green leafy vegetables, broccoli, turnip greens, romaine lettuce, cabbage	• Regulates normal blood clotting • Important for production of prothrombin, a protein essential for blood coagulation	Hemorrhagic disease of newborn, prolonged bleeding time

ciency if they are fed whole cow's milk, which may irritate the intestine and cause gastrointestinal blood loss. Older children who eat insufficient quantities of iron-containing foods are also at risk for developing iron-deficiency anemia. This is especially true of children who are raised on milk or formulas without iron supplementation or without enriched cereals. Iron-deficiency anemia occurs most frequently in children between 6 months and 3 years of age (American Academy of Pediatrics, Committee on Nutrition Staff, 1993). Symptoms include irritability, listlessness, anorexia, diminished spontaneous activity, and decreased interest in the environment. Although scores on motor tests in children revert to normal after nutritional rehabilitation, there are residual effects of early iron-deficiency anemia in areas of emotionality, cognitive processing, and attention (Lozoff, Jimenez, & Wolf, 1991; Morgane, Austin-Lafarance, Bronzino, et al., 1993). In order to avoid iron deficiency, supplementation of iron-enriched formula or iron compounds providing 1 milligram per kilogram per day should be started in full-term infants by 4 months of age, and introduction of iron-fortified cereals should occur between 4 and 6 months of age. Iron supplementation should continue until 3 years of age. For preterm infants, the recommendation is to begin supplements of 2 milligrams per kilogram per day by 2 months of age (American Academy of Pediatrics, Committee on Nutrition Staff, 1993). It should be emphasized that treatment of iron deficiency requires both replacement therapy and the identification of its underlying cause.

NONTRADITIONAL ALTERNATIVE DIETS

To this point, we have focused on the most common diets of children who consume a wide variety of animal and plant foods. However, there are a number of alternative diets. Some of these, such as vegetarian diets, are acceptable substitutes provided certain adjustments are made. Others, such as macrobiotic diets and megavitamin therapy, can be harmful to a child. Still others, such as certain elimination diets, may have no adverse effects but claim unproven benefits. This section touches on some of these nontraditional diets.

Vegetarian Diets

A balanced vegetarian diet with a vitamin supplement can meet all the average child's nutritional requirements. Interest in vegetarian diets has increased in the United States for cultural, religious, philosophical, and health reasons. Vegetarians classify themselves as lacto-ovovegetarian (eats vegetables plus dairy products and eggs), lacto-vegetarian (eats no eggs), or vegan (eats plant foods only). People in many societies have practiced vegetarianism for centuries and have remained healthy, especially when they have supplemented their diet with milk or eggs. In older children and adults, vegan diets can be as nourishing as diets containing meats, as long as individuals select their foods carefully and make sure they receive sufficient calories and essential amino acids and vitamins. Advantages of a vegetarian diet include a low incidence of obesity and low cholesterol levels.

Yet, there may be problems with a vegetarian diet for young children. A vegan nursing mother may not adequately supply her infant with calcium, vitamin D, vitamin B_{12}, zinc, and iron. The infant should receive a daily multivitamin/mineral supplement. Following weaning, the child may have difficulties ingesting sufficient calories for growth. A vegetarian diet is very high in bulk foods and fiber (fruits and vegetables) that may rapidly fill the stomach before the toddler has obtained adequate calories. The protein content also may be low but can be countered by providing increased quantities of legumes (beans, peas, and soy). An older child can usually eat a sufficient balance of legumes, wheatgerm products, nuts, seeds, and dark green leafy vegetables to achieve an adequate caloric intake. This still may not meet the requirement for vitamins and minerals, however, so a daily multivitamin/mineral supplementation is prudent.

Macrobiotic Diets

Although a vegetarian diet may permit typical growth and development, a macrobiotic diet is definitely detrimental to growing children. The goals of such a diet are largely spiritual. One must follow 10 stages of dietary restriction beginning with the gradual elimination of animal products and leading to the elimination of fruits and vegetables. The highest level diets allow only cereals and the caloric intake is very low. Strict adherence to such a diet may result in scurvy, rickets, anemia, hypocalcemia, malnutrition, and even death in infancy and childhood (Dagnelie, Vergote, van-Staveren, et al., 1990).

Organic Food Diets

Natural or organic food diets are not restricted in their content but in how the plants are grown or the animals raised. To qualify as organic, plants must be grown in soil enriched with humus and compost in which no pesticides, herbicides, or inorganic fertilizers have been used. Animals must be reared on natural feeds and not treated with hormones or antibiotics. Although proponents of these diets laud their results, no long-term study has shown the nutritional superiority of organically grown crops over those grown under standard conditions. Nevertheless, concerns about hormones and additives may be valid and, for some individuals, are sufficient reason to buy only organic foods. One important consideration is that organically grown foods are more costly than standard foods.

Megavitamin Diets

While the Feingold diet is restrictive (see Chapter 22), megavitamin diets involve supplementation. Large doses of certain vitamins, usually 10 times or more the RDA, are advocated. The foundation for megavitamin or orthomolecular diets is the finding that certain individuals with rare inborn errors of metabolism benefit from high doses of specific vitamins that stimulate residual enzymatic activity (see Chapter 19). Orthomolecular psychiatry—developed by Drs. Pauling, Cott, and others—has extrapolated this finding to suggest that individuals with a host of other diseases and brain malfunctions can be treated by augmenting normally occurring vitamins (Cott, 1972). Megavitamins have been used in treating mental retardation, Down syndrome, hyperactivity, autism, and learning disorders. However, these efforts have not survived scientific scrutiny. For example, Haslam (1992) found no beneficial effects of megavitamins on ADHD in a controlled crossover study. Of even more concern is that there were abnormalities in liver function tests, suggesting toxicity.

NUTRITIONAL ASSESSMENT

Nutritional assessment of the child with developmental disabilities is required if there are signs of undernutrition (Scott, Artman, & St. Jean, 1992). This assessment consists of a review of the dietary intake, medical status, **anthropometric** data, and medication list. It considers not only what the child eats, but also the child's eating abilities. When assessing a child's diet, the parent/caregiver needs to be specific about the type and amount of food and liquid the child actually consumes, the way it was prepared, the type of utensils used, feeding difficulties, the time needed to finish a meal, the schedule of feeding, where the meals are eaten, and whether a vitamin and mineral supplement is given. The most frequent method of collecting this information is either by a 24-hour food recall or a 3–5 day diet diary, which gives a more accurate picture of the child's eating habits.

The medical status of the child, including issues that affect the acquisition and utilization of nutrients, also must be reviewed. Specific laboratory investigations are based on the individual's condition but most commonly include an assessment of hematological status, kidney and liver function, acid-base and electrolyte balance, and vitamin and mineral levels. In some medical centers, more complex measures of resting energy expenditure can be made using specialized equipment (Thomson, Bucolo, Quirk, et al., 1995).

Anthropometric studies consist of measurements of height, weight, head circumference, and skinfold thickness (Hammer, Kraemer, Wilson, et al., 1991). Physically disabling conditions can make it difficult to measure height accurately, especially if there are contractures or abnormal development of limbs. Measuring upper arm and lower leg length are reliable alternatives for stature when children with disabilities are nonambulatory (Spender, Cronk, Charney, et al., 1989; Stevenson, 1995). Once obtained, the anthropometric measurements should be plotted on growth charts and compared with standards. In addition to the growth charts developed by the National Center for Health Statistics (NCHS), there are specialized growth charts for children with Down syndrome, Prader-Willi syndrome, Turner syndrome, sickle-cell disease, meningomylocele, cerebral palsy, and prematurity (Cronk, Crocker, Pueschel, et al., 1988; Ekvall, 1993; Krick, Murphy-Miller, Zeger, et al., 1996).

Consistent growth along a given percentile is ideal; however, during development there may be times when height increases with no concomitant increase in weight or vice versa. To deal with this issue, weight/height charts compare the weight of a child with other children of the same length/height, rather than to other children of the same age.

When assessing a child's nutritional status, especially for those below the 10th percentile, it is also important to evaluate the composition of lean and fat tissue. This can be done by measuring the triceps and subscapular skinfold thickness (Frisancho, 1974). Triceps skinfold measurement in relation to arm circumference is used to determine cross-sectional midarm muscle and fat areas. Abnormal anthropometric measurements are an early indicator of malnutrition as they occur before clinical symptoms become apparent (Ekvall, 1993).

INTERVENTIONS FOR NUTRITIONAL PROBLEMS

Treatment plans are based on the chronicity of the problem and focus on modifying both the content and mode of delivery of the nutrition. Attention must be addressed to underlying medical, neurodevelopmental, psychosocial, and economic factors (Ekvall, 1993). The child's unique metabolic needs, nutritional requirements, and ability to ingest or digest nutrients also must be considered. Table 10.3 provides caloric requirements for children with selected developmental disorders.

Table 10.3.   Caloric requirements of children with selected disorders

Disorder	Factors	Daily caloric needs
Cerebral palsy	Increased/decreased tone, increased/decreased movement	13.9 Kcal/cm: 5–11 years for mild to moderate activity, 11.1 Kcal/cm: 5–11 years for inactivity
Meningomyelocele	Restricted activity, oromotor dysfunction	9–11 Kcal/cm height for maintenance, 7 Kcal/cm height for weight loss
Prader-Willi syndrome	Genetic predisposition	10–11 Kcal/cm for maintenance 8–9 Kcal/cm for weight loss
Down syndrome	Genetic predisposition	Boys: 16.1 Kcal/cm height Girls: 14.3 Kcal/cm height
Premature infant	Increased metabolic needs	90–120 Kcal/kg

Sources: Ekvall (1993), Queen & Lang (1993), Rokusek & Neinrichs (1992).
Key: 1 inch = 2.54 centimeters; 1 pound = 2.2 kilograms; Kcal = Kilocalorie; cm = centimeters; kg = kilograms.

Routes of Acquiring Nutrition

Liquid Oral Nutrition

In the first months of life, nutrition is provided as oral liquids. Most infants will do well with either breast milk or standard infant formula that contains 20 calories per ounce. Some infants will need caloric supplements, however, either because of a metabolic disturbance (e.g., an inborn error of metabolism) or increased need (e.g., prematurity). In these cases, 24 calories per ounce of formula may be necessary; concentrating the formula further is not usually recommended as it increases the protein load to the kidneys. Caloric density also can be increased by adding carbohydrate (e.g., Polycose) and/or fat (e.g., Microlipids, medium-chain triglyceride oil) as they do not increase the load to the kidneys. Breast milk also can be expressed and fortified to provide more calories per ounce. When these manipulations are done, distribution of calories needs to be monitored so that 7%–16% of calories come from protein, 30%–55% from fat, and 35%–65% from carbohydrates.

Solid Oral Nutrition

There is a natural developmental progression in a child's ability to handle solid foods, starting with strained foods and progressing to more complex textures. Examples of strained foods include vanilla pudding, "stage 1" commercial baby food, and blenderized foods. Unfortunately, children with disabilities who have impaired oromotor skills (e.g., cerebral palsy) may have difficulties handling even these smooth textures (Croft, 1992). This problem often can be overcome by using commercially available thickeners, such as Thick-it and Thick and Easy, or other foods such as dried baby cereal, instant potatoes, instant pudding, and ground cracker crumbs.

Once a child is ready to progress from strained foods, the next stage is "junior foods" that introduce small lumps and some texture. These foods can be swallowed without chewing but do require some "munching." Examples include mashed potatoes and "stage 2" baby food. As a child gains more experience and skills, he or she can tolerate more and more lumps and is ready for "stage 3" baby food. Finally, when the child is ready for finger feeding, foods such as macaroni or soft cooked carrots can be introduced. Hard foods should be offered cautiously until the child has passed the stage of increased risk of choking, usually 3–5 years.

Enteral Feedings

Enteral or tube-feedings into the gut may be required on a short-term basis for refeeding malnourished children or on a long-term basis for children who cannot safely ingest sufficient food to maintain adequate nutrition. Short-term enteral feeding generally involves the insertion of a nasogastric or a nasojejunal tube. Long-term enteral feedings require the placement of a gastrostomy or a jejunostomy feeding tube (see Chapter 31).

In planning tube-feeding, the first objective is to establish tolerance to the feeding solution and to its rate of flow (Nardella, 1995). The tube-feedings are started slowly and gradually advanced. It is prudent not to increase both 24-hour volumes and concentrations simultaneously. Feedings are based on the nutritional requirements and gastrointestinal tolerance of the child, so the choice of formula must be individualized. There are many factors to consider in selecting a tube-feeding formula including the nutrient and fluid requirements; route of delivery (gastric, jejunal); osmolality (concentration); viscosity (thickness); medical condition; age of the child; cost; family lifestyle; and feeding schedule.

For infants younger than 1 year of age, human milk or a commercial infant formula is the most appropriate for tube-feeding. Standard infant commercial formulas or specialized casein hydrolysate formulas can be used (Table 10.4). For older children, specific tube-feeding formulas are available, such as Jevity or Ensure. Alternately, some families choose to blenderize their meals, a process that is more economical but also more labor-intensive. Blenderized meals also increase the risk of an unbalanced diet and bacterial contamination. Furthermore, the thickness of the blenderized meals may impair flow through small bore feeding tubes.

Parenteral Feeding

Some children cannot meet their nutritional needs enterally because of chronic diarrhea, congenital or acquired bowel abnormalities, or hypermetabolic states. An example is a former premature infant who has had a significant portion of the small bowel removed because of necrotizing enterocolitis (see Chapter 7). In these children, parenteral nutrition may be required for extended periods of time. This involves the delivery of water, electrolytes, carbohydrates, fats, protein, vitamins, and minerals through a central venous line. Although started in the hospital, these infusions can be delivered in the home setting once the child is medically stable. Close collaboration and monitoring by a team consisting of nutrition, medical, and home nursing professionals are essential. The most common complications are clotting of the venous line and infection. Rarer complications include liver or pancreatic damage or worsening intestinal malfunction.

Nutritional Treatment of Specific Disorders

Many disorders require specific nutritional therapy as part of their management (Yadrick & Sneed, 1994), for example, malnutrition, obesity, and inborn errors of metabolism.

Nutritional Replenishment in Malnutrition

Planning nutritional rehabilitation of malnutrition requires careful assessment of its etiology, be it failure of ingestion, abnormal digestion, or unusual requirements. A diet must be planned that is high in calories and protein and replaces essential minerals and vitamins. Malnourished children may require twice the usual caloric intake to begin gaining weight.

Table 10.4. Examples of infant and pediatric formulas

Manufacturer	Classification	Characteristics	Use
		Infant formulas	
Breast milk Similac (Ross) Enfamil (Mead Johnson)	Standard milk based	Intact milk protein Lactose-containing, long-chain triglycerides Moderate residue Low to moderate osmolality .67 cal/ml	Normally functioning gastrointestinal tract
Isomil (Ross) Prosobee (Mead Johnson)	Standard lactose free	Intact soy protein Low to moderate residue Low to moderate osmolality .67 cal/ml	Lactose intolerant, milk intolerant
Lacto-free (Mead Johnson)	Lactose free	Intact milk protein Lactose free .67 cal/ml	When lactose intolerance is suspected
Portagen (Mead Johnson)	Lactose free Modified fat	Intact protein Fat content is 88% Medium-chain triglycerides (MCT) and 12% long-chain triglycerides .67 cal/ml	Intestinal malabsorption
Pregestimil (Mead Johnson) Alimentum (Ross) Nutramigen (Mead Johnson) Carnation Good Start (Nestlé)	Semi elemental	Hydrolyzed protein Lactose free Low to moderate osmolality (320 mOsm/kg H_2O) Partial MCT content .67 Kcal/ml	Intestinal malabsorption Short gut Cystic fibrosis Chronic liver disease Inflammatory bowel disease Allergy to cow's milk and soy protein

(continued)

Table 10.4. (continued)

Manufacturer	Classification	Characteristics	Use
Pediatric formulas			
Pediasure (Ross)	Standard	Intact protein Virtually lactose free Ready to feed 1 Kcal/ml	Tube or oral feeding for children 1–10 years of age; may be used as sole source of nutrition or as a supplement
Ensure (Ross) Nutren 1.0 (Clintec) Isocal (Mead Johnson) Sustacal (Mead Johnson)	Standard	Intact protein Virtually lactose free Ready to feed 1 Kcal/ml	Tube or oral feeding for children age 10 and older; may be used as sole source of nutrition or as a supplement
Pediasure with fiber (Ross) Kindercal (Mead Johnson)	Standard with fiber	Intact protein Lactose free, gluten free Low osmolality 1.2 gm total fiber/8 oz. Ready to feed 1 Kcal/ml	Tube or oral feeding for children 1–10 years of age; may be used as sole source of nutrition or as a supplement
Sustacal with fiber (Mead Johnson) Ensure with fiber (Ross) Nutren 1.0 with fiber (Clintec) Ultracal (Mead Johnson) Jevity (Ross)	Standard with fiber	Intact protein Lactose free Low to moderate osmolality 3.2–3.4 gm total fiber/8 ounces Ready to feed, 1 Kcal/ml	Tube or oral feeding for children age 10 and older; may be used as sole source of nutrition or as a supplement
Peptamin Jr. (Clintec)	Elemental	Peptide based (100% whey) MCT oil Ready to feed 1 Kcal/ml	Impaired gastrointestinal function
Pediatric Vivonex (Sandoz)	Elemental	Lactose free Free amino acid based Low osmolality MCT oil, Powder, .8 Kcal/ml	Impaired gastrointestinal function
Neocate One (Scientific Hospital Supplies)	Elemental	Free amino acid based Whey, soy, and milk free High osmolality MCT oil Ready to feed 1 Kcal/ml	Impaired gastrointestinal function
Electrolyte replacement			
Pedialyte (Ross) Lytren (Mead Johnson) Suralyte (Mead Johnson)	Electrolyte formula	Balanced electrolyte solution .10 Kcal/ml	Acute treatment of diarrhea

200

With appropriate nutritional rehabilitation, weight gain can be established in children with moderate malnutrition within a few days. The child usually starts to show increased alertness and responsiveness by 1 week. In replenishing nutrition, however, close attention must be paid to the route and rate of delivery of nutrients as well as to their composition and volume. Oral refeeding, for example, may result in aspiration, and excessive volume of a feeding may lead to vomiting or diarrhea (Fee, Charney, & Robertson, 1988).

Although oral refeeding may be sufficient to treat moderate malnutrition, severe malnutrition may require the use of nasogastric tube-feedings. In this case a predigested lactose-free formula with vitamin and mineral supplements (especially iron and zinc) should be used. Refeeding must be done slowly to avoid potentially severe complications. With rapid refeeding, metabolism suddenly shifts from **catabolic** to **anabolic** with an accompanying dramatic redistribution of minerals and electrolytes. The most prominent change is in phosphorus, although sodium, potassium, magnesium, and calcium are also involved. These shifts may adversely affect the child's cardiac, neurological, respiratory, and gastrointestinal systems. Rebound hypoglycemic seizures, edema, and diarrhea may occur. These complications can be avoided by slower refeeding rates and close monitoring of fluid and electrolyte balance (Havala & Shronts, 1990; Solomon & Kirby, 1990).

Yet, if management of malnutrition is focused solely on nutritional replenishment, and the underlying developmental and psychosocial causes are not identified and corrected, the condition is likely to recur. Treatment therefore should include parental training in an interdisciplinary setting that provides nursing, medical, nutrition, and psychosocial services. In addition, early intervention services should be provided to promote the child's neurodevelopmental progress. Home-based intervention services have proven more successful than solely hospital-based programs (Maggioni & Lifshitz, 1995).

Weight Reduction in Obesity

Weight loss is generally a difficult process. To be successful, management of moderate to severe obesity requires a multidisciplinary approach including a balanced low-calorie diet, behavior management program, exercise regimen, counseling, and parental education (Grundy & Barnett, 1994). The individual and family both must be motivated to participate in the program.

An individualized weight reduction diet developed by a nutritionist involves a low-calorie but balanced diet that may have added vitamins and nutrients, combined with an exercise program that increases the caloric expenditure of the child. A behavior management program should be instituted that rewards the child for compliance and achievement of weight goals. Food craving as well as hoarding and stealing behaviors also may need to be addressed, and, especially in adolescents, issues of self-esteem should be explored. Appetite suppressant medication is not a usual part of a weight reduction program in moderately overweight children. Perhaps the most important issue in treatment of obesity is maintenance of the weight loss once it has been achieved. This requires a change in lifestyle; food must become a less prominent part of a child's life. A maintenance diet should be prescribed and the exercise program continued on a long-term basis.

In treating potentially life-threatening morbid obesity, a more intensive program is required. If there is **sleep apnea,** these children may require continuous positive airway pressure (CPAP) overnight (see Chapter 31). Parenteral feedings, a protein-sparing modified fast, and even gastric bypass surgery have been used to produce weight loss (Collier & Walker, 1991). Anorexiant medications also may be employed to enhance weight loss. The combination of fenfluramine (Pondimin) and phentermine (Fastin) has been proposed as effective in treating adults with morbid obesity (Goldstein & Potvin, 1994; Weintraub, Sundaresan, Madan, et al., 1992). Fenfluramine acts through the serotonin neurotransmitter system, slowing eating and increasing satiety. Phentermine, a stimulant medication, suppresses appetite through noradrenergic and dopamine mechanisms, much like methylphenidate. These drugs are being tested for use in adolescents with morbid obesity. Fluoxetine, naltrexone, and polypeptide infusions have been used to treat overeating in certain genetic disorders associated with severe obesity such as Prader-Willi syndrome (Benjamin & Buot-Smith, 1993; Berntson, Zipf, O'Dorisio, et al., 1993; Dech & Budow, 1991). In these situations, the use of drugs in conjunction with diet and exercise has been found to be more successful than medication alone (Weintraub et al., 1992).

Nutritional Management in Inborn Errors of Metabolism

Inborn errors of metabolism may require long-term restriction of certain nutrients (especially protein-containing foods) in order to avoid life-threatening metabolic crises (see Chapter 19). Nutritional balance may be further compromised by intermittent infections and metabolic derangements (Tranms, 1995). It takes a coordinated effort among the metabolic team, primary physician, nutritionist, family, school, and other caregivers to provide a diet that will promote growth and development and yet avoid metabolic decompensation with its risk of further brain damage (Goldberg & Slonim, 1993). Suggestions for facilitating acceptance of the diet are outlined in Table 10.5. Because of accompanying developmental disabilities, anorexia, and food refusal, some of these children will need to have their nutrition provided partially or entirely as tube-feedings.

HAZARDOUS INGESTIONS

While nutrients are needed for good nutrition, the ingestion of lead, certain medications, and infectious agents contained in food can impede normal growth and development.

Lead

One of the best-studied effects of ingested toxins on neurodevelopment involves lead. Very high levels of lead in blood (more than 70 micrograms per deciliter) cause seizures and coma; long-term sequelae include neurological and cognitive impairments. Moderate toxicity (blood lead levels 45–69 micrograms per deciliter) can cause nonspecific symptoms such as fatigue, irritability, lethargy, abdominal discomfort, inattention, headache, tremor, vomiting, and weight

Table 10.5.   Tips to help with acceptance of a special diet

- Involve the entire family in the teaching and observance of the diet restrictions.
- Involve the child in the management of the diet, if possible.
- It is better if the child is not allowed to sample restricted foods.
- When traveling, remember to take more formula than the child needs.
- Adding flavoring to a formula may increase acceptance. Suggested flavors are strawberry, chocolate, and vanilla flavorings and peppermint or lemon extracts.
- Children drinking formula from a cup generally prefer it cool.

Source: Rokusek & Neinrichs (1992).

loss (Chao & Kikano, 1993). This level of lead also has been shown to affect the neuroendocrine system and thereby have a suppressive effect on growth (Huseman, Varma, & Angle, 1992). There is more controversy about the effects of lower lead exposure (blood lead 10–44 micrograms per deciliter) on the developing child. Studies have been criticized for confounding developmental and psychosocial variables, but most evidence supports a modest association between an increased lead burden and lowered IQ score at school age (Bellinger & Deitrich, 1994). Language impairments and ADHD also have been attributed to early lead exposure (Needleman, 1993, 1994).

At present, by far the biggest risk for lead exposure, especially in the child with developmental disabilities, is pica, or the eating of nonfood items. Although lead has been removed from external house paint for many years, it remains a problem for children who live in old homes in the inner city and munch on flaking paint chips and plaster. This is a particular concern in children with pervasive developmental disorders (Shannon & Graef, 1996).

With the advent of lead-free gasoline in the United States, airborne lead has become only a minor cause of exposure, except around heavy industry. Lead content in food also has markedly decreased, although there are still potential sources including food grown in soil with high lead content (urban gardens), and food from cans that may contain lead solder. Diets high in fat, however, result in increased absorption of lead through the gastrointestinal tract. Storage of food in open cans, storage of acidic foods in ceramic containers, food processed in lead-contaminated water, and "non-Western medicines" also may increase lead exposure (Philip & Gerson, 1994; Schonfeld, 1993).

Treatment of lead toxicity requires both deleading the child and removing lead from the house (American Academy of Pediatrics, Committee on Drugs, 1995). If the level is high enough to cause clinical symptoms, treatment of the child requires chelation using intravenous ethylene diaminetetraacetic acid (EDTA) or BAL (dimercaprol), which bind to lead and result in its elimination in the urine. If the blood lead level is 35–45 micrograms per deciliter and the child does not have symptoms, oral chelation therapy with succimer, a new medication, is now being advocated (Besunder, Anderson, & Super, 1995). When a child has a blood lead level around 25 micrograms per deciliter, he or she does not require therapy but should be removed from the source of the lead intoxication. Iron deficiency often complicates lead poisoning because iron competes with lead for absorption from the intestine. Thus, a deficiency in iron results in increased lead absorption as well as anemia. Therefore, iron supplementation may be an important part of chelation therapy.

Combating lead poisoning requires a combination of chelation therapy, a behavior management program, and lead abatement of the house. During the abatement procedure, the family must leave the house while lead-containing paint is removed from the surfaces the child contacts.

In terms of prophylaxis, dietary calcium and phosphorus competitively inhibit lead absorption, probably by binding to lead in the small intestine. This suggests that regular meals providing nutritional sources of calcium and phosphorus, such as milk and yogurt, may decrease the risk of lead intoxication in lead-exposed children. Surveillance for iron deficiency also should be maintained and iron supplements added if appropriate.

Drug–Nutrient Interactions

It is well known that the effectiveness of oral medications can be influenced by the food present in the gastrointestinal tract. Conversely, medication can affect the synthesis, absorption, distribution, and excretion of nutrients (Britzee, 1992). Medication also can have an adverse effect on nutritional status by causing nausea, vomiting, or diarrhea or by altering the taste of food. Children with developmental disabilities often receive medications known to have drug–nutrient interactions. Examples include phenytoin (Dilantin), which affects the utilization of vitamin D, and another antiepileptic drug, valproate (Depakene), which alters carnitine metabolism (Coulter, 1991). It is recommended that these children have annual nutritional and biochemical assessments to determine if a nutrient supplement is needed. Table 10.6 provides examples of drug–nutrient interactions involving medications commonly taken by children with developmental disabilities.

Table 10.6.   Drug–nutrient interactions common to children with developmental disabilities

Medications—generic name (trade name)	Potential nutrient reactions
Antiepileptic drugs	
Phenytoin (Dilantin) Phenobarbital Carbamazepine (Tegretol) Primidone (Mysoline)	• Decreases serum folic acid levels • Decreases vitamin D levels leading to decreased calcium absorption
Valproic acid (Depakene)	• As above, plus may decrease carnitine levels in serum and tissue
Corticosteroids	
Prednisone	• Increased appetite • Sodium and fluid retention • Decreased calcium and phosphorus absorption • Occasional glucose intolerance
Diuretics	
Furosemide (Lasix) Spironalactone (Aldactone)	• Increased excretion of potassium, calcium, and magnesium • Decreased carbohydrate tolerance • Fluid and electrolyte imbalance • Increased serum glucose
Anticonstipation	
Mineral oil Milk of Magnesia	• Interferes with absorption of vitamins A, D, E, and K • With the decreased absorption of vitamin D, calcium and phosphorus absorption can be impaired • Long-term use: decreased thiamin, phosphate, calcium, and iron absorption
Antireflux	
Metoclopramide (Reglan) Cisapride (Propulsid)	• Nausea, abdominal pain, diarrhea, constipation, flatulence
Antacid	
Omeprazole (Prilosec) Ranitidine (Zantac) Famotidine (Pepcid)	• Long-term use decreases vitamin B_{12} and can lead to anemia

Food-Borne Pathogens

In certain settings, food can be a vehicle for transmission of bacterial, viral, and parasitic infections. These can cause a range of illnesses including **bacteremia,** gastroenteritis, hepatitis, malabsorption, encephalitis, and meningitis. Children with developmental disabilities are at increased risk for exposure to food-borne pathogens because they are often cared for in group settings, may have impaired immunity due to malnutrition, and may not have ideal personal hygiene (e.g., fecal-oral transmission of infectious agents). Good hygiene of the child and caregivers, including proper handwashing technique and the use of universal precautions in handling fecal material, can greatly decrease this risk.

SUMMARY

Children with developmental disabilities have unique problems in the acquisition and maintenance of adequate nutrition. Furthermore, inadequacy of nutrition may contribute to or exacerbate the developmental disability. An understanding of nutrition principles and clinical management options is vital in maximizing children's well-being and developmental outcome.

REFERENCES

Acosta, P.B., & Yannicelli, S. (1993). Nutrition support of inherited disorders of amino acid metabolism: Part I. *Topics in Clinical Nutrition, 9,* 65–82.

Agostoni, C., Trojan, S., Bellu, R., et al. (1995). Neurodevelopment quotient of healthy term infants at 4 months and feeding practice: The role of long-chain polyunsaturated fatty acids. *Pediatric Research, 38,* 262–266.

American Academy of Pediatrics, Committee on Drugs. (1995). Treatment guidelines for lead exposure in children. *Pediatrics, 96,* 155–160.

American Academy of Pediatrics, Committee on Nutrition Staff. (1993). *Pediatric nutrition handbook* (3rd ed.). Evanston, IL: Author.

Atencio-LaFollette, P., Ekvall, S.W., Oppenheimer, S., et al. (1992). Effect of level of lesion and quality of ambulation on growth chart measurements in children with myelomeningocele: A pilot study. *Journal of the American Dietetic Association, 92,* 858–861.

Bellinger, D., & Deitrich, K.N. (1994). Low-level lead exposure and cognitive function in children. *Pediatric Annals, 23,* 600–605.

Benjamin, E., & Buot-Smith, T. (1993). Naltrexone and fluoxetine in Prader-Willi syndrome. *Journal of the American Academy of Child and Adolescent Psychiatry, 32,* 870–873.

Berntson, G.G., Zipf, W.B., O'Dorisio, T.M., et al. (1993). Pancreatic polypeptide infusions reduce food intake in Prader-Willi syndrome. *Peptides, 14,* 497–503.

Besunder, J.B., Anderson, R.L., & Super, D.M. (1995). Short-term efficacy of oral dimercaptosuccinic acid in children with moderate lead intoxication. *Pediatrics, 96,* 683–687.

Britzee, L. (1992). Drug-nutrient interacts: Concerns for children with special health care needs. *Nutrition Focus of the Washington Child Development and Mental Retardation Center, 7,* 1–6.

Brown, J.L., & Pollitt, E. (1996, February). Malnutrition, poverty, and intellectual development. *Scientific American, 284,* 38–43.

Chao, J., & Kikano, G.E. (1993). Lead poisoning in children. *American Family Physician, 47,* 113–120.

Collier, S.B., & Walker, W.A. (1991). Parenteral protein-sparing modified fast in an obese adolescent with Prader-Willi syndrome. *Nutrition Reviews, 49,* 235–238.

Colombo, M., dela Parra, A., & Lopez, I. (1992). Intellectual and physical outcome of children undernourished in early life is influenced by later environmental conditions. *Developmental Medicine and Child Neurology, 34,* 661–662.

Cott, A. (1972). Megavitamins: The orthomolecular approach to behavioral disorders and learning disabilities. *Academic Therapy, 7,* 245–249.

Coulter, D. (1991). Carnitine, valproate, and toxicity. *Journal of Child Neurology, 6,* 7–14.

Croft, R.D. (1992). What consistency of food is best for children with cerebral palsy who cannot chew? *Archives of Diseases of Childhood, 67,* 269–271.

Cronk, C., Crocker, A.C., Pueschel, S.M., et al. (1988). Growth charts for children with Down's syndrome: 1 month to 18 years of age. *Pediatrics, 81,* 102–110.

Crosby, W.M. (1991). Studies in fetal malnutrition. *American Journal of Diseases of Childhood, 145,* 871–876.

Dagnelie, P.C., Vergote, F.J., van-Staveren, W.A., et al. (1990). High prevalence of rickets in infants on macrobiotic diets. *American Journal of Clinical Nutrition, 51,* 202–208.

Dech, B., & Budow, L. (1991). The use of fluoxitine in an adolescent with Prader-Willi syndrome. *Journal of the American Academy of Child and Adolescent Psychiatry, 30,* 298–302.

DeLong, G.R. (1993). Effects of nutrition on brain development in humans. *American Journal of Clinical Nutrition, 57*(2), 286S–290S.

Ekvall, S.W. (1993). *Pediatric nutrition in chronic diseases and developmental disorders: Prevention, assessment, and treatment.* New York: Oxford University Press.

Fee, M.A., Charney, E.B., & Robertson, W.W. (1988). Nutritional assessment of the young child with cerebral palsy. *Infants and Young Children, 1,* 33–40.

Finn, R. (1992). Food allergy: Fact or fiction: A review. *Journal of the Royal Society of Medicine, 85,* 560–564.

Frisancho, A.R. (1974). Tricep skinfold and upper arm muscle size norm for assessment of nutritional status. *American Journal of Clinical Nutrition, 27,* 1052–1058.

Goldberg, T., & Slonim, A.E. (1993). Nutrition therapy for hepatic glycogen storage disease. *Journal of the American Dietetic Association, 12,* 1423–1430.

Goldstein, D.J., & Potvin, J.H. (1994). Long-term weight loss: The effect of pharmacologic agents. *American Journal of Clinical Nutrition, 60,* 647–657.

Grundy, S.M., & Barnett, J.P. (1994). Metabolic and health complications of obesity. *Disease-a-Month, 36,* 641–731.

Guo, S., Roche, A.F., Fomon, S.J., et al. (1991). Reference data on gains in weight and length during the first two years of life. *Journal of Pediatrics, 119,* 355–362.

Hack, M., Breslau, N., Weissman, B., et al. (1991). Effect of very low birth weight and subnormal head size on cognitive abilities at school age. *New England Journal of Medicine, 325,* 231–237.

Halaas, J.L., Gajiwala, K.S., Maffel, M., et al. (1995). Weight-reducing effects of the plasma protein encoded by the obese gene. *Science, 269,* 543–546.

Hamill, P.V., Drizd, T.A., Johnson, C.L., et al. (1977). NCHS growth curves for children, birth–18 years. *Vital and Health Statistics, 11*(165), 56–61. Hyattsville, MD: U.S. Department of Health, Education, and Welfare, Public Health Service.

Hammer, L.D., Kraemer, H.C., Wilson, D.M., et al. (1991). Standardized percentile curves of body-mass index for children and adolescents. *American Journal of Diseases of Children, 145,* 259–263.

Hardy, S.C., & Kleinman, R.E. (1994). Fat and cholesterol in the diet of infants and young children: Implications for growth, development and long-term health. *Journal of Pediatrics, 125,* 69–77.

Haslam, R.H. (1992). Is there a role for megavitamin therapy in the treatment of attention deficit hyperactivity disorder? *Advances in Neurology, 58,* 303–310.

Havala, T., & Shronts, E. (1990). Managing the complications associated with refeeding. *Nutrition in Clinical Practice, 5,* 23–29.

Hokken-Koelega, A.C.S., De Ridder, M.A.J., Lemmen, R.J., et al. (1995). Children born small for gestational age: Do they catch up? *Pediatric Research, 38,* 267–271.

Huseman, C.A., Varma, M.M., & Angle, C.R. (1992). Neuroendocrine effects of toxic and low blood lead levels in children. *Pediatrics, 90,* 186–189.

Karlberg, P., Engstrom, I., Lichtenstein, H., et al. (1968). The development of children in a Swedish urban community: A prospective longitudinal study: III. Physical growth during the first three years of life. *Acta Paediatrica Scandinavica, 187*(Suppl.), 48–66.

Klish, W.J. (1990). Special infant formulas. *Pediatrics in Review, 12,* 55–61.

Krick, J., Murphy-Miller, P., Zeger, S., et al. (1996). Pattern of growth in children with cerebral palsy. *Journal of the American Dietetic Association, 96,* 680–685.

Lozoff, B., Jimenez, E., & Wolf, A.W. (1991). Long-term effects of iron deficiency anemia in infancy. *New England Journal of Medicine, 325,* 687–694.

Luke, A., Roizen, N.J., Sutton, M., et al. (1994). Energy expenditure in children with Down syndrome: Correcting metabolic rate for movement. *Journal of Pediatrics, 125,* 829–838.

Maggioni, A., & Lifshitz, F. (1995). Nutritional management of failure to thrive. *Pediatric Clinics of North America, 42,* 791–810.

Moffatt, M.E.K., Longstaffe, S., Besant, J., et al. (1994). Prevention of iron deficiency and psychomotor decline in high-risk infants through use of iron-fortified infant formula: A randomized clinical trial. *Journal of Pediatrics, 125,* 527–534.

Morgane, P.J., Austin-Lafarance, R., Bronzino, J., et al. (1993). Prenatal malnutrition and development of the brain. *Neuroscience and Biobehavioral Reviews, 17,* 91–128.

Nardella, M.T. (1995). Practical tips on tube-feedings for children. *Nutrition Focus, 10,* 1–8.

National Academy of Sciences, National Research Council. (1989). *Recommended dietary allowances* (10th ed.). Washington, DC: National Academy Press.

National Cholesterol Education Program. (1990). *Report of the expert panel on population strategies for blood cholesterol reduction* (DHHS Publication No. NIH 90-3046). Washington, DC: U.S. Government Printing Office.

Needleman, H.L. (1993). The current status of childhood lead toxicity. *Advances in Pediatrics, 40,* 125–139.

Needleman, H.L. (1994). Childhood lead poisoning. *Current Opinion in Neurology, 7,* 187–190.

Nutrition Labeling and Education Act Amendments of 1993, PL 103-80, 21 U.S.C. §107 *et seq.*

Opala, G., Winter, S., Vance, C., et al. (1991). The effect of valproic acid on plasma carnitine levels. *American Journal of Diseases of Children, 145,* 999–1001.

Perrone, L., Del Gaizo, D., D'Angelo, E., et al. (1994). Endocrine studies in children with myelomeningocoele. *Journal of Pediatric Endocrinology, 7,* 219–223.

Philip, A.T., & Gerson, B. (1994). Lead poisoning: Part I. Incidence, etiology, and toxicokinetics. *Clinics in Laboratory Medicine, 14,* 423–444.

Pollitt, E., Gorman, K.S., Engle, P.L., et al. (1995). Nutrition in early life and the fulfillment of intellectual potential. *Journal of Nutrition, 125,* 1111S–1118S.

Queen, P.M., & Lang, C.E. (1993). *Handbook of pediatric nutrition.* Rockville, MD: Aspen Publishers, Inc.

Rokusek, C., & Neinrichs, E. (1992). *Nutrition and feeding for persons with special needs* (2nd ed.).

Sioux Falls: South Dakota University Affiliated Program.

Rothman, K.J., Moore, L.L., Singer, M.R., et al. (1995). Teratogenicity of high vitamin A intake. *New England Journal of Medicine, 333,* 1369–1373.

Schonfeld, D.J. (1993). New developments in pediatric lead poisoning. *Current Opinion in Pediatrics, 5,* 537–544.

Scott, B.J., Artman, H., & St. Jean, S.T. (1992). Growth assessment in children: A review. *Topics in Clinical Nutrition, 8,* 5–31.

Shannon, M., & Graef, J.W.E. (1996). Lead intoxication in children with pervasive developmental disorders. *Journal of Toxicology and Clinical Toxicology, 34,* 177–181.

Shepherd, K., Roberts, D., Golding S., et al. (1991). Body composition in myelomeningocoele. *American Journal of Clinical Nutrition, 53,* 1–6.

Shils, M.E., Olson, J.A., & Shike, M. (1994). *Modern nutrition in health and disease* (8th ed.). Philadelphia: Lea & Febiger.

Smith, D.W. (1977). *Growth and its disorders: Basics and standards, approach and classifications, growth deficiency disorders, growth excess disorders, obesity.* Philadelphia: W.B. Saunders.

Solomon, S.M., & Kirby, D.F. (1990). The refeeding syndrome: A review. *Journal of Parenteral and Enteral Nutrition, 14,* 90–97.

Spender, Q., Cronk, C., Charney, E., et al. (1989). Assessment of linear growth of children with cerebral palsy: Use of alternative measures to height or length. *Developmental Medicine and Child Neurology, 31,* 206–214.

Stein, Z., & Susser, M. (1975). The Dutch famine, 1944–45, and the reproductive process. I: Effects on six indices at birth. *Pediatric Research, 9,* 70–76.

Stevenson, R.D. (1995). Use of segmental measures to estimate stature in children with cerebral palsy. *Archives of Pediatric and Adolescent Medicine, 149,* 658–662.

Stevenson, R.D., Hayes, R.P., Carter, L.V., et al. (1994). Clinical correlates of linear growth in children with cerebral palsy. *Developmental Medicine and Child Neurology, 36,* 135–142.

Suskind, R.M., & Lewind-Suskind, L. (1993). *Textbook of pediatric nutrition.* New York: Raven Press, Ltd.

Thomson, M.A., Bucolo, S., Quirk, P., et al. (1995). Measured versus predicted resting energy expenditure in infants: A need for reappraisal. *Journal of Pediatrics, 126,* 21–27.

Thorp, F.K., Peirce, P., & Deedwania, C. (1987). Nutrition in the infant and young child. In S.L. Halpern (Ed.), *Quick reference to clinical nutrition* (2nd ed., pp. 72–101). Philadelphia: J.B. Lippincott.

Tranms, C.M. (1995). Overview of assessment of nutritional status for children with metabolic disorders. *Nutrition Focus of the Washington Child Development and Mental Retardation Center, 10,* 1–8.

Vargas, A., & Tenore, A. (1993). Nutritional considerations in the development and treatment of psychosocial-deprivation dwarfism. In R.M. Suskind & L. Lewind-Suskind (Eds.), *Textbook of pediatric nutrition* (2nd ed.). New York: Raven Press, Ltd.

Warshaw, J.B. (1994). Intrauterine growth retardation. *Pediatric Rounds, 3,* 1–4.

Weintraub, M., Sundaresan, P.R., Madan, M., et al. (1992). Long-term weight control study I (weeks 0–34). *Clinical Pharmacological Therapy, 51,* 586–594.

Williams, C., Bollella, M., & Wynder, E.L. (1995). A new recommendation for dietary fiber in childhood. *Pediatrics, 96,* 985–988.

Winick, M. (Ed.). (1979). *Nutrition: Pre- and postnatal development.* New York: Plenum.

Winikoff, B. (1990). Breastfeeding. *Current Opinion in Obstetrics and Gynecology, 2,* 548–555.

Winikoff, B., Myers, D., Laukaran, V.H., et al. (1987). Overcoming obstacles to breastfeeding in a large municipal hospital: Applications of lessons learned. *Pediatrics, 80,* 423–433.

Winter, S.C., Szabo-Aczel, S., Curry, C.J.S., et al. (1987). Plasma carnitine deficiency: Clinical observations in 51 pediatric patients. *American Journal of Children, 141,* 660–665.

Yadrick, K., & Sneed, J. (1994). Nutrition services for children with developmental disabilities and chronic illnesses in education programs. *Journal of the American Dietetic Association, 94,* 1122–1128.

Zhang, Y., Proenca, R., Maffel, M., et al. (1994). Positional cloning of the mouse obese gene and its human homologue. *Nature, 372,* 425–432.

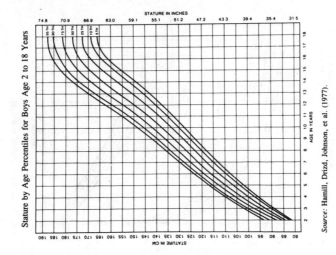

Stature by Age Percentiles for Boys Age 2 to 18 Years

Source: Hamill, Drizd, Johnson, et al. (1977).

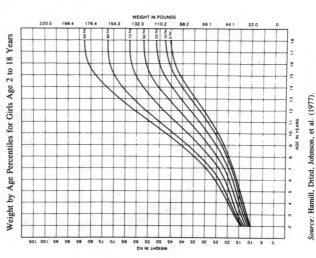

Weight by Age Percentiles for Girls Age 2 to 18 Years

Source: Hamill, Drizd, Johnson, et al. (1977).

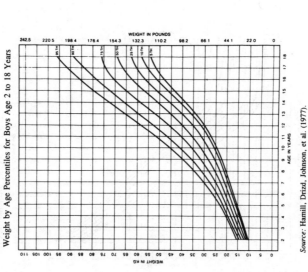

Weight by Age Percentiles for Boys Age 2 to 18 Years

Source: Hamill, Drizd, Johnson, et al. (1977).

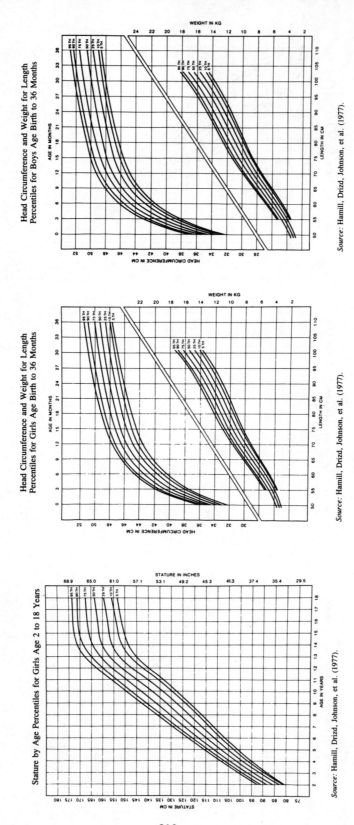

Head Circumference and Weight for Length Percentiles for Boys Age Birth to 36 Months

Source: Hamill, Drizd, Johnson, et al. (1977).

Head Circumference and Weight for Length Percentiles for Girls Age Birth to 36 Months

Source: Hamill, Drizd, Johnson, et al. (1977).

Stature by Age Percentiles for Girls Age 2 to 18 Years

Source: Hamill, Drizd, Johnson, et al. (1977).

11 | Vision

Our Window to the World

Sheryl J. Menacker
Mark L. Batshaw

Upon completion of this chapter, the reader will:

- be able to describe the anatomy of the eye
- know the function and common problems of the major parts of the eye
- be aware of some of the tests used to determine visual acuity
- understand how a child typically develops visual skills
- know the definition and some of the causes of visual impairment in children
- recognize some of the ways in which the development of a child with visual impairment differs from that of a sighted child and some approaches to intervention

Vision may be the most important sense for interpreting the world around us. When sight is impaired in childhood, it can have detrimental effects on physical, neurological, cognitive, and emotional development. Visual impairment in childhood is often part of a multiple disability disorder. Even as an isolated disability, severe visual impairment causes delays in walking and talking and affects behavior and socialization. If visual loss is identified early, however, effective interventions can be instituted. This chapter explores the embryonic development of the eye along with its structure and function. It also examines disorders of the eye and common visual problems of the child with disabilities. Finally, the effects of blindness on a child's development are discussed.

STRUCTURE OF THE EYE

In many ways, the structure of the eye is similar to that of a camera (Figure 11.1). In the eye, the thick, white fibrous covering called the sclera functions as the camera body, while the iris, the colored area that opens and closes in response to changes in light conditions, serves as the shutter. The pupil is the aperture in the center of the iris. Light rays entering the eye through the

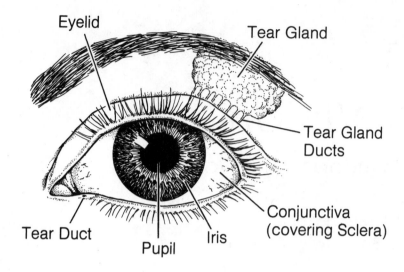

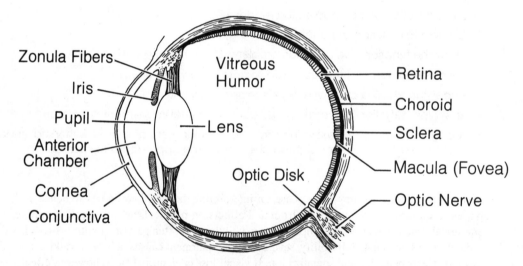

Figure 11.1.   The structure of the eye is similar to that of a camera.

pupil are focused first by the cornea, the clear dome that covers and protects the iris, and then by the lens, which lies behind the pupil. The cornea is the most important refracting surface of the eye. The lens further deflects light rays toward the retina, the photographic film of the eye, which lines the inner surface of the eye. The retina records the image in an upside-down, back-to-front format and sends the image via the optic nerve to the brain for interpretation.

The eye is primarily maintained in a ball shape by two substances: the aqueous humor, which is contained in the area between the cornea and the iris (the anterior chamber), and the translucent jelly-like vitreous humor, which fills the space between the lens and retina.

The eye itself sits in a bony socket of the skull, the orbit, which provides support and protection. This space also is occupied by blood vessels; extraocular muscles that move the eye; a lacrimal gland that produces tears; and the optic nerve that sends images from the eye to the brain. Additional protection for the eyeball is provided by the eyelids, eyelashes, and conjunctiva. Blinking the eyelids wipes dust and other foreign bodies from the surface of the eye. Eyelashes help to protect the eye from airborne debris. The conjunctiva, a thin, transparent layer covering the sclera, contains tiny nutritive blood vessels that give a "bloodshot" appearance to the eye when it is inflamed or infected (conjunctivitis).

DEVELOPMENT OF THE EYE

In the human embryo, the structures that will develop into eyes first appear at 4 weeks' gestation as two spherical bulbs at the side of the head (Figure 11.2). These bulbs gradually indent to form the optic cups. Three specialized cell layers in these cups subsequently develop into the various parts of the eye. By 7 weeks' gestation, when the embryo is only 1-inch long, the eyes have already assumed their basic form (Isenberg, 1988; Sadler, 1990). As fetal growth continues, the eyes gradually move from the side of the head to the center of the face. Any deviation from the path of typical development can lead to a wide variety of ocular defects, ranging from **anophthalmia,** a lack of eyes, to subtle abnormalities such as irregularly shaped pupils.

To illustrate the origin of malformations of the eye, consider a **coloboma,** a defect in the ocular tissue. Early in gestation, the developing eye is cup shaped. In order for the eye to become ball shaped, the edges of this cup must come together and form a "seam" that then must close imperceptibly during the seventh week of gestation. A coloboma results from any defect in the closure of this seam. Depending on the location and extent of the defect, it may result in anything from a keyhole shaped pupil, causing no visual impairment, to a malformation of the optic nerve and retina, causing severe visual impairment (Cook, Sulik, & Wright, 1995). As is true of most other eye malformations, a coloboma may occur as an isolated defect or as part of a syndrome, for example, as part of trisomy 13 or 18.

Abnormalities occurring later in embryogenesis, when the eyes usually migrate closer together, may lead to abnormal facial features such as **hypertelorism.** Finally, intrauterine infections (see Chapter 4) can cause **chorioretinitis,** cataracts, glaucoma, and/or other anomalies that lead to both an abnormal facial appearance and severe visual impairment (Table 11.1).

DEVELOPMENT OF VISUAL SKILLS

As in the acquisition of language and motor skills, vision has developmental milestones (Friendly, 1993). Although the eyes have good optical clarity within days of birth, the visual system remains immature in many respects (Simons, 1993). The **fovea,** the part of the retina that is responsible for fine visual acuity, is not well-developed at birth. Cells in this region undergo a process of growth and organization that does not reach maturity until approximately 4 years of age (Boothe, Dobson, & Teller, 1985). Similarly, the connections between the eye and the brain mature over several years. At birth, visual acuity is estimated to be 20/400 according to behavioral measures (Teland & Dweck, 1989), reaching adult levels of 20/20 only by 3–5 years of age (Boothe et al., 1985). Fixation and following motions are usually present by approximately 3 months of age (Friendly, 1989), and binocular function develops between 3 and 7 months of age (Boothe et al., 1985; Braddick & Atkinson, 1982). Because of the lack of binocular vision prior to this age, misalignment of the eyes (strabismus) is not uncommon or necessarily abnormal.

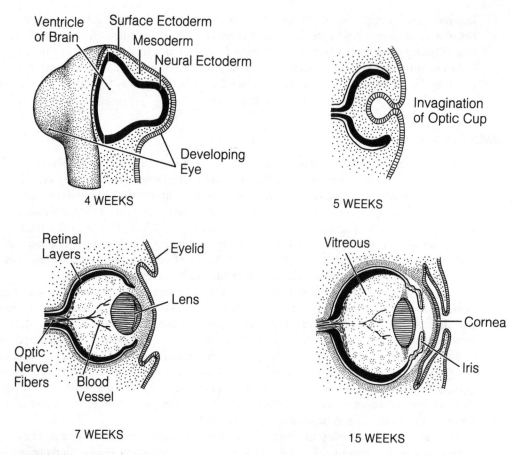

Figure 11.2. Embryonic development of the eye. The eyes first appear at 4 weeks' gestational age as two spherical bulges at the side of the head. They indent in the next week to form the optic cups. By 7 weeks, the eyes have already assumed their basic form. The eye is completely formed by 15 weeks.

Amblyopia

During childhood, visual development is an ongoing process. As an important part of this process, the brain must learn how to put together information sent from both eyes and make one picture. If the image from one eye is clear and the other blurry or if the eyes are misaligned and send two different pictures, however, the brain will ignore the picture sent from one eye. A condition called amblyopia results when the brain consistently ignores the information from the same eye. Amblyopia means that there is subnormal visual acuity despite the typical physical appearance of an eye (Rubin & Nelson, 1993; von Noorden, 1996). Using the analogy of the eye as a camera and the brain as the photo-processing machinery, the problem causing amblyopia is not that the camera (eye) is defective, but that the photo processor (brain) is not properly developing the "film" it is receiving.

It has been estimated that amblyopia affects more than 2% of the general population and causes loss of vision in more people under age 45 than all ocular diseases and trauma combined

Table 11.1.   Selected genetic syndromes associated with eye abnormalities

Syndrome	Eye abnormality
Lowe	Cataracts, glaucoma
Zellweger	Cataracts, retinitis pigmentosa
Marfan	Dislocated lens
Homocystinuria	Dislocated lens, glaucoma
Osteogenesis imperfecta	Blue sclera, cataract
Osteopetrosis	Cranial nerve palsies, optic atrophy
Aicardi	Retinal abnormalities
Tuberous sclerosis	Retinal defects, iris depigmentation
Tay-Sachs disease	Cherry red spot of macula, optic nerve atrophy
Hurler	Cloudy cornea
Galactosemia	Cataract
CHARGE association	Coloboma, microphthalmos
Trisomy 13, trisomy 18	Microphthalmos, corneal opacities, coloboma

(Magramm, 1992; von Noorden, 1996). With early recognition and treatment of the underlying cause of amblyopia, however, visual loss can be minimized or even completely restored. The extent of visual impairment resulting from amblyopia ranges from mild to profound and depends on the underlying defect, the age of onset, and the delay in identification and treatment.

Because the visual system matures with age, the risk of developing amblyopia is greatest in early childhood and decreases as visual maturity is approached. Although the age of visual maturation has not been definitively determined in humans, it is generally believed to occur by 7 years of age (von Noorden, 1996). Early treatment of the problem causing amblyopia, combined with occlusive patching of the better eye, has been shown to improve visual acuity. Treatment may range from correcting a refractive error with glasses to surgically removing a cataract. After age 9, however, it is unusual for intervention to significantly improve visual acuity in an amblyopic eye (von Noorden, 1996; Woodruff, Hiscox, Thompson, et al., 1994).

Visual Development in Children with Disabilities

Many of the causes of developmental disabilities can also affect maturation of the visual system. Accordingly, the prevalence of significant ocular disorders among individuals with developmental disabilities has been reported to range from 48% to 75%. Processes governing eye motions, alignment, visual acuity, and visual perception may mature slowly, partially, or abnormally in these children. Refractive errors, ocular misalignment, and eye movement disorders are especially frequent (Edwards, Price, & Weisskopf, 1972; Henry, 1980; Jacobson, 1988; Landau & Berson, 1971; Maino, Maino, & Maino, 1990; Orel-Bixler, Haegerstrom-Portnoy, & Hall,

1989). Because of these associations, it is important to include an ophthalmic evaluation in the overall assessment of children with disabilities.

FUNCTION AND DISEASES OF THE EYE

In this section, the functions of the cornea, anterior chamber, lens, retina, optic nerves, visual cortex, and eye muscles are reviewed, along with some of the common disorders that affect them.

The Cornea

The cornea focuses an image on the most light-sensitive part of the retina, the fovea centralis. This is accomplished in the following manner: When a person looks at a tree, a series of parallel rays of light leave the tree and reach the dome-shaped surface of the cornea, where they are refracted, or bent, toward a focal point on the retina. If everything works properly, the rays are further deflected by the lens and come into focus on the fovea, resulting in a sharp image that is transmitted to the brain (Figure 11.3). However, if the cornea is cloudy or deformed, the images will be blurred and indistinct. This requires prompt evaluation and treatment to avoid amblyopia. The most common causes of a cloudy cornea are birth trauma, certain inborn errors of metabolism, and congenital glaucoma.

The Anterior Chamber

In the anterior chamber, located behind the cornea and in front of the iris, pressure is kept within typical limits by drainage of the aqueous humor through a passageway at the angle where the cornea meets the iris, called Schlemm's canal (Figure 11.4). If this canal is blocked or provides slow drainage, the intraocular pressure rises and causes glaucoma.

Glaucoma

In children, glaucoma most commonly represents a congenital abnormality (Wagner, 1993). It also can occur, however, as a result of an intrauterine infection, retinopathy of prematurity (ROP), eye trauma, or chronic inflammation. Glaucoma also has been observed in certain genetic syndromes (e.g., neurofibromatosis) and inborn errors of metabolism (e.g., homocystinuria).

Glaucoma causes approximately 4% of all blindness in children (Nelson, Calhoun, & Harley, 1991). The hallmarks of this condition are an enlarged hazy cornea, excessive tearing, light sensitivity, and eye pain. Once the diagnosis has been made, oral or ophthalmic medication may be used to decrease the intraocular pressure until surgery can be performed. This entails a microsurgical procedure, in which the meshwork in the anterior chamber angle is cut to open a passageway, permitting drainage of the aqueous humor. Early treatment results in successful preservation of vision in 90% of affected children (Franks & Taylor, 1989). Additional surgery may be required over time, however, so the child needs to be followed carefully for signs of elevated intraocular pressure throughout life. Delayed treatment can result in blindness of the affected eye.

The Lens

The lens, the second refracting surface of the eye, is a translucent, globular body located behind the iris, about one third of the way between the cornea and retina. It is convex on both sides and is attached by ciliary muscles to the inside of the eye. Stretching or relaxing these muscles changes the shape of the lens, fine tuning the focus to accommodate changes in the distance of

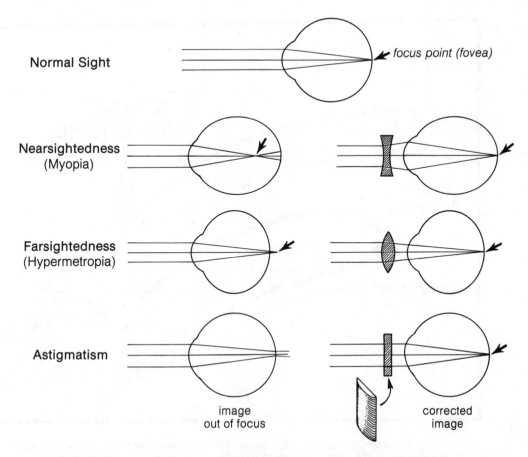

Figure 11.3.   Refractive errors. If the eyeball is too long, images are focused in front of the retina (myopia). A concave lens deflects the rays, correcting the problem. If the eyeball is too short, the image focuses behind the retina and is again blurred (hypermetropia). A convex lens corrects this. In astigmatism, the eyeball is the correct size, but typically the cornea is misshapen. A cylindrical lens is required to compensate. (From *Your child has a disability: A complete sourcebook of daily and medical care* by Mark Batshaw [p. 164]. Copyright © 1991 by M.L. Batshaw; illustrations copyright © 1991 by Lynn Reynolds. Boston: Little, Brown; reprinted by permission.)

an object from the eye (Figure 11.5). When light comes from a distant object, the rays are close together and well focused. Because little refraction is needed, the ciliary muscles tighten and pull the lens so that it is stretched to minimally refract the light rays (Figure 11.5). To see a nearby object, where the rays are more dispersed, the ciliary muscles relax so that the lens assumes a more globular shape and has greater refractive power. As a person ages, the lens becomes less flexible and therefore less able to accommodate, causing near vision to become blurred (**presbyopia**). Wearing bifocals or reading glasses helps to compensate for this loss of flexibility.

Cataracts

The major disorder affecting the lens is a **cataract.** This term refers to any defect in clarity of the lens. Small cataracts often remain stable and do not need to be removed. A cataract, however, of-

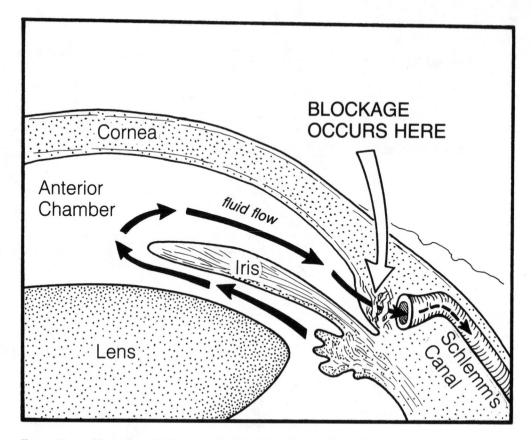

Figure 11.4. Glaucoma. Fluid normally drains from the anterior chamber through Schlemm's canal. A blockage in this passage leads to the accumulation of fluid and pressure, a condition called glaucoma.

ten becomes dense enough to be visible as a white object in the pupil. At this point, it is likely to significantly obscure vision (Figure 11.6). Although cataracts are primarily seen in adults, they also occur in about 1 in 250 infants, accounting for about 15% of blindness in children (Moore, 1994). A cataract may be an isolated abnormality or part of a syndrome or disease. For example, children with galactosemia, congenital rubella, and eye trauma may develop cataracts (Endres & Shin, 1990).

If a cataract is large enough to interfere with vision, it should be removed immediately to avoid amblyopia (Potter, 1993). A congenital cataract, for example, should be removed in the first months of life. This is done by a microsurgical procedure in which the contents of the lens are cut up and then aspirated, leaving only the outer shell of the lens intact. The surgery is quite safe and can be performed as an outpatient procedure. When the lens is removed, however, one of the two refracting mechanisms of the eye is eliminated. To compensate for the loss of the natural lens, a contact lens, thick glasses, or an intraocular lens implant is used. Contact lenses are used in both very young and older children with unilateral or bilateral cataract extraction. Thick glasses are quite often employed for very young children with bilateral cataracts. Intraocular

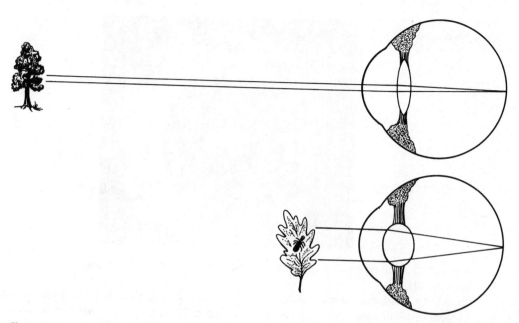

Figure 11.5. Accommodation. The lens changes shape to focus on a near or far object. The lens becomes thin and less refractive for distant objects, but rounded and more refractive for near vision.

lenses are generally reserved for older children with unilateral cataracts. The prognosis for vision depends both on how long the cataract has been affecting vision prior to its removal and on how compliant the child and parents are with visual rehabilitation by way of contact lenses, glasses, and/or patching following surgery.

The Retina

The retina is the light-sensitive "film" of the eye on which visual images are focused before transmission to the brain. Two layers, the sclera and the choroid, underlie the retina, providing support, protection, and nourishment (Figure 11.1). Within the retina are two types of light sensitive cells, or **photoreceptors:** rods and cones. Both types of cells respond to light by undergoing a chemical reaction.

For detailed vision, such as reading, seeing distant objects, and color vision, cones are needed. They are located primarily in the fovea centralis, or macula, where central vision is processed. Each cone is sensitive to one of three distinct colors: red, green, or blue (Figure 11.7). The light from a colored object elicits a different response from each type of cone and leads to a patchwork pattern that is interpreted in the brain as shades of color and shape. In the more peripheral areas of the retina, rods predominate. Rods function in conditions of diminished light and are therefore necessary for night vision (Figure 11.7).

Disorders of Photoreceptors

A number of disorders involve abnormalities in the rods or cones. The most common is color blindness in which one of the three types of cones is either abnormal or missing from birth. Red-

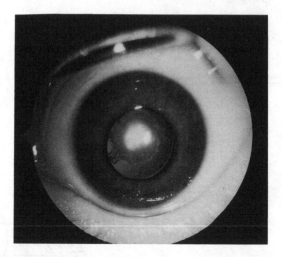

Figure 11.6.   Photograph of a cataract, the white body seen through the pupil.

green color blindness, the most common form, is typically inherited as an X-linked trait and affects about 8% of men and 1% of women (see Chapter 2). Although affected individuals are able to correctly identify the color of common moderate-to-large size items, such as automobiles, solid colored carpets, and walls, they will have great difficulty identifying colors in small objects and in the lines of a plaid. When viewing traffic lights, the red and yellow lights will be indistinguishable. However, the green traffic light falls on the blue side of the spectrum and appears white or colorless, easily distinguishable from the red and yellow lights (Breton & Nelson, 1983). Ordinary color blindness does not cause a decrease in vision.

Other diseases can affect the cones or rods after birth. For example, a dietary deficiency of vitamin A may cause impairment of night vision, which may improve after replenishment of the vitamin impairment (Haynes & Pulido, 1995). In retinitis pigmentosa, a group of related genetic disorders, the rods and/or cones undergo a process of degeneration. Night blindness is usually the first symptom, followed by generalized and more severe visual impairment (Kimura, Drack, & Stone, 1995).

Retinopathy of Prematurity

In infants, the most common cause of retinal damage is ROP. Nearly two thirds of infants weighing less than 1,251 grams (less than 3 pounds) at birth will develop some degree of ROP (Keith & Doyle, 1995). Although the incidence of this disorder has remained stable in the 1990s, the prevalence of affected infants has increased because of the increase in survival among very low birth weight infants (Phelps, 1993).

ROP results from vascular damage to the retina. During the fourth month of gestation, retinal blood vessels begin their growth at the optic nerve in the back of the eye. By the ninth month they have reached the furthest edges of the retina toward the front of the eye (Cook et al., 1995). In preterm infants, however, maturation of the retinal blood vessels is not yet complete, predisposing these infants to retinopathy and its consequences, which include nearsightedness (**my-**

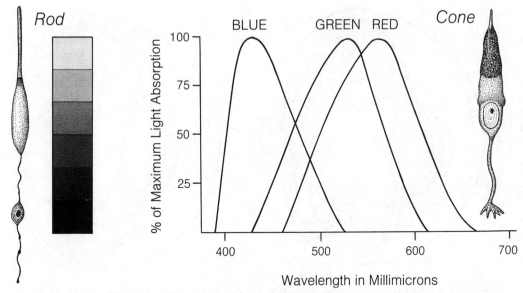

Figure 11.7.   Rods react in low light conditions, allowing night vision. Cones are needed for color vision. There are three types of cones, each of which is sensitive to one of the three spectra of color: red, blue, or green. The absence of or damage to one type of cone leads to color blindness.

opia), strabismus, glaucoma, and blindness (Figure 11.8) (Birch & Spencer, 1991; Quinn, 1992; Quinn, Dobson, Barr, et al., 1991; Quinn, Dobson, Repka, et al., 1992; Schaffer, Quinn, & Johnson, 1984).

The cause of ROP is not completely known, although the oxygen supplementation used to treat respiratory distress syndrome plays a major role. The best way to prevent the problem is to delay delivery of a premature infant so that the retinal blood vessels have more time to mature (see Chapter 7). Other preventive measures include providing surfactant replacement therapy to mitigate the severity of respiratory distress syndrome and to use the lowest concentrations of oxygen supplementation possible. Initial enthusiasm for using large doses of vitamin E, an antioxidant, as a prophylaxis has waned (Johnson, Quinn, Abbasi, et al., 1989).

Although ROP cannot be completely prevented, early detection permits effective treatment. An ophthalmologist should examine the retina of the premature infant at specified intervals during the first months of life. If abnormal blood vessel development progresses to meet specific criteria, **cryo,** or laser, therapy can be used to cauterize the **avascular** area of the retina. This decreases the likelihood of macular distortion and retinal detachment and has considerably reduced the risk of blindness resulting from ROP. There remains a high frequency of nearsightedness, but this can usually be corrected with glasses.

Besides ROP, the retina can be damaged by brain trauma in which there is a retinal hemorrhage or tear. In addition, certain inborn errors of metabolism, such as Tay-Sachs disease, are associated with deposits of toxic material in the choroid and retina. Finally, retinal tumors, such as retinoblastoma, can lead to blindness. Diagnosis of a retinal disorder is made by an ophthalmological examination and/or electroretinogram.

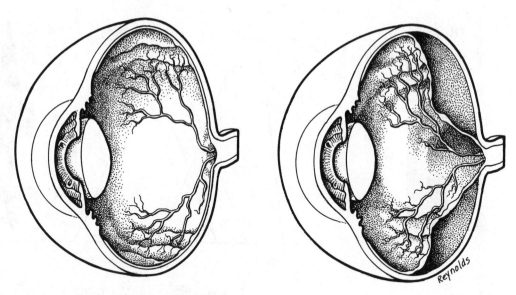

Figure 11.8.   Retinopathy of prematurity. Blood vessels in the retina proliferate (left figure). Eventually they stop growing, leaving a fibrous scar that contracts in the most severe cases and pulls the retina away from the back of the eye, causing blindness (right figure). (From *Your child has a disability: A complete sourcebook of daily and medical care* by Mark Batshaw [p. 165]. Copyright © 1991 by M.L. Batshaw; illustrations copyright © 1991 by Lynn Reynolds. Boston: Little, Brown; reprinted by permission.)

The Optic Nerves

The surface of the retina contains more than 1 million optic nerve fibers that are connected to the rods and cones. The fibers come together at the back of the eye in an area called the optic disc. This region is also known as the blind spot because it contains nerve fibers but no rods or cones; therefore, no vision occurs when light rays are projected onto this area of the eye (Figure 11.1).

One optic nerve emerges from behind each eye and begins its journey toward the brain. Some of the fibers from each nerve cross at a point called the optic chiasm that rests within the skull just before the nerves enter the brain (Figure 11.9). Each optic nerve (now called a tract) continues through the cerebral hemisphere to the occipital lobe (Figure 11.9). Here the image received by the retina is perceived and coordinated with the sounds transmitted from the ears to form a complete message that can be interpreted. Because some nerve fibers from each eye cross to the opposite side, each eye sends information to both the right and left sides of the brain. Therefore, damage to either the right or left optic tract at any point after the optic chiasm will cause an impairment in the visual field of both eyes (Figure 11.9). By identifying the part of a visual field affected, an ophthalmologist often can determine where the damage has occurred.

The Visual Cortex

The visual cortex is the region of the occipital lobe responsible for receiving and decoding information sent by the eyes. Damage to this area can result in a type of visual loss called cortical visual impairment (CVI), which in children is most commonly caused by oxygen deprivation (hypoxia), infections of the central nervous system, brain trauma, and hydrocephalus (Brodsky, Baker, & Hamed, 1996; Good, Jan, DeSa, et al., 1994; Hoyt, 1987; Lambert, 1995; Whiting, Jan, Wong, et al., 1985). CVI is one of the major causes of visual impairment in children in the de-

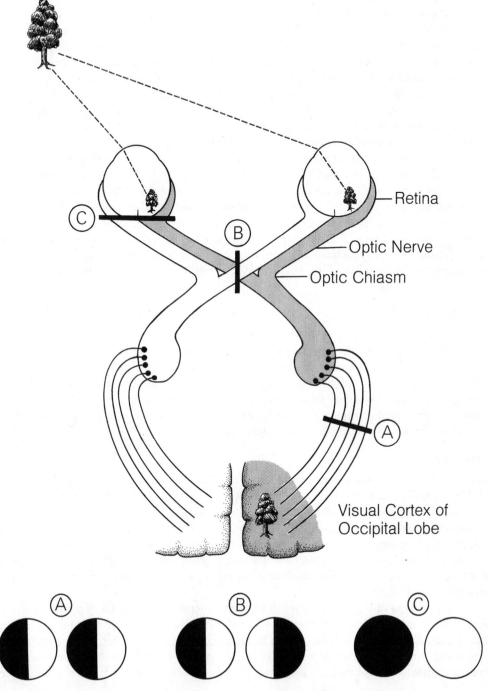

Figure 11.9.   The visual pathway. One optic nerve emerges from behind each eye. A portion of the fibers from each crosses at the optic chiasm. An abnormality at various points along the route (upper figure) will lead to different patterns of visual loss (lower figure). These are illustrated: A) abnormality at the cortical pathway; B) damage to the optic chiasm; C) retinal damage.

veloped world. Advances in neonatal care have resulted in saving the lives of an increased number of infants with cortical damage at the same time that advances in ophthalmology have resulted in a decrease in blindness from treatable causes. Together, these two factors have increased the proportion of blindness in children due to CVI (Brodsky et al., 1996). Although vision testing initially may indicate extremely poor vision in such cases, most children do recover some visual function (Hoyt, 1986a; Lambert, 1995). Most do not bump into objects when walking and do not have visual self-stimulation behavior, such as eye pressing, that is commonly associated with retinal blindness (Whiting et al., 1985). It is not fully understood why vision may improve in children with CVI, but it has been hypothesized that alternate neuronal pathways or cortical areas take over some visual function.

It is important to differentiate CVI from delayed visual maturation (DVM) in the infant with visual inattention. As with CVI, infants with DVM do not show a response to visual stimuli. In general, however, these children have normal gestational and birth histories, normal ocular examinations, no cortical abnormalities, and usually only mild to moderate developmental delays (Brodsky et al., 1996; Lambert, Kriss, & Taylor, 1989; Skarf, 1989). As the name of the condition implies, those with DVM generally have an excellent visual prognosis, with improvement of visual function spontaneously occurring in infancy as overall development of the child progresses (Brodsky et al., 1996; Skarf, 1989). The etiology of DVM is poorly understood (Brodsky et al., 1996).

The Eye Muscles

Six eye muscles direct the eye toward an object and maintain binocular vision (Figure 11.10). Four of these muscles lie along the upper, lower, inner, and outer portions of the eye and are responsible primarily for moving it up, down, in, and out. The other two are placed obliquely and help rotate the eye. Three nerves originating in the brainstem control the movement of these six muscles (one nerve drives four muscles, and the other two nerves drive one muscle each). The complex, coordinated movement of these eye muscles allows us to look in all directions without turning our heads and to maintain proper alignment of the eyes.

Strabismus

The loss of this coordinated movement leads to misalignment of the eyes, or strabismus. Overall, this occurs in about 3%–4% of children. However, it occurs in 15% of former premature infants and in 40% of children with cerebral palsy (Nelson et al., 1991). Two main forms of strabismus exist: **esotropia,** in which the eyes turn in, and **exotropia,** in which the eyes turn out (Figure 11.10). Esotropia is the more common of the two. Strabismus may be apparent all the time or intermittently, such as when the child tires. Intermittent strabismus is unlikely to cause amblyopia; however, uncorrected, ongoing deviations in a child younger than the age of 9 years may lead to amblyopia.

Misalignment of the eyes may result from an abnormality in eye focusing, in the nerves supplying the eye muscles, or in the brain (Wright, 1995). In terms of eye focusing, quite often farsightedness is the cause of esotropia. In this case, corrective glasses improve both the child's vision and esotropia (Lavrich & Nelson, 1993). In cerebral palsy, brain damage may alter the brain's signals to the eye muscles and cause strabismus. Here, corrective eye muscle surgery

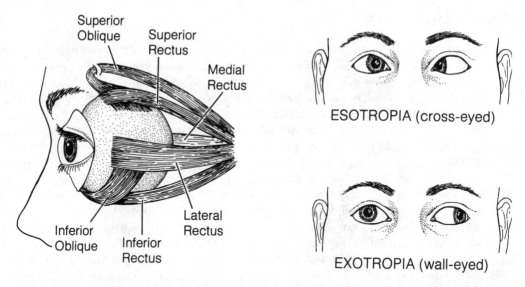

Figure 11.10.   The eye muscles. Six muscles move the eyeball. A weakness of one of these muscles causes strabismus. In esotropia, the eye turns in, while in exotropia, the eye turns out. Esotropia and exotropia of the left eye are illustrated.

may be necessary to realign the eyes. This is also true for the child with hydrocephalus who develops strabismus as a result of nerve palsy caused by increased intracranial pressure. Approximately 75% of children show good ocular alignment following surgery.

REFRACTIVE ERRORS IN CHILDREN

As discussed previously, light entering the eye is focused by the cornea and lens. Under optimal conditions, the light rays will be perfectly refracted onto the retina, resulting in a clearly focused image. If the eye is too long or the refracting mechanisms of the eye are too strong, the focused image falls in front of the retina, and the picture is blurred (Figure 11.3). This is called myopia, or nearsightedness. If the eye is too short or the refracting mechanisms are too weak, the image is focused behind the retina, also producing a blurred image (Figure 11.3). In this instance, the person has **hyperopia,** or farsightedness. The other common refractive problem is **astigmatism** (Figure 11.3). Astigmatism typically occurs when the surface of the cornea has an elliptical rather than spherical shape. Because of this, light rays entering the eye do not focus on a single point and the image is blurred.

Hyperopia is the most common refractive error of childhood. The important difference between myopia and hyperopia is that with hyperopia, the eye can use its power of accommodation to further focus light rays onto the retina. As a result, most children with hyperopia will have excellent visual acuity. With myopia, there is no such mechanism to fine tune the improperly focused distant images. Therefore, children with hyperopia generally will not have problems with visual acuity at distance or near, while children with myopia will have blurred distant vision.

Prescribing Glasses for Children

Glasses are usually prescribed for children if blurred vision interferes with daily functions, if there is a risk of amblyopia, or if there is misalignment of the eyes. Because the eye is able to use its power of accommodation to correct mild to moderate farsightedness, glasses are not usually necessary unless the eyes also turn in or if the level of hyperopia exceeds the amount the eye can comfortably accommodate. Although the eye is not able to compensate for myopia, glasses may not be necessary for children with mild myopia, because good visual acuity should be present within a comfortable near range, and the visual demands required for sustained viewing conditions at distance (e.g., driving, looking across the room at a blackboard) are not required in the young child's daily routine. Similarly, correction of mild astigmatic errors may not be necessary if visual acuity without correction is adequate for the child's visual needs. When there is a significant difference in refractive error between eyes (**anisometropia**), however, glasses should be prescribed to avert amblyopia. In these cases, glasses promote equal clarity of the images focused on the retina of each eye and ultimately sent to the brain.

Glasses are also used to treat strabismus, especially when the eyes are turning in to accommodate for farsightedness. In this case, the eyeglasses must be worn at all times, and the eyes will usually turn inward when the glasses are removed. However, over time, gradual changes in the prescription may allow good alignment even without glasses. Glasses are less commonly prescribed when the eyes turn out and the patient is myopic, although they may help to decrease the amount or frequency of the exotropia (Caltrider & Jampolsky, 1983).

Eyeglasses can be prescribed even for the youngest infant and the child with multiple disabilities. This is because a method exists for assessing refractive errors that relies completely on objective measures rather than on subjective input from the child. After instillation of eyedrops, which dilate the pupils and paralyze accommodation, the ophthalmologist looks at the child's eyes through a retinoscope and can determine, using lenses of varying powers, the refractive error and the required correction. Eyeglasses can then be prescribed.

Eyeglasses in children should be made of polycarbonate plastic rather than glass. Although plastic lenses scratch more easily, they are lighter, safer, and last longer. Frames with cable temples and spring hinges tend to fit best in smaller children. Contact lenses are used in infants and children when a cataract has been extracted from one eye, because glasses with one very strong lens and one regular lens will not provide normal binocular vision. Although contact lenses also may be preferred by teenagers, the age at which they may be worn depends on the child's commitment and ability to accept responsibility for cleaning and inserting the lenses. Whether glasses or contacts are used, testing should be repeated at least once a year because the child's eyes are likely to grow, causing the prescription to change.

VISION TESTS

Assessing the visual function of children with developmental disabilities is critical in helping to determine the best interventions (Mackie, McCulloch, Saunders, et al., 1995). On the one hand, if testing shows that a child has poor vision, educational interventions based principally on visual learning will be frustrating and ineffective. On the other hand, testing may show that the child has better visual function than anticipated, allowing for a more visually based approach to meet therapeutic and educational objectives. Vision testing can be quite effective even when the child will not cooperate. Tests of visual acuity fall into two general categories: those based on an examiner's assessment through observation or eye charts, which can be conducted by any careful and patient observer, and those utilizing higher technology, for which special training and equipment are required.

Assessing Visual Function Through Acuity Charts and Observation

For the verbal and cooperative child who can identify characters on an eye chart, determination of visual acuity is relatively easy. Visual acuity in nonverbal children also can be successfully evaluated by having them point to a figure on a hand-held near card on request (Figure 11.11) (Allen, 1957). Although this may not accurately reflect visual acuity at a distance, it is a good indication of function within the range where vision is most important for children (Ipata, Cioni, Bottai, et al., 1994). Although it is easier to test visual acuity by showing characters one at a time rather than in groups, this tends to underestimate amblyopia because acuity is better for single symbols than groups, a phenomenon called the crowding effect (von Noorden, 1996). This problem is avoided by a method of visual acuity testing for both verbal and nonverbal children that uses a distance chart in which only the letters H, O, T, and V appear, with black bars beside the letters allowing characters to be shown individually (Jenkins, Prager, Mazow, et al., 1983). A card containing the letters H, O, T, and V is placed on the child's lap. As each letter is presented on the distance chart, the child is asked to point to the corresponding character on the lap card. It does not require familiarity with the alphabet but does entail comprehension, coordination, and cooperation on the part of the child.

Another type of acuity testing, called *contrast sensitivity,* measures the minimal amount of contrast required to resolve objects of various sizes from the background and represents a more sensitive test of visual function. In conditions such as cerebral lesions and amblyopia, ordinary high-contrast visual acuity testing may report normal functioning, but contrast sensitivity testing often reveals abnormalities (Stout & Wright, 1995). Identifying decreased contrast sensitivity allows those involved in the child's care to choose high-contrast visual stimuli in order to best meet therapeutic, educational, and even recreational needs. Several different charts and tests are available to assess contrast sensitivity in children. They are recognizable by optotypes, ranging in contrast from black to very light gray.

Although ophthalmic evaluation of the verbal, cooperative child may be relatively easy, a good assessment can be achieved even in children who are minimally interactive due to age or disability. When the child is alert and calm, much information can be ascertained by observation alone. Does the child gaze at the surrounding environment and fixate on objects or people? Or do the eyes wander aimlessly, have unusual motions, or remain directed in one position? Making good eye contact with the examiner as well as steadily fixating and following a face or toy indicate the presence of some functional vision. Wandering eye motions, to-and-fro oscillations of the eyes, and eyes that always gaze in one direction are warning flags for significant visual dysfunction. Children who display any of these actions should receive a comprehensive evaluation by an ophthalmologist.

Assessing Visual Function Through Higher Technology

The ophthalmologist is often consulted to determine whether a child with disabilities can see and, if so, to what degree. There are several techniques available for testing visual function without relying on verbal responses or character recognition. These techniques are well suited to as-

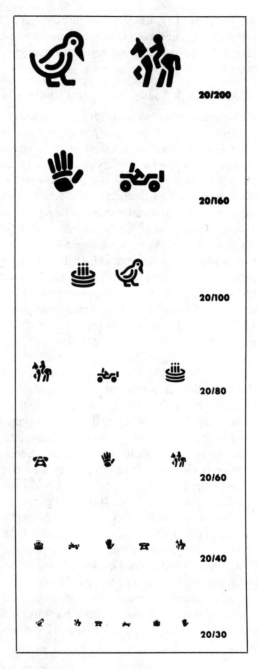

Figure 11.11.   Allen Kindergarten Chart (actual size). The child names the various pictures down as far as he or she can go on a card held 18" away from face. The smallest line that can be named indicates visual acuity. (Courtesy of Richmond Products, Inc.)

sessing vision in children with developmental disabilities and include optokinetic nystagmus, preferential looking, and electrophysiological testing.

Optokinetic Nystagmus

The optokinetic nystagmus (OKN) response is determined by rotating a black-and-white striped cylinder in front of the child's eyes. Similar to the effect of watching a picket fence from a passing car, the child's eyes should jiggle back and forth (nystagmus) as he or she slowly follows the movement of one stripe and then quickly jerks back to fixate on another. OKN is an involuntary response that should be present soon after birth (Boothe et al., 1985; Lewis, Maurer, & Brent, 1989). It is estimated that the minimum vision necessary for an OKN response is perception of fingers held in front of the eyes (Burde, Savino, & Trobe, 1985). OKN also may be employed to assess quality of visual acuity by using progressively thinner stripes and ascertaining the thinnest that produce a response.

Although the presence of an OKN response is reassuring, its absence does not necessarily indicate poor visual function. It may simply be due to inattention to the stripes that are held too far away or moved too quickly to produce a response (Friendly, 1989; Hoyt, 1986b; Lewis et al., 1989). Despite its shortcomings, OKN testing is a quick, easy, inexpensive, and noninvasive method of evaluating visual function in infants, nonverbal children, and those with disabilities.

Preferential Looking Techniques

One of the exciting advances in visual acuity testing has been the advent of preferential looking (PL) techniques. PL testing relies on the fact that an infant will preferentially fixate on a boldly patterned striped target rather than an on equally luminous blank target (Teller, McDonald, Preston, et al., 1986). The child is shown a series of cards containing a pattern of black-and-white stripes, or gratings, on one side and a blank gray target of equal luminance on the other side (Dobson, Quinn, Saunders, et al., 1995). The stripe widths become progressively thinner on successive cards, creating finer gratings that require better visual resolution (Figure 11.12). The tester presents the cards at a predetermined distance and watches the child's fixation through a peephole in the center of each card. The finest set of stripes for which the child reliably looks to the patterned side is called the grating visual acuity.

Acuity card testing has been shown to correlate well with traditional estimates of visual acuity (Quinn, Berlin, & James, 1993). Despite the fact that it relies on the clinical judgment and possible bias of the tester, there is good interobserver agreement (Hertz & Rosenberg, 1992; Mohn, van Hof-van Duin, Fetter, et al., 1988; Teller et al., 1986). The overall success rate for being able to perform PL testing in children with developmental disabilities ranges from 82% to 99% (Bane & Birch, 1992; Hertz & Rosenberg, 1992; Hertz, Rosenberg, Sjo, et al., 1988; Mohn et al., 1988). To its advantage, PL testing can be accomplished in minutes, requires no devices to be attached to the child, does not require speech or recognition behavior, and is relatively inexpensive. It may, however, overestimate visual acuity in cases of amblyopia (Friendly, 1989; Mohn et al., 1988; Teller et al., 1986) or underestimate visual acuity in children with eye movement abnormalities, and it requires some level of cooperation. Despite these limitations, PL testing is a useful and easily performed method of evaluating acuity in infants and children with developmental disabilities.

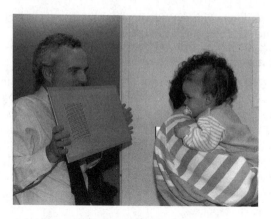

Figure 11.12.   Teller preferential looking cards. The infant is held and a grating pattern on a card is shown on one side and a gray color card on the other. The baby prefers the grating to a plain color. The sides are switched to ensure the baby is looking at the pattern. Successively smaller gratings are shown until the child no longer shows a preference, indicating that he or she cannot differentiate the stripes from the solid color. The smallest discriminable size determines the grating visual acuity. (Courtesy of Graham Quinn, M.D., Children's Hospital of Philadelphia.)

Electrophysiological Testing: Electroretinogram and Visual Evoked Potential

Electrophysiological testing of the visual system is an important part of the clinical investigation when visual disability is suspected. This testing can determine whether the problem lies primarily in the eyes or the brain. The electroretinogram (ERG) tests retinal functioning, whereas the visual evoked potential (VEP) analyzes the pathway between the eye and the visual cortex in the brain.

Electroretinogram   In ERG testing, modified contact lenses are placed on the corneas of the child after instillation of topical anesthetic drops. Depending on the type of equipment used, 1–3 electrodes are also affixed to the face and/or body. Lights are momentarily flashed in the child's eyes under different conditions while a computer analyzes the information received from the electrodes and from the leads attached to the contact lenses. In order for the ERG to evaluate both the retinal rods, which function in the dark, and the cones, which function in conditions of light, individuals are dark adapted prior to testing by wearing an opaque black blindfold for approximately 30 minutes. Sedation may be necessary in some children for optimal cooperation and results.

The ERG is particularly useful in demonstrating diseases of the retina such as retinitis pigmentosa and its related syndromes, several of which are associated with developmental disabilities (e.g., Laurence-Moon-Biedl syndrome, neuronal ceroid-lipofuscinoses, infantile phytanic acid storage disease, Usher syndrome). In certain types of retinal disorders, including some associated with nystagmus and many in the retinitis pigmentosa family, the retina of affected children will appear normal on physical examination, yet the ERG will be markedly abnormal or nonrecordable. Therefore, the ERG may indicate not only that retinal dysfunction is the cause of visual impairment, but it may also implicate a specific disease.

Visual Evoked Potential   In the electrophysiological evaluation of an individual with visual impairment, VEP testing is the next step once an ERG indicates that the retina is functioning normally. The VEP is used to evaluate the pathway between the eye and the brain in children suspected of having cortical visual impairment and to test visual acuity in infants and children with severe disabilities (Granet, Hertle, Quinn, et al., 1993; Taylor & McCulloch, 1992). To perform the test, the child is seated in front of a television screen on which checkerboard patterns or grated lines of various sizes are alternated at various rates. Scalp electrodes affixed to the back of the head receive impulses as the child watches the screen. Computer-analyzed results reflect activity in the visual cortex and are used to obtain an estimate of visual acuity. If the child's level of cooperation or attention precludes fixation on a television screen, a bright light can be flashed into the child's eye as a stimulus for measuring VEP. This can ascertain the general integrity of the pathway between the eye and the brain but will not establish visual acuity.

There has been considerable controversy regarding the reliability of VEPs in predicting future visual functioning of children with cortical visual impairment. Although past studies have suggested there is little correlation (Granet, Hertle, Breton, et al., 1992; Hoyt, 1986b, 1987; McCulloch, Taylor, & Whyte, 1991; Nawratzki, Landau, & Auerbach, 1969), some investigations have reported a higher degree of success with VEPs predicting the degree of visual recovery in children with acquired cortical visual impairment (Lambert, 1995). Interpretation of VEP results must also take into account that they may be inaccurate when evaluating children who have seizure disorders or nystagmus or are under sedation (Hoyt, 1984).

BLINDNESS

The definition of blindness from both a legal and federal educational standpoint is visual acuity of 20/200 or worse in the better eye with correction, or a visual field that subtends to an angle of not greater than 20° instead of the usual 105° (Bishop, 1991; Individuals with Disabilities Education Act [IDEA] of 1990, PL 101-476). Individuals with low vision (partially sighted) are defined as having a visual acuity better than 20/200 but worse than 20/70 with correction (Buncic, 1987; Education for All Handicapped Children Act of 1975, PL 94-142). Both of these categories of students are considered to have visual impairments. Some people who are "legally blind" may nevertheless have considerable useful vision and be able to detect objects, define color, and even read large print texts. They may, in fact, function as people with sight. Other people with blindness, however, do not even have light and dark perception. Associated visual deficits also must be considered when labeling someone as having a visual impairment. A child who has both a visual loss and myopia, for example, has more limited functional vision than a child with visual loss alone. This dual impairment is often the case with ROP.

The overall incidence of blindness in children is about 1 in 3,000; 46% of these children were born blind, and an additional 38% lost their sight before 1 year of age (Foster, 1988). Among children with severe visual impairments, approximately 25% are totally blind, 25% have some light perception, and the remaining 50% may have enough vision to read large type (Buncic, 1987). The most common sites of the visual impairment are the retina (36%), the optic nerve or pathways to the brain (22%), the lens (17%), and the eye (16%) (Nelson et al., 1991).

Causes of Blindness

In childhood, the causes of blindness are many and varied. The most common congenital causes are intrauterine infections and malformations. Intrauterine infections, such as rubella and toxoplasmosis, may cause severe retinal damage. Malformations of the visual system range from colobomas of the retina to optic nerve hypoplasia and cerebral malformations. Other causes of blindness include ROP, brain trauma, anoxic events, severe eye infections, and tumors. Blindness is far more prevalent in developing countries where nutritional disorders such as vitamin A deficiency and infections including trachoma, measles, and tuberculosis are common (Foster & Johnson, 1990). Public health measures, including the use of silver nitrate drops at birth to prevent infections in infants' eyes and immunization programs, are gradually making an inroad into this tragic situation.

Identifying the Child with a Severe Visual Impairment

Blindness can be an isolated disability or part of a condition involving multiple disabilities. For example, visual impairment caused by an inherited disorder such as albinism may be an isolated finding, while impairment caused by congenital rubella is usually associated with congenital heart disease, hearing loss, cerebral palsy, and mental retardation. About half of children with severe visual impairments have other associated developmental disabilities (Warburg, Frederiksen, & Rattleff, 1979).

Several clues may indicate that an infant has severe visual impairment, even when the blindness is an isolated disability. The child will not visually fixate on a parent's face or show interest in following brightly colored objects. Parents also may notice abnormalities in the movement of the child's eyes, including wandering eye motions, nystagmus, or eyes that always gaze in one particular direction. In addition, the infant may not blink or cry when a threatening gesture is made or a bright light is shined in the eyes. Any of these findings should lead to a thorough examination by an ophthalmologist.

Development of the Child with Severe Visual Impairment

Even with typical intelligence, a child who is blind from birth or early childhood has significant developmental delays (Cass, Sonkesen, & McConachie, 1994; Dekker & Koole, 1992). Muscle tone is decreased, partly because its maintenance depends on visual perception. As a result, gross motor skills tend to be delayed; the child may not sit until after 8 months and usually does not crawl at all (Figure 11.13). The child may not take steps until 2–2 ½ years of age and tends to have a wide-based gait to help provide support in the absence of visual cues. Fine motor skills also are delayed or unusual. For example, reaching for objects may occur at 9 months rather than at 4 months, and the child will reach toward a sound rather than turning toward it. Self-feeding skills are similarly delayed (Warren, 1994).

Because speech is aided by imitating mouth movements as well as by listening to sounds, language development may be delayed (Dunlea, 1989). The child must learn to speak using auditory cues alone, which is a slow and painstaking process. The child also may imitate noises in the environment (e.g., cars, flushing toilets) rather than use words and may have difficulty differentiating "I" from "you." In the child with average intelligence, speech and language become more typical by school age. However, speech is accompanied by less body and facial expression, and the child lacks age-appropriate conversation skills.

In addition to developmental delays, there frequently are behavioral mannerisms that have been termed "blindisms." These self-stimulatory behaviors include eye pressing, blinking forcefully, gazing at lights, waving fingers in front of the face, rolling the head, and swaying the body (Good & Hoyt, 1989). Eye pressing seems to occur only in children with retinal disease, in whom it produces visual stimulation. These behaviors may persist into adulthood, especially in

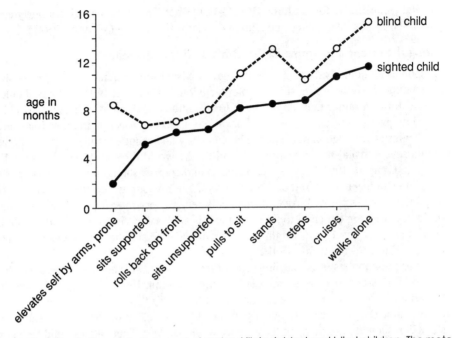

Figure 11.13.   Chart of age of attainment of motor skills in sighted and blind children. The motor development of a blind child is delayed. (From Fraiberg, S. [1977]. *Insights from the blind.* Copyright © 1977 by Selma Fraiberg; reprinted by permission of HarperCollins Publishers, Inc.)

children who also have mental retardation or hearing loss (Jan, 1991). They often can be controlled using behavior management techniques.

The development of play and social interaction skills is often delayed or impaired as well (Zell Sacks, Kekelis, & Gaylord-Ross, 1992). Play may be less imaginative and more stereotypical than in sighted children. This may be a consequence of being unable to read "body language" and to respond to facial expressions and other nonverbal communication. It is interesting that the child with congenital blindness may be unaware of any sensory impairment until 4–5 years of age. In the school-age child, however, social skills impairments may be related to social isolation and poor self-image. Inclusion in a program with typically developing children is helpful, provided there is an agenda to promote socialization (Warren, 1994). Professionals also can help parents who have become discouraged by their child's slow development or who are overprotective.

Because the Bayley Scales of Infant Development (Bayley, 1994) and other infant developmental tests are based primarily on performance of visual skills, they are not very useful in evaluating infants with severe visual impairment. Alternative non–visually based developmental scales include the Reynell Zinkin Scales (Reynell & Zinkin, 1979), PAVI, and the Oregon Project (Brown, Simmons, & Methwin, 1994). By school age, the verbal subtests of the Wechsler Intelligence Scale for Children (WISC–III) (Wechsler, 1991) can give a fairly accurate picture of the child's intelligence and help in educational planning (Wodrich, 1997).

Stimulating the Infant and Young Child with Visual Impairment

As soon as an infant is diagnosed with a severe visual impairment, the caregivers should begin stimulating him or her using sensorimotor techniques (Harrison, 1993). Infants should be placed on the stomach rather than on the back to strengthen neck and trunk muscles and should be talked to quietly before being touched or picked up so that it is not an unpleasant surprise. This also begins an association between the human voice and change (Moller, 1993). The young child with a severe visual impairment must explore the world through touch and sound (Pogrund, Fazzi, & Lampert, 1992). Therefore, parents and therapists should place or store toys at a height the child can reach. Textured and sound-producing toys are generally favored, although some children will be tactile defensive. In such children, sensory integration techniques may be helpful in desensitizing the child to touch. If there is any usable vision, the child should be encouraged to take advantage of it. Bright colors should be used and the child's vision and attention directed verbally toward them (Moller, 1993).

For preschoolers, it is very important for the parents, teachers, and therapists to provide a running verbal commentary of what is happening (Nixon, 1991). For example, the child should be addressed by name whenever someone passes by, so that the footsteps carry meaning. The child's name should be used frequently to encourage inclusion in conversations and so that he or she will respond to questions in the absence of verbal cues. There also should be an explanation before, during, and after a task is performed. While moving from one space to another, the purpose of the move and the orientation of the space should be explained.

Orientation refers to such skills as laterality and directionality. In terms of orientation and mobility, the child is first taught to locate familiar objects within the home, then progresses to travel outdoors. The child should be urged to walk despite the risks of scrapes and bruises. Poor peripheral vision (tunnel vision) is more of a problem in walking than the loss of central vision. Any residual vision, however, is better than none. The use of mobility aids for walking should be encouraged, including push toys. For older children, canes or laser-guided obstacle devices can be used (Sonksen, Petrie, & Drew, 1991).

Educating the Child with Severe Visual Impairment

The educational placement for a child depends on age, extent of visual impairment, and associated impairments (Torres & Corn, 1990; Warren, 1994). Intervention should begin as soon as the diagnosis is made. For the infant, an early intervention program can be started in the first month of life. Usually, this entails a once-a-week, home-based program in which the early childhood educator or therapist visits and works with the parent to set up a stimulating environment. In addition to language and exploration, the teacher works on motor skills and stimulation of residual vision (Sonksen et al., 1991).

By 3 years of age, the child is usually ready for a school-based program. Over the next few years, listening, concept development, conversation, and daily living skills (e.g., dressing, eating, personal hygiene) are emphasized. Self-dressing should be encouraged by using loose clothing and Velcro straps to fasten shoes, pants, and shirts. Play and social skills training and behavior modification of "blindisms" are also an important part of the program.

By the time the child with visual impairment reaches school age, the extent of the visual loss is usually clear. A child with better than 20/200 vision may be able to read large print books or use optical aids and devices to read regular print text. This child often can be integrated into a general education classroom with the use of visual aids and resource help.

For the child with less than 20/200 vision, reading readiness for braille begins in kindergarten. Braille is a written language formed as a series of raised dots on a page and read from left to right. Fine motor skills and tactile sensitivity are taught first. When the child is able to recognize small shapes, differentiate between rough and smooth, and follow a line of small figures across a page, the learning of the braille alphabet can begin (Jan, Sykanda, & Groenveld, 1990).

Children with severe visual impairments should learn to type on a computer by fourth grade. No modifications are needed, except they cannot use a "mouse." In addition to computers, there is a great deal of other technology assistance available. Text can be converted to braille using a machine called an Optacon that scans typed text and converts it into a tactile stimulus of vibrating pins. Another system, VersaBraille, converts material received by a computer into braille. Computer printouts can also be converted into speech using a Kurzweil Reading Machine; and TotalTalk and other software programs provide speech capacity to a personal computer. There are also verbal note-taking devices and talking calculators. In addition, books on tape are generally available from Recordings for the Blind and at bookstores and libraries.

It is critical to make sure that the child has all the appropriate equipment needed for learning and independence. With these tools, children with severe visual impairments and typical intelligence often can follow a general curriculum. They may need certain special services, however, such as classes on promoting listening skills, which range from auditory discrimination, to following complex directions, to using accelerated or compressed speech in recorded textbooks.

Intervention in Children with Multiple Disabilities

The incidence of blindness in children with multiple developmental disabilities is more than 200 times that found in the general population (Warburg et al., 1979). One third of children with partial sight and two thirds of children with blindness have other developmental disabilities, including mental retardation, hearing impairments, seizure disorders, and cerebral palsy. Two thirds of these children have two or more disabilities in addition to visual impairment (Curtis & Donlon, 1984). Treatment of these children must address all the disabilities and use all the senses and abilities that remain. A multidisciplinary approach involving a range of educational and health care professionals is essential.

Prognosis for Severe Visual Impairment

The prognosis for the child with severe visual impairment depends most on the amount of residual vision, the child's intellectual functioning, the motivation of the child and family, and the skills of the involved teachers and therapists. In general, the less the visual impairment and the higher the IQ score, the better the prognosis for independence. In a classical study of 82 blind children (18 also had mental retardation), 33 did well in an inclusive school setting, 41 had a mixed school performance, and 8 did poorly. At 25 years of age, 17 were married, and 43 still lived at home; 66 traveled independently, and 27 were gainfully employed (Warburg, 1983).

SUMMARY

Abnormalities of the visual system are among the many obstacles children with developmental disabilities may face. The visual challenges encountered may range from minor to severe, transient to permanent, stable to progressive, and ocular to cortical. Children with developmental disabilities, as a group, are at higher risk for visual impairment than those in the general population. Because the visual system is undergoing a process of maturation during childhood, early recognition of visual disorders is essential to ensure prompt treatment and to optimize visual outcome. Therefore, careful visual assessment is important for all children and can be performed regardless of a child's level of impairment or ability to cooperate. To a great extent, the prognosis for children with visual impairments depends on the degree of the visual loss, developmental status, motivation of child and family, and skill of involved teachers and therapists.

REFERENCES

Allen, H.F. (1957). A new picture series for preschool vision testing. *American Journal of Ophthalmology, 44,* 38.

Bane, M.C., & Birch, E.E. (1992). VEP acuity, FPL acuity, and visual behavior of visually impaired children. *Journal of Pediatric Ophthalmology and Strabismus, 29,* 202–209.

Batshaw, M.L. (1991). *Your child has a disability: A complete sourcebook of daily and medical care.* Boston: Little, Brown.

Bayley, N. (1994). *The Bayley Scales of Infant Development–Second edition manual.* San Antonio, TX: The Psychological Corporation.

Birch, E.E., & Spencer, R. (1991). Visual outcome in infants with cicatricial retinopathy of prematurity. *Investigative Ophthalmology and Visual Science, 32,* 410.

Bishop, V.E. (1991). Preschool visually impaired children: A demographic study. *Journal of Visual Impairment and Blindness, 85,* 69–74.

Boothe, R.G., Dobson, V., & Teller, D.Y. (1985). Postnatal development of vision in human and nonhuman primates. *Annual Review of Neuroscience, 8,* 495.

Braddick, O., & Atkinson, J. (1982). The development of binocular function in infancy. *Acta Ophthalmologica, 157,* 27.

Breton, M.E., & Nelson, L.B. (1983). What do color blind children really see? Guidelines for clinical prescreening based on recent findings. *Survey of Ophthalmology, 27,* 306–312.

Brodsky, M.C., Baker, R.S., & Hamed, L.M. (1996). The apparently blind infant. In *Pediatric neuro-ophthalmology* (pp. 1–41). New York: Springer-Verlag.

Brown, L.B., Simmons, J.C., & Methwin, E. (1994). *Oregon Project Curriculum for Visually Impaired and Blind Preschool Children (OPC).* Medford, OR: Jackson County Education Service District.

Buncic, J.R. (1987). The blind child. *Pediatric Clinics of North America, 34,* 1403–1414.

Burde, R.M., Savino, P.J., & Trobe, J.D. (1985). Nystagmus and other periodic eye disorders. In *Clinical decisions in neuro-ophthalmology* (pp. 197–220). St. Louis: C.V. Mosby.

Caltrider, N., & Jampolsky, A. (1983). Overcorrecting minus lens therapy for treatment of intermittent exotropia. *Ophthalmology, 90,* 1160.

Cass, H.D., Sonkesen, P.M., & McConachie, H.R. (1994). Developmental setback in severe visual impairment. *Archives of Diseases of Childhood, 70,* 192–196.

Cook, C.S., Sulik, K.K., & Wright, K.W. (1995). Embryology. In K.W. Wright (Ed.), *Pediatric ophthalmology and strabismus* (pp. 3–43). St. Louis: C.V. Mosby.

Curtis, W.S., & Donlon, E.T. (1984). A ten-year follow-up study of deaf-blind children. *Exceptional Child, 50,* 449–455.

Dekker, R., & Koole, F.D. (1992). Visually impaired children's visual characteristics and intelligence. *Developmental Medicine and Child Neurology, 34,* 123–133.

Dobson, V., Quinn, G.E., Saunders, R.A., et al. (1995). Grating visual acuity in eyes with retinal residua of retinopathy of prematurity. *Archives of Ophthalmology, 113,* 1172–1177.

Dunlea, A. (1989). *Vision and the emergence of meaning: Blind and sighted children's early language.* New York: Cambridge University Press.

Education for All Handicapped Children Act of 1975, PL 94-142, 20 U.S.C. § 1400 *et seq.*

Edwards, W.C., Price, W.D., & Weisskopf, B. (1972). Ocular findings in developmentally handicapped children. *Journal of Pediatric Ophthalmology, 9,* 162.

Endres, W., & Shin, Y.S. (1990). Cataract and metabolic disease. *Journal of Inherited Metabolic Disease, 13,* 509–516.

Foster, A. (1988). Childhood blindness. *Eye, 2*(Suppl.), S27–S36.

Foster, A., & Johnson, G.J. (1990). Magnitude and causes of blindness in the developing world. *International Ophthalmology, 14,* 135–140.

Fraiberg, S. (1977). *Insights from the blind.* New York: Basic Books.

Franks, W., & Taylor, D. (1989). Congenital glaucoma: A preventable cause of blindness. *Archives of Diseases in Childhood, 64,* 649–650.

Friendly, D.S. (1989). Visual acuity assessment of the preverbal patient. In S.J. Isenberg (Ed.), *The eye in infancy* (pp. 48–56). Chicago: Yearbook Medical Publishers.

Friendly, D.S. (1993). Development of vision in infants and young children. *Pediatric Clinics of North America, 40,* 693–704.

Good, W.V., & Hoyt, C.S. (1989). Behavioral correlates of poor vision in children. *International Ophthalmology Clinics, 29,* 57–60.

Good, W.V., Jan, J.E., DeSa, L., et al. (1994). Cortical visual impairment in children. *Survey of Ophthalmology, 38,* 251–264.

Granet, D.B., Hertle, R.W., Breton, M.E., et al. (1992, February 9–13). *The visual evoked response in infants with central visual impairment* [Poster]. Maui, HI: The American Association for Pediatric Ophthalmology and Strabismus.

Granet, D.B., Hertle, R.W., Quinn, G.E., et al. (1993). The visual evoked response in infants with central visual impairment. *American Journal of Ophthalmology, 116,* 437–443.

Harrison, F. (1993). *Living and learning with blind children: A guide for parents and teachers of visually impaired children.* Toronto, Canada: University of Toronto Press.

Haynes, W.L., & Pulido, J.S. (1995) Infectious, inflammatory, and toxic diseases of the retina and vitreous. In K.W. Wright (Ed.), *Pediatric ophthalmology and strabismus* (pp. 541–544). St. Louis: C.V. Mosby.

Henry, J.G. (1980). The ophthalmological assessment of the severely retarded child. *Australia and New Zealand Journal of Ophthalmology, 8,* 1.

Hertz, B.G., & Rosenberg, J. (1992). Effect of mental retardation and motor disability on testing with visual acuity cards. *Developmental Medicine and Child Neurology, 34,* 115–122.

Hertz, B.G., Rosenberg, J., Sjo, O., et al. (1988). Acuity card testing of patients with cerebral visual impairment. *Developmental Medicine and Child Neurology, 30,* 632.

Hoyt, C.S. (1984). The clinical usefulness of the visual evoked response. *Journal of Pediatric Ophthalmology and Strabismus, 21,* 231.

Hoyt, C.S. (1986a). Cortical blindness in infancy. In (Eds.), *Pediatric ophthalmology and strabismus: Transactions of the New Orleans Academy of Ophthalmology* (pp. 235–243). New York: Raven Press.

Hoyt, C.S. (1986b). Objective techniques of visual acuity assessment in infancy. *Australia and New Zealand Journal of Ophthalmology, 14,* 205.

Hoyt, C.S. (1987). Neurovisual adaptations to subnormal vision in children. *Australia and New Zealand Journal of Ophthalmology, 15,* 57.

Individuals with Disabilities Education Act (IDEA) of 1990, PL 101-476, 20 U.S.C. § 1400 *et seq.*

Ipata, A.E., Cioni, G., Bottai, P., et al. (1994). Acuity card testing in children with cerebral palsy related to magnetic resonance images, mental levels and motor abilities. *Brain and Development, 16,* 195–203.

Isenberg, S.J. (1988). *The eye in infancy.* Chicago: Yearbook Medical Publishers.

Jacobson, L. (1988). Ophthalmology in mentally retarded adults. *Acta Ophthalmologica, 66,* 457.

Jan, J.E. (1991). Head movements of visually impaired children. *Developmental Medicine and Child Neurology, 33,* 645–647.

Jan, J.E., Sykanda, A., & Groenveld, M. (1990). Habilitation and rehabilitation of visually impaired and blind children. *Pediatrician, 17,* 202–207.

Jenkins, P.F., Prager, P.C., Mazow, M.L., et al. (1983). Preliterate vision screening: A comparative study. *American Orthoptic Journal, 33,* 91.

Johnson, L., Quinn, G.E., Abbasi, S., et al. (1989). Effect of sustained pharmacologic vitamin E levels on incidence and severity of retinopathy of prematurity: A controlled clinical trial. *Journal of Pediatrics, 114,* 827–838.

Keith, C.G., & Doyle, L.W. (1995). Retinopathy of prematurity in extremely low birth weight infants. *Pediatrics, 95,* 42–45.

Kimura, A.E., Drack, A.V., & Stone, E.M. (1995). Retinitis pigmentosa and associated disorders. In K.W. Wright (Ed.), *Pediatric ophthalmology and strabismus* (pp. 449–466). St. Louis: C.V. Mosby.

Lambert, S.R. (1995). Cerebral visual impairment. In K.W. Wright (Ed.), *Pediatric ophthalmology and strabismus* (pp. 801–805). St. Louis: C.V. Mosby.

Lambert, S.R., Kriss, A., & Taylor, D. (1989). Delayed visual maturation: A longitudinal and electrophysiological assessment. *Ophthalmology, 96,* 524–528.

Landau, L., & Berson, D. (1971). Cerebral palsy and mental retardation: Ocular findings. *Journal of Pediatric Ophthalmology, 8,* 245.

Lavrich, J.B., & Nelson, L.B. (1993). Diagnosis and treatment of strabismus disorders. *Pediatric Clinics of North America, 40,* 737–752.

Lewis, T.L., Maurer, D., & Brent, H.P. (1989). Optokinetic nystagmus in normal and visually deprived children: Implications for cortical development. *Canadian Journal of Psychology, 43,* 121–140.

Mackie, R.T., McCulloch, D.L., Saunders, K.J., et al. (1995). Comparison of visual assessment tests in multiply handicapped children. *Eye, 9,* 136–141.

Magramm, I. (1992). Amblyopia: Etiology, detection and treatment. *Pediatrics in Review, 13*(1), 7–14.

Maino, D.M., Maino, J.H., & Maino, S.A. (1990). Mental retardation syndromes with associated ocular defects. *Journal of the American Optometrists Association, 61,* 707–716.

McCulloch, D.L., Taylor, M.J., & Whyte, H.E. (1991). Visual evoked potentials and visual prognosis following perinatal asphyxia. *Archives of Ophthalmology, 109,* 229.

Mohn, G., van Hof-van Duin, J., Fetter, W.P., et al. (1988). Acuity assessment of non-verbal infants and children: Clinical experience with the acuity card procedure. *Developmental Medicine and Child Neurology, 30,* 232.

Moller, M.A. (1993). Working with visually impaired children and their families. *Pediatric Clinics of North America, 40,* 881–890.

Moore, B.D. (1994). Pediatric cataracts: Diagnosis and treatment. *Optometry and Vision Science, 71,* 168–173.

Nawratzki, I., Landau, L., & Auerbach, E. (1969). Belated visual maturation in a mentally retarded child. *Journal of Pediatric Ophthalmology, 6,* 39.

Nelson, L.B., Calhoun, J.H., & Harley, R.D. (1991). *Pediatric ophthalmology* (3rd ed.). Philadelphia: W.B. Saunders.

Nixon, H.L. (1991). *Mainstreaming and the American dream: Sociological perspectives on parental coping with blind and visually impaired children.* New York: American Foundation for the Blind.

Orel-Bixler, D., Haegerstrom-Portnoy, G., & Hall, A. (1989). Visual assessment of the multiply handicapped patient. *Optometry and Visual Science, 66,* 530.

Phelps, D.L. (1993). Retinopathy of prematurity. *Pediatric Clinics of North America, 40,* 705–714.

Pogrund, R.L., Fazzi, D.L., & Lampert, J.S. (Eds.). (1992). *Early focus: Working with young blind and visually impaired children and their families.* New York: American Foundation for the Blind.

Potter, W.S. (1993). Pediatric cataracts. *Pediatric Clinics of North America, 40,* 841–854.

Quinn, G.E. (1992). Retinopathy of prematurity: Natural history and classification. In J.T. Flynn & W. Tasman (Eds.), *Retinopathy of prematurity* (pp. 7–22). New York: Springer-Verlag.

Quinn, G.E., Berlin, J.A., & James, M. (1993). The Teller acuity card procedure: Three testers in a clinical setting. *Ophthalmology, 100,* 488–494.

Quinn, G.E., Dobson, V., Barr, C.C., et al. (1991). Visual acuity in infants after vitrectomy for severe retinopathy of prematurity. *Ophthalmology, 98,* 5.

Quinn, G.E., Dobson, V., Repka, M.X., et al. (1992). Development of myopia in infants with birth weights less than 1251 grams. *Ophthalmology, 99,* 329–340.

Reynell, J., & Zinkin, P. (1979). *Reynell Zinkin Scales.* Wood Dale, IL: Soelting Co.

Rubin, S.E., & Nelson, L.B. (1993). Amblyopia: Diagnosis and management. *Pediatric Clinics of North America, 40,* 727–736.

Sadler, T.W. (1990). *Langman's medical embryology* (6th ed.). Baltimore: Williams & Wilkins.

Schaffer, D.B., Quinn, G.E., & Johnson, L. (1984). Sequelae of arrested mild retinopathy of prematurity. *Archives of Ophthalmology, 102,* 373.

Simons, K. (Ed.). (1993). *Early visual development normal and abnormal.* New York: Oxford University Press.

Skarf, B. (1989). Discussion of Lambert, Kriss, & Taylor article. *Ophthalmology, 96,* 529.

Sonksen, P.M., Petrie, A., & Drew, K.J. (1991). Promotion of visual development of severely visually impaired babies: Evaluation of a developmentally based programme. *Developmental Medicine and Child Neurology, 33,* 320–335.

Stout, A.U., & Wright, K.W. (1995). Pediatric eye examination. In K.W. Wright (Ed.), *Pediatric ophthalmology and strabismus* (pp. 63–72). St. Louis: C.V. Mosby.

Taylor, M.J., & McCulloch, D.L. (1992). Visual evoked potentials in infants and children. *Journal of Clinical Neurophysiology, 9,* 357–372.

Teland, V., & Dweck, H.S. (1989). The eye of the newborn: A neonatologist's perspective. In S.J. Isenberg (Ed.), *The eye in infancy* (pp. 3–8). Chicago: Yearbook Medical Publishers.

Teller, D.Y., McDonald, M., Preston, K., et al. (1986). Assessment of visual acuity in infants and children: The acuity card procedure. *Developmental Medicine and Child Neurology, 28,* 779.

Torres, I., & Corn, A.L. (1990). *When you have a visually handicapped child in your classroom.* New York: American Foundation for the Blind.

von Noorden, G.K. (1996). Examination of patient: III. Sensory signs, symptoms, and adaptations in strabismus. In *Binocular vision and ocular motility* (5th ed., pp. 206–296). St. Louis: C.V. Mosby.

Wagner, R.S. (1993) Glaucoma in children. *Pediatric Clinics of North America, 40,* 855–867.

Warburg, M. (1983). Why are the blind and severely visually impaired children with mental retardation much more retarded than the sighted children? *Acta Ophthalmologica, 157*(Suppl.), 72–81.

Warburg, M., Frederiksen, P., & Rattleff, J. (1979). Blindness among 7,720 mentally retarded children in Denmark. *Clinics in Developmental Medicine, 73,* 56–67.

Warren, D.H. (1994). *Blindness and children: An individual differences approach.* New York: Cambridge University Press.

Wechsler, D. (1991). *Wechsler Intelligence Scale for Children–Third edition.* San Antonio, TX: The Psychological Corporation.

Whiting, S., Jan, J.E., Wong, P.K., et al. (1985). Permanent cortical visual impairment in children. *Developmental Medicine and Child Neurology, 27,* 730–739.

Wodrich, D.L. (1997). *Children's psychological testing: A guide for nonpsychologists* (3rd ed.). Baltimore: Paul H. Brookes Publishing Co.

Woodruff, G., Hiscox, F., Thompson, J.R., et al. (1994). Factors affecting the outcome of children treated for amblyopia. *Eye, 8,* 627–631.

Wright, K.W. (Ed.). (1995). *Pediatric ophthalmology and strabismus.* St. Louis: C.V. Mosby.

Zell Sacks, S., Kekelis, L.S., & Gaylord-Ross, R.J. (Eds.). (1992). *The development of social skills by blind and visually impaired students: Exploratory studies and strategies.* New York: American Foundation for the Blind.

12 Hearing

Sounds and Silences

Annie G. Steinberg
Carol A. Knightly

Upon completion of this chapter, the reader will:

- be able to describe the anatomy of the ear
- know the different types of hearing losses and their causes
- be aware of various hearing tests and their uses
- understand the multidimensional aspects of the assessment of a child with a hearing loss
- understand the treatment options for the child with a hearing loss
- be able to discuss the educational options and potential outcomes for the child with a hearing loss

For most people, the sense of hearing is integral to one of the most fundamental of human activities: the use of language for communication. It is through hearing that the child acquires a linguistic system to both transmit and receive information. In this chapter, hearing impairment, its effect on the development of a child's communication skills, and various approaches to treatment and education are discussed.

DEFINING SOUND

When we hear a sound, we are actually interpreting a pattern of vibrating air molecules. An initial vibration sets successive rows of air molecules into motion in oscillating concentric circles, or waves. This movement of the molecules is described in terms of the **frequency** with which the oscillations occur and the amplitude of the oscillations from the resting point (Figure 12.1).

The frequency of a sound is perceived as pitch and is measured in cycles per second or Hertz (Hz). The more cycles that occur per second, the higher the frequency, or pitch, of the sound. Middle C, on the musical scale, is 256 Hz, while the ring of a cellular phone is approxi-

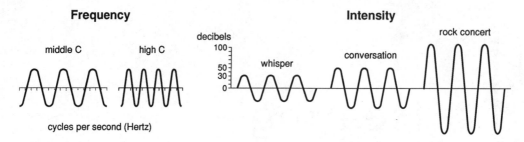

Figure 12.1.   Frequency and intensity of sound waves. The pitch of a sound, or its frequency, is expressed as cycles per second, or Hertz (Hz). Middle C is 256 Hz; one octave above is 512 Hz. Intensity of sound is expressed as dB and varies from a whisper at 30 dB to a rock music concert at 100 dB or more.

mately 2,000 Hz. The human ear can detect frequencies ranging from 20 Hz to 20,000 Hz but is most sensitive to sounds in the 500- to 6,000-Hz range, in which most of the sounds of speech occur (Bluestone, Stool, & Kenna, 1996).

The amplitude of the molecular oscillation is perceived as the loudness, or **intensity,** of the sound and is measured in decibels (dB). The softest sound an individual with normal hearing can usually detect is defined as 0 dB HL (hearing level). A whisper is about 30 dB HL, while typical conversation is 45 dB–50 dB HL. A lawn mower or chain saw is measured at about 100 dB HL.

Speech, however, does not occur at a single intensity or frequency. In general, vowel sounds are low frequency in nature and more intense; while consonants, particularly the voiceless consonants (e.g., *s, sh, t, th, k, p, h*) are composed of higher frequencies and are the least intense. Furthermore, during a conversation, the speaker will change the intensity of speech by talking in a louder or softer voice to express emotion or emphasis. This adversely affects an individual with a hearing loss, especially if the loss is not consistent at all frequencies. If an individual has a high-frequency hearing loss but normal hearing in the low-frequency region, that individual will be able to hear speech (because of the relative loudness of vowels) but will not be able to understand it (because of the softness of voiceless consonants). That person hears only parts of words and often is unable to follow a conversation.

THE HEARING SYSTEM

The mechanism for hearing is a complex system (B.C.J. Moore, 1995). It is divided into a peripheral auditory mechanism, which starts at the external ear and ends at the auditory nerve, and a central auditory system, which extends from the auditory nerve to the brain. A defect in the peripheral system results in a hearing loss, while a central auditory problem interferes with the interpretation of what is heard.

The peripheral auditory system is divided into the external, middle, and inner ear. The external ear includes the **auricle** and the ear canal (Figure 12.2). The auricle channels sound into the ear canal and then to the middle ear. The ear canal in adults is roughly 1½–2 inches long. The skin along the lateral portion of the canal contains hair and glands that produce **cerumen** and function together to prevent foreign bodies from entering the canal.

At the end of the ear canal lies the eardrum, or tympanic membrane, which separates the external and middle ear. The tympanic membrane serves as a barrier between the middle and external ears and is attached to the first of a series of small bones of the middle ear: the malleus, in-

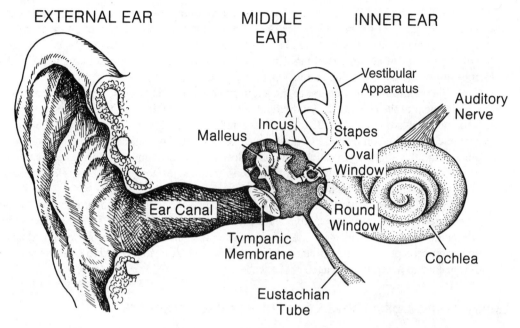

EXTERNAL EAR   MIDDLE   INNER EAR
                        EAR

Vestibular
Apparatus

Auditory
Nerve

Incus   Stapes

Malleus   Oval
                 Window

Ear Canal   Round
                   Window

Tympanic   Cochlea
Membrane

Eustachian
Tube

Figure 12.2.   Structure of the ear. The middle ear is composed of the tympanic membrane, or eardrum, and the three ear bones: the malleus, the incus, and the stapes. The stapes lies next to the oval window, the gateway to the inner ear. The inner ear contains the cochlea and the vestibular apparatus, collectively called the labyrinth.

cus, and stapes, collectively called the ossicles. The end of the ossicular chain, the stapes foot-plate, is attached by ligaments to the oval window, which serves as the boundary between the middle ear and the bony housing of the inner ear, the cochlea.

The eustachian tube is also part of the middle ear. This tube runs from the floor of the middle ear space down to the nasopharynx. The eustachian tube is usually closed but opens during a swallow or yawn, allowing a small amount of air from the nasopharynx into the middle ear to equalize the pressure and provide a new supply of oxygen for the mucous membrane lining.

When sound waves strike the tympanic membrane, the membrane vibrates and thus sets the ossicular chain into motion. Because the tympanic membrane has a larger surface area than the oval window and because the ossicles act as a lever system, the incoming sound pressure is amplified by about 30 dB.

The inner ear is composed of the vestibular system and the cochlea. The vestibular system houses the organ of balance, while the cochlea houses the organ of hearing. The cochlea is a snail-shaped structure, approximately 35 millimeters in length, which is divided into three chambers by the membranous labyrinth (Figure 12.3a). The actual end organ of hearing, the organ of Corti, is housed on the floor of the interior chamber or basilar membrane of the scala media and runs the entire length of the cochlea.

The organ of Corti consists of multiple rows of delicate hair cells that are the actual receptors for the auditory nerve. The cochlea is arranged **tonotopically;** that is, hair cells located at the base of the cochlea, near the oval window, respond to high-frequency sounds (above 2,000 Hz), while those in the middle and top respond to gradually lower frequency sounds (Figure

12.3b). The organ of Corti converts the mechanical energy arriving from the middle ear into electrical energy, or the nerve impulse. As the ossicular chain is set into motion by the vibrating tympanic membrane, the movement is transmitted through the chambers of the cochlea and results in release of neurotransmitters from the hair cells. This generates a nerve impulse that is transmitted via the ascending auditory pathway to the brain.

The organizational structure of the auditory nerve itself is orderly, much like the tonotopic arrangement of the cochlea. The individual nerve fibers leave the cochlea via the spiral ganglion and then wrap around one another to form the auditory nerve, with the fibers from the **basal** end of the cochlea (which respond to high-frequency sounds) located around the outside, and the fibers from the **apical** end (which respond to low-frequency sounds) arranged nearer the center of the nerve. About half of the fibers respond to frequencies above 2,000 Hz, yielding hearing that is most sensitive for higher pitched sounds.

From the inner ear, sound is carried to the auditory cortex in the temporal lobe of the brain. The route from ear to cortex involves four relay stations (Figure 12.4). The final destination is the auditory cortex, in which the sound is combined with other sensory information and memory to permit perception and interpretation. The auditory cortex is not needed to perceive sound, but it is needed to interpret language.

EMBRYOLOGICAL DEVELOPMENT OF THE HEARING APPARATUS

Knowledge of the origins of auditory structures can be helpful in predicting and diagnosing hearing loss if the clinician recognizes syndromes that are associated with altered ear develop-

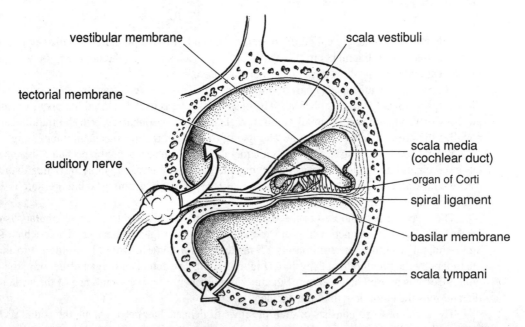

Figure 12.3. a) The cochlea. Cross-section of the cochlea, showing the scala vestibuli, the scala media, the scala tympani, and the organ of Corti.

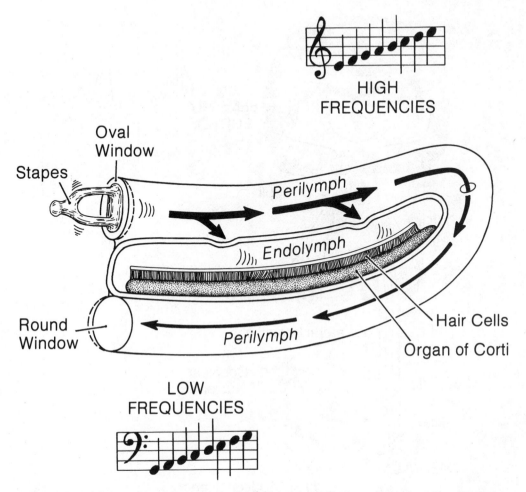

Figure 12.3.   b) The cochlea has been "unfolded" for simplicity. Sound vibrations from the stapes are transmitted as waves in the perilymph. This leads to the displacement of hair cells in the organ of Corti. These hair cells lie above and attach to the auditory nerve, and the impulses generated are fed to the brain. Low-frequency sounds stimulate hair cells close to the oval window, while high-frequency sounds stimulate the end of the organ. The sound wave in the perilymph is rapidly dissipated through the round window, and the cochlea is ready to accept a new set of vibrations.

ment, such as in the CHARGE association or Waardenburg syndrome (see Appendix B). In addition, if the timing of a prenatal insult or possible fetal injury is close to the timing of ear development, the clinician should also suspect hearing loss.

The differentiation of the normal hearing apparatus from the three primitive cell types, the ectoderm, mesoderm, and endoderm, begins in the first weeks of life (Romand, 1992). By 4½ weeks, a tubular extension known as the endolymphatic duct can be recognized as the early vestibular portion of the labyrinth; and by 6 weeks, three outpockets have an arch-shaped configuration and represent the early derivatives of the semi-circular canals (i.e., the vestibular system). Although sensory end-organ cells are visible by the seventh week, maturation of the sen-

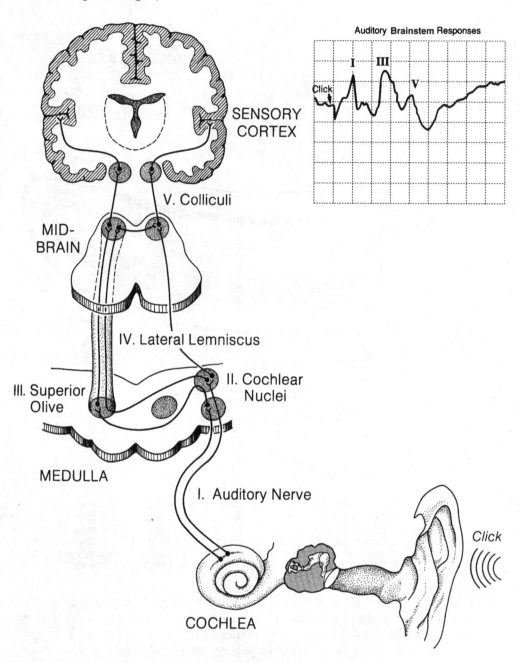

Figure 12.4.   The auditory pathway and auditory brainstem responses (ABR). The auditory nerve carries sounds to the cochlear nuclei in the medullary portion of the brainstem. Here most impulses cross over to the superior olivary body and then ascend to the opposite inferior colliculus and ultimately the sensory cortex, where the sound is perceived. The function of this pathway can be measured by ABR. Each wave corresponds to a higher level of the pathway (denoted by Roman numerals in the reporting of ABRs).

sory cells in the cochlea does not occur until the fifth month. The middle ear has a different developmental process, with the tympanic cavity and auditory tube derived from an endodermal-lined pouch between the first and second branchial arches and the ossicles derived from these arches. By the 15th week, the form of the ear is completed, and the cartilaginous structures begin to ossify over the ensuing 4 months. The auricle begins to develop by the third or fourth week of gestation (Figure 12.5) and by the 20th week has an adult configuration but continues to develop until the seventh year of life.

HEARING LOSS

Normal hearing requires intact functioning of both the peripheral and central components of the auditory pathway. The location and nature of the dysfunction in the auditory pathway will determine the degree and type of the hearing loss. Because it is through hearing that a child develops the comprehension of speech, a hearing loss commonly affects both the receptive and expressive development of spoken language. This is particularly true if the hearing loss occurs prior to 2 years of age, during the period of most rapid language acquisition. When hearing is impaired, the child typically compensates through the use of vision. This can consist of close observation of the visual environment, speechreading for those who are able to do so, or use of a sign language.

There is some disagreement among professionals regarding basic terminology. Most audiologists reserve the term "deaf" for those individuals whose hearing loss is in the profound range (hearing sounds only above 90 dB); below that level an individual would be called "hearing impaired" or "hard of hearing." Others use the term "deaf" to describe any person with a hearing impairment who does not benefit from the use of hearing aids and/or who uses sign language or other manual forms of communication, regardless of the degree of hearing loss. In this chapter, we use "hearing impaired" or "deaf" interchangeably to refer to all children with significant hearing loss.

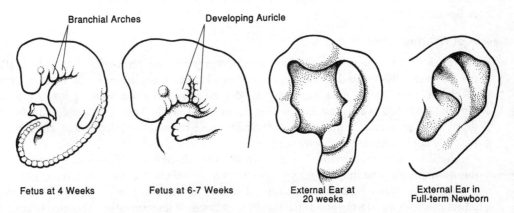

Figure 12.5.   Embryological development of the ear showing stages from the fourth week of gestation to the newborn period. The ear is functional by 20 weeks' gestation.

Types of Hearing Loss

Dysfunction of the external or middle ear causes a *conductive hearing loss.* If the cochlea or auditory nerve malfunctions, a *sensorineural hearing loss* results. Occasionally, the term sensorineural will be broken down further into the terms sensory hearing loss, implicating the cochlea, or neural hearing loss, implicating the auditory nerve. A *mixed hearing loss* indicates that there are both conductive and sensorineural components to the loss.

The effect of a hearing loss on speech and language depends on a number of variables, including severity, age at onset, age at discovery, and age at intervention. Hearing losses acquired after language has been well established have less of an impact on language and speech skills and later academic achievement than hearing losses occurring in infancy. Hearing loss may affect one ear (unilateral loss) or both ears (bilateral loss). Although more subtle, unilateral hearing loss can have a significant impact on communication, interpersonal relationships, and the educational achievement of the child. Progressive hearing losses can be insidious and challenging to recognize early (Levi, Tell, & Feinwesser, 1993).

Prevalence and Incidence of Hearing Loss

Approximately 10%–15% of children who receive hearing screenings at school fail; however, the majority of these children have a transient conductive hearing loss. A 1994 estimate of prevalence in the United States reported that slightly less than 1 million or 1.8% of youth under the age of 18 years have a hearing impairment (Holt & Hotto, 1994; National Center for Health Statistics, 1994). One frequently reported estimate is that approximately 1 in 1,000 infants is born with a severe to profound hearing loss, and that this incidence doubles during infancy and childhood (Kvaerner & Arnesen, 1994). Inconsistencies in assessing the incidence of hearing impairment in childhood result from the lack of clear parameters for and definitions of hearing impairment. The specific age of onset of hearing impairment is often difficult to determine, particularly between birth and 2½ years, because the early identification of hearing loss has not yet been addressed with universal screening. Another largely unrecognized population are those children with minimal hearing loss or unilateral hearing loss, which may go undetected and/or misdiagnosed well into adolescence despite mandatory school-based screening programs (Dobie & Berlin, 1979).

Causes of Hearing Loss

Hearing loss can occur as a result of an event or injury *in utero,* perinatally, or after birth (Parving & Hauch, 1994). The determination of etiology is often complicated by the delay in diagnosis and because the specific contributing factors are often unknown. Hearing losses present at birth are described as congenital, regardless of causation, while those that develop after birth are described as acquired. Confusion exists regarding those hereditary etiologies that, albeit congenital, may not be revealed until later in life.

Traditionally, the literature has reported that the etiology of hearing loss is approximately one third genetic, one third acquired, and one third of unknown causes (Peckham, 1986). The genetic causes of hearing loss include some disorders in which deafness is the sole disability and others in which the hearing loss is but part of a spectrum of abnormalities. Acquired hearing loss can result from both prenatal and postnatal infections; anoxia; prematurity; prenatal and postnatal exposures to ototoxic agents (e.g., certain antibiotics); and trauma. Because middle-ear infections have been shown to contribute to so many cases of acquired conductive hearing loss (Bluestone & Klein, 1995), they are discussed in some detail later in this chapter.

Genetic Causes

Hereditary deafness occurs in approximately 1 in 2,000 to 1 in 6,000 children. There are more than 70 documented inherited syndromes associated with deafness, some of which manifest later in life. About 90% of children who have hereditary deafness inherit it as an autosomal recessive disorder; often a child's sibling is also affected (McKusick, 1994). Hereditary disorders can affect the formation or function of any part of the hearing mechanism (Gorlin, Toriello, & Cohen, 1995). Table 12.1 describes some of the most common genetic disorders associated with hearing loss.

Cleft palate, in which the roof of the mouth fails to close during embryological development, is a malformation with associated conductive hearing loss. It has a multifactorial inheritance pattern and an incidence of about 1 in 900. It may occur alone or together with cleft lip. Of children with a cleft palate, 50%–90% are susceptible to severe and persistent middle-ear infections (Muntz, 1993). Because of the absence of closure of the palate, the tensor veli palatini muscle does not have a normal midline attachment and functions poorly in opening the eustachian tube (Potsic, Handler, Wetmore, et al., 1995). Many children with cleft palate develop a conductive hearing loss, while others have a sensorineural or mixed type hearing loss. Close monitoring and myringotomy and tube insertions are necessary to address remediable etiologies of hearing loss. (See Chapter 13 for further discussion of cleft palate.)

Pre-, Peri-, and Postnatal Factors and Prematurity

Environmental exposures to viruses, bacteria, and other toxins such as drugs prior to or following birth can result in hearing loss. During delivery or in the newborn period, a number of other complications such as hypoxia may cause damage to the hearing mechanism, particularly the cochlea (Razi & Das, 1994). Neonatal hyperbilirubinemia and intracranial hemorrhage also have been associated with subsequent sensorineural hearing loss. Premature infants, especially those born weighing less than 1,500 grams, have an increased susceptibility to all three of these problems. Of these infants, 2%–5% will demonstrate significant hearing loss (Herregard, Karjalainen, Martikainen, et al., 1995; Weisglas-Kuperus, Baerts, de Graaf, et al., 1993). (See Chapters 6 and 7 for further discussion of neonatal complications and prematurity.)

Infections

Infections, both intrauterine and following birth, are common causes of hearing loss. A mother who contracts rubella during the first trimester of pregnancy has about a 30% risk of bearing an infant who has a severe to profound sensorineural hearing loss, microcephaly, cardiac malformations, retinal abnormalities, and other disabilities (Bale, 1992). Other infections during pregnancy, including toxoplasmosis, herpes virus, syphilis, and cytomegalovirus (CMV), may cause similar hearing losses (Henderson & Weiner, 1995; Veda, Tokugawa, & Kusuhara, 1992). The most prevalent of these is CMV, with an incidence of 5–25 per 1,000 in newborn infants (Hanshaw, 1994). Among children with clinically detectable CMV at birth, 80% have nervous system sequelae, including hearing loss. As many as 90% of CMV infections, however, are thought to be subclinical (Schildroth, 1994). Among these children, only 5%–15% will develop central ner-

Table 12.1. Examples of genetic disorders associated with hearing loss

Examples of syndromes	Inheritance pattern	Type of hearing loss	Other characteristics
Treacher-Collins syndrome	Autosomal dominant	Conductive or mixed	Abnormal facial appearance, deformed auricles, defects of ear canal and middle ear
Waardenburg syndrome	Autosomal dominant	Sensorineural, stable	Unusual facial appearance, irises of different colors, white forelock, absent organ of Corti
Laurence-Moon-Biedl syndrome	Autosomal recessive	Sensorineural, progressive	Retinitis pigmentosa, mental retardation, obesity, extra fingers or toes
Usher syndrome	Autosomal recessive	Sensorineural, progressive in Usher III	Retinitis pigmentosa; CNS effects including vertigo, loss of smell, mental retardation, epilepsy; half have psychosis
CHARGE association	Sporadic	Mixed, progressive	Eye, gastrointestinal, and other malformations
Down syndrome	Chromosomal	Conductive, occasionally sensorineural	Small auricles, narrow ear canals, high incidence of middle-ear infections
Trisomy 13, trisomy 18	Chromosomal	Sensorineural	CNS malformations
Cleft palate	Multifactorial	Conductive	Cleft lip

vous system manifestations, although these children are still at risk for late-onset hearing loss that is usually symmetrical and may worsen over time (Williamson, Demmer, & Percy, 1992).

Infections of infancy and childhood also can lead to a sensorineural hearing loss. Bacterial meningitis carries a 10% risk of hearing loss from damage to the cochlea (Fortnum & Davis, 1993). The hearing loss may progress further if the weakened cochlea degenerates and ossifies. Among the common viral diseases of childhood, unilateral hearing loss has been reported after mumps, while bilateral involvement has occurred after measles and chickenpox (Nussinovitch, Volovitz, & Varsano, 1995).

Middle Ear Disease

The most common type of hearing impairment is a mild conductive hearing loss secondary to a chronic middle ear disease or **effusion.** Such hearing loss often goes undiagnosed and usually does not result in a permanent hearing loss. Middle-ear infection (acute otitis media) is most common in very young children, with 76%–95% of all children having at least one middle-ear infection during their first 2 years of life (Shapiro & Bluestone, 1995). Members of certain ethnic groups appear to be at greater risk than usual to develop recurrent or chronic otitis media, especially Native Americans and the Inuit (Bluestone & Klein, 1995). This increased prevalence may be due to reduced access to health care and exposure to other sick children in the child care setting, and it underscores the importance of rapid detection and treatment of middle-ear disease.

Although some children with otitis media are asymptomatic, in most cases, fever or irritability is the first sign of an infection. The older child may pull at the external ear or fluid may drain from the ear. Hearing may be obviously decreased, and the child may appear ataxic. On examination with an otoscope, the eardrum looks red and opaque rather than white and translucent. Fluid or effusion is usually present behind the eardrum. Pneumatic otoscopy, or the use of an insufflation bulb to detect the degree of movement of the tympanic membrane, reveals stiffness and decreased mobility; the diagnosis can be supported by **tympanometry** that shows a flat rather than "tented" pattern.

Trauma

Trauma to the cochlea, as might occur following a blow to the skull, may lead to a sensorineural hearing loss (Zimmerman, Ganzel, Windwill, et al., 1993), while blood in the middle ear or damage to the ossicles may result in a conductive hearing loss. Mild to moderate sensorineural hearing losses also may result from traumatic noise levels. In children and adolescents, sources of excessive impact noise include firecrackers, fireworks, and air guns. Transient or permanent sensorineural hearing loss may occur with the use of stereo headphones at high-intensity levels and attendance at rock concerts where noise levels may exceed 100 dB–110 dB. Any sustained noise level above 90 dB is potentially damaging to the cochlea and should be avoided (Brookhouser, Worthington, & Kelly, 1992). Noise levels in incubators containing premature infants also have been a concern because they may reach intensities of 60 dB–80 dB (Northern & Downs, 1991).

Ototoxic Agents

Certain antibiotics used to treat severe bacterial infections may be toxic to the cochlea (Aran, 1995). This is especially true of the aminoglycosides: neomycin, kanamycin, gentamicin, vancomycin, and tobramycin (listed in descending order of toxicity). They destroy the outer row of hair cells. Fortunately, physicians can monitor blood levels of the antibiotics during treatment to avoid the development of toxic levels. Other drugs that can damage the inner ear include diuretics, nonsteroidal anti-inflammatory drugs, and chemotherapeutic agents.

Identification of Hearing Loss

There is often considerable delay in identifying a child with hearing impairment (Coplan, 1987). Although many parents first suspect a hearing loss during infancy and it is possible to reliably test auditory system function hours after birth, the average age of a child at the time of identification of a significant hearing loss is 2½ years (Goldberg, 1996), with the average initiation of appropriate intervention at 3½ years. Many factors are involved in this delay of diagnosis. In general, the more severe the hearing loss and the greater its association with other disabilities, the earlier its identification. The reported age of identification of congenital hearing loss of severe to profound degree in children in the United States ranges from under 6 months of age to 16–18 months of age (Stein, Kraus, McGee, et al., 1995). This delay in part is the consequence of hearing loss being a silent disability; it is not usually accompanied by pain, fever, or physical abnormalities. During the first 6 months of life, development occurs on the foundation of a nonverbal and prelinguistic communication system; after that, on a visual gestural system as well. It is only when expectations of and demands for verbal communication are placed on the child that the sensory impairment becomes more obvious. Furthermore, while children with sudden onset hearing loss (e.g., secondary to meningitis) may become frustrated and angry, infants or young children who are completely deaf may not appear upset.

The importance of early identification of hearing loss (until recently usually defined as occurring before 2 years of age) is analogous to the need for early detection of a vision loss. The brain pathways for both of these senses are still immature at birth and develop normally only when stimulated early. Although the degree to which auditory training can improve residual functioning is unclear and the benefits of amplification for a child with a hearing loss vary, the conventional wisdom is that amplification should be used as early as possible. This gives the child the maximum opportunity to utilize residual hearing in the development of speech and language skills during the critical early stages. In addition, many professionals strongly recommend augmenting auditory input with visual forms of communication in the early years.

Hearing Milestones

There are specific milestones that are helpful in detecting a hearing loss. The hearing mechanism is functional by 20 weeks' gestation, particularly for low-pitched sound, making it quite likely that the fetus has an appreciation of and the ability to distinguish familiar from nonfamiliar sounds. It has been shown that a newborn infant will suck preferentially to the recorded voice of his or her mother. The infant also will awaken from sleep specifically to the loud voice of his or her parent (Northern & Downs, 1991).

The newborn infant clearly prefers to listen to speech as opposed to other environmental sounds, just as the infant prefers to fixate visually on a face rather than an object. By 2 months of age, the typically developing infant can distinguish vowel from consonant sounds; and by 4 months, the infant shows a preference for speech patterns that have varied rhythm and stress (Northern & Downs, 1991). The child prefers listening to prolonged discourse rather than repetitive baby talk.

Up to 5 months of age, the speech sounds a baby makes are not influenced by the sounds the baby hears. This is why the early babbling of infants from different countries sounds alike.

After 5 months of age, the infant's babbling starts to imitate the parents' speech patterns (Northern & Downs, 1991). Thus, the babbling of a French-speaking infant becomes different from that of an English-speaking child. For all hearing children, however, listening to spoken language during early life is a critical prerequisite for the normal development of speech. This is likely to explain why children who acquire a hearing loss after learning to speak have both better speech and better command of the language spoken in their community than do children with congenital deafness. Helen Keller was an example of a child who lost hearing (and vision) as a result of meningitis at 18 months of age and ultimately developed effective speech, presumably because her brain had been exposed to spoken language in her early life.

Signs of Hearing Impairment

With the usual milestones in mind, the variations in development seen in deaf infants are easier to understand. An early sign of severe hearing loss is a sleeping infant who does not awaken to loud noises, although even an infant who is deaf may react to the vibration alone, leading family members to assume that he or she has actually heard the noise. Between 3 and 4 months of age, infants who are deaf coo and laugh normally, yet babbling seems to be delayed (Oller & Eilers, 1988). In children with unaffected hearing, babbling noises become more varied and eventually are attached to meanings (e.g., the babble "dadadadada" becoming the word, "dada"), while the vocalizations of infants who are deaf show less variety in articulation and are less likely to become meaningful and recognizable words. Between the ages of 5 months and 17 months, while hearing infants increase their repertoire of consonant sounds, their deaf counterparts demonstrate a reduction in consonant variety (Stoel-Gammon & Otomo, 1986). It is this failure to develop comprehensible speech that leads parents to suspect a hearing loss.

Receptive language also lags. By 4 months of age, the hearing child turns toward his or her parents' voices; the child with a hearing loss may or may not do this, depending on the severity and configuration of the loss. At around 12 months of age, infants receive verbal instructions accompanied by gestures, such as waving "bye-bye." The deaf child of this age may seem to understand the message because he or she can often figure out the command by watching mouth movements, following gestures, and understanding the context. For example, a deaf toddler may get his jacket when others do, whether or not he has understood "Get your coat." By about 16 months of age, the hearing child responds to more complex instructions by words alone. The child with an undiagnosed hearing loss, however, may have great difficulty in doing this and may stop following instructions unless they can be inferred from context or are accompanied by gestures. This failure to respond to verbal instructions may lead parents to suspect a hearing loss but also can be misperceived as an oppositional or behavior disorder. Hearing children with mental retardation also are delayed in the achievement of these language milestones. However, in these children, speech, motor, and cognitive skills are similarly delayed, while the child with hearing impairment has slow development of speech and language skills but not of other abilities.

HEARING SCREENING

Screening for hearing loss can facilitate early identification (McCormick, 1995). As with any screening procedure, hearing screening is designed to separate those individuals with a higher risk of the target condition (hearing loss) from the general population. An individual either passes a screening or is referred for diagnostic evaluation. While a screening alerts the professional to the possibility of hearing loss, the diagnostic evaluation serves to confirm whether a hearing loss is present and provides additional information regarding the hearing loss. Some groups of children, such as premature infants, those with complicated pre-, peri-, and postnatal periods, and children with family histories of deafness, should be screened routinely for signs of hearing loss. In 1982, the Joint Committee on Infant Hearing published "risk factors" for hearing loss that included 1) a positive family history of hearing loss; 2) congenital perinatal infection, such as rubella or syphilis; 3) bacterial meningitis; 4) congenital malformations of the head and neck; 5) prematurity, with a birth weight of less than 1,500 grams; 6) anoxia; and 7) hyperbilirubinemia requiring exchange transfusion. Unfortunately, evaluating the hearing of children who meet these criteria would identify only about half of children with hearing impairments. To improve early identification further, the National Institutes of Health (NIH) (1993) issued a consensus statement recommending universal screening for hearing loss in all infants within the first 3 months of life. The updated Joint Committee on Infant Hearing Position Statement in 1994 endorsed universal screening, with high-risk indicators guiding assessment when universal screening is not possible. The 1994 position statement contains an expanded list of risk indicators, including those resulting in conductive hearing loss, and those factors specifically associated with late-onset hearing loss.

In addition to observing the guidelines found in the NIH consensus and Joint Committee statements, clinicians should monitor the achievement of developmental language milestones and obtain a hearing test in any child who appears to have delays in speech and/or language development. A child's hearing can be tested at any age, even within 24 hours of birth, so parental concern should prompt an immediate referral for testing.

Screening Infants Younger Than 6 Months of Age

In infants, formal behavioral observation audiometry often can detect a hearing loss but cannot determine precisely the degree of the impairment or its type. Noisemakers, such as horns or bells, are sounded near the baby and the observer looks for a change in behavior, including limb movements or eye widening. Generally, the stimulus required to elicit a response, even in a child with normal hearing sensitivity, must be rather intense, often in the range of 80 dB–90 dB. Thus, a positive response serves only to rule out a severe or profound hearing loss but does not distinguish among lesser degrees or unilateral hearing loss or between conductive and sensorineural hearing loss. Furthermore, the absence of a response does not necessarily mean that the child has a hearing loss. Infants do adjust to repeated loud environmental noise, and this habituation limits the interpretation of behavioral observation audiometry.

Because of these problems, the NIH consensus statement endorses evoked otoacoustic emissions (EOAE) testing as the preferred method of screening for hearing loss in infants (Meredith, Stephens, Hogan, et al., 1994). EOAE testing is a rapid, noninvasive, and inexpensive method of assessing cochlear function based on the cochlea's capability of not only transmitting sound to the brain, but also generating low-level sound in response to a stimulus (Champlin, 1996). In this test, the infant's ear canal is sealed with a plastic probe that includes a microphone and a receiver. Clicks or tones of various frequencies are introduced into the ear canal, and the microphone records responses that are evoked from the cochlea. If a hearing loss exists that is greater than about 25 dB–30 dB, no response is obtained. A limitation of the use of EOAE procedures is that the stimulus intensity and response may be reduced in the presence of the stiff ear drum and middle ear fluid in otitis media. Thus, the child's ear needs to be checked for middle ear disease before the EOAE procedure is done (Brass & Kemp, 1994).

Another method of screening infants is auditory brainstem response (ABR) audiometry, also called brainstem auditory evoked response (BAER) audiometry (American Speech-Language-Hearing Association, 1989; Stein et al., 1995). Like EOAE testing, this procedure does not require the infant's cooperation. Unlike EOAE testing, which assesses only the cochlea, ABR testing assesses the auditory nerve as well. EEG electrodes are pasted to the forehead and behind each ear of the sleeping or sedated child. Using earphones, tones or clicks are presented separately to each ear, stimulating bursts of neural activity from the auditory pathway within the brainstem. The electrodes detect this activity; a computer averages the responses from the auditory nerve and displays a waveform that reflects activity in the auditory brainstem pathway. In infants, the waveform is composed of three distinct waves, numbered I, III, and V (Figure 12.4) that represent successively higher levels of the ascending auditory pathway. An absence of a waveform at a given intensity suggests a hearing loss, while the complete absence of a particular wave suggests an abnormality in a particular location of the brainstem pathway. ABR audiometry is a highly sensitive test for both hearing loss and neural disruption of the auditory pathway (McClelland, Watson, Lawless, et al., 1992).

Hearing Tests

In addition to hearing screening, both EOAE and ABR measurements also can be used as part of a diagnostic battery of tests and are particularly useful in assessing older children with severe developmental disabilities who are unable to respond to conventional audiometric testing (Gorga, Stover, Bergman, et al., 1995; Richardson, Williamson, & Lenton, 1995). However, these methods of assessment can be costly and limited in the information they provide, particularly when compared with the information that can be obtained with behavioral hearing testing (Gravel, 1994). Formal behavioral hearing testing is performed to 1) determine whether there is a hearing loss; 2) differentiate a conductive from a sensorineural hearing loss; 3) determine the configuration of the hearing loss in each ear (i.e., the degree of the hearing impairment at specific frequencies); and 4) estimate the clarity with which speech sounds can be discriminated. The age of the child need not interfere with the successful completion of audiological assessment, although the methodology and specific techniques must be modified for the developmental age of the child (Gans & Gans, 1993).

Testing Children with Developmental Ages from 6 Months to 2½ Years

Between 6 months and 2½ years of age, as a child's responses to auditory stimuli become more predictable, visual reinforcement audiometry (VRA) can be used to assess hearing sensitivity (Gravel & Traquina, 1992; J.M. Moore, 1995). VRA enables identification of the magnitude and configuration of the hearing loss. The tones are presented through speakers (i.e., in soundfield), and information is limited to responses from the better hearing ear (in cases of asymmetrical hearing loss). This method does not provide ear-specific information as both of the child's ears are uncovered and receiving the sound information together.

VRA uses visual reinforcers to elicit consistent responses to auditory stimuli. Typically, the child is seated on the parent's lap in the middle of a sound-treated audiometric booth. At a 90° angle to one side of the child is a speaker. Above the speaker is a darkened plexiglass box that contains an animated toy. To establish conditioning, an acoustic stimulus (e.g., a tone or voice) is presented from the speaker and at the same time the box above the speaker is illuminated to reveal the animated toy inside. Thus, the child is conditioned to associate the presence of the sound with the pleasurable experience of viewing the toy. Once the child has revealed an awareness of the relationship between the acoustic stimulus and the visual "reward," the box is not illuminated until the child responds by turning toward the sound in anticipation of viewing the toy.

Conditioned orienting response (COR) audiometry differs from VRA in that it requires the child not only to show an awareness of the stimuli but to localize the sound source. In this case, speakers are usually placed at 45° angles to the front of the child and the plexiglass boxes containing the toys are positioned above or near each speaker. After conditioning, the child must turn toward the correct speaker before receiving reinforcement. COR can also be used with earphones to obtain ear-specific information.

Testing Children with Developmental Ages Greater Than 2½ Years

Conditioned play audiometry can be used for testing children between the ages of 2½ and 4 years. In this approach, the child usually wears earphones and is conditioned to perform a play task whenever the stimulus is heard. For example, the child may stack blocks, put rings on a peg, or perform some other motor task in response to hearing the auditory stimulus. By about 4 years of age, the child can respond to requests to press a button or raise a hand, in response to the stimulus. If conditioning of the child is successful, audiometric testing results are as complete as from a mature child or adult, although all preschool children require developmentally appropriate reinforcement and praise.

When a child's hearing is assessed via speakers or earphones (i.e., air conduction) and a hearing loss is identified, it is not possible to determine whether the loss is conductive or sensorineural. The sounds must then also be presented through a vibrator placed on the mastoid bone behind the ear (i.e., bone conduction) (Figure 12.6). While air conduction testing involves the contribution of the external, middle, and inner ear, bone conduction testing effectively bypasses the external and middle ear and stimulates the inner ear directly. Therefore, if the child demonstrates a hearing loss by air conduction but hearing is normal by bone conduction, the hearing loss is conductive in nature. Likewise, if the child evidences hearing loss of equal magnitude by air and bone conduction, the hearing loss is sensorineural (Figure 12.7).

Assessing Middle Ear Function

To evaluate objectively the function of the middle ear system, immittance measures are used because any significant change to the immittance characteristics of the middle ear will affect transmission of energy to the cochlea (Page, Kramer, Novak, et al., 1995). The immittance battery of tests includes tympanometry and acoustic reflex measures. Tympanometry indirectly assesses middle ear pressure, tympanic membrane compliance, mobility of the ossicles, and eustachian tube function. Acoustic reflex measurements provide an assessment of the functional integrity of the afferent auditory and efferent facial nerve (Figure 12.8) (Hall & Baer, 1993).

Assessing Cortical Function

In order to assess how well the brain receives auditory messages and interprets or retains what is heard, complex psycholinguistic tests are used (Martin, Schwegler, Gleeson, et al., 1994). These address central auditory processing disorders, which are most often diagnosed in older children (i.e., older than 7 years of age) and adults (for whom test norms exist) with learning disabilities

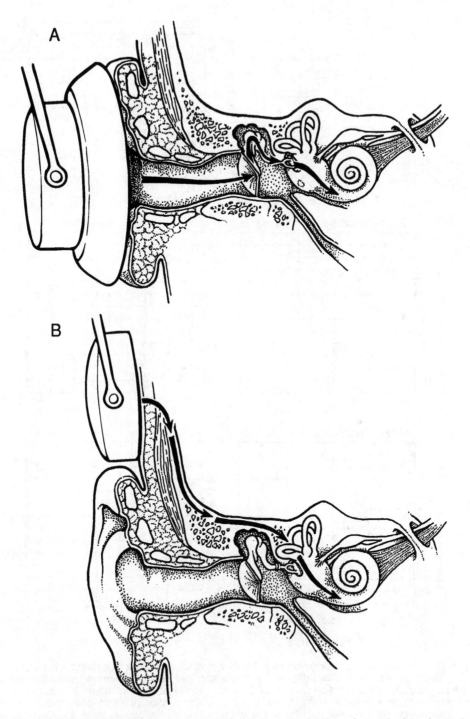

Figure 12.6. Approaches to testing air and mastoid bone conduction of sound. a) In air conduction, the sound comes through the ear canal and middle ear to reach the inner ear. b) In bone conduction, the sound bypasses the external and middle ear and comes directly to the inner ear.

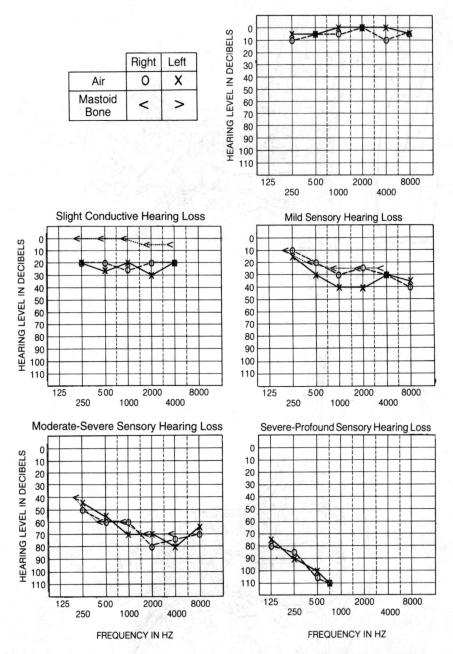

Figure 12.7.   Audiograms showing normal hearing and various degrees of hearing loss. Note that, in most cases, both ears are equally affected. In a conductive hearing loss, bone conduction is found to be better than air conduction because it bypasses the external and the middle ear where the damage lies. In sensorineural hearing loss, bone and air conduction produce similar results because the problem lies with the inner ear. The range of hearing loss is as follows: slight, 16 dB–25 dB; mild, 26 dB–40 dB; moderate, 41 dB–55 dB; moderate to severe, 56 dB–70 dB; severe, 71 dB–90 dB; profound, greater than 90 dB. (Audiograms courtesy of Brad Friedrich, Ph.D.)

or traumatic brain injury. Children with hearing impairments should not be administered these psycholinguistic tests, as the tests themselves degrade the incoming auditory signals. It would be impossible to determine whether a poor score on a specific test was the result of a true central auditory processing disorder or a combination of degradation of the incoming signal by the test procedure and the individual's own hearing loss.

DEGREES OF HEARING LOSS

In general, the degree of hearing loss is meant to predict the difficulty the child will have in understanding speech through hearing alone and, therefore, in acquiring language and information through hearing. Typically, the more severe the hearing loss, the more the individual is apt to rely on vision for receiving information; the less severe the loss, the more effective amplification is likely to be. These generalizations, however, include many individual exceptions. Many variables other than the degree of hearing loss affect the child's acquisition of language and educational progress. These include age of onset, frequency configuration of the hearing loss, speech discrimination, general intelligence, and family support, among others. It is therefore not possible to state definitively the educational and therapeutic interventions appropriate for all children evidencing a specific degree of hearing loss.

Degree of hearing loss is categorized from slight to profound (Chan, 1994). Although most often described in one of four categories, slight to mild, moderate, severe, or profound, the degree of hearing loss can be better understood as a continuum. Albeit convenient, generalizations of ranges of hearing levels often result in misperceptions of the consequences of the loss. For example, a "mild" hearing loss has potentially serious implications for the language and emotional development of a preverbal child, whereas a similar loss in an adolescent may have less of an impact (Crandell, 1993). A description of the functional impact of the hearing loss is the best

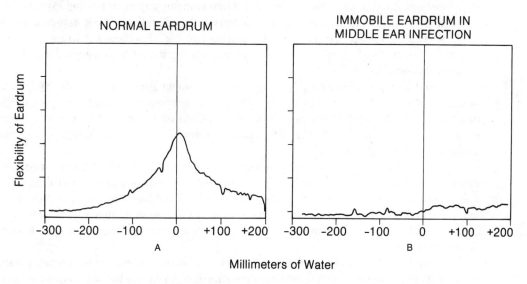

Figure 12.8.   Tympanogram. a) A normal "tent-shaped" tympanogram. b) During otitis media (middle-ear infection), a flattened function may be obtained. (Courtesy of Brad Friedrich, Ph.D.)

measure of the degree of hearing loss for a specific child and should accompany any interpretation of audiometrical testing.

Although not completely accurate, the degree of hearing loss frequently is determined by measuring and averaging the minimum response levels at three different frequencies (500 Hz, 1,000 Hz, and 2,000 Hz). A slight loss (i.e., threshold of 16 dB–25 dB HL) is usually associated with a middle-ear infection and typically has no significant effect on development, especially if the loss is transitory. The child may have difficulty hearing faint or distant speech, however, missing up to 10% of speech when the teacher is at a distance of greater than 3 feet or when the classroom is noisy (Anderson & Matkin, 1991). Some clinicians believe that intermittent or recurrent slight hearing loss can be more confusing to a child than a consistent loss to which the child most often can accommodate. A slight loss should be monitored, and if there is evidence of problems in school or in social interactions, a hearing aid or personal FM system may be necessary. At the minimum, these children should be seated in the front of the classroom and may need academic supports.

A child with a mild hearing impairment can hear only sounds that are at least 26 dB–40 dB in intensity. This magnitude of hearing loss is also commonly associated with chronic otitis media. This child typically has difficulty hearing distant sounds or soft speech, missing 25%–40% of speech at typical conversational loudness. The child has difficulty perceiving the unvoiced consonants *s, p, t, k, th, f,* and *sh,* which are soft, high-frequency sounds. As a result, the child may miss some of the content of class and home discussions. In addition, if there is a significant loss in the low frequencies, the child may have difficulty discriminating differing tones and the stress patterns of speech.

Sounds must register at least 41 dB–55 dB to be heard by children with a moderate hearing loss. This amount of loss affects the ability to hear even loud conversation without intervention. In the absence of amplification, a child with a moderate to severe loss (56 dB–70 dB) misses almost all conversation. Nonetheless, no assumptions can be made about the vocabulary, speech production, or voice quality of children with any degree of hearing loss, but learning difficulties often result from the significantly reduced auditory input associated with a moderate hearing loss. Academic supports, hearing aids and classroom amplification, speech-language therapy, tutoring, and a special education setting should be considered based on the needs of the individual child.

A child with a severe hearing loss perceives only sound greater than 71 dB–90 dB. Functionally, this means that the child may hear close, loud environmental sounds without amplification but not speech of typical conversational volume. Even with amplification, certain consonant sounds are likely to be missed. If the loss occurred before 2 years of age, language and speech may not develop spontaneously.

A profound hearing impairment indicates a loss greater than 91 dB. Although a child with this loss may react to very loud sounds, it is not possible for unaided hearing to be the primary avenue by which the child learns and communicates. The child has little awareness of tonal patterns; and although amplification may help the child to distinguish rhythm, accent, and patterns of speech and to recognize environmental sounds, he or she cannot comprehend speech without visual input.

Spoken language is not the sole language option available to children with hearing impairments and their families. Visual communication strategies, including but not limited to sign language, are very important to individuals with significant hearing loss. Signed languages are accessible to the child with a hearing impairment, and many families opt to raise their child in a signing environment to foster the development of language both with or in the absence of strong speech or speechreading skills. The need for visual communication is not limited to those children with profound deafness. Many children with moderate or severe losses have enough difficulty in receiving and processing information auditorily that they benefit from visual communication as well.

TREATMENT OF MIDDLE-EAR DISEASE

If hearing is tested during an infection (acute otitis media), a mild or moderate conductive hearing loss is frequently found. Even if only temporary, this loss may affect speech and language development and scholastic achievement. The infection usually clears up within a week or two. If the infection persists or recurs, however, it may cause a permanent hearing loss. This loss may be a mixed type, with a sensorineural loss caused by damage to the organ of Corti from bacterial toxins superimposed on the initial conductive loss (Brookhouser, Worthington, & Kelly, 1993). Therefore, aggressive treatment and follow-up of middle-ear infections are now standard practice and involve the use of an antibiotic, usually amoxicillin or ampicillin, for 1 week. Although decongestants have been used in the past, experimental studies indicate that they make little difference in the duration or outcome of a middle-ear infection and are no longer recommended (Bluestone & Klein, 1995). Clinical improvement generally occurs in 48–72 hours, but the ears should be rechecked in 1–2 weeks to make certain that the fluid is gone.

Following otitis media, monitoring for less common complications such as the formation of a **cholesteatoma** or the development of **mastoiditis** should occur. A cholesteatoma can develop during chronic otitis media in which severe retraction or perforation of the tympanic membrane has occurred (Potsic et al., 1995). Under these conditions, skin tissue lining the ear canal can migrate through the perforated eardrum into the middle ear forming a mass. If not surgically removed, this cholesteatoma can destroy the ossicles, erode the temporal bone, or invade the meninges.

Mastoiditis involves the extension of middle-ear infection into the mastoid air cells of the temporal bone, which contains the cochlea. It can lead to a permanent sensorineural hearing loss by damaging the cochlea. Treatment involves antibiotics and, if unsuccessful, surgical drainage of the abscessed mastoid air cells. Although a major cause of hearing loss in the preantibiotic era (i.e., before 1950), mastoiditis is now very uncommon.

These complications point to the importance of aggressive treatment and follow-up of middle-ear disease. If the infection is recurrent or persistent, it often must be treated with a 1- to 2-month course of antibiotics. This is particularly true if the first infection occurred before 6 months of age, if there have been three episodes of otitis media within a 6-month period, or if the child has had fluid in the middle ear for at least 3 months.

Surgical Management of Middle-Ear Disease

If antibiotics are not effective in treating persistent fluid in the middle ear (chronic otitis media), an otolaryngology (ENT) surgeon may need to perform a myringotomy, a minor surgical procedure in which an incision is made in the eardrum and the fluid is suctioned from the middle ear system. The surgeon may also insert a pressure-equalization (PE) tube in the incision (Figure

12.9). This tube serves in place of the malfunctioning eustachian tube, equalizing the pressure between the middle ear and the ear canal and allowing the fluid in the middle ear cavity to drain. A tube will generally remain in the eardrum for at least 6 months, after which time it usually falls out, and the eardrum closes over the incision. The use of tubes has significantly reduced the risk of permanent hearing loss in children with chronic otitis media (Briggs & Luxford, 1994). There is also some evidence that removal of the adenoids (but not the tonsils) decreases the occurrence of recurrent middle-ear infections in children who have enlarged adenoids (Bluestone & Klein, 1995). Therefore, the procedures of myringotomy and tube placement may be combined with an adenoidectomy. These day surgery procedures require general anesthesia; complications are rare but include infection and bleeding.

TREATMENT OF HEARING LOSS

The diagnosis of permanent hearing impairment in an infant or child can have a profound psychological impact on the family (Gregory, 1995). Yet, it is during this diagnostic period that parents must make treatment decisions that will affect the life and the language of the child and family. Successful passage through this stage requires the coping mechanisms of the extended and immediate family, the child's adaptability, and nonjudgmental and knowledgeable professional support and assistance.

Professionals' views about hearing loss often affect the information, treatment options, and recommendations presented to parents (Densham, 1995). When a child has a loss ranging from mild to severe, the choices will focus on a variety of aural/oral methodologies. However, when a child has a profound loss (i.e., is deaf), his or her family will want to learn about the positions of both the aural/oral and deaf communities. A bitter, 200-year controversy has existed about the recommended approach for communication with and education of deaf infants and children.

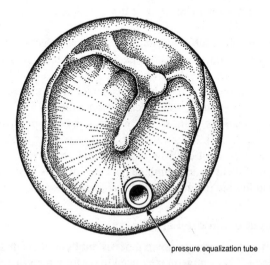

pressure equalization tube

Figure 12.9.   The procedure of myringotomy and tube placement involves the surgical incision of the tympanic membrane. The effusion is withdrawn and a plastic tube is then inserted through the opening to permit ongoing drainage of fluid and equilibration of air pressure.

There continues to exist a heated debate among proponents of oralism, who emphasize the development of speech, speechreading, and the use of residual hearing, and advocates of total communication, who support the use of visually accessible forms of communication including sign language. Proponents of the oral/aural approach argue that access to sign language will limit a child's comfort and presence in the "hearing world," and thereby lessen the likelihood that the child will learn to speak and later integrate into that world. Supporters of manual communication argue that sign language allows the child access to communication and aids in the development of meaningful language at the earliest possible age. Parents often encounter ardent proponents of one of these positions and are further polarized by endorsements of specific interventions. The intensity of the argument, and the lack of scientific basis for specific recommendations often made to parents, has impeded the objective examination of options, obstacles, and outcomes (Rushmer, 1994).

Early Intervention

Once the diagnosis of hearing impairment has been made, the infant or child should be referred for involvement in a multidisciplinary, comprehensive early intervention program (O'Hare, Grigor, & Cowan, 1993). Guidelines for early intervention have been established in Part H of the Education of the Handicapped Act Amendments of 1986, PL 99-457 (Joint Committee of ASHA and Council on Education of the Deaf, 1994). Following the diagnosis, parents need support in integrating conflicting expert opinions in their child-rearing decisions. Regardless of the theoretical approach, the goals for a successful intervention include family adaptation to and acceptance of the child's special communication needs and the provision of a linguistically accessible home and school environment that enhances the child's self-esteem (Ramkalawan & Davis, 1992). Optimally, programs should be flexible in their orientation and include family supports and integration with community services. Parent education materials, support groups, and national information centers are now available to assist the parent in selecting an appropriate intervention site and a language acquisition strategy.

Amplification

Amplification (i.e., hearing aids, assistive listening devices) is an important part of the services required by the child with hearing loss (Alpiner & McCarthy, 1993; McCracken & Bamford, 1995). Hearing aids can be used by children of any age and should be fitted as soon as a permanent hearing loss has been identified, even if all of the information about the hearing loss is not yet available. Assistive listening devices, such as FM systems, are most commonly used in conjunction with hearing aids in difficult listening situations, such as the classroom (Madell, 1992). Professionals are using FM systems as the primary amplification option, however, particularly when using the newer, all-in-one hearing aid FM combinations. FM systems are designed to reduce the amount of background noise that is heard by the child. The system includes a microphone and a wireless transmitter, about the size of an electronic pager, worn by the speaker. The listener wears a receiver similar in size to the transmitter. The output of the receiver is delivered to the child's ears in a variety of ways, including plugging directly into the hearing aids or sending an electromagnetic signal to the aids.

Audiologists are responsible for the appropriate fitting of amplification devices. The selection and utilization of amplification for children, particularly preverbal children, differs significantly from the procedures used in adult fittings (Palmer, 1994). First, the selection of hearing aids for a child is an ongoing process that extends far beyond the identification of hearing loss and the initial fitting of an amplification device. Second, the settings of the system are subject to change, as new information regarding the hearing loss and verification of the fit is obtained. Moreover, the degree of hearing loss is not the only consideration in determining a child's candidacy for amplification. Profiles of the child's existing speech and language skills, intellectual ability, commonly encountered listening situations, and school performance are all important factors in determining the appropriateness of hearing aid use and specific fitting.

Hearing aids have three components: a microphone that changes the acoustic signal into electrical energy, one or more amplifiers that increase the intensity of the electrical signal, and a receiver that converts the electrical signal back to an amplified acoustical signal. The amplified sound is channeled into the ear canal through an earmold. The hearing aid is powered by a battery, and the loudness of the aid can be adjusted by the volume control. Children's aids should also permit direct audio input to allow coupling to an FM system, tamper-resistant battery compartments, and a cover for the volume dial, to prevent inadvertent changing of the setting.

Hearing aids can be adjusted to the specific characteristics of a hearing loss, providing amplification to the frequencies where the hearing loss exists. Four categories of hearing aids exist: behind-the-ear (BTE) aids, in-the-ear (ITE) aids, body aids, and bone conduction aids.

BTE hearing aids, because of their casing size, can accommodate more circuitry and controls, allowing for more flexibility than an ITE hearing aid (Figure 12.10). This is especially important if audiometric information is incomplete or if the possibility of progressive hearing loss exists. Programmable hearing aids have permitted the user to modify settings based on listening environments. Such devices may be beneficial to older children and adolescents who might otherwise reject standard aids in certain situations.

The microphone on an ITE hearing aid benefits from its location relative to the pinna that directs sound toward the microphone. As the child grows, however, the aid will need to be re-cased, which can be costly once the manufacturer's warranty expires. In addition, the relatively smaller size of an ITE hearing aid limits the controls that can be built in and therefore the flexibility of the aid. The advantage of ITE hearing aids is primarily cosmetic; these aids are used in older children who are likely to reject the more visible hearing aids and who are less likely to misplace or lose the device.

Body hearing aids are less frequently used now than in the past. Initially, body aids provided more power with less acoustical feedback than BTE hearing aids, but that is not necessarily the case with the improved electronic and acoustic modifications available for use with BTE hearing aids. The chest-level placement of the microphone in a body aid is also a disadvantage. The child's body can act as a baffle against receiving sound, and clothing may rub on the microphone, causing interference. Body hearing aids are the least cosmetically appealing of the four types, and noncompliance is a significant factor in older children.

Bone conduction hearing aids can be used with children who have long-term conductive hearing loss or who have a medical condition such as chronic drainage into the external ear canal, which would prevent use of an ITE hearing aid or an earmold with a BTE instrument. The receiver of the bone conduction hearing aid is actually a vibrator approximately 1 inch in size. The vibrator is attached to a headband that holds it in place, usually on the mastoid. The signal is then sent via bone conduction to the cochlea, in much the same way that bone conduction testing is performed.

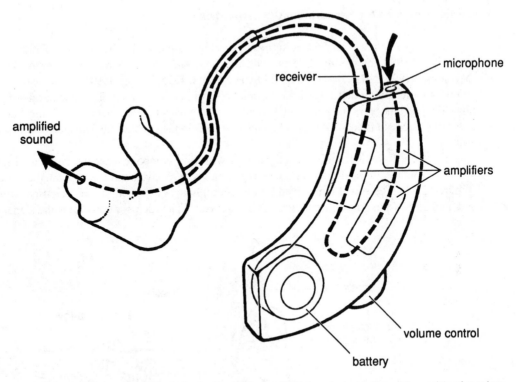

Figure 12.10. The components of a behind-the-ear (BTE) hearing aid. The aid consists of a microphone, an amplifier power supply, and a receiver that projects the amplified sound through the earmold into the ear canal.

Binaural fittings should be used in children, unless there are contraindications to fitting both ears, such as structural abnormalities or in the absence of any usable hearing in an ear. In cases of asymmetrical hearing loss in adults, binaural amplification has, on occasion, been shown to improve speech understanding in the poorer ear. The same phenomenon is likely to be true in children. Close monitoring of the child's use of binaural amplification must be followed in cases of significant asymmetry.

Although hearing aids are a valuable tool, it is important to understand that they do not correct hearing loss in the same way that glasses correct vision loss. Hearing aids simply make sounds louder; they do not make sounds clearer nor do they selectively amplify speech or other necessary sounds. Therefore, when sensorineural hearing loss is present, the child may have difficulty understanding what is said, even when the hearing aids provide sounds that are comfortably loud. The individual and family must be counseled regarding realistic expectations from amplification, as well as the importance of speech and language therapy and the need to modify the listening environment of the child. Unfortunately, even with technological advances, some children derive limited auditory benefit and report disturbing background noise, in which case the aid may not be sufficiently beneficial to justify its continued use.

Surgical Interventions for Sensorineural Hearing Loss

Cochlear implantation is an elective surgical procedure approved by the Food and Drug Administration in 1990 for use in children who are deaf and do not benefit from amplification (Miyamoto, 1995; NIH Consensus Development Panel, 1995; Young, 1994). A cochlear implant is a prosthetic device that electrically stimulates the cochlea via an electrode surgically implanted in the inner ear. The reasoning behind the use of a cochlear implant is that many auditory nerve fibers remain functional even when the hair cells in the cochlea are damaged or reduced in number.

The device provides auditory information with four components: a microphone, a signal processor that electronically encodes incoming sounds, a receiver, and the implanted electrodes (Figure 12.11). The sound is received by the microphone, converted into its electrical equivalent, and sent by the transmitter to the signal processor. The processor transforms the signal into

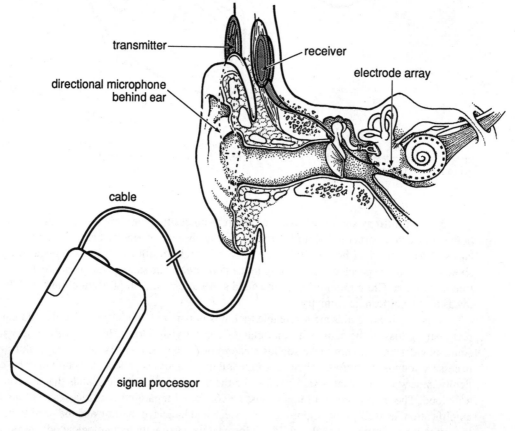

Figure 12.11.   Cochlear implant. The device has four components: a microphone to capture sound, a signal processor that electronically encodes the incoming sounds, a receiver, and the electrodes that have been surgically threaded through the cochlea. The electrodes stimulate nerve fibers along the cochlea and the child perceives sound.

individually programmed electrical information. This information is sent to the implanted receiver and then sent through the electrodes, which have been surgically threaded through the cochlea. These electrodes can stimulate nerve fibers at different locations along the cochlea, taking advantage of its tonotopic organization.

The information that is perceived by the child does not imitate normal hearing (Manrique, Paloma, Cervera-Paz, et al., 1995). It can, however, improve detection of environmental and speech sounds and speech patterns, speech recognition, and speech production (Coerts & Mills, 1995). The degree of improvement is extremely variable and dependent on numerous factors including the age of the child at onset of hearing loss, number of residual auditory fibers, the quality of the therapy and educational program, and the motivation of the child and family (Osberger, Maso, & Sam, 1993; Robbins, Osberger, Miyamoto, et al., 1995). As with hearing aids, the family must be counseled as to realistic expectations and the limited outcome data regarding its impact on meaningful language and psychosocial functioning in childhood and adolescence (Moog & Geers, 1995; NIH Consensus Development Panel, 1995; Ruben, 1995).

Although controversies abound relating to the timing, age, and inclusionary and exclusionary criteria for implantation, the need for educational and rehabilitative services such as auditory and speech instruction that utilize the auditory information offered by the implant is well-documented. Some professionals believe that sign language can augment auditory information from the cochlear implant, while others believe this negatively affects the development of auditory and oral skills (Cohen, 1995).

Communication and Education

Communication and education are inextricably linked for the child with a hearing impairment because educational curricula are language based (Volterra, Pace, Penacci, et al., 1995). Without adequate language skills, a child with a hearing impairment is at a functional disadvantage in all academic arenas. The goal of the speech-language pathologist, the educational audiologist, and the educator should be the facilitation of optimal communication, utilizing whatever is most beneficial for the individual child, based on his or her cognitive, attentional, and sensory profile and other related variables, including familial considerations (e.g., the family's language selection, communication modality) (Kelly, Kelly, & Jones, 1993).

In order to improve communication, treatment focuses on developing listening skills and all aspects of language including syntax and grammar, increasing speech or sign language production, improving vocabulary skills, and expanding vocabulary. The roles of the therapists are variable and dependent on the context of the service provision. Some speech-language pathologists and educational audiologists work in the classroom along with a special educator; others work as teachers in preschool programs; and still others work as independent contractors either in school-linked consultations or as providers of therapy. The variety of available services is likely dependent on the child's age, degree of hearing and communication impairment, local and regional educational philosophy, and other external factors such as the family's financial resources (Kvam, 1993).

Speech-language therapy service models often incorporate a specific type of communication modality, according to the preference of the therapist, center, school, or family. Ideally, parents and professionals should review the child's development and arrive at a consensus regarding a common modality for all environments to support the achievement of the child's potential.

Different options include oralism, English-based sign system, total communication, and the bilingual-bicultural approach (Dolman, 1992).

Aural/oral educational methods emphasize the teaching of listening skills, speech- and lipreading, and speech articulation. Many therapists and educators who utilize this approach believe that sign language use will inhibit speech development. Subspecialized oral approaches include cued speech, which utilizes a limited number of hand shapes to express phonetic sounds with spoken language, and unimodal speech, which emphasizes the training of residual hearing without reliance on visual stimuli. English-oriented sign systems are intended to facilitate the learning of English by combining American Sign Language (ASL) vocabulary, coined signs, and fingerspelling in an attempt to represent English sentence structure. Proponents of total communication incorporate aural/oral and manual communication modes such as listening skills, speechreading, English-oriented or ASL systems, gesture, mime, or essentially anything that facilitates the child's comprehension of what is spoken and/or signed. Advocates of the bilingual-bicultural approach propose that children must first be immersed in ASL so that they have full access to and can acquire the meaningful use of a language before they can attain a less available (spoken) language. ASL has been shown to have its own unique grammatical patterns and is structurally different from a spoken language, as it is visually received and spatially expressed. The bilingual-bicultural approach teaches English as a second language, once the sign language foundation is well established (Wood, 1992).

Remediation for a deaf child goes beyond amplification and speech-language therapy. Deafness is an inability to hear, not an inability to speak or to learn. Not only does a child who is unable to hear fail to develop speech and spoken language in a typical fashion, but he or she also misses interpersonal interactions and world knowledge that is transmitted auditorily. Educators, therefore, must address this larger communication issue and reduce the information gaps that currently exist.

The Individuals with Disabilities Education Act (IDEA) of 1990, PL 101-476, and Section 504 of the Rehabilitation Act of 1973, PL 93-112, mandate early intervention and free, appropriate educational services for all infants and children who have hearing impairments. The public school district is responsible for all programs, services, and safeguards (Afzali-Nomani, 1995). Mandated services include but are not limited to hearing assessment, hearing aid fittings, speech-language therapy, and special education. Services should begin shortly after the diagnostic assessment, with home visits by early intervention specialists as well as center-based services with other families and children. Education includes both specialized instruction and related services necessary for the student to benefit from the instruction; therefore, ongoing in-school therapies such as speech and language, communication, occupational, and audiology services are part of the school day. Perhaps the area of most controversy is the matter of "appropriateness," or what is often referred to as the least restrictive environment for the child with a hearing impairment. While some view full inclusion with hearing children (i.e., mainstreaming) as the least restrictive alternative for a deaf child, others maintain that a deaf residential or day school, in which educational, social, and athletic activities are fully accessible, is in fact less restrictive than a setting in which deaf students face a constant communicative disadvantage in interaction with hearing students both in the classroom and in extracurricular activities.

Supportive Therapy

Hearing impairment exerts a tremendous influence on important aspects of child rearing (Cohen, 1994; Medwid & Westom, 1995). First, parents must learn how to communicate with their child who is hearing impaired beyond the early nonverbal and prelinguistic modes (Densham, 1995). Frustration and discomfort may accompany efforts to communicate because of the limits of what can be expressed and understood. Without the availability of verbal explanations, parents often find it difficult to establish early behavioral expectations of their deaf child. This is further complicated by differences in the typical behavior of deaf children; in the absence of verbal language, children often resort to motoric displays or responses to their emotional experiences. In addition, the child's and family's sense of self and self-esteem are often deeply affected by perceptions and beliefs about hearing impairment that are held by family and community members (Hindley, Hill, McGuigan, et al., 1994). Family dynamics often shift due to the increased need for parental involvement in the early intervention and ongoing treatment of the child who has a hearing impairment. Supporting the family in their adaptation to their child's deafness involves the use of multimodal therapies, including behavior management, supportive-expressive family therapy, and most important, the facilitation of family communication and dialogue (Greenberg & Kusche, 1993).

AMY: A CHILD WHO IS DEAF

Amy had a typical newborn period and infancy. She was cuddly and responsive to parental care and impressed all her caregivers with her intelligent facial expressions and visual alertness. She smiled at 2 months, cooed at 3 months, babbled spontaneously and in response to others' talking with her, and achieved motor developmental milestones at age-appropriate intervals. Her family had concerns about her hearing for about as long as they could remember and reported their concerns to their pediatrician at 6- and 9-month visits. Yet, despite inconsistent responses to the sound of a bell ringing, responses that were attributed to recurrent ear infections, Amy was not referred for audiological evaluation until she was 12 months old.

The initial audiological testing revealed a mild hearing loss, but reliability was questioned because Amy cried and vocalized throughout the session. A month later, another test was delayed because Amy had another ear infection. Finally, after completion of antibiotic treatment for the ear infections, an ABR test was performed, revealing a bilateral severe to profound hearing loss.

Her parents were distraught and pursued all diagnostic evaluations, including several trips to out-of-state ENT surgeons and cochlear implant programs. Amy's family lived in a distant suburb of a large metropolitan area, not near any self-contained preschool classes for deaf children, so they promptly enrolled in a correspondence program emphasizing oral communication, as well as a local, church-based, early intervention program. The early intervention program provided several in-home visits and booklets about hearing aids, parent support groups, and options in special education.

Amy was fitted with binaural hearing aids at 15 months of age, and a difficult adjustment period was reported for 4 months. By her second birthday, she tolerated wearing her aids through the day, although tantrums and frustration were evident when she was unable to communicate her needs or wishes. When Amy was 3 years of age, her parents, eager to provide her with social experiences and with hearing playmates after whom she could model her communication, enrolled her in a local preschool three mornings a week. The correspondence program provided training materials to familiarize Amy's teachers with methods of encouraging oral communication. In addition, Amy received private speech-language therapy.

By age 5, Amy was very compliant in using her hearing aids, despite occasional discomfort from the earmolds. She was viewed as a bright, eager, and inquisitive student and was liked by all teachers and therapists. Both her expressive and receptive speech, however, lagged behind expectations. A speech-language therapist recommended trying sign language, but Amy's parents chose to continue with an oral approach, enrolling her for kindergarten as the only child with a hearing impairment in the neighborhood elementary school.

Amy fared reasonably well in kindergarten, with the support of an itinerant teacher for children with hearing impairments and the school's speech-language therapist. She played readily with other children, adapted rapidly to classroom routine, had an evident aptitude for art, and excelled at craft projects. As Amy progressed through elementary school, however, she found it increasingly difficult to keep up, particularly in language arts. Unable to follow rapid turn taking, she missed much of what transpired in classroom discussions. By the fourth grade, her difficulties in participating in casual conversation were causing her to become socially isolated.

Concerned about both Amy's deteriorating academic performance and her increasing withdrawal from social interactions, her teacher requested a psychological evaluation. Although the school psychologist had little knowledge of deafness, the speech-language therapist, called in for a consultation, suggested that Amy be transferred to a school in a neighboring suburb that housed a regional program for deaf students. This program used signed communication, providing both a resource room with a teacher of students with hearing impairments and classroom interpreters. Reluctantly, Amy's parents eventually agreed to the transfer. Amy herself was not consulted but was compliant.

After an initially difficult transition, Amy began learning to sign rapidly; within a few months, she acquired manual skills that enabled her to communicate fairly effectively with deaf classmates, interpreters, and signing teachers. Her reading and writing skills improved rapidly, although they did not reach grade level. At least equally striking was the improvement in her self-confidence. At 18, Amy still has reading and writing skills that lag behind those of her hearing peers, her speech remains comprehensible only to those who are accustomed to it, and she prefers to communicate in sign. She has a number of deaf friends, but few hearing ones. Amy continues to excel in art and is preparing to enter the local community college to study graphic design; the college has a small program for deaf students and provides interpreting and tutorial services.

PROGNOSIS

The wide range of audiological, familial, linguistic, social, and environmental factors such as age of onset and severity of hearing loss, familial response and resources, age of exposure to a language system, psychosocial supports, and the nature of other disabling or comorbid conditions all can affect speech development, English literacy, language competence, social development, and, ultimately, educational outcome and career options (Schilling & DeJesus, 1993).

Formulating a prognosis for the child's ultimate language, educational, and psychosocial development based on any single variable, however, is not possible with our current level of knowledge. Instead, the focus should be on the early identification of hearing loss and the prompt initiation of individually tailored and carefully monitored rehabilitation efforts.

SUMMARY

Hearing loss can be temporary or permanent, conductive or sensorineural, congenital or acquired. It may affect one or both ears and may exist alone or with other disabilities. Regardless of the degree or the etiology of the hearing loss, it is important for the professional working with children who have a hearing impairment to understand the anatomy and physiology of the hearing mechanism and the impact of the hearing loss on the perception and processing of spoken language.

Hearing loss in childhood offers a unique opportunity to witness adaptation to perceptual impairment and resilience in the face of a disruption in communication channels. The child's and family's innate strengths, capacities, and vulnerabilities must be viewed within a larger social, linguistic, educational, cultural, and environmental context. Hearing impairment need not impede typical development, place an individual at a functional disadvantage, or alter ultimate outcome. Clinicians who wish to address the needs of the child with a hearing impairment must recognize and make recommendations based on the unique needs of the individual child.

REFERENCES

Afzali-Nomani, E. (1995). Educational conditions related to successful full inclusion programs involving deaf and hard of hearing children. *American Annals of the Deaf, 140,* 396–401.

Alpiner, J.G., & McCarthy, P.A. (1993). *Rehabilitative audiology: Children and adults.* Baltimore: Williams & Wilkins Co.

American Speech-Language-Hearing Association. (1989). Audiologic screening of infants who are at risk for hearing impairment. *Asha, 31,* 89–92.

Anderson, K.L., & Matkin, N.D. (1991). Hearing conservation in the public schools revisited. *Seminars in Hearing, 12,* 340–364.

Aran, J.M. (1995). Current perspectives on inner ear toxicity. *Otolaryngology Head and Neck Surgery, 112,* 133–144.

Bale, J.F., Jr. (1992). Congenital infections and the nervous system. *Pediatric Clinics of North America, 39,* 669–690.

Bluestone, C.D., & Klein, J.O. (1995). *Otitis media in infants and children* (2nd ed.). Philadelphia: W.B. Saunders.

Bluestone, C.D., Stool, S.E., & Kenna, M.A. (1996). *Pediatric otolaryngology* (3rd ed.). Philadelphia: W.B. Saunders.

Brass, D., & Kemp, D.T. (1994). The objective assessment of transient evoked otoacoustic emission in neonates. *Ear and Hearing, 15,* 371–377.

Briggs, R.J., & Luxford, W.M. (1994). Correction of conductive hearing loss in children. *Otolaryngologic Clinics of North America, 27,* 607–620.

Brookhouser, P.E., Worthington, D.W., & Kelly, W.J. (1992). Noise-induced hearing loss in children. *Laryngoscope, 102,* 645–655.

Brookhouser, P.E., Worthington, D.W., & Kelly, W.J. (1993). Middle ear disease in young children with sensorineural hearing loss. *Laryngoscope, 103,* 371–378.

Champlin, C.A. (1996). Physiologic measures of auditory and vestibular function. In F. Martin & J.G. Clark (Eds.), *Hearing care for children.* Needham, MA: Allyn & Bacon.

Chan, K.H. (1994). Sensorineural hearing loss in children: Classification and evaluation. *Otolaryngologic Clinics of North Ameria, 27,* 473–486.

Coerts, J., & Mills, A. (1995). Spontaneous language development of young deaf children with a cochlear implant. *Annals of Otology, Rhinology and Laryngology, 166*(Suppl.), 385–387.

Cohen, L.H. (1994). *Train go sorry: Inside a deaf world.* Boston: Houghton Mifflin.

Cohen, N.L. (1995). The ethics of cochlear implants in young children. *Advances in Oto-Rhino-Laryngology, 50,* 1–3.

Coplan, J. (1987). Deafness: Ever heard of it? Delayed recognition of permanent hearing loss. *Pediatrics, 79,* 206–213.

Crandell, C.C. (1993). Speech recognition in noise by children with minimal degrees of sensorineural hearing loss. *Ear and Hearing, 14,* 210–216.

Densham, J. (1995). *Deafness, children and the family: A guide to professional practice.* Brookfield, VT: Ashgate Publishing Company.

Dobie, R.A., & Berlin, C.I. (1979). Influence of otitis media on hearing and development. *Annals of Otology, Rhinology, and Laryngology, 80*(Suppl. 60), 48–53.

Dolman, D. (1992). Some concerns about using whole language approaches with deaf children. *American Annals of the Deaf, 137,* 278–282.

Education of the Handicapped Act Amendments of 1986, PL 99-457, 20 U.S.C. § 1400 *et seq.*

Fortnum, H., & Davis, A. (1993). Hearing impairment in children after bacterial meningitis: Incidence and resource implications. *British Journal of Audiology, 27,* 43–52.

Gans, D., & Gans, K.D. (1993). Development of a hearing test protocol for profoundly involved multi-handicapped children. *Ear and Hearing, 14,* 128–140.

Goldberg, D. (1996). Early intervention. In F. Martin & J.G. Clark (Eds.), *Hearing care for children.* Needham, MA: Allyn & Bacon.

Gorga, M.P., Stover, L., Bergman, B.M., et al. (1995). The application of otoacoustic emissions in the assessment of developmentally delayed patients. *Scandinavian Audiology, 41*(Suppl.), 8–17.

Gorlin, R.L., Toriello, H.V., & Cohen, M.M., Jr. (1995). *Hereditary hearing loss and its syndromes.* New York: Oxford University Press.

Gravel, J. (1994) Auditory assessment of infants. *Seminars in Hearing, 15,* 100–113.

Gravel, J.S., & Traquina, D.N. (1992). Experience with the audiologic assessment of infants and toddlers. *International Journal of Pediatric Otorhinolaryngology, 23,* 59–71.

Greenberg, M.T., & Kusche, C.A. (1993). *Promoting social and emotional development in deaf children: The PATHS project.* Seattle: University of Washington Press.

Gregory, S. (1995). *Deaf children and their families.* New York: Cambridge University Press.

Hall, J.W., III, & Baer, J.E. (1993). Current concepts in hearing assessments of children and adults. *Comprehensive Therapy, 19,* 272–280.

Hanshaw, J.B. (1994). Congenital cytomegalovirus infection. *Pediatric Annals, 23,* 124–128.

Henderson, J.L., & Weiner, C.P. (1995). Congenital infection. *Current Opinion in Obstetrics and Gynecology, 7,* 130–134.

Herregard, E., Karjalainen, S., Martikainen, A., et al. (1995). Hearing loss at the age of 5 years of children born preterm: A matter of definition. *Acta Paediatrica, 84,* 1160–1164.

Hindley, P.A., Hill, P.D., McGuigan, S., et al. (1994). Psychiatric disorder in deaf and hearing impaired children and young people: A prevalence study. *Journal of Child Psychology and Psychiatry and Allied Disciplines, 35,* 917–934.

Holt, J., & Hotto, S. (1994). *Demographic aspects of hearing impairment: Questions and answers* (3rd ed.).Washington, DC: Gallaudet University, Center for Assessment and Demographic Studies.

Individuals with Disabilities Education Act (IDEA) of 1990, PL 101-476, 20 U.S.C. § 1400 *et seq.*

Joint Committee on Infant Hearing. (1982). Position statement. *Asha, 24,* 1017–1018.

Joint Committee on Infant Hearing. (1994). Position statement. *Audiology Today, 6,* 6–9.

Joint Committee of ASHA and Council on Education of the Deaf. (1994). Service provision under the Individuals with Disabilities Education Act, Part H, as amended to children who are deaf and hard of hearing, ages birth to 36 months. *Asha, 36,* 117–121.

Kelly, D.P., Kelly, B.J., & Jones, M.L. (1993). Attention deficits in children and adolescents with hearing loss: A survey. *American Journal of Diseases of Children, 147,* 737–741.

Kvaerner, K.J., & Arnesen, A.R. (1994). Hearing impairment in Oslo born children 1989–1991: Incidence, etiology, and diagnostic delay. *Scandinavian Audiology, 23,* 233–239.

Kvam, M.H. (1993). Hard-of-hearing pupils in ordinary schools: An analysis based on interviews with integrated hard-of-hearing pupils and their parents and teachers. *Scandinavian Audiology, 22,* 261–267.

Levi, H., Tell, L., & Feinwesser, M. (1993). Progressive hearing loss in hard-of-hearing children. *Audiology, 32,* 132–136.

Madell, J.R. (1992). FM systems as primary amplification for children with profound hearing loss. *Ear and Hearing, 13,* 102–107.

Manrique, M., Paloma, V., Cervera-Paz, F.J., et al. (1995). Pitfalls in cochlear implant surgery in children. *Advances in Oto-Rhino-Laryngology, 50,* 45–50.

Martin, W.K., Schwegler, J.W., Gleeson, A.L., et al. (1994). New techniques of hearing assessment. *Otolaryngologic Clinics of North America, 27,* 487–510.

McClelland, R.J., Watson, D.R., Lawless, V., et al. (1992). Reliability and effectiveness of screening for hearing loss in high risk neonates. *British Medical Journal, 304,* 806–809.

McCormick, B. (1995). *The medical practitioner's guide to paediatric audiology.* New York: Cambridge University Press.

McCracken, W.M., & Bamford, J.M. (1995). Auditory prostheses for children with multiple handicaps. *Scandinavian Audiology, 41*(Suppl.), 51–60.

McKusick, V.A. (1994). *Mendelian inheritance in man: A catalog of human genes and genetic disorders* (11th ed.). Baltimore: Johns Hopkins University Press.

Medwid, D.K., & Westom, D.C. (1995). *Kid-friendly parenting with deaf and hard of hearing children.* Washington, DC: Clerk Books.

Meredith, R., Stephens, D., Hogan, S., et al. (1994). Screening for hearing loss in an at-risk neonatal population using evoked otoacoustic emissions. *Scandinavian Audiology, 23,* 187–193.

Miyamoto, R.T. (1995). Cochlear implants. *Otolaryngologic Clinics of North America, 28,* 287–294.

Moog, J., & Geers, A. (1995). Rehabilitation and educational issues in children. *NIH Consensus Development Panel on Cochlear Implants in Adults and Children,* 71–73.

Moore, B.C.J. (1995). *Hearing.* San Diego: Academic Press.

Moore, J.M. (1995). Behavioural assessment procedures based on conditioned head-turn responses for auditory detection and discrimination with low-functioning children. *Scandinavian Audiology, 41*(Suppl.), 36–42.

Muntz, H.R. (1993). An overview of middle ear disease in cleft palate children. *Facial Plastic Surgery, 9,* 177–180.

National Center for Health Statistics. (1994). *Data from the National Health Survey, Series 10*(188), 24–25.

National Institutes of Health (NIH). (1993). Early identification of hearing impairment in infants and young children: Conference statement. *International Journal of Pediatric Otorhinolaryngology, 27,* 215–227.

NIH Consensus Development Panel. (1995). Cochlear implants in adults and children. *Journal of the American Medical Association, 274,* 1955–1961.

Northern, J.L., & Downs, M.P. (1991). *Hearing in children* (4th ed.). Baltimore: Williams & Wilkins Co.

Nussinovitch, M., Volovitz, B., & Varsano, I. (1995). Complications of mumps requiring hospitalization in children. *European Journal of Pediatrics, 154,* 732–734.

O'Hare, A.E., Grigor, J., & Cowan, D. (1993). Screening and assessment of childhood deafness: Experience from a centralized multi-disciplinary service. *Child: Care, Health and Development, 19,* 239–249.

Oller, D.K., & Eilers, R.E. (1988). The role of audition in infant babbling. *Child Development, 59,* 441–466.

Osberger, M.J., Maso, M., & Sam, L.K. (1993). Speech intelligibility of children with cochlear implants, tactile aids, or hearing aids. *Journal of Speech and Hearing Research, 36,* 186–203.

Page, A., Kramer, S., Novak, J., et al. (1995). Tympanometric screening in elementary school children. *Audiology, 34,* 6–12.

Palmer, C.V. (1994). Variables to consider when interpreting the impact of monaural amplification. *Journal of the American Academy of Audiology, 5,* 286–290.

Parving, A., & Hauch, A.M. (1994). The causes of profound hearing impairment in a school for the deaf: A longitudinal study. *British Journal of Audiology, 28,* 63–69.

Peckham, C.S. (1986). Hearing impairment in childhood. *British Medical Bulletin, 42,* 145–149.

Potsic, W.P., Handler, S.D., Wetmore, R.F., et al. (1995). *Primary care pediatric otolaryngology* (2nd ed.). Andover: J. Michael Ryan Publishing.

Ramkalawan, T.W., & Davis, A.C. (1992). The effects of hearing loss and age of intervention on some language metrics in young hearing-impaired children. *British Journal of Audiology, 26,* 97–107.

Razi, M.S., & Das, V.K. (1994). Effects of adverse perinatal events on hearing. *International Journal of Pediatric Otorhinolaryngology, 30,* 29–40.

Rehabilitation Act of 1973, PL 93-112, 29 U.S.C. § 701 *et seq.*

Richardson, M.P., Williamson, T.J., & Lenton, S.W. (1995). Otoacoustic emissions as a screening test for hearing impairment in children. *Archives of Disease in Childhood, 72,* 294–297.

Robbins, A.M., Osberger, M.J., Miyamoto, R.T., et al. (1995). Language development in young children with cochlear implants. *Advances in Oto-Rhino-Laryngology, 50,* 160–166.

Robertson, C., Aldridge, S., Jarman, F., et al. (1995). Late diagnosis of congenital sensorineural hearing impairment: Why are detection methods failing? *Archives of Disease in Childhood, 72,* 11–15.

Romand, R. (Ed.). (1992). *Development of auditory and vestibular systems* (2nd ed.). New York: Elsevier.

Ruben, R. (1995). *Language: The outcome measure for the linguistically developing cochlear implant patient.* Paper presented at the NIH Consensus Development Conference on Cochlear Implants in Adults and Children, Rockville, MD.

Rushmer, N. (1994). Supporting families of hearing impaired infants and toddlers. *Seminars in Hearing, 15,* 160–172.

Schildroth, A. (1994). Congenital cytomegalovirus and deafness. *American Journal of Audiology, 3,* 27–38.

Schilling, L.S., & DeJesus, E. (1993). Developmental issues in deaf children. *Journal of Pediatric Health Care, 7,* 161–166.

Shapiro, A.M., & Bluestone, C.D. (1995). Otitis media reassessed: Up-to-date answers to some basic questions. *Postgraduate Medicine, 97,* 73–76, 79–82.

Stein, L., Kraus, N., McGee, T., et al. (1995). New developments in the clinical application of auditory evoked potentials with children with multiple handicaps. *Scandinavian Audiology, Supplementum, 41,* 18–30.

Steinberg, A.G. (1997). Deafness. In J. Noshpitz (Eds.), *Handbook of child and adolescent psychiatry.* New York: John Wiley & Sons.

Stoel-Gammon, C., & Otomo, K. (1986). Babbling development of hearing-impaired and normally hearing subjects. *Journal of Speech and Hearing Disorders, 51,* 33–41.

Veda, K., Tokugawa, K., & Kusuhara, K. (1992). Perinatal viral infections. *Early Human Development, 29,* 131–135.

Volterra, V., Pace, C., Penacchi, B., et al. (1995). Advanced learning technology for a bilingual education of deaf children. *American Annals of the Deaf, 140,* 402–409.

Weisglas-Kuperus, N., Baerts, W., de Graaf, M.A., et al. (1993). Hearing and language in preschool very low birthweight children. *International Journal of Pediatric Otorhinolaryngology, 26,* 129–140.

Williamson, W.D., Demmer, G.J., & Percy, A.K. (1992). Progressive hearing loss in infants with asymptomatic congenital cytomegalovirus infection. *Pediatrics, 89,* 862–866.

Wood, D. (1992). Total communication in the education of deaf children. *Developmental Medicine and Child Neurology, 34,* 266–269.

Young, N.M. (1994). Cochlear implants in children. *Current Problems in Pediatrics, 24,* 131–138.

Zimmerman, W.D., Ganzel, T.M., Windwill, I.M., et al. (1993). Peripheral hearing loss following head trauma in children. *Laryngoscope, 103,* 87–91.

13 Language

A Code for Communicating

Paul P. Wang
Marleen Ann Baron

Upon completion of this chapter, the reader will:

- be able to describe the different elements of speech and of language
- understand the typical course of language development
- be familiar with the biological processes that underlie speech and language
- know the major types of speech and language disorders and their causes
- be aware of the methods of speech and language assessment
- recognize the treatment alternatives for these communication disorders

Parents, biologists, and philosophers all recognize that language, more than any other skill, differentiates humans from other animals. In fact, children's language development often is used as a gauge of their more general development, and many referrals for developmental evaluation start with the parents' concern about their child's language skills. Conversely, many developmental disabilities (including mental retardation, autism, learning disabilities, and cerebral palsy) result in some impairment of language or speech skills. In this chapter, the nature of speech and language, their typical course of development, commonly seen deviations from that typical course, and methods of diagnosis and treatment for disorders of communication are discussed.

LANGUAGE AND SPEECH: TWO SIDES OF A COIN

Language and speech, together, allow people to communicate through the medium of sound. *Speech* refers to the sounds that we use to transmit ideas from one person to another. *Language* refers to the code that gives meaning to the sounds, telling us that specific sounds mean specific things and indicating what order the sounds should be in. People from different countries use different codes (i.e., they use different languages). Some codes are visual rather than acoustic (e.g., American Sign Language), bypassing speech entirely. So, communication can occur without speech, but it would be very limited without language.

The Domains of Language

Both speech and language have component parts. The components of language are **phonology, grammar, semantics,** and **pragmatics.** The first two domains, phonology and grammar, give language its form. The phonology of a language is the distinct set of sounds that it employs and the rules for using those sounds. For example, Spanish and English share many sounds, but English does not use the trilled *r*, and Spanish does not use the *ng*. The grammar of a language specifies how the different words and parts of words are arranged. In English, for example, we put the plural "s" at the end of the word, and we put adjectives before the nouns they modify. In Spanish, however, plurals are formed similarly, but adjectives go after the noun.

The semantics of a language tell us what the different words mean: In English, *soo* is a female name (Sue), but in Spanish, *soo* means "his," "her," or "your" (su). Semantics thus gives language its content. Finally, the pragmatics of a language describe how language should be adapted to specific social situations, to convey emotion, and to emphasize meanings. Discourse and narrative skills (conversational turn taking, organizing a story, etc.) and prosody (the use of pitch, rhythm, and stress) are included in this domain. A spellbinding storyteller is one of the best illustrations of the masterful use of pragmatics.

The Domains of Speech

Speech is commonly characterized along four domains: **articulation, resonance, voice,** and **fluency/rhythm.** The most familiar of these is articulation, the production of consonant and vowel sounds by the lips, tongue, and teeth. Resonance refers to the balance of airflow between the nose and the mouth. The consonant sounds *m, n,* and *ng* require air to flow through the nasal tract, and disorders of resonance cause either a hypernasal or hyponasal sound.

The vibration of the vocal cords in the larynx yields the speech quality known as "voice." Disturbances in laryngeal control can cause the voice to be unusually high, deep, or hoarse. The fourth domain of speech is fluency. Typical fluency entails a certain rate and rhythm. Disorders of fluency, often known as stuttering, disrupt that rate and rhythm.

LANGUAGE DEVELOPMENT: A COMMONPLACE MIRACLE

Language is the most complex skill that people acquire. Unlike calculus, abstract painting, chess, or many other very difficult skills, no animal or machine has ever been able to "do" language like people do. And yet, despite the complexity of language, the vast majority of people develop from nonverbal, noncomprehending infants to become fluent and skilled listeners and talkers. Although science does not yet understand how children acquire language so well, it is known that children from all cultures appear to follow the same general course of language development.

Even before they are born, children begin to learn about the sounds of their native language. Psychologists have found that very young infants can distinguish between a foreign language and the language their mothers spoke to them in the womb. In the first few months after birth, children further tune their ears to the specific sounds used in their language (its phonology) and start shutting out foreign sounds (Werker & Tees, 1992). That is why, later in life, we often have difficulty hearing just how foreign words are pronounced. Parallel with these receptive skills, children begin developing their expressive skills. Social smiling is regarded as one of the first expressive milestones, followed by cooing (using the voice box) around 2 or 3 months of age. Starting around 6 months, infants use their oral articulators to babble consonant sounds. Infants who are "spoken" to in sign language also babble around that time—with their hands (Petitto & Marentette, 1991)!

In the second year of life, semantic development usually comes to the fore. Although "mama," "dada," and a few other words may be used earlier, vocabulary acquisition does not really accelerate until around 1½ years. Between then and 2 years old, children seem to figure out that everything has a name, and they may expand their vocabulary by many words each day. They demonstrate their new vocabulary both by speaking the words and by pointing to or retrieving things that are requested. When children learn new words, they often show overgeneralization (e.g., calling all animals "doggie") or undergeneralization (e.g., using the word "dog" for their own pet but not realizing that other canines also are "dogs"). Most utterances during this period consist of single words, though this is also the time that children produce profuse jargon, a form of speech that mimics the intonation of real language but does not use real words or carry meaning.

In the third year, semantic ability continues to develop with the emergence of grammar taking center stage. Now, children begin to speak in phrases—two words at first ("more milk"), followed by longer and longer phrases ("Daddy go bye-bye car"). Later in the year, children start to utter full sentences; use pronouns correctly; and use prepositions, plurals, and verb conjugations (e.g., sleep-ing). Psychologists have found that children who speak a single language typically gain mastery of these morphemes in a specific order. In English, for example, "-ing" is learned, followed by "-s" and then "-ed." And again, overgeneralizations (e.g., "runned" instead of "ran") may be produced before final mastery of all the correct forms occurs.

During the preschool years, children continue to acquire vocabulary and to produce more complex grammatical constructions. By the time children reach early school age, they already have become masters of their native language, capable of understanding and producing almost all the grammatical constructions that adults use. These preschoolers also acquire the pragmatics of language, learning how to alternate turns during conversation, how to tell a cohesive story, and how to modulate the tone and pitch of their speech to match their conversational partners. When speaking to younger children, for example, preschoolers will spontaneously slow down their speech, overemphasize their enunciation, and repeat words frequently (Shatz & Gelman, 1973). Put another way, they speak "motherese" to younger children.

Not all children strictly adhere to the pattern of language acquisition outlined in the preceding paragraphs. For example, some children may start speaking in short phrases, rather than with single words (Bates, Bretherton, & Snyder, 1988). The age at which children achieve specific language milestones also varies. But for most, the age at which the first word is spoken (or the age for other milestones) has little bearing on later academic performance. Perhaps more surprisingly, the ages at which these milestones are reached are only minimally related to the environment in which the child is raised. Whether both parents work or the child attends child care, most children show remarkable resilience in their language development. Attesting to this is the fact that almost all adults speak grammatically and with a vocabulary of tens of thousands of words, despite the wide variations that exist in child-rearing environments. (For a general review of language acquisition and of introductory linguistics, see Burling, 1992.)

THE BIOLOGICAL BASIS OF LANGUAGE: EARS TO BRAIN TO LIPS

What are the mechanisms that underlie this uniquely human skill? How are we all able to master such complex behaviors as language and communication, when the fastest, most powerful computers still cannot understand human speech? The answer is that the human brain is a wonderfully complex biological machine. Although we are far from a full understanding of its workings, we know that a rich network of neurons distributed widely across different brain regions is devoted to the processing of language.

Ears and Auditory Pathways: Antenna and Tuner

In contrast to the sound made by a tuning fork or even the sound made by an orchestra, the sounds of speech are extraordinarily complex. Acoustically, human speech features multiple sounds that occur simultaneously across many frequencies, with rapid transitions from one frequency to another (Figure 13.1). The ear must tune into this complex auditory signal, decipher it, and translate it into electric impulses. These impulses are then sent by nerve cells to the auditory areas of the cerebral cortex, which lie in the brain's temporal lobe (see Chapter 14). The primary auditory cortex then processes the impulses further, passes them along to language areas of the cortex, and probably stores a version of the acoustic signal for a brief period of time. Dysfunction in any of these steps can interfere with the comprehension of language.

Brain: A Neural Network for Understanding

How does the brain take these processed acoustic signals and interpret them into thoughts and concepts? The starting point is in the areas that surround the primary auditory cortex. This re-

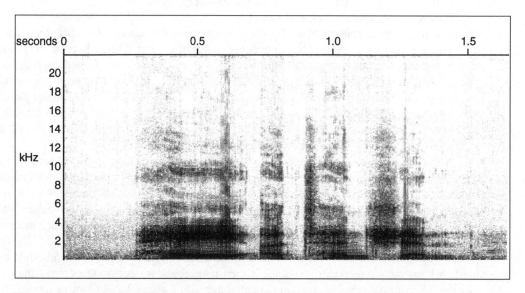

Figure 13.1.   An acoustic spectrogram of the phrase "Pay attention." Like all human speech, this phrase is an acoustically complex signal, consisting of multiple simultaneous sounds at different frequencies and amplitudes and rapid transitions from one set of frequencies to another.

gion, known as Wernicke's area, is believed to recognize the pattern of the auditory signals. For each different signal (i.e., for every different word), a distinct set of neurons becomes activated (Figure 13.2). Thus, when a person hears the word "cup," auditory pathways transmit the signal to Wernicke's area, where neurons that correspond to the sound *kup* become activated. These neurons then activate other neurons (perhaps in the inferior temporal lobe) that store a visual picture of a cup and still other neurons (perhaps in the parietal lobe) that store concepts about how cups are used. According to this model, a person's knowledge (auditory, visual, and conceptual) about "cup" is stored in a **neural network** that encompasses many brain regions, not in a single central processing unit (Damasio & Damasio, 1992).

When we think a thought and then try to verbalize it, a reverse process is believed to occur. For example, if a person was asked to describe a cup, he or she would first activate an internal representation of a cup, including its shape, its uses, and related concepts (glass, saucer, liquid, drinking, spilling, etc.). Then, these thoughts would be channeled through a speech area of the brain, known as Broca's area, in the inferior frontal lobe. Broca's area is believed to be responsible for somehow converting these thoughts into the patterns of neuron activation that are needed to produce speech. Another theory, that is compatible with newer neural network models, suggests that Broca's area may also participate in the perception of sounds as well as the production

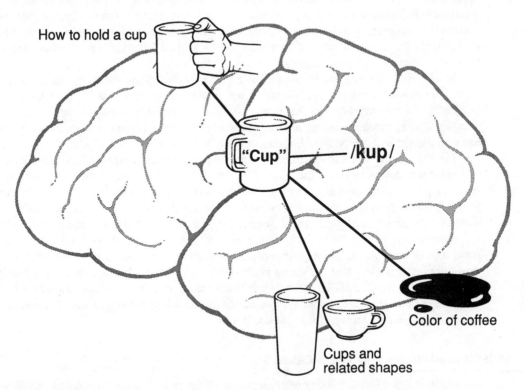

Figure 13.2.   The complex concept of "cup." Our concept of the word "cup" consists of many different but related ideas. These include shapes that cups can have; the sound of the word "kup"; knowledge of how to hold a cup; and associated ideas such as the taste, smell, color, and temperature of coffee. Many regions of the brain participate in this complex understanding of "cup."

of speech. This "motor theory of speech perception" is supported by some studies using functional neuroimaging techniques (Liberman, Shankweiler, Fischer, et al., 1974; Zattore, Evans, Meyer, et al., 1992).

Lips and More: Speech Output Devices

Like the other aspects of communication, the act of speech production is terrifically complex. After all, the lips alone cannot speak; they must be coordinated with the tongue, palate, jaw, larynx (which itself has many muscles), and even the diaphragm. In sum, the coordination of the motor apparatus used for talking is considerably more difficult than the coordination of the muscles needed for walking. Conditions affecting motor planning and control, such as cerebral palsy, can thus cause impairments in speech output.

Other Biological Considerations

Studies of adults who have had strokes have provided much of our knowledge on how the brain handles language (Damasio & Damasio, 1989). For example, strokes in Broca's area cause impairment in language output, and strokes in Wernicke's area cause difficulties in language comprehension. It also is known that strokes in the left hemisphere of the brain cause language impairment much more often than strokes in the right hemisphere. It is estimated that the left hemisphere is dominant for language in about 90% of the population. The right hemisphere does contribute to language processing, however, especially to aspects of pragmatics (Code, 1987). Research also suggests that adult women may show less rigid left-right specialization than men (Shaywitz, Shaywitz, Pugh, et al., 1995).

In addition to Broca's and Wernicke's areas, other brain regions, including the auditory and motor control areas, participate in language function. Also involved are the brain regions that are responsible for memory. Memory function is essential for remembering the thread of a story, for recalling who a pronoun refers to, and for processing lengthy and complex sentences (e.g., "The boy who the girl with the ponytail hugged is crying") (Just & Carpenter, 1992).

Finally, it is important to remember that the brain is a dynamic organ that constantly adapts to new information. As a result, the areas of the brain that serve language differ at least slightly from one person to the next and even from one language to the next in people who are multilingual (Ojemann, 1991). Furthermore, it is not known whether the adult language areas are the same as those areas used by children to acquire language (Thal, Marchman, Stiles, et al., 1991). It is possible that some parts of the brain are used only during the period of language development, but not later, just as training wheels may be used to learn how to ride a bike but are not used later on. It is clear that the young brain shows more plasticity and adaptability than the adult brain. As a result, children recover more readily from brain injuries than do adults, whether language or other areas are injured. (A more extensive review of the brain basis of language and speech is provided by Damasio & Damasio, 1992.)

SPEECH DISORDERS AND THEIR CAUSES

Speech disorders affect the ability to produce speech but not the ability to express or to understand language. They may involve any of the previously discussed components of speech, and they may occur as isolated speech problems or together with language and other developmental disabilities (Ruscello, St. Louis, & Mason, 1991; Van Dyke, Yeager, McInerney, et al., 1984).

Estimates of the prevalence of speech disorders vary from one study to another, depending on the populations screened, the methods used for screening, and the precise definitions or levels of impairment used as diagnostic criteria. One study, a very comprehensive screening conducted in urban and suburban Canada, found evidence for pure speech disorders in about 6% of boys and girls in kindergarten. Another 3%–8% had both language and speech disorders (Beitchman, Nair, Clegg, et al., 1986).

Articulation

Articulation problems are much more common than disorders of voice, resonance, or fluency. As anyone who has played with toddlers knows, children typically go through a developmental progression in their articulation skills. Some sounds are correctly pronounced before other sounds, for example, the "b" sound before "t" and "sh." As a rule of thumb, 1-year-olds are 25% understandable by non–family members, 2-year-olds are 50% understandable, and 4-year-olds are 100% understandable. Most children with impaired articulation have no known cause for their problems, but hearing impairments should be considered when there are multiple articulation errors. In children who are "tongue tied," movement of the tongue is restricted by an extremely short frenulum, which is the band of tissue connecting the underside of the tongue to the floor of the mouth. Although this condition can cause articulation problems, it does not cause language delays, and the articulation problems are usually treatable without surgery.

Resonance

Disorders of resonance occur when the soft or hard palate is dysfunctional. Cleft palates cause an obvious problem in the regulation of airflow between the mouth and the nose. Some children without obvious clefts also can have palatal dysfunction, with consequent hypernasality. An example is found in children with velocardiofacial (VCF) syndrome. These children may have either overt cleft palates or "submucus clefts," in which the palate appears to be intact, but the underlying muscles are cleft and do not work properly. Hyponasal speech can be encountered in children with nasal obstruction, which can result from chronic allergic congestion, septal deviation in the nose, enlargement of the **adenoids,** or from other causes.

Voice

Voice disorders (abnormalities in pitch, loudness, softness, and hoarseness) usually result from some sort of injury to the laryngeal apparatus. Possible causes of injury include viral infection (causing laryngitis), polyps on the vocal cords (which also are caused by viruses), and abusive vocal patterns (e.g., excessive shouting, deliberate alterations of pitch). Neurological injuries can cause paralysis of one or both sides of the voice box, with resultant abnormalities of pitch, loudness and, possibly, voice quality (hoarseness).

Fluency

Stuttering is a general term that refers to abnormalities in the fluency and rhythm of speech. These dysfluencies can take the form of unusual hesitations or pauses, repetition of words or syllables, and the interjection of nonspeech sounds. Typically developing children and adults often have some dysfluencies, but they are not psychologically upset by these dysfluencies as stutterers are. No underlying anatomical or physiological defect has been identified definitively, but dysfluency can have more pervasive and devastating psychological consequences than other speech disorders. The early identification of a significant dysfluency and careful efforts to encourage the child's confidence in his or her speaking ability are central to the successful treatment of stuttering (Leung & Robson, 1990).

Dysarthria and Dyspraxia

Dysarthria refers to dysfunction in the neuromotor control of the muscles used for speech. It may occur either in isolation or as part of a general condition such as cerebral palsy or traumatic brain injury (TBI). Articulation is most often affected, although resonance, voicing, and other components of speech may be affected as well, depending on the particular muscles involved. **Dyspraxia** is a somewhat similar condition in which voluntary but not reflexive control of muscles is impaired. Here, too, articulation is commonly affected (Aram & Horwitz, 1983). The precise neurological mechanisms of dyspraxia are unknown, though it may follow TBI. The term **developmental apraxia** is also used to refer to these conditions.

Cleft Palate

The most common congenital malformation affecting the jaw region is cleft lip and palate. These defects occur when the palatal shelves fail to fuse typically during the sixth to eighth week of fetal development. The resultant opening, known as a cleft (Figure 13.3), occurs in about 1 of 700 live-born infants. Cleft lip and palate may occur alone or as part of a complex genetic syndrome, such as VCF syndrome. When a cleft lip or palate occurs in isolation, the risk that subsequent children will be born with cleft lip or palate is estimated to be 1%–3%.

In addition to the hypernasal speech that characterizes children with cleft lip and palate, problems with articulation can be expected if surgical correction is not performed. Another primary concern is difficulty with feeding. Surgical repair of the cleft lip is therefore performed around 2–3 months of age in most children, so that they may suck more effectively. A second surgery to repair the soft and hard palates is performed at around 1 year of age. Earlier repair of the palate can distort facial structure, and later repair would interfere more with articulation. Multiple surgical procedures may be required later in childhood to enhance jaw size, dental arch stability, tooth position, and bite (Kaufman, 1991). In addition, because middle-ear dysfunction frequently accompanies cleft lip and palate, affected children often require placement of pressure equalizing tubes to prevent frequent ear infections and the hearing problems that can accompany the infections.

Figure 13.3. Cleft lip and palate result from incomplete fusion of the palatal arches.

LANGUAGE DISORDERS AND THEIR CAUSES

Until the mid-1970s, language disorders were thought to occur less frequently than speech disorders. However, several studies suggest this may not be the case. For example, the Beitchman et al. study (1986) found evidence for language disorders in about 8% of all 5-year-olds tested. Although language disorder may not have been the primary concern for all the diagnosed children, the study points out that language disorders may be more common than generally appreciated.

Unlike the disorders of speech, disorders of language generally are not classified according to the component of language that is affected. This is because children do not present with disorders that are restricted to only one component of language. Although Rapin and Allen (1988) have suggested a component-based classification scheme, their "lexical-syntactic" and "semantic-pragmatic" groupings can be difficult to describe and to recognize, and their classification is not in wide clinical use. Instead, childhood language disorders commonly are classified according to 1) whether the disorder is specific to language or is part of a more general cognitive disorder; and 2) whether comprehension, expression, or both are affected.

General Impairments Cause Language Impairments

Children who have mental retardation or global developmental delays almost always have language delays as well (see Chapter 16). Regardless of the etiology of their general impairments, it is extremely rare for a child's language level to be more advanced than his or her general ability level. This fact and other evidence have led many psychologists to hypothesize that language development depends on certain underlying cognitive skills and cannot advance beyond the level of those skills. However, the identity of those skills has not been established with certainty. Children with pervasive developmental disorders (e.g., autism; see Chapter 21) also have language impairments as part of their primary diagnoses.

Expressive versus Receptive Language Disorders

Children whose language skills are significantly below their general cognitive abilities are said to have a specific language impairment (SLI). If their difficulties are primarily in the expression of thoughts and ideas, they are said to have an expressive language disorder. If they also have difficulties in understanding language, then they are said to have a mixed receptive-expressive language disorder. It is rare for children to have only a receptive language disorder (American Psychiatric Association, 1994).

For each of these disorders, the severity and particular language functions affected greatly vary. One child may have severe difficulties comprehending lengthy, grammatically complex sentences, while another may have no trouble in grammatical comprehension but have difficulty in finding the right word to express his or her thoughts. A third child might have particular difficulty in using prepositions that indicate spatial relationships ("through," "beside," "into"). Therefore, every child with a language disorder should have a thorough individualized evaluation.

Causes of Language Disorders

Just as childhood language disorders are heterogeneous in their manifestations, so too are the factors that underlie them. Because of the complexity of language and the neural mechanisms that underlie it, how these and other factors relate to each other is not yet known.

Language disorders may be subdivided into those that are acquired and those that are congenital (present from birth, which are far more frequent). For acquired language disorders, the etiology is often apparent from the child's medical history. One common cause is TBI (see Chapter 27). Here, the etiology is clear, although exactly how brain processing has been disturbed is not. A rare cause of acquired language disorder is the Landau-Kleffner syndrome (LKS) (Paquier, Van Dongen, & Loonen, 1992). In LKS, language skills deteriorate after initially typical development. Children with LKS often have abnormal electroencephalograms (EEGs) (see Chapter 26) and also may have obvious seizures. It is hypothesized that the EEG abnormalities in LKS underlie the loss of the ability to process complex auditory signals such as speech. The resulting impairment of receptive language is accompanied by an impairment of expressive language. Children with LKS, as well as other children with language disorders, may be misdiagnosed as having autism. Children with autism, however, typically show other distinctive symptoms that should differentiate them from children with language impairments only. These include impairments in nonverbal communication as well as verbal communication, stereotyped and perseverative behaviors, unusually focused interests, and social skills impairments (see Chapter 21). Otitis media by itself is highly unlikely to cause significant language delays. Within a psychologically impoverished home environment, however, frequent ear infections are associated with language delays (Roberts, Burchinal, Medley, et al., 1995).

The etiology of congenital language disorders is less well understood. Some children with delayed language development have significant hearing impairments, but most do not. Whereas mild hearing loss is not a common cause of language impairment, impaired phonological processing may be a significant contributing factor. Tallal and colleagues (1996) suggest that the fundamental impairment for many children with SLI lies in their inability to process rapidly changing auditory stimuli despite normal hearing, an abnormality called a "temporal processing deficit" (Anderson, Brown, & Tallal, 1993). Human speech consists of just such complex, rapidly changing auditory stimuli. The fact that many children with SLI subsequently display reading disabilities may be related to these findings, because phonological processes are believed to be very important in the acquisition of reading skills (Catts, 1993; Scarborough, 1990). Tallal, Miller, Bedi, et al. (1996) have reported that these basic phonological impairments and the associated language impairments may be correctable with the use of carefully designed, computer-based remediation programs. This explicit identification of a fundamental processing impairment is much more helpful than the vague notion of a "central auditory processing deficit" that some children with SLI are said to have.

Magnetic resonance imaging studies of live subjects and pathological studies of autopsy brains have identified differences between the brains of people with and without SLI (Jernigan, Hesselink, Sowell, et al., 1991). These include abnormal patterns of left-right symmetry in language areas of the brain and the presence of neuronal heterotopias—cortical neurons in inappropriate places (see Chapter 14) (Galaburda, Sherman, Rosen, et al., 1984). A genetic contribution to the development of SLI is strongly supported by other studies. Bishop, North, and Donlan (1995) reported that identical (monozygotic) twins have close to 100% concordance for speech-language disorders. Familial studies have shown a much higher incidence of speech-language disorders in the parents of affected children than in parents of unaffected children (Tallal, Ross, & Curtiss, 1989; Tomblin, 1989). In one family, it has been suggested that there is a specific inherited inability to form the past tense of verbs (Gopnik & Crago, 1991). Further supportive evidence of a genetic influence comes from the study of children with reading disabilities. There is clear evidence for the familial transmission of reading disabilities, and geneticists have suggested that a specific locus on chromosome #6 is linked to reading disability (Cardon, Smith, Fulker, et al., 1994).

Some genetic syndromes that cause general cognitive impairment also show a characteristic pattern of language development. For example, individuals with Down syndrome often show greater impairment in their grammatical skills than in their vocabulary skills and general cognitive abilities (Fowler, 1990). In contrast, individuals with Williams syndrome typically show grammatical skills that are commensurate with their general cognitive skills. They sometimes show very specific impairments in grammar, however, such as the inappropriate over-regularization of verbs, for example, using "knowed" instead of "knew" (Bellugi, Wang, & Jernigan, 1994; Pinker, 1991). Continued study of syndromes such as these will further our knowledge of the genetic, neurological, and psychological bases of language impairments.

WHO SHOULD SEE A SPEECH-LANGUAGE THERAPIST?

Early identification and treatment of children with communication impairments increases the likelihood that later disabling conditions will be minimized. Therefore, educators and therapists should always be alert to parental concerns about communicative development, and physicians should include screening of communication skills in their regular well-child visits. Children who are at high risk for impairment in communication skills, such as those who were born prematurely or who have hearing loss or other developmental delays, should be assessed at regular intervals for language function. Referral to a speech-language pathologist can then be made whenever a delay or impairment in communication skills is suspected.

Impairments and delays can occur in any one of the domains of speech and language or in combination. These impairments can occur either with or without associated physical disabilities, behavioral issues, or other medical problems. The trajectory of the child's development should also be taken into account when considering a referral. Children who are progressing quickly after an initial period of delay are less worrisome than children who have plateaued or who are regressing (losing skills that they previously had). Table 13.1 lists some general guidelines for referring young children to a speech-language pathologist. Generally, children who are not producing 20 words by age 2 should be considered for evaluation. In older children, referral is warranted when parents or other caregivers are concerned about vocabulary or grammatical development, comprehension, changes in vocal quality or fluency, or any other disruption in the communication process.

SPEECH-LANGUAGE ASSESSMENT

Speech-language pathologists utilize an array of instruments and techniques in their evaluations. For the initial determination of the existence of a communication problem, parental reports and direct observations of the child in less-structured contexts are often most helpful. Information gleaned from these sources can be compared informally with the language and speech behaviors of children of similar ages. There are also systematic and norm-referenced methods for analyzing children's spontaneous speech, whether it is observed by parents or by the speech-language

Table 13.1.   Indications for speech-language evaluation

Age at which referral is indicated	Indication for referral
Birth–6 months	No response to environmental sounds or voices
3–4 months	No cooing or comfort sounds, crying only
1 year	No response to the sound of people talking No babbling or stopped babbling
2 years	No comprehension when spoken to Fewer than 10–20 words
2½ years	No phrases of two or more words Very limited vocabulary Not beginning to answer simple questions Speech entirely unintelliglbe
3 years	No short sentences Not engaging in simple conversation Speech largely unintelligible
4 years	Difficulty learning new concepts Difficulty explaining events No complete sentences Difficulty following two-step directions Still echoing speech Speech unclear

specialist. The MacArthur Communicative Development Inventories (Fenson, Dale, Resnick, et al., 1993) is a parent questionnaire that assesses communication skills in infants and toddlers, which appears to correlate well with standardized clinician assessments.

Clinicians generally do not rely on a single standardized measure to determine the existence of a communication impairment (Smith & Damico, 1995). Instead, a combination of measures is used to probe many parameters of communicative competency. Examples of comprehensive measures of communication skills are the Preschool Language Scale (3rd edition) (PLS–3) (Zimmerman, Steiner, & Pond, 1992) and the Clinical Evaluation of Language Fundamentals (3rd edition) (Semel, Wiig, & Secord, 1995). These instruments include measures of the ability to 1) understand and use various grammatical forms, 2) follow spoken directions, and 3) formulate expressive language. When indicated, children with suspected language impairments also should undergo evaluation of their skills in articulation, concept acquisition, and pragmatic skills. Some of the more commonly used tests of speech and language skills are listed in Table 13.2. Most of these measures can be used to obtain both qualitative and quantitative descriptions of a child's skills, including age-equivalent scores and standard scores.

The cultural diversity present in the United States requires speech-language pathologists to consider the linguistic background of the children being assessed. For children whose primary language is not English, interviewing the parents and administering norm-referenced tests can present considerable challenges. Few standardized measures for bilingual children are available, and most of these are for Spanish speakers. In some cases, the services of an interpreter may be required. Beyond linguistic differences, cultural differences in language pragmatics also must be considered. In some cases, the language assessment may provide only a gross estimate of the child's skills. Such children probably are best served by a bilingual speech-language pathologist, when one is available.

Table 13.2.   Some frequently used measures of speech and language skills

Test name	Age (years)	Description
Preschool Language Scale–Third Edition (PLS–3) (Zimmerman, Steiner, & Pond, 1992)	Birth–6	Subscales include auditory comprehension and expressive communication; Spanish version available
Clinical Evaluation of Language Fundamentals–Third Edition (CELF–3) (Semel, Wiig, & Secord, 1995)	6–21	Multiple subtests of expressive and receptive language, tapping grammar semantics, phonology, sentence recall, and paragraph comprehension; Spanish version available
Clinical Evaluation of Language Fundamentals–Preschool (CELF–Preschool) (Wiig, Secord, & Semel, 1992)	3–6	Downward extension of CELF–3, assessing semantics, morphology, syntax, and auditory memory
Peabody Picture Vocabulary Test–Revised (PPVT–R) (Dunn & Dunn, 1981)	2½–40	Test of receptive vocabulary
Expressive One Word Picture Vocabulary Test–Revised (EOWPVT–R) (Gardner, 1990)	2–15	Test of expressive vocabulary
Goldman-Fristoe Test of Articulation–Revised (Goldman & Fristoe, 1986)	2–16	Assesses articulation of consonant sounds

SPEECH-LANGUAGE THERAPY

Speech-language therapy services can be provided for preventive, remedial, or compensatory indications. Preventive therapies are administered for young children whose underlying medical conditions put them at high risk for speech-language impairments. Remedial therapies are designed to increase functioning in areas that already show impairment. Compensatory therapies allow children to adjust and use alternative strategies to bypass their communicative limitations. Remedial or compensatory therapy is indicated whenever there is a significant discrepancy between chronological age and communicative skill level or between general developmental skills and communicative skills.

Therapy may be administered individually, in a group setting, or in consultation with other professionals (e.g., teachers) and family members. The frequency of therapy may vary from daily to once every other week, depending on the type and severity of impairment. For example, a child with mild articulation impairments may receive direct therapy only once a week; while a child with language and communication skills that are significantly below general cognitive skills might receive direct therapy several times a week. It is important to keep in mind that communication is an interactive social process. Learning occurs naturally throughout the day, and optimal language learning will occur when families, teachers, and other caregivers are integrated into the therapy process on a daily basis.

ALTERNATIVE MODES OF COMMUNICATION

Social interaction and purposeful communication are essential for children's emotional health and development. Therefore, children who are unable to communicate through the auditory-verbal channel should be provided with an alternative mode of communication. The selection and development of the alternative communication system must take into account the child's cognitive, sensory, and motor abilities, as well as the anticipated communicative partners.

Four types of alternative systems are commonly used: sign language, low-tech communication boards, high-tech computer systems, and the Picture Exchange Communication System (PECS) (Frost & Bondy, 1992). The first of these, sign language, refers to a collection of distinct methods for communicating with designated hand gestures (see Chapter 12). Sign language is an actual language; American sign language even has its own grammar and sentence structure. Obviously, children who use sign language must have communicative partners who can sign with them. When sign language is used for children without severe hearing impairments, parents often express concern that it will delay the development of spoken language. The available evidence, however, suggests that this is not true (Miller, 1992). Rather, sign language allows richer social interaction and decreases the children's level of frustration, while spoken language continues to develop at the rate it would have.

Communication boards (Figure 13.4) vary in complexity from simple two-object picture boards to high-tech computer systems. Selection among these systems depends again on the children's cognitive, visual, and motor abilities. The low-tech systems may include miniature objects, photographs, and Blissymbols (a picture/symbol code system). High-tech systems may include a keyboard; touch panel; or switch input and print, voice, or visual output. Prosthetic device modifications include headstick pointers and electronic scanning devices.

PECS requires an individual to give a picture of a desired item to a communicative partner in exchange for a desired item or activity. Children who use this system must have the cognitive ability to understand cause and effect and to associate pictures and symbols with meaning; and they must have the visual and motoric abilities to distinguish among pictures and to pick up and give the pictures to somebody, abilities that are generally present by a mental age of 18 months. Children with autism, who may communicate primarily to obtain desired outcomes, often benefit from this system.

DOUG: A BOY WITH AN EXPRESSIVE LANGUAGE DISORDER

When Doug was 2½ years old, his parents reported that he spoke very few words and no phrases or sentences. His medical history and other aspects of his development were typical, and he had normal hearing on audiometric testing. During his speech-language evaluation, Doug demonstrated good social and play skills. He scored at age level on the Peabody Picture Vocabulary Test–Revised (PPVT–R) (Dunn & Dunn, 1981), a test of receptive vocabulary, and on the Comprehension subtest of the PLS–3. However, Doug's expressive language was limited to a five-word vocabulary that was intelligible only in context. He preferred grunting and pointing to make his desires known. His oral anatomy appeared normal, but Doug would not cooperate with oral-motor or speech-imitation assessments.

The diagnostic impression was that Doug had age-appropriate receptive language, but expressive language that was delayed at the 12- to 13-month level with a limited phonemic reper-

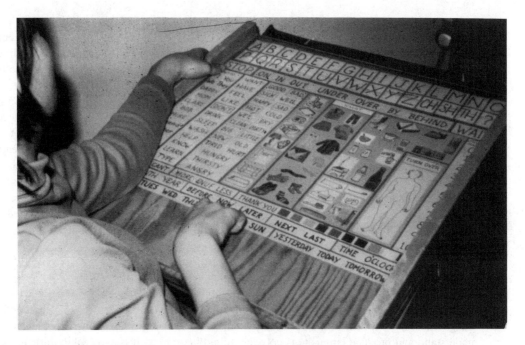

Figure 13.4.   A communication board being used by a child with cerebral palsy. A combination of pictures, letters, and words is used to allow this child to communicate with other people.

toire. It appeared that Doug had oral-motor planning difficulties or dyspraxia, which would require speech-language therapy.

The modes of therapy were multifaceted. Doug was provided with individual speech therapy sessions twice weekly to facilitate mastery of new oral-motor postures and new and varied phonemes. Doug was encouraged by his early successes, and he quickly carried over his new sounds to a larger number of words. As his vocabulary expanded, therapy focused on sequencing of words into phrases and sentences, and the refinement of sequencing of sounds within words. It was recommended that elements of Doug's therapy be incorporated into his home and school. To this end, Doug's speech-language therapist consulted regularly with his parents and teachers, to provide additional practice and reinforcement for Doug's newly learned skills.

At age 5, Doug's vocabulary, sentence structure, discourse, and narrative skills are now acceptable for his chronological age. He continues, however, to exhibit mild articulation errors and unusual prosody. Nonetheless, he is doing well in kindergarten, and speech-language therapy has been discontinued for the present time. A follow-up evaluation will be performed in 6 months to assess future therapy needs.

PROGNOSIS

The underlying etiology for a communication impairment is the single most important factor in determining the "shape" that a child's language will later take. For example, in a child with cerebral palsy and severe oral-motor apraxia, a computerized communication board may permit good language expression. Dysphasia due to TBI tends to improve with recovery, but subtle impairments may persist (Ewing-Cobbs, Levin, Eisenberg, et al., 1987). For children with a communication disorder superimposed on a general cognitive impairment, language may improve greatly with therapy but should not be expected to surpass the general cognitive level. In children with autism, if expressive language has not developed by 6 years, it is unlikely to be functional in the future (Harris, Handelman, Gordon, et al., 1991).

For children with impairments in articulation, it is common to see resolution with appropriate therapy by the mid-elementary school years. Children with specific language impairments have a more variable prognosis (Bashir & Scavuzzo, 1992). Although the majority show substantial improvements, most retain subtle impairments in language and other aspects of learning that persist through adolescence and into adulthood (Aram & Hall, 1989). In particular, children with receptive language impairments are at a higher risk for reading disabilities than those with expressive impairments alone (Beitchman, Brownlie, Inglis, et al., 1994; Fenson, Dale, Reznick, et al., 1994). Because reading and language are so important for the acquisition of knowledge on other topics, many of these children show a global underachievement in later school years (Rissman, Curtiss, & Tallal, 1990).

SUMMARY

Human communication is a complex phenomenon, with two primary facets: speech and language. Each is composed of multiple components. The neurological machinery that allows us to understand and produce language is correspondingly complex. It is a veritable miracle that so many children acquire language as easily as they do. When the process of language acquisition goes awry, it may be part of a general developmental impairment, or it may be an isolated problem. Regardless, children who have communicative impairments should have a comprehensive evaluation, including assessment of their general cognitive abilities, their hearing, and their many speech and language skills. An individualized therapy plan should then be constructed. With appropriate therapy and maturation, most speech and language skills are likely to improve, although there may be associated learning disabilities and residual impairments.

REFERENCES

American Psychiatric Association. (1994). *Diagnostic and statistical manual of mental disorders* (4th ed.). Washington, DC: Author.

Anderson, K.C., Brown, C.P., & Tallal, P. (1993). Developmental language disorders: Evidence for a basic processing deficit. *Current Opinion in Neurology and Neurosurgery, 6*, 98–106.

Aram, D.M., & Hall, N.E. (1989). Longitudinal follow-up of children with preschool communication disorders: Treatment implications. *School Psychology Review, 18*, 487–501.

Aram, D.M., & Horwitz, S.J. (1983). Sequential and non-speech praxic abilities in developmental verbal apraxia. *Developmental Medicine and Child Neurology, 25*, 197–206.

Bashir, A.S., & Scavuzzo, A. (1992). Children with language disorders: Natural history and academic success. *Journal of Learning Disabilities, 25*, 53–65.

Bates, E., Bretherton, I., & Synder, L. (1988). *From first words to grammar: Individual differences and dissociable mechanisms.* New York: Cambridge University Press.

Beitchman, J.H., Brownlie, E.B., Inglis, A., et al. (1994). Seven-year follow-up of speech-language-impaired and control children: Speech-language stability and outcome. *Journal of the American Academy of Child and Adolescent Psychiatry, 33*, 1322–1330.

Beitchman, J.H., Nair, R., Clegg, M., et al. (1986). Prevalence of speech and language disorders in 5-

year-old kindergarten children in the Ottawa-Carleton region. *Journal of Speech and Hearing Disorders, 51,* 98–110.

Bellugi, U., Wang, P.P., & Jernigan, T.L. (1994). Williams syndrome: An unusual neuropsychological profile. In S. Broman & J. Grafman (Eds.), *Atypical cognitive deficits in developmental disorders: Implications for brain function* (pp. 23–56). Hillsdale, NJ: Lawrence Erlbaum Associates.

Bishop, D.V.M., North, T., & Donlan, C. (1995). Genetic basis of specific language impairment: Evidence from a twin study. *Developmental Medicine and Child Neurology, 37,* 56–71.

Burling, R. (1992). *Patterns of language: Structure, variation, change.* San Diego: Academic Press.

Cardon, L.R., Smith, S.D., Fulker, D.W., et al. (1994). Quantitative trait locus for reading disability on chromosome 6. *Science, 266,* 276–279.

Catts, H.W. (1993). The relationship between speech-language impairments and reading disabilities. *Journal of Speech and Hearing Research, 36,* 948–958.

Code, C. (1987). *Language, aphasia, and the right hemisphere.* New York: John Wiley & Sons.

Damasio, A.R., & Damasio, H. (1992). Brain and language. *Scientific American, 267,* 88–109.

Damasio, H., & Damasio, A.R. (1989). *Lesion analysis in neuropsychology.* New York: Oxford University Press.

Dunn, L.M., & Dunn, L.M. (1981). *Peabody Picture Vocabulary Test–Revised.* Circle Pines, MN: American Guidance Service.

Ewing-Cobbs, L., Levin, H.S., Eisenberg, H.M., et al. (1987). Language functions following closed-head injury in children and adolescents. *Journal of Clinical and Experimental Neuropsychology, 9,* 575–592.

Fenson, L., Dale, P.S., Reznick, J.S., et al. (1993). *The MacArthur Communicative Development Inventories: User's guide and technical manual.* San Diego: Singular Publishing Group.

Fenson, L., Dale, P.S., Reznick, J.S., et al. (1994). Variability in early communicative development. *Monographs of the Society for Research in Child Development, 59,* 1–189.

Fowler, A.E. (1990). Language abilities in children with Down syndrome: Evidence for a specific syntactic delay. In D. Cicchetti & M. Beeghly (Eds.), *Children with Down syndrome: A developmental perspective* (pp. 302–328). Cambridge, England: Cambridge University Press.

Frost, L.A., & Bondy, A.S. (1992). *The Picture Exchange Communication System (PECS) training manual.* (Available from Pyramid Educational Consultants, Inc., 5 Westbury Drive, Cherry Hill, NJ 08003; 1-888-732-7462.)

Galaburda, A.M., Sherman, G.F., Rosen, G.D., et al. (1984). Developmental dyslexia: Four consecutive patients with cortical anomalies. *Annals of Neurology, 18,* 222–233.

Gardner, M.F. (1990). *Expressive One Word Picture Vocabulary Test–Revised.* Novato, CA: Academic Therapy Publications.

Goldman, R., & Fristoe, M. (1986). *Goldman-Fristoe Test of Articulation.* Circle Pines, MN: American Guidance Service.

Gopnik, M., & Crago, M.B. (1991). Familial aggregation of a developmental language disorder. *Cognition, 39,* 1–50.

Harris, S.L., Handelman, J.S., Gordon, R., et al. (1991). Changes in cognitive and language functioning of preschool children with autism. *Journal of Autism and Developmental Disorders, 21,* 281–290.

Jernigan, T.L., Hesselink, J.R., Sowell, E., et al. (1991). Cerebral structure on magnetic resonance imaging in language- and learning-impaired children. *Archives of Neurology, 48,* 539–545.

Just, M.A., & Carpenter, P.A. (1992). A capacity theory of comprehension: Individual differences in working memory. *Psychological Review, 99,* 122–149.

Kaufman, F.L. (1991). Managing the cleft lip and palate. *Pediatric Clinics of North America, 38,* 1127–1147.

Leung, A.K., & Robson, W.L. (1990). Stuttering. *Clinical Pediatrics, 29,* 498–502.

Liberman, I.Y., Shankweiler, D., Fischer, F.W., et al. (1974). Explicit syllable and phoneme segmentation in the young child. *Journal of Experimental Child Psychology, 18,* 201–202.

Miller, J.F. (1992). Development of speech and language in children with Down syndrome. In I.T. Lott & E.E. McCoy (Eds.), *Down syndrome: Advances in medical care* (pp. 39–50). New York: John Wiley & Sons.

Ojemann, G.A. (1991). Cortical organization of language. *Journal of Neuroscience, 11,* 2281–2287.

Paquier, P.F., Van Dongen, H.R., & Loonen, C.B. (1992). The Landau-Kleffner syndrome or "Acquired Aphasia with Convulsive Disorder." *Archives of Neurology, 49,* 354–359.

Petitto, L.A., & Marentette, P.F. (1991). Babbling in the manual mode: Evidence for the ontogeny of language. *Science, 251,* 1493–1496.

Pinker, S. (1991). Rules of language. *Science, 253,* 530–535.

Rapin, I., & Allen, D.A. (1988). Syndromes in developmental dysphasia and adult aphasia. In F. Plum (Ed.), *Language, communication, and the brain* (pp. 57–75). New York: Raven Press.

Rissman, M., Curtiss, S., & Tallal, P. (1990). School placement outcomes of young language impaired children. *Journal of Speech Language Pathology and Audiology, 14,* 49–58.

Roberts, J.E., Burchinal, M.R., Medley, L.P., et al. (1995). Otitis media, hearing sensitivity, and maternal responsiveness in relation to language during infancy. *Journal of Pediatrics, 126,* 481–489.

Ruscello, D.M., St. Louis, K.O., & Mason, N. (1991). School-aged children with phonologic disorders: Coexistence with other speech-language disorders. *Journal of Speech and Hearing Research, 34,* 236–242.

Scarborough, H.S. (1990). Very early language deficits in dyslexic children. *Child Development, 61,* 1728–1743.

Semel, E., Wiig, E.H., & Secord, W. (1995). *Clinical Evaluation of Language Fundamentals* (3rd ed.). San Antonio, TX: The Psychological Corporation.

Shatz, M.J., & Gelman, R. (1973). The development of communication skills: Modifications in the speech of young children as a function of listener. *Monographs of the Society for Research in Child Development, 38,* 1–37.

Shaywitz, B.A., Shaywitz, S.E., Pugh, K.R., et al. (1995). Sex differences in the functional organization of the brain for language. *Nature, 373,* 607–609.

Smith, M.D., & Damico, J.S. (Eds.). (1995). *Childhood language disorders: Current therapy of communication disorders.* New York: Thieme.

Tallal, P., Miller, S.L., Bedi, G., et al. (1996). Language comprehension in language-learning impaired children improved with acoustically modified speech. *Science, 271,* 81–84.

Tallal, P., Ross, R., & Curtiss, S. (1989). Familial aggregation in specific language impairment. *Journal of Speech and Hearing Disorders, 54,* 167–173.

Thal, D.J., Marchman, V., Stiles, J., et al. (1991). Early lexical development in children with focal brain injury. *Brain and Language, 40,* 491–527.

Tomblin, J.B. (1989). Familial concentration of developmental language impairment. *Journal of Speech and Hearing Disorders, 54,* 287–295.

Van Dyke, D.C., Yeager, D.J., McInerney, J.F., et al. (1984). Speech and language disorders in children. *American Family Physician, 29,* 257–268.

Werker, J.F., & Tees, R.C. (1992). The organization and reorganization of human speech perception. *Annual Review of Neuroscience, 15,* 377–402.

Wiig, E.H., Secord, W., & Semel, E. (1992). *Clinical Evaluation of Language Fundamentals: Preschool.* San Antonio, TX: The Psychological Corporation.

Zattore, R.J., Evans, A.C., Meyer, E., et al. (1992). Lateralization of phonetic and pitch discrimination in speech processing. *Science, 256,* 846–849.

Zimmerman, I.L., Steiner, V.G., & Pond, R.E. (1992). *Preschool Language Scale–3.* San Antonio, TX: The Psychological Corporation.

14 The Brain and Nervous System

Our Computer

David R. Lynch
Mark L. Batshaw

Upon completion of this chapter, the reader will:

- be able to trace the development of the central nervous system and understand the potential deviations

- know the structure of the neuron, how it operates, and how messages are transmitted

- be aware of the lobes of the cerebral hemispheres and their functions

- know the location and purpose of the basal ganglia, thalamus, and the cerebellum and how each interacts with the cerebral cortex

- comprehend the workings of the peripheral nervous system and how it aids in movement

- know the function of the autonomic nervous system

- be able to describe the origin and function of cerebrospinal fluid and its associated blockage in hydrocephalus

The nervous system is the body's computer; yet it is far more complex than the most advanced computer ever built. It coordinates and directs various body systems via billions of cells, which connect in the brain to carry out conscious and unconscious functions. Its major components are the central nervous system (CNS), consisting of the brain and spinal cord, and the peripheral nervous system. The peripheral nervous system is further divided into the **somatic** nervous system, which includes sensory and motor nerves, and the **autonomic** nervous system, which controls automatic functions such as the beating of the heart. Each component of the nervous system controls some aspect of behavior and affects our interaction with the world around us. An impairment of any part of this system makes us less able to adapt to the environment and can lead to disorders as diverse as mental retardation, learning disabilities, cerebral palsy, meningomyelocele, and epilepsy. This chapter provides an overview of the structure and function of this intricate system.

DEVELOPMENT OF THE CENTRAL NERVOUS SYSTEM

The CNS begins to form during the third week of gestation, when the embryo is a mere 1.5 millimeters long (Singer, Chiu, Meiri, et al., 1994). Part of the ectodermal, or outer, layer forms an elongated, shoe-shaped body called the **neural plate.** With further development, this plate expands and rises to become the **neural fold,** which then closes to form the neural tube (Figure 14.1). At this time, the CNS looks like a closed tubular structure with a tail and a head. The tail portion eventually will become the spinal cord, while the broader head portion will form the brain. The hollow tube will persist as the ventricular system of the mature brain.

The head portion of this tubular structure has three distinct bulges that eventually form the basic subdivisions of the brain: the forebrain or prosencephalon, which will form the **cerebral hemispheres,** the basal ganglia, and the thalamus; the midbrain or mesencephalon, which will form the midbrain; and the hindbrain or rhombencephalon, which will become the majority of the brainstem and the cerebellum (Figure 14.2). These parts of the brain start to bend into their adult shape approximately 5 weeks after fertilization. The cerebral hemispheres rest on top of the brainstem, and the cerebellum lies behind it. The cerebellum is the last part of the CNS to be formed and is still immature at birth (Figure 14.2).

When the fetus is 3 months old, all of the basic brain structures are in place. Yet, internally, enormous changes continue to occur especially at the level of the neuron, the basic functional unit of the nervous system (Noback, 1991).

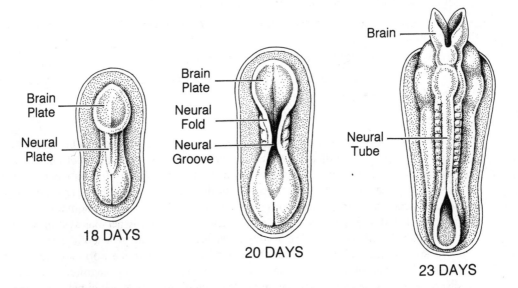

Brain
Plate

Neural
Plate

18 DAYS

Brain
Plate

Neural
Fold

Neural
Groove

20 DAYS

Brain

Neural
Tube

23 DAYS

Figure 14.1.   Development of the CNS during the first month of fetal life. This is a longitudinal view showing the gradual closure of the neural tube to form the spinal column and the rounding up of the head region to form the primitive brain.

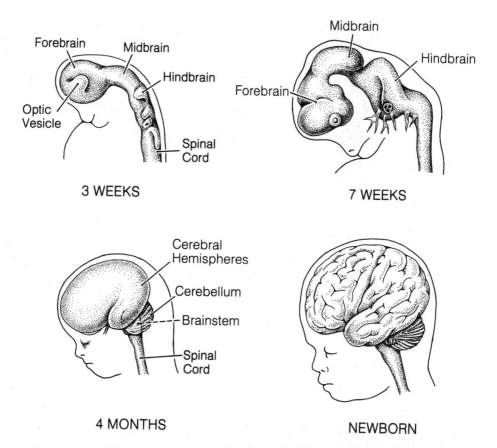

Figure 14.2. Development of the brain during fetal life. This is a side view illustrating the increasing complexity of the brain over time. The forebrain or prosencephalon develops into the cerebral hemispheres, the midbrain or mesencephalon into the brainstem, and the hindbrain or rhomben-cephalon into the cerebellum. Although all brain structures are formed by 4 months, the brain grows greatly in size and complexity during the final months of prenatal development.

Genetics versus Environment

Creating a system as complex as the nervous system is an amazing event. Scientists have long debated whether the processes involved in such an event result from genetic or environmental influences. Not surprisingly, there is ample evidence that both influence the developing nervous system. For example, certain genes are thought to cause particular cells of the nervous system to differentiate or migrate in specific ways to form the embryonic brain. If these genes are abnormal, development and differentiation of the brain will proceed abnormally. Thus, the genetic makeup of an individual can directly influence the formation of specific brain structures. However, not all modifications in brain development are genetically programmed. The formation of **synapses**—the connections among nerve cells—is very responsive to environmental cues (Figure 14.3). In the portion of the brain that serves vision, each cell usually is "dominantly" responsive to one eye more than the other. If input from one eye is removed at birth, the cells in the brain will respond to the open eye better, forming more synapses. This shows that environmental

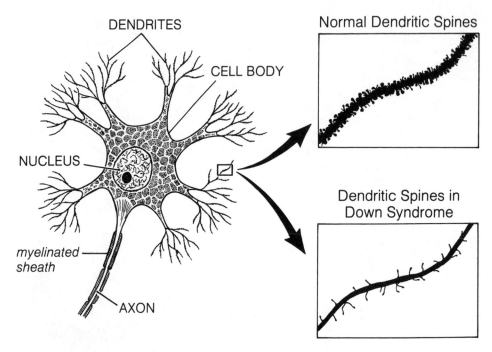

Figure 14.3.   Illustration of a nerve cell showing its component elements. The enlargements show the minute dendritic spines that increase the number of synapses or junctures among nerve cells. Note the diminished size and number of dendritic spines in a child with Down syndrome.

cues can alter the programmed development of the brain and explains the importance of correcting abnormal inputs of the visual system, such as congenital cataracts and strabismus, so that normal vision can develop (see Chapter 11).

In adulthood, the ability of the environment to modify the brain is not as great as earlier, but similar changes in the number and structure of synapses are probably involved in the process of learning. As of 1997, our knowledge is insufficient to understand such changes in synapses at a microscopic level. Indeed, as many questions remain as have been answered. For example, children with both Down syndrome (trisomy 21) and fragile X syndrome have mental retardation. Exactly how these specific genetic abnormalities cause mental retardation and why it varies so much among individuals with similar genetic problems, however, is unclear. Somehow, each genetic syndrome must hinder formation of new memories in a specific way. Thus, there is still much to learn about how genetic abnormalities influence prenatal and postnatal brain development and how these are also affected by environmental events.

In order to discuss these processes and problems in more detail, the six stages of brain development—neurulation, prosencephalic development, neuronal proliferation, neuronal migration, organization, and myelination—are discussed in some detail (Table 14.1) (Volpe, 1995).

Neurulation

The time from 3 to 7 weeks' gestation is termed the period of neurulation, or neural tube formation (Van Allen, Kalousek, Chernoff, et al., 1993). If the neural tube does not form correctly dur-

Table 14.1. Peak time period of human brain development

Gestational age	Stage	Normal event	Adverse effect
3–7 weeks	Neurulation	Neural tube formation and closure	Anencephaly, meningomyelocoele
2–3 months	Prosencephalic development	Formation of face, cleavage of cerebral hemisphere and lateral ventricles	Holoprosencephaly, trisomy 13
3–4 months	Neuronal proliferation	Division of embryonic neurons before migration	Microcephaly as seen in fetal alcohol syndrome, irradiation, intrauterine infection
3–5 months	Neuronal migration	Radial migration in cortex and cerebellum	Heterotopias as in tuberous sclerosis, Hurler disease, lissencephaly
5 months–childhood	Organization	Growth of dendritic and axonal spines, synapses, glia, selective elimination of processes	Down syndrome, fragile X syndrome, prematurity
Birth–18 months	Myelination	Mature myelination of the CNS	Periventricular leukomalacia, congenital hypothyroidism

Source: Volpe (1995).

ing this time, the child will be born with meningomyelocele (spina bifida) or anencephaly (see Chapter 25). The formation of the neural tube requires the correct anterior-posterior positioning of cells along the tube, a process that is controlled by a developmental gene called PAX. Although a defect in this gene has been shown to lead to problems with neurulation in animal models, there are probably many other factors involved in neural tube defects (NTDs). For example, during the first trimester of pregnancy, a maternal deficiency of folic acid or excessive intake of vitamin A results in an increased risk of NTDs (see Chapter 25). The mechanism, however, is not yet known.

Prosencephalic Development

During the second and third months' gestation, called the period of prosencephalic development, the five cerebral vesicles develop from the forebrain (Volpe, 1995). The formation of the face and the cleavage of the hemispheres and ventricles occur during this time. The most common defect occurring in this period is holoprosencephaly, which has an incidence of 6–12 per 100,000 (Muenke, Gurrieri, Bay, et al., 1994). This disorder ranges in severity from a nonviable cyclops (presence of only one eye) to a child with an unusual facial appearance involving closely spaced eyes, a single incisor, and cleft lip and palate. Other characteristics of this defect include a single cerebral ventricle, incomplete development of the cerebral lobes, and absence of the corpus callosum. The degree of the facial malformation usually correlates with the severity of the brain malformation and resultant mental retardation. Holoprosencephaly can occur as part of a major chromosomal disorder such as trisomy 13 or 18, or it may be an isolated defect. A gene for isolated holoprosencephaly (called sonic hedgehog) has been located (Muenke et al., 1996).

Neuronal Proliferation

During the third and fourth months' gestation, the embryonic nerve cells rapidly divide (proliferate) prior to their migration into the developing upper layers of the brain. From this point onward, defects occur primarily at the level of the neuron. Similar to other cells, the neuron has a cell body consisting of a nucleus and cytoplasm. Unlike other cells, however, it also has a long process called an axon, which extends from the cell body, and many, shorter, jutting processes called dendrites (Figure 14.3). If proliferation of the neurons is inhibited during this critical period, the fetus will develop a small brain, or microcephaly. This malformation is usually associated with mental retardation. Common teratogens that affect neuronal proliferation include alcohol, irradiation, and intrauterine infections (see Chapter 4). Regardless of the agent involved, malformations incurred during this particular period of brain development are usually quite similar. Thus, it may be very difficult to determine the specific etiology of microcephaly in a particular child.

Neuronal Migration

Between 3 and 5 months' gestation, the neurons migrate radially into the cortex and cerebellum. During early fetal life, there is only one nerve cell layer in the brain. As the brain expands in size, so too does the complexity of the nerve cell layers. By early adulthood, nerve cells in the cerebral cortex are arranged in six layers. The nerve cell bodies migrate from the bottom layer toward the top layer (Figure 14.4). Supporting cells called glia are important in directing the paths that neurons take in migration (Rakic, 1989). Incomplete migration of nerve cell bodies has been discovered in a variety of conditions causing mental retardation and seizures, for example tuberous sclerosis (Sarnat, 1987). In this autosomal dominant disorder, calcified nodules or tubers are present in the brain. Although the mechanism for the associated migration defects is unknown, some speculate that physical impediments—the small tubers—get in the way of the migrating neurons. When the neuron hits one of these obstacles, migration stops and differentiation takes place at the site of the obstacle rather than at the correct location. The result is heterotopias, or misplaced neurons, that do not function correctly.

Organization

Brain organization begins at 5 months' gestation and proceeds through early childhood. This period of brain development involves the outgrowth of axons and dendrites, the formation of synapses, and the selective elimination of neuronal processes. Defects at this period have been found in disorders as diverse as Down syndrome, fragile X syndrome, inborn errors of metabolism, and prematurity (Sarnat, 1991).

Axons and dendrites have different functions. The axon carries impulses away from the nerve cell body, often for a distance greater than 1 meter. Dendrites receive impulses from other neurons and carry them a short distance toward the cell body. Size and shape of dendrites may change with activity, suggesting that these changes represent the anatomical basis of memory. Attached along the length of the axon and dendrites are tiny projections, or spines, that increase the surface area and enable a more elaborate transmission of messages. During the first 2 years of life, increases in the complexity of dendrites change the appearance of the neural network from that of a barren sapling to an arboreal structure of great beauty and complexity. Children with Down syndrome have dendritic spines that are fewer in number and narrower than those of unaffected children (Huttenlocher, 1991). The narrower the spine, the more difficult it is to communicate messages because the resistance to electrical current is increased (Figure 14.3).

Impulses are transmitted from one neuron to another across a synapse (Becker, 1991). Here, the terminal of the axon of one neuron almost touches either the dendrite or the cell body of another neuron (Figure 14.5). When an impulse traveling down the axon reaches the presynaptic membrane at the end of the axon, it cannot cross the synaptic cleft without a bridge, a

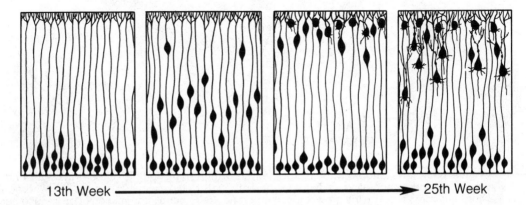

13th Week ⟶ 25th Week

Figure 14.4.   Growth of nerve cells in the cortex between 3 and 6 months' gestation. The cell bodies climb toward the upper layers of the cortex and sprout dendrites. There is an increase both in the number of cells and in the complexity of their projections.

chemical called a neurotransmitter. Each neuron uses one or more specific neurotransmitters, including glutamate, norepinephrine, acetylcholine, dopamine, serotonin, and gamma aminobutyric acid (GABA). These substances are contained in small pouches near the presynaptic membrane. Upon stimulation by an electrical impulse, the pockets open and release the neurochemical into the synaptic cleft. The electrical energy, now transformed into chemical energy, is carried across the synapse to a receptor at the postsynaptic membrane, where binding of the neurotransmitter to the receptor triggers an electrical impulse in the postsynaptic nerve (Gilman & Winans-Newman, 1987). The impulse is carried along the postsynaptic nerve to the next synapse, eventually reaching its final destination. This entire process, called synaptic transmission, is important in developmental disabilities because many of the drugs used to treat seizures, movement disorders, and attention-deficit/hyperactivity disorder (ADHD) act on specific neurotransmitters or their receptors during the process of synaptic transmission. Abnormalities in neurotransmitters have been found in infants with hypoxic-ischemic encephalopathy, Down syndrome, and a number of inborn errors of metabolism, including phenylketonuria, Lesch-Nyhan syndrome, nonketotic hyperglycinemia, and urea cycle disorders (see Chapter 19).

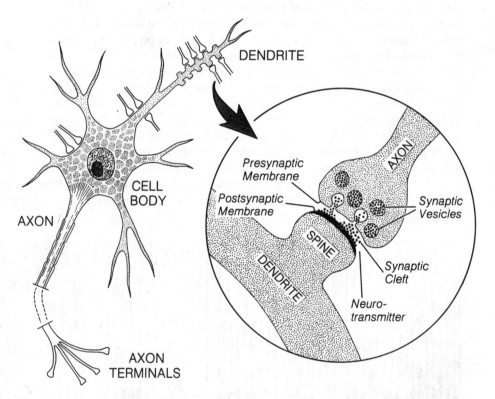

Figure 14.5.   CNS synapse. The enlargement shows the abutting of an axon against a dendritic spine. The space separating the two is the synaptic cleft. Neurotransmitter bundles are released into the cleft from vesicles in the presynaptic membrane. These permit transmission of an impulse across the juncture.

Myelination

The neurons of the brain and spinal cord form two distinct regions of the CNS called the gray and the white matter. The gray matter contains the nerve cell bodies; it appears grayish in color. The white matter is made up of axons sheathed with a protective covering called myelin that aids in more rapid conduction of nerve impulses. During fetal life, most of the axons have no myelin coating. They gradually develop this glistening casing after birth, from a central region outward. Effective myelination is necessary for the development of gross and fine motor movement and the suppression of primitive reflexes. Myelination is usually completed by 18 months of age, around the time a child can run (Volpe, 1995). Deficient myelin formation has been found in premature infants as a sequela of periventricular leukomalacia (see Chapter 7), in congenital hypothyroidism, in postnatal undernutrition, and in a number of inborn errors of amino acid and organic acid metabolism (Rodriguez-Pena, Ibarrola, Iniguez, et al., 1993).

THE MATURE CENTRAL NERVOUS SYSTEM: BRAIN AND SPINAL CORD

The mature CNS consists of the brain and the spinal cord. In an adult, the brain weighs about 3 pounds and has four main components: the cerebral hemispheres, the basal ganglia and thalamus, the brainstem, and the cerebellum (Waxman & de Groot, 1995).

The Cerebral Hemispheres

The cerebral hemispheres, which make up the largest part of the brain, are joined together in the middle by a group of axons called the corpus callosum (Figure 14.6a). The corpus callosum permits the exchange of information between the two hemispheres. The importance of this exchange is emphasized by the results of a surgical procedure called a corpus callostomy (see Chapter 26). In this operation, a portion of the corpus callosum is cut in an attempt to control a severe seizure disorder. It has proven quite effective in decreasing the spread of seizure activity but in some adults has resulted in a decline in language and in manual dexterity, probably because the operation interferes with interhemispheric exchange of information (Madsen, Carmant, Holmes, et al., 1995).

Each cerebral hemisphere is anatomically divided into four lobes: The frontal lobe occupies the front, or anterior, third of the hemisphere; the occipital lobe takes up the back, or posterior, fourth of each hemisphere; the parietal lobe sits in the middle-upper part of the hemisphere; and the temporal lobe is in the lower-middle region (see Figure 14.6c).

In the premature fetus, the cerebral surface appears smooth. As the complexity of the brain increases, indentations gradually appear. These are present by birth. The surface of the mature brain is very convoluted with many furrows and humps, called sulci and gyri. In a few children, a smooth, unconvoluted cerebral surface, called **lissencephaly,** is seen and is associated with severe mental retardation (Dobyns, Reiner, Carrozzo, et al., 1993).

The surface of the cerebral hemisphere is called the cortex and is composed mainly of nerve cell bodies, or gray matter. Below the gray matter lie the nerve fibers, or the white matter. The cerebral cortex initiates motion and thought and adds flexibility to the more reflexive and involuntary brainstem. Each cortical lobe takes care of particular activities and functions.

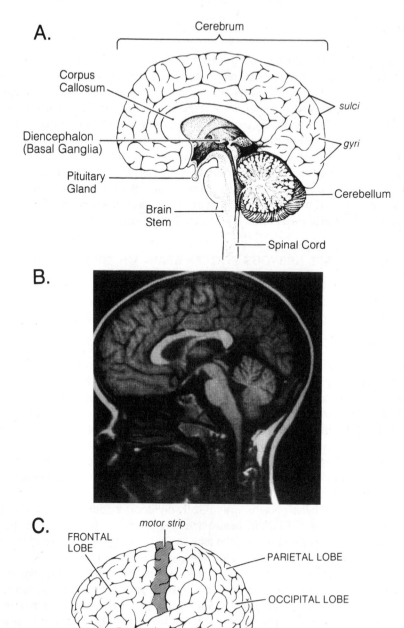

A.

Cerebrum

Corpus Callosum

sulci

gyri

Diencephalon (Basal Ganglia)

Pituitary Gland

Cerebellum

Brain Stem

Spinal Cord

B.

C.

motor strip

FRONTAL LOBE

PARIETAL LOBE

OCCIPITAL LOBE

TEMPORAL LOBE

Figure 14.6.   a) Lateral view of the brain showing the component elements: cerebral hemispheres, diencephalon, cerebellum, brainstem, and spinal cord. b) Lateral view of brain by MRI scan. Note the excellent reproduction of the structures of the brain. c) Side view of the left hemisphere. The cortex is divided into four lobes: frontal, parietal, occipital, and temporal. The motor strip, lying at the back of the frontal lobe, is highlighted. It initiates voluntary movement and is damaged in spastic cerebral palsy.

The Frontal Lobe

The frontal lobe is involved both in initiating voluntary muscle movement and in cognition (Brodal, 1992). The motor strip of the frontal lobe, lying just in front of the parietal lobe, controls voluntary motor activity. The different areas of the body are represented topographically along this strip. The tongue and larynx, or voice box, are controlled from the lowest point, followed in an upward sequence by the face, hand, arm, trunk, thigh, and foot (Figure 14.7). The tongue, larynx, and hand occupy a particularly large area along this strip because the motor activities involved in speech and fine motor dexterity are very complex and require elaborate control.

Voluntary movement begins with stimulation of a nerve impulse in this strip. This impulse passes down the pyramidal, or **corticospinal,** tract, which connects the cortex with the spinal cord. At the spinal cord, the impulse is passed across a synapse to an anterior horn cell. This motor neuron sends its axon into a peripheral nerve that leads to a particular muscle. The end result is voluntary movement of that specific muscle. In the adult condition of amyotrophic lateral sclerosis (Lou Gehrig disease) and in the spinal muscular atrophy disease of childhood (Werdnig Hoffman disease), these motor neurons die, resulting in flaccid weakness (see Chapter 15). Conversely, if there is damage to either the motor cortex or the pyramidal tract, spasticity results. The underlying involuntary (reflexive) muscle contractions controlled by the brainstem and spinal cord are no longer counterbalanced by voluntary pyramidal activity. Voluntary movement becomes difficult, and muscle tone is increased, as seen in spastic cerebral palsy (see Chapter 24).

In addition to controlling voluntary movement, the frontal lobe also contains areas that are involved in abstract thinking (Barkley, Grodzinsky, & DuPaul, 1992). Years ago, some people with severe psychosis or with antisocial behavior were treated with a prefrontal leukotomy, an operation in which part of the frontal lobe was cut. This diminished the number of aggressive outbursts, but the people became messy, lost some of their initiative, were easily distracted, and

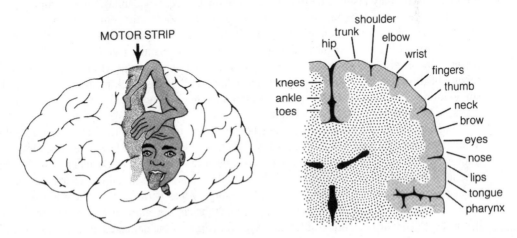

Figure 14.7.   The motor strip. This cartoon shows a representation of body parts at various points on the strip. Note that the areas of facial and hand muscles are very large. This is because of the intricate control necessary for speech and fine motor coordination. A cross-sectional view of the motor strip is shown at right.

demonstrated poor judgment (Benson, Stuss, Naeser, et al., 1981). Because of these side effects, leukotomies are now rarely performed.

The Occipital Lobe

In the occipital lobe, which is primarily concerned with vision, visual stimuli are deciphered and "analyzed" in an area called the visual-receptive area. The image is processed further in another part of the occipital lobe and then is passed on to the temporal and parietal lobes, where the location in space and the identity of the object are determined. In both the temporal and parietal lobes, the image is related to what has been heard and felt so that an intelligent interpretation can be made. Severe damage to the occipital region can lead to "cortical blindness" (Good, Jan, DeSa, et al., 1994). Although the eyes can see, the occipital lobe does not receive the image. As a result, the person is functionally blind (see Chapter 11).

The Parietal Lobe

Besides aiding in vision, the parietal lobe integrates other stimuli, making a whole impression, or gestalt, from various inputs received from the different senses. Within this lobe are distinct areas for visual, auditory, touch, pain, smell, and temperature sensations. Few specific diseases have been associated with damage to this lobe. However, some researchers believe that the visual-perceptual problems experienced by children with learning disabilities are the result of abnormal functioning in this lobe (Flowers, 1993). In addition, the difficulty that a child with ADHD has in performing fine motor tasks may result from changes in this area of the brain.

The Temporal Lobe

The temporal lobe of the cerebral hemisphere is primarily involved in communication and sensation. In the dominant hemisphere (usually the left side), it helps to form and understand language and stores visual and auditory experiences. When the temporal lobe malfunctions, a number of disorders may result. The two most common are receptive aphasia and complex partial seizures. In receptive aphasia, which is usually an adult disorder, the temporal lobe is damaged by a tumor, stroke, or traumatic injury (Nolte, 1993). The person cannot understand the words he or she hears but is able to speak, although in a nonsensical manner (see Chapter 13). Complex partial seizures also arise in the temporal lobe (Plate, Wieser, Yasargil, et al., 1993). Before the seizure begins, the individual may experience a "déjà vu," or flashback phenomenon, caused by stimulation of this area of the brain. The person also may see strange images, smell unpleasant odors, or hear bizarre sounds (see Chapter 26).

In some children whose seizures have been resistant to antiepileptic drugs, a portion of the temporal lobe may be removed. The results from this type of surgery have been encouraging in improving seizure control, and side effects have been few (Haglund & Ojemann, 1993). Adults who have received the same surgery for intractable seizures occasionally experience memory loss and/or decreased spontaneous speech if the surgery was performed on the dominant hemisphere (Devinsky & Pacia, 1993). This suggests that the child's brain, in which the nondominant hemisphere can take over some of the language functions of the damaged area, is more resilient than the adult brain.

The Basal Ganglia and Thalamus

Resting beneath the cortex, in the center of the brain, is an area called the diencephalon (Figure 14.6a). Adjacent to the diencephalon are the basal ganglia and related structures. In lower vertebrates, this area controls motor activity. In humans, this primitive part of the brain modifies and alters the instructions from the motor cortex that call for voluntary movement (Roberts, 1992). As a result, damage to the basal ganglia leads to movement disorders. Voluntary movement is possible, but it may be exaggerated in a twisting, squirming pattern called choreoathetosis. In addition, a plastic or "lead pipe" rigidity rather than spasticity characterizes the changes in tone and is the hallmark of dyskinetic cerebral palsy (see Chapter 24) (Cote & Crutcher, 1991).

Adjacent to the basal ganglia is the thalamus. All information traveling toward the cortex stops in the thalamus. The thalamus is believed to act as a gateway for the cerebral cortex and may be involved in a variety of disorders, including absence epilepsy (petit mal seizures).

The Brainstem

The brainstem connects the cerebral hemispheres to the spinal cord. It has three regions: the medulla, the pons, and the midbrain (Figure 14.8). Together, these parts send out 12 cranial nerves that control such diverse functions as breathing, swallowing, seeing, and hearing (Klemm & Vertes, 1990). These nerves also affect facial expression, eye and tongue movements, and salivation. The brainstem also contains sections of the corticospinal tract as well as other nerve tracts that flow from the cortex to the spinal cord and sensory tracts that go from the spinal cord to the brain. Children with cerebral palsy often have damage to the brainstem or to pathways that end in the brainstem. This explains why these children have, in addition to gross motor problems, a high incidence of sucking and swallowing problems, strabismus, excessive salivation, and speech disorders (see Chapter 24).

The Cerebellum

The cerebellum develops from a portion of the brainstem and rests just below the cerebral hemispheres and behind the pons (Figure 14.6a). The cerebellum coordinates the action of the voluntary muscles and times their contractions so that movements are performed smoothly and accurately.

For us to move efficiently, the work of the cerebellum must be integrated with the work of the cerebral hemispheres and the basal ganglia. Although voluntary movement can occur without the presence of the cerebellum, such movement is clumsy and disorganized. The walk of a person with abnormal cerebellar functioning is called **ataxic** and is most commonly seen in an inebriated person. Also, the hands of a person with cerebellar damage tremble, the eyes twitch (also called nystagmus), and the individual overshoots the mark when reaching for an object. In a child, the most common cause of cerebellar dysfunction is drug intoxication (Menkes, 1995). For example, a child with a seizure disorder who receives too much phenytoin (Dilantin) weaves while walking and has difficulty reaching precisely. This is because phenytoin has a direct effect on cerebellar function. When the drug level returns to normal, these problems disappear. Other antiepileptic medicines can have similar toxic effects.

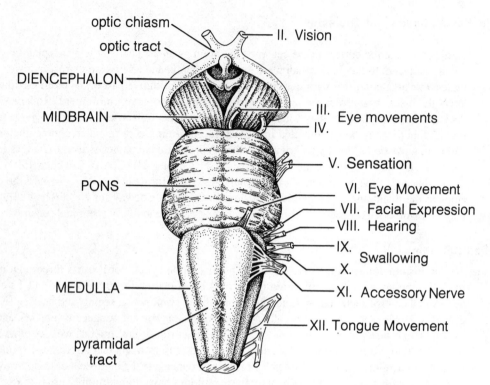

optic chiasm
optic tract
DIENCEPHALON
MIDBRAIN
PONS
MEDULLA
pyramidal tract

II. Vision
III. Eye movements
IV.
V. Sensation
VI. Eye Movement
VII. Facial Expression
VIII. Hearing
IX.
    Swallowing
X.
XI. Accessory Nerve
XII. Tongue Movement

Figure 14.8.   The brainstem. The three regions are shown: midbrain, pons, and medulla. The place-ment and function of 11 of the 12 cranial nerves are illustrated. (The first cranial nerve [smell] is not shown. It lies in front of the second cranial nerve, below the frontal lobe.) Note that the pyramidal tract runs from the cortex into the brainstem. The pyramidal fibers cross over in the medulla. Thus, the right hemisphere controls left-side movement.

The Spinal Cord

Extending from the brainstem to the lower back is the cylindrical spinal cord. A three-layer cov-ering called the meninges surrounds both the brain and the spinal cord (Figure 14.9). The spinal cord is enlarged in the neck, or cervical, region and in the lumbar, or lower back area. These en-larged areas contain motor neurons, which send messages to the peripheral nerve fibers that lead to the arms and legs.

Primarily a conduit, the spinal cord transmits motor and sensory messages. If the spinal cord is damaged—for example, because of trauma or a congenital malformation such as meningomyelocele—messages from the brain are short-circuited before they reach the periph-eral nerves below the **lesion** or area of injury. The result may be the loss of both sensation and movement in the affected limbs.

Damage to the spinal cord also can result from an infection. The polio virus, now virtually eradicated in the United States, led to paralysis in many children during the 1950s because it destroyed the motor neurons of the spinal cord (Mulder, 1995). Although the sensory pathways remained intact, the motor path was interrupted. The child could feel touch and pain but could not move.

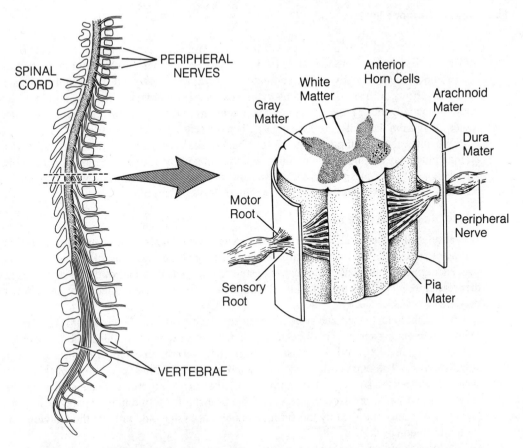

Figure 14.9.   The spinal column. The spinal cord extends from the neck to the lower back. It is pro-tected by the bony vertebrae that form the spinal column. The enlargement to the right shows a section of the cord taken from the upper back region. Note the meninges (the dura, arachnoid, and pia mater) surrounding the cord and the peripheral nerve on its way to a muscle. This nerve contains both motor and sensory components. The spinal cord, like the brain, has both gray and white matter. The gray matter consists of various nerve cells, most important of which are the ante-rior horn cells. These are destroyed in polio. The white matter contains nerve fibers wrapped in myelin, which gives the cord its glistening appearance.

THE PERIPHERAL NERVOUS SYSTEM

For movement to occur, the nerve impulse that passes from the motor cortex to the motor neu-rons in the spinal cord must connect with a peripheral nerve, which carries the impulse to the muscle. Peripheral nerves have fibers that run in both directions. The motor, or efferent, fibers bring signals from the brain to the muscles and cause movement. The sensory, or afferent, fibers carry signals from the muscle to the brain that indicate the position of a joint and the tone of the muscle following the movement. The interaction between these two types of nerves allows smooth movement. Nerves of the peripheral nervous system control both voluntary and involun-tary movement.

The Somatic Nervous System

The somatic nervous system is the part of the peripheral nervous system that controls voluntary movement. For normal muscle tone to occur, the proper relationship between the motor and the sensory fibers must exist. Even when at rest, muscles have some tone because of the balance between the efforts of the motor and sensory nerves. In other words, it is not the muscle itself, but rather the activity of the nervous system, that maintains muscle tone. Tone is decreased when the motor fibers from the spinal cord are cut or when the sensory fibers are affected.

When the motor neurons or the motor fibers of the peripheral nervous system are injured, an individual may lose both the voluntary and the reflexive qualities of the muscle. The affected muscle not only becomes paralyzed, it also loses its tone and becomes floppy, or hypotonic. After a while, the affected muscle and limb begin to shrink, or atrophy.

The Autonomic Nervous System

An entirely different part of the peripheral nervous system takes care of involuntary activities. The autonomic nervous system controls the functioning of the cardiovascular, respiratory, digestive, endocrine, urinary, and reproductive systems. The tracts that control this system start in the diencephalon, proceed to the spinal cord, and then move on to the particular organ with which they are involved.

While the somatic nervous system is concerned with individual muscle movements, the autonomic nervous system has an all-or-none effect. The best example of this is the "fight or flight" response (Figure 14.10). When a person is frightened, several physiological changes take place simultaneously. The pupils dilate, the hair stands on end, and the functioning of the digestive system is suspended so that blood can be diverted to more important areas, such as the brain. Heart rate and blood pressure increase, and the bronchioles of the lung expand in size. All of these changes are controlled by the autonomic nervous system and prepare the individual to react to the emergency.

A more common function of the autonomic nervous system is the control of bladder and bowel function in infants: When the bladder or bowel fills, the outlet muscles release, and the child urinates or defecates. Between the ages of 12 and 18 months, the child gradually gains control over these activities. The cerebral cortex starts sending impulses to the spinal cord and, from there, to the muscles of the bladder and bowel. These impulses inhibit the autonomic nervous system's response so that the reflexive action of urinating or defecating is reduced. Thus, when an older child feels the need to urinate or defecate, he or she can tighten the necessary muscles until reaching a bathroom. Individuals who have damage to either the corticospinal tract or the spinal cord cannot inhibit the autonomic nervous system in this way (Low, 1994). This is why some children with cerebral palsy, spina bifida, and mental retardation have great difficulty controlling bladder and bowel function.

THE CEREBROSPINAL FLUID AND HYDROCEPHALUS

The cerebrospinal fluid is a clear, watery liquid that bathes the spinal cord and flows through the ventricles, or cavities, within the brain (Figure 14.11). Totaling about 4 ounces in an adult, this fluid serves to buffer the CNS against sudden pressure changes and also helps to provide this system with nutrition. Produced in a tangle of cells that hang from the roof of the ventri-

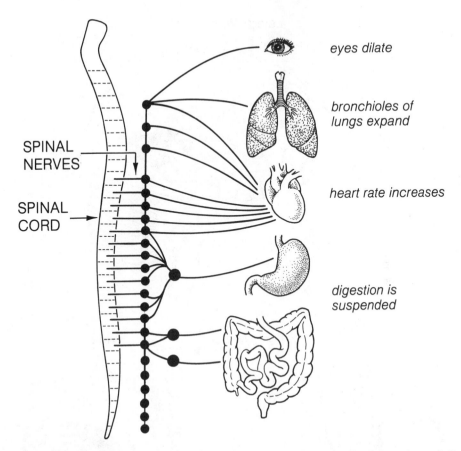

eyes dilate

bronchioles of lungs expand

heart rate increases

digestion is suspended

SPINAL NERVES

SPINAL CORD

Figure 14.10.   Autonomic nervous system. These nerves control such involuntary motor activities as breathing, heart rate, and digestion. This system is involved in "fight or flight" reactions.

cles, called the choroid plexus, and absorbed on the surface of the brain, this fluid is constantly recycled.

After it is produced in the roof of the lateral ventricles, the cerebrospinal fluid flows from the lateral ventricle to the third ventricle, and then into the fourth ventricle via a narrow passageway called the aqueduct. Three openings in the roof of the fourth ventricle allow some of the cerebrospinal fluid to move into the small space surrounding the brain. Much of the fluid, however, goes from the fourth ventricle down the meninges surrounding the spinal cord to the base of the spine.

If this flow is obstructed, it backs up in the ventricles and leads to increased intracranial pressure. This condition is called hydrocephalus (Figure 25.6) (Schurr & Polkey, 1993). In an infant, a significant increase in intracranial pressure is prevented because the brain can expand by pushing open the unfused bones of the skull, which increases the infant's head circumference. In an older child, however, the cranial bones are fused, and the brain has no room to expand. If untreated, this intracranial pressure builds and can cause the child to vomit, become lethargic, and

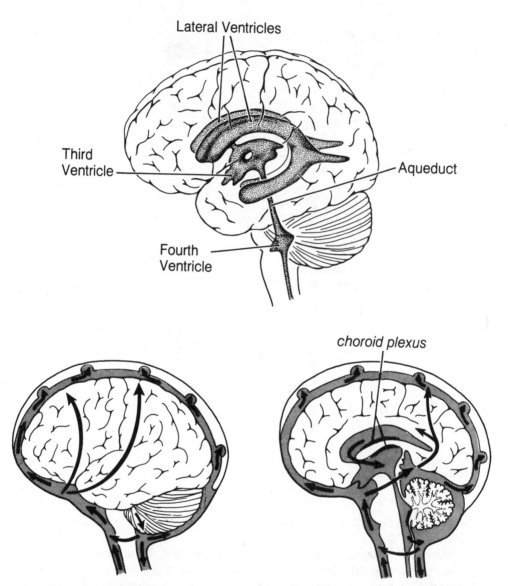

Figure 14.11.   The ventricular system of the brain. The major parts of the ventricular system are shown above. The flow of cerebrospinal fluid is shown below. The fluid is produced by the choroid plexus in the roof of the lateral and third ventricles. Its primary route is through the aqueduct, into the fourth ventricle, and then into the spinal column, where it is absorbed. A secondary route is around the surface of the brain. A blockage, most commonly of the aqueduct, leads to hydrocephalus. (Lower illustration redrawn with permission from Milhorat, T.H. [1972]. *Hydrocephalus and the cerebrospinal fluid*. Baltimore: Williams & Wilkins Co. Copyright 1972, The Williams & Wilkins Co., Baltimore.)

go into a coma. Such a situation requires emergency treatment at the first sign of increased intracranial pressure.

Hydrocephalus has many causes. In some children, it is congenital and can be associated with other abnormalities such as meningomyelocele (see Chapter 25). In others, meningitis or an intraventricular hemorrhage causes a blockage of the openings on the surface of the brain or of the aqueduct. Both abnormalities hinder the flow of the cerebrospinal fluid, thereby causing hydrocephalus. In some children, the cause of the hydrocephalus is unknown.

Children with hydrocephalus are usually treated with medication or the surgical placement of a permanent bypass, usually a ventriculo-peritoneal (V-P) shunt (Vintzileos, Ingardia, & Nochimson, 1983), which drains the fluid into the peritoneal cavity, where it can be reabsorbed by the body. This prevents the buildup of intracranial pressure and further enlargement of the head (Figure 25.7). Hydrocephalus is not necessarily associated with mental retardation or other disabilities, and many children with hydrocephalus grow up to lead typical lives (Prigatano, Zeiner, Pollay, et al., 1983).

IMAGING THE BRAIN

In the 1990s, neuroimaging techniques have allowed us to more fully understand the living brain (Lyon & Rumsey, 1996). Neuroimaging procedures provide high-resolution functional or anatomical information about the brain without placing the child at significant risk. The first imaging technique to be developed was computed tomography (CT). It uses conventional X-ray beams to visualize brain "slices" that are analyzed by a computer, which provides precise anatomical information about the brain. The technology is based on differences in density among various parts of the brain. Although the images are not as detailed as other imaging techniques, CT scans are relatively easily performed and provide all the basic anatomical information needed to diagnose most neurological conditions.

More recently, magnetic resonance imaging (MRI) has become available for evaluating the brain (Figure 14.6b). This method exploits subtle magnetic differences in water and other molecules of the brain to evaluate regions in great anatomical detail. MRI scanning, which uses no radiation, is very safe and usually provides better resolution than CT scanning. It is, however, more expensive and time consuming than CT scanning and more difficult to perform under emergency situations. It also provides slightly different information so that, in some instances, the techniques are complementary. Still, MRI has replaced the CT scan in many cases as the preferred tool for anatomically evaluating the CNS (Leonard, Voeller, Lombardino, et al., 1993).

Other neuroimaging procedures have become available for assessing the functional state of the CNS (Messa, Fazio, Costa, et al., 1995). Single photon emission computed tomography (SPECT) and positron emission tomography (PET) both use radioactively labeled compounds, most commonly glucose, which are selectively taken up by the most active regions of the brain. The label permits visualization of the regions of the brain that are most active (e.g., using up the most glucose) during the performance of a particular task such as finger movement or reading. This has been used in clinical research to study children with ADHD, learning disabilities, and other developmental disabilities. As of 1997, these tests have been most useful in clinically evaluating children with seizure disorders, as the technology differentiates those areas that are hyperactive because of seizure activity from those that are damaged from structural lesions and are thus hypoactive (Figure 31.9). The most recent neuroimaging technique, called functional magnetic resonance imaging (fMRI), combines the safety and superior anatomic resolution of MRI with functional assessments, to evaluate nervous system capability (Figure 14.12). It is likely to be used in situations similar to those in which PET scans are used.

SUMMARY

The nervous system has two major subunits: the CNS and the peripheral nervous system. Within the CNS are the cerebral hemispheres, the thalamus, the basal ganglia, the brainstem, the cerebellum, and the spinal cord. The CNS is responsible for cognition and for controlling the peripheral nervous system, which is composed of the somatic and autonomic nervous systems. Mistakes at various stages of nervous system development can lead to developmental disabilities including mental retardation.

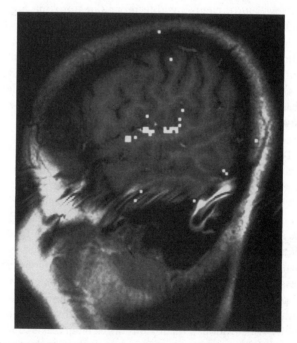

Figure 14.12.   Functional MRI. The image shows a side view of the left hemisphere of an adult who is being asked to perform an auditory memory task during the scan. The white dots indicate "activation" (increased use of glucose) during performance of the task. As expected, the auditory areas of the temporal lobe are activated.

REFERENCES

Barkley, R.A., Grodzinsky, G., & DuPaul, G.J. (1992). Frontal lobe functions in attention deficit disorder with and without hyperactivity: A review and research report. *Journal of Abnormal Child Psychology, 20,* 163–188.

Becker, L.E. (1991). Synaptic dysgenesis. *Canadian Journal of Neurological Sciences, 18,* 170–180.

Benson, D.F., Stuss, D.T., Naeser, M.A., et al. (1981). The long-term effects of prefrontal leukotomy. *Archives of Neurology, 38,* 165–169.

Brodal, P. (1992). *The central nervous system: Structure and function.* New York: Oxford University Press.

Cote, L., & Crutcher, M.D. (1991). The basal ganglia. In E.R. Kandel & J.H. Schwartz (Eds.), *Principles of neural science* (pp. 647–659). Norwalk, CT: Appleton and Lange.

Devinsky, O., & Pacia, S. (1993). Epilepsy surgery. *Neurologic Clinics, 11,* 951–971.

Dobyns, W.B., Reiner, O., Carrozzo, R., et al. (1993). Lissencephaly: A human brain malformation associated with deletion of the LIS1 gene located at chromosome 17p13. *Journal of the American Medical Association, 270,* 2838–2842.

Flowers, D.L. (1993). Brain basis for dyslexia: A summary of work in progress. *Journal of Learning Disabilities, 26,* 575–582.

Gilman, S., & Winans-Newman, S. (Eds.). (1987). *Manter and Gatz's essentials of clinical neuroanatomy and neurophysiology* (7th ed.). Philadelphia: F.A. Davis.

Good, W.V., Jan, J.E., DeSa, L., et al. (1994). Cortical visual impairment in children. *Survey of Ophthalmology, 38,* 351–364.

Haglund, M.M., & Ojemann, L.M. (1993). Seizure outcome in patients undergoing temporal lobe resections for epilepsy. *Neurosurgery Clinics of North America, 41,* 337–344.

Huttenlocher, P.R. (1991). Dendritic and synaptic pathology in mental retardation. *Pediatric Neurology, 7,* 79–85.

Klemm, W.R., & Vertes, R.P. (Eds.). (1990). *Brainstem mechanisms of behavior.* New York: John Wiley & Sons.

Leonard, C.M., Voeller, K.K., Lombardino, L.J., et al. (1993). Anomalous cerebral structure in dyslexia revealed with magnetic resonance imaging. *Archives of Neurology, 50,* 461–469.

Low, P.A. (1994). Autonomic neuropathies. *Current Opinion in Neurology, 7,* 402–406.

Lyon, G.R., & Rumsey, J.M. (Eds.). (1996). *Neuroimaging: A window to the neurological foundations of learning and behavior in children.* Baltimore: Paul H. Brookes Publishing Co.

Madsen, J.R., Carmant, L., Holmes, G.L., et al. (1995). Corpus callostomy in children. *Neurosurgery Clinics of North America, 6,* 541–548.

Menkes, J.H. (1995). *Textbook of child neurology* (5th ed.). Baltimore: Williams & Wilkins.

Messa, C., Fazio, F., Costa, D.C., et al. (1995). Clinical brain radionuclide imaging studies. *Seminars in Nuclear Medicine, 25,* 111–143.

Milhorat, T.H. (1972). *Hydrocephalus and the cerebrospinal fluid.* Baltimore: Williams & Wilkins.

Muenke, M., Gurrieri, F., Bay, C., et al. (1994) Linkage of a human brain malformation, familial holoprosencephaly, to chromosome 7 and evidence for genetic heterogeneity. *Proceedings of the National Academy of Sciences: U.S.A., 91,* 8102–8106.

Mulder, D.W. (1995). Clinical observations on acute poliomyelitis. *Annals of the New York Academy of Sciences, 753,* 1–10.

Noback, C.R. (1991). *The human nervous system: Introduction and review* (4th ed.). Philadelphia: Lea & Febiger.

Nolte, J. (1993). *The human brain: An introduction to its functional anatomy* (3rd ed.). St. Louis: C.V. Mosby.

Plate, K.H., Wieser, H.G., Yasargil, M.G., et al. (1993). Neuropathological findings in 224 patients with temporal lobe epilepsy. *Acta Neuropathologica, 86,* 433–438.

Prigatano, G.P., Zeiner, H.K., Pollay, M., et al. (1983). Neuropsychological functioning in children with shunted uncomplicated hydrocephalus. *Child's Brain, 10,* 112–120.

Rakic, P. (1989). Specification of cerebral cortical areas. *Science, 241,* 170–176.

Roberts, P.A. (1992). *Neuroanatomy* (3rd ed.). New York: Springer-Verlag.

Rodriguez-Pena, A., Ibarrola, N., Iniguez, M.A., et al. (1993). Neonatal hypothyroidism affects the timely expression of myelin-associated glycoprotein in the rat brain. *Journal of Clinical Investigation, 91,* 812–818.

Sarnat, H.B. (1987). Disturbances of late neuronal migrations in the perinatal period. *American Journal of Diseases of Children, 141,* 969–980.

Sarnat, H.B. (1991). Cerebral dysplasias as expressions of altered maturational processes. *Canadian Journal of Neurological Sciences, 18,* 196–204.

Schurr, P.H., & Polkey, C.E. (Eds.). (1993). *Hydrocephalus.* New York: Oxford University Press.

Singer, H.S., Chiu, A.Y., Meiri, K.F., et al. (1994). Advances in understanding the development of the nervous system. *Current Opinion in Neurology, 7,* 153–159.

Van Allen, M.I., Kalousek, D.K., Chernoff, G.F., et al. (1993). Evidence for multi-site closure of the neural tube in humans. *American Journal of Medical Genetics, 47,* 723–743.

Vintzileos, A.M., Ingardia, C.J., & Nochimson, D.J. (1983). Congenital hydrocephalus: A review and protocol for perinatal management. *Obstetrics and Gynecology, 62,* 539–549.

Volpe, J.J. (1995). *Neurology of the newborn.* Philadelphia: W.B. Saunders.

Waxman, S.G., & de Groot, J. (1995). *Correlative neuroanatomy* (22nd ed.). Norwalk, CT: Appleton and Lange.

15 Muscles, Bones, and Nerves

The Body's Framework

John P. Dormans
Mark L. Batshaw

Upon completion of this chapter, the reader will:

- be able to explain the structure and development of bone
- recognize the various types of joints
- know the function of tendons and ligaments
- understand how the musculoskeletal and neuromuscular systems work together to produce movement
- know some of the most common bony deformities and their treatments
- be able to identify some of the major musculoskeletal and neuromuscular disorders of childhood

Although the central nervous system (CNS) initiates the commands for movement, nothing would happen if motor neurons, nerves, neuromuscular junctions, muscles, bones, and joints did not respond in a concerted manner to these signals. Together, these components make up the musculoskeletal and neuromuscular systems and are responsible for our physical strength and movement. Without them, we would be immobile. This chapter explores how these systems function and examines what can go wrong.

THE MUSCULOSKELETAL SYSTEM

The musculoskeletal system is composed of bone, muscles, and joints, as well as their associated ligaments and tendons, which work together to permit movement. Defects within this system are a major cause of disability in childhood.

Common Musculoskeletal Terms

Before discussing how the musculoskeletal system works, it is important to understand the terms used to describe different kinds of movement. These terms are illustrated in Figure 15.1.

Flexion refers to the bending of a limb or body part at a joint. **Extension,** the opposite of flexion, means to straighten. When a part of the body moves away from the midline of the body, it is called **abduction;** movement toward the midline is called **adduction.** The midline also is called the **median plane;** the outer parts of the body are the **lateral** sections. **Anterior** refers to the front of a flat surface, whereas **posterior** is the rear or under part. Thus, the chest is anterior, while the back is posterior. The word **superior** means up or above; **inferior** means below. The head is superior and the feet are inferior to the shoulders. For the extremities, **proximal** means toward the center of the body and **distal** away from the center of the body. The hands are distal and the shoulders are proximal.

Supine refers to lying on one's back, prone to lying on one's stomach. A foot is **everted** when the sole faces outward, or away from the midline, and **inverted** when the sole turns inward. **Valgus** denotes a condition in which the distal body part is angled away from the midline of the body. The opposite of valgus is a **varus** condition, in which the distal body part is angled toward the midline. Valgus or varus may be either normal (physiological) or abnormal. An example of normal valgus is the heel, or hindfoot, which is usually angled away from the midline. An example of abnormal valgus is talipes valgus, in which the hindfoot is turned outward excessively from the midline.

Equinus refers to a condition in which the sole of the foot is downwardly displaced, such that the child walks on tiptoes, like a horse. **Dislocation** refers to the complete displacement of one **articular** surface from its opposing articular surface. **Subluxation** is an incomplete or partial dislocation of a joint.

Spasticity is a state of increased muscle tone and is often a major feature of children with cerebral palsy. **Athetosis** refers to slow, writhing, involuntary movements, especially in the hands. **Ataxia** implies an incoordination of muscular movement such as walking, usually resulting from abnormalities in the cerebellum. Athetosis and ataxia are also seen in individuals with cerebral palsy.

Bone

The bones of the skeleton form the internal scaffolding of our body. They range in size from the 0.5-inch bones of the finger (**phalanges**) to the thigh bone (**femur**), which is roughly 18 inches long. Some bones, such as the skull, are flat; others, such as the femur, are tubular. Even though bones are hard and immobile, they are a dynamic organ system contributing not only to structural support, but also to the **hematopoietic** and metabolic systems. Just as the body is dependent on the skeleton for support, the skeletal system relies on the body for its maintenance and growth. Bone is the only tissue in the body that does not heal with scar tissue.

Structure and Development

The height of a child increases because of growth of the spine and the long, tubular bones of the lower extremities. To understand how this works, it is helpful first to examine the structure of a bone. Consider the femur as an example. This bone consists of a shaft, or **diaphysis,** composed mostly of **cortical** bone; a spongy, upper portion called a **metaphysis,** composed mostly of **can-**

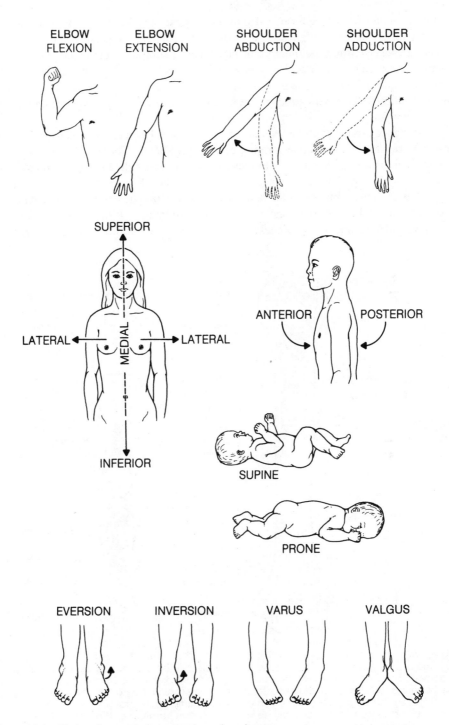

Figure 15.1.   Various types of movements and postures.

cellous bone; the end of the bone, called the **epiphysis;** and a growth plate, or **physis,** that separates the metaphysis and epiphysis (Figure 15.2). Surrounding the bone is a tough, fibrous layer called the **periosteum.** Calcium crystals embedded in a protein compound make up about two thirds of a bone. The remainder is composed of living cells. It is the mineral-protein mixture that lends strength to the bone. The central core, the bone marrow, is where blood cells are formed. Weaving through the bone's structure are blood vessels that supply oxygen and nutrients necessary for growth.

New bone originates at the level of the growth plate. Here, cartilage cells are laid down and are then transformed into bone-forming cells (**osteoblasts**). These cells contain calcium and gradually transform the cartilage into bone. This process is called **enchondral ossification.** As both ends of the long bone lengthen, the child grows taller (Figure 15.2).

As growth takes place and the bone is subject to different stresses, it begins to remodel or change in shape. These changes increase the tensile strength and stability of the bone, making it less susceptible to fracture. Remodeling and growth involve formation of new bone by the os-

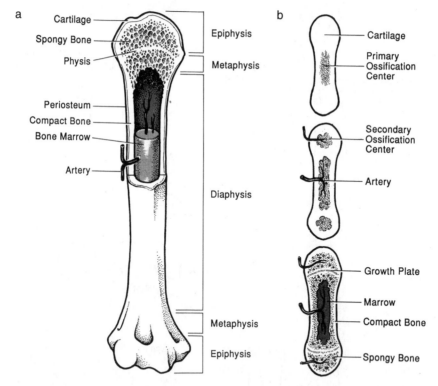

Figure 15.2.   a) The structure of a typical long bone, the humerus. New bone arises from the physis, and the arm lengthens. The upper portion of the bone is the metaphysis, and the shaft is called the diaphysis. The bone marrow, which produces blood cells, lies in the center of the shaft. Surrounding the bone is a fibrous sheath, the periosteum. The bone facing the joint space is covered by articular cartilage. b) The long bone starts off as a mass of cartilage in fetal life. Gradually the center is invaded by osteoblasts. These cells lay down minerals that form bone. The ossification centers spread and the bone enlarges. After birth, further bone growth occurs only from the physis.

teoblast cells as well as the breakdown and resorption of bone by **osteoclast** cells. The osteoblast produces **osteoid** that calcifies or crystallizes, and the osteoclast removes the crystals from already-formed bone and returns the calcium to the bloodstream. Thus, a part of the bone is constantly disappearing as new bone is being laid down in its place. On average, a section of a child's bone lasts about a year and is then replaced by new bone. In an adult, the reshaping continues although growth has stopped. The average bone segment of an adult lasts about 7 years. In other words, bone is a living organ that constantly grows and reshapes in response to physiological stresses.

Bony Malformations

Bone diseases may be congenital or acquired and may involve only one limb or the entire skeleton. One example of a bony malformation is achondroplasia, an autosomal dominantly inherited form of short-limbed dwarfism. Individuals with achondroplasia have a shortening in the proximal portion of their limbs. There is some evidence that this defect may be related to an abnormality in a receptor for fibroblast growth factor, resulting in defective enchondral ossification (Rousseau, Bonaventure, Legeai-Mallet, et al., 1994). The affected individual has shortened arms and legs and a disproportionately large head and trunk (Figure 15.3). The average height in adulthood is 4 feet (American Academy of Pediatrics, Committee on Genetics, 1995). Motor development is delayed, but cognitive development is usually unaffected. Complications can include airway obstruction, hydrocephalus, spinal deformity, and spinal cord compression. The incidence is about 1 in 10,000. Trials of growth hormone treatment during childhood have been generally ineffective in increasing height (Horton, Hecht, Hood, et al., 1992), although limb lengthening procedures may be helpful in selected cases (Green, 1991).

Figure 15.3.   Achondroplasia, an autosomal dominant form of short-limbed dwarfism.

Another genetic bone disease is **osteopetrosis,** an autosomal recessively inherited disorder with an incidence of about 1 in 200,000 that is caused by an abnormality of the osteoclasts (Gerritsen, Vossen, van Loo, et al., 1994). As the osteoclasts fail to resorb the bone, the bone becomes very dense, and the bone marrow space becomes very narrow. This in turn results in anemia because the space for blood cell production is reduced. In addition, there is progressive thickening of the bones of the skull with eventual impingement of the cranial nerves that emerge through holes in the skull. This may cause blindness and deafness. Growth is delayed and most affected children die in the first decade. Bone marrow transplantation has been used to provide normal osteoclasts to children with osteopetrosis; it has been shown to reverse many of the symptoms and permit prolonged survival.

Deformities of Bone

Two of the more common extremity deformities seen in infants and children are **club foot** and **developmental dislocation of the hip (DDH).** These are complex deformities that involve both bone and soft tissues. Both deformities are thought to be multifactorial in nature, having both genetic and environmental influences (see Chapter 2).

Club foot occurs in 1 in 1,000 births and affects twice as many males as females (Bleck, 1993; Morrissy, 1990). It may be an isolated deformity without a known cause (idiopathic), or it may be part of a generalized neurological disorder (neurogenic) such as cerebral palsy or meningomyelocele. The cause may be endogenous, as a consequence of an abnormality or arrest of embryonic development; or it may be extrinsic, resulting from lack of room during intrauterine development.

At approximately the ninth week of gestation, the typical fetal foot has musculoskeletal changes similar to those of club foot; by the eleventh week, however, the foot assumes a more functional position. One theory asserts that if there is a developmental arrest at 9 weeks, club foot results (Coleman, 1993; Kawashima & Uhthoff, 1990). "Fetal packing" can also contribute to the formation of club foot, particularly when there are multiple births or decreased amniotic fluid production. In these situations, the fetus may have little room to move, and the foot may get "stuck" in one position for prolonged periods of time and become deformed.

The club foot deformity, or **talipes equinovarus,** has three components: equinus of the foot, varus of the heel, and forefoot adduction. One or both feet may be affected. Treatment should start at birth with serial casting (Ikeda, 1992). Surgical correction, if needed, is usually carried out at 4–6 months. This approach leads to a positive outcome for 60%–95% of affected children.

Although club foot is more common in boys, DDH occurs more frequently in girls (Coleman, 1994). It results from a disruption of the normal ball-and-socket relationship between the femoral head and the acetabulum (Figure 15.4). DDH ranges in severity from acetabular **dysplasia,** in which the acetabulum is shallow and does not hold the femoral head well, to subluxation, in which the head has slipped partially out of the acetabulum, to dislocation, in which there is a complete loss of contact between the femoral head and the acetabulum. DDH was once called congenital dislocation of the hip, which implied a congenital etiology. It is now known, however, that the disorder may occur gradually after birth. In most infants, successful treatment is achieved with a Pavlik harness that is worn for 3–6 months. This holds the hip in flexion and abduction, keeping the femoral head securely in place and allowing for better formation of the joint. Use of the Pavlik harness often averts the need for corrective surgery.

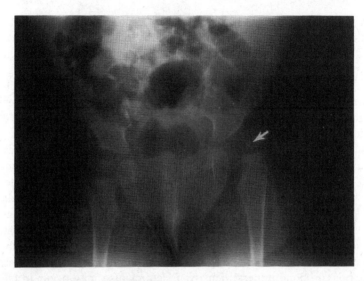

Figure 15.4.   Developmental dislocation of the hip. The arrow points to the proximal femoral epiphysis that is dislocated from the acetabulum. (X ray courtesy of Dr. Sandra Kramer, Department of Pediatric Radiology, The Children's Hospital of Philadelphia.)

Bony deformities also may develop after birth. For example, in cerebral palsy, muscle imbalance due to spasticity can cause contractures, dislocations of joints, or scoliosis (Dormans, 1993). In addition, children with osteogenesis imperfecta (OI) and **rickets** have underlying abnormalities of musculoskeletal development that are present from early in fetal development; these bony deformities often progress after birth.

Disorders Causing Fractures

Any person may fracture a bone if sufficient force is brought to bear against the bone, causing it to break (Figure 15.5). The most common causes of fractures in children are household, automobile, and playground accidents; sports injuries; and physical abuse. In some children with disabilities, however, a fracture can occur with little or no trauma, even from being lifted out of bed. These are called "pathological" fractures and can be associated with significant weakness of the bone (e.g., OI); a nutritional or metabolic deficiency (e.g., rickets); a secondary effect of a medication (e.g., antiepileptic drugs); disuse weakness (e.g., from cerebral palsy); or invasion of bone (e.g., tumor). In each of these cases, the underlying medical disorder causes the bone to be more brittle than usual and thereby more susceptible to fracture (Shaw, White, Fraser, et al., 1994). This brittleness, or **osteopenia,** results from too little or abnormal bony matrix.

OI is an inherited skeletal dysplasia with an incidence of 1 in 20,000 and is usually associated with brittle bones that fracture easily (Byers & Steiner, 1992). Individuals with OI have a mutation in one of the genes required for the production of collagen (Bachinger, Morris, & Davis, 1993). Impaired collagen synthesis leads to abnormal or decreased cartilage formation and reduced bone strength. These children may sustain fractures during birth and may have as many as 20–30 fractures of their long bones during childhood. Additional musculoskeletal problems include bowing of the legs, spinal deformities, joint laxity, contractures, and muscle weakness (Binder, Conway, & Gerber, 1993). Children with OI often experience low back pain caused by vertebral compression fractures. There is no cure for OI as of 1997, but combined treatment using medication, surgery, and rehabilitation therapy has improved functional outcome. For example, calcitonin, a bone hormone, improves tensile bone strength and decreases the frequency of fractures (Nishi, Hamamoto, Kajiyama, et al., 1992). Bowing of the legs can be treated with surgical straightening and internal fixation of the femur and/or tibia. Rehabilitation therapy focuses on preventing joint contractures and disuse weakness and keeping the child ambulatory. It includes leg bracing as well as weight-bearing and strengthening/conditioning exercises (Binder, Conway, Hanson, et al., 1993).

Conditions with disruption of normal bone mineralization also may be associated with deformity and pathogenic fractures. For example, because of a lack of or abnormal metabolism of vitamin D, which usually aids in calcium absorption, children with rickets do not form normal calcium phosphorus mineral deposits in their bones (see Chapter 10). Some antiepileptic drugs, especially phenytoin (Dilantin) and phenobarbital, also have been found to cause vitamin D deficiency or to interfere with the utilization of vitamin D. This places nonambulatory children with seizure disorders at increased risk for fractures. Nonambulatory children with cerebral palsy or meningomyelocele also tend to have frail bones, resulting from disuse and associated with severe reductions in bone mineral density. Fractures also may occur in children who have leukemia, osteosarcoma, or other tumors that invade the bone and weaken its internal structure. Children with pathological fractures may present with swelling and increased warmth of the fractured extremity, which can occasionally be confused with osteomyelitis.

For proper healing to occur, fractures must be aligned properly and immobilized by casting. Casts are made of plaster or fiberglass (the lighter and stronger of the two). The cast stabilizes the bone fragments, which makes the child more comfortable and holds the bones in satisfactory position and alignment. Children's bones usually heal in 4–6 weeks. Healing takes place by a process called **callus** formation (Figure 15.5). The callus begins as a blood clot, the result of bleeding from blood vessels inside and around the bone. This stimulates the formation of cartilage within the blood clot at the fracture site. In a few weeks, osteoblasts start to lay down new bone on the cartilage framework. After 4–6 weeks, healing has usually progressed to the point that the cast can be removed and there can be a gradual return of function. The remodeling process, however, continues. Eventually, the bulging callus remodels and disappears, and by 6–12 months the bone appears normal on X ray (Morrissy, 1990).

Joints

A joint is defined as the connection of two or more bones, for example, at the knee. It is composed of 1) the epiphysis and cartilage of the two connecting bones; 2) the small, lubricated space between the cartilage ends called the joint cavity; and 3) the ligaments and muscles that bind the bones together and make the joint stable (Figure 15.6).

Joints may be immobile, partly mobile, or completely mobile. The **sutures** of the skull are examples of immobile joints. The wrist and hand are composed of both slightly mobile joints and completely mobile joints. Mobile joints include hinge, pivot, and ball-and-socket types. The knee is an example of a hinge joint that can flex and extend (Figure 15.6). At this joint, movement of 145° back and forth is possible. At the elbow (which is a pivot and hinge joint), rotation as well as hinge movement occurs. The hip, a ball-and-socket joint, can move in all three planes—flexion, rotation, and abduction.

A common disorder of joints is **arthritis.** Actually, arthritis is a group of disorders, each with its own characteristics and challenges. In general, however, arthritis involves damage to the

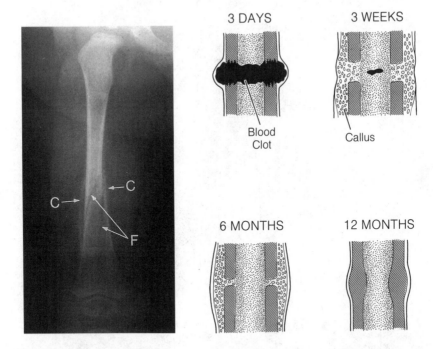

Figure 15.5.   Bone fracture. The X ray shows the fracture line (F). This was taken 3 weeks after the accident, and callus formation can be seen (C). The mechanism of healing is outlined to the right. Initially, there is bleeding from the bone and surrounding soft tissues damaged in the accident. Soon this blood clot is invaded by osteoblasts that lay down bony tissue forming a callus. In addition, the covering of the bone, the periosteum, lays down new bone. By 6 months, the bones are almost fused, but the bone structure is still enlarged. At 12 months, fusion is complete, and the bone is strong and looks fairly normal. Further reshaping over time will make all signs of fracture disappear.

cartilage surrounding the joint space. Inflammation occurs, and with time the bones in the joint space grind against each other and may eventually fuse (Figure 15.6), resulting in pain and loss of motion. Although arthritis most commonly occurs in adults, it can also occur in children. For example, a child with spastic cerebral palsy who develops a dislocation of the hip may, over a number of years, develop painful arthritis of the hip. Surgery is directed at preventing or correcting the dislocation and lessening the risk of arthritis and pain.

Ligaments are the fibrous tissues that attach one bone to another across a joint (Figure 15.6). **Tendons,** which attach muscles to bones, are similar in composition and function to ligaments but have looser fibers. Both ligaments and tendons are flexible, resilient, and essential to keeping joints moving properly. In comparison with bone, these tissues have a more limited capacity to regenerate. Thus, damage to tendons or ligaments (all too common in sports injuries) often requires surgical repair.

Muscle

The main function of muscle is to contract. Cells called muscle fibers comprise muscle. The muscle fiber's contractile machinery consists of two proteins, **actin** and **myosin** (Figure 15.7), which form highly organized subunits called **sarcomeres.** These subunits are stimulated by nerve impulses to contract. Smooth movement requires that all the muscle groups around a joint act in concert. Most joints have attached muscles that pull in different directions. **Antagonist**

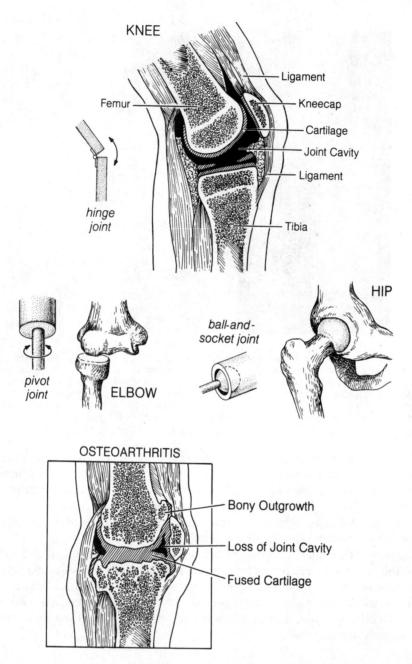

Figure 15.6. Joints. A typical knee joint is compared with an arthritic knee joint. Usually there is a lubricated joint cavity separating the femur and tibia bones. Muscles cross the joint attached to the
ligaments. In the diseased joint, the cartilage is abnormal and has disappeared in places, and there
may be fusion of the opposing bones. This severely limits movement. The different types of joints are
also illustrated: hinge (knee), pivot (elbow), and ball-and-socket (hip).

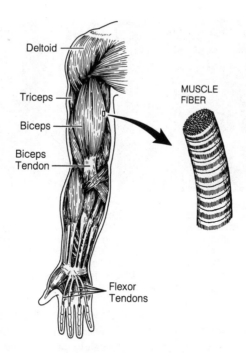

Figure 15.7.   Muscles. The major muscles in the arm. Note that the biceps and triceps are antagonists. The enlargement shows a muscle fiber, which is the unit of muscle tissue.

muscles oppose one another in the movement of a joint, while **agonist** muscles pull together to produce movement. For example, when the arm is flexed, the biceps contracts, as does the **brachialis.** The **triceps,** however, relaxes (Figure 15.7). If both muscle groups contracted simultaneously, the arm would be held stiffly in "isometric" contraction. Thus, when the brain tells the arm to move, it actually sends a number of messages that tell some muscles to contract and others to relax.

Muscular Dystrophy

Diseases of the muscle obviously affect movement. The best known of these disorders is muscular dystrophy. The most common form of this disease is Duchenne muscular dystrophy (DMD). Inherited as a sex-linked disorder (see Chapter 2), DMD has a lifetime incidence of about 1 in 3,000 males (Emery, 1993). The principal clinical features are proximal muscle weakness, **pseudohypertrophy** of the calf muscles, and characteristic contractures of the hips and feet. In addition, these children may have learning disabilities or cognitive impairments. The underlying defect is decreased or absent production of dystrophin, a protein that stabilizes the muscle membrane during contraction. When dystrophin is deficient, the muscle degenerates.

Parents are usually unaware of any problem until their son is between 2 and 5 years of age. Then the child's ambulation skills deteriorate; he develops a waddling gait and has difficulty climbing steps or getting up from a lying down position. Over several years, the child becomes weaker and less mobile and requires a wheelchair, usually by age 12. As a consequence of the gradual destruction of muscle fibers and scarring (Figure 15.8), the muscles develop pseudo-

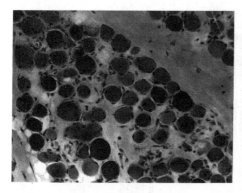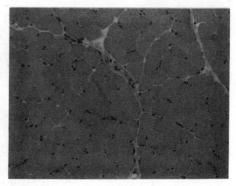

Figure 15.8.   Example of a muscle biopsy from a child with Duchenne muscular dystrophy (left), and from a child who does not have the disorder (right). Note that the muscle biopsy from the child with muscular dystrophy has decreased numbers of muscle fibers and increased fat and fibrous tissue compared with the normal biopsy. (Photographs courtesy of John Sladky, M.D., Emory University.) (From *Your child has a disability: A complete sourcebook of daily and medical care* by Mark Batshaw [p. 194]. Copyright © 1991 by M.L. Batshaw; illustrations copyright © 1991 by Lynn Reynolds. Boston: Little, Brown; reprinted by permission.)

hypertrophy. All muscles are affected, but leg weakness precedes arm weakness. Scoliosis is common around the time the boy begins to use a wheelchair. In addition to causing flaccid weakness in the voluntary muscles, this disease ultimately damages the involuntary muscles of the heart and diaphragm as well, often leading to respiratory and heart failure. At this point, a decision of whether to prolong life by mechanical ventilation must be made.

Diagnosing muscular dystrophy depends on finding a markedly elevated level of creatine kinase (CK) in the blood (Miller & Wessel, 1993). This enzyme is released by damaged muscle cells. A muscle biopsy may be necessary to demonstrate the pattern consistent with breakdown and regeneration of muscle cells and the loss of dystrophin. Molecular diagnosis is possible by examination of DNA from a blood test for a mutation in the dystrophin gene (Nicholson, Johnson, Bushby, et al., 1993; Roberts, Bobrow, & Bentley, 1992).

A multidisciplinary team should be involved in the care of children with DMD. This team ideally should include a physical therapist, occupational therapist, orthopedic surgeon, physiatrist, neurologist, and social worker. In fact, interdisciplinary clinics have been supported throughout the country by the Muscular Dystrophy Association. These clinics use multimodal treatment approaches that include rehabilitation therapy, orthopedic surgery, medication, educational planning, and family counseling. Rehabilitative therapy is directed at minimizing contractures, maximizing muscle strength, and compensating for weakness. Therapists should encourage the child to avoid the use of a wheelchair for as long as possible and to be involved in an active exercise program. Passive stretching and night splints may delay contractures. Self-care skills also should be stressed. This may require the use of assistive devices to maintain independence.

The orthopedic surgeon works with occupational and physical therapists to determine the need for bracing or surgery. The most common surgical procedures are spinal fusion for scoliosis and lengthening of contracted tendons (Galasko, Delaney, & Morris, 1992; Roberts & Evans, 1993). Spinal bracing, however, is not appropriate for children with scoliosis as it can interfere with breathing efforts. Instead, early surgery consisting of posterior spinal instrumentation and fusion should be performed if there is progressive spinal deformity. After surgery, these children are mobilized as soon as possible to maintain and prolong ambulation.

In terms of medical management, the use of the corticosteroid, prednisone, appears to increase muscle mass and strength, somewhat slowing the progression of the disease and improving lung function and walking (Griggs, Moxley, Mendell, et al., 1993; Khan, 1993). A new immunosuppressant, deflazacort, may have fewer side effects than prednisone and is under investigation (Roland, 1994). Despite medical therapy, the prognosis for these boys in 1997 is inevitable progression to respiratory insufficiency and death before adulthood. As these children tend to have learning disabilities or cognitive impairments, planning for special education services is important. Counseling is equally important for the child and his family. Issues of depression and coping with approaching mortality will need to be addressed.

Two innovative treatments are being explored in an attempt to alter this poor prognosis: myoblast transplantation and gene therapy. Myoblast transplantation attempts to provide the missing dystrophin protein by intramuscular injection of normal immature muscle cells (myoblasts). Ideally, these muscle cells will provide the missing gene and/or replace the fatty muscle. The results of initial clinical trials, however, have not been encouraging (Mendell, Kissel, Amato, et al., 1995). Gene therapy involves injecting either the naked DNA coding for dystrophin or a viral vector containing portions of the dystrophin gene into fatty muscles (see Chapter 19). Preliminary results in a mouse model of muscular dystrophy look encouraging, and human clinical trials are planned (Dunckley, Piper, & Dickson, 1995; Vincent, Ragot, Gilgenkrantz, et al., 1993).

Congenital Myopathies

Congenital myopathies are another group of childhood muscle diseases, marked by decreased muscle tone and strength (Dubowitz, 1995). Children with congenital myopathies are distinguished from those with muscular dystrophy because their levels of CK are normal or only mildly elevated. They also have a different pattern of abnormalities on muscle biopsy. There are many forms of congenital myopathies, and the causes of most remain unknown. A fair amount is known, however, about one group of congenital myopathies called **mitochondrial myopathies** (Wallace, 1992). Mitochondria are small cellular organelles that are inherited maternally. They have their own circular DNA (see Chapter 1). Mitochondria serve as the cell's power plants by converting certain nutritional elements into a chemical that contains high-energy phosphate groups that are used by the cell in all types of metabolic processes. This conversion involves a complex series of enzymatic steps, and a deficiency in any of the enzymes in this pathway impairs energy production. Because muscles use enormous amounts of energy to contract, one result of a mitochondrial defect is muscle weakness. Some children with mitochondrial disorders have catastrophic illnesses beginning at birth and leading to death in the first month of life. Others may have milder disorders that impair typical muscle function. At this point, there is no specific medical therapy for these disorders.

THE NEUROMUSCULAR SYSTEM

In order for a muscle to produce movement across a joint, a signal begins in the brain, passes through the spinal cord to the anterior horn cell, then to the peripheral nerve, and ends at a neuromuscular junction. The electrical impulse then jumps the gap or synapse at this junction using the neurotransmitter acetylcholine. The message then passes to the muscle fiber, stimulating it to contract or relax, and movement results. Defects anywhere in the neuromuscular system lead to weakness and decreased movement (Menkes, 1995).

The Anterior Horn Cell

Anterior horn cells, or motor neurons, are nerve cells in the spinal cord that transmit messages to the peripheral nerves. Abnormalities of the anterior horn cell lead to severe weakness or paralysis. The two diseases most commonly associated with damage to the anterior horn cells are **polio** and the **spinal muscular atrophies.** The polio virus selectively destroys the anterior horn cells, creating a functional gap between the CNS and the peripheral nerves. Paralysis occurs below the part of the brainstem and/or spinal cord that has been damaged by the infection. Polio has not been a significant health problem in the United States since the polio vaccine was first introduced in 1955 by Dr. Jonas Salk. Later, Dr. Albert Sabin developed an oral vaccine that is used worldwide. Now, infants receive immunizations that include three doses of oral polio vaccine in addition to a series of diphtheria, whooping cough (pertussis), and tetanus (DPT) shots (Kimpen & Ogra, 1990).

Spinal muscular atrophy involves a clinically diverse group of inherited disorders with a lifetime incidence of approximately 8 per 100,000 (MacKenzie, Jacob, Surh, et al., 1994). Children with spinal muscular atrophy have severely decreased numbers of anterior horn cells throughout the brainstem and down the entire length of the spinal cord (Iannaccone, Brown, Samaha, et al., 1993), presumably due to inadequate neuronal development and possibly accelerated cell death of anterior horn cells (Roland, 1994; Russman & Schwartz, 1993). Microscopic examination of the spinal cord reveals a severe decrease in anterior horn cells, which leads to atrophy of the muscle. Children with the severe form of this disorder (called Werdnig-Hoffmann disease) are very floppy soon after birth, and their life expectancy is quite short because of breathing problems caused by weak diaphragmatic muscles and recurrent lung infections. There are later onset forms of the disease that are less severe (Russman, Iannaccone, Buncher, et al., 1992). The characteristic physical signs are muscle atrophy, weakness, and loss of deep tendon reflexes. Muscle weakness is symmetric, with proximal muscles being more involved than distal muscle groups. There is also cranial nerve involvement, which may interfere with feeding and speech. Unlike muscular dystrophy, there is no involvement of the heart (cardiac muscle). As of 1997, no specific treatment is available, although animal studies suggest that administering nerve growth factors may hold promise for the future (Forger, Roberts, Wong, et al., 1993). Rehabilitative therapy and adaptive seating are important as they can decrease contractures and loss of function due to immobility.

The Peripheral Nerve

The peripheral nerve is responsible for carrying signals from the motor neuron to the neuromuscular junction. Guillain-Barré syndrome, an illness primarily affecting adults, involves an immune mediated attack on the myelin sheath and axon of the peripheral nerve (Jones, 1996). It affects approximately 1 in 100,000 people per year (Ropper, 1992). Also called acute inflammatory demyelinating polyneuropathy, this disease causes paralysis similar to that seen in polio. About two thirds of individuals with Guillain-Barré syndrome have a history of a preceding acute infectious illness (Arnason & Soliven, 1993; Hartung, Pollard, Harvey, et al., 1995b). The most common association appears to be with *Campylobacter jejuni* (*C. jejuni*), a common bacterial cause of diarrheal illness (Rees, Soudain, Gregson, et al., 1995). Other predisposing infections include cytomegalovirus, vaccinia, human immunodeficiency virus (HIV), and the Epstein-Barr (mononucleosis) virus. Guillain-Barré syndrome generally occurs a few weeks after the illness and, unlike polio (which is asymmetric), involves both sides of the body equally. It often involves the legs first, with progression to the upper extremities and diaphragm over a few days to 2 weeks. Thirty percent of individuals require short-term mechanical ventilation because of breathing impairment, and there is a 3% mortality rate. The acute illness lasts 2–4 weeks and is followed by a period of plateauing of symptoms and then gradual improvement for 2–12 months (Russman & Schwartz, 1993). More than three quarters of people recover completely; the remainder, most commonly those with a *C. jejuni* infection, are left with some permanent weakness (Korinthenberg & Mönting, 1996).

Guillain-Barré syndrome results from an **autoimmune** response to an infection. Peripheral nerves are thought to share antigen sites with the infecting organism. Following the infection, the body mistakenly identifies the nerves as a foreign body and develops myelin-directed antibodies that try to destroy them. A new treatment directed at this autoimmune response is called **plasmapheresis** (Jansen, Perkin, & Ashwal, 1993; Van der Meché, Schnitz, & The Dutch Guillain-Barré Study Group, 1992). This procedure involves removing some of the individual's blood plasma, clearing the antibodies through a dialysis machine, and then reinfusing the plasma. Studies have shown that titers of the antibody significantly decline after this procedure (Bradshaw & Jones, 1992; Hartung et al., 1995a, b). Individuals treated quickly with plasmapheresis improve more rapidly, need shorter periods of mechanical ventilation, and spend less time in the hospital. It also has been shown that high-dose intravenous immunoglobulin G results in a similarly improved outcome by diminishing the autoimmune response (Dwyer, 1992).

In addition to medical management, rehabilitation is a critical part of therapy. During the acute episode, range of motion exercises and proper positioning can prevent the development of contractures. During recovery, strengthening exercises and gait retraining will be required. Bracing also may be needed.

The Neuromuscular Junction

The peripheral nerve ends at the neuromuscular junction. For a nerve impulse to "jump" across the synapse separating the nerve and muscle, it requires a chemical neurotransmitter (see Chapter 14). Impaired neurotransmitter activity prevents the impulse from generating muscle movement. **Myasthenia gravis** is the classic example of a disease of the neuromuscular junction. There are both acquired and inherited forms of myasthenia. The rare inherited form presents in infancy and results from a mutation affecting a subunit of the acetylcholine neurotransmitter receptors on skeletal muscles (Engle, Hutchinson, Nakano, et al., 1993). As a result, there is a 70%–90% reduction in the number of functional acetylcholine receptors. In the absence of these receptors, the neurotransmitter is unable to stimulate the muscle.

Individuals with the more common acquired form of myasthenia experience an autoimmune phenomenon akin to Guillain-Barré syndrome that targets the acetylcholine receptor on the skeletal muscle rather than the nerve. As a consequence, nerve impulses do not effectively bridge the neuromuscular junction and muscle does not receive a signal to contract. This form of disease occurs more commonly in girls and young women.

Unusual fatigability of voluntary muscles is the main characteristic of both forms of myasthenia. A muscle may be strong with the first effort at contraction but rapidly weakens. Myasthenia often affects the muscles of the face first with droopy eyelids (ptosis) or indistinct speech. It may then progress to involve other muscle groups, interfering with eating, walking, or even breathing. Because the weakness increases with repeated muscle contractions, a person with myasthenia gravis usually feels stronger in the morning and increasingly weakens as the day progresses.

Treatment of acquired myasthenia has been directed at both removing the offending antibody and increasing the level of acetylcholine in the synaptic cleft (Drachman, McIntosh, Reim, et al., 1993). The immunological approach has employed corticosteroid medication, immunoglobulin, plasmapheresis, and the surgical removal of the thymus gland. Corticosteroids, specifically prednisone, and intravenous immunoglobulin are used to decrease the immune response (Edam & Landgraf, 1994). Plasmapheresis is used on an emergency basis in an individual with myasthenia who is having difficulty breathing because of weak respiratory muscles. Yet, unlike Guillain-Barré syndrome, which is a self-limited postinfectious disease, myasthenia gravis is a lifelong illness; thus, plasmapheresis usually is not a permanent solution. Instead, long-term suppression of autoimmunity is necessary, much like immunosuppression is required after an organ transplant. This often involves performing an operation in which the thymus is removed, called a thymectomy (Blossom, Ernstoff, Howells, et al., 1993). The thymus, a small gland resting under the sternum or breast plate, plays an important role in the autoimmune response. Lymphocytes that initiate this response develop in this gland. Although most individuals will continue to require immunosuppression after thymectomy, the proportion of individuals achieving long-term remission increases. It should be noted that, because immune cells that develop in the thymus early in life serve a critical surveillance function, removal of the thymus may increase the risk of cancer and increase the susceptibility to some infections (Genkins, Sivak, & Tartter, 1993).

Immune therapy will not be helpful in congenital myasthenia. Here, treatment involves increasing neurotransmitter levels in the synaptic cleft. This requires the use of a medication called **pyridostigmine** (Mestinon) that helps minimize the weakness for virtually all individuals. This drug delays the breakdown of acetylcholine so that more of the neurochemical is available to aid in the transmission of the nerve impulse. Strength improves within minutes of taking this drug and improvement lasts about 4 hours. This drug is also used in acquired myasthenia in combination with immune therapy. Overall, using these various treatment approaches, individuals with myasthenia can lead quite typical lives.

SUMMARY

The musculoskeletal and neuromuscular systems both support the physical structure of the body and help to carry out movement. Abnormalities of the musculoskeletal system can lead to deformities or malformations, such as club foot or short-limbed dwarfism, or diseases, such as arthritis and muscular dystrophy. Abnormalities in the neuromuscular system can affect the peripheral nerve and anterior horn cell, resulting in paralysis, or the neuromuscular joints, causing muscle weakness. Because many of these diseases are difficult to treat, it is consoling to note that their occurrence is rare.

REFERENCES

American Academy of Pediatrics, Committee on Genetics. (1995). Health supervision for children with achondroplasia. *Pediatrics, 95,* 443–451.

Arnason, B.G.W., & Soliven, B. (1993). Acute inflammatory demyelinating polyradiculoneuropathy. In P.J. Dyck, P.K. Thomas, J.W. Griffin, P.A. Low, & J. Poduslo (Eds.), *Peripheral neuropathy* (3rd ed., pp. 1437–1497) Philadelphia: W.B. Saunders.

Bachinger, H.P., Morris, N.P., & Davis, J.M. (1993). Thermal stability and folding of the collagen triple helix and the effects of mutations in osteogenesis imperfecta on the triple helix of type I collagen. *American Journal of Medical Genetics, 45,* 152–162.

Batshaw, M.L. (1991). *Your child has a disability: A complete sourcebook of daily and medical care.* Boston: Little, Brown.

Binder, H., Conway, A., & Gerber, L.H. (1993). Rehabilitation approaches to children with osteogenesis imperfecta: A ten-year-experience. *Archives of Physical Medicine and Rehabilitation, 74,* 386–390.

Binder, H., Conway, A., Hanson, S., et al. (1993) Comprehensive rehabilitation of the child with osteogenesis imperfecta. *American Journal of Medical Genetics, 45,* 265–269.

Bleck, E.E. (1993). Club foot. *Developmental Medicine and Child Neurology, 35,* 927–931.

Blossom, G.B., Ernstoff, R.M., Howells, G.A., et al. (1993). Thymectomy for myasthenia gravis. *Archives of Surgery, 128,* 855–862.

Bradshaw, D.Y., & Jones, H.R. (1992). Guillain-Barré syndrome in children: Clinical course, diagnoses, electrodiagnosis, and prognoses. *Muscle and Nerve, 15,* 500–506.

Byers, P.H., & Steiner, R.D. (1992). Osteogenesis imperfecta. *Annual Review of Medicine, 43,* 269–282.

Coleman, S.S. (1993). *Complex foot deformities in children.* Philadelphia: Lea & Febiger.

Coleman, S.S. (1994). Developmental dislocation of the hip: Evolutionary changes in diagnosis and treatment. *Journal of Pediatric Orthopedics, 14,* 1–2.

Dormans, J.P. (1993). Orthopaedic management of children with cerebral palsy. *Pediatric Clinics of North America, 40,* 645–657.

Drachman, D.B., McIntosh, K.R., Reim, J., et al. (1993). Strategies for treatment of myasthenia gravis. *Annals of the New York Academy of Sciences, 681,* 515–528.

Dubowitz, V. (1995). *Muscle disorders in childhood* (2nd ed.). Philadelphia: W.B. Saunders.

Dunckley, M.G., Piper, T.A., & Dickson, G. (1995). Toward a gene therapy for Duchenne muscular dystrophy. *Mental Retardation and Developmental Disabilities Research Reviews, 1,* 71–78.

Dwyer, J.M. (1992). Manipulating the immune system with immune globulin. *New England Journal of Medicine, 326,* 107–116.

Edam, G., & Landgraf, F. (1994). Experience with intravenous immunoglobin in myasthenia gravis: A review. *Journal of Neurology, Neurosurgery, and Psychiatry, 57*(Suppl.), 55–56.

Emery, A.E.H. (1993). *Duchenne muscular dystrophy* (2nd ed.). Oxford, England: Oxford University Press.

Engle, A.G., Hutchinson, D.O., Nakano, S., et al. (1993). Myasthenic syndromes attributed to mutations affecting the epsilon subunit of the acetylcholine receptor. *Annals of the New York Academy of Sciences, 681,* 496–508.

Forger, N.G., Roberts, S.L., Wong, V., et al. (1993). Ciliary neurotrophic factor maintains motor meurons and their target muscles in developing rats. *Journal of Neuroscience, 13,* 4720–4726.

French Cooperative Group of Plasma Exchange in Guillain-Barré Syndrome. (1992). Plasma exchange in Guillain-Barré syndrome: One-year follow-up. *Annals of Neurology, 32,* 94–97.

Galasko, C.S., Delaney, C., & Morris, P. (1992). Spinal stabilization in Duchenne muscular dystrophy. *Journal of Bone and Joint Surgery (Bri.), 74,* 210–214.

Genkins, G., Sivak, M., & Tartter, P.I. (1993). Treatment strategies in myasthenia gravis. *Annals of the New York Academy of Sciences, 681,* 603–608.

Gerritsen, E.J., Vossen, J.M., van Loo, I.H., et al. (1994). Autosomal recessive osteopetrosis: Variability of findings at diagnosis and during the natural course. *Pediatrics, 93,* 247–253.

Green, S.A. (1991). Limb lengthening. *Orthopedic Clinics of North America, 22,* 555–735.

Griggs, R.C., Moxley, R.T., Mendell, J.R., et al. (1993). Duchenne dystrophy: Randomized controlled trial of prednisone (18 months) and azathiaprine (12 months). *Neurology, 43,* 520–527.

Hartung, H.P., Pollard, J.D., Harvey, G.K., et al. (1995a). Immunopathogenesis and treatment of the Guillain-Barré syndrome: Part I. *Muscle and Nerve, 18,* 137–153.

Hartung, H.P., Pollard, J.D., Harvey, G.K., et al. (1995b). Immunopathogenesis and treatment of the Guillain-Barré syndrome: Part II. *Muscle and Nerve, 18*, 154–164.

Horton, W.A., Hecht, J.T., Hood, O.J., et al. (1992). Growth hormone therapy in achondroplasia. *American Journal of Medical Genetics, 42*, 667–670.

Iannaccone, S.T., Brown, R.H., Samaha, F.J., et al. (1993). A prospective study of spinal muscular atrophy before age six years. *Pediatric Neurology, 9*, 187–193.

Ikeda, K. (1992). Conservative treatment of idiopathic clubfoot. *Journal of Pediatric Orthopaedics, 12*, 217–223.

Jansen, P.W., Perkin, R.M., & Ashwal, S. (1993). Guillain-Barré syndrome in childhood: Natural course and efficacy of plasmapheresis. *Pediatric Neurology, 9*, 16–20.

Jones, H.R. (1996). Childhood Guillain-Barré syndrome: Clinical presentation, diagnosis, and therapy. *Journal of Child Neurology, 11*, 4–12.

Karpati, G., Ajdukovic, D., Arnold, D., et al. (1993). Myoblast transfer in Duchenne muscular dystrophy. *Annals of Neurology, 34*, 8–17.

Kawashima, T., & Uhthoff, H.K. (1990). Development of the foot in prenatal life in relation to idiopathic club foot. *Journal of Pediatric Orthopaedics, 10*, 232–238.

Khan, M.A. (1993). Corticosteroid therapy in Duchenne muscular dystrophy. *Journal of the Neurological Sciences, 120*, 8–14.

Kimpen, J.L., & Ogra, P.L. (1990). Poliovirus vaccines: A continuing challenge. *Pediatric Clinics of North America, 37*, 627–649.

Korinthenberg, R., & Mönting, J.S. (1996). Natural history and treatment effects in Guillain-Barré syndrome: A multicentre study. *Archives of Diseases in Childhood, 74*, 281–287.

MacKenzie, A.E., Jacob, P., Surh, L., et al. (1994). Genetic heterogeneity in spinal muscular atrophy: A linkage analysis-based assessment. *Neurology, 44*, 919–924.

Mendell, J.R., Kissel, J.T., Amato, A.A., et al. (1995). Myoblast transfer in the treatment of Duchenne's muscular dystrophy. *New England Journal of Medicine, 333*, 832–838.

Menkes, J.H. (1995). *Textbook of child neurology* (5th ed.). Baltimore: Williams & Wilkins.

Miller, G., & Wessel, H.B. (1993). Diagnosis of dystrophinopathies: Review for the clinician. *Pediatric Neurology, 9*, 3–9.

Morrissy, R.T. (1990). *Lovell and Winter's pediatric orthopaedics* (3rd ed.). Philadelphia: J.B. Lippincott.

Nicholson, L.V., Johnson, M.A., Bushby, K.M., et al. (1993). Functional significance of dystrophin positive fibres in Duchenne muscular dystrophy. *Archives of Diseases of Childhood, 68*, 632–636.

Nishi, Y., Hamamoto, K., Kajiyama, M., et al. (1992). Effect of long-term calcitonin therapy by injection and nasal spray on the incidence of fractures in osteogenesis imperfecta. *Journal of Pediatrics, 121*, 477–480.

Rees, J.H., Soudain, S.E., Gregson, N.A., et al. (1995). Campylobacter jejuni infection and Guillain-Barré syndrome. *New England Journal of Medicine, 333*, 1374–1379.

Roberts, A., & Evans, G.A. (1993). Orthopedic aspects of neuromuscular disorders in children. *Current Opinion in Pediatrics, 5*, 374–383.

Roberts, R.G., Bobrow, M., & Bentley, D.R. (1992). Point mutations in the dystrophin gene. *Proceedings of the National Academy of Science USA, 89*, 2331–2335.

Roland, E.H. (1994). Neuromuscular disorders in childhood. *Current Opinion in Pediatrics, 6*, 636–641.

Ropper, A. (1992). The Guillain-Barré syndrome. *New England Journal of Medicine, 326*, 1130–1136.

Rousseau, F., Bonaventure, J., Legeai-Mallet, L., et al. (1994). Mutations in the gene encoding fibroblast growth factor receptor-3 in achondroplasia. *Nature, 371*, 252–254.

Russman, B.S., Iannaccone, S.T., Buncher, C.R., et al. (1992). New observations on the natural history of spinal muscular atrophy. *Journal of Child Neurology, 7*, 347–353.

Russman, B.S., & Schwartz, R.C. (1993). Neuromuscular diseases of childhood. *Current Opinion in Pediatrics, 5*, 669–674.

Shaw, N.J., White, C.P., Fraser, W.D., et al. (1994). Osteopenia in cerebral palsy. *Archives of Disease in Childhood, 71*, 235–238.

Van der Meché, F.G., Schnitz, P.I.M., & The Dutch Guillain-Barré Study Group. (1992). A randomized trial comparing intravenous immune globulin and plasma exchange in Guillain-Barré syndrome. *New England Journal of Medicine, 326*, 1123–1129.

Vincent, N., Ragot, T., Gilgenkrantz, H., et al. (1993). Long-term correction of mouse dystrophic degeneration by adenovirus-mediated transfer of a minidystrophin gene. *Nature Genetics, 5*, 130–134.

Wallace, D.C. (1992). Diseases of the mitochondrial DNA. *Annual Review of Biochemistry, 61*, 1175–1212.

Developmental Disabilities

16 Mental Retardation

Mark L. Batshaw
Bruce K. Shapiro

Upon completion of this chapter, the reader will:

- know the developmental milestones children attain
- be acquainted with Piaget's theory of intellectual development
- understand the definition and implications of the term mental retardation
- be aware of the various causes of mental retardation
- know the advantages and disadvantages of the principal intelligence tests used with children
- recognize the various approaches to intervention in mental retardation
- be aware of the different levels of functioning and independence that individuals with mental retardation can achieve

At birth, a newborn responds in an involuntary, or reflexive, way to the environment. Over the next few years, a combination of brain growth and learning experiences enables the child to move from complete dependence on parents to active participation in the world. This development occurs in a sequential fashion. Yet, some of the steps are steeper than others, and some children cannot manage all of them. This chapter discusses the principles of typical and atypical development. It also identifies different causes of mental retardation and reviews approaches to intervention.

EARLY DEVELOPMENT

Development is an ongoing process that begins with embryogenesis and continues throughout the life span. This process is closely linked to the maturation of the central nervous system (CNS). Consequently, the most rapid intellectual development corresponds to the time of fastest brain growth, the first few years of life (see Chapter 14). Development progresses from head to foot, or in a cephalocaudal fashion. Thus, a child first gains head control, then sits, then crawls, and finally walks. Furthermore, development follows a fixed sequence. Children usually roll before sitting, sit before crawling, and crawl before walking. This sequential development permits the early assessment of children. By comparing rates of attaining developmental milestones with norms, professionals can identify those children with atypical development or developmental delay.

When discussing early developmental milestones (birth to 2 years), four major types of skills are usually considered: gross motor, fine motor, language, and social-adaptive. Language, the best predictor of future intellectual functioning, is further broken down into expressive and receptive skills (see Chapter 13). The early developmental history of Jamal, a child born of an uncomplicated pregnancy, illustrates the typical sequence of developmental milestones children pass as they grow from birth to 2 years of age (Table 16.1).

Gross Motor Development

As is generally true of children, Jamal's activity during the first 3 months of life reflected the influence of primitive reflexes. During early infancy, when Jamal's mother stroked the side of his lips, he rooted, or turned toward her. When she placed her breast at his lips, he began to suck vigorously. If Jamal turned his head to the right, his right arm and leg shot out involuntarily while his left arm and leg flexed into an asymmetric tonic neck reflex. He usually held his hands in a clenched position and, when pried open, his fingers automatically grasped his mother's fingers.

Yet, within 2 months he began to gain some control over his movements. For example, when pulled to a sitting position, he managed to hold his head upright for a few seconds before it fell to rest on his chest. Also, when placed face down, Jamal turned his head to one side or the other, which allowed him to breathe more comfortably.

As Jamal grew, his actions became more purposeful. He was able to roll over from stomach to back at 4 months of age. To perform this action, his brain had to suppress certain primitive reflexes. If Jamal had cerebral palsy, the primitive reflexes would have persisted and interfered with rolling (see Chapter 24).

Continuing to develop on schedule, Jamal next progressed to sitting up without support at 7 months of age. This accomplishment required passage through a series of developmental steps. Earlier, Jamal had been unable to sit because he could not maintain his balance. A primitive reflex, called the tonic labyrinthine response, interfered with sitting by making Jamal retract his shoulders and extend his arms whenever he lifted his head. He would then fall over. By 5 months of age, however, this reflex had been suppressed, and Jamal could sit with support. The next step was to develop propping responses in which his hands would reach out to help him balance whenever he began to topple over as he sat. Once this was perfected, he could sit with confidence.

Not satisfied with sitting, Jamal next began the evolution to walking. At 8 months, he could stand when held, bearing weight on his feet. Then, at 9 months, he began to crawl, alternating his legs. He was also able to move from crawling to the sitting position. He was able to pull himself up to a standing position at 10 months and started to walk around objects, or cruise, at 11 months. At last, at 12 months, Jamal took his first independent steps. Five months later, he was running and, by 2 years of age, he could jump and walk up steps.

Fine Motor Development

Jamal's fine motor development paralleled his gross motor development. During his first 2–3 months, he could do very little with his hands because they were usually clenched tight. Once they opened at 3 months, he started to reach toward his colorful mobile and pull at his clothing.

Table 16.1. Development in the first 2 years of life (approximate ages of skill attainment)

Month	Gross motor	Fine motor	Language	Social-adaptive
1	Partial head control Primitive reflexes predominate	Clenched fists	Alerts to sound Makes small sounds	Fixates objects and follows 90°
2	Good head control Lifts chin in prone			Follows 180° Smiles responsively
3	Lifts chest off bed Primitive reflexes less prominent	Hands held open Reaches toward objects Pulls at clothing	Coos	Follows 360° Recognizes mother
4	Swimming movements	Hands come to midline	Laughs aloud Produces different sounds for different needs	Shakes rattle Anticipates food Belly laughs
5	Rolls over stomach to back Holds head erect		Orients toward sound Gives a "raspberry"	Frolics when played with
6	Anterior propping response	Transfers objects Holds bottle Palmar grasp	Babbles Recognizes friendly and angry voices	Looks after lost toy Mirror play
7	Bounces when standing Sits without support	Feeds self cookie	Imitates noise Responds to name	Drinks from cup
8	Lateral propping responses	Rings bell Radial raking grasp	Uses nonspecific "Mama" Understands "no"	Separation anxiety begins Tries to gain attention
9	Crawls		Recognizes familiar words	Mouths objects

(continued)

Table 16.1. (continued)

Month	Gross motor	Fine motor	Language	Social-adaptive
10	Stands with support	Plays with bell Claps	Says specific "Da-da, Ma-ma"	Waves "bye-bye" Plays pat-a-cake
11	Cruises around objects	Uses pincer grasp	Follows gesture command	
12	Makes first steps	Throws objects Puts objects in containers	Says two or three specific words	Aids in dressing Turns papers Takes turns
15	Climbs up stairs	Marks with pencil	Speaks low jargon Follows 1-step commands Speaks four to six words Identifies 1 body part	Indicates when wet Spoon-feeds Builds tower with blocks Gives kisses Imitates chores
18	Runs stiffly Handedness is determined	Constructive play with toys Scribbles Imitates lines Places objects in formboard	Speaks high jargon Follows 2-step commands Points to 1 picture in book Uses 10 words	Places formboard Turns pages Parallel play Takes off shoes Does puzzles
24	Walks up and down steps, both feet on each step	Imitates vertical lines	Uses "I" Identifies four body parts Can form three-word sentences Says "yes" and "no"	Puts on and takes off shoes Plays alongside other children Is negativistic Uses fork Indicates toileting needs

In the fourth month, he would clasp his hands together and then put them in his mouth, often chortling when he did this.

By 5 months of age, Jamal could transfer objects from one hand to the other. This gave him slightly more independence; he could feed himself a cookie and hold a bottle. Over the next few months, he started to explore his environment actively, reaching out and examining anything in sight. For example at 8 months, if placed near a bell, Jamal would grab and ring it until one of his parents successfully substituted a quieter instrument. When he could crawl, at 9 months, he explored all the nooks and crannies of his house. At 11 months, his pincer grasp (i.e., using his thumb and forefinger) was refined and enabled him to pick up small objects. These objects usually ended up in his mouth, whether they were edible or not. When he reached 18 months of age, he could scribble with a pencil, creating many abstract works of art.

Language Skills

From birth, Jamal began to explore the world with his eyes. If his mother was lucky, she could hold his attention for a few seconds. He responded to loud noises by stopping his movement for an instant and then returned to his seemingly random motion. When Jamal was 2 months old, he rewarded his father's attention with a smile.

As a newborn, Jamal communicated his needs mainly by crying. As time went on, he developed more complex communication skills. He cooed in the third month and gave a "raspberry" in the fourth. Jamal also started to turn his head toward a conversation as if to take part in it. In the sixth month, he started making babbling sounds. Four weeks later, he tried to imitate the sounds his parents made and responded to his name with a smile and a turn of the head. By the time Jamal was 8 months old, he understood the command "no," although understanding it did not ensure his following it for very long. He began saying "dada" to everything and everyone in sight. At 11 months, Jamal spoke a few specific words ("ma," "bye") and could follow a simple command if it was accompanied by a gesture.

In comparison with his motor skills, which were simply being refined during the second year of life, Jamal's language skills exploded. At 15 months, he had a 5- to 10-word vocabulary and used jargon (word-like sounds that do not carry meaning) all the time. He also closed the door or sat down when commanded, without a gesture as a guide. When he was 18 months old, Jamal could point to different parts of his body when asked to name them. He spoke unintelligible monologues, interspersing real words with jargon. By 2 years of age, he could name some pictures in a book, follow 2-step commands such as "take the bell and put it on the table," and referred to himself as "I." Soon, he began to put together three-word phrases such as "I am hungry" or "I go outside."

Social-Adaptive Skills

In addition to gaining motor and language skills, Jamal developed the ability to relate to the important people in his life and to differentiate some of their emotional responses. By the time he was 2 months old, Jamal started to distinguish his mother from other people, giving her his best smiles. During his fourth month, he began to laugh heartily. By 6 months, he would reach for his bottle when it was brought into sight.

Jamal's social interactions also became more sophisticated. Before he was a year old, he could play "peekaboo" and "pat-a-cake," wave "bye-bye," and throw a ball. During his second year, Jamal started to help push his arms through a shirt and take off most of his clothes. He also began to play alongside other children, not yet wanting to share with them. When he was separated from his parents, he became upset. By age 2, he became quite independent, feeding himself with a spoon and fork. Like his communication skills, his social skills had become much more refined.

PIAGET'S THEORY OF INTELLECTUAL DEVELOPMENT

Jamal illustrates that neurodevelopment involves a series of steps that build on one another to eventually enable a person to reason and solve problems. It is the inability to complete all of the steps that typifies mental retardation. This lifelong limitation interferes with the person's ability to adapt to his or her world. To explain typical and atypical cognitive development, the Swiss educator Jean Piaget divided the process into four sequential stages: 1) the sensorimotor period, 2) the preoperational stage, 3) the stage of concrete operations, and 4) the period of formal operations (Gruber & Voneche, 1977; Spreen, Risser, & Edgell, 1995). As a child progresses through these stages, he or she gains more and more abilities. Although some theorists have objected to Piaget's classifications, such delineations provide a framework to help in understanding both the sequence of intellectual development and the limitations associated with different levels of mental retardation.

The Sensorimotor Stage: Birth to Approximately 18 Months

During the first 18 months of life, thinking is linked to overt sensorimotor schemes involving grasping, reaching, and vocalizing. The infant's poorly myelinated nerves are slow to process information; even at this stage, however, primitive forms of intelligence are evident. The child begins to coordinate activities to reach certain goals, such as pulling a string to reach a brightly colored ring attached to it. In addition, the child gradually becomes less self-absorbed and more interested in the external world. Through experimentation, the child explores the environment, finding ways of acting and relating to achieve goals. For example, if an 18-month-old wants something out of reach, he or she finds a chair or stool and climbs on it to get the desired object. The child is beginning to find solutions to concrete problems. However, the child still cannot generalize what is learned to new situations. Most "discoveries" are made through trial and error. A child with mental retardation requiring extensive supports usually does not progress beyond this stage.

The Preoperational Stage: Approximately 2–7 Years of Age

As children grow, they gradually develop cognitive schemes for solving problems as all six layers of the cortex and of the structures that link the two hemispheres of their brains mature. Language improves during this stage. Beginning around 2 years of age, the child can use symbols to represent objects that are not present. For example, a child may pretend a mud pie is a chocolate bar and also may pretend to eat it. A child at age 4 can make up a story and may reconstruct the recent past and project into the very near future.

Even with the use of language and the ability to think in more abstract terms, the child's intelligence remains relatively primitive during the preoperational stage of development. Although the child is beginning to classify and group objects, he or she is not yet proficient at this task. Also, although the child can distinguish between certain quantities (e.g., big versus little), he or she is not yet able to understand the concept of conservation. A child of 4, for example, believes that when water is poured from a tall, thin glass into a wide-mouthed, shorter glass, there is less water. He or she is taken in by the appearance of less water. The ability to understand that quantity cannot be judged by appearance alone is refined during the stage of concrete operations. A child with mental retardation requiring limited supports, however, rarely progresses beyond the preoperational stage.

The Stage of Concrete Operations: Approximately Ages 7–12 Years

During the stage of concrete operations, occurring in proximity to the late maturation of the frontal lobes of the brain, a child becomes better able to order and classify numbers, classes, relations, and other aspects of the physical world. For example, a 9-year-old can speak of one object as being wider than another and shorter than something else. This child can also arrange objects according to size or weight and can divide something into its parts. Children in this stage of development are able to solve some mathematical problems and to read well. They also are able to generalize learning to new situations and begin to appreciate another person's point of view. They can understand right from wrong. These children, however, still have difficulty dealing with hypothetical problems. In addition, although in this stage children are better able to understand the concept of past and future, this understanding is somewhat limited. Individuals with mental retardation requiring intermittent supports usually remain at this level of development.

The Stage of Formal Operations: After 12 Years of Age

Piaget's final stage of intellectual development proceeds from age 12 throughout adulthood. During this stage of formal operations, thinking is no longer limited to concrete events; individuals are able to project themselves into the future and to think about long-term goals. They also develop a sensitivity to the feelings of others and become, at the same time, increasingly self-conscious. Perhaps the most notable characteristic, however, is the development of an ability to reason using hypotheses. A classic example is Cyril Burt's (1959) test: If Edith is fairer than Susan and darker than Lilly, who is the darkest of all three? To solve this problem, a person must be able to formulate a system that includes all possible combinations of each element. This ability is developed during the stage of formal operations. The use of higher mathematics is also possible. In other words, development of formal thought involves the ability to isolate a problem, review it systematically, and figure out all possible solutions to that problem. This is also the time for developing executive functions, which are important for higher learning. These higher cortical activities include strategic planning, impulse control, organized search, flexibility of thought and action, and self-monitoring of behavior (Borkowski, 1985). These functions are linked in the brain to the prefrontal cortex and its connections to the limbic and arousal systems (Trevarthen, 1990). They are commonly impaired in children with learning disabilities.

Thus, Piaget's perspective on intellectual development involves the addition of more complex and abstract abilities with each stage. The child typically progresses from one stage to the next. A person who is unable to progress through all the stages is limited in his or her ability to adapt as an adult. Such a person has mental retardation.

DEVELOPMENTAL DELAY

Developmental delay is the term used to indicate atypical neurodevelopment in which there is the failure to achieve age-appropriate milestones (Brown & Elksnin, 1994). To illustrate, consider the story of David, whose mother, Maria, noticed many signs in his early development that indicated atypical development. (In the following paragraphs, the typical ages for these developmental milestones are indicated in parentheses after the age at which David achieved them.)

As an infant, David showed little interest in his environment and was not very alert. He would sit in an infant seat for hours without complaint. Although Maria tried to breast-feed him, his suck was weak, and he frequently regurgitated his formula. He was floppy and had poor head control. His cry was high-pitched, and he was difficult to comfort. In terms of gross motor development, David could hold his head up at 4 months (1 month), roll over at 8 months (5 months), and sit up at 14 months (7 months).

In social and fine motor development, David also lagged behind the norm. He smiled at 5 months (2 months) and was not very responsive to his parents' attention. He transferred objects from one hand to the other at 14 months (6 months). In language skills, he did not start babbling until 13 months (6 months).

David's parents, concerned about their child's lack of progress at 15 months, consulted their pediatrician, who confirmed a significant developmental delay and referred the family to the local Infant and Toddler program for early intervention services. When given the Bayley Scales of Infant Development–Second Edition (BSID–2) (Bayley, 1993) at 16 months, David's mental age was found to be 7 months, and he received a Mental Developmental Index (MDI, similar to an IQ score) score of less than 50. He progressed from the early intervention program to a special preschool program and then, prior to school entry at age 6, David was retested on the Stanford-Binet Intelligence Scale (Terman & Merrill, 1985). His score indicated a mental age of 2 years 8 months and an IQ score of 40. Concomitant impairments in adaptive behavior were demonstrated by the Vineland Adaptive Behavior Scales (VABS) (Sparrow, Balla, & Cicchetti, 1984).

To summarize, developmental delay is recognized by the failure to meet age-appropriate expectations that are based on the typical sequence of development previously illustrated. In the first months of life, delayed development is often indicated by an inadequate sucking response, floppy or spastic muscle tone, and/or a lack of visual or auditory response. Later in the first year, motor delays in sitting and walking and lack of language may suggest a developmental delay. When the child is significantly delayed in all developmental spheres, mental retardation is the likely diagnosis. Although developmental delay is the most common presenting concern in children who turn out to have mental retardation (as well as sensory impairments and cerebral palsy), it does not always indicate a severe disability. Isolated mild delays in expressive language (particularly in boys) or gross motor abilities usually resolve over time. These mild early delays, however, usually signal an increased risk of learning disability that will become evident on school entry.

EARLY IDENTIFICATION

The rationale for early identification of developmental delay is to intervene while the CNS is malleable and responsive to habilitation. Parents usually seek an evaluation for developmental delay once their child fails to meet specific developmental milestones. In early infancy, these include a lack of responsiveness, unusual muscle tone or posture, and feeding difficulties. After 6 months of age, motor delay is the most common complaint. Language and behavior problems are common concerns after 18 months.

Early identification of atypical development is more likely to occur with severe impairments. The child with mental retardation requiring extensive supports is likely to be identified in infancy, while the child with mental retardation requiring only intermittent supports may not be identified until he or she has failed kindergarten or first grade. In order to facilitate early identification, all children should receive developmental screening as part of their routine pediatric care. Unfortunately, too many children live in poverty and receive medical care episodically or move so frequently that follow-up records are unavailable to make this goal achievable. Even when followed in a clinic, there may be little time for the staff to take a developmental history or perform a developmental screening test. Furthermore, the available developmental screening tests themselves are not always effective in detecting developmental disabilities. The most commonly used test in physicians' offices, the Denver II Developmental Screening Test (Frankenburg, Dodds, Archer, et al., 1992), has been shown to have a low sensitivity for detecting mental retardation.

It is important to emphasize that screening tests are not designed to supplant a formal neurodevelopmental and psychological assessment. They are meant to be applied to asymptomatic populations in order to identify individuals at risk. The usefulness of a screening instrument is determined by its ability to appropriately classify children—or its sensitivity and specificity. Sensitivity is the ability of the screening test to correctly detect children who, on further testing, are found to have significant developmental delays; it is measured by the true positive rate. Specificity is the ability to appropriately determine individuals who do not require further assessment; it is measured by the true negative rate. The ideal screening instrument would detect all the children who require further assessment and none of those who do not. Unfortunately, most available screening instruments misclassify too many children (i.e., have too many false positives and false negatives) to be clinically useful.

Given these difficulties, the best approach to early identification is multifaceted. Infants at high risk (e.g., those with prematurity, maternal drug abuse, perinatal insult) should be registered in newborn follow-up programs in which they are evaluated periodically for developmental lags during the first 2 years of life. All parents should be educated to look for and report delays in the typical development sequence. Clinic staff and physicians should routinely note developmental milestones much like they note height and weight. In addition, children should receive a developmental screening battery and tests of vision and hearing every 6–12 months during early childhood (Shapiro, 1996).

If there is evidence of a significant developmental delay over time, the child should then be sent for a comprehensive evaluation. Ideally, the evaluation should include an examination by a neurodevelopmental pediatrician, a clinical psychologist, and a social worker. Depending on the child's age and impairments, he or she also may need to be seen by a special educator, speech-language pathologist, audiologist, and behavioral psychologist. If the child displays motor impairments, physical and occupational therapists should also be involved. Following the assessment of an infant or preschooler, an individualized family service plan (IFSP) is developed in the context of an early intervention program.

EARLY INTERVENTION SERVICES

Traditionally, education programs for children with developmental disabilities began in the primary grades. The efforts of parents and professionals combined with scientific data supporting the value of early identification and intensive early intervention, however, have led to the establishment of education programs for infants and young children (Campbell & Ramey, 1994). The

Education of the Handicapped Act Amendments of 1986, PL 99-457, and its reauthorization, as the Individuals with Disabilities Education Act Amendments of 1991, PL 102-119, mandate that early identification and intervention be initiated in the preschool years (3–5 years) for children who have been identified as having disabilities and for children at risk for developmental disabilities.

In addition, many states have developed discretionary early intervention programs that deal with infants with special needs under age 3. In these early intervention (also called Infant and Toddler) programs, each child undergoes a comprehensive assessment that results in an IFSP. The IFSP must contain 1) a statement of the child's present level of development; 2) a statement of the family's concerns, priorities, and resources related to enhancing the child's development; 3) a statement of major outcomes expected to be achieved for the child and family and the criteria, procedures, and timelines for determining progress; 4) the specific early intervention services required to meet the needs of the child and family, including the frequency, intensity, and expected duration; 5) the name of the service coordinator responsible for implementing the plan; and 6) the procedures for transition from early intervention to preschool services.

At age 3, children make the transition from Infant and Toddler programs to preschool education programs. Federal legislation (Individuals with Disabilities Education Act [IDEA] of 1990, PL 101-476) entitles students from age 3 to 21 years to a free, individualized educational program that is appropriate to the child's needs and abilities and is delivered in the least restrictive environment. The focus of the education program shifts from the family to the individual, and continued service is predicated on establishing an educationally disabling diagnosis. An individualized education program (IEP) replaces the IFSP (see Chapter 23).

MENTAL RETARDATION

Defining Mental Retardation

Although the definition of mental retardation (and even the use of this term) is currently controversial, there is general agreement that a person with mental retardation must have 1) significantly subaverage intellectual functioning; 2) an impairment resulting from an injury, disease, or abnormality that existed before age 18; and 3) an impairment in adaptive abilities (Table 16.2). Despite this general agreement, disagreements over the details of these definitions have arisen for both biological and philosophical reasons.

IQ Scores

The first controversial issue involves IQ scores. The definition of mental retardation relates to a statistical interpretation of "normal" intellectual functioning. The average, or mean, level of intellectual functioning in a population corresponds to the apex of a bell-shaped curve. Two standard deviations on either side of the mean encompass 95% of a population sample and approximately define the range of normal (Figure 16.1). By definition, the average intelligence quotient, or IQ score, is 100, and the standard deviation of most IQ tests is 15 points. Typically, a person scoring more than 2 standard deviations below the mean, or below 70, has been considered to have mental retardation.

However, statisticians point out that there is a measurement error of approximately 5 points in assessing IQ by most psychometric tests. In other words, repeated testing of the same individ-

Table 16.2.   Diagnostic criteria for mental retardation

- Significantly subaverage intellectual functioning: an IQ score of approximately 70 or below on an individually administered IQ test (for infants, a clinical judgment of significantly subaverage intellectual functioning)
- Concurrent deficits or impairments in present adaptive functioning (i.e., the person's effectiveness in meeting the standards expected for his or her age by his or her cultural group) in at least two of the following areas: communication, self-care, home living, social/interpersonal skills, use of community resources, self-direction, functional academic skills, work, leisure, health, and safety
- Onset before 18 years of age

Code-based on degree of severity reflecting level of intellectual impairment:

317 Mild mental retardation (requiring intermittent support)	IQ level 50–55 to approximately 70
318.0 Moderate mental retardation (requiring limited support)	IQ level 35–40 to 50–55
318.1 Severe mental retardation (requiring extensive support)	IQ level 20–25 to 35–40
318.2 Profound mental retardation (requiring pervasive support)	IQ level below 20–25

American Psychiatric Association. (1994). *Diagnostic and statistical manual of mental disorders* (4th ed., p. 46). Washington, DC: Author; reprinted by permission.

ual will produce scores that vary by as much as 5 points (American Psychiatric Association, 1994). Thus, it has been proposed that the demarcation of mental retardation be changed from an IQ score of 70 to a range of 65–75. Within this "borderline" range, the presence or absence of significant impairments in adaptive skills would be used to make the diagnosis. Using this schema, mental retardation would be diagnosed in an individual with an IQ score between 70–75 who exhibits significant impairments in adaptive behavior, while it would not be diagnosed in an individual with an IQ of 65–70 who does not have impairments in adaptive skills. This lack of precision, unfortunately, presents a problematic overlap between the definitions of learning disability and mental retardation.

Beyond any measurement variability, a more fundamental concern of some theorists is the underlying value of an IQ score. Gardner (1983) challenged the dichotomous (verbal versus performance) structure of intelligence assessed by most IQ tests. He proposed that intelligence comprises a wider range of abilities, not only the traditional linguistic and logical-mathematical skills, but musical, spatial, bodily-kinesthetic, and interpersonal characteristics as well. This approach has not gained wide acceptance as it does not have a clear neuropsychological or neuroanatomical basis. And, while it is acknowledged that a single IQ score averages a person's cognitive abilities and may not capture all forms of intelligence, it is still felt that a significantly subnormal IQ score is a meaningful predictor of future cognitive functioning.

Yet, it must be acknowledged that cognitive functioning is not always uniform across all neurodevelopmental domains. An example is found in the study by Wang and Bellugi (1993) comparing neuropsychological testing results in children with Down syndrome and Williams syndrome. Although the full scale IQ scores in both groups were similar, the pattern of cognitive strengths and weaknesses was very different. The individuals with Williams syndrome had much stronger skills in language than did the children with Down syndrome, but much poorer visual-perceptual abilities. Neuroimaging studies in individuals with Williams syndrome showed selective preservation of the prefrontal cortex, the auditory association cortex, and the neocerebellum, all of which are important in language. Conversely, neuroimaging studies in individuals with Down syndrome showed preservation of the brain structures (basal ganglia and thalamus) that

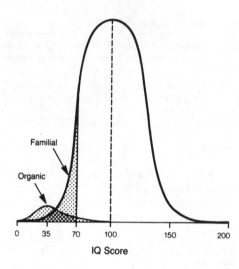

Figure 16.1.   Bimodal distribution of intelligence. The mean IQ score is 100. An IQ score of less than 70, or 2 standard deviations below the mean, can indicate mental retardation. The second, smaller curve takes into account those individuals who have mental retardation because of birth trauma, infection, inborn errors, or other "organic" causes. This explains why more individuals have mental retardation requiring extensive to pervasive support than are predicted by the "familial" curve alone. (From Zigler, E. [1967]. Familial retardation: A continuing dilemma. *Science, 155*, 292–298, Figure 1; reprinted by permission. Copyright 1967 by the American Association for the Advancement of Science.)

are needed for visual-spatial reasoning. Finally, there are the concerns over predictive validity and cultural bias. Infant psychological tests are notoriously poor predictors of adult IQ, although they clearly differentiate severe impairments from normal functioning. And cultural bias has been suggested as one explanation for differences in IQ scores found among various racial and ethnic groups and socioeconomic classes.

Age of Onset

The second requirement for a diagnosis of mental retardation is onset during childhood. If a 3-year-old boy were in a car accident resulting in severe brain damage, he would be considered to have mental retardation because the injury occurred during his developmental years. If his mother also sustained traumatic brain injury in this accident, however, she would have organic brain damage, not mental retardation, because she was no longer in her developmental years. The underlying premise is that the brain of the child and adult are different and that mental retardation must be present during developmental brain growth.

Adaptive Impairments

Finally, individuals with mental retardation not only must have limitations in their intellectual abilities but also must be impaired in their ability to adapt or function in daily life. The classic definition of mental retardation did not elaborate on the specifics of these adaptive impairments. However, both the American Association on Mental Retardation (AAMR) (Luckasson, Coulter, Polloway, et al., 1992) and the American Psychiatric Association (1994) define mental retardation as including at least two of the following impairments in adaptive behavior: communication, self-care, home living, social/interpersonal skills, use of community resources, self-direction, functional academic skills, work, leisure, health, and safety (Table 16.2).

It is important to recognize that there are both philosophical and political underpinnings to this part of the definition. Implied in it is the suggestion that, through education and training of adaptive skills, a child can emerge from mental retardation. It is therefore used to argue for inclusion of children with mental retardation within general education classroom settings, based on evidence that adaptive functioning can be significantly influenced by education, motivation, personality, and social and vocational opportunities. Adaptive skills, however, may not be entirely independent of cognitive skills. Furthermore, their measurement is difficult; imprecise; and requires a great deal of effort, time, and expense. As a result, many developmental disabilities specialists have not routinely applied this criterion in diagnosing mental retardation, even though it is required for provision of educational services.

Degrees of Mental Retardation

There is also controversy about defining the levels of mental retardation. The classical model has been to subdivide mental retardation into four degrees of severity. Each subgroup represents one additional standard deviation (i.e., 15 points) below the mean in IQ score. *The Diagnostic and Statistical Manual of Mental Disorders, Fourth Edition* (DSM-IV) definition has modified this criterion somewhat to take into account test variability: An individual is classified as having mild mental retardation if his or her IQ score is 50–55 to approximately 70; moderate retardation, IQ 35–40 to approximately 50; severe retardation, IQ 20–25 to approximately 35; and profound retardation, IQ below 20–25 (Table 16.2) (American Psychiatric Association, 1994). This classification has met with widespread acceptance, although it has also been suggested that mental retardation be simply dichotomized into mild (IQ score of 50 to approximately 70) and severe (IQ score below 50) because of the discrete biological division between mild retardation and the more severe forms of mental retardation, with different etiologies and outcomes. This dichotomy has not been widely accepted for clinical purposes because the medical, educational, and habilitative needs are quite different within the moderate to profound retardation group.

AAMR takes a different approach in defining the degree of severity of mental retardation, relying not on IQ scores but rather on the patterns and intensity of supports needed (i.e., intermittent [mild], limited [moderate], extensive [severe], or pervasive [profound]) (Luckasson et al., 1992). This definition marks a philosophical shift from an emphasis on degree of impairment to a focus on the abilities of individuals to function in an inclusive environment. This is controversial, as it assumes that adaptive behavior is independent of cognition and does not provide clear guidelines for establishing eligibility of children with IQ scores in the upper limits of the range connoting mental retardation (MacMillan, Gresham, & Siperstein, 1995). Despite recognizing these limitations, we have chosen to use this terminology throughout the book to emphasize the capabilities, rather than the impairments, of individuals with mental retardation.

A final controversy concerns the continued use of the rather perjorative term "mental retardation." In a sense, this term is like the term "cancer." Both carry appropriate meanings—intellectual disability and neoplastic growth, respectively. Both, however, also carry stigmas that are no longer warranted—the need for segregation and the assumption of rapid death, respectively. Furthermore, both of these terms encompass subgroups of disorders with different causes, biological origins, and outcomes. For example, an infant diagnosed with mental retardation due to a nutritional deficit may end up with typical intelligence, while a child with Down syndrome will retain his or her genetically based intellectual disability despite intensive early intervention. Perhaps it would be better to discard the term mental retardation altogether. Already there is a host of new terms waiting to be anointed, including intellectual disability, cognitive disability, and learning disability.

It is likely that innovative approaches to neuropsychological testing combined with new medical tests, including neuroimaging and DNA studies, will profile an individual's cognitive strengths and weaknesses and their biological origin more precisely. This may lead to more appropriate terms and prove helpful in developing new habilitation strategies that may include neurotransmitter medication, gene therapy, and/or neural transplantation. In sum, the concept of mental retardation is in a period of transition. The final outcome of the name, definition, and subtyping may not be determined for a number of years. The battle is likely to be fought on biological, philosophical, and political fronts.

Prevalence of Mental Retardation

Based on the previous discussion, the prevalence of mental retardation depends on the definition used, the method of ascertainment, and the population studied. According to statistics, based on the classic definition, 2.5% of the population should have mental retardation, and another 2.5% superior intelligence (Figure 16.1). Of those with mental retardation, the IQ scores of 85% should fall 2–3 standard deviations below the mean, in the range of mental retardation requiring intermittent support. If individuals who score low on IQ tests because of cultural or social disadvantage are excluded from the count of those with "mild" mental retardation, however, the prevalence is about half of what was predicted, somewhere between 0.8% and 1.2% (McLaren & Bryson, 1987). Whatever the prevalence, it appears to peak at 10–14 years of age, acknowledging that children with mental retardation requiring intermittent support are identified significantly later than those with more severe impairments.

Overall, mental retardation occurs more frequently in boys than in girls. The ratio of males to females is 2:1 in mental retardation requiring intermittent supports and 1.5:1 in mental retardation requiring extensive supports (McLaren & Bryson, 1987). This is thought to be the consequence of sex-linked disorders, such as fragile X syndrome (see Chapter 18).

The prevalence of mental retardation requiring extensive supports has not changed appreciably since the 1940s. This is likely a result of the natural balance between improved health care and the emergence of new diseases. For example, while the morbidity rate of premature infants weighing 1,500–2,500 grams has declined markedly, there is improved survival of much smaller premature infants, weighing less than 1,000 grams, who have a relatively high prevalence of disability (see Chapter 7) (Wolke, Ratschinski, Ohrt, et al., 1994). Prenatal diagnosis has led to a decrease in the number of births of children with Down syndrome, and neonatal screening and early dietary management have helped to eradicate mental retardation caused by phenylketonuria. Both of these preventive measures have been counterbalanced, however, by the increased prevalence of prenatal exposure to drugs of abuse (including alcohol) and congenital human immunodeficiency virus infection (see Chapters 8 and 9). In addition, many of the causes of mental retardation requiring extensive support result from genetic or congenital brain malformations that, as of 1997, can neither be anticipated nor treated.

Overall, the recurrence risk in families with one child who has mental retardation requiring extensive support of unknown origin is 3%–9% (Costeff & Weller, 1987; Louhiala, 1995). A family whose child has mental retardation following neonatal meningitis does not have a significantly increased risk of having future affected children, while a woman who has had one child with fetal alcohol syndrome (FAS) has a 30%–50% risk of having other affected children if she continues to drink. The risk of recurrent Down syndrome ranges from less than 1% for trisomy 21 to more than 10% for a balanced translocation (see Chapter 1) (Mikkelsen, Poulsen, & Tommerup, 1989; Wolff, Back, Arleth, et al., 1989). If the cause of mental retardation is a Mendelian disorder, such as neurofibromatosis (an autosomal dominant trait), Hurler syndrome (an autosomal recessive trait), or fragile X syndrome (an X-linked trait), the risk ranges from 0% to 50%, depending on the inheritance pattern of the specific disorder.

Associated Impairments

While mental retardation requiring intermittent supports is frequently an isolated disability, mental retardation requiring extensive supports is often accompanied by associated impairments that further limit the child's adaptive abilities and adversely affect outcome. The prevalence of these associated impairments correlates with the severity of the mental retardation (Kiely, 1987; Pollak, 1993; Steffenburg, Hagberg, & Kyllerman, 1995; Steffenburg, Hagberg, Viggedal, et al., 1995). These associated impairments include cerebral palsy, visual impairments, seizure disorders, communication impairments, feeding difficulties, psychiatric disorders, and attention-deficit/hyperactivity disorder (ADHD) (Table 16.3). More than half of children with mental retardation requiring extensive supports and one quarter of children with mental retardation requiring intermittent supports have sensory impairments, of which vision impairments, especially strabismus and refractive errors, are the most common. Speech and language impairments (beyond other cognitive impairments) also are frequent. Approximately 20% of children with mental retardation requiring extensive supports have cerebral palsy, which may be associated with feeding problems and failure to thrive. Seizure disorders also occur in about 20% of children with mental retardation. Finally, psychiatric (e.g., pervasive developmental disorder) and behavior disorders (e.g., self-injurious behavior) occur in up to half of these children. In considering intervention strategies, it is essential to identify these additional impairments and work toward their treatment.

Associated impairments may make it difficult to distinguish mental retardation from other developmental disabilities. However, certain distinguishing factors usually exist. In isolated mental retardation, language and nonverbal reasoning skills usually are significantly delayed, while motor skills are less affected. Conversely, in cerebral palsy, motor impairments tend to be more prominent than cognitive impairments. In communication disorders, expressive and/or receptive language skills are more delayed than motor and nonverbal reasoning skills. In perva-

Table 16.3. Percentages of children with mental retardation who have associated developmental disabilities

	Extensive support (%)	Intermittent support (%)
None	17	63
Cerebral palsy	19	6
Seizure disorders	21	11
Sensory impairments	55	24
Psychological/behavioral	50	25

From Kiely, M. (1987). The prevalence of mental retardation. *Epidemiology Reviews, 9,* 194; adapted by permission.

sive developmental disorders, social skills impairments and aberrant behaviors are superimposed on cognitive (especially communication) impairments. In some instances, repeated assessments may be necessary to determine the primary developmental disability.

Causes of Mental Retardation

The epidemiology of mental retardation suggests that there are two overlapping populations. Mental retardation requiring intermittent supports is associated with lower socioeconomic status and more deprived environments. Mental retardation requiring extensive supports, however, is more typically linked to a biological cause. There is also often an interaction between nature and nurture. For example, a child may have an initial biological insult (e.g., intrauterine growth retardation), which is compounded by environmental variables (e.g., poor nutrition, maternal neglect). Mothers who never finished high school are four times more likely to have children with mental retardation requiring intermittent supports than women who completed high school (Capute & Accardo, 1996; Drews, Yeargin-Allsopp, Decoufle, et al., 1995). The explanation for this is unclear but may involve a genetic component (i.e., children may inherit a cognitive impairment) and socioeconomic factors (i.e., poverty, neglect, undernutrition). While African American children appear to be more than twice as likely to have mental retardation requiring intermittent support than Caucasian children, at least half of the mental retardation is attributable to poverty or other adverse social conditions (Yeargin-Allsopp, Drews, Decoufle, et al., 1995). The interaction of nature and nurture can also be beneficial. For example, application of early intervention services to children at risk has resulted in improved cognitive outcomes.

In children with mental retardation requiring extensive supports, a biological origin of the condition can be identified in about two thirds of cases. The most common diagnoses are fragile X syndrome (see Chapter 18), Down syndrome (see Chapter 17), and FAS (see Chapter 8), which together account for almost one third of all identifiable cases of mental retardation requiring extensive supports (Table 16.4) (Moser, 1995; Wellesley, Hockey, & Stanley, 1991).

One way of dividing the biological origins of mental retardation is by their timing in the developmental sequence (Crocker, 1989). In general, the earlier the problem exists, the more severe its consequence. Chromosomal disorders (e.g., Down syndrome) and hereditary multiple anomaly syndromes (e.g., de Lange syndrome), which affect early embryogenesis, are both the most common, accounting for half of identifiable causes, and the most severe (see Chapter 1). Insults occurring in the first and second trimesters as a result of drugs (e.g., FAS); infections (e.g., cytomegalovirus); and other pregnancy problems (e.g., intrauterine growth retardation)

Table 16.4. Identifiable etiologies of mental retardation requiring extensive support (%)

Chromosomal	35
Multiple congenital anomalies	16
Early pregnancy problems	11
Perinatal insults	10
Single-gene defect	10
Postnatal brain damage	5
Other	13

Source: Crocker (1989).

(see Chapter 4) occur in 10% of cases. Complications of the third trimester and perinatal period (see Chapter 5) now account for less than 10% of cases of mental retardation requiring extensive supports. Ten percent are attributable to single-gene defects (e.g., inborn errors of metabolism) (see Chapter 19). Five percent are the result of postnatal brain damage, most commonly brain infections and traumatic brain injury (see Chapter 27).

In contrast to mental retardation requiring extensive support, the origins of mental retardation requiring intermittent support are currently identifiable in less than 20% of individuals (Akesson, 1986). The most common biological causes are perinatal insults, intrauterine exposure to drugs of abuse (especially alcohol), and sex chromosomal abnormalities (Matilainen, Airaksinen, Mononen, et al., 1995).

Medical Diagnostic Testing

No single method exists for detecting all causes of mental retardation. As a result, diagnostic testing should be based on historical information and a physical examination (Majnemer & Shevell, 1995). For example, a child with an unusual facial appearance or multiple congenital anomalies should have a chromosome study performed. A child with clinical features of autism and/or a family history of mental retardation should probably be tested for fragile X syndrome. A child with a progressive neurological disorder will need extensive metabolic investigation; and a child with seizure-like episodes should have an electroencephalogram (EEG). Finally, children with abnormal head growth or asymmetrical neurological findings warrant a neuroimaging procedure (Levy & Hyman, 1993).

Although these are the most common reasons for performing diagnostic tests, it now seems clear that some children with subtle physical or neurological findings also may have determinable biological causes of their mental retardation. It has been shown that about 6% of unexplained mental retardation can be accounted for by small chromosomal abnormalities that require extensive testing to identify (Flint, Wilkie, Buckle, et al., 1995). Affected children have no obvious abnormal physical findings. Furthermore, normal test results do not necessarily rule out an abnormality (e.g., neuroimaging studies are not sensitive enough to detect microscopic developmental brain abnormalities) (Huttenlocher, 1991).

How intensively the physician investigates the cause of a child's mental retardation is based on a number of questions. First, what is the degree of mental retardation? One is less likely to find a cause in a child with mental retardation requiring intermittent support. Second, is there a specific diagnostic path to follow? If there is historical information, a family history, or physical findings pointing to a specific cause, a diagnosis is more likely to be made. Conversely, in the absence of these indicators, it is difficult to choose specific tests to run. Third, are the parents planning to have additional children? If so, one would be more likely to intensively seek disorders for which prenatal diagnosis or a specific early treatment option is available. Finally, what are the parents' wishes? Some parents have little interest in searching for the cause and focus exclusively on treatment. Others will be so focused on obtaining a diagnosis that they will have difficulty accepting intervention until a cause has been found. Both extremes and everything in between must be respected, but rational guidance should be provided to families.

Psychological Testing

The routine evaluation for mental retardation includes the performance of an individual intelligence test. The most commonly used test in infants is the BSID. For children over 2 years of age, the Stanford-Binet Intelligence Scale (Terman & Merrill, 1985), the Wechsler Intelligence Scales (Wechsler, 1974), and the Kaufmann Assessment Battery for Children (Kaufman & Kaufman, 1985) are most commonly used (Wodrich, 1997) (Table 16.5).

Infant Developmental Tests

The BSID is used to assess fine motor, gross motor, language, visual problem-solving skills, and behavior of children between 1 month and 3½ years of age. An MDI and a Psychomotor Development Index score (PDI, a measure of motor competence) are derived from the results. Less commonly used infant tests include the Battelle and the Mullen Scales of Early Language.

In infants and young children with typical development, there is substantial variability on repeated cognitive testing and consequently poor predictive validity until around 10 years of age. Accuracy is enhanced if repeated testing confirms a stable rate of cognitive development. The predictive value of infant tests is further limited because they are primarily dependent on nonlanguage items, while language items remain the best predictors of future IQ scores (Bayley, 1958). These tests do permit the differentiation of infants with mental retardation requiring extensive support from typical infants but are less helpful in distinguishing between a typical child and one with mental retardation requiring intermittent support (Maisto & German, 1986). In general, however, there is less variability seen with cognitive growth in children with mental retardation than in children with typical development so predictive validity is enhanced.

Intelligence Tests in Children

One of the most established of the psychological tests used in children older than 18 months is the Stanford-Binet Intelligence Scale (Terman & Merrill, 1985). It comprises 15 subtests that as-

Table 16.5. Psychometric tests (IQ tests) used in diagnosing mental retardation

Name of test	Age range	Description
Bayley Scales of Infant Development (BSID) (Bayley, 1993)	1–42 months	Verbal, motor, and behavior scales. Measures sensory motor development. Limited predictability of future development. Also gives motor development index and behavior rating scale.
Stanford-Binet Intelligence Scale (4th edition) (Terman & Merrill, 1985)	1½ years–adult	Designed for measuring verbal reasoning, abstract visual reasoning, quantitative and short-term memory skills. Few motor tasks.
Wechsler Preschool and Primary Scale of Intelligence–Revised (WPPSI–R) (Wechsler, 1989)	3–7 years	General intelligence scale for young children. Information, similarities, arithmetic, vocabulary, comprehension, sentences, object assembly, picture completion, geometric design, block design, animal pegs, mazes. Focus on motor and processing skills.
Wechsler Intelligence Scale for Children–Third Edition (WISC–III) (Wechsler, 1991)	6–17 years	Standard measure of intelligence in children. Subtests: information, similarities, arithmetic, vocabulary, comprehension, digit span, picture completion, picture arrangement, block design, object assembly, symbol search, coding, mazes. Focus on approach to problem solving.

Source: Wodrich (1997).

sess four areas of intelligence: verbal abilities, abstract/visual thinking, quantitative reasoning, and short-term memory. This permits the evaluator to determine, using some caution, areas of relative strength and weakness. Unfortunately the Stanford-Binet is rather lengthy and difficult to administer and therefore is generally not the first test of choice. Furthermore, it underdiagnoses mental retardation (Wodrich, 1997).

The most commonly used psychological tests for children older than 3 years of age are the Wechsler Scales. The Wechsler Preschool and Primary Scale of Intelligence (WPPSI–R) (Wechsler, 1989) was revised in 1989 and is used for children with mental ages of 3–7 years. The Wechsler Intelligence Scale for Children (WISC–III, revised in 1991) is used for children who function above a 6-year mental age. Both scales contain a number of subtests in the areas of verbal and performance skills. Although children with mental retardation usually score below average on all subscale scores, they occasionally score in the normal range in one or more performance areas. Overall, the Stanford-Binet and Wechsler Scales are quite accurate in predicting adult IQ scores when given to school-age children. The evaluator, however, must ensure that situations that may lead to falsely low IQ scores are not confounding the test performance. Conditions such as motor impairments, communication disorders, sensory impairments, speaking a language other than English, extremely low birth weight, or severe sociocultural deprivation may invalidate certain intelligence tests, require modification of others, and always involve caution in interpretation.

Tests of Adaptive Functioning

As noted in the DSM-IV definition of mental retardation, in addition to intelligence testing, adaptive skills also should be measured. The most commonly used test of adaptive behavior is the VABS. This test involves parental and/or caregiver/teacher semi-structured interviews that assess adaptive behavior in four domains: communication, daily living skills, socialization, and motor skills. There are three forms of the test with between 244 and 577 items. Other tests of adaptive behavior include the Woodcock-Johnson Scales of Independent Behavior (Bruinicks, Woodcock, Weatherman, et al., 1996) and the American Association on Mental Deficiency Adaptive Behavior Scale (ABS) (Wodrich, 1997). There is usually (but not always) a good correlation between scores on the intelligence and adaptive scales (Bloom & Zelko, 1994). Adaptive abilities, however, are more responsive to remedial efforts than is the IQ score.

Intervention Approaches for Mental Retardation

The most useful approach for children with mental retardation consists of multidisciplinary efforts directed at many aspects of the child's life—education, social, and recreational activities; behavior problems; and associated impairments (Colozzi & Pollow, 1984). Counseling for parents and siblings may also be needed (see Chapters 3 and 34).

Educational Services

Education is the single most important discipline involved in the treatment of children with mental retardation. The achievement of "good outcomes" is dependent on the interaction of the student and teacher. Educational programs must be relevant to the child's needs and address the child's individual strengths and weaknesses. The child's developmental level and his or her requirements for support and goals for independence provide a basis for establishing an educational plan. In general, the child with mental retardation requiring intermittent support needs to gain academic and vocational skills for independent living, while the child with mental retardation requiring limited to extensive support needs "survival" skills that can be used in supported employment and alternate living units.

Leisure and Recreational Needs

In addition to education, the child's social and recreational needs should be addressed (Dattilo & Schleien, 1994). In the ideal world, children with mental retardation would participate as equals in recreation and leisure activities. While young children are not excluded from play activities, adolescents frequently do not have opportunities for appropriate social interaction and are not competitive in extracurricular sports activities. Yet, participation in sports should be encouraged as it offers many benefits, including weight management, development of physical coordination, maintenance of cardiovascular fitness, and improvement of self-image (Eichstaedt & Lavay, 1992). Social activities are equally important. These include dances, trips, dating, and other typical social and recreational events.

Control of Behavior Disorders

To facilitate the child's socialization, significant behavior problems must be addressed (Walker, 1993). Although most children with mental retardation do not have behavior disorders, these problems do occur with a greater frequency in this population than among children with typical development (Fraser & Rao, 1991). Behavior problems may result from inappropriate parental expectations, organic problems, and/or family difficulties. Alternately, they may represent attempts by the child to gain attention or avoid frustration. In assessing the behavior, one must consider whether it is inappropriate for the child's mental age, rather than for his or her chronological age. Thus, the "terrible twos" in a 6-year-old with mental retardation requiring extensive support may be appropriate for the child's mental age and may not require professional intervention. When intervention is needed, an environmental change, such as a more appropriate classroom setting, may improve certain behavior problems. For some children, behavior management techniques (see Chapter 30) and/or the use of medication may be necessary.

Use of Medication

Medication is not useful in treating the core symptoms of mental retardation; no drug has been found to improve intellectual function. Medication may be very helpful, however, in treating associated behavior and psychiatric problems. These drugs are generally directed at specific symptom complexes including ADHD (e.g., methylphenidate [Ritalin]); self-injurious behavior (e.g., haloperidol [Haldol]); aggression (e.g., carbamazepine [Tegretol]); and depression (e.g., fluoxetine [Prozac]) (Aman, 1993). These drugs are discussed in detail in Chapters 20 and 22. Before long-term therapy with any psychopharmacological agent is initiated, a short trial should be conducted. Ideally, the child's teacher should agree to be a "blinded" observer in which she or he is unaware of the treatment condition but keeps a record of attention, behavior, and activity level (Conners & Wells, 1986). Even if a medication proves successful, its use should be reevaluated at least yearly to determine the need for continued treatment.

Treating Associated Impairments

If there are associated impairments—cerebral palsy; visual or hearing impairments; seizure disorders; speech disorders; autism; and other disorders of language, behavior, and perception—they must also be treated to achieve an optimal outcome. This may require ongoing physical therapy, occupational therapy, speech-language therapy, adaptive equipment, glasses, hearing aids, antiepileptic medication, and so on. Failure to adequately identify and treat these problems may hinder successful habilitation and result in difficulties in the school, home, or neighborhood environment.

Family Counseling

Many families adapt well to having a child with mental retardation, but some do not. Among the factors that have been associated with family coping skills are stability of the marriage, age of the parents, parental self-esteem, number of siblings, socioeconomic status, degree of disability, parental expectations and acceptance of the diagnosis, supportive extended family members, and availability of community programs and respite care services. In those families in which the emotional burden of having a child with mental retardation is great, family counseling should be an integral part of treatment (see Chapter 34).

Periodic Reevaluation

Although mental retardation is considered a static disorder, the needs of the child and his or her family change over time. As the child grows, more information must be provided to parents, goals must be reassessed, and programming will need to be adjusted. A periodic review should include information about the child's health status as well as his or her functioning at home, at school, and in other settings. Other information, such as formal psychological or educational testing, may be needed. Although the Education for All Handicapped Children Act of 1975, PL 94-142, mandates reevaluation every 3 years, it should be undertaken any time the child is not meeting expectations and when he or she is moving from one service provision system to another. This is especially true during adolescence and in the transition to adulthood when fewer services may be available (see Chapter 35).

PROGNOSIS

The prognosis for individuals with mental retardation depends on the underlying cause, the degree of mental retardation, the presence of associated medical and developmental disabilities, and the capabilities of the families. As adults, many people with mental retardation requiring intermittent support are able to gain economic and social independence with the equivalent of up to a fifth-grade education (i.e., functional literacy). They may need periodic supervision, however, especially under social and economic stress. Most marry and live successfully in the community, either independently or in supervised settings (American Psychiatric Association, 1994). Life expectancy is not adversely affected.

For individuals with mental retardation requiring limited support, the goals of education are to enhance adaptive abilities, "survival" academics, and vocational skills so they are better able to live in the adult world. They may achieve up to a second-grade education. Contemporary gains including the concept of supported employment have benefited these individuals the most. Supported employment challenges the view that "prerequisite" skills must be taught before there can be successful vocational adaptation. Instead, individuals are trained by a coach to do a specific job in the setting in which the person is to work. This bypasses the need for a sheltered workshop experience and has resulted in successful work adaptation in the community for many people with mental retardation. Outcome studies have documented the effectiveness of this approach. People with mental retardation requiring limited support generally live at home or in a supervised setting in the community. Individuals with Down syndrome generally fit in this group.

As adults, people with mental retardation requiring extensive to pervasive support function at the preschool level. They may perform simple tasks in closely supervised workshop settings. However, these individuals frequently have associated impairments such as cerebral palsy and sensory impairments that further limit their adaptive functioning. Most people with this level of mental retardation live in the community, usually in their parents' homes. Some individuals with severe medical problems, behavioral disturbances, or disrupted families, however, live in out-of-home settings including foster homes, alternative living units, group homes, nursing homes, residential schools, and institutions. Life span appears to be shortened in individuals with mental retardation requiring extensive to pervasive support (Figure 16.2) (Eyman, Grossman, Chaney, et al., 1990).

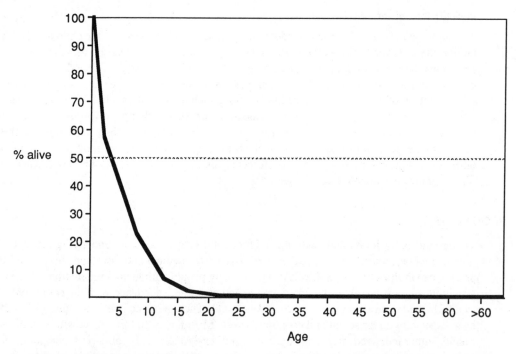

Figure 16.2.   Life table for 1,550 people receiving services from the California Department of Developmental Services from 1984 through 1987 who had mental retardation; were immobile; were not toilet trained; and required tube feeding. (From Eyman, R.K., Grossman, H.J., Chaney, R.H., et al. [1990]. The life expectancy of profoundly handicapped people with mental retardation. *New England Journal of Medicine, 323,* 587; reprinted by permission.)

SUMMARY

Development is a step-by-step process that is linked to the maturation of the CNS. With mental retardation, development is altered so that intellectual and adaptive skills are impaired. In most cases of mental retardation requiring intermittent support, the underlying cause is unclear. In two thirds of individuals with mental retardation requiring extensive support, however, there is a definable cause. The vast majority of people with mental retardation require only intermittent support, though, and are often able to achieve economic and social independence. The early identification of a developmental delay is important to ensure appropriate treatment and to enable the child to develop and use all of his or her capabilities.

REFERENCES

Akesson, H.O. (1986). The biological origin of mild mental retardation: A critical review. *Acta Psychiatrica Scandinavica, 74,* 3–7.

Aman, M.G. (1993). Efficacy of psychotropic drugs for reducing self-injurious behavior in the developmental disabilities. *Annals of Child Neurology, 5,* 171–188.

American Psychiatric Association. (1994). *Diagnostic and statistical manual of mental disorders* (4th ed., DSM-IV). Washington, DC: Author.

Bayley, N. (1958). Value and limitations of infant testing. *Children, 5,* 129–133.

Bayley, N. (1993). *Bayley Scales of Infant Development–Second edition manual.* San Antonio, TX: The Psychological Corporation.

Bloom, A.S., & Zelko, F.A. (1994). Variability in adaptive behavior in children with developmental delay. *Journal of Clinical Psychology, 50,* 261–265.

Borkowski, J.G. (1985). Signs of intelligence: Strategy generalization and metacognition. In S.R. Yussen (Ed.), *The growth of reflection in children* (pp. 105–144). Orlando, FL: Academic Press.

Bricker, D., Squires, J., & Mounts, L. (1995). *Ages & Stages Questionnaires (ASQ): A parent-completed, child-monitoring system.* Baltimore: Paul H. Brookes Publishing Co.

Brown, F.R., III, & Elksnin, N. (1994). *An introduction to developmental disabilities.* San Diego: Singular Publishing Group.

Bruinicks, R.H., Woodcock, R.W., Weatherman, R.F., et al. (1996). *Scales of Independent Behavior–Revised.* Chicago: Riverside Publishing.

Burt, C. (1959). General ability and special aptitudes. *Educational Research, 1,* 3–16.

Campbell, F.A., & Ramey, C.T. (1994). Effects of early intervention on intellectual and academic achievement: Follow-up of children from low-income families. *Child Development, 65,* 684–698.

Capute, A.J., & Accardo, P.J. (Eds.). (1996). *Developmental disabilities in infancy and childhood: Vols. 1 & 2. Neurodevelopmental diagnosis and treatment and the spectrum of developmental disabilities* (2nd ed.). Baltimore: Paul H. Brookes Publishing Co.

Colozzi, G.A., & Pollow, R.S. (1984). Teaching independent walking to mentally retarded children in a public school. *Education and Training of the Mentally Retarded, 19,* 97–101.

Conners, C.K., & Wells, A.C. (1986). *Hyperactive children.* Beverly Hills: Sage Publications.

Costeff, H., & Weller, L. (1987). The risk of having a second retarded child. *American Journal of Medical Genetics, 27,* 753–766.

Crocker, A.C. (1989). The causes of mental retardation. *Pediatric Annals, 18,* 623–635.

Dattilo, J., & Schleien, S.J. (1994). Understanding leisure services for individuals with mental retardation. *Mental Retardation, 32,* 53–59.

Drews, C.D., Yeargin-Allsopp, M., Decoufle, P., et al. (1995). Variation in the influence of selected sociodemographic risk factors for mental retardation. *American Journal of Public Health, 85,* 329–334.

Education for All Handicapped Children Act of 1975, PL 94-142, 20 U.S.C. § 1400 *et seq.*

Education of the Handicapped Act Amendments of 1986, PL 99-457, 20 U.S.C. § 1400 *et seq.*

Eichstaedt, C.B., & Lavay, B.W. (1992). *Physical activity for individuals with mental retardation.* Champaign, IL: Human Kinetics Books.

Eyman, R.K., Grossman, H.J., Chaney, R.H., et al. (1990). The life expectancy of profoundly handicapped people with mental retardation. *New England Journal of Medicine, 323,* 584–589.

Flint, J., Wilkie, A.O.M., Buckle, V.J., et al. (1995). The detection of subtelomeric chromosomal rearrangements in idiopathic mental retardation. *Nature Genetics, 9,* 132–140.

Frankenburg, W.K., Dodds, J.B., Archer, P., et al. (1992). The Denver II: A major revision and restandardization of the Denver developmental screening test. *Pediatrics, 89,* 91–97.

Fraser, W.I., & Rao, J.M. (1991). Recent studies of mentally handicapped young people's behavior. *Journal of Child Psychology and Psychiatry, 32,* 79–108.

Gardner, H. (1983). *Frames of mind: The theory of multiple intelligences.* New York: Basic Books.

Glascoe, F.P., Byrne, K.E., Ashford, L.G., et al. (1992). Accuracy of the Denver II in developmental screening. *Pediatrics, 89,* 1221–1225.

Gruber, H.E., & Voneche, J.J. (Eds.). (1977). *The essential Piaget.* New York: Basic Books.

Huttenlocher, P.R. (1991). Dendritic and synaptic pathology in mental retardation. *Pediatric Neurology, 7,* 79–85.

Individuals with Disabilities Education Act (IDEA) of 1990, PL 101-476, 20 U.S.C. § 1400 *et seq.*

Individuals with Disabilities Education Act Amendments of 1991, PL 102-119, 20 U.S.C. § 1400 *et seq.*

Kaufman, A.S., & Kaufman, N.L. (1985). *Kaufman Test of Educational Achievement.* Circle Pines, MN: American Guidance Services.

Kiely, M. (1987). The prevalence of mental retardation. *Epidemiology Reviews, 9,* 194–218.

Levy, S.E., & Hyman, S.L. (1993). Pediatric assessment of the child with developmental delay. *Pediatric Clinics of North America, 40,* 465–477.

Louhiala, P. (1995). Risk indicators of mental retardation: Changes between 1967 and 1981. *Developmental Medicine and Child Neurology, 37,* 631–636.

Luckasson, R., Coulter, D.L., Polloway, E.A., et al. (1992). *Mental retardation: Definition, classification, and systems of supports.* Washington, DC: American Association on Mental Retardation.

Macmillan, D.L., Gresham, F.M., & Siperstein, G.N. (1995). Heightened concerns over the 1992 AAMR definition: Advocacy versus precision. *American Journal on Mental Retardation, 100,* 87–97.

Maisto, A.A., & German, M.L. (1986). Reliability, predictive validity, and interrelationships of early assessment indices used with developmentally delayed infants and children. *Journal of Clinical Child Psychiatry, 15,* 547–554.

Majnemer, A., & Shevell, M.I. (1995). Diagnostic yield of the neurologic development of the developmentally delayed child. *Journal of Pediatrics, 127,* 193–199.

Matilainen, R., Airaksinen, E., Mononen, T., et al. (1995). A population-based study on the causes of mild and severe mental retardation. *Acta Paediatrica, 84,* 261–266.

McLaren, J., & Bryson, S.E. (1987). Review of recent epidemiological studies of mental retardation: Prevalence, associated disorders, and etiology. *American Journal on Mental Retardation, 92,* 243–254.

Mikkelsen, M., Poulsen, H., & Tommerup, N. (1989). Genetic risk factors in human trisomy 21. *Progress in Clinical and Biological Research, 311,* 183–197.

Moser, H.W. (1995). A role for gene therapy in mental retardation. *Mental Retardation and Developmental Disabilities Research Reviews, 1,* 4–6.

Pollak, M. (1993). *Textbook of developmental paediatrics.* Edinburgh, Scotland: Churchill Livingstone.

Shapiro, B.K. (1996). Neurodevelopmental assessment of infants and young children. In A.J. Capute & P.J. Accardo (Eds.), *Developmental disabilities in infancy and childhood: Vol. 1. Neurodevelopmental diagnosis and treatment* (2nd ed., pp. 311–322). Baltimore: Paul H. Brookes Publishing Co.

Sparrow, S., Balla, D., & Cicchetti, D. (1984). *Vineland Adaptive Behavior Scales (VABS).* Circle Pines, MN: American Guidance Service.

Spreen, O., Risser, A.H., & Edgell, D. (1995). *Developmental neuropsychology.* New York: Oxford University Press.

Steffenburg, U., Hagberg, G., & Kyllerman, M. (1995). Active epilepsy in mentally retarded children: II. Etiology and reduced pre- and perinatal optimality. *Acta Paediatrica, 84,* 1153–1159.

Steffenburg, U., Hagberg, G., Viggedal, G., et al. (1995). Active epilepsy in mentally retarded children: I. Prevalence and additional neuroimpairments. *Acta Paediatrica, 84,* 1147–1152.

Terman, L.M., & Merrill, M.A. (1985). *Stanford-Binet Intelligence Scale: Manual for the fourth revision.* Boston: Houghton Mifflin.

Trevarthen, C. (1990). Growth and education in the hemispheres. In C. Trevarthen (Ed.), *Brain circuits and functions of the mind* (pp. 334–363). New York: Cambridge University Press.

Walker, G.R. (1993). Noncompliant behavior of people with mental retardation. *Research in Developmental Disabilities, 14,* 87–105.

Wang, P.P., & Bellugi, U. (1993). Williams syndrome, Down syndrome, and cognitive neuroscience. *American Journal of Diseases of Childhood, 147,* 1246–1251.

Wechsler, D. (1967). *Manual for the Wechsler Preschool and Primary Scale of Intelligence.* New York: The Psychological Corporation.

Wechsler, D. (1974). *Weschler Intelligence Scale for Children.* New York: The Psychological Corporation.

Wechsler, D. (1989). *Wechsler Preschool and Primary Scale of Intelligence–Revised.* New York: The Psychological Corporation.

Wechsler, D. (1991). *Wechsler Intelligence Scale for Children–Third edition.* New York: The Psychological Corporation.

Wellesley, D., Hockey, A., & Stanley, F. (1991). The aetiology of intellectual disability in Western Australia: A community-based study. *Developmental Medicine and Child Neurology, 33,* 963.

Wodrich, D.L. (1997). *Children's psychological testing: A guide for nonpsychologists* (3rd ed.). Baltimore: Paul H. Brookes Publishing Co.

Wolff, G., Back, E., Arleth, S., et al. (1989). Genetic counseling in families with inherited balanced translocations: Experience with 36 families. *Clinical Genetics, 35,* 404–416.

Wolke, D., Ratschinski, G., Ohrt, B., et al. (1994). The cognitive outcome of very preterm infants may be poorer than often reported: An empirical investigation of how methodological issues make a big difference. *European Journal of Pediatrics, 153,* 906–915.

Yeargin-Allsopp, M., Drews, C.D., Decoufle, P., et al. (1995). Mild mental retardation in black and white children in metropolitan Atlanta: A case-control study. *American Journal of Public Health, 85,* 324–328.

Zigler, E. (1967). Familial retardation: A continuing dilemma. *Science, 155,* 292–298.

17 Down Syndrome

Nancy J. Roizen

Upon completion of this chapter, the reader will:

- be aware of the methods used in prenatal screening and diagnosis of Down syndrome
- recognize the physical characteristics of Down syndrome
- understand the medical complications of this disorder
- know the typical cognitive, developmental, and behavioral characteristics of a child with Down syndrome
- understand approaches to intervention

Down syndrome was one of the first symptom complexes associated with mental retardation to be identified as a syndrome. In fact, evidence of the syndrome dates back to ancient times. Archaeological excavations have revealed a skull from the 7th century that displays the physical features of an individual with Down syndrome. Portrait paintings from the 16th century depict children with a Down-like facial appearance. In 1866, Dr. John Langdon Down, for whom the syndrome is named, published the first complete physical description of Down syndrome, including the similarity of facial features among affected individuals (Figure 17.1). In 1959, researchers identified the underlying chromosomal abnormality (an additional #21 chromosome) that causes Down syndrome (Lejeune, Gautier, & Turpin, 1959).

CHROMOSOMAL ABNORMALITIES

Three types of chromosomal abnormalities lead to Down syndrome: trisomy 21 (which accounts for about 95% of individuals with the disorder), translocation (which accounts for 4%), and mosaicism (which accounts for 1%). Trisomy 21 results from nondisjunction, most commonly during meiosis I of the egg (see Chapter 1). Translocation Down syndrome involves the attachment of the long arm of an extra chromosome #21 to chromosome #14, #21, or #22. Mosaic trisomy implies that some but not all cells have the defect, resulting from nondisjunction during mitosis of the fertilized egg.

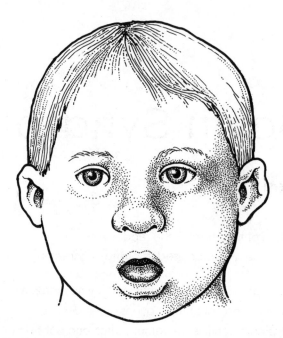

Figure 17.1.   The physical features of a child with Down syndrome include a small head with flatten-ing of the back and face. The nose is recessed, and there is an upward slant to the eyes with epi-canthal folds at the inner corners. The ears and mouth are small, as are the hands and feet. The fin-gers are short and stubby, with incurving of the fifth digit. There is often a simian crease on the palm. The neck is broad and the skin may appear mottled.

Studies indicate that children with translocation Down syndrome do not differ cognitively or medically from those with trisomy 21 (Johnson & Abelson, 1969). Children with mosaic Down syndrome, perhaps because their trisomic cells are interspersed with normal cells, typi-cally score 10–30 points higher on IQ tests and have fewer medical complications than children with translocation or trisomy 21 Down syndrome (Fishler & Koch, 1991).

PREVALENCE

The prevalence of Down syndrome births has decreased from 1.33 per 1,000 to 0.92 per 1,000 since the 1970s, presumably as a result of prenatal diagnosis (Down Syndrome Prevalence, 1994). Many women opt to terminate a pregnancy in which the fetus is identified as having Down syndrome. In defining prevalence, maternal age has been consistently linked to Down syndrome. In fact, at 20 years of age, women have about a 1 in 2,000 chance of having a child with trisomy 21; but at 45 years of age, the likelihood increases to 1 in 20 (Trimble & Baird, 1978) (Figure 3.2). There is no age effect in translocation Down syndrome, but one third of these individuals inherit the translocation from their parents, who are carriers (Jones, 1996). A chro-mosome analysis can identify those parents who are at risk of producing other children with translocation Down syndrome. Although trisomic Down syndrome occurs in more males (59%) than females (41%), translocation Down syndrome more often occurs in females (74%) (Staples, Sutherland, Haan, et al., 1991). The reason for these phenomena is unclear.

ETIOLOGY

When an individual has three copies of a "critical region" on chromosome #21, he or she will present with the clinical features of Down syndrome (Figure 17.2). Although it is not exactly known how three copies of this region produce this syndrome, researchers believe that defects on a closely related group of 50 genes together contribute to the clinical picture, a condition called a contiguous gene syndrome (Korenberg, Chen, Schipper, et al., 1994; Sinet, Theophile, Rahmani, et al., 1994). One of these genes, for example, codes for the enzyme DYRK (dual specificity tyrosine phosphorylation-related kinase), which plays an important role in how the neuronal pathways are put together. Although the underlying mechanism remains unclear, much has been learned about the embryology and neuropathology of Down syndrome since the 1980s. It is likely that the trisomy causes malformations as a result of incomplete rather than deviant development of the embryo. For example, although the heart may be normally formed, the wall separating the two sides of the heart may not close completely. Similarly, the separation of the trachea and esophagus may be incomplete, resulting in a tracheo-esophageal fistula or connection.

Examination of the brain tissue of individuals with Down syndrome reveals multiple developmental brain abnormalities including delayed myelination, fewer neurons, decreased synaptic density, and decreased acetylcholine neurotransmitter receptors (see Chapter 14) (Florez, del Arco, Gonzalez, et al., 1990; Zigman, Silverman, & Wisniewski, 1996). Furthermore, a gene for amyloid, an abnormal protein found in the brain of individuals with Alzheimer's disease, is located on chromosome #21, which may explain why adults with Down syndrome are at an increased risk for developing Alzheimer's disease. As more is learned about the genes contained

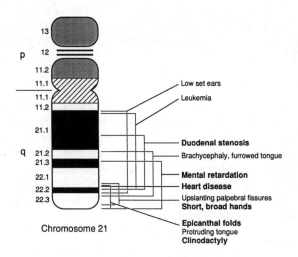

Figure 17.2. The "critical region" for the Down syndrome phenotype is on the long arm (q11.1-q22.3) of chromosome #21. Specific malformations are noted as being localized to the bracketed regions. The most clear associations are bolded. (From Epstein, C.E. [Ed.]. [1991, January 17–18]. *The morphogenesis of Down syndrome [Proceedings of the National Down Syndrome Society Conference on Morphogenesis and Down Syndrome, New York]* [p. 44]. Copyright © 1991 John Wiley & Sons; adapted by permission.)

on chromosome #21, it is likely that the origins of additional clinical manifestations of Down syndrome will be better understood.

EARLY IDENTIFICATION

Typically, women 35 years of age and older are offered prenatal diagnostic testing for Down syndrome. In addition, most obstetricians utilize a blood screening test for advising prenatal diagnosis for Down syndrome in younger women (see Chapter 3) (Grudzinskas, Chard, Chapman, et al., 1995; Rose, 1996; Rose, Palomaki, Haddow, et al., 1994). Identification of Down syndrome prior to birth enables the physician to provide genetic counseling to the family and appropriate medical evaluation of the newborn infant, if the pregnancy is continued to term.

Because of the distinctive pattern of physical features, infants with Down syndrome can be identified fairly easily at birth. An index developed by Rex and Preus (1982) bases the diagnosis on eight phenotypic characteristics, including three palm print (dermatoglyphic) patterns, Brushfield spots (colored speckles in the iris of the eye), ear length, internipple distance, neck skinfold, and widely spaced first toes, and can predict Down syndrome with an accuracy rate of 75%. Individuals with XXXY, XXXXY, and XXXX syndromes (see Chapter 3), however, bear a physical resemblance to individuals with Down syndrome in the newborn period (Jones, 1996). Therefore, all children suspected of having Down syndrome should have a chromosomal analysis performed in order to ensure a correct diagnosis and to provide accurate genetic counseling about future pregnancies.

MEDICAL COMPLICATIONS IN DOWN SYNDROME

Children with Down syndrome have an increased risk of abnormalities in almost every organ system (Roizen, 1996). A knowledge of the possible complications enables the caregiver to evaluate the child for the more common disorders and increase vigilance for other potential medical problems (Table 17.1).

Congenital Heart Disease

In one study of unselected newborns with Down syndrome, two thirds of children had congenital heart defects detected by echocardiogram, the most common lesions being an endocardial cushion defect (resulting in a connection between the atria and ventricles), ventricular septal defect, and atrial septal defect (Marino & Pueschel, 1996; Wells, Barker, Finley, et al., 1994). A major complication of congenital heart disease is pulmonary vascular obstructive disease leading to congestive heart failure. Progression of this potentially fatal complication is more rapid in children with Down syndrome than in children with the same heart defects and normal chromosomes (Clapp, Perry, Farooki, et al., 1990).

Sensory Impairments

Both vision and hearing problems occur with increased frequency in children with Down syndrome. A survey of 77 unselected children with Down syndrome found that more than 60% had ophthalmic disorders requiring treatment or monitoring. The most common of these disorders were refractive errors, strabismus, nystagmus, blepharitis (inflammation of the eyelids), tear duct

Table 17.1.   Medical complications in Down syndrome

Disorder	Percentage affected
Congenital heart defect	66
Endocardial cushion defect	19
Ventricular septal defect	15
Atrial septal defect	14
Other	18
Ophthalmic disorders (often more than 1)	60
Refractive errors	35
Strabismus	27
Nystagmus	20
Blepharitis	9
Tear duct obstruction	6
Cataracts	5
Ptosis	5
Hearing loss	60–80
Endocrine abnormalities	50–90
Subclinical hypothyroidism	30–50
Overt hypothyroidism	7
Diabetes	0.4
Obesity	60
Short stature	50–90
Orthopedic abnormalities	
Subclinical atlanto-axial subluxation	15
Symptomatic atlanto-axial subluxation	1
Dental problems, periodontal disease, malocclusion	60–100
Gastrointestinal malformations	5
Seizure disorder	6
Leukemia	0.01
Skin conditions	50
Alzheimer's disease after 40 years	15–20

obstruction, cataracts, and ptosis (droopy eyelids) (Roizen, Mets, & Blondis, 1994). In children with no ophthalmic abnormalities observed during general pediatric checkups, 35% actually had an identified disorder on exam by an ophthalmologist. Thus, in the first few weeks of life, and subsequently at periodic intervals, all children with Down syndrome need an ophthalmological examination.

Hearing loss occurs in approximately two thirds of children with Down syndrome. It can be conductive, sensorineural, or both and can be unilateral or bilateral (see Chapter 12) (Roizen, Wolters, Nicol, et al., 1993). Conductive hearing problems result from a combination of narrow posterior throat structures and a subtle immune deficiency that predispose these children to recurrent ear infections. These children also may develop sleep apnea (brief periods of arrested respiration during sleep) as a consequence of upper airway obstruction from enlarged tonsils and adenoids (Stebbens, Dennis, Samuels, et al., 1991).

Endocrine Abnormalities

Congenital hypothyroidism is found in 1 in 141 infants with Down syndrome, a rate about 28 times that seen in the general population (Fort, Lifshitz, Bellisario, et al., 1984). In addition, between 30% and 50% of older children with Down syndrome manifest subclinical **hypothyroidism**. In one study, 7% of these children were found to ultimately develop overt hypothyroidism (Rubello, Pozzan, Casara, et al., 1995). Diabetes occurs in 1 in 250 children with Down syndrome, more than twice the usual prevalence (Milunsky & Neurath, 1968).

In terms of growth pattern, children with Down syndrome tend to be lightweight for their height during the first year of life. During the next few years, however, the children gain relatively more weight than height, and by early childhood, half are overweight (Cronk, Crocker, Pueschel, et al., 1988). Yet, compared with children of the same size, they have similar activity levels and consume fewer calories (Luke, Roizen, Sutton, et al., 1994). The mechanism for the obesity therefore appears to be a lower resting metabolic rate; they require fewer calories to gain weight.

In addition to being overweight, individuals with Down syndrome have short stature. The average adult height is 5 feet in males and 4½ feet in females (Cronk et al., 1988). A few studies have examined the effect of growth hormone in children with Down syndrome and documented accelerated short-term growth (Torrado, Bastian, Wisniewski, et al., 1991). However, it remains unclear whether the eventual height of children with Down syndrome treated with growth hormone will be significantly increased. There also is a need for further assessing the safety (including concerns about leukemia) and ethical ramifications of growth hormone treatment before it is more commonly used in this population (Lawson Wilkins Pediatric Endocrine Society Board of Directors and Drug and Therapeutics Committee, 1993).

Orthopedic Problems

Children with Down syndrome have an increased prevalence of orthopedic problems that are probably related to ligament abnormalities. These include atlanto-axial subluxation or instability (Figure 17.3), hip dislocation, patella instability, and flat feet. They also can develop a juvenile rheumatoid arthritis-like disorder (Pueschel & Pueschel, 1992).

Atlantoaxial subluxation (partial dislocation of the upper spine) is the most controversial and perplexing of these problems, occurring in approximately 15% of children with Down syndrome (American Academy of Pediatrics, Committee on Sports Medicine and Fitness, 1995). However, only 1% of children with Down syndrome become symptomatic, and the subluxation rarely leads to paralysis (Pueschel, Scola, & Pezzullo, 1992). Symptoms of subluxation include easy fatigability, difficulties in walking, abnormal gait, neck pain, limited neck mobility, torticollis or head tilt, a change in hand function, the new onset of urinary retention or incontinence, incoordination and clumsiness, sensory impairments, spasticity, hyperreflexia, and clonus (American Academy of Pediatrics, Committee on Sports Medicine and Fitness, 1995).

Dental Problems

The most serious dental problem is periodontal disease that is early in onset and rapidly progressive. This involves gingivitis (gum inflammation) with loss of alveolar bone (see Chapter 29). The periodontal disease is a manifestation of the general low resistance to infection in children with Down syndrome. In addition to periodontal disease, almost all of the children have maloc-

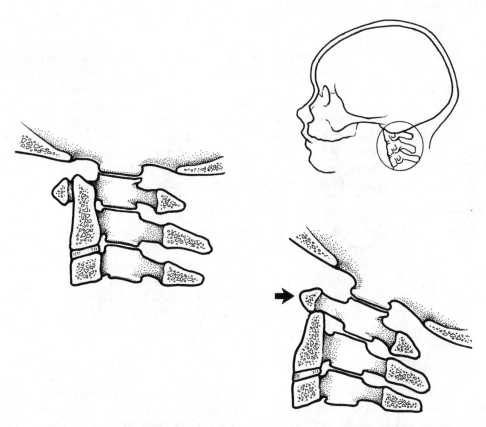

Figure 17.3.   Children with Down syndrome are at risk to develop subluxation (partial dislocation) of the atlanto-axial or atlanto-occipital joint, as shown in this illustration (right side). A typical neck region is shown for comparison (left side). This subluxation predisposes these children to spinal injury with trauma. This abnormality can be detected by X ray or MRI scan of the neck.

clusions and many have a variety of dental anomalies including missing teeth, microdontia (small teeth), and fused teeth. In the majority of children, both the primary and permanent teeth erupt 1–2 years later than usual. The average age of eruption of the first tooth is 13 months rather than the usual 6 months. Dental caries occurs in children with Down syndrome with a lower prevalence than in the general population (Pueschel & Pueschel, 1992); the reason for this is unclear.

Gastrointestinal Malformations

Gastrointestinal malformations are found in approximately 5% of children with Down syndrome. Most of these abnormalities present with symptoms of poor feeding, vomiting, or aspiration pneumonia in the newborn period. The malformations include stenosis (narrowing) or atresia (blockage) of the duodenum (3%), imperforate (closed) anus (0.9%), Hirschsprung disease (congenitally enlarged colon) (0.5%), tracheo-esophageal fistula (an abnormal connection between the trachea and esophagus) or esophageal atresia (0.4%), and pyloric stenosis (narrowing of the stomach outlet) (0.3%) (Pueschel & Pueschel, 1992).

Seizure Disorders

Epilepsy occurs in 6% of individuals with Down syndrome. This is more common than in the general population but about average for children with mental retardation requiring limited support. Seizure types include generalized tonic-clonic (55% of all seizures), infantile spasms (13%), myoclonic (6%), atonic plus tonic-clonic (6%), and simple partial (6%) (see Chapter 26). The age of onset of seizures has a bimodal distribution, occurring under 3 years and after age 13. Sixty-two percent of the seizures have an identifiable cause, the most common of which are infections and hypoxia, resulting from congenital heart disease (Stafstrom, Patxot, Gilmore, et al., 1991). Infantile spasms in children with Down syndrome have a more benign prognosis than in the general population (Stafstrom & Konkol, 1994).

Hematologic Disorders

Although there is little information about the specific mechanisms of the abnormalities, almost every cellular element of the hematopoietic (blood) system has been found to be at risk for an abnormality in Down syndrome. For example, erythrocytosis (too many red blood cells) can be found in the newborn or in the older child with cyanotic ("blue baby") heart disease. Platelets may be either increased or decreased (Pueschel & Pueschel, 1992). Although these hematologic abnormalities rarely lead to severe problems, children with Down syndrome have a 1 in 150 risk of developing leukemia as compared with 1 in 2,800 in children at large (Avet-Loiseau, Mechinaud, & Harousseau, 1995).

Skin Conditions

Several skin conditions, mostly of immune origin, are observed more frequently in individuals with Down syndrome than in the general population. Some of these conditions noticeably affect the appearance, and therefore the quality of life of the child, and thus require treatment. By puberty, half or more of these individuals will experience atopic dermatitis (eczema), cheilitis (inflammation of the lips), ichthyosis (dry and scaly skin), onychomycosis (fungal infection of the nails), seborrheic dermatitis (dandruff), vitiligo (patches of depigmentation), and or xerosis (dryness of eyes). Less commonly, they have syringomas (sweat gland cysts) and alopecia areata (patchy hair loss) (Pueschel & Pueschel, 1992; Scherbehske, Benson, Rotchford, et al., 1990).

NEURODEVELOPMENTAL AND BEHAVIOR IMPAIRMENTS

Infants with Down syndrome typically have central hypotonia (floppiness without weakness) and, as a consequence, gross motor skills are delayed. Most children with Down syndrome do not sit up until 1 year of age or walk until 2 years. The early developmental milestones of boys tend to occur slightly later than those of girls. On average, boys walk at 26 months, while girls walk at 22 months (Melyn & White, 1973). Although continued progress in the gross motor area is slow, significant physical disabilities are rare. Children with Down syndrome learn to run, ride bicycles, and participate in sports.

In the first 2 years of life, the child with Down syndrome, primarily because of his or her social responsiveness, appears to have fewer cognitive impairments than he or she actually does (Brown, Greer, Aylward, et al., 1990). By 2 years of age, however, significant language delays become evident; children with Down syndrome often do not speak their first word until

24 months: Their receptive language is generally better than their expressive language (Kumin, 1996; Mundy, Kasari, Sigman, et al., 1995; Van Dyke, Lang, Lang, et al., 1990). Formal psychological testing at school age shows that 85% of children with Down syndrome have IQ scores that range from 40 to 60 (Connolly, 1978), which label them as having mental retardation requiring intermittent to limited support. Although these children generally have poor verbal short-term memory skills, their visual-motor skills are relatively strong (Wang, 1996). This cognitive pattern is consistent with functional neuroimaging studies that reveal impairments within and between the frontal and parietal lobes including the inferior frontal gyrus, which includes Broca's speech area (see Chapter 13) (Horwitz, Schapiro, Grady, et al., 1990).

Children with Down syndrome are stereotyped as being amiable and happy. However, temperament studies actually have shown them to have profiles comparable to typically developing children (Vaughn, Contreras, & Seifer, 1994). In addition, a survey of 261 children with Down syndrome found the following prevalence of behavior and psychiatric disorders: attention-deficit/hyperactivity disorder (ADHD) (6%), conduct/oppositional disorder (5%), aggressive behavior (7%), phobias (2%), eating disorders (1%), elimination difficulties (2%), Tourette syndrome (0.4%), stereotypic behavior (3%), self-injurious behavior (1%), and autism (1%) (Cuskelly & Dadds, 1992; Myers & Pueschel, 1991).

Some individuals with Down syndrome may experience a deterioration of cognitive or psychological functioning in adolescence, often evidenced with worsening of behavior or academic performance. Many times, this deterioration can be attributed to unrecognized hypothyroidism or depression. If confirmed, medical and psychiatric treatment can reverse these problems. Mental deterioration in the fourth and fifth decades of life, however, is more likely a sign of Alzheimer's disease. It appears that virtually all individuals with Down syndrome older than the age of 50 have pathological plaques and tangles in their brain, which are the hallmarks of Alzheimer's disease. However, only 15%–20% of individuals with Down syndrome older than the age of 40 demonstrate clinical signs of this disorder (Holland & Oliver, 1995). Nevertheless, this prevalence is much greater than that found in the general population.

EVALUATION AND TREATMENT

Several of the aforementioned conditions occur with sufficient frequency that all children with Down syndrome should be periodically evaluated for them. These include congenital heart disease, ophthalmic disorders, hearing loss, and hypothyroidism. An outline of the suggested periodic evaluation of children with Down syndrome is shown in Figure 17.4.

Congenital heart disease in children with Down syndrome may be difficult to identify based on physical findings alone as it is not always accompanied by a cardiac murmur nor does it commonly produce a "blue baby" (Wells et al., 1994). Yet, because these children tend to develop pulmonary vascular disease sooner than other children with the same defect, early identification and treatment are essential. Although children with Down syndrome were once considered poor risks for cardiac surgery, data indicate that they have a similar prognosis as other children with the same heart defect (Baird & Sadovinick, 1987). A cardiac evaluation, including an echocardiogram, is the standard of care in the newborn period.

Within the first 6 months of life, all children with Down syndrome need an ophthalmologic evaluation to identify cataracts and strabismus. Subsequently, they should be evaluated annually or semi-annually to detect refractive errors and other ophthalmic disorders (Roizen et al., 1994).

	Infancy						Early Childhood					Late Childhood					Adolescence			
Age	1	2	4	6	9	12	15	18	24	3	4	5	6	8	10	12	14	16	18	21
	(in months)									*(in years)*										
History	●[1]	●[1]	●[1]	●	●	●	●[2]	●[2]	●[2]	●[2]	●[2]	●	●	●	●	●	●[3]	●[3]	●[3]	●[3]
Measurements	●[4]	●	●	●	●	●	●	●	●	●	●	●	●	●	●	●	●	●	●	●
Developmental/ behavioral assessment	●	●	●	●	●	●	●[5]	●	●	●	●	●[6]	●	●[6]	●	●[6]	●	●[6]	●	●
Physical exam	●[7]	●[7]	●[7]	●[7]	●[7]	●[7]	●[7]	●[7]	●[8]	●[8]	●[8]	●	●[8]	●	●[8]	●	●	●	●[9]	●[9]
Procedures																				
Karyotype	●																			
Thyroid screen	●					●			●	●	●	●	●	●	●	●	●		●	●
Echocardiogram	●[10]																			
Neck X rays										●[11]					●			●		
Sensory																				
Vision	○[12]	S	S	S	S	S	S	S	○	○	○	○	○	○	○	○	○	○	○	○
Hearing	○[13]	S	S	○	S	S	○	S	○	○	S	○	○	○	○	○	○	○	○	○
Consultation																				
Cardiology	●																			
Opthalmology		●				●				●	●	●	●			●	●	●		●
Ear, nose, and throat		●				●				●	●		●	●		●	●	●		●
Genetic	●																			
Down clinic		●				●			●	●	●	●	●	●	●	●	●	●	●	
Dental									●	●	●	●	●	●	●	●	●	●	●	●
Referrals																				
Early intervention	●——————————→																			
Supplemental Security Income (SSI)	●					●													●	
State mental retardation agency	●——————————————————————————————→																			
Anticipatory guidance[14]	●[14]	●	●	●	●	●	●	●	●	●	●	●	●	●	●	●	●[15]	●	●	●

(continued)

Figure 17.4.   (*continued*)

• = to be performed;   S = subjective, by history;   o = objective, by a standard testing method

1. Special attention to GI/cardiac systems
2. Special attention to sleep/behavior problems
3. Special attention to thyroid, seizures
4. Based on growth curves developed for DS (Cronk et al., 1988)
5. Special attention to speech evaluation begins at this time

6. Psychoeducational evaluation
7. Check tympanic membrane
8. Neurological exam regarding atlanto-axial instability
9. GYN exam
10. Even in absence of murmur
11. Earlier, if having surgery

12. Must see red reflex to rule out cataracts
13. Neonatal screening, ABRs
14. Information on medical problems, educational programs, tax deductions, SSI, local services, wills, vaccinations (including hepatitis)
15. Information on vocational programs, sexuality, independent living, hepatitis vaccine

Figure 17.4.   Recommendations for preventive health care for children and adolescents with Down syndrome. (Based on the format of the American Academy of Pediatrics recommendations for preventive health care, the recommendations from the publication *Down Syndrome, Papers and Abstracts for Professionals*, the DS Preventive Medical Check List compiled by the DS Center of Western Pennsylvania, and the consensus derived from the first conference on DS Health Care sponsored by the National DS Society in San Diego, March 1990.)

Clarification of the hearing status of infants with Down syndrome requires an auditory brainstem response (ABR) test (see Chapter 12). An initial ABR test is recommended by 6 months of age in order to demonstrate the baseline hearing status of the child and to rule out a unilateral hearing loss. It also can determine whether a hearing loss is conductive or sensorineural (Roizen et al., 1993). Because these children are at increased risk for recurrent middle-ear infections, leading to a conductive hearing loss, hearing evaluation should be repeated every 6 months until age 3 and annually thereafter (American Academy of Pediatrics, Joint Committee on Infant Hearing, 1995).

If there is the suspicion of sleep apnea, a **polysomnogram** should be performed. If the diagnosis is confirmed and found to be associated with enlarged adenoids, antibiotic treatment is used and the adenoids are subsequently removed surgically. If the adenoidectomy does not correct the mechanical obstruction, further surgical procedures (e.g., tracheostomy to bypass the obstruction) or sleeping with CPAP (breathing air under pressure) to keep the airway open may be necessary.

As with all newborns, children with Down syndrome are routinely screened for congenital hypothyroidism (see Chapter 19). In addition, they should have thyroid function tests performed at 4–6 months of age, at 1 year, and then annually (American Academy of Pediatrics, Committee on Genetics, 1994). More frequent thyroid function tests are indicated if the child displays the onset of behavior problems, plateauing of height, accelerated weight gain, or an unexpected lack of cognitive progress. If there is laboratory evidence of hypothyroidism, treatment with thyroxine (thyroid hormone) is indicated.

Because of the high prevalence of periodontal disease, daily cleaning of teeth should begin as soon as they erupt. As with all children, introduction of regular dental visits should also begin at this time. Orthodontic intervention is needed by most of the children and becomes possible when the child is able to cooperate with and tolerate the therapy.

The evaluation of children for atlantoaxial subluxation by x-ray studies is customarily done on entrance to preschool and sometimes prior to elective surgery. If the child participates in Special Olympics activities, an additional radiograph is usually obtained at that time to make sure there has not been progression of the subluxation, placing the child at increased risk for sports injuries. Signs and symptoms of spinal cord compression such as the onset of weakness in gait, torticollis, neck pain, or bowel and bladder incontinence indicate the need for further studies (American Academy of Pediatrics, Committee on Sports Medicine and Fitness, 1995). Children with radiologic findings indicating neck instability of an unacceptable degree and children with symptomatic subluxation are treated surgically with a neck fusion.

Several other medical problems, for example diabetes and leukemia, occur more frequently in children with Down syndrome than in the general population. Although screening for these disorders is not routinely done, it is appropriate to lower the threshold for evaluation. The clinician also should be alert to symptoms of psychiatric illness (e.g., depression) and refer the child for appropriate evaluation and treatment when indicated (see Chapter 20).

EARLY INTERVENTION

The parents of a newborn with Down syndrome should be made aware of a variety of services including early intervention educational programs, Supplemental Security Income (SSI), local and national parent support/advocacy programs such as the National Down Syndrome Society and the National Down Syndrome Congress, and respite care options. Children with Down syndrome have a long history of involvement in early intervention programs. Studies of the effect of early intervention indicate improved motor and developmental function (Connolly, Morgan, Russell, et al., 1993; Hines & Bennett, 1996).

As there is no cure for Down syndrome and the cognitive and medical problems may significantly interfere with a child's function, parents are vulnerable to proponents of alternative therapeutic modalities who promise improved function. During the years, alternative therapies have included mixtures of vitamins, minerals, and hormones; cell therapy or injections of fetal lamb brains; and, most recently, piracetam, a stimulant drug. Scientifically designed studies of vitamin, mineral, and cell therapies for children with Down syndrome have not shown improvement in appearance, growth, health, or developmental function (Bennett, McClelland, Kriegsmann, et al., 1983; Smith, Spiker, Peterson, et al., 1984; Van Dyke, Lang, van Duyne, et al., 1990). Piracetam has resulted in improved reading speed in children with dyslexia, but no controlled study has been conducted in children with Down syndrome or other causes of mental retardation.

PROGNOSIS

Since the 1970s, the prognosis for a productive and positive life experience for individuals with Down syndrome has increased substantially, largely due to the efforts of parent advocacy groups (Carr, 1994, 1995; Pueschel, 1996). Previously physicians would often endorse or even recommend institutionalization for newborn infants with Down syndrome, and they sometimes would hesitate to recommend life-saving cardiac and gastrointestinal surgery. Now, when a child is born with Down syndrome, the physician routinely refers the family to early intervention programs and parent support groups and performs surgery as a matter of course (Haslam & Milner, 1992). Parents are encouraged to raise their children at home as it has been demonstrated that children with Down syndrome develop better when raised with their family instead of in an institution (Brown et al., 1990). Children with Down syndrome were among the first children with disabilities to be "mainstreamed" in the public schools and thus have been the "pioneers" in the trend toward inclusion.

Life expectancy and the quality of life for individuals with Down syndrome also has improved greatly in the 1980s and 1990s (Strauss & Eyman, 1996). In the first 5 years of life, 87% of children with Down syndrome without congenital heart disease survive, as do 76% of those with congenital heart disease. By 30 years of age, 79% of individuals without congenital heart disease are surviving, although only 50% of those with cardiac defects are (Baird & Sadovnick, 1987).

Following the introduction in the 1980s of supported employment (in which individuals have a job coach), adults with Down syndrome often hold real jobs with decent pay and benefits and good working conditions (Kingsley & Levitz, 1994; Nadel & Rosenthal, 1995). To ensure success in supported employment, the person needs to have a healthy sense of self-esteem nurtured from early childhood, an ability to complete tasks without assistance, a willingness to separate emotionally from parents and family members, and personal recreational activities (Pueschel, 1996; Turnbull & Turnbull, 1985; Unruh, 1994). All of these should be some of the goals of educational programs.

JASON

In most ways, Jason is like all of the other 8-year-old boys in the neighborhood. He plays soccer, skates, swims, is a boy scout, and is in the second grade. But, he has had experiences that most of the other children haven't. He has had operative procedures in his ears, a hernia repair, and surgical correction of his congenital heart defect. He had a unilateral hearing loss discovered on auditory brainstem response testing when he was 2 years of age. He is nearsighted and recently began to wear glasses. In addition, Jason has ADHD, which has improved on methylphenidate (Ritalin). In his school, Jason was the first child with Down syndrome to be included in the general education kindergarten. His reading skills are at a pre-primer level. His most recent medical challenge was the discovery of obstructive sleep apnea. This resolved with the removal of his adenoids.

SUMMARY

Down syndrome is a disorder characterized by a recognizable pattern of physical features, an increased risk for specific medical problems, and mental retardation requiring intermittent to limited supports. As children with Down syndrome are usually identified at birth, the early intervention system frequently has them as their youngest enrollees. Although much remains to be learned and done, the educational and medical systems are probably more knowledgeable and comfortable with the special needs of children with Down syndrome than with any other single diagnostic group.

The American Academy of Pediatrics, Committee on Genetics (1994) and the Down Syndrome Medical Interest Group (Ohio/Western Pennsylvania Down Syndrome Network, 1992) have proposed standards of medical care that include periodic monitoring for medical problems that occur frequently in children with Down syndrome. By ensuring optimal audiologic, cardiac, endocrinologic, ophthalmologic, and orthopedic functioning, children with Down syndrome have the opportunity for good health and developmental functioning.

REFERENCES

American Academy of Pediatrics, Committee on Genetics. (1994). Health supervision for children with Down syndrome. *Pediatrics, 93,* 855–859.

American Academy of Pediatrics, Committee on Sports Medicine and Fitness. (1995). Atlantoaxial instability in Down syndrome: Subject review. *Pediatrics, 96,* 151–154.

American Academy of Pediatrics, Joint Committee on Infant Hearing. (1995). 1994 position statement. *Pediatrics, 95,* 152–156.

Avet-Loiseau, H., Mechinaud, F., & Harousseau, J-L. (1995). Clonal hematologic disorders in Down syndrome: A review. *Journal of Pediatric Hematology and Oncology, 17,* 19–24.

Baird, P.A., & Sadovnick, A.D. (1987). Life expectancy in Down syndrome. *Journal of Pediatrics, 110,* 849–854.

Bennett, F.C., McClelland, S., Kriegsmann, E.A., et al. (1983). Vitamin and mineral supplementation in Down's syndrome. *Pediatrics, 72,* 707–713.

Brown, F.R., Greer, M.K., Aylward, E.H., et al. (1990). Intellectual and adaptive functioning in individuals with Down syndrome in relation to age and environmental placement. *Pediatrics, 85,* 450–452.

Carr, J. (1994). Long-term-outcome for people with Down's syndrome. *Journal of Child Psychology and Psychiatry and Allied Disciplines, 35,* 429–439.

Carr, J.H. (1995). *Down's syndrome: Children growing up.* New York: Cambridge University Press.

Clapp, S., Perry, B.L., Farooki, Z.Q., et al. (1990). Down's syndrome, complete atrioventricular canal, and pulmonary vascular obstructive disease. *Journal of Thoracic and Cardiovascular Surgery, 100,* 115–121.

Connolly, B.H., Morgan, S.B., Russell, F.F., et al. (1993). A longitudinal study of children with Down syndrome who experienced early intervention programming. *Physical Therapy, 73,* 170–179.

Connolly, J.A. (1978). Intelligence levels on Down's syndrome children. *American Journal of Mental Deficiency, 83,* 193–196.

Cronk, C.E., Crocker, A.C., Pueschel, S.M., et al. (1988). Growth charts for children with Down syndrome: 1 month to 18 years of age. *Pediatrics, 81,* 102–110.

Cuskelly, M., & Dadds, M. (1992). Behavioural problems in children with Down's syndrome and their siblings. *Journal of Child Psychology and Psychiatry, 33,* 749–762.

Down syndrome prevalence at birth: United States, 1983–1990. (1994). *Morbidity and Mortality Weekly Report, 43,* 617–622.

Epstein, C.E. (Ed.). (1991). The morphogenesis of Down syndrome [Proceedings of the National Down Syndrome Society Conference on Morphogenesis and Down Syndrome, New York]. New York: John Wiley & Sons.

Fishler, K., & Koch, R. (1991). Mental development in Down syndrome mosaicism. *American Journal of Mental Retardation, 96,* 345–351.

Florez, J., del Arco, C., Gonzalez, A., et al. (1990). Autoradiographic studies of neurotransmitter receptors in the brains of newborn infants with Down syndrome. *American Journal of Medical Genetics, 7*(Suppl.), 301–305.

Fort, P., Lifshitz, F., Bellisario, R., et al. (1984). Abnormalities of thyroid functioning in infants with Down syndrome. *Journal of Pediatrics, 104,* 545–549.

Grudzinskas, T., Chard, M., Chapman, M., et al. (Eds.). (1995). *Screening for Down's syndrome.* New York: Cambridge University Press.

Haslam, R.H.A., & Milner, R. (1992). The physician and Down syndrome: Are attitudes changing? *Journal of Child Neurology, 71,* 304–310.

Hines, S., & Bennett, F. (1996). Effectiveness of early intervention for children with Down syndrome. *Mental Retardation and Developmental Disabilities Research Reviews, 2,* 96–101.

Holland, A.J., & Oliver, C. (1995). Down's syndrome and the links with Alzheimer's disease. *Journal of Neurology, Neurosurgery, and Psychiatry, 59,* 111–114.

Horwitz, B., Schapiro, M.B., Grady, C.L., et al. (1990). Cerebral metabolic pattern in young adult Down's syndrome subjects: Altered intercorrelations between regional rates of glucose utilization. *Journal of Mental Deficiency Research, 34,* 237–252.

Johnson, R.C., & Abelson, R.B. (1969). Intellectual, behavioral, and physical characteristics associated with trisomy, translocation, and mosaic types of Down's syndrome. *American Journal of Mental Deficiency, 73,* 852–855.

Jones, K.L. (1996). *Smith's recognizable patterns of human malformation* (5th ed.). Philadelphia: W.B. Saunders.

Kingsley, J., & Levitz, M. (1994). *Count us in: Growing up with Down syndrome.* San Diego: Harcourt Brace Jovanovich.

Korenberg, J.R., Chen, X.N., Schipper, C.R., et al. (1994). Down syndrome phenotypes: The consequences of chromosomal imbalance. *Proceedings of the National Academy of Sciences of the United States, 91,* 4997–5001.

Kumin, L. (1996). Speech and language skills in children with Down syndrome. *Mental Retardation and Developmental Disabilities Research Reviews, 2,* 109–115.

Lawson Wilkins Pediatric Endocrine Society Board of Directors and Drug and Therapeutics Committee. (1993). Growth hormone for children with Down syndrome. *Journal of Pediatrics, 123,* 742–743.

Lejeune, J., Gautier, M., & Turpin, R. (1959). Etude des chromosomes somatiques de neuf enfants mongoliens. *Compte Rendu d'Academy de Science, 248,* 1721–1722.

Luke, A.H., Roizen, N.J., Sutton, M., et al. (1994). Energy expenditure in Down syndrome. *Journal of Pediatrics, 125,* 829–836.

Marino, B., & Pueschel, S.M. (Eds.). (1996). *Heart diseases in persons with Down syndrome.* Baltimore: Paul H. Brookes Publishing Co.

Melyn, M.A., & White, D.T. (1973). Mental and developmental milestones of noninstitutionalized Down's syndrome children. *Pediatrics, 52,* 542–545.

Miller, J.F., & Paul, R. (1995). *The clinical assessment of language comprehension.* Baltimore: Paul H. Brookes Publishing Co.

Milunsky, A., & Neurath, P.W. (1968). Diabetes mellitus in Down's syndrome. *Archives of Environmental Health, 17,* 372–376.

Msall, M.E., Digaudio, C., & Malone, A.F. (1990). Healthy developmental and psychosocial aspects of Down syndrome. *Infants and Young Children, 4,* 35–45.

Mundy, P., Kasari, C., Sigman, M., et al. (1995). Nonverbal communication and early language acquisition in children with Down syndrome and in normally developing children. *Journal of Speech and Hearing Research, 38,* 157–167.

Myers, B.A., & Pueschel, S.M. (1991). Psychiatric disorders in persons with Down syndrome. *Journal of Nervous and Mental Diseases, 179,* 609–613.

Nadel, L., & Rosenthal, D. (1995). *Down syndrome: Living and learning in the community.* New York: John Wiley & Sons.

Ohio/Western Pennsylvania Down Syndrome Network. (1992). Down syndrome preventive medical check list. *Down Syndrome Papers and Abstracts for Professionals, 15,* 1–9.

Pueschel, S.M. (1996). Young people with Down syndrome: Transition from childhood to adulthood. *Mental Retardation and Developmental Disabilities Research Reviews, 2,* 90–95.

Pueschel, S.M., & Pueschel, J.K. (Eds.). (1992). *Biomedical concerns in persons with Down syndrome.* Baltimore: Paul H. Brookes Publishing Co.

Pueschel, S.M., Scola, F.H., & Pezzullo, J.C. (1992). A longitudinal study of atlanto-dens relationships in asymptomatic individuals with Down syndrome. *Pediatrics, 89,* 1194–1198.

Pueschel, S.M., & Šustrová, M. (Eds.). (1997). *Adolescents with Down syndrome: Toward a more fulfilling life.* Baltimore: Paul H. Brookes Publishing Co.

Rex, A.P., & Preus, M. (1982). A diagnostic index for Down syndrome. *Journal of Pediatrics, 100,* 903–906.

Roizen, N.J. (1996). Down syndrome and associated medical disorders. *Mental Retardation and Developmental Disabilities Research Reviews, 2,* 85–89.

Roizen, N.J., Mets, M.B., & Blondis, T.A. (1994). Ophthalmic disorders in children with Down syndrome. *Developmental Medicine and Child Neurology, 36,* 594–600.

Roizen, N.J., Wolters, C., Nicol, T., et al. (1993). Hearing loss in children with Down syndrome. *Journal of Pediatrics, 123,* S9–S12.

Rose, N.C. (1996). Pregnancy screening and prenatal diagnosis of fetal down syndrome. *Mental Retardation and Developmental Disabilities Research Reviews, 2,* 80–84.

Rose, N.C., Palomaki, G.E., Haddow, J.E., et al. (1994). Maternal serum alpha-fetoprotein screening for chromosomal abnormalities: A prospective study in women aged 35 and older. *American Journal of Obstetrics and Gynecology, 170l,* 1073–1080.

Rubello, D., Pozzan, G.B., Casara, D., et al. (1995). Natural course of subclinical hypothyroidism in Down's syndrome: Prospective study results and therapeutic considerations. *Journal of Endocrinologic Investigation, 17,* 35–40.

Scherbehske, J.M., Benson, P.M., Rotchford, J.P., et al. (1990). Cutaneous and ocular manifestations of Down syndrome. *Journal of the American Academy of Dermatology, 22,* 933–938.

Sinet, P.M., Theophile, D., Rahmani, Z., et al. (1994). Mapping of the Down syndrome phenotype on chromosome 21 at the molecular level. *Biomedicine and Pharmacotherapy, 48,* 247–252.

Smith, G.F., Spiker, D., Peterson, C.P., et al. (1984). Use of megadoses of vitamins with minerals in Down syndrome. *Journal of Pediatrics, 105,* 228–234.

Stafstrom, C.E., & Konkol, R.J. (1994). Infantile spasms in children with Down syndrome. *Developmental Medicine and Child Neurology, 36,* 576–585.

Stafstrom, C.E., Patxot, O.F., Gilmore, H.E., et al. (1991). Seizures in children with Down syndrome: Etiology, characteristics and outcome. *Developmental Medicine and Child Neurology, 33,* 191–200.

Staples, A.J., Sutherland, G.R., Haan, E.A., et al. (1991). Epidemiology of Down syndrome in South Australia, 1960–89. *American Journal of Human Genetics, 49,* 1014–1024.

Stebbens, V.A., Dennis, J., Samuels, M.P., et al. (1991). Sleep related upper airway obstruction in a cohort with Down's syndrome. *Archives of Disease in Childhood, 66,* 1333–1338.

Strauss, D., & Eyman, R. (1996). Mortality of people with mental retardation in California with and without Down syndrome, 1986–1992. *American Journal on Mental Retardation, 100,* 643–653.

Torrado, C., Bastian, W., Wisniewski, K.E., et al. (1991). Treatment of children with Down syndrome and growth retardation with recombinent human growth hormone. *Journal of Pediatrics, 119,* 478–483.

Trimble, B.K., & Baird, P.A. (1978). Maternal age and Down syndrome: Age-specific incidence rates by single-year intervals. *American Journal of Medical Genetics, 2,* 1–5.

Turnbull, A.P., & Turnbull, H.R. (1985). Developing independence. *Journal of Adolescent Health Care, 6,* 108–119.

Unruh, J.F. (1994). *Down syndrome: Successful parenting of children with Down syndrome.* Eugene, OR: Fern Ridge Press.

Van Dyke, D.C., Lang, D.J., Lang, D.J., et al. (1990). *Clinical perspectives in the management of Down syndrome.* New York: Springer-Verlag.

Van Dyke, D.C., Lang, D.J., van Duyne, S., et al. (1990). Cell therapy in children with Down syndrome: A retrospective study. *Pediatrics, 85,* 79–84.

Vaughn, B.E., Contreras, J., & Seifer, R. (1994). Short-term longitudinal study of maternal ratings of temperament in samples of children with Down syndrome and children who are developing normally. *American Journal of Mental Retardation, 98,* 607–618.

Wang, P. (1996). A neuropsychological profile of Down syndrome: Cognitive skills and brain morphology. *Mental Retardation and Developmental Disabilities Research Reviews, 2,* 102–108.

Wells, G.L., Barker, S.E., Finley, S.C., et al. (1994). Congenital heart disease in infants with Down's syndrome. *Southern Medical Journal, 87,* 724–727.

Zigman, W., Silverman, W., & Wisniewski, H.M. (1996). Aging and Alzheimer's disease in Down syndrome: Clinical and pathological changes. *Mental Retardation and Developmental Disabilities Research Reviews, 2,* 73–79.

18 Fragile X Syndrome

Mark L. Batshaw

Upon completion of this chapter, the reader will:

- understand this most frequent *inherited* cause of mental retardation
- recognize its different clinical presentations in boys and girls
- be aware of the behavior and cognitive impairments associated with the syndrome
- know the underlying molecular genetic abnormalities and the diagnostic tests available
- be familiar with intervention strategies for individuals with this disorder
- understand issues concerning outcome

The discovery of fragile X syndrome was incremental (Hagerman, McBogg, & Hagerman, 1983). In the early 1940s, Martin and Bell (1943) observed 11 males and 2 females in two generations of a family with a number of similar clinical symptoms. The affected men had severe mental retardation, language impairments, and behavior problems, while the women had mild mental retardation and a "highly nervous temperament." In the early 1960s, Robert Lehrke predicted in a dissertation study the presence of a common X-linked form of mental retardation (Lehrke, 1972). His hypothesis was confirmed in the 1970s when Sutherland noted a linkage between "fragile" sites on the X chromosome and X-linked mental retardation (Sutherland, 1977). He and colleagues were performing chromosomal studies on residents in a mental retardation facility using a new growth medium that was low in folic acid. They found that a number of the males had a previously unrecognized abnormality of the X chromosome that caused the bottom tip of the long arm to become constricted and threadlike (Figure 18.1). When the cells were grown in media with a folic acid supplement, this fragility was not evident, explaining why it had been missed previously. Many of these men had a family history consistent with an X-linked disorder. In 1991, the underlying gene defect, an abnormality in the so-called FMR1 (fragile X mental retardation) gene, was found in all individuals with fragile X syndrome (Verkerk, Pieretti, Sutcliffe, et al., 1991). In 1995, this gene defect was found to be associated with decreased or absent production of a protein dubbed FMRP (FMR1 protein), which is thought to be important in brain development (Feng, Zhang, Lokey, et al., 1995). Since its recognition as a distinct genetic disorder, fragile X syndrome has rapidly become the most frequent diagnosed in-

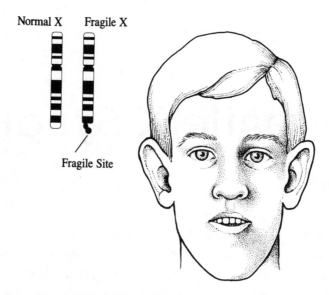

Figure 18.1.   An adolescent boy with fragile X syndrome has an unusual, elongated face, large ears, and a prominent jaw. He usually develops enlarged testicles. Younger children have more sub-tle facial alterations. The fragile X chromosome is shown, with the terminal pinched off portion.

herited cause of mental retardation. It also gives a partial explanation for why mental retardation occurs more frequently in males than in females.

PREVALENCE

Fragile X syndrome now represents one third of all X-linked causes of mental retardation. Stud-ies suggest that 0.4–0.8 per 1,000 males and 0.2–0.6 per 1,000 females have fragile X syndrome (Brown & Jenkins, 1992; Morton, Rindl, Bullock, et al., 1995). Those with the syndrome ac-count for 11 per 1,000 children receiving special education services (Hagerman, Wilson, Stan-ley, et al., 1994; Meadows, Pettay, Newman, et al., 1996; Slaney, Wilkie, Hirst, et al., 1995). Be-tween 6% and 14% of all males with mental retardation requiring extensive supports and 3%–6% of individuals with autism (see Chapter 21) have fragile X syndrome (Bailey, Bolton, Butler, et al., 1993; Hagerman & Cronister, 1996). Furthermore, fragile X syndrome is account-able for about 7% of females with mental retardation requiring intermittent support. It also may account for a significant percentage of non–language learning disabilities and avoidant or schizoid personality disorders in females.

THE GENETICS OF FRAGILE X SYNDROME

In a typical sex-linked disorder, such as hemophilia or muscular dystrophy, a carrier mother will pass on the defective gene on average to half of her sons and daughters. All the sons with the gene defect will be affected while the daughters will carry the gene but remain unaffected (see Chapter 2). With fragile X syndrome, however, transmission is more complex and outcomes are not so strictly defined (Oostra & Halley, 1995). Of males who carry the FMR1 gene defect, 20%

are clinically unaffected, and their chromosomes do not have the fragile X site. These individuals are called "transmitting males" because, although unaffected, they can transmit fragile X syndrome to their children. Meanwhile, 30% of carrier females manifest symptoms of fragile X syndrome, although they are generally less severely affected than manifesting males. This variation is primarily due to the degree of expansion of a triplet repeat.

There is typically some perseveration in the genetic code (i.e., the repetition of a series of three nucleotide base pairs at certain places along the chromosome; see Chapter 2). If there is marked expansion of these so-called triplet repeats, the result may be a physically unstable or "fragile site" on the chromosome—a thin, threadlike segment containing the expanded triplet repeats. There are many fragile sites on human chromosomes; however, only two of these (both on the X chromosome) have been associated with developmental disabilities: the FRAXA site for fragile X syndrome and the FRAXE site, a much less common cause of mental retardation (Mulley, Yu, Loesch, et al., 1995; Warren & Nelson, 1994).

At the FRAXA site, there are typically 6–50 repeats of the triplet base pair sequence cytosine-guanine-guanine (CGG). Transmitting males have 50–90 CGG repeats, and asymptomatic carrier females have 50–200 triplet repeats. Both of these groups are said to have a "premutation," because they are asymptomatic and there is no physically visible fragile site on the X chromosome (Loesch, Hay, & Mulley, 1994). Approximately 1 in 500 males and 1 in 250 females in the general population have premutations (Reiss, Kazazian, Krebs, et al., 1994; Rousseau, Heitz, Tarleton, et al., 1994). Symptomatic female carriers and affected males have at least 200–3,000 CGG repeats, a "full mutation." These individuals manifest clinical symptoms and have fragile sites on the X chromosome of some cells. Half of the females and all males with this full mutation will have mental retardation. It has been reported that there is a correlation between the number of CGG repeats and the severity of the clinical findings, but this finding remains controversial (Stanley, Hull, Mazzoco, et al., 1993).

The clinical manifestations of fragile X syndrome typically become more severe in subsequent generations of a family because the expanded triplet repeat in premutations is unstable and likely to be further amplified in successive generations, a concept called **anticipation.** Premutations involving more than 100 CGG repeats almost always expand into full mutations when transmitted to the next generation (Imbert & Mandel, 1995). The larger the number of triplet repeats, the more unstable is the fragile X site, making it likely to further expand during cell division of the fertilized egg (Eichler, Holden, Popovich, et al., 1994). Because transmitting males usually have less than 100 CGG repeats, they tend to produce daughters with the premutation who are also asymptomatic. These females, however, are likely to have expanded to 90–200 CGG repeats. As a result, their children (both sons and daughters) who inherit the trait are likely to have the full mutation, with expansions of more than 1,000 (Fisch, Snow, Thibodeau, et al., 1995; Pintado, DeDiego, Hmadcha, et al., 1995). Thus, transmitting males tend to have grandchildren manifesting fragile X syndrome, a very unusual pattern for an X-linked disorder!

A concept related to anticipation is genomic imprinting, which implies that a trait will be influenced by which parent passes it on. For example, if the fragile X trait is passed from an unaffected transmitting male to his daughter, the daughter will not be affected. If the trait is passed, however, from an asymptomatic carrier female to her daughter, there is a 30% chance that the daughter will express the full mutation and have clinical symptoms. Thus, the expression of this disorder depends on which parent passes on the trait. The expansion to a full mutation only occurs when the gene is imprinted by a female.

CLINICAL FINDINGS IN AFFECTED MALES

Once fragile X syndrome was identified as a discrete entity, it soon became clear that affected men have a characteristic appearance (Bailey & Nelson, 1995; Hagerman, Amiri, & Cronister, 1991). They have elongated faces, prominent jaws and foreheads, large protruding ears, a high-arched palate, hyperextensible joints, and flat feet (Figure 18.1). Almost all of these men have markedly enlarged testicles and many have a prolapse of the mitral heart valve. Some of these characteristics, such as large ears, are subtle during childhood and become more pronounced with age, making early identification difficult based on physical features alone. At school age, an affected boy generally has a somewhat enlarged head, protruding ears, and a high-arched palate (Table 18.1). Like children with Down syndrome, they may have epicanthal folds and simian creases. These boys also tend to be hypotonic and clumsy. Although they grow rapidly during childhood, they have short stature as adults.

More prominent than the physical appearance are the cognitive, communicative, and behavior impairments of boys with the fragile X full mutation (Table 18.2). Their developmental delays are evident in infancy; they typically begin to walk at 19 months and speak at 26–30 months (Dykens, Hodapp, & Leckman, 1994; Freund, Peebles, Aylward, et al., 1995). Most young boys with fragile X syndrome have IQ scores that identify them as having mental retardation requiring intermittent supports. By adolescence, though, these scores tend to decline, indicating a slowing in development but not a loss of skills (Dykens, Hodapp, & Leckman, 1987; Hagerman, 1995; Kemper, Hagerman, & Altshul-Stark, 1988; Maes, Fryns, Van Walleghem, et al., 1994; Wright, Tolamante, & Cheema, 1996). Simultaneous processing, the synthesis of separate elements into groups when all parts of the task are presented at once and must be integrated, is actually a specific strength for affected males (Maes et al., 1994). Their daily living

Table 18.1. Physical findings in males with fragile X syndrome

Finding	Percentage of males affected
Prepubescent[a]	
Protruding ears	70
High arched palate, flattened nasal bridge	50
Macrocephaly	40
Epicanthal folds, simian creases	40
Poor coordination	50
Hyperextensible joints/hypotonia	20
Postpubescent[b]	
Elongated face/prominent jaw	48
Long ears	80
Macro-orchidism	92
Mitral valve prolapse	80

Sources: [a]Simko, Horstein, Soukup, et al. (1989); [b]Hagerman (1995).

Table 18.2. Cognitive and behavioral characteristics of fragile X syndrome in young children

Parental concern	Percentage of children affected
Boys	
Mental retardation	95
Communication disorder	95
Hyperactivity	65
Poor eye contact	80
Self-stimulatory/ autistic-like behavior	60
Discipline problems	60
Seizures	20
Girls	
Learning disability	20
Mild mental retardation	10
Abnormal speech patterns	30
Emotional disturbance	30

Sources: Maes et al. (1994); Simko, Horstein, Soukup, et al. (1989).

skills are also relatively strong in relation to their communication and socialization skills (Dykens, 1995; Dykens, Hodapp, & Evans, 1994; Fisch, Simeonsen, Tarleton, et al., 1996).

Evidence of speech and language delays beyond those predicted by cognitive functioning is usually present from the preschool period (Reiss, Abrams, Greenlaw, et al., 1995). Speech tends to be echolalic, cluttered, and perseverative, with word-finding problems and irrelevant associations, especially when the child is anxious; he will talk incessantly in a cluttered manner, and often to himself (Ferrier, Bashir, Meryash, et al., 1991; Sudhalter, Cohen, Silverman, et al., 1990). There also is poor auditory memory and reception.

Three quarters of boys with fragile X syndrome manifest significant behavior problems by school age (Baumgardner, Reiss, & Freund, 1995). These include stereotypic behavior (e.g., hand flapping); poor eye contact; unusual responses to sensory stimuli including tactile defensiveness; ADHD; aggression; and disciplinary problems (Lachiewicz, Spiridigliozi, Gullion, et al., 1994). The combination of mental retardation, nonverbal and verbal communication impairments, self-stimulatory behavior, poor eye contact, and a lack of sociability defines many of these children as having a **pervasive developmental disorder** (Baumgardner et al., 1995; Cohen, 1995; Cohen, Fisch, Sudhalter, et al., 1988; Reiss & Freund, 1992). In contrast to boys with autism, however, those with fragile X syndrome do not show problems in developing attachment behaviors to caregivers (Fisch, Holden, Simensen, et al., 1994).

CLINICAL FINDINGS IN AFFECTED FEMALES

Among female carriers of fragile X syndrome, 70% have the premutation and do not manifest significant physical or cognitive-behavior abnormalities (Reiss, Freund, Abrams, et al., 1993). The other 30% have the full mutation and show a spectrum of symptoms (Abrams, Reiss, Freund, et al., 1994; Sobesdy, Taylor, Pennington, et al., 1996; Taylor, Safanda, Fall, et al.,

1994). In general, affected women have only a slightly altered physical appearance, with a narrow face and large ears.

The cognitive and behavioral abnormalities of women with the full mutation are usually less severe than those observed in affected males. About half of these females have typical intellectual functioning and exhibit non–language-based learning disabilities. The other half have mental retardation, usually requiring intermittent supports (Fisch et al., 1995). All of these women, however, seem to have cognitive impairments that originate in the right hemispheric and frontal lobe regions of the brain, resulting in abnormalities in visual-spatial perceptual skills, **executive function**, attention, and simultaneous processing (Lachiewicz, 1995). Affected women, however, do better with sequential processing, in which information is organized or in temporal order. They have relative strengths in verbal memory and reading but weaknesses in mathematics. On the Weschsler (1974) Intelligence Scale for Children–Revised (WISC–R) IQ tests, they tend to score particularly low in the math computation and block design subtests (Mazzocco, Pennington, & Hagerman, 1993). They also have an unusual speech pattern, which may be perseverative and cluttered.

Their personalities tend to be shy and withdrawn with odd communication patterns and mannerisms. Specific features include stereotypic behavior, **tangential speech,** impulsivity, distractibility, and difficulty with transitions. Psychiatric disorders have been diagnosed in 20%–60% of females with the full mutation (Franke, Maier, Hautzinger, et al., 1996; Freund, Reiss, & Abrams, 1993; Sobesky, Pennington, Porter, et al., 1994). The most common diagnoses are depression, schizoid personality disorder, pervasive developmental disorder, avoidant personality disorder, and anxiety disorder (Reiss et al., 1993).

ORIGINS OF ABNORMALITIES

Most of the physical characteristics of fragile X syndrome, such as hyperextensible ligaments and mitral valve prolapse, likely relate to connective tissue abnormalities. And although it is not entirely clear how the triplet repeat expansion leads to mental retardation, research is beginning to uncover the mechanism involved (Abrams & Reiss, 1995). In 1993, scientists showed that the presence of more than 230 CGG repeats leads to the **hypermethylation** and turning off of the FMR1 gene, resulting in decreased or absent production of FMRP, which appears to be important in early brain development (McConkie-Rosell, Lachiewicz, Spiridigliozzi, et al., 1993). FMRP is usually found in high levels in the following brain regions: the caudate (which governs affect, impulse control, and executive function); the thalamus (which is involved in sensory integration); the cerebellum (which is involved in motor planning); the hippocampus (which directs memory and attention); the superior temporal gyrus (which directs language); and the cerebral cortex (which directs goal-directed behavior and working memory) (see Chapter 14) (Abitbol, Menini, Delezoide, et al., 1993; Cohen, 1995). Abnormalities in these regions are associated with the specific behavior and cognitive impairments of fragile X syndrome. Neuroimaging and neuropathology studies of people with fragile X syndrome confirm abnormalities in these regions consistent with deficient FMRP (Hinton, Brown, Wisniewski, et al., 1991; Reiss et al., 1995; Reiss, Aylward, Freund, et al., 1991; Schapiro, Murphy, Hagerman, et al., 1995).

A number of these findings have been confirmed in a mouse model of fragile X syndrome, which was produced by "knocking out" the FMR1 gene in the mouse embryos (Willems, Reyniers, & Oostra, 1995). The animals show some of the same abnormalities seen in humans, suggesting that the absence of FMR1 is likely to be the underlying cause of the neurodevelopmental abnormalities in humans. This is quite exciting as it raises the future possibility of gene therapy. Gene therapy in which only one gene must be "added" is much more plausible than therapy involving multiple genes, as is the case in Down syndrome.

DIAGNOSING FRAGILE X SYNDROME

The approach to diagnosing fragile X syndrome has evolved since the mid-1980s, based both on the identification of the specific gene defect and on the recognition of the frequency of its occurrence (Oostra, Jacky, Brown, et al., 1993). Initially, the diagnosis was made only in affected males. Individuals with a family history consistent with an X-linked disorder and a specific profile of physical features and cognitive-behavior impairments were identified as possible candidates, and a chromosome study was performed using a special culture medium deficient in folic acid. This induced the appearance of the fragile site on the X chromosome; 1%–50% of cells in males with the full mutation showed the fragile site. This approach was quite successful in the identification of affected males, but the karyotyping of the chromosomes was expensive and could be done only in specialized laboratories. Furthermore, women with the premutation and transmitting males were missed by this test, as they do not express the fragile X chromosome. Even some women and mildly affected males with the full mutation were missed because of the low percentage of cells with the fragile X chromosome.

With the identification of the FMR1 gene as the underlying defect in fragile X syndrome, a more specific and less costly blood test (the DNA blood test for fragile X) was developed to detect the amplification of the CGG triplet repeats in both full mutations and permutations (Brown, Houck, Jeziorowska, et al., 1993). This blood test can also be used for prenatal diagnosis (Castellví-Bel, Milà, Soler, et al., 1995). Some developmental specialists have suggested that DNA testing for fragile X syndrome should be done on any male or female with mental retardation of uncertain etiology.

In 1995, a blood antibody test that seeks the presence of FMRP and can be used to detect individuals with the full mutation was developed (Willemsen, Monkamsing, DeVries, et al., 1995). The availability of this test raises the possibility (and the ethical dilemma) of newborn screening for fragile X syndrome (Brown, 1996).

INTERVENTION STRATEGIES

Children with fragile X syndrome should receive all routine pediatric care, including immunizations (American Academy of Pediatrics, Committee on Genetics, 1996). In addition, ophthalmic disorders, orthopedic abnormalities, serous otitis, mitral valve prolapse, seizure disorders, and **macro-orchidism** should be assessed during the examination. Ophthalmic disorders include strabismus, myopia, ptosis, and nystagmus. The most common of these is strabismus; if present, refraction or patching may help prevent amblyopia from developing. Orthopedic abnormalities relate to the underlying connective tissue problem and include flat feet, scoliosis, and loose joints; surgery is rarely indicated. Inguinal hernias are another manifestation of the connective tissue laxity. Recurrent middle-ear infections may require antibiotic prophylaxis or, if persistent, surgical aspiration and placement of pressure-equalizing tubes. An audiological examination also should be performed. If there is a cardiac murmur or click, an echocardiogram should be obtained. Antibiotic prophylaxis should be considered if there is a mitral valve prolapse. Seizures, most commonly complex partial or generalized tonic-clonic types, occur in about 20% of affected males, who generally respond well to antiepileptic drugs (see Chapter 26) (Wisniewski, Segan, Miezejeski, et al., 1991). An EEG is only indicated if there is the suspicion of a seizure disorder. Macro-orchidism may become evident before adolescence; parents should be reassured that this does not require treatment or lead to any symptoms, including precocious puberty.

Intervention strategies for boys with the full mutation and resultant fragile X syndrome are directed at the various cognitive, communicative, and behavior impairments they exhibit. A structured learning environment and behavior management techniques can be used to intervene with hyperactive and stereotypic behavior. A sight-word approach to reading, using visual cues and repetition, has been useful to assist in processing new, sequential information and visual-motor integration. Computer learning also may be helpful in promoting visual learning and attention. In addition, these children benefit from speech-language therapy that focuses on learning to follow short commands. They do well using a shaping approach to learning daily living skills. In addition, many benefit from social skills training. If ADHD is a problem, some improvement has been reported by using stimulant medication (Hagerman, Murphy, & Wittenberger, 1988).

The educational needs of girls with fragile X syndrome depend on the degree and type of cognitive impairments (Hagerman, Jackson, Amiri, et al., 1992). Those with mental retardation will benefit from a similar approach to boys with the full mutation. Girls with typical development but learning disabilities require appropriate special education services for non–language-based learning disabilities. Counseling and psychopharmacological agents have been helpful in treating associated psychiatric disorders (Hagerman, Fulton, Leaman, et al., 1994) (see Chapter 20). They also benefit from social skills training.

Folic acid has been proposed to treat both boys and girls with fragile X syndrome based on the finding that it prevents the fragile X change in their chromosomes. There has been controversy about whether this has value; most studies do not demonstrate consistent benefit to behavior or cognition (Hagerman & Silverman, 1991).

OUTCOME

Because fragile X syndrome is a newly recognized disorder, the long-term outcomes are not yet clear. Individuals with the fragile X permutation generally appear to be clinically unaffected (Hagerman, Stanley, O'Conner, et al., 1996). Males with the full mutation, however, have mental retardation requiring limited to extensive supports. Furthermore, they tend to be less independent than would be expected from their cognitive impairment because of their associated communicative, behavior, and social skills impairments. Longevity is likely to be unaffected.

The most prominent long-term problem facing females with the full mutation is psychiatric disorder (Hagerman et al., 1992). Shyness and social anxiety superimposed on mild cognitive impairments can significantly interfere with independence.

TONY

When he was 4 years old, Tony was identified as having fragile X syndrome during his evaluation for entry into a preschool program for children with special needs. He had been diagnosed as having mental retardation requiring limited supports, marked hyperactivity, self-stimulatory behavior, and language skills that were more delayed than his other cognitive abilities. The family history was significant in that his half-brother, 3-year-old Vincent, was similarly but more severely affected. His mother, Sylvia, who is single, had received resource help in high school for a non–language-based learning disability and is currently being treated for depression. Fragile X testing was done on all three members of this family; Sylvia was found to have 250 CGG repeats, Vincent 1,500, and Tony 1,000, establishing the diagnosis of fragile X syndrome with the full mutation in all three and illustrating the genetic principle of anticipation. As a result of further neurodevelopmental testing, both Tony and Vincent were placed in preschool programs that focused on language development and used behavior management techniques. Tony also began taking dexedrine, which has significantly decreased his hyperactivity. Sylvia is also coping better; her social worker arranged for wrap-around services, including an in-home aide for 2 hours a day.

SUMMARY

Fragile X syndrome is the most common inherited cause of mental retardation. It is an X-linked disorder in which most affected boys present with a characteristic pattern of physical, cognitive, and behavior impairments, while a fraction of carrier girls manifest less severe symptoms. Caused by an expansion of a triplet base pair repeat, CGG, that creates a fragility of the X chromosome and inactivates the FMR1 gene, individuals with fragile X syndrome have decreased or absent production of FMRP, a protein important in early brain development. Although there is currently no specific treatment for this disorder, special education, behavior management techniques, social skills training, and pharmacotherapy can improve the prognosis of affected individuals. Because this disorder is associated with a single gene defect, the possibility of gene therapy exists in the future.

REFERENCES

Abitbol, M., Menini, C., Delezoide, A-L., et al. (1993). Nucleus basalis magnocellularis and hippocampus are the major sites of FMR1 expression in the human fetal brain. *Nature Genetics, 4,* 147–153.

Abrams, M.T., & Reiss, A.L. (1995). The neurobiology of fragile X syndrome. *Mental Retardation and Developmental Disabilities Research Reviews, 1,* 269–275.

Abrams, M.T., Reiss, A.L., Freund, L.S., et al. (1994). Molecular–neurobehavioral association in females with the fragile X full mutation. *American Journal of Medical Genetics, 51,* 317–327.

American Academy of Pediatrics, Committee on Genetics. (1996). Health supervision for children with fragile X syndrome. *Pediatrics, 98,* 297–300.

Bailey, A., Bolton, P., Butler, L., et al. (1993). Prevalence of the fragile X anomaly amongst autistic twins and singletons. *Journal of Child Psychology and Psychiatry, 34,* 673–688.

Bailey, D.B., Jr., & Nelson, D. (1995). The nature and consequences of fragile X syndrome. *Mental Retardation and Developmental Disabilities Research Reviews, 1,* 238–244.

Baumgardner, T.L., Reiss, A.L., & Freund, L.S. (1995). Specification of the neurobehavioral phenotype in males with fragile X syndrome. *Pediatrics, 95,* 744–752.

Brown, W.T. (1996). The FRAXE syndrome: Is it time for routine screening? *American Journal of Human Genetics, 58,* 903–905.

Brown, W.T., Houck, G.E., Jr., Jeziorowska, A., et al. (1993). Rapid fragile X carrier screening and prenatal diagnosis using a nonradioactive PCR test. *Journal of the American Medical Association, 270,* 1569–1575.

Brown, W.T., & Jenkins, E.C. (1992). The fragile X syndrome. *Molecular and Genetic Medicine, 2,* 39–66.

Castellví-Bel, S., Milà, M., Soler, A., et al. (1995). Prenatal diagnosis of fragile X syndrome: (CGG)n expansion and methylation of chorionic villus samples. *Prenatal Diagnosis, 15,* 801–807.

Cohen, I.L. (1995). A theoretical analysis of the role of hyperarousal in the learning and behavior of fragile X males. *Mental Retardation and Developmental Disabilities Research Reviews, 1,* 286–291.

Cohen, I.L., Fisch, G.S., Sudhalter, V., et al. (1988). Social gaze, social avoidance, and repetitive behavior in fragile X males: A controlled study. *American Journal of Mental Retardation, 92,* 436–446.

Dykens, E.M. (1995). Adaptive behavior in males with fragile X syndrome. *Mental Retardation and Developmental Disabilities Research Reviews, 1,* 281–284.

Dykens, E.M., Hodapp, R.M., & Evans, D.W. (1994). Profiles and development of adaptive behavior in children with Down syndrome. *American Journal of Mental Retardation, 98,* 580–587.

Dykens, E.M., Hodapp, R.M., & Leckman, J.F. (1987). Strengths and weaknesses in the intellectual functioning of males with fragile X syndrome. *American Journal of Mental Deficiency, 92,* 234–236.

Dykens, E.M., Hodapp, R.M., & Leckman, J.F. (1994). *Behavior and development in fragile X syndrome.* Beverly Hills: Sage Publications.

Eichler, E.E., Holden, J.A., Popovich, B.W., et al. (1994). Length of uninterrupted CGG repeats determines instability in the FMR1 gene. *Nature Genetics, 8,* 88–94.

Feng, Y., Zhang, F., Lokey, L.K., et al. (1995). Translational suppression by trinucleotide repeat expansion at FMR1. *Science, 268,* 731–734.

Ferrier, L.J., Bashir, A.S., Meryash, D.L., et al. (1991). Conversational skills of individuals with fragile X syndrome: A comparison with autism and Down syndrome. *Developmental Medicine and Child Neurology, 33,* 776–788.

Fisch, G.S., Holden, J.J.A., Simensen, R., et al. (1994). Is fragile X syndrome a pervasive developmental disorder? Cognitive ability and adaptive behavior in males with the full mutation. *American Journal of Medical Genetics, 51,* 346–352.

Fisch, G.S., Simenson, R., Tarleton, J., et al. (1996). Longitudinal study of cognitive abilities and adaptive behavior levels in fragile X males: A prospective multicenter analysis. *American Journal of Medical Genetics, 64,* 356–361.

Fisch, G.S., Simensen, R., Arinami, T., et al. (1994). Longitudinal changes in IQ among fragile X females: A preliminary multicenter analysis. *American Journal of Medical Genetics, 51,* 353–357.

Fisch, G.S., Snow, K., Thibodeau, S.N., et al. (1995). The fragile X premutation in carriers and its effect on mutation size in offspring. *American Journal of Human Genetics, 56,* 1147–1155.

Franke, P., Maier, W., Hautzinger, M., et al. (1996). Fragile X carrier females: Evidence for a distinct psychopathological phenotype? *American Journal of Medical Genetics, 64,* 334–339.

Freund, L.S., Peebles, C.D., Aylward, E., et al. (1995). Preliminary report on cognitive and adaptive behaviors of preschool aged males with fragile X. *Developmental Brain Dysfunction, 8,* 242–251.

Freund, L.S., Reiss, A.L., & Abrams, M.T. (1993). Psychiatric disorders associated with fragile X in the young female. *Pediatrics, 91,* 321–329.

Hagerman, R.J. (1995). Molecular and clinical correlations in fragile X syndrome. *Mental Retardation and Developmental Disabilities Research Reviews, 1,* 276–280.

Hagerman, R.J., Amiri, K., & Cronister, A. (1991). Fragile X checklist. *American Journal of Medical Genetics, 38,* 283–287.

Hagerman, R.J., & Cronister, A. (Eds). (1996). *Fragile X syndrome: Diagnosis, treatment and research* (2nd ed.). Baltimore: The Johns Hopkins University Press.

Hagerman, R.J., Fulton, M.J., Leaman, A., et al. (1994). Fluoxetine therapy in fragile X syndrome. *Developmental Brain Dysfunction, 7,* 155–164.

Hagerman, R.J., Jackson, C., Amiri, K., et al. (1992). Girls with fragile X syndrome: Physical and neurocognitive status and outcome. *Pediatrics, 89,* 395–400.

Hagerman, R.J., McBogg, P., & Hagerman, P.J. (1983). The fragile X syndrome: History, diagnosis, and treatment. *Journal of Developmental and Behavioral Pediatrics, 4,* 122–130.

Hagerman, R.J., Murphy, M.A., & Wittenberger, M.D. (1988). A controlled trial of stimulant medication in children with the fragile X syndrome. *American Journal of Medical Genetics, 30,* 241–262.

Hagerman, R.J., & Silverman, A.C. (Eds.). (1991). *Fragile X syndrome: Diagnosis, treatment, and research.* Baltimore: The Johns Hopkins University Press.

Hagerman, R.J., Stanley, L.W., O'Conner, R., et al. (1996). Learning disabled males with a fragile X CGG expansion in the upper premutation size range. *Pediatrics, 97,* 122–126.

Hagerman, R.J., Wilson, P., Stanley, L.W., et al. (1994). Evaluation of school children at high risk for fragile X syndrome utilizing buccal cell FMR1 testing. *American Journal of Medical Genetics,* *51,* 474–481.

Hinton, V.J., Brown, W.T., Wisniewski, K., et al. (1991). Analysis of neocortex in three males with the fragile X syndrome. *American Journal of Medical Genetics, 41,* 289–294.

Imbert, G., & Mandel, J.L. (1995). The fragile X mutation. *Mental Retardation and Developmental Disability Research Reviews, 1,* 251–262.

Kemper, M.B., Hagerman, R.J., & Altshul-Stark, D. (1988). Cognitive profiles of boys with the fragile X syndrome. *American Journal of Medical Genetics, 30,* 191–200.

Lachiewicz, A.M. (1995). Females with fragile X syndrome: A review of the effects of an abnormal FMR1 gene. *Mental Retardation and Developmental Disabilities Research Reviews, 1,* 292–297.

Lachiewicz, A.M., Spiridigliozi, G.A., Gullion, C.M., et al. (1994). Aberrant behaviors of young boys with fragile X syndrome. *American Journal of Mental Retardation, 98,* 567–579.

Lehrke, R. (1972). Theory of X-linkage of major intellectual traits. *American Journal of Mental Deficiency, 76,* 611–619.

Loesch, D.Z., Hay, D.A., & Mulley, J. (1994). Transmitting males and carrier females in fragile X–revisited. *American Journal of Medical Genetics, 51,* 392–399.

Maes, B., Fryns, J.P., Van Walleghem, M., et al. (1994). Cognitive functioning and information processing of adult mentally retarded men with fragile-X syndrome. *American Journal of Medical Genetics, 50,* 190–200.

Martin, J.P., & Bell, J. (1943). A pedigree of mental defect showing sex-linkage. *Journal of Neurology and Psychiatry, 6,* 154–157.

Mazzocco, M.M., Pennington, B.F., & Hagerman, R.J. (1993). The neurocognitive phenotype of female carriers of fragile X: Additional evidence for specificity. *Journal of Developmental and Behavioral Pediatrics, 14,* 328–335.

McConkie-Rosell, A., Lachiewicz, A.M., Spiridigliozzi, G.A., et al. (1993). Evidence that methylation of the FMR1 locus is responsible for variable phenotypic expression of the fragile X syndrome. *American Journal of Human Genetics, 53,* 800–809.

Meadows, K.L., Pettay, D., Newman, J., et al. (1996). Survey of the fragile X syndrome and the fragile XE syndrome in a special education needs population. *American Journal of Medical Genetics, 64,* 428–443.

Morton, J.E., Rindl, P.M., Bullock, S., et al. (1995). Fragile X syndrome is less common than previously estimated. *Journal of Medical Genetics, 32,* 144–145.

Mulley, J.C., Yu, S., Loesch, D.Z., et al. (1995). FRAXE and mental retardation. *Journal of Medical Genetics, 32,* 162–169.

Oostra, B.A., & Halley, D.J.J. (1995). Complex behavior of simple repeats: The fragile X syndrome. *Pediatric Research, 38,* 629–637.

Oostra, B.A., Jacky, P.B., Brown, W.T., et al. (1993). Guidelines for the diagnosis of fragile X syndrome. *Journal of Medical Genetics, 30,* 410–413.

Pintado, E., DeDiego, Y., Hmadcha, A., et al. (1995). Instability of the CGG repeat at the FRAXA locus and variable phenotypic expression in a large fragile X pedigree. *Journal of Medical Genetics, 32,* 907–908.

Reiss, A.L., Abrams, M.T., Greenlaw, R., et al. (1995). Neurodevelopmental effects of the FMR1 full mutation in humans. *Nature Medicine, 1,* 159–167.

Reiss, A.L., Aylward, E., Freund, L.S., et al. (1991). Neuroanatomy of fragile X syndrome: The posterior fossa. *Annals of Neurology, 29,* 26–32.

Reiss, A.L., & Freund, L. (1992). Behavioral phenotype of fragile X syndrome: DSM-IIIR autistic behavior in male children. *American Journal of Medical Genetics, 43,* 35–46.

Reiss, A.L., Freund, L., Abrams, M.T., et al. (1993). Neurobehavioral effects of the fragile X premutation in adult women: A controlled study. *American Journal of Human Genetics, 52,* 884–894.

Reiss, A.L., Kazazian, H.H., Jr., Krebs, C.M., et al. (1994). Frequency and stability of the fragile X premutation. *Human and Molecular Genetics, 3,* 393–398.

Rousseau, F., Heitz, O., Tarlton, J., et al. (1994). A multicenter study on genotype-phenotype correlation in the fragile X syndrome, using direct diagnosis with probe StB12.3: The first 2,253 cases. *American Journal of Human Genetics, 55,* 225–237.

Rousseau, F., Rouillard, P., Morel, M.L., et al. (1995). Prevalence of carriers of premutation-size alleles of the FMRI gene and implications for the population genetics of the fragile X syndrome. *American Journal of Human Genetics, 57,* 1006–1018.

Schapiro, M.B., Murphy, D.G.M., Hagerman, R.J., et al. (1995). Adult fragile X syndrome: Neuropsychology, brain anatomy and metabolism. *American Journal of Medical Genetics, 60,* 480–493.

Simko, A., Horstein, L., Soukup, S., et al. (1989). Fragile X syndrome: Recognition in young children. *Pediatrics, 83,* 547–552.

Simon, E.W., Rappaport, D.A., Papka, M., et al. (1995). Fragile-X and Down's syndrome: Are there syndrome-specific cognitive profiles at low IQ levels? *Journal of Intellectual Disability Research, 39,* 326–330.

Slaney, S.F., Wilkie, A.O.M., Hirst, M.D., et al. (1995). DNA testing for fragile X syndrome in schools for learning difficulties. *Archives of Disease in Childhood, 72,* 33–37.

Sobesky, W.E., Pennington, B.F., Porter, D., et al. (1994). Emotional and neurocognitive deficits in fragile X. *American Journal of Medical Genetics, 51,* 378–384.

Sobesky, W.E., Taylor, A.K., Pennington, B.F., et al. (1996). Molecular/clinical correlations in females with fragile X. *American Journal of Medical Genetics, 64,* 340–345.

Stanley, L.W., Hull, C.E., Mazzocco, M.M.M., et al. (1993). Molecular-clinical correlations in children and adults with fragile X syndrome. *American Journal of Diseases of Childhood, 147,* 723–726.

Sudhalter, V., Cohen, I.L., Silverman, W., et al. (1990). Conversational analyses of males with fragile X, Down syndrome, and autism: Comparison of the emergence of deviant language. *American Journal of Mental Retardation, 94,* 431–441.

Sutherland, G.R. (1977). Fragile sites on human chromosomes: Demonstration of their dependence on the type of tissue culture medium. *Science, 197,* 265–266.

Taylor, A.K., Safanda, J.F., Fall, M., et al. (1994). Molecular predictors of cognitive involvement in female carriers of fragile X syndrome. *Science, 271,* 507–514.

Verkerk, A.J.M.H., Pieretti, M., Sutcliffe, J.S., et al. (1991). Identification of a gene (FMR1) containing a CGG repeat coincident with a breakpoint cluster region exhibiting length variation in fragile X syndrome. *Cell, 65,* 905–914.

Warren, S.T., & Nelson, D.L. (1994) Advances in molecular analysis of fragile X syndrome. *Science, 271,* 536–542.

Wechsler, D. (1974). *Wechsler Intelligence Scale for Children–Revised.* New York: The Psychological Corporation.

Willems, P.J., Reyniers, E., & Oostra, B.A. (1995). An animal model for fragile X syndrome. *Mental Retardation and Developmental Disabilities Research Reviews, 1,* 298–302.

Willemsen, R., Monkamsing, S., DeVries, B., et al. (1995). Rapid antibody test for fragile X syndrome. *Lancet, 345,* 1147–1148.

Wisniewski, K.E., Segan, S.M., Miezejeski, C.M., et al. (1991). Fragile-X syndrome: Neurological, electrophysiological and neuropathological abnormalities. *American Journal of Medical Genetics, 38,* 476–480.

Wright-Talamante, C., Cheema, A., Riddle, J.E., et al. (1996). A controlled study of longitudinal IQ changes in females and males with fragile X syndrome. *American Journal of Medical Genetics, 64,* 350–355.

19 PKU and Other Inborn Errors of Metabolism

Mark L. Batshaw

Upon completion of this chapter, the reader will:

- understand what is meant by the term inborn error of metabolism
- know the differences among a number of these inborn errors, including amino acid disorders, organic acidemias, and lysosomal storage diseases
- identify the clinical symptoms and diagnostic tests associated with these disorders
- know which of these disorders have newborn screening tests available
- recognize the different approaches to treatment, including the prospects for gene therapy
- understand the outcome and range of developmental disabilities associated with inborn errors of metabolism

To receive adequate nutrition, the food we eat must be broken down into fats, proteins, and carbohydrates and then metabolized by hundreds of enzymes that work to maintain equilibrium in body functions (Figure 19.1). Approximately 3 in 1,000 children are born deficient in an enzyme that normally catalyzes an important biochemical reaction in the body (Scriver, Kaufman, Eisensmith, et al., 1995). These children are said to have an inborn error of metabolism. The enzyme deficiency can result in the accumulation of a toxic **substrate** behind the enzyme block or lead to the impaired formation of a product normally produced by the deficient enzyme. The result may be organ damage (principally of the brain) or even death. For example, children with phenylketonuria (PKU) have a deficiency in the enzyme that normally converts the amino acid phenylalanine to tyrosine. An enzyme deficiency leads to the toxic accumulation of phenylalanine, which adversely affects a neurotransmitter system in the brain and, if untreated, leads to mental retardation. Conversely, in children with congenital hypothyroidism, an enzyme deficiency leads to decreased synthesis of thyroid hormone, which is essential for brain growth. Here too, if left untreated, this disorder results in mental retardation. Fortunately, for both of these disorders, newborn screening tests and early treatment have permitted affected children to grow up with their intellectual functioning intact. Not all inborn errors of metabolism are as easily treated, however, because of delays in diagnosis or lack of effective intervention. This chap-

389

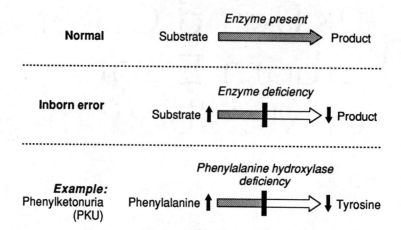

Figure 19.1.   Inborn errors of metabolism are genetic disorders involving an enzyme deficiency. This enzyme block leads to the accumulation of a toxic substrate and/or the deficient synthesis of a product needed for normal body function. In phenylketonuria (PKU) there is a toxic accumulation of phenylalanine behind the deficient enzyme, phenylalanine hydroxylase (PH).

ter provides examples of inborn errors of metabolism to explain diagnostic and therapeutic advances that are improving the prognosis of these disorders.

TYPES OF INBORN ERRORS OF METABOLISM

Inborn errors of metabolism are a relatively newly discovered group of diseases. PKU was one of the first, described by Fölling in 1934. About 300 additional disorders have been identified since the 1950s, and a number of new ones are described each year (Scriver et al., 1995). The majority of these enzyme deficiencies are inherited as autosomal recessive traits, although a few are transmitted as sex-linked or mitochondrial disorders (see Chapter 2). Prenatal diagnosis is available for most of them (see Chapter 3).

Inborn errors of metabolism can be divided into those that are "silent," those that produce acute toxicity, and those that cause progressive neurological deterioration (Table 19.1). Among silent disorders are certain amino acid and hormone abnormalities. Those disorders producing acute toxicity include inborn errors of amino acid, organic acid, fatty acid, and carbohydrate metabolism. Inborn errors of metabolism causing progressive neurological deterioration include peroxisomal and lysosomal storage disorders. The names of the disorders are often derivatives of the deficient enzyme (e.g., ornithine transcarbamylase [OTC] deficiency, an inborn error of the urea cycle). Silent disorders do not manifest life-threatening crises but, if untreated, lead to brain damage and developmental disabilities. This contrasts with inborn errors that cause acute symptoms that may be life threatening in infancy. In both cases, affected children are generally protected *in utero* because the maternal circulation can provide the missing product or remove the toxic substrate. However, after birth, the infant must rely on his or her own metabolic pathways and if abnormal, toxicity occurs rapidly or over time. In progressive neurological disorders, there is the gradual accumulation, beginning *in utero,* of large molecules that cannot cross the placental membrane. These molecules are stored in the cells of various body organs, including

Table 19.1.   Examples of inborn errors of metabolism

Type I.   Silent disorders
- Phenylketonuria
- Congenital hypothyroidism

Type II.   Disorders presenting in acute metabolic crisis
- Urea cycle disorders (OTC deficiency)
- Organic acidemias (multiple carboxylase deficiency)

Type III.   Disorders with progressive neurological deterioration
- Tay Sachs disease
- Gaucher disease
- Metachromatic leukodystrophy

the brain, where they ultimately destroy the neurons, leading to neurological deterioration (Scriver et al., 1995).

CLINICAL MANIFESTATIONS

The clinical manifestations of the various inborn errors of metabolism fall along a continuum. Silent disorders (e.g., the amino acid disorder PKU) do not manifest such symptoms as lethargy, coma, or regression of skills. Instead, affected children develop very slowly; they are typically not identified as having mental retardation until later in childhood.

Life-threatening crises characterize a second group of inborn errors of metabolism. Infants with these disorders appear to be unaffected at birth, but by a few days of age they develop vomiting, respiratory distress, and lethargy before slipping into coma. These symptoms, however, mimic those observed in other severe newborn illnesses such as sepsis (blood-borne infection), intracerebral hemorrhage, cardiopulmonary abnormalities, and gastrointestinal obstruction (see Chapter 6), which can make an accurate diagnosis difficult. If specific metabolic tests of the blood and urine are not performed, the disease will go undetected. Undiagnosed and untreated, virtually all affected children will die quickly. One study reported that 60% of children with inborn errors of the urea cycle had at least one sibling who died before it was correctly diagnosed in a second affected child (Batshaw, Brusilow, Waber, et al., 1982). Even with heroic treatment, which may include dialysis to "wash out" the toxin, many infants do not survive, and severe developmental disabilities are common in those who do (Msall, Batshaw, Suss, et al., 1984).

In children with neonatal onset disease, DNA analysis typically shows that these children have mutations that cause the formation of a nonfunctional enzyme (see Chapter 2). Enzyme activity levels are generally undetectable. Some children with the same inborn error of metabolism, however, have mutations that produce enzymes that are only partially dysfunctional. These children have later developing and more variable symptoms. Here, symptoms of vomiting and lethargy are often provoked in childhood by excessive protein intake or intercurrent infections. Although these children have a better prognosis than those with neonatal onset disease, they remain at risk for life-threatening metabolic crises throughout life. And although their developmental disabilities may be less severe than those children with neonatal onset disease, they rarely escape without some residual impairments, ranging from attention-deficit/hyperactivity disorder (ADHD) and learning disabilities to mental retardation.

The third clinical presentation of inborn errors of metabolism is a neurodegenerative disorder. Examples include lysosomal storage disorders, such as Tay-Sachs disease, Hurler disease, Gaucher disease, and metachromatic leukodystrophy. In these disorders, there is a gradual and progressive loss of motor and cognitive skills beginning in early childhood, resulting in a nonresponsive state by the preschool years and culminating in death by adolescence (Kaback, Lim-Steele, Dabholkar, et al., 1993). In the case of Tay-Sachs disease, for example, the affected child appears to develop typically until 3–6 months of age, at which point skill development is arrested. For the next 1–2 years, the child gradually loses all skills and begins having seizures and exhibiting decreased muscle tone, vision, hearing, and cognition. Death usually results from malnutrition or aspiration pneumonia. Unfortunately, no effective treatment currently exists for this group of disorders, although organ transplantation and gene therapy hold some hope for the future.

MECHANISM OF BRAIN DAMAGE

The causes of brain damage in the various inborn errors of metabolism are not completely understood. However, research is starting to provide some clues that may eventually lead to improved treatment. For example, thyroid hormone has been found to be necessary for the normal growth of neurons, their processes, and surrounding myelin. A thyroid hormone deficiency is thought to lead to poor postnatal brain growth and resultant microcephaly (Rodriguez-Pena, Ibarrola, Iniguez, et al., 1993).

Neurotoxins appear to play a role in certain other metabolic disorders. In nonketotic hyperglycinemia, an inborn error of amino acid metabolism, an accumulation of glycine leads to uncontrolled seizures (Tada, Kure, Takayanagi, et al., 1992). Glycine appears to produce excitotoxicity at a neurotransmitter receptor (McDonald & Johnston, 1990), leading to the influx of calcium ions and water into the neuron. This causes swelling of the neuron and, eventually, cell death. Experimental drugs are being tested to partially block the receptor overstimulation (Hamosh, McDonald, Valle, et al., 1992).

In some disorders, more than one neurotoxin may be involved. Scientists believe that in inborn errors of the urea cycle (another group of amino acid disorders), the accumulating toxin, ammonia, directly causes the nerve cells to swell and also indirectly causes excitotoxic damage to the brain (Batshaw, 1994). If children are rescued from the ammonia-induced coma in a few days, the neurotoxic effect can be arrested and their outcome can be fairly good (Msall et al., 1984). If coma is prolonged, however, irreversible brain damage occurs (Batshaw, Robinson, Hyland, et al., 1993).

ASSOCIATED DISABILITIES

The toxic accumulation of metabolic substrates or deficient production of essential products results in a spectrum of developmental disabilities in children with inborn errors of metabolism. The most common are mental retardation and cerebral palsy. However, there are also rather unique disabilities, sometimes associated with distinctive pathological features, which may eventually help us to better understand brain development and function. For example, boys with the sex-linked Lesch-Nyhan syndrome, a defect in purine metabolism, exhibit both choreoathetosis (a form of dyskinetic cerebral palsy) and a compulsive self-injurious behavior (Anderson & Ernst, 1994). Children with glutaric acidemia type I, an organic acidemia, have dystonic cerebral palsy associated with calcifications in their basal ganglia (Hoffmann, Trefz, Barth, et al., 1991). And in Zellweger syndrome, a disorder of the peroxisome, children exhibit multiple malformations more commonly associated with chromosomal disorders, including an abnormal facial appearance, kidney cysts, and congenital heart defects (Brown, Voight, Singh, et al., 1993).

DIAGNOSTIC TESTING

A child with developmental disabilities of unknown origin should be referred for metabolic evaluation if he or she has any of the following: cyclical vomiting and lethargy, evidence of neurological deterioration, and/or a suggestive family history. Available tests can lead to a correct diagnosis and possibly improved therapy and outcome. Even in untreatable disorders, a knowledge of the diagnosis may permit effective genetic counseling. A metabolic workup, however, is not recommended to be performed routinely on all children with mental retardation.

Diagnoses of inborn errors of metabolism rely primarily on blood and urine tests to detect accumulation of toxins. The most common tests performed include blood tests for ammonia, lactic acid, carnitine, and amino acids and urine tests for organic acids and orotic acid. The metabolic evaluations are based on the specific biochemical pathway that is suspected to be defective (Winter, 1993). OTC deficiency, the most common inborn error of the urea cycle, illustrates this (Figure 19.2). When protein is broken down into its component amino acids, ammonia is normally released. The ammonia is then converted into the nontoxic product urea through the five enzymatic steps in the urea cycle. (OTC is the second enzyme in the urea cycle.) Urea is then excreted in the urine. If any one of these five enzymes is deficient, ammonia will accumulate and can cause severe neurological symptoms (Batshaw, 1994). To diagnose this disorder, levels of ammonia and amino acids are measured in blood; and orotic acid is measured in the urine. Many other inborn errors of amino acid and organic acid metabolism can be identified using similar types of blood and urine tests.

Tests to detect lysosomal storage disorders typically examine the blood or skin for the deficient enzyme. Neuroimaging studies (magnetic resonance imaging [MRI] and computed tomography [CT] scans), electroencephalograms (EEGs), and other neurophysiological measures (e.g., nerve conduction velocity, electromyography) may also prove helpful in diagnosing these disorders.

NEWBORN SCREENING

Because individual inborn errors of metabolism are rare (usually less than 1 in 10,000 births) and their diagnosis is easily missed, efforts have been directed at developing population screening methods for the detection of a number of the more common and treatable disorders. Rapid diagnosis and treatment is important if the goal is a good outcome. As a result, screening efforts have focused on newborns, a captive population. The first newborn screening test was developed for PKU in 1959 (Guthrie & Susi, 1963). It was successful in detecting more than 90% of affected children. Subsequently, methods were established for testing a number of other inborn errors of metabolism including congenital hypothyroidism, galactosemia, homocystinuria, biotinidase deficiency, and maple syrup urine disease, as well as certain other genetic disorders not

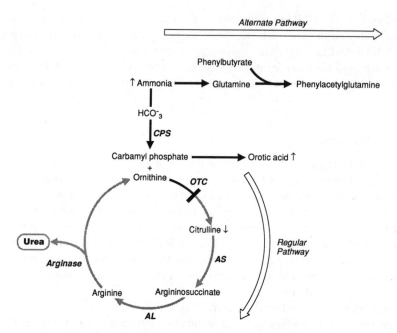

Figure 19.2.   The urea cycle and alternate pathway therapy. There are five enzymes in this cycle that convert toxic ammonia, a breakdown product of protein, to nontoxic urea, which is excreted in the urine. The enzymes are CPS (carbamyl phosphate synthetase), OTC (ornithine transcarbamylase), AS (argininosuccinate synthetase), AL (argininosuccinate lyase), and arginase. Inborn errors at each step of the urea cycle have been described, with the most common one being OTC deficiency. In OTC deficiency there is accumulation behind the block of orotic acid, ammonia, and glutamine and deficient production of citrulline. Treatment has been directed at providing an alternate pathway for waste nitrogen excretion by giving the drug sodium phenylbutyrate that combines with glutamine to form phenylacetylglutamine, a nontoxic product that can be excreted in the urine. This results in a decrease in the accumulation of ammonia.

associated with developmental disabilities, including cystic fibrosis, sickle cell anemia, and alpha-1-antitrypsin deficiency (a disorder affecting liver and lung). This testing is offered to all families in the newborn nurseries; the specific inborn errors of metabolism tested for vary among states.

To perform the test, a few drops of blood are taken from the baby's heel and placed on filter paper. The blood sample is mailed to the state screening laboratory, where the staff can obtain results before the child is 2 weeks old. The blood sample is analyzed either for specific biochemical abnormalities or mutations (McCabe, 1994). Because of the possibility of false positive results, confirmation of the diagnosis is essential before starting treatment. Although these tests have proven to be remarkably effective, parents should be reminded that they can detect only a fraction of the inborn errors of metabolism that cause developmental disabilities. Parents sometimes incorrectly assume that these tests are diagnostic for mental retardation.

THERAPEUTIC APPROACHES

Diagnosis is most valuable if it leads to effective treatment. Figure 19.3 illustrates the varying approaches to treating inborn errors of metabolism. These methods include 1) limiting intake of

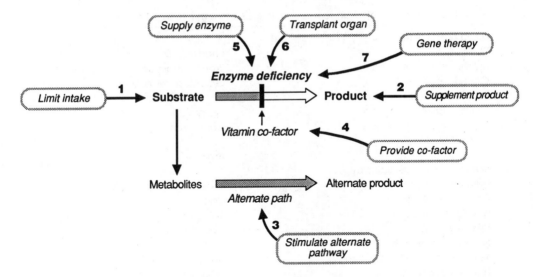

Figure 19.3.   Approaches to treatment of inborn errors. Treatment can be directed at 1) limiting the intake of a potentially toxic compound, 2) supplementing the deficient product, 3) stimulating an alternate metabolic pathway, 4) providing a vitamin co-factor to activate residual enzyme activity, 5) supplying the enzyme itself, 6) transplanting a body organ containing the deficient enzyme, and 7) gene therapy.

a potentially toxic substrate, 2) supplying the deficient product, 3) stimulating an alternate metabolic pathway, 4) providing vitamin co-factors to activate residual enzyme activity, 5) providing enzyme replacement therapy, 6) transplanting a body organ containing the deficient enzyme, and 7) gene therapy. Each of these approaches is illustrated by a specific disorder in Table 19.2.

Limiting Intake of a Potentially Toxic Substrate

A relatively straightforward way to correct an inborn error of metabolism is to establish dietary restrictions that limit the child's intake of a potentially toxic substrate. For example, children with PKU are placed on a phenylalanine-restricted diet in order to prevent the phenylalanine accumulation that causes brain damage (Scriver et al., 1995). As infants, they receive a special formula that contains only small amounts of phenylalanine but normal amounts of other essential amino acids. Once on table foods, they are restricted to small quantities of high-protein foods, such as meats, cheeses, and poultry, which contain phenylalanine. One study showed that the IQ scores of children who began this treatment in the first month of life hovered around 100, while those initially treated later in childhood scored between 20 and 50 points lower (Table 19.3) (Hanley, Linsao, & Netley, 1971).

Scientists initially thought that only children with PKU under 6 years of age needed to follow a phenylalanine-restricted diet. For older children, the high cost and peer rejection of this rather unpleasant and restrictive diet made continuation difficult. Initial studies to determine whether children with PKU experienced a loss in intellectual functioning following dietary discontinuation suggested that IQ scores did not decline over time (Waisbren, Mahon, Schnell, et al., 1987). However, in a subsequent study, researchers found that children with PKU who

Table 19.2.   Examples of treatment approaches for inborn errors of metabolism

Dietary restriction

PKU	Phenylalanine restriction
Maple syrup urine disease	Branch chain amino acid restriction
Galactosemia	Galactose restriction

Supplement deficient product

Congenital hypothyroidism	Synthroid
Glycogen storage disease	Cornstarch
Urea cycle disorders (except argininemia)	Arginine

Stimulate alternate pathway

Urea cycle disorders	Sodium phenylbutyrate
Organic acidemias	Carnitine
Isovaleric acidemia	Glycine
Wilson disease	Penicillamine

Supply vitamin co-factors

Multiple carboxylase deficiency	Biotin
Homocystinuria	Pyridoxine
Methylmalonic acidemia	Vitamin B_{12}

Organ transplantation

Metachromatic leukodystrophy	Bone marrow
OTC deficiency	Liver
Tyrosinemia	Liver
Glycogen storage disease	Liver

Enzyme replacement therapy

ADA deficiency	PEG-ADA
Gaucher disease	Glucocerebrosidase

Gene therapy

Ornithine transcarbamylase deficiency	*In vivo* adenovirus
ADA deficiency	*Ex vivo* retrovirus

maintained the diet through age 10 actually experienced a modest gain in IQ scores compared with children who stopped the diet at age 6. The differences in IQ scores between the two groups were statistically significant (Michals, Azen, Acosta, et al., 1988; Waisbren, Brown, de Sonneville, et al., 1994). Thus, most metabolic specialists suggest that the phenylalanine-restricted diet be continued indefinitely (Azen, Koch, Friedman, et al., 1991).

This therapy, while improving outcomes for numerous individuals, poses a serious complication for women of childbearing age with PKU (Levy, Waisbren, Lobbregt, et al., 1994). At one time, women with PKU had mental retardation requiring extensive supports and did not often bear children. With the specialized diet, there now exists a generation of women with PKU who have average intelligence and bear children; most of them have stopped following the phenylalanine-restricted diet. Unexpectedly, almost all of the children born to these women have been found to have mental retardation. These children, however, do not have PKU; they are only carriers. Instead, their mental retardation is caused by the high levels of phenylalanine in their mothers, which has a teratogenic effect on the developing fetal brain. Studies indicate that low-

Table 19.3.   Results of treating PKU diagnosed at various stages

	Age at diagnosis (months)				
	Birth–2	2–6	6–12	12–24	24+
Number of cases	38	6	11	19	20
IQ scores					
90+	27	0	0	1	2
80–89	6	3	0	2	1
70–79	4	1	3	2	0
Under 70	1	2	8	14	17
Mean IQ score	93.5	71.6	54.5	55.5	40.8

From Hanley, W.B., Linsao, L.S., & Netley, C. (1971). The efficiency of dietary therapy for phenylketonuria. *Canadian Medical Association Journal, 104,* 1089; reprinted by permission of the publisher.

ering the phenylalanine levels in the pregnant mother with PKU significantly improves the chances for typical development of her offspring. As a result, it is now advised that women with PKU resume the phenylalanine-restricted diet prior to conception or as soon as they discover that they are pregnant (Levy et al., 1994).

Supplying the Deficient Product

Some children with inborn errors of metabolism are given replacements for the enzyme product they are missing. For example, children with congenital hypothyroidism receive a thyroid supplement to compensate for the thyroid hormone they lack. This treatment, if administered early, effectively corrects the metabolic disorder, and children treated in the first months of life develop average cognitive functioning (Kooistra, Laane, Vulsma, et al., 1994). Treatment using a thyroid extract has been available since the late 1800s, but its use was limited until newborn screening became available in the 1970s (Fisher, 1987).

Stimulating an Alternative Metabolic Pathway

Physicians are able to treat some metabolic disorders by stimulating an alternative pathway that detours around the enzymatic block. For example, children with inborn errors of the urea cycle cannot convert potentially toxic ammonia, a byproduct of protein breakdown, to nontoxic urea. Treatment by dietary protein restriction alone has proven unsuccessful as the level required to prevent an accumulation of ammonia is insufficient to sustain growth or prolonged survival (Shih, 1976). A novel approach to the problem is to use the drug sodium phenylbutyrate to stimulate an alternate pathway for ammonia excretion. By providing a detour around the enzyme block and converting the ammonia to an alternate nontoxic product, phenylacetylglutamine, instead of urea (Figure 19.2), this drug allows the majority of children with these disorders to survive, although many have developmental disabilities (Brusilow & Horwich, 1995).

Providing a Vitamin Co-factor to Activate Residual Enzyme Activity

For a few inborn errors, providing large doses of a vitamin co-factor results in amplification of residual enzyme activity and clinical improvement. This approach has been most effective in treating children with an organic acidemia, multiple carboxylase deficiency (Michalski, Berry, & Segal, 1989). These children, who develop symptoms of acidosis and coma because of a defect in their enzyme holocarboxylase synthetase, can show marked improvement if biotin (vitamin B complex) is provided at a very high (but nontoxic) dose.

This therapy, which can also help children with certain forms of methylmalonic acidemia (using vitamin B_{12}) and homocystinuria (using vitamin B_6) (Scriver et al., 1995), has unfortunately spawned a "quick fix" approach to treating everything from cancer, to Down syndrome, to schizophrenia although there is no evidence that "megavitamin" therapy is effective in treating any of these disorders (Nutrition Committee of the Canadian Paediatric Society, 1990). Thus, although rare diseases teach us much about normal body chemistry, they have also been used inappropriately to advocate unproven therapy in unrelated disorders.

Providing Enzyme Replacement Therapy

All of the previously discussed methods of therapy are indirect attempts to improve the child's condition. Supplying the missing enzyme is a direct approach to actually treat the inborn error. Injections of a commercially produced synthetic enzyme have proven successful in treating the lysosomal storage disorder, Gaucher disease, which is associated with the accumulation of glucocerebroside in cells of the liver, spleen, and bone marrow (with severe infantile Gaucher disease, it accumulates in the brain as well). Individuals who receive biweekly injections show marked improvements, including significant shrinkage of the liver and spleen (Rosenthal, Doppelt, Mankin, et al., 1995). This enzyme, however, cannot cross the blood-brain barrier, making it ineffective for those children with the severe infantile form of Gaucher disease.

Although replacement therapy seems ideal for those with the milder form of Gaucher disease, it is not without problems. The necessary synthetic enzyme is the most expensive drug in the world, and therapy for one adult costs more than $300,000 per year. Unless these costs can be reduced by improved methods of manufacture or decreased dosage requirements, it seems unlikely that enzyme replacement therapy will come into more general use. Even if enzyme replacement therapy becomes cost effective, it is not a "cure." The enzyme must be injected at frequent intervals throughout the individual's life, and antibodies can develop against the foreign protein, just as insulin resistance develops in some individuals with diabetes.

Transplanting a Body Organ Containing the Deficient Enzyme

Some deficient enzymes can be replaced by transplanting a body organ that contains the enzyme. For example, bone marrow transplants have been attempted in individuals with certain lysosomal storage disorders, such as juvenile metachromatic leukodystrophy. This disorder, marked by dementia, loss of speech, quadriparesis, and early death, is caused by the deficiency of the enzyme arylsulfatase A, which can be found in many body organs including bone marrow cells. In a few affected children, bone marrow transplantation has resulted in the arrest of or improvement in symptoms (Dhuna, Toro, Torres, et al., 1991; Pridjian, Humbert, Willis, et al., 1994).

In addition to bone marrow transplant, liver transplantation has been used to treat certain inborn errors of amino acid metabolism, most notably OTC deficiency and tyrosinemia, with associated biochemical correction and improvement in symptoms. However, organ transplantation is a very expensive (more than $100,000) procedure with significant mortality and morbidity rates and the requirement for immunosuppression therapy throughout life. Unless organ transplantation becomes more effective, safer, and less expensive, it will remain an infrequent procedure in treating inborn errors of metabolism.

Gene Therapy

In theory, the ideal treatment for an inborn error of metabolism would involve the insertion of a normal gene to compensate for a defective one. This insertion would allow for the production of a normal enzyme, thereby permanently correcting or curing the disorder. In 1983, scientists successfully inserted the first gene. In this experiment, the gene for rat growth hormone was injected into a mouse embryo (Palmiter, Norstedt, Gelinas, et al., 1983), causing the mouse to grow to twice the size of its siblings (Figure 19.4). In human experiments, however, initial gene therapy trials begun in the early 1990s have been less successful; both efficacy and duration have been limited.

There are two basic approaches to gene therapy using viral vectors: **ex vivo** and **in vivo.** With *ex vivo* gene therapy, the genetically engineered gene is inserted into cells that have been removed from the body, whereas with *in vivo* gene therapy, the gene is delivered directly to the cells in the body. Each approach has its advantages and disadvantages.

Ex vivo gene therapy is further along in development than *in vivo* gene therapy (Suhr & Gage, 1993; Wolfe, 1994). The process is as follows (Figure 19.5): The normal gene for the defective enzyme is isolated and then spliced onto a retrovirus that will serve as a "taxi" to transport the new gene into the individual's cells. (Retroviruses are useful for gene therapy because

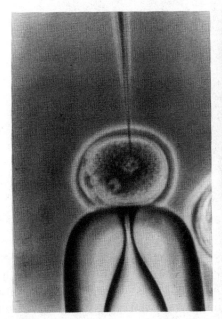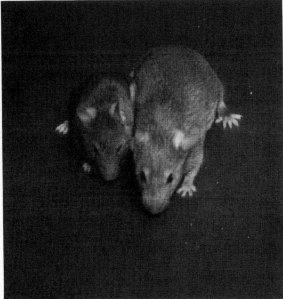

Figure 19.4.   Gene transfer in a mouse embryo. Left panel: Microscopic photograph of fertilized mouse egg being injected with the gene for rat growth hormone. Right panel: The mouse on the left is untreated. The mouse on the right received the growth hormone gene as an embryo and is twice normal size. (Photograph of mice provided by R.L. Brinster, Ph.D. University of Pennsylvania School of Veterinary Medicine, Philadelphia.)

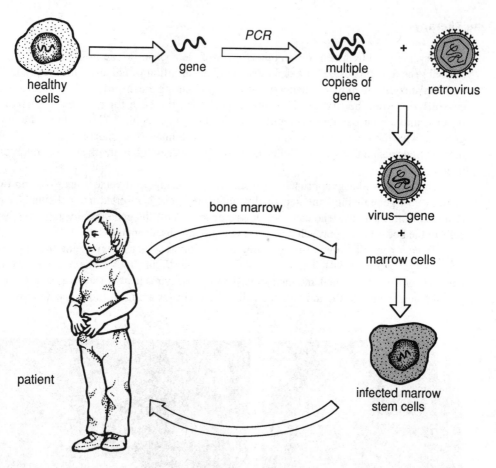

Figure 19.5. *Ex vivo* gene therapy. The gene coding for the deficient enzyme is obtained from healthy cells. Millions of copies of the gene are generated using a polymerase chain reaction (PCR) machine. These genes are then spliced onto the DNA of a retrovirus. For treatment of ADA deficiency (Bubble Baby syndrome), bone marrow cells are removed from the child and infected with the genetically modified virus. As a result the new gene is incorporated into the child's chromosomes and starts to code for the production of the missing ADA enzyme. The marrow cells are reinjected into the child's bone marrow. If things have gone according to plan, ADA will be produced by the child who will then be more resistant to infection.

they are inserted into the DNA of the cells that they infect.) This recombinant retrovirus is then used to infect cells that have been removed from the individual, typically bone marrow cells. If successful, the virus inserts the normal gene into these cells. These genetically altered cells are then reinfused into the individual with the expectation that they will express the gene and correct the metabolic derangement.

The first inborn error in which *ex vivo* gene therapy has been tested is adenosine deaminase (ADA) deficiency, a cause of severe combined immunodeficiency, also called Bubble Baby syndrome. *Ex vivo* gene therapy has proven successful in correcting this disorder, and the treated children appear to be less susceptible to infection (Blaese, Culver, Miller, et al., 1995).

Although the effects of *ex vivo* gene therapy appear to be long lasting, perhaps even permanent, the fact that only a small fraction of cells are corrected may limit efficacy. In addition, the theoretical risk of an individual developing cancer as new DNA is incorporated into the host DNA during the treatment is also worrisome.

An alternate approach is *in vivo* gene therapy, which is currently being developed for a number of inborn errors, including cystic fibrosis, muscular dystrophy, and OTC deficiency (Robinson, Batshaw, Ye, et al., 1995). In *in vivo* gene therapy, a genetically modified virus, most commonly an adenovirus (which is a cause of the common cold), is directly injected into the bloodstream. This approach does not require a surgical procedure, and virtually every cell in the body can be infected by the virus. However, with *in vivo* gene therapy, the virus is not incorporated into the individual's DNA, a feature that has both advantages and disadvantages. On the one hand, there is little risk of chromosomal damage, which could theoretically lead to cancer. On the other hand, because the gene is not permanently incorporated and there can be a host immune response to the virus, the gene is likely to be lost over time, making repeated gene transfers necessary.

Despite these technical problems and the fact that its importance as a treatment for inborn errors of metabolism remains to be proven, there is a great deal of enthusiasm for the prospects of gene therapy.

OUTCOME

The range of outcomes in inborn errors of metabolism varies enormously. In disorders that can be detected by newborn screening, affected children have generally done well. Their intellectual functioning falls within the average range, if somewhat lower than that of their parents; they are, however, at increased risk for having learning disabilities and ADHD (Levy et al., 1994). Less optimistic outcomes occur in inborn errors of amino acid and organic acid metabolism that are not detected early. Although these children are surviving longer, many manifest both mental retardation and cerebral palsy (Msall et al., 1984). Among children with metabolic disorders associated with progressive neurological disorders, such as lysosomal storage diseases, there has not been a significant improvement in mortality or morbidity.

A 1995 study attempted to evaluate the overall effectiveness of therapies for 65 inborn errors of metabolism (Treacy, Childs, & Scriver, 1995) by examining a number of parameters: longevity, reproductive ability, growth, intelligence, and ability to work independently (Figure 19.6). The study showed that about half of the disorders were completely or partially ameliorated by treatment.

LISA

Lisa was discharged from the hospital at 3 days of age. Her parents were surprised and upset to be called back a week later after doctors found Lisa to have a positive PKU screening test. Amino acid studies confirmed the diagnosis, and Lisa was placed on a low-phenylalanine formula. Her parents could hardly believe there was a problem because she looked and acted well and achieved her developmental milestones on time. The visits to the metabolism clinic were difficult reminders of her "silent disorder." Once Lisa entered elementary school, she began re-

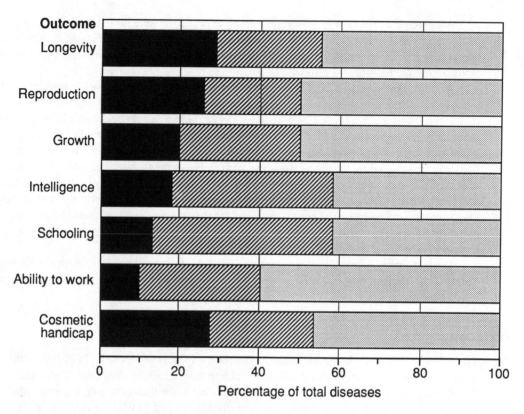

Figure 19.6.   Outcome studies in 1995 showed that about half of individuals with inborn errors of metabolism have benefited from therapy approaches in terms of improved longevity, reproduction, growth, intelligence, or ability to hold a job as adults. (Key: ■ = prevented adverse effects; ▨ = modified adverse effects; ▨ = unchanged adverse effects.)

sisting the restrictions on her diet, and her parents had difficulty maintaining good metabolic control. Lisa was born in 1970, when the importance of strict dietary control was not widespread knowledge. She stopped her diet at 7 years of age. Psychometric testing at 10 years of age showed that she had an IQ score of 85. Despite learning difficulties in school she graduated from high school and began a clerical job. She soon became pregnant but was not placed back on a low-phenylalanine diet. Her child was born with microcephaly and, at age 5, has mental retardation requiring limited supports. Fortunately, Lisa's younger sister Barbara, who also has PKU, is likely to have a happier story. She has remained on the low-phenylalanine diet continuously and intends to remain on the diet through her pregnancies.

DARNEL

Darnel babbled at 6 months and sat without support shortly thereafter. However, his parents became concerned by 1 year when he made no further progress. If anything, he seemed less steady in sitting and more uninvolved with his surroundings. His pediatrician worried that Darnel might have autism. By 18 months, there were graver concerns. Darnel was no longer able to roll over;

he was very floppy and did not appear to respond to light or sound. His pediatrician referred Darnel to a genetics clinic where an extensive workup eventually diagnosed Tay-Sachs disease. Over the next 3 years, Darnel slipped into an unresponsive condition and required tube-feeding. He finally succumbed to aspiration pneumonia. As a result of the diagnosis, his mother was able to undergo prenatal diagnosis in subsequent pregnancies. She now has two unaffected children and underwent one termination of an affected fetus.

SUMMARY

Although inborn errors of metabolism are rare, their consequences are often devastating. Fortunately, therapy is effective for a number of these disorders. However, affected children often must continue treatment for the rest of their lives, which may prove difficult to accomplish. For therapy to succeed, it must be started early. Researchers continue to look for new therapeutic strategies for these diseases, focusing on gene and enzyme replacement. It is hoped that these new therapeutic approaches will continue to improve outcomes for children with these disorders.

REFERENCES

Anderson, L.T., & Ernst, M. (1994). Self injury in Lesch-Nyhan disease. *Journal of Autism and Developmental Disorders, 24*(1), 67–81.

Azen, C.G., Koch, R., Friedman, E.G., et al. (1991). Intellectual development in 12-year-old children treated for phenylketonuria. *American Journal of Diseases of Children, 145,* 35–39.

Batshaw, M.L. (1994). Inborn errors of urea synthesis: A review. *Annals of Neurology, 35,* 133–141.

Batshaw, M.L., Brusilow, S., Waber, L., et al. (1982). Treatment of inborn errors of urea synthesis: Activation of alternative pathways of waste nitrogen synthesis and excretion. *New England Journal of Medicine, 306,* 1387–1392.

Batshaw, M.L., Robinson, M.B., Hyland, K., et al. (1993). Quinolinic acid in children with congenital hyperammonemia. *Annals of Neurology, 34,* 676–681.

Blaese, R.M., Culver, K.W., Miller, A.D., et al. (1995). T lymphocyte-directed gene therapy for ADA-SCID: Initial trial results after 4 years. *Science, 270,* 475–480.

Brown, F.R., Voigt, R., Singh, A.K., et al. (1993). Peroxisomal disorders. *American Journal of Diseases of Children, 147,* 617–626.

Brusilow, S.W., & Horwich, A.L. (1995). Urea cycle enzymes. In C.R. Scriver, A.L. Beaudet, W.S. Sly, & D. Valle (Eds.), *The metabolic and molecular bases of inherited disease* (7th ed., pp. 1187–1232). New York: McGraw-Hill.

Dhuna, A., Toro, C., Torres, F., et al. (1991). Longitudinal neurophysiologic studies in a patient with metachromatic leukodystrophy following bone marrow transplantation. *Archives of Neurology, 49*(10), 1088–1092.

Fisher, D.A. (1987). Effectiveness of newborn screening programs for congenital hypothyroidism: Prevalence of missed cases. *Pediatric Clinics of North America, 34,* 881–890.

Fölling, A. (1934). Excretion of phenylalanine in urine: An inborn error of metabolism associated with mental retardation. *Hoppe-Seyler's Z. Physiologie Chemistrie, 227,* 169–176.

Grossman, M., Raper, S.E., Kozarsky, K., et al. (1994). Successful ex vivo gene therapy directed to liver in a patient with familial hypercholesterolemia. *Nature Genetics, 6,* 335–341.

Guthrie, R., & Susi, A. (1963). A simple method for detecting phenylketonuria in large populations of newborn infants. *Pediatrics, 32,* 338–343.

Guttler, F. (1994, May 23–25). Phenylketonuria: Past, present, future: Preface of the proceedings of a symposium held in Elsinore, Denmark. *Acta Paediatrica, 83,* 1–3.

Hamosh, A., McDonald, J.W., Valle, D., et al. (1992). Dextromethorphan and high-dose benzoate therapy for nonketotic hyperglycinemia in an infant. *Journal of Pediatrics, 121,* 131–135.

Hanley, W.B., Linsao, L.S., & Netley, C. (1971). The efficiency of dietary therapy for phenylketonuria.

Canadian Medical Association Journal, 104, 1089.

Hoffmann, G.F., Trefz, F.K., Barth, P.G., et al. (1991). Glutaryl-CoA dehydrogenase deficiency: A distinct encephalopathy. Pediatrics, 88, 1194.

Kaback, M., Lim-Steele, J., Dabholkar, D., et al. (1993). Tay-Sachs disease-carrier screening, prenatal diagnosis, and the molecular era: An international perspective, 1970 to 1993: The International TSD Data Collection Network. Journal of the American Medical Association, 270(19), 2307–2315.

Kooistra, L., Laane, C., Vulsma, T., et al. (1994). Motor and cognitive development in children with congenital hypothyroidism: A long-term evaluation of the effects of neonatal treatment. Journal of Pediatrics, 124(6), 909.

Levy, H.L., Waisbren, S.E., Lobbregt, D., et al. (1994). Maternal mild hyperphenylalaninemia: An international survey of offspring outcome. Lancet, 344(8937), 1589–1594.

McCabe, E.R. (1994). DNA techniques for screening of inborn errors of metabolism. European Journal of Pediatrics, 153(Suppl. 7), S84–S85.

McDonald, J.W., & Johnston, M.V. (1990) Nonketotic hyperglycinemia: Pathophysiological role of NMDA-type excitatory amino acid receptors. Annals of Neurology, 27, 449–450.

Michals, K., Azen, C., Acosta, P., et al. (1988). Blood phenylalanine levels and intelligence of 10-year-old children with PKU in the national collaborative study. Journal of the American Dietetic Association, 88, 1226–1229.

Michalski, A.J., Berry, G.T., & Segal, S. (1989). Holocarboxylase synthetase deficiency: 9-year follow-up of a patient on chronic biotin therapy and a review of the literature. Journal of Inherited Metabolic Diseases, 5, 49.

Msall, M., Batshaw, M.L., Suss, R., et al. (1984). Neurologic outcome in children with inborn errors of urea synthesis: Outcome of urea-cycle enzymopathies. New England Journal of Medicine, 310, 1500–1505.

Nutrition Committee of the Canadian Paediatric Society. (1990). Megavitamin and megamineral therapy in childhood. Canadian Medical Association Journal, 143(10), 1009–1013.

Palmiter, R.D., Norstedt, G., Gelinas, R.E., et al. (1983). Metallothionein-Human GH fusion genes stimulate growth of mice. Science, 222, 809–814.

Pridjian, G., Humbert, J., Willis, J., et al. (1994). Presymptomatic late-infantile metachromatic leukodystrophy treated with bone marrow transplantation. Journal of Pediatrics, 125, 755–758.

Robinson, M.B., Batshaw, M.L., Ye, S., et al. (1995). Prospects for gene therapy in ornithine carbamoyltransferase deficiency and other urea cycle disorders. Mental Retardation and Developmental Disabilities Research Reviews, 1, 62–70.

Rodriguez-Pena, A., Ibarrola, N., Iniguez, M.A., et al. (1993). Neonatal hyperthyroidism affects the timely expression of myelin-associated glycoprotein in the rat brain. Journal of Clinical Investigation, 91(3), 812–818.

Rosenthal, D.I., Doppelt, S.H., Mankin, H.J., et al. (1995). Enzyme replacement therapy for Gaucher disease: Skeletal responses to macrophage-targeted glucocerobrosidase. Pediatrics, 96, 629–637.

Scriver, C.R., Kaufman, S., Eisensmith, R.C., et al. (1995). The hyperphenylaninemias. In C.R. Scriver, A.L. Beaudet, W.S. Sly, & D. Valle (Eds.), The metabolic and molecular bases of inherited disease (7th ed., pp. 1015–1076). New York: McGraw-Hill.

Shih, V.E. (1976). Hereditary urea-cycle disorders. In S. Grisolia, R. Baguena, & F. Mayor (Eds.), The urea cycle (pp. 367–414). New York: John Wiley & Sons.

Suhr, S.T., & Gage, F.H. (1993). Gene therapy for neurologic disease. Archives of Neurology, 50, 1252–1268.

Tada, K., Kure, S., Takayanagi, M., et al. (1992). Nonketotic hyperglycinemia: A life-threatening disorder in the neonate. Early Human Development, 29(1–3), 75–81.

Treacy, E., Childs, B., & Scriver, C.R. (1995). Response to treatment in hereditary metabolic disease: 1993 survey and 10-year comparison [Review]. American Journal of Human Genetics, 56(2), 359–367.

Waisbren, S.E., Brown, M.J., de Sonneville, L.M., et al. (1994). Review of neuropsychological functioning in treated phenylketonuria: An information processing approach. Acta Paediatrica (Suppl.), 407, 98–103.

Waisbren, S.E., Mahon, B.E., Schnell, R.R., et al. (1987). Predictors of intelligence quotient and intelligence quotient change in persons treated for phenylketonuria early in life. Pediatrics, 79, 351–355.

Winter, S.C. (1993). Diagnosing metabolic disorders: One step at a time. Contemporary Pediatrics, 10, 35–63.

Wolfe, J.H. (1994). Recent progress in gene therapy for inherited diseases. Current Opinion in Pediatrics, 6(2), 213–218.

20 Dual Diagnosis
Mental Retardation and Psychiatric Disorders

Mark Reber
Breck G. Borcherding

Upon completion of this chapter, the reader will:

- understand why individuals with mental retardation have a relatively high prevalence of psychiatric disorders
- be able to describe the types of psychiatric disorders and symptomatology among people with mental retardation
- be knowledgeable about interventions for children who have a dual diagnosis

Children with mental retardation may be affected not only by their cognitive impairments, but also by emotional and behavioral disturbances that limit their ability to adapt, learn, develop socially, and become independent. When these disturbances are of sufficient severity, they may constitute a diagnosable psychiatric disorder, a cluster of symptoms associated with a significant impairment in thought, feelings, or behavior. Accepted definitions of, and criteria for, specific psychiatric disorders are contained in the *Diagnostic and Statistical Manual of Mental Disorders, Fourth Edition* (DSM-IV) (American Psychiatric Association, 1994). Some of the more common or disabling psychiatric disorders are described in this chapter.

For decades, emotional and behavior problems in people with mental retardation were simplistically attributed to nonspecific behavior problems or symptoms of the mental retardation. Since the 1980s, however, the concept of a **dual diagnosis** has evolved to refer to individuals with mental retardation who also have a separately diagnosed psychiatric disorder (Lovell & Reiss, 1993). This conceptualization of coexisting developmental and psychiatric diagnoses has been a step forward, opening up an array of treatment options. It is important that professionals who work with children with mental retardation consider the possibility of a second, psychiatric, diagnosis, especially when new behavior or emotional problems arise (Dosen, 1993), although an individual's cognitive impairments might make delineation of psychiatric symptoms difficult. Left untreated, psychiatric disorders create great difficulties for both the individual and his or her family, and they are the most common cause for out-of-home placement of children with mental retardation.

A HISTORICAL PERSPECTIVE

In the early part of the 20th century, therapeutic pessimism prevailed among mental health professionals with regard to individuals with mental retardation. The treatment approaches used by most psychiatrists were thought to be inappropriate for people with cognitive impairments. Individuals with mental retardation requiring extensive support were commonly housed in wards of mental hospitals or special residential facilities and given tranquilizing drugs to control aberrant behaviors. With the exception of a few practitioners, most psychiatrists did not attempt to make careful diagnoses in people with mental retardation, and many individuals were inappropriately classified as having schizophrenia. Since the 1960s, however, there has been a more rigorous attempt to diagnose and appropriately treat psychiatric disorders in the general population, which has influenced the care of individuals with mental retardation as well (Ratey & Gualtieri, 1991).

PREVALENCE AND CAUSES OF PSYCHIATRIC DISORDERS

In their landmark study of the epidemiology of childhood psychiatric disorders on the Isle of Wight, Rutter, Graham, and Yule (1970) found emotional disturbances in 7%–10% of typically developing children. Yet 30%–42% of children with mental retardation demonstrated psychiatric disorders (Rutter et al., 1970). Additional studies have confirmed these results (Borthwick-Duffy, 1994; Bregman, 1991; Crews, Bonaventura, & Rowe, 1994). Epidemiological studies have further indicated that psychiatric problems do not decline in severity as these children grow into adulthood.

Children both with and without mental retardation are at risk for the same types of psychiatric disorders. Maladaptive behavior disorders, however—stereotypic movement disorder (i.e., repetitive, self-stimulating, self-injurious behavior [SIB]) and pica (i.e., the persistent ingesting of nonfood items)—are found principally among individuals with mental retardation requiring extensive to pervasive supports.

In some cases, psychiatric disorders in individuals with mental retardation are a direct result of a biochemical abnormality. For example, in Lesch-Nyhan syndrome, an inborn error of metabolism, there are abnormalities in the dopamine neurotransmitter system causing affected individuals to exhibit a compulsive form of SIB. Psychiatric disorders, however, are typically more likely to be caused by an interaction among biological, environmental, and psychosocial factors. For example, an adolescent boy recovering from traumatic brain injury (TBI) may develop depression as a result of a combination of neurotransmitter alterations induced by the brain injury, a familial predisposition to depression, and his concern about postinjury peer acceptance.

In other cases, biological factors merely increase an individual's vulnerability to life's stresses. Phenomena that often accompany mental retardation, such as traumatic social experiences (e.g., stigmatization, rejection by age mates and society at large); certain temperamental features (e.g., inadequate adaptability to new situations, poor concentration); and educational failure may increase the likelihood of psychiatric disorders. It also has been suggested that the kinds of family dysfunction and social adversity that can contribute to emotional disturbances in typically developing children have a greater impact on children with mental retardation because of their limited understanding and problem-solving abilities, greater need for support, and temperaments that make them less able to cope with such stress. Their family structures, in turn, may be more fragile because of the experience of having a child with mental retardation (Corbett, 1985). Limited availability of, or access to, community resources and services may increase stress on families and exacerbate minor emotional disturbances. Finally, individuals with mental retardation often experience genuine powerlessness, which greatly increases psychosocial distress. Individuals with severe impairments may have difficulty communicating their needs and desires, and many are at increased risk for emotional and sexual exploitation and abuse (Menolascino, 1990).

DIAGNOSIS

Children and adolescents with mental retardation are an extremely diverse group with widely varying skills and impairments and an enormous number of accompanying medical and neurological disorders (or no organic illness at all). Each person with mental retardation is unique, as are the ways in which psychiatric disturbances manifest themselves. Certain generalities, however, can be drawn. Children and adolescents with mental retardation requiring intermittent to limited support, for example, usually exhibit the same psychiatric symptoms as typically developing children. Thus, the same diagnostic criteria and descriptors prescribed in the DSM-IV can be used. Among people with mental retardation requiring extensive or pervasive supports, psychiatric disorders may present atypically, making diagnosis much more difficult. Some argue that the DSM-IV diagnoses are not valid for this population and have proposed that a new system of diagnostic categories and descriptors be developed (Einfeld & Aman, 1995). Although some experts have offered modified formulations of diagnostic criteria to be used specifically with people with mental retardation (Sovner, 1986), most psychiatrists diagnose all individuals according to DSM-IV criteria. The following sections describe symptoms of several major psychiatric diagnoses and severe behavior disorders that may present in young people with mental retardation.

AFFECTIVE DISORDERS

Affective or mood disorders have been well described in individuals with mental retardation (Johnson, Handen, Lubetsky, et al., 1995). Researchers estimate that 5%–15% of individuals with mental retardation, compared with 2%–5% of the general population, have affective or mood disorders. There are three classical syndromes of disturbed mood: **dysthymia, major depression,** and **bipolar disorder.**

Dysthymia is characterized in DSM-IV by 2 years of chronic low-grade depressive symptoms (1 year in children and adolescents) that lead to significant functional impairments (American Psychiatric Association, 1994; Jancar & Gunaratne, 1994). These symptoms are typically of a lesser magnitude than those required for a diagnosis of major depression.

Major depression, a common diagnosis, can present as a single episode or a repetitive series of discrete episodes. Prominent symptoms include emotional withdrawal, diminished interest in activities of daily living, problems with sleep and appetite, poor concentration, feelings of worthlessness, inappropriate guilt, and recurrent thoughts of death or suicide (Table 20.1). When

Table 20.1. Symptoms of psychiatric disorders in children with mental retardation

---

Major depression (in mental retardation requiring extensive support)
Change in pattern of physical activity
Change in sleep pattern
Feeding problems
Increase in challenging behaviors (aggression, self-injury, stereotypies)
Loss of interest or pleasure in daily routines
Persistent depressed or irritable mood
Withdrawal from social interactions

Major depression (in mental retardation requiring intermittent to limited support)
Change in appetite and/or weight
Diminished ability to concentrate
Fatigue or loss of energy
Feelings of worthlessness or guilt
Insomnia or excessive sleeping
Loss of interest in school and extracurricular activities
Persistent feelings of sadness, despair
Recurrent irritable or withdrawn behavior
Recurrent thoughts of death or suicide

Mania
Decreased frustration tolerance and increased aggression
Decreased need for sleep
Elevation of mood together with grandiose or paranoid thoughts
Heightened sexual arousal (increased masturbatory or inappropriate sexual activity)
Increased motor restlessness and agitation

Schizophrenia
Catatonic behavior
Delusions
Flat or inappropriate emotional expression
Hallucinations
Loosening of associations in speech

Obsessive-compulsive disorder
Repetitive purposeful behaviors performed in response to obsessions
Persistent thoughts that are senseless

---

severe, major depression can be associated with psychosis and suicidal behavior. While vulnerability to depression has a hereditary component, a depressive episode is commonly precipitated by life stresses.

Bipolar disorder (commonly called manic-depression) refers to a condition in which a person has episodes of both **mania** and depression. During a manic phase, an individual experiences an altered state of mood and behavior for a distinct period of time. Symptoms include an elevated, expansive, or irritable mood. For example, an individual might have inflated self-esteem, decreased need for sleep, excessive or pressured talking, distractibility, a feeling that one's thoughts are racing, and excessive involvement in pleasurable activities that have potentially harmful consequences (e.g., promiscuous sexual behavior). During a depressed phase, a person may experience all the symptoms of major depression. Periods of mania typically alternate with periods of depression, although in children symptoms of a mixed mood state may be present. Bipolar disorder appears to have a strong hereditary component, and a gene locus has been reported in certain families (Byerley, Holik, Hoff, et al., 1995).

Syndromes of disturbed mood may be hidden or overlooked in people with mental retardation (Johnson et al., 1995). Sleep or appetite problems often go unnoticed, and fluctuations in such symptoms as noncompliance, social withdrawal, aggressiveness, irritability, self-injury, or crying spells are often assumed to be components of the mental retardation rather than a separate disorder. In order to identify mood disorders in people with mental retardation, professionals should question individuals and their caregivers about changes in, or the episodic nature of, symptoms (Rojahn, Warren, & Ohringer, 1994).

ANXIETY DISORDERS

Anxiety disorders, among the most common psychiatric problems, are associated with feelings of emotional uneasiness and a sense of anticipated danger. Clinical findings include excessive fear, **phobias,** general anxiety, and excessive vigilance. There is a strong hereditary component to the development of anxiety disorders and children and adolescents with mental retardation can develop **panic** symptoms and phobias much like their typically developing siblings. However, these symptoms must be distinguished from usual but delayed stages in the child's emotional development (e.g., persistence of a preschooler's typical social anxiety, fear of separation from parents). At times, however, these children may exhibit **separation anxiety** that is unacceptable for their developmental level, most commonly presenting as school phobia.

The prevalence of **obsessive-compulsive disorder (OCD),** an anxiety disorder with a biological basis, has historically been underestimated but is now receiving increasing notice (Bodfish, Crawford, Powell, et al., 1995). Individuals with OCD have recurrent and persistent thoughts or ideas that may be quite bizarre but cannot be suppressed, even when the individual is aware of their inappropriate nature. Often these obsessive thoughts are associated with compulsive behaviors or repetitive rituals, such as compulsive touching or excessive hand washing.

PSYCHOSIS

The classical symptoms of psychosis—confused thinking, delusions, and hallucinations—may be seen with severe depression, mania, or **delirium.** (Delirium is the sudden onset of confusion associated with TBI, drug toxicity, or severe medical disorders such as encephalitis that acutely affect brain function.) Although these symptoms also can occur in typically developing individuals as a reaction to an extremely stressful situation, they are usually symptomatic of **schizophrenia.**

Schizophrenia is a chronic condition, typically characterized by a deterioration in functional level; prominent hallucinations; delusions (i.e., false beliefs that are often quite bizarre); incoherence; catatonia (i.e., muscle rigidity and stupor); and grossly inappropriate emotional expression. An individual must exhibit these symptoms for at least 6 months to receive a diagnosis of schizophrenia. The more severe manifestations are usually preceded by a period of social withdrawal, apparent loss of skills, peculiar behaviors, altered thought and speech, poor self-care, lack of initiative, and odd ideas. In individuals with mental retardation requiring extensive support, behavior deterioration and severe disorganization may be the only presenting symptoms. Adolescence is the typical age for the onset of schizophrenia, although it can occur in younger children. Many children formerly diagnosed as having "childhood schizophrenia," however, are now understood to have had pervasive developmental disorders (PDDs) (Werry, 1996).

DISORDERS OF SOCIAL COMMUNICATION (PERVASIVE DEVELOPMENTAL DISORDERS)

PDDs involve poor reciprocal social interactions, problems with communication, and impaired imagination (according to one's mental-age level). It is estimated that one fourth of the individuals with mental retardation requiring extensive supports have PDDs (see Chapter 21) (Bregman, 1991).

ATTENTION-DEFICIT/HYPERACTIVITY DISORDER

Children with mental retardation are diagnosed as having attention-deficit/hyperactivity disorder (ADHD) (see Chapter 22) if they exhibit hyperactivity, impulsivity, and inattentiveness that are developmentally inappropriate for their mental ages and associated with marked functional impairments (Handen, McAuliffe, Janosky, et al., 1994). Approximately 11% of individuals with mental retardation have ADHD, almost double the prevalence in typically developing children (Gillberg, Persson, Grufman, et al., 1986). Physicians and psychologists experienced in evaluating children with mental retardation use clinical examinations, parent and teacher behavior rating scales, clinical history, and, when indicated, direct observations in school to establish the diagnosis (see Chapter 22).

ADJUSTMENT DISORDERS

Acute short-term reactions to stress are classified in the DSM-IV as **adjustment disorders** and defined by anxiety or disturbances in conduct or mood (American Psychiatric Association, 1994). These maladaptive reactions to an identifiable stressful event include mildly disturbed emotions or behaviors that lead to short-term functional impairment. Although not proven, it seems likely that these disorders are more common in individuals with mental retardation because of their decreased ability to adapt to stress.

POSTTRAUMATIC STRESS DISORDER

An individual may experience a stressor that is severe enough to involve the threat of serious harm or death and is associated with feelings of intense fear or helplessness. If subsequently the individual develops recurrent and intrusive recollections of the stressful event, nightmares, and intense emotional distress in situations or at times that remind the individual of the trauma, then he or she is diagnosed as having **posttraumatic stress disorder (PTSD)** (Ryan, 1994). Diagnosis of this disorder often depends on a description of the symptoms, which may be difficult to elicit from a person with mental retardation who has limited verbal skills. As a result, the prevalence of PTSD among children and adolescents with mental retardation is unclear. As these individuals are prone to victimization, however, the disorder is probably not uncommon. Symptoms of PTSD may follow rape, sexual molestation, physical abuse, or a terrifying situation that is beyond the individual's capacity to understand or a caregiver's ability to explain. In all instances, efforts must be made to try to determine the cause and nature of the traumatic event and to protect the child from its recurrence.

CONDUCT DISORDERS

Children with conduct disorders display aggressive, destructive, and rule-violating behaviors in repetitive and persistent patterns. These behaviors include bullying, intimidating others, initiating fights, setting fires, deliberately destroying other people's property, stealing, and truancy. Children tend to have conduct disorders when there are models for this kind of behavior in their families or communities, inadequate educational and extracurricular programming in their schools, social neglect or abuse, or detrimental peer influences.

The term conduct disorder, which is defined as the violation of social norms and rules, should not be used to describe someone who cannot comprehend the nature of such rules; these are usually referred to as conduct problems. It is estimated that 12%–45% of individuals with mental retardation have conduct problems. This generally presents as episodic aggressive, destructive, and disruptive behavior (Bregman, 1991). These problems often result from their inability to verbalize feelings and poor impulse control (Lovell & Reiss, 1993). Depression, pain, fear, and impaired communication skills may also lead to conduct problems in these children. It is important to interpret the behaviors in light of the child's mental age (i.e., tantrums that usually disappear after the preschool years may typically persist into adolescence and lead to aggressive and destructive behavior in a child with mental retardation requiring extensive supports).

SUBSTANCE ABUSE DISORDERS

Substance abuse (e.g., alcohol abuse) is a problem among individuals with mental retardation requiring intermittent supports, especially during adolescence. The same genetic and familial factors that make typically developing adolescents susceptible to substance abuse also influence those with mental retardation (see Chapter 8). In addition, certain conditions associated with mental retardation, primarily fetal alcohol syndrome, appear to confer a predisposition to substance abuse. Furthermore, immature judgment, impulsiveness, and a desire for social acceptance may lead individuals with mental retardation to experiment with alcohol or other drugs of abuse (Tyas & Rush, 1993).

There is, however, no evidence that the prior use of psychoactive drugs, such as stimulant medications for ADHD, increases the risk of later substance abuse. The best treatment for substance abuse is prevention through education, starting in elementary school. Once an alcohol or other drug abuse problem does arise, however, the individual should be immediately referred to competent substance abuse specialists.

MALADAPTIVE BEHAVIOR DISORDERS

Some individuals with mental retardation requiring extensive supports develop severe behavioral symptoms that simply cannot be classified by the diagnostic schema for people without developmental disabilities. These symptoms, which include repetitive self-stimulating behavior, SIB, and pica in fact, rarely occur in the typically developing population.

Individuals who engage in SIB generally display a specific pattern for producing injury. They may bang their heads, bite their hands, pick at their skin, hit themselves with their fists, or poke their eyes. They may do this once or twice a day, in association with tantrums, or up to several hundred times an hour. Tissue destruction, infection, internal injury, loss of vision, and even death may result. These behaviors may be accompanied by additional repetitive, stereotyped behaviors, such as hand waving and body rocking. When these repetitive behaviors interfere with activities of daily living or result in significant injury to the individual, a diagnosis of **stereotypic movement disorder** (formerly called stereotypy-habit disorder) is made.

Although serious SIB occurs in fewer than 5% of people with mental retardation, these behaviors are important to recognize and diagnose because they cause enormous distress to the individuals and their caregivers, can result in severe body injury, and may lead to institutionalization, with the separation of the individual from the family and from other social contacts. Some children with SIB also demonstrate severe aggressive behavior toward their caregivers or peers.

The underlying cause of SIB varies among individuals and may include both environmental and biological factors (Buitelaar, 1993). Some children may exhibit SIB as a result of environmental events (i.e., operant control) (Loschen & Osman, 1992). For example, a nonverbal girl's head banging may be reinforced once she learns that this action captures the attention she craves. Some children manifest symptoms of SIB because of a co-morbid psychiatric disorder such as autism, depression, mania, or schizophrenia. A third group of children may exhibit SIB as a consequence of a medical condition. For example, a painful middle-ear infection may lead to head banging. Defining the subgroup is important in designing effective treatment (Sternberg, Taylor, & Babkie, 1994).

Although the brain mechanisms underlying most forms of SIB remain unknown, several neurotransmitters are thought to be involved. These include dopamine, which mediates certain reinforcement systems in the brain; serotonin, depletion of which is sometimes associated with violent behavior; gamma-aminobutyric acid (GABA), an inhibitory neurotransmitter; and opioids, the brain's natural painkillers. This information can be used in choosing specific pharmacotherapy for behavior that appears to be under biological rather than behavioral control.

Pica, the persistent craving and ingesting of nonfood items, is a typical behavior for toddlers. When children older than 2 years display pica, professionals should explore the possibility that the child has a psychiatric disorder or nutritional deficiency, although pica in older children can also be a typical behavior in mental retardation requiring extensive supports. Irrespective of the cause, pica can seriously affect a child's well-being. It can result in toxicity from ingested materials such as lead-containing plaster or paint chips or medications. It also can cause physical damage to the individual's gastrointestinal tract, for example, when an obstruction from an ingested hair ball blocks the intestine or swallowing corrosive cleaning chemicals causes esophageal damage (Decker, 1993). Behavior management techniques have been found to be the most effective treatment for pica (Johnson, Hunt, & Siebert, 1994).

ASSOCIATED MEDICAL PROBLEMS

It is important to note that many of the symptoms of a psychiatric disorder can actually be caused by a variety of medical disorders or treatments. For example, hypothyroidism, common in individuals with Down syndrome, can cause emotional disturbances that are exhibited as anxiety or depression. In excessive doses, drugs used to treat associated impairments (e.g., antiepileptic drugs) can cause symptoms that appear as hyperactivity or depression. Careful evaluation for medical conditions or drug reactions should be a part of any assessment of new-onset behavioral or psychiatric symptoms.

GENETIC SYNDROMES AND BEHAVIORAL PHENOTYPES

There are several genetic syndromes that have behavioral phenotypes (a group of psychiatric symptoms that occurs in most affected individuals) including fragile X syndrome, Rett syndrome, Prader-Willi syndrome, and Lesch-Nyhan syndrome (O'Brien & Yule, 1996).

Males with fragile X syndrome (see Chapter 18) have mental retardation and a behavioral phenotype that includes poor eye contact, communication impairments, and stereotyped movements. They also may exhibit hyperactivity and SIB. Heterozygous females, who manifest a less severe form of the syndrome and have only modest cognitive impairments, often exhibit shyness, impulsivity, distractibility, and a personality disorder. It remains to be determined whether the differing amounts of abnormal genetic material in males and females with fragile X syndrome correlate with the severity of the behavioral phenotype.

Girls with Rett syndrome, an X-linked dominant progressive neurological disorder (see Chapter 21), display certain features of autism early in the course of the disorder. The most prominent characteristic behaviors are a loss of purposeful hand movements and the onset of stereotypical hand wringing and hand flapping, often accompanied by hyperventilation.

Prader-Willi syndrome, which is associated with a microdeletion of chromosome #15 (Knoll, Wagstoff, & Lalande, 1993), is usually accompanied by decreased muscle tone, short stature, obesity, mental retardation requiring limited supports, underdeveloped gonads, and a particular facial appearance with almond-shaped, upslanting eyes, and a narrow forehead. Behavioral symptoms relate to the striking obesity seen in these children who will demand, steal, and even forage for food. These feeding behaviors are often accompanied by impulsiveness, obstinacy, and disinhibition (Curfs & Fryns, 1992). Research indicates that the insatiable overeating results from a lack of a feeling of satiation, derived from an abnormality in the hypothalamic region of the brain. Their overeating is treated with diet, behavior management techniques, and anorexogenic medications.

Lesch-Nyhan syndrome is an X-linked disorder associated with a disturbance in the metabolism of purines, the building blocks of DNA. In addition to having mental retardation and a progressive neurological disorder, affected boys compulsively bite their lips and fingers (Anderson & Ernst, 1994; Matthews, Solan, & Barabas, 1995). Studies of brain chemistry have found specific abnormalities in the neurotransmitters dopamine and serotonin, which are known to cause self-injury in animal models. Unfortunately, medications that affect these neurotransmitters have not achieved much success (Roscioni, Farnetani, Pagini, et al., 1994).

Other examples of genetic disorders with characteristic behavioral phenotypes are Williams syndrome, in which affected individuals demonstrate mental retardation requiring limited support and a superficial sociability described as "cocktail party" speech (Udwin & Yule, 1990), and Down syndrome, which may be associated with the development of dementia in young adulthood (see Chapter 17) (Holland, 1994).

EVALUATION

Psychiatric needs can be met only if parents, teachers, and other staff who work with children with disabilities are attuned to the possible existence of emotional disturbances. Ideally, the referral for evaluation should be made to mental health professionals (psychiatrists, psychologists, social workers) with specific training, experience, and expertise in the psychiatric problems of children with mental retardation and other developmental disabilities. Often this requires referral to a specialized, tertiary care center with a multidisciplinary team. Less experienced mental health professionals who undertake such evaluations should have the opportunity to obtain consultation from a specialized center if needed.

The mental health professional will first take a detailed history of the current symptoms and aberrant behaviors from parents or other caregivers. For example, identification of recent changes in sleep pattern, appetite, or mood provides important evidence of depression. In addition, an individual and family medical history should be obtained. The family history may reveal, for example, other members with depression. A review of the individual's past medical and psychological assessments may indicate prior behavior or psychiatric problems. Following the history taking, an interview is conducted posing both structured and open-ended questions to the child and parents. If communication and cognitive skills impairments are significant, the professional can still gain important information from the direct observation of the child both alone and in the presence of the parents (King, DeAntonio, McCracken, et al., 1994).

The evaluation should also focus on the social system in which the psychiatric problem occurs. Thus, the professional should evaluate the current level of family functioning by assessing 1) the family's ability to cope with both the child's psychiatric disorder and therapy; 2) their current morale, problem-solving abilities, external social supports, and practical resources (e.g., finances, insurance); 3) the system of beliefs that sustains their efforts; and 4) the marital stability of the parents. It is important to understand how individual family members are reacting and adjusting to the child's underlying developmental disability as well as any current mental health problems (see Chapter 34).

Following the psychiatric interview, the child may be referred for psychological testing or behavior assessment. Although psychiatric rating scales are available for use in people with mental retardation, they are inadequate by themselves as diagnostic tools (Demb, Brier, Huron, et al., 1994; Linaker & Helle, 1994; Reiss & Valenti-Hein, 1994). The range of developmental levels and behavioral baselines exhibited by these individuals cannot be covered by a single structured psychological testing instrument. However, these instruments are useful in confirming information obtained from the history and interview. They also are helpful in assessing changes that occur during the course of treatment.

This testing may be combined with a functional behavior analysis. This type of assessment is extremely helpful for children with severe behavioral abnormalities for which specific family or behavior therapies are being considered. Behavior analysis provides direct observation of the child in a natural setting, yielding a clear description of the abnormal behavior itself and its antecedents and consequences (see Chapter 30).

After the evaluations have been completed, the professional can begin to work to formulate a treatment plan based not only on the psychiatric diagnosis, but also on the developmental level of the child, accompanying medical conditions, and the family's strengths and weaknesses.

TREATMENT

The foundation for treating a child or adolescent with both mental retardation and a psychiatric disorder is a comprehensive plan that addresses rehabilitation and education, the child's emotional needs, social stressors, the family's need for support, and the specific psychiatric diagnosis and behavior problems (Dosen, 1993). Implementing such a plan involves interdisciplinary teamwork incorporating various treatment approaches including special education programs, rehabilitation therapy, psychotherapy, social skills training, behavior therapy, and pharmacological management.

Special Education Programs

Because the educational setting can help or hinder therapy, it is essential that the school be part of the therapy program and that collaboration and communication among teachers, parents, and therapists be encouraged. Small class size with one-to-one supervision is most advantageous to children with dual diagnoses because, in these settings, the teacher can record behaviors, incorporate behavior management techniques, and provide emotional support. Teachers can also modify the curriculum to decrease stress and give the student a positive learning experience. The guidance counselor also may be able to provide supportive counseling. If the class is large and the teacher is unaware of the child's emotional problems, the child may experience school failure, which can have adverse consequences on behavior and emotions.

Rehabilitation Therapy

Rehabilitation therapy programs can have a positive impact on the child with dual diagnosis. There is evidence that language impairments significantly contribute to the development of certain behavior problems. Some aggressive and self-injurious behaviors have been linked to the inability to communicate needs, and it has been shown that SIB can be decreased by teaching functional communication skills. Thus, speech-language therapy and alternative communication systems may be an important part of the therapy program. Similarly, if the child has a physical disability, the pain from contractures, an inability to ambulate, or difficulty reaching for desired objects may lead to behavior and mood alterations. Physical and occupational therapy may result in an improvement in motor function, with associated improvement in behavior and mood.

Psychotherapy

There is ample evidence that psychotherapy (individual, group, and family) can benefit children and adolescents with dual diagnoses if it is adapted to the child's mental age and communication abilities (Hollins, Sinason, & Thompson, 1994; Nezu & Nezu, 1994; Sigman, 1985). Regrettably, individuals with mental retardation are seriously underserved in this area, despite the fact that psychotherapy can provide a supportive relationship, help restore self-esteem, promote social skills, and enhance the capacity to recognize and master emotional conflicts and solve problems. Psychotherapy also can be an adjunctive treatment, added to behavior therapy and pharmacotherapy when these approaches have not produced adequate resolution of symptoms or a good quality of life. Ideally, the therapist should be one who has expertise in working with individuals with mental retardation.

Social Skills Training

Social skills involve the ability to interact appropriately with parents, peers, teachers, other caregivers, and community members. Social skills impairments may be secondary to developmental delay or disability, or part of a psychiatric disorder (e.g., PDD). Social skills training may include practice in maintaining eye contact, smiling, and sharing with peers. It also may involve learning to display appropriate signs of affection and to become aware of others' emotions and feelings (Lovell & Reiss, 1993). Social skills training generally is provided in groups to give a social context for the modeling (Cox & Schopler, 1991).

Behavior Therapy

Behavior therapy is perhaps the most widely researched therapeutic intervention for children and adolescents with mental retardation (see Chapter 30). This approach comprises many different types of treatment that complement and enhance education and rehabilitation. Behavior therapy involves the data-based assessment of individual behaviors as they occur in a person's natural social environment, with attention paid to prior conditions and subsequent events. The underlying assumption is that all behavior is functional and exists only because it effects a purpose or results in a rewarding consequence. The general strategy of behavior therapy is to minimize the reinforcement that has been shown to support inappropriate behavior and to provide rewards for adaptive responses that compete with this behavior. This kind of therapy has been effective in treating problems such as SIB (Matson & Gardner, 1991) and is also used to teach self-help, vocational, leisure, social, community survival, and communication skills.

Behavior therapy, which is based on an **operant model,** is commonly called behavior management (or modification). With this model, behavior therapists use an assessment called a functional analysis to attempt to quantitatively identify the variables that maintain the behavior. They then manipulate these variables to confirm that they are, in fact, controlling the behavior. Interventions are then designed based on the functional analysis.

Another conditioning model for behavior, **cognitive-behavior therapy,** can be combined with behavior management in treating individuals with emotional disorders. This type of treatment can be used, for example, with individuals with mental retardation who have a relatively high level of functioning but experience anxiety disorders, such as phobias, OCD, or depression. In a cognitive-behavioral approach, emotional responses that have been learned or conditioned by past experiences are relieved by a variety of techniques. For example, children who engage in compulsive rituals, such as excessive hand washing, learn cognitive techniques (helpful thoughts) to master feelings of anxiety that arise when they are not permitted to wash their hands. They are then exposed to a situation that would usually lead to hand washing but resist the compulsion while using the cognitive techniques until they begin to experience a lessening or "deconditioning" of the anxiety. When effective, the result is a diminished compulsion to wash.

There is extensive literature supporting the effectiveness of behavioral approaches in psychiatric disorders (National Institutes of Health, 1989). When used in conjunction with comprehensive assessment, accurate medical and psychiatric diagnoses, and programmatic intervention, behavior therapy is among the most powerful available interventions. However, like psychotherapy and pharmacotherapy, it should be implemented only under the supervision of licensed professionals who have been specifically trained in this methodology.

Pharmacological Management

Since the 1970s, pharmacotherapy has become an established mode of treatment for psychiatric disorders in children and adolescents (Baumeister, Todd, & Sevin, 1993; Campbell & Cueva, 1995a, b). Although most guidelines for using psychoactive medicines come from studies performed with adults without mental retardation, a few well-controlled studies of the efficacy of pharmacological treatment of psychiatric disorders among children with and without mental retardation have been conducted. It appears that both typically developing children and children with mental retardation may respond to drug treatments for psychiatric disorders in much the same way.

There is concern about the overuse or inappropriate use of psychoactive medications with individuals with mental retardation because of incidents in the 1950s involving the abuse of major tranquilizers in institutions for the purpose of behavior control (Aman & Singh, 1988). Now, appropriate use of pharmacotherapy assumes that a comprehensive medical and psychiatric evaluation has been completed, a psychiatric diagnosis has been made, and the medication has been selected because of its known effects in relieving target symptoms associated with the psychiatric diagnosis. As indicated previously, the use of medicine should be only one part of a comprehensive treatment plan (Schaal & Hackenberg, 1994). Still, it is impossible to predict whether a particular medicine will be helpful to a specific patient or whether side effects may prove to be intolerable in that individual. In the clinical situation, even medicines that have been appropriately selected are used empirically, with ongoing observation to determine if they have the intended salutary effect and are well tolerated by the patient (Towbin, 1995).

Antidepressants are used to treat major depression, dysthymia, anxiety disorders, and ADHD in children. Unfortunately, most studies of antidepressant use in people with mental retardation have not been well controlled (see Bregman, 1995, for a comprehensive review of these agents). There are mixed results reported with the use of older antidepressant agents such as imipramine (Tofranil) and desipramine (Norpramin) for treating depression and anxiety in individuals with mental retardation, as well as with newer agents such as the **serotonin reuptake inhibitor** drugs fluoxetine (Prozac), sertraline (Zoloft), and paroxetine (Paxil) (Bodfish & Madison, 1993; Troisi, Vicario, Nuccetelli, et al., 1995). These newer medications, however, appear to have much lower risks and fewer serious side effects, making fluoxetine or sertraline common treatments for depression.

Obsessive-compulsive behaviors in otherwise typical adults and children are significantly lessened by the use of clomipramine (Anafranil), an agent that affects the neurotransmitter serotonin (Garber, McGonigle, Slomka, et al., 1992). Similarly, some stereotypic behavior problems seen in autism and in the more severe forms of mental retardation are also responsive to serotonergic medications (Bodfish & Madison, 1993; Cook, Rowlett, Jaselskis, et al., 1992; Gordon, State, Nelson, et al., 1993), and it is now common to use serotonin reuptake inhibitors to treat these symptoms.

Stimulant medications such as methylphenidate (Ritalin) and dextroamphetamine (Dexedrine), known to be effective in treating symptoms of ADHD in typically developing children, have also been proven effective in children with mental retardation requiring intermittent to limited supports (Aman, Kern, McGee, et al., 1993; Handen, Janosky, McAuliffe, et al., 1994; Quintana, Birmaher, Stedge, et al., 1995). However, the side effects of these drugs (irritability, sleep disturbance, and worsening stereotypies) may negate the therapeutic benefit for some children. Also, stimulant medication may be ineffective in children with mental retardation requiring extensive to pervasive supports. Therefore, treatment with stimulants must be individualized.

Antipsychotic drugs such as thioridazine (Mellaril) and haloperidol (Haldol) that are indicated for the treatment of psychotic disorders such as mania and schizophrenia are subject to considerable debate when prescribed for individuals with mental retardation, particularly when used to treat behavior problems such as aggression, irritability, noncompliance, and self-injury in individuals with mental retardation requiring extensive support. Although these medications may be appropriate for use in treating self-injury and other stereotypic behavior (Aman, 1993), they should not be used to "control" noncompliant behavior. This is a form of "chemical restraint" and is not ethically defensible when given to an individual who cannot understand and consent to its use and who poses no immediate threat to the safety of self or others.

Several of these antipsychotic drugs carry a significant risk of serious side effects when used on a long-term basis. These side effects include **supersensitivity psychosis, tardive dyskinesia, akathisia,** and **neuroleptic malignant syndrome.** Supersensitivity psychosis involves the acute worsening of symptoms as doses of antipsychotic medication are decreased (Kirkpatrick, Alphs, & Buchanan, 1992). This may lead the physician to incorrectly increase the medication to higher and higher levels when the medication should actually be gradually withdrawn over an extended period of time. Tardive dyskinesia is a condition involving involuntary movements, caused by chronic treatment with antipsychotic medication. Because tardive dyskinesia is usually masked by the drug that caused the disorder, it might not be observed until the medication is decreased or withdrawn. The abnormal movements occur around the mouth and face especially but at times involve the limbs and trunk as well. These movements can be incapacitating and disfiguring and are permanent in about half of people who develop them. Akathisia, a motor restlessness, is another worrisome side effect that occurs in up to 20% of people with mental retardation who take antipsychotic medicines (Blasdell, 1994). Akathisia is reversible, however, and can be controlled with other medications. Neuroleptic malignant syndrome is a rare idiosyncratic, toxic reaction to antipsychotic medicines, characterized by fever, muscular rigidity, and altered consciousness (Bambrick & Wilson, 1992). New antipsychotics such as risperidone (Risperdal) and clozapine (Clozaril) are thought to be less likely to cause movement disorders, but this has yet to be confirmed (Chouinard, Vainer, Belanger, et al., 1994; Cohen & Underwood, 1994).

Mood stabilizers such as lithium and the antiepileptic drugs carbamazepine (Tegretol) and valproic acid (Depakene, Depakote) are used to treat bipolar disorder and other cyclic mood disturbances in individuals with mental retardation (Campbell, Gonzalez, & Silva, 1992). There is some evidence that lithium is useful for controlling self-injury and aggression toward others in individuals with cyclic mood disorders (Alessi, Naylor, Ghaziuddin, et al., 1994; Campbell, Kafantaris, & Cueva, 1995). Studies also have suggested the use of carbamazepine for episodic aggression (Friedman, Kastner, Plummer, et al., 1992; Patterson, 1987), and valproic acid in affective disorders of individuals with mental retardation (Kastner, Friedman, Plummer, et al., 1990).

Other potentially useful pharmacological agents for treating SIB and aggression include **opiate antagonists** and **beta adrenergic blockers** (Aman, 1993; Osman & Loschen, 1992). The use of opiate antagonists such as naltrexone (Trexan) is based on a hypothesis linking certain subtypes of SIB to the release of endogenous opiate-like substances into the central nervous system. Opiates are highly reinforcing, and this hypothesis postulates that SIB occurs at a high rate in certain individuals because it is reinforced by the release of opiate-like substances. Opiate antagonists block the chemical effects of opiates. However, studies of the use of these agents for SIB have not demonstrated consistent results (Buzan, Dubovsky, Treadway, et al., 1995). Another group of agents that has shown some usefulness in decreasing aggressive and impulsive behaviors is beta adrenergic blockers such as propranolol (Inderal). These have an unclear mechanism of action but are safe when used and monitored appropriately and can be helpful for some individuals with sudden and impulsive violent outbursts.

Several principles are important to consider if psychoactive medications are being used as part of a treatment plan. First, the psychiatric disorder and symptoms must be correctly identified and periodically reevaluated. Second, an adequate trial (in terms of period of time and amount) of one medication should occur before switching to a new drug. Third, polypharmacy, or the use of multiple medications for the same condition, should be avoided if possible. Exceptions to this rule do exist, particularly when individual treatments do not have sufficient efficacy on multiple symptoms. Because of the complexity in adjusting the doses and assessing side effects, individuals receiving multiple psychoactive drugs must be carefully monitored, with ongoing attention to the risk–benefit ratio. Finally, a decision about changing or adding medications should be made only after careful explanation of anticipated benefits and potential harmful effects to the family and, if developmentally appropriate, the child. Carefully used, pharmacotherapy has become an integral part of the management of psychiatric disorders in individuals with dual diagnoses.

JOHN

John is a 16-year-old with mental retardation requiring extensive support. His disabilities were recognized at age 2 when language and social skills delays became apparent. He was subsequently placed in a preschool program for children with special needs and then in special education classes in the public school. Until several months before his referral for psychiatric evaluation, he had been developing at a slow but steady pace without behavior difficulties. His caregivers explained that his new behavioral disturbances coincided with a change in his school placement. He had recently transferred to an educational day program with an emphasis on daily living and early vocational skills. In this program John had difficulties indicating his needs to the new teachers. His speech was minimal and often unintelligible, and he had developed only a few useful signs.

Four weeks into his new day placement, he was noted to be irritable and aggressive with others and began exhibiting SIB. He began shoving his worksite supervisor and started hitting his own head with his fist and, at times, on door frames. A behavioral psychologist was consulted and completed a behavior analysis, which suggested that the SIB served to gain attention. A positive reinforcement schedule was set up to give John more attention for positive and cooperative behavior. After approximately 2 months of this program, however, there was only a slight improvement in his self-injurious and aggressive behavior.

At a school conference, his parents reported that there also had been behavior changes at home over the past few months. John showed a decreased appetite and had lost 5 pounds. Furthermore, he was isolating himself from other family members, awakening at about 4 A.M., and exhibiting SIB at home for the first time. At the conference, it was decided to refer John to a child and adolescent psychiatrist who had experience in treating children with developmental disabilities.

The psychiatrist discovered a maternal family history of members with significant depressive episodes and developmental disabilities. On examination, John's appearance was notable for large ears and a large jaw, poor eye contact, unresponsiveness to questions, and a flat affect. He persisted throughout the interview in slapping his head and turning away from his interviewer. He did understand, however, simple requests that the interviewer made of him.

The psychiatrist decided that John's acute symptoms, which included sleep and appetite problems and mood changes at both home and school, met the criteria for an episode of major depression. Given the family history of depressive episodes, John was treated with the antidepressant medication sertraline (Zoloft) at 50 milligrams per day. It was recommended that his behavior management program be continued at the educational worksite. He also was referred to a speech-language therapist to work on the development of a picture exchange communication system. Finally, John was referred to a geneticist for workup of a possible biological basis of his behavioral phenotype. Given the family history of developmental disabilities and his physical appearance, a diagnosis of fragile X syndrome was considered and subsequently confirmed by DNA testing. Appropriate genetic counseling was then given to family members (see Chapter 18).

Three weeks after antidepressant medication was initiated, John's SIB ceased. His appetite, sleep, and mood returned to baseline over the succeeding months. His day placement staff continued to give him positive attention for his more appropriate behaviors in the school setting. John also started using a communication board to express his desires. He remained on antidepressant medication for 1 year without recurrence, after which time the medication was tapered off. His risk for a future episode of depression is somewhat increased based on his family history, genetic diagnosis, and early age of onset of the psychiatric disorder.

This story illustrates the usefulness of having multiple informants about behavioral and psychiatric symptoms. Although the staff at his new program may have interpreted John's problems as a continuation of chronic behavior difficulties, his parents were able to help the psychiatrist recognize the relationship between these new behaviors and the changes that they were observing at home. Recognition of a change from previous functioning helped to define a clear episode of major depression. Making the diagnosis of depression permitted appropriate medication to be started. In the absence of the historical information, one might have treated John with other behavioral or pharmacological agents without recognizing that his SIB was a depressive symptom in a nonverbal patient. This story also shows the importance of exploring other related problems, such as genetic syndromes that have prognostic importance for the family, and communication problems that increased John's stress and decreased his ability to adjust to the change in his school placement.

SUMMARY

Children with mental retardation are at an increased risk for developing psychiatric disorders because of intrinsic biological and developmental factors and extrinsic environmental and psychosocial factors. Although they may exhibit the same psychiatric disorders as a typically developing child, their developmental and neurological status may alter the way these problems are expressed. Therefore, caregivers must recognize their range of psychiatric problems. Once problems are recognized, help with diagnosis and treatment should be sought from a mental health professional who has expertise in working with people with developmental disabilities. The professional also should be knowledgeable about appropriate evaluation procedures and the breadth of available treatment strategies. It is often desirable to have diagnosis and treatment undertaken from a multidisciplinary point of view. The challenges that children and adolescents with dual diagnoses present can often be overcome with appropriate interventions and therapies.

REFERENCES

Alessi, N., Naylor, M.W., Ghaziuddin, M., et al. (1994). Update on lithium carbonate therapy in children and adolescents. *Journal of the American Academy of Child and Adolescent Psychiatry, 33,* 291–304.

Aman, M.G. (1993). Efficacy of psychotropic drugs for reducing self-injurious behavior in the developmental disabilities. *Annals of Clinical Psychiatry, 5,* 171–188.

Aman, M.G., Kern, R.A., McGee, E.E., et al. (1993). Fenfluramine and methylphenidate in children with mental retardation and ADHD. *Journal of the American Academy of Child and Adolescent Psychiatry, 32,* 851–859.

Aman, M.G., & Singh, N.N. (Eds.). (1988). *Psychopharmacology of the developmental disabilities.* New York: Springer-Verlag.

American Psychiatric Association. (1994). *Diagnostic and statistical manual of mental disorders* (4th ed.). Washington, DC: Author.

Anderson, L.T., & Ernst, M. (1994). Self-injury in Lesch-Nyhan disease. *Journal of Autism and Developmental Disorders, 24,* 67–81.

Bambrick, M., & Wilson, D. (1992). Recurrent neuroleptic malignant syndrome in a man with mild mental handicap. *Journal of Intellectual Disability Research, 36,* 377–381.

Baumeister, A.A., Todd, M.E., & Sevin, J.A. (1993). Efficacy and specificity of pharmacological therapies for behavioral disorders in persons with mental retardation. *Clinical Neuropharmacology, 16,* 271–294.

Blasdell, G.D. (1994). Akathisia: A comprehensive review and treatment summary. *Pharmacopsychiatry, 27,* 139–146.

Bodfish, J.W., Crawford, T.W., Powell, S.B., et al. (1995). Compulsions in adults with mental retardation: Prevalence, phenomenology, and comorbidity with stereotypy and self-injury. *American Journal on Mental Retardation, 100,* 183–192.

Bodfish, J.W., & Madison, J.T. (1993). Diagnosis and fluoxetine treatment of compulsive behavior disorder of adults with mental retardation. *American Journal on Mental Retardation, 98,* 360–367.

Borthwick-Duffy, S.A. (1994). Epidemiology and prevalence of psychopathology in people with mental retardation. *Journal of Consulting and Clinical Psychology, 62,* 17–27.

Bregman, J.D. (1991). Current developments in the understanding of mental retardation: Part II. Psychopathology. *Journal of the American Academy of Child and Adolescent Psychiatry, 30,* 861–872.

Bregman, J.D. (1995). Psychopharmacological treatment of neuropsychiatric conditions in mental retardation. *Child and Adolescent Psychiatric Clinics of North America, 4,* 401–433.

Buitelaar, J.K. (1993). Self-injurious behavior in retarded children: Clinical phenomena and biological mechanisms. *Acta Paedopsychiatrica, 56,* 105–111.

Buzan, R.D., Dubovsky, S.L., Treadway, J.T., et al. (1995). Opiate antagonists for recurrent self-injurious behavior in three mentally retarded adults. *Psychiatric Services, 46,* 511–512.

Byerley, W., Holik, J., Hoff, M., et al. (1995). Search for a gene predisposing the manic depression on chromosome 21. *American Journal of Medical Genetics, 60,* 231–233.

Campbell, M., & Cueva, J.E. (1995a). Psychopharmacology in child and adolescent psychiatry: Part I. A review of the past seven years. *Journal of the American Academy of Child and Adolescent Psychiatry, 34,* 1124–1132.

Campbell, M., & Cueva, J.E. (1995b). Psychopharmacology in child and adolescent psychiatry: Part II. A review of the past seven years. *Journal of the American Academy of Child and Adolescent Psychiatry, 34,* 1262–1272.

Campbell, M., Gonzalez, N.M., & Silva, R.R. (1992). The pharmacological treatment of conduct disorders and rage outbursts. *Psychiatric Clinics of North America, 15,* 69–85.

Campbell, M., Kafantaris, V., & Cueva, J.E. (1995). An update on the use of lithium carbonate in aggressive children and adolescents with conduct disorder. *Psychopharmacology Bulletin, 31,* 93–102.

Chouinard, G., Vainer, J.L., Belanger, M.C., et al. (1994). Risperidone and clozapine in the treatment of drug-resistant schizophrenia and neuroleptic-induced supersensitivity psychosis. *Progress in Neuro-Psychopharmacology and Biological Psychiatry, 18,* 1129–1141.

Cohen, S.A., & Underwood, M.T. (1994). The use of clozapine in a mentally retarded and aggressive population. *Journal of Clinical Psychiatry, 55,* 440–444.

Cook, E., Rowlett, R., Jaselskis, C., et al. (1992). Fluoxetine treatment of children and adults with autistic disorder and mental retardation. *Journal of the American Academy of Child and Adolescent Psychiatry, 31,* 739–745.

Corbett, J.A. (1985). Mental retardation: Psychiatric aspects. In M. Rutter & L. Hersov (Eds.), *Child and adolescent psychiatry: Modern approaches* (2nd ed., pp. 661–678). Oxford, England: Blackwell Scientific Publications.

Cox, R., & Schopler, E. (1991). Social skills training for children. In M. Lewis (Ed.), *Child and adolescent psychiatry: A comprehensive textbook* (pp. 903–909). Baltimore: Williams & Wilkins Co.

Crews, W.D., Jr., Bonaventura, S., & Rowe, F. (1994). Dual diagnosis: Prevalence of psychiatric disorders in a large state residential facility for individuals with mental retardation. *American Journal on Mental Retardation, 98,* 724–731.

Curfs, L.M., & Fryns, J.P. (1992). Prader-Willi syndrome: A review with special attention to the cognitive and behavioral profile. *Birth Defects: Original Article Series, 28,* 99–104.

Decker, C.J. (1993). Pica in the mentally handicapped: A 15-year surgical perspective. *Canadian Journal of Surgery, 36,* 551–554.

Demb, H.B., Brier, N., Huron, R., et al. (1994).The adolescent behavior checklist: Normative data and sensitivity and specificity of a screening tool for diagnosable psychiatric disorders in adolescents with mental retardation and other developmental disabilities. *Research in Developmental Disabilities, 15,* 151–165.

Dosen, A. (1993). Diagnosis and treatment of psychiatric and behavioural disorders in mentally retarded individuals: The state of the art. *Journal of Intellectual Disability Research, 37,* 1–7.

Einfeld, S.L., & Aman, M. (1995). Issues in the taxonomy of psychopathology in mental retardation. *Journal of Autism and Developmental Disorders, 25,* 143–167.

Friedman, D.L., Kastner, T., Plummer, A.T., et al. (1992). Adverse behavioral effects in individuals with mental retardation and mood disorders treated with carbamazepine. *American Journal on Mental Retardation, 96,* 541–546.

Garber, H.J., McGonigle, J.J., Slomka, G.T., et al. (1992). Clomipramine treatment of stereotypic behaviors and self-injury in patients with developmental disabilities. *Journal of the American Academy of Child and Adolescent Psychiatry, 31,* 1157–1160.

Garth, A. (1990). Down syndrome children and their families. *American Journal of Medical Genetics, 7*(Suppl.), 314–316.

Gillberg, C., & Coleman, M. (1996). Autism and medical disorders: A review of the literature. *Developmental Medicine and Child Neurology, 38,* 191–202.

Gillberg, C., Persson, E., Grufman, M., et al. (1986). Psychiatric disorders in mildly and severely mentally retarded urban children and adolescents: Epidemiological aspects. *British Journal of Psychiatry, 149,* 68–74.

Gordon, C.T., State, R., Nelson, J., et al. (1993). A double blind comparison of clomipramine, desipramine, and placebo in the treatment of autistic disorder. *Archives of General Psychiatry, 50,* 441–447.

Handen, B.L., Janosky, J., McAuliffe, S., et al. (1994). Prediction of response to methylphenidate among children with ADHD and mental retardation. *Journal of the American Academy of Child and Adolescent Psychiatry, 33,* 1185–1193.

Handen, B.L., McAuliffe, S., Janosky, J., et al. (1994). Classroom behavior and children with mental retardation: Comparison of children with and without ADHD. *Journal of Abnormal Child Psychology, 22,* 267–280.

Holland, A. (1994). Down syndrome and Alzheimer disease. In N. Bouras (Ed.), *Mental health in mental retardation.* Cambridge, MA: Cambridge University Press.

Hollins, S., Sinason, V., & Thompson, S. (1994). Individual, group and family psychotherapy. In N. Bouras (Ed.), *Mental health in mental retardation.* Cambridge, MA: Cambridge University Press.

Jancar, J., & Gunaratne, I.J. (1994). Dysthymia and mental handicap. *British Journal of Psychiatry, 164,* 691–693.

Johnson, C.R., Handen, B.L., Lubetsky, M.J., et al. (1995). Affective disorders in hospitalized children and adolescents with mental retardation: A retrospective study. *Research in Developmental Disabilities, 16,* 221–231.

Johnson, C.R., Hunt, F.M., & Siebert, M.J. (1994). Discrimination training in the treatment of pica and food scavenging. *Behavior Modification, 18,* 214–229.

Kastner, T., Friedman, D.L., Plummer, A.T., et al. (1990). Valproic acid for the treatment of children with mental retardation and mood symptomatology. *Pediatrics, 86,* 467–472.

King, B.H., DeAntonio, C., McCracken, J.T., et al. (1994). Psychiatric consultation in severe and profound mental retardation. *American Journal of Psychiatry, 151,* 1802–1808.

Kirkpatrick, B., Alphs, L., & Buchanan, R.W. (1992). The concept of supersensitivity psychosis. *Journal of Nervous and Mental Disease, 180,* 265–270.

Knoll, J.H., Wagstoff, J.R., & Lalande, M. (1993). Cytogenetic and molecular studies in the Prader-Willi and Angelman syndromes: An overview. *American Journal of Medical Genetics, 46,* 2–6.

Linaker, O.M., & Helle, J. (1994). Validity of the schizophrenia diagnosis of the psychopathology instrument for mentally retarded adults (PIMRA): A comparison of schizophrenic patients with and without mental retardation. *Research in Developmental Disabilities, 15,* 473–486.

Loschen, E.L., & Osman, O.T. (1992). Self-injurious behavior in the developmentally disabled: Assessment techniques. *Psychopharmacology Bulletin, 28,* 433–438.

Lovell, R.W., & Reiss, A.L. (1993). Dual diagnoses: Psychiatric disorders in developmental disabilities. *Pediatric Clinics of North America, 40,* 579–592.

Matson, J.L., & Gardner, W.I. (1991). Behavioral learning theory and current applications to severe behavior problems in persons with mental retardation. *Clinical Psychology Review, 11,* 175–183.

Matthews, W.S., Solan, A., & Barabas, G. (1995). Cognitive functioning in Lesch-Nyhan syndrome. *Developmental Medicine and Child Neurology, 37,* 715–722.

Menolascino, F.J. (1990). The nature and types of mental illness in the mentally retarded. In M. Lewis & S. Miller (Eds.), *Handbook of developmental psychopathology.* New York: Plenum.

National Institutes of Health. (1989). Treatment of destructive behaviors in persons with developmental disabilities. *NIH Consensus Development Conference Statement, 7*(9), 1–14.

Nezu, C.M., & Nezu, A.M. (1994). Outpatient psychotherapy for adults with mental retardation and concomitant psychopathology: Research and clinical imperatives. *Journal of Consulting and Clinical Psychology, 62,* 34–42.

O'Brien, G., & Yule, W. (Eds.). (1996). *Behavioural phenotypes: Clinics in developmental medicine.* Cambridge, MA: Cambridge University Press.

Osman, O.T., & Loschen, E.L. (1992). Self-injurious behavior in the developmentally disabled: Pharmacological treatment. *Psychopharmacology Bulletin, 28,* 439–449.

Patterson, J.F. (1987). Carbemazepine for assaultive patients with organic brain disease. *Psychosomatics, 38,* 579–581.

Philips, I. (1966). Children, mental retardation, and emotional disorder. In I. Philips (Ed.), *Prevention and treatment of mental retardation.* New York: Basic Books.

Quintana, H., Birmaher, B., Stedge, D., et al. (1995). The use of methylphenidate in the treatment of children with autistic disorder. *Journal of Autism and Developmental Disorders, 25,* 283–294.

Ratey, J., & Gualtieri, T. (1991). Neuropsychiatry and mental retardation. In J. Ratey (Ed.), *Mental retardation: Developing pharmacotherapies.* Washington, DC: American Psychiatric Press.

Reiss, S., & Valenti-Hein, D. (1994). Development of a psychopathology rating scale for children with mental retardation. *Journal of Consulting and Clinical Psychology, 62,* 28–33.

Rojahn, J., Warren, V.J., & Ohringer, S. (1994). A comparison of assessment methods for depression in mental retardation. *Journal of Autism and Developmental Disorders, 24,* 305–313.

Roscioni, G., Farnetani, M.A., Pagani, R., et al. (1994). Plasma and urinary oxypurines in Lesch-Nyhan patient after allopurinol treatment. *Advances in Experimental Medicine and Biology, 370,* 357–361.

Rutter, M. (1981). Psychological sequelae of brain damage in children. *American Journal of Psychiatry, 138,* 1533–1544.

Rutter, M., Graham, P., & Yule, W. (1970). *A neuropsychiatric study in childhood.* London, England: Spastics International.

Ryan, R. (1994). Posttraumatic stress disorder in persons with developmental disabilities. *Community Mental Health Journal, 30,* 45–54.

Schaal, D.W., & Hackenberg, T. (1994). Toward a functional analysis of drug treatment for behavior problems of people with developmental disabilities. *American Journal on Mental Retardation, 99,* 123–140.

Sigman, M. (1985). Individual and group psychotherapy with mentally retarded adolescents. In M. Sigman (Ed.), *Children with emotional disorders and developmental disabilities* (pp. 259–276). New York: Grune & Stratton.

Smith, D.A., & Perry, P.J. (1992). Nonneuroleptic treatment of disruptive behavior in organic mental syndromes. *Annals of Pharmacotherapy, 26,* 1400–1408.

Sovner, R. (1986). Limiting factors in the use of DSM-III criteria with mentally ill/mentally retarded persons. *Psychopharmacology Bulletin, 22,* 1055–1059.

Sternberg, L., Taylor, R.L., & Babkie, A. (1994). Correlates of interventions with self-injurious behavior. *Journal of Intellectual Disability Research, 38,* 475–485.

Towbin, K.E. (1995). Evaluation, establishing the treatment alliance, and informed consent. *Child and Adolescent Psychiatric Clinics of North America, 4,* 1–14.

Troisi, A., Vicario, E., Nuccetelli, F., et al. (1995). Effects of fluoxetine on aggressive behavior of adult inpatients with mental retardation and epilepsy. *Pharmacopsychiatry, 28,* 73–76.

Tyas, S., & Rush, B. (1993). The treatment of disabled persons with alcohol and drug problems: Results of a survey of addiction services. *Journal of Studies on Alcohol, 54,* 275–282.

Udwin, O., & Yule, W. (1990). Expressive language of children with Williams syndrome. *American Journal of Medical Genetics, 6*(Suppl.), 108–114.

Werry, J. (1996). Childhood schizophrenia. In F. Volkmar (Eds.), *Psychoses and pervasive developmental disorders in childhood and adolescence* (pp. 1–48). Washington, DC: American Psychiatric Press.

21 Autism

And Other Pervasive Developmental Disorders

Joyce Elizabeth Mauk
Mark Reber
Mark L. Batshaw

Upon completion of this chapter, the reader will:

- be familiar with the three central features of all pervasive developmental disorders
- appreciate the spectrum of pervasive developmental disorders
- know how to distinguish autism from other developmental disabilities
- be familiar with interventions for these disorders

Autism is a severe form of a group of disorders termed pervasive developmental disorders (PDDs) (Bauer, 1995; Frith, 1993). PDDs are characterized by impairments in social relatedness and communication skills and by the presence of unusual activities and interests such as rituals, **stereotypies,** and poor play skills. PDDs appear to be brain-based neurological disorders of multiple origins and may co-exist with other developmental disabilities such as mental retardation, attention-deficit/hyperactivity disorder (ADHD), and epilepsy. Although these disorders are usually regarded as lifelong, advances in defining the underlying impairments and novel treatment approaches have improved the prognosis.

A HISTORICAL PERSPECTIVE

Dr. Leo Kanner, a child psychiatrist, published the first description of what he called "autistic disturbances of affective contact" (1943, p. 217). In the 1990s, his description remains as apt as when it was written a half century ago. Based on a group of children who exhibited symptoms that isolated them from their environment and who had abnormal language or did not speak at all, Kanner believed that these children had one fundamental disturbance: "an inability to relate themselves in the ordinary way to people and situations from the beginning of life" (p. 242). He observed that as infants, they did not seek to be held, ignored or shut out any social approaches, treated people as objects, and made minimal eye contact. In addition, as children they required such a sameness in their environment that even a minor change—for example, the repositioning of a chair—threw them into a rage. Among those children who could speak, unusual features of language included parrot-like repetition of phrases, sometimes uttered long after they were heard; literalness of usage; and a tendency to repeat pronouns as heard. Play was repetitive and stereotyped, with little imaginative use of toys and other objects. In terms of cause, Kanner noted that the parents of these children tended to be cold and formal in their interpersonal relationships but speculated that the disorder was an "inborn disturbance" (p. 250). In the 1950s and 1960s, "cold" and "aloof" parents were increasingly identified as the cause of autism. In the 1990s, however, autism is understood to be a disturbance that arises early in life and originates in the child's own biology. The aloofness witnessed in some families may indicate that the parent is exhibiting a milder form of the condition.

DEFINING PERVASIVE DEVELOPMENTAL DISORDER

In the past, terms such as childhood psychosis, autism, PDD, and atypical development were used to describe children with a triad of 1) impairments in communication; 2) impairments in reciprocal social interaction skills; and 3) the presence of stereotyped patterns of behavior, interests, and activities (Volkmar & Rutter, 1995). This symptomatology is presently grouped under the terminology PDDs and includes five syndromes: autistic disorder, Asperger disorder, pervasive developmental disorder-not otherwise specified (PDD-NOS), Rett syndrome, and childhood disintegrative disorder (CDD). The following descriptions of these disorders are based on the diagnostic schema outlined in the *Diagnostic and Statistical Manual of Mental Disorders, Fourth Edition* (DSM-IV) (American Psychiatric Association, 1994).

Autistic Disorder

Autism is the most severe expression of a PDD, although individual manifestations greatly vary in severity. In order to be diagnosed with autistic disorder, a child must have onset of symptoms prior to 3 years of age and meet 6 of the 12 criteria listed in the DSM-IV (Table 21.1) (American Psychiatric Association, 1994). These specific clinical features also apply, more or less, to the other PDDs.

Communication Impairments

In children with autism, the development of language is severely delayed and deviant, hindering both expressive and receptive communication. Cooing and babbling may develop in the first 6 months of life but then be lost. Speech may develop late or not at all. Although about half of children with autism remain mute throughout their lives and may be unable even to use gestures or signs to communicate, many of them may be taught to use alternative communication systems such as sign language or communication cards (Prizant, 1996).

When spoken language does develop, the first word is often spoken between 2 and 3 years of age. However, it becomes quickly evident that speech pragmatics is impaired (see Chapter 13). Speech in autism is idiosyncratic and **echolalic,** rather than creative or spontaneous. The echolalia may be immediate (i.e., repeating the last part of a question) or delayed (i.e., repeating stock phrases, songs, or long commercial jingles). Although it may seem that they are understanding what they are saying, children with autism may just be parroting what they have heard.

Table 21.1. Diagnostic criteria for autistic disorder

A. A total of six (or more) items from the following groups:

Group 1[a]	Group 2[b]	Group 3[c]
1. Marked impairment in the use of multiple nonverbal behaviors such as eye-to-eye gaze, facial expression, body postures, and gestures to regulate social interaction	1. Delay in, or total lack of, the development of spoken language (not accompanied by an attempt to compensate through alternative modes of communication such as gesture or mime)	1. Encompassing preoccupation with one or more stereotyped and restricted patterns of interest that is abnormal either in intensity or focus
2. Failure to develop peer relationships appropriate to developmental level	2. In individuals with adequate speech, marked impairment in the ability to initiate or sustain a conversation with others	2. Apparently inflexible adherence to specific, nonfunctional routines or rituals
3. A lack of spontaneous seeking to share enjoyment, interests, or achievements with other people (e.g., by a lack of showing, bringing, or pointing out objects of interest)	3. Stereotyped and repetitive use of language or idiosyncratic language	3. Stereotyped and repetitive motor mannerisms (e.g., hand or finger flapping or twisting, complex whole-body movements)
4. Lack of social or emotional reciprocity	4. Lack of varied, spontaneous make-believe play or social imitative play appropriate to developmental level	4. Persistent preoccupation with parts of objects

B. Delays or abnormal functioning in at least one of the following areas with onset prior to age 3 years:

  1. Social interaction
  2. Language as used in social communication
  3. Symbolic or imaginative play

C. The disturbance is not better accounted for by Rett syndrome or childhood disintegrative disorder.

Adapted from American Psychiatric Association (1994).
[a]Qualitative impairments in social interaction, as manifested by at least two criteria from Group 1.
[b]Qualitative impairments in communication as manifested by at least one criterion from Group 2.
[c]Restricted, repetitive, and stereotyped patterns of behavior, interests, and activities, as manifested by at least one criterion from Group 3.

427

There is often confusion of personal pronouns (using "you" to refer to oneself) and verbal perseveration (dwelling on a specific subject). Abnormalities of prosody may be evident; that is, their voices are often high pitched, with unusual speech rhythm and intonation, which makes their speech sound sing-song, monotonous, or pedantic. In sum, children with autistic disorder usually have an accompanying severe expressive language disorder and tend to use language in a very stereotyped, rote fashion, exhibiting relatively better memorization skills but frequently communicating very little, if any, meaning. In higher functioning children with autism or Asperger disorder, the echolalia may disappear by school entry, accompanied by a marked increase in spontaneous vocabulary. Their basic problems with pragmatics, however, remain.

Receptive language is impaired in these children as well, and sometimes they appear deaf. Children with autism may respond to brief phrases, but they find it very difficult to understand more complex commands. As infants, they tend not to engage in imitation games or do so only in a mechanical way. They learn better with visual, rather than auditory, cues. Eye contact, body posture, gestures, and other nonverbal aspects of communication are also severely impaired. Although other aspects of language may improve over time, nonverbal communication impairments remain prominent, unless specific behavioral interventions to address these problems are provided (Frea, 1995).

Impaired Reciprocal Social Interactions

Wing (1988) described three types of social interaction impairments: impaired social recognition, communication, and understanding or imagining. Impaired social recognition, in its mild form, appears as a lack of empathy (an interest in the feelings and thoughts of others) and an absence of eye contact. Individuals with autism generally demonstrate aloofness and indifference to other people except for one or two caregivers; they do not often form friendships. Impaired social communication is characterized by an absence of pleasure in the exchange of smiles and feelings (i.e., body language). This characteristic may be obvious as early as the first 2–3 months of life, though it often goes unrecognized until other impairments become more obvious (Siegel, 1996; Stone, Lemanek, Fishel, et al., 1990). Impaired social communication also implies a lack of desire to communicate with others or communication that is limited to the simple expression of needs. Impaired social imagination and understanding refers to the inability to imitate others, to engage in pretend play, or to imagine another's thoughts and feelings. For example, infants with this impairment do not copy their mothers' facial expressions, a trait that has been termed *mind blindness* (Baron-Cohen, Allen, & Gillberg, 1992; Hobson, 1993; Tager-Flusberg, 1993). Other social impairments include not seeking comfort when hurt and lacking interest in forming friendships.

Behavioral Abnormalities

Individuals with autism have a desire for sameness and resist change. This is marked by restricted, perseverative, and stereotyped patterns of behaviors, interests, and activities and lack of representational or pretend play. Obsessive rituals and strict adherence to routines are common, including, for example, rigid insistence on eating at the same time each day or eating a restricted menu of foods, sitting in exactly the same position at the table, placing objects in a particular location, or touching every door knob one passes. Young children with autistic disorder may show intense attachment to unusual objects, such as a piece of string, rather than a cuddly item like a teddy bear. They may not use toys in their intended manner but focus instead on a part of a toy, such as the wheels on a toy truck, which they may spin endlessly. A common form of play is to line objects up in rows. Shining surfaces, rotating fans, and people's hair or beards may fascinate young children with autism. Older, more cognitively advanced children may become intensely preoccupied with train schedules, calendars, or particular patterns of numerical relationships. They will focus on these things to the exclusion of other activities such as make-believe games.

Frequently, children with autism become upset and have intense temper tantrums if anything interrupts these rituals and preoccupations. Similar tantrums can be provoked by trivial departures from daily routines or changes in the environment. Stereotyped movements and self-stimulating behaviors, such as rocking, hand waving, arm flapping, spinning, toe walking, head banging, and other forms of self-injurious behavior, are also common, especially among children with autism who also have mental retardation requiring extensive supports. Other behavior problems associated with autism include sleep disturbances (especially in younger children), short attention span, rapid mood changes, hyperactivity, phobias, and aggressiveness. Unusual responses to sensory input are also common. These include insensitivity to pain or heat and overreaction to environmental noises, touch, or odors. For example, although the child may appear "deaf" to parental questions or commands, he or she may cover the ears and scream when close to a vacuum cleaner. Food selectivity, food refusal, or resistance to certain food textures may lead to compromised nutrition or constipation.

Associated Impairments

In addition to the core symptoms of autism, affected children have an increased risk for other developmental disabilities, most commonly mental retardation, ADHD, and seizures. Approximately three quarters of individuals with autistic disorder have mental retardation, most commonly requiring limited to extensive supports (American Psychiatric Association, 1994). The profile of cognitive skills is generally uneven; they tend to perform better on tests of visual-spatial skills and rote memory and poorer on tasks requiring symbolic and logical reasoning. It is important to note that test scores can also vary dramatically depending on the motivational conditions in the testing situation.

Some children with autism have restricted areas of higher functioning, called islets of ability or splinter skills (O'Connor & Hermelin, 1991). These include decoding skills manifesting as hyperlexia; musical skills, such as perfect pitch; exceptional rote memory; an unusual capacity for jigsaw puzzles; or the ability to do rapid calculations, such as finding the day of the week for distant dates. The biological origin of these skills is unclear. Usually, these splinter skills relate to the individual's selected area of preoccupation and do not help him or her solve problems in daily life. However, skillful therapists and teachers can build on these inherent interests as a basis for developing functional skills.

ADHD is also common in children with autism. The principal findings are hyperactivity, impulsive behavior, and inattention. These may be difficult to differentiate from the core symptoms of autism but should be assessed because they will affect intervention strategies. Treatment with stimulant medications in children with PDD is controversial.

There is also controversy as to whether seizure disorders are more common in autism than in the overall population of individuals with mental retardation. The prevalence of seizures in autism has been cited as 14%, with peaks in infancy and adolescence (Tuchman, Rapin, & Shinnar, 1991). This prevalence, however, is significantly higher in individuals with mental retardation requiring extensive supports and motor disability (30%–40%). Studies that have taken into account the increased risk of seizures in all children with mental retardation note that the risk in autism is not significantly increased.

Asperger Disorder

The term Asperger disorder describes individuals with behavioral and social features of autism but no significant delays in language development or impairments in cognition (Szatmari, 1991). In fact, some aspects of cognitive development may appear advanced. The child may recognize letters by 3 years and brand-name logos or car models by age 4. Some children have hyperlexia and are able to read before age 5, although they usually comprehend little. The major features of Asperger disorder are the severe and sustained impairment in social interaction and the development of restricted, repetitive patterns of behavior, interests, and activities (American Psychiatric Association, 1994; Bonnet, 1996). For instance, spoken language may be unusually pedantic and formal, and the nonverbal aspects of communication such as eye contact and body position may be abnormal. Older children with Asperger disorder exhibit unusual activities and interests in maps, sports statistics, train schedules, and so forth. Some of these preoccupations may prove to be adaptive and lead to future careers, for example in computing. Their social ineptitude, however, prevents them from developing friendships and other close personal relationships (Grandin, 1995; Klin, 1994; Williams, 1992). Delayed motor milestones and clumsiness are additional characteristics. Overall, the disorder causes significant impairment in social and occupational functioning. Yet because of good language and cognitive skills, this disorder is frequently not recognized until later in childhood.

Pervasive Developmental Disorder-Not Otherwise Specified

PDD-NOS is a term reserved for those individuals with abnormal social and communication skills and stereotyped behaviors that are of relatively brief duration, develop later in life, or are of insufficient severity to warrant another PDD diagnosis. It is not uncommon for a child who ultimately is diagnosed with a language-based learning disability to be diagnosed as PDD-NOS at age 2 or 3, but later to exhibit few or no autistic features. In practice, this term is often used to describe individuals with mild autistic features.

Rett Syndrome

Rett syndrome is listed as a PDD but is unlikely to remain in this classification once its etiology is clarified. This progressive neurological disorder, which appears to affect only girls, is characterized by transient autistic behavior, stereotypic hand use, progressive spasticity of the lower extremities, dementia, seizures, acquired microcephaly, and mental retardation (Hagberg, 1995). Individuals often appear to develop typically during the first year of life, although, in retrospect, there may have been subtle neurodevelopmental abnormalities present in infancy. At variable ages older than 1 year, they experience rapid deterioration of behavior, language, and mental status; lose purposeful hand movements; and develop ataxia and seizures. A prominent feature is continuous "hand washing" movements, often accompanied by hyperventilation. By 6 years of age, an affected girl commonly has mental retardation requiring extensive to pervasive supports, spasticity, and seizures. The condition then stabilizes over a period of many years, generally following a clinical staging system (Table 21.2). Although its early presentation may be indistin-

Table 21.2.   Clinical stages in Rett syndrome

Early onset stagnation stage (6–18 months)
Arrest of developmental progress
Deceleration of head growth
Diminishing play interest
Possible deterioration of eye contact and loss of communication

Rapid destructive stage (1–4 years)
Apraxic/ataxic gait
Irregular breathing; hyperventilation
Loss of purposeful hand use
Rapid developmental deterioration over weeks to months
Seizures
Severe dementia with autistic features
Stereotyped hand movements

Pseudostationary stage (preschool through early school years)
Less prominent autistic features
Mental retardation
Prominent gait apraxia and truncal ataxia
Seizures
Variable motor dysfunction

Late motor deterioration stage (5–15 years)
Decreasing mobility
Growth retardation, cachexia
Secondary neurotrophic changes: scoliosis, foot deformities
Seizures less problematic
Spasticity
Staring in an unfathomable gaze

Adapted from Hagberg & Witt-Engerström (1985).

guishable from autistic disorder, the particular characteristics of Rett syndrome usually become evident in the preschool years.

Childhood Disintegrative Disorder

CDD, also called Heller syndrome, is a rare disorder of childhood typified by a loss in multiple areas of functioning after at least 2 years of typical development (Volkmar & Rutter, 1995). The areas of regression include language, social or adaptive skills, bowel and bladder functioning, play, and motor skills. Children with this disorder develop the social and communicative impairments and behavioral features typically observed in autistic disorder. They also usually have mental retardation. Because of the progressive nature of this disorder, however, these children should be evaluated for metabolic and neurodegenerative diseases. CDD is considered a diagnosis of exclusion following workup for known neurodegenerative disorders. Some researchers believe that a specific inborn error of metabolism ultimately will be identified in individuals diagnosed with CDD.

PREVALENCE AND ORIGIN OF PDD

The overall prevalence of the PDDs is about 22 per 10,000 births. Autistic disorder occurs in 10 per 10,000 live births (Costello, 1996). Rett syndrome and CDD are rarer, each occurring in less than 1 per 10,000 live births. Except for Rett syndrome, which has been described only in females, the male to female ratio for the other PDDs is 3–4:1.

The biological basis of the PDDs can best be understood as the result of a combination of genetic and developmental factors operating through one or more genes (Lander & Schort, 1994; Smalley & Collins, 1996). Autistic disorder, Asperger disorder, and PDD-NOS are often thought of as a single entity with various gradations of severity. Multiple studies have identified an increased risk of these PDDs as well as other cognitive, social, and psychiatric disorders in certain families (DeLong, 1994; DeLong & Nohria, 1994; Ritvo, Freeman, Pingree, et al., 1989). In these studies, the recurrence risk of autism in subsequent pregnancies ranged from 2% to 9% (Jorde, Mason-Brothers, Waldmann, et al., 1990; Ritvo et al., 1989). Twin studies have shown a 95% concordance for identical twins and 24% for fraternal twins (Ritvo, Freeman, Mason-Brothers, et al., 1985). Transmission, however, does not follow a strictly Mendelian pattern of inheritance. Studies of families with numerous affected members are likely to be fruitful in determining an underlying genetic cause. It should be noted that the genetics of Rett syndrome are probably unrelated to the other PDDs; it may be explained by an X-linked process that is lethal in males.

There are several known medical disorders associated with an increased risk of PDD (Gillberg & Coleman, 1996), which may give clues to the defect underlying PDD. Children with genetic disorders such as phenylketonuria and congenital hypothyroidism (when untreated) (Gillberg, Gillberg, & Kopp, 1992); neurocutaneous syndromes including tuberous sclerosis and neurofibromatosis (Gillberg, Gillberg, & Ahlsen, 1994); and other syndromes such as Cornelia de Lange (Reiss, Feinstein, & Rosenbaum, 1986) all have an increased risk of PDD. In the past, fragile X syndrome (see Chapter 18) was thought to be a common cause of autism, but in the 1990s this association is being questioned (Einfeld, Maloney, & Hall, 1989; Fisch, 1992). Complications during fetal development are also associated with PDD, including exposure to thalidomide and intrauterine infections including rubella and cytomegalovirus (Stromland, Nordin, Miller, et al., 1994). Contrary to expectations, complications in late pregnancy and the perinatal period do not appear to increase the risk of PDD (Cryan, Bryne, O'Donovan, et al., 1996; Nelson, 1991). Overall, 10% of children with mental retardation requiring extensive supports have a PDD (Nordin & Gillberg, 1996).

As of 1997, the neurobiological underpinnings of autism have eluded our efforts at understanding (Bauman & Kemper, 1994; Gillberg & Coleman, 1996). Neuroimaging studies, electroencephalograms (EEGs), autopsy studies, and neurochemical investigations have not revealed a consistent pattern of abnormalities. This may be the result of investigators lumping together a number of different disorders with variant origins. Alternatively, researchers may not as yet have hit on the single underlying cause of autism.

The most interesting studies to date have focused on neurochemistry and neuroimaging. Neurochemical studies suggest alterations in the serotonin, dopamine, and opioid transmitter systems (Bailey, Phillips, & Rutter, 1996; Lotspeich & Ciaranello, 1993). The correction of these abnormalities underlies the approaches to drug therapy. Magnetic resonance imaging

(MRI) and neuropathology studies have identified abnormalities in the limbic region of the cortex (which controls emotions) and underdevelopment of the brainstem and cerebellum (Filipek, 1995; see also Bachevalier, 1994; Courchesne, Townsend, & Saitoh, 1994; Haas, Townsend, Courchesne, et al., 1996; Piven, Arndt, Bailey, et al., 1995). Studies attempting to correlate these MRI and anatomical findings with positron emission tomography (PET) metabolic studies have revealed low metabolic activity in these regions (Schifter, Hoffman, Hatten, et al., 1994). Yet, how these findings link to the abnormalities in communication, social skills, and behavior found in PDD remains unclear.

DISTINGUISHING AUTISM FROM OTHER DISABILITIES

It is important to differentiate autism from other childhood developmental disorders such as mental retardation, childhood schizophrenia, sensory impairments, communication disorders, and neurodegenerative disorders. Autism can be distinguished from mental retardation by its characteristic social and behavior problems and by a somewhat different pattern of cognitive impairments. Children with autism typically shun social interactions, while children with mental retardation generally enjoy social contacts. Children with autism have more prominent language impairments, whereas children with mental retardation usually have similar delays in language, cognitive, and visual-perceptual skills. It must be acknowledged, however, that most children with autism also have mental retardation, and many individuals with mental retardation requiring extensive supports display autistic features, such as stereotyped movements and self-injurious behavior (Capute, Derivan, Chauvel, et al., 1975).

Autism may also be confused with psychiatric disorders, most commonly childhood schizophrenia (American Psychiatric Association, 1994). Although the child with autism may behave in a bizarre manner, he or she will not have the delusions and hallucinations that are characteristic of schizophrenia. In addition, while a child with autism lacks imagination, a child with schizophrenia may live in a fantasy world. Finally, individuals with schizophrenia do not usually have mental retardation.

Children with sensory impairments may also demonstrate autistic features. For example, congenital blindness (e.g., as a result of retinopathy of prematurity; see Chapter 11) often is associated with eye-poking behaviors and impaired interpersonal skills (Janson, 1993). Children with blindness, however, do not have the global language disorder that typifies children with autism. Severe to profound hearing impairment also may mimic autism because of inconsistent responses to verbal commands and social interaction. However, social interaction and cognition are usually unaffected. It is therefore important to test vision and hearing in children with a suspected PDD.

Similarly, children with developmental language disorders may display shyness, echolalia, and some social withdrawal, but they typically do not show other deviant behaviors typical of autism, including stereotyped utterances, abnormal social interactions, bizarre behaviors, and absence of a desire to communicate (Rutter, 1985a).

Neurodegenerative disorders, such as Tay-Sachs disease (see Chapter 19), may initially present with features of autism and must be differentiated from Rett syndrome and CDD. Over time, however, there is a clear loss of motor and cognitive skills. The children also may develop blindness and deafness. They rarely survive adolescence.

EARLY IDENTIFICATION OF AUTISM

By definition, the symptoms of autistic disorder must be manifest by 3 years of age. Yet, this does not necessarily mean that the diagnosis is made by this age; some children may escape detection until school entry. Studies have shown that even when parents express an early concern, there is often a 2- to 3-year lag before a firm diagnosis is made (Siegel, Pliner, Eschler, et al., 1988). As with many other disorders, the more severe the symptoms, the earlier the diagnosis.

The core symptoms of delay in language development, aberrant behavior, and lack of socialization are, in order, the most common presenting complaints of parents. Infants with autism often have poor eye contact and are irritable and stiffen when held. In the first and second years of life, they may be unresponsive to nursery tricks; are generally difficult to care for; and have frequent temper tantrums, often including head banging. Speech may not develop, and commands will not be followed. During the preschool years, severe disruptive behaviors may emerge, including aggression, hyperactivity, and self-injury. At this time, affected children often manifest stereotypies, social withdrawal, and emotional lability to a degree that the diagnosis is seriously considered. Even children with the milder PDD-NOS or Asperger disorder have poorly developed play skills, and pretend play is usually absent.

Although autism is generally not diagnosed before 2–3 years, systematic review of early videotapes demonstrates prelinguistic communication abnormalities in infancy (Adrien, Lenoir, Martineau, et al., 1993; Osterling & Dawson, 1994). Furthermore, parent questionnaires, such as the Checklist for Autism in Toddlers (CHAT; Baron-Cohen, Allen, & Gillberg, 1992) and the Autism Behavior Checklist (ABC; Krug, Arick, & Almond, 1980), often retrospectively reveal impairments in pretend play, protodeclarative pointing, joint-attention, social interest, and social play as early as 18 months (Figure 21.1).

EVALUATION

The diagnosis of a PDD is based on clinical rather than laboratory findings. The clinical assessment should include an evaluation of communication, cognition, and social skills as well as the repertoire of behaviors, activities, and interests. This requires an assessment by a clinical psychologist, speech-language pathologist, social worker, and physician (developmental pediatrician, child psychiatrist, or child neurologist). Observation in multiple settings—for example, home, school, and clinic—is optimal and may be obtained using video cameras.

Standardized psychological testing (both IQ and adaptive scales) should be administered, as well as behavioral questionnaires and observational scales (e.g., the Childhood Autism Rating Scale [CARS; Schopler, Reichler, DeVellius, et al., 1980] or the Autism Diagnostic Interview [ADI; LeCouteur, Rutter, Lord, et al., 1989]). In general, psychological tests show that children with PDD have relatively high nonverbal skills and depressed language skills. The adaptive rating scales will show impairments in play, social interactions, and behavior, and the autism rating scales will further specify these abnormalities.

Speech and language testing should demonstrate communication impairments typical of PDD, especially in pragmatics and nonverbal communication. It should be emphasized that all children suspected of having autism also should have a hearing test, using either behavioral audiology or auditory brainstem response (see Chapter 12).

Questions for the parent:

1. Does your child ever pretend, for example, to make a cup of tea using a toy cup and teapot or pretend other things?
2. Does your child ever use his or her index finger to point and indicate interest in something?
3. Does your child take an interest in other children?
4. Does your child enjoy playing Peekaboo or Hide-and-Seek?
5. Does your child ever bring objects to you or show you something?

If the answer to two or more of these questions is "no," autism is suspected (except in the presence of severe generalized developmental delays).

Physician's observations:

1. During the appointment, has the child made eye contact with you?
2. Get the child's attention, then point across the room at an interesting object and say, "Oh look! There's a [name object]." Watch the child's face. Does the child look across to see what you are pointing at?
3. Get the child's attention, then give the child a miniature toy cup and teapot and say, "Can you make a cup of tea?" Does the child pretend to pour out the tea, drink it, and so forth? (may use other objects for pretend play)
4. Ask the child, "Where's the light?" or say, "Show me the light." Does the child point with his or her index finger at the light?

If the answer to two or more of these is "no," autism is suspected.

Figure 21.1.   The CHAT (Checklist for Autism in Toddlers). This screening questionnaire is designed to use with children who are approximately 18 months old to detect signs of autism. (From Baron-Cohen, S., Cox, A., Baird, G., et al. [1996]. Psychological markers in the detection of autism in infancy in a large population. *British Journal of Psychiatry, 168,* 160; adapted by permission.)

A social worker should evaluate the child's social setting and caregivers. Even though family and social problems are not thought to cause autism, children who are severely neglected or depressed can appear autistic. Furthermore, the coping abilities and strategies of the family need to be assessed and strengthened. Appropriate services should be identified in the child's community.

The physician should focus on obtaining historical information suggestive of the diagnosis and perform a physical, neurological, and developmental examination to exclude other diagnoses. A positive family history may lead to genetic testing. In most cases, the developmental history will be supportive of the diagnosis, although the physical and neurological examination will be nonspecific. During the testing session, the physician also will note abnormalities in the child's interactions with the environment and with other people. Abnormalities may include hypersensitivity to sound and unusual environmental exploration such as sniffing or licking.

Medical testing generally is not helpful; there are no specific screening tests for PDD. However, if the history suggests developmental regression (e.g., CDD, Rett syndrome) or the physical examination supports a neurological disease (e.g., tuberous sclerosis) or a genetic syndrome (e.g., fragile X), these options should be explored. Evidence of regression may prompt a metabolic evaluation, and an unusual appearance may lead to chromosomal testing. Other nonspecific findings may also warrant study. For example, a very large or small head circumference may prompt a brain imaging study. Evidence of seizures or consideration of Rett syndrome should prompt an EEG. Many children with PDD are evaluated for fragile X syndrome using a molecular test for expanded triplet repeats (Cohen, Sudhalter, Jenkins, et al., 1991; Einfeld et al., 1989).

TREATMENT

Management of children with PDDs can be frustrating for families and other caregivers. Treatment must be intensive, continuous, and multidisciplinary. Rutter (1985b), an eminent British child psychiatrist, has outlined five main goals of the treatment of autism: 1) the fostering of development, 2) the promotion of learning, 3) the reduction of rigidity and stereotypy, 4) the elimination of nonspecific maladaptive behaviors, and 5) the alleviation of family distress. This usually requires a combination of behavior treatment, education, speech-language therapy, pharmacotherapy, and family support.

Behavior Treatment

Behavioral interventions in PDD are designed to decrease maladaptive behaviors while increasing adaptive ones. Specific foci of treatment will depend on the target behaviors, the reinforcers used, and the severity of the symptoms (see Chapter 30) (Howlin, 1993). Stereotypies, tantrums, noncompliance, and poor socialization are common target behaviors. Positive reinforcement is the method of choice, although mild punishments such as time-out also may be required. As an example, transitions from one activity to another are particularly difficult for children with PDD and often lead to tantrums. Reinforcement techniques can be used to first teach predictable schedules and routines of change in activities. Subsequently, the child can be taught to anticipate change in an incremental fashion, ultimately leading to increased flexibility.

Individuals with autism often have distinctly different problem behaviors, although behavior analysts contend that each behavior serves a function for that child. The trick is to eliminate the problematic behavior and replace its function with a more socially acceptable behavior. The efficacy of behavior treatment in leading to improved functioning depends on the severity of the behavior problem, the age treatment is started, the intensity of the treatment, and the involvement of the family and school. Behavioral approaches should be integrated into the home and school setting to promote acquisition of both social and academic skills. The importance of parental involvement as therapists cannot be overemphasized.

Education

Ideally, educational programs should start as soon as the child is diagnosed (i.e., in the preschool years). Early intervention programs focus on the teaching of social and communication skills.

Effective early intervention has been shown to be intensive and highly structured and to involve a small teacher-to-student ratio. An occupational therapist and speech-language therapist should be an integral part of this team. There should be opportunities to generalize and practice skills, and parents should be trained as treatment providers. The educational program may use incidental teaching and a natural language paradigm to take advantage of learning situations as they occur throughout the day. Extensive use of visual cues helps these children who do not learn well auditorially.

Autism is now included as a special category of educational disability under the Individuals with Disabilities Education Act (IDEA) of 1990, PL 101-476. This law mandates that specific academic goals relate both to the child's cognitive and functional level and that the educational program be provided in the least restrictive environment. This last provision has led to controversy regarding inclusion versus a specialized educational setting for children with autism. For high-functioning older children with autism or Asperger disorder, inclusion is very appropriate (Minshew, Goldstein, Taylor, et al., 1994). For younger and lower-functioning children with autism, inclusion may be a future goal rather than a starting point. Even in these cases, some interaction with typically developing peers is optimal. The level of academic achievement attained by the large group of individuals diagnosed with PDD is quite variable.

One of the commonly used behavior curricula in special education programs for children with PDD is termed TEACCH (Treatment and Education of Autistic and related Communications Handicapped Children). TEACCH is a comprehensive educational approach that includes classroom teaching, parent training, and other support services (Cox & Schopler, 1993). The approach is eclectic and involves the use of behavioral strategies to reinforce communication and social interaction. It also heavily emphasizes the parents' role as co-therapists.

Individualized educational programming based on the practices of Lovaas have become popular. Lovaas developed and reported on a model of intensive (40 hours per week), comprehensive, individualized (one-to-one) teaching. Therapy relies on the introduction, prompting, and reinforcement of a behavior. The curriculum includes hundreds of individual lessons to teach specific language, academic, and social behaviors. Treatment is generally initiated at 2 years of age. Goals of the first year of treatment include developing language; increasing social behavior; promoting cooperative play; and decreasing excessive rituals, tantrums, and aggressive behavior. In the second year, treatment focuses on expressive and abstract language and interactive play with peers. In his initial study, Lovaas (1993) reported an almost 50% recovery rate (i.e., the children did not need special support services or aids in a general classroom). Lovaas reported significant gains in IQ scores, preacademic skills, and adaptive functioning. This pilot study is being replicated at a number of centers. Controversy over the Lovaas method has raged over both the claims of success and the expense of the program ($20,000–$60,000 annually per child), which places the Lovaas method out of reach of the general population. As a result, several parents have legally challenged their school systems to enroll their children in this still-experimental program. Parents have generally won reimbursement for Lovaas therapy only when they have convinced a hearing officer or court both that the school's program was inappropriate and that the Lovaas method was appropriate.

Speech-Language Therapy

Fostering development must include speech-language therapy with an emphasis on the pragmatics of language. Interactive and meaningful conversations should be modeled and practiced. Research has shown that all verbal productions in young individuals with autism should be rewarded socially or in other ways to foster language development (Carr, Levin, McConnachie, et al., 1995; Koegel, O'Dell, & Dunlap, 1988). Sign language can also be attempted but is often difficult for children with autism who may have poor fine motor skills. Augmentative communication using a computer or story board can be useful (see Chapter 13). Art and music therapy have also been used in attempts to communicate nonverbally with these children.

Pharmacological Management

Despite the intense interest in structural and biochemical brain abnormalities in autism, a specific medication has not been identified as effective in treating the core symptoms (Gilman & Tuchman, 1995). Pharmacological management should be considered secondary to educational and behavioral interventions and is clearly not indicated for all affected children. Medications should be used to target specific symptoms that may interfere with the child's global functioning.

Prescribing psychotropic medications for these children requires careful evaluation of treatment goals and side effects (McDougle, Price, & Volkmar, 1994). Once a drug is selected, the dosage should be maximized until either a good response or significant side effects occur. Multiple drug use should be avoided if possible. It may take a number of weeks for the maximum drug effects to become evident. Some medication will require periodic monitoring of blood pressure, electrocardiogram (EKG), liver function, or blood count. As a result of these complexities, medication should be prescribed by a physician with extensive experience with children who have PDD.

Hyperactivity

Overactivity and abnormal ability to focus on an activity (i.e., symptoms of ADHD) are particularly common behavioral concerns in individuals with PDD-NOS and Asperger disorder. Some individuals respond favorably to conventional stimulants, such as methylphenidate (Ritalin), but there is a significant risk of side effects including a worsening of stereotypies, self-injury, or withdrawal, and the development of excessive irritability (Aman, Marks, Turbott, et al., 1991). Clonidine (Catapres), a second-line drug for treatment of ADHD, has been used with some success and fewer side effects to control overactivity and sleep problems in children with PDD (Jaselskis, Cook, Fletcher, et al., 1992). Clonidine is available orally and as a transdermal patch, which can be helpful when compliance is an issue (Fankhauser, Karumanchi, German, et al., 1992). The principal side effects are drowsiness and postural hypotension. Guanfacine (Tenex), which is in the same class as clonidine, may have similar benefits and produces less sedation.

Aggression

Aggression is common in children with PDD. Haloperidol (Haldol), a high-potency neuroleptic agent, has been found to be effective in reducing aggression as well as decreasing stereotypies, hyperactivity, and self-injury and increasing vocalizations and social interactions in some individuals with PDD (Locascio, Malone, Small, et al., 1991; Perry, Campbell, Adams, et al., 1989). Although Haldol has no beneficial effect on learning, it can calm children without sedation (Anderson, Campbell, Adams, et al., 1989). Unfortunately, the high incidence of movement disorders including dyskinesia, dystonia, and akathisia has limited its usefulness (Malone, Ernst, Godfrey, et al., 1991; Shay, Sanchez, Cueva, et al., 1993). The concomitant use of the anti-

Parkinsonian drug, benztropine (Cogentin), has somewhat decreased this risk, especially if haloperidol is used for only a few months at a time. Newer neuroleptic drugs such as clozapine (Clozaril) and risperidone (Risperdal), with reportedly less dyskinetic symptoms, may prove safer for longer-term use. Other drugs that have been used to control aggression include the beta-blocker propranolol (Inderal), the antiepileptic drugs carbamazepine (Tegretol) and valproic acid (Depakene, Depakote), the anxiolytic drug buspirone (Buspar), and the mood disorder drug lithium.

Self-Injury

As with aggression, self-injury is most often under behavioral control or a combination of behavior and biological control. When there appears to be a significant biological component, the same drugs used to treat aggression are used for self-injury. Neuroleptics have been most effective (Schroeder, Hammach, Mulich, et al., 1995), although lithium, propranolol, and serotonin reuptake inhibitors also have been helpful (Mace & Mauk, 1995). In addition, naltrexone (Trexan), a synthetic opiate antagonist, has been utilized to treat self-injurious and aggressive behavior in children with autism (Campbell, Anderson, Small, et al., 1993; Gonzalez, Campbell, Small, et al., 1994). It also has mildly beneficial effects on the autistic symptoms of overactivity and stereotypies.

Stereotypies and Rigid Behaviors

Serotonin reuptake inhibitors such as fluoxetine (Prozac) have been investigated to treat ritualistic behaviors in individuals with PDD. Because many autistic features are similar to characteristics of individuals with obsessive-compulsive disorder (OCD), the tricyclic antidepressant clomipramine (Anafranil), which has been found to be useful in OCD, may be effective in correcting ritualistic behaviors as well (Brasic, Barnett, Kaplan, et al., 1994). Another drug with a complex effect on serotonin, fenfluramine (Pondimin), was initially felt to improve many symptoms of autism (Geller, Ritvo, Freeman, et al., 1982). However, a number of studies subsequently showed that fenfluramine has few benefits and considerable side effects (Ritvo, Freeman, Yuwiler, et al., 1984). These include hyperactivity, agitation, decreased appetite, and insomnia (Leventhal, Cook, Morford, et al., 1993).

Depression

Mood disorders, most commonly depression, may complicate PDD, especially in adolescents with Asperger disorder (Lainhart & Folstein, 1994). Tricyclic antidepressants such as imipramine (Tofranil), nortriptyline (Pamelar), and desipramine (Norpramin) may be useful. Serotonin uptake inhibitors can also be used (Cook, Rowlett, Jaselskis, et al., 1992); and if there is a manic component, lithium may be effective (Steingard & Biederman, 1987).

Seizure Disorders

As with other children with developmental disabilities, generalized tonic-clonic seizures are the most common form of epilepsy in children with PDD. Antiepileptic drugs used in these children include carbamazepine (Tegretol) and valproic acid (Depakene, Depakote). Phenobarbital and phenytoin (Dilantin) are generally avoided because they tend to produce significant behavioral side effects, including hyperactivity and irritability (Gillberg, 1991).

Sleep Disorders

Sleep-related problems are often evident in children with PDDs. Preliminary studies suggest that melatonin may be helpful (Jan, Espezel, & Appleton, 1994). Tricyclic antidepressants such as imipramine (Tofranil), sedatives such as chloral hydrate, and alpha adrenergic agonists such as clonidine (Catapres) have also been used.

Family Support

Parents need emotional support and advocacy and, most important, should be included in the treatment process as teachers and co-therapists of their children (Koegel & Koegel, 1995; Koegel, Koegel, & Dunlap, 1996). There is no doubt that having a child with PDD is enormously stressful for the family (Barron & Barron, 1992; Hart, 1993; Moes, 1995). In addition to the usual difficulties of having a child with disabilities, there are many additional demands as well as frustrations of caring for a child who provides few emotional rewards, requires intense supervision, has disturbed sleep, and exhibits behavior that is difficult to manage. If emotional problems arise, family counseling is indicated (see Chapter 34).

Unproven Therapies

The eagerness to find a treatment or cure often leads to the rapid acceptance and promotion of therapeutic techniques before they have undergone adequate trials, particularly among individuals with autism. Currently used unproven treatments include immune therapy, megavitamin therapy, facilitated communication, auditory integration training, and multiple medications. None of these has been shown to be effective.

Rimland (1987) described positive responses in children with autism who were treated with high dose vitamin B_6 (pyridoxine, 3 grams per day) and magnesium. His success has not, however, been replicated by other investigators (Martineau, Barthelemy, Garreau, et al., 1985). In addition, megavitamin therapy has potential neurotoxicity (Albin, Albers, Greenberg, et al., 1987).

The steroid hormones ACTH and prednisone have been proposed to treat children with autistic features who have Landau-Kleffner syndrome (Stefanatos, Grover, & Geller, 1995), a seizure disorder associated with an acquired aphasia (Paquier, Van Dongen, & Loonen, 1992). This very rare disorder is evaluated using specialized EEG (Stefanatos, 1993). Other investigators believe that autism can be differentiated clinically from Landau-Kleffner syndrome because there is evidence of a developmental language disorder in autism versus language regression in Landau-Kleffner. In terms of treatment, long-term steroid administration carries considerable risks, including hypertension, diabetes, and osteoporosis.

A synthetic analogue of ACTH (ORG 2766) has been more broadly proposed to treat the core symptoms of autism. In a pilot study, high-dose prolonged treatment was associated with significant increases in social interactions, improved verbal communications, and positive changes in play behavior (Buitelaar, Van Engeland, deKogel, et al., 1992). Further studies are ongoing. This experimental medication is not available in the United States.

Facilitated communication involves a "facilitator" providing physical support under the arm of a child with autism to permit the typing of messages on a keyboard communicator. It has been claimed that nonverbal individuals previously diagnosed as having mental retardation can actually type sophisticated messages using facilitated communication (Biklen, 1990). Controlled studies, however, have discredited this method by showing that the facilitator is (often unintentionally) the source of the communication (Jacobson, Mulick, & Schwartz, 1995).

Auditory integration training is another unproven method based on the theory that in autism there is a primary disturbance in the auditory system. Treatment involves having the child listen through earphones to sounds in which specific frequencies have been filtered out. This is supposed to improve both behavior and language. There have been no scientifically valid studies published in support of this treatment.

Gluten avoidance, immune therapy, piracetam, treatment for fungal infections, and the use of special tinted glasses have all been popularized as treatments for autism and related disorders. Most of these approaches are based on an unscientifically founded association of autism with other conditions. Children may be exposed to unwarranted treatment side effects, and parents may spend a great deal of time and money on these ineffective treatments.

IAN: A CHILD WITH AUTISM

Ian was initially evaluated when he was 26 months old because his parents noticed that he was not yet talking. His birth, the first to his young parents, was much anticipated and uncomplicated. However, he was fussy and not cuddly as an infant. His grandparents attributed this to his parents' inexperience. He was an attractive, strong, blond child who rolled over early and sat and walked at the usual times. He did not begin to make sounds, however, until he was about 12 months old, and he did not participate in any baby games such as So Big. When he still did not respond consistently to his name at 18 months, his parents brought up concerns about deafness to their pediatrician. Although Ian was uncooperative with the hearing testing, he did not appear to have a significant hearing loss.

At his second birthday, Ian was still not speaking and avoided eye contact. Rather than play with toys, he lined them up in rows or twirled them. He was hyperactive and had frequent temper tantrums that included head banging. These most commonly occurred during transitions from one activity to another. He could not make his needs known, and his parents were exhausted from caring for him. Ian also stopped eating most table foods and limited his intake to oatmeal and peanut butter sandwiches. This was the final straw, and the parents sought help.

He was evaluated by a multidisciplinary team that included a developmental pediatrician, speech-language therapist, child psychologist, and early childhood educator. At the family conference that followed the evaluation, his parents were devastated to learn that Ian was diagnosed as having autistic disorder and severe developmental delays. They were told he was at high risk for mental retardation and were referred to an early intervention program.

Initially, the teacher at the intervention program had difficulty working with Ian. He was not interested in imitating in order to learn new skills, and his temper tantrums interfered with his participation in activities. He had difficulty sitting quietly and was uninterested in interacting with the other children. The family then consulted a behavioral specialist. She prescribed a set daily schedule and trained his parents to safely ignore the tantrums. She assisted the teachers in working with Ian to attend and sit quietly in the classroom. They set up a system of rewards (tickles) for vocalizations and eye contact. Ian's parents practiced this at home in both structured and unstructured settings. At age 5, Ian entered a specialized program for children with autism that used the TEACCH curriculum and incorporated some of the behavioral strategies that had seemed to help him. He made good progress within the constraints of his cognitive impairments.

Now at age 10, Ian's tantrums are rare, and he is able to go shopping with his mother without causing a scene. He speaks in short phrases and has many self-care skills. As suspected earlier, he has mental retardation requiring extensive supports with a mental age of 4 years. It is apparent that as a result of his communication impairments and mental retardation he will need lifelong supervision. However, his family feels he is much happier, more interactive, and has gained many language and self-help skills.

JULIO: A CHILD WITH ASPERGER SYNDROME

Julio was the first boy in a family of three girls. Pregnancy and childbirth were uncomplicated, and Julio appeared to be a beautiful and happy baby. He rolled, sat, and walked at the usual times and was quite physically active although somewhat clumsy. He began to speak at the usual time, but he tended to use stereotypic language, repeating nursery rhymes and commercial jingles.

As the only boy and youngest child, he received a great deal of attention at home. Yet, although he had many potential playmates, he seemed to prefer to be alone. He also perseverated in special interests, particularly dinosaurs, and resisted transitions to new activities. His parents were not concerned about him until he went to nursery school. At that time, his teacher told them that although Julio seemed to be doing well academically, he interacted poorly socially. He spoke well, but his speech was stilted, and he would get terribly upset if he were interrupted from his monologues. Julio appeared disengaged from the kidding and joking of the other children, and he reacted with severe tantrums when the class routine was altered in any way. He was also described as hyperactive and inattentive.

In kindergarten there were similar problems, and he was referred for evaluation. The school psychologist found that Julio had typical intelligence but believed there was something unusual about him and recommended a referral to a developmental disabilities center. The specialists there diagnosed Julio as having Asperger syndrome and expressed some concern about the father's social isolation, speculating that he too was affected. Clonidine was prescribed to control both Julio's overactivity and ritualistic behaviors. The family also was advised to obtain social skills programming for their son. This program focused on teaching Julio to integrate more socially with his peers and to carry on an interactive conversation. In addition, a speech therapist worked with him to help modulate his voice, and she tried to teach and reinforce eye contact.

At age 14, Julio has no close friends but gets B's in school. He is preoccupied by sports statistics and computer games. His family nervously is considering allowing him to take an early morning job delivering newspapers. The school guidance counselor feels that after graduation Julio will be capable of going to college and then engaging in independent employment, providing the position does not require much social interaction. This is consistent with Julio's budding interest in computer science.

PROGNOSIS

The prognosis of a child with PDD is closely linked to his or her verbal abilities and intelligence. In general, predictions of adult intellectual functioning should be deferred until age 5 or 6. Earlier predictions tend to be inaccurate, and the more prominent autistic symptomatology often resolves over time. Higher functioning people with Asperger disorder may "grow out" of a diagnosis of autism but retain abnormalities in social function (Gonzalez, Alpert, Shay, et al., 1993).

Independent functioning is more difficult to predict as it is related to social ability and behavioral issues. It is increasingly recognized that major barriers to social function may be related to lack of opportunity and instruction as much as to intrinsic impairments (Grenot-Scheyer, Coots, & Falvey, 1990). Evidence suggests that individuals with PDD will continue acquiring new adaptive skills throughout their life span. A small percentage of higher functioning individuals will be self-supporting, but two thirds of adults with PDD require supervised living arrangements (Rumsey, Rapoport, & Sceery, 1985).

SUMMARY

Autism and the other PDDs are organically determined disorders that generally present in infancy or early childhood. They are all characterized by abnormalities in communication, social interaction, and activities and interests. Those children with autism are more likely to have associated mental retardation and severe communication impairments. Individuals with Asperger disorder or PDD-NOS have a better prognosis but still may have substantial difficulties, particularly in interpersonal relationships. Multidimensional treatment has resulted in a significant improvement in outcome.

REFERENCES

Adrien, J.L., Lenoir, P., Martineau, J., et al. (1993). Blind ratings of early symptoms of autism based upon family home movies. *Journal of the American Academy of Child and Adolescent Psychiatry, 32,* 617–626.

Albin, R.L., Albers, J.W., Greenberg, H.S., et al. (1987). Acute sensory neuropathy from pyridoxine overdose. *Neurology, 37,* 1729–1732.

Aman, M.G., Marks, R.E., Turbott, S.H., et al. (1991). Methylphenidate and thioridazine in the treatment of intellectually subaverage children: Effects on cognitive-motor performance. *Journal of the American Academy of Child and Adolescent Psychiatry, 30*(5), 816–824.

American Psychiatric Association. (1994). *Diagnostic and statistical manual of mental disorders* (4th ed.). Washington, DC: Author.

Anderson, L.T., Campbell, M., Adams, P., et al. (1989). The effects of haloperidol on discrimination learning and behavioral symptoms in autistic children. *Journal of Autism and Developmental Disorders, 19,* 227–239.

Bachevalier, J. (1994). Medial temporal lobe structures and autism: A review of clinical and experimental findings. *Neuropsychologia, 32,* 627–648.

Bailey, A., Phillips, W., & Rutter, M. (1996). Autism: Towards an integration of clinical, genetic, neuropsychological, and neurobiological perspectives. *Journal of Child Psychology and Psychiatry and Allied Disciplines, 37,* 89–126.

Baron-Cohen, S., Cox, A., Baird, G., et al. (1996). Psychological markers in the detection of autism in infancy in a large population. *British Journal of Psychiatry, 168,* 158–163.

Barron, J., & Barron, S. (1992). *There's a boy in here.* New York: Simon & Schuster.

Bauer, S. (1995). Autism and the pervasive developmental disorders. *Pediatrics in Review, 16,* 130–136, 168–176.

Bauman, M.L., & Kemper, T.L. (Eds.). (1994). *The neurobiology of autism.* Baltimore: The Johns Hopkins University Press.

Biklen, D. (1990). Communication unbound: Autism and praxis. *Harvard Educational Review, 60,* 291–314.

Bonnett, K., & Gao, X-K. (1996). Asperger syndrome in neurologic perspective. *Journal of Child Neurology, 11,* 483–487.

Brasic, J.R., Barnett, J.Y., Kaplan, D., et al. (1994). Clomipramine ameliorates adventitious movements and compulsions in prepubertal boys with autistic disorder and severe mental retardation. *Neurology, 44,* 1309–1312.

Buitelaar, J.K., Van Engeland, H., deKogel, K., et al. (1992). The adrenocorticotrophic hormone analog ORG 2766 benefits autistic children: Report on a second controlled clinical trial. *Journal of the*

American Academy of Child and Adolescent Psychiatry, 31, 1149–1156.

Campbell, M., Anderson, L.T., Small, A.M., et al. (1993). Naltrexone in autistic children: Behavioral symptoms and attentional learning. *Journal of the American Academy of Child and Adolescent Psychiatry, 32*(6), 1283–1291.

Capute, A.J., Derivan, A.T., Chauvel, P.J., et al. (1975). Infantile autism: I. A prospective study of the diagnosis. *Developmental Medicine and Child Neurology, 17,* 58–62.

Carr, E.G., Levin, L., McConnachie, G., et al. (1995). *Communication-based intervention for problem behavior: A user's guide for producing positive change.* Baltimore: Paul H. Brookes Publishing Co.

Cohen, I.L., Sudhalter, V., Jenkins, E.C., et al. (1991). Why are autism and the fragile-X syndrome associated? Conceptual and methodological issues. *American Journal of Human Genetics, 48,* 195–202.

Cook, E.H., Rowlett, R., Jaselskis, C., et al. (1992). Fluoxetine treatment of children and adults with autistic disorder and mental retardation. *Journal of the American Academy of Child and Adolescent Psychiatry, 31,* 739–745.

Costello, E.J. (1996). State of the science in autism: Report to the National Institutes of Health: Epidemiology. *Journal of Autism and Developmental Disorders, 26,* 126–129.

Courchesne, E., Townsend, J., & Saitoh, O. (1994). The brain in infantile autism: Posterior fossa structures are abnormal. *Neurology, 44,* 214–223.

Cox, R.D., & Schopler, E. (1993). Aggression and self-injurious behaviors in persons with autism: The TEACCH (Treatment and Education of Autistic and related Communications Handicapped Children) approach. *Acta Paedopsychiatrica, 56,* 85–90.

Cryan, E., Bryne, M., O'Donovan, A., et al. (1996). Brief report: A case control study of obstetric complications and later autistic disorder. *Journal of Autism and Developmental Disorders, 26*(4), 453–460.

DeLong, R. (1994). Children with autistic spectrum disorder and a family history of affective disorder. *Developmental Medicine and Child Neurology, 36,* 674–687.

DeLong, R., & Nohria, C. (1994). Psychiatric family history and neurological disease in autistic spectrum disorders. *Developmental Medicine and Child Neurology, 36,* 441–448.

Einfeld, S., Moloney, H., & Hall, W. (1989). Autism is not associated with the fragile X syndrome. *American Journal of Medical Genetics, 34,* 187–193.

Fankhauser, M.P., Karumanchi, V.C., German, M.L., et al. (1992). A double-blind, placebo-controlled study of the efficacy of transdermal clonidine in autism. *Journal of Clinical Psychiatry, 53,* 77–82.

Filipek, P.A. (1995). Quantitative magnetic resonance imaging in autism: The cerebellar vermis. *Current Opinion in Neurology, 8,* 134–138.

Fisch, G.S. (1992). Is autism associated with the fragile X syndrome? *American Journal of Medical Genetics, 43,* 47–55.

Frea, W.D. (1995). Social-communicative skills in higher-functioning children with autism. In R.L. Koegel & L.K. Koegel (Eds.), *Teaching children with autism: Strategies for initiating positive interactions and improving learning opportunities* (pp. 53–66). Baltimore: Paul H. Brookes Publishing Co.

Frith, U. (1993). Autism. *Scientific American, 268,* 108–114.

Geller, E., Ritvo, E.R., Freeman, B.J., et al. (1982). Preliminary observations on the effect of fenfluramine on blood serotonin and symptoms in threee autistic boys. *New England Journal of Medicine, 307,* 165–169.

Gillberg, C. (1991). The treatment of epilepsy in autism. *Journal of Autism and Developmental Disorders, 21,* 61–77.

Gillberg, C., & Coleman, M. (1996). Autism and medical disorders: A review of the literature. *Developmental Medicine and Child Neurology, 38,* 191–202.

Gillberg, I.C., Gillberg, C., & Ahlsen, G. (1994). Autistic behaviour and attention deficits in tuberous sclerosis: A population-based study. *Developmental Medicine and Child Neurology, 36,* 50–56.

Gillberg, I.C., Gillberg, C., & Kopp, S. (1992). Hypothyroidism and autism spectrum disorders. *Journal of Child Psychology and Psychiatry and Allied Disciplines, 33,* 531–542.

Gilman, J.T., & Tuchman, R.F. (1995). Autism and associated behavioral disorders: Pharmacotherapeutic intervention. *Annals of Pharmacotherapy, 29,* 47–56.

Gonzalez, N.M., Alpert, M., Shay, J., et al. (1993). Autistic children on followup: Change of diagnosis. *Psychopharmacology Bulletin, 29*(3), 353–358.

Gonzalez, N.M., Campbell, M., Small, A.M., et al. (1994). Naltrexone plasma levels, clinical response and effect on weight in autistic children. *Psychopharmacology Bulletin, 30,* 203–208.

Grandin, T. (1995). *Thinking in pictures: And other reports from my life with autism.* New York: Doubleday.

Grenot-Scheyer, M., Coots, J., & Falvey, M.A. (1989). Developing and fostering friendships. In M.A. Falvey (Ed.), *Community-based curriculum: Instructional strategies for students with severe handicaps* (2nd ed., pp. 345–358). Baltimore: Paul H. Brookes Publishing Co.

Haas, R.H., Townsend, J., Courchesne, E., et al. (1996). Neurological abnormalities in infantile autism. *Journal of Child Neurology, 11,* 84–92.

Hagberg, B. (1995) Rett syndrome: Clinical peculiarities and biological mysteries. *Acta Paediatrica, 84,* 971–976.

Hagberg, B., & Witt-Engerström, I. (1985). *Rett syndrome: A suggested staging system for describing impairment profile with increasing age towards adolescence.* Paper presented at the International Workshop on Rett syndrome, Baltimore.

Hart, C. (1993). *A parents' guide to autism.* New York: Pocket Books.

Hobson, R.P. (1993). *Autism and the development of mind.* Hillsdale, NJ: Lawrence Erlbaum Associates.

Howlin, P. (1993). Behavioural techniques to reduce self-injurious behavior in children with autism. *Acta Paedopsychiatrica, 56,* 74–84.

Individuals with Disabilities Education Act (IDEA) of 1990, PL 101-476, 20 U.S.C. § 1400 *et seq.*

Jacobson, J.W., Mulick, J.A., & Schwartz, A.A. (1995). A history of facilitated communication. *American Psychologist, 50,* 750–765.

Jan, J.E., Espezel, H., & Appleton, R.E. (1994). The treatment of sleep disorders with melatonin. *Developmental Medicine and Child Neurology, 36,* 97–107.

Janson, U. (1993). Normal and deviant behavior in blind children with ROP. *Acta Ophthalmologica, 210*(Suppl.), 20–26.

Jaselskis, C.A., Cook, E.H., Fletcher, K.E., et al. (1992). Clonidine treatment of hyperactive and impulsive children with autistic disorder. *Journal of Clinical Psychopharmacology, 12,* 322–327.

Jorde, L.B., Mason-Brothers, A., Waldmann, R., et al. (1990). The UCLA–University of Utah epidemiologic survey of autism: Genealogical analysis of familial aggregation. *American Journal of Medical Genetics, 36,* 85–88.

Kanner, L. (1943). Autistic disturbances of affective contact. *Nervous Child, 2,* 217–250.

Klin, A. (1994). Asperger syndrome. *Child and Adolescent Psychiatric Clinics of North America, 3*(1), 131–148.

Koegel, L.K., Koegel, R.L., & Dunlap, G. (Eds.). (1996). *Positive behavioral support: Including people with different behavior in the community.* Baltimore: Paul H. Brookes Publishing Co.

Koegel, R.L., & Koegel, L.K. (1995). *Teaching children with autism: Strategies for initiating positive interactions and improving learning opportunities.* Baltimore: Paul H. Brookes Publishing Co.

Koegel, R.L., O'Dell, M.C., & Dunlap, G. (1988). Producing speech use in nonverbal autistic children by reinforcing attempts. *Journal of Autism and Developmental Disabilities, 17,* 187–199.

Krug, D.A., Arick, J.R., & Almond, P. (1980). Behavior checklist for identifying severely handicapped individuals with high levels of autistic behavior. *Journal of Child Psychiatry, 21,* 221–229.

Lainhart, J.E., & Folstein, S.E. (1994). Affective disorders in people with autism: A review of published cases. *Journal of Autism and Developmental Disorders, 24,* 587–601.

Lander, E.S., & Schort, N.J. (1994). Genetic dissection of complex traits. *Science, 265,* 2037–2048.

LeCouteur, A., Rutter, M., Lord, C., et al. (1989). Autism diagnostic interview: A standardized investigator-based instrument. *Journal of Autism and Developmental Disorders, 19,* 363–387.

Leventhal, B.L., Cook, E.H., Jr., Morford, M., et al. (1993). Clinical and neurochemical effects of fenfluramine in children with autism. *Journal of Neuropsychiatry and Clinical Neurosciences, 5,* 307–315.

Locascio, J.J., Malone, R.P., Small, A.M., et al. (1991). Factors related to haloperidol response and dyskinesias in autistic children. *Psychopharmacology Bulletin, 27,* 119–126.

Lotspeich, L.J., & Ciaranello, R.D. (1993). The neurobiology and genetics of infantile autism. *International Review of Neurobiology, 35,* 87–129.

Lovaas, O.I. (1993). The development of a treatment-research project for developmentally disabled and autistic children. *Journal of Applied Behavior Analysis, 26*(4), 617–630.

Mace, F.C., & Mauk, J.E. (1995) Bio-behavioral diagnosis and treatment of self-injury. *Mental Retardation and Developmental Disabilities Research Reviews, 1*(2), 104–110.

Malone, R.P., Ernst, M., Godfrey, K.A., et al. (1991). Repeated episodes of neuroleptic-related dyskinesias in autistic children. *Psychopharmacology Bulletin, 27,* 113–117.

Martineau, J., Barthelemy, C., Garreau, B., et al. (1985). Vitamin B$_6$, magnesium, and combined B$_6$–Mg: Therapeutic effects in childhood autism. *Biological Psychiatry, 20,* 467–478.

McDougle, C.J., Price, L.H., & Volkmar, F.R. (1994). Recent advances in the pharmacotherapy of autism and related conditions. *Child and Adolescent Psychiatric Clinics of North America, 3*(1), 71–89.

Minshew, N.J., Goldstein, G., Taylor, H.G., et al. (1994). Academic achievement in high functioning autistic individuals. *Journal of Clinical and Experimental Neuropsychology, 16,* 261–270.

Moes, D. (1995). Parent education and parenting stress. In R.L. Koegel & L.K. Koegel (Eds.), *Teaching children with autism: Strategies for initiating positive interactions and improving learning opportunities* (pp. 79–94). Baltimore: Paul H. Brookes Publishing Co.

Nelson, K.B. (1991). Prenatal and perinatal factors in the etiology of autism. *Pediatrics, 87*(Suppl. 5), 761–766.

Nordin, V., & Gillberg, C. (1996). Autism spectrum disorders in children with physical or mental disability or both: I. Clinical and epidemiological aspects. *Developmental Medicine and Child Neurology, 38,* 297–313.

O'Connor, N., & Hermelin, B. (1991). Talents and preoccupations in idiot-savants. *Psychological Medicine, 21,* 959–964.

Osterling, J., & Dawson, G. (1994). Early recognition of children with autism: A study of first birthday home videos. *Journal of Autism and Developmental Disorders, 24,* 247.

Paquier, P.F., Van Dongen, H.R., & Loonen, M.C.B. (1992). The Landau-Kleffner syndrome or "acquired aphasia with convulsive disorder." *Archives of Neurology, 49,* 354–359.

Perry, R., Campbell, M., Adams, P., et al. (1989). Long-term efficacy of haloperidol in autistic children: Continuous versus discontinuous drug administration. *Journal of the American Academy of Child and Adolescent Psychiatry, 28,* 87–92.

Piven, J., Arndt, S., Bailey, J., et al. (1995). An MRI study of brain size in autism. *American Journal of Psychiatry, 152*(8), 1145–1149.

Prizant, B.M. (1996). Brief report: Communication, language, social, and emotional development. *Journal of Autism and Developmental Disorders, 26*(2), 173–178.

Reiss, A.L., Feinstein, C., & Rosenbaum, K. (1986). Autism and genetic disorders. *Schizophrenia Bulletin, 12,* 724–738.

Rimland, B. (1987). Megavitamin B$_6$ and magnesium in the treatment of autistic children and adults. In E. Schopler & G.B. Mesibov (Eds.), *Neurobiological issues in autism* (pp. 389–405). New York: Plenum.

Ritvo, E.R., Freeman, B.J., Mason-Brothers, A., et al. (1985). Concordance for the syndrome of autism in 40 pairs of afflicted twins. *American Journal of Psychiatry, 142,* 74–77.

Ritvo, E.R., Freeman, B.J., Pingree, C., et al. (1989). The UCLA–University of Utah epidemiologic survey of autism: Prevalence. *American Journal of Psychiatry, 146*(2), 194–199.

Ritvo, E.R., Freeman, B.J., Yuwiler, A., et al. (1984). Study of fenfluramine in outpatients with the syndrome of autism. *Journal of Pediatrics, 105,* 823–828.

Rumsey, J.M., Rapoport, J.L., & Sceery, W.R. (1985). Autistic children as adults: Psychiatric, social and behavioral outcomes. *Journal of the American Academy of Child Psychiatry, 24,* 465–473.

Rutter, M. (1985a). Infantile autism and other pervasive developmental disorders. In M. Rutter & L. Hersov (Eds.), *Child and adolescent psychiatry: Modern approaches* (pp. 545–566). Oxford, England: Blackwell Scientific Publications.

Rutter, M. (1985b). The treatment of autistic children. *Journal of Child Psychology and Psychiatry and Allied Disciplines, 26,* 193–214.

Schifter, T., Hoffman, J.M., Hatten, H.P., Jr., et al. (1994). Neuroimaging in infantile autism. *Journal of Child Neurology, 9,* 155–161.

Schopler, E., & Mesibov, G.B. (1995). *Learning and cognition in autism.* New York: Plenum.

Schopler, E., Reichler, R.J., DeVellius, R., et al. (1980). Toward objective classification of childhood autism: Childhood Autism Rating Scale (CARS). *Journal of Autism and Developmental Disorders, 10,* 91–102.

Schroeder, R.S., Hammach, R.J., Mulich, J.A., et al. (1995). Clinical trials of D1 and D2 dopamine modulating drugs and self-injury in mental retardation and developmental disability. *Mental Retardation and Developmental Disabilities Research Reviews, 1,* 120–130.

Shay, J., Sanchez, L.E., Cueva, J.E., et al. (1993). Neuroleptic-related dyskinesias and stereotypies in autistic children: Videotaped ratings. *Psychopharmacology Bulletin, 29,* 359–363.

Siegel, B. (1996). *The world of the autistic child.* New York: Oxford University Press.

Siegel, B., Pliner, C., Eschler, J., et al. (1988). How children with autism are diagnosed: Difficulties in identification of children with multiple developmental delays. *Developmental and Behavioral Pediatrics, 9,* 199–204.

Smalley, S.L., & Collins, F. (1996). Genetic, prenatal and immunologic factors. *Journal of Autism and Developmental Disorders, 26,* 195–198.

Stefanatos, G.A. (1993). Frequency modulation analysis in children with Landau-Klessner syndrome. *Annals of the New York Academy of Sciences, 692,* 412–414.

Stefanatos, G.A., Grover, W., & Geller, E. (1995). Case study: Corticosteroid treatment of language regression in pervasive developmental disorder. *Journal of the American Academy of Child and Adolescent Psychiatry, 34,* 1107–1111.

Steingard, R., & Biederman, J. (1987). Lithium responsive manic-like symptoms in two individuals with autism and mental retardation: Case report. *Journal of the American Academy of Child and Adolescent Psychiatry, 26,* 932–935.

Stone, W.L., Lemanek, K.L., Fishel, P.T., et al. (1990). Play and imitation skills in the diagnosis of autism in young children. *Pediatrics, 86,* 267–272.

Stromland, K., Nordin, V., Miller, M., et al. (1994). Autism in thalidomide embryopathy: A population study. *Developmental Medicine and Child Neurology, 36,* 351–356.

Szatmari, P. (1991). Asperger's syndrome: Diagnosis, treatment, and outcome. *Psychiatric Clinics of North America, 14,* 81–93.

Tager-Flusberg, H. (1993). *Understanding other's minds: Perspectives from autism.* New York: Oxford University Press.

Tuchman, R.F., Rapin, I., & Shinnar, S. (1991). Autistic and dysphasic children: II. Epilepsy. *Pediatrics, 88,* 1219–1225.

Volkmar, F., & Rutter, M. (1995) Childhood disintegrative disorder: Results of the DSM-IV autism field trial. *Journal of the American Academy of Child and Adolescent Psychiatry, 34,* 1092–1095.

Williams, D. (1992). *Nobody nowhere: The extraordinary autobiography of an autistic.* New York: Times Books.

Wing, L. (1988). The continuum of autistic characteristics. In E. Schopler & G.B. Mesibov (Eds.), *Diagnosis and assessment in autism* (pp. 91–110). New York: Plenum.

22 Attention-Deficit/ Hyperactivity Disorder

Nathan J. Blum
Marianne Mercugliano

Upon completion of this chapter, the reader will:

- be familiar with the characteristics of attention-deficit/hyperactivity disorder
- be aware of some of the causes of inattention and hyperactivity
- understand the components of the diagnostic process
- know the different approaches to management

A short attention span, impulsivity, distractibility, and hyperactivity are the cardinal features of attention-deficit/hyperactivity disorder (ADHD). Although these are also common behavioral characteristics that occur to a greater or lesser degree in many individuals, when a parent, teacher, or physician has concerns that these symptoms interfere with a child's academic or interpersonal development, evaluation and treatment are warranted. An evaluation requires an assessment of both the symptoms of ADHD and their severity, as well as medical, neurological, academic, psychosocial, and/or psychiatric conditions that may be present instead of or in addition to ADHD. Coping with these symptoms on an ongoing basis can be stressful and demoralizing for the child and his or her family. Treatment includes an individualized, multimodal approach aimed at minimizing symptoms and their negative impact on learning, interpersonal relationships, and self-esteem. This chapter focuses on children diagnosed with ADHD and discusses its management and prognosis.

CHARACTERISTICS OF ATTENTION-DEFICIT/HYPERACTIVITY DISORDER

The disorder known as ADHD has been called by many names over the years, including minimal brain damage, minimal cerebral dysfunction, hyperactive child syndrome, and attention deficit disorder with or without hyperactivity. The term attention-deficit/hyperactivity disorder has evolved as the understanding of the disorder has improved. There remains, however, much to be learned.

ADHD is the most common neurodevelopmental disorder of childhood, with an estimated prevalence of 3%–5% among school-age children and a male to female ratio of 4:1–9:1 (American Psychiatric Association, 1994; Sandberg, 1996). In addition to a short attention span, impulsivity, distractibility, and hyperactivity, affected children also display a low frustration tolerance, a lack of motivation for all but the most stimulating activities, a tendency to become bored very easily or often, and a relative inability to recognize future consequences of behavior or learn from mistakes. Although most children with ADHD exhibit hyperactivity and impulsivity, some children are primarily inattentive. These children may even be slow-moving and slow to respond. They are more likely to have difficulties for several years before being correctly diagnosed. Despite these difficulties, some children with ADHD have the ability to be highly successful in areas of interest to which they devote their motivation, energy, and enthusiasm. ADHD occurs in individuals with a range of intellectual and social abilities. Although some have good social skills, many have great difficulty due to impairments in "reading" the nuances of social behavior or inhibiting impulsive responses (Barkley, 1990; Whalen & Henker, 1992).

The characteristics of and the difficulties for a child with ADHD frequently change with age. Although children with hyperactivity often display symptoms during the preschool years, those who are primarily inattentive may not have difficulties until the elementary school years, when the persistent demands of the school day tax their limited attention span. Young school-age children with ADHD often have difficulty following classroom rules and teachers' instructions. As they become older, these problems may lead to difficulty completing seatwork and homework independently. Social difficulties, especially in less structured situations such as the lunchroom and playground, are common, and peer rejection can be a significant problem. In the majority of individuals, symptoms of ADHD persist to some degree into adolescence and adulthood (Hill & Schoener, 1996). Adolescents often have difficulty with the organization, planning, and self-management required for longer-term projects and college work; and adults may express concerns about completing projects; handling job stress; interacting with work colleagues; and juggling the demands of marriage, family, and work (Barkley, 1990; Wender, 1995; Werry, 1992).

ADHD frequently coexists with other disorders of learning, behavior, or emotion. These disorders are defined in the *Diagnostic and Statistical Manual of Mental Disorders, Fourth Edition* (DSM-IV) (American Psychiatric Association, 1994). The "disruptive behavior disorders" category, coexisting with ADHD in 30%–50% of clinic-referred individuals, includes oppositional defiant disorder (characterized by noncompliance and defiance of authority) and conduct disorder (characterized by more serious antisocial behaviors) (American Psychiatric Association, 1994). Studies of the co-occurrence of learning disabilities with ADHD show a range of results, likely due in part to variability in the definition of learning disability. Using a rigorous definition of learning disability, approximately 25% of children with ADHD also have a learning disability (Barkley, 1990; Shaywitz & Shaywitz, 1988). An additional 25% have other academic problems. Children and adults with ADHD are also at increased risk for mood disorders, including depression and anxiety, although the percent of comorbidity varies greatly from study to study (American Psychiatric Association, 1994; Barkley, 1990; Biederman, Faraone, Keenan, et al., 1992; Biederman, Newcorn, & Sprich, 1991).

CAUSES OF ATTENTION-DEFICIT/HYPERACTIVITY DISORDER

Early in the 20th century, it was noted that children who recovered from encephalitis exhibited behavior characterized by a short attention span, impulsivity, and disinhibition. In addition, reports from the field of neuropsychology demonstrated that individuals with other types of brain injuries had similar behaviors. Thus, in the 1950s, it was surmised that children who exhibited these symptoms in the absence of a known brain insult must have had "minimal brain damage." Over the subsequent years, however, it became clear that most children with ADHD do not show evidence of brain injury. ADHD is now thought to have a genetic basis (Faraone & Biederman, 1994), although the specific way in which the gene or genes that contribute to ADHD are passed on is not known. Some researchers are using molecular genetic techniques to identify genes that may be important (Cook, Stein, Krasowski, et al., 1995).

The causes of ADHD are related to how the brain functions to regulate behavior. Multiple lines of evidence suggest that subtle structural and functional differences exist in the brains of individuals with ADHD (reviewed in Mercugliano, 1995). The frontal lobes of the brain serve as the "executive center," processing incoming stimuli and selecting the appropriate emotional and motor response. It is hypothesized that the frontal lobes of individuals with ADHD may be compromised in their "executive" role because of altered communication with other brain regions. In particular, it is thought that the catecholamine neurotransmitters, dopamine and norepinephrine, are involved in this altered communication because the stimulant medications that are helpful in treating the symptoms of ADHD are known to increase the availability of these neurotransmitters. Consistent with this is the finding that in certain families with a history of ADHD, there is a defect in the dopamine transporter gene (Cook et al., 1995).

Some researchers are using neuroimaging techniques to study the brains of individuals with ADHD, while others are developing animal models to test basic science hypotheses about ADHD and potential drug treatments. In the studies using neuroimaging techniques, results have differed among laboratories, possibly because the ideal methodology is not yet clear. One approach uses magnetic resonance imaging with volumetric analyses to compare the size of certain brain regions in individuals with ADHD versus controls. Several studies suggest that certain brain regions including the frontal lobes, basal ganglia, and corpus callosum (which carries fibers from one cortical hemisphere to the other) may differ in size between individuals with ADHD and controls (Mercugliano, 1995). A second neuroimaging approach uses techniques that analyze functional, rather than structural, aspects of the brain. For example, positron emission tomography (PET) scans provide information about blood flow or glucose utilization, which correlate closely with metabolic activity in different brain regions. Some PET studies suggest that individuals with ADHD have a mildly decreased rate of metabolism in several brain regions including parts of the frontal lobes and basal ganglia (Mercugliano, 1995). Advances in functional neuroimaging technology and the increasing understanding of the cellular and molecular biology of the catecholamine neurotransmitter systems should make the near future very fruitful in terms of advancing knowledge about the neurobiology of ADHD.

Although it appears that the most common etiology for ADHD is genetic, other conditions known to affect brain development may predispose a child to developing this disorder (Table 22.1). These include prenatal exposures to lead (Bellinger & Needleman, 1983), alcohol (Steinhausen, Willms, & Spohr, 1993), and probably cocaine (Giacoia, 1990); prematurity (Szatmari, Saigal, Rosenbaum, et al., 1990); low birth weight at term (Hawdon, Hey, Klovin, et al., 1990); brain infections; inborn errors of metabolism (Shaywitz & Shaywitz, 1988); sex chromosome abnormalities, such as Klinefelter syndrome, Turner syndrome, and fragile X syndrome (Borghgraef, Fryns, & van den Berghe, 1990); and certain other genetic syndromes such as neurofibromatosis type 1 and Tourette syndrome (Comings & Comings, 1990; Shaywitz & Shaywitz,

Table 22.1.   Conditions predisposing a child to develop ADHD

Brain infections
Fragile X syndrome
Inborn errors of metabolism
Low birth weight
Neurofibromatosis type I
Perinatal insults
Prenatal exposure to lead, alcohol, or cocaine
Sex chromosome abnormalities
Tourette syndrome

1988). In addition, there appears to be an increased incidence of a variety of complications during labor, delivery, and infancy in children with nonfamilial ADHD, although the nature of their relationship to ADHD is unclear (Sprich-Buckminster, Biederman, Milberger, et al., 1993). The disparate group of disorders associated with ADHD suggests that many factors present during development may influence the way the brain later functions to organize thinking and behavior.

A number of medical, neurological, and/or psychiatric conditions that require very different treatment can cause some symptoms similar to those of ADHD (Table 22.2). A careful history and examination can help to rule these "in" or "out" or suggest the need for further specific testing. Medical conditions that can impair behavior or academic performance include thyroid disease, anemia, lead intoxication, and metabolic disorders. In addition, behavior may be affected by certain medications, such as many of those used to treat asthma and seizures. Neurological disorders that are associated with ADHD-like symptoms include sensory impairments (see Chapters 11 and 12); seizure disorders (see Chapter 26); syndromes (e.g., tuberous sclerosis); and certain neurodegenerative disorders (e.g., childhood-onset metachromatic leukodystrophy). Unaddressed cognitive impairments, such as mental retardation (see Chapter 16) or learning disabilities (see Chapter 23); psychiatric disorders, including anxiety disorders, depression, and manic-depressive disorder; and pervasive developmental disorders can also present with academic and behavioral difficulties. Sometimes the symptoms of ADHD are part of the primary diagnosis; for example, these symptoms may be present with a neurodegenerative disorder, pervasive developmental disorder, or untreated but treatable medical conditions, such as thyroid disease. At other times, however, ADHD symptoms coexist with the primary disorder, making it important to sort out the symptoms. For example, a child with mental retardation or learning disabilities also may have ADHD. In these instances, the combination of hyperactivity, short attention span, impulsive behavior, frustration intolerance, and poor school performance is beyond

Table 22.2.   Disorders that may simulate ADHD

Anemia
Lead intoxication
Progressive neurological disorders
Psychiatric disorders
Seizure disorders and antiepileptic drugs
Sensory impairments
Thyroid disease

that expected for the child's cognitive age or academic abilities (American Psychiatric Association, 1994; Shaywitz & Shaywitz, 1988).

DIAGNOSING ATTENTION-DEFICIT/HYPERACTIVITY DISORDER

Because a variety of conditions can present with the symptoms of ADHD, the diagnostic process requires the clinician to consider not only whether the criteria for ADHD are met, but also whether there are signs and symptoms of any other disorder present instead of, or in addition to, ADHD. Proper diagnosis is important because it dictates approaches to therapy. The diagnostic process involves a comprehensive review of the child's behavioral, academic, psychosocial, developmental, medical, and family history. This information is obtained primarily by parent interview, medical and school records, and one or more standardized rating scales designed to be completed by parents, teachers, and the child (Achenbach, 1991; Barkley, 1990; Reiff, Banez, & Culbert, 1993). The clinician will also interview the child in order to understand the child's perceptions, concerns, and self-reported symptoms of ADHD and other disorders, as well as to obtain information about language and thought processes. The evaluation will also include a medical/neurological examination and a psychoeducational assessment. Other individuals with relevant information about the child's functioning, especially educators, should provide input. A variety of clinicians may be involved in ADHD evaluations including a primary care physician, developmental or behavioral pediatrician, child neurologist, child psychiatrist, child psychologist, speech-language therapist, educator, and/or social worker.

Most clinicians use the diagnostic criteria developed by the American Psychiatric Association (1994) as a starting point for diagnosing ADHD (Table 22.3) as there are no laboratory measures or physical examination findings that confirm a diagnosis of ADHD. Some clinicians may use computerized continuous performance tests (e.g., coding) to assess attention and impulsivity, but these tests have a high rate of false negatives (Barkley, 1991). The diagnosis requires that symptoms be present in more than one setting, thus information from both the home and (usually) school is critical. A thorough physical examination is required to rule out other medical/neurological diagnoses. Soft neurological signs, although not specific to ADHD, occur with increased frequency in children with this disorder. Some clinicians may check laboratory tests for anemia, lead poisoning, and/or thyroid disease if the possibility of these disorders is suggested by history or examination. In the absence of specific neurological abnormalities, EEGs and neuroimaging scans are not indicated because they do not show specific abnormalities related to ADHD. Finally, a psychoeducational evaluation of intelligence and academic achievement may be required if contributing learning difficulties are suspected (Barkley, 1990).

A typical activity level in the clinician's office cannot be used to rule out ADHD because children often behave differently in an unfamiliar environment (American Psychiatric Association, 1994). Likewise, a positive response to stimulant medications should not be used to make a diagnosis, because individuals without ADHD also have improved concentration and productivity when receiving these medications (Rapoport, Buchsbaum, Zahn, et al., 1978).

MANAGEMENT OF ATTENTION-DEFICIT/HYPERACTIVITY DISORDER

The management of children with ADHD is most effective when a combination of approaches is used (Culbert, Banez, & Reiff, 1994). This section reviews educational interventions, counsel-

Table 22.3.   Diagnostic criteria for ADHD

I. Symptoms of inattention
    1.   Often fails to give attention to detail or makes careless mistakes
    2.   Often has difficulty sustaining attention
    3.   Often does not seem to listen
    4.   Often does not follow through on instructions and fails to finish tasks
    5.   Often has difficulty organizing tasks and activities
    6.   Often avoids or dislikes tasks that require sustained mental effort
    7.   Often loses things
    8.   Is often easily distracted
    9.   Is often forgetful

II. Symptoms of hyperactivity/impulsivity
    1.   Often fidgets or squirms
    2.   Often leaves seat when remaining seated is expected
    3.   Often runs about or climbs excessively in inappropriate situations
    4.   Often has difficulty engaging in activities quietly
    5.   Is often "on the go" or "driven by a motor"
    5.   Often talks excessively
    7.   Often blurts out answers before questions have been completed
    8.   Often has difficulty waiting a turn
    9.   Often interrupts or intrudes on others

III. At least 6 of 9 from category I (ADHD-inattentive type) or category II (ADHD-impulsive/ hyperactive type) or both (ADHD-combined type)

IV. Additional criteria: Symptoms are
    1.   Present for at least 6 months
    2.   Of a degree that is maladaptive and inconsistent with developmental level
    3.   Present before age 7
    4.   Present in more than one setting
    5.   Not due to pervasive developmental disorder or a psychotic disorder or primarily due to another mental disorder

Reprinted with permission from the *Diagnostic and statistical manual of mental disorders* (4th ed., pp. 83–85). Copyright © 1994 by American Psychiatric Association.

ing, behavior management, and medication for ADHD as well as various nonconventional therapies that have been advocated for children with ADHD.

Educational Interventions

Appropriate school programs are extremely important for children with ADHD, many of whom have coexisting learning disabilities that need appropriate intervention (Klein & Rapin, 1990) (see Chapter 23). Even those without a specific learning disability may experience frequent frustration in their attempts to master new material and therefore require some educational assistance. A well-trained teacher who is interested in providing special help and an educational program suited to the needs of the child is invaluable. The teacher may need to use behavior management techniques to maintain the child's attention on tasks and improve behavior, teach the child organizational skills, and modify classwork or assignments to help manage the child's comorbid learning disabilities. Tutoring outside of school will be helpful in some cases. When children with ADHD are in need of more educational assistance than is typically provided in the general education classroom, they qualify for accommodations within their general classes or in other special education services under both the Individuals with Disabilities Education Act (IDEA) of 1990, PL 101-476, and Section 504 of the Rehabilitation Act of 1973, PL 93-112 (DuPaul & Stoner, 1994).

Counseling

Counseling for both the child and the family is a key element of the intervention program (Barkley, 1995). Typically it should include discussions about the disorder, implementation of behavior management strategies, and emotional support for the child and family. For some children, interventions to address social skills impairments (Sheridan, Dee, Morgan, et al., 1996) or comorbid conditions such as anxiety or depression will be needed. Parents should receive information on the characteristics, effective treatments, and natural history of ADHD. They often need help in understanding how inattention, impulsivity, and hyperactivity lead to impairments in acquiring new skills and to inconsistencies in the performance of skills the child has already mastered. Children with ADHD must understand that having the disorder does not mean they are stupid, sick, or alone (Kelly, Cohen, Walker, et al., 1989).

Counseling for most children with ADHD should include the use of behavior management procedures to increase the frequency with which the child engages in desired behaviors. These procedures have consistently been found to be one of the most effective approaches to teaching and motivating children with ADHD to engage in appropriate behaviors (Barkley & Murphy, 1991). Usually behavior management counseling will focus on specific times of the day or specific behaviors that are difficult for the family or child. These will vary from family to family but often include difficulty getting up and ready for school on time, problems doing homework, failing to complete tasks, or engaging in disruptive behaviors. (The basic principles and procedures used in behavior management are discussed in Chapter 30.) Although these principles are not difficult to understand, instituting effective behavior management interventions and maintaining the effect over time often requires professional guidance. This guidance may be provided by a psychologist, social worker, pediatrician, psychiatrist, or school counselor with expertise in ADHD and behavior management.

At the time families seek help, many children with ADHD will have already experienced repeated failures both at home and in school. Thus, one of the most important goals of intervention is to increase the child's chances of experiencing success. Environmental modifications will often help to achieve this goal. For example, if a child who is easily distracted is sitting near a window or noisy hallway, moving the child's seat to another area of the room may decrease the chance of the child being distracted. A child who frequently talks to friends in class may do better when not sitting near those friends. A child who leaves books needed for homework assignments in school is more likely to have the opportunity to complete assignments if a second set of books is kept at home. Clearly these are but a few of the more common environmental modifications that may be helpful to children with ADHD.

Behavior management also involves providing positive reinforcers for desired behaviors. Again it is important that the child experience frequent success. If a reinforcer is offered, but the child rarely earns it, it is not likely to provide much motivation for the child to change his or her behavior. For children with ADHD, it is also important that the reinforcers be offered consistently and as soon after the behavior as possible. Studies suggest that children with ADHD will usually choose small, frequent reinforcers over larger, less frequent ones (Rapport, Tucker, Du-Paul, et al., 1986).

One commonly used strategy is the daily school–home note. With this procedure, the child and parents receive daily feedback from the teacher on how the child did in selected areas of classroom functioning. The child's **baseline** level of performance is determined and then home-based reinforcers are offered for improvement in the child's performance. This procedure facilitates parent–teacher communication. In addition, it establishes clear goals for the child and allows the child to receive frequent feedback and reinforcement about his or her classroom performance.

Counseling should also provide emotional support for the family. Parents, the child, or siblings may need to talk about their anxieties, frustrations, or anger. Parents and siblings may need help in understanding the implications that ADHD may have for them (Silver, 1989). For example, parents may need help in balancing the demands of the child with ADHD with the needs of siblings or other responsibilities. In addition, both parents may not agree on the nature or severity of their child's difficulties, or they may feel blamed by others for their child's problems and hopeless about their ability to help their child. Siblings may be angry about "double standards" in the home or embarrassed by the behavior of their brother or sister. Stress in the family and in the marriage can exacerbate behavior problems and should be addressed for everyone's benefit (see Chapter 34).

A number of national and local parent groups exist that can provide support and education for individuals with ADHD and their families. The national parent support group Children and Adults with Attention Deficit Disorder (CHADD) has local chapters through which a parent can meet the parents of other children with ADHD. Membership in such organizations can be extremely helpful in supplementing what is provided by professionals and in giving parents an organized forum to advocate for their children's needs.

Medication

Medication is often used in addition to educational and behavioral strategies for children who have ADHD (American Academy of Pediatrics, Committee on Children with Disabilities and Committee on Drugs, 1996). Stimulants (Table 22.4) are the most effective and most commonly prescribed medications for ADHD. Other medications such as the alpha-2 adrenergic agonists, antidepressants, and neuroleptics may be used with children with ADHD who do not benefit from stimulants, have significant side effects from stimulants, or have ADHD as well as another condition that is better treated by one of these medications. Although combinations of these medications are sometimes used, there is little research available concerning the efficacy and safety of polydrug use in ADHD.

Stimulant Treatment of Attention-Deficit/Hyperactivity Disorder

The short-term efficacy of stimulant medication in improving attention span and decreasing hyperactivity and impulsivity cannot be disputed. Since 1937 when Dr. Charles Bradley first reported the beneficial effects of stimulants on children's behavior, hundreds of well-designed studies have confirmed these effects (Jacobvitz, Sroufe, & Stewart, 1990). In addition, stimulants have been found to improve academic productivity and accuracy, improve parent–child interactions, and decrease aggression (Barkley, 1988; Barkley, DuPaul, & McMurray, 1991; Du-Paul & Rapport, 1993; Elia, Borcherding, Rapoport, et al., 1991; Gadow, Nolan, Sverd, et al.,

Table 22.4.   Medications used to treat ADHD

Stimulants
Dextroamphetamine (Dexedrine)
Methylphenidate (Ritalin)
Pemoline (Cylert)

Alpha-2 adrenergic agonists
Clonidine (Catapres)
Guanfacine (Tenex)

Tricyclic antidepressants
Desipramine (Norpramin)
Imipramine (Tofranil)
Nortriptyline (Pamelor)

Other antidepressants
Bupropion (Wellbutrin)

Neuroleptics
Chlorpromazine (Thorazine)
Haloperidol (Haldol)
Thioridazine (Mellaril)

1990). In the 1990s, 1%–3% of children in the United States receive a stimulant medication for ADHD (Safer & Krager, 1994).

Methylphenidate (Ritalin) is the most frequently prescribed stimulant. Most but not all children with ADHD show significant improvements in behavior on methylphenidate. The demonstration of efficacy depends, at least in part, on the measures that are used to assess response. When teacher ratings of behavior are used, from 70% to more than 80% of children will demonstrate improvements on methylphenidate (Rapport, Denney, DuPaul, et al., 1994). The effect of stimulants on academic performance is less clear. When measures of academic productivity or learning are used to assess response, only about half of the children with ADHD show significant improvements (Rapport et al., 1994). Because not all children improve on the medicine and the response rate differs with the problem behaviors chosen, it is important to document the efficacy of the medicine in treating the target behaviors. This is most frequently done by having the teacher or parent note the frequency of the problem behaviors on rating scales before starting the medication and after the child has been on the medication for a few weeks (Cohen, Kelly, & Atkinson, 1989). Because stimulants are quick acting, improvements in behavior are often seen the first day the child starts on the medication.

As with other drugs, there are side effects, but they are usually mild and rarely require discontinuing the medication (Barkley, McMurray, Edelbrock, et al., 1990). The most common side effect is loss of appetite after taking the medication. Some children, especially those receiving three doses per day, may require caloric supplementation to prevent weight loss (Stein, Blondis, Schnitzler, et al., 1996). As many as 25%–35% of children on methylphenidate may complain of headaches or stomachaches. One must be cautious about attributing these symptoms to the medication, however, as 10%–20% of children with ADHD complain of these same concerns while on placebo (Ahmann, Waltonen, Olson, et al., 1993; Barkley et al., 1990). Stimulants may cause insomnia, but usually only when they are given late in the day or in long-acting forms.

Some children may have difficulty with irritability, increased activity, or mood swings at the end of the day. This phenomenon is called **rebound** and seems to represent a temporary worsening of symptoms as the medication wears off. In some cases, it may be difficult to distinguish whether the child is experiencing rebound or if the child's behavior is simply returning to its baseline state (Johnston, Pelham, Hoza, et al., 1988). When rebound effects are reported, a low dose of stimulant medication in the late afternoon or use of a slow-release preparation will often ameliorate the symptoms.

Tics, which are brief repetitive movements (e.g., eye blinks, throat clearing) that resemble nervous habits, occur in approximately 9% of children treated with stimulants (Lipkin, Goldstein, & Adesman, 1994). Use of a stimulant medication may need to be stopped if the child develops tics. If tics are mild and the medication resulted in dramatic behavioral improvements (or if other medications are not effective), however, physicians and families may elect to continue the stimulants. Long-term studies that clarify the relationship between stimulant treatment and the persistence of tics are lacking.

Because of concerns about the potential for stimulants to be abused, they are classified as controlled substances by the federal government. They have been used by college students to "pull all-nighters," by truckers to maintain vigilance while driving, and by dieters to curb their appetites. There has been increased attention to the fact that adolescents or adults may abuse methylphenidate or dextroamphetamine by injecting it or taking it intranasally to produce a "high." As a result, when stimulant medication is needed to treat ADHD in an adolescent with a history of substance abuse or drug dealing, one should consider the use of pemoline (Cylert) as it is not water soluble and thus cannot be injected or inhaled. In the past, there also have been concerns that the use of methylphenidate for ADHD increases the risk for later substance abuse. Long-term follow-up studies, however, have not supported this idea (Hechtman, Weiss, & Perlman, 1984a, b).

During long-term treatment with stimulants, questions often arise about how many times per day a child should receive the medication; whether he or she should receive the medicine on weekends and over the summer; whether tolerance (i.e., decreased medication effectiveness over time) to the medication will require increased doses; and how long the child will need to be on the medication. Decisions regarding after-school, weekend, and summer doses need to be made on an individual basis, balancing the benefits the child receives from the medicine with the side effects he or she may experience. This usually involves comparing beneficial effects of the medicine on homework completion (or summer school), social or peer relations, and family interactions, versus potential side effects of the medicine on appetite, growth, and sleep. A study suggests that in most cases, a late afternoon dose of methylphenidate will not adversely affect sleep (Kent, Blader, Koplewicz, et al., 1995). If a child experiences a decrease in the rate of growth during treatment, it may be necessary to stop the medication on weekends and over the summer to allow for "catch-up" growth (Klein, Landa, Mattes, et al., 1988). With this approach, final height is not usually affected as a result of long-term therapy with stimulants (Klein & Mannuzza, 1988).

The need for stimulant medications should be reassessed on a yearly basis, as some children "outgrow" the need for the medication. However, others will continue to benefit from stimulant medications even as adults (Wender, Wood, & Reimherr, 1985). Children do not usually develop tolerance to stimulant medications (Safer & Allen, 1989) but in some cases may require higher doses consistent with their increase in size.

Outcome of Stimulant Treatment

Although the short-term benefits of stimulants are clear and the side effects generally mild, many questions remain about their long-term efficacy. Studies generally have failed to show significant improvement in academic achievement (DuPaul & Rapport, 1993; Jacobvitz et al., 1990; Rapport et al., 1994). However, the conclusions that can be drawn from these studies are limited by a number of methodological problems. The studies have not randomly assigned children into medication and placebo groups; thus, it is possible that those children with the greater impairments are more likely to get treated with stimulants, which would bias the results toward the conclusion that medication is ineffective in achieving academic gains (Schachar & Tannock, 1993). Furthermore, often children have been treated with stimulants for relatively short periods of time, which diminishes the chances of achieving long-term gains. Finally, conclusions from these studies are limited by high attrition rates. One study does suggest that intensive treatment of ADHD with a combination of behavioral, educational, and pharmacological approaches individualized to the needs of the child can decrease the long-term risk of delinquency when compared with treatment with medication alone (Satterfield, Satterfield, & Schell, 1987). Further long-term studies are needed to determine the treatments necessary to improve outcome for children with ADHD (Richters, Arnold, Jensen, et al., 1995).

Treatment of Stimulant Nonresponders

Children who do not respond to methylphenidate may benefit from one of the other stimulants. Elia et al. (1991) found that if children were given a range of doses of both methylphenidate and dextroamphetamine, 96% of them responded to at least one of the medications. Nevertheless, some children will not benefit from any of the stimulants or will have adverse side effects that will preclude their use. Antidepressants or alpha-2 adrenergic agonists should be used to treat these children.

Several different types of antidepressants (Table 22.4) have been found to be effective in children with ADHD. The tricyclic antidepressants (desipramine, imipramine, and nortriptyline) have been the most extensively studied. In general, when tricyclic antidepressants are compared with placebo and stimulants, the antidepressants are found to be more effective than placebo, but slightly less effective than stimulants in improving attention span, improving teacher ratings of behavior, and decreasing impulsivity (Garfinkel, Wender, & Sloman, 1983; Rapport, Carlson, Kelly, et al., 1993; Werry, Aman, & Diamond, 1980). As many as 60%–70% of the children with ADHD who do not respond to a stimulant will respond to a tricyclic antidepressant (Biederman, Baldessarini, Wright, et al., 1989).

Unlike stimulants, tricyclic antidepressants must be administered continuously in order to be effective. One potential advantage of tricyclic antidepressants is that the therapeutic effect lasts throughout the day rather than for only a few hours after a dose as occurs with stimulants. However, tricyclic antidepressants have more problematic side effects than stimulants (see Appendix C). Drug levels should be checked as there can be large inter-individual differences in the metabolism of these medications (Green, 1995). EKGs must be monitored for cardiovascular side effects as a few cases of sudden death, presumably from cardiac arrhythmias, have occurred in children taking desipramine (Green, 1995; Riddle, Nelson, Kleinman, et al., 1991). Thus, many clinicians elect to use alternative tricyclic antidepressants instead of desipramine in young children (Werry, 1995), although others believe that with EKG monitoring desipramine can be used safely (Biederman, Thisted, & Greenhill, 1995).

Other types of antidepressants may also be effective for children with ADHD. Like the tricyclic antidepressants, bupropion, a chemically distinct antidepressant, has been shown to be about as effective as stimulants for treatment of ADHD (Barrickman, Perry, Allen, et al., 1995). Case reports have suggested that a new class of antidepressants, the serotonin reuptake inhibitors (fluoxetine [Prozac], sertraline [Zoloft], paroxetine [Paxil]), also may have a role in the treatment of some children with ADHD (Barrickman, Noyes, Kuperman, et al., 1991; Frankenburg & Kando, 1994; Gammon & Brown, 1993), but further studies are needed to better define this role.

The alpha-2 adrenergic agonists (Table 22.4) have been reported to improve hyperactivity (Hunt, Arnsten, & Asbell, 1995; Hunt, Minderaa, & Cohen, 1985), but they tend to have less effect on attention and concentration. The best responders seem to be children with ADHD who are extremely hyperactive and impulsive.

Treatment of Attention-Deficit/Hyperactivity Disorder Subtypes

The DSM-IV divides ADHD into three subtypes: a primarily inattentive type, a primarily hyperactive-impulsive type, and a combined type. Although there has been limited research into the effectiveness of different medications on these subtypes, some evidence indicates that among children with the primarily inattentive type of ADHD, fewer respond to methylphenidate, and those who do respond to a lower dose of the medication (Barkley et al., 1991; Cantwell & Baker, 1992). Children with the primarily inattentive type of ADHD who do not respond to stimulants may be treated with one of the antidepressant medications but would not be good candidates for treatment with alpha-2 adrenergic agonists. There has not been any research into whether the responses of children with the hyperactive-impulsive subtype to the medications are different from those of children with ADHD combined type.

Treatment of Children with ADHD and Mental Retardation

Studies suggest that stimulants have similar effects in children with ADHD and mental retardation requiring intermittent to limited supports and children with ADHD and average intelligence (Aman, Marks, Turbott, et al., 1991; Handen, Breaux, Janosky, et al., 1992). Children with mental retardation, however, may have an increased risk of side effects such as tics and social withdrawal (Handen, Feldman, Gosling, et al., 1991; Helsel, Hersen, & Lubetsky, 1989). Individuals with mental retardation requiring extensive or pervasive supports do not respond to stimulants as well as children with mental retardation requiring only intermittent or limited supports. Some studies have not found any benefit from stimulant medications in this group (Aman et al., 1991; Aman & Singh, 1982), but one study suggests that at least some children with mental retardation requiring extensive or pervasive supports will demonstrate decreased disruptive behaviors when treated with stimulants (Blum, Mauk, McComas, et al., 1996).

Neuroleptic medications have been frequently used to treat hyperactivity in individuals with mental retardation (Baumeister, Todd, & Sevin, 1993; Handen, 1993). Although neuroleptics are often effective in decreasing hyperactivity, their usefulness is limited by a high frequency and severity of side effects, including movement disorders (see Chapter 20). In addition, they have a sedating effect, often reduce concentration, and as a result may interfere with progress in academic and other skills.

Treatment of ADHD and Tic Disorders

The alpha-2 adrenergic agonists, clonidine (Catapres) and guanfacine (Tenex), are often the first medications used because they may improve both hyperactivity and tics (Chappell, Riddle, Scahill, et al., 1995; Hunt et al., 1995; Steingard, Biederman, Spencer, et al., 1993). Some children's ADHD symptoms, however, will improve more when given stimulants or antidepressants (Singer, Brown, Quaskey, et al., 1995); while other children are better treated for tics with neuroleptics (Chappell, Leckman, & Riddle, 1995). In many cases, one will need to consider whether one or both of the disorders is in need of pharmacological treatment before determining the medication to use.

The tricyclic antidepressants, desipramine and nortriptyline, also have been used to treat ADHD in children with chronic tics or Tourette syndrome (Singer et al., 1995; Spencer, Biederman, Wilens, et al., 1993). In most children, these medications appear to improve ADHD symptoms without exacerbating the tics. It has been thought that the use of stimulants in children with ADHD and tics or Tourette syndrome was contraindicated because the stimulants would worsen the tics. This is not true for all children, however (Gadow, Nolan, Sprafkin, et al., 1995; Gadow, Sverd, Sprafkin, et al., 1995). Thus, if other treatment strategies fail and ADHD is a more functionally relevant problem for the child than the tics, a judicious trial of stimulants may be warranted.

Treatment of Children with ADHD and Internalizing Disorders

Many children with ADHD also experience depression or anxiety disorders (i.e., internalizing disorders). Studies suggest that compared with children with ADHD alone or ADHD and disruptive behavior disorders, children with ADHD and comorbid internalizing disorders may be less likely to benefit from methylphenidate (DuPaul, Barkley, & McMurray, 1994; Pliszka, 1989). Nonetheless, stimulants remain the first-line medication for these children as no research suggests a better response to other medications in this population. For those who do not respond to stimulants, antidepressants may be helpful.

Nonconventional Treatments for ADHD

Nonconventional treatments are those that are not considered to be proven effective in the peer-reviewed medical literature. It is particularly common for a variety of such treatments to evolve for childhood disorders that are incurable, complex to treat, and chronic, especially when aspects of diagnosis and conventional treatment are controversial. Three of the most common nonconventional treatments for ADHD are reviewed here: vitamin and mineral supplementation, elimination diets, and EEG biofeedback training.

Vitamin and Mineral Supplementation

In the 1950s, a theory was proposed that some individuals have a genetic defect in the handling of vitamins or minerals such that they need to ingest excessive doses in order to maintain normal CNS function. The term "orthomolecular psychiatry" was coined in the 1970s to describe this approach to treatment. Since that time, the theory has been applied to numerous disorders including ADHD. Practitioners of this approach order extensive laboratory analyses of vitamin and mineral levels in blood and hair and then prescribe supplements based on the results. In the 1970s, both the American Psychiatric Association and the American Academy of Pediatrics published position statements concluding that there was no scientific support for this treatment approach, and there has been no subsequent research to challenge this conclusion. Furthermore, excessive doses of certain vitamins and minerals can have deleterious effects on several organ systems (Goldstein & Ingersoll, 1992; Silver, 1991).

Elimination Diets

The relationship of food and food additives to behavior is a complex subject with a long and controversial history. Although there is good evidence that some individuals have allergic symptoms (i.e., eczema, wheezing, gastrointestinal disturbances) in response to foods and/or additives that they ingest, there is far less evidence that ingestion of foods or food additives is a common cause of the behavioral disturbances associated with learning disabilities or ADHD. Nevertheless, numerous researchers have proposed that elimination of certain foods from the diet can alleviate some behavioral symptoms. Elimination diets fall into three general categories according to the foods eliminated: allergenic foods; artificial colors, preservatives, and salicylates; and sugar and artificial sweeteners.

In the 1950s, Speer introduced the concept that allergies could lead to a diverse group of behavioral symptoms, characterized as the tension-fatigue syndrome. Affected children (and adults) frequently showed allergic upper respiratory signs, excessive fatigue, and restlessness/nervousness. Since that time, several other researchers have attempted to show that elimination of certain allergenic foods could lead to behavior improvements. The results of these studies have been criticized because of weaknesses in methodology and statistical analyses (Crook, 1975; Egger, Carter, Soothill, et al., 1992; Egger, Stolla, & McEwen, 1992). A more rigorously designed study (Kaplan, McNichol, Conte, et al., 1989) suggests behavior improvements may occur in some (particularly younger) children on diets that eliminate both highly allergenic foods and a variety of food additives.

In 1975, Dr. Benjamin Feingold published a book detailing his observations of the relationship among food additives, allergy, and behavior, which became the basis for the Feingold diet. Later, Feingold extended his elimination diet to include all artificial colors and preservatives as well as foods that contain natural salicylates (aspirin-like compounds), and he extended his treatment group to children with hyperactivity and/or learning disabilities. The concept of food *allergy* shifted to one of food *sensitivity,* although the physiological basis for the proposed sensitivity remains obscure (Conners, 1989; Feingold, 1975; NIH Consensus Development Conference, 1982). It has been hypothesized that small molecules (e.g., red dye) may affect behavior by interfering with dopamine uptake when given in large quantities (NIH Consensus Development Conference, 1982).

The Feingold Association is now an international organization of parents and some professionals with the primary goal of supporting families who wish to try this approach with information and resources. The diet itself is not harmful; although because many common vegetables and fruits contain small amounts of salicylates, careful attention must be taken to ensure adequate intake of essential nutrients, especially vitamin C. Furthermore, it is difficult for the average family to institute and maintain the diet, particularly because food labeling practices allow preservatives to go unlisted when they are components of an ingredient rather than a direct ingredient. It may also add stress to children who already sense that they are "different" from their peers.

Many studies have attempted to prove or disprove the efficacy of Feingold's diet (Conners, 1989; Weiss, 1982; Wender, 1986). Initial open clinical trials generated substantial support for Feingold's hypothesis. However, two of the more carefully controlled, double-blind studies that followed (Conners, Goyette, & Southwick, 1976; Harley, Ray, Tomasi, et al., 1978) as well as several other studies (Conners, 1989; Wender, 1986) did not. An NIH consensus panel convened in 1982 concluded that there was little evidence to support the widespread claims of efficacy of this approach (NIH Consensus Development Conference, 1982). Specific children, however, did appear to respond well in these studies, suggesting that elimination diets may be useful for a subgroup of children. Thus, it has been suggested that studies using single-subject experimental designs may more validly assess response to elimination diets (Weiss, 1982). It is also possible that the improvements seen are not specifically linked to ADHD but may relate to restlessness, irritability, sleep, and physical symptoms that may exacerbate ADHD.

The link between dietary sugar and artificial sweeteners to hyperactivity has also been mired in controversy. Although a few studies have found small deteriorations in behavior or laboratory measures after a sugar or aspartame challenge, the majority have not (Shaywitz, Sullivan, Anderson, et al., 1994; Wender & Solanto, 1991; Wolraich, Lindgren, Stumbo, et al., 1994; Wolraich, Wilson, & White, 1995). Additional studies have found that children with ADHD may not have immediate behavior responses to sugar challenges but do have altered neuroendocrine responses, and the relationship of these alterations to behavior remains to be determined (Conners, 1989; Girardi, Shaywitz, Shaywitz, et al., 1995).

EEG *Biofeedback Training*

EEG biofeedback training is a relatively new approach to ADHD treatment that has gained popularity in the 1990s but has received very little empirical study. There is a certain brainwave pattern associated with alert, attentive mental states and a different brainwave pattern associated with drowsiness and daydreaming, which can be identified and quantified by EEG measurements. Children can be trained using positive reinforcement to generate the "good" brainwaves for longer periods of time (Lubar, 1991). Although biofeedback techniques have been used to treat a variety of disorders and there is perhaps some scientific rationale for its investigation in individuals with ADHD, it is premature to identify it as a treatment. Specific questions relate to the generalizability of the biofeedback effects seen in the laboratory and their clinical significance. It is an expensive and time-consuming process and, thus far, has been studied in combination with counseling and tutoring; thus, the efficacy of each specific treatment is unclear (Barkley, 1992).

These, as well as other nonconventional treatments, continue to be promoted in the media. The clinician should be sufficiently knowledgeable about them to assist families in making decisions about intervention choices for their child and should continue to assist families in rigorously assessing their positive and negative effects, just as is customary for more traditional treatments.

MATTHEW

Matthew was the third child in his family. The labor and delivery were uncomplicated, although his mother noted that Matthew seemed more active *in utero* than her other children. As an infant, he did not like to be held or cuddled, and he slept fitfully.

Developmentally, Matthew reached the various milestones at the typical times. His parents commented that he "ran before he walked." His language development was somewhat slower than that of his two siblings. Both his sister and his brother had spoken in phrases by 2 years of age, but Matthew did not do this until several months later.

By the time he was 3 years old, Matthew's parents were quite concerned about his marked hyperactivity. He was not merely curious; he was a terror, running aimlessly from one room to the next. He would pull out all the pots and pans, tear the curtains, and write on the walls. Matthew would disrupt three or four rooms in a matter of minutes. His parents, always worn out, nicknamed him "The Little Hurricane."

As he grew up, Matthew knew no fears. He could not be left alone, even for a few moments. He was just as likely to turn on the stove as he was to run outside and into the street. Matthew also had trouble sharing things. He showed little interest in playing cooperatively and was easily frustrated in his dealings with other children. Children began to avoid playing with him.

In first grade, Matthew did poorly. His printing was messy, and many letters were reversed. He did not know his alphabet and had great difficulty with phonics. He frequently forgot lessons he had been taught only moments earlier. Socially, he was ostracized by the other children, who called him "retarded." At home, he did no better. He was punished constantly for his uncontrollable behavior and poor school performance. Matthew was unhappy most of the time and had many mood swings.

At the end of the first grade, Matthew was evaluated by a multidisciplinary team. On the Wechsler Intelligence Scale for Children–III (WISC–III; Wechsler, 1991), he earned an IQ of 105. Psychoeducational testing found that, although his math skills were at a first-grade level, his reading skills were at a preprimer level. He was very slow writing letters and often needed to have instructions repeated. His ability to pay attention was markedly decreased. A thorough medical history was obtained and a neurological exam showed clumsiness and other "soft neurological signs." Also, it was clear that Matthew had a poor self-image and expected to fail at everything he tried.

This information led to a diagnosis of both ADHD and a learning disability (see Chapter 23). It was the beginning of a coordinated effort to help Matthew. His treatment program involved a combination of various therapies. At the end of first grade, because his hyperactivity was so severe, Matthew began to take 10 milligrams of methylphenidate before school and at lunchtime. His behavior and attention improved. Together, Matthew's teacher and parents outlined a behavior management program. He also received extra help in reading and his writing assignments were shortened. Within 6 months, Matthew changed from a withdrawn, rather somber child to one who was interested in making friends and attending school.

In physical activities, he had other problems. Because Matthew's clumsiness persisted, it was difficult for him to do well in sports, and the other children teased him. His father took him to special physical education classes to help improve his coordination. There, he met other children with similar problems. This discovery helped Matthew feel less alone and encouraged him to keep trying. He did particularly well in swimming. Even so, he continued to have "two left feet" and to be accident prone over the years.

Matthew continued to get extra help throughout his elementary school years. He began to meet regularly with a counselor at school who helped him better understand and cope with his problems and frustrations. His parents frequently participated in these discussions. Some years were better than others. By 12 years of age, he was much less hyperactive but continued to take were better than others. By 12 years of age, he was much less hyperactive but continued to take methylphenidate for his short attention span and impulsive behaviors. He maintained a "C" average. Matthew received tutoring throughout junior and senior high school to help him master new material by improving his organizational and study skills.

Now an adult, Matthew is entering the job market. He will make it in society but how well is uncertain. He continues to be at a disadvantage because of his disabilities. Yet he has tasted success and is willing to work hard to make a go of it.

ADHD IN YOUNG ADULTS

The story of Matthew is typical of many children with ADHD. As adolescents, more than half of these children improve, if they have not developed motivation and conduct problems (Hill & Schoener, 1996; Klein & Mannuzza, 1991). They are less hyperactive, although they still have problems with organization and planning (Thorley, 1988; Wender, 1995). The majority become well-adjusted, well-functioning adults, but they often do not attain as high an academic level as their siblings (Weiss & Hechtman, 1986). Individuals with ADHD may have problems with maintaining stability in their interpersonal relationships and jobs and may exhibit a higher incidence of antisocial behavior and psychiatric disorders as adults (Barkley, 1990; Satterfield et al., 1987).

SUMMARY

Attention problems and hyperactivity are symptoms common to many disorders. The cause of the symptoms must be determined before effective intervention is possible. If the diagnosis is ADHD, a program combining behavior management techniques, educational intervention, stimulant medication, and counseling is usually helpful. If the symptoms stem from a problem such as mental retardation, a neurological disease, deafness, or a psychiatric disturbance, the underlying disorder determines the type of intervention and the prognosis. For the child with ADHD who is diagnosed early and treated comprehensively, the likelihood of a favorable outcome is good.

REFERENCES

Achenbach, T.M. (1991). *Manual for the Child Behavior Checklist.* Burlington: University of Vermont, Department of Psychiatry.

Ahmann, P.A., Waltonen, S.J., Olson, K.A., et al. (1993). Placebo-controlled evaluation of Ritalin side effects. *Pediatrics, 91,* 1101–1106.

Aman, M.G., Marks, R.E., Turbott, S.H., et al. (1991). Clinical effects of methylphenidate and thioridazine in intellectually subaverage children. *Journal of the American Academy of Child and Adolescent Psychiatry, 30,* 246–256.

Aman, M.G., & Singh, N.N. (1982). Methylphenidate in severely retarded residents and the clinical significance of stereotypic behavior. *Applied Research in Mental Retardation, 3,* 345–358.

American Academy of Pediatrics, Committee on Children with Disabilities and Committee on Drugs. (1996). Medication for children with attentional disorders. *Pediatrics, 98,* 301–303.

American Psychiatric Association. (1994). *Diagnostic and statistical manual of mental disorders* (4th ed.). Washington, DC: Author.

Barkley, R.A. (1988). The effects of methylphenidate on the interaction of preschool ADHD children with their mothers. *Journal of the American Academy of Child and Adolescent Psychiatry, 27,* 336–341.

Barkley, R.A. (1990). *Attention deficit hyperactivity disorder: A handbook for diagnosis and treatment.* New York: Guilford Press.

Barkley, R.A. (1991). The ecological validity of laboratory and analogue assessment methods of ADHD symptoms. *Journal of Abnormal Child Psychology, 19,* 149–178.

Barkley, R.A. (1992, April). *CHADDer Box: Newsletter from C.H.A.D.D., the National Organization for Children and Adults with Attention Deficit Disorder.* Plantation, FL: C.H.A.D.D.

Barkley, R.A. (1995). *Taking charge of ADHD.* New York: Guilford Press.

Barkley, R.A., DuPaul, G.J., & McMurray, M.B. (1991). Attention deficit disorder with and without hyperactivity: Clinical response to three dose levels of methylphenidate. *Pediatrics, 87,* 519–531.

Barkley, R.A., McMurray, M.B., Edelbrock, C.S., et al. (1990). Side effects of methylphenidate in children with attention deficit hyperactivity disorder: A systematic, placebo-controlled evaluation. *Pediatrics, 86,* 184–192.

Barkley, R.A., & Murphy, J.V. (1991). Treating attention-deficit hyperactivity disorder: Medication and behavior management training. *Pediatric Annals, 20,* 256–266.

Barrickman, L., Noyes, R., Kuperman, S., et al. (1991). Treatment of ADHD with fluoxetine: A preliminary trial. *Journal of the American Academy of Child and Adolescent Psychiatry, 30,* 762–767.

Barrickman, L.L., Perry, P.J., Allen, A.J., et al. (1995). Bupropion versus methylphenidate in the treatment of attention-deficit hyperactivity disorder. *Journal of the American Academy of Child and Adolescent Psychiatry, 34,* 649–657.

Baumeister, A.A., Todd, M.E., & Sevin, J.A. (1993). Efficacy and specificity of pharmacologic therapies for behavioral disorders in persons with mental retardation. *Clinical Neuropharmacology, 16,* 271–294.

Bellinger, D.C., & Needleman, H.L. (1983). Lead and the relationship between maternal and child intelligence. *Journal of Pediatrics, 102,* 523–527.

Biederman, J., Baldessarini, R.J., Wright, V., et al. (1989). A double-blind placebo controlled study of desipramine in the treatment of ADD: I. Efficacy. *Journal of the American Academy of Child and Adolescent Psychiatry, 28,* 777–784.

Biederman, J., Faraone, S.V., Keenan, K., et al. (1992). Further evidence for family-genetic risk factors in attention deficit hyperactivity disorder. *Archives of General Psychiatry, 49,* 728–738.

Biederman, J., Newcorn, J., & Sprich, S. (1991). Comorbidity of attention deficit hyperactivity disorder with conduct, depressive, anxiety, and other disorders. *American Journal of Psychiatry, 148,* 564–577.

Biederman, J., Thisted, R., & Greenhill, L. (1995). Resolved: Cardiac arrhythmias make desipramine an unacceptable choice in children. *Journal of the American Acadamy of Child and Adolescent Psychiatry, 34,* 1239–1248.

Blum, N.J., Mauk, J.E., McComas, J.J., et al. (1996). Separate and combined effects of methylphenidate and a behavioral intervention on disruptive behavior in children with mental retardation. *Journal of Applied Behavior Analysis, 29,* 305–319.

Borghgraef, M., Fryns, J.P., & van den Berghe, H. (1990). The female and the fragile X syndrome: Data on clinical and psychological findings in 7 fra (x) carriers. *Clinical Genetics, 37,* 341–346.

Brown, R.T., Coles, C.D., Smith, I.E., et al. (1991). Effects of prenatal alcohol exposure at school age: II. Attention and behavior. *Neurotoxicology and Teratology, 13,* 1–8.

Cantwell, D.P., & Baker, L. (1992). Attention deficit disorder with and without hyperactivity: A review and comparison of matched groups. *Journal of the American Academy of Child and Adolescent Psychiatry, 31,* 432–438.

Chappell, P.B., Leckman, J.F., & Riddle, M.A. (1995). The pharmacologic treatment of tic disorders. *Child and Adolescent Psychiatric Clinics of North America, 4,* 197–216.

Chappell, P.B., Riddle, M.A., Scahill, L., et al. (1995). Guanfacine treatment of comorbid attention-deficit hyperactivity disorder and Tourette's syndrome: Preliminary clinical experience. *Journal of the American Acadamy of Child and Adolescent Psychiatry, 34,* 1140–1146.

Cohen, M.L., Kelly, P.C., & Atkinson, A.W. (1989). Parent, teacher, child: A trilateral approach to attention deficit disorder. *American Journal of Diseases of Children, 143,* 1229–1233.

Comings, D.E., & Comings, B.G. (1990). A controlled family history study of Tourette syndrome: I. Attention deficit hyperactivity disorder and learning disorders. *Journal of Clinical Psychiatry, 51,* 275–280.

Conners, C.K. (1989) *Feeding the brain: How foods affect children.* New York: Plenum.

Conners, C.K., Goyette, C.H., & Southwick, D.A. (1976). Food additives and hyperkinesis: A controlled double-blind experiment. *Pediatrics, 58,* 154–165.

Cook, E.H., Stein, M.A., Krasowski, M.D., et al. (1995) Association of attention-deficit disorder and the dopamine transporter gene. *American Journal of Human Genetics, 56,* 993–998.

Crook, W.G. (1975) Food allergy: The great masquerader. *Pediatric Clinics of North America, 22,* 227–238.

Culbert, T.P., Banez, G.A., & Reiff, M.I. (1994). Children who have attentional disorders: Interventions. *Pediatrics Reviews, 15,* 5–14.

DuPaul, G.J., Barkley, R.A., & McMurray, M.B. (1994). Response of children with ADHD to methylphenidate: Interaction with internalizing symptoms. *Journal of the American Academy of Child and Adolescent Psychiatry, 33,* 894–903.

DuPaul, G.D., & Rapport, M.D. (1993). Does methylphenidate normalize the classroom performance of children with attention deficit disorder. *Journal of the American Academy of Child and Adolescent Psychiatry, 32,* 190–198.

DuPaul, G.J., & Stoner, G. (1994). *ADHD in the schools: Assessment and intervention strategies.* New York: Guilford Press.

Egger, J., Carter, C.H., Soothill, J.F., et al. (1992). Effect of diet therapy on enuresis in children with migraine or hyperkinetic behavior. *Clinical Pediatrics, 31,* 302–307.

Egger, J., Stolla, A., & McEwen, L.M. (1992). Controlled trial of hyposensitization in children with food-induced hyperkinetic syndrome. *Lancet, 339,* 1150–1153.

Elia, J., Borcherding, B.G., Rapoport, J.L., et al. (1991). Methylphenidate and dextroamphetamine: Are there true nonresponders? *Psychiatric Research, 36,* 141–155.

Faraone, S.V., & Biederman, J. (1994). Genetics of attention-deficit hyperactivity disorder. *Child and Adolescent Psychiatric Clinics of North America, 3,* 285–301.

Feingold, B. (1975). *Why your child is hyperactive.* New York: Random House.

Frankenburg, F.R., & Kando, J.C. (1994). Sertraline treatment of attention deficit hyperactivity disorder and Tourette's syndrome. *Journal of Clinical Psychopharmacology, 14,* 359–360.

Gadow, K.D., Nolan, E., Sprafkin, J., et al. (1995). School observation of children with attention-deficit hyperactivity disorder and comorbid tic disorder: Effects of methylphenidate treatment. *Journal of Developmental and Behavorial Pediatrics, 16,* 167–176.

Gadow, K.D., Nolan, E.E., Sverd, J., et al. (1990). Methylphenidate in aggressive-hyperactive boys: Effects on peer aggression in public school settings. *Journal of the American Academy of Child and Adolescent Psychiatry, 29,* 710–718.

Gadow, K.D., Sverd, J., Sprafkin, J., et al. (1995). Efficacy of methylphenidate for attention-deficit hyperactivity disorder in children with tic disorder. *Archives of General Psychiatry, 52,* 444–455.

Gammon, G.D., & Brown, T.E. (1993). Fluoxetine and methylphenidate in combination for treatment of attention deficit hyperactivity disorder and comorbid depressive disorder. *Journal of Child and Adolescent Psychiatry, 3,* 1–10.

Garfinkel, B.D., Wender, P.H., & Sloman, L. (1983). Tricyclic antidepressant and methylphenidate treatment of attention deficit disorder in children. *Journal of the American Academy of Child and Adolescent Psychiatry, 22,* 343–348.

Giacoia, G.P. (1990). Cocaine in the cradle: A hidden epidemic. *Southern Medical Journal, 83,* 947–951.

Girardi, N.L., Shaywitz, S.E., Shaywitz, B.E., et al. (1995). Blunted catecholamine responses after glucose ingestion in children with attention deficit disorder. *Pediatric Resource, 38,* 539–542.

Goldstein, S., & Ingersoll, B. (1992, Fall/Winter). Controversial treatments for children with attention deficit hyperactivity disorder. *CHADDER,* 19–22.

Green, W.H. (1995). The treatment of attention-deficit hyperactivity disorder with nonstimulant medications. *Child and Adolescent Psychiatric Clinics of North America, 4,* 169–195.

Handen, B.L. (1993). Pharmacotherapy in mental retardation and autism. *School Psychology Review, 22,* 162–183.

Handen, B.L., Breaux, A., Janosky, J., et al. (1992). Effects and noneffects of methylphenidate in children with mental retardation and ADHD. *Journal of the American Academy of Child and Adolescent Psychiatry, 31,* 455–461.

Handen, B.L., Feldman, H., Gosling, A., et al. (1991). Adverse side effects of methylphenidate among mentally retarded children with ADHD. *Journal of the American Academy of Child and Adolescent Psychiatry, 30,* 241–245.

Harley, J.P., Ray, R.S., Tomasi, L., et al. (1978). Hyperkinesis and food additives: Testing the Feingold hypothesis. *Pediatrics, 61,* 818–828.

Hawdon, J.M., Hey, E., Klovin, I., et al. (1990). Born too small: Is outcome still affected? *Developmental Medicine and Child Neurology, 32,* 943–953.

Hechtman, L., Weiss, G., & Perlman, T. (1984a). Hyperactives as young adults: Past and current substance abuse and antisocial behavior. *American Journal of Orthopsychiatry, 54,* 415–425.

Hechtman, L., Weiss, G., & Perlman, T. (1984b). Young adult outcome of hyperactive children who received long-term stimulant treatment. *Journal of the American Academy of Child Psychiatry, 23,* 261–269.

Helsel, W.J., Hersen, M., & Lubetsky, M.J. (1989). Stimulant medication and the retarded. *Journal of the American Academy of Child and Adolescent Psychiatry, 28,* 138–139.

Hill, J.C., & Schoener, E.P. (1996). Age-dependent decline of attention deficit hyperactivity disorder. *American Journal of Psychiatry, 153,* 1143–1146.

Hunt, R.D., Arnsten, A.F.T., & Asbell, M.D. (1995). An open trial of guanfacine in the treatment of attention-deficit hyperactivity disorder. *Journal of the American Academy of Child and Adolescent Psychiatry, 34,* 50–54.

Hunt, R.D., Minderaa, R.B., & Cohen, D.J. (1985). Clonidine benefits children with attention deficit disorder and hyperactivity: Report of a double-blind placebo-crossover therapeutic trial. *Journal of the American Academy of Child Psychiatry, 24,* 617–629.

Individuals with Disabilities Education Act (IDEA) of 1990, PL 101-476, 20 U.S.C. § 1400 *et seq.*

Jacobvitz, D., Sroufe, L.A., & Stewart, M. (1990). Treatment of attentional and hyperactivity problems in children with sympathomimetic drugs: A comprehensive review. *Journal of the American Academy of Child Psychiatry, 29,* 677–688.

Johnston, C., Pelham, W.E., Hoza, J., et al. (1988). Psychostimulant rebound in attention deficit disordered boys. *Journal of the American Academy of Child and Adolescent Psychiatry, 27,* 806–810.

Kaplan, B.J., McNichol, J., Conte, R.A., et al. (1989). Dietary replacement in preschool hyperactive boys. *Pediatrics, 83,* 7–17.

Kelly, P.C., Cohen, M.L., Walker, W.O., et al. (1989). Self-esteem in children medically managed for attention deficit disorder. *Pediatrics, 83,* 211–217.

Kent, J.D., Blader, J.C., Koplewicz, H.S., et al. (1995). Effects of late afternoon methylphenidate on behavior and sleep in attention-deficit hyperactivity disorder. *Pediatrics, 96,* 320–325.

Klein, R.G., Landa, B., Mattes, J.A., et al. (1988). Methylphenidate and growth in hyperactive children: A controlled withdrawal study. *Archives of General Psychiatry, 45,* 1127–1130.

Klein, R.G., & Mannuzza, S. (1988). Hyperactive boys almost grown up: III. Methylphenidate effects on ultimate height. *Archives of General Psychiatry, 45,* 1131–1134.

Klein, R.G., & Mannuzza, S. (1991). Long-term outcome of hyperactive children: A review. *Journal of the American Academy of Child and Adolescent Psychiatry, 30*(3), 383–387.

Klein, S.K., & Rapin I. (1990). Clinical assessment of pediatric disorders of higher cerebral function. *Current Problems in Pediatrics, 20,* 1–60.

Lipkin, P.H., Goldstein, I.J., & Adesman, A.R. (1994). Tics and dyskinesias associated with stimulant treatment in attention-deficit hyperactivity disorder. *Archives of Pediatric and Adolescent Medicine, 148,* 859–861.

Lubar, J.F. (1991). Discourse on the development of EEG diagnostics and biofeedback for attention-deficit/hyperactivity disorders. *Biofeedback and Self-Regulation, 16,* 201–225.

Mercugliano, M. (1995). Neurotransmitter alterations in attention deficit hyperactivity disorder. *Mental Retardation and Developmental Disorders Research Reviews, 1,* 220–226.

NIH Consensus Development Conference. (1982). Defined diets and childhood hyperactivity: Report of the National Advisory Committee on Hyperkinesis and Food Additives. *Journal of the American Medical Association, 248,* 290–292.

Pliszka, S.R. (1989). Effect of anxiety on cognition, behavior, and stimulant response in ADHD. *Journal of the American Academy of Child and Adolescent Psychiatry, 28,* 882–887.

Rapoport, J.L., Buchsbaum, M.S., Zahn, T.P., et al. (1978). Dextroamphetamine: Cognitive and behavioral effects in normal prepubertal boys. *Science, 199,* 560–563.

Rapport, M.D., Carlson, G.A., Kelly, K.L., et al. (1993). Methylphenidate and desipramine in hospitalized children: Separate and combined effects on cognitive function. *Journal of the American Academy of Child and Adolescent Psychiatry, 32,* 333–342.

Rapport, M.D., Denney, M.A., DuPaul, G.J., et al. (1994). Attention deficit disorder and methylphenidate: Normalization rates, clinical effectiveness, and response prediction in 76 children. *Journal of the American Academy of Child and Adolescent Psychiatry, 33,* 882–893.

Rapport, M.D., Tucker, S.B., DuPaul, G.J., et al. (1986). Hyperactivity and frustration: The influence of size and control over rewards in delaying gratification. *Journal of Abnormal Child Psychology, 14,* 191–204.

Rehabilitation Act of 1973, PL 93-112, 29 U.S.C. § 701 *et seq.*

Reiff, M.I., Banez, G.A., & Culbert, T.P. (1993) Children who have attentional disorders: Diagnosis and evaluation. *Pediatrics in Review, 14,* 455–464.

Richters, J.E., Arnold, L.E., Jensen, P.S., et al. (1995). NIMH collaborative multisite multimodal treatment study of children with ADHD: Background and rationale. *Journal of the American Academy of Child and Adolescent Psychiatry, 34,* 987–1000.

Riddle, M.A., Nelson, J.C., Kleinman, C.S., et al. (1991). Sudden death in children receiving norpramin: A review of three reported cases and commentary. *Journal of the American Academy of Child and Adolescent Psychiatry, 30,* 104–108.

Safer, D.J., & Allen, R.P. (1989). Absence of tolerance to the behavioral effects of methylphenidate in hyperactive and inattentive children. *Journal of Pediatrics, 115,* 1003–1008.

Safer, D.J., & Krager, J.M. (1994). The increased rate of stimulant treatment for hyperactive/inattentive students in secondary schools. *Pediatrics, 94,* 462–464.

Safer, D.J., Zito, J.M., & Fine, E.M. (1996). Increased methylphenidate usage for attention deficit disorder in the 1990s. *Pediatrics, 98*(6), 1084–1085.

Sandberg, S. (Ed.). (1996). *Hyperactivity disorders of childhood. Cambridge monographs on child and adolescent psychiatry 2.* New York: Cambridge University Press.

Satterfield, J.H., Satterfield, B.T., & Schell, A.M. (1987). Therapeutic interventions to prevent delinquency in hyperactive boys. *Journal of the American Academy of Child and Adolescent Psychiatry, 26,* 56–64.

Schachar, R., & Tannock, R. (1993). Childhood hyperactivity and psychostimulants: A review of extended treatment studies. *Journal of Child and Adolescent Psychopharmacology, 3,* 81–97.

Shaywitz, B.A., Sullivan, C.M., Anderson, G.M., et al. (1994). Aspartame, behavior, and cognitive function in children with attention deficit disorder. *Pediatrics, 93,* 70–75.

Shaywitz, S.E., & Shaywitz, B.A. (1988). Attention deficit disorder: Current perspective. In J.F. Kavanagh & T.J. Truss, Jr. (Eds.), *Learning disability: Proceedings of the national conference* (pp. 369–523). Baltimore: York Press.

Sheridan, S.M., Dee, C.C., Morgan, J.C., et al. (1996). A multimethod intervention for social skills deficits in children with ADHD and their parents. *School Psychology Review, 25,* 57–76.

Silver, L.B. (1989). Psychological and family problems associated with learning disabilities: Assessment and intervention. *Journal of the American Academy of Child and Adolescent Psychiatry, 28,* 319–325.

Silver, L.B. (1991). Nonstandard therapies of learning disabilities. *Seminars in Neurology, 11,* 57–63.

Singer, H.S., Brown, J., Quaskey, S., et al. (1995). The treatment of attention-deficit hyperactivity disorder in Tourette's syndrome: A double-blind placebo-controlled study with clonidine and desipramine. *Pediatrics, 95,* 74–81.

Spencer, T., Biederman, J., Wilens, T., et al. (1993). Nortriptyline treatment of children with attention-deficit hyperactivity disorder and tic disorder or Tourette syndrome. *Journal of the American Academy of Child and Adolescent Psychiatry, 32,* 201–210.

Sprich-Buckminster, S., Biederman, J., Milberger, S., et al. (1993). Are perinatal complications relevant to the manifestations of ADD? Issues of comorbidity and familiarity. *Journal of the American Academy of Child and Adolescent Psychiatry, 32,* 1032–1037.

Stein, M.A., Blondis, T.A., Schnitzler, E.R., et al. (1996). Methylphenidate dosing: Twice daily versus three times daily. *Pediatrics, 98,* 748–756.

Steingard, R., Biederman, J., Spencer, T., et al. (1993). Comparison of clonidine response in the treatment of attention-deficit hyperactivity disorder with and without comorbid tic disorders. *Journal of the American Academy of Child and Adolescent Psychiatry, 32,* 350–353.

Steinhausaen, H-C., Willms, J., & Spohr, H-L. (1993). Long-term psychopathological and cognitive outcome of children with fetal alcohol syndrome. *Journal of the American Academy of Child and Adolescent Psychiatry, 32,* 990–994.

Szatmari, P., Saigal, S., Rosenbaum, P., Campbell, D., & King, S. (1990). Psychiatric disorders at five years among children with birthweights <1000 g: A regional perspective. *Developmental Medicine and Child Neurology, 32,* 954–962.

Thorley, G. (1988). Adolescent outcome for hyperactive children. *Archives of Disease in Childhood, 63,* 1181–1183.

Wechsler, D. (1991). *Wechsler Intelligence Scale for Children–Third edition.* San Antonio, TX: The Psychological Corporation.

Weiss, B. (1982). Food additives and environmental chemicals as sources of childhood behavior disorders. *Journal of the American Acadamy of Child and Adolescent Psychiatry, 21,* 144–152.

Weiss, G., & Hechtman, L. (1986). *Hyperactive children grown up.* New York: Guilford Press.

Wender, E.H. (1986). The food additive-free diet in the treatment of behavior disorders: A review. *Journal of Deviant Behavioral Pediatrics, 7,* 35–42.

Wender, E.H., & Solanto, M.V. (1991). Effects of sugar on aggressive and inattentive behavior in children with attention deficit disorder with hyperactivity and normal children. *Pediatrics, 88,* 960–966.

Wender, P.H. (1995). *Attention-deficit hyperactivity disorder in adults.* New York: Oxford University Press.

Wender, P.H., Wood, D.R., & Reimherr, F.W. (1985). Pharmacological treatment of attention deficit disorder, residual type (ADD, RT, "minimal brain dysfunction," "hyperactivity") in adults. *Psychopharmacology Bulletin, 21,* 222–231.

Werry, J.S. (1992). History, terminology, and manifestations at different ages. *Child and Adolescent Psychiatric Clinics of North America, 1,* 297–310.

Werry, J.S. (1995). Resolved: Cardiac arrhythmias make desipramine an unacceptable choice in children: Affirmative. *Journal of the American Academy of Child and Adolescent Psychiatry, 34,* 1239–1248.

Werry, J.S., Aman, M.G., & Diamond, E. (1980). Imipramine and methylphenidate in hyperactive children. *Journal of Child Psychology and Psychiatry, 21,* 27–35.

Whalen, C.K., & Henker, B. (1992). The social profile of attention-deficit hyperactivity disorder. *Child and Adolescent Psychiatric Clinics of North America, 1,* 395–410.

Wolraich, M.L., Lindgren, S.D., Stumbo, P.J., et al. (1994). Effects of diets high in sucrose or aspartame on the behavior and cognitive performance of children. *New England Journal of Medicine, 330,* 301–307.

Wolraich, M.L., Wilson, D.B., & White, J.W. (1995). The effect of sugar on behavior and cognition in children: A meta-analysis. *Journal of the American Medical Association, 274,* 1617–1621.

23 Learning Disabilities

Robin P. Church
M.E.B. Lewis
Mark L. Batshaw

Upon completion of this chapter, the reader will:

- know the definitions of learning disability
- be aware of impairments associated with learning disabilities
- recognize some of the methods of early identification
- be aware of various intervention strategies
- be knowledgeable about outcome for children with learning disabilities

A child may have difficulty learning for many reasons. Mental retardation, cerebral palsy, seizure disorders, and hearing and vision impairments all can interfere with learning. This chapter focuses on the child whose difficulty with learning is not primarily the result of any of these disorders. Instead, these children appear to have an impairment in some aspect of language and/or visual-perceptual development that interferes with learning. Specific reading disability is the principal focus of discussion as it is both the most common learning disability and the one about which the most is known.

DEFINING LEARNING DISABILITIES

The Individuals with Disabilities Education Act (IDEA) of 1990, PL 101-476, defines a learning disability as a disorder in one or more of the basic psychological processes involved in understanding or in using language, spoken or written, which may manifest itself in an imperfect ability to listen, think, speak, read, write, spell, or do mathematical calculations. The term includes such conditions as perceptual disabilities, brain injury, minimal brain dysfunction, dyslexia, and developmental aphasia. The term, however, excludes learning problems that are primarily the result of visual, hearing, or motor disabilities and those resulting from mental retardation; emotional disturbance; or environmental, cultural, or economic disadvantage.

Unfortunately, there are several problems with this federally mandated definition. First, it focuses on exclusionary criteria while failing to define the core features of a learning disability. The exclusionary clause requires that all other possible causes for the learning problems be ruled out. This is problematic because it is well known that learning disabilities can coexist with other conditions, most notably attention-deficit/hyperactivity disorder (ADHD). In addition, this definition does not address etiology and treatment response (Shapiro & Gallico, 1993). Furthermore, the definition fails to provide guidelines regarding what the "basic psychological processes" of learning are or how marked an "imperfect ability" to learn must be to constitute a disability.

The way this definition has been operationalized is also problematic. The commonly accepted approach for determining the existence of a learning disability has been to document a severe discrepancy between ability and achievement. This is done by demonstrating a significant difference between a child's potential to learn, or IQ score, and his or her actual educational achievement (Wallach & Butler, 1994). For a specific reading disability, however, evidence now suggests that this discrepancy approach has poor sensitivity and specificity in discriminating students with reading disability from those with low ability and poor reading (Lyon, 1996). In one study, it correctly identified less than half of children who were currently receiving special education services, particularly underidentifying young and African American students (Shapiro, 1996). In fact, children with high IQ scores who have a specific reading disability do not differ from those with lower IQ scores in reading skills (Fletcher, Shaywitz, Shankweiler, et al., 1994; Pennington, 1995; Shankweiler, Crain, Katz, et al., 1995; Stanovich & Siegel, 1994). Discrepancy formulas also have shown poor validity in projecting the child's later school performance in reading. Only 17% of children classified as having a specific reading disability in the first grade on the basis of ability–achievement discrepancy remained in this classification by sixth grade (Shaywitz, Escobar, Shaywitz, et al., 1992). In addition, the discrepancy model is flawed by the assumption that IQ score is a good predictor of phonological decoding and word recognition, the basic skills involved in reading. In many studies, the discrepancy formula was no better in identifying a learning disability than simply applying a low achievement criterion (Fletcher et al., 1994). For all these reasons, there is now serious doubt about the utility and validity of the discrepancy concept for a specific reading disability. It is less clear whether the discrepancy model works for other learning disabilities (Berninger, 1994; Lyon, 1994; Lyon, Gray, Kavanagh, et al., 1993).

In an attempt to deal with these limitations, the National Joint Committee on Learning Disabilities has proposed the following amended definition:

> Learning disability is a generic term that refers to a heterogeneous group of disorders manifested by significant difficulties in the acquisition and use of listening, speaking, reading, writing, reasoning, or mathematical abilities. These disorders are intrinsic to the individual and are presumed to be due to a dysfunction of the central nervous system. Even though a learning disability may occur concomitantly with other disabling conditions (e.g., sensory impairment, mental retardation, social and emotional disturbance) or environmental influences (e.g., cultural differences, insufficient/inappropriate instruction), it is not the direct result of those conditions or influences. (Hammill, 1990, pp. 77–78)

This definition has a number of advantages: It emphasizes the heterogeneous nature of learning disabilities; it recognizes that the impairments extend beyond childhood; it acknowledges cultural disadvantage; and it states that there can be comorbidity with other developmental disabilities.

SUBTYPES OF LEARNING DISABILITIES

Just as there are different definitions of learning disabilities, so too are there different approaches to subtyping the disorder. The Office of Education (1977) specifies seven areas in which a child might exhibit a specific learning disability: oral expression, written expression, listening comprehension, basic reading skills, reading comprehension, math calculation, and math reasoning. Unfortunately, this subdivision is incomplete as it does not address the underlying impairments. Another approach has been to grade learning impairments from mild to severe and to differentiate an impairment in a single academic area (e.g., reading) from a combined disability (e.g., a reading disability associated with impairments in spelling and written expression) or a global learning problem (e.g., reading, writing, mathematics) (Shafrir & Siegel, 1994). This is useful but also incomplete as it does not take into account the biological underpinnings of specific reading disability (i.e., dyslexia). As there are a number of steps involved in reading, it is likely that many biological subtypes of dyslexia will be identified. In an attempt to address this, the Yale University Learning Disability Research Center (Lyon, 1995) has proposed three subtypes of reading disability: one based on phonological impairment, a second based on phonological and short-term memory impairments, and a third based on general cognitive impairment.

Using a similar approach, learning disabilities involving written expression have been grouped into those with a language disorder, those with a spatial disorder, those with memory and attention impairments, and those with motor impairments. Learning disabilities in mathematics are identified as isolated (dyscalculia) or as part of a combined disability involving reading or written expression (Gross-Tsur, Manor, & Shalev, 1996). As our knowledge increases, it is likely that these subgroupings will be modified further to reflect their biological bases.

PREVALENCE

Over the years, there has been a significant increase in the number of students identified by school systems as having a learning disability. Although this expansion may represent early or improved diagnosis, it also may be the result of poor diagnostic practices, teachers too willing to label a student with a learning difference as "disabled," or the inclusion of children with more subtle learning problems into a category previously reserved for students with more obvious disabilities.

According to figures provided by the U.S. Department of Education, Office of Special Education Programs (1995), half of all students served in special education programs are identified as having a specific learning disability. This category has more than doubled since its original creation in 1977, with a particularly high rate of increase in the 1990s.

The actual prevalence of learning disabilities in the school-age population (6–17 years) has been estimated to be 4%–5%, accounting for approximately 2 million children (Macmillan, 1993; Roush, 1995). If children with both ADHD and a learning disability are included, this rate increases to 11% (Epstein, Shaywitz, Shaywitz, et al., 1991; Pennington, Groisser, & Welsh, 1993). It should be emphasized, however, that prevalence figures depend on the definition of the disability. Because the definition of specific learning disability is problematic, it follows that prevalence figures may be unreliable and may vary from author to author or study to study.

Another area of dispute is gender effects. Studies have traditionally suggested a multifold gender predominance (4–5 times) of learning disabilities among males. However, it is now thought that because girls manifest attention and learning problems differently from boys and tend not to exhibit oppositional-defiant behavior, they may escape the teacher's attention. Research suggests that the actual ratio may be closer to 1:1 (Duane, 1991; Guerin, Griffen, Gottfried, et al., 1993).

GENETICS OF LEARNING DISABILITIES

Since the turn of the 20th century, it has been hypothesized that learning disabilities are heritable (Thomas, 1905). Often several members of a family have a specific reading disability, and the underlying phonological processing impairments in this disorder appear to be highly heritable. Studies of identical twins have found that more than half of reading performance impairments are a consequence of heritable influences (DeFries & Alarcon, 1996; Wolff, Melngailis, Obregon, et al., 1995). Furthermore, the recurrence rate of reading disability in susceptible families has been found to be 35%–45%, suggesting that a single gene may be involved (Pennington, 1995). In fact, a major gene locus for reading disability has been identified in a small region on the short arm of chromosome #6 (Cardon, Smith, Fulker, et al., 1994).

Children with certain genetic syndromes also may have an increased risk of specific types of learning disabilities, although less commonly a specific reading disability (Light & DeFries, 1995). Girls with Turner syndrome and fragile X syndrome and boys with Klinefelter syndrome tend to have visual-perceptual–based learning disabilities (Pennington, Heaton, Karzmark, et al., 1985; Reiss & Freund, 1990). Children with neurofibromatosis type 1 have both visual-perceptual and language-based learning disabilities (Denckla, 1996).

THE CAUSES OF SPECIFIC READING DISABILITY

Specific reading disability is by far the most common form of learning disability, accounting for approximately 80% of affected children (Flynn & Rabar, 1994; Roush, 1995). Theoretically, any defect in the processing and interpretation of written words can lead to a specific reading disability. Efficient reading depends on rapidly, accurately, and fluently decoding and recognizing the phonemes of single words (Lyon & Chhabra, 1996). Phonological awareness includes a metacognitive understanding of word boundaries within spoken sentences, of syllable boundaries within spoken words, and of how to isolate these phonemes to establish their location within syllables and words (Clark & Uhry, 1995). Phoneme awareness manifests in the ability to analyze and manipulate sounds within syllables: to count, delete, and reorder them. If a child is not able to comprehend that syllables and words are composed of phonemes and that these segments can be divided according to their acoustic boundaries, reading will be slow, labored, and inaccurate; and comprehension will be poor (Fletcher et al., 1994; Lyon, 1995). This represents an impairment in phonological awareness. Such an impairment also could result from impaired rapid sequential processing across both auditory and visual modalities (Kraus, McGee, Carrell, et al., 1996; Tallal, Miller, Bedi, et al., 1996). In addition, a child may have a defect in phonetic representation in working memory, so that he or she can understand the syntactic structure of a sentence but is unable to maintain it in working memory long enough to comprehend the meaning (Mann, 1994).

Taking these findings into account, the Orton Dyslexia Society Research Committee proposed a biologically based definition of specific reading disability:

> A language-based disorder of constitutional origin characterized by difficulties in single word decoding, usually reflecting insufficient phonological processing. These difficulties in single word decoding are often unexpected in relation to age and other cognitive and academic abilities; they are not the result of a generalized developmental disability or sensory impairment. Dyslexia is manifest by variable difficulty with different forms of language, often including, in addition to problems with reading, a conspicuous problem with acquiring proficiency in writing and spelling. (Lyon, 1995, p. 9)

NEUROANATOMY OF SPECIFIC READING DISABILITY

To understand the neurological impairments underlying specific reading disability, the normal neural pathways involved in reading must be explained. When one reads, the visual pathways of both eyes pass the print image (written language) to the visual cortex in the occipital lobes of the brain (Figure 14.6). From here, the information is transferred forward to the left angular gyrus of the temporal lobe and to Wernicke's area, which both appear to be critical for phonological coding (i.e., the translation of written language into its speech sound equivalents) (Rumsey, 1996). Data from the right occipital (visual) cortex cross over to the left through the corpus callosum and are interpreted in the dominant left temporal lobe of the brain (Hynd, Hall, Novey, et al., 1995a,b). Consistent with evidence that the left temporal lobe is a center for language processing, there is typically an asymmetry, with structures being larger on the left than on the right.

Neuropathological studies of young adults with dyslexia who died of unrelated causes have found altered asymmetries in these language-related brain regions. Structures in the temporal-parietal region (i.e., the planum temporale) and the parieto-occipital region were found to be of equal size on the right and left sides, and the corpus callosum was decreased in size (Filipek, 1995). Other studies of adults with dyslexia have found microscopic developmental abnormalities in the parietal lobe of the brain, which is involved in auditory processing and language syntax, and in the lateral geniculate body, which is sensitive to processing visual information (Duffy, Denckla, McAnulty, et al., 1988; Galaburda, 1993; Galaburda & Livingstone, 1993; Galaburda, Menard, & Rosen, 1994; Schultz, Cho, Staib, et al., 1994). These abnormalities involve **ectopias** and **architectonic dysplasias,** which occurred during early brain development.

Functional neuroimaging studies using positron emission tomography (PET) and magnetic resonance imaging (MRI) (see Chapter 14) have yielded results consistent with the above information. The findings have included 1) decreased activation of the left temporal-parietal cortex and superior temporal cortex during rhyme detection, a measure of phonological awareness and semantic processing; 2) dysfunction of the central visual pathways (Eden, VanMeter, Rumsey, et al., 1996; Lehmkuhle, Garzia, Turner, et al., 1993; Livingstone, Rosen, Drislane, et al., 1991; Rumsey, Berman, Denckla, et al., 1987); and 3) abnormalities in the thalamus, which is normally involved in attention and planning (Pennington, 1991). These findings suggest that reading involves the simultaneous activation of multiple associated cortical regions in a neural network involved in language and visual processing and in attention and planning. A defect anywhere in the network would be expected to result in a specific reading disability. This supports the idea that there are subtypes of reading disability associated with specific neurocognitive impairments in phonological decoding, visual processing, and so forth. This is also consistent with the findings by Tallal et al. (1996) that difficulty with rapid temporal processing of phonemes affects reading.

ASSOCIATED IMPAIRMENTS

Because so many brain regions are affected, it is not surprising that one quarter to one half of children with learning disabilities have additional impairments that interfere with school functioning. These may include executive function impairments, ADHD, social skills impairments, and emotional and behavior disorders (Capute, Accardo, & Shapiro, 1994). These behavior and emotional problems may be externalizing (e.g., aggression, oppositional/defiant) or internalizing (e.g., shyness, depression).

As comorbid conditions may adversely affect outcome, it may be most appropriate to categorize children not only on the basis of their learning impairments, but also on comorbid conditions (McConaughy, Mattison, & Peterson, 1994; McKinney, 1987, 1989; Pennington, 1991; Rock, Fessler, & Church, 1996).

Impairments in Executive Functions

According to Pennington (1991), executive functions involve the ability to maintain an appropriate problem-solving set of procedures for attaining a future goal. This includes the ability to inhibit or defer a response; to formulate a sequential, strategic plan of action; and to encode relevant information in memory for future use (Welsh & Pennington, 1988). These metacognitive abilities are necessary for organizational skills, planning, future-oriented behavior, maintaining an appropriate problem-solving set of procedures, impulse control, selective attention, vigilance, inhibition, and creativity in thinking (Denckla & Reader, 1993). They also involve an awareness of what skills, strategies, and resources are needed to perform a task effectively and the ability to use self-regulatory mechanisms to ensure the successful completion of the task. Yet students with learning disabilities are often impulsive rather than reflective when presented with a problem-solving task. This failure to consider alternative solutions often results in errors or poor quality in the solution (Lyon & Krasnegor, 1996). Executive functions become essential in middle school to complete homework and long-term projects, to sustain attention during lectures, and to set future goals. Disruption in this organization and control of behavior often manifests itself as disruption in the classroom.

Memory Impairments

Impairments in the ability to listen, remember, and repeat auditory stimuli have been associated with reading disability. A number of studies comparing children with equivalent IQ scores but low or high reading abilities report impairments in the poor readers on the Digit Span subtest of the Wechsler Intelligence Scale for Children, Third Edition (WISC–III; Wechsler, 1991) (Clark & Uhry, 1995). This involves retaining the beginning of a word in memory while decoding the middle and end parts so that all the sounds can be blended. The holding of information in immediate and working memory is essential to learning to read. Individuals with impaired phonological processing have impaired memory skills.

Attention-Deficit/Hyperactivity Disorder

Approximately one third of children with learning disabilities also have ADHD, making this the most common comorbidity (Light & DeFries, 1995; Shaywitz, Fletcher, & Shaywitz, 1995; Shaywitz & Shaywitz, 1991). The symptoms typically include inattention, impulsivity, and hyperactivity (see Chapter 22).

Social Skills Impairments

Children with learning disabilities, especially of the nonverbal type, may have perceptually based impairments in social skills. They tend to be socially isolated, have few close friends, and infrequently participate in social activities. In turn, they are often overlooked or rejected by their peers because of their odd behavior and poor school and/or athletic performance. Teachers tend to rate these children as having social adjustment difficulties and being easily led. There may be many reasons for these problems, including poor social comprehension, inability to take the perspective of others, poor pragmatic language skills, and misinterpretation of body language (Shapiro & Gallico, 1993).

Emotional and Behavior Disorders

Although associated impairments may represent endogenous biological conditions, they also may result from the child's external experiences of school failure (Fessler, Rosenberg, & Rosenberg, 1991; Gallico, Burns, & Grob, 1988; Spafford & Grosser, 1993). Children with learning disabilities can exhibit a range of emotional and behavior disturbances, including conduct disorders, withdrawal, poor self-esteem, and depression. These individuals are less likely to take pride in their successes and more likely to be overcome by their failures. More than one third of students with learning disabilities receive a failing grade in one or more courses each school year. These children often exhibit chronic frustration and anxiety as they attempt to meet the demands of skill-based tasks such as phonological decoding, comprehension, spelling, and math. This school failure, combined with social skills impairments, may lead to peer rejection, poor self-image, and withdrawal from participating in school activities (Bender & Wall, 1994; McKinlay, Ferguson, & Jolly, 1996). Eventually, the child may avoid going to school all together or act out in class to obtain the attention he or she does not receive through good grades. The overall dropout rate of children with a learning disability is twice that found in the general population (U.S. Department of Education, Office of Special Education Programs, 1991).

EARLY IDENTIFICATION

The age at which a child is identified as having a learning disability is a function of the type of disability, its severity, associated medical problems, the child's intelligence, parental concerns, and surveillance methods (Richards & Hammitte, 1993). In general, the more severe or global the disability, the earlier it will be detected. Parental concern, often resulting from another family member having a learning disability, also may lead to early identification. A medical history of a condition (e.g., prematurity) that places the child at increased risk for developing a learning disability may lead to early diagnosis. In addition, there is an inverse correlation between intelligence and age at detection; intellectually gifted children tend to be identified late because their cognitive abilities often compensate for their learning disabilities in elementary school.

Because federal educational definitions of learning disability are still based on discrepancy formulas, the identification of an affected child traditionally has awaited school entry. Yet, studies have shown that the core symptoms of learning disabilities are present from the preschool years (Catts, 1991; Scanlon & Vellutino, 1996). They may manifest as delays in language, attention, and behavior and may be associated with impairments in social interactions, impulse control, and motor skills (Reynolds, Elksnin, & Brown, 1996). The most prominent predictor of a specific reading disability is weakness in the comprehension of semantics and syntax. Conversely, strengths in phoneme awareness and verbal memory are predictors of good reading ability. Scarborough (1990) found that at 30 months of age, children who later developed reading disabilities had decreased length of utterances, syntactic complexity, and pronunciation accuracy. By age 3, these children showed weaknesses in receptive vocabulary and object naming, and by age 5 they had impairments in phonological awareness and letter-sound knowledge.

Unfortunately, the items most commonly asked on school readiness education tests (e.g., the Metropolitan Readiness Test, Pediatric Examination of Educational Readiness, Wide Range Achievement Test [Jastak & Wilkinson, 1984]) are not good predictors of which students will develop specific learning disabilities (Badian, McAnulty, Duffy, et al., 1990). Newer tests of language and memory function, employing grapheme-phoneme associations and rapid retrieval from long-term memory, appear to be more helpful in early identification (Badian, 1995; Badian et al., 1990). Measures of phonological awareness include the Test of Phonological Awareness (Torgesen & Bryant, 1994); the Test of Awareness of Language Segments (Sawyer, 1987); and the Lindamood Auditory Conceptualization Test (Lindamood & Lindamood, 1979). Other useful tests include measures of verbal short-term memory, such as the Digit Span subtest of the WISC–III, and comparison of memory for rote material with memory for meaningful material as measured by the Memory for Words versus Memory for Sentences Test (Woodcock-Johnson Revised Battery [Woodcock & Johnson, 1989]). Rapid automatic recall of information can be measured by the Rapid Automatized Naming Test (Denckla & Rudel, 1976). Impairments in both short-term auditory memory and retrieval of phonological information also have been good predictors of future learning disabilities (Brady, Fowler, Stone, et al., 1994; Felton & Wood, 1989; Stone & Brady, 1993).

Impairments in visual-perceptual skills are more difficult to diagnose in the preschool period than are language delays. However, tests can indicate problems in drawing and understanding shape concepts. For example, a 3-year-old should be able to draw a circle and a cross and match colors. A 4-year-old typically can draw a "stick figure," and a 6-year-old should be able to copy a number of the pictures in the Bender Visual Motor Gestalt Test (Figure 23.1) (Bender, 1938). Many kindergarten and first-grade teachers believe that difficulty with certain perceptual-motor tasks, such as tying shoes and skipping, are red flags in predicting poor academic success. However, other visual-perceptual signs may not show up until a child is older than 7 years of age. For example, although letter reversal is common in children with learning disabilities, it is not uncommon for typically developing children under 7 years of age to reverse letters such as "b" for "d." Although an inability to distinguish right from left may be a marker for learning disability, it is not until 6 years of age that an average child can accomplish this task consistently. Other so-called "soft" neurological signs such as difficulty with rapid alternating movements do not appear until after 6 years of age, and their importance in diagnosing a learning disability at any time is questionable.

SCHOOL PROBLEMS SIMULATING LEARNING DISABILITIES

Some children who do not have a specific learning disability may demonstrate learning differences in school as a consequence of another developmental disability, a chronic illness, or psychosocial problems. If these children are misdiagnosed as having a specific learning disability, efforts directed solely at treating the learning problem will have limited benefit. Instead, the un-

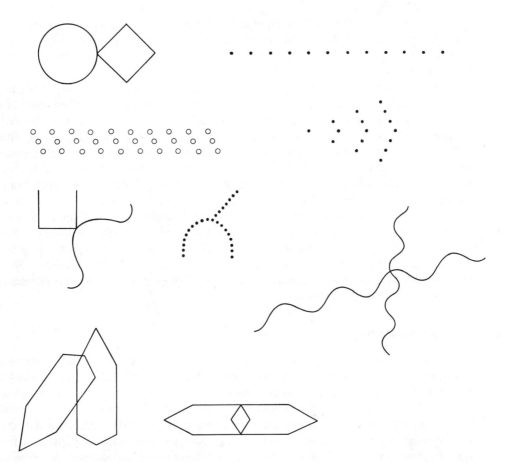

Figure 23.1.   Figures used in the Bender-Gestalt test of visual-perceptual abilities. The individual is asked to copy the nine figures. (From Bender, L. [1946]. *Instructions for the use of Visual Motor Gestalt Test, Plate I.* New York: American Orthopsychiatric Association, 1946; reprinted by permission. Copyright © 1946 by Lauretta Bender and The American Orthopsychiatric Association, Inc.)

derlying problem must be identified and addressed. Once this problem has been treated, the learning problem may well improve. For example, if a child has an unidentified sensory impairment, learning is likely to be impaired. The provision of hearing aids to a child with hearing loss or glasses to the child with visual impairment may make a significant difference in school performance. Children with epilepsy also may have problems in school resulting either from poorly controlled seizures or from side effects of antiepileptic drugs. Modifying the drug regimen may significantly improve both attention and learning. Children with psychiatric disorders also may fail in school. The use of psychotropic drugs and psychotherapy often leads to significantly improved school performance, although some of these drugs have an adverse effect on attention.

An increased incidence of learning problems also has been described in children with such chronic illnesses as diabetes (Rovet, Ehrlich, Czuchta, et al., 1993); acquired immunodeficiency syndrome (Armstrong, Seidel, & Swales, 1993); cancer (Brown & Madan-Swain, 1993); and chronic kidney and liver disease (Hobbs & Sexson, 1993). In these situations, learning difficulties may result from some combination of biochemical disturbance, excessive school absences, attention impairments, or depression. A secondary learning problem rather than a primary learning disability is suggested if learning improves once the medical condition is brought under control (Sexson & Madan-Swain, 1993).

Acute disorders such as meningitis, encephalitis, and traumatic brain injury (TBI) also can result in the subsequent development of learning problems. TBI is the most common of these and is an increasingly recognized cause of behavior and learning problems in children (see Chapter 27). The injury may result in either temporary or permanent neurological impairments. Affected children present special challenges in the classroom as a result of the evolving nature of their recovery (Savage & Wolcott, 1994). Because of this, TBI has been identified as a separate category of special education programs under IDEA, to distinguish it from learning disabilities and other related disorders.

Finally, psychosocial influences can affect the child's ability to learn. A child who is hungry cannot pay attention or learn well (Durkin, 1989). A child who comes from a home that does not value learning rarely achieves well in school. And a home beset with family problems or abuse is a poor setting to encourage the child's school performance (Coles, 1987; Maslow, 1970). Improvement in these psychosocial areas would likely result in improved school performance but has proven very difficult to achieve.

ASSESSMENT PROCEDURES

Psychological and educational tests are the mainstay of assessment for learning disabilities in school-age children. However, a complete medical, behavioral, educational, and social history also should be taken to consider confounding variables that may simulate or worsen a learning disability (Shapiro & Gallico, 1993). After determining that no other physical or emotional disorder is responsible for the learning problem, a comprehensive psychoeducational evaluation that assesses cognitive, visual-perceptual, and linguistic processes should be performed. In addition, the implementing regulations of IDEA require assessment of the following seven academic areas: oral expression, listening comprehension, written expression, basic reading skills, reading comprehension, mathematical calculation, and mathematical reasoning. This assessment theoretically permits the diagnosis of an ability–achievement discrepancy and a strategy for intervention. As noted previously, though, the validity of this discrepancy approach is now being questioned (Hooper, 1996).

Assessment of cognitive functioning should include the relevant areas of discrimination, generalization, motor behavior, general information, vocabulary, induction, comprehension, sequencing, detail recognition, analogies, abstract reasoning, memory, and pattern completion (Table 23.1) (Salvia & Ysseldyke, 1995). This is accomplished using IQ tests such as the WISC–III and the Kaufman–Assessment Battery for Children (K–ABC; Kaufman & Kaufman, 1983) (Wodrich, 1997).

The WISC–III is divided into six verbal and six performance subtests, none of which requires reading or spelling. These subtests consist of a series of increasingly difficult questions ranging from a 6- to 16-year-old level. On each subtest, the child is asked to perform up to the level at which he or she consistently fails. Each subtest is then scored, with 10 being an average score. It is possible to determine a child's strengths and weaknesses by examining the subtest scores. The verbal subtests of the WISC–III include information, comprehension, arithmetic,

Table 23.1.   Commonly used tests for evaluating cognitive and executive functioning

Name of test	Consists of	Assesses
Wechsler Intelligence Scale for Children–Third Edition (Wechsler, 1991)	Six verbal and six performance subscales	General information, verbal comprehension, abstract reasoning, memory, spatial abilities
Woodcock-Johnson Psycho-Educational Battery–Revised Tests of Cognitive Ability (Woodcock & Johnson, 1989)	21 subtests measuring visual and auditory processing	Verbal comprehension, perceptual organization, processing speed, attention and memory
California Verbal Learning Test–Children's Version (Delis & Fridlund, 1994)	Lists of words randomly related	Amount of verbal information learned and how it is learned
Gordon Diagnostic System (Gordon, 1983)	Computerized activity in which child must react to stated stimuli and not react to others	Vigilance and inhibition of impulsivity
Test of Variables of Attention (Greenberg, 1990)	Computerized activity in which child must react to stated stimuli and not react to others	Inhibition of impulsivity and selective attention
Wisconsin Card Sorting Test (Grant & Berg,1993)	Patterns that must be recognized and categorized by attributes that shift and change	Perseveration and abstract reasoning

similarities, vocabulary, and digit span. The performance subtests include picture completion, picture arrangement, block design, object assembly, coding, and mazes. The child with a learning disability may have a scattering of abilities (Branch, Cohen, & Hynd, 1995; Stanford & Hynd, 1994). For example, the examiner may find specific strengths in verbal areas or particular weaknesses in the visual-performance area. Such information is helpful in setting up an individualized education program (IEP).

A newer test, the K–ABC, is designed to measure both intelligence and achievement through mental processing and achievement scales. It yields four global scales: Sequential Processing, Simultaneous Processing, Mental Processing Composite, and Achievement.

Methods for assessing executive functioning vary and are reviewed in Table 23.1. These tasks challenge the person to tolerate boredom, to operate independently, and to generate active plans to solve puzzles or problems. Such tasks tap the child's ability to initiate problem-solving activities, to maintain sustained attention, to inhibit off-track behavior, and to organize and carry out successful and flexible problem-solving strategies (Campione, 1989; Denckla & Reader, 1993; Haywood & Wingenfeld, 1992; Palinscar, Brown, & Campione, 1991).

These tests are usually combined with tests of visual perception, language, and academic achievement (Table 23.2). Tests that measure visual-perceptual abilities include the Bender Gestalt figures and the Goodenough-Harris Drawing Test (Harris, 1963). Language functioning may be tested by the Clinical Evaluation of Language Fundamentals–Revised (Semel, Wiig, & Secord, 1995). Finally, there is a group of academic achievement tests, the most prominent of which is the Woodcock-Johnson Psycho-Educational Battery–Revised (Woodcock & Johnson, 1989), which measures oral reading/comprehension, spelling, and arithmetic.

Table 23.2.   Commonly used tests for evaluation of achievement and related areas

Name of test/author	Description of contents and areas assessed
Visual-Perceptual Tests	
Bender Gestalt Test (Bender, 1942)	The child is asked to copy nine drawings measuring visual-perceptual skills and eye–hand coordination
Goodenough-Harris Drawing (Harris, 1963)	Points given for number of body parts, accuracy and detail in drawing (of a person) by the child, measuring visual-perceptual skills and self-image
Comprehensive Academic Achievement Tests	
Woodcock-Johnson Psycho-Educational Battery–Revised (Woodcock & Johnson, 1989)	Selected items from grades 1–12 measuring word recognition, comprehension, math calculation and reasoning, spelling, and written expression
Wechsler Individual Achievement Test (WIAT) (Wechsler, 1992)	Graded items from grades 1–12 designed to match up with seven areas outlined in federal legislation: oral expression, basic reading (recognition) comprehension, math calculation and reasoning, listening comprehension, and written expression
Kaufman Test of Educational Achievement (KTEA) (Kaufman & Kaufman, 1985)	Selected items from grades 1–12 measuring word recognition and comprehension, math calculation and reasoning, and spelling
Peabody Individual Achievement Test–Revised (PIAT–R) (Markwardt, 1989)	Graded items ranging from grades 1–12 measuring word recognition and comprehension, math calculation and reasoning, spelling and written expression
Standardized Tests of Reading	
Stanford Diagnostic Reading Test (Karlsen, Madden, & Gardner, 1985)	
Gates-MacGinitie Reading Test (MacGinitie, 1989)	Vocabulary words and stories with questions to assess comprehension
Gray Oral Reading Test–Revised (Wiederholt & Bryant, 1992)	Assesses a variety of reading skills including oral reading fluency, word attack, and word recognition
Nelson-Denny Reading Test (Brown, Bennett, & Hanna, 1985)	Designed for use with ages 9–16; assesses reading skills, comprehension
Standardized Tests of Math	
Key Math–Revised (Connolly, 1988)	Designed for use with kindergarten–grade 9; measures basic math concepts, operations, and applications
Standardized Tests of Written Expression	
Test of Written Spelling–Second Edition (Larsen & Hammill, 1986)	Designed for grades 1–12; assesses spelling of phonetically regular and irregular words

The results of the combined psychoeducational testing indicate the child's IQ score, executive functioning, visual-perceptual and language abilities, and levels of achievement in various academic subjects. From these findings, IEPs are developed. Federal legislation requires psychoeducational testing to be repeated every 3 years; however, annual retesting in academic subjects is important to determine the progress the child has made and the effectiveness of the program.

INTERVENTION STRATEGIES

The goals of intervention are to achieve academic competence, treat associated impairments, and prevent adverse mental health outcomes. This requires the cooperation of educators, healthcare professionals, and parents. If children with a specific reading disability are not provided with an intervention program composed of instruction in phoneme awareness, sound–symbol relations, and contextual reading skills before the third grade, at least three quarters will show little improvement in reading throughout their school years (Shaywitz & Shaywitz, 1991). In addition to treating the core learning disability, intervention strategies also must focus on associated cognitive, attentional, perceptual, and sensory impairments. Immaturity, lack of motivation, and poor impulse control also must be considered in determining the child's needs for remediation (Bakker, 1992). Professionals continue to debate the most effective intervention strategies. A major consideration is whether to teach to the child's abilities (i.e., compensatory strategies) or to the disabilities (i.e., rehabilitation strategies). Little evidence supports the superiority of one approach over the other. It is generally agreed, however, that there must be a combination of instructional and cognitive interventions (Deshler, Ellis, & Lenz, 1995).

Instructional Interventions

The following is a review of instructional interventions focusing on the areas of reading, writing, and mathematics.

Reading

Reading proficiency depends on phonological processing and alphabetical mapping. Phonics instruction, however, is different from phonological awareness training. Clark and Uhry (1995) define phonics as a low level of rote knowledge of the association between letters and sounds, while phonological awareness includes a range of higher-level metacognitive understandings of word boundaries within spoken sentences, of syllable boundaries in spoken words, and of how to isolate the phonemes and establish their location within syllables and words. Regardless of the method chosen, the major goal of reading instruction is to improve phonological awareness so that there is effective word recognition and comprehension of meaning. Reading activities focus on helping the child become attuned to the sound characteristics of language (phoneme awareness) and the utility of letter–sound relationships (the alphabetic principle).

In elementary school, reading instruction includes methods designed to increase skills in acquiring vocabulary, using syntax, and understanding meaning (Maggart & Zintz, 1993; Newby, Recht, & Caldwell, 1993). Explicit phonics training programs teach individual grapheme–phoneme correspondences before they teach blending these sounds together to form syllables and words. The cornerstone of these programs is the Orton-Gillingham approach (Gillingham & Stillman, 1973; Orton, 1937; Sheffield, 1991). Newer remedial programs adapted from this method are commonly used today with students with reading disabilities. Examples of such programs include Alphabetic Phonics (Cox, 1985); Recipe for Reading (Traub & Bloom, 1975); and the Wilson Reading System (Wilson, 1988).

Along with knowledge of phonics, a rapid sight vocabulary is essential to efficient reading. Different word recognition strategies include analysis of sound (phonics or phonetics), analysis for structure (visual configuration), and use of memory skills to recognize words as total entities (whole word approach). Comprehension strategies center on developing the ability to draw meaning from text, often using a sequence of books that introduces words and concepts in a gradual progression. This skill requires symbolic processing memory, visual-processing fluency, and rapid automatized naming (Korhonen, 1995; Watson & Willows, 1995). An example of a program designed to deliver this kind of systematic direct instruction is Project Read (Calfee & Henry, 1986).

As students progress to middle and high school, the reading process connects with other skills needed for mastering content-related matter in subjects such as social studies, geography, higher-level mathematics, and sciences. Study, organizational, and problem-solving skills must blend with the processing skills involved in obtaining meaning from words, sentences, charts, maps, books, poetry, and dramatic or narrative literature. Meaning is easier to teach in the elementary and middle grades than in high school where it may become buried in nuances of language, such as humor, sarcasm, and metaphor (Englert & Hiebert, 1984).

Many students with a reading disability will need an adjustment in the curriculum or placement in a specialized class setting (Lewis, 1993). Some methods of teaching reading such as Orton-Gillingham and Fernald (Denning, 1990; Silberberg, Iverson, & Goins, 1975) employ multisensory approaches to the remediation of difficulties in efficient sound–symbol processing. Other approaches include whole language (reinforcing a spectrum of language arts) (Edelsky, Atwerger, & Flores, 1991); thematics (uniting content areas conceptually) (Lewis, 1993); literature based (using trade books to build on basal program skills); individualized reading (using trade books and alternative literature forms to build personal reading) (Fielding & Roller, 1992); and language experience (having students generate their own reading material) (Tierney, Readence, & Dishner, 1995). An emphasis on functional skills involves the use of daily living materials (e.g., forms, notices, directions).

As more is known about the neuropsychological impairments of dyslexia, it is likely that new methods will emerge that focus on the underlying brain impairments. One example of such an experimental approach has been reported by Tallal et al. (1996). Based on evidence that certain children with language-based reading disabilities have difficulty discriminating rapidly successive phonetic elements and nonspeech sound stimuli, computer games have been designed to improve these "temporal processing" skills (Merzenich, Jenkins, Johnston, et al., 1996).

Writing

Students with **dysgraphia** have specific disabilities in processing and reporting information in written form. Writing is firmly connected to reading and spelling because comprehension and exposition of these skills are demonstrated through production of written symbols as indicators of understanding. Although writing is a representation of oral language (Maggart & Zintz, 1993), it also must convey meaning without the benefit of vocal intonation or stress. This makes additional demands on the writer.

Problems in writing may result from either an inability to manipulate a pen and paper to produce a legible representation of ideas or an inability to express oneself on paper. Word processors assist with disabilities related to the manipulation of the writing implements (Bain, Bailet, & Moats, 1991). Remedial and instructional techniques helpful with problems of written expression include the use of open-ended sentences (Mercer, Hughes, & Mercer, 1985); probable passages (a strategy used to draw on a student's prior knowledge of a topic while incorporating writing into a basic reading lesson) (Wood, 1984); journal keeping (Beach & Anson, 1993; Taylor, 1991); employment of modified writing systems using rebus or other symbols (Newcomer, Nodine, & Barenbaum, 1988); and subscription to newspapers and other print media to demonstrate various writing styles and organizational models.

Writing is also a sociocultural endeavor, representing a cognitive process learned through dialogic interactions, expressing the social and cultural perspectives of the student (Englert, 1992). The difficulties that a student with learning disabilities may have with social perception and awareness of cultural aspects of personal development may influence the written product as well as the writing process.

Content area literacy calls for connections between reading and writing (Mason, 1989; Vacca & Vacca, 1993). Study skills and organization of written materials so they are retrievable for later use are both vital elements to the success of the student with learning disabilities (Barr, Kamil, Mosenthal, et al., 1991).

Mathematics

Students whose learning disabilities center around arithmetic functioning are called dyscalculic. This problem involves an inability to perform basic math operations (i.e., addition, subtraction, multiplication, division) or to apply those operations to daily situations. For some of these children, a calculator may prove helpful as an aid. However, often the problem is in understanding the abstract concepts of mathematical usage. When students with **dyscalculia** have only written math problems to solve, the concepts remain vague; but when functional applications are used (e.g., involving money or time), the student can connect the concepts to their practical application and demonstrate greater understanding (Schwartz & Budd, 1983). Thus, teaching may focus on the use of money in fast-food restaurants (e.g., making change); grocery shopping (e.g., comparing prices per unit of weight); banking (e.g., balancing a checkbook, calculating interest); cooking (e.g., measurement); and transportation (e.g., reading, keeping to schedules).

Hutchinson (1992) and Montague (1992) have demonstrated the effectiveness of an approach that emphasizes executive functions for solving mathematical word problems and complex operations (i.e., multiplication). This approach involves rehearsal, practice, and mastery of math skills, in combination with corrective and positive feedback throughout the process of instruction. This can give students with dyscalculia hope for greater success and facility in progressing to higher and more complex mathematical levels (Hutchinson, 1990; Montague & Bos, 1986).

For many students with mathematical disabilities, the more abstract levels of mathematics, such as algebra, geometry, and calculus, may remain mysteries forever; however, these students can still become facile with basic mathematical functions in daily life (Mercer, 1991). Many schools teach students how and when to use calculators so that more complex problems can be simplified or homework checked for accuracy. In addition, the computer is now a common part of a school's equipment, and computer-assisted instruction in math may provide opportunities for practice and reinforcement (Okolo, 1992).

Social Skills Training

The maintenance of self-esteem and development of social skills are important in preventing adverse mental health outcomes. The teacher can encourage this by giving the child special jobs in the classroom and by supporting participation in extracurricular activities such as sports, scouting, music, drama, arts and crafts, and so forth. Social skills training also can be provided in a group setting using role-playing techniques.

Counseling

Counseling may be required to treat underlying psychological disorders. This can be provided individually or in groups. Family-centered counseling also may be appropriate. Issues to be discussed may include homework, behavior management techniques, discipline, parental expectations, and the child's self-esteem. Families also should be provided a source of information about learning disabilities, a support group, and knowledge about their legal rights and responsibilities in the education of their child.

Vocational Training and Career Education

Vocational training, which usually begins in high school, consists of counseling, assessment, and training in the hands-on skills that future jobs require. The U.S. Department of Labor (1992) publishes competencies determined to be necessary for employment. These SCANS (Secretary's Commission on Achieving Necessary Skills) reports have been translated into curriculum areas that deemphasize specific job-related tasks while teaching general competencies that cross all job markets. Programs for adolescents with learning disabilities will need to carefully consider these issues if they are to adequately prepare young adults for employment.

Vocational training for students with learning disabilities begins with realistic counseling resulting from a comprehensive assessment of abilities and aptitudes. Without appropriately directed training, students are at risk to become adults unable to support themselves in an independent manner (Michaels, 1994). If vocational rehabilitative services are delayed until adulthood they are less likely to be effective (Dowdy, Smith, & Nowell, 1992).

Career and technology education is equally important if students are to be ready for the jobs that will be available in the 21st century. Career education is a concept that should be part of educational programming from the primary grades. Even as adults, individuals with learning disabilities have poor retention of verbal instructions and other problems that may interfere with effectiveness in their jobs. They also may be hesitant to ask questions and seek assistance. Social immaturity, clumsiness, and poor judgment may make social interactions more difficult. The skills taught in career education are those required to overcome these impairments and enhance success in the work environment, be it the classroom or the adult marketplace. Cooperation, respect, responsibility, teamwork, organization, and how to seek information to solve one's problems are part of career education (U.S. Department of Labor, 1992).

Medication

Although learning disabilities cannot be "cured" through the use of medication, certain associated impairments that affect learning, such as ADHD and related behavior and emotional problems, can be improved with the use of psychoactive drugs (Forness, Swanson, Cantwell, et al., 1992). If any of these drugs is used, its effectiveness must be monitored carefully (see Chapter 22). Medication should never be a substitute for sound educational programming.

Nontraditional Treatment Approaches

Because there is no cure for learning disabilities, it is not surprising that a host of nontraditional therapies have gained advocates from time to time. The most commonly used of these approaches have been directed at correcting underlying perceptual impairments. These treatment methods include optometric approaches and sensory integration. Neither has been proven effective.

Some optometrists propose that children with dyslexia should use visual training exercises to overcome visual-perceptual impairments. Yet, research does not link the physical structure of the eye or any peripheral visual aspect to learning disabilities as a whole or dyslexia in particular (American Academy of Pediatrics Committee on Learning Disabilities, American Association for Pediatric Opthamology and Strabismus, and American Academy of Opthamology, 1992). In addition, individuals with dyslexia were not found to have significant differences in visual fixation or smooth pursuit of a stimulus (Eden, Stein, Wood, et al., 1994; Eden, Stein, Wood, et al., 1995). No research has found that eye muscle exercises have any beneficial effect on reading (Metzger & Werner, 1984).

Another visual hypothesis focuses on "scotopic sensitivity" of the retina. It was hypothesized that certain children are highly sensitive to particular frequencies and wavelengths of the white light spectrum. This impairment was postulated to cause fatigue, resulting in reading disability, poor coordination and depth perception, eye strain, and sensitivity to glare (O'Connor, Sofo, Kendall, et al., 1990). The proposed treatment involves wearing colored lenses that filter out offending light frequencies. Research conducted on the colored lenses, however, has not proven them to be effective in improving reading facility (Hoyt, 1990).

Another treatment approach attempts to overcome perceptual problems by sensory integration training (Ayres, 1972). This theory suggests that the ability of the cortex to respond to auditory and visual stimuli depends on the organization of the stimuli in the brainstem. Ayres noted that other abnormalities connected with the functioning of the brainstem are apparent in children with learning disabilities. These include clumsiness and poor eye muscle coordination. To deal with this, she proposed activities that involve balancing and fine motor coordination aimed at improving brainstem functioning. Studies suggest that although this method may be helpful in improving coordination and self-confidence (see Chapter 32), it is not successful in treating the underlying learning disability (Hoehn & Baumeister, 1994).

OTHER INTERVENTION ISSUES

Individualized Education Programs

An IEP must be developed for each child with a learning disability who receives special education services. This program details the student's specific disabilities and the remedial activities, including goals and objectives, for the academic year. The program is designed by a team of professionals in consultation with parents. The prescribed services can be provided in general education "inclusion" classes or in "resource" programs in which the student leaves the general education classroom to be instructed separately. This continuum of services was originally mandated in 1975 by the Education for All Handicapped Children Act, PL 94-142 (reauthorized in 1990 as IDEA). Although states can determine how these services are delivered, the goal is always education in the "least restrictive environment," ideally with peers and in community schools. A child's IEP is evaluated at least annually, at which time changes are made to reflect the student's progress. Parents have the right to appeal if they do not agree with the goals and objectives of their child's IEP.

Instructional interventions must be viewed in light of where and how they are performed. In terms of "where," the placement can range from inclusion in a general education class, to resource room assistance (4–6 students with a specialized teacher for 30–45 minutes, 3–5 times per week), to special classes (part or full time), to transfer to a specialized school. The movement in education is clearly toward inclusion, which is defined as the development of instructional programming within a general educational environment that can support and develop learning skills for students of all ability levels. To be successful, this approach requires collaboration between special educators and general educators in designing instruction. Accommodations for inclusion of students with learning disabilities must be recognized as strategies, not special treatment. The success of inclusion is influenced by the availability of 1) a range of learning environments, 2) appropriate class sizes, 3) input from special educators in the general education program, 4) specialized methods and strategies, and 5) a student-centered program that recognizes severity of need as an important factor in placement (Vaughn & Schumm, 1995).

Homework

Taking into account weekends and summer vacations, students spend less than one fifth of their waking hours in school. Thus, planning for successful educational interventions requires open and ongoing communication between home and school. Influences within the community, recreational and leisure choices, family resources, and expectations all must be factored into the educational plan. Accommodations then can be made so that assignments are meaningful and appropriately challenging without being too demanding, and beneficial routines at home can be established. The home and school should be able to function in partnership so that the hours spent at home do not lead to tension among family members or misunderstanding of the teacher's intent in providing the home assignment. This may require training the parent to set up a workable system and schedule at home (Kay, Fitzgerald, Paradee, et al., 1994). Students with learning disabilities often feel that homework is an imposition, providing no personal fulfillment or advancement (Nicholls, McKenzie, & Shufro, 1994), and so individualization of assignments and creative use of them is essential for homework to fulfill its reinforcing purpose. Techniques to facilitate homework performance include reading and reviewing difficult material with the child and minimizing the need for boring exercises, such as copying. Homework should be limited to a specific time allotment.

Periodic Reevaluations

The treatment programs for learning disabilities are complex, and many potential gaps exist. Furthermore, the child is a developing organism whose needs and abilities change from year to year. Therefore, ongoing monitoring is essential. The goal of periodic reassessments is to evaluate parent–child relationships, psychosocial issues, and academic progress. It is also an opportunity to convey new information to the family and ensure that they are obtaining appropriate resources. Finally, it is a time for retesting the child and revising the educational program. These reevaluations should occur yearly, usually in the spring, so planning for the next school year can occur.

DAVID: A CHILD WITH DYSLEXIA

David developed typically as a young child and seemed as bright and alert as his sisters, although he began to talk somewhat later than they had. He was not hyperactive, nor did he seem particularly clumsy. In kindergarten, however, he began to have some difficulties. He had particular problems learning the alphabet and the sound of each letter. On the Metropolitan Readiness Test, he scored well below average in reading skills, although his math skills fell within the average range.

In first grade, David entered a general education class and soon began to fail. He could not learn phonetic skills, and reading remained difficult. His spelling errors were bizarre. Yet, he learned to add and subtract easily. David went through a battery of tests that identified a specific reading disability. His full-scale IQ score on the WISC–III was 120.

The school decided to keep David in a general class but to have an itinerant special education teacher give him extra help. This approach was not effective. David fell further and further behind the other children in language arts. He started misbehaving in school and avoiding going to school, using headaches as an excuse. At the end of first grade, his reading was more than 1 year delayed, while his arithmetic skills were above age-appropriate level.

When he entered second grade, David was anxious and unhappy. This time, he went to a reading resource room daily for 45 minutes, where he found only five other children. The reading specialist was kind but firm; the approach was very structured. Soon David began to learn. It was a slow, arduous process. Besides the special class in school, his parents worked with him at night. He remained a poor reader, but he could feel the excitement of gaining new knowledge. He developed friendships with the other children in the resource room, although his less sensitive schoolmates continued to tease him.

At the end of second grade, David was retested and found to have made 1 year's progress during the previous school year. He remained a little more than a year behind in reading, but his rate of learning had accelerated. He continued to attend the resource room daily for 2 more years. By this time, he was an expert mathematician, which helped to offset his difficulty with reading and spelling. He still found school difficult, but he stopped avoiding it. His behavior problems also faded. With the continued support of his teachers and parents, David has a good prognosis. He is bright, and the early help he received kept significant emotional problems from developing.

MARIA: A CHILD WITH DYSGRAPHIA AND DYSCALCULIA

Maria is a 12-year-old who attends a general education middle school in her neighborhood. She has received resource services since second grade. Although Maria has always maintained adequate grades, especially in reading, her teachers have noted her struggle with note taking, written assignments, and copying from the board. Maria also has had difficulty in arithmetic instruction, finding it impossible to memorize math facts and apply them to problem solving. These weaknesses were documented in a comprehensive educational assessment. The evaluator predicted that as Maria entered middle school, her impairments in written expression would have an increasing impact on her academic functioning because more writing and study strategies would be required. This has proven to be the case.

The WISC–III showed verbal skills of 105 and performance skills of 90. The evaluator noted a high degree of frustration whenever Maria had to contend with written demands or math calculations. This has begun to manifest itself both in the classroom, with a falling attendance rate, and at home, with more frequent complaints of stomachaches and headaches.

The school decided to provide Maria with specific resource assistance in the area of organization and study skills. She began using a word processor for longer written assignments and a calculator during math class. Maria also was assigned a "buddy" to take notes for her whenever she could not keep up with the demands of the written work. In addition, teachers were advised not to penalize her for spelling errors but rather to require her to correct them.

Maria's difficulties seem manageable because the school staff have been willing to be flexible and creative in accommodating her needs. Since this program was implemented, Maria's attendance has improved and her increasing willingness to attempt more difficult assignments has met with success. As she progresses through middle school and enters high school, she will continue to need assistance in organizing her study skills, in using word processing, and in developing math coping strategies. Given these compensations, her prognosis is good.

OUTCOME

Long-term outcome appears to depend less on the specific method used to help the student than on the severity of the learning disability, the age at diagnosis and intervention, the IQ score, the presence of a comorbid condition, the socioeconomic status of the family, the child's motivation to learn, and family support systems (Gottesman, 1991). For example, children with comorbid conditions, such as ADHD, have a less bright outcome than individuals with an isolated learning disability. By middle and secondary school, these students may have acquired "learned helplessness," lacking confidence in their own ability to solve learning and social problems independently (Bryan, 1986). They also are at risk for making poor choices in their postsecondary education, employment, and independent living. In one study, during the years following high school, only 5% had professional- or managerial-level jobs (Brown, Aylward, & Keogh, 1996).

Adolescence is often a time when even well-compensated children with learning disabilities may experience difficulty. Some children are able to compensate for organizational and study skills impairments during elementary school. However, things tend to deteriorate during middle school when they encounter schedules and the need for time management, organization of materials, and completing multiple assignments and long-term projects (Shapiro & Gallico, 1993). In addition, the demands for sustained attention are greater as classes increase in length and complexity. If intervention is not provided, these students may show dramatic worsening of behavior and academic performance in high school.

As adults, the prognosis for most individuals with an isolated learning disability is good (Kurzweil, 1992). Although they may never perform at grade level, most gain the academic skills required for everyday function. Some students who do not achieve this functional literacy during traditional education may still do so as young adults. Academic preparation of students with learning disabilities is permitting more and more students to pursue postsecondary education (Gajar, 1992; Shaw & Shaw, 1989). However, the average college student with dyslexia reads only at about a tenth-grade level (Hughes & Smith, 1990). These students also read more slowly, make more spelling errors, and acquire less information from texts. They tend to have difficulty in writing essays, completing heavy reading assignments, scoring well on timed tests, and learning foreign languages (Denckla, 1993). Many colleges now offer adjustments to program load and schedules as well as tutorial and other support services, which have permitted students with learning disabilities to complete college at an increasing rate (Brinckerhoff, Shaw, & McGuire, 1992; Durlak, Rose, & Bursuck, 1994; Scott, 1994; Spillane, McGuire, & Norlander, 1992; Vogel & Adelman, 1992).

SUMMARY

A learning disability is a disorder in which a healthy child with typical intelligence fails to learn adequately in one or more subjects. The underlying cause of the most common of these disorders, specific reading disability, appears to be an impairment in phonetical decoding. Neuroimaging and neuropathological studies in specific reading disability suggest developmental abnormalities in the parietal and occipital lobes of the brain. There also appears to be a significant genetic component.

Early detection of a specific learning disability is important because, if untreated, the child may develop secondary emotional and behavior problems that hinder progress. If a learning disability is suspected, a psychoeducational evaluation should be performed to identify areas of strengths and weaknesses. Then the school can develop an IEP. Results of the program must be assessed at the end of each year and appropriate changes made. No one treatment method is best for all children, so a trial-and-error approach may be needed to find the most useful method. Career and vocational education should be integrated into the general educational program. The prognosis for the child with a learning disability is often good, but the individual usually carries his or her learning deficiency into adulthood.

REFERENCES

American Academy of Pediatrics Committee on Children with Disabilities, American Association for Pediatric Ophthalmology and Strabismus, and American Academy of Ophthalmology. (1992). Learning disabilities, dyslexia, and vision. *Pediatrics, 90,* 124–126.

Armstrong, F.D., Seidel, J.F., & Swales, T.P. (1993). Pediatric HIV infection: A neuropsychological and educational challenge. *Journal of Learning Disabilities, 26,* 92–103.

Ayres, A.J. (1972). Improving academic scores through sensory integration. *Journal of Learning Disabilities, 5,* 338–343.

Badian, N.A. (1995). Predicting reading ability over the long term: The changing roles of letter naming, phonological awareness, and orthograhpic processing. *Annals of Dyslexia, 14,* 79–96.

Badian, N.A., McAnulty, G.B., Duffy, F.H., et al. (1990). Prediction of dyslexia in kindergarten boys. *Annals of Dyslexia, 40,* 152–169.

Bain, A.M., Bailet, L.L., & Moats, L.C. (1991). *Written language disorders: Theory into practice.* Austin, TX: PRO-ED.

Bakker, D.J. (1992). Neuropsychological classification and treatment of dyslexia. *Journal of Learning Disabilities, 2,* 102–109.

Barr, R., Kamil, M.L., Mosenthal, P.B., et al. (Eds.). (1991). *Handbook of reading research: Vol. II.* New York: Longman.

Beach, R., & Anson, C.M. (1993). Using peer-dialogue journals to foster response. In G. Newell & R.K. Durst (Eds.), *The role of discussion and writing in the teaching and learning of literature.* Norwood, MA: Christopher-Gordon Publishers.

Bender, L. (1938). *The Bender Visual Motor Gestalt Test for Children.* New York: American Orthopsychiatric Association.

Bender, L. (1946). *Instructions for the Use of Visual Motor Gestalt Test, Plate 1.* New York: American Orthopsychiatric Association.

Bender, W.N., & Wall, M.E. (1994). Social-emotional development of students with learning disabilities. *Learning Disabilities Quarterly, 17,* 323–341.

Berninger, V.W. (1994) Re-defining learning disabilities: Moving beyond aptitude-achievement discrepancies to failure to respond to validated treatment protocols. In G.R. Lyon (Ed.), *Frames of reference for the assessment of learning disabilities: New views on measurement issues* (pp. 163–184). Baltimore: Paul H. Brookes Publishing Co.

Boder, E. (1973). Developmental dyslexia: A diagnostic approach based on three typical reading-spelling patterns. *Developmental Medicine and Child Neurology, 15,* 663–687.

Brady, S., Fowler, A., Stone, B., et al. (1994). Training phonological awareness: A study with inner-city kindergarten children. *Annals of Dyslexia, 114,* 26–59.

Branch, W.G., Cohen, M.J., & Hynd, G.W. (1995). Academic achievement and attention-deficit/hyperactivity disorder in children with left- or right-hemisphere dysfunction. *Journal of Learning Disabilities, 28,* 35–43, 64.

Brinckerhoff, L.C., Shaw, S.F., & McGuire, J.M. (1992). Promoting access, accommodations, and independence for college students with learning disabilities. *Journal of Learning Disabilities, 25,* 417–429.

Brown, F.R., Aylward, E., & Keogh, B.K. (Eds.). (1996). *Diagnosis and management of learning disabilities: An interdisciplinary lifespan approach* (3rd ed.). San Diego: Singular Publishing Group.

Brown, J.I., Bennett, J.M., & Hanna, G.S. (1985). *The Nelson-Denny Reading Test.* Chicago: Riverside.

Brown, R.T., & Madan-Swain, A. (1993). Cognitive, neuropsychological, and academic sequelae in children with leukemia. *Journal of Learning Disabilities, 26,* 74–90.

Bryan, T.H. (1986). Self-concept and attributions of the learning disabled. *Learning Disability Focus, 1,* 82–89.

Calfee, R., & Henry, M. (1986). Project READ: An inservice model for training classroom teachers in effective reading instruction. In J.V. Hoffman (Ed.), *Effective teaching of reading: Research and practice* (pp. 199–229). Newark, DE: International Reading Association.

Campione, J.C. (1989). Assisted assessment: A taxonomy of approaches and an outline of strengths and weaknesses. *Journal of Learning Disabilities, 22,* 151–165.

Capute, A.J., & Accardo, P.J. (Eds.). (1996). *Developmental disabilities in infancy and childhood* (2nd ed.). Baltimore: Paul H. Brookes Publishing Co.

Capute, A.J., Accardo, P.J., & Shapiro, B.K. (Eds.). (1994). *Learning disabilities.* New York: Spectrum Publications.

Cardon, L.R., Smith, S.D., Fulker, D.W., et al. (1994). Quantitative trait locus for reading disability on chromosome 6. *Science, 226,* 276–279.

Catts, H.W. (1991). Early identification of dyslexia: Evidence from a follow-up study of speech-language impaired children. *Annals of Dyslexia, 41,* 163–177.

Clark, D.B., & Uhry, J.K. (1995). *Dyslexia theory and practice of remedial instruction* (2nd ed.). Baltimore: York Press.

Coles, G. (1987). *The learning mystique: A critical look at learning disabilities.* New York: Fawcett.

Connolly, A.J. (1988). *KeyMath Diagnostic Arithmetic Test.* Circle Pines, MN: American Guidance Service.

Cox, B.A. (1985). Alphabetic phonics: An organization and expansion of Orton-Gillingham. *Annals of Dyslexia, 35,* 187–198.

DeFries, J.C., & Alarcon, M. (1996). Genetics of specific reading disability. *Mental Retardation and Developmental Disabilities Research Reviews, 2,* 39–47.

Delis, D., & Fridlund, A. (1994). *The California Verbal Learning Test–Children's Version.* San Antonio, TX: The Psychological Corporation.

Denckla, M.B. (1993). The child with developmental disabilities grown up: Adult residua of childhood disorders. *Neurology Clinics, 11,* 105–125.

Denckla, M.B. (1996). Neurofibromatosis type 1: A model for the pathogenesis of reading disability. *Mental Retardation and Developmental Disabilities Research Reviews, 2,* 48–53.

Denckla, M.B., & Reader, M.J. (1993). Education and psychosocial interventions: Executive dysfunction and its consequences. In R. Kurlan (Ed.), *Handbook of Tourette's syndrome and related tic and behavioral disorders* (pp. 431–451). New York: Marcel Dekker.

Denckla, M.B., & Rudel, R.G. (1976). Rapid automatized naming (R.A.N.): Dyslexia differentiated from other learning disabilities. *Neuropsychologia, 14,* 471–479.

Denning, E.M. (1990). *A comparison of nonoral and an oral method of teaching reading association skills to children with language learning disabilities.* Unpublished doctoral dissertation, The Johns Hopkins University, Baltimore.

Deshler, D., Ellis, E.S., & Lenz, B.K. (Eds.). (1995). *Teaching the learning disabled adolescent: Strategies and methods.* Denver, CO: Love Publishing.

Dowdy, C.A., Smith, T.E.C., & Nowell, C.H. (1992). Learning disabilities and vocational rehabilitation. *Journal of Learning Disabilities, 25,* 442–447.

Duane, D.D. (1991). Biological foundations of learning disabilities. In J.E. Obrzut & G.W. Hynd (Eds.), *Neuropsychological foundations of learning disabilities: A handbook of issues, methods, and practice* (pp. 7–28). New York: Academic Press.

Duffy, F.H., Denckla, M.B., McAnulty, G.B., et al. (1988). Neurophysiological studies in dyslexia. In F. Plum (Ed.), *Language, communication, and the brain* (pp. 149–170). New York: Raven Press.

Durkin, D. (1989). *Teaching them to read.* Needham, MA: Allyn & Bacon.

Durlak, C.M., Rose, E., & Bursuck, W.D. (1994). Preparing high school students with learning disabilities for the transition to postsecondary education: Teaching the skills of self-determination. *Journal of Learning Disabilities, 27,* 51–59.

Edelsky, C., Atwerger, B., & Flores, B. (1991). *Whole language: What's the difference?* Portsmouth, NH: Heineman.

Eden, G.F., Stein, J.F., Wood, H.M., et al. (1994). Differences in eye movements and reading problems in dyslexic and normal children. *Vision Research, 34,* 1345–1358.

Eden, G.F., Stein, J.F., Wood, H.M., et al. (1995). Verbal and visual problems in reading disability. *Journal of Learning Disabilities, 28,* 272–290.

Eden, G.F., VanMeter, J.W., Rumsey, J.M., et al. (1996). Abnormal processing of visual motion in dyslexia revealed by functional brain imaging. *Nature, 382,* 66–69.

Education for All Handicapped Children Act of 1975, PL 94-142, 20 U.S.C. § 1400 *et seq.*

Englert, C.S. (1992). Writing instruction from a sociocultural perspective: The holistic, dialogic, and social enterprise of writing. *Journal of Learning Disabilities, 25,* 153–172.

Englert, C.S., & Hiebert, E.H. (1984). Children's developing awareness of text structure in expository material. *Journal of Educational Psychology, 76,* 65–74.

Epstein, M.A., Shaywitz, S.E., Shaywitz, B.A., et al. (1991). The boundaries of attention deficit disorder. *Journal of Learning Disabilities, 24,* 78–86.

Felton, R.H., & Wood, F.B. (1989). Cognitive deficits in reading disability and attention deficit disorder. *Journal of Learning Disabilities, 22*(1), 3–22.

Fessler, M.A., Rosenberg, M.S., & Rosenberg, L.A. (1991). Concomitant learning disabiities and learning problems among students with behavioral/emotional disorders. *Behavioral Disorders, 16,* 97–106.

Fielding, L., & Roller, C. (1992). Making difficult books accessible and easy books acceptable. *Reading Teacher, 45,* 678–685.

Filipek, P.A. (1995). Neurobiologic correlates of developmental dyslexia: How do dyslexics' brains differ from those of normal readers? *Journal of Child Neurology, 10*(Suppl. 1), S62–S69.

Fletcher, J.M., Francis, D.J., Rourke, B.P., et al. (1992). The validity of discrepancy-based definitions of reading disabilities. *Journal of Learning Disabilities, 25,* 555–561.

Fletcher, J.M., Shaywitz, S.E., Shankweiler, D., et al. (1994). Cognitive profiles of reading disability: Comparisons of discrepancy and low achievement definitions. *Journal of Educational Psychology, 86,* 6–23.

Flynn, J.M., & Rabar, M.H. (1994) Prevalence of reading failure in boys compared with girls. *Psychology in Schools, 31,* 66.

Forness, S.R., Swanson, J.M., Cantwell, D.P., et al. (1992). Stimulant medication and reading performance: Follow-up on sustained dose in ADHD boys with and without conduct disorders. *Journal of Learning Disabilities, 25,* 115–123.

Gajar, A. (1992). Adults with learning disabilities: Current and future research priorities. *Journal of Learning Disabilities, 25,* 507–519.

Galaburda, A.M. (Ed.). (1993). *Dyslexia and development: Neurobiological aspects of extraordinary brains.* Cambridge, MA: Harvard University Press.

Galaburda, A.M., & Livingstone, M. (1993). Evidence for a magnocellular defect in developmental dyslexia. *Annals of the New York Academy of Science, 682,* 70–82.

Galaburda, A.M., Menard, M.T., & Rosen, G.D. (1994). Evidence for aberrant auditory anatomy in developmental dyslexia. *Proceedings of the National Academy of Sciences of the United States of America, 91,* 8010–8013.

Gallico, R.P., Burns, T.J., & Grob, C.S. (1988). *Emotional and behavioral problems in children with learning disabilities.* Boston: College-Hill Press.

Gillingham, A., & Stillman, B. (1973). *Remedial training for children with specific disabilities in reading, spelling, and penmanship.* Cambridge, MA: Educators Publishing Service.

Gordon, M. (1983). *The Gordon Diagnostic System.* Dewitt, NY: Gordon Systems.

Gottesman, R.L. (1991). Prognosis: The adult with a learning disability. *Seminars in Neurology, 11,* 64–74.

Grant, D., & Berg, F. (1993). *Wisconsin Card Sorting Test.* Odessa, FL: Psychological Assessment Resources.

Greenberg, L. (1990). *Test of Variables of Attention.* Minneapolis, MN: Attention Technology Systems.

Gross-Tsur, V., Manor, O., & Shalev, R.S. (1996). Developmental dyscalculia: Prevalence and demographic features. *Developmental Medicine and Child Neurology, 38,* 25–33.

Guerin, D.W., Griffin, J.R., Gottfried, A.W., et al. (1993). Dyslexic subtypes and severity levels: Are there gender differences? *Optometry/Vision/Science, 70,* 348–351.

Hammill, D.D. (1990). On defining learning disabilities: An emerging consensus. *Journal of Learning Disabilities, 23*(2), 74–84.

Harris, D.B. (1963). *Children's drawings as measures of intellectual maturity: A revision and extension of the Goodenough Draw-A-Man Test.* New York: Harcourt, Brace, & World.

Haywood, H.C., & Wingenfeld, S.A. (1992). Interactive assessment as a research tool. *Journal of Special Education, 26,* 253–268.

Hobbs, S.A., & Sexson, S.B. (1993). Cognitive development and learning in the pediatric organ transplant recipient. *Journal of Learning Disabilities, 26,* 104–13.

Hoehn, T.P., & Baumeister, A.A. (1994). A critique of the application of sensory integration therapy to children with learning disabilities. *Journal of Learning Disabilities, 27,* 338–350.

Hooper, S.R. (1996). Subtyping specific reading disabilities: Classification approaches, recent advances, and current status. *Mental Retardation and Developmental Disabilities Research Reviews, 2,* 14–20.

Hoyt, C.S. (1990). Irlen lenses and reading difficulties. *Journal of Learning Disabilities, 23,* 624–627.

Hughes, C.A., & Smith, J.O. (1990). Cognitive and academic performance of college students with learning disabilities: A synthesis of the literature. *Learning Disabilities Quarterly, 13,* 66–79.

Hutchinson, N.L. (1990). *Problem representation and algebra problem solving of students with LD.* Paper presented at the Council for Exceptional Children, International Conference, Toronto, Ontario, Canada.

Hutchinson, N.L. (1992). The challenges of componential analysis: Cognitive and metacognitive instruction in mathematical problem solving. *Journal of Learning Disabilities, 25,* 249–252.

Hynd, G.W., Hall, J., Novey, E.S., et al. (1995a). Dyslexia and corpus callosum morphology. *Archives of Neurology, 47,* 919–926.

Hynd, G.W., Hall, J., Novey, E.S., et al. (1995b). Dyslexia and the corpus callosum. *Archives of Neurology, 52,* 32–38.

Individuals with Disabilities Education Act (IDEA) of 1990, PL 101-476, 20 U.S.C. § 1400 *et seq.*

Jastak, S., & Wilkinson, G.S. (1984). *Wide Range Achievement Test–Revised.* Wilmington, DE: Jastak Associates.

Karlsen, B., Madden, R., & Gardner, E.F. (1985). *Stanford Diagnostic Reading Test.* San Antonio, TX: The Psychological Corporation.

Kaufman, A.S., & Kaufman, N.L. (1983). *Kaufman Assessment Battery for Children.* Circle Pines, MN: American Guidance Service.

Kay, P.J., Fitzgerald, M., Paradee, C., et al. (1994). Making homework work at home: The parent's perspective. *Journal of Learning Disabilities, 27,* 550–561.

Korhonen, T.T. (1995). The persistence of rapid naming problems in children with reading disabilities: A nine-year follow-up. *Journal of Learning Disabilities, 28,* 232–239.

Kraus, N., McGee, T.J., Carrell, T.D., et al. (1996). Auditory neuropsychologic responses and discrimination deficits in children with learning problems. *Science, 273,* 971–973.

Kurzweil, S.R. (1992). Developmental reading disorder: Predictors of outcome in adolescents who re-

ceived early diagnosis and treatment. *Journal of Developmental and Behavioral Pediatrics, 13,* 399–404.

Lehmkuhle, S., Garzia, R.P., Turner, L., et al. (1993). A defective visual pathway in children with reading disability. *New England Journal of Medicine, 328,* 989–996.

Lewis, M.E.B. (1993). *Thematic methods and strategies for learning disabled students.* San Diego, CA: Singular Publishing Group.

Light, J.G., & DeFries, J.C. (1995). Comorbidity of reading and mathematics disabilities: Genetic and environmental etiologies. *Journal of Learning Disabilities, 28,* 96–106.

Lindamood, C.H., & Lindamood, P.C. (1979). *The Lindamood Auditory Conceptualization Test.* Chicago: Riverside.

Livingstone, M.S., Rosen, G.D., Drislane, F.W., et al. (1991). Physiological and anatomical evidence for a magnocellular defect in developmental dyslexia. *Proceeding of the National Academy of Sciences, USA, 88,* 7943–7947.

Lyon, G.R. (Ed). (1994). *Frames of reference for the assessment of learning disabilities: New views on measurement issues.* Baltimore: Paul H. Brookes Publishing Co.

Lyon, G.R. (1995). Toward a definition of dyslexia. *Annals of Dyslexia, 45,* 3–31.

Lyon, G.R. (1996). Learning disabilities. In E.J. Mash & R.A. Barkley (Eds.), *Child psychology* (pp. 390–435). New York: Guilford Press.

Lyon, G.R., & Chhabra, V. (1996). The current state of science and the future of specific reading disability. *Mental Retardation and Developmental Disabilities Research Reviews, 2,* 2–9.

Lyon, G.R., Gray, D.B., Kavanagh, J.F., et al. (Eds.). (1993). *Better understanding learning disabilities: New views from research and their implications for education and public policies.* Baltimore. Paul H. Brookes Publishing Co.

Lyon, G.R., & Krasnegor, N.A. (Eds.). (1996). *Attention, memory, and executive function.* Baltimore: Paul H. Brookes Publishing Co.

MacGinitie, W. (1989). *The Gates-MacGinitie Reading Diagnostic Tests.* Boston: Houghton Mifflin.

Macmillan, D.L. (1993). Development of operational definitions in mental retardation: Similarities and differences with the field of learning disabilities. In G.R. Lyon, D.B. Gray, J.F. Kavanagh, & N.A. Krasnegor (Eds.), *Better understanding learning disabilities: New views from research and their implications for education and public policies* (pp. 117–152). Baltimore: Paul H. Brookes Publishing Co.

Maggart, Z.R., & Zintz, M. (1993). *The reading process: The teacher and the learner* (6th ed.). Dubuque, IA: William C. Brown.

Mann, V. (1994). Phonological skills and the prediction of early reading problems. In N.C. Jordan & J. Goldsmith-Phillips (Eds.), *Learning disabilities, new directions for assessment and intervention* (pp. 67–84). Needham, MA: Allyn & Bacon.

Markwardt, F. (1989). *Peabody Individual Achievement Test–Revised.* Circle Pines, MN: American Guidance Services.

Mason, J.M. (Ed.). (1989). *Reading and writing connections.* Needham, MA: Allyn & Bacon.

Maslow, A. (1970). *Motivation and personality.* New York: HarperCollins.

McConaughy, S.H., Mattison, R.E., & Peterson, R.L. (1994). Behavior/emotional problems of children with serious emotional disturbance and learning disabilities. *School Psychology Review, 23,* 81–98.

McKinlay, I., Ferguson, A., & Jolly, C. (1996). Ability and dependency in adolescents with severe learning disabilities. *Developmental Medicine and Child Neurology, 38,* 48–58.

McKinney, J.D. (1987). Research on conceptually and empirically derived subtypes of specific learning disabilities. In M.C. Wang, M.C. Reynolds, & H.J. Walberg (Eds.), *Handbook of special education: Research and practice* (Vol. 11, pp. 253–282). Elmsford, NY: Pergamon.

McKinney, J.D. (1989). Longitudinal research on the behavioral characteristics of children with learning disabilities. *Journal of Learning Disabilities, 22,* 141–150.

Mercer, C.D. (1991). *Students with learning disabilities* (4th ed.). New York: Merrill-Macmillan Co.

Mercer, C.D., Hughes, C.A., & Mercer, A.R. (1985). Learning disabilities definitions used by state education departments. *Learning Disability Quarterly, 8,* 45–55.

Merzenich, M.M., Jenkins, W.M., Johnston, P., et al. (1996). Temporal processing deficits of language learning impaired children ameliorated by training. *Science, 271,* 77–81.

Metzger, R.L., & Werner, D.B. (1984). Use of visual training for reading disabilities: A review. *Pediatrics, 73,* 824–829.

Michaels, C.A. (1994). *Transition strategies for persons with learning disabilities.* San Diego, CA: Singular Publishing Group.

Montague, M. (1992). The effects of cognitive and metacognitive strategy instruction on the mathematical problem solving of middle school students with learning disabilities. *Journal of Learning Disabilities, 25,* 230–248.

Montague, M., & Bos, C.S. (1986). The effect of cognitive strategy training on verbal math problem solving performance of learning disabled adolescents. *Journal of Learning Disabilities, 19,* 26–33.

Newby, R.F., Recht, D., & Caldwell, J. (1993). Empirically tested interventions for subtypes of reading disabilities. In M.G.Tramontana & S.R. Hooper (Eds.), *Advances in child neuropsychology* (Vol. 2, pp. 201–232). New York: Springer-Verlag.

Newcomer, P., Nodine, B., & Barenbaum, E. (1988). Teaching writing to exceptional children: Reaction and recommendations. *Exceptional Children, 54,* 559–564.

Nicholls, J.G., McKenzie, M., & Shufro, J. (1994). Schoolwork, homework, life's work: The experience of students with and without learning disabilities. *Journal of Learning Disabilities, 27,* 562–569.

O'Connor, P.D., Sofo, F., Kendall, L., et al. (1990). Reading disabilities and the effects of colored filters. *Journal of Learning Disabilities, 23,* 597–603.

Office of Education. (1977). Assistance to states for education for handicapped children: Procedures for evaluating specific learning disabilities. *Federal Register, 42*(250), 62,082–62,085.

Okolo, C.M. (1992). The effects of computer-based attribution retraining on the attributions, persistence, and mathematics computation of students with learning disabilities. *Journal of Learning Disabilities, 25,* 327–334.

Orton, S.T. (1937). *Reading, writing, and speech problems in children: A presentation of certain types of disorders in the development of the language faculty.* New York: Norton.

Palinscar, A., Brown, A., & Campione, J. (1991). Dynamic assessment. In H.L. Swanson (Ed.), *Handbook on the assessment of learning disabilities: Theory, research and practice* (pp. 75–94). Austin, TX: PRO-ED.

Pennington, B.F. (1991). Genetics of learning disabilities. *Seminars in Neurology, 11,* 28–34.

Pennington, B.F. (1995). Genetics of learning disabilities. *Journal of Child Neurology, 10,* 69–77.

Pennington, B.F., Groisser, D., & Welsh, M.C. (1993). Contrasting cognitive deficits in attention deficit hyperactivity disorder versus reading disability. *Developmental Psychology, 29,* 511–523.

Pennington, B.F., Heaton, R.K., Karzmark, P., et al. (1985). The neuropsychological phenotype in Turner syndrome. *Cortex, 21,* 391–404.

Reiss, A.L., & Freund, L. (1990). Fragile-X syndrome. *Biological Psychiatry, 27,* 223–240.

Reynolds, A.M., Elksnin, N., & Brown, F.R., III. (1996). Specific reading disabilities: Early identification and long-term outcome. *Mental Retardation and Developmental Disabilities Research Reviews, 2,* 21–27.

Richards, S., & Hammitte, D.J. (1993). The assessment of preschoolers in reference to the learning disabilities label. *Learning Disabilities Forum, 18,* 27–30.

Rock, E.E., Fessler, M.A., & Church, R.P. (1996). The concomitance of learning disabilities and emotional/behavioral disorders: A conceptual model. *Journal of Learning Disabilities, 30,* 245–265.

Roush, W. (1995). Arguing over why Johnny can't read. *Science, 267,* 1896–1898.

Rovet, J.F., Ehrlich, R.M., Czuchta, D., et al. (1993). Psychoeducational characteristics of children and adolescents with insulin-dependent diabetes mellitus. *Journal of Learning Disabilities, 26,* 7–22.

Rumsey, J. (1996). Developmental dyslexia: Anatomic and functional neuroimaging. *Mental Retardation and Developmental Disabilities Research Reviews, 2,* 28–38.

Rumsey, J.M., Berman, K.F., Denckla, M.B., et al. (1987). Regional cerebral blood flow in severe developmental dyslexia. *Archives of Neurology, 44,* 144–1150.

Salvia, J., & Ysseldyke, J.E. (1995). *Assessment* (6th ed.). Boston: Houghton-Mifflin.

Savage, R.C., & Wolcott, G.F. (Eds.). (1994). *Educational dimensions of acquired brain injury.* Austin, TX: PRO-ED.

Sawyer, D.J. (1987). *Test of Awareness of Language Segments.* Austin, TX: PRO-ED.

Scanlon, D.M., & Vellutino, F.R. (1996). Prerequisite skills, early instruction, and success in first-grade reading: Selected results from a longitudinal study. *Mental Retardation and Developmental Disabilities Research Reviews, 2,* 54–63.

Scarborough, H.S. (1990). Very early language deficits in dyslexic children. *Child Development, 61,* 1728–1743.

Schultz, R.T., Cho, N.K., Staib, L.H., et al. (1994) Brain morphology in normal and dyslexic children: The influence of sex and age. *Annals of Neurology, 35,* 732–742.

Schwartz, S.E., & Budd, D. (1983). Mathematics for handicapped learners: A functional approach for adolescents. In E. Meyer, G.A. Vergason, & B.P. Whelan (Eds.), *Promising practices for exceptional children: Curriculum implications* (pp. 321–340). Denver, CO: Love Publishing.

Scott, S.S. (1994). Determining reasonable academic adjustments for college students with learning disabilities. *Journal of Learning Disabilities, 27,* 403–412.

Semel, E., Wiig, E., & Secord, W. (1995). *Clinical evaluation of language fundamentals* (3rd ed.). San Antonio, TX: The Psychological Corporation, Harcourt Brace Jovanovich.

Sexson, S.B., & Madan-Swain, A. (1993). School reentry for the child with chronic illness. *Journal of Learning Disabilities, 26,* 115–125, 137.

Shafrir, U., & Siegel, L.S. (1994). Subtypes of learning disabilities in adolescents and adults. *Journal of Learning Disabilities, 27,* 123–134.

Shankweiler, D., Crain, S., Katz. L., et al. (1995).Cognitive profiles of reading-disabled children: Comparison of language skills in phonology, morphology, and syntax. *Psychological Science, 6,* 149–156.

Shapiro, B.K. (1996). The prevalence of specific reading disability. *Mental Retardation and Developmental Disabilities Research Reviews, 2,* 10–13.

Shapiro, B.K., & Gallico, R.P. (1993). Learning disabilities. *Pediatric Clinics of North America, 40,* 491–505.

Shaw, S.F., & Shaw, S.R. (1989). Learning disabilities and college programming: A bibliography. *Journal of Postsecondary Education and Disability, 6,* 77–85.

Shaywitz, B.A., Fletcher, J.M., & Shaywitz, S.E. (1995). Defining and classifying learning disabilities and attention-deficit/hyperactivity disorder. *Journal of Child Neurology, 10,* S50–S57.

Shaywitz, B.A., & Shaywitz, S.A. (1991). Comorbidity: A critical issue in attention deficit disorder. *Journal of Child Neurology, 6*(Suppl.), S13–S22.

Shaywitz, S.E., Escobar, M.D., Shaywitz, B.A., et al. (1992). Evidence that dyslexia may represent the lower tail of a normal distribution of reading ability. *New England Journal of Medicine, 326,* 145–150.

Sheffield, B.B. (1991). The structured flexibility of Orton-Gillingham. *Annals of Dyslexia, 41,* 41–54.

Silberberg, N.E., Iverson, I.A., & Goins, J.T. (1975). Which reading method works best? *Journal of Learning Disabilities, 6,* 547–556.

Spafford, C.S., & Grosser, G.S. (1993). The social misperception syndrome in children with learning disabilities: Social causes versus neurological variables. *Journal of Learning Disabilities, 26,* 178–189, 198.

Spillane, S.A., McGuire, J.M., & Norlander, K.A. (1992). Undergraduate admission policies, practices, and procedures for applicants with learning disabilities. *Journal of Learning Disabilities, 25,* 665–670, 677.

Stanford, L.D., & Hynd, G.W. (1994). Congruence of behavioral symptomatology in children with ADD/H, ADD/WO, and learning disabilities. *Journal of Learning Disabilities, 27,* 243–253.

Stanovich, K.E., & Siegel, L.S. (1994). Phenotypic performance profile of children with reading disabilities: A regression-based test of phonological-core variable-difference model. *Journal of Educational Psychology, 86,* 24–53.

Stone, B., & Brady, S. (1993, October). *Evidence for basic phonological deficits in less-skilled readers.* Paper presented at the International Association for Research on Learning Disabilities Conference, Boston.

Tallal, P., Miller, S.L., Bedi, G., et al. (1996). Language comprehension in language-learning impaired children improved with acoustically modified speech. *Science, 271,* 81–84.

Taylor, D.F. (1991). Literature letters and narrative response: Seventh and eighth graders write about their reading. In J. Feeley, D. Strickland, & S. Wepner (Eds.), *Process reading and writing: A literature-based approach.* New York: Teachers College Press.

Thomas, C.J. (1905). Congenital word-blindness and its treatment. *Ophthalmoscope, 3,* 380–385.

Tierney, R.J., Readence, J.E., & Dishner, E.K. (1995). *Reading strategies and practices: A compendium.* Needham, MA: Allyn & Bacon.

Torgesen, J.K., & Bryant, B.R. (1994). *Test of phonological awareness.* Austin, TX: PRO-ED.

Traub, N., & Bloom, F. (1975). *Recipe for reading.* Cambridge, MA: Educators Publishing Service.

U.S. Department of Education, Office of Special Education Programs. (1991). *Youth with disabilities: How are they doing? The first comprehensive report from the National Longitudinal Transition Study of Special Education Students.* Menlo Park, CA: SRI International.

U.S. Department of Education, Office of Special Education Programs. (1995). *To assure the free appropriate education of all children with disabilities: 17th annual report to Congress on the implementation of the Individuals with Disabilities Education Act.* Washington, DC: U.S. Government Printing Office.

U.S. Department of Labor, The Secretary's Commission on Achieving Necessary Skills. (1992). *Learning a living: A blueprint for high performance: A SCANS report for AMERICA 2000.* Washington, DC: U.S. Government Printing Office.

Vacca, R.T., & Vacca, J.A.L. (1993). *Content area reading* (4th ed.). New York: HarperCollins.

Vaughn, S., & Schumm, J.S. (1995). Responsible inclusion for students with learning disabilities. *Journal of Learning Disabilities, 28,* 264–270.

Vogel, S.A., & Adelman, P.B. (1992). The success of college students with learning disabilities: Factors related to educational attainment. *Journal of Learning Disabilities, 25,* 430–441.

Wallach, G., & Butler, K. (Eds.). (1994). *Language learning disability in school age children and adolescents: Some underlying principles and applications.* Columbus, OH: Charles E. Merrill.

Watson, C., & Willows, D.M. (1995). Information-processing patterns in specific reading disability. *Journal of Learning Disabilities, 28,* 216–231.

Wechsler, D. (1991). *Wechsler Intelligence Scale for Children: Third edition.* San Antonio, TX: The Psychological Corporation.

Wechsler, D. (1992). *Wechsler Individual Achievement Test.* San Antonio, TX: The Psychological Corporation.

Welsh, M.C., & Pennington, B.F. (1988). Assessing frontal lobe functioning in children: Views from developmental psychology. *Developmental Neuropsychology, 4*(3), 199–230.

Wiederholt, J.L., & Bryant, B.R. (1992). *Gray Oral Reading Test–Three.* Austin, TX: PRO-ED.

Wilson, B.A. (1988). *Wilson Reading System Program Overview.* Millbury, MA: Wiulson Language Training.

Wodrich, D.L. (1997). *Children's psychological testing: A guide for nonpsychologists* (3rd ed.). Baltimore: Paul H. Brookes Publishing Co.

Wolff, P.H., Melngailis, I., Obregon, M., et al. (1995). Family patterns of developmental dyslexia: Part II. Behavioral phenotypes. *American Journal of Medical Genetics, 60,* 494–505.

Wood, K. (1984). Probable passages: A writing strategy. *The Reading Teacher, 37,* 496–499.

Woodcock, R., & Mather N. (1989). *Woodcock-Johnson Tests of Cognitive Ability.* Allen, TX: DLM.

Woodcock, R.W. (1991). *Woodcock Language Proficiency Battery–Revised.* Chicago: Riverside.

Woodcock, R.W., & Johnson, M.B. (1989). *Woodcock-Johnson Psycho-Educational Battery–Revised.* Allen, TX: DLM.

24 Cerebral Palsy

Louis Pellegrino

Upon completion of this chapter, the reader will:

- be aware of some early clues to the diagnosis of cerebral palsy
- know the various types of cerebral palsy and their characteristics
- understand how cerebral palsy is diagnosed
- know the sensory, cognitive, and medical problems commonly associated with cerebral palsy
- understand the role of primitive reflexes and automatic movement reactions in motor function
- recognize habilitation as an interdisciplinary strategy to maximize function for children with cerebral palsy
- be knowledgeable about the prognoses for the different forms of cerebral palsy

Cerebral palsy refers to a disorder of movement and posture that is due to a nonprogressive abnormality of the immature brain. Although the brain continues to grow into early adulthood, the crucial events of its development occur during intrauterine life and early childhood. Events or conditions that disturb the usual unfolding of this process can result in cerebral palsy and may also produce several other associated disabilities, including mental retardation, seizures, visual and auditory impairments, learning difficulties, and behavior problems.

Cerebral palsy may result from numerous conditions. Genetic abnormalities may lead to brain malformation in the early stages of embryonic development. Intrauterine infection may damage the developing nervous system of the fetus. Pregnancy-related abnormalities may lead to preterm delivery and related complications that are associated with the later emergence of cerebral palsy. Adverse conditions during labor and delivery may deprive vulnerable areas of the immature brain of oxygen and blood. A previously healthy child may experience traumatic brain injury in a car accident and show symptoms of cerebral palsy following recovery from a coma. In each case, typical developmental processes are disturbed or actual brain damage occurs, resulting in a set of motor abnormalities and functional impairments termed cerebral palsy. The damage or dysfunction generally occurs during an early period of the brain's development and is not progressive. This distinguishes cerebral palsy from other ongoing disorders of movement and posture, such as a brain tumor or a progressive neurological disorder.

CAUSES OF CEREBRAL PALSY

The most common causes of cerebral palsy are listed in Table 24.1. Until the 1980s, it was thought that most cases of cerebral palsy resulted from birth trauma. It is now clear, however, that only a small fraction result from this cause (Nelson & Ellenberg, 1986). Prematurity and problems during intrauterine development account for the majority of known causes of cerebral palsy (Scher, Belfar, Martin, et al., 1991). Although children with cerebral palsy are more likely to have had difficult deliveries, this appears to be more likely the result of preexisting brain abnormalities rather than the cause of it.

Epidemiological studies suggest that children who develop cerebral palsy unrelated to postnatal infection or trauma tend to fall into one of two groups based on the circumstances of pregnancy and birth. The first group includes those born prematurely. Although the overall prevalence of cerebral palsy has remained fairly constant for many years at 1.4–2.4 per 1,000 (Cummins, Nelson, Grether, et al., 1993; Hagberg, Hagberg, & Olow, 1993; Stanley, Blair, Hockey, et al., 1993), the proportion of former premature infants among all children with cerebral palsy has steadily increased to 40%–50% since the 1970s (Cummins et al., 1993). As of 1997, this trend seems to be leveling off (Figure 24.1) (Hagberg et al., 1993; Meberg & Broch, 1995). Infants with birth weights of less than 1,500 grams are especially vulnerable, although it should be emphasized that the vast majority of low birth weight infants do not develop cerebral palsy (Grether, Nelson, Emery, et al., 1996). The relationship of premature birth to cerebral palsy is beginning to be understood. Many lines of investigation have suggested that an area of

Table 24.1.   Causes of cerebral palsy

Time period (Percentage of cases)	Causes
Prenatal (44)	
First trimester	Teratogens
	Genetic syndromes
	Chromosomal abnormalities
	Brain malformations
Second–third trimester	Intrauterine infections
	Problems in fetal/placental functioning
Labor and delivery (19)	Preeclampsia
	Complications of labor and delivery
Perinatal (8)	Sepsis/central nervous system infection
	Asphyxia
	Prematurity
Childhood (5)	Meningitis
	Traumatic brain injury
	Toxins
Not obvious (24)	

Adapted from Hagberg & Hagberg (1984).

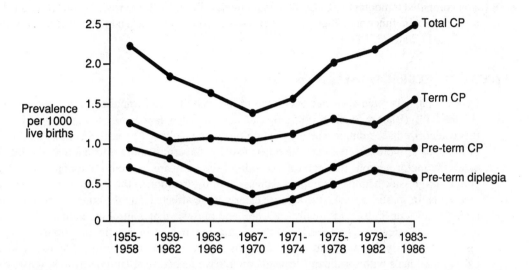

Figure 24.1. Prevalence of cerebral palsy 1955–1986. Over a 30-year period, there has not been a significant decrease in the occurrence of cerebral palsy (Hagberg et al., 1993).

the brain near the lateral ventricles is especially vulnerable to injury at 26–32 weeks' gestation (Volpe, 1990). The blood vessels in this area bleed easily during this time, resulting in damage to the adjacent white matter, which contains neuronal connections important in many aspects of motor control. Disruption of these connections most commonly results in problems of muscle tone and motor control in the legs, called spastic diplegia. Thus, abnormalities that disrupt regulation and maintenance of the latter stages of pregnancy may set into motion a series of parallel or synergistic pathological events that result in both preterm birth and periventricular white matter injury (periventricular leukomalacia) and subsequent cerebral palsy (see Chapter 7) (Adinolfi, 1993; Leviton, 1993).

The second group of children with cerebral palsy includes those born at term. Compared with those born prematurely, these children are more often small for gestational age or have malformations inside and outside the central nervous system (CNS), suggesting a problem with early fetal development (Krageloh-Mann, Hagberg, Meisner, et al., 1995). In addition, if a full-term infant experiences severe birth asphyxia, he or she may develop athetoid or dystonic cerebral palsy, reflecting damage to deep brain structures (the basal ganglia). In the past, high bilirubin in the immediate postnatal period resulted in a condition called kernicterus, which also caused athetoid cerebral palsy. However, improvements in the care of infants have made this condition rare in developed countries.

A number of brain-imaging techniques are available to help define the anatomical correlates of cerebral palsy (Barnes, 1992). Ultrasonography is used for fetal and neonatal screening and can distinguish gross malformations of the brain and abnormalities related to brain hemorrhage (i.e., intraventricular hemorrhage, periventricular leukomalacia). Computed tomography (CT) and especially magnetic resonance imaging (MRI) provide more detailed resolution of anatomical structures than ultrasound and may help to define the cause of cerebral palsy in individuals. New techniques, such as positron emission tomography (PET) and single photon emission computed tomography (SPECT), complement CT and MRI by providing information about brain metabolic function, which in some cases is abnormal even when brain structure appears to be normal (Chugani, 1992).

TYPES OF CEREBRAL PALSY

Cerebral palsy is often classified according to the type of motor impairment that predominates (Figure 24.2) (Blair & Stanley, 1985). Spastic cerebral palsy is the most common type; it is further categorized according to the distribution of limbs involved. In spastic hemiplegia, one side of the body is more affected than the other; usually, the arm is more affected than the leg. Because the motor neurons that control one side of the body are located in the opposite cerebral cortex, a right-side hemiplegia implies damage to or dysfunction of the left side of the brain, and vice versa. In spastic diplegia, the legs are clearly more affected than the arms. In **spastic quadriplegia,** all four limbs, and usually the trunk and muscles that control the mouth, tongue, and pharynx, are affected. The severity of the motor impairment in spastic quadriplegia implies wider cerebral dysfunction and worse prognosis than for the other forms of spastic cerebral palsy. Individuals with spastic quadriplegia often have mental retardation, seizures, sensory impairments, and medical complications as well.

Dyskinetic cerebral palsy is characterized by tonal abnormalities that involve the whole body. Changing patterns of muscle tone from hour to hour and day to day are common. These children will often exhibit rigid muscle tone while awake and normal or decreased muscle tone

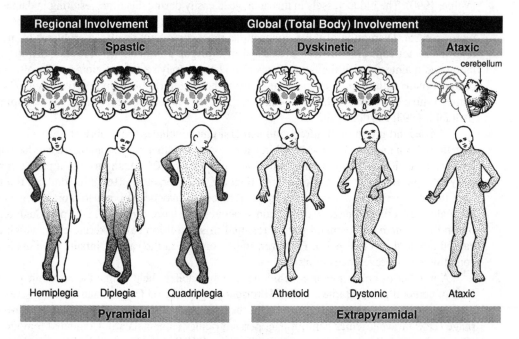

Figure 24.2.   Different regions of the brain are affected in various forms of cerebral palsy. The darker the shading, the more severe the involvement.

while asleep. Involuntary movements are often present, though sometimes difficult to detect, and are the hallmark of this type of cerebral palsy. Rapid, random, jerky movements (chorea) and slow, writhing movements (athetosis) are seen in **athetoid cerebral palsy,** a subtype of dyskinetic cerebral palsy. In **dystonic cerebral palsy,** rigid posturing centered in the trunk and neck is characteristic.

Ataxic cerebral palsy is characterized by abnormalities of voluntary movement involving balance and position of the trunk and limbs in space. For children who can walk, this is noted most especially as a wide-based, unsteady gait. Difficulties with controlling the hand and arm during reaching (overshooting or past-pointing) and problems with the timing of motor movements are also seen. Ataxic cerebral palsy may be associated with increased or decreased muscle tone.

The term **mixed cerebral palsy** is used when more than one type of motor pattern is present and should be used only when one pattern does not clearly predominate over another. The term total body cerebral palsy is sometimes used to emphasize that certain types of cerebral palsy (dyskinetic, ataxic, mixed, and spastic quadriplegia) involve the entire musculoskeletal system to a greater or lesser degree; other forms of spastic cerebral palsy (diplegia, hemiplegia) are localized to particular regions of the body. The terms *pyramidal* (i.e., spastic) and *dyskinetic* (i.e., nonspastic) cerebral palsy also are often applied, "pyramidal" implying abnormalities in the brain pathways originating in the cerebral gray matter, called the corticospinal (pyramidal) pathways, and "dyskinetic" implying pathological involvement of the basal ganglia or cerebellum. The physiological mechanisms suggested by these terms are presumptive and, in some cases, controversial (Young, 1994); thus, the clinically descriptive terms spastic, dyskinetic, and ataxic are preferred.

EARLY DIAGNOSIS OF CEREBRAL PALSY

Certain groups of newborns at high risk, especially infants who weigh less than 1,500 grams, twins, and small for gestational age infants, merit close neurodevelopmental monitoring to detect cerebral palsy early (Cummins et al., 1993; Grether, Nelson, & Cummins, 1993; Peterson, Stanley, & Henderson, 1990). Tests, such as the Denver Developmental Screening Test (Frankenburg, Dodds, Archer, et al., 1992), which have traditionally been used by pediatricians to screen infants in developmental follow-up programs, often fail to detect cerebral palsy during the first 12 months of life (Nickel, Renken, & Gallenstein, 1989). For this reason, a number of neuromotor tests have been developed to evaluate the quality of movement skills in young infants (Paban & Piper, 1987). They assess both the presence of normal movement patterns and the absence of primitive reflexes and abnormal tone.

In addition to these formal tests, a group of behavioral symptoms may suggest cerebral palsy. Children with cerebral palsy may sleep excessively, be irritable when awake, have weak cries and poor sucks, and show little interest in their surroundings. Their resting position is also different. Instead of lying in a semiflexed position, they may lie in a floppy, rag doll way; alternatively, they may have markedly increased tone and lie in an extended, arched position, called **opisthotonos.**

When examining such a child, a physician looks for abnormalities in muscle tone and deep tendon reflexes (DTR). Muscle tone may be increased, decreased, or variable. It also may be asymmetrical, because one side of the body may be more affected than the other side. Also, the deep tendon reflexes, such as the knee jerk, may be too brisk, or the child may have tremors, or clonus, in the arms and legs.

The persistence of primitive reflexes is also a sign of cerebral palsy. Primitive reflexes are those typically seen only in the first 6–12 months of life. Their persistence beyond this time interferes with the expression of what are called automatic, or protective movement, reactions which are necessary for such motor skills as sitting, standing, and walking. As a result, the child with cerebral palsy does not attain motor skills at the appropriate age. Although motor development is significantly delayed in children with cerebral palsy, cognitive and language skills may progress at more typical rates. Thus, a discrepancy between the rates of motor and intellectual development is another clue to the existence of cerebral palsy.

As children with cerebral palsy grow from infancy to 2 years of age, other signs become evident. Typically, 3-month-old infants hold their hands open most of the time. In a child with cerebral palsy, the hands often remain clenched in fists. Also, a child does not typically become right-handed or left-handed until around 18 months of age, whereas a child with spastic hemiplegia may do so before 6 months of age. This suggests that one side of the child's body is weaker than the other. As the child grows, this may become more obvious because the spastic limbs atrophy, becoming smaller both in circumference and in length.

Not all of these signs are found in every infant with cerebral palsy, and not all infants who have these signs develop cerebral palsy (Allen & Capute, 1989; Nelson & Ellenberg, 1982). Diagnostic errors are greatest in the group of children who exhibit mild abnormalities. For example, slightly more than half of those infants suspected to be at high risk of having cerebral palsy at 12 months of age are considered neurologically unimpaired by 2 years of age (Piper, Mazer, Silver, et al., 1988).

Primitive Reflexes

One of the chief diagnostic signs of cerebral palsy, as noted previously, is the persistence of primitive reflexes. These reflexes cause changes both in muscle tone and in movement of the limbs. They are called primitive because they are present in early life (in some cases during intrauterine development) and because they are controlled by the primitive regions of the nervous system: the spinal cord, the labyrinths of the inner ear, and the brainstem. As the cortex matures, these reflexes are gradually suppressed and integrated into voluntary movement patterns. During early infancy, such primitive reflexes as the **Moro** and **tonic neck reflex** dominate movement; by 12 months of age, integration of the primitive reflexes should be complete (Capute, 1986).

This is not true of the child with cerebral palsy. In such a child, primitive reflexes are stronger than usual and often last into adult life (especially in dyskinetic cerebral palsy). In a previously unaffected child, primitive reflexes may reemerge following traumatic brain injury or during a coma.

There are many primitive reflexes, three of which are considered in this section: the asymmetrical tonic neck reflex (ATNR), the tonic labyrinthine reflex (TLR), and the positive support reflex (PSR). Each of these significantly affects posture and movement, and each is elicited by a different stimulus (Capute, Accardo, Vining, et al., 1978; Illingworth, 1987).

The ATNR is stimulated by the active or passive rotation of the head. When the head is turned, the ATNR causes the arm and leg on the same side as the chin to extend further, while the opposite arm and leg become more flexed (Figure 24.3). Changes in muscle tone may occur in

Full-term Infant
Resting Position

Asymmetrical Tonic
Neck Reflex

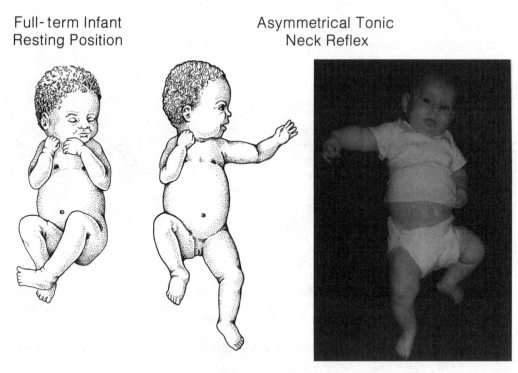

Figure 24.3.   Asymmetrical tonic neck reflex, or fencer's response. As the head is turned, the arm and leg on the same side as the chin extend, and the other arm and leg flex.

the trunk as well. Thus, the ATNR causes an increase in muscle tone and also frequently brings about a change in position. Infants under 3 months of age typically show the ATNR. Yet, even in infancy, a child can overcome the reflex (i.e., flex and move the arm once it is reflexively extended). Children with cerebral palsy often cannot; they remain in the extended position until the head turns and releases the reflex. This predicament illustrates the obligatory nature of the primitive reflexes in cerebral palsy.

The TLR is stimulated by the position of the labyrinth inside the inner ear. The response is present at birth, is more notable in prematurely born infants, and is seen in some children with cerebral palsy. It is typically integrated by 4 months of age. When the child is lying on his or her back and the neck is extended, the legs extend and the shoulders retract, or pull back (Figure 24.4). When the child is lying on his or her stomach and the neck is flexed, the hips and knees flex while the shoulders protract, or roll forward. Flexing or extending the neck in either position may modify the response (e.g., flexing the neck when the infant is supine may decrease extensor tone in the truck and legs, extending the neck may enhance these responses). When the reflex is present but is not as strong (in many newborn infants and some children with cerebral palsy), muscle tone may change without any change in the position of the limbs.

The third primitive reflex is the PSR. When the balls of the feet come in contact with a firm surface, the child extends the legs (Figure 24.5). This reflex enables the typical newborn infant to support weight while standing. The increased response in a child with cerebral palsy, however,

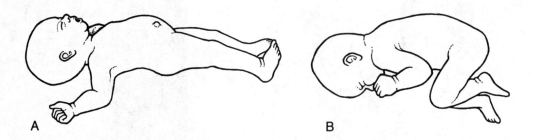

Figure 24.4.   Tonic labyrinthine reflex. When the child is in the supine position (a) with the head slightly extended, retraction of the shoulders and extension of the legs is observed. The opposite occurs when the infant is in the prone position (b) with the head slightly flexed.

leads to a rigid extension of the legs and feet. Rather than helping, this reflex then interferes with standing and walking.

Because these primitive reflexes result in changes in muscle tone and in position of the limbs, their persistence interferes with the development of voluntary motor activity. For example, to be able to roll over (typically accomplished at 4–5 months of age), the ATNR must be fairly well suppressed. If the ATNR persists, as the infant turns his or her head, the extended arm and leg hinder the start of the roll. Once the roll is begun, the flexed arm of the strong ATNR prevents its completion.

A similar problem occurs with the TLR and sitting. To sit independently, equilibrium reactions must be present. These reactions require constant, fine changes in muscle tone to maintain balance. If a strong TLR is present, changes in the position of the head cause patterns of flexion and extension throughout the body that are incompatible with maintaining equilibrium and balance in a sitting position, and the child falls over.

Automatic Movement Reactions

As primitive reflexes diminish in intensity in the typical child, postural reactions, also known as automatic movement reactions, are developing (Figure 24.6). Some of the more important of these reactions include righting, equilibrium, and protective reactions, which enable the child to have more complex voluntary movement and better control of posture.

Up to 2 months of age, a baby's head tilts passively in the same direction that the body is leaning. However, by 3 months of age, the baby should be able to compensate and hold the head upright even if the body is tilted. This is called head righting.

Before 5 months of age, if a child is placed in a sitting position and starts to fall forward, he or she will tumble over without trying to regain balance. At 5 months, when the child begins to

Positive Support Reflex

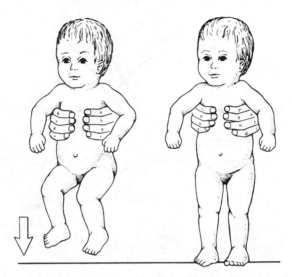

Figure 24.5.   Positive support reflex. As the baby is bounced, the legs straighten to support the child's weight.

fall forward, he or she will push out the arms to prevent the fall. This is called the anterior protective (or propping) response. By 7 months, a similar response, the lateral protective response, occurs when the child starts to fall sideways (Capute et al., 1978). Combined, these equilibrium reactions enable the child to sit and move comfortably by automatically compensating when the center of gravity is shifted. In children with cerebral palsy, not only do the primitive reflexes persist, but the development of the automatic movement reactions may lag behind or never occur.

Walking

Many children with cerebral palsy first come to professional attention because of delayed walking. This developmental milestone has a powerful intrinsic meaning for parents and professionals alike. Most adults know that children begin walking at about 1 year of age, and there is an implicit understanding that a child's first steps mark the transition from infancy to toddlerhood. When a child fails to make this transition at the expected time, it is more difficult to ignore than other delays in development.

To walk, a child must be able to maintain an upright posture, move forward in a smoothly coordinated manner, and demonstrate protective responses for safety when falling. Even a child with the mildest form of cerebral palsy has difficulty attaining the continuous changes in muscle tone that are required for typical walking. The child's walk or gait is affected in many ways. Scissoring, the most common gait disturbance, occurs because of increased tone in the muscles that control adduction and internal rotation of the hips. Toe walking results from an equinus position of the feet (Figure 24.7) and an increased flexor tone in the legs. In children without cerebral palsy, a protective reaction called the parachute response develops by 10 months of age. This is analogous to the anterior protective response and is manifest by forward extension of the

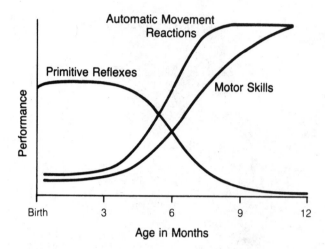

Figure 24.6.   Relationship of primitive reflexes, automatic movement reactions, and motor skills. (From Capute, A.J., Accardo, P.J., Vining, E.P.G., et al. [1978]. *Primitive reflex profile* [p. 10]. Baltimore: University Park Press; adapted by permission.)

arms when falling forward. Children with cerebral palsy have delayed or absent development of this response, making walking inherently unsafe.

ASSOCIATED IMPAIRMENTS IN CEREBRAL PALSY

All children with cerebral palsy have problems with movement and posture. Many also have other impairments associated with damage to the CNS. The most common associated disabilities are mental retardation, visual impairments, hearing impairments, speech-language disorders, seizures, feeding and growth abnormalities, and behavior and emotional disorders (Table 24.2).

Assessment of intellectual functioning in children with cerebral palsy may be difficult, because most tests of cognition require motoric or verbal responses. Even taking this into account, approximately one half to two thirds of children with cerebral palsy have mental retardation, and many of those with typical intelligence exhibit some degree of perceptual impairment and learning disability. The particular type of cerebral palsy influences the risk and degree of mental retardation. Hemiplegia, the most common type of cerebral palsy, is associated with the best intellectual outcome; more than 60% of these children have typical intelligence. Spastic diplegia, the form of cerebral palsy associated with prematurity, also has a fairly good intellectual outcome. Less than 30% of individuals with the "total body" forms of cerebral palsy, however, have typical intelligence. Among those children with cerebral palsy and mental retardation, 15% have mental retardation requiring intermittent supports, 35% have mental retardation requiring limited supports, and 50% have mental retardation requiring extensive to pervasive supports (Crothers & Paine, 1959).

Visual impairments are also common and diverse in children with cerebral palsy (Black, 1982; Schenk-Rootlieb, van Nieuwenhuizen, van der Graaf, et al., 1992). The premature infant may have severe visual impairment caused by retinopathy of prematurity (see Chapter 11). Nystagmus, or involuntary oscillating eye movements, may be present in the child with ataxia. Chil-

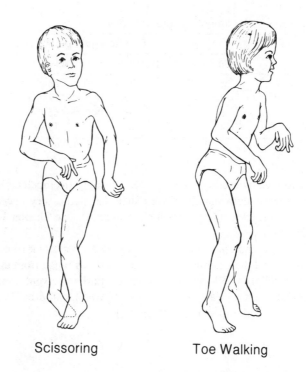

Scissoring   Toe Walking

Figure 24.7.   Scissoring results from increased tone in the muscles that control adduction and internal rotation of the hip. Toe walking is due to an equinus position of the feet and increased flexor tone in the legs.

dren with hemiplegia frequently present with homonomous hemianopsia, a condition causing loss of one part of the visual field. Strabismus, or squint, is seen in a majority of children with cerebral palsy.

Hearing, speech, and language impairments are also common, occurring in about 30% of children with cerebral palsy. Children with congenital rubella or other intrauterine viral infections often have a high-frequency hearing loss (see Chapter 12). Dyskinetic cerebral palsy is associated with articulation problems, as choreoathetosis affects tongue and vocal cord movements. Expressive or receptive language disorders are commonly observed among children with cerebral palsy who do not have mental retardation and may be a harbinger of a learning disability, such as a specific reading disorder (see Chapter 23).

Roughly 50% of children with cerebral palsy also develop a seizure disorder (Aksu, 1990; Delgado, Riela, Mills, et al., 1996). Spastic forms of cerebral palsy carry the highest incidence of seizures. Tonic-clonic seizures occur frequently in individuals with hemiplegia, while minor-motor seizures are common in those with quadriplegia or rigidity (see Chapter 26).

Feeding and growth difficulties are often present in people with cerebral palsy (Azcue, Zello, Levy, et al., 1996; Stallings, Charney, Davies, et al., 1993b) and may be secondary to a variety of problems, including hypotonia, weak suck, poor coordination of the swallowing mechanism, tonic bite reflex, hyperactive gag reflex, and exaggerated tongue thrust (Jones, 1989; Reilly, Skuse, & Poblete, 1996). These problems may lead to poor nutrition and may require the

Table 24.2.   Associated impairments in cerebral palsy

Impairment	Percentage with specific impairment				
	Quadriplegia	Hemiplegia	Diplegia	Dyskinetic	Mixed
Visual impairment	55	23	38	50	64
Auditory impairment	22	8	17	17	21
Mental retardation	67	38	56	92	79
Seizure disorder	45	12	12	45	12

Source: Robinson (1973).

use of alternative feeding methods, such as tube-feeding (Rempel, Colwell, & Nelson, 1988). Although these interventions may improve nutritional status, they may complicate other problems, such as the management of gastroesophageal reflux (see Chapter 10) (Heine, Reddihough, & Catto-Smith, 1995).

Finally, behavior and emotional disorders play an important role in the lives of children with cerebral palsy and their families. Behavior disorders range from attention-deficit/hyperactivity disorder (ADHD) to self-injurious behavior. Early intervention programs and agencies, such as the United Cerebral Palsy Associations (UCPA), can provide invaluable support and training for preschool children and their families.

HABILITATION

Cerebral palsy is a lifelong disability that has different functional implications at different stages of the human life cycle (McCuaig & Frank, 1992). For families and professionals involved in the care of children with cerebral palsy, the ultimate goal of any treatment or intervention is to maximize functioning while minimizing any disability-related disadvantages. This is accomplished by recognizing the specific abilities and needs of the individual child as they occur within the context of his or her family and community. Habilitation is an intervention strategy that is family focused and community based. Ideally, it is conceived and implemented as a comprehensive program designed to facilitate adaptation to and participation in an increasing number and variety of societal settings, including home, school, clinic, child care, neighborhood, and day treatment programs (Pellegrino, 1995). The ultimate goal of intervention is to enhance participation in these settings and to afford access to new settings in a manner that is mutually satisfying for the individual and the community.

Traditional models of multidisciplinary and interdisciplinary care recognize the need for the involvement of many different professionals in the care of the child with cerebral palsy but may be cumbersome, costly, and often place inappropriate emphasis on the clinic setting and professional priorities. Interdisciplinary care works best when family members and professionals interact across a variety of settings and keep the goals of habilitation firmly in mind. This is best accomplished under the direction of a care or service coordinator. The care coordinator's job is to keep the "big picture" in mind and to represent the child's best interest to everyone involved. The care coordinator may be a social worker, nurse practitioner, teacher, physician, or a member of a number of other disciplines; the key requirements of the role are regular contact with the family and mobility across settings (home, school, clinic, etc.).

PREVENTING IMPAIRMENT: MANAGING THE MUSCULOSKELETAL COMPLICATIONS OF CEREBRAL PALSY

Orthotics: Braces and Splints

Orthotic devices, including braces and splints, are integrated into the habilitation plans of physical and occupational therapists in an effort to maintain range of motion, prevent **contractures** at specific joints, provide stability, and control involuntary movements that interfere with functioning (Nuzzo, 1980). Contractures may develop when muscles consistently have increased tone and remain in shortened positions for prolonged periods of time. Orthoses may be used to maintain a specific group of muscles in a lengthened or less contracted state so that the function of the joint is improved (see Chapter 15).

One of the most commonly prescribed orthotics is the short leg brace that prevents permanent shortening of the heel cords, often avoiding the need for an operation to lengthen the Achilles, or ankle, tendon. This brace usually consists of a plastic splint worn inside the shoe, called a molded ankle-foot orthosis (MAFO) (Figure 32.2) (Sankey, Anderson, & Young, 1989).

A variety of splints may be used to improve hand function. In the common resting hand splint, the thumb is held in an abducted position and the wrist in a neutral or slightly extended position. This helps the child keep his or her hand open to prevent a deformity. Other splints are designed to position the arm and hand in such a way as to reduce tone and to allow greater functional gains during therapy (Figure 32.2).

Most pediatric braces and splints are custommade of plastic materials that are molded directly on the child. They must be monitored closely and modified as the child grows or changes abilities. A new type of brace, called a "body splint," is made of a flexible, porous material and controls abnormal tone and involuntary movements by stabilizing the trunk and proximal limbs (Blair, Ballantyne, Horsman, et al., 1995).

The use of casts has become increasingly popular as an adjunct to more traditional methods of managing spasticity (Hanson & Jones, 1989; Smith & Harris, 1985). Tone-reducing, or "inhibitive," casts are made for upper or lower extremities and can be designed either for immobilization or to be used during weight-bearing activities. Casts position the extremities so that spastic muscles are in lengthened positions, being gently stretched. Application of serial casts can allow the therapist to increase range of motion gradually when contractures are present. After maximal range and position have been achieved, the cast is worn intermittently to maintain the improvement. Benefits of inhibitive casting include improved gait and weight-bearing, increased range of motion, and improved functional hand use (Bertoti, 1986; Smelt, 1989; Yasukawa, 1990).

Positioning

Proper positioning geared to the age and functional status of the child is often a key intervention in addressing the tone and movement abnormalities associated with cerebral palsy. A variety of adaptive devices are available to this end (Perin, 1989). Static positioning devices, including sidelyers, prone wedges, and standers (Figure 24.8), may be used to promote skeletal alignment, to compensate for abnormal postures, or to prepare the child for independent mobility. For children who must sit for extended periods of time or who are dependent on a wheelchair for mobility, a carefully designed seating system becomes an all-important component of their habilita-

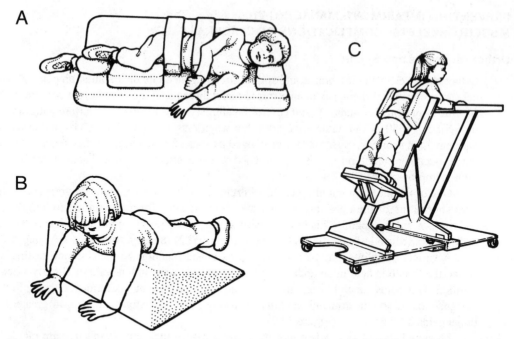

Figure 24.8. a) Child in sidelyer, b) child in prone wedge, and c) child in prone standing device.

tion. Careful attention to functional seating may also have long-term benefits in the prevention of contractures and joint deformities related to spasticity (Myhr, von Wendt, Norrlin, et al., 1995).

Other devices, including scooters, tricycles, and wheelchairs, provide the child with the means to move independently within the environment and increase opportunities for exploratory play and social interaction.

Medication

As of 1997, medications have shown limited usefulness in improving muscle tone in children with spasticity and rigidity (Pranzatelli, 1996). No drug has proved helpful for treating choreoathetosis. Both carbidopa-levodopa (Sinemet) and trihexyphenidyl (Artane), medications used effectively in Parkinson's disease, have been helpful for some children with dystonic cerebral palsy. The medications most commonly used to control spasticity and rigidity are diazepam (Valium), baclofen (Lioresal), and dantrolene (Dantrium). Diazepam and its derivative compounds, lorazepam and clonazepam, have been used most frequently. They affect brain control of muscle tone, beginning within half an hour after ingestion and lasting about 4 hours. Withdrawal of these drugs should be gradual, as physical dependency can develop. Side effects include drowsiness and excessive drooling, which may interfere with feeding and speech.

Baclofen is also a CNS inhibitor. It has been most commonly used to treat adults with multiple sclerosis and traumatic damage to the spinal cord. Drowsiness, nausea, headache, and low blood pressure are the most common side effects of this oral medication in children with cerebral palsy. About 10% of children treated with baclofen experience side effects unpleasant enough to require discontinuation of the medication. Care must be taken when stopping the medication, as rapid withdrawal may lead to severe side effects, including hallucinations (Glenn & Whyte, 1990).

Dantrolene works on muscle cells directly as a calcium channel blocker to inhibit their contraction. About half of the children with spasticity who were treated with this drug showed modest improvement (Joynt & Leonard, 1980). It is usually given 2–3 times daily. Side effects include drowsiness, muscle weakness, and increased drooling. A rare side effect of this drug is severe liver damage.

Although a variety of additional medications are becoming available for the treatment of spasticity, most cause problematic side effects similar to those described for diazepam, baclofen, and dantrolene; and none is clearly superior to these medications for use in children with cerebral palsy (Coward, 1994; Young, 1994).

Nerve Blocks, Motor Point Blocks, and Botulinum Toxin

In contrast to medication therapy, which has both systemic effects and side effects, several injectable agents are available that can be used to target spasticity in particular muscle groups. Local anesthetic agents injected into the nerves that supply spastic muscles produce a temporary, reversible conduction block and are used for diagnostic purposes (Bleck, 1987). More long-lasting effects are achieved by injecting chemical agents, such as diluted alcohol or phenol, which denature muscle and nerve protein at the point of injection (Koman, Mooney, & Smith, 1996). Direct injections of denaturing agents into motor nerves, called **nerve blocks,** are sometimes used but carry the risk of sensory loss due to damaged sensory nerves fibers that are bundled together with motor fibers. A **motor point block** effectively interrupts the nerve supply at the entry site to a spastic muscle without compromising sensation. The main side effect of the procedure is localized pain that may persist for a few days after the injection. Inhibition of spasticity lasts for 4–6 months, and the procedure can be repeated after the initial effect has worn off. This temporary reduction of spasticity allows for more effective application of physical therapy to improve range of motion and function and may make it possible to postpone orthopedic surgery when this is desirable.

Injectable botulinum toxin has been introduced as an alternative to motor point blocks (Calderon-Gonzalez, Calderon-Sepulveda, Rincon-Reyes, et al., 1994; Cosgrove, Corry, & Graham, 1994; Denislic & Meh, 1995; Koman, Mooney, Smith, et al., 1993). Botulinum toxin is produced by the bacterium that causes **botulism** and is among the most potent neurotoxins known. It works by irreversibly blocking the nerve–muscle junction. When the toxin is absorbed into the general circulation (as with botulism), death may result from paralysis of respiratory muscles. However, small quantities can be safely injected directly into spastic muscles without significant spread of the toxin into the bloodstream. This results in weakening of the muscle and reduction of spasticity for 3–6 months (i.e., the effects of the injections are reversible with time). The main advantage of botulinum toxin over motor point blocks is its relative ease of administration with less pain and discomfort. The main disadvantage is the prohibitive cost of the drug and lack of information regarding the long-term benefits of treatment and the efficacy and potential toxicity of repeat doses.

Neurosurgery

Selective posterior rhizotomy has become an accepted treatment option for the reduction of spasticity in selected children with severe lower extremity involvement, especially spastic diplegia (Abbott, 1996; Park, Phillips, & Peacock, 1989). In spasticity, the deep tendon (or stretch) reflex is overactive. This reflex has a motor (**efferent**) component and a sensory (**afferent**) component (Figure 24.9) When a muscle is stretched rapidly, special sensory organs in the muscle (called **muscle spindles**) send nerve impulses via the afferent nerve fibers to the spinal cord. Impulses are then directed from the spinal cord through the efferent nerve fibers, which end in the muscle and stimulate it to contract, thus completing a feedback loop and counteracting the original stretch. In selective dorsal rhizotomy, the specific afferent fibers (or rootlets) that make the greatest contribution to spasticity are discerned by observing that these rootlets, when stimulated directly with electrical current in the operating room, result in the largest spastic motor response. These rootlets are cut. Because only carefully selected rootlets are cut, touch and position sense remain intact. Postoperatively, spasticity is reduced and is associated with variable degrees of

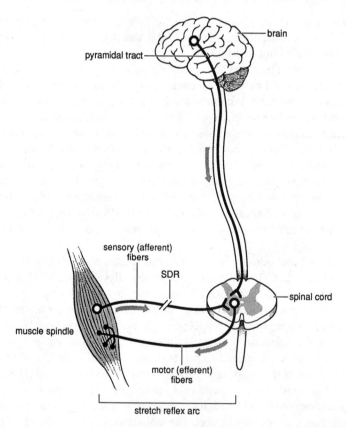

Figure 24.9.   Selective dorsal rhizotomy (SDR). Spasticity results from an overactive stretch reflex. When a muscle is stretched, sensory organs (muscle spindles) initiate nerve impulses that are transmitted via sensory (afferent) fibers to the spinal cord. This signal is then modified by input from the pyramidal tract in the brain and relayed back to the muscle via motor (efferent) fibers, causing the muscle to contract. In spastic cerebral palsy, the pyramidal tract is impaired and this leads to increased muscle contraction. In SDR, the stretch reflex is interrupted by cutting afferent fibers that supply the muscles that exhibit the greatest degree of spasticity. This results in a decrease in muscle tone.

weakness. Functional improvement in sitting, standing, and walking has been reported in some studies (Abbott, Forem, & Johann, 1989; Berman, Vaughan, & Peacock, 1990; Peacock & Staudt, 1990), but others have emphasized the great variability in functional outcomes and the need for more rigorous clinical trials (McLaughlin, Bjornson, Astley, et al., 1994).

A newer neurosurgical procedure allows for the direct delivery of antispasticity medication into the spinal fluid (intrathecal) space, where it can inhibit motor nerve conduction at the level of the spinal cord (Albright, 1996; Albright, Barron, Fasick, et al., 1993). A disk-shaped pump is placed beneath the skin of the abdomen, and a catheter is tunneled below the skin around to the back, where it is inserted through the lumbar spine into the intrathecal space. The intrathecal medication most often used is baclofen, which is stored in a reservoir in the disk and which may be refilled with a needle inserted into the reservoir through the skin. The medication is delivered at a continuous rate that is computer controlled and adjustable. Because the drug is delivered directly to its site of action (the cerebrospinal fluid), much lower doses may be used to achieve benefit, with less risk of systemic side effects. The main benefit of the method is dramatic reduction in spasticity and adjustable dosing (Albright, 1997). The main disadvantages are complications related to mechanical failures and infection and the need for intensive and reliable medical follow-up.

Some other neurosurgical procedures that were used in the past to treat cerebral palsy, including placement of cerebellar or dorsal column stimulators, have largely fallen out of favor due to lack of efficacy and problems with complications (Davis, Schulman, Nanes, et al., 1987; Hugenholtz, Humphreys, McIntyre, et al., 1988; Park & Owen, 1992).

Orthopedic Surgery

Because of the abnormal or asymmetrical distribution of muscle tone, children who have cerebral palsy are susceptible to the development of joint deformities (Dormans, 1993). The most common of these result from permanent shortening or contracture of one or more groups of muscles around a joint, which limits joint mobility. Orthopedic surgery is done to increase the range of motion by lengthening a tendon, by cutting through muscle or tendon ("release"), or by moving the point of attachment of a tendon on bone. For example, a partial release or transfer of the hip adductor muscles may improve the child's ability to sit and walk and may lessen the chances of a hip dislocation (Binder & Eng, 1989). A partial hamstring release, involving the lengthening or transfer of muscles around the knee, also may facilitate sitting and walking. A lengthening of the Achilles tendon at the ankle improves walking (Figure 24.10). All of these procedures require the use of a cast or splint for 6–8 weeks after surgery and a brace at night for at least several more months (Bleck, 1987).

More complicated orthopedic procedures may be required for correction of a dislocated hip (Cooke, Cole, & Carey, 1989; Scrutton, 1989). If this is diagnosed when there is a partial dislocation (called subluxation), release of the hip adductor muscles alone can be effective (Figure 24.11) (Moreau, Drummond, Rogala, et al., 1979). If the head of the femur is dislocated more than one third to one half of the way out of a hip joint socket, a more complex procedure, a varus osteotomy, may be necessary. In this operation, the angle of the femur (the thigh bone) is changed surgically to place the head of the femur back into the hip socket (Figure 24.12). In some cases, the hip socket also must be reshaped to ensure that the hip joint remains functional.

Before performing surgery, the orthopedist is careful to evaluate and explain to the parents both the potential risks and benefits of an operation. Computerized gait analysis conducted prior

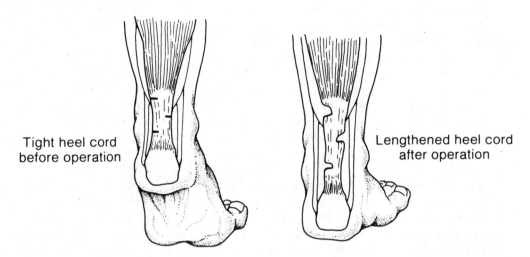

Tight heel cord
before operation

Lengthened heel cord
after operation

Figure 24.10.   Achilles tendon lengthening operation. When the heel cord is tight, the child walks on his or her toes. Surgery lengthens the heel cord and permits a more flat-footed gait.

to surgical intervention to improve ambulation has become increasingly common. Precise measurements obtained through motion analysis, force plates, and electromyography offer detailed information relating to specific abnormalities at each lower extremity joint as well as the muscle activity that controls motion through all phases of the gait cycle (Cahan, Adams, Perry, et al., 1990; Russman & Gage, 1989). Such precise definition is not possible through clinical observation alone. Preoperative gait analysis helps to determine exactly which procedures are likely to be successful. Postoperative analysis can provide an objective measure of outcome.

Besides treating contractures and dislocations, orthopedic surgeons also are involved in the care of scoliosis, a complication of both spastic and nonspastic forms of cerebral palsy. If untreated, a spinal curvature can interfere with sitting, walking, and self-care skills. If severe enough, it also can affect respiratory efforts. Treatment of significant scoliosis ranges from a molded plastic jacket or chair insert to surgery in an effort to straighten the spine as much as possible. The surgery involves using rods and wires to hold the spine in an improved alignment while bone graft material fuses the spine in position (Bulman, Dormans, Ecker, et al., 1996) (Figure 24.13). With an improved surgical technique, called a Lucque procedure, scoliosis surgery now is being pursued more aggressively (Ferguson & Allen, 1988).

PREVENTING DISABILITY: PROMOTING OPTIMAL FUNCTION

Early Intervention Services

The key to success in any therapy program is the consistency of its delivery and the early involvement of parents so that they can learn to manage their child at home (Miller, Bacharach, Boos, et al., 1995). Legislation governing public education for children with disabilities has provided guidelines and financial incentives for the development of statewide early intervention

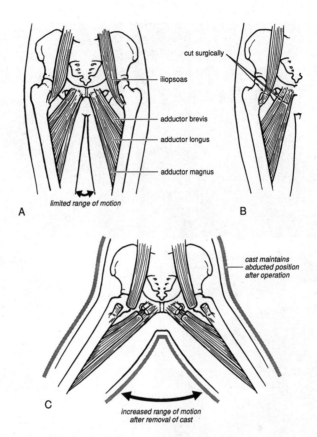

Figure 24.11.   Adductor tenotomy. This operation is done to improve scissoring (Figure 24.7) and to prevent hip dislocation caused by contractures of the adductor muscles in the thigh. In this procedure, the iliopsoas, adductor brevis, and adductor longus muscles are cut, leaving the adductor magnus intact. The child is then placed in a cast for 6–8 weeks to maintain a more open (abducted) position. The muscles eventually grow together in a lengthened position, allowing improved sitting and/or walking.

systems. Parents are encouraged to participate actively in planning and implementing services and in developing competence in advocacy for their child. Programs are individualized according to the specific needs of the family and may include a combination of consultative, home-based, or center-based intervention.

Neurodevelopmental Therapy

The primary method of physical and occupational therapy for the young child with cerebral palsy is neurodevelopmental therapy (NDT), an approach designed to provide the child with sensorimotor experiences that enhance the development of normal movement patterns (see Chapter 32) (Bobath, 1980; Perin, 1989). An individualized program of positioning, therapeutic handling, and play is developed for the child. Program goals include the normalization of tone and control of movement during functional activities.

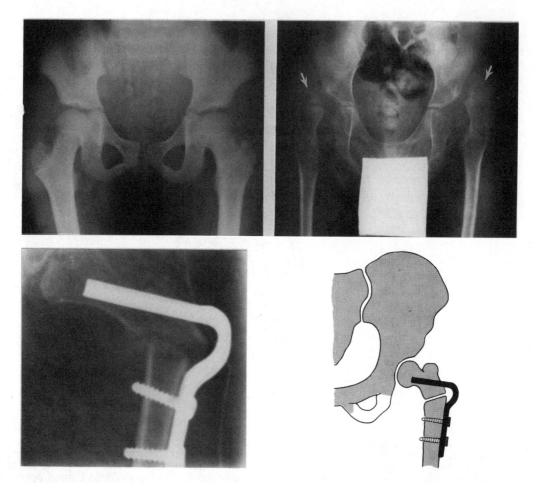

Figure 24.12.   Dislocation of the hip. The upper X rays show a normal hip to the left and a hip dislocated on both sides on the right. The arrows indicate the points of dislocation. The lower picture shows the results of a varus osteotomy to correct the left-side dislocation. The femur has been cut and realigned so that it now fits into the acetabulum. Pins, which are later removed, hold the bone in place until it heals.

A controversial approach to treating children with cerebral palsy is called patterning. Patterning involves putting the child through a series of exercises designed to improve "neurological organization." Three to five volunteers simultaneously manipulate the child's limbs and head for hours daily in patterns that are supposed to simulate prenatal and infantile movement of typically developing children. Proponents believe that if a child repeats certain motions frequently enough, undamaged brain cells will be reprogrammed to take over the functions of the damaged cells (Zigler, 1981). The American Academy of Pediatrics (1982) has stated its opposition to this treatment, as it has found no evidence to support its effectiveness. In addition, the regimen prescribed is so demanding and restrictive that it places considerable stress on the child, parents, and siblings (Matthews, 1988).

Figure 24.13.   Treatment of scoliosis may require a spinal fusion. This X ray shows improved scoliosis following a Lucque procedure. During this surgery the position of the spine is improved using metal hooks, rods, and wires while bone graft material fuses the spine in position.

Functional Mobility and Equipment

One of the questions of greatest concern to parents of young children with cerebral palsy is whether their child will ever walk. Early factors that may predict prognosis for ambulation include type of cerebral palsy, age of independent sitting, and postural and tonic reflex activity. A diagnosis of hemiplegia or ataxia and attainment of independent sitting by 2 years of age generally predict eventual ability to walk distances. A diagnosis of spastic quadriplegia or absence of postural reactions and obligatory persistence of primitive reflexes at 2 years of age carries a poor prognosis for ambulation (Trahan & Marcoux, 1994; Watt, Robinson, & Grace, 1989). Treatment interventions commonly used for ambulation training include a combination of physical therapy; assistive devices, such as walkers or crutches; orthotics; and surgery. For children with limited walking skills, wheelchairs are essential for maximizing mobility and function (Hulme, Shaver, Acher, et al., 1987; Schultz-Hurlburt & Tervo, 1982).

A wheelchair with a solid seat and back is usually recommended. Some children, however, have difficulty using this type of chair unless modifications are made. The addition of head and trunk supports or a tray may be needed for the child who lacks postural control due to low tone. The child with limited head control or with feeding difficulties may benefit from a high-backed chair that can be tilted back 10°–15° (Figure 24.14a). This helps to maintain the child's body and head in proper alignment.

Special seating cushions or custom-molded inserts that conform to the contours of the body can offer necessary support for the child with orthopedic deformities such as scoliosis (Katz, Liebertal, & Erken, 1988). Motorized wheelchairs can enhance the independence of children who are able to use them. Although these usually employ an easily manipulated joystick for controlling both speed and direction, other types of switches are available for children who cannot control their hand movements (see Figure 24.14b).

Special supportive strollers are an alternative to wheelchairs for mobility within the community or for the young child whose potential for ambulation has yet to be determined. These are lightweight and collapsible yet support the back and keep the hips properly aligned (see Figure 24.14c).

Walkers, crutches, and canes may be appropriate for the child with milder forms of cerebral palsy. Walkers are available with or without wheels and offer a stable base of support to the child who can maintain correct positional alignment while in a standing position (Logan, Byers-Hinkley, & Ciccone, 1990). However, they are difficult to maneuver around obstacles or over rough terrain. Crutches and canes are easier to maneuver but require considerable strength, endurance, and balance for functional use. They are recommended rarely.

Car seats are essential to the safety of all children who ride in automobiles. Several manufacturers offer adapted car seats that meet federal safety guidelines as well as provide proper support for the child with cerebral palsy. Often these models include a base that allows the seat to be used as a stroller or positioning chair outside of the car.

Physical Activity and Sports

Physical exercise is important to strengthen muscles and bones, enhance motor skills, and prevent contractures. In addition, the social and recreational aspects of organized physical activities can be highly beneficial (Humphrey, 1985). Many popular activities, including swimming, dancing, and horseback riding, can be modified so that people with cerebral palsy can participate (Jones, 1987). In addition, the Special Olympics has enabled thousands of children with disabilities to take part in various sporting events. The rewards of engaging in competitive sports are invaluable for enhancing self-esteem and providing a sense of belonging to a peer group. Parents and professionals should encourage all children to participate in whatever physical activities their interests, motivation, and capabilities allow.

Assistive Technology

Assistive technology devices are often an important part of the habilitation plan for children with cerebral palsy. The technology involved may be as simple as Velcro or as complex as the computer chip. Although it is generally true that the simplest intervention is the best, it cannot be denied that the computer has become the hero of assistive technology. Computers can be used to control the environment, provide a lifeline with the outside world, enable a person to work at home, facilitate artificial speech and sight, and provide entertainment (Cole & Dehdashti, 1990; Levy, 1983; Treviranus & Tannock, 1987). The real potential of this technology to improve the quality of life for children with disabilities is just beginning to be realized. Our enthusiasm for its use is tempered by problems with access related to the cost and availability of durable hardware and well-designed software (see Chapter 32).

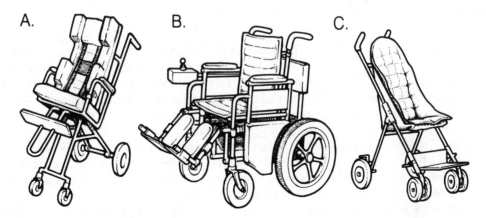

Figure 24.14.   Wheelchairs. a) High-backed, tilting chair with lateral inserts and head supports. b) Motorized wheelchair with joystick control. c) Supportive collapsible stroller.

School

For many children with cerebral palsy, entry into school represents the first major step into the wider community. Difficulties are often encountered in accommodating the physical, nutritional, and medical needs of these children at school. Whereas motor impairments tend to receive the most attention in the early years after the initial diagnosis of cerebral palsy, associated disabilities such as learning difficulties, attention and behavior problems, mental retardation, and sensory impairments tend to come to the fore in the setting of elementary school. For many children, it is these associated problems, rather than their motor disability, that put them at greatest disadvantage relative to their peers.

The special education model has long been used to address the educational issues of children with special needs. Children with cerebral palsy have traditionally been segregated into classrooms with designations such as "multiply disabled" and "orthopedically impaired," sometimes without proper regard for their cognitive skills. The trend is now, however, toward inclusive classrooms, which under ideal circumstances can accommodate the needs of children with a range of abilities. The original legislative support for inclusion in education was provided by the Education for All Handicapped Children Act of 1975, PL 94-142, which recognized the right of children with disabilities to an education and provided a mandate that this should occur in the least restrictive classroom environment possible. Additional impetus has been given to this trend by the adoption of the Americans with Disabilities Act (ADA) of 1990, PL 101-336 (Kalscheur, 1992). This law mandates equal opportunities for people with disabilities at all ages.

Inclusive settings require a significant collaboration between the general and special education models and work best when a team of educators and paraprofessional aides is associated with each classroom. Unfortunately, economic priorities can work against this necessary collaboration and create the temptation to use "inclusion" as an excuse to increase classroom size and reduce the level of support given to children with disabilities.

TOMMY

Tommy's birth was traumatic. His mother had an abruptio placenta, which necessitated an emergency cesarean section and caused her to lose a great deal of blood. The physician could not detect a fetal heartbeat during the 3 minutes before birth. Tommy's Apgar scores were 1 at 1 minute and 2 at 5 minutes. An injection of adrenaline into his heart and artificial ventilation were required. The doctors were able to stabilize Tommy within the first day of life, but they were afraid that significant brain damage had already occurred.

Their concern was justified. As an infant, Tommy fed poorly and slept most of the time. When he was awake, he was irritable and screamed. His muscle tone remained floppy. At 3 months of age, he still held his hands in fists and could not hold his head upright. He had intermittent minor-motor seizures. By 6 months of age, Tommy still made no attempt to roll over and was only beginning to make cooing sounds. When he was 12 months old, he started having choreoathetoid movements of his arms, and his muscle tone was variable (i.e., sometimes decreased and other times increased). At 2 years of age, he rolled over and reached for objects. Because of the choreoathetosis, Tommy could not grasp objects; instead, he batted at them. He responded inconsistently to sounds and was later found to have a severe sensorineural hearing loss.

For Tommy's parents, the situation became progressively more difficult emotionally as they realized he also had mental retardation requiring extensive supports and would never be self-sufficient. However, with the support of relatives and the use of special schools and respite care, they were able to cope over the years. Now, at 21 years of age, Tommy still lives at home and attends a cerebral palsy activity center. He is happy at the center and enjoys the company of others. His cerebral palsy continues to make it impossible for him to feed or dress himself. He can now sit without support but remains in a wheelchair. His parents worry about his future when they are no longer able to care for him.

TINA

Tina, a premature infant, weighed less than 2 pounds when she was born in the seventh month. She had a rocky newborn period with hypoglycemia, respiratory distress syndrome, and a patent ductus arteriosus. When finally released from the hospital at 3 months of age, however, she was an alert, active, and happy baby. Yet her legs were spastic and were held in a scissored position. She started to receive physical therapy at this time.

Apart from her motor development, many of her other developmental milestones were typical, especially considering her prematurity. At 1 year of age, she said "mama" to everyone and followed one-step commands. She also could drink from a cup. She would roll over from stomach to back, but she could not sit or stand. Her primitive reflexes persisted, and the muscle tone, especially in her legs, was increased. Her hips were subluxed. Although her intellectual skills fell around the 9-month level, her gross motor skills were at a 4-month level.

By 2 years of age, the scissoring of her legs became more and more troublesome, and the problem with her hips was more prominent. Dressing and sitting were difficult. Orthopedic surgery successfully released the adductor muscles of her hips. After intensive physical therapy, she learned to roll over and sit. By 4 years of age, she was walking with short leg braces and canes. Her language development continued right on course, and IQ testing at 6 years of age showed a verbal score of 110 and a performance score of 82. In children with cerebral palsy, such a discrepancy is common. For Tina, it was the first clue to the presence of a learning disability that became more apparent in the first grade.

Another problem, a squint, was corrected surgically, and Tina's appearance improved and her bilateral vision was preserved. She was a vibrant, pretty, and happy child. However, her difficulties were not over. In the second grade, she had a number of generalized tonic-clonic seizures. An electroencephalogram confirmed the diagnosis of a seizure disorder, and she was placed on carbamazepine (Tegretol). Tina is now 9 years old and has had only one seizure in the last year.

Right now, Tina is doing well in a public school setting. She is in a general education classroom for most of her subjects and gets help in a resource room for her reading problems. She also continues to have physical and occupational therapy. Emotionally, both she and her parents have done well coping with her disabilities.

PROGNOSIS

Prognosis is most simply defined in terms of longevity. Although most children with cerebral palsy will live to adulthood, their projected life expectancy is somewhat less than that of the general population (Crichton, Mackinnon, & White, 1995; Hutton, Cooke, & Pharoah, 1994). The prognosis varies for each type of cerebral palsy. A child with a mild left hemiplegia probably will have a typical life expectancy, while a child with spastic quadriplegia may not live beyond age 40.

Prognosis may also be defined in terms of functional outcome and ability to participate in a variety of societal settings (O'Grady, Crain, & Kohn, 1995). In this sense, prognosis becomes a complex function of a child's profile of abilities and disabilities as these occur within a specific set of environmental circumstances. Prognosis is also a matter of perception. A child who is unlikely to walk may have a "worse prognosis" than a child who will eventually walk; yet, he or she may have better functional mobility because of an excellent wheelchair, a supportive family, and an accessible community. Judgments about prognosis are also biased by an understandable tendency to emphasize mobility issues when developing plans for habilitation for children with cerebral palsy. Yet, when asked, parents identify communication and socialization as the functional areas of greatest concern to them. A child's ability to integrate successfully into society is probably more strongly related to cognitive strengths than to physical ability.

Although about 40% of the individuals who have cerebral palsy have typical intelligence, most have difficulty leading completely "typical" lives (Murphy, Molnar, & Lankasky, 1995). Studies suggest that employability is not related solely to the degree of disability, but to a variety of other factors including family support, quality of educational programs, and the availability of community-based training and technical support (Russman & Gage, 1989). As adults, only 10% are entirely self-supporting. Another 40% work in sheltered workshops or supported employment programs. An additional 35% have sufficient self-help skills to be partially independent at home. The remaining 15% are dependent on others; a few of these individuals live in institutions (Table 24.3) (O'Grady, Nishimura, Kohn, et al., 1985). It is hoped that these figures will improve as a result of new federal mandates, such as the ADA, which define the rights of people with disabilities and begin to make inroads into societal perceptions of disability. Once society recog-

Table 24.3.   Outcome of cerebral palsy in adults

Outcome	Percentage with specific outcomes		
	Complete	Partial	Very little
Independence at home	55	28	17
Independence in community	48	23	29
Competitive employment	59	18	23
Use of hands	86	7	7
Speech	78	12	10

Adapted from O'Grady, Nishimura, Kohn, et al. (1985).

nizes that functional outcomes are related as much to societal conditions as they are to the characteristics of a particular child with a disability, our perception of prognosis will undergo a major shift. Ultimately, strengthening supports to families, improving schools, increasing opportunities for employment, and changing attitudes about disabilities in society at large may do as much for children with cerebral palsy as traditional therapy and medical interventions.

SUMMARY

Cerebral palsy is a developmental disability that results from damage to or dysfunction of the developing brain. The impairments associated with cerebral palsy are nonprogressive but permanent. Varying degrees of disability related to functional mobility, daily living skills, and communication/socialization skills result from these impairments. Habilitation is an interdisciplinary strategy that seeks to maximize function and minimize the disadvantage a person experiences as a consequence of disability or societal circumstances. Efforts founded on the principles articulated in the ADA will create new opportunities for greater participation and enhanced quality of life for people with cerebral palsy.

REFERENCES

Abbott, R. (1996). Sensory rhizotomy for the treatment of childhood spasticity. *Journal of Child Neurology, 11*(1), S36–S42.

Abbott, R., Forem, S.L., & Johann, M. (1989). Selective posterior rhizotomy for the treatment of spasticity: A review. *Child's Nervous System, 5,* 337–346.

Adinolfi, M. (1993). Infectious diseases in pregnancy, cytokines and neurological impairment: An hypothesis. *Developmental Medicine and Child Neurology, 351,* 549–558.

Aksu, F. (1990). Nature and prognosis of seizures in patients with cerebral palsy. *Developmental Medicine and Child Neurology, 32,* 661–668.

Albright, A.L. (1996). Intrathecal baclofen in cerebral palsy movement disorders. *Journal of Child Neurology, 11*(1), S29–S35.

Albright, A.L., Barron, W.B., Fasick, M.P., et al. (1993). Continuous intrathecal baclofen infusion for spasticity of cerebral origin. *Journal of the American Medical Association, 270,* 2475–2477.

Albright, A.L. (1997). Baclofen in the treatment of cerebral palsy. *Journal of Child Neurology, 11,* 77–83.

Allen, M.C., & Capute, A.J. (1989). Neonatal neurodevelopmental examination as a predictor of neuromotor outcome in premature infants. *Pediatrics, 83,* 498–506.

American Academy of Pediatrics. (1982). The Doman-Delacato treatment of neurologically handicapped children. *Pediatrics, 70,* 810–812.

Americans with Disabilities Act (ADA) of 1990, PL 101-336, 42 U.S.C. § 12101 *et seq.*

Arens, L.J., Peacock, W.J., & Peter, J. (1989). Selective posterior rhizotomy: A long-term follow-up study. *Child's Nervous System, 5,* 148–152.

Azcue, M.P., Zello, G.A., Levy, L.D., et al. (1996). Energy expenditure and body composition in children with spastic quadriplegic cerebral palsy. *Journal of Pediatrics, 129,* 870–876.

Barnes, P.D. (1992). Imaging of the central nervous system in pediatrics and adolescence. *Pediatric Clinics of North America, 39*(4), 743–776.

Berman, B., Vaughan, C.L., & Peacock, W.J. (1990). The effect of rhizotomy on movement in patients with cerebral palsy. *American Journal of Occupational Therapy, 44,* 511–516.

Bertoti, D.B. (1986). Effect of short-leg casting on ambulation in children with cerebral palsy. *Physical Therapy, 66,* 1522–1529.

Binder, H., & Eng, G.D. (1989). Rehabilitation management of children with spastic diplegic cerebral palsy. *Archives of Physical Medicine and Rehabilitation, 70,* 482–489.

Black, P. (1982). Visual disorders associated with cerebral palsy. *British Journal of Ophthalmology, 66,* 46–52.

Blair, E., Ballantyne, J., Horsman, S., et al. (1995). A study of a dynamic proximal stability splint in the management of children with cerebral palsy. *Developmental Medicine and Child Neurology, 37,* 544–554.

Blair, E., & Stanley, F. (1985). Intraobserver agreement in the classification of cerebral palsy. *Developmental Medicine and Child Neurology, 25,* 615–622.

Bleck, E.E. (1987). *Orthopedic management of cerebral palsy.* Philadelphia: J.B. Lippincott.

Bobath, K. (1980). A neurophysiological basis for the treatment of cerebral palsy. *Clinics in Developmental Medicine, 75,* 77–87.

Bulman, W.A., Dormans, J.P., Ecker, M.L., et al. (1996). Posterior spinal fusion for scoliosis in patients with cerebral palsy: A comparison of luque rod and unit rod instrumentation. *Journal of Pediatric Orthopedics, 16,* 314–323.

Cahan, L.D., Adams, J.M., Perry, J., et al. (1990). Instrumented gait analysis after selective dorsal rhizotomy. *Developmental Medicine and Child Neurology, 32,* 1037–1043.

Calderon-Gonzalez, R., Calderon-Sepulveda, R., Rincon-Reyes, M., et al. (1994). Botulinum toxin A in management of cerebral palsy. *Pediatric Neurology, 10,* 284–288.

Capute, A.J. (1986). Early neuromotor reflexes in infancy. *Pediatric Annals, 15,* 217–218, 221–223, 226.

Capute, A.J., Accardo, P.J., Vining, E.P.G., et al. (1978). *Primitive reflex profile.* Baltimore: University Park Press.

Chugani, H.T. (1992). Functional brain imaging in pediatrics. *Pediatric Clinics of North America, 39*(4), 777–799.

Cole, E., & Dehdashti, P. (1990). Interface design as a prosthesis for an individual with brain injury. *SIGCHI (Special Interest Group on Computer and Human Interaction) Bulletin, 22,* 28–32.

Cooke, P.H., Cole, W.G., & Carey, R.P. (1989). Dislocation of the hip in cerebral palsy: Natural history and predictability. *Journal of Bone and Joint Surgery (British Volume), 71,* 441–446.

Cosgrove, A.P., Corry, I.S., & Graham, H.K. (1994). Botulinum toxin in the managment of the lower limb in cerebral palsy. *Developmental Medicine and Child Neurology, 36,* 386–396.

Coward, D.M. (1994). Tizanidine: Neuropharmacology and mechanism of action. *Neurology, 44*(Suppl. 9), S6–S11.

Crichton, J.U., Mackinnon, M., & White, C.P. (1995). The life-expectancy of persons with cerebral palsy. *Developmental Medicine and Child Neurology, 37,* 567–576.

Crothers, B., & Paine, R.S. (1959). *The natural history of cerebral palsy.* Cambridge, MA: Harvard University Press.

Cummins, S.K., Nelson, K.B., Grether, J.K., et al. (1993). Cerebral palsy in four northern California counties, births 1983 through 1985. *Journal of Pediatrics, 123,* 230–237.

Davis, R., Schulman, J., Nanes, M., et al. (1987). Cerebellar stimulation for spastic cerebral palsy: Double-blind quantitative study. *Applied Neurophysiology, 50,* 451–452.

Delgado, M.R., Riela, A.R., Mills, J., et al. (1996). Discontinuation of antiepileptic drug treatment after two seizure-free years in children with cerebral palsy. *Pediatrics, 97,* 192–197.

Denislic, M., & Meh, D. (1995). Botulinum toxin in the treatment of cerebral palsy. *Neuropediatrics, 26,* 249–252.

Dormans, J.P. (1993). Orthopedic management of children with cerebral palsy. *Pediatric Clinics of North America, 3,* 645–652.

Education for All Handicapped Children Act of 1975, PL 94-142, 20 U.S.C. § 1400 *et seq.*

Ferguson, R.L., & Allen, B.L., Jr. (1988). Considerations in the treatment of cerebral palsy patients with spinal deformities. *Orthopedic Clinics of North America, 19,* 419–425.

Frankenburg, W.K., Dodds, J., Archer, P., et al. (1992). The Denver II: A major revision and restandardization of The Denver Developmental Screening Test. *Pediatrics, 89,* 91–97.

Glenn, M.B., & Whyte, J. (1990). *The practical management of spasticity in children and adults.* Philadelphia: Lea & Febiger.

Grether, J.K., Nelson, K.B., & Cummins, S.K. (1993). Twinning and cerebral palsy: Experience in four Northern California counties, births 1983 through 1985. *Pediatrics, 92,* 854–858.

Grether, J.K., Nelson, K.B., Emery, E.S., et al. (1996). Prenatal and perinatal factors and cerebral palsy in very low birth weight infants. *Journal of Pediatrics, 128,* 407–414.

Hagberg, B., Hagberg, G., & Olow, I. (1993). The changing panorama of cerebral palsy in Sweden: VI. Prevalence and origin during the birth year period 1983–1986. *Acta Paediatrica, 82,* 387–393.

Halpern, D., & Meelhuysen, F.E. (1966). Phenol motor point block in the management of muscular hypertonia. *Archives of Physical Medicine and Rehabilitation, 47,* 659–664.

Hanson, C.J., & Jones, L.J. (1989). Gait abnormalities and inhibitive casts in cerebral palsy. *Journal of the American Podiatric Medical Association, 79,* 53–59.

Heine, R.G., Reddihough, D.S., & Catto-Smith, A.G. (1995). Gastro-oesophageal reflux and feeding problems after gastrostomy in children with severe neurological impairment. *Developmental Medicine and Child Neurology, 37,* 320–329.

Hugenholtz, H., Humphreys, P., McIntyre, W.M., et al. (1988). Cervical spinal cord stimulation for spasticity in cerebral palsy. *Neurosurgery, 22,* 707–714.

Hulme, J.B., Shaver, J., Acher, S., et al. (1987). Effects of adaptive seating devices on the eating and drinking of children with multiple handicaps. *American Journal of Occupational Therapy, 41,* 81–89.

Humphrey, F. (1985). Therapeutic recreation. In D.A. Umphred (Ed.), *Neurological rehabilitation* (Vol. 3, pp. 653–662). St. Louis: C.V. Mosby.

Hutton, J.L., Cooke, T., & Pharoah, P.O.D. (1994). Life expectancy of children with cerebral palsy. *British Medical Journal, 309,* 4315.

Illingworth, R.S. (1987). *The development of the infant and young child: Normal and abnormal* (9th ed.). New York: Churchill Livingstone.

Jones, J.A. (Ed.). (1987). *Training guide to cerebral palsy sports* (3rd ed.). Champaign, IL: Human Kinetics Publishers.

Jones, M.H. (1975). Differential diagnosis and natural history of the cerebral palsied child. In R.L. Samilson (Ed.), *Orthopaedic aspects of cerebral palsy.* Philadelphia: J.B. Lippincott.

Jones, P.M. (1989). Feeding disorders in children with multiple handicaps. *Developmental Medicine and Child Neurology, 31,* 404–406.

Joynt, R.L., & Leonard, J.A., Jr. (1980). Dantrolene sodium suspension in treatment of spastic cerebral palsy. *Developmental Medicine and Child Neurology, 22,* 755–767.

Kalscheur, J.A. (1992). Benefits of the Americans with Disabilities Act of 1990 for children and adolescents with disabilities. *American Journal of Occupational Therapy, 46,* 419–425.

Katz, K., Liebertal, M., & Erken, E.H.W. (1988). Seat insert for cerebral-palsied children with total body involvement. *Developmental Medicine and Child Neurology, 30,* 222–226.

Koman, L.A., Mooney, J.F., Smith, B., et al. (1993). Management of cerebral palsy with botulinum A toxin: Preliminary investigation. *Journal of Pediatric Orthopaedics, 13,* 489–495.

Koman, L.A., Mooney, J.F., & Smith, B.P. (1996). Neuromuscular blockade in the management of cerebral palsy. *Journal of Child Neurology, 11*(1), S23–S28.

Krageloh-Mann, I., Hagberg, G., Meisner, C., et al. (1995). Bilateral spastic cerebral palsy: A collaborative study between South-West Germany and Western Sweden: III. Aetiology. *Developmental Medicine and Child Neurology, 37,* 191–203.

Leviton, A. (1993). Preterm birth and cerebral palsy: Is Tumor Necrosis Factor the missing link? *Developmental Medicine and Child Neurology, 35,* 549–558.

Levy, R. (1983). Interface modalities of technical aids used by people with disability. *American Journal of Occupational Therapy, 37,* 761–765.

Logan, L., Byers-Hinkley, K., & Ciccone, C.D. (1990). Anterior versus posterior walkers: A gait analysis study. *Developmental Medicine and Child Neurology, 32,* 1044–1048.

Matthews, D.J. (1988). Controversial therapies in the management of cerebral palsy. *Pediatric Annals, 17,* 762–764.

McCuaig, M., & Frank, G. (1992). The able self: Adaptive patterns and choices in independent living for a person with cerebral palsy. *American Journal of Occupational Therapy, 45,* 224–234.

McLaughlin, J.F., Bjornson, K.F., Astley, S.J., et al. (1994). The role of selective dorsal rhizotomy in cerebral palsy: Critical evaluation of a prospective clinical series. *Developmental Medicine and Child Neurology, 36,* 755–769.

Meberg, A., & Broch, H. (1995). A changing pattern of cerebral palsy: Declining trend for incidence of cerebral palsy in the 20-year period 1970–89. *Journal of Perinatal Medicine, 23,* 395–402.

Miller, F., Bacharach, S.J., Boos, M.L., et al. (1995). *Cerebral palsy: A complete guide for caregiving.* Baltimore: The Johns Hopkins University Press.

Moreau, M., Drummond, D.S., Rogala, E., et al. (1979). Natural history of the dislocated hip in spastic cerebral palsy. *Developmental Medicine and Child Neurology, 21,* 744–753.

Murphy, K.P., Molnar, G.E., & Lankasky, K. (1995). Medical and functional status of adults with cerebral palsy. *Developmental Medicine and Child Neurology, 37,* 1075–1084.

Myhr, U., von Wendt, L., Norrlin, S., et al. (1995). Five-year follow-up of functional sitting position in children with cerebral palsy. *Developmental Medicine and Child Neurology, 37,* 587–596.

Nelson, K.B., & Ellenberg, J.H. (1982). Children who "outgrew" cerebral palsy. *Pediatrics, 69,* 529–536.

Nelson, K.B., & Ellenberg, J.H. (1986). Antecedents of cerebral palsy: Multivariate analysis of risk. *New England Journal of Medicine, 315,* 81–86.

Nickel, R.E., Renken, C.A., & Gallenstein, J.S. (1989). The infant motor screen. *Developmental Medicine and Child Neurology, 31,* 35–42.

Nuzzo, R.M. (1980). Dynamic bracing: Elastics for patients with cerebral palsy, muscular dystrophy and myelodysplasia. *Clinical Orthopaedics and Related Research, 148,* 263–273.

O'Grady, R.S., Crain, L.S., & Kohn, J. (1995). The prediction of long-term functional outcomes of children with cerebral palsy. *Developmental Medicine and Child Neurology, 37,* 997–1005.

O'Grady, R.S., Nishimura, D.M., Kohn, J.G., et al. (1985). Vocational predictions compared with present vocational status of 60 young adults with cerebral palsy. *Developmental Medicine and Child Neurology, 27,* 775–784.

Paban, M., & Piper, M.C. (1987). Early predictors of one-year neurodevelopmental outcome for "at risk" infants. *Physical and Occupational Therapy in Pediatrics, 7,* 17–34.

Park, T.S., & Owen, J.H. (1992). Surgical management of spastic diplegia in cerebral palsy. *New England Journal of Medicine, 326,* 745–749.

Park, T.S., Phillips, L.H., & Peacock, W.J. (1989). *Management of spasticity in cerebral palsy and spinal cord injury.* Philadelphia: Hanley & Belfus.

Peacock, W.J., & Staudt, L.A. (1990). Spasticity in cerebral palsy and the selective posterior rhizotomy procedure. *Journal of Child Neurology, 5,* 179–185.

Pellegrino, L. (1995). Cerebral palsy: A paradigm for developmental disabilities. *Developmental Medicine and Child Neurology, 37,* 834–839.

Perin, B. (1989). Physical therapy for the child with cerebral palsy. In J.S. Tecklin (Ed.), *Pediatric physical therapy* (pp. 68–105). Philadelphia: J.B. Lippincott.

Peterson, B., Stanley, F., & Henderson, D. (1990). Cerebral palsy in multiple births in western Australia: Genetic aspects. *American Journal of Medical Genetics, 37,* 346–351.

Piper, M.C., Mazer, B., Silver, K.M., et al. (1988). Resolution of neurological symptoms in high-risk infants during the first two years of life. *Developmental Medicine and Child Neurology, 30,* 26–35.

Pranzatelli, M.R. (1996). Oral pharmacotherapy for the movement disorders of cerebral palsy. *Journal of Child Neurology, 11*(1), S13–S22.

Reilly, S., Skuse, D., & Poblete, X. (1996). Prevalence of feeding problems and oral motor dysfunction in children with cerebral palsy: A community survey. *Journal of Pediatrics, 129,* 877–882.

Rempel, G.R., Colwell, S.O., & Nelson, R.P. (1988). Growth in children with cerebral palsy fed via gastrostomy. *Pediatrics, 82,* 857–862.

Robinson, R.O. (1973). The frequency of other handicaps in children with cerebral palsy. *Developmental Medicine and Child Neurology, 15,* 305–312.

Russman, B.S., & Gage, J.R. (1989). Cerebral palsy. *Current Problems in Pediatrics, 19,* 65–111.

Sankey, R.J., Anderson, D.M., & Young, J.A. (1989). Characteristics of ankle-foot orthoses for management of the spastic lower limb. *Developmental Medicine and Child Neurology, 31,* 466–470.

Schenk-Rootlieb, A.J.F., van Nieuwenhuizen, O., van der Graaf, Y., et al. (1992). The prevalence of cerebral visual disturbance in children with cerebral palsy. *Developmental Medicine and Child Neurology, 34,* 473–480.

Scher, M.S., Belfar, H., Martin, J., et al. (1991). Destructive brain lesions of presumed fetal onset: Antepartum causes of cerebral palsy. *Pediatrics, 88,* 898–906.

Schultz-Hurlburt, B., & Tervo, R.C. (1982). Wheelchair users at a children's rehabilitation center: Attributes and management. *Developmental Medicine and Child Neurology, 24,* 54–60.

Scrutton, D. (1989). The early management of hips in cerebral palsy. *Developmental Medicine and Child Neurology, 31,* 108–116.

Smelt, H.R. (1989). Effect of an inhibitive weight-bearing mitt on tone reduction and functional performance in a child with cerebral palsy. *Physi-*

cal and Occupational Therapy in Pediatrics, 9, 53–80.

Smith, L.H., & Harris, S.R. (1985). Upper extremity inhibitive casting for a child with cerebral palsy. *Physical and Occupational Therapy in Pediatrics, 5,* 71–79.

Stallings, V.A., Charney, E.B., Davies, J.C., et al. (1993a). Nutritional status and growth of children with diplegic or hemiplegic cerebral palsy. *Developmental Medicine and Child Neurology, 35,* 997–1006.

Stallings, V.A., Charney, E.B., Davies, J.C., et al. (1993b). Nutrition-related growth failure of children with quadriplegic cerebral palsy. *Developmental Medicine and Child Neurology, 35,* 126–138.

Stanley, F.J., Blair, E., Hockey, A., et al. (1993). Spastic quadriplegia in Western Australia: A genetic epidemiological study: I. Case population and perinatal risk factors. *Developmental Medicine and Child Neurology, 35,* 191–201.

Trahan, J., & Marcoux, S. (1994). Factors associated with the inability of children with cerebral palsy to walk at six years: A retrospective. *Developmental Medicine and Child Neurology, 36,* 787–795.

Treviranus, J., & Tannock, R. (1987). A scanning computer access system for children with severe physical disabilities. *American Journal of Occupational Therapy, 41,* 733–738.

Volpe, J.J. (1990). Brain injury in the premature infant: Is it preventable? *Pediatric Research, 27,* S28–S33.

Watt, J.M., Robinson, C.M., & Grace, M.G. (1989). Early prognosis for ambulation of neonatal intensive care survivors with cerebral palsy. *Developmental Medicine and Child Neurology, 31,* 766–773.

World Health Organization. (1980). *International classification of impairments, disabilities, and handicap.* Geneva, Switzerland: Author.

Yasukawa, A. (1990). Upper extremity casting: Adjunct treatment for a child with hemiplegia cerebral palsy. *American Journal of Occupational Therapy, 44,* 840–846.

Young, R.R. (1994). Spasticity: A review. *Neurology, 44*(Suppl.), 512–520.

Zigler, E. (1981). A plea to end the use of the patterning treatment for retarded children. *American Journal of Orthopsychiatry, 51,* 388–390.

25 Neural Tube Defects

Gregory S. Liptak

Upon completion of this chapter, the reader will:

- be able to define spina bifida and meningomyelocele
- know the incidence and multifactorial causes of neural tube defects
- be knowledgeable about the effects of meningomyelocele on the spinal cord and brain
- understand the variability and secondary effects of meningomyelocele
- understand strategies for intervention, the need for multidisciplinary care, and goals for independence

Neural tube defects (NTDs) refer to a group of malformations of the spinal cord, brain, and vertebrae. The resulting disorders vary in severity according to their location, the extent of bony opening, and the exposure of spinal cord or brain. The three major NTDs are **spina bifida, encephalocele,** and **anencephaly.** The most common of these is spina bifida, which refers to a split of a section of the **vertebral arches.** This split may be isolated or may occur with a protruding **meningeal** sac that may contain a part of the spinal cord. The most common form of spina bifida, **spina bifida occulta,** is also the most benign. Approximately 10% of the general population has this hidden separation at the beginning of their central nervous systems, a portion of the vertebral arches. It is often accompanied by a fat pad, dermal sinus, hairy tuft, or dimple in the lower back (lumbo-sacral) region. Individuals with spina bifida occulta do not have a sac or protruding spinal cord and do not have any symptoms. Some individuals may be born with a membranous covering of the spinal cord, called a **meningocele.** Because the spinal cord itself is not entrapped, these individuals usually have no symptoms during childhood. When spina bifida is associated with both a sac and a malformed spinal cord, the condition is called meningomyelocele (or myelomeningocele). This disorder is associated with a complex array of symptoms that includes flaccid paralysis, sensory loss below the lesion, and hydrocephalus. Most meningomyeloceles are "open," and a portion of the spinal cord is visible at birth as an open sac overlying part of the vertebral column (Figure 25.1).

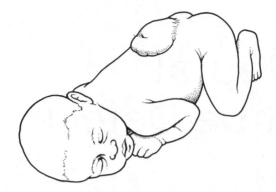

Figure 25.1.   A newborn with meningomyelocele. The sac (meningocele) covers the malformed spinal cord and rests above the defect in the vertebral column (spina bifida).

The other two forms of NTDs are both less common and more severe than spina bifida and meningomyelocele. Encephalocele refers to a malformation of the skull that allows a portion of the brain, which is usually malformed, to protrude. The vast majority of encephaloceles occur in the occipital region of the brain (Adetioloye, Dare, & Oyelami, 1993). Affected children have mental retardation, hydrocephalus, spastic diplegia, and seizures. Anencephaly indicates an even more severe congenital malformation of the skull and brain in which no neural development occurs above the brainstem. About half of fetuses with anencephaly are spontaneously aborted; those who are liveborn rarely survive infancy.

This chapter focuses on the disabilities associated with meningomyelocele. It also discusses approaches to treatment, the effects of the disability on psychosocial and cognitive development, and the psychological and economic stress that can affect the families of children with this disorder.

PREVALENCE OF NEURAL TUBE DEFECTS

The prevalence of NTDs varies remarkably among countries. In the United States, the prevalence of meningomyelocele is approximately 60 in 100,000 births; of encephalocele, 10 in 100,000; and of anencephaly, 20 in 100,000. In Wales and Ireland, the prevalence is 3–4 times higher, yet in Africa it is much lower (Shurtleff & Lemire, 1995; Yen, Khoury, Erickson, et al., 1992). This variability is probably a reflection of both genetic influences in certain ethnic groups and environmental factors. In addition, females are affected 3–7 times as frequently as males. The incidence also increases with maternal age and with lower socioeconomic status.

The prevalence of NTDs worldwide is falling as a result of a number of factors. Developed countries are now using maternal serum testing to screen prenatally for NTDs (Roberts, Moore, Cragan, et al., 1995). Approximately 40% of couples, upon discovering that they are carrying an affected fetus, choose to terminate the pregnancy. In addition, the association of NTDs with folic acid deficiency has caused obstetricians to generally recommend folic acid supplementation during pregnancy. The decline in the incidence of NTDs, however, preceded these innovations, suggesting that other factors, including improved nutrition, may be operative (Shurtleff & Lemire, 1995). In the 1990s, the overall incidence of NTDs is only half what it was in the 1960s.

THE ORIGIN OF NEURAL TUBE DEFECTS

The malformation causing NTDs occurs by 26 days after fertilization of the egg during the period of neurulation (Figure 25.2) (see Chapter 14). By this time, the neural tube has folded over to become the spinal cord and vertebral arches, the beginnings of the central nervous system (CNS). During this process, if a portion of the neural tube does not close completely, a NTD results, and the spinal cord is malformed. There may be as little as 2 days separating the development of anencephaly and meningomyelocele. Although the mechanism of neural tube closure is not fully understood, it seems likely that it does not simply close like a zipper but has multiple sites of closure (Van Allen, Kalousek, Chernoff, et al., 1993). Each of these sites may be under separate genetic control with differential sensitivity to various environmental factors (Golden & Chernoff, 1995; Urui & Oi, 1995).

Abnormalities in two genes, PAX3 and 5,10-methylene tetrahydrofolate reductase, have been associated with the development of NTDs (Chatkupt, Hol, Shugart, et al., 1995; Scott, Weir, Molloy, et al., 1994; van der Put, Steegers-Theunissen, Frosst, et al., 1995). PAX3 is a transcription control gene involved in anterior-posterior closure of the body axis (Baldwin, Hoth, Macina, et al., 1995). 5,10-methylene tetrahydrofolate reductase is an enzyme involved in

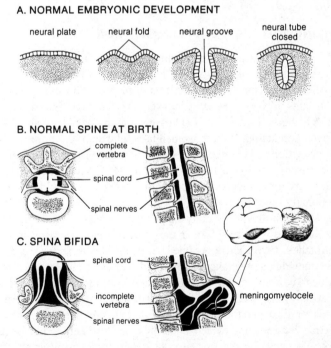

A. NORMAL EMBRYONIC DEVELOPMENT

neural plate   neural fold   neural groove   neural tube closed

B. NORMAL SPINE AT BIRTH

complete vertebra
spinal cord
spinal nerves

C. SPINA BIFIDA

spinal cord
incomplete vertebra
spinal nerves
meningomyelocele

Figure 25.2.   Spina bifida with meningomyelocele. a) The typical formation of the neural tube (i.e., the precursor of the spinal column) during the first month of gestation. b) Complete closure of the neural groove has occurred, and the vertebral column and spinal cord appear normal in the cross-section on the left and in the longitudinal section on the right. c) Incomplete closure of an area of the spine is called spina bifida and may be accompanied by a sac-like abnormality of the spinal cord, the meningomyelocele. As nerves do not normally form below this malformation, the child is paralyzed below that point.

the conversion of the amino acid homocysteine to methionine. It is not known how a deficiency of this enzyme predisposes to NTDs, but supplementation with its co-factor, folic acid, reduces the risk of NTD in both affected families and in the general population (Daly, Kirke, Malloy, et al., 1995; Steegers-Theunissen, 1995). Other conditions that have been associated with the development of NTDs include chromosomal disorders (trisomy 13 and 18); maternal exposure to the antiepileptic drugs valproic acid (Depakene, Depakote) and carbamazepine (Tegretol); and to the acne medication isotretinoin (Accutane) (Davis, Peters, & McTavish, 1994); excessive maternal use of alcohol or hyperthermia (e.g., saunas) during pregnancy; and maternal diabetes (Sadler, Robinson, & Msall, 1995). Excessive free radical formation has been suggested as a teratogenic factor in a number of these predisposing conditions (Shurtleff & Lemire, 1995).

It is unclear whether the neural damage in NTDs results simply from the malformed spinal cord or the combination of malformation and the inflammatory effects of chronic exposure of the open cord to amniotic fluid. In an intriguing experiment, surgeons performed intrauterine surgery during the second trimester on sheep fetuses that had an induced spina bifida. In the surgery, they covered the open spine with a patch so that it would be protected from prolonged exposure to potentially corrosive amniotic fluid (Meuli, Meuli-Simmen, Hutchins, et al., 1995). After birth, these sheep were found to have less neural damage than the control group. This suggests the possibility that prenatal surgery in the future may be able to preserve some neurological function in affected human fetuses.

PREVENTION USING FOLIC ACID SUPPLEMENTATION

Although this chapter focuses on the treatment of children with meningomyelocele, prevention is possible because of the apparent strong link between NTDs and folic acid (also called folate) deficiency. Although the mechanism of action of the vitamin folic acid is unclear, it may protect against NTDs in its role as a free radical scavenger (Chatkupt, Skurnick, Jagg, et al., 1994). Couples who have had one child with a NTD have a recurrence risk about 30 times higher (3 in 100) than the general population. If these women take folic acid (0.4 milligrams per day) at or before the time of conception and continue this supplementation for the first 3 months of the pregnancy, however, their recurrence risk is reduced by 70% (MRC Vitamin Study Research Group, 1991). (Women who have a first-degree relative with a NTD also should take 0.4 milligrams per day peri-conceptionally.)

Studies also have shown that daily supplemental doses of folic acid can reduce the incidence of new cases of NTDs by at least 50% in the general population (Bower & Stanley, 1992; Werler, Shapiro, & Mitchell, 1993). Therefore, the U.S. Public Health Service recommends that all women who are contemplating a pregnancy take 0.4 milligrams of supplemental folic acid per day while they are trying to conceive and for the first 12 weeks of pregnancy (Centers for Disease Control, 1992; Daly et al., 1995). Because many pregnancies are unplanned, however, efforts are underway to supplement certain staple foods such as bread, flour, and rice with folic acid. (It is intriguing to note that there is experimental evidence that this may also help to reduce the occurrence of heart disease among the general population [Boushey, Beresford, Owens, et al., 1995; Motulsky, 1996].)

PRENATAL DIAGNOSIS

NTDs can be diagnosed prenatally by several methods (see Chapter 3) (Main & Mennuti, 1986). Most programs first measure levels of alpha-fetoprotein (AFP) in the mother's serum during the

16th–18th week of pregnancy (Bock, 1992; Candenas, Villa, Fernandez Collar, et al., 1995). AFP is a chemical typically found in fetal spinal fluid. In the presence of an open meningomye-locele, encephalocele, or anencephaly, AFP will leak from the open spine into the amniotic fluid. Some AFP will subsequently enter the maternal circulation where it can be detected. Because there are other conditions in both mother and fetus that can lead to elevated AFP levels, maternal serum AFP (MSAFP) is used only to screen for NTDs. After a positive AFP screen has been obtained, a high-resolution ultrasound is used to detect specific abnormalities of the fetal head and back consistent with a NTD (Babcock, 1995; Ennever & Lave, 1995). If no abnormalities are observed on ultrasound but a NTD is still suspected, amniocentesis is performed, and the levels of two substances in the amniotic fluid—AFP and an enzyme specific for NTDs called acetylcholinesterase (ACH)—are measured. ACH can be found in fetal cerebrospinal fluid (CSF) and its presence in the amniotic fluid suggests leakage from an open spinal cord. The combination of elevated levels of AFP and ACH together with abnormal ultrasonographic findings make the diagnosis of NTD in the fetus quite certain. Even if a family is not considering a therapeutic abortion, obtaining a prenatal diagnosis can help members plan for the special needs of their child with a NTD. For example, they may opt to deliver the child at a specialty center via a cesarean section and to have the back lesion closed early, precautions that some believe may decrease the severity of paralysis in infants with meningomyelocele (Shurtleff, Luthy, Nyberg, et al., 1994).

TREATMENT IN THE NEWBORN PERIOD

When an infant is born with meningomyelocele, the first two priorities are to prevent infection from occurring through the soft tissue defect on the back and to protect exposed nerves and structures from physical injury. Both of these goals can be accomplished by the surgical closure of the defect within the first few days of life (Charney, Weller, Sutton, et al., 1985). In addition, a shunting procedure is often required shortly after the back closure to prevent CSF, which can no longer leak from an open meningomyelocele, from accumulating and causing a potentially life-threatening hydrocephalus (McLone, 1992).

PRIMARY NEUROLOGICAL IMPAIRMENTS IN CHILDREN WITH MENINGOMYELOCELE

The malformation leading to meningomyelocele can affect the entire CNS (Dahl, Ahlsten, Carlson, et al., 1995; Gilbert, Jones, Rorke, et al., 1986). Table 25.1 illustrates some of the brain abnormalities commonly found in children with meningomyelocele. These include multiple disorders of the cranial nerve nuclei (e.g., the visual gaze centers of the brain can be affected, leading to strabismus) (Lennerstrand, Gallo, & Samuelsson, 1990); excessive fluid or splitting of the spinal cord above the primary lesion resulting in additional motor impairment (Dias & Pang, 1995); and diffuse changes in the brain's cortex associated with cognitive impairments. The primary neurological abnormalities, however, are paralysis, loss of sensation, and Chiari malformation with associated hydrocephalus.

Paralysis and Loss of Sensation

The extent of motor paralysis and sensory loss in meningomyelocele depends on the location of the defect in the spinal cord (Figure 25.3), as sensory and motor function below that point are

Table 25.1. Malformations of the brain frequently seen in children with meningomyelocele

Malformation	Prevalence (%)
Dysplasia of cerebral cortex	92
Displaced nerve cells	44
Small gyri with abnormal layers	40
Abnormalities of layers	24
Profound primitive development	24
Small gyri with normal layers	12
Malformations of the brainstem	76
Malformations of the cerebellum	72

Adapted from Gilbert, Jones, Rorke, et al. (1986).

typically impaired. Children with defects at the thoracic (chest) or high-lumbar (L1 or L2, upper back) level have paralysis that affects the legs and causes variable weakness and sensory loss in the abdomen and lower body region (Figure 25.4). Children with defects at L3 can flex their hips and extend their knees, but their ankles and toes are paralyzed. Children with low-lumbar (L4 or L5, low back) lesions can flex their hips and extend their knees and ankles but typically have weak or absent ankle-toe flexion and hip extension. Children with sacral (low back-buttocks) lesions usually have only mild weakness of their ankles or toes.

All individuals with meningomyelocele experience a loss of sensation that is more marked on the back of the legs than on the front. Furthermore, most affected children lose sensation around the anus, genitalia, and feet. The loss of motor and sensory function is not always symmetrical; one side may have better motor function or sensation than the other (Figure 25.5).

Chiari Malformation and Hydrocephalus

Almost all children with meningomyelocele above the sacral level have a Chiari type II (also called Arnold-Chiari) malformation of the brain (Griebel, Oakes, & Worley, 1991; Rauzzino & Oakes, 1995). In this abnormality, the brainstem and part of the cerebellum are displaced downward toward the neck, rather than remaining within the skull (Figure 25.6), as if the spinal cord had been pulled downward prior to birth. Symptoms and signs of spinal cord compression can result, including difficulty swallowing, choking, hoarseness, breath-holding, apnea, stiffness in the arms, and a tendency to hold the head arched backward (opisthotonos). There also have been rare deaths from cardiorespiratory arrest (Charney, Rorke, Sutton, et al., 1987). Fortunately, although most children with meningomyelocele have a Chiari malformation, few develop symptoms of compression. When symptoms develop, they can be treated surgically by a decompression procedure, in which the lower back of the skull and the arches of some of the cervical vertebral bodies are removed to provide additional space for the brainstem. Because these procedures are done rarely, the long-term outcome remains uncertain.

Associated with the Chiari malformation is hydrocephalus (Table 25.2). This complication occurs in 60%–95% of children with meningomyelocele and is more common in higher-level lesions (Griebel et al., 1991). Hydrocephalus develops as a result of an abnormal CSF flow pattern and can be diagnosed by ultrasonography in the prenatal period and infancy and by computed tomography (CT) or magnetic resonance imaging (MRI) in older children. These neuroimaging studies will show enlarged ventricular spaces in the brain if hydrocephalus is present.

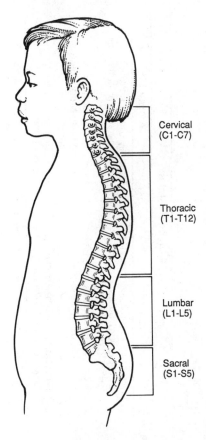

Figure 25.3.   The vertebral column is divided into seven neck (cervical), twelve chest (thoracic), five back (lumbar), and five lower-back (sacral) vertebrae. Meninogmyelocele most commonly affects the thoraco-lumbar region.

Hydrocephalus is treated with a shunting procedure. Shunting diverts cerebrospinal fluid from the enlarged ventricular system to another place in the body where it can be better absorbed. The most common type of shunt, a ventriculo-peritoneal (V-P) shunt, drains fluid into the child's abdominal cavity (Figure 25.7). Shunts can become blocked or infected, especially during the first year of life. By 2–3 years of age, approximately half the shunts inserted have failed and have been replaced (Liptak & McDonald, 1986). In infants, signs of a blocked shunt may include excessive head growth and a tense "soft spot" (anterior fontanelle) on the head. In children older than 2 years, the skull bones will have fused, and a blocked shunt results in symptoms of lethargy, headache, vomiting, and irritability as the pressure builds inside the head. Increased intracranial pressure can lead to paralysis of the sixth cranial nerve (VI) and resultant strabismus and double vision; paralysis of upward gaze also may occur. A child with an infected shunt will display similar symptoms but will also have a fever and an elevated white blood cell count. More subtle symptoms of a partial shunt failure include a change in personality, decline in school performance, or weakness of the arms or legs.

Table 25.2. Degree of paralysis and functional implications

Degree of paralysis	Hydrocephalus (%)	Mobility status	
		Childhood	Adulthood
Thoracic (T1–T12) or high lumbar (L1, L2)	90	Will require extensive orthosis like parapodium, reciprocal gait orthosis, or HKAFO[a]	Typically use wheelchairs; community ambulation rare
Lumbar, L3, L4	80	Will ambulate with less extensive orthotics, using crutches	Most use wheelchairs; community ambulation is uncommon
Low lumbar, L5, and sacral (S1–S4)	65	Will ambulate with minimal or no bracing, with or without crutches	Most continue to be community ambulators

From Charney, E.B. (1990). Myelomeningocele. In M.W. Schwartz (Ed.), *Pediatric primary care: A problem oriented approach* (p. 663). St. Louis: C.V. Mosby; reprinted by permission.

[a]HKAFO = Hip-knee-ankle-foot orthosis.

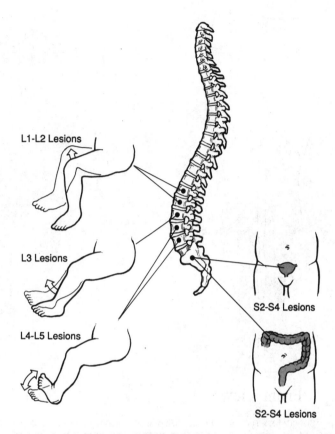

L1-L2 Lesions

L3 Lesions

L4-L5 Lesions

S2-S4 Lesions

S2-S4 Lesions

Figure 25.4.   The effects of various levels of meninogmyelocele on the child's ability to move lower extremities and to control bowel and bladder function.

Early recognition of shunt failure or infection is critical, as both can be life threatening. A child who develops new neurological symptoms should be evaluated immediately for shunt failure. If a blocked shunt is suspected, the physician may order a neuroimaging study as well as radiographs of the shunt system (shunt series) to determine if the ventricles have increased in size or if the tubing is broken or kinked. To detect increased intracranial pressure, a neurosurgeon may insert a needle into the shunt tubing to measure CSF pressure. If the shunt is found to be obstructed, the blocked portion will be replaced surgically with a new catheter and/or valve.

As an interim measure to treat shunt failure, the oral medications acetazolamide (Diamox), furosemide (Lasix), or dexamethasone (Decadron) may be given. These drugs inhibit CSF production and thereby lower the intracranial pressure until surgery can be performed. The long-term effects of these medications on children with hydrocephalus has not been evaluated. If the shunt is infected, the child needs to receive intravenous antibiotics. It also may be necessary to remove the infected shunt and, after antibiotic treatment, replace it with a new one. It is important to emphasize that the individual with hydrocephalus will require a working shunt throughout the life span.

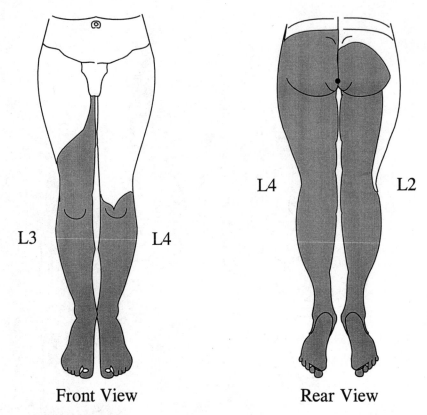

Front View   Rear View

Figure 25.5.   Sensory loss in child with L3- to L4-level meningomyelocele. The back of legs has more loss than the front. Asymmetry of sensory or motor loss is common; sensory loss may not completely correlate with loss of motor function.

ASSOCIATED IMPAIRMENTS AND MEDICAL COMPLICATIONS

The combination of the NTD, hydrocephalus, and other malformations of the brain leads to associated impairments and places the individual at risk for a number of medical complications. The associated impairments involve mobility, cognitive impairments, seizure disorders, and visual impairment, while medical complications include musculoskeletal deformities, spinal curvatures and humps, urinary and bowel dysfunction, skin sores, weight and stature abnormalities, sexual dysfunction, and allergy to latex. Many of these impairments and complications can be prevented or their impact lessened by painstaking clinical care and monitoring by the family, the child, and healthcare professionals.

Mobility

In discussing mobility, it is important to remember that the higher the level of the meningomyelocele and the greater the muscle weakness, the more ambulation will be impaired (McDonald, 1995). Even in children with low-level lesions (L4 and below), however, there is likely to be a significant impairment in mobility. Many infants with meningomyelocele have delayed rolling and sitting skills. Most affected infants, regardless of their level of lesion, learn to belly crawl com-

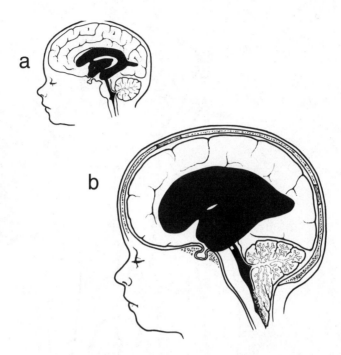

Figure 25.6.   a) The typical brain. b) The Chiari II malformation and hydrocephalus. The brainstem and part of the cerebellum are displaced downward toward the neck region, which can cause symptoms such as difficulty swallowing and hoarseness.

mando style as their first means of mobility. Infants with strong voluntary hip flexion and some knee movement may eventually assume the all-fours crawl, but often not until after 1 year of age.

Children with sacral (S1, S2) lesions generally learn to walk well by 2 or 3 years of age with bracing at the ankles or no bracing at all. Children with mid-lumbar (L3) paralysis often require crutches and bracing up to the hip (Table 25.2). Children with thoracic or high-lumbar (L1 and L2) paralysis may eventually stand upright and walk but only with support of the hips, knees, and ankles. This support may be provided by extensive bracing and/or mobility devices such as a parapodium (an external flexible skeleton, shown in Figure 25.8a); reciprocal gait orthosis (RGO) (Guidera, Smith, Raney, et al., 1993); or hip-knee-ankle-foot orthosis (HKAFO) used with crutches or walker (Figure 25.8b).

As children with L3- and L4-level lesions approach adolescence and their center of gravity and relative strength change, most will rely increasingly on wheelchairs for mobility (Table 25.2) (Hunt & Poulton, 1995; McDonald, Jaffe, Mosca, et al., 1991). Because most children with meningomyelocele will not become effective community ambulators, the supplemental or primary use of a wheelchair should be considered by early adolescence as it offers the advantages of speed, efficiency, and attractiveness (Liptak, Shurtleff, Bloss, et al., 1992).

The likelihood of ambulation is not only a function of the height of the lesion and associated muscle weaknesses, but also of the cognitive functioning of the child, the involvement of the parents, and the therapy program. Children with high-level paralysis are more likely to stand upright and walk, at least for exercise, if they have typical intelligence, regular ambulation therapy, and

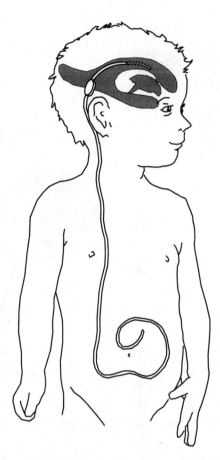

Figure 25.7.   Ventriculo-peritoneal shunt, which has been placed for hydrocephalus. A plastic tube is inserted into one of the lateral ventricles and connected to a one-way valve. Another tube runs under the skin from the valve to the abdominal cavity. Enough extra tubing is left in the abdomen to uncoil as the child grows.

parents who are committed to carrying out walking therapy at home (Charney, Melchionni, & Smith, 1991). For those children with a combination of high-level lesion and mental retardation, walking may not be a realistic goal, and wheelchair training should start early. Motorized wheelchairs can be used beginning at a 24-month developmental level (McDonald, 1995).

Cognitive Impairments

Approximately three quarters of children with meningomyelocele have intelligence that falls within the low-average range (Friedrich, Lovejoy, Shaffer, et al., 1991). Most of the remaining one quarter have mental retardation requiring intermittent supports. The few children with meningomyelocele who have mental retardation requiring extensive supports usually have had a complicating brain infection resulting from an infected shunt or prenatal hydrocephalus with a head circumference at birth well above the 95th percentile (Brumfield, Aronin, Cloud, et al., 1995).

Although the majority of affected children have average intellectual function, they tend to show significant impairments in perceptual skills, organizational abilities, attention, speed of motor response, memory, and hand function (Snow, 1994; Wills, Holmbeck, Dillon, et al., 1990). As a result, many of these children have learning disabilities (see Chapter 23) (Williamson, 1987). All children with meningomyelocele and hydrocephalus should have a formal psychoeducational evaluation prior to school entry. This assessment can identify their capabilities and weaknesses and allow modification of the school environment (Rowley-Kelly & Reigel, 1992).

Seizure Disorders

Similar to individuals with other significant developmental disabilities such as mental retardation and cerebral palsy, approximately 15% of individuals with meningomyelocele develop a seizure disorder (Noetzel, 1989). The seizures usually are generalized tonic-clonic and respond well to antiepileptic medication (see Chapter 26). If a new seizure develops, however, a blocked shunt or shunt infection should be investigated.

Visual Impairments

Strabismus is present in about 20% of children with meningomyelocele and often requires surgical correction. This may result from abnormalities of the visual gaze center or from increased intracranial pressure caused by a malfunctioning ventricular shunt.

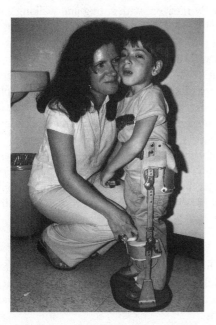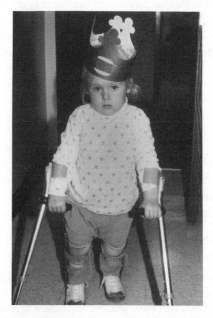

Figure 25.8.   Children using the parapodium (left) and hip-knee-ankle-foot orthosis (HKAFO) with crutches (right).

Musculoskeletal Deformities

With partial or total paralysis, muscle imbalances and lack of mobility may lead to deformities around joints (Westcott, Dynes, Remer, et al., 1992). This can occur even prior to birth. For example, children with meningomyelocele may develop a club foot as a result of the foot being stuck in one position pressed against the uterine wall. Treatment of club foot involves using serial casting during the first 3–4 months of life to gradually straighten the deformity. Corrective surgery can then follow at 4 months to 1 year of age (Swank & Dias, 1992). Other ankle and foot deformities may require surgical intervention to facilitate proper foot placement in shoes. Bracing is used to help maintain physiological positioning of joints and should be monitored to minimize the likelihood of skin breakdown over bony prominences.

Muscle imbalance and lack of movement also can lead to hip deformities. Surgical correction is controversial and may be appropriate only for those children with low lumbar–level paralysis who have the potential for functional ambulation (Roberts & Evans, 1993; Sherk, Uppal, Lane, et al., 1991). In general, surgery should be used only to improve function and not for cosmetic reasons (Karol, 1995). It should be noted that loss of muscle strength and inactivity may predispose affected children to pathological fractures.

Spinal Curvatures and Humps

Almost 90% of children with a meningomyelocele above the sacral level have spinal curvatures and humps (Mayfield, 1991). These deformities include scoliosis (a spinal curvature), kyphosis (a spinal hump), and kyphoscoliosis (a combination of both conditions) (Figure 25.9). Scoliosis and kyphosis may be present before birth (congenital) or develop in later childhood (acquired). If untreated, spinal deformities may eventually interfere with sitting and walking and may even decrease the functional capacity of the lungs. Scoliosis greater than 25° requires an orthotic (molded plastic shield-like jacket) support (see Chapter 15). Despite this, the curvature often progresses, and surgery may be necessary (Mayfield, 1991). Surgical correction involves a spinal fusion with bone grafts, often with two surgical procedures—one anterior and one posterior—and the use of metal rods (internal fixation) for stabilization of the spinal column (Vivani, Raducan, Bednar, et al., 1993). Children with congenital rather than developmental scoliosis generally respond poorly to orthotic treatment and may require spinal fusion at younger ages.

Kyphosis is generally located in the lumbar spine and may measure as much as 80°–90° at birth. The hump on the spine may be rigid and may worsen over time. Surgical removal of the deformity (called a kyphectomy) in infancy has had a high incidence of complications and recurrences (Mayfield, 1991). When performed in school-age children, however, kyphectomy has been quite effective (Lintner & Lindseth, 1994).

Urinary Dysfunction

Because the bladder, urinary outlet, and rectum are all controlled by nerves that leave the spinal cord in the lower sacrum (Figure 25.4), bladder and bowel dysfunction are present in virtually all children with meningomyelocele. Even children with sacral lesions and normal leg movement often have bladder and bowel problems.

The bladder has two major functions: to store urine that has been produced by the kidney and to empty the urine once the bladder is full. Children with meningomyelocele often have dif-

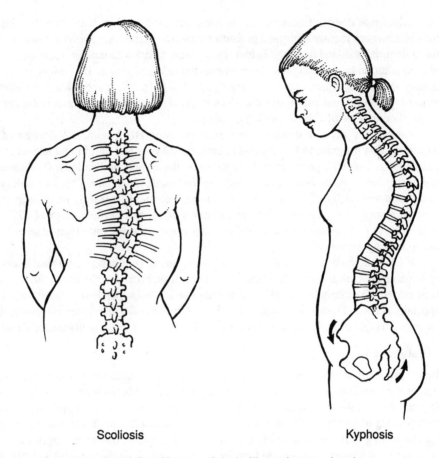

Scoliosis   Kyphosis

Figure 25.9.   Common spinal deformities associated with meningomyelocele.

ficulty with both functions and are consequently incontinent (Vereecken, 1992). In addition, the inability to completely empty the bladder of urine may predispose the child to infection of the bladder and/or kidneys. The combination of a tight bladder outlet and increased tone in the bladder also may produce severe kidney damage (Anderson & Travers, 1993).

In order to detect early structural damage, the urinary tract is imaged using ultrasonography at 6- to 12-month intervals from infancy. Ultrasound examination also permits the identification of malformations, such as horseshoe kidneys, which are more common in children with meningomyelocele.

Bladder function is evaluated using a cystometrogram. If elevated pressure is found in the bladder it must be reduced to avoid permanent kidney damage. For many years, surgeons performed an ileostomy, a surgical procedure in which urine is diverted from the bladder, through the abdominal wall, and into an external collection vessel (Krahn & Johnson, 1993). Now, reducing bladder pressure is accomplished by teaching clean intermittent catheterization (CIC). In this procedure, parents are taught to insert a clean, but not sterile, catheter (tube) through the urethra and into the bladder. This commonly is done four times a day to drain urine. Using CIC correctly, urine does not accumulate, become infected, or flow back into the kidneys. Some infants, however, require a surgical procedure called a vesicostomy, in which an opening through the abdominal wall and into the bladder allows urine to drain directly into the diaper.

In addition to assessing bladder pressure, the infant also is monitored for the occurrence of urinary infections, which occur in at least half of individuals. If these happen frequently, long-term prophylactic oral antibiotics are given to prevent infections. Alternatively, antibiotics can be instilled into the bladder through the catheter.

Attempts to achieve urinary continence are generally begun at 3–4 years of age. For a catheterization program to be successful, both the parents and child must adhere to the recommendations. This CIC program may be aided by the use of medications. Oxybutynin chloride (Ditropan) can be given orally or instilled into the bladder to diminish bladder wall contractions, and pseudoephedrine (Sudafed) or imipramine chloride (Tofranil) may be given orally to enhance storage of urine. About 70% of children who receive a combination of CIC and medications achieve continence during the elementary school years despite their bladder dysfunctions due to meningomyelocele.

If CIC and medication are unsuccessful in producing continence, a surgical intervention may be undertaken. One approach is a bladder augmentation procedure in which the bladder capacity is increased (Cher & Allen, 1993). Another approach is an appendico-vesicostomy, in which the appendix is used to connect the bladder to the abdominal wall, permitting catheterization through the appendix (Keating, Rink, & Adams, 1993). These approaches are often used simultaneously.

Bowel Dysfunction

Bowel problems in children with meningomyelocele are related to uncoordinated propulsive action of the intestines and an ineffectual anal sphincter, combined with a lack of rectal sensation (Agnarsson, Warde, McCarthy, et al., 1993). Constipation is common and may be interspersed with periods of overflow diarrhea. Lack of sensation and failure of external sphincter function lead to soiling that can be socially devastating. Attempts at bowel management can begin as soon as the child starts eating solid food by encouraging foods that are high in fiber. Between 2½ and 4 years of age, timed potty-sitting can be tried after every meal to take advantage of the post-feeding gastrocolic reflex. If, after several months, bowel control has not been achieved, parents may be instructed to administer a daily stool softener (e.g., dioctyl sodium [Colace]); a laxative containing senna (e.g., Senokot); a fiber supplement (e.g., Metamucil); or a nightly rectal suppository (e.g., bisacodyl [Dulcolax]) that will facilitate more complete bowel emptying. Daily enemas using water also have been successful (Liptak & Revell, 1992). Two newer surgical procedures, one that connects the appendix to the colon and the other that provides a direct connection between the abdominal wall and the colon, allow forward-flowing irrigation of the colon on a regular basis. These approaches show promise for some children in whom more conventional bowel techniques have failed (Squire, Kiely, Ransley, et al., 1993). For older children with low-level (sacral) meningomyeloceles, biofeedback may be used to improve rectal sensation (Benninga, van der Hoeven, Wijers, et al., 1994).

Achievement of bladder and bowel continence is both a realistic and critical part of a child's development (King, Currie, & Wright, 1994). Competence in toileting, a basic activity of daily living, is necessary for social growth toward independence. Prevention of soiling, wetness, and odor also enhances the child's self-esteem.

Skin Sores

Skin sores or decubitus ulcers frequently occur in children with meningomyelocele, whose weight-bearing surfaces (e.g., feet, buttocks) are not sensitive to pain (Wood, Evans, Schall-reuter, et al., 1993). These children may sustain injuries that they do not feel. This problem becomes more frequent during adolescence and, if not caught early, may require prolonged hospitalizations for **debridement,** skin grafting, and intravenous antibiotics. The best treatment is prevention. Certain common-sense rules should be followed: Use sunscreen to prevent sunburn, replace tight-fitting shoes or braces, avoid giving the child hot baths, and do not let him or her crawl about on rough or hot surfaces. For children in wheelchairs, pressure sores on the buttocks or coccyx can be prevented by modifying the wheelchair with an adaptive seating system, by performing regular wheelchair pushups to relieve pressure, and by frequently changing position. Existing small sores should be treated by alleviating pressure and using wet-to-dry saline-soaked dressings or artificial skin preparations such as Tegaderm or Duoderm. If ulcers do not heal in a reasonable amount of time, an underlying infection of soft tissue or bone may be present, requiring surgical debridement and intravenous antibiotic treatment.

Weight and Stature Abnormalities

Children with meningomyelocele, particularly those with thoracic to L-2 lesions, are at increased risk for obesity as a result of their decreased energy expenditure (Polito, DelGaizo, Di-Manso, et al., 1995). About two thirds of these children are significantly overweight. Attention should be directed at increasing involvement in physical activities such as stretching; aerobic conditioning (e.g., wheelchair sports); and strength training (e.g., the lifting of free weights). Exercise should be combined with dietary restrictions on sweets and fats (Duncan & Ogle, 1995). Affected children also are likely to have short stature. This results from a combination of failure of growth of the legs, spinal curves, and, occasionally, deficiency of growth hormone (Roten-stein, Adams, & Reigel, 1995).

Sexual Dysfunction

Although 75% of postpubertal males with meningomyelocele can have erections, most do not have control of them. Furthermore, retrograde ejaculations, in which the semen is discharged into the bladder, are common. Penile implants; injection or application of prostaglandin prior to coitus (Kim & McVary, 1995); and the use of vacuum devices (Chen, Godschalk, Katz, et al., 1995) can help males achieve erections.

Females with meningomyelocele have normal fertility and, if sexually active, should use the same precautions as the general population. They have approximately a 4% risk of having a child with a NTD (McDonald, 1995). Although many are able to experience orgasm during sexual intercourse, they usually have decreased genital sensation and less sexually stimulated lubrication. As a result, frequent intercourse without adequate lubrication may lead to vaginal sores. Precocious puberty (e.g., breast development 1–2 years before usual) is a common occurrence in females due to a disorder of the hypothalamus (Elias & Sadeghi-Nejad, 1994). This can be treated with leuprolide (Lupron), a synthetic sex-hormone analogue (Kappy, Stuart, & Perelman, 1988).

Allergy to Latex

More than half of children with meningomyelocele have an allergy to latex (Pearson, Cole, & Jarvis, 1994). Although the reason for this is unclear, the allergy seems to be more common in children who have had frequent surgical procedures (Ellsworth, Merguerian, Klein, et al., 1993). This allergic reaction can be life threatening, leading to **anaphylaxis** (Dormans, Templeton, Schreiner, et al., 1995). As a result, all surgical procedures, including dental procedures, should occur in latex-free settings. Children who demonstrate latex sensitivity generally receive anti-anaphylaxis medications prior to operative procedures. Prophylaxis may also be possible. Early contact of the infant with latex should be avoided, if possible, in an effort to prevent the development of allergy (Emans, 1992). Catheterization should be performed with nonlatex catheters, and nonlatex gloves should be used during care. Toys that contain significant amounts of latex, such as balloons and rubber balls, should be avoided as should products that come into contact with the skin, such as Band-Aids and Ace bandages.

Neurological Deterioration

Neurological deterioration is not part of the natural history of meningomyelocele. Therefore, if a child's strength, bowel and bladder function, or daily living skills deteriorate, a reason should be sought. The origin of the deterioration may be a malfunctioning or blocked ventricular shunt, a tethered spinal cord, or, rarely, swelling or splitting of the spinal cord. A tethered spinal cord may result from scarring at the site of the initial surgery to close the back, from scoliosis, or from pressure of a **lipoma** (Liptak, 1996; Yamada, Iacono, Andrade, et al., 1995). Pressure or stretch on the tethered cord leads to poor circulation and diminished motor functioning.

All children who present with neurological deterioration should be evaluated for structure and function of the ventricular shunt, bladder, and spinal cord. This usually involves performing a MRI of the head and spine and a cystometrogram. A blocked shunt can be replaced, a bladder problem corrected with improved CIC or surgery, a tethered cord released, and a lipoma removed. If these complications are evaluated and treated early, additional neurological damage can be avoided.

EDUCATIONAL PROGRAMS

Referral to an early intervention program should occur by 6 months of age. Sensorimotor assessment during the child's first year should include evaluations of range of motion of joints, muscle tone, muscle strength, muscle bulk, sensation, movement skills, postural control, and sensory-integrative skills (Williamson, 1987). Treatment should focus on maintaining range of motion, enhancing strength, and moving toward standing and ambulation. Because of the considerable diversity in the degree of motor delay among these children, individualized intervention plans must be developed. Adaptive equipment should be provided as needed.

As the child moves toward school entry, it is important to perform psychoeducational testing. This permits the identification of the child's cognitive strengths and weaknesses and the development of an individualized education program and realistic expectations that will optimize the child's learning (Hurley, 1993). Physical therapy should be provided as part of the school program. Yearly reassessments will permit modification of the program based on the child's changing needs.

PSYCHOSOCIAL ISSUES FOR THE CHILD

There are many psychosocial issues for the child with meningomyelocele. During the preschool years, the achievement of independence (Erikson, 1959) may be thwarted by problems with mobility and bladder and bowel control. A sense of industry that develops in the school-age child may be reduced by the child's learning impairments as well as by his or her failure to compete with peers in sports. Difficulty in the school setting may exacerbate a preexisting poor self-image that many of these children have as a result of their physical disabilities. The feeling of being different can impair the establishment of peer relationships in both school and community (Hayden, 1985). The child's self-esteem also may be lowered if he or she must continue to wear diapers or care for an ostomy. During adolescence, lowered self-esteem also may relate to a poor body image and difficulty in dealing with the sexual changes and feelings (Blum, Resnick, Nelson, et al., 1991; Rinck, Berg, & Hafeman, 1989). Problems for the young adult with meningomyelocele may include increasing social isolation, a realization that the disability is permanent, and sexual dysfunction.

MULTIDISCIPLINARY MANAGEMENT

The goals of therapy are to improve functioning and independence and to prevent or correct secondary physical or emotional problems. This generally involves surgical intervention, adaptive equipment, special education programs, and psychosocial support for the child and family. As a result of the complexity of the resultant disabilities, a multidisciplinary approach to treating the child with meningomyelocele is essential (McDonald, 1995). The team of health care professionals should include a physician (e.g., neurodevelopmental pediatrician, pediatric neurologist, physiatrist) with particular interest and expertise in the care of meningomyelocele; a nurse specialist; physical and occupational therapists; a social worker; consulting orthopedic, urological, and neurosurgeons; and an **orthotist.** Other team members or consultants may include a psychologist, plastic surgeon, dentist, special educator, speech-language therapist, genetic counselor, and financial counselor. The services the child needs and receives should be coordinated by a designated service coordinator (or case manager). Efforts should be made to empower the child and family by involving them in the design of a management plan that is both appropriate and realistic.

The successful development of children with meningomyelocele is largely dependent on how well the family is able to meet the needs of the child. This requires emotional support, realistic expectations, limits on behavior, and the provision of coordinated services in the community. The care of a child with meningomyelocele is expensive. Direct medical expenses have been estimated to total more than $100,000 over the individual's lifetime (Waitzman, Romano, & Scheffler, 1994); indirect costs, such as loss of parental income and survivor productivity effects, are estimated to total $250,000 over the life span (Centers for Disease Control, 1990). Therefore, one of the priorities of care is to provide financial counseling to families of an affected child.

JESSICA

Jessica was born at term to her 20-year-old mother, who had not received prenatal care. At the time of birth, a thoracic-level spina bifida with meningomyelocele was evident. This was surgically closed at 2 days of age, and a ventriculo-peritoneal shunt was inserted at 8 days of age to correct the associated hydrocephalus.

During her first year of life, Jessica received weekly in-home early intervention services, including physical therapy and an early childhood development program. She made good progress; at 12 months, she was speaking several single words, sitting independently, and crawling about commando style by propelling herself with her arms. A month later, she began to stand in a parapodium and started working on ambulation. Because of recurrent urinary tract infections that did not respond to preventive antibiotics and catheterization, a vesicostomy was placed surgically at age 18 months to allow urine to drain continuously into her diaper.

By 3 years of age, Jessica was independently using the parapodium for mobility. At age 4, she suddenly developed headaches, vomiting, and lethargy and was diagnosed as having ventricular shunt blockage. This was corrected surgically, and although she had a brief period of neurological deterioration, she subsequently recovered well.

Prior to school entry at age 6, psychoeducational testing was performed, which indicated that she had average intelligence (an IQ score of 90) but learning impairments. She was placed in an inclusion class with an aide and resource help in reading and arithmetic. She was successful in her CIC and bowel program and her improved continence gave her confidence in interacting with the other children.

During her school years, she has had several medical setbacks related to recurrent urinary tract infections and scoliosis. She ultimately required a bladder augmentation and a spinal fusion. Despite this, she has done well. Now at age 20, she attends a community college where she is majoring in psychology. She uses a wheelchair for mobility and self-administers a saline enema every other day to maintain bowel continence. She catheterizes herself four times a day and is generally dry between catheterizations. She has a limited social life and still depends on her family for transportation but is learning to drive through the state office of vocational rehabilitation.

PROGNOSIS

The survival rate of children with meningomyelocele has improved dramatically since the 1950s when survival to adulthood was less than 10% (Dunne & Shurtleff, 1986; Hunt & Poulton, 1995; Steinbok, Irvine, Cochrane, et al., 1992). In the 1990s, about 85% of children with meningomyelocele survive to adulthood as a result of many factors including the use of ventriculo-peritoneal shunts to control hydrocephalus and the prevention of kidney damage by CIC and urological surgery (McLone, 1989).

Outcome data for adults are incomplete, and the population is quite heterogeneous. In one study, Hunt (1990) found that half the individuals with meningomyelocele were still able to walk 50 yards or more in adulthood. Half also were able to maintain urinary and bowel continence. Overall, 12% had minimal disabilities, with average intelligence, community ambulation, and well-managed continence; 52% had moderate disability with borderline intelligence and the ability to attend to toilet needs independently and use a wheelchair with the ability to transfer. Severe disability involving mental retardation, incontinence, and dependence for most self-help skills was found in 37% of the individuals. Only about one quarter of the individuals were employed, and few married and had children.

SUMMARY

In meningomyelocele, an overlying sac protruding from the spine contains a malformed spinal cord and leads to the most complex birth defect compatible with life. Paralysis and loss of sensation occur below the level of the spinal cord defect, and there is usually an associated hydrocephalus. Numerous disabilities arise as a consequence of this condition, including paralysis, musculoskeletal abnormalities, bowel and bladder incontinence, impotence, obesity, and cognitive impairments. Meningomyelocele should be considered a nonprogressive condition, and any deterioration in function should lead to a search for a treatable cause, such as a tethered spinal cord or a blocked ventricular shunt. Advances in surgical and medical care have enhanced the survival and physical well-being of these individuals but have not completely corrected the associated impairments. In order to help these individuals reach their potential, professionals must advocate for the child and family in the areas of education and psychosocial adjustment while providing integrated, high-quality health care.

REFERENCES

Adetioloye, V.A., Dare, F.O., & Oyelami, O.A. (1993). A ten-year review of encephalocele in a teaching hospital. *International Journal of Gynaecology and Obstetrics, 41,* 241–249.

Agnarsson, U., Warde, C., McCarthy, G., et al. (1993). Anorectal function of children with neurological problems: I. Spina bifida. *Developmental Medicine and Child Neurology, 35,* 893–902.

Anderson, P.A., & Travers, A.H. (1993). Development of hydronephrosis in spina bifida patients: Predictive factors and management. *British Journal of Urology, 72,* 958–961.

Babcock, C.J. (1995). Ultrasound evaluation of prenatal and neonatal spina bifida. *Neurosurgery Clinics of North America, 6,* 203–218.

Baldwin, C.T., Hoth, C.F., Macina, R.A., et al. (1995). Mutations in PAX3 that cause Waardenburg syndrome type I: Ten new mutations and review of the literature. *American Journal of Medical Genetics, 58,* 115–122.

Benninga, M.A., van der Hoeven, C.W., Wijers, O.B., et al. (1994). Treatment of fecal incontinence in a child with sacral agenesis: The use of biofeedback training. *Developmental Medicine and Child Neurology, 36,* 518–527.

Blum, R.W., Resnick, M.D., Nelson, R., et al. (1991). Family and peer issues among adolescents with spina bifida and cerebral palsy. *Pediatrics, 88,* 280–285.

Bock, J.L. (1992). Current issues in maternal serum alpha-fetoprotein screening. *American Journal of Clinical Pathology, 97,* 541–554.

Boushey, C.J., Beresford, S.A.A., Owens, G.S., et al. (1995). A quantitative assessment of plasma homocysteine as a risk factor for vascular disease. *Journal of the American Medical Association, 274,* 1049–1057.

Bower, C., & Stanley, F.J. (1992). Periconceptional vitamin supplementation and neural tube defects: Evidence from a case-control study in Western Australia and a review of recent publications. *Journal of Epidemiology and Community Health, 46,* 157–161.

Brumfield, C.G., Aronin, P.A., Cloud, G.A., et al. (1995). Fetal myelomeningocele: Is antenatal ultrasound useful in predicting neonatal outcome? *Journal of Reproductive Medicine, 40,* 26–30.

Candenas, M., Villa, R., Fernandez Collar, R., et al. (1995). Maternal serum alpha-fetoprotein screening for neural tube defects: Report of a program with more than 30,000 screened pregnancies. *Acta Obstetricia et Gynecologica Scandinavica, 74,* 266–269.

Centers for Disease Control. (1990). Economic burden of spina bifida: United States, 1980–1990. *Morbidity and Mortality Weekly Reports, 38*(15), 264–267.

Centers for Disease Control. (1992). Recommendations for the use of folic acid to reduce the number of cases of spina bifida and other neural tube defects. *Morbidity and Mortality Weekly Reports, 41*(RR-14), 1–7.

Charney, E.B. (1990). Meningomyelocele. In M.W. Schwartz, E.B. Charney, T.A. Curry, et al. (Eds.),

Pediatric primary care: A problem oriented approach (2nd ed.). Chicago: Yearbook Medical Publishers.

Charney, E.B., Melchionni, J.B., & Smith, D.R. (1991). Community ambulation by children with meningomyelocele and high level paralysis. *Journal of Pediatric Orthopaedics, 11,* 579–582.

Charney, E.B., Rorke, L.B., Sutton, L.N., et al. (1987). Management of Chiari II complications in infants with MM. *Journal of Pediatrics, 111,* 364–371.

Charney, E.B., Weller, S.C., Sutton, L.N., et al. (1985). Management of the newborn with meningomyelocele: Time for a decision making process. *Pediatrics, 75,* 58–64.

Chatkupt, S., Hol, F.A., Shugart, Y.Y., et al. (1995). Absence of linkage between familial neural tube defects and PAX3 gene. *Journal of Medical Genetics, 32,* 200–204.

Chatkupt, S., Skurnick, H.H., Jagg, L.M., et al. (1994). Study of genetics, epidemiology, and vitamin usage in familial spina bifida in the United States, the 1990's. *Neurology, 44,* 65–70.

Chen, J., Godschalk, M.F., Katz, P.G., et al. (1995). Combining intracavernous injection and external vacuum as treatment for erectile dysfunction. *Journal of Urology, 153,* 1476–1477.

Cher, M.L., & Allen, T.D. (1993). Continence in the myelodysplastic patient following enterocystoplasty. *Journal of Urology, 149,* 1103–1106.

Dahl, M., Ahlsten, G., Carlson, H., et al. (1995). Neurological dysfunction above cele level in children with spina bifida cystica: A prospective study to three years. *Developmental Medicine and Child Neurology, 37,* 30–40.

Daly, L.E., Kirke, P.N., Malloy, A., et al. (1995). Folate levels and neural tube defects: Implications for prevention. *Journal of the American Medical Association, 274,* 1698–1702.

Davis, R., Peters, D.H., & McTavish, D. (1994). Valproic acid: A reappraisal of its pharmacological properties and clinical efficacy in epilepsy. *Drugs, 47,* 332–372.

Dias, M.S., & Pang, D. (1995). Split cord malformations. *Neurosurgery Clinics of North America, 6,* 339–358.

Dormans, J.P., Templeton, J., Schreiner, M.S., et al. (1995). Intraoperative latex anaphylaxis in children: Early detection, treatment, and prevention. *Contemporary Orthopaedics, 30,* 342–347.

Duncan, C.C., & Ogle, E.M. (1995). Spina bifida. In B. Goldberg (Ed.), *Sports and exercise for children with chronic health conditions* (pp. 79–88). Champaign, IL: Human Kinetics.

Dunne, K.B., & Shurtleff, D.B. (1986). The adult with meningomyelocele: A preliminary report. In R.L. McLaurin (Ed.), *Spina bifida* (pp. 38–51). New York: Praeger.

Elias, E.R., & Sadeghi-Nejad, A. (1994). Precocious puberty in girls with myelodysplasia. *Pediatrics, 93,* 521–522.

Ellsworth, P.I., Merguerian, P.A., Klein, R.B., et al. (1993). Evaluation and risk factors of latex allergy in spina bifida patients: Is it preventable? *Journal of Urology, 150*(2), 691–693.

Emans, J.B. (1992). Allergy to latex in patients who have myelodysplasia. *Journal of Bone and Joint Surgery, 74*(A), 1103–1109.

Ennever, F.K., & Lave, L.B. (1995). Parent preferences and prenatal testing for neural tube defects. *Epidemiology, 6,* 8–16.

Erikson, E.H. (1959). Identity and the life cycle. *Psychological Issues, 1,* 1–171.

Friedrich, W.N., Lovejoy, M.C., Shaffer, J., et al. (1991). Cognitive abilities and achievement status of children with myelomeningocele: A contemporary sample. *Journal of Pediatric Psychology, 16,* 423–428.

Gilbert, J.N., Jones, K.L., Rorke, L.B., et al. (1986). Central nervous system anomalies associated with meningomyelocele, hydrocephalus, and the Arnold-Chiari malformation: Reappraisal of theories regarding the pathogenesis of posterior neural tube closure defects. *Neurosurgery, 18,* 559–564.

Golden, J., & Chernoff, G.F. (1995). Multiple sites of anterior neural tube closure in humans: Evidence from anterior neural tube defects (anencephaly). *Pediatrics, 95,* 506–510.

Griebel, M.L., Oakes, W.J., & Worley, G. (1991). The Chiari malformation associated with meningomyelocele. In H.L. Rekate (Ed.), *Comprehensive management of spina bifida* (pp. 67–92). Boca Raton, FL: CRC Press.

Guidera, K.J., Smith, S., Raney, E., et al. (1993). Use of the reciprocating gait orthosis in myelodysplasia. *Journal of Pediatric Orthopography, 13,* 341–348.

Hayden, P.W. (1985). Adolescents with meningomyelocele. *Pediatrics in Review, 6,* 245–252.

Hol, F.A., Geurds, M.P.A., Chatkupt, S., et al. (1996). PAX genes and human neural tube defects: An amino acid substitution in PAX1 in a patient with spina bifida. *Journal of Medical Genetics, 33,* 655–660.

Hunt, G.M. (1990). Open spina bifida: Outcome for a complete cohort treated unselectively and followed into adulthood. *Developmental Medicine and Child Neurology, 32,* 108–118.

Hunt, G.M., & Poulton, A. (1995). Open spina bifida: A complete cohort reviewed 25 years after closure. *Developmental Medicine and Child Neurology, 37,* 19–29.

Hurley, A.D. (1993) Conducting psychological assessments. In F.L. Rowley-Kelly & D.H. Reigel (Eds.), *Teaching the student with spina bifida* (pp. 107–123). Baltimore: Paul H. Brookes Publishing Co.

Kappy, M.S., Stuart, T., & Perelman, A. (1988). Efficacy of leuprolide therapy in children with central precocious puberty. *American Journal of Diseases of Children, 142,* 1061–1064.

Karol, L.A. (1995). Orthopedic management in myelomeningocele. *Neurosurgery Clinics of North America, 6,* 259–268.

Keating, M.A., Rink, R.C., & Adams, M.C. (1993). Appendicovesicostomy: A useful adjunct to continent reconstruction of the bladder. *Journal of Urology, 149,* 1091–1094.

Kim, E.D., & McVary, K.T. (1995). Topical prostaglandin-E1 for the treatment of erectile dysfunction. *Journal of Urology, 153,* 1828–1830.

King, J.C., Currie, D.M., & Wright, E. (1994). Bowel training in spina bifida: Importance of education, patient compliance, age, and reflexes. *Archives of Physical Medicine and Rehabilitation, 75,* 243–247.

Krahn, C.G., & Johnson, H.W. (1993). Cutaneous vesicostomy in the young child: Indications and results. *Urology, 41,* 558–563.

Lennerstrand, G., Gallo, J.E., & Samuelsson, L. (1990). Neuro-ophthalmological findings in relation to CNS lesions in patients with myelomeningocele. *Developmental Medicine and Child Neurology, 32,* 423–431.

Lintner, S.A., & Lindseth, R.E. (1994). Kyphotic deformity in patients who have a myelomeningocele. *Journal of Bone and Joint Surgery, 76*(A), 1301–1307.

Liptak, G.S. (1996). Tethered spinal cord: Update of an analysis of published articles. *European Journal of Pediatric Surgery, 5,* 21–23.

Liptak, G.S., & McDonald, J. (1985/1986) Ventriculoperitoneal shunts in children with hydrocephalus: Factors affecting shunt survival. *Pediatric Neuroscience, 12,* 289–293.

Liptak, G.S., & Revell, G.M. (1992). Management of bowel dysfunction in children with spinal cord disease or injury by means of the enema continence catheter. *Journal of Pediatrics, 120,* 190–194.

Liptak, G.S., Shurtleff, D.B., Bloss, J.W., et al. (1992). Mobility aids in children with high-level meningomyelocele: Parapodium versus wheelchair. *Developmental Medicine and Child Neurology, 34,* 787–796.

Main, D.M., & Mennuti, M.T. (1986). Neural tube defects: Issues in prenatal diagnosis and counselling. *Obstetrics and Gynecology, 67,* 1–16.

Mayfield, J.K. (1991). Comprehensive orthopedic management in meningomyelocele. In H.L. Rekate (Ed.), *Comprehensive management of spina bifida* (pp. 113–163). Boca Raton, FL: CRC Press.

McDonald, C.M. (1995). Rehabilitation of children with spinal dysraphism. *Neurosurgery Clinics of North America, 6,* 393.

McDonald, C.M., Jaffe, K.M., Mosca, V.S., et al. (1991). Ambulatory outcome of children with myelomeningocele: Effect of lower extremity muscle strength. *Developmental Medicine and Child Neurology, 33,* 482–490.

McLone, D.G. (1989). Spina bifida today: Problems adults face. *Seminars in Neurology, 9,* 169–175.

McLone, D.G. (1992). Continuing concepts in the management of spina bifida. *Pediatric Neurosurgery, 18,* 254–256.

Meuli, M., Meuli-Simmen, C., Hutchins G.M., et al. (1995). In utero surgery rescues neurological function at birth in sheep with spina bifida. *Nature Medicine, 1,* 142–147.

Motulsky, A.G. (1996). Nutritional ecogenetics: Homocysteine-related arteriosclerotic vascular disease, neural tube defects, and folic acid. *American Journal of Human Genetics, 58,* 17–20.

MRC Vitamin Study Research Group. (1991). Prevention of neural tube defects: Results of the Medical Research Council Vitamin Study. *Lancet, 338,* 131–137.

Noetzel, M.J. (1989). Meningomyelocele: Current concepts of management. *Clinics in Perinatology, 16,* 311–329.

Pearson, M.L., Cole, J.S., & Jarvis, W.R. (1994). How common is latex allergy? A survey of children with myelodysplasia. *Developmental Medicine and Child Neurology, 36,* 64–69.

Polito, C., DelGaizo, G., DiManso, D., et al. (1995). Children with myelomeningocele have shorter stature, greater body weight, and lower bone mineral content than healthy children. *Nutrition Research, 15,* 161–162.

Rauzzino, M., & Oakes, W.J. (1995). Chiari II malformation and syringomyelia. *Neurosurgery Clinics of North America, 6,* 293–309.

Rinck, C., Berg, J., & Hafeman, C. (1989). The adolescent with meningomyelocele: A review of parent experiences and expectations. *Adolescence, 24,* 699–710.

Roberts, A., & Evans, G.A. (1993). Orthopedic aspects of neuromuscular disorders in children. *Current Opinion in Pediatrics, 5,* 379–383.

Roberts, H.E., Moore, C.A., Cragan, J.D., et al. (1995). Impact of prenatal diagnosis on the birth prevalence of neural tube defects, Atlanta, 1990–1991. *Pediatrics, 96,* 880–883.

Rotenstein, D., Adams, M., & Reigel, D.H. (1995). Adult stature and anthropomorphic measurement of patients with myelomeningocele. *European Journal of Pediatrics, 154,* 398–402.

Rowley-Kelly, F., & Reigel, D.H. (Eds.). (1992). *Teaching the student with spina bifida.* Baltimore: Paul H. Brookes Publishing Co.

Sadler, L.S., Robinson, L.K., & Msall, M.E. (1995). Diabetic embryopathy: Possible pathogenesis. *American Journal of Medical Genetics, 55,* 363–366.

Scott, J.M., Weir, D.G., Molloy, A., et al. (1994). Folic acid metabolism and mechanisms of neural tube defects. *Ciba Foundation Symposium, 181,* 180–187.

Sherk, H.H., Uppal, G.S., Lane, G., et al. (1991). Treatment versus non-treatment of hip dislocations in ambulatory patients with meningomyelocele. *Developmental Medicine and Child Neurology, 33,* 491–494.

Shurtleff, D.B., & Lemire, R.J. (1995). Epidemiology, etiologic factors, and prenatal diagnosis of open spinal dysraphism. *Neurosurgery Clinics of North America, 6,* 183–193.

Shurtleff, D.B., Luthy, D.A., Nyberg, D.A., et al. (1994). Meningomyelocele: Management in utero and post natum. *Ciba Foundation Symposium, 181,* 270–280.

Snow, J.H. (1994). Memory functions for children with spina bifida: Assessment in rehabilitation and exceptionality. *Pediatrics, 1,* 20–27.

Squire, R., Kiely, E.M., Ransley, P.G., et al. (1993). The clinical application of the Malone antegrade colonic enema. *Journal of Pediatric Surgery, 28,* 1012–1015.

Steegers-Theunissen, R.P. (1995). Folate metabolism and neural tube defects: A review. *European Journal of Obstetrics, Gynecology, and Reproductive Biology, 61,* 39–48.

Steinbok, P., Irvine, B., Cochrane, D.D., et al. (1992). Long-term outcome and complications of children born with meningomyelocele. *Child's Nervous System, 8,* 92–96.

Swank, M., & Dias, L. (1992). Myelomeningocele: A review of the orthopaedic aspects of 206 patients treated from birth with no selection criteria. *Developmental Medicine and Child Neurology, 34,* 1047–1052.

Urui, S., & Oi, S. (1995). Experimental study of embryogenesis of open spinal dysraphism. *Neurosurgery Clinics of North America, 6,* 195–202.

Van Allen, M.I., Kalousek, D.K., Chernoff, G.F., et al. (1993). Evidence for multi-site closure of the neural tube in humans. *American Journal of Medical Genetics, 47,* 723–743.

van der Put, N.M.J., Steegers-Theunissen, R.P.M., Frosst, P., et al. (1995). Mutated methylenetetrahydrofolate reductase as a risk factor for spina bifida. *Lancet, 346,* 1070–1071.

Vereecken, R.L. (1992). Bladder pressure and kidney function in children with myelomeningocele. *Paraplegia, 30,* 153–159.

Vivani, G.R., Raducan, V., Bednar, D.A., et al. (1993). Anterior and posterior spinal fusion: Comparison of one-stage and two-stage procedures. *Canadian Journal of Surgery, 36,* 468–473.

Waitzman, N.J., Romano, P.S., & Scheffler, R.M. (1994). Estimates of the economic costs of birth defects. *Inquiry, 31,* 188–205.

Werler, M.M., Shapiro, S., & Mitchell, A.A. (1993). Periconceptional folic acid exposure and risk of occurrent neural tube defects. *Journal of the American Medical Association, 269,* 1257–1261.

Westcott, M.A., Dynes, M.C., Remer, E.M., et al. (1992). Congenital and acquired orthopedic abnormalities in patients with myelomeningocele. *Radiographics, 12,* 1155–1173.

Williamson, G.G. (Ed.). (1987). *Children with spina bifida: Early intervention and preschool programming.* Baltimore: Paul H. Brookes Publishing Co.

Wills, K.E., Holmbeck, G.N., Dillon, K., et al. (1990). Intelligence and achievement in children with meningomyelocele. *Journal of Pediatric Psychology, 15,* 161–176.

Wood, J.M., Evans, P.E., Schallreuter, K.U., et al. (1993). A multicenter study of direct current for healing of chronic stage II and stage III decubitus ulcers. *Archives of Dermatology, 129,* 999–1009.

Yamada, S., Iacono, R.P., Andrade, T., et al. (1995). Pathophysiology of tethered cord syndrome. *Neurosurgery Clinics of North America, 6,* 311–324.

Yen, I.H., Khoury, M.J., Erickson, J.D., et al. (1992). The changing epidemiology of neural tube defects: United States, 1968–1989. *American Journal of Diseases of Children, 146,* 857–861.

26 Seizure Disorders

Lawrence W. Brown

Upon completion of this chapter, the reader will:

- understand what constitutes a seizure and how it originates
- know the various types of seizures
- be able to identify the drugs used to treat seizures
- realize what acute care is needed in case of a seizure
- be aware of the prognosis for children with seizure disorders

About 8% of all children in the United States will have at least one seizure by 15 years of age (Annegars, 1993; O'Donohoe, 1994). More than half of these seizures will be isolated events associated with high fever or brain injury in early childhood. This type of seizure rarely recurs and does not require specific treatment. Even among children with **afebrile seizures,** only about 40% will have a recurrence within the next 3 years (Shinnar, Berg, Moshe, et al., 1990). In contrast with these isolated seizures, epilepsy is defined as repeated unprovoked seizures. Seizure recurrence is best predicted by an abnormal electroencephalogram (EEG) obtained shortly after the **ictal** episode (Figure 26.1). About half of all children with epilepsy have typical intelligence; the other half have various degrees of mental retardation. Children with seizure disorders have a high incidence of learning disabilities as well as behavior and psychological problems (Aldenkamp, Alpherts, Dekker, et al., 1990). Children with learning disabilities, however, are not at increased risk of having a seizure disorder.

Childhood seizures are generally well controlled with appropriate antiepileptic drugs (AEDs). Many children will enter a sustained remission, and drugs can usually be stopped if the child has remained seizure-free for at least 2 years. Children with significant developmental disabilities in addition to a seizure disorder, however, often require prolonged treatment. They tend to have complex seizure patterns, metabolic disturbances, or structural brain abnormalities—all of which make seizure control more difficult. This chapter defines seizure disorders and describes various types of seizures, diagnostic tests, AEDs and other forms of treatment, and prognosis.

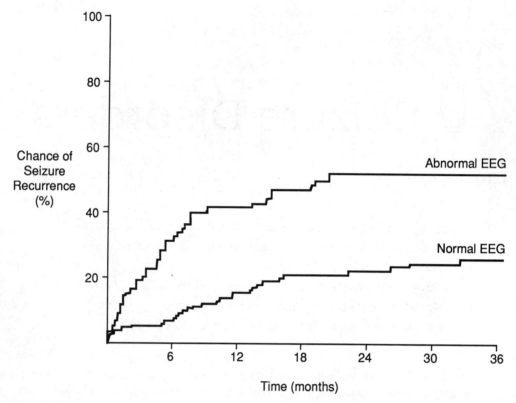

Figure 26.1.   Percentage risk of seizure recurrence in the 3 years following a first nonfebrile seizure. Overall, about 40% of children had a second seizure. However, while those with normal EEGs had a 26% chance of recurrence, those with abnormal EEG patterns had a 56% chance of recurrence. (From Shinnar, S., Berg, A.T., Moshe, S.L., et al. [1990]. Risk of seizure recurrence following a short unprovoked seizure in childhood: A prospective study. *Pediatrics, 85,* 1076; reprinted by permission of *Pediatrics,* Copyright 1990.)

WHAT IS A SEIZURE?

A seizure is defined as any sudden attack of altered behavior, consciousness, sensation, or autonomical function that is produced by a self-limited disruption of brain activity due to repetitive, simultaneous electrical discharges from hyperexcitable neurons in the cortex (Clancy, 1990). From this initiating region, the discharge spreads and recruits neurons surrounding the seizure focus, causing them to discharge in an excessively **synchronous** fashion. It is this hypersynchronous, periodic discharge that produces a seizure. Depending on the initial location and spread of the abnormal discharge within the brain, the seizure may present with loss of consciousness, behavior changes, involuntary movements, altered muscle tone, or abnormal sensory phenomena.

At its most fundamental level, a seizure is caused by disturbances in the normal **ionic** currents across the nerve cell membrane (Lothman, 1993). This involves an abnormal cascade of inward currents carried by sodium and calcium ions that can become self-sustaining. If this localized discharge is intensive enough in a sufficiently large population of neurons, it can spread by excitatory connections to surrounding brain regions and lead to behavioral alterations identified as a clinical seizure. Although this mechanism is best worked out for seizures of **focal** onset, primary generalized epilepsy appears to share a similar mechanism.

Instability leading to seizure discharge can occur if there is either too much excitation or insufficient inhibition of the neurons. As the central nervous system (CNS) matures, many children with epilepsy develop a more finely tuned equilibrium between excitatory and inhibitory influences. This new balance may explain why children may "grow out of" a seizure disorder.

PRECIPITANTS OF SEIZURES

Seizures may be caused by developmental brain abnormalities, anoxia, hypoglycemia, inborn errors of metabolism, trauma, and infections, all of which also cause other developmental disabilities. Thus, it is not surprising that the incidence of epilepsy in children with mental retardation is 16%, in cerebral palsy 25%, and in spina bifida 25% (Wallace, 1990). Chromosomal disorders are less likely causes of seizures, unless there are associated cerebral malformations. Children with spastic cerebral palsy are more likely to have seizures than those with the dyskinetic form. Children with mental retardation requiring extensive supports are more likely to have seizures than those with mental retardation requiring intermittent supports (Goulden, Shinnar, Koller, et al., 1990; Steffenburg, Hagberg, & Kyllerman, 1995; Steffenburg, Hagberg, Viggedal, et al., 1995). In general, males are at greater risk for seizures than females.

Once there is an established focus, spontaneous seizures may occur at any time. Certain circumstances, however, make a seizure more likely. Fever, sleep deprivation, minor brain injury, and emotional excitement often prompt seizures. Actually, anyone can have a seizure, providing the fever is high enough, blood glucose low enough, or brain trauma severe enough to exceed the individual's seizure threshold.

TYPES OF SEIZURES

Seizure classification is important because it helps to provide a clearer basis for understanding the underlying cause as well as a practical guide to effective treatment. The International League Against Epilepsy (ILAE) classifies seizures based on clinical observation and EEG findings. The two basic types of seizures are generalized and partial (Dreifuss, 1989). The generalized seizure appears to involve the entire cortex from the outset, whereas the partial seizure begins in a single location with signs and symptoms dependent on specific brain function (Pellock, 1990). Partial seizures may remain limited, or they may spread to become secondarily generalized. An individual may have both generalized and partial seizures, which is called a mixed seizure disorder. A revised ILAE classification system was introduced in 1981, and new terms replaced the traditional grand mal, petit mal, and temporal lobe seizures. Generalized seizures were divided into tonic-clonic, absence, atypical absence, myoclonic, and atonic forms. Partial seizures were separated into simple and complex, based on whether there is a disturbance in consciousness (Table 26.1). There is also a category of syndromes, such as Aicardi syndrome, lissencephaly, and certain inborn errors of metabolism, in which seizures play a principal role. Some seizures that exist in early childhood (i.e., neonatal seizures, febrile convulsions) are somewhat different from

Table 26.1.   Comparison of complex partial and absence seizures

	Complex partial	Absence
Incidence	Common	Uncommon
Duration	30 seconds–5 minutes	Less than 10 seconds
Frequency of occurrence	Occasional	Multiple times daily
Aura	Present	Absent
Consciousness	Partial amnesia and confusion	Immediate return to consciousness
EEG pattern	Temporal lobe focus	Generalized
History of tonic-clonic seizures	Yes	No
Primary AED	Carbamazepine	Ethosuximide

other seizure disorders. Finally, there are habits and conditions that simulate epilepsy but are not seizures. These are also discussed in this chapter.

Generalized Seizures

Generalized seizures affect both hemispheres of the brain simultaneously. They account for about 40% of all cases of epilepsy (Niedermeyer, 1990).

Tonic-Clonic Seizures

The generalized tonic-clonic seizure (formerly called grand mal, major motor seizure, or convulsion) is the most common variant in childhood and the prototype of the epileptic seizure. This is the most nonspecific type of seizure that can occur at any age (Figure 26.2) and may result from a fever, CNS infection, metabolic disturbance, tumor, developmental brain abnormality, or hereditary tendency. It involves excessive firing of neurons from both hemispheres in a symmetrical and simultaneous manner. Primary generalized seizures appear to originate simultaneously in all areas of the brain, while **secondary** generalized seizures evolve from initially localized events. This localized event is often indicated by a brief, sometimes nonspecific aura or warning preceding the overt portion of the seizure. The convulsive seizure itself generally starts with eye deviation upward or to one side, sudden loss of consciousness, and rigidity. This tonic stage lasts for about 30 seconds to 1 minute, during which time the individual may stop breathing and bite the tongue. A clonic phase follows with rhythmic jerking of the body, lasting 1–3 minutes (Figure 26.3). The clonic phase is usually followed by lethargy or sleep. Incontinence may occur during this **postictal** period. Upon recovery, the person typically has no memory of the seizure itself. Some individuals have purely tonic or clonic seizures.

Tonic-clonic seizures can occur as often as several times a day or as seldom as once in a lifetime. Most clinicians will treat children who have more than one unprovoked attack with an AED until they are seizure-free for at least 2 years. Withdrawing medication after this time is successful in about two thirds of these children depending on the particular epileptic syndrome and underlying etiology (Shinnar, Berg, Moshe, et al., 1994). Unfortunately, children with mental retardation requiring extensive supports are much less likely to enter remission or remain seizure-free when medication is discontinued.

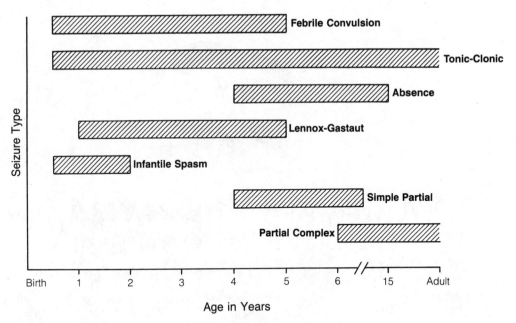

Figure 26.2.   Common ages of occurrence of various types of seizures.

Absence Seizures

Absence seizures (formerly called petit mal) are much less common than tonic-clonic seizures, accounting for less than 5% of all seizure disorders (Pearl & Holmes, 1993). Childhood absence epilepsy is usually hereditary with an autosomal dominant pattern showing variable expression and penetrance. Onset is in the first decade of life, usually between 3 and 7 years of age (Holmes, 1987). During this type of seizure, the child abruptly stops all activity, assumes a glazed look, stares, and remains unaware of surroundings for several seconds (Figure 26.4). The maintenance of normal muscle tone protects the child from falling. Careful video EEG observation has shown a high degree of subtle eyeblinking, muscle twitching, or repetitive movements (**automatisms**) (Holmes, McKeever, & Adamson, 1987). Unlike simple daydreaming, absence seizures cannot be interrupted by verbal or tactile stimulation.

It may be difficult to identify an absence seizure because the brevity of the event without any postictal confusion or sleepiness often allows the child to respond almost immediately to a question. Unaware of the episode, the child usually continues to read at the point where he or she left off or picks up a conversation begun just prior to the seizure. Yet, some children recognize that they lost a period of time. One boy described his life as like a movie in which certain scenes have been cut out (Freeman, Vining, & Pillas, 1990). Recurrent absence spells may be misinterpreted not only as simple daydreaming, but also as a learning disability or oppositional behavior. If the seizures remain undetected and untreated, hundreds of episodes may occur daily, interfering with schoolwork and other activities and leading to school failure and low self-esteem. Children with absence epilepsy generally have typical intelligence. Hyperventilation in the untreated patient can usually induce an event within seconds to a few minutes that can be

Tonic-Clonic

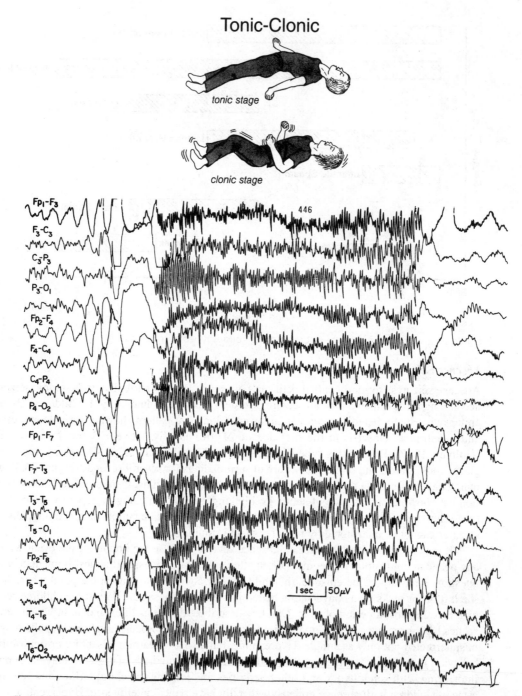

Figure 26.3.   EEG pattern of a child with tonic-clonic seizures. There is a burst of spike activity over the entire cortex during the course of the seizure. (EEG from Niedermeyer, E., & Lopes da Silva, F. [1987]. *Electroencephalography: Basic principles, clinical applications, and related fields* [2nd ed., p. 441]. Baltimore: Urban & Schwarzenberg; reprinted by permission of Williams & Wilkins Co.)

Absence

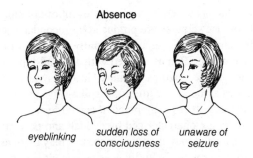

eyeblinking   sudden loss of   unaware of
consciousness   seizure

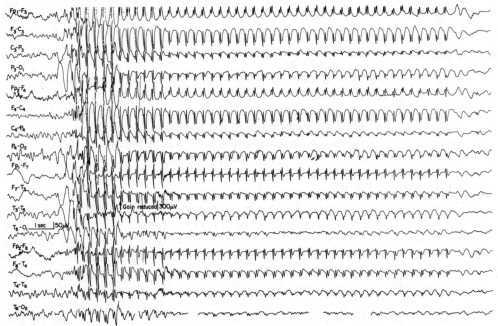

Figure 26.4.   EEG pattern in absence seizures shows a regular, slow spike and wave pattern that lasts less than 30 seconds. (EEG from Niedermeyer, E., & Lopes da Silva, F. [1987]. *Electroencephalography: Basic principles, clinical applications, and related fields* [2nd ed., p. 416]. Baltimore: Urban & Schwarzenberg; reprinted by permission of Williams & Wilkins Co.)

recorded on an EEG as spike and wave disturbances with a frequency of 2.5–3.5 hertz (Hz; cycles per second). Using the antiepileptic drug ethosuximide (Zarontin), 80% of absence epilepsy can be successfully controlled; most cases of childhood onset absence epilepsy achieve remission by mid-adolescence (Holmes, 1987). The outcome is less favorable when absence epilepsy starts around puberty (juvenile absence epilepsy), when there is associated myoclonus (juvenile myoclonic epilepsy), or when the spike-wave discharge is significantly faster than 3 Hz.

Atypical Absence, Myoclonic, and Atonic Seizures

Atypical absence seizures involve complex staring spells and associated focal features. Compared with typical absence seizures, this type of seizure usually starts gradually, lasts longer, and terminates with postictal confusion. Furthermore, the underlying mechanism is very different from typical absence that is caused by a primary event originating in deep midline structures of the brain. Atypical absence seizures are produced by secondary generalization and carry a more ominous prognosis than absence seizures. Usually seen in children with mental retardation, atypical absence seizures are often associated with a mixed-type seizure pattern including tonic-clonic, myoclonic, and atonic seizures. Lennox-Gastaut syndrome is another name for these intractable mixed seizures associated with a slow spike-wave pattern on an EEG (less than 2.5 Hz) and mental retardation and other developmental disabilities.

Myoclonic seizures are characterized by sudden and powerful involuntary contractions of muscles. For example, a hand may fling out or spasms may involve the entire body and cause the child to be thrown to the ground. Infantile spasms is a classic example of a myoclonic seizure. Atonic seizures produce sudden loss of muscle tone without warning. In these seizures, head nods or crashing falls may be followed by tonic stiffening or unconsciousness (Lockman, 1989).

Partial Seizures

Partial seizures are the most common type of seizure disorder, accounting for almost 60% of all cases (Wallace, 1990). About three quarters of affected children have a structural brain abnormality, most commonly of prenatal origin. Signs and symptoms of partial seizures depend on the localization of the seizure focus in a restricted area of one hemisphere. These seizures are further classified as simple partial seizures when the child remains fully aware and complex partial seizures when consciousness is impaired (Kotagal & Rothner, 1993).

Simple Partial Seizures

Simple partial seizures can occur at any age but are commonly first identified after 4 years of age. When the seizure focus involves the motor cortex, the result is usually rhythmic clonic activity of the face, arm, or leg. Psychic symptoms such as visual hallucinations or illusions may occur with simple partial seizures originating in the occipital or parietal lobes, while more auditory hallucinations or **olfactory sensations** indicate localization in the temporal lobe. These symptoms are also seen in complex partial seizures.

One of the most common simple partial disorders in childhood is benign rolandic epilepsy. In this disorder, typical seizures include nighttime awakenings, twitching of the facial muscles that may spread to one hand, and speech arrest. The seizure focus may spread to involve larger areas of the brain, resulting in tonic-clonic seizures involving all extremities. The seizures are usually easily controlled with AEDs, such as carbamazepine (Tegretol), and always resolve completely by puberty.

The aura that may precede a generalized tonic-clonic or complex partial seizure is another common example of a simple partial seizure. It is not surprising to find descriptions of a sudden fearful feeling or déjà vu, because these psychic phenomena arise in the temporal lobe. The individual can often remember these sensations, because consciousness is not lost until there is localized spread or secondary generalization (Figure 26.5). Isolated twitching of one extremity is yet another example of a simple partial seizure. This focal motor seizure may start in one hand and move up the arm to involve the entire body (called a "jacksonian march") (Wyllie, Rothner, & Luders, 1989). This example implies a focus in the primary motor cortex of the frontal lobe. A completely different form of simple partial seizure is associated with involuntary symptoms such as pallor, flushing, rapid heart beat, and chest pain. In this case, the seizure is localized in deeper subcortical nuclei that control the autonomic nervous system (see Chapter 14).

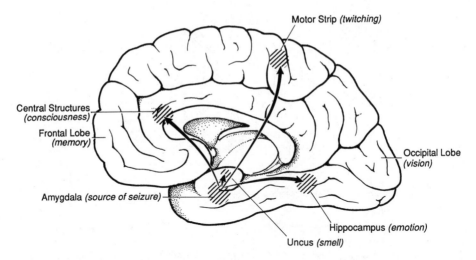

Motor Strip *(twitching)*

Central Structures
(consciousness)

Frontal Lobe
(memory)

Occipital Lobe
(vision)

Amygdala *(source of seizure)*

Hippocampus *(emotion)*

Uncus *(smell)*

Figure 26.5.   Spread of a simple partial seizure. A simple partial seizure may begin anywhere, in this case in the amygdala of the temporal lobe. The initial feature may be the child smelling an unusual odor. The seizure may stop there or project out to the hippocampus, which might trigger feelings of fearfulness or abdominal queasiness. Memory and visual perception may be affected if the frontal or occipital lobe is involved. It might ultimately extend to the motor strip, resulting in twitching of a limb, which may spread to other limbs or to central structures causing loss of consciousness, converting it into a complex partial seizure. Finally, it may cross the corpus callosum to the other cerebral hemisphere, converting the partial into a generalized seizure.

EEG abnormalities in simple partial seizures reflect the specific region containing the seizure focus. A routine EEG can be normal, however, if the focus is restricted to a small region that is not readily projected to the surface scalp electrodes. Approximately 70% of simple partial seizures can be controlled with AEDs, most commonly carbamazepine or phenytoin (Holmes, 1987).

Complex Partial Seizures

The complex partial seizure (once called psychomotor, limbic, or temporal lobe seizure) is the most common seizure type in older children and adolescents but may be seen at any age including infancy (Wyllie, Chee, Granstrom, et al., 1993). These focal seizures resemble generalized absence seizures. Distinguishing characteristics of complex partial seizures include the presence of an aura preceding the staring spell, duration longer than 10 seconds, and postictal confusion or actual sleeping.

Most complex partial seizures originate in the temporal lobe. Because this cortical region controls primary senses (e.g., smell, sound, taste) and is also responsible for integrating visual input with other senses, language processing, and memory, the individual may experience a variety of psychic phenomena. Auras may include a sudden familiar odor, an odd taste, or a visual hallucination (Figure 26.6). There also may be unprovoked emotional outbursts such as anger, laughter, or fear.

The seizure itself often includes eye blinking, lip smacking, facial grimaces, groaning, chewing, unbuttoning and buttoning clothing, or other motor automatisms. The child may even wander aimlessly. Automatic motor movements also can occur with absence seizures, but they

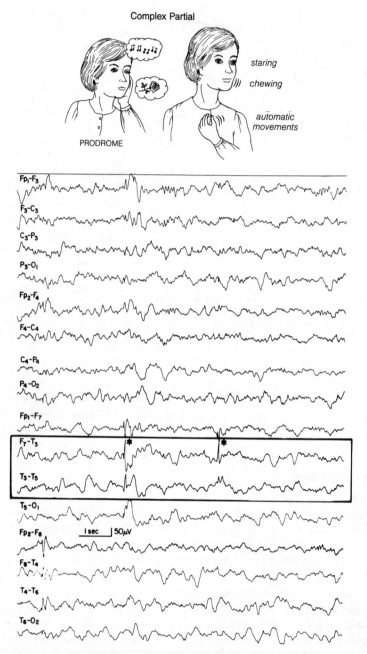

Figure 26.6.   In complex partial seizures, the abnormal spike discharges (noted by the asterisks) are confined to the temporal lobe of the brain, leads F7–T3 and T3–T5. The remainder of the EEG record appears normal. (EEG from Niedermeyer, E., & Lopes da Silva, F. [1987]. *Electroencephalography: Basic principles, clinical applications, and related fields* [2nd ed., p. 466]. Baltimore: Urban & Schwarzenberg; reprinted by permission of Williams & Wilkins Co.)

are less common. There are a number of other differences that distinguish partial complex from absence seizures (Table 26.1) (Gomez & Klass, 1983). Most children with partial complex seizures respond to AEDs, but the prognosis is less favorable than for the primary generalized epilepsies. Spontaneous remission occurs only in about 20% of cases as compared with 90% in childhood absence epilepsies (Kotagal, Rothner, Erenberg, et al., 1987; Loiseau, Duche, & Pedespan, 1995). Even if the child has an apparent permanent remission, there is a risk of recurrence in late adolescence or early adulthood. Those teenagers or young adults whose seizures return after a period of seizure-freedom often become resistant to AEDs. Complex partial epilepsy can also become intractable early in its course. There are occasional instances in childhood and even in infancy in which standard medical management is unsuccessful, and epilepsy surgery needs to be considered.

EPILEPTIC SYNDROMES

Epileptic syndromes are seizure disorders characterized by specific clinical features and characteristic EEG findings (Aicardi, 1994). Examples include infantile spasms and Lennox-Gastaut syndrome. These disorders can be considered catastrophic when they are associated with mental retardation as well as a high incidence of difficult-to-control seizures. Other specific neurological syndromes such as tuberous sclerosis (and other neurocutaneous syndromes), Aicardi syndrome, and malformations such as lissencephaly are associated with epilepsy of variable severity. There are also some epileptic syndromes that are much less severe, the best example being benign rolandic epilepsy (see discussion of simple partial seizures).

Infantile Spasms

Infantile spasms (also known as West syndrome or infantile myoclonic epilepsy) commonly start at 4–8 months of age. They can occur in infants with a variety of brain disorders (called symptomatic infantile spasms) as well as in typically developing infants without any predisposing conditions (called cryptogenic infantile spasms) (Bobele & Bodensteiner, 1990). Individual massive myoclonic spasms can look like an exaggerated Moro reflex. They occur primarily during periods of drowsiness or arousal from sleep. The spasms usually take the form of a sudden jackknifing jolt with bending forward at the waist with arms and legs outstretched (Figure 26.7). They generally occur in clusters of five or more, each separated by a few seconds; clusters often last for up to 5 minutes. In their most extreme form, repetitive clusters interrupt activity throughout the day. Neurodevelopmental arrest or regression with loss of skills is common. Infantile spasms are often associated with a severe underlying brain disorder. However, even cryptogenic infantile spasms with a benign history, normal neurological examination, and normal neuroimaging studies often lead to permanent neurological abnormalities or evolve into other epilepsy syndromes such as Lennox-Gastaut syndrome.

About 1 in 6,000 children have infantile spasms (Bobele & Bodensteiner, 1990). Any condition that affects the developing CNS can lead to symptomatic infantile spasms. Common genetic etiologies include tuberous sclerosis, Tay-Sachs disease, untreated phenylketonuria, and Down syndrome. Environmental etiologies such as birth asphyxia and congenital infections also can predispose the infant to the development of infantile spasms. In about half of these children, the cause of the seizures is unknown even after extensive evaluation.

Infantile Spasm

sudden jackknifing of body

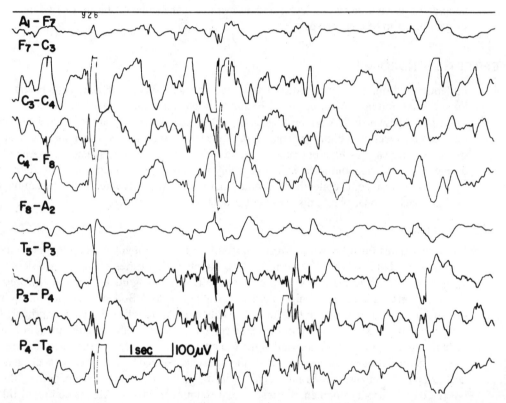

Figure 26.7.   EEG pattern of a child with infantile spasms. Note the disorganized high-voltage activity. This pattern is called hypsarrhythmia. (EEG from Niedermeyer, E., & Lopes da Silva, F. [1987]. *Electroencephalography: Basic principles, clinical applications, and related fields* [2nd ed., p. 438]. Baltimore: Urban & Schwarzenberg; reprinted by permission of Williams & Wilkins Co.)

Treatment with adrenocorticotropic hormone (ACTH), prescribed daily as an intramuscular gel preparation, often stops the spasms within days or weeks (Baram, Mitchell, Tournay, et al., 1996; Snead, 1990). Yet, more than 90% of children with symptomatic infantile spasms develop mental retardation despite effective treatment, and about two thirds of the cryptogenic group also develop mental retardation (Glaze, Hrachovy, Frost, et al., 1988). Functional neuroimaging (using positron emission tomography [PET]) has revealed that the vast majority of children with intractable infantile spasms have a focal abnormality in the brain (Chugani, Shewmon, Shields, et al., 1993). This has led to successful surgery to remove the defective area in selected individuals. There is also enthusiasm about vigabatrin, an AED under investigation in the United States. In European trials, this agent compared very favorably with ACTH in its effectiveness and had fewer side effects, but more experience is necessary to determine its safety and if this treatment will prevent mental retardation (Aicardi, the Coordinating Peer Review Group, & the European Infantile Spasms Vigabatrin Group, 1995).

Lennox-Gastaut Syndrome

Lennox-Gastaut syndrome describes a mixed seizure pattern (including atypical absence, tonic-clonic, myoclonic, and atonic seizures) with an EEG pattern of slow spike-wave activity (Niedermeyer, 1986). Often affecting children with a prior history of infantile spasms, it generally begins between 1 and 8 years of age. Seizures in Lennox-Gastaut syndrome are notoriously difficult to control with AEDs. Valproic acid (Depakene/Depakote) is the first-line drug because its wide spectrum of action can be effective against all the types of seizures seen in this syndrome. Secondary medications directed against the most disabling seizure type also may be added. Sometimes multiple drug therapy may be needed; however, polypharmacy carries its own problems. For example, a drug may improve one type of seizure while worsening another. Although felbamate (Felbatol) was specifically released for the treatment of Lennox-Gastaut syndrome, its relatively high risk of generating liver toxicity and bone marrow suppression has severely limited its use. Early results with some of the newly released AEDs (i.e., lamotrigine [Lamictal]) and investigational new drugs (i.e., vigabatrin) hold promise for more effective treatment in the future. A course of ACTH or prednisone can be extremely effective in selected individuals, but relapse is frequent when these drugs are withdrawn. The ketogenic diet (see pp. 581–582) has also been found to be successful in some cases (Kinsman, Vining, & Quaskey, 1992). Surgical intervention can be considered in cases of severe intractable epilepsy with Lennox-Gastaut syndrome.

Neurocutaneous Syndromes: Tuberous Sclerosis and Sturge-Weber

Neurocutaneous syndromes refer to a group of inherited disorders in which there is a combination of skin abnormalities and CNS disturbances. The most common example is tuberous sclerosis, which can present in early life with infantile spasms and accounts for about 0.5% of all children with mental retardation requiring extensive supports. Characteristic skin abnormalities include depigmented white birthmarks (called ash leaf spots because of their shape) and round, beige-colored areas (called café au lait spots because of their color). The principal finding in the brain is the presence of **tubers,** which are large areas of disorganized cortex and white matter that represent a developmental brain malformation. They can be seen best on magnetic resonance images (MRIs), although computed tomography (CT) can also demonstrate associated calcifications, glial tumors, and hydrocephalus. Because there may also be benign retinal tumors, all individuals should be examined by an ophthalmologist. The syndrome may involve other organs, including the heart, kidney, and lungs. Inheritance is usually autosomal dominant but can be sporadic. Gene identification has not yet been completed, but there are several candidate genes under active investigation on chromosomes #9 and #16.

About 90% of individuals with tuberous sclerosis develop seizures at some point, although some children with typical skin findings remain asymptomatic for years (Roach, Smith, Huttenlocher, et al., 1992). Infantile spasms are most common in infants, but tonic-clonic seizures become more frequent after 1 year of age. Complex partial, tonic, atonic, and atypical absence seizures also are seen, especially in those children with an EEG pattern suggestive of Lennox-Gastaut syndrome.

There is no specific treatment approach to tuberous sclerosis. Management is directed at the seizure types, which are usually multiple and often frustratingly difficult to control. There is also an increased risk for certain benign brain tumors, particularly subependymal giant cell astrocytomas. These tumors grow near the ventricles and can cause blockage leading to hydrocephalus.

In the 1990s, the thinking about treatment options for tuberous sclerosis has evolved. Children with tuberous sclerosis and intractable epilepsy are increasingly being considered candidates for surgical removal of the seizure focus provided the majority of seizures originate in one region of the brain (Bebin, Kelly, & Gomez, 1993). In addition, the ketogenic diet can be successful in this condition. There is also considerable enthusiasm about vigabatrin. In early studies of its use with infantile spasms, the group with tuberous sclerosis had the highest response rate (90%). This compares favorably with ACTH and other treatment modalities with more serious side effects (Aicardi et al., 1995).

Sturge-Weber syndrome is a second relatively common neurocutaneous disorder. It is characterized by a congenital port wine stain involving one side of the face (Pascual-Castroviejo, Diaz-Gonzalez, Garcia-Melian, et al., 1993). These blood vessel malformations affect the brain as well as the skin. Venous angiomas (benign blood vessel tumors) in the membranes surrounding the brain are associated with neurological impairments and progressive cortical atrophy. Severe partial or generalized seizures occur in almost all individuals; and hemiparesis on the side opposite to the port wine stain is common. Seizures are often difficult to control with AEDs. The early subtotal or complete surgical removal of one of the cerebral hemispheres has been shown to prevent progressive mental retardation in some severe cases. However, not all children with Sturge-Weber syndrome are appropriate candidates for this hemispherectomy (Roach, Riela, Chugani, et al., 1994).

Aicardi Syndrome

Aicardi syndrome occurs only in girls. It is associated with absence of the corpus callosum and congenital abnormalities of the eye (Neidich, Nussbaum, Packer, et al., 1990). These children have mental retardation requiring extensive supports and infantile spasms that are often difficult to control.

SELF-LIMITED AND EPILEPTIC-LIKE DISORDERS

Not all seizures are classified as epilepsy, and not all paroxysmal disorders represent epileptic seizures. Newborn infants may have symptomatic seizures as a consequence of a difficult delivery, transient metabolic disturbance, or systemic infection. These infants may never again experience seizure activity. Toddlers and young children can have febrile convulsions that they outgrow prior to entering elementary school. Neither of these conditions is considered epilepsy. Furthermore, some children have behavioral habits or other paroxysmal events that superficially resemble seizures. These include breath-holding, fainting, and temper tantrums. These conditions must be distinguished from epilepsy so that AEDs are not prescribed indiscriminately. These conditions are described in the following sections.

Febrile Convulsions

According to the 1980 Consensus Development Conference, febrile seizures usually occur between 3 months and 5 years of age in association with fever, but in the absence of evidence of an intracranial infection or other defined cause. By definition, seizures with fever in children who previously experienced an afebrile convulsion are not considered benign febrile convulsions. Epidemiological studies have shown a prevalence of febrile convulsions of 3%–5% in North America and Western Europe. The peak age is 8–24 months, with most children having their first febrile convulsions before 3 years of age (Figure 26.2). Upper respiratory illnesses, middle-ear infections, gastroenteritis, and viruses associated with skin rashes (e.g., roseola) are precipitants for the vast majority of these convulsions. Bacteria have been cultured in only about 5% of children having febrile convulsions. The most common diagnoses are urinary tract infections and diarrhea associated with the bacterial organism shigella (Ferry, Banner, & Wolf, 1986). Immunization also has been implicated as a cause of febrile convulsions. DPT (diphtheria, pertussis, tetanus) and rubeola (measles) immunizations are the most likely to produce fever and precipitate a febrile seizure. In general, however, a febrile convulsion should not be interpreted as evidence of immunization-related encephalopathy and a reason to put off further immunizations. Only standard pertussis (whooping cough) immunization may be deferred in children who have had febrile convulsions. Even in these cases, an alternate immunization exists; the acellular pertussis vaccine can be given together with acetaminophen (Tylenol) to prevent high fever (American Academy of Pediatrics, Committee on Infectious Diseases, 1994).

Febrile convulsions occur most often with temperature elevations above 39°C (102°F). The typical simple febrile seizure is brief (usually far less than 5 minutes), generalized tonic-clonic in type, ends with a rapid return to typical mental status, and does not recur the same day. Atypical febrile seizures include prolonged events lasting longer than 15 minutes and focal seizures. There is often an abnormal neurological or developmental history or a family history of epilepsy. The recurrence risk for simple febrile seizures without any of the above risk factors is approximately 33%. Age of onset influences the recurrence rate: The risk of a second febrile seizure is more than 50% in infants under 1 year of age, while only 11% in children older than 3 years (Berg, Shinnar, Hauser, et al., 1990). It is unclear why some children are more likely to develop febrile convulsions than others. Genetic factors are suggested because some families have multiply affected members (Wallace, 1988).

By the time the child is brought to the pediatrician's office or emergency room following a febrile seizure, the seizure has almost always ended and the child is either sleeping or back to normal. Examination reveals no abnormalities other than the infection that led to the seizure. A lumbar puncture (spinal tap) is often performed for the initial seizure, especially in children younger than 2 years of age, in order to exclude the possibility of meningitis (Hirtz, 1989). Brain imaging studies are not required and should yield normal results if performed. There is no evidence that an EEG helps to predict outcome, but many clinicians prefer to exclude epileptiform features by performing an EEG before making the diagnosis of atypical febrile seizures. It is unusual to hospitalize a child following a febrile seizure unless there are other compelling medical reasons. Antiepileptic medication is not indicated under routine conditions. No evidence exists that febrile seizures increase the risk for later development of mental retardation, cerebral palsy, or learning disabilities.

Overall, about 2% of children with febrile convulsions subsequently develop seizure disorders. However, children with family histories of seizure disorders, abnormal neurological development before their first febrile convulsion, or atypical febrile convulsions have a 10% risk of developing epilepsy. Clearly, it is the subsequent development of unprovoked afebrile seizures that is the most important concern about febrile seizures. Retrospective analyses of adults with intractable complex partial seizures show a high incidence of earlier febrile convulsions (Harvey, Grattan-Smith, Desmond, et al., 1995). There is great interest in finding any markers to identify those children who are destined to have a poor prognosis. Prospective studies are beginning to follow cohorts of children with febrile convulsions. The temporal lobe is now being studied using sophisticated neuroimaging techniques because there is an association between mesial temporal sclerosis (damage to the hippocampal region of the brain) and complex partial seizures following febrile seizures earlier in childhood.

After the second febrile convulsion, prophylactic AED is sometimes considered (Consensus Development Conference, 1980). Use of anticonvulsants for febrile convulsions has been controversial for many years, particularly in the absence of risk factors for the subsequent development of epilepsy. It has been repeatedly shown that chronic AED administration can prevent further febrile convulsions but does not appear to influence the risk for the development of subsequent epilepsy. Daily administration of phenobarbital was the treatment of choice in the past. Studies have shown that it reduces the risk of recurrence of febrile convulsions from 30% to less than 10%. Unfortunately, side effects are common, including fatigue, hyperactivity, irritability, and attention problems. There is a single report that associates phenobarbital with a small decline in IQ score months after discontinuation of the medication (Farwell, Lee, Hirtz, et al., 1990). Intermittent treatment with phenobarbital is ineffective because adequate blood levels are not achieved in time to offer protection. Furthermore, approximately 20% of children have seizures as the first sign of their acute illness. The trend is to avoid daily treatment in cases of febrile convulsions unless there are frequent recurrences, the child has a developmental disability, or there is overwhelming parental anxiety concerning the threat of future seizures (Berg et al., 1990). The only effective intermittent prophylaxis is oral diazepam [Valium] administered every 8 hours during a febrile illness (Rosman, Colton, Labazzo, et al., 1993). A popularized alternative is rectal diazepam administered within 5–10 minutes of seizure onset to prevent the development of status epilepticus. There is rapid absorption of rectal diazepam with peak blood levels reached within 5 minutes. Clinical studies have not shown any risk of cardiorespiratory compromise with this treatment (Camfield, Camfield, Smith, et al., 1989).

Neonatal Seizures

Seizures in the newborn period are most often a consequence of acute metabolic abnormalities, birth trauma, or hypoxia. These are often isolated seizures that typically do not require long-term AED once acute disturbances have resolved. (A complete discussion of neonatal seizures appears in Chapter 6.)

Conditions that Mimic Seizures

A number of conditions can mimic seizures. These occur in typically developing children as well as in those with developmental disabilities. Some of the most common nonepileptic paroxysmal events simulating seizures include breath-holding spells, fainting, migraine headaches, drug reactions, tics, night terrors, gastroesophageal reflux, rage reactions, and masturbation.

Breath-Holding

Breath-holding is the most common nonepileptic cause of spells that are confused with seizures. It occurs in about 4% of children between the ages of 6 and 18 months (Brenningstall, 1996). Episodes begin with prolonged crying, followed by the arrest of breathing in expiration. This may last close to a minute with associated blueness of the lips, back arching, and loss of consciousness. It ends with a sudden gasping for breath and rapid neurological recovery. Prolonged episodes can be associated with brief generalized convulsive movements followed by lethargy. Breath-holding can be distinguished from a seizure by a normal EEG between attacks and a characteristic pattern associated with bradycardia during the attack. Breath-holding episodes are often precipitated by unexpected pain, anger, or frustration. It is inappropriate to treat breath-holding spells with AEDs. Instead, therapy should include parental education and behavior management techniques.

Sleep Disorders

Sleep disorders also may resemble seizures. Sudden attacks of daytime sleep may occur in children who are sleep deprived, whose nighttime sleep is severely disturbed by frequent arousals, or in those with narcolepsy. Narcolepsy is a sleep disorder characterized by daytime sleep attacks, sudden loss of postural tone called cataplexy (usually triggered by strong emotion), and sleep paralysis. The sleep attacks associated with narcolepsy can mimic absence seizures, while cataplexy may closely resemble atonic seizures. The diagnosis of narcolepsy is suggested by the clinical findings of excessive daytime sleepiness plus the appearance of one or more REM (rapid eye movement) episodes on the Multiple Sleep Latency Test (Brown & Billiard, 1995). An overnight EEG usually shows no other disorders.

Parasomnias are another type of primary sleep disorder often confused with epilepsy. Night terrors are the most frightening form of these non-REM partial arousals, which also include confusional arousals, sleepwalking, and sleeptalking (Mahowald & Throrpy, 1995). Sporadic confusional arousals are extremely common in typically developing children between 2 and 5 years of age. The child awakens suddenly 1–3 hours after falling asleep, cries out inconsolably, appears disoriented, and may run through the house in an agitated state. The episode ends within a few minutes as the child either fully awakens or quietly returns to sleep. Often, the only treatment needed is reassurance to the parents that this is a normal phenomenon. Frequent events can be disrupting to the family, however, and self-endangering behavior can occur (e.g., falling down stairs). In these situations, treatment options include nightly benzodiazepine medication (e.g., diazepam) or nonpharmacological techniques such as planned arousals 15–30 minutes before the expected attack. This may prevent attacks by reducing the depth of the first deep sleep cycles (Lask, 1988; Rosen, Mahowald, & Ferber, 1995). An overnight EEG in a sleep laboratory can be performed to exclude a seizure disorder or an underlying physiological disturbance such as apnea, cardiac arrhythmia, or myoclonus, which can trigger the event. Even though most children do not show their full characteristic events in the sleep laboratory, minor arousals from slow-wave sleep are typically seen and are generally sufficient to make a firm diagnosis.

Tics

Tics are repetitive, brief, stereotypic movements or vocalizations (Cohen & Leckman, 1994). Motor tics typically involve the head and neck and may include facial twitches, head shaking, eye blinking, and shoulder shrugging. Vocal tics, which are characterized by coughing, humming, sniffing, or repetitive grunts or other sounds, become more common in older children. Tics often begin in primary school-age children and can be intensified by anxiety, fatigue, or excitement. Simple, transient tics occur in approximately 15% of children. The most severe tic disorder is called Tourette syndrome and occurs in approximately 1 in 2,000 children. The criteria for diagnosis of Tourette syndrome are met when motor mannerisms are combined with vocal tics and the history of symptoms exceeds 1 year. More than 60% of children with Tourette syndrome also demonstrate attention-deficit/hyperactivity disorder (ADHD). These symptoms sometimes antedate the onset of tics by years. Therefore, it is not uncommon for tics to become prominent after initiation of methylphenidate (Ritalin) or other stimulant medication for the treatment of ADHD. These medications should be avoided in children with a personal or family history of tics (see Chapter 22). Obsessive or compulsive behavior occurs in 30% of children with Tourette syndrome, although few have sufficient symptoms to fulfill the criteria for obsessive-compulsive disorder. Repetitive tics may occasionally resemble partial or myoclonic seizures. However, tics are not associated with loss of consciousness and can be suppressed temporarily, suggesting that they are under partial voluntary control. Medical treatment of tics is entirely different from treatment of seizure disorders. They do not respond to AEDs, which primarily enhance activity of the neurotransmitter gamma-aminobutyric acid (GABA) but rather to drugs that affect the neurotransmitter dopamine such as haloperidol (Haldol) or alpha-2 adrenergic agonists such as clonidine (Catapres). The EEG in Tourette syndrome may have nonspecific abnormalities of background activity but does not show epileptiform features.

Migraine Headaches

The visual phenomena, hemiplegia, speech impairment, and mood changes of complex migraine headaches can be confused with the aura of a partial seizure (Hockaday, 1990). Headache, vomiting, and lethargy can simulate the postictal state. An EEG obtained between migraine attacks does not typically show epileptiform activity, but diffuse abnormalities can be seen in up to half of individuals who suffer from migraine headaches. Studies taken during migraine attacks may show a variety of EEG findings, but not an actual seizure pattern. Still, there is some overlap of migraines and seizures. The diagnosis of pediatric migraine is made by a consistent history of episodic, pulsatile, unilateral headaches, associated with nausea, vomiting, photophobia, and sound sensitivity. A positive family history is found in more than 80% of these children.

Fainting

Fainting (also called syncope) is caused by a brief decrease in blood supply to the brain. It can be the result of a variety of problems, most of which are benign. These include blood drawing, viral illness, standing in a line on a hot day, fasting, hyperventilating, or highly emotional activities (e.g., attending a rock concert). It occurs most commonly in adolescent girls. Fainting may mimic an atonic seizure but has a somewhat different clinical picture. The child feels dizzy and becomes pale and sweaty; vision is impaired, and the room seems to spin; then the child gradually slips to the floor, but not forcefully as in a seizure. Recovery is within seconds and without amnesia. An EEG is not indicated and if performed will not show the typical features of a seizure.

Gastroesophageal Reflux

Gastroesophageal reflux results from an incompetent muscular valve at the junction of the stomach and esophagus. This leads to backflow of acidic stomach contents into the esophagus. In young children, especially those with cerebral palsy, this may result in the child assuming a back-arched position (called Sandifer syndrome) that may resemble a tonic seizure. This position appears to decrease the reflux and relieve the associated pain. Episodes usually stop when appropriate antireflux treatment is initiated.

Behavior Disturbances

Certain behaviors may resemble seizures. In uncontrolled rage reactions, the child may appear to be disoriented, and events often end with exhaustion. Sudden mood changes and the onset of violent behavior can be sufficiently abrupt as to resemble a partial complex seizure. In contrast to epilepsy, however, these episodes are usually provoked by anger or frustration. Furthermore, intentional and directed violence almost never occurs as part of a seizure. In addition, there is no loss of consciousness or amnesia with a rage reaction. However, with both conditions some children are exhausted and sleep after the event. Rage reaction can often be controlled using behavior management techniques and family counseling. Effective pharmacotherapy has included lithium, propranolol, carbamazepine, and valproic acid.

In children with mental retardation requiring extensive supports, certain self-stimulatory or self-injurious behaviors may also resemble complex partial seizures. In addition, jitteriness and **sleep myoclonus** can be confused with seizures, particularly in neonates. Last, masturbation, especially with its shuddering climax and subsequent sleepiness, may resemble a seizure in infant girls or children with developmental disabilities in whom it may be unsuspected (Fleisher & Morrison, 1990).

STATUS EPILEPTICUS

A single, brief seizure is not usually dangerous unless the child falls; is exposed to physical danger (e.g., a tonic-clonic seizure while swimming); or aspirates on food. Status epilepticus, however, can become life threatening or result in brain damage. Status epilepticus is defined as a single seizure or cluster of seizures that is sufficiently prolonged or repeated at sufficiently brief intervals to produce an unvarying and enduring epileptic condition (Working Group on Status Epilepticus, 1993). Although this definition does not establish a precise duration, most clinicians consider 20–30 minutes of continuous seizures or repetitive seizures without a full return of consciousness to represent status. Certainly, one would not withhold treatment until a seizure meets the minimal time duration for status epilepticus. There is increasing evidence that early treatment is more effective than if it is initiated later in the course.

Status epilepticus occurs most frequently during the first 3 years of life. Disorders predisposing to status include birth asphyxia, traumatic brain injury, inborn errors of metabolism, progressive neurological disorders, neurocutaneous syndromes, and brain tumors (Brown & Hussain, 1991a). Equally common are acute, symptomatic causes such as meningitis, electrolyte disturbances, prolonged febrile convulsions, and subtherapeutic AED levels in a child known to have epilepsy.

Studies have documented the possibility of permanent neurological impairment following prolonged status epilepticus. Fortunately, morbidity and mortality following status epilepticus have decreased significantly in the 1980s and 1990s as a result of a combination of more aggressive treatment and improvements in supportive care in the emergency room and intensive care unit (Appleton, Sweeney, Choonara, et al., 1995; Brown & Hussain, 1991b).

DIAGNOSING EPILEPSY

The diagnosis of epilepsy begins with a history of recurrent seizures. Almost any paroxysmal or sudden episodic behavior can represent a seizure if it is associated with abnormal electrical discharges on an EEG. Even headaches, fainting spells, apneic episodes, and sleep attacks may occasionally be a symptom of epilepsy. Specific abnormalities on the EEG can help determine the type of epilepsy and localize the region in the brain where the seizure focus originates (Figure 26.8). In addition, brain-imaging techniques have become increasingly important in evaluating seizure disorders.

The Electroencephalogram

An EEG should be performed on any child suspected of having a seizure disorder as soon as possible after the event. Approximately 80% of all children with seizure disorders have abnormal EEG patterns between seizures (Holmes, 1989). The abnormalities, however, may disappear with treatment. Generalized tonic-clonic epilepsy produces an interictal pattern of widespread bursts of spike and wave activity simultaneously throughout the whole brain (Figure 26.3). In contrast, typical absence seizures show a normal interictal background with the discharge during a seizure consisting of repetitive spike and slow waves at a frequency of 2.5–3.0 Hz (Figure 26.4). Each paroxysmal burst lasts only a few seconds but often recurs throughout the EEG. Unlike those general seizures, partial seizures are typified by seizure activity that occurs only in one part of a hemisphere (most commonly the temporal lobe), with seizure spikes restricted to the affected region (Figure 26.6). The EEG of infantile spasms typically shows chaotic bursts of epileptiform activity throughout the brain, known as hypsarrhythmia (Figure 26.7).

Abnormal EEGs, even those with frequent abnormal discharges, do not necessarily correlate with the clinical diagnosis of epilepsy. Up to 35% of completely asymptomatic first-degree relatives of children with generalized epilepsy will demonstrate spike-wave activity on a routine EEG. For this reason, most neurologists do not treat an abnormal EEG in the absence of clinically apparent seizures. Conversely, a normal EEG does not preclude a definite diagnosis of clinical seizures. Sometimes the identification of epileptiform EEG disturbances requires activation procedures, including sleep, photic stimulation, or hyperventilation to bring out an underlying seizure tendency.

Sleep often acts as a powerful force to increase epileptiform EEG activity, and the transition from sleep to wake is a common time for seizures to occur. Therefore, every routine EEG study should attempt to include natural sleep and arousal. When indicated, hypnotics such as chloral hydrate may be used to induce sleep, although they are not part of a routine pediatric EEG protocol. Overnight sleep deprivation is known to double the frequency of epileptiform abnormalities in both children and adults and is often used in EEG studies (Declerck, 1986). There are no specific guidelines for sleep deprivation in infants or young children. Even a few hours of

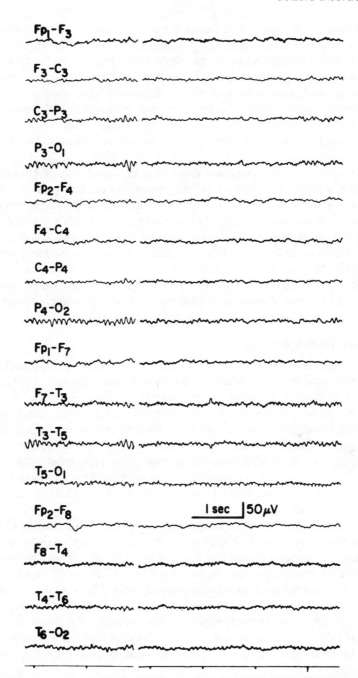

Figure 26.8.   Appearance of a normal electroencephalogram (EEG). Note the relatively regular, undulating brain wave pattern. (From Niedermeyer, E., & Lopes da Silva, F. [1987]. *Electroencephalography: Basic principles, clinical applications, and related fields* [2nd ed., p. 100]. Baltimore: Urban & Schwarzenberg; reprinted by permission of Williams & Wilkins Co.)

missed sleep on the night before the study may permit easier identification of important abnormalities. Older children should be encouraged to remain awake all night. Photosensitive epilepsy can be brought out by intense strobe light (photic stimulation) at various frequencies. Hyperventilation typically produces EEG activation characterized by generalized high-voltage slow waves in all children, but nonepileptic individuals rarely show actual spike or sharp waves. Hyperventilation also can lead to clinical seizures, particularly in the newly diagnosed or undertreated child with absence seizures. Occasionally, the EEG laboratory can reproduce the conditions that evoke seizures. For example, in the susceptible child a sudden loud noise can provoke seizures.

When there is still a diagnostic dilemma after a routine study, prolonged EEG monitoring can lead to a proper diagnosis. Ambulatory recordings can now provide studies under naturalistic settings at home and school. Video EEG, which permits prolonged simultaneous monitoring of behavior in conjunction with EEG recording, is also widely available. Analysis of events identified by caregivers can be supplemented by computer-assisted spike and seizure detection. A 4- to 8-hour outpatient video EEG can often capture events in order to provide accurate diagnosis. Video EEG monitoring also can be performed as long as necessary in the inpatient setting in order to clarify the nature of events. Long-term monitoring to capture clinical seizures is necessary prior to surgical removal; in addition to surface recording, implanted intracranial leads may be invaluable for precise localization of the seizure focus.

Brain Imaging Techniques

Advanced neuroimaging technology is increasingly important in the identification of discrete areas of brain abnormality in children with seizure disorders (Shields, 1993). These techniques include CT, MRI, PET, and single photon emission computer tomography (SPECT). These techniques can be used to identify tumors, aneurysms, calcifications, atrophy, and developmental brain malformations. They are most likely to yield positive findings in children with uncontrolled epilepsy, more than one type of seizure, and other developmental disabilities. CT combines X-ray techniques with computer technology to create serial images (slices) of the brain. MRI makes use of the intrinsic magnetic characteristics of the molecules of the brain to produce images that are even better than CT scans in defining structural abnormalities and differentiating gray and white matter.

PET and SPECT produce images that reveal metabolic activity of the brain (Chugani, Shields, Shewmon, et al., 1990). They can localize a seizure focus by identifying areas of the brain that have decreased blood flow between seizures and increased blood flow during a seizure (Figure 26.9). This is a prerequisite for seizure surgery. Both PET and SPECT scans require injection of small amounts of radioactive material. SPECT has the advantage of utilizing commercially available reagents, while PET requires rapidly decaying tracers that must be produced on site by a cyclotron, an extremely expensive piece of equipment that is not widely available. As a result, SPECT has become more widely available then PET and should become even more popular in the future with the advent of more advanced imaging technology and tracers with longer shelf lives.

Other rapidly developing technologies include functional MRI and magnetic resonance spectroscopy that have the potential to demonstrate brain activity without the need for radioactive tracers. Magneto-electroencephalography is another noninvasive modality that may permit

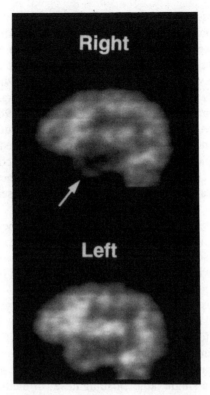

Figure 26.9.   These PET images were obtained following the intravenous administration of 18-F-Deoxyglucose. Tomographic scans reveal significant hypometabolism in the right temporal lobe (arrow), compared with the left. This finding is consistent with a seizure focused in the right temporal lobe.

an additional window on brain function by measuring magnetic activity of the cortex to provide three-dimensional localization of a seizure focus.

TREATMENT OF SEIZURE DISORDERS

Most seizure disorders can be treated effectively with one or more of the widely available AEDs (Buchanan, 1995). Alternative therapies for intractable seizures include unusual AEDs or alternative medications, investigational new drugs, the ketogenic diet, and surgery.

Antiepileptic Drugs

Once epilepsy is diagnosed, treatment with an AED is usually started in order to prevent further seizures. The most commonly used medications, dosages, and side effects are listed in Appendix C. Surprisingly, there is no significant difference in effectiveness among a number of drugs used to treat certain seizure types. For example, carbamazepine, phenobarbital, phenytoin, primidone, and valproic acid all appear to be equally effective in treating generalized tonic-clonic seizures. As a result, the reason for choosing a specific AED for a specific type of seizure is often based more on side effects, cost, and the doctor's experience than anything else (Brodie & Dichter, 1995). In terms of cost, phenobarbital and phenytoin are the least expensive, while carbamazepine, valproic acid, and three more recently released drugs (lamotrigine, gabapentin, and felbamate) are the most expensive. In terms of side effects, phenobarbital, phenytoin, lamotrigine, and felbamate have the most toxicity, while valproic acid and carbamazepine have the least among the standard AEDs (Collaborative Group for Epidemiology of Epilepsy, 1988; Herranz, Armijo, & Arteaga, 1988).

In a child with a single type of seizure, there is up to a 90% success rate in controlling the seizures using a single AED (Herranz et al., 1988). Once a drug is chosen, the dosage is adjusted so that seizures are controlled and side effects are minimized (Dodson, 1989; Pellock, 1989). AED drug levels, complete blood count (CBC), and liver function tests (LFT) are the most common routine surveillance studies performed. In addition, most child neurologists ask the child and family to maintain a diary to document the frequency of seizures and to determine the effectiveness of treatment.

The child who has mental retardation or other developmental disabilities, a structural brain malformation, mixed seizure types, or recurrent infantile spasms is more likely to require two or more AEDs to achieve seizure control. Not only is the risk of toxicity higher in this situation, but the likelihood of achieving complete elimination of seizures is far lower than in the uncomplicated child.

When a child is first started on a maintenance dose of any AED, he or she is unprotected for a number of days. It takes 4–5 half-lives (the time it takes for half of the drug dose to be eliminated from the body) to achieve steady state blood levels (Figure 26.10). Steady state exists when the rate of elimination equals the rate of input. Because AEDs have half-lives ranging from 6 to 48 hours, it can take up to 2 weeks before the child achieves steady state. Thus, after a seizure has occurred, a single large "loading dose" of medication may be given in order to achieve therapeutic drug levels more rapidly. The risks of sedation and ataxia resulting from this loading dose must be weighed against the need for immediate protection against a future seizure. However, not all AEDs are amenable to loading; in fact, only phenobarbital and phenytoin are commonly initiated in this way. This likely accounts for their ongoing wide acceptance even though other AEDs are now available that are equally effective and have fewer side effects.

Drug levels are measured at least 4–5 half-lives after an AED has been started or after the dose has been changed. Periodic levels should be measured consistently relative to the dose, either by measuring peak levels, usually reached about 2 hours after oral administration of most drugs, or trough levels, the point when drug levels are lowest, usually just before the morning dose (Schoenberger, Milenko, Ashish, et al., 1995). If there is concern about drug toxicity, peak levels are more helpful. If the physician is worried about breakthrough seizures or possible noncompliance, however, trough levels are preferred. Ordinarily, trough or lowest drug levels are obtained several times per year to ensure that they remain within an acceptable range. Some children may need and are able to tolerate higher than usual drug levels without toxicity while others will show side effects within the therapeutic range. If significant side effects develop, a blood level should be taken immediately to ensure that the level is in a range that was previously well tolerated.

Phenytoin

Phenytoin (Dilantin) appears to control seizures by inactivating the sodium channel that normally permits depolarization of the neuron. It also prevents the release of excitatory neurotransmitters from the synapse so that the impulse cannot pass from one neuron to another. This pre-

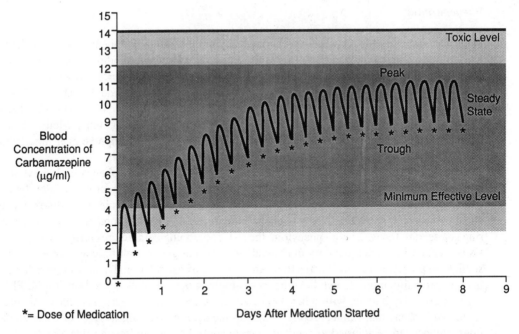

15
14   Toxic Level
13
12   Peak
11
10   Steady
9   State
8
Blood
Concentration of   7   Trough
Carbamazepine   6
(μg/ml)   5   Minimum Effective Level
4
3
2
1
0 *   1   2   3   4   5   6   7   8   9

*= Dose of Medication   Days After Medication Started

Figure 26.10. Achieving steady state with carbamazepine (Tegretol) in a child being dosed three times a day. The medication has been started on Day 1. Peak serum level is achieved approximately 1 hour after each dose, and it declines over the next 8 hours, at which time the second dose is given. After each successive dose, peak levels increase until leveling out at 4–5 half-lives when steady state is reached. By 1 week of treatment, the child should be well protected against seizures. For a drug with a shorter half-life (e.g., valproate), it takes less time to achieve a steady state, and for one with a longer half-life (e.g., phenobarbital), it can take up to 3 weeks. (Key: * = dose of medication.)

vents the recruitment of nerve cells that surround the focus of the seizure, thereby stopping its spread (Matsuda, Higashi, & Inotsume, 1989). Thus, although phenytoin does not prevent the discharge of a seizure focus, it restricts the spread of the electrical abnormality so that there is insufficient cortical involvement to produce a clinical seizure.

Phenytoin can be used to control both generalized tonic-clonic and partial seizures. Young children usually take it twice a day, although older children can sometimes be given a single daily dose of proprietary Dilantin Kapseals. Among the common side effects of phenytoin are gum swelling, excessive hairiness, worsening of acne, and coarsening of facial features. Signs of acute toxicity include vomiting, lethargy, and ataxia. Nonambulatory individuals are at risk of developing osteoporosis related to folic acid and vitamin D deficiencies. Phenytoin also can have an adverse effect on learning and behavior (American Academy of Pediatrics, Committee on Drugs, 1995). All of these symptoms disappear when the dosage is lowered or stopped. Generally, phenytoin is considered to be safe and effective, but it does have a relatively high incidence of bothersome side effects. Also, exposure during early pregnancy can lead to malformations in the developing embryo (see Chapter 4).

Phenobarbital

Phenobarbital is no longer widely prescribed beyond infancy. Like phenytoin, it is primarily used to treat tonic-clonic and partial seizures. It has the advantage of administration in a single daily dose. However, side effects including drowsiness, sleep disturbance, irritability, and skin rash are so common that they limit its usefulness in older children and adults. About 20%–40% of the children who take phenobarbital become significantly hyperactive or experience other behavior and learning problems that lead to discontinuing the medication (Vining, Mellits, Dorsen, et al., 1987). It should be noted that adverse behavioral effects may improve over time and are less apparent if the drug is started at a low dose and gradually increased.

The mechanism of action of phenobarbital is quite different from phenytoin. It prevents the onset of a seizure by raising the intensity of the stimulus needed to trigger the seizure. Its main action is at the N-methyl-D aspartate (NMDA) glutamate receptor. This is an excitotoxic neurochemical receptor, and inhibition by phenobarbital decreases the likelihood of a discharge occurring at a seizure focus. As with phenytoin, the risk of pathological fractures related to osteoporosis is increased in nonambulatory individuals who do not get enough folic acid or exposure to sunlight to promote vitamin D activation. An overdose of phenobarbital leads to severe lethargy, but this generally improves within 24 hours of stopping the medication (Dodson, 1989). Phenobarbital also may interact with other AEDs, affecting their blood levels. This most commonly occurs with phenytoin, carbamazepine, and valproic acid. As a result, dosages of these medications may need to be adjusted to maintain seizure control while minimizing side effects.

Primidone

Primidone (Mysoline) is structurally related to phenobarbital and normal metabolism generates therapeutic phenobarbital levels. This drug is primarily used to treat partial and secondarily generalized tonic-clonic seizures. It appears to be somewhat better in controlling complex partial seizures than phenobarbital alone, but toxicity is more common. Behavioral side effects disappear when the drug is discontinued (Aicardi, 1994). Because of its frequent side effects, primidone is now infrequently prescribed.

Carbamazepine

Carbamazepine (Tegretol) is the drug of choice for most cases of tonic-clonic and partial seizures; however, it may actually worsen absence seizure activity (Snead & Hosey, 1985). Its mechanism of action is thought to be similar to that of phenytoin. Side effects are generally milder and less frequent than phenytoin or phenobarbital, making it the initial drug of choice for many neurologists. Side effects are uncommon, and they can be minimized if the drug is started at a low dosage and gradually increased to therapeutic levels. However, ataxia, double vision, drowsiness, slurred speech, tremor, headache, and nausea can occur and be troublesome. Swallowable tablets of proprietary Tegretol XR can be given twice a day without leading to excessive variability in blood levels, but generic preparations as well as the oral suspension and other preparations of Tegretol are best administered three times daily. Bone marrow suppression is an uncommon idiosyncratic problem, but asymptomatic minor lowering of the white blood cell count is common. Carbamazepine has only modest adverse effects on behavior and cognitive function.

Ethosuximide

Ethosuximide (Zarontin) is used primarily for treating absence seizures. It is the drug of choice when absences are the only manifestations of primary generalized epilepsy. It may also be effective as an adjunctive drug to valproic acid or benzodiazepines in refractory generalized epilepsy. Side effects include drowsiness, dizziness, gastric distress, insomnia, rash, headache, and depression.

Benzodiazepines

Effective AEDs in the benzodiazepine family include clonazepam (Klonopin), lorazepam (Ativan), nitrazepam, and clorazepate (Tranxene). Diazepam (Valium) is rarely used in the chronic treatment of seizures because clonazepam and clorazepate are far more effective; lorazepam, with its sustained blood levels for 12–24 hours, make it better for treating status epilepticus (Lockman, 1990). Clonazepam, clorazepate, and nitrazepam are most often used to treat infantile spasms, Lennox-Gastaut syndrome, and absence seizures and are occasionally used to treat generalized and partial complex seizures (Chamberlain, 1996). They act by indirectly stimulating the GABA receptors that are inhibitory to seizure activity. Drowsiness and irritability are common when the medication is first started but usually subside after a few weeks. In children with cerebral palsy, other side effects include decreased muscle tone, excessive drooling, and increased swallowing difficulties (Eadie, 1984).

Valproic Acid

Valproic acid (Depakene/Depakote) is a broadly effective AED that can be used to treat all types of seizures. However, it is most often prescribed for primary generalized epilepsy with tonic-clonic seizures or absence attacks. It can also be effective in treating Lennox-Gastaut syndrome, and studies compare it favorably to other major AEDs for partial onset seizures with or without secondary generalization. It works in part by decreasing the breakdown of GABA so more neurotransmitter is available to suppress seizure activity. Side effects are seen in about 12% of treated children and include nausea, drowsiness, excessive weight gain, and hair loss (Vining et al., 1987). These problems usually improve over time and will stop if the drug is discontinued. Certain metabolic abnormalities, including elevated levels of ammonia and glycine, also may develop. These do not appear, however, to be associated with clinical symptoms in most cases. Supplements of carnitine are sometimes used to correct these alterations (Coulter, 1995). Potentially fatal hepatic toxicity and pancreatitis have been reported but are very rare; experience shows that only 1 in 35,000 individuals who take this drug develop severe, irreversible liver failure or pancreatitis (Bryant & Dreifuss, 1996). However, these complications are more common (approximately 1 in 600) in children under 2 years of age receiving multiple AEDs and in older individuals with metabolic disorders or severe developmental disabilities. In these children, valproic acid should be used with caution and preferably as the only AED; many clinicians will start these children on carnitine supplementation in hopes of avoiding these severe complications. Despite these potential hazards, valproic acid is considered to be an excellent and quite safe AED.

New Antiepileptic Drugs

In the 1990s, there has been a flurry of newly released drugs and a number of other novel medications being considered by the Food and Drug Administration (FDA) (Dichter & Brodie, 1996;

Marson, Kadir, & Chadwick, 1996; Richens & Perucca, 1995). Felbamate (Felbatol), gabapentin (Neurontin), and lamotrigine (Lamictal) are already on the market, although only felbamate has a pediatric indication (Besag, Wallace, Dulac, et al., 1995; Khurana, Riviello, Helmers, et al., 1996). There was initial excitement about the use of felbamate in treating Lennox-Gastaut syndrome and other seizure disorders. This has been muted by reports of severe liver toxicity and aplastic anemia, and it is now indicated only for refractory epilepsy. Other drugs far along in the development process include vigabatrin, topiramate, and tiagabine (Uldall, Alving, Gram, et al., 1995). Each appears to have an excellent safety and efficacy profile. Although some of these drugs act in similar ways to the AEDs described previously, they may be more powerful and have fewer side effects. Others, such as gabapentin and vigabatrin, appear to have novel mechanisms of action (Meldrum, 1996). It is too soon to know which of these drugs will eventually end in the first-line treatment of epilepsy and which in the epileptologist's armamentarium for drug-resistant seizures.

ACTH *and Corticosteroids*

ACTH, a steroid-releasing hormone, is used primarily to treat infantile spasms and Lennox-Gastaut syndrome, although it also can be used to treat other intractable seizure disorders. This drug has the disadvantage of requiring daily intramuscular injections. Treatment is usually tapered within a few weeks if it has been effective in stopping the seizures, but some clinicians continue it at low doses on a long-term basis. ACTH is effective in stopping about 80% of cryptogenic infantile spasms if started within 1 month of their onset (Bobele & Bodensteiner, 1990). It is less effective in controlling symptomatic infantile spasms from identifiable causes and Lennox-Gastaut syndrome. ACTH has potentially severe side effects including osteoporosis, high blood pressure, diabetes, gastric ulcers, cataracts, and increased risk of infection. Thus, it is used with extreme caution. It is also unclear whether stopping the seizures has any beneficial effect on neurodevelopmental outcome. Oral prednisone has been used in the same conditions as ACTH, and results are quite similar. Often the decision to use one or the other agent is a result of local custom.

Maintaining AED Control

The most common cause of poorly controlled seizures is noncompliance in taking prescribed AEDs. This may range from a teenager's rebellious behavior to parents who frequently forget to give the medication to their young child. Thus, when faced with increased seizure activity, the physician's first thought should be to determine whether the child is receiving the prescribed dosage before deciding to increase the dosage or change the medication. AED blood levels are very useful in determining compliance. A weekly pill box may help ensure compliance. There are even containers with built in alarms that ring each day at the proper time for the medication.

Administering the proper dosage of AED may be a problem even if the parent follows the prescribed schedule. The child may spit out or throw up the medication. The parent may then be concerned about overdosing the child by repeating the medication. In general, if the child spits out or vomits most of the medication within 1 hour, the dose should be repeated.

Generic brands are available for most AEDs. Although nominally equivalent in strength, they may vary in absorption rate, leading to variable drug levels. Therefore, low AED blood levels also may result from a change in the brand of medication.

If compliance appears to be good and the seizures are still poorly controlled, the physician may decide to increase the dosage of the medication. The medication can be increased until the child develops side effects or there are significant biochemical abnormalities found on blood tests. It is always preferable to use a single AED rather than two or more. This prevents drug interactions, but the concept of "rational polypharmacy" has become popular for difficult-to-control epilepsy. This approach combines drugs with different mechanisms of action or synergistic effects at the same synaptic sites for improved effectiveness.

When to Stop Antiepileptic Drugs

For most children, epilepsy will eventually go into spontaneous remission although the EEG may not completely normalize. It is no longer believed that most individuals with epilepsy will require AED administration for life. A number of studies have reported the effects of stopping AED therapy in children who have been completely seizure-free for 2–4 years (Delgado, Riela, Mills, et al., 1996). Shinnar, Vining, Mellits, et al. (1985) followed children for 4 years after stopping treatment and found that more than two thirds remained seizure-free (Figure 26.11). Recurrences tended to occur within a year after stopping AED therapy, most frequently in the early months while the medication was being withdrawn. The risk for recurrent seizures was higher in children with mental retardation, in those with onset of epilepsy before 2 years of age, in individuals with a history of more than 30 seizures (Figure 26.12), and in those with abnormal EEG patterns when they stopped treatment (Figure 26.1). A more recent prospective study following children for seizure recurrence after discontinuation of medication found that 64% remained seizure-free after a mean follow-up period of 58 months (Shinnar et al., 1994). This study found that etiology, family history, age at onset, EEG findings, epileptic syndrome, and seizure type were useful in defining prognosis. In another study, individuals were followed for 15–23 years after termination of treatment (Thurston, Thurston, Hixon, et al., 1982). They found a 72% chance of remaining seizure-free in general and virtually a 100% chance if no seizure occurred within 5 years after stopping the medication. Overall, about 50% of children with mental retardation and seizures remain seizure-free without medication. It also has been shown that the removal of medication has led to some improvement in cognitive function (Siemes, Spohr, Michael, et al., 1988). Therefore, even for a child who has a combination of a seizure disorder, mental retardation, and an abnormal EEG, stopping medication after 2 seizure-free years should be considered.

The Ketogenic Diet

The ketogenic diet is an approach to treating seizures that has been available since the 1920s. Until losing popularity in the 1970s (following the release of carbamazepine and valproic acid), it was one of the few available safe and effective treatment options. In the 1990s, it has regained popularity (Wheless, 1995). It is most often used to treat intractable infantile spasms, atypical absences, tonic-clonic seizures, and Lennox-Gastaut syndrome. The ketogenic diet is high in fats and low in carbohydrates. To compensate for the deficiency in carbohydrates, fat becomes an important fuel source and releases ketone bodies. **Ketosis** is associated with a decrease in seizure activity in about half of the children treated, and AEDs can often be reduced or eliminated (Schwartz, Eaton, Bower, et al., 1989). The mechanism of action is thought to involve stimulation of the inhibitory neurotransmitter GABA.

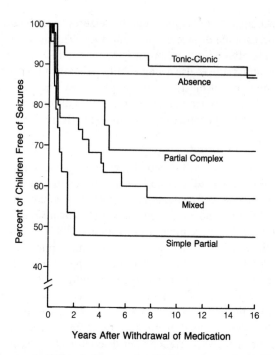

Figure 26.11.   Percentage of children who remained seizure-free after withdrawal of AEDs. More than 80% of children with tonic-clonic seizures or absence seizures remained seizure-free compared with 50%–70% of children with other types of seizures. All children had been free of seizures for at least 4 years before stopping the medication. (From Thurston, J.H., Thurston, D.L., Hixon, B.B., et al. [1982]. Prognosis in childhood epilepsy: Additional follow-up of 148 children 15 to 23 years after withdrawal of anticonvulsant therapy. *New England Journal of Medicine, 306,* 833; adapted by permission of *New England Journal of Medicine.*)

The diet regimen starts with a brief period of starvation under hospital supervision, to prevent hypoglycemia and excessive dehydration. The high-fat diet is gradually initiated once ketosis has been established. Butter and heavy cream provide the basis for the classic ketogenic diet. This diet is surprisingly well tolerated by most children. It has fewer side effects than more developed modifications based on medium chain triglyceride (MCT) oil or corn oil. Noncompliance can be an issue in older children who have access to cookies and other carbohydrate treats. Seizures can return abruptly if ketosis is not maintained.

Like any other medical treatment, the diet has risks. Multivitamins and minerals must be provided to supplement the ketogenic diet that is deficient in calcium, the B vitamins, and trace minerals. Constipation and dehydration are usually easily managed with increased fluids. Renal stones, neutropenia, and other complications are rare. The diet is calculated to provide the minimal protein requirements for growth, and, therefore, the child will not gain much weight or height. The 4:1 ketogenic diet is generally limited to no more than 2 years of full use with another year of gradual liberalization.

Surgical Treatment of Seizure Disorders

Surgical approaches to intractable epilepsy have become a well-accepted treatment option for some pediatric seizure disorders in the 1990s (Duchowny, 1989; Engel, 1996). Surgery should

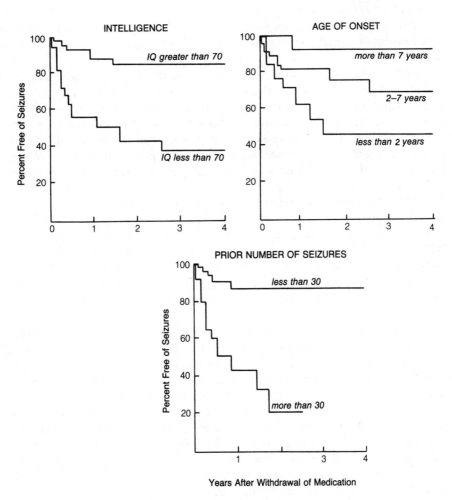

Figure 26.12.   Percentage of children who remained free of seizures for 4 years after withdrawal of AEDs. The risk of recurrence of seizures was higher in children with mental retardation, in those with onset of seizures before 2 years of age, and in those with histories of many seizures. All children had been free of seizures for 4 years before stopping medications. (From Emerson, R.D., D'Souza, B.J., Vining, E.P., et al. [1981]. Stopping medication in children with epilepsy: Predictors of outcome. *New England Journal of Medicine, 304,* 1127–1128; adapted by permission of *New England Journal of Medicine.*)

be considered if the seizures have proved resistant to AEDs and if the burdens of inadequately controlled epilepsy or side effects of medication are significantly interfering with the child's life. For example, in children with intractable seizures complicating Sturge-Weber syndrome, surgery should be performed before the onset of inevitable intellectual deterioration. Three types of surgical procedures have been used to treat various forms of epilepsy: focal resection, hemispherectomy, and corpus callostomy.

Focal Resection

Focal resection is considered when partial seizures (with or without secondary generalization) can be localized to one brain region. The most commonly performed focal surgery, and the procedure with the best outcome, is the excision of an abnormal region of one temporal lobe for treatment of partial complex seizures (Hopkins & Klug, 1991; Shields, Duchowny, & Holmes, 1993).

Appropriate candidates for focal excision are children who have had partial complex seizures that have been unresponsive to adequate trials of AEDs for at least 2 years. Epilepsy surgery requires a team approach emphasizing a comprehensive evaluation including neuropsychological and psychosocial assessments (Mizrahi, Kellaway, Grossman, et al., 1990). In carefully selected children and young adults, almost 80% of previously uncontrollable partial complex seizures are fully controlled or significantly improved by surgery (Walczak, Radtke, McNamara, et al., 1990). Virtually all individuals show a marked improvement in psychosocial and school function but no change in IQ score.

Risks of the procedure include memory impairment, visual field loss, and speech impairment. These risks can be minimized by 1) prior neuroimaging mapping of the cortical regions important in language or motor function so these can be avoided during surgery, 2) performing a Wada (intracarotid amytal) test to document that the temporal lobe on the opposite side can support language and memory functions, and 3) stimulating and testing the affected region in the awake older child prior to its removal during surgery. The risk of surgery itself is low, with a mortality rate less than 1 in 1,000 and the remote possibility of infection or stroke (Walczak et al., 1990).

Focal excisions also have been used to control partial seizures in areas of the brain other than the temporal lobe (Adler, Erba, Winston, et al., 1991). The best candidates are children with typical intelligence and a single type of seizure that can be localized to a brain region that is not necessary for speech, motor function, vision, and so forth. Some surgical candidates who have seizures of anterior temporal origin, supportive imaging results, and a positive Wada test may proceed directly to surgery. However, all extratemporal candidates must undergo invasive EEG recordings employing subdural or depth electrodes. This is necessary both to localize the seizure focus and to avoid the production of a new disability by resection of a portion of the cortex involved in speech. Approximately 70% of children undergoing extratemporal resection show improvement following surgery, but complete cessation of seizure activity is less likely to occur than with temporal lobe excision (Wyllie, 1991).

Corpus Callosotomy

The corpus callosum is the major band of white matter that connects the two hemispheres and permits rapid transmission of messages between the two sides of the brain (Sass, Spencer, Spencer, et al., 1988). However, it also allows spread of seizure discharges by permitting a focal event to cross over and become a generalized seizure. Subtotal surgical division of the corpus callosum has been most effective in treating drop attacks (atonic seizures). This procedure also has been helpful in certain individuals with poorly controlled generalized seizures and partial seizures with secondary generalization (Reutens, Bye, Hopkins, et al., 1993). Callosotomy is not intended as a cure for epilepsy but rather palliative treatment in stopping disabling and dangerous seizures.

Transient side effects of callosotomy including mutism, left hemiparesis (mostly affecting the leg), and depression usually resolve within days or weeks after surgery. Rarely, manual dexterity may be impaired on a permanent basis. However, attention, behavior, and performance on cognitive tasks are usually improved (Mizrahi et al., 1990). Overall, between 25% and 75% of treated people show significant improvement in seizure control (Wyllie, 1988).

Hemispherectomy

Hemispherectomy is the most drastic, but also one of the most successful, surgical procedures for the treatment of certain forms of intractable epilepsy. Most surgeons now perform a variation of the original procedure called a functional hemispherectomy. This procedure removes the majority, but not all, of one cerebral hemisphere; portions of the frontal and occipital lobes are left in place but are disconnected. This variation was developed to avoid a serious late complication of complete hemispherectomy called **hemosiderosis** in the brain that resulted from recurrent subdural hemorrhages (Lindsay, Ounsted, & Richards, 1987). Functional hemispherectomy is considered only in children with the most severe, uncontrolled seizure disorders. It is most commonly considered in children with partial seizures who have **hemiplegia,** suggesting that one hemisphere is already damaged. The vast majority of these children also have significant behavior problems and cognitive impairments. About 85% of children treated with functional hemispherectomy become seizure-free, with associated improvement in behavior and cognitive function (Wyllie, 1991). Fortunately, hemiplegia rarely becomes worse, and postoperative hydrocephalus is an unusual complication (Lindsay et al., 1987).

WHAT TO DO IN THE EVENT OF A SEIZURE

Although AEDs and surgery are very effective, some individuals will not become entirely seizure-free. Seizures may occur as infrequently as once per year or as often as hundreds of times per day. The need for intervention by parents or professionals depends on the seizure type and duration. Repeated absence seizures require no immediate action, provided they stop within 15 minutes. Increasing frequency of the seizures, however, signals the possible need for adjustment in medication.

Tonic-clonic seizures are a more difficult problem because the child may fall and sustain serious injury even with brief spells. The appropriate first aid procedure follows simple, common-sense guidelines. The child should be placed on the floor or a bed. He or she should be turned to one side in order to prevent choking or aspirating from vomiting. The child should not, however, be tightly restrained. Clothing should be loosened around the neck. Fingers, tongue-blades, spoons, or other instruments should not be inserted between the child's teeth to prevent "swallowing of the tongue," which is physically impossible. The most common result of trying to insert an object is a bitten finger or a broken tooth. There have been reports of aspiration of blood from a resulting laceration or even blunt injury to the internal carotid artery that lies behind the tonsils. Emergency medical services should be called only if the seizure lasts more than 10–15 minutes, which is very uncommon in children. Home administration of rectal diazepam has become an accepted treatment for prevention of status epilepticus in those children who are prone to prolonged seizures. It is given as a retention enema within the first 10 minutes of a seizure at a dose of 0.5 milligrams per killigram with a maximum dose of 20 milligrams. Effective blood levels are reached within 5 minutes, and there have been no reports of cardiorespiratory compromise. Obviously, the child should be attended until fully awake and alert. Reassurance and comforting are often needed, and the child should be encouraged to resume activities once fully recovered.

MULTIDISCIPLINARY INTERVENTION

The care of the child with epilepsy involves more than medical and surgical treatment of the seizures. Education, psychosocial support, and involvement of the entire family are all critical to the effective management of the child (Hermann & Seidenberg, 1989). For these reasons, it is wise to have the child with difficult seizures followed at a comprehensive epilepsy program. These multidisciplinary clinics are staffed with a team of neurologists, nurses, psychologists, social workers, and other therapists working together (Vining, 1989). They are usually found at children's hospitals and university medical centers.

Educational Setting

From an educational perspective, the student's basic needs are dictated by his or her cognitive and learning abilities. In addition, teachers must be alert for signs of difficulty attributable to seizures or their treatment. The child with absence seizures who suddenly begins to do poorly in class may have unsuspected increased seizure activity. Alternatively, new or worsening school problems may develop as a result of increased drug dosage or the switch to a new medication. Behavioral side effects may include fatigue, inattention, irritability, or aggression. Teachers and parents must be alert to these signs for they may indicate the need to check drug levels or to change the dosage schedule. Alternatively, these nonspecific features may point to intercurrent illness, peer problems, new learning difficulties, or the need to reevaluate the entire educational program.

There are also the psychological side effects of a child having a seizure in class. A tonic-clonic seizure may make quite a spectacle, including the embarrassment of bowel and bladder incontinence during the seizure. The best approach is anticipatory education of classmates about seizures so that they know what to expect and do not ostracize their affected peer. A towel and a fresh change of clothing should also be kept in the classroom.

Psychosocial Issues

The child with epilepsy must be educated about the cause of the seizures. The more epilepsy can be accepted as a matter of fact, the better it is for everyone. Even in the case in which seizures become rare after achieving proper medication dosage, full discussion is appropriate.

The issue of sports has been controversial. At one time, children with epilepsy were precluded from participation in many sports; now it is felt that most sports are permissible once seizures are well controlled. Most clinicians continue to recommend that children with epilepsy avoid heavy contact sports such as tackle football as well as unusually dangerous activities such as rock climbing and scuba diving. Of course, routine precautions recommended for all children should be taken. For example, the child with epilepsy should not swim or dive in the absence of an experienced lifeguard; and helmets should be worn when bicycling, skateboarding, roller blading, playing baseball, and similar activities.

Like sports, family vacations and camping trips need not be curtailed in the child with well-controlled seizures. However, excessive fatigue should be avoided, as it may precipitate a seizure, and the family should travel with an adequate supply of antiepileptic medication. The decision to wear a medical identification bracelet optimally should be made with the child's assent; its value is considerably diminished if it is felt to be stigmatizing.

The family structure and routine should be kept intact as much as possible, and it is important not to overprotect the child (Lechtenberg, 1984). As the child moves toward adulthood, independence should be encouraged as much as possible. This includes independent living, driving if seizure-free for a suitable time period, and pursuing any appropriate job opportunity. The one exception is the epilepsy syndromes, which do not usually resolve, such as juvenile myoclonic epilepsy. In this case, it is important for the teenager to learn to accept long-term treatment, because medication-free remission is unlikely.

Several other issues should be addressed as the child approaches adulthood. Alcohol and illicit drugs should be avoided, if only for their effect on lowering seizure threshold and their interaction with AEDs. Some AEDs may decrease the effectiveness of birth control pills, resulting in contraceptive failure. As noted previously, AEDs taken during pregnancy have been associated with an increased risk of fetal malformations. In addition, during pregnancy, there may be altered drug metabolism and an increased risk of seizure activity. Overall, these risks are low; more than 90% of pregnancies in women with epilepsy are uneventful and have successful outcomes (see Chapter 4).

TIFFANY

Tiffany was 15 months old when she had her first seizure at the onset of a nonspecific viral illness. Her mother was giving her a sponge bath, trying to bring down her fever of 103°F, when she began having tonic-clonic convulsive movements. Her parents rushed her to a nearby hospital. When she arrived there 15 minutes later, she was no longer convulsing; in fact, she was sleeping. Within 2 hours, she was back to normal. Routine blood tests, urinalysis, and lumbar puncture were normal. Her EEG showed no paroxysmal features several hours after the event. The physician told Tiffany's parents that she had experienced a febrile convulsion. She indicated that this was not dangerous but might recur before Tiffany was 4 years old. She reassured the parents that Tiffany was fine and had not sustained any brain damage. The parents were instructed that the best prevention of future seizures was to keep her fever from going above 102°F by using acetaminophen (Tylenol) plus sponge baths. They were not advised to use any AEDs. Tiffany subsequently had two brief febrile convulsions in the next year, but her parents felt better prepared, and the seizures were not as traumatic for them. She has been well since then and is now an "A" student in the second grade.

JUANITA

Like Tiffany, Juanita's first seizure was tonic-clonic. It was not associated with fever, however, and occurred when she was 5 years old. There was no infection or injury to explain the seizure. Unlike Tiffany's normal EEG, Juanita's EEG showed focal spike and sharp waves. She was placed on carbamazepine to control the seizures. Despite therapeutic levels of the medication, Juanita's seizures continued. The family had difficulty coping with the illness, and they found it hard to give her the support and encouragement they knew she needed. Juanita felt ostracized in school; she was self-conscious about her disability, and she developed few friendships. Phenytoin was soon added to the carbamazepine, and her seizures became less frequent. However, the physician had difficulty achieving the desired level of phenytoin. Sometimes it was too high, and she was lethargic and ataxic; other times, it was too low, and she had seizures. Finally, the right dose was obtained and her seizures came under control. Unfortunately, the emotional problems for Juanita and her family persisted. Eventually, they were referred to a social worker for family counseling. Juanita began to feel better about herself and gained self-esteem. Her parents developed ways of coping with her illness and began to handle the situation more effectively. At 8 years of age, Juanita is doing well in school. She now attends Brownies and dancing classes; although still shy, she is making more friends.

YOSHI

Yoshi is a 3-year-old boy. For him, seizures are but one part of a more complex and serious condition. Yoshi was born prematurely at 33 weeks' gestation. Sepsis with meningitis complicated his neonatal course. He developed infantile spasms at 4 months of age, by which time he also showed poor head growth with microcephaly. The diagnosis of spastic cerebral palsy and mental retardation requiring extensive supports was made by 12 months of age. His seizures were poorly controlled despite therapeutic blood levels of valproic acid. By 16 months of age, he averaged 20–30 seizures of multiple types each day. His mother preferred not to administer additional medication because she found doing so made him lethargic and uninterested in his environment. The family elected not to attempt the ketogenic diet because they could not accept the demanding nature of the required close monitoring and the restricted variety of allowed foods.

His parents know Yoshi has mental retardation, and they worry about his future. He is now in a preschool program for children with cerebral palsy, and his parents are strengthened by the support of the teacher, physical therapist, and other professionals who work with him. For now, both Yoshi and his family are coping. Yet, his seizures continue.

PROGNOSIS

Most individuals with seizure disorders have typical intelligence. There has been controversy as to whether repeated seizures themselves or chronic antiepileptic drug treatment can lead to subtle brain injury, limiting the child's potential over time (Vermeulen & Aldenkamp, 1995). However, repeated IQ tests have not shown a decline in intellectual abilities unless the child is being overmedicated or has had a prolonged episode of status epilepticus (Ellenberg, Hirtz, & Nelson, 1986).

Prognosis most depends on the seizure type and the underlying brain pathology. Virtually all children with absence seizures have typical intelligence, while virtually all children with Lennox-Gastaut syndrome have mental retardation (Holmes, 1987). Yet, prognosis does not depend solely on intelligence. It also depends on how the child and family handle this chronic illness. If the seizures come under control easily and drug reactions are few, the family is likely to cope well. If the seizures prove resistant to treatment and drug side effects are many, additional stresses may interfere with the functioning of both the child and family.

Finally, there are emotional issues. Some children with seizure disorders have low self-esteem and depression leading to absenteeism in school and overdependence on their parents. When combined with subtle impairments in memory or learning, school failure may result. Yet, if these issues are approached in an effective manner, the prognosis is generally good. Because a majority of seizure disorders enter remission during childhood, it is critically important to allow each individual to achieve his or her maximal potential. Those who make it psychologically intact through school are likely to do well later in life. For those who have seizure disorders as but one feature of a multiple disability disorder, the eventual outcome is more commonly a function of the other disabilities than of the seizures.

SUMMARY

Seizure disorders are conditions in which there are abnormally functioning neurons that discharge at the least provocation to cause seizures. Generalized seizures include those classified as tonic-clonic, absence, myoclonic, and atonic. Partial seizures are defined as simple or complex, depending on whether there is loss of consciousness. Seizures may occur singly or in combination and may start in the newborn period, in infancy, or in later childhood. For about half of affected children, the seizures are an isolated disability. Most can be controlled by a single AED and these children can lead almost typical lives. For a child with multiple disabilities, the prognosis is generally more a function of the other disabilities than of the seizures.

REFERENCES

Adler, J., Erba, G., Winston, K.R., et al. (1991). Results of surgery for extratemporal partial epilepsy that began in childhood. *Archives of Neurology, 48,* 133–140.

Aicardi, J. (1994). *Epilepsy in children* (2nd ed.). New York: Raven Press.

Aicardi, J., the Coordinating Peer Review Group, & the European Infantile Spasms Vigabatrin Group. (1995, December). *European experience on the use of vigabatrin as first-line monotherapy in infantile spasms.* Paper presented at the annual meeting of the American Epilepsy Society, Baltimore.

Aldenkamp, A.P., Alpherts, W.C., Dekker, M.J., et al. (1990). Neuropsychological aspects of learning disabilities in epilepsy. *Epilepsia, 31*(Suppl. 4), S9–S20.

American Academy of Pediatrics, Committee on Drugs. (1995). Behavioral and cognitive effects of anticonvulsant therapy. *Pediatrics, 96,* 538–540.

American Academy of Pediatrics, Committee on Infectious Diseases. (1994). *Report of the committee on infectious diseases.* Elk Grove Village, IL: Author.

Annegars, J.E. (1993). Epidemiology of childhood onset seizures. In W.E. Dodson & J.M. Pellock (Eds.), *Pediatric epilepsy: Diagnosis and therapy* (pp. 57–61). New York: Demos Publications.

Appleton, R., Sweeney, A., Choonara, I., et al. (1995). Lorazepam versus diazepam in the acute treatment of epileptic seizures and status epilepticus. *Developmental Medicine and Child Neurology, 37,* 682–688.

Baram, T.Z., Mitchell, W.G., Tournay, A., et al. (1996). High-dose corticotropin (ACTH) versus prednisone for infantile spasms: A prospective, randomized, blinded study. *Pediatrics, 97,* 375–379.

Bebin, E.M., Kelly, P.J., & Gomez, M.R. (1993). Surgical treatment for epilepsy in cerebral tuberous sclerosis. *Epilepsia, 34,* 651–657.

Berg, A.T., Shinnar, S., Hauser, W.A., et al. (1990). Predictors of recurrent febrile seizures: A metaanalytic review. *Journal of Pediatrics, 116,* 329–337.

Besag, F.M.C., Wallace, S.J., Dulac, O., et al. (1995). Lamotrigine for the treatment of epilepsy in childhood. *Pediatrics, 127,* 991–997.

Bobele, G.B., & Bodensteiner, J.B. (1990). Infantile spasms. *Neurologic Clinics, 8,* 633–645.

Brenningstall, G.N. (1996). Breathholding spells. *Pediatric Neurology, 15,* 91–97.

Brodie, M.J., & Dichter, M.A. (1995). Antiepileptic drugs. *New England Journal of Medicine, 334,* 168–175.

Brown, J.K., & Hussain, J.H. (1991a). Status epilepticus: I. Pathogenesis. *Developmental Medicine and Child Neurology, 33,* 3–17.

Brown, J.K., & Hussain, J.H. (1991b). Status epilepticus: II. Treatment. *Developmental Medicine and Child Neurology, 33,* 97–109.

Brown, L.W., & Billiard, M. (1995). Narcolepsy, Kleine-Levin syndrome, and other causes of sleepiness in children. In R. Ferber & M. Kryger (Eds.), *Principles and practice of sleep medicine in the child* (pp. 125–134). Philadelphia: W.B. Saunders.

Bryant, A.E., & Dreifuss, F.E. (1996). Valproic acid hepatic fatalities: III. U.S. experience since 1986. *Neurology, 46,* 465–469.

Buchanan, N. (1995). *Epilepsy: A handbook.* Philadelphia, W.B. Saunders.

Camfield, C.S., Camfield, P.R., Smith, E., et al. (1989). Home use of rectal diazepam to prevent status epilepticus in children with convulsive disorders. *Journal of Child Neurology, 4,* 125–126.

Chamberlain, M.C. (1996). Nitrazepam for refractory infantile spasms and the Lennox-Gastaut syndrome. *Journal of Child Neurology, 11,* 31–34.

Chugani, H.T., Shewmon, D.A., Shields, W.D., et al. (1993). Surgery for intractable infantile spasm:

Neuroimaging perspectives. *Epilepsia, 34,* 764–771.

Chugani, H.T., Shields, W.D., Shewmon, D.A., et al. (1990). Infantile spasms: I. PET identifies focal cortical dysgenesis in cryptogenic cases for surgical treatment. *Annals of Neurology, 27,* 406–413.

Clancy, R.R. (1990). Valproate: An update: The challenge of modern pediatric seizure management. *Current Problems in Pediatrics, 20,* 161–233.

Cohen, D.J., & Leckman, J.F. (1994). A prospective longitudinal study of Gilles de la Tourette's syndrome. *Journal of the American Academy of Child and Adolescent Psychiatry, 33,* 377–385.

Collaborative Group for Epidemiology of Epilepsy. (1988). Adverse reactions to antiepileptic drugs: A follow-up study of 355 patients with chronic antiepileptic drug treatment. *Epilepsia, 29,* 787–793.

Consensus Development Conference. (1980). Febrile seizures: Long-term management of children with fever-associated seizures. *Pediatrics, 66,* 1009–1012.

Coulter, D.L. (1995). Carnitine deficiency in epilepsy: Risk factors and treatment. *Journal of Child Neurology, 10,* S2.

Declerck, A.C. (1986). Interaction sleep and epilepsy. *European Neurology, 25*(Suppl. 2), 117–127.

Delgado, M.R., Riela, A.R., Mills, J., et al. (1996). Discontinuation of antiepileptic drug treatment after two seizure-free years in children with cerebral palsy. *Pediatrics, 97,* 192–197.

Dichter, M.A., & Brodie, M.J. (1996). New antileptic drugs. *New England Journal of Medicine, 334,* 1583–1590.

Dodson, W.E. (1989). Medical treatment and pharmacology of antiepileptic drugs. *Pediatric Clinics of North America, 36,* 421–433.

Dreifuss, F.E. (1989). Classification of epileptic seizures and the epilepsies. *Pediatric Clinics of North America, 36,* 265–278.

Duchowny, M.S. (1989). Surgery for intractable epilepsy: Issues and outcome. *Pediatrics, 84,* 886–894.

Eadie, M.J. (1984). Anticonvulsant drugs: An update. *Drugs, 27,* 328–363.

Ellenberg, J.H., Hirtz, D.G., & Nelson, K.B. (1986). Do seizures in children cause intellectual deterioration? *New England Journal of Medicine, 314,* 1085–1088.

Emerson, R.D., D'Souza, B.J., Vining, E.P., et al. (1981). Stopping medication in children with epilepsy: Predictors of outcome. *New England Journal of Medicine, 304,* 1125–1129.

Engel, J., Jr. (1996). Surgery for seizures. *New England Journal of Medicine, 334,* 647–652.

Farwell, J.R., Lee, Y.J., Hirtz, D.G., et al. (1990). Phenobarbital for febrile seizures: Effects on intelligence and on seizure recurrence. *New England Journal of Medicine, 322,* 364–369.

Ferry, P.C., Banner, W., Jr., & Wolf, R.A. (Eds.). (1986). *Seizure disorders in children.* Philadelphia: J.B. Lippincott.

Fleisher, D.R., & Morrison, A. (1990). Masturbation mimicking abdominal pain or seizures in young girls. *Pediatrics, 116,* 810–814.

Freeman, J.M., Vining, E.P.G., & Pillas, D.J. (1990). *Seizures and epilepsy in childhood: A guide for parents.* Baltimore: The Johns Hopkins University Press.

Glaze, D.G., Hrachovy, R.A., Frost, J.D., Jr., et al. (1988). Prospective study of outcome of infants with infantile spasms treated during controlled studies of ACTH and prednisone. *Journal of Pediatrics, 112,* 389–396.

Gomez, M.R., & Klass, D.W. (1983). Epilepsies of infancy and childhood. *Annals of Neurology, 13,* 113–124.

Goulden, K.J., Shinnar, S., Koller, H., et al. (1990). Epilepsy in children with mental retardation: A cohort study. *Epilepsia, 32,* 690–697.

Harvey, A.S., Grattan-Smith, J.D., Desmond, P.M., et al. (1995). Febrile seizures and hippocampal sclerosis: Frequent and related findings in intractable temporal lobe epilepsy of childhood. *Journal of Child Neurology, 12,* 201–206.

Hermann, B.P., & Seidenberg, M. (Eds.). (1989). *Childhood epilepsies: Neuropsychological, psychosocial and intervention aspects.* New York: John Wiley & Sons.

Herranz, J.L., Armijo, J.A., & Arteaga, R. (1988). Clinical side effects of phenobarbital, primidone, phenytoin, carbamazepine, and valproate during monotherapy in children. *Epilepsia, 29,* 794–804.

Hirtz, D.G. (1989). Generalized tonic-clonic and febrile seizures. *Pediatric Clinics of North America, 36,* 365–382.

Hockaday, J.M. (1990). Management of migraine. *Archives of Diseases in Childhood, 65,* 1174–1176.

Holmes, G.L. (1987). *Diagnosis and management of seizures in children.* Philadelphia: W.B. Saunders.

Holmes, G.L. (1989). Electroencephalographic and neuroradiologic evaluation of children with epilepsy. *Pediatric Clinics of North America, 36,* 395–420.

Holmes, G.L., McKeever, M., & Adamson, M. (1987). Absence seizures in children: Clinical and electrographic features. *Annals of Neurology, 21,* 268–273.

Hopkins, I.J., & Klug, G.L. (1991). Temporal lobectomy for the treatment of intractable complex partial seizures of temporal lobe origin in early childhood. *Developmental Medicine and Child Neurology, 33,* 26–31.

Khurana, D.S., Riviello, J., Helmers, S., et al. (1996). Efficacy of gabapentin therapy in children with refractory partial seizures. *Journal of Pediatrics, 128,* 829–833.

Kinsman, S.L., Vining, E.P.G., & Quaskey, S.A. (1992). Efficacy of the ketogenic diet for intractable seizure disorders: Review of 58 cases. *Epilepsia, 33,* 1132–1136.

Kotagal, P., & Rothner, A.D. (1993). Localization-related epilepsies: Simple partial seizures, complex partial seizures, benign focal epilepsy of childhood, and epilepsia partialis continua. In W.E. Dodson & J.M. Pellock (Eds.), *Pediatric epilepsy: Diagnosis and therapy* (pp. 183–196). New York: Demos Publications.

Kotagal, P., Rothner, A.D., Erenberg, G., et al. (1987). Complex partial seizures of childhood onset: A five-year follow-up study. *Archives of Neurology, 44,* 1177–1180.

Lask, B. (1988). Novel and non-toxic treatment for night terrors. *British Medical Journal, 306,* 1477.

Lechtenberg, R. (1984). *Epilepsy and the family.* Boston: Harvard University Press.

Lindsay, J., Ounsted, C., & Richards, P. (1987). Hemispherectomy for childhood epilepsy: A 36–year study. *Developmental Medicine and Child Neurology, 29,* 592–600.

Lockman, L.A. (1989). Absence, myoclonic, and atonic seizures. *Pediatric Clinics of North America, 36,* 331–341.

Lockman, L.A. (1990). Treatment of status epilepticus in children. *Neurology, 40*(Suppl. 2), 43–46.

Loiseau, P., Duche, B., & Pedespan, J.M. (1995). Absence epilepsies. *Epilepsia, 36,* 1182–1186.

Lothman, E.W. (1993). Pathophysiology of seizures and epilepsy in the mature and immature brain: Cells, synapses, and circuits. In W.E. Dodson & J.M. Pellock (Eds.), *Pediatric epilepsy: Diagnosis and therapy* (pp. 57–61). New York: Demos Publications.

Mahowald, M.W., & Throrpy, M.J. (1995). Nonarousal parasomnias in the child. In R. Ferber & M. Kryger (Eds.), *Principles and practice of sleep medicine in the child* (pp. 115–124). Philadelphia: W.B. Saunders.

Marson, A.G., Kadir, Z.A., & Chadwick, D.W. (1996). New antiepileptic drugs: A systematic review of their efficacy and tolerability. *British Medical Journal, 313,* 1169–1174.

Matsuda, I., Higashi, A., & Inotsume, N. (1989). Physiologic and metabolic aspects of anticonvulsants. *Pediatric Clinics of North America, 36,* 1099–1111.

Meldrum, B.S. (1996). Update on the mechanism of action of antiepileptic drugs. *Epilepsia, 37* (Suppl. 6), S4–S11.

Mizrahi, E.M., Kellaway, P., Grossman, R.G., et al. (1990). Anterior temporal lobectomy and medically refractory temporal lobe epilepsy of childhood. *Epilepsy, 31,* 302–312.

Neidich, J.A., Nussbaum, R.L., Packer, R.J., et al. (1990). Heterogeneity of clinical severity and molecular lesions in Aicardi syndrome. *Journal of Pediatrics, 116,* 911–917.

Niedermeyer, E. (1986). The Lennox-Gastaut syndrome and its frontiers. *Clinical Electroencephalography, 17,* 117–126.

Niedermeyer, E. (1990). *The epilepsias.* Baltimore: Urban & Schwarzenberg.

Niedermeyer, E., & Lopes da Silva, F. (1987). *Electroencephalography: Basic principles, clinical applications, and related fields* (2nd ed.). Baltimore: Urban & Schwarzenberg.

O'Donohoe, N.V. (1994). *Epilepsies of childhood* (3rd ed.). Oxford, England: Butterworth-Heinemann.

Pascual-Castroviejo, I., Diaz-Gonzalez, C., Garcia-Melian, R.M., et al. (1993). Sturge-Weber syndrome: Study of 40 patients. *Pediatric Neurology, 9,* 283–288.

Pearl, P.L., & Holmes, G.L. (1993). Absence seizures. In W.E. Dodson & J.M. Pellock (Eds.), *Pediatric epilepsy: Diagnosis and therapy* (pp. 57–61). New York: Demos Publications.

Pellock, J.M. (1989). Efficacy and adverse effects of antiepileptic drugs. *Pediatric Clinics of North America, 36,* 435–448.

Pellock, J.M. (1990). The classification of childhood seizures and epilepsy syndromes. *Neurologic Clinics, 8,* 619–632.

Reutens, D.C., Bye, A.M., Hopkins, I.J., et al. (1993). *Epilepsia, 34,* 904–909.

Richens, A., & Perucca, E. (1995). Clinical pharmacology and medical treatment. In J. Laidlaw, A. Richens, & D. Chadwick (Eds.), *A textbook of epilepsy* (4th ed., pp. 498–559). London: Churchill Livingstone.

Roach, E.S., Riela, A.R., Chugani, H.T., et al. (1994). Sturge-Weber syndrome: Recommendations for surgery. *Journal of Child Neurology, 9,* 190–192.

Roach, E.S., Smith, M., Huttenlocher, P., et al. (1992). Diagnostic criteria: Tuberous sclerosis complex. *Journal of Child Neurology, 7,* 221–224.

Rosen, G., Mahowald, M.W., & Ferber, R. (1995). Sleepwalking, confusional arousals, and sleep terrors in the child. In R. Ferber & M. Kryger (Eds.), *Principles and practice of sleep medicine in the child* (pp. 99–106). Philadelphia: W.B. Saunders.

Rosman, N.P., Colton, T., Labazzo, J., et al. (1993). A controlled trial of diazepam administered during febrile illness to prevent recurrence of febrile seizures. *New England Journal of Medicine, 329,* 79–84.

Sass, K.J., Spencer, D.D., Spencer, S.S., et al. (1988). Corpus callostomy for epilepsy: II. Neurologic and neuropsychological outcome. *Neurology, 38,* 24–28.

Schoenberger, R., Milenko, T., Ashish, J., et al. (1995). Appropriateness of antiepileptic drug level monitoring. *Journal of the American Medical Association, 274,* 1622–1626.

Schwartz, R.H., Eaton, J., Bower, B.D., et al. (1989). Ketogenic diets in the treatment of epilepsy: Short-term clinical effects. *Developmental Medicine and Child Neurology, 31,* 145–151.

Shields, W.D. (1993). Neuroimaging in the diagnosis and management of pediatric epilepsy. In W.E. Dodson & J.M. Pellock (Eds.), *Pediatric epilepsy: Diagnosis and therapy* (pp. 99–108). New York: Demos Publications.

Shields, W.D., Duchowny, M.S., & Holmes, G.L. (1993). Surgically remedial syndromes of infancy and early childhood. In J. Engel, Jr. (Ed.), *Surgical treatment of the epilepsies* (pp. 35–48). New York: Raven Press.

Shinnar, S., Berg, A.T., Moshe, S.L., et al. (1990). Risk of seizure recurrence following a short unprovoked seizure in childhood: A prospective study. *Pediatrics, 85,* 1076–1085.

Shinnar, S., Berg, A.T., Moshe, S.L., et al. (1994). Discontinuing antiepileptic drugs in children with epilepsy: A prospective study. *Annals of Neurology, 35,* 534–545.

Shinnar, S., Vining, E.P., Mellits, E.D., et al. (1985). Discontinuing antiepileptic medication in children with epilepsy after two years without seizures: A prospective study. *New England Journal of Medicine, 313,* 976–980.

Siemes, H., Spohr, H.L., Michael, T., et al. (1988). Therapy of infantile spasms with valproate: Results of a prospective study. *Epilepsia, 29,* 553–560.

Snead, O.C. (1990). Treatment of infantile spasms. *Pediatric Neurology, 6,* 147–150.

Snead, O.C., III, & Hosey, L.C. (1985). Exacerbation of seizures in children by carbamazepine. *New England Journal of Medicine, 313,* 916–921.

Steffenburg, U., Hagberg, G., & Kyllerman, M. (1995). Active epilepsy in mentally retarded children: II. Etiology and reduced pre- and perinatal optimality. *Acta Paediatrica, 84,* 1153–1159.

Steffenburg, U., Hagberg, G., Viggedal, G., et al. (1995). Active epilepsy in mentally retarded children: I. Prevalence and additional neuroimpairments. *Acta Paediatrica, 84,* 1147–1152.

Thurston, J.H., Thurston, D.L., Hixon, B.B., et al. (1982). Prognosis in childhood epilepsy: Additional follow-up of 148 children 15 to 23 years after withdrawal of anticonvulsant therapy. *New England Journal of Medicine, 306,* 831–836.

Uldall, P., Alving, J., Gram, L., et al. (1995). Vegabatrin in childhood epilepsy: 5-year follow-up study. *Neuropediatrics, 26,* 253–256.

Vermeulen, J., & Aldenkamp, A.P. (1995). Cognitive side-effects of chronic antiepileptic drug treatment: A review of 25 years of research. *Epilepsy Research, 22,* 65–95.

Vining, E.P. (1989). Educational, social, and life-long effects of epilepsy. *Pediatric Clinics of North America, 36,* 449–461.

Vining, E.P., Mellits, E.D., Dorsen, M.M., et al. (1987). Psychologic and behavioral effects of antiepileptic drugs in children: A double-blind comparison between phenobarbital and valproic acid. *Pediatrics, 80,* 165–174.

Walczak, T.S., Radtke, R.A., McNamara, J.O., et al. (1990). Anterior temporal lobectomy for complex partial seizures: Evaluation, results, and long-term follow-up in 100 cases. *Neurology, 40,* 413–418.

Wallace, S.J. (1990). Risk of seizures (Annotation). *Developmental Medicine and Child Neurology, 32,* 645–649.

Wallace, S.T. (1988). *The child with febrile seizures.* Stoneham, VT: Butterworth-Heinlein.

Wheless, J.W. (1995). The ketogenic diet: Fa(c)t or fiction. *Journal of Child Neurology, 10,* 419–423.

Working Group on Status Epilepticus. (1993). Treatment of convulsive status epilepticus: Recommendations of the Epilepsy Foundation of America's Working Group on Status Epilepticus. *Journal of the American Medical Association, 270,* 854–859.

Wyllie, E. (1988). Corpus callostomy for intractable generalized epilepsy. *Journal of Pediatrics, 113,* 255–261.

Wyllie, E. (1991). Cortical resection for children with epilepsy: Perspectives in pediatrics. *American Journal of Diseases of Children, 145,* 314–320.

Wyllie, E., Chee, M., Granstrom, M.L., et al. (1993). Temporal lobe epilepsy in early childhood. *Epilepsia, 34,* 859–868.

Wyllie, E., Rothner, A.D., & Luders, H. (1989). Partial seizures in children: Clinical features, medical treatment, and surgical considerations. *Pediatric Clinics of North America, 36,* 343–364.

27 Traumatic Brain Injury

Linda Michaud
Ann-Christine Duhaime
Mary F. Lazar

Upon completion of this chapter, the reader will:

- know the definition and major causes of traumatic brain injury in children
- be aware of the major types of brain injuries
- understand some of the problems that result from traumatic brain injuries of varying severity
- be able to discuss the components of care for a child with a traumatic brain injury
- be able to identify prognostic factors

Most head trauma in children is minor and not associated with persisting impairments. However, severe head injury (with associated brain injury) occurs with sufficient frequency to make it the most common cause of acquired disability in childhood (Kraus, Rock, & Hemyari, 1990). Even when obvious physical complications are minimal, neuropsychological impairments may lead to chronic academic, behavior, and interpersonal difficulties that pose an enormous challenge to the child, family, and society. Effective acute management and long-term rehabilitation are vital after traumatic brain injury (TBI) in order to optimize the child's outcome.

INCIDENCE OF HEAD INJURIES

Each year, approximately 1 in 25 children receive medical attention because of a head injury (Brookes, MacMillan, Cully, et al., 1990). These injuries range from confined areas of scalp or skull trauma to more diffuse and severe brain damage. TBI, defined as trauma sufficient to result in a change in level of consciousness and/or an anatomical abnormality of the brain, occurs in approximately 1 in 500 children per year (Baker, O'Neill, & Karpf, 1984). Head injuries most commonly occur in the spring and summer, on weekends, and in the afternoons, when children are most likely to be outside playing or riding in cars.

CAUSES OF TRAUMATIC BRAIN INJURY

Common causes of TBI include falls from heights; sports and recreation-related injuries; motor vehicle crashes; and assaults, including child abuse. The frequency of these types of brain injuries varies with age (Figure 27.1). Young children are more likely to sustain brain injuries as a result of falls, while teenagers are more often involved in motor vehicle crashes (Centers for Disease Control, 1990; Sasin, Sachs, & Webb, 1996). The frequency of gunshot wounds to the head is increasing dramatically in children from the inner city (Ordog, Wasserberger, Schatz, et al., 1988).

Certain psychosocial factors may increase the risk of childhood head trauma. Children with a conduct disorder or hyperactive, impulsive behavior (as seen in children with attention-deficit/hyperactivity disorder [ADHD]) may act in a dangerous manner, although hyperactive behavior itself does not necessarily increase the risk of injury (Davidson, Hughes, & O'Connor, 1988; Davidson, Taylor, Sandberg, et al., 1992). Adolescents who are severely depressed may attempt suicide (Holinger, 1990). Social factors, such as poverty, living in congested residential areas, and marital instability, have also been associated with an increased risk of brain injury in children as a result of physical abuse or neglect (Alexander, Sato, Smith, et al., 1990; Braddock, Lapidus, Gregorio, et al., 1991).

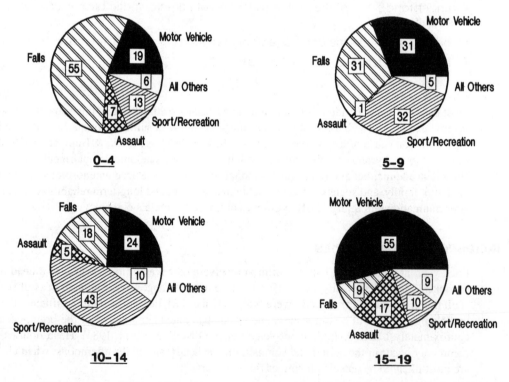

Figure 27.1.   Causes of TBI in children by age and percentage. (*Source:* Centers for Disease Control [1990].)

TYPES OF BRAIN INJURIES

The type of brain injury that a child sustains depends primarily on the nature of the force that caused the injury and the severity of the injury. Head trauma can be caused by both impact and inertial forces. Impact, or contact, forces occur when the head strikes a surface or is struck by a moving object. Impact forces can result in scalp injuries; skull fractures; focal brain bruises (contusions); or blood collections beneath the skull (i.e., epidural hematomas). Inertial forces occur when the brain undergoes violent motion inside the skull, which tears the nerve fibers and blood vessels. The severity of injuries caused by inertial forces depends on the magnitude and the direction of the motion. Angular acceleration-deceleration forces, such as those that might occur in a high-speed motor vehicle crash, cause much more serious damage than do straight-line (translational) forces, such as those that might occur in a fall. Injuries caused by inertial forces range from relatively mild concussions to more serious injuries, such as subdural hematomas and diffuse axonal injuries (DAI).

Most clinical brain injuries include both impact and inertial components, with several injury types occurring simultaneously. Thus, the injuries discussed in the following sections do not usually occur singly.

Scalp and Skull Injuries

Impact forces cause scalp and skull injuries. Although scalp injuries sometimes cause considerable blood loss, they have no neurological consequence. Skull fractures can be either benign or serious. A linear fracture, in which there is no visible injury but a crack in the skull on an X ray, is sometimes seen in young children who have fallen from low heights. These fractures do not cause significant neurological damage. A depressed fracture, in which the skull is broken and presses against the underlying brain tissue, however, may be associated with significant brain injury and associated disabilities. For example, a depressed fracture directly over the motor cortex (the part of the brain that controls movement) may result in weakness of the opposite side of the body.

Brain Contusions

Brain contusions, or bruises of the brain, most often result from direct impact to the head. As is true of bruises in other areas of the body, brain contusions often evolve during the first few days after the injury, such that clinical symptoms may worsen. Associated hemorrhages occasionally require surgical removal. Impairments depend on the extent of the bruise and resultant damage to the brain.

Epidural Hematomas

Although epidural hematomas can lead to serious impairments or even death, if detected promptly they can be treated effectively, increasing the chance for a favorable outcome. A hematoma, or blood clot, forms between the skull and the outer covering of the brain (i.e., dura) and may originate in either an artery or a vein (Figure 27.2). An arterial hematoma occurs when the brain's covering, usually containing the middle meningeal artery, is torn due to impact. This is usually associated with a skull fracture and is the only life-threatening brain injury to result from a low-height fall in young children. In older children, epidural hematomas may occur from falls and other contact injuries, such as sports injuries. Venous epidural hematomas occur when there is bleeding from a fractured bone or from a tear in a large vein in the dura. Because veins

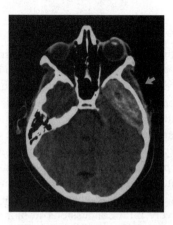

Figure 27.2.   Epidural hematoma (see arrow) in the right temporal region of an 8-year-old boy who fell from his bicycle. He was initially dazed but awake and conversant but became progressively less responsive during the subsequent few hours. Upon arrival at the hospital, he was comatose with a dilated right pupil. He made a complete recovery after neurosurgical removal of the blood clot.

generally bleed more slowly than arteries, venous epidural hematomas are usually self-limited and less serious than arterial hematomas.

The classic clinical hallmark of an arterial epidural hematoma is delayed onset of symptoms. Thus, when a child sustains the injury, neurological symptoms may be minimal or absent. As the hematoma enlarges, however, secondary injury, caused by increased pressure on the brain, may occur. This can lead to headaches; confusion; vomiting; focal neurological impairment (e.g., one-sided weakness); and agitation. It may progress to lethargy, coma, and even death if left untreated. Specific symptoms associated with arterial epidural hematoma vary, depending on other concomitant injuries and/or the age of the individual. Venous epidural hematomas, which typically occur from bleeding at a fracture in the skull, may be asymptomatic or present with more delayed symptomatology. These do not always require surgical intervention. If surgery is performed before secondary injury becomes irreversible, outcome is remarkably favorable (Dhellemmes, Lejeune, Christiaens, et al., 1985), and these children quickly return to normal functioning. If surgery is delayed, various physical and cognitive impairments are likely to persist.

Concussions

Concussions are brain injuries sufficient to cause a brief loss of consciousness or amnesia for the event. Physiologically, a concussion indicates a relatively mild injury to the nerve fibers in the brain. In children, concussions occur most commonly from falls and represent one of the most frequent reasons for trauma admissions to the hospital (Kraus, Fife, & Conroy, 1987). Usually, a brief loss of consciousness (typically a few minutes) is followed by a complete return to a normal mental status and behavior. In some children, however, a period of headache, drowsiness, confusion, or irritability will occur, often several hours after the injury; these symptoms may last for a few days. The computed tomography (CT) scan of a child with a concussion will be normal, differentiating him or her from the child whose deterioration is caused by a blood clot requiring surgery.

Diffuse Axonal Injuries

While concussion is at the mild end of the spectrum of diffuse injuries, people with more severe symptoms are classified as having sustained DAI, in which nerve fibers (i.e., axons) throughout the brain have been damaged or torn, usually by violent motion (e.g., during motor vehicle crashes). The individual may have been a passenger, pedestrian, or bicycle rider. People who have sustained DAI lapse into immediate unconsciousness. For practical purposes, a diagnosis of DAI is given if unconsciousness lasts at least 6 hours without other causes, such as seizures or increased intracranial pressure from a hematoma. Depending on the severity of the injury, people also may exhibit abnormal movements (i.e., posturing); abnormal reactions of the pupils; and difficulty regulating breathing and blood pressure. CT and magnetic resonance imaging (MRI) scans of these individuals will reveal small, scattered brain tissue tears and hemorrhages (Figure 27.3). In more mild cases, the CT scan may show no abnormalities. Because of the large mechanical forces involved in this type of injury, trauma to other organ systems or to the spine is not uncommon, and lack of oxygen or blood loss may exacerbate the primary insult to the central nervous system.

Recovery from DAI occurs over weeks to years, depending on the severity of injury. Long-lasting impairments may include motor, communicative, cognitive, and behavior problems and range from mild to severe. A few individuals with severe injuries may remain in a chronic unresponsive state, but the majority regain consciousness.

Acute Subdural Hematomas

Acute subdural hematomas are blood clots that form beneath the dura, over the surface of the brain itself (Figure 27.4; see also Figure 6.5). Unlike an epidural hematoma, hemorrhages in the subdural compartment occur not from impact, but from shearing forces applied to the veins that course between the brain surface and the large, draining dural veins. Tremendous angular

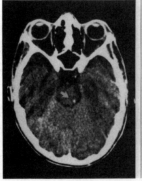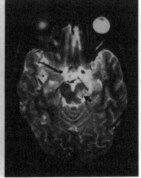

Figure 27.3.   Computed tomography (CT) scan (left) and magnetic resonance image (MRI) (right) of the brain of a 9-year-old boy who was struck by a car. He was immediately unresponsive with abnormal posturing movements. Both the CT and MRI studies show changes typical of diffuse axonal injury (DAI). The MRI is much more sensitive to white matter injury, displaying the extent and degree of damage. In these images, the small white dot in the center of the CT scan (see arrow) is a brainstem hemorrhage. This area appears as a more extensive white region on MRI, which also shows the surrounding tissue disruption and swelling.

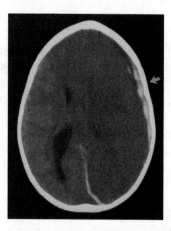

Figure 27.4.   Subdural hematoma (see arrow) in an 11-month-old girl who was the victim of inflicted injury. She was comatose upon hospital admission and remained so after surgery to remove the blood clot. The right hemisphere of the brain was extremely swollen. Follow-up studies show massive brain damage, and the child has severe cognitive and motor impairments.

acceleration-deceleration forces are required to displace the brain from the dura sufficiently to rupture these bridging veins. As a result, a large acute subdural hematoma usually accompanies a major generalized injury to the brain itself. The damage done by direct pressure from the overlying blood clot thus adds to the damage from the primary injury, explaining why morbidity and mortality rates are so high among children with subdural hematomas and why surgical removal of the clot often appears to make only a small difference in the clinical status of the individual. This contrasts with the epidural hematoma, for which prompt surgical removal of the blood clot markedly improves the prognosis.

Recovery from a subdural hematoma is quite similar to that from a DAI; in fact, the two injuries often occur together. A subdural hematoma may cause major brain swelling and stroke and is almost always unilateral (i.e., on one side of the brain). Individuals with subdural hematomas often have a large area of brain damage on the affected side, in addition to the DAI throughout the brain.

DETECTING SIGNIFICANT BRAIN INJURY

As noted previously, most head trauma is minor and does not require treatment or result in significant consequences. But how does a parent or teacher know whether head trauma warrants treatment? Generally speaking, if a child hits his or her head and does not lose consciousness, no treatment is necessary unless the child develops symptoms. Medical evaluation (a visit to a physician or the emergency room) is needed, however, if the child becomes lethargic, confused, or irritable; has a severe headache; demonstrates acute impairments in speech, vision, or movements of the arms or legs; has significant bleeding from the wound; or vomits repeatedly.

If the child is momentarily unconscious and then resumes activities, he or she may have a mild concussion. If there has been more than a momentary loss of consciousness or confusion, the child should be taken to the emergency room, where a neurological examination will be performed. A brain-imaging study may be performed to be certain there is no brain injury. If there are no abnormal neurological or radiological findings, the child may then be sent home. Parents will be given instructions to make sure the child can be roused from sleep, is not confused, and develops no new neurological symptoms.

If the child remains unconscious for more than a few minutes, the paramedics should be called. If, upon arrival at the hospital, the child is still unconscious, he or she will be stabilized in the emergency room and then usually transferred to the intensive care unit. Immediate coma after head trauma is the result of primary injury to neural pathways. There may be worsening in the subsequent 24 hours as a consequence of secondary hemorrhaging or brain swelling.

SEVERITY OF BRAIN INJURY

The duration and severity of coma indicate the seriousness of a brain injury. The most frequently used scale for coma severity is the Glasgow Coma Scale (GCS) (Jennett, Teasdale, Galbraith, et al., 1977). Although this scale was devised for use in adults and can be difficult to apply to very young children, it remains the most useful method available for classifying severe brain injuries in the early phase after trauma. Using this scale within the first 6 hours after injury, the trauma team assigns the child a score based on the degree and quality of movement, vocalization, and eye opening (Table 27.1). Individuals receive a score between 3 and 15. The best score is 15, representing the least severe brain injury. An individual with a score of 3 would have no eye opening, movement, or verbal response and would be in deep coma. An individual who looks about, moves limbs in response to requests, and is oriented to the environment receives a score of 15. Someone who opens his or her eyes when physically prodded, withdraws a limb that is touched, and makes only incomprehensible sounds receives a score of 8. Severe brain injury is defined as a score of 8 or less (Langfitt & Gennarelli, 1982). Scores of 9–12 reflect moderate

Table 27.1.   Glasgow Coma Scale

Response	Score
Eye opening	
Spontaneous	4
To speech	3
To pain	2
Nil	1
Best motor response	
Obeys	6
Localizes	5
Withdraws	4
Abnormal flexion	3
Extensor response	2
Nil	1
Verbal response	
Oriented	5
Confused conversation	4
Inappropriate words	3
Incomprehensible sounds	2
Nil	1

From Jennett, B., Teasdale, G., Galbraith, S., et al. (1977). Severe head injuries in three countries. *Journal of Neurology, Neurosurgery, and Psychiatry, 40,* 293; reprinted by permission.

brain injury, and scores of 13–15 reflect minor brain injury. Fatality rate after severe brain injury is about 33% (Michaud, Rivara, Grady, et al., 1992).

TREATMENT APPROACHES

Approaches to therapy depend on the stage of recovery from coma and associated medical and physical problems. Treatment can be divided into an acute medical phase and a later rehabilitative phase. Initial rehabilitation, which may last for weeks to months, is often provided in an inpatient setting after severe injury. Subsequent outpatient rehabilitation can be provided in a hospital, rehabilitation center, or school. Unfortunately, due to caps on insurance policies, rehabilitative services are often time limited. Furthermore, schools may be ill-prepared to care for these children who may have complex neuropsychological impairments. These problems can adversely affect recovery and outcome.

Acute Medical Management

The first priority in the emergency room is to address the "ABCs" of pediatric advanced life support: airway, breathing, and circulation. Immediate goals are to stop any hemorrhaging, aid respiration, and support blood pressure. Once vital signs are stable, the attending physician identifies fractures and damage to various internal body organs. A neurological examination is also performed that includes an assessment of the child's level of consciousness. The physician directs a light into the child's eyes to see if his or her pupils constrict equally in bright light and dilate equally in the dark. If these responses are absent, delayed, or asymmetrical, brain swelling or injury is likely. Movement of limbs and reflexes are also tested to see if there are tone changes or asymmetry that would indicate brain injury. For example, left-sided weakness usually indicates damage to the right side of the brain.

Certain physical findings suggest damage to a specific region of the skull or brain. Blood behind the eardrum, cerebrospinal fluid drainage from the nose or ear, and bruising around the orbits of the eye all suggest the presence of a fracture at the base of the skull. Hemorrhages in the retina of the eye may be associated with subdural hematoma (Raimondi & Hirschauer, 1984) and are nearly always associated with child abuse.

Neurosurgical consultation is recommended for all children who have sustained more than mild head trauma. A child with an open-skull fracture may require surgery to prevent infection of the brain. Children with epidural or subdural hematomas also may require surgery to prevent or treat potentially life-threatening increased intracranial pressure (Dhellemmes et al., 1985). Concern over increased intracranial pressure also may lead the neurosurgeon to insert a device to monitor intracranial pressure or a drainage tube (ventriculostomy) to both monitor and reduce intracranial pressure.

A CT scan is used routinely following significant head trauma to diagnose intracranial hemorrhage, swelling, DAI, and skull fractures. MRI scans are used during recovery to determine more clearly the extent of residual brain damage (Gentry, Godersky, & Thompson, 1988).

The medical management of coma primarily aims to prevent or limit secondary brain damage, which can result from a buildup of intracranial pressure, a lack of oxygen, a lack of sufficient metabolic energy supply, or an accumulation of neurotoxins. Intracranial pressure often builds as a result of brain swelling. If this is found, drainage of spinal fluid, control of breathing rate, or medications (e.g., mannitol, barbiturates) may be used to decrease the pressure within the head. Blood flow to the brain affects both pressure within the brain and the supply of nutrients and oxygen. Thus, blood supply must be carefully controlled (Ghajar & Hariri, 1992). Research suggests that brain damage following TBI is, at least in part, intensified by excitatory neurotransmitters that are released in toxic amounts at the time of injury (Siesjö, 1992). These neurotoxins lead to swelling and death of nerve cells. Experimental trials with drugs that block receptors for these chemicals have shown some promise in protecting the brain. Other strategies to protect the brain against delayed cellular processes are also being investigated.

The occurrence of seizures immediately after the injury or within the first few days after a brain injury is rather common, even in children with only mild concussions. Less than 2% of these children, however, will subsequently develop a seizure disorder (Ylvisaker, 1985). Factors that increase this risk include bleeding into the brain and penetrating injury that may cause the formation of scar tissue. Antiepileptic medication may be given preventively for a week after the injury, but prolonged treatment is generally used only if the child develops a persistent seizure disorder (see Chapter 26).

Recovery from Coma

Although type and severity of injuries differ, certain patterns of behavior are observed in children recovering from TBI. Initially, the child may not respond at all to external stimuli or may respond in stereotypical ways. For example, the child's response to a painful stimulus administered to one extremity may be generalized, with movement of all the extremities and an elevation in blood pressure and intracranial pressure. The child may not respond to a voiced command, such as "open your eyes." Or the child may open his or her eyes spontaneously, a sign that does not by itself signify wakefulness.

Fortunately, most children with TBI regain consciousness, and only a very small number remain in a permanent unresponsive state. Emergence from coma does not occur suddenly or smoothly but typically follows a saw-toothed pattern of waxing and waning levels of consciousness. The first signs are often heightened responses to external stimuli, especially to the voices of family members. Eye opening that occurs as a response to external stimuli reflects improving neurological status.

At about this time in recovery, the child may become intermittently agitated and combative —for instance, pulling at tubes, moaning, and trying to sit up. Although his or her eyes may be open, there appears to be little meaningful perception of the environment. This stage can be extremely difficult for family members, who should be reassured that this is expected during recovery and that the child will not remember these events. Occasionally, medications can be helpful in reducing agitation (e.g., narcotics, especially if other injuries make it likely that the child is in pain; sedatives; sympathetic blocking agents such as propranolol [Inderal]).

As agitation subsides, the child will show increasing awareness of the environment. He or she will usually begin to visually fixate, with clear recognition and memory of familiar objects and people. Speech begins with short words or phrases, with delayed responses. These responses are usually inconsistent in the early stages of recovery.

Return of consciousness can be defined functionally as the ability to follow commands reliably. In preverbal or aphasic children, more general responsiveness must be used to ascertain the end of coma. Once consciousness has returned, therapeutic strategies increasingly utilize active participation by the individual with TBI. At variable rates, children with TBI become increasingly oriented to the environment, and behavior becomes progressively more age appropriate, purposeful, and complex. Motor, communicative, cognitive, sensory, and behavior impairments can be assessed and long-range goals set at this stage.

Rehabilitation

The goals of rehabilitation are to limit secondary damage, relearn lost skills, and learn new skills that will be needed to compensate for disabilities. Rehabilitation begins almost immediately after vital signs have been stabilized, often while the child is still in coma.

Acute rehabilitative care following TBI aims to limit secondary musculoskeletal damage by passive range of motion exercises, positioning, and splinting of limbs. These efforts can help to prevent the later development of contractures, which could interfere with seating, ambulation, and participation in daily activities (Blasier & Letts, 1989). Other important acute rehabilitative measures include changing body position and caring for the skin in order to prevent the development of pressure sores (Jaffe & Hays, 1986). In addition, adequate nutrition promotes wound healing. These measures, taken together, appear to shorten hospitalization and improve outcome.

As the child begins to recover from coma, physical, cognitive, and emotional problems may become evident (Hall, Johnson, & Middleton, 1990). Rehabilitation aims to 1) avert complications that arise from immobilization, disuse, and neurological dysfunction; 2) augment the use of abilities regained as a result of recovery from coma; 3) teach adaptive compensation for impaired or lost function; and 4) alleviate the effect of chronic disability on the process of growth and development (Molnar & Perrin, 1983).

FUNCTIONAL IMPAIRMENTS

The nature and severity of functional impairments will determine the rehabilitative strategies. Severe DAI is likely to result in impairment in all areas of functioning, while focal damage may result in more localized abnormalities. Interdisciplinary services typically include medical, nutritional, physical, occupational, speech-language, and recreational therapies, as well as rehabilitation, nursing, psychological, special education, and social services (Jaffe & McDonald, 1992). Services are discussed in relation to the specific impairments that they are intended to remediate.

Motor Impairments

The site(s) of brain injury determines the type of motor dysfunction that occurs. Spasticity, ataxia, and tremor are the most common motor abnormalities, indicating damage to the corticospinal (pyramidal) tract, basal ganglia, and cerebellum (see Chapter 14) (Mysiw, Corrigan, & Gribble, 1990).

Medication and surgery have had varying success in treating motor impairments. As of 1997, there is no effective medical or surgical approach to ataxia, although both approaches have proven somewhat helpful in controlling spasticity. Useful medications to treat spasticity include those that are used to treat spastic cerebral palsy: diazepam (Valium), baclofen (Lioresal), and dantrolene (Dantrium) (see Chapter 24).

Management of spasticity may also include nerve blocks—injecting anesthetic agents at a variety of sites in the peripheral nervous system—and selective dorsal rhizotomy (see Chapter 24). The effects of nerve blocks last for a number of weeks or months, but repeated injections are required if spasticity persists. Intramuscular injections of botulinum-A toxin (Botox) also appear safe and effective in reducing localized spasticity in children (Koman, Mooney, Smith, et al., 1994).

Orthopedic surgery may be required in some cases. Long-term contractures or dislocations may need to be treated by performing tendon releases, femoral osteotomies, or scoliosis surgery (see Chapter 24). Serial casting may be used to correct a limb deformity in some cases of spasticity.

Medical and surgical approaches may be helpful, but they offer no cure. The child may continue to have motor impairments that interfere with the ability to ambulate and to participate in self-care skills. Furthermore, cognitive and visual-perceptual impairments may exacerbate motor deficits. Active physical and occupational therapy is needed to assist the child in regaining motor function. Exercises and activities are designed to increase strength, balance, and coordination; to reduce spasticity; and to prevent contractures and dislocations. The child may need to relearn ambulation and may require crutches, walkers, or wheelchair training (see Chapter 32).

Feeding Disorders

Feeding disorders often accompany motor impairments (Ylvisaker & Weinstein, 1989). Food intake may decrease if the child is unable to communicate when hungry; if the ability to obtain food or to eat is compromised because of impaired motor skills; or if there are problems with swallowing or gastroesophageal reflux.

Nutritional treatment during coma may involve hyperalimentation, in which a solution containing protein, carbohydrates, and fats is given intravenously. Even after coma has resolved, children who are unable to take in sufficient sustenance by mouth will require temporary or long-term nasogastric or gastrostomy tube-feedings with high-caloric formulas.

A number of rehabilitation therapies also are involved in treating feeding disorders. An occupational therapist may work on proper positioning for feeding. A speech-language pathologist may use desensitization techniques; stimulation of the swallowing reflex; and facilitation of tongue, lip, and jaw control to improve swallowing. Nutritionists provide advice concerning the textures, taste, temperature, and caloric density of the food. Finally, medication to control reflux may improve the child's ability to eat and gain weight (see Chapter 28).

Sensory Impairments

Vision and hearing can both be affected by TBI. The most common vision complication is diplopia (i.e., double vision), caused by eye muscle palsy. Nystagmus, caused by injury to the cerebellum, is also quite common among children with severe TBI. Less commonly, a crush injury (e.g., blunt object) damages an eye, or a missile injury (e.g., gun shot) severs a portion of the visual pathway; both cause irreversible damage. Finally, a TBI accompanied by severe brain swelling can result in a stroke or cortical blindness. Cortical blindness involves an abnormality in the visual cortex, but not the eye itself, and partial or complete recovery can occur (see Chapter 11). As a result of these problems, vision testing should be included in the evaluation after recovery from coma.

Sensorineural hearing loss after TBI most commonly results from a fracture of the temporal bone and is usually unilateral. Longitudinal fractures involving the middle-ear structures are associated with a conductive hearing loss. Transverse fractures can affect the cochlea and result in sensorineural hearing loss (Healy, 1982). Formal hearing assessment should be conducted following severe TBI because of the frequency with which hearing loss occurs. Because involvement is usually unilateral, deafness does not generally result. Even a mild hearing loss, however, should be identified and corrected with amplification so that the child can benefit maximally from all of his or her senses in working toward recovery (see Chapter 12).

Communication Impairments

If the left hemisphere of the brain is damaged, speech and language impairments are likely. Language disorders may be expressive, receptive, or mixed. Dysarthria and dysphasia are the most common expressive language problems in children with TBI (see Chapter 13). Receptive language impairments most commonly involve auditory-perceptual problems. Recovery of speech motor function often is more complete than recovery of receptive language abilities (Brink, Garrett, Hale, et al., 1970). Usually when language is disordered, cognition also is affected (Chapman, 1995; Chapman, Levin, Matejka, et al., 1995). Intervention by a speech-language pathologist is directed at improving both the speech disorder and the language and cognitive impairments. Initially, this involves using simple commands and discussing uncomplicated topics related to the surroundings. The speech-language pathologist will also help to train the nursing staff and parents to use simple commands and, if needed, alternate means of communication.

Cognitive Impairments

Recovery of cognitive functioning is typically not as complete as recovery of motor functioning following severe TBI (Brink et al., 1970; Eiben, Anderson, Lockman, et al., 1984; Massagli, Michaud, & Rivara, 1996). Furthermore, children who are preschoolers at the time of injury may have delayed manifestation of cognitive impairments, showing difficulty handling more complex tasks as they get older (Lazar & Menaldino, 1995).

Investigations of mild TBI in children have demonstrated no significant long-term adverse consequences on cognitive functioning (Bijur, Haslum, & Golding, 1990; Fay, Jaffe, Polissar, et al., 1993). Studies of children who have sustained moderate to severe TBI, however, document significant cognitive impairments (Dalby & Obrzut, 1991; Jaffe, Polissar, Fay, et al., 1995). Intellectual and neuropsychological impairment is increased with greater severity of injury (Jaffe et al., 1995). The cognitive sequelae most often associated with pediatric TBI are lowered performance on visual-spatial and visual-motor tasks as compared with verbal tasks; problems with attention, learning, and memory (Dalby & Obrzut, 1991); and diminished speed of information processing (Hanson & Clippard, 1992). Impairments in judgment, problem-solving, reasoning, and organizational skills have also been demonstrated (Hanson & Clippard, 1992).

In order to identify impairments, neuropsychologists evaluate children using measures of intelligence as well as assessments of more discrete and/or subtle impairments in cognition that typically result from significant brain injury (Goldstein & Levin, 1985). This assessment involves a series of standardized tests that measure concept formation, reasoning, adaptive problem-solving skills, language, memory, concentration, visual-spatial skills, sensory-perceptual/sensory-motor abilities, and academic performance (Fay & Janesheski, 1986). Results of such evaluations are used in planning appropriate rehabilitation programs and educational curricula (Goldstein & Levin, 1985).

Performance on cognitive tasks varies in different settings (Cohen, 1986). In a typical neuropsychological evaluation, the examiner meets individually with the child in a quiet room under very structured conditions. Because this situation is unlike the typical classroom with its many distractions, these tests alone may not accurately represent the child's ability to function in a general classroom setting. For this reason, it is recommended that such evaluations be augmented by contextual assessments (Telzrow, 1991) as well as by the use of functional assessment measures (Milton, Scaglione, Flanagan, et al., 1991).

Impairments in intellectual and neuropsychological functioning are generally proportional to the severity of the injury (Jaffe et al., 1995). Although significant recovery occurs during the first year after severe injury in children, the recovery rate slows down subsequently (Figure 27.5). Much remains to be learned about the role of rehabilitative and educational interventions in influencing the rate and extent of recovery of specific cognitive functions.

Interventions to address cognitive impairments may be useful even during the inpatient phase of management. Multidisciplinary cognitive remediation may use a combination of memory training exercises (psychology), language therapy (speech-language pathology), and educational programming (special education). The strategy is to improve areas of impairment and encourage the development of compensatory techniques (Volpe & McDowell, 1990), such as assistive technology (including computer-assisted learning) (Fay & Janesheski, 1986; Ried, Strong, Wright, et al., 1995). Impairments in communication and cognition often are the main deterrents to successful reintegration into home, school, and community. Social inclusion (i.e., full, meaningful inclusion in the social fabric of the culture [Ried et al., 1995]) should be a major goal of provision of assistive technology for children with impairments after TBI.

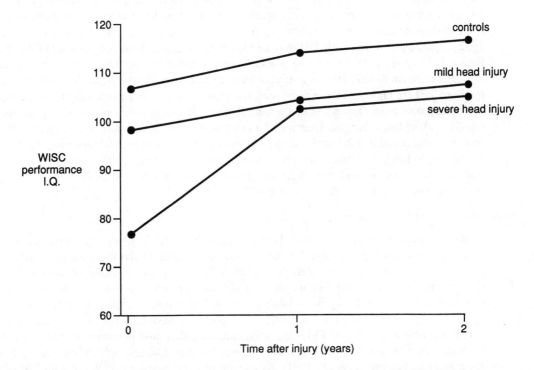

Figure 27.5.   Recovery of cognitive function following head injuries of variable degrees of severity in children. (From Chadwick, O., Rutter, M., Brown, G., et al. [1981]. A prospective study of children with head injuries: II. Cognitive sequelae. *Psychological Medicine, 11,* 53; reprinted by permission.)

Academic Impairments

Research has consistently documented that children who have sustained a moderate to severe TBI tend to experience academic problems (Brink et al., 1970; Klonoff, Low, & Clark, 1977). Although these difficulties may be demonstrated in a particular area such as reading or math (Goldstein & Levin, 1985), impairments in attention, problem solving, and speed of information processing more typically compromise all academic performance (Carney & Schoenbrodt, 1994). Therefore, these children often require at least modifications to the general education setting and often need some degree of special education support, which may range from self-contained, special education classes to assistance in a resource room or in the general classroom (Savage, 1991). Focused instruction based on each child's specific skill or memory impairments will be most useful, especially when the instruction is both highly structured and motivating with feedback and correction. In addition, physical, occupational, and/or speech-language therapies may be provided as part of the child's individualized education program (IEP).

TBI is now recognized as a specific category of disability within special education, as mandated by the Education for All Handicapped Children Act of 1975, PL 94-142, reauthorized as the Individuals with Disabilities Education Act (IDEA) of 1990, PL 101-476. There has been, however, a lag between the passage of this legislation and its actual implementation, and the definition of brain injury has not been interpreted consistently on a state-by-state basis. Because there are so few children with TBI in any given school, and so many school systems lack adequate resources (e.g., funding, school personnel with training in TBI), these children often receive inadequate educational programming (Carney & Schoenbrodt, 1994; Hanson & Clippard, 1992). Although children with TBI may be identified as having behavior disorders (Michaud, Rivara, Jaffe, et al., 1993) or learning problems, their patterns of cognitive impairment are actually quite different from ADHD or a specific learning disability. Unlike these disorders, two hallmarks of TBI are highly variable performance within and across academic subjects and continued change over time. Depending on the time since the injury, recovery may still be proceeding rapidly, with abilities changing from month to month. As a result, an appropriate educational approach in September may be outdated by November. Thus, flexibility and innovative approaches are needed to teach the child who is recovering from TBI (Telzrow, 1987). Above all, careful management of school reentry and long-term monitoring are essential in facilitating a successful academic outcome (Hanson & Clippard, 1992).

Psychobehavioral Impairments

Changes in personality and behavior also may follow TBI (Filley, Cranberg, Alexander, et al., 1987). Even with adequate cognitive functioning, significant behavior challenges can be expected (Dalby & Obrzut, 1991; Perrott, Taylor, & Montes, 1991; Williams & Mateer, 1992). Changes may include inattention, increased or decreased activity, impulsivity, irritability, lowered frustration tolerance, emotional lability, apathy, aggression, and/or social withdrawal (Filley et al., 1987; Hanson & Clippard, 1992). These problems have been documented most clearly in children who sustain severe TBI; behavioral outcomes after mild to moderate injuries seem to be more varied (Asarnow, Satz, Light, et al., 1991; Fletcher, Ewing-Cobbs, Miner, et al., 1990; Knights, Ivan, Ventureyra, et al., 1991). As a result of these problems, children with TBI often develop problems with peer relationships. Treatment for behavior problems may include counseling, behavior management, medication, or a combination of these approaches.

Social and Family Difficulties

The effects of severe TBI on the family can be enormous (Urbach & Culbert, 1991). In many ways, they are similar to the challenges faced by all families of children newly diagnosed with a developmental disability (see Chapter 34). Parents of children with TBI, in addition, may face overwhelming feelings of guilt and remorse, particularly if the child was in the parent's care when the injury occurred or if the parents feel otherwise responsible. Siblings also may feel guilty that they were left unharmed or did not protect their brother or sister (Florian, Katz, & Lahav, 1989). In addition, prolonged hospitalization and rehabilitation can place a heavy financial burden on the family. One parent may be forced to take a leave of absence from work to be with the child. This loss of income combined with the additional costs of modifying a home or providing outpatient rehabilitation can have a devastating effect on family finances (McMordie & Barker, 1988).

Even after less severe TBI, psychosocial problems may develop. The family may rush to put the experience behind them and thus deny or ignore mild but persistent impairments, especially if the child appears to have recovered well. This can lead parents (and teachers) to expect normal achievement by the child, even if subtle cognitive impairments persist. If these impairments go undetected, they can lead to frustration, behavior problems, and poor learning.

Studies have shown that the family's preinjury level of functioning was predictive of family functioning 1 year after the child's TBI (Rivara, Fay, Jaffe, et al., 1992). Family functioning, in combination with injury severity and the child's preinjury functioning, was also predictive of the child's functioning 1 year after injury (Rivara, Jaffe, Fay, et al., 1993). These investigations strongly support the need to identify families at risk very early in the rehabilitation process. Families can be assisted by individual and family counseling, participation in support groups, and by teachers and health professionals (Rivara et al., 1993). In addition, families may need ongoing service coordination, especially if they are having difficulty gaining access to resources (Rivara, Jaffe, Polissar, et al., 1994).

TBI also may have a major effect on the child's vocational development and outcome. In one follow-up study of Finnish adults who had sustained severe TBI during their preschool years, only one fourth were able to work full time, although half had achieved average school performance (Koskiniemi, Kyykka, Nybo, et al., 1995). That study also found that the individual's sense of identity was a major predictor of the capability to care for oneself in adulthood. Vocational services for children and adolescents with TBI have generally not been provided through either the medical rehabilitation or educational systems. IDEA, however, mandates provision of transition services, defined to include vocational evaluation and training, for students with disabilities beginning no later than age 16. This legislation is too recent for its impact to be known but is certainly a step in the right direction in aiding children with disabilities, including those with TBI, to achieve the ability to work and live independently in adulthood.

PREVENTION

Most head trauma to children is preventable (American Academy of Pediatrics, Committee on Accident and Poison Prevention, 1987; Rivara, 1984). Because a number of factors contribute to the risk of injury, however, no single intervention will be completely effective. Rather, specific preventive strategies must be employed for each major category of TBI (i.e., motor vehicle accidents, including those associated with pedestrian and bicycle injuries; assaults and abuse; household incidents, including falls and drownings; sports and recreation-related injuries; suicide attempts). Prevention also is important in children who have already sustained TBI, as the effect of subsequent injury is cumulative. Persistent neurological impairments that result in impulsivity or hyperactivity place these children at high risk for additional injury.

Laws in all states requiring restraint of children who are passengers in motor vehicles have been highly (but not completely) effective in lowering the frequency and severity of TBI (Margolis, Wagenaar, & Liu, 1988). Nevertheless, the number of motor vehicle crashes in which teenagers sustain brain injuries continues to be too high. Education about the risks of drinking and driving has had some impact. Many experts believe, however, that further effective prevention efforts must include nighttime curfews and other graduated licensing measures, delaying licensure to 17 years of age, eliminating driver education courses that allow teenagers to obtain their licenses at younger ages (Agran, Castillo, & Winn, 1990), and random breath testing for alcohol.

Efforts also should be supported to improve pedestrian safety. Although street-crossing skills in children can improve somewhat with training, children younger than 11–12 years of age have developmental limitations in their ability to assess distances and speeds and negotiate traffic safely (Rivara, 1994). Reducing the speed of traffic, separating pedestrians from traffic, and enforcing laws that govern motor vehicle–pedestrian interactions have been recommended as community strategies to reduce childhood pedestrian injuries (Rivara, 1994).

Bicycle helmets have been found to reduce the risk of TBI due to bicycle-related trauma by 88%, and their use should be strongly promoted (Thompson, Rivara, & Thompson, 1989). Individuals riding on motorcycles, as well as those who participate in contact sports (e.g., football, hockey) and certain recreational activities (e.g., horseback riding, roller blading, skateboarding) should also wear helmets (Rivara, 1994).

Falls could be reduced through measures including maximizing safety of playground surfaces and reducing the height of playground equipment and increasing house safety by placing bars on windows (Rivara, 1994). Use of infant walkers increases exposure to household hazards, such as stairs, and should be discouraged (Rivara, 1994).

Although assaults and physical abuse theoretically represent entirely preventable causes of childhood TBI, society is making little progress in preventing them (Christoffel, 1990). Programs that provide in-home support and teaching of parenting skills to young mothers have been used in an attempt to decrease the risk of child abuse (Olds, Henderson, Chamberlin, et al., 1986).

Most suicides in children also are preventable. A suicide attempt in a child is usually an impulsive act, a cry for help. If caregivers are attuned to recognize signs of depression, drug abuse, or other problems leading to this gesture, many suicide attempts could be prevented. Parent and teacher awareness needs to improve in this area. Reduced availability of firearms to children and adolescents could also reduce pediatric suicide (and homicide) rates. Gun control legislation represents one important attempt to limit access to lethal weapons, but enactment has proven a political minefield. Finally, parents, teachers, and community groups need to be educated in the prevention of falls from heights, playground injuries, pool drownings, and sports injuries (Rivara, 1984).

CARMEN

When Carmen was 9 years old, she fell during her summer vacation from the top of a 6-foot ladder. She hit her head on the concrete pavement and immediately lost consciousness. Paramedics rushed her to the hospital, where she opened her eyes on command, withdrew her feet to pain, and spoke some garbled words. Physicians then administered the GCS (Table 27.1); Carmen scored a 10. Her neurological examination and cranial CT scan were normal with no evidence of hemorrhage or edema. Carmen improved so rapidly that in 1 week she seemed back to "normal" and was discharged.

Yet, after returning home, Carmen's parents noticed that she was very irritable, which was unusual for her. They initially attributed this to her stay in the hospital. They became concerned, however, when the irritability persisted for the next 2 months. They also noticed that Carmen was becoming quite aggressive toward her brother, her friends, and her dog.

When Carmen returned to school in the fall, her teachers also noticed these changes in her behavior. In addition, they were concerned by deterioration in her school performance. She had previously been a straight "A" student but was now receiving "C's" and "D's" in most subjects. Carmen's teachers requested a conference with her parents to discuss these changes.

Her parents, wondering whether the changes in her personality, behavior, and school performance could be attributed to her brain injury, consulted a neurologist who was unable to detect any neurological abnormalities. The physician then referred Carmen for a neuropsychological assessment. Her score on the Weschler Intelligence Scale for Children–Revised (Wechsler, 1991) indicated average intellectual functioning with no significant verbal–performance discrepancy. Her scores were also average in arithmetic, spelling, and reading achievement tests. The tests, however, did indicate impairments in auditory memory, abstract problem-solving abilities, and attention span.

As a result of this evaluation, Carmen was provided special educational support in math and social studies, the subjects that were most difficult for her. Her behavior and school performance gradually improved over the next few months, and it was expected that resource help would not be required during the next school year. Also, Carmen's parents thought that her personality was gradually returning to normal.

ETHAN

Ethan was 7 years old when he was hit by a car while riding his bicycle without a helmet. Minutes after the collision, medics arrived and found him unresponsive and with an abnormal flexion motor response. A cranial CT scan performed on admission to the hospital showed a large subdural hematoma over the left frontal, temporal, and parietal lobes. There were no other injuries. Ethan was taken to the operating room within an hour and the neurosurgeon removed the hematoma and placed an intracranial pressure monitor in him. He was found to have elevated intracranial pressure that was eventually controlled with mannitol and hyperventilation.

Ethan remained in coma for 10 weeks, at which point he began to respond to the command "move your hand" by opening his left hand. He also followed objects placed in his field of vision but did not speak. He was transferred to the neurorehabilitation service, where he received physical, occupational, and speech-language therapy twice daily. Gradually, over the next 12 weeks, his motor control improved, although he had spasticity on the right side of his body. He began to walk with an ankle orthosis (brace) and was able to complete self-care activities independently, primarily using his left arm, with some assistance from the right. Communication remained a major problem, as both expressive and receptive language impairments were evident. Cognitive testing revealed persisting impairments, with scores on both verbal and performance subtests more than 2 standard deviations below the norms.

Ethan was eventually discharged and enrolled in an outpatient rehabilitation program, in which he received physical and occupational therapy weekly and speech-language therapy three times weekly. Three months later he returned to school in a self-contained class for children with communication disorders; he also received physical and occupational therapy.

At 1-year follow-up, Ethan's right hand functioning had gradually improved, but he continued to prefer using his left hand. Both expressive and receptive language skills had significantly increased. His IEP for the next school year included continued placement in a class for children with communication disorders, with participation in a general education third-grade class for 20% of the day. He continued to receive physical and occupational therapies. Ethan has not been able to keep up with his old friends but is making new ones. It is likely that he will continue to have disabilities, but he will also continue to gain new skills and knowledge that should help him cope with his disabilities.

PROGNOSIS

Almost 95% of children admitted to a hospital following a TBI survive. For these children, a number of factors have been identified as predictors of outcome. Lower GCS scores generally indicate greater severity of TBI and a poorer outcome (Luerssen, Klauber, & Marshall, 1988; Michaud et al., 1992; Walker, Mayer, Storrs, et al., 1985). As in the cases of Carmen and Ethan, the duration of coma is a major index of the severity of the TBI (Eiben et al., 1984; Filley et al., 1987; Massagli et al., 1996). Children who come out of coma within 6 weeks have a good prognosis for recovery; when coma duration is between 6 weeks and 3 months, outcome is variable; and when the duration of coma is longer than 3 months, prognosis for recovery of functioning is generally poor (Brink & Hoffer, 1978). Those children who do recover motor functioning after prolonged coma have impairments in cognitive functioning and changes in personality (Brink & Hoffer, 1978). The duration of posttraumatic amnesia (PTA), which includes the period of coma and the subsequent period during which the individual with TBI is unable to store and remember new events, is also a prognostic indicator (Ewing-Cobbs, Levin, Fletcher, et al., 1990). Longer duration of PTA indicates more severe TBI and is associated with worse outcome. Duration of PTA in children can be reliably and validly measured using the Children's Orientation and Amnesia Test (COAT; Ewing-Cobbs et al., 1990).

The type of brain injury also is important in determining prognosis. Children with focal lesions in addition to DAI have been observed to have poorer outcomes than those with only DAI (Filley et al., 1987). Outcomes are usually good for children who have epidural hematomas but poor for those with subdural hematomas (Raimondi & Hirschauer, 1984). Injuries resulting in multiple organ damage also carry a poor prognosis, as the associated oxygen deprivation and low blood pressure cause secondary hypoxic-ischemic injury to the brain (Walker et al., 1985).

The impact of age is complex, and the results of different studies have been inconsistent (Ewing-Cobbs, Duhaime, & Fletcher, 1995). In some studies, poorer outcomes have been observed in children who are quite young at the time of injury (Koskiniemi et al., 1995; Luerssen et al., 1988; Mahoney, D'Souza, Haller, et al., 1983). In other studies, however, outcome has been found to be unrelated to age at the time of injury (Berger, Pitts, Lovely, et al., 1985; Zuccarello, Facco, Zampieri, et al., 1985). These contrasting findings may reflect the fact that different areas of functional outcome were being assessed. The brain of the young child may have a greater degree of plasticity than that of the older child or adult. Yet, this advantage may be offset by the fact that brain injury impairs new learning more than the retention of prior information. The young child has had less time to store knowledge before the injury and therefore may experience a greater impairment in cognitive functioning. Younger children with brain injuries due to physical abuse (e.g., shaken impact syndrome) have significantly worse cognitive and motor outcomes than age-matched children with brain injury from other causes (e.g., motor vehicle accidents) (Kriel, Krach, & Panser, 1989).

Finally, one must consider any preexisting developmental disability in predicting outcome. If ADHD or mental retardation is evident in a child after recovery from TBI, it is important to know whether this predated the injury. Similarly, cognitive impairments following an injury should be compared with any preexisting cognitive test scores.

SUMMARY

Head trauma is a common childhood event and the spectrum of consequences is broad. Depending on the severity, type, and location of the injury, outcome may range from complete recovery to severe functional disability. Persistent motor, communication, cognitive, behavior, and sensory impairments may result from TBI. Restoration of function in affected areas is the goal of rehabilitation and requires the participation of multiple medical specialists, allied health professionals, and educators. Although treatment is important, most head injuries in children are preventable. Injury prevention programs must be supported if there is to be a significant decrease in TBI in the future.

REFERENCES

Agran, P., Castillo, D., & Winn, D. (1990). Childhood motor vehicle occupant injuries. *American Journal of Diseases of Children, 144,* 653–662.

Alexander, R., Sato, Y., Smith, W., et al. (1990). Incidence of impact trauma with cranial injuries ascribed to shaking. *American Journal of Diseases of Children, 144,* 724–726.

American Academy of Pediatrics, Committee on Accident and Poison Prevention. (1987). *Injury control for children and youth.* Elk Grove Village, IL: Author.

Asarnow, R.F., Satz, P., Light, R., et al. (1991). Behavior problems and adaptive functioning in children with mild and severe closed head injury. *Journal of Pediatric Psychology, 16,* 543–555.

Baker, S.P., O'Neill, B., & Karpf, R.S. (1984). *The injury fact book.* Lexington, MA: Lexington Books.

Berger, M.S., Pitts, L.H., Lovely, M., et al. (1985). Outcome from severe head injury in children and adolescents. *Journal of Neurosurgery, 62,* 194–199.

Bijur, P.E., Haslum, M., & Golding, J. (1990). Cognitive and behavioral sequelae of mild head injury in children. *Pediatrics, 86,* 337–344.

Blasier, D., & Letts, R.M. (1989). The orthopaedic manifestations of head injury in children. *Orthopaedic Review, 18,* 350–358.

Braddock, M., Lapidus, G., Gregorio, D., et al. (1991). Population, income, and ecological correlates of child pedestrian injury. *Pediatrics, 88,* 1242–1247.

Brink, J.D., Garrett, A.L., Hale, W.R., et al. (1970). Recovery of motor and intellectual function in children sustaining severe head injuries. *Developmental Medicine and Child Neurology, 12,* 565–571.

Brink, J.D., & Hoffer, M.M. (1978). Rehabilitation of brain injured children. *Orthopedic Clinics of North America, 9,* 451–454.

Broman, S.H., & Michel, M.E. (Eds.). (1995). *Traumatic head injury in children.* New York: Oxford University Press.

Brookes, M., MacMillan, R., Cully, S., et al. (1990). Head injuries in accident and emergency departments: How different are children from adults? *Journal of Epidemiology and Community Life, 44,* 147–151.

Bruce, D.A. (1990). Head injury in the pediatric population. *Current Problems in Pediatrics, 20,* 61–107.

Butterworth, J.F., & DeWitt, D.S. (1989). Severe head trauma: Pathophysiology and management. *Critical Care Clinics, 5,* 807–820.

Carney, J., & Gerring, J. (1990). Return to school following severe closed head injury: A critical phase in pediatric rehabilitation. *Pediatrician, 17,* 222–229.

Carney, J., & Schoenbrodt, L. (1994). Educational implications of traumatic brain injury. *Pediatric Annals, 23,* 47–52.

Centers for Disease Control. (1990). Childhood injuries in the United States. *American Journal of Diseases of Children, 144,* 627–646.

Chadwick, O., Rutter, M., Shaffer, D., et al. (1981). A prospective study of children with head injuries: IV. Specific cognitive deficits. *Journal of Clinical Neuropsychology, 3,* 101–120.

Chadwick, O., Rutter, M., Thompson, J., et al. (1981). Intellectual performance and reading skills after localized head injury in childhood. *Journal of Child Psychology and Psychiatry and Allied Disciplines, 22,* 117–139.

Chapman, S.B. (1995). Discourse as an outcome measure in pediatric head-injured populations. In S.H. Broman & M.E. Michel (Eds.), *Traumatic head injury in children.* New York: Oxford University Press.

Chapman, S.B., Levin, H.S., Matejka, J., et al. (1995). Discourse ability in children with brain injury: Correlations with psychosocial, linguistic, and cognitive factors. *Journal of Head Trauma Rehabilitation, 10*(5), 36–54.

Christoffel, K.K. (1990). Violent death and injury in U.S. children and adolescents. *American Journal of Diseases of Children, 144,* 697–706.

Cohen, S.B. (1986). Educational reintegration and programming for children with head injuries. *Journal of Head Trauma Rehabilitation, 1*(4), 22–29.

Costeff, H., Groswasser, Z., & Goldstein, R. (1990). Long-term follow-up of 31 children with severe closed head trauma. *Journal of Neurosurgery, 73,* 684–687.

Craft, A.W., Shaw, D.A., & Cartlidge, N.E. (1972). Head injuries in children. *British Medical Journal, 4,* 200–203.

Dalby, P.R., & Obrzut, J.E. (1991). Epidemiologic characteristics and sequelae of closed head-injured children and adolescents: A review. *Developmental Neuropsychology, 7,* 35–68.

Davidson, L.L., Hughes, S.J., & O'Connor, P.A. (1988). Preschool behavior problems and subsequent risk of injury. *Pediatrics, 82,* 644–651.

Davidson, L.L., Taylor, E.A., Sandberg, S.T., et al. (1992). Hyperactivity in school-age boys and subsequent risk of injury. *Pediatrics, 90,* 697–702.

Dhellemmes, P., Lejeune, J.P., Christiaens, J.L., et al. (1985). Traumatic extradural hematomas in infancy and childhood: Experience with 144 cases. *Journal of Neurosurgery, 62,* 861–864.

Duhaime, A-C., Alario, A.J., Lewander, W.J., et al. (1992). Head injury in very young children: Mechanisms, injury types, and ophthalmologic findings in 100 hospitalized patients younger than 2 years of age. *Pediatrics, 90,* 179–185.

Education for All Handicapped Children Act of 1975, PL 94-142, 20 U.S.C. § 1400 *et seq.*

Eiben, C.F., Anderson, T.P., Lockman, L., et al. (1984). Functional outcome of closed head injury in children and young adults. *Archives of Physical Medicine and Rehabilitation, 65,* 168–170.

Ewing-Cobbs, L., Duhaime, A-C., & Fletcher, J.M. (1995). Inflicted and noninflicted traumatic brain injury in infants and preschoolers. *Journal of Head Trauma Rehabilitation, 10*(5), 13–24.

Ewing-Cobbs, L., Fletcher, J.M., & Levin, H.S. (1986). Neurobehavioral sequelae following head injury in children: Educational implications. *Journal of Head Trauma Rehabilitation, 1*(4), 57–65.

Ewing-Cobbs, L., Levin, H.S., Fletcher, J.M., et al. (1990). The Children's Orientation and Amnesia Test: Relationship to severity of acute head injury and to recovery of memory. *Neurosurgery, 27,* 683–691.

Fay, G.C., Jaffe, K.M., Polissar, N.L., et al. (1993). Mild pediatric traumatic brain injury: A cohort study. *Archives of Physical Medicine and Rehabilitation, 74,* 895–901.

Fay, G., & Janesheski, J. (1986). Neuropsychological assessment of head-injured children. *Journal of Head Trauma Rehabilitation, 1*(4), 16–21.

Filley, C.M., Cranberg, L.D., Alexander, M.P., et al. (1987). Neurobehavioral outcome after closed head injury in childhood and adolescence. *Archives of Neurology, 44,* 194–198.

Fletcher, J.M., Ewing-Cobbs, L., Miner, M., et al. (1990). Behavioral changes after closed head injury in children. *Journal of Consulting and Clinical Psychology, 58,* 93–98.

Florian, V., Katz, S., & Lahav, V. (1989). Impact of traumatic brain damage on family dynamics and functioning: A review. *Brain Injury, 3,* 219–233.

Gentry, L.R., Godersky, J.C., & Thompson, B. (1988). MR imaging of head trauma: Review of the distribution and radiopathologic features of traumatic lesions. *American Journal of Roentgenology, 150,* 663–672.

Gerring, J.P. (1986). Psychiatric sequelae of severe closed head injury. *Pediatrics in Review, 8,* 115–121.

Ghajar, J., & Hariri, R.J. (1992). Management of pediatric head injury. *Pediatric Clinics of North America, 39,* 1093–1125.

Goldstein, F.C., & Levin, H.S. (1985). Intellectual and academic outcome following closed head injury in children and adolescents: Research strategies and empirical findings. *Developmental Neuropsychology, 1,* 195–214.

Greenspan, A.I., & MacKenzie, E.J. (1994). Functional outcome after pediatric head injury. *Pediatrics, 94,* 425–432.

Gualtieri, C.T. (1988). Pharmacotherapy and the neurobehavioral sequelae of traumatic brain injury. *Brain Injury, 2,* 101–129.

Hall, D.M., Johnson, S.L., & Middleton, J. (1990). Rehabilitation of head injured children. *Archives of Disease in Childhood, 65,* 553–556.

Hanson, S.L., & Clippard, D. (1992). Assessment of children with traumatic brain injury: Planning for school reentry. *Physical Medicine and Rehabilitation: State of the Art Reviews, 6,* 483–494.

Healy, G.B. (1982). Current concepts in otolaryngology: Hearing loss and vertigo secondary to head injury. *New England Journal of Medicine, 306,* 1029–1031.

Holinger, P.C. (1990). The causes, impact, and preventability of childhood injuries in the United States: Childhood suicide in the United States. *American Journal of Diseases of Children, 144,* 670–676.

Individuals with Disabilities Education Act (IDEA) of 1990, PL 101-476, 20 U.S.C. § 1400 *et seq.*

Jacobson, M.S., Rubenstein, E.M., Bohannon, W.E., et al. (1986). Follow-up of adolescent trauma victims: A new model of care. *Pediatrics, 77,* 236–241.

Jaffe, K.M., & Hays, R.M. (1986). Pediatric head injury: Rehabilitative medical management. *Journal of Head Trauma Rehabilitation, 1*(4), 30–40.

Jaffe, K.M., & McDonald, C.M. (1992). Rehabilitation following childhood injury. *Pediatric Annals, 21,* 438–439, 443–447.

Jaffe, K.M., Polissar, N.L., Fay, G.C., et al. (1995). Recovery trends over three years following pediatric traumatic brain injury. *Archives of Physical Medicine and Rehabilitation, 76,* 17–26.

Jennett, B., & Teasdale, G. (1981). *Management of head injuries.* Philadelphia: F.A. Davis.

Jennett, B., Teasdale, G., Galbraith, S., et al. (1977). Severe head injuries in three countries. *Journal of Neurology, Neurosurgery, and Psychiatry, 40,* 291–298.

Kaufman, B.A., & Dacey, R.G., Jr. (1994). Acute care management of closed head injury in childhood. *Pediatric Annals, 23,* 18–20, 25–28.

Klonoff, H. (1971). Head injuries in children: Predisposing factors, accident conditions, accident proneness, and sequelae. *American Journal of Public Health, 61,* 2405–2417.

Klonoff, H., Low, M.D., & Clark, C. (1977). Head injuries in children: A prospective five year follow-up. *Journal of Neurology, Neurosurgery, and Psychiatry, 40,* 1211–1219.

Knights, R.M., Ivan, L.P., Ventureyra, E.C.G., et al. (1991). The effects of head injury in children on neuropsychological and behavioural functioning. *Brain Injury, 5,* 339–351.

Koman, L.A., Mooney, J.F., III, Smith, B.P., et al. (1994). Management of spasticity in cerebral palsy with botulinum-A toxin: Report of a preliminary, randomized, double-blind trial. *Journal of Pediatric Orthopaedics, 14,* 299–303.

Koskiniemi, M., Kyykka, T., Nybo, T., et al. (1995). Long-term outcome after severe brain injury in preschoolers is worse than expected. *Archives of Pediatrics and Adolescent Medicine, 149,* 249–254.

Kraus, J.F., Fife, D., & Conroy, C. (1987). Pediatric brain injuries: The nature, clinical course, and early outcomes in a defined United States' population. *Pediatrics, 79,* 501–507.

Kraus, J.F., Rock, A., & Hemyari, P. (1990). Brain injuries among infants, children, adolescents, and young adults. *American Journal of Diseases of Children, 144,* 684–691.   ·

Kriel, R.L., Krach, L.E., & Jones-Saete, C. (1993). Outcome of children with prolonged unconsciousness and vegetative states. *Pediatric Neurology, 9*, 362–368.

Kriel, R.L., Krach, L.E., & Panser, L.A. (1989). Closed head injury: Comparison of children younger and older than 6 years of age. *Pediatric Neurology, 5*, 296–300.

Kriel, R.L., Krach, L.E., & Sheehan, M. (1988). Pediatric closed head injury: Outcome following prolonged unconsciousness. *Archives of Physical Medicine and Rehabilitation, 69*, 678–681.

Langfitt, T.W., & Gennarelli, T.A. (1982). Can the outcome from head injury be improved? *Journal of Neurosurgery, 56*, 19–25.

Lazar, M.F., & Menaldino, S. (1995). Cognitive outcome and behavioral adjustment in children following traumatic brain injury: A developmental perspective. *Journal of Head Trauma Rehabilitation, 10*(5), 55–63.

Luerssen, T.G., Klauber, M.R., & Marshall, L.F. (1988). Outcome from head injury related to patient's age: A longitudinal prospective study of adult and pediatric head injury. *Journal of Neurosurgery, 68*, 409–416.

Mahoney, W.J., D'Souza, B.J., Haller, J.A., et al. (1983). Long-term outcome of children with severe head trauma and prolonged coma. *Pediatrics, 71*, 756–762.

Margolis, L.H., Wagenaar, A.C., & Liu, W. (1988). The effects of a mandatory child restraint law on injuries requiring hospitalization. *American Journal of Diseases of Children, 142*, 1099–1103.

Massagli, T.M., & Jaffe, K.M. (1994). Pediatric traumatic brain injury: Prognosis and rehabilitation. *Pediatric Annals, 23*, 29–30, 33–36.

Massagli, T.L., Michaud, L.J., & Rivara, F.P. (1996). Association between injury indices and outcome after severe traumatic brain injury in children. *Archives of Physical Medicine and Rehabilitation, 77*, 125–132.

Masters, S.J., McClean, P.M., Arcarese, J.S., et al. (1987). Skull X-ray examinations after head trauma. Recommendations by a multidisciplinary panel and validation study. *New England Journal of Medicine, 316*, 84–91.

Mayes, S.D., Pelco, L.E., & Campbell, C.J. (1989). Relationships among pre- and post-injury intelligence, length of coma and age in individuals with severe closed-head injuries. *Brain Injury, 3*, 301–313.

McDonald, C.M., Jaffe, K.M., Fay, G.C., et al. (1994). Comparison of indices of traumatic brain injury severity as predictors of neurobehavioral outcome

in children. *Archives of Physical Medicine and Rehabilitation, 75*, 328–337.

McMordie, W.R., & Barker, S.L. (1988). The financial trauma of head injury. *Brain Injury, 2*, 357–364.

Michaud, L.J., Duhaime, A-C., & Batshaw, M.L. (1993). Traumatic brain injury in children. *Pediatric Clinics of North America, 40*, 553–565.

Michaud, L.J., Rivara, F.P., Grady, M.S., et al. (1992). Predictors of survival and severity of disability after severe brain injury in children. *Neurosurgery, 31*, 254–264.

Michaud, L.J., Rivara, F.P., Jaffe, K.M., et al. (1993). Traumatic brain injury as a risk factor for behavioral disorders in children. *Archives of Physical Medicine and Rehabilitation, 74*, 368–375.

Milton, S.B., Scaglione, C., Flanagan, T., et al. (1991). Functional evaluation of adolescent students with traumatic brain injury. *Journal of Head Trauma Rehabilitation, 6*, 35–46.

Molnar, G.E., & Perrin, J.C.S. (1983). Rehabilitation of the child with head injury. In K. Shapiro (Ed.), *Pediatric head trauma* (pp. 241–269). Mt. Kisco, NY: Futura Publishing.

Mysiw, W.J., Corrigan, J.D., & Gribble, M.W. (1990). The ataxic subgroup: A discrete outcome after traumatic brain injury. *Brain Injury, 4*, 247–255.

Olds, D.L., Henderson, C.R., Jr., Chamberlin, R., et al. (1986). Preventing child abuse and neglect: A randomized trial of nurse home visitation. *Pediatrics, 78*, 65–78.

Oppenheimer, D.R. (1968). Microscopic lesions in the brain following head injury. *Journal of Neurology, Neurosurgery, and Psychiatry, 31*, 299–306.

Ordog, G.J., Wasserberger, J., Schatz, I., et al. (1988). Gunshot wounds in children under 10 years of age: A new epidemic. *American Journal of Diseases of Children, 142*, 618–622.

Parmelee, D.X. (1989). Neuropsychiatric sequellae of traumatic brain injury in children and adolescents. *Psychiatric Medicine, 7*, 11–16.

Perrott, S.B., Taylor, H.G., & Montes, J.L. (1991). Neuropsychological sequelae, familial stress, and environmental adaptation following pediatric head injury. *Developmental Neuropsychology, 7*, 69–86.

Pittman, T., Bucholz, R., & Williams, D. (1989). Efficacy of barbiturates in the treatment of resistant intracranial hypertension in severely head-injured children. *Pediatric Neuroscience, 15*, 13–17.

Raimondi, A.J., & Hirschauer, J. (1984). Head injury in the infant and toddler: Coma scoring and outcome scale. *Child's Brain, 11*, 12–35.

Ried, S., Strong, G., Wright, L., et al. (1995). Computers, assistive devices, and augmentative communication aids: Technology for social inclusion.

Journal of Head Trauma Rehabilitation, 10(5), 80–90.

Rivara, F.P. (1984). Childhood injuries. III: Epidemiology of non-motor vehicle head trauma. *Developmental Medicine and Child Neurology, 26,* 81–87.

Rivara, F.P. (1994). Epidemiology and prevention of pediatric traumatic brain injury. *Pediatric Annals, 23,* 12–17.

Rivara, J.B., Fay, G.C., Jaffe, K.M., et al. (1992). Predictors of family functioning one year following traumatic brain injury in children. *Archives of Physical Medicine and Rehabilitation, 73,* 899–910.

Rivara, J.B., Jaffe, K.M., Fay, G.C., et al. (1993). Family functioning and injury severity as predictors of child functioning one year following traumatic brain injury. *Archives of Physical Medicine and Rehabilitation, 74,* 1047–1055.

Rivara, J.B., Jaffe, K.M., Polissar, N.L., et al. (1994). Family functioning and children's academic performance and behavior problems in the year following traumatic brain injury. *Archives of Physical Medicine and Rehabilitation, 75,* 369–379.

Sasin, D.M., Sachs, J.J., & Webb, K.W. (1996). Pediatric head injuries and deaths from bicycling in the United States. *Pediatrics, 98,* 868–870.

Savage, R.C. (1991). Identification, classification, and placement issues for students with traumatic brain injuries. *Journal of Head Trauma Rehabilitation, 6*(1), 1–9.

Shurtleff, H.A., Massagli, T.L., Hays, R.M., et al. (1995). Screening children and adolescents with mild or moderate traumatic brain injury to assist school reentry. *Journal of Head Trauma Rehabilitation, 10*(5), 64–79.

Siesjö, B.K. (1992). Pathophysiology and treatment of focal cerebral ischemia: Part II. Mechanisms of damage and treatment. *Journal of Neurosurgery, 77,* 337–354.

Telzrow, C.F. (1987). Management of academic and educational problems in head injury. *Journal of Learning Disabilities, 20,* 536–545.

Telzrow, C.F. (1991). The school psychologist's perspective on testing students with traumatic brain injury. *Journal of Head Trauma Rehabilitation, 6*(1), 23–34.

Thompson, N.M., Francis, D.J., Stuebing, K.K., et al. (1994). Motor, visual-spatial, and somatosensory skills after closed head injury in children and adolescents: A study of change. *Neuropsychology, 8,* 333–342.

Thompson, R.S., Rivara, F.P., & Thompson, D.C. (1989). A case-control study of the effectiveness of bicycle safety helmets. *New England Journal of Medicine, 320,* 1361–1367.

Urbach, J.R., & Culbert, J.P. (1991). Head-injured parents and their children. Psychosocial consequences of a traumatic syndrome. *Psychosomatics, 32,* 24–33.

Volpe, B.T., & McDowell, F.H. (1990). The efficacy of cognitive rehabilitation in patients with traumatic brain injury. *Archives of Neurology, 47,* 220–222.

Walker, M.L., Mayer, T.A., Storrs, B.B., et al. (1985). Pediatric head injury: Factors which influence outcome. *Concepts in Pediatric Neurosurgery, 6,* 84–97.

Wechsler, D. (1991). *Wechsler Intelligence Scale for Children–Third edition.* New York: The Psychological Corporation.

White, R.J., & Likavec, M.J. (1992). The diagnosis and initial management of head injury. *New England Journal of Medicine, 327,* 1507–1511.

Williams, D., & Mateer, C. (1992). Developmental impact of frontal lobe injury in middle childhood. *Brain and Cognition, 20,* 196–204.

Winn, D.G., Agran, P.F., & Castillo, D.N. (1991). Pedestrian injuries to children younger than 5 years of age. *Pediatrics, 88,* 776–782.

Ylvisaker, M. (Ed.). (1985). *Head injury rehabilitation: Children and adolescents.* San Diego: College-Hill Press.

Ylvisaker, M., & Weinstein, M. (1989). Recovery of oral feeding after pediatric head injury. *Journal of Head Trauma Rehabilitation, 4*(4), 51–63.

Zuccarello, M., Facco, E., Zampieri, P., et al. (1985). Severe head injury in children: Early prognosis and outcome. *Child's Nervous System, 1,* 158–162.

IV Interventions, Families, and Outcomes

28 Feeding

Peggy S. Eicher

Upon completion of this chapter, the reader will:

- be able to describe the typical swallowing process
- be aware of the influence of developmental, respiratory, and gastrointestinal dysfunction on swallowing in children
- recognize some of the common feeding problems of children with developmental disabilities
- understand the basic components of a treatment approach to feeding problems

Children with developmental disabilities frequently face special problems in obtaining adequate nutrition (Rudolph, 1994; Stevenson, 1995; Sullivan & Rosenbloom, 1996). These problems may arise from motor or sensory dysfunction that makes it difficult to accept new food textures or that interferes with the preparation of food for swallowing or from other medical conditions that interfere with swallowing or digestion. The continuous pressure on children and their caregivers to maintain adequate nutrition often leads to stressful mealtimes and behavior problems. In this chapter, the typical anatomy and physiology of the swallowing process is described so that the influences of various medical and developmental conditions on it can be understood. Specific feeding and digestive disorders are discussed, along with approaches to therapy.

THE FEEDING PROCESS

Swallowing

Swallowing can be divided into four phases (Figure 28.1). During the **oral preparatory** phase, food is taken into the mouth, processed to a manageable consistency, and then collected into a small parcel or bolus. Once a bolus is formed, **oral transport** begins when the tongue propels the bolus backward into the pharynx. Movement of the bolus past the faucial (throat) arches marks the start of **pharyngeal transfer** and triggers what is called the swallowing cascade, an involuntary sequence of highly coordinated movements of the pharyngeal and esophageal muscles. With each swallow, respiration ceases as the nasopharynx and trachea are covered by the

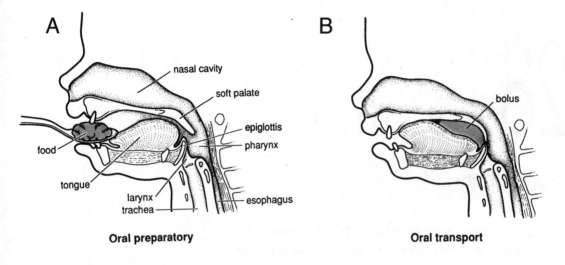

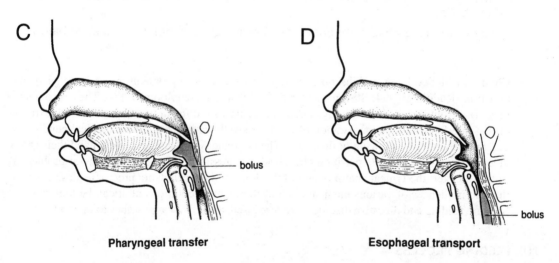

Figure 28.1.   The four phases of swallowing. a) Oral preparatory: Food is taken into the mouth, processed to a manageable consistency, and then collected into a small parcel or bolus. b) Oral transport: The bolus is then pushed backward by the tongue toward the pharynx. c) Pharyngeal transfer: As swallowing begins, the epiglottis normally folds over the opening of the trachea to direct food down the esophagus and not into the lungs. d) Esophageal transport: The peristaltic wave moves the bolus down the esophagus toward the stomach.

soft palate and epiglottis, respectively, so that food does not slip into the airway. A peristaltic wave originating in the posterior wall of the hypopharynx propels the bolus past the airway and into the esophagus. During the **esophageal transport** phase, the wave continues to move the bolus down the esophagus and into the stomach.

Neurological Control

Neurological control of the swallowing process resides in the upper medullary region of the brainstem in an area referred to as the "swallowing center" (Figure 28.2) (Miller, 1993). Cranial nerves V, VII, IX, and X transmit sensory information from the mouth and pharynx to the nucleus tractus solitarius (NTS), which serves as a relay station for taste input as well as sensory input from the heart, lungs, stomach, and esophagus. Descending neurons from cortical centers also project here to provide further control (Martin & Sessel, 1993). Master neurons in the NTS control the coordination of respiration with swallowing and are able to evoke pharyngeal and esophageal swallows. Patterns of output from the master neurons activate the central rhythm generator (CRG), which initiates the swallowing cascade. The CRG is a group of interneurons that generates bursts of sequential activity even in the absence of sensory feedback. The CRG signals are translated in the nucleus ambiguous (NA) where switching neurons transmit timed output from the CRG to the proper motor neurons at various brainstem levels. Output from the NA can be modified directly by sensory feedback from the NTS or from descending cortical projections to the NA. There is a hierarchy of organizational control of swallowing. The lowest level is the local sensory input related to the food bolus itself. Next is the reflexive control through the brainstem relay station and the CRG. The highest level of control is provided by the descending cortical pathways (Kennedy & Kent, 1988). Any abnormality in the cranial nerves V, VII, IX, X, or XII can alter sensory input and potentially motor output, disrupting coordination and function of the swallowing process. Because of the importance of descending projections on modification of swallowing, cortical injuries can also significantly impair its safe execution.

Influence of Development

The process of swallowing is greatly affected by the development and growth of the child (Casas, McPherson, & Kenny, 1995; Koch, 1993). As the nervous system matures, reflexive patterns are integrated into learned motor patterns through practice. With cortical maturation, more specific and finely graded movements under volitional control develop, similar to the sequential development of gross motor skills observed in the growing child.

Suckling

Suckling is the most primitive oral pattern. The suckle pattern involves wide, rhythmic excursions of the jaw. The tongue rides up and down with the jaw but moves in and out creating a wave-like motion. Although suckling motions are evident earlier, they do not result in swallowing until 34 weeks' gestation, and only at full term does the pattern become coordinated with breathing to allow functional feeding. This is why premature infants typically require tube-feedings. Initially, suckling is a reflexive activity that is elicited involuntarily whenever something enters the child's mouth. With brain maturation, the reflex is integrated and the pattern is refined to the voluntary act of sucking.

Sucking

During sucking, the lips purse, jaw movements are more finely graded, and the tongue is raised and lowered independent of the jaw. When sucking replaces the anterior-posterior pattern of suckling, usually around 5 months of age, the child can progress to spoon-feeding. If spoon-

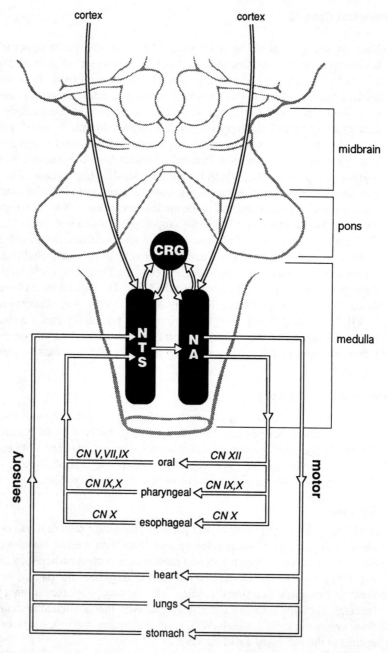

Figure 28.2.   Neurological control of swallowing. The "swallowing center" is located in the upper medullary region of the brainstem. Cranial nerves (CN) V, VII, IX, and X transmit sensory information from the mouth and pharynx to the nucleus tractus solitarius (NTS), which is a relay station for sensory input from the heart, lungs, stomach, and esophagus. Descending neurons from the cortex also project here. Output from the neurons in the NTS activates the central rhythm generator (CRG), which initiates the swallowing cascade. The CRG signals are translated to the nucleus ambiguous (NA), where switching neurons transmit output to various brainstem levels.

feeding is tried earlier, the food will ride out of the mouth on the tongue instead of being swallowed.

Munching

With munching, the next stage in oral-motor development, small pieces of food are broken off, flattened, and then collected for swallowing. Munching consists of a rhythmical bite-and-release pattern with a series of well-graded jaw openings and closings. The emergence of tongue lateralization at this stage enables the child to move food from side to side and back to midline. Chewing of the food and breaking it into smaller pieces does not occur until the child acquires a rotary component to jaw movement. This emerges as early as 9 months and is gradually modified with practice to the adult pattern by around 3 years of age (Gisel, 1994).

Structures and Growth

Typically, the attainment of new oral-motor skills is timed to integrate perfectly with the change in oral-motor structures occurring with growth. The infant, for example, is perfectly equipped for nipple feeding. The buccal fat pads in the cheeks confine the oral cavity laterally. The soft tissue structures, tongue, soft palate, and epiglottis fill much of the oropharyngeal cavity, making it easier to generate the negative intraoral pressure necessary to draw fluids out of the nipple. The larynx is positioned high and anterior, almost tucked under the tongue, necessitating less intrapharyngeal control to guide the liquid past the airway and into the esophagus (Bosma, 1986).

With growth, the jaw and palate enlarge in relation to the soft tissue structures, allowing room for teeth (Figure 28.3). The larger oral cavity (even without teeth) is not as efficient for nipple feeding but facilitates spoon entry and lateralization. The larynx descends and moves posteriorly as the neck elongates. This necessitates increased postural control for correct head and neck alignment, manifested by the child developing volitional control of head and neck movement and the ability to sit independently. Laryngeal descent is accompanied by increased propulsive control to safely guide the bolus past the airway. Delay in gross motor or oral-motor development can interfere with the integration of oral-motor skill acquisition with growth, resulting in decreased feeding efficiency (Stevenson & Allaire, 1991).

Any anatomical defect involving the oral or nasal cavities, pharynx, or esophagus can adversely affect swallowing. Clefts in the lip or palate prevent the sealing off of the oral cavity. This decreases the ability to generate negative pressure and interferes with bolus collection. A structural change that affects coordination also can be significant, for example **choanal atresia** or **adenoidal hypertrophy,** which renders the child dependent on his or her mouth as an airway.

INFLUENCE OF MEDICAL CONDITIONS

Successful feeding is dependent not only on the anatomy and function of the oral and pharyngeal structures involved in swallowing, but also on the child's medical status especially with regard to respiration and digestion (Gisel & Alphonce, 1995). The heart and lungs send information directly to the swallowing center. Thus, a child with breathing difficulty (e.g., when wheezing) may start to drool because his or her swallowing frequency is decreased to allow more frequent respirations (Timms, Defiore, Martin, et al., 1993).

Input from the gastrointestinal tract also significantly influences the feeding process. Typically as the bolus of food travels to the stomach, the lower esophageal sphincter works as a one-way valve to

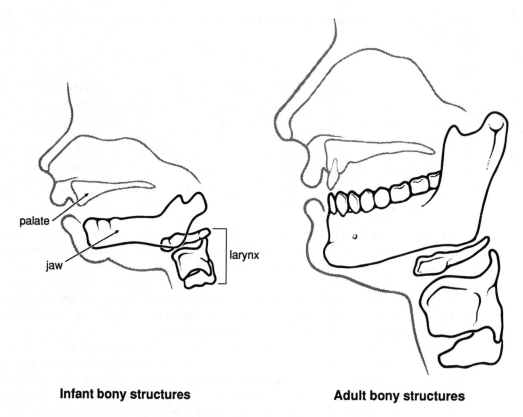

Infant bony structures　　　　　**Adult bony structures**

Figure 28.3.　The influence of growth on the bony structures of the oropharynx. The mandible (jaw) enlarges, enabling room for teeth and a larger oral cavity. The larynx descends and moves posteriorly, necessitating increased control of bolus propulsion to guide it past the airway.

prevent the backward flow, or reflux, of food after it has entered the stomach. Meanwhile, the stomach secretes acids to further break down the food. Contractions of the stomach wall mix the food, acids, and added fluids and push this mass gradually into the duodenum, the upper part of the small intestine (Figure 28.4). (Incidentally, the intestines are referred to as small or large because of their diameter, not their length.) Enzymes and other substances from the pancreas and bile ducts are released into the duodenum and aid in the breakdown of food particles into their major components: proteins, fats, and carbohydrates. These compounds are further simplified into sugars, such as lactose, fatty acids, amino acids, vitamins, and minerals. The jejunum and ileum, the middle and lower portions of the small intestine, absorb these digested nutrients.

The nonabsorbable nutrients, often called bulk or fiber, pass to the large intestine or colon. Movement through the colon is much slower than through the rest of the digestive tract and is influenced by the volume of nonabsorbable nutrients contained in the food. Although movement from the stomach to the end of the ileum may take only 30–90 minutes, passage through the colon may require 1–7 days. Rapid movement, which happens, for example, during a stomach flu, leads to diarrhea. Conversely, slower movement causes more water to be absorbed and

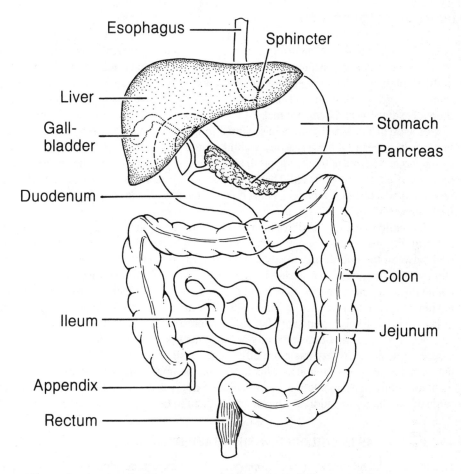

Figure 28.4.   After food enters the stomach, it is mixed with acid and is partially digested. Then it passes through the three segments of the small intestine (duodenum, jejunum, and ileum). There, digestive juices are added, and nutrients are removed. The remaining water and electrolytes pass through the colon where water is removed. Voluntary stooling is controlled by the rectal sphinctor muscles.

results in hard stools and constipation. Constipation can lead to slower transit through the entire system and even vomiting. For proper bowel evacuation to take place, an individual needs fluid, fiber, and coordinated propulsive muscle activity. This includes control of the rectal sphincter muscles that facilitate voluntary defecation.

Any medical condition that impairs the function of the respiratory or gastrointestinal tracts can influence the swallowing process. Reactive airway disease (asthma) with recurrent exacerbations; gastroesophageal reflux (GER), the backward flow of stomach contents into the esophagus; renal disease; or inborn errors of metabolism, such as cystic fibrosis or a urea cycle defect, can contribute to development of a feeding problem. In addition, if oral feeding is precluded for prolonged periods of time for any reason, the child may lose oral-motor skills and may require gradual retraining in how to eat (Monahan, Shapiro, & Fox, 1988).

INFLUENCE OF DEVELOPMENT

A child's developmental function influences the feeding process in several ways. Abnormal muscle tone and/or persistent primitive reflex activity frequently interfere with trunk support and body alignment. Lack of adequate trunk support greatly hinders rib cage expansion, which interferes with respiration, and increases pressure on the stomach and abdominal cavity. Improper head and neck alignment make it harder to guide a bolus past the airway, increasing the risk of **aspiration.** Malalignment also limits tongue movement, thereby interfering with oral-motor patterns. For all these reasons, a child should be seated during feedings, with a firm base of support and adequate trunk support to allow neutral alignment of the head and neck. This may require a slight recline if the child has not yet accomplished independent sitting. The child's fine motor and adaptive skills influence the choice of utensils and level of independence at mealtime (see Chapter 32).

The child's cognitive abilities help to shape how he or she interacts with the mealtime environment. Because children are dependent on their caregivers for nutrition, effective communication between the two during meals is crucial. This is facilitated by an understanding of the child's cognitive level and a sensitivity to nonverbal cues. The absence of effective, constructive communication increases the likelihood that expression will take the form of maladaptive behaviors at mealtime, such as expelling, refusal, or having tantrums. Approaching the child at his or her cognitive level also engages the child's interest and makes meals more enjoyable.

Many feeding transitions typically occur in the first 3 years of life. Frequently a child with a developmental disability has more difficulty adjusting to changes that include new textures, new utensils, and new situations. This heightens the importance of a stable mealtime environment and consistent interactions between the caregiver and the child. Consistency imparts a sense of familiarity to children, which enables them to be comfortable and more tolerant.

FEEDING PROBLEMS IN CHILDREN WITH DISABILITIES

One third of all children with a developmental disability will develop a feeding problem significant enough to interfere with their nutrition, medical well-being, or social integration (Rogers, Arvedson, Buck, et al., 1994; Waterman, Koltai, Downey, et al., 1992). The problem may result from structural anomalies affecting the mouth, nose, respiratory or gastrointestinal tract, or from a neurological impairment, medical condition, or developmental delay that affects feeding. Manifestation of a feeding problem can be subtle, such as increased congestion or gagging with meals, or it can be dramatic (e.g., total food refusal, choking, failure to thrive). An explanation of some of the more common feeding problems follows.

Increased Oral Losses

Loss of food from the mouth signals oral-motor dysfunction (Chigira, Omoto, Mukai, et al., 1994). The child may have poor lip closure or jaw instability related to abnormal tone in the facial muscles. Once in the mouth, food may be carried out on the tongue or as a result of a persistent suckle pattern. Sometimes food may be exhaled out of the mouth if the oral cavity also serves as the primary airway. It must be remembered that a diet history will not accurately reflect a child's caloric intake in the presence of increased oral losses (Stallings, Zemel, Davies, et al., in preparation).

Prolonged Feeding Time

Prolonged feeding time of greater than 30 minutes usually results from a combination of factors. Oral transport may be slowed related to difficulty with bolus collection or weakened tongue movements. The child may need more time between bites if pharyngeal transfer is weak or uncoordinated. This will prevent the child from clearing the bolus from the pharynx with a single swallow. Similarly, the child may slow the meal to allow more time for breathing between bites or to complete transport through the esophagus. Prolonged feeding time is very difficult for the child and the caregiver and signals the need for an evaluation.

Pocketing

Food pocketing (i.e., holding food in the cheeks or front of the mouth for prolonged periods) suggests a problem with either oral transport or food refusal. Often children who have difficulty with tongue lateralization have trouble bringing food back to the midline before a swallow. As a result, mashed food or chunks migrate toward the cheeks. If a child does not want to swallow a food because of its texture or taste, he or she may trap it in the cheeks, out of the way of the active transport pattern.

Coughing, Gagging, and Choking

Coughing and gagging indicate difficulty with swallowing. Both are normal defense mechanisms to prevent aspiration. The time at which coughing and gagging occurs during the meal may indicate which texture is troublesome (Casas, Kenny, & McPherson, 1994). For example, gagging on lumpy foods but not purées suggests difficulty adequately processing the higher texture. Coughing with liquids indicates difficulty controlling flow through the pharynx and past the airway. In addition, if coughing or gagging occurs at the end of or after a meal but not during the meal, GER should be considered. Coughing or gagging with meals that persists over several weeks is a serious warning signal and requires thorough evaluation as soon as possible (Rogers, Arvedson, Msall, et al., 1993).

Aspiration

Aspiration refers to the entry of food or foreign substance into the airway (Figure 28.5). It may occur before, during, or after a swallow or as a result of GER. Everyone aspirates small amounts occasionally, but protective responses such as a gag or cough help to clear it from the airway. Children with developmental disabilities that affect sensory or motor coordination of the oropharynx, larynx, or trachea are at increased risk for recurrent aspiration. These children also frequently have impaired protective responses that limit their ability to clear their airway once aspiration has occurred. Signs of aspiration are influenced by the age of the child. Aspiration in infants may present as apnea and bradycardia. In older infants and children, symptoms commonly include coughing, increased congestion, or wheezing during meals. Some children can aspirate without evoking any protective response; this is called silent aspiration. The accumulation of foodstuffs in the airway causes irritation and inflammation. Depending on the amount and frequency of aspiration, the child can develop recurrent pneumonia, bronchitis, or tracheitis (Loughlin & Lefton-Greif, 1994).

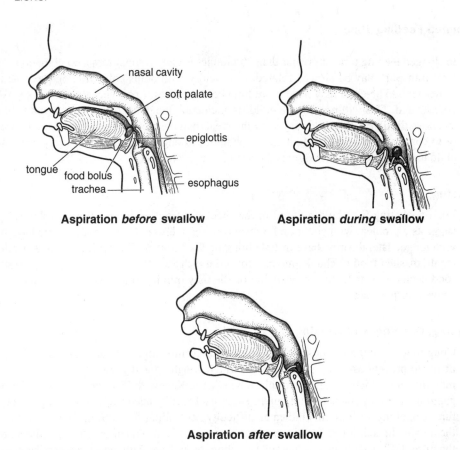

Aspiration *before* swallow   **Aspiration *during* swallow**

Aspiration *after* swallow

Figure 28.5.   Aspiration. a) If a part of the bolus "leaks" past the soft palate before a swallow is triggered, it can flow past the open epiglottis and into the trachea. b) If the epiglottis is not competently closed as the bolus passes, aspiration can also occur. c) Food residua in the pharynx after a swallow can be carried into the airway with the next breath, resulting in aspiration after the swallow.

Gastroesophageal Reflux

GER involves the backward flow of stomach contents into the esophagus (Figure 28.6). Reflux can result in vomiting and/or recurrent respiratory symptoms such as coughing, wheezing, or even pneumonia if the stomach contents enter the airway (Bagwell, 1995). In addition, the escape of stomach acid can cause an inflammation of the esophagus (esophagitis) that makes eating uncomfortable. GER can result from a number of abnormalities. The most common problem is a weakened sphincter muscle at the end of the lower esophagus, which does not close adequately to prevent reflux of gastric contents. Reflux also may result from increased abdominal pressure caused by hypertonia, posturing, or constipation. Increased intra-abdominal pressure can push food up through even a normally functioning gastroesophageal sphincter. Finally, delayed stomach emptying, resulting from abnormal stomach contractions or poor intestinal motility, may lead to stomach distension, which increases sphincter relaxation and creates the opportunity for reflux.

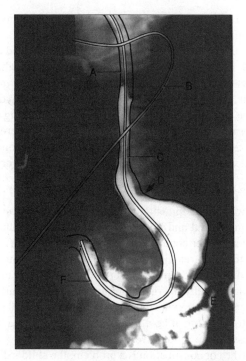

Figure 28.6.   Gastroesophageal reflux. Food passes down the esophagus (A), through the lower esophageal sphincter (D), and into the stomach (E) and duodenum (F). If the sphincter does not remain closed after the passage of food, reflux (C) occurs as shown in this barium study in a child with a nasogastric tube (B) in place.

Not all vomiting is a consequence of GER. Increased intracranial pressure, obstruction of the stomach's outflow tract, kidney disease, and food allergies are some of the other medical conditions that can present with symptoms of vomiting and gastric intolerance similar to reflux. Therefore, appropriate medical evaluation is important. Sometimes the pattern or content of emesis can suggest an etiological agent (i.e., bilious emesis suggests obstruction; emesis immediately after a certain food on several occasions suggests an allergy). But these are not specific differentiating factors.

Digestion: The Small Intestine

Although children with disabilities often have problems sucking and swallowing, they usually are able to absorb nutrients once the food reaches the small intestine. Occasionally, however, there may be malabsorption that interferes with adequate nutrition (Brady, Richard, Fitzgerald, et al., 1986).

The most common malabsorptive disorder is lactose intolerance. Approximately 10%–20% of African American and Jewish children have this problem (Rings, Grand, & Buller, 1994). Symptoms include vomiting and diarrhea after ingesting milk products. The cause of the intolerance is an inherited deficiency of the enzyme lactase, which normally breaks down milk sugar (lactose) and allows its absorption. Unabsorbed lactose irritates the gastrointestinal wall and causes vomiting and diarrhea. An individual with this disorder can prevent or at least decrease the symptoms by taking lactase in a capsule form before ingesting a milk product or by using lactase-containing milk.

The function of the small intestine also can be compromised by the "dumping syndrome," in which the stomach is emptied too rapidly. When this happens, the duodenal receptors are presented with an excess of gastric contents. Symptoms of dumping may include nausea, vomiting, diarrhea, palpitations, and weakness. Children receiving carbohydrate-based high-calorie supplements or formulas are particularly at risk. Avoiding dumping requires slowing the rate of stomach emptying or decreasing the concentration of food delivered to the duodenum. This can be accomplished by slowing the feeding rate with continuous feeding, using fat instead of carbohydrate calorie supplements, or changing to a formula with a lower concentration.

Constipation: The Large Intestine

For many children with developmental disabilities, constipation is a major problem. This is caused by an inadequate fluid and fiber intake combined with uncoordinated muscle contractions and poor rectal sphincter control. The result is the retention of stool for prolonged periods of time. The longer the stool remains in the colon, the more water is absorbed, and the harder and more immobile the stool becomes. The end result is constipation. Besides increasing intra-abdominal pressure and thereby the risk of reflux, constipation can be associated with cramping and discomfort that can interfere with appetite, positioning, and sleep.

Overly loose stools also can be a problem. This may be caused by lack of dietary fiber, dumping, overaggressive use of laxatives or enemas, or passage of loose stool around an impaction. If either diarrhea or constipation is a problem, the child's diet and bowel regimen should be evaluated and adjusted.

Failure to Thrive

Failure to thrive is the term used to describe inadequate growth, which is a falling away from the normal growth curve or from the child's previously established growth curve. Failure to thrive results from inadequate caloric intake, excessive caloric expenditures, or an inability to use the calories ingested. Children with developmental disabilities are at increased risk of failure to thrive for both nutritional and nonnutritional reasons (see Chapter 10).

EVALUATION

Because of the complexity of the process and the multiple influences on it, evaluation of a feeding problem should include a medical history and examination, neurodevelopmental assessment, oral-pharyngeal evaluation, feeding history, and mealtime observation (Couriel, Bisset, Miller, et al., 1993; Parrott, Selley, Brooks, et al., 1992). The information gleaned may be enough to identify the problem and the factors contributing to it. Diagnostic procedures may be needed, however, to provide further information to support or clarify clinical hypotheses.

If aspiration or GER is suspected, several tests are available to further define the problem (Kramer & Eicher, 1993). For GER, an upper gastrointestinal (GI) series may be done to rule out anatomical problems in the GI tract. In the upper GI series, a milk-like substance is either ingested by the child or infused into the stomach by a nasogastric tube. The barium in this substance is visible on X-ray film as the fluid courses through the esophagus, stomach, and small intestine, allowing the radiologist to identify structural abnormalities (Morton, Bonas, Fourie, et al., 1993; Taniguchi & Moyer, 1994). Reflux from the stomach into the esophagus also may be seen (Figure 28.6).

A second procedure, a milk scan, provides information about frequency of GER as well as rate of gastric emptying (Figure 28.7) (Heyman, Eicher, & Alavi, 1995). Delayed gastric emptying can lead to vomiting and aspiration, while an increased rate of gastric emptying can lead to diarrhea. For this study, the child swallowed a milk formula to which is added small amounts of a radioactive tracer, enabling the radiologist to track the milk as it moves through the GI tract. The milk scan is also valuable if aspiration from GER is suspected. If radioactive tracer is found in the lung after several hours, it suggests that aspiration has occurred during a reflux episode.

The final two studies, the pH probe and gastroesophageal duodenoscopy (endoscopy), are considered the gold standards in the evaluation of GER and esophagitis (Willging, 1995). For the pH probe study, a nasogastric-like tube is inserted through the nose and passed down the esophagus to just above the junction of the stomach and esophagus. At the tip of the tube is a small sensor, which measures the pH or acidity above the gastroesophageal junction. If acid in

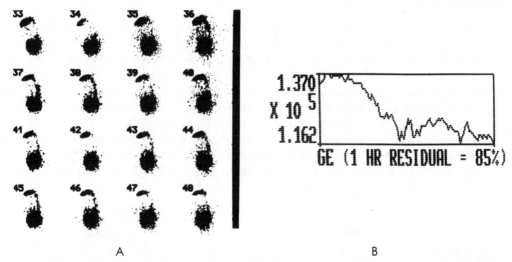

A   B

Figure 28.7.   a) Milk scan. In this study, the child is given a formula/milk feeding containing minute amounts of a radioactive label that can be seen on scanning. Shown here is a sequence of images taken after the child drinks the milk. The images are generated by a computer from information obtained by the scanner every 120 seconds. The area of radioactivity at the top of each image represents residual in the mouth while the lower area of radioactivity is the stomach. Images 34–39 show increased activity in the mouth and esophagus reflecting a reflux episode to the mouth and descending back to the stomach. In frames 44–48, radioactivity can be seen flowing up from the stomach into the mid esophagus, indicating another episode of gastroesophageal reflux. A repeat scan after the child was placed on antireflux medication would show an absence of stomach reflux. b) In addition to diagnosing reflux, the milk scan can also evaluate whether the stomach is emptying food into the small intestine at a normal rate. If there is delayed gastric emptying, this increases stomach pressure and the possibility of reflux or vomiting. In the above study, residual gastric radioactivity decreased by 15% 1 hour after the labeled milk was ingested (decreasing from 1.370 × 10^5 counters per minute to 1.162). This 85% 1 hour residual is high, the normal being 67% or less. Prokinetic agents such as cisipride (Propulsid) not only decrease gastroesophageal reflux directly but also indirectly by increasing gastric emptying. Following effective medication, the gastric emptying would be expected to increase, potentially to normal levels.

the stomach refluxes through an incompetent sphincter, the sensor records a sudden drop in the pH level, signaling GER (Figure 28.8). Reflux is most likely to occur in the hour following a meal or during sleep, when the child is reclining. For this reason, the pH probe is left in place for 24 hours to record the presence of reflux and the circumstances of its occurrence. This may have important therapeutic implications in terms of positioning after feeding. Endoscopy entails passing a fiberoptic tube through the mouth down the esophagus and into the stomach while the child is sedated. The gastroenterologist can then visualize the tissues and take small biopsy specimens to examine for inflammation of the esophagus and stomach.

If aspiration of oral feedings is suspected, a modified barium swallow with videofluoroscopy is the best test to use. In this study, the child is positioned in the usual feeding position and offered foods that contain barium. The radiologist uses a video fluoroscope to visualize the pharynx and watch how food is guided by the muscles past the airway. The texture of the food and liquids can be changed to evaluate whether the child has more difficulty with one texture than another (Fox, 1990).

MANAGING FEEDING PROBLEMS

Because feeding difficulties in children with developmental disabilities usually result from the interaction of multiple factors, managing them can be difficult, time consuming, and frustrating. Effective treatment usually requires intervention from more than one therapeutic discipline. The treatment team, which should include the child's caregiver, needs to prioritize the goals of treatment and outline an integrated plan to approach these goals. The primary care provider, with input from the team, oversees the plan and monitors progress toward the goals. This is done in the context of the child's medical, nutritional, and developmental well-being. Components of a successful treatment strategy include minimizing negative medical influences, optimizing positioning for feeding, facilitating oral-motor function, improving the mealtime environment, being consistent, and constantly monitoring the child's progress. The management recommendations that follow illustrate this approach.

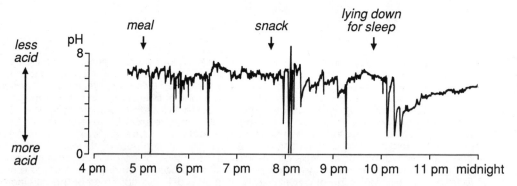

Figure 28.8.   A pH probe study is done by passing a tube containing a pH electrode down the esophagus and positioning it just above the stomach. If there is reflux, the pH should drop as the acid contents of the stomach reach the lower esophagus where the probe is placed. Shown here is an abnormal study with multiple episodes of low pH, occurring about half an hour after feeding or when the child is laid down to sleep. (From *Your child has a disability: A complete sourcebook of daily and medical care* [p. 224] by M.L. Batshaw. Copyright © 1991 by Mark L. Batshaw; illustrations copyright © 1991 by Lynn Reynolds. By permission of Little, Brown.)

Decrease Gastroesophageal Reflux

GER can adversely affect respiratory and GI function as well as positioning of the body and the child's level of comfort. A number of therapeutic modalities, including proper positioning, meal modification, medications, and surgery, may be needed to control these difficulties (Lewis, Khoshoo, Pencharz, et al., 1994). The goal of each of these interventions is to protect the esophagus from reflux of stomach acid, either by decreasing the amount of food in the stomach at any one time or by decreasing the amount of acidic stomach juices that are excreted.

Small, frequent meals and/or medications that promote stomach emptying help to decrease the volume of food in the stomach. In addition, studies have found that whey-based formulas improve stomach emptying and decrease vomiting in children with spastic quadriplegia (Fried, Khoshoo, Secker, et al., 1992). Upright positioning and thickened feedings use gravity to help keep stomach contents from refluxing into the esophagus. Medications, such as urecholine (Bethanechol), metoclopramide (Reglan), and cisipride (Propulsid), increase the tone in the esophageal sphincter, making it harder for reflux to occur (McCallum, 1990). Cimetidine (Tagamet), ranitidine (Zantac), or famotidine (Pepcid) often are added to decrease stomach acidity and thereby lower the risk of inflammation of the esophagus from reflux (see Appendix C) (Wiseman & Faulds, 1994).

When GER cannot be controlled by positioning and medication alone, surgery may be necessary in order to prevent problems associated with prolonged reflux: failure to thrive, recurrent aspiration pneumonia, and/or gastroesophageal bleeding. The most common procedure is a fundal plication (Fonkalsrud, Ellis, Shaw, et al., 1995), in which the top of the stomach is wrapped around the opening of the esophagus (Figure 28.9). This decreases reflux while permitting continued oral feeding. An alternative to fundal plication is the surgical placement of a gastrojejunostomy (G-J) tube that allows access to the stomach as well as the jejunum, permitting some portion of the feeds to bypass the stomach, thereby decreasing the risk of reflux (Figure 28.10) (Albanese, Towbin, Ulman, et al., 1993).

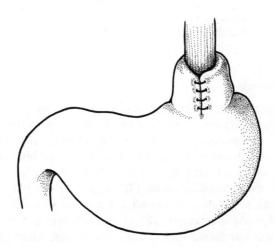

Figure 28.9.   In the surgical procedure of fundal plication, the upper stomach is wrapped around the lower esophagus to create a muscular valve that prevents reflux.

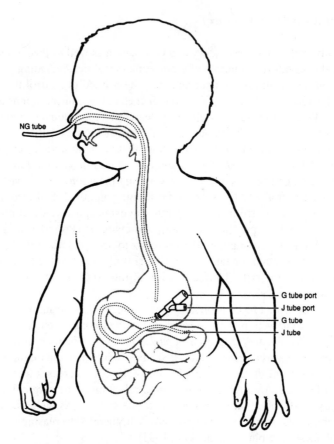

Figure 28.10.   Enteral feeding tubes. The NG tube is placed through the nostril and into the stomach. A NG tube is helpful when problems with the child's oral function are the primary obstacle to adequate nutrition and are temporary. A G-J tube allows access to the stomach as well as directly into the intestine. A G-J tube can be helpful when the stomach is unable to tolerate the quantity of nutrients needed for adequate growth.

Avoid and Treat Constipation

Constipation is a long-term problem for most children with severe developmental disabilities. In addition to being uncomfortable, it may decrease the child's appetite and possibly increase GER. Although no cures for constipation are known, the following suggestions may be helpful. As much fluid as possible should be added to the diet. Bulky and high-fiber foods, such as whole grain cereals, bran, and raw fruits and vegetables, should also be included in the diet to increase movement through the gastrointestinal tract (Hillemeier, 1995; Williams, Bollella, & Wynder, 1995). Prune, apricot, or papaya juice can act as a mild laxative and can be especially helpful if the child is in need of additional calories. Stool softeners, such as Colace or Kondremul, may be used regularly to help coat the stool and facilitate its movement through the intestines. Active or passive physical exercise will also aid movement of the stool.

When constipation is present, additional measures may be needed. Laxatives and suppositories can be used, including Milk of Magnesia, Maltsupex, Senokot, Dulcolax, or glycerine suppositories. Enemas, such as Fleet's pediatric enema, also may help; but constant use of enemas can interfere with normal rectal sphincter control and should be avoided. A combination of these approaches may be needed to establish regular bowel movements.

Ensure Proper Positioning

Feeding is a flexor activity that requires good breath support. Appropriate positioning maximizes the child's ability to both flex and breathe (Larnert & Ekberg, 1995). The child should be firmly supported though the hips and trunk to provide a stable base. The head and neck should be aligned in a neutral position, which decreases extension through the oral musculature while maintaining an open airway. Such positioning allows improved coordination and more control of the steps in oral-motor preparation and transport. This in turn results in more positive feedback to the child and caregiver from good feeding experiences (Kerwin, Osborne, & Eicher, 1994).

Optimize Oral-Motor Function

Facilitating jaw and lip closure when necessary may help make the child's oral feeding pattern more effective, as well as accustom the child to the proper position for accepting food (Gisel, Applegate-Ferrante, Benson, et al., 1996; Takada, Miyawaki, & Tatsuta, 1994). Spoon placement with gentle pressure on the mid-tongue region can help remind the child to keep the tongue inside the mouth. Chewing may be enhanced by placing food between the upper and lower back teeth. This encourages the child to move the jaw and use the tongue in an effort to dislodge the food.

Food textures can be manipulated to facilitate safe, controlled swallowing (Gisel, 1994). Thickening of liquids slows their rate of flow, allowing more time for the child to organize and initiate a swallow. Thickening agents (e.g., Thick-it, instant pudding powders) can transform any thin liquid into a nectar-, honey-, or milkshake-like consistency. This provides children who have difficulty drinking more options to ensure adequate hydration. Almost any food can be chopped fine or puréed to a texture that the child can more competently manage.

It is important to remember that the primary goal of eating is to achieve adequate nutrition. Thus, when a child is first learning to accept a higher texture of foods, these foods should be presented during snacktime, when volumes are smaller. At mealtimes, easier textures should be used to ensure consumption of adequate calories during this transition period.

Make the "Work" of Mealtimes More Inviting

Eating requires more coordination among muscle groups than any other motor activity. Failure to perform the work competently may result in aspiration, which is unpleasant, frightening, and dangerous. Therefore, it is important to make eating as easy as possible (Babbitt, Hoch, Coe, et al., 1994; Kerwin, Ahearn, Eicher, et al., 1995). This can be accomplished by increasing the child's focus on the meal and including foods in each meal that are more desirable and easier for the child to control (Luiselli, 1994). Let the child know that mealtime is coming so he or she can prepare for the "work" to be done. This may entail a premeal routine of going to a special corner of the room and putting on a bib or napkin or some relaxation therapy followed by oral stimulation to get the needed muscles ready for eating. Children with feeding difficulties usually eat better in one-to-one situations or in small groups because there is less distraction and they are better able to focus on the eating process. Undivided attention also makes mealtimes more reinforcing.

A number of adaptive devices can promote independence in feeding. These include bowls with high sides, spoons with built-up or curved handles, and cups with rocker bottoms (see Chapter 32). The satisfaction children get from eating can be increased by social attention during the meal or providing a favorite food after the meal is completed.

Promote Appetite

Some children have little appetite. Alternately, they may be unable to communicate that they are hungry. If speech is impaired or limited, signing or a communication board may prove helpful. If this does not work, try feeding the child at different times of the day to find out at which hour he or she eats best. The child may eat the largest meal at breakfast or lunch rather than at dinner. Foods the child likes can be paired with less favored ones. Regular bowel movements can improve motility and appetite.

Consider Alternative Methods of Feeding

In some cases, oral feeding may not be safe or sufficient to permit adequate nutrition. For these children, nasogastric tube feedings or the placement of a gastrostomy (GT) feeding tube is required (Figure 28.10). A commercially prepared enteral formula (e.g., Ensure, Pediasure) can be used with any of these tubes. Although blenderized feedings can be given through an NG- or G-tube, they are not appropriate for a J-tube because they will obstruct it. With an NG- or G-tube, feedings can be given as single large volumes (bolus) of 3–8 ounces every 3–6 hours or as a continuous drip throughout the day or overnight. J-tube feedings must be given continuously, not as a bolus. The advantage of large-volume feedings is that they do not interfere with typical daily activities. The feeding itself takes about 30 minutes. However, the large volume may be difficult for the child to tolerate and may lead to vomiting or abdominal discomfort. If this happens, continuous drip feedings can be instituted. A Kangaroo or similar type pump is then used to deliver the formula at a set rate (Figure 28.11). Sometimes tube feedings are used to supplement oral feedings. In this case, the tube feedings generally are used at night, so that the child remains hungry for oral feedings during the day.

HECTOR

Hector is a 16-month-old boy with cerebral palsy, mental retardation, and failure to thrive. He was referred for evaluation of feeding intolerance manifested by frequent gagging, choking, and vomiting with any oral feeding and worse on more highly textured foods.

Hector was the product of a 34-week gestation complicated by respiratory distress syndrome and periventricular leukomalacia. Oral feedings were initiated in the nursery, and by discharge at 1 month of age, Hector was feeding well. However, vomiting after feeds began at 2 months of age. An upper GI study showed evidence of esophageal dysmotility without reflux; but a milk scan showed two episodes of reflux into the upper esophagus. After antireflux medications were initiated, the vomiting stopped, and Hector started eating and growing well for several months.

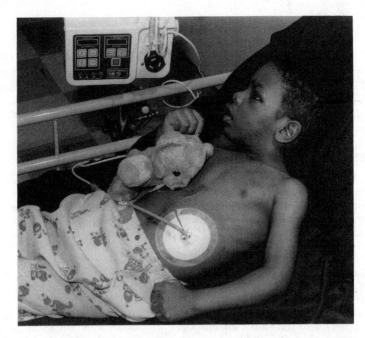

Figure 28.11.   This child is receiving his feedings by continuous drip through his G-tube using a Kangaroo pump.

Unfortunately, between 7 and 10 months of age, Hector gradually decreased his oral intake and had intermittent vomiting and feeding refusal. At 10 months of age, his weight was less than the 5th percentile, even taking into account his prematurity. A modified barium swallow at that time revealed aspiration on all textures that cleared with coughing or repeated swallowing. As a result of concerns about aspiration pneumonia, he was placed on continuous NG-tube feedings and antireflux medications were restarted. There was again a period of improvement and spoon-feeding sessions were started using puréed table food. This training focused on improving oral transport of small volumes while Hector was seated in a variable tilt-in-space chair that provided adequate head and trunk support needed for effective eating. Bottle sessions were conducted recumbent using a bottle with a variable volume flow nipple to pace Hector and match formula flow to his suck and endurance. Hector showed steady improvement in oral-motor skills and after 4 weeks of therapy was consuming orally 75% of his total daily calories; he received the remainder through NG feedings overnight.

Hector could not advance further because he could not tolerate without vomiting the increased bolus size needed per feeding to allow adequate calories for growth. Treatment plan options were discussed with his parents who chose using NG feeds for 3 months at home to see if the GER would slowly improve. Hector continued to gain weight well on this regimen, and his growth parameters have improved to the 10th percentile. However, it is likely that he will ultimately require a surgical procedure such as a G-tube placement with a fundal plication or a G-J tube placement. With this in place, he should continue to do well nutritionally.

SUMMARY

Feeding a child with a developmental disability often requires the implementation of a number of creative approaches and the involvement of a variety of health care professionals. When effective and well integrated, these methods allow the child not only to have optimal oral feeding experiences with their positive social and developmental ramifications but also to receive the necessary combination of nutrients and fluids to grow and remain healthy.

REFERENCES

Albanese, C.L., Towbin, R.B., Ulman, T., et al. (1993). Percutaneous gastrojejunostomy versus Nissen fundoplication for enteral feeding of the neurologically impaired child with gastroesophageal reflux. *Journal of Pediatrics, 123,* 371–375.

Babbitt, R.L., Hoch, T.A., Coe, D.A., et al. (1994). Behavioral assessment and treatment of pediatric feeding disorders. *Journal of Developmental and Behavioral Pediatrics, 15,* 278–291.

Bagwell, C.E. (1995). Gastroesophageal reflux in children. *Surgery Annual, 27,* 133–163.

Batshaw, M.L. (1991). *Your child has a disability: A complete sourcebook of daily and medical care.* Boston: Little, Brown.

Bosma, J.F. (1986). Development of feeding. *Clinical Nutrition, 5,* 210–218.

Brady, M.S., Richard, K.A., Fitzgerald, J.F., et al. (1986). Specialized formulas and feedings for infants with malabsorption or formula intolerance. *Journal of the American Dietetic Association, 86,* 191–200.

Casas, M.J., Kenny, D.J., & McPherson, K.A. (1994). Swallowing/ventilation interactions during oral swallow in normal children and children with cerebral palsy. *Dysphagia, 9,* 40–46.

Casas, M.J., McPherson, K.A., & Kenny, D.J. (1995). Durational aspects of oral swallow in neurologically normal children and children with cerebral palsy: An ultrasound investigation. *Dysphagia, 10,* 155–159.

Chigira, A., Omoto, K., Mukai, Y., et al. (1994). Lip closing pressure in disabled children: A comparison with normal children. *Dysphagia, 9,* 193–198.

Couriel, J.M, Bisset, R., Miller, R., et al. (1993). Assessment of feeding problems in neurodevelopmental handicap: A team approach. *Archives of Disease in Childhood, 69,* 609–613.

Fonkalsrud, E.W., Ellis, D.G., Shaw, A., et al. (1995). A combined hospital experience with fundoplication and gastric emptying procedure for gastroesophageal reflux in children. *Journal*

of the American College of Surgeons, 180, 449–455.

Fox, C.A. (1990). Implementing the modified barium swallow evaluation in children who have multiple disabilities. *Infants and Young Children, 3,* 67–77.

Fried, M.D., Khoshoo, V., Secker, D.J., et al. (1992). Decrease in gastric emptying time and episodes of regurgitation in children with spastic quadriplegia fed a whey-based formula. *Journal of Pediatrics, 120,* 569–572.

Gisel, E.G. (1994). Oral motor skills following sensorimotor intervention in the moderately eating-impaired child with cerebral palsy. *Dysphagia, 9,* 180–192.

Gisel, E.G., & Alphonce, E. (1995). Classification of eating impairments based on eating efficiency in children with cerebral palsy. *Dysphagia, 10,* 268–274.

Gisel, E.G., Applegate-Ferrante, T., Benson, J., et al. (1996). Oral-motor skills following sensorimotor therapy in two groups of moderately dysphagic children with cerebral palsy: Aspiration versus nonaspiration. *Dysphagia, 11,* 59–71.

Heyman, S., Eicher, P.S., & Alavi, A. (1995). Radionuclide studies of the upper gastrointestinal tract in children with feeding disorders. *Journal of Nuclear Medicine, 36,* 351–354.

Hillemeier, C. (1995). An overview of the effects of dietary fiber on gastrointestinal transit. *Pediatrics, 96,* 997–999.

Kennedy, J.G., III, & Kent, R.D. (1988). Physiological substrates of normal deglutition. *Dysphagia, 3,* 24–37.

Kerwin, M.E., Ahearn, W.H., Eicher, P.S., et al. (1995). The costs of eating: A behavioral economic analysis of food refusal. *Journal of Applied Behavior Analysis, 28,* 245–260.

Kerwin, M.E., Osborne, M., & Eicher, P.S. (1994). Effect of position and support on oral-motor skills of a child with bronchopulmonary dysplasia. *Clinical Pediatrics, 33,* 8–13.

Koch, W.M. (1993). Swallowing disorders: Diagnosis and therapy. *Medical Clinics of North America, 77,* 571–582.

Kramer, S.S., & Eicher, P.M. (1993). The evaluation of pediatric feeding abnormalities. *Dysphagia, 8,* 215–224.

Larnert, G., & Ekberg, O. (1995). Positioning improves the oral and pharyngeal swallowing function in children with cerebral palsy. *Acta Paediatrica, 84,* 689–692.

Lewis, D., Khoshoo, V., Pencharz, P.B., et al. (1994). Impact of nutritional rehabilitation on gastroesophageal reflux in neurologically impaired children. *Journal of Pediatric Surgery, 29,* 167–170.

Loughlin, G.M., & Lefton-Greif, M.A. (1994). Dysfunctional swallowing and respiratory disease in children. *Advances in Pediatrics, 41,* 135–162.

Luiselli, J.K. (1994). Oral feeding treatment of children with chronic food refusal and multiple developmental disabilities. *American Journal on Mental Retardation, 98,* 646–655.

Martin, R.E., & Sessel, B.J. (1993). The role of the cerebral cortex in swallowing. *Dysphagia, 8,* 195–202.

McCallum, R.W. (1990). Gastric emptying in gastroesophageal reflux and the therapeutic role of prokinetic agents. *Gastroenterology Clinics of North America, 19,* 551–564.

Miller, A.J. (1993). The search for the central swallowing pathway: The quest for clarity. *Dysphagia, 8,* 185–194.

Monahan, P., Shapiro, B., & Fox, C. (1988). Effect of tube feeding on oral function. *Developmental Medicine and Child Neurology, 30,* 7.

Morton, R.E., Bonas, R., Fourie, B., et al. (1993). Videofluoroscopy in the assessment of feeding disorders of children with neurological problems. *Developmental Medicine and Child Neurology, 35,* 388–395.

Parrott, L.C., Selley, W.G., Brooks, W.A., et al. (1992). Dysphagia in cerebral palsy: A comparative study of the Exeter Dysphagia Assessment Technique and a multidisciplinary assessment. *Dysphagia, 7,* 209–219.

Rings, E.H., Grand, R.J., & Buller, H.A. (1994). Lactose intolerance and lactase deficiency in children. *Current Opinion in Pediatrics, 6,* 562–567.

Rogers, B., Arvedson, J., Buck, G., et al. (1994). Characteristics of dysphagia in children with cerebral palsy. *Dysphagia, 9,* 69–73.

Rogers, B.T., Arvedson, J., Msall, M., et al. (1993). Hypoxemia during oral feeding of children with severe cerebral palsy. *Developmental Medicine and Child Neurology, 35,* 3–10.

Rudolph, C.D. (1994). Feeding disorders in infants and children. *Journal of Pediatrics, 125,* S116–S124.

Stallings, V.A., Zemel, B.S., Davies, J.C., et al. (in preparation). Energy expenditure of children and adolescents with severe disabilities: A cerebral palsy model. *Journal of the American Medical Association.*

Stevenson, R.D. (1995). Feeding and nutrition in children with developmental disabilities. *Pediatric Annals, 24,* 255–260.

Stevenson, R.D., & Allaire, J.H. (1991). The development of normal feeding and swallowing. *Pediatric Clinics of North America, 38,* 1439–1453.

Sullivan, P.B., & Rosenbloom, L. (1996). *Feeding the disabled child: Clinics in developmental medicine.* New York: Cambridge University Press.

Takada, N., Miyawaki, S., & Tatsuta, M. (1994). The effects of food consistency on jaw movement and posterior temporalis and inferior orbicularis oris muscle activities during chewing in children. *Archives of Oral Biology, 39,* 793–805.

Taniguchi, M.H., & Moyer, R.S. (1994). Assessment of risk factors for pneumonia in dysphagic children: Significance of videofluoroscopic swallowing evaluation. *Developmental Medicine and Child Neurology, 36,* 495–502.

Timms, B.J.M., Defiore, J.M., Martin, R.J., et al. (1993). Increased respiratory drive as an inhibitor of oral feeding of preterm infants. *The Journal of Pediatrics, 123,* 127–131.

Waterman, E.T., Koltai, P.J., Downey, J.C., et al. (1992). Swallowing disorders in a population of children with cerebral palsy. *International Journal of Pediatric Otorhinolaryngology, 24,* 63–71.

Willging, J.P. (1995). Endoscopic evaluation of swallowing in children. *International Journal of Pediatric Otorhinolaryngology, 32,* S107–S108.

Williams, C.L., Bollella, M., & Wynder, E.L. (1995). A new recommendation for dietary fiber in childhood. *Pediatrics, 96,* 985–988.

Wiseman, L.R., & Faulds, D. (1994). Cisipride: An updated review of its pharmacology and therapeutic efficacy as a prokinetic agent in gastrointestinal motility disorders. *Drugs, 47,* 116–152.

29 Dental Care

Beyond Brushing and Flossing

Mark L. Helpin
Howard M. Rosenberg

Upon completion of this chapter, the reader will:

- understand the usual pattern of formation and emergence of the teeth and potential problems affecting their development
- know how dental decay and periodontal diseases occur and what preventive steps can be taken to reduce or eliminate these problems
- be aware of the specific dental problems common to children with disabilities
- understand procedures commonly used during routine dental checkups

Children with disabilities are at an increased risk for both dental malformations and oral disease. Maintaining the health of the **primary** and **secondary** teeth and associated soft tissues influences the child's ability to chew, speak, look attractive, and position teeth in their proper locations. Thus, those who care for children with developmental disabilities should be aware that oral health is an important part of the child's overall well-being. This chapter introduces basic concepts of dentistry for children, with a focus on the child with special needs. It describes the formation and emergence of teeth; the causes, prevention, and treatment of common dental diseases; and the relationship between developmental disabilities and dental problems.

FORMATION AND EMERGENCE OF TEETH

Human tooth formation begins when the embryo is only 4–6 weeks old (Figure 29.1). Initially, the oral ectodermal layer of tissue forms the **dental lamina,** a thickened band of cells along the future dental arches. At specific points along the dental lamina, rapid growth of cells occurs. This forms small knobs that press downward into the underlying mesodermal layer of tissue. There is one such knob (**dental organ, tooth bud**) for each of the 20 primary teeth, 10 in the **maxilla** and 10 in the **mandible** (Figure 29.2) (Sicher, 1991). With time, permanent incisors, canines, and premolars will develop from the corresponding primary tooth predecessors. In contrast, permanent molars develop from the dental lamina itself.

For the most part, primary teeth develop before birth, while most permanent teeth develop after birth. Calcification of primary teeth begins at approximately 14 weeks *in utero;* permanent teeth begin to develop around the time of birth, and the vast majority of calcification occurs during early childhood (McDonald & Avery, 1994).

The calcified layer of the tooth is made up of **enamel,** which arises from the outer layer of the tooth bud (Figure 29.1). The layer under the enamel, called **dentin,** arises from the mesodermal cells. The soft tissue under the dentin, called the **pulp,** also arises from the mesoderm. The

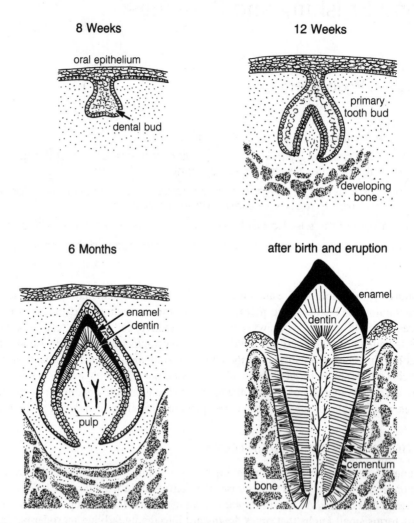

Figure 29.1.   Development of teeth. By the time the fetus is 8 weeks old, the dental (tooth) bud has formed, and by 12 weeks it is beginning to assume a tooth-like shape. At 6 months' gestation, the layers of the tooth—enamel, dentin, and pulp—are evident. After birth, when the child is about 16 months old, the primary cuspid, completely formed, erupts.

pulp contains the vital parts of the tooth, its blood vessels, lymphatics, connective tissue, and nerve fibers (Sicher, 1991).

The first primary tooth begins to erupt around 6 months of age. The full complement of primary teeth (20), however, takes 2–3 years to appear. The first permanent tooth emerges around 6 years of age, and most permanent teeth generally have erupted by 12–13 years of age (Figure 29.2). The third molars ("wisdom teeth"), however, erupt between 17 and 21 years of age, making a total of 32 permanent teeth.

When a permanent tooth emerges, a primary tooth is shed, except in the case of first, second, and third molars that develop independently from the primary teeth (McDonald & Avery, 1994). Caution should be taken when evaluating tooth eruption in relation to tables and time schedules (Table 29.1), especially in children with developmental disabilities, as each child has

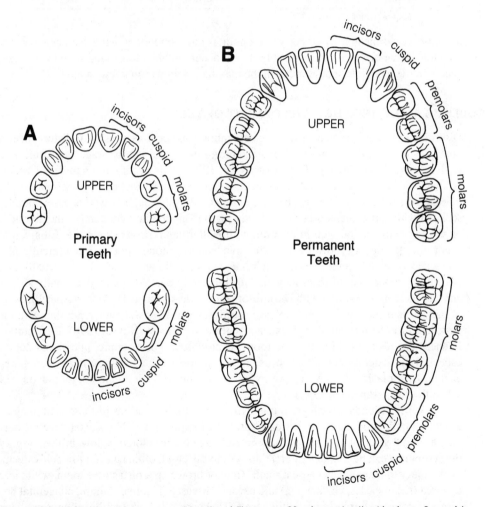

Figure 29.2.   Primary and permanent teeth. A) There are 20 primary teeth: 4 incisors, 2 cuspids, and 4 molars on the top and on the bottom of the mouth. B) There are 32 permanent teeth: 4 incisors, 4 premolars, and 6 molars on the top and on the bottom.

Table 29.1.   Timetable for emergence and shedding of teeth

	Age (months) at emergence		Age (years) at shedding	
	Lower	Upper	Lower	Upper
Central incisor	6	7½	6–7	7–8
Lateral incisor	7	9	7–8	8–9
Cuspid	16	18	9–10	11–12
First molar	12	14	6–7	6–7
Second molar	20	24	11–13	12–13
Incisors	Range = ±2 months			
Molars	Range = ±4 months			

Source: Lunt and Law (1974).

his or her own timetable. Symmetry in eruption is more important than adherence to a strict time schedule. What occurs on the right side should occur, within a few months, on the left; and what occurs in the mandible should occur in the maxilla, again within a few months.

PROBLEMS AFFECTING THE DEVELOPMENT OF TEETH

Disorders of number, size, shape, and calcification can occur as a result of disturbances at various times of tooth development. Problems during the dental lamina stage can result in missing teeth or extra teeth (Poole & Redford-Badwal, 1991). This occurs in a number of genetic syndromes. Anodontia, the absence of all teeth, is rare but can be found in ectodermal dysplasia, an inherited disorder of skin-related tissues. Ectodermal dysplasia, however, is more commonly associated with partial anodontia. Oligodontia (partial anodontia, hypodontia), the absence of one or several teeth, can be seen in children with Hallermann-Streiff syndrome, Ellis-van Creveld syndrome, Williams syndrome, Crouzon syndrome, achondroplasia, incontinentia pigmenti, orofacial digital syndrome, Seckel syndrome, and cleft lip and palate (Lyons, 1988). Disorders affecting development of teeth may also lead to thinly enameled and abnormally shaped teeth and can be seen in children with chromosomal disorders such as Down syndrome, inborn errors of metabolism such as the mucopolysaccharidoses and Lesch-Nyhan syndrome, and inherited disorders of bone formation such as osteogenesis imperfecta (Buyse, 1990). Environmental influences can also affect intrauterine tooth development. For example, nutritional deficiencies, especially of calcium and phosphorus, and vitamins A, C, and D, may result in generalized enamel hypoplasia. Also, excessive exposure to fluoride can create a hypoplastic condition called fluorosis (Pinkham, 1994).

Because secondary teeth are formed after birth, malformations of these teeth may occur as a result of childhood illness or its treatment. For example, if a child takes tetracycline between 4 months and 8 years of age, the permanent teeth may be discolored yellow, brown, or gray when they erupt and can be a source of great distress to the child, often causing low self-esteem. Traumatic injury to a tooth may cause a small white or brown spot on a single tooth, while infectious diseases (i.e., measles, chickenpox) and chronic diseases (i.e., liver failure, congenital heart disease) can cause **hypoplasia** of multiple teeth (Pinkham, 1994). All of these abnormalities can increase both the risk of tooth decay and of malocclusion.

ORAL DISEASES

There are two basic types of oral diseases: **dental caries** and **periodontal diseases.** Both are usually initiated by specific bacteria and, therefore, can be considered infectious in nature, although some periodontal problems are associated with systemic diseases (e.g., diabetes, leukemia).

Dental Caries

Dental caries, commonly called dental decay or cavities, occurs mainly in children and adolescents and is related to the presence of the bacteria *Streptococcus mutans* and *Lactobacillus acidophilus.* Decay is a multifactorial process that involves the teeth themselves, bacteria, diet, saliva, the immune system, biochemistry, and physiology (Figure 29.3). The "chain of decay" is as follows (Figure 29.4): Bacteria in the mouth break down food, creating acid as a by-product. The acid damages the integrity of the enamel, and cavity formation begins. Tooth breakdown and ultimately abscess formation can occur when caries is left untreated (Stewart, Barber, Troutman, et al., 1982). Bacteria adhere to the teeth in an organized mass called **dental plaque.** Plaque consists of bacteria, bacterial by-products, **epithelial** cells, and food particles (Pinkham, 1994). Although the oral cavity contains more than 300 bacterial species, only a few of these are found in plaque. When plaque becomes calcified, it is called calculus or tartar. Plaque as well as unremoved tartar can cause inflammation, tenderness, and swelling of the gums. This is one phase of periodontal or gum disease and can lead to loss of stability of the teeth. The process of decay is one of demineralization of enamel and dentin. The prevalence of dental caries has been cited as more than 40% in 5-year-olds and 85% in 17-year-olds (Edelstein & Douglas, 1995). Caries is more common in children who do not receive systemic fluoride, either from water or from supplements.

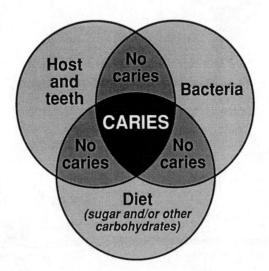

Figure 29.3.   Dental caries results from a multifactorial process involving the interaction of three factors: 1) the teeth and other host factors including the child's immune system, biochemistry, and physiology; 2) bacteria; and 3) dietary carbohydrates.

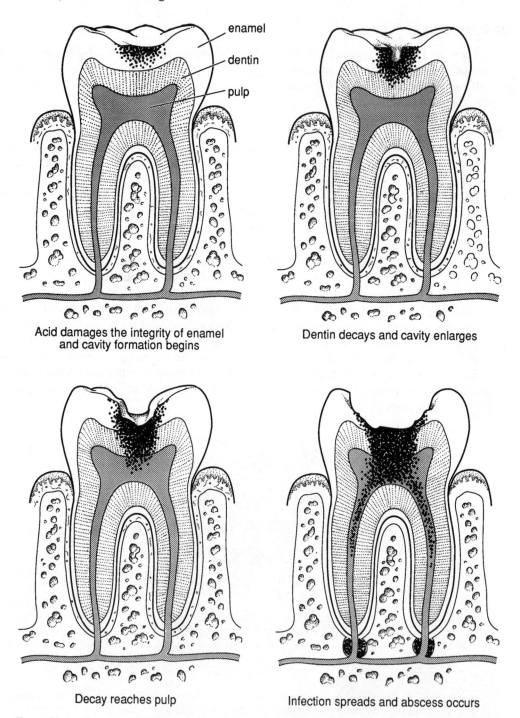

Figure 29.4.   The chain of decay. In the presence of these adverse factors, the "chain of decay" follows: Acids formed from the action of bacteria on carbohydrates damage the enamel, leading to cavity formation. If untreated, the decay eventually affects the dentin and pulp layers of the tooth and may lead to abscess formation.

One form of caries that merits special attention is nursing caries syndrome (i.e., baby bottle tooth decay). This is a pattern of highly destructive, rapidly progressive decay, caused by the carbohydrates in the bottle contents or in breast milk. Typically associated with prolonged nursing bottle use or sleeping with a bottle in the mouth, it should also be emphasized that nursing caries can occur with breast feeding (Dilley, Dilley, & Machen, 1990). The primary maxillary incisors are the first teeth to show severe breakdown. Often portions of these teeth break off as a result of structural weakness caused by the decay. Nursing caries can be prevented by mouth cleaning after each feeding once primary teeth have started to emerge and by eliminating the bottle feedings when the infant is asleep. If bottles must be used, water is the only liquid that is safe. This issue is a particular concern in children with developmental disabilities who may remain on bottle feedings well beyond the typical 12 months. If a medical condition or nutritional requirement dictates that a child feed with a bottle beyond 12 months of age, particular attention must be given to proper cleaning of the mouth.

Periodontal Diseases

Periodontal diseases are a group of disorders affecting the tissue supporting the teeth. These include gingivitis; acute primary herpetic gingivostomatitis (APHG, a herpes simplex viral infection); and acute necrotizing ulcerative gingivitis (ANUG, or Vincent disease). The most frequent form is gingivitis. Like caries, it is associated with plaque and specific bacterial organisms (Matthewson & Primosch, 1995). This pathological process begins with an inflammation and resultant bleeding of the gums. It is often an insidious process that can go unrecognized for years, leading to involvement of the underlying tissues and bone. When there is bone loss, gingival tissue may recede, the tooth may loosen in its socket, and ultimately the tooth may be lost. Studies have shown that gingivitis can be found in 50% of children 6–12 years old (Bimstein, 1991; Pinkham, 1994).

Initial exposure to the herpes simplex virus can cause an acute inflammation of the gingiva (APHG). This primary infection usually occurs in children under 5 years of age and can include fever, malaise, irritability, pain, fiery red gingiva, and blister (vesicle) formation anywhere in the mouth. Treatment is usually supportive because the disease is self-limited and resolves within 10–14 days. It is contagious, however, and children should be isolated. Children who are immune-compromised should consult a physician; often, they require a much more aggressive program of treatment and intervention.

Vincent disease is an infection caused by spirochete and fusiform bacteria. In contrast to APHG, this condition is usually seen in children 6–12 years of age. The clinical picture is one of pain, foul mouth odor, the presence of a gray pseudomembrane on the gingiva, and gingival breakdown and bleeding. Treatment consists of oral antibiotic therapy, usually penicillin, combined with thorough cleaning of the teeth and removal of the injured gingival tissues. Chlorhexidine (Peridex) rinses may also help (McDonald & Avery, 1994; Pinkham, 1994).

Some children who take phenytoin (Dilantin) or phenobarbitol, antiepileptic drugs; cyclosporin (Sandimmune, an immune supressant drug); or nifedipine (Procardia, an antihypertensive agent) present with hypoplastic and fibrotic gingival overgrowth. While the exact cause of this condition is unknown, it is generally regarded as an exaggerated response to a local irritant. Withdrawal of the drug may bring about some return to normal physical architecture, but surgical intervention may also be required.

MALOCCLUSION

Malocclusion is the improper interdigitation or relationship of the teeth or jaws. Malocclusion can interfere with oral functions such as speech and chewing and may also increase the risk of dental caries and periodontal diseases. In addition, it can create problems with facial appearance and self-image. Although many malocclusions are minor and require attention only for cosmetic reasons, others are more severe and debilitating. The prevalence of severe malocclusion has been reported to be as high as 14%; children with certain developmental disabilities, such as cerebral palsy, have an even higher prevalence (McDonald & Avery, 1994). In these cases, the correction of this improper alignment of the teeth by orthodontic treatment to position the teeth properly also decreases the risk of dental disease by making routine oral hygiene easier.

DENTAL TRAUMA

It is estimated that half of all children experience traumatic injury to the primary or permanent teeth prior to graduation from high school. Injuries to the primary teeth are more frequent than injuries to permanent teeth. Although the incidence of primary tooth injury is approximately equal in boys and girls, males have twice as many injuries to permanent teeth (Andreasen & Andreasen, 1994). The risk of dental trauma in children with cerebral palsy and seizure disorders is increased because of their more frequent falls. The maxillary incisors, both primary and permanent, are the teeth most frequently traumatized. The presence of prominent maxillary anterior "buck" teeth, a consequence of malocclusion, is an important predisposing factor to injury. Trauma to primary teeth generally causes tooth displacement. This is a result of the softer, spongier quality of the young bone that supports the teeth. Trauma to permanent teeth most often results in fracture of tooth structure (chipped teeth) (Andreasen & Andreasen, 1994).

Most dental injuries merit evaluation immediately after the incident occurs. Although primary teeth are not replanted, a permanent tooth that has been knocked out should be replaced into the tooth socket by a caregiver as soon as possible after the accident. Replantation within 30 minutes maximizes the likelihood of successful tooth retention. If immediate replantation is not possible, the tooth should be kept in cold milk, saliva, or a commercial kit that is now available for tooth transport until a dentist can reimplant it (available from Sav-A-Tooth, Biological Rescue Products, Conshohocken, Pennsylvania, 19428). The use of milk or a commercial kit, which contains Hank's solution, appears to extend the time a tooth may be out of the mouth before successful reimplantation.

In fracture and avulsion (knock out) injuries, care must be taken to find any missing piece of tooth or to take a chest X ray to rule out aspiration into the lung. Injury to a primary or permanent tooth can result in damage to its pulp or the ligament tissue that joins the tooth to underlying bone. If the pulp is not able to recover, this may lead to pulp death and a "black tooth." This situation indicates a nonvital tooth that will require endodontic (root canal) therapy or extraction.

Because many dental injuries can be avoided, prevention is extremely important. Athletic mouth guards, when they can be tolerated, significantly decrease the risk of dental injuries in children participating in contact sports and in those with developmental disabilities who are at high risk for falls or self-injury (Andreasen & Andreasen, 1994; Joselle & Abrams, 1982).

DENTAL CARE AND TREATMENT

The initial dental examination should be performed soon after the emergence of the first tooth or by 12 months of age. The goals of these early visits are 1) anticipatory guidance; 2) establishment of a "home base" for dental care; 3) examination of the oral cavity, both teeth and soft tissues; 4) education of the family about proper oral hygiene (brushing and flossing), home care techniques, diet, nutrition, and nursing caries syndrome; 5) discussion regarding the need for fluoride supplementation; and 6) determination of the child's risk of dental disease. Usually, very little if any treatment is necessary at this time (American Academy of Pediatric Dentistry, 1996/1997; Edelstein, 1994; Griffen & Goepferd, 1991; Newbrun, 1992; Shelton & Ferretti, 1982).

This visit should be followed by checkups at regular intervals, depending on the child's risk for oral disease. During these checkups, cleaning and topical fluoride application will be performed to help minimize the risk of caries and periodontal disease. Consideration of the need for home fluoride treatments will also be given. Care must be taken, however, because young children tend to swallow rather than spit out fluoride rinses or gels and could receive an overdose. Symptoms of an overdose may vary from stomach upset to delirium. In addition, some children will benefit from the use of chlorhexidine gluconate, an antibacterial mouth rinse (Anderson, Bales, & Omnell, 1993). However, chlorhexidine can occasionally cause excess **calculus** buildup and surface discoloration of teeth. **Dental sealants,** a plastic coating that is bonded to the teeth in order to prevent initiation of decay, may be recommended. In this technique, the biting surface of the molars and premolars is etched with a mild acid and coated with a plastic material. This covering bonds to the tooth surface, providing protection to the pit and grooved surfaces of the teeth that are most susceptible to cavities (Johnsen, 1991). If, despite all preventive efforts, caries does appear, the dentist will treat this by removing the decay and placing a filling material or a crown. The newest dental materials offer the advantages of good strength, aesthetics, and anticaries activity.

In order to minimize anxiety and help the child cope with the stress of treatment, the dentist may employ behavior management techniques or use sedation agents (e.g., nitrous oxide [laughing gas], sedative medications). The dentist will also take into account the special needs related to the child's primary medical condition. For example, individuals with congenital heart disease may require antibiotic prophylaxis to minimize the risk of infective **endocarditis** resulting from dental procedures. Individuals with extensive treatment needs and an inability to cooperate in the outpatient setting may have their treatment performed in the operating room under general anesthesia (American Academy of Pediatric Dentistry, 1996/1997; American Dental Association, 1995).

Equally important to dental checkups is daily preventive treatment. Some highlights of these techniques follow:

1. *Brushing*—Children under the age of 6 years generally have not developed the manual dexterity to effectively remove plaque from teeth. They should be encouraged to participate in their own oral hygiene; however, adults must take an active role and be responsible for adequately cleaning the teeth and gum regions. A soft, nylon bristle brush with polished, rounded ends works best. A scrubbing motion of the brush is a quick and easy method with which to begin. An electric toothbrush can be helpful. Furthermore, studies have shown that

the newer types of electric brushes may be advantageous for gingival health (Barnes, Weatherford, & Menaker, 1993). When brushing, a small, pea-sized amount of toothpaste with fluoride may be used. If bubbles and foam from the paste cause a problem for the child, however, use water alone. Positioning the child in a supine position facilitates good vision, access, and head control and will be helpful for the adult doing the brushing. A dentist can demonstrate the positions that might be best for an individual child (McDonald & Avery, 1994; Pinkham, 1994).

2. *Flossing*—Adults should floss for a child until he or she has demonstrated facility with this procedure. Improper flossing can harm gingival tissues. Flossing should be performed wherever teeth are in contact with each other and the toothbrush cannot clean between the teeth. Unwaxed floss is preferred; however, any floss may be used. Floss-holding devices are available and can be employed by parents and/or caregivers when dexterity is a problem or when the child may close or bite (McDonald & Avery, 1994).

3. *Fluoride*—Water fluoridation is the single greatest anticaries measure available to large segments of the population. Studies have demonstrated that fluoride in water can decrease the prevalence of tooth decay by up to 60% (Pinkham, 1994). Fluoride makes enamel more resistant to decay and remineralizes new carious lesions, making them hard again. Fluoride supplementation should be considered (Table 29.2) if fluoride is not available in the community drinking water or in the water where child care is provided or if the family uses a home water filter or bottled water. Excessive systemic fluoride, however, can cause fluorosis, a condition in which permanent teeth are discolored or malformed. In addition, the dentist may apply a local, topical fluoride. This offers benefits that go beyond those of systemic fluorides alone (McDonald & Avery, 1994).

4. *Diet*—Children with chewing and/or swallowing difficulties may require dietary modifications that place them at increased risk for dental disease. Often their diet will be soft or puréed. Also, some medical conditions (e.g., failure to thrive) will require frequent meals or sweet, sucrose-containing foods and snacks to provide calories. If either of these situations exists, more frequent toothbrushing should be performed. Table 29.3 lists a number of healthy snacks that are good for teeth. When children eat snacks, adults should realize that the consistency, frequency, and timing contribute to their potential for decay. Snacks that are sticky (not just caramels, but foods such as sweet rolls, pretzels, and potato chips); eaten frequently; and eaten between meals have a high potential for causing dental decay (Gustafsson, Quensel, & Lanket, 1954).

Table 29.2.   Daily fluoride supplementation schedule as a function of fluoridation of water: Fluoride concentration in water

Age	Less than 0.3 ppm	0.3–0.6 ppm	More than 0.6 ppm
Birth–6 months	NR	NR	NR
6 months–3 years	0.25 milligrams	NR	NR
3 years–6 years	0.50 milligrams	0.25 milligrams	NR
6 years–16 years	1.0 milligrams	0.50 milligrams	NR

Source: American Dental Association (1995).
Key: NR = supplementation not required; ppm = parts per million.

Table 29.3.   Foods that are good to use as snacks to maintain dental health

Raw vegetables

Carrot sticks	Green pepper rings
Celery sticks	Lettuce wedges
Cauliflower bits	Radishes
Cucumber sticks	Tomatoes

Drinks

Milk	Unsweetened vegetable juices
Sugar-free carbonated beverages	

Other snacks

Nuts	Unsweetened peanut butter
Popcorn	Cheese
Unsweetened plain yogurt	Sugarless gum or candy

Source: American Dental Association (1983).

DENTAL CARE FOR CHILDREN WITH DEVELOPMENTAL DISABILITIES

The basic principles of pediatric dental care and oral health just discussed apply to all children. There are, however, specific issues related to several common developmental disabilities, including cerebral palsy, seizure disorders, mental retardation, attention-deficit/hyperactivity disorder (ADHD), and pervasive developmental disorders; certain genetic disorders such as Down syndrome; meningomyelocele; and human immunodeficiency virus (HIV) infection.

Cerebral Palsy

Poor motor control and altered muscle tone may interfere with routine dental care in children with cerebral palsy (see Chapter 24). Although no specific oral problems are unique to children with cerebral palsy, several findings are more common or more severe in this population. Malocclusion is more likely to occur as a consequence of the uncoordinated movements of the muscles of the jaws, lips, and tongue (e.g., tongue thrusting). The predilection for falling and the frequent prominence of the maxillary incisors place these children at increased risk for dental trauma. In addition, mouth breathing and **bruxism** are often present (Cooley & Sanders, 1991; McDonald & Avery, 1994; Nowak, 1976). Bruxism may lead to enamel and dentin wear (Petersen & Schneider, 1991). The incidence of periodontal disease is also higher, due to difficulty in brushing and flossing and the soft, sticky, high-carbohydrate diet that may be needed to maintain adequate nutrition. In addition, the incidence of enamel hypoplasia is increased among children with cerebral palsy; however, the incidence of dental decay is not necessarily increased.

A number of treatment approaches can help; providing dental care in the child's wheelchair or the use of positioning supports such as pillows in the dental chair itself add to the comfort of the child. If brushing after eating is not possible, wiping soft food debris from the mouth using a moistened face cloth or gauze pad is of benefit. In older children, an adapted toothbrush with handle modifications, an electric toothbrush, and floss holders can be of assistance in maintaining good oral hygiene.

Seizure Disorders

In children with seizure disorders, the major issues are side effects from certain antiepileptic drugs and dental trauma (see Chapter 26). Approximately half of the children receiving the antiepileptic drug phenytoin, and occasionally those receiving phenobarbital, develop over-growth of the gingiva. In this condition, the gums become enlarged and fibrotic. This is both un-aesthetic and can prevent teeth from erupting or push them out of their normal position. Stopping the medication may begin to reverse the problem, but often the child will require surgical removal of the overgrown tissue. The second problem is an increased risk of dental trauma from seizure-induced falls. In children with poorly controlled generalized tonic-clonic seizures, the use of a helmet may be appropriate until seizure control is gained. Fortunately, if dental fractures occur, they can usually be repaired so that it is often difficult to distinguish the injured tooth from a noninjured one (Cooley & Sanders, 1991; McDonald & Avery, 1994; Nowak, 1976).

Mental Retardation, Attention-Deficit/Hyperactivity Disorder, and Pervasive Developmental Disorders

Children with mental retardation, ADHD, and PDDs generally do not have dental problems that are significantly different from typically developing children. It is important, however, that they be treated according to their mental age and attention level rather than their chronological age. If these children require extensive dental care, the procedure often must be done in an operating room under general anesthesia (McDonald & Avery, 1994).

Down Syndrome

In addition to mental retardation, children with Down syndrome have congenital anomalies that place them at increased risk for oral disease. Their midface deficiency and extra, missing, or small teeth contribute to the development of malocclusion. These children may also have hypoplastic enamel, although their risk of caries is low (Cooley & Sanders, 1991). Their open-mouth posture with mouth breathing and calculus formation can lead to inflammation of the gums and periodontal disease. An additional important medical consideration is congenital heart disease that places these children at increased risk for infective endocarditis and requires antibiotic prophylaxis prior to dental procedures.

Meningomyelocele

Individuals with meningomyelocele have a caries rate similar to that found in the general population; however, because of compromised oral hygiene, they have a high level of periodontal disease. As a result of the spinal curvatures so often seen in these individuals and considering that many are confined to a wheelchair, positioning and comfort are important in pediatric dental care. The presence of hydrocephalus with a shunt may also have a bearing on the child's dental treatment, depending on the specific type of shunt. Individuals with ventriculo-atrial shunts require antibiotic prophylaxis. Also important, individuals with meningomyelocele have an increased risk of developing an allergic reaction to latex (Engibous, Kittle, & Jones, 1993). Because many common items in the dental office contain latex, this allergy influences the delivery of even the most simple and routine dental care.

Human Immunodeficiency Virus Infection

Individuals who are HIV seropositive or who have HIV infection often encounter great difficulty in gaining access to dental care (see Chapter 9). Fortunately, the Americans with Disabilities Act

(ADA) of 1990, PL 101-336, has helped to ease the situation. Furthermore, the American Dental Association has formally stated that a decision not to treat a patient based solely on HIV status is unethical. Healthcare providers should know that there are a number of oral manifestations, some painful, which are seen in children and adolescents who have HIV infection. These include 1) gingivitis and other periodontal diseases often caused by herpes virus, 2) fungal infection (thrush) and ulcers of the mouth, 3) painful swelling of the salivary glands, 4) dry mouth, 5) tongue lesions, and 6) toothaches. Depending on the child's immune status, antibiotic coverage, and/or use of antibacterial/antifungal mouth rinse (chlorhexidine) may be indicated. Bleeding abnormalities and anemia may also influence treatment. Emphasis on all aspects of prevention is vital. It is important that the healthcare provider be aware that dental infection in this population can become life threatening (American Dental Association, 1996; Greenspan & Greenspan, 1993; McDonald & Avery, 1994; Pinkham, 1994).

SUMMARY

Oral health is an important component of overall health. It contributes to wellness of the child, eliminates pain and discomfort, and enhances the quality of life. Furthermore, good oral health maximizes the chances for adequate nutrition, speech, and appearance. The emphasis in oral care for the child with a developmental disability should be the same as it is for a typically developing child: prevention through home dental care and regular office checkups.

REFERENCES

American Academy of Pediatric Dentistry. (1996/1997). American Academy of Pediatric Dentistry reference manual. *Pediatric Dentistry, 18*(6), 30–81.

American Dental Association. (1983). *Diet and dental health.* Chicago: American Dental Association, Bureau of Health Education and Audiovisual Services.

American Dental Association. (1995). Caries diagnosis and risk assessment: A review of preventive strategies and management. *Journal of American Dental Association, 126,* 1S–24S.

American Dental Association. (1996, January). Dental management of the HIV-infected patient. *Journal of American Dental Association* (Suppl.), 6–40.

Americans with Disabilities Act (ADA) of 1990, PL 101-336, 42 U.S.C. § 12101 *et seq.*

Anderson, M.H., Bales, D.J., & Omnell, K. (1993). Modern management of dental caries. *Journal of American Dental Association, 124,* 37–44.

Andreasen, J.O., & Andreasen, F.M. (1994). *Textbook and color atlas of traumatic injuries to the teeth* (3rd ed.). St. Louis: C.V. Mosby.

Barnes, C.M., Weatherford, T.W., & Menaker, L. (1993). A comparison of the Braun Oral-B plaque remover electric and a manual toothbrush in af-

fecting gingivitis. *Journal of Dentistry for Children, 4,* 48–51.

Bimstein, E. (1991). Periodontal health and disease in children and adolescents. *Pediatric Clinics of North America, 38,* 1183.

Buyse, M.I. (1990). *Birth defects encyclopedia.* Dover, DE: Center for Birth Defects Information Services, Inc.

Cooley, R.O., & Sanders, V.J. (1991). The pediatrician's involvement in prevention and treatment of oral disease in medically compromised children. *Pediatric Clinics of North America, 38,* 1265–1288.

Dilley, J.G., Dilley, D.H., & Machen, J.B. (1990). Prolonged nursing habit: A profile of parents and their families. *Journal of Dentistry for Children, 47,* 102–108.

Edelstein, B.L. (1994). Medical management of dental caries. *Journal of American Dental Association, 125,* 31S–39S.

Edelstein, B.L., & Douglas, C.W. (1995). Dispelling the myth that 50% of U.S. school children have never had a cavity. *Public Health Report, 110,* 6–13.

Engibous, P.J., Kittle, P.E., & Jones, H.L. (1993). Latex allergy in patients with spina bifida. *Pediatric Dentistry, 15,* 364–366.

Greenspan, J.S., & Greenspan, D. (1993). *Oral manifestations of HIV infection: Proceedings of the Second International Workshop.* Chicago: Quintessence Publishing.

Griffen, A.L., & Goepferd, S.J. (1991). Preventive oral health for the infant, child, and adolescent. *Pediatric Clinics of North America, 38,* 1209–1226.

Gustafsson, B.E., Quensel, C.E., Lanket, L.S., et. al. (1954). The Vipeholm dental caries study. *Acta Odontalogica Scandinavica, 11,* 232–364.

Johnsen, D.C. (1991). The role of the pediatrician in identifying and treating dental caries. *Pediatric Clinics of North America, 38,* 1173–1181.

Joselle, S.D., & Abrams, R.G. (1982). Traumatic injuries to the dentition and its supporting structures. *Pediatric Clinics of North America, 29,* 717–741.

Lunt, R.L., & Law, D.B. (1974). A review of the chronology of eruption of deciduous teeth. *Journal of American Dental Association, 89,* 872–879.

Lyons, K.L. (1988). *Smith's recognizable patterns of human malformation.* Philadelphia: W.B. Saunders.

Matthewson, R.J., & Primosch, R.E. (1995). *Fundamentals of pediatric dentistry* (3rd ed.). Chicago: Quintessence Publishing.

McDonald, R.E., & Avery, D.R. (1994). *Dentistry for the child and the adolescent* (6th ed.). St. Louis: C.V. Mosby.

Newbrun, E. (1992). Preventing dental caries: Current and prospective strategies. *Journal of American Dental Association, 123,* 68–73.

Nowak, A.J. (1976). *Dentistry for the handicapped patient.* St. Louis: C.V. Mosby.

Nowak, A.J., Johnson, D., Waldman, H.B., et al. (1992). *Pediatric oral health.* Washington, DC: George Washington University, The Center for Health Policy Research.

Petersen, J.E., Jr., & Schneider, P.E. (1991). Oral habits: A behavioral approach. *Pediatric Clinics of North America, 38,* 1289–1307.

Pinkham, J.R. (1994). *Pediatric dentistry: Infancy through adolesence* (2nd ed.). Philadelphia: W.B. Saunders.

Poole, A.E., & Redford-Badwal, D.A. (1991). Structural abnormalities of the craniofacial complex and congenital malformations. *Pediatric Clinics of North America, 38,* 1089–1125.

Shelton, P.G., & Ferretti, G.A. (1982). Maintaining oral health. *Pediatric Clinics of North America, 29,* 653–668.

Sicher, H. (1991). *Orban's oral histology and embryology* (11th ed.). St. Louis: C.V. Mosby.

Stewart, R.E., Barber, T.K., Troutman, K.C., et al. (1982). *Pediatric dentistry: Scientific foundations and clinical practice.* St. Louis: C.V. Mosby.

30 Behavior Management

Promoting Adaptive Behavior

John M. Parrish

Upon completion of this chapter, the reader will:

- have a basic understanding of common challenging behaviors
- be acquainted with selected principles and methods of improving child behavior, including effective instruction and discipline
- be familiar with the contexts in which specific instructional and behavior management strategies are applicable, and the (contra)indications, advantages, and disadvantages of each

What constitutes a challenging behavior depends on who is doing what, who is observing it, under what circumstances it is occurring, and how frequently it happens. Thus, the "terrible twos" are less acceptable in a 5 year old, grandparents may be less tolerant of rambunctious behavior than young parents, acceptable behavior in church differs from acceptable behavior at home, and infrequent tantrums are of less concern than constant tantrums. All children are, at times, disruptive, impulsive, noncompliant, and aggressive. About half of children with disabilities display challenging behaviors like these with enough frequency or severity that they impede their interpersonal relationships, educational progress, functioning in the home, or medical management (Table 30.1). Parents, teachers, and other professionals tend to use informal principles of behavior management in attempts to modify these behaviors or develop adaptive behavior. With specific instruction, however, these attempts can result in a better level of care and can help to ensure an optimal outcome. This chapter provides an overview of selected principles of applied behavior analysis and gives a description of the steps taken by behavior managers in assessing and treating problem behaviors and promoting adaptive behaviors in children with disabilities.

Table 30.1   Common behavioral excesses and impairments in children with disabilities

Aerophagia (excessive swallowing of air)

Aggression

Attentional impairments

Disruptive behavior

Elopement

Excessive activity

Feeding problems (e.g., food selectivity by type or texture)

Hair pulling

Impulsivity

Inappropriate sexual behavior

Lack of community survival skills (e.g., crossing streets safely)

Lack of self-help skills (e.g., dressing, feeding, toileting)

Medical noncompliance (refusal to complete prescribed regimens)

Noncompliance with parental or teacher instructions

Obesity

Pica

Property destruction

Rumination

Self-injury

Sleep disturbances (e.g., spontaneous awakenings)

Social skills impairments

Somatic complaints (e.g., recurrent abdominal pain)

Stereotypies (e.g., hand flapping, arm waving, body rocking)

Tantrums

Thumb sucking

Truancy

ORIGIN OF BEHAVIOR PROBLEMS

Surprisingly little is known about the origin of behavior problems. They are likely to arise from a complex interaction of genetic, biological, and environmental factors. To date, environmental events that trigger and serve to maintain challenging behavior have received the most scrutiny. For example, receipt of reinforcers (e.g., adult attention, desired objects) and escape from or avoidance of unpleasant tasks (e.g., chores, assigned seatwork) sometimes result in behavior difficulties. Limitations in the child's communication skills (e.g., nonfunctional speech) also may be a causative factor. In some children with disabilities, specific genetic defects may contribute to problem behaviors. Examples include self-injury in Lesch-Nyhan syndrome, tics in Tourette syndrome, an eating disorder in Prader-Willi syndrome, and hand-wringing behavior in Rett syndrome.

DEFINITIONS

A fundamental assumption underlying applied behavior analysis is that behavior problems are typically learned (i.e., the child's behavior is largely a function of its immediate **antecedents** and **consequences**). Antecedents are those events that "trigger" a behavior (e.g., teasing that provokes aggression). Consequences are those events that follow the behavior (e.g., aggression results in loss of a privilege). Other concurrent events (e.g., the child's level of arousal or fatigue) and historical events (e.g., a recent argument) also may influence the child's behavior. Problem behaviors frequently serve multiple purposes, even for the same child. For example, aggression (or tantrums) may serve to gain access to what the child wants (e.g., an extra turn in a game), to escape from work or unpleasant situations (e.g., not doing an assigned chore or delaying bedtime), or to attain desired objects or attention.

The goal of behavior management is to enable the child to live as independently as possible while being fully included in least restrictive settings. Priority is assigned to supporting the child's overall development and quality of life, not merely to manage the child's problem behavior(s). Accordingly, behavior management plans emphasize instruction as well as modification of challenging behavior.

Effective instruction and management require accurate identification of events that instigate and maintain problem behaviors. These events are subsequently altered to decrease problem behaviors while at the same time teaching **prosocial** behaviors. The behavior selected for assessment and management is termed the **target behavior.** Interventions typically involve multiple components.

FUNDAMENTAL PRINCIPLES AND PROCEDURES OF APPLIED BEHAVIOR ANALYSIS

There are four principal approaches to behavior management termed **positive reinforcement, planned ignoring (extinction), negative reinforcement,** and **punishment.** Figure 30.1 presents a simplified graphical model of each, and they are discussed in more detail throughout the chapter.

Positive Reinforcement

Positive reinforcement is said to occur when consequences following a behavior result in an increase in that behavior in the future (Alberto & Troutman, 1982). For example, when Paul, a 9-year-old boy with mental retardation requiring limited supports, receives a compliment for using his utensils correctly during mealtimes, subsequent use of utensils is likely to increase. Such consequences are referred to as **positive reinforcers.** Events that function as positive reinforcers may center on social activities, toys, or food (Miller, 1980). Table 30.2 presents examples of common positive reinforcers.

Positive Side Effects of Positive Reinforcement

Effective use of positive reinforcement not only serves to increase appropriate behavior, it also tends to reduce problem behavior (Parrish, Cataldo, Kolko, et al., 1986). For instance, as Paul's parents acknowledge his display of "manners" during mealtimes and involve him in casual conversation about his preferred topics, Paul will be less likely to be disruptive (e.g., by interrupting adult-to-adult conversations) in order to attract attention.

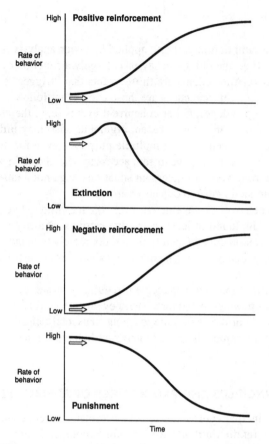

Figure 30.1.   The four principal approaches to behavior management are illustrated. Positive and negative reinforcement both result in an increase in the rate of occurrence of a behavior over time, while extinction and punishment procedures reduce the behavior. The arrows indicate baseline observation periods and the arrowhead, the start of the behavior management procedure.

Variation in Positive Reinforcers

Reinforcers vary widely in type (i.e., what events the child prefers) and value (i.e., how much the child prefers them) among different children and within each child over time. Reinforcers are defined solely on the basis of their effect on a given child's behavior, not on their form, content, appearance, or assumed value. A common mistake is to assume that some children with developmental disabilities do not have any positive reinforcers. Every child, without exception, has preferences that can be identified by asking or observing the child, asking others familiar with the child, and/or by structuring systematic reinforcer assessments (Berg & Wacker, 1991; Fisher, Piazza, Bowman, et al., 1992; Green, Reid, Canipe, et al., 1991; Mason, McGee, Farmer-Dougan, et al., 1989; Pace, Ivancic, Edwards, et al., 1985). Specific events and items become positive reinforcers for the given child because they have been paired previously with biological essentials (e.g., food, water, warmth) and/or with other events that are already positive reinforcers for the child (e.g., the presence of a friend).

Table 30.2. Examples of positive reinforcers

Social reinforcers	Manipulative reinforcers
Affection	Bicycles
Allowing child to be left alone on child's request	Books, magazines
Arranging for demonstration by child of a mastered skill	Computers
Casual conversation	Games
	Gifts
Descriptive praise	Money
Gesture of approval	Musical instruments
Offering assistance on child's request	Pencils, pens, crayons
Physical proximity	Small toys (e.g., dolls, ball)
Talking about topics of interest to child	Tickets to preferred events
Activity reinforcers	**Edible reinforcers**
Assembling a puzzle	Celery, carrots
Dining at a restaurant	Chips
Going to an arcade	Cookies
Painting with watercolors	Crackers
Playing outside	Dry cereals
Singing	Fruit
Talking on the telephone	Ice cream
Visiting friends	Juice or soft drinks
Watching a video	Popcorn
	Raisins

Importance of Selecting Age-Appropriate Reinforcers

It is important to select positive reinforcers that are appropriate for the child's chronological and/or developmental age. For example, given Paul's age and cognitive disability, it would be appropriate to provide him with opportunities to listen to music, look at picture books, or enjoy time with friends. Selection of everyday positive reinforcers also is important. For instance, when teaching Paul to say "give me bread," it is better to provide bread as a reinforcer than some other arbitrary reinforcer. Selection and use of natural reinforcers increase the likelihood that the newly learned behavior will continue to occur in appropriate, everyday situations.

Factors Influencing Effectiveness of Positive Reinforcement

Several factors influence the effectiveness of an item or event as a positive reinforcer (Miller, 1980). Effectiveness will be enhanced if the event or item is delivered only when the targeted appropriate behavior occurs, but not when an alternative inappropriate behavior occurs. Another key factor is the child's degree of **deprivation** in relation to the "reinforcing" item or event being presented. For instance, if Paul is hungry, a snack may be an effective reinforcer. Offering Paul a snack, however, just after he has had a meal is likely to be ineffective. It also is important to vary the positive reinforcers offered to the child.

Another critical dimension is the **timing** of reinforcer delivery. Reinforcers may be delivered immediately after a target behavior or on a delayed basis. In general, immediate reinforcement is more effective than delayed reinforcement. With a prolonged time interval, the child may have difficulty understanding the relationship between his or her behavior and the delivery of positive reinforcement. Also, delayed reinforcement for appropriate behavior is likely to unintentionally reinforce inappropriate behavior that may have occurred during the interim.

The amount of reinforcement provided is also important. If the child receives a lot of a reinforcer, **satiation** can occur and the reinforcing effect of an item or event is diminished or temporarily lost. In general, the amount of positive reinforcement provided should be proportional to the effort required of the child to behave appropriately. At the beginning of a program designed to strengthen the child's prosocial behavior, larger amounts of reinforcement may be needed to establish a desired behavior because more initial effort by the child is required.

A fourth factor pertains to the **schedule** of reinforcement. Positive reinforcement can be provided after a set number of responses have occurred (i.e., **ratio schedules**) or after passage of a certain amount of time relative to the child's performance (i.e., **interval schedules**). Ratio schedules are typically appropriate when the behavior being reinforced has a definite beginning and end. For instance, Paul receives praise after he puts each toy away or solves two spelling problems. Interval schedules are more suitable when behaviors are continuous or of extended duration. For example, Paul receives praise for playing appropriately with a peer for 3 minutes. Positive reinforcement can also be administered on a continuous or intermittent basis. Continuous reinforcement involves provision of positive reinforcement following every occurrence of a targeted appropriate behavior. All other schedules are intermittent. Continuous reinforcement is often necessary to establish new behaviors. However, satiation needs to be avoided. Once a behavior is established, intermittent reinforcement may effectively maintain it.

The quality or value of the positive reinforcer is also important. The more highly valued a reinforcer is to the child, the more effective it is likely to be. This varies immensely with the individual and within the individual across situations and time. The value of a reinforcer is always relative to other available reinforcers. Positive reinforcers are typically more effective if they are novel and varied. Introducing new reinforcers periodically, and otherwise varying reinforcers previously administered, better ensures that the child does not get too much of any reinforcer.

Misplaced Positive Reinforcement Can Cause Harm

Although positive reinforcement procedures can be designed to promote the child's prosocial behavior, in everyday life the process of positive reinforcement also may increase inappropriate behavior unintentionally. For instance, if Paul's father pays attention to Paul's persistent demands for attention, he may inadvertently increase the likelihood of "bossy" behavior by Paul in the future. A teacher who publicly scolds Paul for disruptive behavior in the classroom may precipitate peer reinforcement for such behavior, thereby compounding the problem. Thus, positive reinforcement, when incorrectly administered, can have unwanted effects.

Planned Ignoring (Extinction)

When a child has received positive reinforcement for misbehavior, that behavior is likely to continue or even intensify. In such situations, a procedure termed planned ignoring has been demonstrated to be effective over time in decreasing the rate of problem behavior (Kazdin, 1989). Planned ignoring is based on the process of extinction, in which positive reinforcement (e.g., adult attention) is withheld when the child's problem behavior occurs. For example, if Mom regularly interrupts her telephone conversations in order to console Paul, he may seek her undivided attention by whining whenever she gets on the telephone. If Mom, however, continues her telephone conversation, withholding her attention from Paul as long as he continues to whine, she is using planned ignoring to minimize the frequency and amount of positive reinforcement he receives for the misbehavior.

Behavior May Worsen Before It Improves

Consistent ignoring of nondangerous, nondestructive behavior (e.g., nagging, whining, crying, complaining, noise-making, talking back) will usually result in an eventual decline in the behavior. The desired effects of planned ignoring, however, are seldom immediate. Often there is a temporary increase or "burst" in the frequency and intensity of the problem behavior before a subsequent reduction occurs. For instance, when Mom first ignores Paul, he is likely to whine persistently or may have a tantrum. Although this burst of inappropriate behavior may appear to be a setback, it actually indicates that previously dispensed positive reinforcement is the culprit, and that planned ignoring is likely to be an effective intervention over time.

Problem Behavior May Reappear

Even after an undesirable behavior has been extinguished, it may recur. This phenomenon, known as **spontaneous recovery**, occurs when the child tests to see whether his or her old behavior (e.g., whining) again will lead to positive reinforcement. When this testing occurs, if the parent continues to ignore the behavior, a rapid and sustained decrease in the problem behavior typically occurs. This illustrates the importance of consistency in behavior management.

Ignoring Problem Behavior Is Challenging

Routine application of planned ignoring may be difficult because many parents confuse planned ignoring with "doing nothing," especially when they hold to the notion that an adult must not allow a child's misbehavior, however minor, to go unpunished. Furthermore, because planned ignoring sometimes results in the problem behavior becoming "worse" before it gets "better," it is not the intervention of choice when the child's problem behavior places someone's safety (including the child's) in jeopardy or may cause property damage or loss.

Negative Reinforcement

As with positive reinforcement, negative reinforcement results in the increased frequency of a target behavior (Iwata, 1987). Negative reinforcement occurs when, as a result of an individual's behavior, an unpleasant event is either avoided or escaped, resulting in an increase in this behavior in the future. Examples of negative reinforcement abound in everyday life, for example when someone chooses to use an umbrella to avoid getting wet or duck his or her head when walking under a low doorway.

Negative Reinforcement Is Not Punishment

Negative reinforcement is often confused with punishment because both processes include an aversive event. Nonetheless, negative reinforcement and punishment are readily distinguishable phenomena, and their effects could not be more different. The key difference is whether the process increases or decreases the behavior that it follows. If the behavior increases in frequency, reinforcement, whether positive or negative, has occurred. If the behavior decreases in frequency, punishment has occurred.

Negative Reinforcement Can Contribute to Problem Behavior

As is true with positive reinforcement, negative reinforcement may function to increase unacceptable as well as acceptable behaviors. For example, when Dad "gives in" to Paul's tantrums in a public place, Paul receives positive reinforcement for oppositional behavior, and Dad's "giving in" is reinforced negatively via the cessation of Paul's difficult behavior. As a result, Paul is more likely to have a tantrum in a public place when Dad denies Paul's request; and Dad is more likely to give in if and when Paul's escalating behavior causes a sufficient public disturbance.

Similarly, negative reinforcement processes are at work when a parent chooses to respond to the child's demanding behavior with threats, yelling, or spanking, and the child concedes. As a result of this negative reinforcement, the parent is more likely to rely on coercive interventions in the future when the child's behavior becomes annoying. Hence, the process of negative reinforcement must be managed judiciously or it can worsen problem behaviors on the part of the child, the care provider, or both.

Punishment

In contrast to positive and negative reinforcement, punishment procedures seek to decrease the occurrence of a behavior. Punishment is frequently thought of as doing something "mean" or "hurtful" to someone because that person made a mistake. Yet, the same event that is a positive reinforcer for one person may be another person's punisher. Thus, generalizations regarding what is a punisher are unwise. Defining an event or action on the basis of its impact on the behavior it follows is more appropriate.

Formats of Punishment

Punishment typically occurs in two formats. A punisher may be applied (**contingent stimulation**) or access to a reinforcer may be withdrawn (**contingent withdrawal**) following the occurrence of a misbehavior. For example, when Paul grabs Mom's eyeglasses, Mom may shout at him, thereby providing punishment via contingent stimulation. When a teacher withdraws recess privileges from Paul after he has broken a classroom rule, she is effecting punishment by contingent withdrawal.

Use of Punishment Is Controversial

The process of punishment is an element of the natural order, just as is gravity. Nonetheless, the purposeful use of punishment of any sort to effect behavior change is controversial. Skillful behavior managers avoid or minimize the use of punishment procedures because 1) positive reinforcement strategies are typically as or more effective, 2) punishment may lead to conflictual relationships, and 3) punishment procedures can be misapplied and cause harm. Reinforcement strategies are almost always attempted first. Exceptions may occur when the behavior puts the child or others at risk for harm.

Purposes of Punishment

The function of punishment procedures is to reduce problem behaviors. On occasion, they may enable a child to learn what not to do. However, they typically provide little direct instruction in regard to what the child is to do. Acquisition and maintenance of adaptive skills require reliance on other behavior management strategies. Thus, punishment procedures should be used infrequently, if at all, and under close monitoring so they are not misused or abused.

Use Reinforcement First

Punishment strategies are generally selected only when positive reinforcement procedures have proven to be ineffective or insufficient across multiple treatments over an extended period of time, and the child continues to be at severe medical, educational, or social risk as a direct result of problem behaviors. When punishment procedures are adopted, they are best implemented in conjunction with positive reinforcement strategies, thereby providing differential consequences for appropriate versus inappropriate behavior. It is important to emphasize the child's acquisition of prosocial skills, strengthening adaptive behaviors that are equivalent in function to aberrant behaviors, and promoting the child's full inclusion in least restrictive environments.

SELECTED INSTRUCTIONAL PROCEDURES

Differential Reinforcement

In many cases, the child with developmental disabilities will have several inappropriate behaviors targeted for change as well as a number of prosocial behaviors that require ongoing positive reinforcement. Correspondingly, positive reinforcement and planned ignoring are often used in combination through a process termed **differential reinforcement.** The purpose of differential reinforcement is to reinforce acceptable behavior while simultaneously withholding reinforcement for unacceptable behavior. This is the essence of managing behavior. For example, the teacher ignores Paul when he speaks out of turn but calls on him when he raises his hand. Table 30.3 presents selected types of differential reinforcement.

Differential reinforcement often is preferred over planned ignoring because it is more effective for teaching the child with disabilities that specific behaviors are appropriate and others are not. The effectiveness of differential reinforcement depends not only on the consistency of its administration, but also on the nonavailability of positive reinforcement for problem behavior. For example, if Paul receives positive reinforcement (e.g., laughter, attention) from his fellow students for speaking out of turn, the teacher's efforts to ignore this behavior will probably be ineffective. Consistent application of differential reinforcement by numerous caregivers across diverse settings and situations is usually required for behavior change to occur and endure.

Instructional and Imitation Training

With many children with disabilities, it is sufficient to simply "show and tell" when teaching new behaviors, while using differential reinforcement procedures. During **instructional training,** the teacher merely describes the behavior he or she wants, asks the child to perform the described action, gives the child a supervised opportunity to initiate/complete the directed activity, and provides positive reinforcement upon satisfactory completion of the task. In **imitation training,** the teacher demonstrates what the child is to do, asks the child to repeat the action, gives the child an opportunity to initiate/complete the targeted activity, and provides the child with positive reinforcement when the task is completed. Imitation training requires less verbal skill and is often used when the child's receptive vocabulary is deficient. When the child learns

Table 30.3.   Selected types of differential reinforcement

Type	Goal	Example
DRO (differential reinforcement of other behavior)	Absence of targeted problem behavior during observation interval	Child allowed to continue to play team sport during recess so long as aggression does not occur
DRA (differential reinforcement of appropriate behavior)	Increased occurrence of targeted appropriate behavior in absence of targeted aberrant behavior	Child acknowledged for sharing, while child's dawdling is ignored
DRC (differential reinforcement of communicative skill)	Increased occurrence of functional communication skill	Child emits functional speech (e.g., "help me . . .") in contrast to being aggressive against teacher to escape from academic demand
DRI (differential reinforcement of incompatible behavior)	Increased occurrence of a targeted appropriate behavior that is incompatible with a targeted problem behavior	Child's "on task" behavior is reinforced; child's "off task" behavior is not reinforced
DRL (differential reinforcement of low rate behavior)	Occurrence of problem behavior at acceptably low rates	Child receives privilege contingent on low rates of complaining

how to follow directions and to imitate what is observed, then the child is better able to learn important daily living and social skills that prevent or replace problem behaviors.

Compliance Training

Some children first need to learn how to follow instructions through highly systematic teaching. **Compliance training** is often a pivotal procedure in the behavior management of children with disabilities. Teaching a child to follow directions and to complete requested actions independently facilitates cooperative learning and has been found to prevent or significantly reduce the occurrence of problem behaviors (Parrish et al., 1986). During compliance training, the instructor orients the child to attend to the instructor and then issues a developmentally appropriate "do" request. A "do" request is a statement that specifies an action (e.g., "give me 10 pennies"). The instructor issues the "do" request using a firm, but matter-of-fact tone. The instructor then waits quietly for about 10–20 seconds (the duration of the wait is dependent on the complexity of the requested action), giving the child an opportunity to follow through. The instructor avoids nagging, lecturing, threatening, yelling, or apologizing for the request. If the child complies with the developmentally appropriate request, the instructor provides praise and perhaps a tangible item (e.g., a raisin) as well.

If the child does not comply, the instructor reissues the request using the same words and tone. The only change in the procedure is that the instructor pairs the repetition of the verbal request with a gesture, such as pointing to the pennies and then to the instructor's outstretched hand. The instructor waits quietly. If the child complies with the first repetition of the request, the instructor provides praise but not a tangible reinforcer. If the child again does not comply, the caregiver immediately uses full or partial graduated guidance to assist the child to complete the requested action. Verbal requests and gestural hints, and contingent reinforcement, are faded gradually as the child increasingly demonstrates independent task completion. (For more explanation, see Forehand & Long, 1996; Forehand & McMahon, 1981.)

Building Momentum

Sometimes, standard methods of teaching the child to follow instructions are unsuccessful. In such cases, it is helpful to identify requests to which the child has complied routinely. These requests are termed "high-p," which is an abbreviation for "high probability." Once "high-p" requests are identified, the instructor issues a few of them one at a time, in sequence, prior to issuing a "low-p" request to which the child has seldom complied. For example, Paul frequently refuses to get ready for bed. Upon request, however, he often agrees to sing his favorite song, go to his bedroom to get a preferred book, and exchange "high fives." Knowing these "high-p" requests, Mom works to build "behavioral momentum" with Paul when redirecting him to begin his bedtime routine. She first issues the three "high-p" requests and excitedly acknowledges his compliance with each. Then, she firmly but matter-of-factly asks him to get dressed for bed. (For more information about building behavioral momentum as a means of promoting compliance, see Mace, Lalli, Shea, et al., 1990.)

Shaping Via Graduated Guidance and Guided Compliance

Among children with more severe disabilities, the desired behavior may not yet be in the child's repertoire at all or may occur quite infrequently. Hence, more is needed than simply issuing an instruction, demonstrating an appropriate behavior, or building momentum, while providing differential reinforcement for prosocial behavior. Often the child exhibits problem behaviors because he or she has not learned how to respond appropriately. Through a systematic procedure known as **shaping,** new prosocial behaviors can be built and added to the child's skill base. Through this process, gradual development of a new behavior is encouraged by reinforcing small advances or improvements in the child's repertoire. Training and reinforcement occur in a step-by-step manner in which each step toward skillful demonstration of the target behavior is reinforced. As steps are performed more and more consistently, they are no longer reinforced. However, reinforcement is provided for performing new or more advanced steps. As the skill is shaped, the amount of structure and degree of direct involvement by the instructor is gradually faded away, so the child demonstrates skill mastery independently.

For instance, Paul is taught to self-feed. Initially, he receives praise paired with a preferred treat for merely touching his spoon. Once Paul consistently touches the spoon, positive reinforcement is discontinued for spoon touching, and he is provided positive reinforcement if and only if he grasps the spoon. When Paul grasps the spoon independently on a consistent basis, he is then required to grasp the spoon and move it toward his mouth in order to receive reinforcement. This procedure continues until the target behavior, self-feeding, is learned.

Prompting

The desired behavior can be developed through the use of **graduated guidance** and **guided compliance.** Here, "graduated" refers to providing only that level of assistance (i.e., guidance) necessary for the child to complete a task satisfactorily. Graduated guidance involves using **prompts** (e.g., verbal, gestural, manual, visual, or auditory cues) that direct the child to participate in a targeted activity (e.g., sharing, waiting, eating, putting on a shirt). Table 30.4 presents examples of prompts. Guided compliance involves the use of graduated guidance in the context of compliance training, which attempts to teach the child to accomplish functional tasks independently.

Teaching in a Functional Context

In order for graduated guidance and guided compliance to be effective, instructors must select developmentally appropriate activities that fit the situation in which instruction is to take place. For example, graduated guidance could be used to teach Paul to select a coat appropriate to current weather conditions. With graduated guidance, "less" is better than "more." The minimum number of cues necessary to accomplish the targeted activity should be provided.

Forward Chaining

Graduated guidance and guided compliance are often used to teach a sequence of skills (Foxx, 1982a), such as toothbrushing, using the toilet, and getting dressed. During **forward chaining,** the first skill in the sequence is typically taught first; the last skill is typically taught last. For instance, when teaching Paul to brush his teeth independently, he would first receive the minimal assistance necessary for him to grasp and hold a toothbrush, at which point he would receive a reinforcer. Next, he would be guided to wet the toothbrush, receive a reinforcer, apply toothpaste, receive a reinforcer, and so forth.

Backward Chaining

Sometimes it is more effective to teach the child skills in the reverse order, a technique called **backward chaining** (Foxx, 1982a). This is particularly appropriate when the child's repertoire is very limited and the last step in the sequence is associated with a potent positive reinforcer. In this event, Paul would first learn the last step in the sequence. For example, when teaching Paul to use a spoon for feeding, he would first be assisted minimally to place a spoon loaded with his preferred food in his mouth. Then he would learn how to balance a loaded spoon when carrying it from a dish to his mouth and place the spoon in his mouth. Then he would learn how to load the spoon and place it in his mouth, and so forth.

Adjusting Amount of Guidance

Usually, when graduated guidance is implemented, the entire skill sequence is completed. Graduated guidance is especially helpful to the child who is unable to understand verbal or gestural

Table 30.4. Selected types of prompts

Prompt	Example
Verbal	"Paul, please turn to page 20 of your math book and complete the word problems."
Gestural	Parent points to pepper shaker while saying "Paul, please pass the pepper."
Manual	Occupational therapist provides hand-over-hand guidance while saying "Paul, pick up your pencil and write your name."
Visual	Teacher scores Paul's completed seatwork with a red pencil. Teacher says "Paul, please rework the problems circled in red."
Auditory	When bell rings, Paul proceeds to his next class.

prompts or the child whose motivation to respond to such prompts is insufficient. During the graduated guidance procedure, the amount of the instructor's gentle guidance is adjusted frequently, depending on the child's behavior. The degree of graduated guidance provided can range from full to partial guidance to **shadowing.** The instructor provides only that amount of gentle guidance required for the child to initiate the requested action and decreases the guidance gradually as the child develops the needed skills.

Moving from Full to Partial Guidance

The degree of required guidance varies from one individual to the next and within each individual over time. During **full graduated guidance,** the instructor keeps his or her hands in full contact with the child's hands throughout the planned activity and provides descriptive praise whenever the child completes the targeted task cooperatively. With **partial graduated guidance,** the instructor does less and less as the child's learning proceeds. The instructor would use minimal physical contact and verbal praise and encouragement as long as the activity is continued independently. In this way, the instructor adjusts his or her effort according to the child's skill and motivational level to complete the task.

Shadowing

Once the child reliably completes the activity while requiring less and less guidance, the instructor begins to shadow. This involves the instructor keeping his or her hands within an inch of the child's hands, as the child proceeds to complete the task. If and when the child ceases to complete the activity or makes a mistake, the caregiver provides only that degree of partial guided compliance necessary for the child to complete the task. During shadowing, the instructor issues verbal prompts, as needed, and provides praise. In this way, the instructor gradually reduces the child's reliance on physical prompts, while increasing the extent to which the child is guided and motivated solely by verbal prompts. Thus, the child simultaneously acquires a skill, learns to demonstrate it more and more independently, and also learns to follow verbal instructions. The use of shadowing is then faded out by gradually increasing the distance between the child's hands and the instructor's hands. (For more detailed information about graduated guidance and graduated compliance, see Foxx, 1982a.)

Fading Prompts and Positive Reinforcement

The long-term use of prompts and positive reinforcement can be time and labor intensive and may foster dependency in the child. Fading is a process by which prompts and/or positive reinforcers are withdrawn gradually, such that the child participates in a target activity competently while being less and less reliant on systematic cues and consequences. For example, initially Mom would verbally prompt Paul to put his lunch money in his pocket prior to leaving home. When Paul complied with her request, she provided him with an extra quarter. Later, he received only praise for doing this without prompts. Eventually, prompts and reinforcers were no longer needed, although Mom would occasionally comment on how pleased she is when Paul is well organized.

Fading will increase the likelihood that desired behaviors will occur spontaneously and in situations other than the one(s) in which training occurred. Fading can be accomplished by decreasing the frequency of prompts preceding a target behavior or by delaying use of prompts. Similarly, fading can be achieved by decreasing the frequency and amount of reinforcement provided following a target behavior or by requiring more occurrences of a target behavior before providing a reinforcer.

PUNISHMENT

Punishment by Contingent Stimulation

In the past, punishment procedures used infrequently by behavior managers have included spraying water mist; placing lemon juice, aromatic ammonia, or mouthwash into the child's mouth; applying mild faradic shock; engaging in exercise contingent on a problem behavior; positioning of protective equipment (e.g., helmets with face shields, gloves) and restraints contingent on self-injurious behavior; spanking; and excessive repetition of the undesirable behavior. Such tactics are currently undergoing in-depth scrutiny and are being increasingly regulated or prohibited altogether by governmental agencies, professional societies, and independent programs. Any use of punishment procedures should be reviewed and approved by a human rights committee prior to its application. Discontinuation criteria (i.e., when punishment is to be stopped) must be in effect prior to any application, and every effort should be expended to fade out the use of punishment as soon as the high-risk behavior becomes manageable.

Statements of Disapproval

Despite their many therapeutic, educational, and ethical limitations, punishment procedures are sometimes implemented under specific circumstances. Undoubtedly, the most common variant of punishment is a negative verbal statement. Adults and children alike often issue warnings, threats, or reprimands. Yet, such statements can have inconsistent effects. Sometimes such remarks suppress ongoing misbehavior. On other occasions, they function as positive reinforcers by way of providing attention. This observation is validated daily in malls, restaurants, schools, and at home. The way by which verbal disapprovals are issued may partially determine their efficacy. For instance, private reprimands delivered softly may be more effective than loud reprimands expressed in the presence of others (O'Leary, Kaufman, Kass, et al., 1970).

Punishment by Contingent Withdrawal

In the context of behavior management programs, punishment by contingent withdrawal is much more prevalent than punishment by contingent stimulation. The former may involve administration of exclusionary **time-out** (e.g., quiet time in a hallway or another room), nonexclusionary time-out (e.g., "time-out ribbons"), or overcorrection.

Time-In

Time-out is removal from time-in. Time-in for a child is said to occur when the child is participating in a preferred activity. The activity may be a reinforcing interpersonal interaction (e.g., being held); an event (e.g., baking cookies); manipulating an object (e.g., pressing a button to hear music); or consuming a favorite snack. Time-in is an essential prerequisite for the effectiveness of most, if not all, instructional strategies. Time-in can be arranged by attending carefully to the child's preferences and by ensuring that these preferences are accessible by the child if and only if he or she is engaged in appropriate behavior. Time-in is typically characterized by enabling the child to select from an array of preferred options; by providing social reinforcement (e.g., praise) or tangibles (e.g., toys, food) as a consequence of acceptable behavior; and by keeping demands placed on the child to a minimum.

Time-Out

Time-out is a procedure whereby positive reinforcement is withdrawn for a predetermined brief amount of time following an occurrence of a targeted problem behavior. Time-out usually occurs in two formats. Exclusionary time-out involves removing the child who misbehaves from "time-in" for a defined time interval. Nonexclusionary time-out occurs when the child is allowed to remain at the site of the infraction but is not allowed to engage in any preferred activities for a prespecified period of time. Exclusionary time-out requires the child to be removed from positive reinforcers, while nonexclusionary time-out requires that these reinforcers be removed from the child.

When Time-Out Makes Sense

Application of time-out makes sense only if the problem behavior is maintained by the positive reinforcement available during time-in. For example, if tantrums have been reinforced by social attention, time-out may be an effective tactic. If the tantrums allow the child to avoid an unwanted activity (e.g., getting dressed), however, then time-out is unlikely to be as effective as some alternative disciplinary strategies and may even be contraindicated. Table 30.5 outlines some of the many prerequisites that must be met for time-out to be effective.

Exclusionary Time-Out

Brief exclusionary time-out works best with children whose developmental age ranges from 2 to 6 years (Forehand & Long, 1996; Forehand & McMahon, 1981). The location of an exclusionary time-out should be predetermined. Important considerations include the extent to which the time-out location is 1) safe, 2) amenable to ongoing monitoring, 3) free of the child's preferred objects and activities, and 4) where the child can serve time-out while being minimally disruptive to others. Practice of the time-out procedure during a few problem-free intervals may facilitate its effective application during problem situations. Some evidence suggests that it may be helpful to issue a single warning that time-out will be started if a labeled misbehavior occurs or persists.

Table 30.5.   Selected prerequisites for effective use of time-out

- Positive reinforcement must be routinely available to the child during time-in.
- Positive reinforcement available to the child during time-out must be kept to a minimum.
- Time-out should be administered only when behaviors previously targeted for treatment occur.
- Time-out should be restricted to dangerous and/or destructive behaviors that occur infrequently.
- Time-out should be applied immediately following the misbehavior.
- During time-out, verbal exchanges with the child should be limited.
- The duration of time-out should be brief and predetermined.
- Access to preferred objects and activities should be precluded during time-out.
- Upon completion of time-out, the child should be returned immediately to the situation in which the problem behavior occurred.
- Record of details surrounding time-out incidents should be maintained.

Managing the Difficult Child

Often the misbehaving child refuses to follow the instruction to go to time-out. The child may ignore, protest, or attempt to negotiate around the instruction. In many instances, the child's unacceptable behavior may intensify. On such occasions, the behavior manager simply provides the minimal physical guidance necessary to escort the child safely and quickly to the chosen site of time-out. Coercive tactics, such as nagging, lecturing, wrestling, verbal reasoning, threatening, and yelling, are to be avoided.

When Exclusionary Time-Out Is Over

When time-out is completed, usually in 5 minutes or less, it is essential to return the child to time-in. No discussion, admonishment, nagging, threatening, yelling, or reminding related to the infraction is necessary. Rather, the behavior manager looks for an opportunity to acknowledge the child's alternative prosocial behavior.

Advantages and Disadvantages of Exclusionary Time-Out

When exclusionary time-out is implemented effectively, it may send a clear and helpful message to the child that an unacceptable behavior has occurred. Use of exclusionary time-out may be especially warranted if and when the child's misbehavior places the child or others at imminent risk for injury. Disadvantages of exclusionary time-out include 1) the risk of providing the child positive reinforcement for inappropriate behavior during implementation of time-out, 2) delaying or allowing escape from completion of a required task while time-out is served, 3) disruption of ongoing prosocial activities, 4) the possible occurrence of dangerous or destructive behavior by the child during time-out, and 5) difficulties in effecting time-out in public places. Exclusionary time-out is a restrictive procedure that is effortful and intrusive. Although it may effectively suppress the targeted behavior, it does not directly help the child to acquire and demonstrate alternative adaptive skills and, therefore, its use should be kept to a minimum or avoided altogether.

Nonexclusionary Time-Out

Nonexclusionary time-out can be implemented in innumerable ways, including contingent removal of a reinforcer (termed **response cost**), **contingent observation,** or the use of **time-out ribbons.**

Response Cost

Response cost involves the loss of a positive reinforcer or the imposition of a penalty if and when the child demonstrates a targeted inappropriate behavior. Removal of the positive reinforcer may be permanent or temporary. To effect response cost, the child must first be accruing positive reinforcement that can be withdrawn. The more the child values the reinforcement, the more effective response cost is likely to be. The precise privilege to be revoked or penalty to be imposed is optimally defined in advance of each problem episode and is applied consistently without extensive explanation.

Point or Token Economies

Response cost is often achieved through star or point systems or token economies in which positive reinforcement is provided contingent on appropriate behavior and withheld (or withdrawn) for inappropriate behavior (Kazdin, 1977). Within these systems, the child earns stars, points, tokens, money, or other currencies by displaying appropriate behavior and is allowed to accumulate across predetermined time intervals a reserve of these reinforcers.

Concurrently, fines are imposed if and when the child engages in targeted inappropriate behavior. Fines are usually small in value in order to increase the probability that the child will earn more "chips" than he or she loses (see Christophersen, 1994). At the end of the intervals, the child is routinely given opportunities to redeem the residual chips for tangible reinforcers or privileges. These are selected from a menu of preferred items and events. Response cost is more likely to have an impact after the child has had an opportunity to spend earned currency and enjoy the resulting privileges. With such experience, the child may be more eager to earn privileges while avoiding response cost. In this way, response cost is seldom achieved in isolation from positive reinforcement contingencies. (For more information about point or token economies, see Christophersen, 1994; Kazdin, 1977.)

Advantages and Disadvantages of Response Cost

Occasionally, response cost strategies may lead to avoidance of or aggression toward the caregiver or escalation of other counter-control behaviors (e.g., tantrums, aggression, property destruction). In such cases, the behavior manager attends to what the child does well, provides positive reinforcement for acceptable behavior, and does not "give in" to the child's demands. Typically, however, response cost procedures are relatively easy to implement and may yield rapid and sizable decreases in problem behaviors, sometimes with long-term effects.

Contingent Observation

Another form of nonexclusionary time-out is contingent observation (Porterfield, Herbert-Jackson, & Risley, 1976), in which the child is asked to "sit at the sidelines" while continuing to observe the ongoing activity from which he or she was withdrawn. The child's participation in time-in is thereby temporarily discontinued. However, the child continues to have an opportunity to observe alternative prosocial behaviors demonstrated by peers and adult supervisors. Contingent observation thus provides an ongoing opportunity for the child to learn adaptive behaviors by way of positive modeling and subsequent imitation of observed skills.

Advantages and Disadvantages of Contingent Observation

Similar to response cost, contingent observation can be used to address a variety of problem behaviors, such as refusal to share or take turns, being disruptive, or failure to remain on task. In some instances, however, contingent observation is contraindicated. Just the opportunity to observe an ongoing activity may be reinforcing. In situations in which inappropriate behavior continues even after the child is withdrawn from the activity, such as ongoing fighting among peers, it may be more reinforcing for the child to observe the activity than to participate in it. Also, negative peer attention is more likely to be available during contingent observation than during exclusionary time-out.

Time-Out Ribbon

Another paradigm for nonexclusionary time-out involves use of a time-out ribbon (Foxx, 1982b). At first, the child is given a ribbon to be worn at the wrist or alternatively a tag or button to be worn on the child's clothing. With the ribbon in place, the child receives positive reinforcement contingent on appropriate behavior. As the child is receiving this reinforcement, the behavior manager describes the appropriate behavior and mentions that the child is wearing the ribbon (or button or tag). This consistent pairing of the ribbon with reinforcement establishes the item as a clear indication to the child, as well as others, that positive reinforcement is available for acceptable behavior. Over time, the child increasingly understands that wearing the ribbon or other item is a prerequisite for delivery of positive reinforcement. Thereafter, the behavior manager can effect a nonexclusionary time-out simply by removing the ribbon or item whenever the child demonstrates a targeted inappropriate behavior. The ribbon or item is withdrawn for the duration of the time-out interval. During this interval, the child's participation in reinforcing activities is discontinued. At the end of time-out, the ribbon or other item is replaced and the behavior manager seeks opportunities to provide positive reinforcement for acceptable behavior.

Advantages and Disadvantages of Time-Out Ribbon

Advantages associated with the use of a time-out ribbon include 1) the program can be implemented effectively with groups of children; 2) misplaced (i.e., inappropriate) peer reinforcement can be curtailed by removing the ribbon of any student who reinforces inappropriate behavior; 3) sequences of inappropriate behavior can be disrupted early by quickly announcing the first occurrence of problem behavior, such as "Paul, you hit Jerry," and removing the ribbon; 4) the presence versus absence of the ribbon is readily discriminable not only by the child and his or her peers, but also by any involved caregiver, family member, or visitor; 5) the presence of the ribbon reminds caregivers to reinforce appropriate behavior; and 6) the ribbon can be worn in many different settings, facilitating the consistent application of nonexclusionary time-out. The disadvantages associated with the time-out ribbon are the same as those associated with response cost and contingent observation.

Overcorrection

Overcorrection is yet another disciplinary method (Epstein, Doke, Sajwaj, et al., 1974; Foxx, 1977; Foxx & Azrin, 1972, 1973). Overcorrection has two components: 1) **restitution,** which involves immediate restoration of any remediable damages caused by the child's misbehavior, and perhaps doing more; and 2) **positive practice,** which requires the child to demonstrate repeatedly a relevant prosocial alternative to the problem behavior. For example, after doodling on the wall with a crayon, Paul is first required to wash the wall (restitution), including an area of the wall not marked by crayons, and is then guided to use crayons on drawing paper (positive practice).

Advantages and Disadvantages of Overcorrection

In conjunction with other treatments, overcorrection is often implemented as a means of strengthening adaptive skills (e.g., toileting) (Foxx & Azrin, 1973). Overcorrection is more likely to be effective if both restitution and positive practice are functionally related to the problem behavior. Overcorrection works best when it is applied immediately after the misbehavior, without fanfare, with the child's preferred objects and activities withheld until overcorrection is completed. However, difficulties may arise during its administration. The child may be unwilling to complete tasks during the restitution and positive practice process. If more than minimal physical guidance is required for the child to engage in the overcorrection procedure, another disciplinary strategy (e.g., response cost) may be indicated.

Cautionary Notes About Use of Punishment

As mentioned previously, use of punishment of any sort, even in conjunction with positive reinforcement, is controversial. Punishment strategies should be used only when positive reinforcement strategies have been shown to have failed to improve a child's severe challenging behavior. If any punishment procedure is used, care must be taken to review the rationale for it with the child's parents or guardians, other care providers, and with the child (when practicable) before the procedure is applied. Each of these individuals should be fully informed of the negative side effects of punishment, such as the risk of modeling inappropriate behaviors, aggression by the child, avoidance of the behavior manager by the child, and the possible suppression of behaviors other than the one(s) targeted for change. Once the "pros" and "cons" of using punishment procedures are understood and informed consent/assent has been obtained, the application of punishment may proceed only if its use is continuously monitored.

Factors Influencing Effectiveness of Punishment

Similar to positive reinforcement, the effectiveness of a given punishment procedure is a function of several variables: its immediacy and intensity, its schedule of occurrence, the availability from others of reinforcement for the punished response, the timing of punishment in the sequence of events leading up to the target problem behavior, and, perhaps most important, the delivery of reinforcement for alternative, appropriate behaviors.

BEHAVIORAL DIAGNOSIS AND TREATMENT

Table 30.6 outlines the steps required for the design and implementation of an effective behavior management program. These steps are differential diagnosis, treatment planning and intervention, fading intervention and programming for generalization, and follow-up assessment/care.

Differential Diagnosis

Assessment techniques include (semi-)structured interviews with key informants (e.g., parents, teachers); administration and scoring of questionnaires and rating scales; viewing of available videotapes; and direct observation of the child's target behavior(s) during interactions with specific individuals and environmental conditions. During interviews, the behavior analyst first obtains an overall evaluation of the child's problem behaviors. Checklists such as the Eyberg Child Behavior Inventory (Eyberg, 1980); the Behavior Problem Checklist (Quay & Peterson, 1979); and the Child Behavior Checklist (Achenbach & Edelbrock, 1979) are often incorporated into the interview.

The behavior analyst then either selects measures focused on a particular problem (e.g., aggression) or a specific diagnosis (e.g., attention-deficit/hyperactivity disorder) or develops individually tailored assessment tools (see Mash & Terdal, 1988). Detailed assessments of the behaviors of greatest concern are then completed. The analyst helps informants describe target behaviors through greater reliance on verbs than adjectives. For instance, the informant may initially describe the child as being "hyperactive," "stubborn," and "lazy." More useful definitions of these concerns may become "leaves seat without permission more than one time per minute," "satisfactorily responds to less than three of every five requested actions," and "does not initiate accurate and timely completion of assigned seatwork or homework."

Table 30.6. Typical steps during construction of behavior management program

1. Differential diagnosis	Review of available records; clinical interviewing; completion of rating scales and questionnaires, viewing videotapes, direct observations; descriptive analyses; functional assessments; and functional analyses in order to 1) define target behaviors operationally, 2) pinpoint conditions under which they occur, 3) collect baseline data, and 4) determine environmental variables that maintain and/or exacerbate problem behavior
2. Treatment planning	Design protocols based on differential diagnosis; protocols specify what is to be done, how, by whom, when; protocols articulate "do's and don'ts" in everyday language, how to assess progress, expected effects, common pitfalls, and clinical/ethical safeguards
3. Intervention	Parents, teachers, other direct service providers undergo training in the effective and safe implementation of recommended protocol(s) prior to intervention; obtain data direct management decisions centered on whether to continue, revise, or discontinue protocol(s) in effect
4. Fading intervention	Upon stabilization of occurrence of newly acquired skills, contingencies are gradually withdrawn
5. Programming generalization	Effort to demonstrate behavioral progress across people, behaviors, settings, other environmental conditions, and time
6. Follow-up assessment/care	Ongoing monitoring of individual's performance, with remedial therapy provided as indicated

The informants are then guided to describe the frequency, duration, and/or intensity of each behavior of concern. Given that the child's behavior is situation specific, the analyst is likely to ask where and under what conditions each behavior does or does not occur. Upon identifying the setting(s) of the target behaviors, the analyst then seeks to ascertain the specific environmental conditions (i.e., variables or factors) that precipitate or maintain the problem behavior. Those events that typically precede or trigger the behavior (i.e., antecedents) are carefully identified. For example, Paul's tantrums may often be preceded by an adult's instruction for him to complete a difficult task or by denial of Paul's request for a toy.

Behavior is also a function of its consequences. The behavior analyst dedicates considerable attention to defining those events or conditions that typically follow the occurrence of the target behavior(s). Many challenging behaviors are followed, and thereby maintained, by positive or negative reinforcement. For instance, Paul's tantrums may be reinforced positively if Mom or Dad consoles him. Alternatively, withdrawal of a request for Paul to complete a task or "giving in" and completing the task for him allows Paul to avoid or escape from the task, thereby providing negative reinforcement. The behavior analyst carefully assesses those consequences that occur in response to target behavior(s). The behavior analyst works to determine the functions served by the problem behavior and the environmental variables that support the continuance of this behavior.

Increasingly, behavior analysts recognize that influences other than those that occur immediately before or after the target behavior are important determinants of that behavior. Events that are more complex or temporally distant also influence current behavior. For example, complex concurrent factors, such as physiological variables including fatigue, deprivation, satiation, infections, discomfort, and pain, influence how the child with disabilities responds. Other complex concurrent factors include the presence or absence of other people, amount of space available, access to alternative or preferred activities, and level of task difficulty or preference. In addition to concurrent factors, prior or historical events influence the child's behavior. For example, Paul's aggression against a classroom peer on a Monday morning may be related to an argument he had with his father during the previous weekend, a previous history of being teased by the peer, or having been corrected for mistakes by his teacher earlier that morning. Such historical events are no longer available as immediate stimuli, but they may nonetheless contribute to current arousal states that continue over time and may compound the influence of current triggering events, such as the peer refusing to share a snack with Paul. Identification of previous or concurrent influences (also referred to as setting events or establishing operations) is important to the selection and use of effective behavior management strategies. (For more information about setting events and establishing operations, see Cooper, Wacker, Thursby, et al., 1992; Kennedy, 1994; Kennedy & Itkonen, 1993; Smith, Iwata, Goh, et al., 1995; and Vollmer & Iwata, 1991.)

Additional relevant information is often obtained, including accounts of previous efforts to teach or manage target behavior(s), prior professional contacts to resolve reported concerns, pertinent medical history, current medications and dosage levels, the child's present school placement and academic status, daily routines, and potential obstacles to delivery of indicated services. Particular attention is dedicated to an understanding of the child's strengths and skills. A focus on the child's endearing qualities and what the child does well serves to orient adult caregivers to use positive reinforcement. The behavior analyst aims to design interventions based on the child's strengths. The behavior analyst also identifies the child's preferred objects, activities, events, and treats, in preparation for development of a contingency management program centered on positive reinforcement.

Whenever practicable, the behavior analyst arranges opportunities to observe videotapes of the child's behavior at home and at school and to observe target behavior(s) directly. Table 30.6 presents definitions and examples of the methods/measures of direct observation typically used.

Behavior analysts increasingly conduct systematic observations of target behavior(s) using the methods of **descriptive and functional analysis** (Bijou, Peterson, & Ault, 1968; Iwata, Dorsey, Slifer, et al., 1982; Iwata, Vollmer, & Zarcone, 1990; Mace & Lalli, 1991; Mace, Lalli, & Pinter-Lalli, 1991; Repp, Felce, & Barton, 1988; Sasso, Reimers, Cooper, et al., 1992). Descriptive analysis involves observation of the child's behavior during routine activities that are often associated with either a very high or a very low frequency of the target behavior(s). The aim is to conduct each activity in a routine manner, while providing typical antecedents and consequences.

Based on interviews, completion of rating scales and questionnaires, as well as direct observations, the behavior analyst develops hypotheses regarding the role different antecedents and consequences play in eliciting (i.e., precipitating) or maintaining the target behavior(s). For example, specific hypotheses may implicate the role of adult or peer attention, access to reinforcers contingent on the problem behavior, or avoidance of/escape from demands. These hypotheses are then tested in relatively well-controlled conditions under which the hypothesized environmental variables are manipulated systematically to determine their effects on the frequency, duration, and intensity of the target behavior(s).

For instance, to test whether Paul's disruptive behavior is precipitated by attention given to him, a series of observational trials may be conducted during which an adult, on an alternating basis, 1) withholds attention until Paul becomes disruptive, 2) enables Paul to avoid or escape from a chore contingent on disruptive behavior, or 3) offers Paul access to a preferred activity or toy contingent on disruptive behavior (Cooper, Wacker, Sasso, et al., 1990; Derby, Wacker, Sasso, et al., 1992; Northup, Wacker, Sasso, et al., 1991). If the rate of disruptive behavior is highest during 1) or 3), then the role of positive reinforcement by way of contingent adult attention or access to preferred events, respectively, is provisionally implicated as a causative factor. If the rate of disruptive behavior is highest during 2), then the role of negative reinforcement is suggested. To obtain more information about the methods of descriptive and functional analysis, the interested reader is referred to O'Neill, Horner, Albin, et al. (1990) and Reichle and Wacker (1993).

Treatment Planning and Intervention

At the conclusion of the initial assessment sequence, the behavior manager consults with the family to discuss whether intervention is warranted and, if so, what form it should take. Every effort is made to incorporate the family's perspectives and desires into the planning of the child's instructional or behavior management program. Family members receive the necessary training and consultation to make informed decisions as advocates for the child. The behavior manager then works with the child and family to develop individually tailored interventions based on the systematic assessments just completed. Once such interventions are defined, the behavior manager provides instruction to empower family members to implement recommended interventions that meet with the family's approval. Interventions typically involve direct learning trials with the child, parent education and training, and teacher/staff consultation. Treatments are typically aimed at the child's specific skill impairments or problem behaviors more so than at the child's diagnosis per se. During parent education and teacher consultation sessions, the behavior manager recommends problem-specific protocols designed to enable these key care providers to implement interventions in home, school, and community settings.

Prioritizing Target Behaviors

Factors frequently considered when prioritizing among target behaviors are 1) the availability of effective treatments, 2) the relative severity of each presenting problem, 3) the degree of effort and skill required of the child and primary care providers to implement the recommended problem-specific protocols, and 4) the preferences of the child and care providers. Behaviors that can be managed solely through positive reinforcement strategies and other positive practices, or dangerous/destructive behaviors that warrant immediate attention, are often selected for intervention first. Treatments for behaviors that are not dangerous or destructive, yet are relatively difficult to manage, such as high-rate self-stimulatory or disruptive behavior, may be delayed until some success has been achieved in implementing basic interventions that work in less difficult behaviors.

Importance of Functional Equivalence

If, as a result of behavior management, the child acquires a prosocial behavior that serves a function equivalent to that of a problematic behavior, then the child will increasingly display acceptable behavior accompanied by a concomitant decrease in problem behavior (Carr, 1988). For example, higher rates of self-injurious behavior are often associated with communication skills impairments (Durand, 1990). The acquisition and use of appropriate communication responses that are functionally equivalent to the problem behavior has been demonstrated to be an effective intervention for many difficult behaviors (Carr & Durand, 1985 a,b; Carr, Levin, McConnachie, et al., 1994; Wacker, Steege, Northup, et al., 1990; Wacker, Wiggins, Fowler, et al., 1988). Through functional communication training, the child learns to exhibit communicative responses (e.g., words, gestures, signs, pressing microswitches) that provide the same positive or negative reinforcement as the problem behavior to be replaced. Typically, speech is the modality of choice because of its universality. If, through differential reinforcement, the child's communicative response results in more positive reinforcement than the problem behavior, then a reduction in the problem behavior should occur. For example, rather than disrupt a peer to acquire the teacher's attention, the student learns to ask "Am I doing good work?" Rather than having a tantrum to avoid work, the student learns to say "Help me, please." Similarly, rather than steal, the child learns to ask "May I have that?" Independent use of communication skills is a pivotal skill that facilitates learning and social relationships. (For more information about the methods of functional communication training as a means of teaching communication skills while managing problem behavior, see Carr et al., 1994; Durand, 1990; and Reichle & Wacker, 1993.)

Parent Education

Parent education and training procedures range from informal tips extended to parents on the telephone to intensive, highly structured curricula presented over a series of sessions. These procedures are often supplemented by "how to" books on child behavior management and articles, lectures, and workshops on effective parenting. Numerous books regarding child behavior management are available for parents (e.g., Baker & Brightman, 1997; Baker, Brightman, Heifetz, et al., 1976; Becker, 1971; Blechman, 1985; Christophersen, 1988; Garber, Garber, & Spizman, 1987; Patterson, 1975, 1976).

Intensive programs usually begin with the behavior manager describing the procedures to be implemented in the home and community, along with a rationale for their use. Predicted effects and possible side effects are reviewed. Common challenges and pitfalls are anticipated. Once the plan of action is determined, a major aspect of many intervention packages is competency-based training of the child care providers. Such training consists of the following steps: 1) identification of target skills; 2) breakdown of these skills into specific steps to be taught; 3) identification of each learner's skills prior to training; and 4) provision of systematic training through verbal description, modeling, and practice. Assessment of the learner's skill acquisition is ongoing, with remedial instruction provided when indicated.

Often, the behavior manager gives the parent(s) a brief written protocol that is procedure or problem specific. These protocols serve as easy-to-use summaries of "do's" and "don'ts." Parents are frequently given homework assignments to implement learned intervention strategies while collecting data to determine the impact of their efforts on the child's target behavior. Homework assignments and obtained data are reviewed during subsequent sessions. When necessary, previously recommended intervention protocols are revised. Ideally, parent education and training sessions continue until the following three criteria are met: 1) the parent(s) demonstrate mastery of requisite intervention strategies; 2) the parent(s) show evidence that such strategies are in routine use; and 3) the child's behavior displays stable improvement.

Case-Centered Consultation

Approaches to the provision of consultation to teachers and care providers are similar to those used with parents. Consultation usually begins with a telephone contact and brief interview, followed by a field visit at the site where care is provided to the child. During a school visit, for example, the behavior expert usually conducts a semi-structured interview and may ask the teacher to respond to selected rating scales and questionnaires. Together, the consultant and teacher examine the key parameters of the child's target behaviors, often observing and recording the target behaviors to obtain objective baseline measures. The consultant recommends observational procedures and periodically returns to the classroom to assist the teacher to obtain valid data regarding the child's behavior.

Once relevant baselines have been established, the consultant collaborates with the teacher to design a behavior management program and, if necessary, demonstrate selected intervention procedures. The teacher is often given an opportunity to practice management strategies while the consultant observes and offers feedback. Consultants often initially choose positive reinforcement interventions designed to increase appropriate behavior. In many cases, the consultant simultaneously collaborates with the child's parent(s) to initiate a home-based program designed to supplement the school-based interventions. The teacher and parent(s) are guided to collaborate effectively with one another via daily school-home communication systems. (See Kelley, 1990, for details regarding design and implementation of school–home communication systems.)

Several works written for professional behavior managers who provide parent education and training and consultation to (para)professional care providers are available (e.g., Barkley, 1990; Carr et al., 1994; Dangel & Polster, 1988; Durand, 1990; Forehand & McMahon, 1981; Foxx, 1982a,b; Gelfand & Hartmann, 1975; Graziano, 1977; Horne & Sayger, 1990; Reichle & Wacker, 1993; Schaefer & Briesmeister, 1989; Sulzer-Azaroff & Mayer, 1977).

Fading Intervention and Programming for Generalization

A child's behavior differs from one situation to the next. If a behavior is reinforced repeatedly (either positively or negatively) in a particular situation, it is likely to recur in that situation. It also may occur in similar situations. Examples of such transfer of behavior across settings (i.e., stimulus generalization) are common in everyday life.

Generalization occurs across behaviors as well as across situations. Changing one behavior often may cause changes in other behaviors. This is termed response generalization. For instance, positive reinforcement of a child's compliance with adult requests also may result in reductions in aggression, disruption, and property destruction (Parrish et al., 1986; Russo, Cataldo, & Cushing, 1981). Reinforcement of a behavior may increase the frequency of behaviors that are similar in form or function.

Behavior managers usually evaluate and address specific target behaviors in specific settings. For example, the behavior manager may target the occurrence of Paul's aggression against a particular peer. The procedures described previously often result in substantive improvements in the behavior of the child with disabilities. Such outcomes are of little benefit, however, if intervention effects do not endure or do not generalize to new situations and behaviors. Unfortunately, the impact of treatment is sometimes highly specific and temporary.

Behavior managers use various strategies to ensure that positive outcomes maintain (i.e., extend over time) and generalize (i.e., transfer, spread) across situations and behaviors (Stokes & Baer, 1977). One of the most common strategies is referred to as **sequential modification.** If desired changes in behavior are not observed to occur across settings and behaviors, concrete steps are taken to introduce the effective intervention (e.g., positive reinforcement) to each of the behaviors or settings to which transfer of effects is inadequate. For instance, Paul is learning to follow instructions issued by each of his five teachers. The initial intervention has been demonstrated to be effective in two of the five classrooms. In this instance, the intervention is refined further and introduced sequentially into each of the other three classrooms. This altered intervention is continued until Paul is following instructions issued by every teacher.

A second strategy is to bring the target behavior under the control of consequences that occur every day. The behavior manager sets "behavior traps." For example, when teaching Paul to share, the instructor may offer praise and tokens each time Paul shares. As Paul increasingly initiates sharing, peers become more cooperative and increasingly reciprocate. Such cooperation and reciprocal reinforcement may be sufficient to sustain (i.e., "trap") Paul's sharing without continuation of the instructor's contingent praise and delivery of tokens.

Offering multiple examples of the desired behavior during training is a third method of increasing maintenance and generalization. This involves providing the child with several opportunities to observe and practice newly acquired skills across slightly altered situations. For example, if the target skill is learning how to engage in conversation, Paul is given opportunities to initiate conversation with many different people in different contexts. The instructor prompts Paul to select one of several available topics for conversation and then introduces Paul to several people with whom Paul is to discuss the chosen topic. This continues until Paul demonstrates a generalized ability to converse capably.

Maintenance and generalization also may be promoted through training "loosely," that is, by teaching a behavior imprecisely in poorly controlled settings. For instance, if Paul learns to speak only when spoken to, Paul will be at a loss when he encounters someone who is reticent to speak. However, if Paul learns to initiate conversation as well as to continue it, Paul's skills may become proficient across diverse, nonstructured (i.e., uncontrolled) settings with different people.

When the instructional focus is to facilitate the child's acquisition of new skills, it is important that the contingencies in effect are clear and consistently applied. However, when the goal is to enhance the maintenance and generalization of an already acquired skill, use of unclear and inconsistent contingencies may be indicated. Here, contingencies are arranged so that the child cannot easily distinguish whether or not the contingencies are in effect. As a result, the child behaves acceptably across many situations and people in hopes of receiving positive reinforcement while avoiding punishment. For example, Paul's dad aims to manage four of Paul's inappropriate behaviors (e.g., tantrums, object-throwing, talking back, cursing) by occasionally putting contingencies in effect for only one or two of these behaviors. Paul is not informed which behaviors do or do not "count." By bedtime, if the rate of occurrence of the target behavior is below a preset criterion frequency, Paul earns a privilege.

Another method to support maintenance and transfer of appropriate behavior is to use the same materials under the same conditions during training as the child will use in everyday situations. This is termed programming for common stimuli. For instance, when teaching a child with physical disabilities how to use a wheelchair, it is optimal to introduce the child to the wheelchair to be used everyday and to teach the child how to maneuver it in the context of daily routines in the child's home, school, and community.

If the child can learn to direct his or her own behavior, lessons learned are more likely to maintain and transfer across relevant settings. This may require teaching children general-case problem-solving and choice-making skills. Teaching children with disabilities to exercise choice and to make sound decisions independently is a major focus of behavior managers (see Bannerman, Sheldon, Sherman, et al., 1990; Guess, Benson, & Siegel-Causey, 1985; Houghton, Bronicki, & Guess, 1987). Research has demonstrated that many children with disabilities can learn to monitor their own behavior, establish performance criteria for reinforcement, and ascertain the amount of positive reinforcement earned. For example, it may be feasible to teach Paul to accomplish assigned seatwork using self-instructions and self-reinforcement across academic tasks.

Near the completion of training, gradual removal (i.e., fading) of positive reinforcement contingencies increases the probability that the child's progress will be maintained. Sudden withdrawal of differential consequences may result in a setback. Gradual withdrawal of reinforcers can be accomplished by altering the amount and timing of reinforcement. For example, Paul may receive fewer points contingent on satisfactory completion of home chores, or Paul may be allowed to earn points every other day only, rather than every day. On alternate days, Paul's performance merely results in praise by his parents.

Gradual withdrawal prepares the child for the "real world," in which consequences for behavior often are not systematic, may be delayed, or may not be provided at all. During the initial phase of skill acquisition or behavior change, it is important that consequences be provided immediately and consistently. However, maintenance of acquired skills or altered behavior is enhanced if consequences are progressively delayed and provided intermittently. Behaviors taught using an intermittent schedule of reinforcement are typically more resistant to extinction than those with continual high levels of reinforcement. Hence, once a new skill is in the child's repertoire or a desired behavior occurs routinely, it is preferable to acknowledge the acceptable behavior every so often rather than each time the behavior occurs. Finally, children can be instructed to exhibit new skills or behaviors at different times in different forms and settings. Parents and teachers often do this by asking the child to change clothes, select a game, complete another math problem, or speak with grandmother on the telephone. These methods of generalization and fading are not mutually exclusive. Each can be employed in isolation or combination.

Follow-Up Assessment/Care

Individually tailored interventions that are applied over time frequently result in substantial improvements that are both clinically significant and socially important. Nonetheless, in many cases, sustained follow-up assessment and care is required because the child's behavioral repertoire and the environments influencing it are everchanging. Learned behavior seldom remains static. Revisions to the management protocol(s) are often indicated in adapting to changing behaviors and environments. In some instances, the impact of previously effective interventions diminishes or new behaviors of concern emerge.

Perhaps one of the most common misconceptions about behavior management is that a permanent "cure" or "fix" can be achieved. In fact, although intervention goals are frequently attained, once a behavior is in a child's repertoire, seldom can it be eliminated altogether. Rather, at best it can be managed under the specific conditions in which it recurs. Thus, the behavior manager develops and implements a plan for ongoing care in anticipation of the continuance or periodic reemergence of the target behavior(s). Periodic assessments and "booster" training sessions are typically provided. In between such planned events, the behavior manager frequently "trouble-shoots" on an as-needed basis.

SUMMARY

Children with developmental disabilities, more often than their typically developing peers, exhibit skill impairments and challenging behaviors. It is exceedingly important to the child's optimal development that these behavioral concerns be addressed. The principles and procedures of effective child behavior management are based on certain fundamental processes, including positive reinforcement, extinction, negative reinforcement, and punishment. Specific interventions often emphasize acquisition and maintenance of prosocial alternate behaviors that enable the child to function independently in least restrictive environments. High priority is assigned to building skills within a framework that promotes the child's self-determination and self-efficacy. A family-centered, community-based approach to care that builds on the child's and family's strengths is essential to the achievement of positive outcomes.

REFERENCES

Achenbach, T.M., & Edelbrock, C.S. (1979). The child behavior profile: II. Boys aged 12–16 and girls 6–11 and 12–16. *Journal of Consulting and Clinical Psychology, 47,* 223–233.

Alberto, P.A., & Troutman, A.C. (1982). *Applied behavior analysis for teachers: Influencing student performance.* Columbus, OH: Charles E. Merrill.

Baer, D.M., Wolf, M.M., & Risley, T.R. (1968). Some current dimensions of applied behavior analysis. *Journal of Applied Behavior Analysis, 1,* 91–97.

Baker, B.L., & Brightman, A.J. (1997). *Steps to independence: Teaching everyday skills to children with special needs.* Baltimore: Paul H. Brookes Publishing Co.

Baker, B.L., Brightman, A.J., Heifetz, L.J., et al. (1976). *Behavior problems.* Champaign, IL: Research Press.

Bannerman, D.J., Sheldon, J.B., Sherman, J.A., et al. (1990). Balancing the right to habilitation with the right to personal liberties: The rights of people with developmental disabilities to eat too many doughnuts and take a nap. *Journal of Applied Behavior Analysis, 23,* 79–89.

Barkley, R.A. (1990). *Hyperactive children: A handbook for diagnosis and treatment.* New York: Guilford Press.

Becker, W.C. (1971). *Parents are teachers.* Champaign, IL: Research Press.

Berg, W.K., & Wacker, D.P. (1991). The assessment and evaluation of reinforcers for individuals with severe mental handicaps. In B. Remington (Ed.), *The challenge of severe mental handicap* (pp. 25–45). West Sussex, England: John Wiley & Sons.

Bijou, S.W., Peterson, R.F., & Ault, M.F. (1968). A method to integrate descriptive and experimental field studies at the level of data and empirical concepts. *Journal of Applied Behavior Analysis, 1,* 175–191.

Blechman, E.A. (1985). *Solving child behavior problems at home and school.* Champaign, IL: Research Press.

Carr, E.G. (1988). Functional equivalence as a mechanism of response generalization. In R. Horner, R. Koegel, & G. Dunlap (Eds.), *Generalization and maintenance: Life-style changes in applied settings* (pp. 221–241). Baltimore: Paul H. Brookes Publishing Co.

Carr, E.G., & Durand, V.M. (1985a). Reducing behavior problems through functional communication training. *Journal of Applied Behavior Analysis, 18,* 111–126.

Carr, E.G., & Durand, V.M. (1985b). The social-communicative basis of severe behavior problems in children. In J. Reiss & R.R. Bootzin (Eds.), *Theoretical issues in behavior therapy* (pp. 219–254). New York: Academic Press.

Carr, E.G., Levin, L., McConnachie, G., et al. (1994). *Communication-based intervention for problem behavior: A user's guide for producing positive change.* Baltimore: Paul H. Brookes Publishing Co.

Christophersen, E.R. (1988). *Little people: Guidelines for common sense child rearing* (3rd ed.). Kansas City, MO: Westport Publishers.

Christophersen, E.R. (1994). *Pediatric compliance: A guide for the primary care physician.* New York: Plenum.

Cooper, L.J., Wacker, D.P., Sasso, G.M., et al. (1990). Using parents as therapists to evaluate the appropriate behavior of their children: Application to a tertiary diagnostic clinic. *Journal of Applied Behavior Analysis, 23,* 285–296.

Cooper, L.J., Wacker, D.P., Thursby, D., et al. (1992). Analysis of the effects of task preferences, task demands, and adult attention on child behavior in outpatient and classroom settings. *Journal of Applied Behavior Analysis, 25,* 823–840.

Dangel, R.F., & Polster, R.A. (1988). *Teaching child management skills.* Elmsford, NY: Pergamon.

Derby, K.M., Wacker, D.P., Sasso, G., et al. (1992). Brief functional assessment techniques to evaluate maladaptive behavior in an outpatient setting: A summary of 79 cases. *Journal of Applied Behavior Analysis, 18,* 713–721.

Durand, V.M. (1990). *Severe behavior problems: A functional communication training approach.* New York: Guilford Press.

Epstein, L.H., Doke, L.A., Sajwaj, T.E., et al. (1974). Generality and side effects of overcorrection. *Journal of Applied Behavior Analysis, 7,* 385–390.

Eyberg, S.M. (1980). Eyberg Child Behavior Inventory. *Journal of Clinical Child Psychology, 9,* 29.

Fisher, W., Piazza, C.C., Bowman, L.G., et al. (1992). A comparison of two approaches for identifying reinforcers for persons with severe and profound disabilities. *Journal of Applied Behavior Analysis, 25,* 491–498.

Forehand, R.L., & Long, N. (1996). *Parenting the strong-willed child.* Chicago: Contemporary Books.

Forehand, R.L., & McMahon, R.J. (1981). *Helping the noncompliant child: A clinician's guide to parent training.* New York: Guilford Press.

Foxx, R.M. (1977). Attention training: The use of overcorrection avoidance to increase eye contact of autistic and retarded children. *Journal of Applied Behavior Analysis, 10,* 489–499.

Foxx, R.M. (1982a). *Decreasing behaviors of severely retarded and autistic persons.* Champaign, IL: Research Press.

Foxx, R.M. (1982b). *Increasing behaviors of severely retarded and autistic persons.* Champaign, IL: Research Press.

Foxx, R.M., & Azrin, N.H. (1972). Restitution: A method of eliminating aggressive-disruptive behavior of retarded and brain damaged patients. *Behavior Research and Therapy, 10,* 15–27.

Foxx, R.M., & Azrin, N.H. (1973). The elimination of autistic, self-stimulatory behavior by overcorrection. *Journal of Applied Behavior Analysis, 6,* 1–14.

Garber, S.W., Garber, M.D., & Spizman, R.F. (1987). *Good behavior.* New York: Villard Books.

Gelfand, D.M., & Hartmann, D.P. (1975). *Child behavior analysis and therapy.* Elmsford, NY: Pergamon.

Graziano, A.M. (1977). *Parents as behavior therapists.* In M. Hersen, R.M. Eisler, & P.M. Miller (Eds.), *Progress in behavior modification* (Vol. 4, pp. 276–294). New York: Academic Press.

Green, C.W., Reid, D.H., Canipe, V.S., et al. (1991). A comprehensive evaluation of reinforcer identification processes for persons with profound multiple handicaps. *Journal of Applied Behavior Analysis, 24,* 537–552.

Gross, A.M., & Drabman, R.S. (1990). *Handbook of clinical behavioral pediatrics.* New York: Plenum.

Guess, D., Benson, H.A., & Siegel-Causey, E. (1985). Concepts and issues related to choice-making and autonomy among persons with severe disabilities. *Journal of The Association for Persons with Severe Handicaps, 10,* 79–86.

Horne, A.M., & Sayger, T.V. (1990). *Treating conduct and oppositional defiant disorders in children.* Elmsford, NY: Pergamon.

Houghton, J., Bronicki, G.J.B., & Guess, D. (1987). Opportunities to express preferences and make choices among students with severe disabilities in classroom settings. *Journal of The Association for Persons with Severe Handicaps, 12,* 18–27.

Iwata, B.A. (1987). Negative reinforcement in applied behavior analysis: An emerging technology. *Journal of Applied Behavior Analysis, 20,* 361–378.

Iwata, B.A., Dorsey, M.F., Slifer, K.J., et al. (1982). Toward a functional analysis of self-injury. *Analysis and Intervention in Developmental Disabilities, 2,* 3–20.

Iwata, B.A., Vollmer, T.R., & Zarcone, J.R. (1990). The experimental (functional) analysis of behavior disorders: Methodology, applications and limitations. In A.C. Repp & N.N. Singh (Eds.), *Perspectives on the use of non-aversive and aversive interventions for persons with developmental disabilities* (pp. 301–330). Sycamore, IL: Sycamore Publishing Co.

Kazdin, A.E. (1977). *The token economy.* New York: Plenum.

Kazdin, A.E. (1989). *Behavior modification in applied settings* (Rev. ed.). Homewood, IL: The Dorsey Press.

Kelley, M.L. (1990). *School–home notes: Promoting children's classroom success.* New York: Guilford Press.

Kennedy, C.H. (1994). Manipulating antecedent conditions to alter the stimulus control of problem behavior. *Journal of Applied Behavior Analysis, 27,* 161–170.

Kennedy, C.H., & Itkonen, T. (1993). Effects of setting events on the problem behavior of students with severe disabilities. *Journal of Applied Behavior Analysis, 26,* 321–327.

Krasnegor, N.A., Arasteh, J.D., & Cataldo, M.F. (1986). *Child health behavior: A behavioral pediatrics perspective.* New York: John Wiley & Sons.

Mace, F.C., & Lalli, J.S. (1991). Linking descriptive and experimental analyses in the treatment of bizarre speech. *Journal of Applied Behavior Analysis, 24,* 553–562.

Mace, F.C., Lalli, J.S., & Pinter-Lalli, E. (1991). Functional analysis and treatment of aberrant behavior. *Research in Developmental Disabilities, 12,* 155–180.

Mace, F.C., Lalli, J.S., Shea, M.C., et al. (1990). The momentum of human behavior in a natural setting. *Journal of the Experimental Analysis of Behavior, 54,* 163–172.

Mash, E.J., & Terdal, L.G. (1988). *Behavioral assessment of childhood disorders* (2nd ed.). New York: Guilford Press.

Mason, S.A., McGee, G.G., Farmer-Dougan, V., et al. (1989). A practical strategy for ongoing reinforcer assessment. *Journal of Applied Behavior Analysis, 22,* 171–179.

Miller, L.K. (1980). *Principles of everyday behavior analysis* (2nd ed.). Monterey, CA: Brooks/Cole.

Northup, J., Wacker, D., Sasso, G., et al. (1991). A brief functional analysis of aggressive and alternative behavior in an outclinic setting. *Journal of Applied Behavior Analysis, 24,* 509–522.

O'Leary, K.D., Kaufman, K.F., Kass, R., et al. (1970). The effects of loud and soft reprimands on the behavior of disruptive students. *Exceptional Children, 37,* 145–155.

O'Neill, R.E., Horner, R.H., Albin, R.W., et al. (1990). *Functional analysis of problem behavior: A practical assessment guide.* Sycamore, IL: Sycamore Publishing Co.

Pace, G.M., Ivancic, M.T., Edwards, G.L., et al. (1985). Assessment of stimulus preference and reinforcer value with profoundly mentally retarded individuals. *Journal of Applied Behavior Analysis, 18,* 249–255.

Parrish, J.M., Cataldo, M.F., Kolko, D.J., et al. (1986). Experimental analysis of response covariation among compliant and inappropriate behaviors. *Journal of Applied Behavior Analysis, 19,* 241–254.

Patterson, G.R. (1975). *Families: Applications of social learning to family life.* Champaign, IL: Research Press.

Patterson, G.R. (1976). *Living with children: New methods for parents and teachers.* Champaign, IL: Research Press.

Patterson, G.R., Reid, J.B., & Dishion, T.J. (1992). *Antisocial boys.* Eugene, OR: Castalia Press.

Porterfield, J.K., Herbert-Jackson, E., & Risley, T.R. (1976). Contingent observation: An effective and acceptable procedure for reducing disruptive behavior of young children in a group setting. *Journal of Applied Behavior Analysis, 9,* 55–64.

Quay, H.C., & Peterson, D.R. (1979). *Manual for the behavior problem checklist.* (Available from 59 Fifth Street, Highland Park, NJ 08904.)

Reichle, J., & Wacker, D.P. (Eds.). (1993). *Communication and language intervention series: Vol. 3. Communicative alternatives to challenging behavior: Integrating functional assessment and intervention strategies.* Baltimore: Paul H. Brookes Publishing Co.

Repp, A.C., Felce, D., & Barton, L.E. (1988). Basing the treatment of stereotypic and self-injurious behaviors on hypotheses of their causes. *Journal of Applied Behavior Analysis, 21,* 281–289.

Routh, D.K. (1988). *Handbook of pediatric psychology.* New York: Guilford Press.

Russo, D.C., Cataldo, M.F., & Cushing, P.J. (1981). Compliance training and behavioral covariation in the treatment of multiple behavior problems. *Journal of Applied Behavior Analysis, 14,* 209–222.

Sasso, G.M., Reimers, T.M., Cooper, L.J., et al. (1992). Use of descriptive and experimental analyses to identify the functional properties of aberrant behavior in school settings. *Journal of Applied Behavior Analysis, 25,* 809–821.

Schaefer, C.E., & Briesmeister, J.M. (1989). *Handbook of parent training: Parents as co-therapists for children's behavior problems.* New York: John Wiley & Sons.

Smith, R.G., Iwata, B.A., Goh, H., et al. (1995). Analysis of establishing operations for self-injury maintained by escape. *Journal of Applied Behavior Analysis, 28,* 515–535.

Stokes, T.F., & Baer, D.M. (1977). An implicit technology of generalization. *Journal of Applied Behavior Analysis, 10,* 349–367.

Sulzer-Azaroff, B., & Mayer, G.R. (1977). *Applying behavior-analysis procedures with children and youth.* New York: Holt, Rinehart and Winston.

Vollmer, T.R., & Iwata, B.A. (1991). Establishing operations and reinforcement effects. *Journal of Applied Behavior Analysis, 24,* 279–291.

Wacker, D., Steege, M., Northup, J., et al. (1990). A component analysis of functional communication training across three topographies of severe behavior problems. *Journal of Applied Behavior Analysis, 23,* 417–429.

Wacker, D., Wiggins, B., Fowler, M., et al. (1988). Training students with profound or multiple handicaps to make requests via microswitches. *Journal of Applied Behavior Analysis, 21,* 331–343.

Watson, L.S. (1967). Application of operant conditioning techniques to institutionalized severely and profoundly retarded children. *Mental Retardation Abstracts, 4,* 1–18.

Weiss, G., & Hechtman, L. (1993). *Hyperactive children grown up: ADHD in children, adolescents, and adults* (2nd ed.). New York: Guilford Press.

White, G.D., Nielson, G., & Johnson, S.M. (1972). Timeout duration and the suppression of deviant behavior in children. *Journal of Applied Behavior Analysis, 5,* 111–120.

31 | Technological Assistance

Innovations for Independence

Susan E. Levy
Maureen O'Rourke

Upon completion of this chapter, the reader will:

- know the definition of medical technology assistance in children
- be aware of the incidence and types of medical technology assistance
- understand conditions leading to medical technology assistance, especially those relating to chronic respiratory failure
- comprehend the psychosocial effects on affected children and their families
- understand what is involved in dealing with such children in early intervention programs, classrooms, and therapy settings

Advances in medical and surgical care have resulted in improved survival of children with complex medical disorders, including complications associated with premature birth; neuromuscular diseases; spinal cord injury; cancer; human immunodeficiency virus (HIV) infection; and chronic diseases of the kidney, respiratory system, gastrointestinal tract, and liver. Some affected children become temporarily or permanently dependent on medical assistive devices, such as mechanical ventilators or feeding tubes. This chapter focuses on the uses of medical assistive technology and the resulting psychological and socioeconomic impact on the child and family.

DEFINITION AND INCIDENCE OF MEDICAL TECHNOLOGY ASSISTANCE

The Office of Technology Assessment (1987) defines a child who receives medical technology assistance as one who requires a mechanical device and substantial daily skilled nursing care to avert death or further disability. These medical devices replace or augment a vital body function and include respiratory technology assistance (e.g., nasal cannulae for provision of oxygen supplementation, mechanical ventilators, positive airway pressure devices, artificial airways such as tracheostomy tubes); surveillance devices (e.g., cardiorespiratory monitors, pulse oximeters);

nutritive assistive devices (e.g., gastrostomy feeding tubes); intravenous therapy (e.g., parenteral nutrition, medication infusion); devices to augment or protect kidney function (e.g., dialysis, urethral catheterization); and ostomies (e.g., colostomy) (Office of Technology Assessment, 1987). Only about 1 in 1,000 children requires medical technology assistance (Palfrey, Walker, Haynie, et al., 1991). The incidence does appear to be increasing in children under 1 year of age, however, primarily as a consequence of improved survival of very low birth weight infants (Palfrey, Haynie, Porter, et al., 1994).

DISORDERS ASSOCIATED WITH MEDICAL TECHNOLOGY ASSISTANCE

Ironically, dependence on medical technology is a consequence of improvements in medical care. Many people are now able to survive what once were rapidly fatal diseases. In a 1987 survey of children who are technology dependent in Massachusetts, more than half of the children (57%) had neurological involvement; 13% had multisystem involvement; 9%, cancer or hematological disorders; 7%, cardiac or respiratory disorders; 7%, gastrointestinal disorders; 4%, kidney disorders; and 3%, musculoskeletal disorders (Palfrey et al., 1991). Table 31.1 lists the requirements for medical assistive devices in a number of these conditions. Approximately half of the children requiring medical technology assistance use some form of respiratory technology (Table 31.2).

Spinal Cord Injury

Children who have sustained severe spinal cord injuries require diverse types of technology assistance. In addition to paralysis below the injury, these children may have respiratory insuffi-

Table 31.1. Conditions requiring medical technology assistance

Conditions	Types of technical assistance
Spinal cord injury	Mechanical ventilation Tube feeding Bladder catheterization
Neuromuscular disorder	Mechanical ventilation Tube feeding
Cerebral palsy	Tube feeding
Prematurity	Mechanical ventilation Oxygen supplementation Tube feeding Intravenous nutrition Ostomy Cardio-respiratory monitor
Kidney failure	Dialysis
Cancer and HIV infection	Intravenous medication Intravenous nutrition Central venous line

Table 31.2.   Types of technology assistance

Assistance	Percentage
Suction, oxygen, tracheostomy care	31
Cardiorespiratory monitoring	25
Mechanical ventilator support	17
Intravenous medications or nutrition	12
Tube feedings	10
Kidney dialysis	1
Other	4

Source: Millner (1991).

ciency resulting from impaired neurological control of the muscles of respiration, as well as impaired swallowing and bowel and bladder dysfunction. Medical technology assistance may include mechanical ventilation, tube feeding, and bladder catheterization.

Neuromuscular Disorders

Neuromuscular disorders, a group of diseases associated with acquired or congenital dysfunction of the central nervous system, spinal cord, peripheral nerves, or muscles, lead to severe weakness. Examples include polio, Guillain-Barré syndrome, Duchenne muscular dystrophy, and spinal muscular atrophy (see Chapter 15). Any of these disorders can severely affect the respiratory muscles, making mechanical ventilation necessary to avert respiratory failure. In addition, if the swallowing musculature is affected, tube feedings may be required.

Cerebral Palsy

Children with cerebral palsy also are at increased risk to develop feeding problems as a consequence of swallowing dysfunction and/or gastroesophageal reflux (GER) (see Chapter 24). Treatment may include the use of tube feedings and special formulas. In addition, children with spastic cerebral palsy may develop scoliosis leading to rib cage distortion and stiffness. This chest wall abnormality can cause a decrease in respiratory muscle power and impede typical lung development. If control of respiratory efforts is seriously impaired or if chronic lung disease develops, assisted ventilation may be required, although this is a rare complication.

Prematurity

Prematurity is associated with immaturity of many organ systems (see Chapter 7). This underdevelopment may lead to dependence on a number of medical assistive technology devices. Immaturity of and subsequent damage to the lung can lead to bronchopulmonary dysplasia (BPD), a disorder that accounts for a significant proportion of mortality and morbidity in low birth weight infants (Farstad & Bratlid, 1994). A child with BPD is frequently dependent on some form of respiratory technology assistance, including oxygen supplementation, tracheostomy tube with continuous positive airway pressure (CPAP), and/or mechanical ventilation (Tammela & Kovisto, 1992).

Tube feedings may be required in very low birth weight infants because of an immature pattern of suck and swallow, which prevents adequate oral intake of formula (Reimers, Carlson, & Lombard, 1992). These infants may even require total parenteral nutrition (i.e., intravenous nutrition) especially after an episode of necrotizing enterocolitis (see Chapter 7). Intravenous nutrition provides a bypass around the gastrointestinal tract. In addition, damage to the gastro-intestinal tract may necessitate the surgical removal of a substantial amount of the small or large bowel, thereby interfering with normal digestion of food. This surgery involves the placement of an ostomy to permit the evacuation of gastrointestinal secretions from the small intestine or fe-ces from the colon through an opening in the abdominal wall.

Premature infants may also have immaturity of the respiratory control centers in the brain-stem. This may lead to apneic episodes. If respiration is not restored quickly, the cardiovascular system may collapse due to lack of oxygen, and the child may have a cardiorespiratory arrest. This is thought to be a precipitant of sudden infant death syndrome (SIDS) or crib death. In or-der to prevent this from occurring, premature infants who have periodic apnea are placed on electronic surveillance using a cardiorespiratory monitor and alarm. This alerts caregivers so they can respond quickly to apneic episodes (see Chapter 7).

Kidney Failure

Renal or kidney failure can occur in children as a result of a congenital malformation, chronic infection, or inherited disease. Chronic kidney failure leads to the accumulation of fluid in the body and metabolic imbalances that can result in poor weight gain and muscle weakness. If se-vere, the accumulation of metabolic toxins can cause coma, brain damage, and death. In many cases, a "cure" is possible with kidney transplantation. However, many children who will even-tually become eligible for a renal transplant may initially be too young or too small or a suitable donor organ may be unavailable (Trompeter, 1990). These children require medical technology assistance through kidney dialysis, a procedure that removes toxic end products of metabolism from the blood. Kidney dialysis may be accomplished by hemodialysis or peritoneal dialysis (see p. 698).

Cancer and HIV Infection

Intravenous medication or nutrition, hemodialysis, or the provision of blood products may be re-quired for weeks or months in children with certain chronic illnesses such as cancer and HIV in-fection (Jayabose, Escobedo, Tugal, et al., 1992). In these situations, a central venous catheter may be surgically placed into a vein and advanced to a position just above the heart. This avoids repeated placement of peripheral intravenous lines. These catheters allow the children to receive chemotherapy, antibiotics, and nutrition at home rather than at the hospital. These lines are more stable than peripheral lines and can be maintained for months or years, provided there is strict adherence to sterile techniques and proper care.

TYPES OF MEDICAL TECHNOLOGY ASSISTANCE

The types of medical technology assistance have been divided into four categories for federally mandated programs (Table 31.3). Of these types, the most frequently used technology is Type IV, which includes cardiorespiratory monitoring.

Respiratory Technology Assistance

Respiratory technology assistance is required by children who have chronic respiratory failure (i.e., the inability of the respiratory system to maintain adequate gas exchange in the lungs). This exchange usually involves the uptake of oxygen [O_2] and the elimination of carbon dioxide

Table 31.3.   Categories of technology assistance

Type	Description
I	Requires mechanical ventilation for at least part of each day
II	Requires prolonged intravenous nutrition or drug therapy
III	Requires support for tracheostomy tube care, suctioning, oxygen supplementation, or tube feeding
IV	Requires cardiorespiratory monitoring, kidney dialysis, or ostomy care

Source: Office of Technology Assessment (1987).

[CO_2]. Oxygen is an essential fuel for energy-generating chemical reactions in the body. Carbon dioxide is a waste product of the chemical reactions and must be eliminated by the lungs and kidneys (Figure 31.1).

Respiratory failure can originate from problems with the respiratory muscle pump or problems with the lungs themselves (Figure 31.2). In order for gas exchange to occur, oxygen and carbon dioxide must be moved in and out of the lungs by the action of the respiratory pump. This consists of the rib cage and the breathing muscles (i.e., diaphragm and muscles of the chest wall) and is driven by the respiratory center in the brainstem (Figure 31.2). Signals from this center are transmitted via the spinal cord and peripheral nerves to the respiratory muscles, which raise and lower the diaphragm and relax and contract the muscles of the chest wall. During inhalation, contraction of the respiratory muscles expands the chest cavity and moves gas into the lungs. With normal breathing, the respiratory muscles then relax and exhalation occurs (gas moves out of the lungs). Dysfunction of any component of the respiratory pump or its neurological control can cause respiratory failure.

In children, respiratory pump failure can be caused by such diseases as spinal cord injury, spinal muscular atrophy, or Duchenne muscular dystrophy (see Chapter 15). This contrasts with BPD and cystic fibrosis, which are disorders that involve damage to the lung itself.

Health care professionals must provide medical support to children with chronic respiratory failure that maintains normal oxygen levels in the blood, prevents ongoing lung injury from recurrent infection, and promotes growth and development (Table 31.4). These goals often can be accomplished using supplemental oxygen, continuous positive airway pressure, chest physiotherapy, medications, and adequate nutrition. When these measures are insufficient, however, mechanical ventilation and tracheostomy tube placement are considered.

Oxygen Supplementation

Oxygen is the single most effective agent in treating the infant with chronic lung disease. In these infants, hypoxia can be precipitated by such simple caregiving activities as handling or feedings. Recurrent hypoxic episodes result in an increased risk of pulmonary hypertension, which may lead to further lung damage (Garg, Kurzner, Bautista, et al., 1988; Long, Philip, & Lucy, 1980; Southall, Samuels, & Talbert, 1990). Continuous oxygen therapy both prevents hypoxia and improves growth and development (Goodman, Perkin, Anas, et al., 1988; Groothius & Rosenberg, 1987). Many infants with chronic respiratory failure require supplemental oxygen

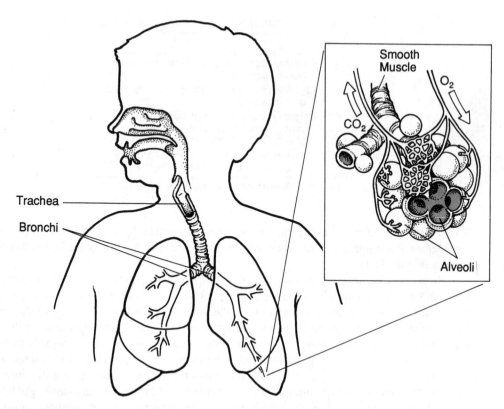

Figure 31.1.   The airways and lungs. The airways conduct inhaled gas from the atmosphere to the alveoli. Air enters the nose (and/or mouth) and then the voice box. It then descends into the chest via the windpipe or trachea. The trachea divides into two bronchi, one serving each lung. The main bronchus to each lung divides repeatedly into a series of progressively smaller tubes that ultimately deliver gas to the alveoli, where gas exchange occurs.

for months or even years. However, too much oxygen can adversely affect the lungs. In order to avoid this, oxygen saturation may be monitored using a device called a pulse oximeter. Oxygen saturation in the blood greater than 90% is optimal for typical growth and well-being. Oxygen can be administered by a **nasal cannula,** face mask, oxygen tent or hood, or an artificial airway (e.g., a tracheostomy). Portable oxygen sources and delivery systems are available so the child is not tethered to the home or hospital room.

Chest Physiotherapy and Suctioning

Children with respiratory illness or failure also may produce excessive secretions and/or be unable to cough effectively. Chest physiotherapy and suctioning, which can be taught to all caregivers, help clear pulmonary secretions. Chest physiotherapy involves the repetitive manual percussion of the chest wall. Secretions are loosened and can then be cleared by coughing or by suctioning in individuals with tracheostomies. This procedure requires the insertion of a **catheter** through the tracheostomy tube and into the trachea. Suction then is applied in order to remove secretions. Typically, supplemental oxygen is administered before and after suctioning

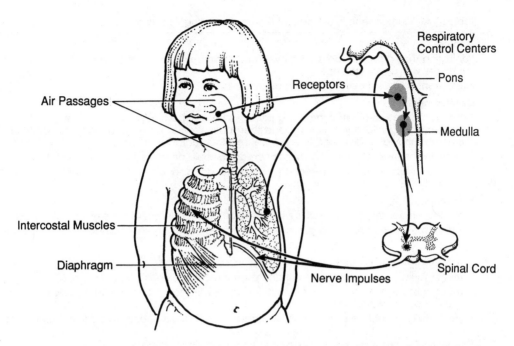

Figure 31.2.   The respiratory muscle pump. Chronic respiratory failure may arise from a defect in any part of the respiratory muscle pump. The respiratory system comprises the respiratory control centers in the brain, the spinal cord and nerves arising from it that transmit signals from the brain, the breathing muscles (diaphragm and intercostal muscles), and the bony and cartilaginous chest cage.

to prevent hypoxia during the procedure. Chest physiotherapy and suctioning are done as often as necessary, usually several times a day.

Positive Airway Pressure

For the child with a moderate disturbance of pulmonary function, such as mild respiratory failure, CPAP may be employed. CPAP is created by a device that imposes resistance to exhalation, thereby preventing recurrent lung collapse. It improves oxygenation by maintaining the alveoli in an open position so they can engage in gas exchange. CPAP can be applied to the child's natural airway (via a tight-fitting mask or nasal pillows) or it can be given through a tracheostomy tube. Mechanical ventilation, when necessary, can be administered between mechanical breaths, in which case it is referred to as positive end expiratory pressure or PEEP.

Mechanical Ventilation and Tracheostomy

Mechanical ventilation is the process by which a device augments or replaces the child's own breaths. Mechanical breaths can be generated either by applying negative pressure to the outside of the chest or by delivering positive pressure through the airway. Negative pressure ventilators are used primarily in children with respiratory muscle pump failure. The "iron lung" is an example of a negative pressure ventilator that was formerly used to treat individuals who had respiratory pump paralysis due to polio. Positive pressure ventilation can be effective for either "pump failure" or lung disease. Positive pressure ventilation can be noninvasive (i.e., applied to the natural airway) or invasive (i.e., delivered via a tracheostomy tube). This chapter focuses on inva-

Table 31.4.   Components in the care of the child requiring ventilator assistance

Medical

Ventilation should support physical growth and minimize shortness of breath and fatigue that can interfere with development.

Intercurrent illnesses should be treated aggressively.

Developmental

Children must be evaluated on a regular basis by an interdisciplinary team of developmental pediatricians, child psychologists, and therapists. Problems are identified, and individualized programs should be designed to enhance developmental functioning.

Early intervention programs with groups of children should be utilized when appropriate.

Physical, occupational, and speech-language therapists should work with children individually as needed.

Environmental

A physical environment that is less restrictive than the typical intensive care unit should be provided.

A regular routine of care, bathing, dressing, mealtimes, play periods, and naps must be provided.

Social

Families may require group and individual psychosocial support.

Families should be encouraged to visit and participate in the child's care.

Families must become an integral part of the caregiving team and should assume an advocacy and decision-making role.

Foster families should be sought when biological families are unable to participate in the child's care.

Primary nursing programs should be used to ensure continuity of care.

sive positive pressure ventilation because it is currently the most commonly used method in children.

A tracheostomy usually involves the insertion of a plastic tube through a surgically created incision in the cartilage of the **trachea** just below the "Adam's apple." It is secured with foam-padded strings around the neck. This open airway is then attached to a ventilator or a CPAP device with tubing that provides humidified air or an air/oxygen mixture. The tracheostomy tube also allows the caregiver to have direct access to the airway, permitting suctioning of secretions or the removal of other blockages (Duncan, Howell, deLorimier, et al., 1992).

Accidental displacement of the tracheostomy tube is the most common complication. This is often a relatively minor problem; the tube can be repositioned and a child who is not completely dependent on the ventilator can breathe spontaneously around the tube. However, it can be life threatening to a child who has a narrowed trachea above the tracheostomy and, as a result, is totally dependent on the device. In this case, a dislodged or blocked tube must be replaced immediately. Children with narrowed tracheas should be closely observed and electronically monitored with a cardiorespiratory monitor and/or pulse oximeter.

Numerous positive pressure ventilators are available and appropriate for children with chronic respiratory failure. Ventilator selection is affected by a number of factors: the child's size, the underlying disorder, where the ventilator will be used (home versus other settings [e.g., hospital, school]), whether portability is necessary (battery-powered ventilators exist), and other special features that may be helpful to the child (Figure 31.3).

The ventilator contains an alarm that sounds under conditions of low or high pressure. The most common reason for a low pressure alarm is accidental disconnection of the tracheostomy tube from the ventilator tubing. This may occur when the child is moved from one position to

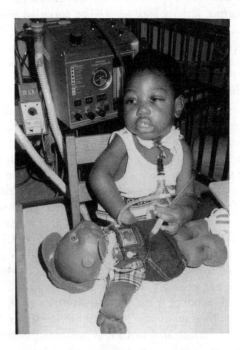

Figure 31.3.   A child with a neuromuscular disease, 2 years old, with a tracheostomy tube and a ventilator, is participating in an early intervention program.

another. It is usually not a serious problem; the tube is simply reattached. A high-pressure alarm most commonly sounds because something is obstructing the flow of gas into the child. This may be external to the child (e.g., kinked or obstructed tubing) or it may be within the child (e.g., mucous inside the tracheostomy tube, a bronchospasm, a cough). Mucous plugging is usually prevented by humidifying the gas mixture that passes through the tubing. If there is a mucous plug, it requires removal by suctioning.

Surveillance Devices

Children with disorders that affect the heart or lungs are likely to require the use of surveillance devices. Although these devices provide no direct therapeutic benefit, they give early warning of problems and thereby improve care indirectly. The two most common types of electronic surveillance devices are pulse oximeters and cardiorespiratory monitors. They can be used individually or in combination in the hospital and at home (Poets & Southall, 1994).

Pulse Oximeters

The oximeter measures oxygen saturation in the arterial blood with a probe that is attached with special tape or bandage to one of the child's fingers or toes. The probe measures the amount of oxygen bound to hemoglobin, the oxygen-carrying protein in blood cells that gives blood its red color. An alarm can be set to sound below a certain oxygen saturation level, which may occur as a result of delivery failure (i.e., the oxygen tank has run out) or a change in the child's condition, such as an increased need for supplemental oxygen because of a respiratory infection. In this latter situation, the current activity may need to be curtailed and the oxygen concentration increased. Because this device reflects how well oxygen is being delivered to vital organs, it is an important monitor; unfortunately, it is quite susceptible to false alarms resulting from probe displacement, movement of the extremity, or electrical interference.

Cardiorespiratory Monitors

The cardiorespiratory (CR) monitor has electrodes that are attached to the child's chest that record heart and respiratory rate (Silvestri, Weese-Mayer, & Kenny, 1994). An alarm is part of the system and is set off by either too high or too low rates. If the alarm sounds, the caregiver should examine the child's respiratory, cardiovascular, and neurological status. Like the oximeter, the CR monitor sounds false alarms, most commonly resulting from the inadvertent detachment of the chest electrodes. However, in the very rare event that the alarm sounds because of a cardiorespiratory arrest (i.e., cessation of breathing and heart rate), cardiopulmonary resuscitation (CPR) must be instituted immediately. All personnel working with children who have special health care needs should be trained in the performance of CPR. As respiratory arrest almost always precedes cardiac arrest in children, proper technique for artificial ventilation is essential. In the child with a tracheostomy, breaths of 100% oxygen should be delivered by attaching a resuscitation bag to the tracheostomy tube. For a child without a tracheostomy or a child whose tube has come out and cannot be reinserted, a tight-fitting mask should be applied to the child's face and oxygen given by resuscitation bag. For further details, the reader is encouraged to review guidelines for the performance of CPR (Christenson, Solimano, & Williams, 1993; Goetting, 1995).

Nutritional Assistive Devices

Good nutrition is a vital component in the medical management of children with chronic illnesses including cancer and HIV infection (Aquino, Smyrl, Hagg, et al., 1995; Miller, Awnetwant, & Evans, 1995). Children with BPD or dyskinetic cerebral palsy may need up to twice the normal caloric intake because of the considerable energy expended in rapid breathing or in engaging in involuntary movements (Kurzner, Garg, Bautista, et al., 1988). Because lung growth parallels linear growth, recovery from BPD is linked to the child's nutritional status. Similarly, development in children with cerebral palsy is often limited by undernutrition (see Chapter 24). Despite needing an increased food intake, these children may be unable to ingest even a normal intake because of oromotor impairments, GER, or behavior problems (Rogers, Arvedson, Msall, et al., 1993). In these instances, nutritional assistance devices may prove helpful.

Children with oral intake that is insufficient to maintain normal growth may require tube feedings temporarily through a tube inserted into one nostril and passed into the stomach (nasogastric) or into the second part of the intestine (nasojejunal). When long-term feedings are required, a permanent tube can be placed directly into the stomach (gastrostomy [G]) or intestine (jejunostomy [J]). A GJ-tube combines a G-tube and a J-tube. The J-tube portion travels through the **pylorus,** the **duodenum,** and into the **jejunum** to prevent reflux of the nutrients (Figure 28.10). New techniques allow insertion of G- and/or J-tubes **percutaneously,** thus avoiding a surgical procedure performed under general anesthesia. This is called a PEG procedure (Albanese, Towbin, Ulman, et al., 1993; Marin, Glassman, Schoen, et al., 1994). If the child has GER, the intervention of choice may be a combination of a surgical antireflux procedure (e.g., a fundoplication) and a G or GJ- tube placed during the abdominal surgery. Once the feeding tube is present, nutrition can be provided as a specially prepared commercially available formula, such as Jevity and Ensure, or blenderized foods that the family eats (see Chapter 10).

Children with feeding tubes require parents, teachers, and other caregivers to possess certain skills (Michaelis, Warzak, Stanek, et al., 1992). If the tube falls out, it must be repositioned. To prevent this from occurring, the tube may be anchored to the stomach and skin by a "button" apparatus or internally by a bulb that is inflated by water or widens in a mushroom shape (Figure 31.4). If the tube comes out, sometimes it is simply because the bulb has deflated. A trained teacher, therapist, nurse, or parent can reinsert the tube and then reinflate the bulb. The gastrostomy tube site must be washed daily with soap and water and the tube changed every few months. Irritation around the gastrostomy site signals that it is infected or that stomach acid is leaking. If an infection has been ruled out, the use of Duoderm or another occlusive ointment such as Vaseline may be applied to protect the area. If the skin around the tube bleeds, it may need to be cauterized using silver nitrate sticks.

Ostomy Care

An ostomy (e.g., gastrostomy) is the connection of an internal organ through the abdominal wall to the outside of the skin. The most common ostomy in older children and adults is a colostomy, an opening that permits the evacuation of bowel contents. As noted previously, a colostomy or **ileostomy** is sometimes necessary in a premature infant who has undergone bowel surgery as a result of necrotizing enterocolitis. In most cases, the bowel can be reattached in a few months

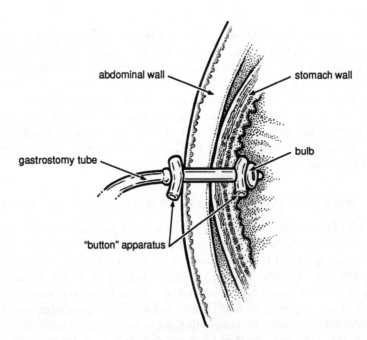

Figure 31.4.   Gastrostomy feeding tube. This tube can be anchored to the stomach and skin by a "button" or an internal "bulb."

after healing has occurred. In older children, a colostomy or ileostomy is often performed for inflammatory bowel disease (ulcerative colitis or Crohn disease). Less common ostomies include a **vesicostomy** and **ureterostomy** that are used to treat urinary tract obstructions. The care of the ostomy site, called the stoma or opening, is similar to the care of the gastrostomy site (Garvin, 1994). In addition, special bags are used to collect feces and secretions and must be emptied and replaced at routine intervals.

Intravenous Therapy

Long-term intravenous therapy, generally provided through a central venous line, is most often required to provide nutrition or to administer medication. Total parenteral nutrition (TPN) involves the provision of a high-calorie, high-protein solution directly into the bloodstream by intravenous administration. Infants who have short bowel syndrome resulting from necrotizing enterocolitis typically require TPN. TPN may also be required by older children with a range of disorders including chronic malabsorption (e.g., cystic fibrosis); intestinal inflammation (e.g., Crohn disease); and cancer (Copeman, 1994; Puntis, 1995). Prolonged intravenous access may also be needed to provide antibiotics (e.g., when a child has osteomyelitis) and chemotherapy (e.g., when a child has leukemia). The parent or nurse is responsible for administering the parenteral nutrition solution or medication at the proper intervals and duration. The caregiver must be trained in the maintenance of sterility of the central venous catheter and be able to recognize catheter detachment and infection. Signs of an infection include redness of the surrounding skin or discharge of pus. Most children with a central venous catheter have a hemostat or clamp that can be placed over the plastic tubing if it becomes detached.

Kidney Dialysis

The two principal forms of kidney dialysis are hemodialysis and peritoneal dialysis. Although home hemodialysis has been used in adults for years, it is not generally used in children. Home peritoneal dialysis, however, has been used since the mid-1980s in children with kidney failure (Alexander & Honda, 1994; Miller, Ruley, & Bock, 1995). To prepare for the child's peritoneal dialysis, a catheter is surgically inserted through the abdominal wall and into the abdominal cavity. This catheter permits dialysis solution to flow into the peritoneal space, equilibrate, and then drain. This procedure eliminates toxins that would usually be metabolized by the kidney. It takes several hours and may be necessary 3–5 days per week. Families can be trained to perform peritoneal dialysis independently at home.

EFFECTS OF MEDICAL TECHNOLOGY ASSISTANCE ON THE CHILD AND FAMILY

Infants with illnesses that require medical technology assistance may be hospitalized for prolonged periods of time among noisy and frightening pieces of machinery. Much of the child's social contact is related to nursing care that may involve unpleasant procedures (Hamlett, Walker, Evans, et al., 1994; Teague, Fleming, Castle, et al., 1993). Prolonged hospitalization places both emotional and financial stresses on the family and may isolate the child from his or her family. Even very involved families may find it difficult to spend extended periods of time in the hospital with their child because of distance or work commitments. Professionals may need to assist families to bond with their infants or provide support for their older children who feel abandoned when parents are unable to visit frequently.

Even once home, social isolation may not disappear. In school, the child is likely to be treated as "different" because of the accompanying machinery and medical/nursing needs. This can be partially offset by educating classmates and providing psychological counseling for the child (Fleming, Challela, Eland, et al., 1994).

The child must also learn to deal with the underlying medical problem that led to the technology dependence. It is generally easier for a child to accept technology dependence on a short-term basis—for example, when intravenous antibiotics are necessary to treat a severe infection or when a temporary ostomy is required following abdominal surgery. However, if the child has a chronic or ultimately fatal disease, such as HIV infection, muscular dystrophy, end-stage renal failure, or cystic fibrosis, adaptation to technology assistance is but one issue among many that must be dealt with by both the child and family (Watson, 1995) (see Chapter 34).

Social issues may also adversely affect the child's emotional well-being. For example, the same factors that led to prematurity (e.g., young maternal age, low socioeconomic status, maternal substance abuse) may also limit the parents' ability to cope with the stress of caring for a child who has an ongoing medical condition (Patterson, Leonard, & Titus, 1992; Petr, Murdock, & Chapin, 1995). Under these circumstances, parental visitation may be infrequent and home care impossible. Nursing and therapy staff then become the primary emotional caregivers in addition to their roles as medical caregivers. In these instances, a pediatric subacute nursing facility or a special medical foster home (individual or group) may be an appropriate alternative to prolonged hospitalization.

In most families, however, the parents remain very involved with their child and are willing to learn to care for their child at home once medically stable. Home care enables the entire family to be together with less disruption but also causes stress for family members who often experience chronic fatigue, financial concerns, and the burden of meeting their child's needs over a prolonged period of time (Bond, Phillips, & Rollins, 1994). Parents may be concerned about making a mistake that could injure or even cause the death of their child. If ongoing home nursing care is required, the lack of privacy caused by the presence of shifts of nurses may be an additional stressor. Studies have suggested that families can do well if the technology assistance lasts less than 2 years. More prolonged periods of time, however, are associated with an increased risk of parental burnout (Ahmann & Bond, 1992).

FUNDING MEDICAL TECHNOLOGY ASSISTANCE

Medical technology assistance can be very expensive, depending on the type of equipment required and the extent of the disability (Parette, 1993). Therefore, before the child needing medical technology can be discharged, a number of financial issues must be addressed (Figure 31.5). The two major issues are nursing care and equipment/supplies. The requirement for nursing care depends on the severity of illness. In individuals requiring mechanical ventilation, nursing care is required for an average of 14 hours per day (Fields, Rosenblatt, Pollock, et al., 1991). Yet, many insurance policies do not provide reimbursement for this much nursing care. Even insurance polices that do reimburse for these needs may have ceilings beyond which they will not pay. Although these ceilings may be many hundreds of thousands of dollars, the benefits can be exhausted in less than a year of intensive nursing care. Yet, the child may require many years of home nursing care and technology assistance.

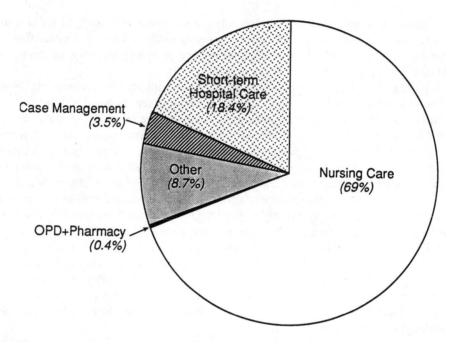

Figure 31.5.   Distribution of annual home care reimbursements for children requiring ventilator assistance in the Medicaid model waiver program. Nursing care includes in-home care with an average of 14 hours per day. Short-term hospital care includes all reimbursements for rehospitalizations during the first year after discharge; outpatient department (OPD) includes physician visits and outpatient hospital charges; and other includes durable medical equipment, disposable medical supplies, transportation, and occupational, physical, and speech-language therapies. (Adapted from Fields, Rosenblatt, Pollock, et al. [1991].)

Prior to 1982, many children who had exhausted their private insurance coverage were deemed ineligible for Medicaid because parental income exceeded Medicaid qualification maximums. In 1982, the case of one child who is ventilator dependent, Katie Beckett, was brought to the attention of President Ronald Reagan, who gave an executive order that allowed the rules regarding eligibility requirements to be waived so that she could return home without losing her Medicaid benefits (Murray, 1989). The 1990 Omnibus Budget Reconciliation Act, PL 101-508, established that each state can apply for up to 200 waiver slots per year. This has helped but not completely solved the funding problem. Because the waiver program limits the number of people who can be funded by each state, some states have long waiting lists and some home health care providers are reluctant to accept the relatively low reimbursement rates that the waiver program offers.

A Supreme Court ruling has provided additional relief to financially pressed families by extending Supplemental Security Income (SSI) to more children with disabilities who require medical technology assistance. A class action suit filed by the family of Brian Zebley, a young child with congenital brain damage who was not found to qualify under the stringent medical severity standards applied by SSI to all children, prompted this legislation. In *Sullivan* (the Secretary of the U.S. Department of Health and Human Services) *v. Zebley* (1990), the Supreme

Court found that the SSI criteria for children were "manifestly contrary to the statute" (Owen, 1991, p. 42) that had created the program. As a result, more individualized criteria are being applied, and many more children with disabilities are receiving funding for medical technology assistance under SSI (Perrin & Stein, 1991; Richardson, Student, O'Boyle, et al., 1992). Whether this improved access will be retained within the evolving health care system is uncertain (see Chapter 36). In addition, there remain certain out-of-pocket expenses that are not compensated for by these federal programs or private insurance policies. These include remodeling of the home, increased utility costs, loss of income from work absences, transportation costs, and child care expenses.

PREPARING FOR HOME CARE

Despite financial and psychosocial problems, more children requiring medical technology assistance are being reintegrated into the community each year (Goldberg, Gardner, & Gibson, 1994; Lewis, Alford-Winston, Billy-Kornas, et al., 1992). One major incentive is that home care can cost half as much as hospital care. But home care, especially when ventilator assistance is required, becomes a viable option only after a number of requirements have been met (Table 31.5). The family must master the child's medical and nursing care (Bakewell-Sachs & Porth, 1995). They need to select a nursing agency if home nursing services are required and a durable medical equipment supplier for equipment, disposable supplies, and in-home support (e.g., equipment maintenance and monitoring). The finances to pay for all these services also must be arranged. In addition, modifications to the family's home may be needed. These may include changing existing electrical systems and adding ramps for wheelchair or stroller accessibility. If mechanical ventilation is required, local electric, ambulance, and telephone companies must be notified that a person dependent on life-support technology will be residing in the family's home so that the household can be placed on a priority list in the event of power failure or medical emergency.

Medical, educational, and rehabilitative services also need to be arranged before discharge. A pediatrician or family physician in the community should be identified to provide general

Table 31.5.   Criteria to be met prior to sending a child home with medical technology assistance

1. The child's medical condition must be stable.
2. The level of support and intervention the child requires must be able to be safely and practically provided in the home.
3. The family must be willing and have demonstrated proficiency in providing all aspects of the child's care.
4. Financial support must be found to fund equipment, supplies, and personnel in the home.
5. A durable equipment company must be identified to provide oxygen and other respiratory equipment and supplies.
6. Nursing services and therapists must be in place prior to discharge.
7. Adequate emotional and respite care resources must be available.

Source: Kettrick and Donar (1985).

medical care. The discharging team contacts this individual prior to the child's hospital discharge to introduce the child and encourage the community physician's active participation in the child's care. If the child requires special rehabilitation therapies after discharge, either center-based or home-based providers should be arranged. Educational services also need to be identified, and the child's health care and rehabilitative plans written into an individualized education program (for school-age children) or an individualized family service plan (for early intervention services) (Abman & Groothius, 1994; Hill, 1993; Palfrey et al., 1994). A center- or school-based educational program offers the child the opportunity to interact with other children in a stimulating environment. This should be encouraged if the child's physical condition permits and appropriate medical or nursing supports are available.

OUTCOME

The prognosis of the child who requires medical technology assistance depends more on the underlying disorder than on the type of technology assistance provided (Stutts, 1994). Therefore, outcome is best discussed for the individual disorders. As the outcomes for cerebral palsy and neuromuscular disorders are discussed in other chapters, the child requiring ventilator assistance is addressed here.

Liberation from Mechanical Ventilation

A child's prognosis for liberation from mechanical ventilation depends on the disease causing the respiratory failure (Canlas-Yamsuan, Sanchez, Kesselman, et al., 1993). Complete liberation from mechanical ventilation is usually a realistic goal for children with BPD. Satisfactory growth, normal gas exchange on the current level of support, sufficient stamina for activities of daily living, and absence of intercurrent illness usually indicate that the child can tolerate a gradual reduction in the level of mechanical support. The speed of weaning is dictated by the child's clinical status and it may occur over months to years (Pilmer, 1994).

Several techniques are used to wean a child from mechanical ventilation. The number of mechanical breaths delivered per minute can be reduced gradually or the child may spend increasingly longer periods of time off the ventilator. The "time off" approach has the advantage of allowing the child greater mobility. Nighttime mechanical ventilation is usually the last support to be withdrawn. After the child has functioned without mechanical ventilation and supplemental oxygen for several months, removal of the tracheostomy tube may be considered.

If the disorder is not expected to improve over time, such as in cases of muscular dystrophy or spinal cord injury, complete liberation from the ventilator may not be a realistic goal; yet partial liberation may still be possible. In order to promote mobility and independence, the child's schedule can be arranged so that ventilation is provided while the child is resting. For the child who is completely dependent on mechanical ventilation, mobility is still possible using a portable ventilator. These devices, with external batteries capable of powering the ventilator for up to 12 hours, can be mounted on specially designed trays attached to wheelchairs or carts. Though somewhat bulky, the portable mechanical ventilator and battery enable the child to attend school and travel with the family.

Developmental and Behavioral Complications
Associated with Long-Term Mechanical Ventilatory Support

Developmental complications associated with long-term mechanical ventilation are most commonly a function of the underlying medical problems associated with respiratory failure and include language, behavior, and feeding problems (Abman & Groothius, 1994; Bregman & Farrell, 1992; Stutts, 1994). A number of studies suggest that some of the impairments in language production, syntax, and articulation are further exacerbated by the presence of a tracheostomy during the critical period of early language development (Hill & Singer, 1990; McGowan, Bleile, Fus, et al., 1993; Singer, Kercsmar, Legris, et al., 1989). Thus, speech-language therapy is very important for these children. Treatment focuses on various augmentative and alternative communication systems as well as encouraging the sounds the child can produce. In the school-age child, the educator and speech-language pathologist collaborate to build a system of communication that incorporates the child's existing means of expression with communication aids. For example, a speaking valve or electrolarynx can be used to enhance esophageal speech at the same time that the therapist encourages the child to use sounds, gestures, and facial expressions. This approach is combined with augmentation or alternative communication systems that use object, graphic, or picture modes of expression displayed in a variety of ways, such as a communication board or wallet, a conversation photograph notebook, a loop tape attached to a cassette recorder, or a computer system with voice or written output. These systems should expand the child's ability to communicate across situations and people.

Few studies have been published concerning the developmental outcome of children requiring long-term mechanical ventilation. One of the most extensive studies describes moderate to severe developmental delay in almost half of premature infants with BPD who require long-term ventilation (Gray, Burns, Mohay, et al., 1995). This is about three times the rate of delay in premature infants who do not require ventilator assistance (Kitchen, Ryan, & Rickards, 1987). The question remains whether prolonged mechanical ventilation itself is causally related to the poorer outcome or is a marker for other preexisting neurological impairments that adversely influence development. For example, the premature infant with severe respiratory distress syndrome (RDS) may have had prolonged hypoxia before intervention was initiated or could have sustained a severe intracerebral hemorrhage. One study provides evidence that neurodevelopmental outcome is a function of previous neurological complications and not the duration of mechanical ventilation (Luchi, Bennett, & Jackson, 1991).

Children who are ventilator dependent may also have behavior problems (Fridy & Lemanek, 1993). The absence of audible speech may lead to frustration in attempts at communication and may result in aggressive or acting-out behavior. Noncompliant behavior may also occur because of inconsistencies in caregiving during prolonged hospitalizations. Some children have developmental disabilities that are associated with perseverative, self-stimulatory, and self-injurious behaviors. Treatment often utilizes behavior management therapy, drug therapy, and supportive counseling for the family and other caregivers (Levy, 1996). In addition, providing alternative communication strategies, which may enhance the ability of caregivers to discern the meaning of the child's messages, is likely to decrease the challenging behavior (Carr, 1994; Reichle & Wacker, 1993).

Children who use ventilators also are at increased risk for GER and resultant vomiting (Sindel, Maisels, & Ballantine, 1989). Over time, the child may associate eating with the subsequent negative experience of vomiting and may refuse to eat. In addition, there may be oral-motor dysfunction and frequent interruptions in periods of oral feeding due to acute illnesses (Starrett, 1991). The young child may lose the skills needed for effective feeding. Usually, the feeding disorder is attributable to an underlying physiological problem such as GER or constipation. Effective treatment includes medical management of any underlying disorder (e.g., surgical treatment of GER) as well as teaching behavior management skills to the child's parents and caregivers.

RAY

Ray is a 3-year-old boy who was hospitalized for the first 2 years of his life for management of chronic respiratory failure. He was born prematurely at 27 weeks' gestation (3 months early) and required oxygen administration and mechanical ventilation at the outset due to RDS. He had a stormy early course in the neonatal intensive care unit (NICU), with a number of the complications commonly associated with small premature infants. At 3 months, a tracheostomy was performed, because his doctors determined that he would require long-term mechanical ventilatory support. Other medical complications included intracerebral hemorrhage, retinopathy of prematurity, and GER.

At 10 months of age, Ray still had BPD and was transferred from the NICU to a pediatric rehabilitation facility with a specialized unit for children requiring mechanical ventilatory support. The medical, nursing, and therapy staff collaborated with the family to develop a plan and a time line to accomplish the goals of enhancing his growth and development and training his parents to care for him at home. Because Ray had been so sick, he had to rely on a feeding tube for nutrition and lacked experience and skills in oral feeding. The tube feedings were effective in helping him grow but made his GER worse, and the doctors and nurses worked closely with the parents adjusting the medications and rate of the tube feeding to minimize the reflux and provide Ray the maximal opportunity to develop his oral skills. As Ray's lungs improved and he grew, the amount of ventilator support could be decreased. By the time Ray was discharged at 2 years, he was able to be placed on a portable ventilator, which could be mounted on an adapted stroller. He could tolerate being off the ventilator for 6 hours during the day, allowing him to attend a special preschool program 3 mornings per week outside of his home. His attendance at the preschool program was important for addressing the delays in development, particularly involving speech and language and gross motor skills.

Ray's parents were active members of the interdisciplinary team. As his medical goals were being addressed, they began to learn his care; and by the time Ray was ready for discharge, they were able to care for him independently. Ray went home with his family with extensive home nursing and therapy support.

One year later, Ray is doing well at home and has not required readmission to the hospital. Important factors in his and his family's success have been the extensive medical, nursing, and therapy supports in the home. Ray now attends an early intervention program 3 mornings per week, where he receives services from speech-language, occupational, and physical therapists. His parents are working closely with the school district and nursing agency to ensure continued provision of developmental services in his school and nursing supervision of his medical problems while in school. His lungs have improved to the extent that he only requires CPAP at night, and his doctors believe that within the next few months this may also be discontinued. The family is optimistic that he may be able to be decannulated by the summer. Despite Ray's complex medical and developmental problems, he has become an integral member of his family.

SUMMARY

A medical technology device replaces or augments a vital bodily function. These devices include respiratory technology assistance, surveillance devices, nutritive assistive devices, devices to augment kidney function, and ostomies. Approximately 1 in 1,000 children will require the long-term use of a medical assistive device, but the incidence among children with developmental disabilities is significantly higher. The requirement for prolonged technology assistance places both financial and emotional stresses on the family. It also provides considerable challenges to health care professionals and other caregivers. Knowledge about the correct use of the medical device and confidence in dealing with potential emergencies is important for both parents and caregivers. Training in medical technology assistance should occur while the child is hospitalized. Arrangement for financial, nursing, and equipment support is essential before the child goes home. Ultimately, the outcome of children who are dependent on medical technology appears to be more a function of the underlying disorder than the type of technology. The role of parents, however, cannot be overemphasized.

REFERENCES

Abman, S.H., & Groothius, J.R. (1994). Pathophysiology and treatment of bronchopulmonary dysplasia: Current issues. *Pediatric Clinics of North America, 41,* 277–315.

Ahmann, E., & Bond, N.J. (1992). Promoting normal development in school-age children and adolescents who are technology dependent: A family centered model. *Pediatric Nursing, 18,* 399–405.

Albanese, C.T., Towbin, R.B., Ulman, I., et al. (1993). Percutaneous gastrojejunostomy versus Nissen fundoplication for enteral feeding of the neurologically impaired child with gastrointestinal reflux. *Journal of Pediatrics, 123,* 371–375.

Alexander, S.R., & Honda, M. (1994). Continuous peritoneal dialysis for children: A decade of worldwide growth and development. *Kidney International, 40*(Suppl.), S65–S74.

Aquino, V.M., Smyrl, C.B., Hagg, R., et al. (1995). Enteral nutritional support by gastrostomy tube in children with cancer. *Journal of Pediatrics, 127,* 58–62.

Bakewell-Sachs, S., & Porth, S. (1995). Discharge planning and home care of the technology-dependent infant. *Journal of Obstetric, Gynecologic, and Neonatal Nursing, 24,* 77–83.

Bond, N., Phillips, P., & Rollins, J.A. (1994). Family-centered care at home for families with children who are technology dependent. *Pediatric Nursing, 20,* 123–130.

Bregman, J., & Farrell, E.E. (1992). Neurodevelopmental outcome in infants with bronchopulmonary dysplasia. *Clinics in Perinatology, 19,* 673–694.

Canlas-Yamsuan, M., Sanchez, I., Kesselman, M., et al. (1993). Morbidity and mortality patterns of ventilator-dependent children in a home care program. *Clinical Pediatrics, 32,* 706–713.

Carr, E.G., Levin, L., McConnachie, et al. (1994). *Communication-based intervention for problem behavior: A user's guide for producing positive change.* Baltimore: Paul H. Brookes Publishing Co.

Christenson, J.M., Solimano, A.J., & Williams, J. (1993). The new American Heart Association guidelines for cardiopulmonary resuscitation and emergency cardiac care: Presented by the Emergency Cardiac Care Subcommittee of the Heart and Stroke Foundation of Canada. *Canadian Medical Association Journal, 149,* 585–590.

Copeman, M.C. (1994). Use of total parenteral nutrition in children with cancer: A review and some recommendations. *Pediatric Hematology and On-cology, 11,* 463–470.

Duncan, B.W., Howell, L.J., deLorimier, A.A., et al. (1992). Tracheostomy in children with emphasis on home care. *Journal of Pediatric Surgery, 27,* 432–435.

Farstad, T., & Bratlid, D. (1994). Incidence and prediction of bronchopulmonary dysplasia in a cohort of premature infants. *Acta Paediatrica, 83*(1), 19–24.

Fields, A.I., Rosenblatt, A., Pollock, M.M., et al. (1991). Home care cost-effectiveness for respiratory technology-dependent children. *American Journal of Diseases of Children, 145,* 729–733.

Fleming, J., Challela, M., Eland, J., et al. (1994). Impact on the family of children who are technology dependent and cared for in the home. *Pediatric Nursing, 20,* 379–388.

Fridy, J., & Lemanek, K. (1993). Developmental and behavioral issues. In K. Bleile (Ed.), *The care of children with long-term tracheotomies* (pp. 141–167). San Diego: Singular Publishing Group, Inc.

Garg, M., Kurzner, S.I., Bautista, D.B., et al. (1988). Clinically unsuspected hypoxia during sleep and feeding in infants with bronchopulmonary dysplasia. *Pediatrics, 81,* 635–642.

Garvin, G. (1994). Caring for children with ostomies. *Nursing Clinics of North America, 29,* 645–654.

Goetting, M.G. (1995). Progress in pediatric cardiopulmonary resuscitation. *Emergency Medicine Clinics of North America, 13,* 291–319.

Goldberg, A.I., Gardner, H.G., & Gibson, L.E. (1994). Home care: The next frontier of pediatric practice. *Journal of Pediatrics, 125*(5), 686–690.

Goodman, G., Perkin, R.M., Anas, N.G., et al. (1988). Pulmonary hypertension in infants with bronchopulmonary dysplasia. *Journal of Pediatrics, 112,* 72–80.

Groothuis, J.R., & Rosenberg, A.A. (1987). Home oxygen promotes weight gain in infants with bronchopulmonary dysplasia. *American Journal of Diseases of Children, 141,* 992–995.

Gray, P.H., Burns, Y.R., Mohay, H.A., et al. (1995). Neurodevelopmental outcome of preterm infants with bronchopulmonary dysplasia. *Archives of Disease in Childhood, 73,* F128–F134.

Hamlett, K.W., Walker, W., Evans, A., et al. (1994). Psychological development of technology-dependent children. *Journal of Pediatric Psychology, 10,* 493–503.

Hill, B., & Singer, L. (1990). Speech and language development after infant tracheostomy. *Journal of Speech and Hearing Disorders, 55,* 15–20.

Hill, D.S. (1993). Coordinating a multidisciplinary discharge for the technology-dependent child based on parental needs. *Issues in Comprehensive Pediatric Nursing, 16,* 229–237.

Jayabose, S., Escobedo, V., Tugal, O., et al. (1992). Home chemotherapy for children with cancer. *Cancer, 69,* 574–579.

Kettrick, R.G., & Donar, M.E. (1985). The ventilator-dependent child: Medical and social care. *Critical Care: State of the Art, 6,* 1–38.

Kitchen, W.H., Ryan, M.M., & Rickards, A.L. (1987). A longitudinal study of very low-birthweight infants: IV. Impairments, health and distance growth to 14 years of age. *Australian Paediatrics Journal, 23,* 23211–23212.

Kurzner, S.I., Garg, M., Bautista, D.B., et al. (1988). Growth failure in infants with bronchopulmonary dysplasia: Nutrition and elevated resting metabolic expenditure. *Pediatrics, 81,* 379–384.

Levy, S.E. (1996). Nonpharmacologic management of disorders of behavior and attention. In A.J. Capute & P.J. Accardo (Eds.), *Developmental disabilities in infancy and childhood* (Vol. 2, pp. 451–457). Baltimore: Paul H. Brookes Publishing Co.

Lewis, C.C., Alford-Winston, A., Billy-Kornas, M., et al. (1992). Case management for children who are medically fragile/technology dependent. *Issues in Comprehensive Pediatric Nursing, 15,* 73–91.

Long, J.G., Philip, A.G., & Lucy, J.F. (1980). Excessive handling as a cause of hypoxemia. *Pediatrics, 65,* 203–207.

Luchi, J.M., Bennett, F.C., & Jackson, J.C. (1991). Predictors of neurodevelopmental outcome following bronchopulmonary dysplasia. *American Journal of Diseases of Children, 145,* 813–817.

Marin, O.E., Glassman, M.S., Schoen, B.T., et al. (1994). Safety and efficacy of percutaneous endoscopic gastrostomy in children. *American Journal of Gastroenterology, 89,* 357–361.

McGowan, J.S., Bleile, K., Fus, L., et al. (1993). Communication disorders. In K. Bleile (Ed.), *The care of children with long-term tracheotomies* (pp. 113–137). San Diego: Singular Publishing Group, Inc.

Michaelis, C.A., Warzak, W.J., Stanek, K., et al. (1992). Parental and professional perceptions of problems associated with long term pediatric home tube feeding. *Journal of the American Dietetic Association, 92,* 1235–1238.

Miller, D.H., Ruley, J., & Bock, G.H. (1995). Current status of pediatric home peritoneal dialysis training in the United States. *Advances in Peritoneal Dialysis, 11,* 274–276.

Miller, T.L., Awnetwant, E.L., & Evans, S. (1995). Gastrostomy tube supplementation for HIV-infected children. *Pediatrics, 96,* 696–702.

Millner, B.N. (1991). Technology-dependent children in New York state. *Bulletin of the New York Academy of Medicine, 67,* 131–142.

Murray, J.E. (1989). Payment mechanisms for pediatric home care. *Caring, 10,* 33–35.

Office of Technology Assessment. (1987). *Technology-dependent children: Hospital versus home care: A technical memorandum* (DHHS Publication No. TM-H-38). Washington, DC: U.S. Government Printing Office.

Omnibus Budget Reconciliation Act of 1990, PL 101-508, 5 U.S.C. § 4712 *et seq.*

Owen, M.J. (1991). What has the Social Security administration done for you lately? *Exceptional Parent, 21*(4), 40–42.

Palfrey, J.S., Haynie, M., Porter, S., et al. (1994). Prevalence of medical technology assistance among children in Massachusetts in 1987 and 1990. *Public Health Reports, 109*(2), 226–233.

Palfrey, J.S., Walker, D.K., Haynie, M., et al. (1991). Technology's children: Report of a statewide census of children dependent on medical supports. *Pediatrics, 87,* 611–618.

Parette, H.P., Jr. (1993). High-risk infant case management and assistive technology: Funding and family enabling perspectives. *Maternal–Child Nursing Journal, 21,* 53–64.

Patterson, J.M., Leonard, B.J., & Titus, J.C. (1992). Home care for medically fragile children: Impact on family health and well-being. *Journal of Developmental and Behavioral Pediatrics, 13,* 248–255.

Perrin, J.M., & Stein, R.E. (1991). Reinterpreting disability: Changes in Supplemental Security Income for children. *Pediatrics, 88,* 1047–1051.

Petr, C.G., Murdock, B., & Chapin, R. (1995). Home care for children dependent on medical technology: The family perspective. *Social Work in Health Care, 21,* 5–22.

Pilmer, S. (1994) Prolonged mechanical ventilation in children. *Pediatric Clinics of North America, 41,* 473–512.

Poets, C.F., & Southall, D.P. (1994). Noninvasive monitoring of oxygenation in infants and children: Practical considerations and areas of concern. *Pediatrics, 93,* 737–746.

Puntis, J.W. (1995). Home parenteral nutrition. *Archives of Disease in Childhood, 72,* 186–190.

Reichle, J., & Wacker, D.P. (1993). *Communication and language intervention series: Vol. 3. Communicative alternatives to challenging behavior: Integrating functional assessment and intervention strategies.* Baltimore: Paul H. Brookes Publishing Co.

Reimers, K.J., Carlson, S.J., & Lombard, K.A. (1992). Nutritional management of infants with bronchopulmonary dysplasia. *Nutrition in Clinical Practice, 7,* 127–132.

Richardson, M., Student, E., O'Boyle, D., et al. (1992). Establishment of a state-supported, specialized home care program for children with complex health-care needs. *Issues in Comprehensive Pediatric Nursing, 15,* 93–122.

Rogers, B.T., Arvedson, J., Msall, M., et al. (1993). Hypoxemia during oral feeding of children with severe cerebral palsy. *Developmental Medicine and Child Neurology, 35,* 3–10.

Silvestri, J.M., Weese-Mayer, D.E., & Kenny, A.S. (1994). Prolonged cardiorespiratory monitoring of children more than twelve months of age: Characterization of events and approach to discontinuation. *Journal of Pediatrics, 125,* 51–56.

Sindel, B.D., Maisels, M.J., & Ballantine, T.V. (1989). Gastroesophageal reflux to the proximal esophagus in infants with bronchopulmonary dysplasia. *American Journal of Diseases of Children, 143,* 1103–1106.

Singer, L.T., Kercsmar, C., Legris, G., et al. (1989). Developmental sequelae of long-term infant tracheostomy. *Developmental Medicine and Child Neurology, 31,* 224–230.

Southall, D.P., Samuels, M.P., & Talbert, D.G. (1990). Recurrent cyanotic episodes with severe arterial hypoxemia and intrapulmonary shunting: A mechanism for sudden death. *Archives of Disease in Childhood, 65,* 953–961.

Starrett, A.L. (1991). Growth in developmental disabilities. In A.J. Capute & P.J. Accardo (Eds.), *Developmental disabilities in infancy and childhood* (pp. 181–187). Baltimore: Paul H. Brookes Publishing Co.

Stutts, A.L. (1994). Selected outcomes of technology dependent children receiving home care and prescribed child care services. *Pediatric Nursing, 20,* 501–505, 507.

Sullivan v. Zebley, 110 S.CT. 885, February 20, 1990.

Tammela, O.K., & Kovisto, M.E. (1992). A 1–year follow-up of low birth weight infants with and without bronchopulmonary dysplasia: Health, growth, clinical lung disease, cardiovascular and neurological sequelae. *Early Human Development, 30,* 109–120.

Teague, B.R., Fleming, J.W., Castle, A., et al. (1993). "High-tech" home care for children with chronic health conditions: A pilot study. *Journal of Pediatric Nursing, 8,* 226–232.

The Technology-Related Assistance for Individuals with Disabilities Act of 1988, PL 100-407, 29 U.S.C. § 2201 *et seq.*

Trompeter, R.S. (1990). Renal transplantation. *Archives of Disease in Childhood, 65,* 143–146.

Watson, A.R. (1995). Strategies to support families of children with end-stage renal failure. *Pediatric Nephrology, 9,* 628–631.

32 Rehabilitation Interventions

Physical Therapy and Occupational Therapy

Lisa A. Kurtz
Susan E. Harryman

Upon completion of this chapter, the reader will:

- recognize the theoretical principles guiding the practices of physical therapy and occupational therapy
- be familiar with some of the common approaches to rehabilitation intervention, including neurodevelopmental therapy, sensory integration, orthotics, and nonmedical assistive technology

Children with physical disabilities or significant developmental delays often benefit from physical and occupational therapy interventions designed to promote the child's integration into the mainstream of society.

A variety of intervention options are available. Therapy may be provided on an individual, group, or consultative basis. It may be delivered in hospital, school, home, or community settings. It may be required daily or on a consultative basis. For example, an early intervention program with frequent physical and occupational therapy is often beneficial for the infant with cerebral palsy; during this period, the child will undergo rapid developmental changes while his or her parents are first learning to cope with their child's impairments. Once the child enters school, therapy may decrease in frequency and assume a more consultative role around the child's specific educational needs. However, the child may periodically benefit from additional short-term therapy to address a specific functional concern, such as the need to improve ambulation following orthopedic surgery or the desire to learn adapted techniques for engaging in a new recreational interest.

FRAMES OF REFERENCE GUIDING PHYSICAL AND OCCUPATIONAL THERAPY

Although physical and occupational therapists receive similar basic educational preparation, tend to hold congruent philosophies regarding approaches to intervention, and may acquire similar levels of skill in the use of selected therapeutic procedures, there are important differences in their primary roles (Kurtz & Scull, 1993). Table 32.1 reviews some of the ways in which occupational and physical therapists might approach similar goals from different perspectives.

Pediatric physical therapy focuses on evaluating and treating sensorimotor development, musculoskeletal alignment, cardiopulmonary status, and neurobehavioral organization in children with physical disabilities or developmental delays that place them at risk for decreased functional mobility or for qualitative problems with mobility or postural control (Heriza & Sweeney, 1994). Pediatric occupational therapy also addresses sensorimotor development and neurobehavioral organization, as well as functional mobility, perceptual maturation, and psychosocial adjustment of children who have or are at risk for disabilities. Occupational therapists particularly focus on those disabilities that limit the child's ability to develop the necessary skills and attitudes for independence in self-care, play, and school performance (the primary "occupations" of childhood) (O'Brien, 1993). Although play is the therapy medium of choice for most young children, both occupational and physical therapy incorporate a wide variety of other modalities, including exercise, sensory stimulation, splinting or casting, use of adaptive aids and equipment, and behavior training.

The nature of rehabilitation services has changed dramatically since the early 1900s, when occupational and physical therapy were in their formative years. Early models for rehabilitation were based in hospital settings and focused on the diagnosis and corrective treatment of pathological conditions resulting from disease or impairment (McNary, 1947; Weiss & Betts, 1967).

Table 32.1.   Differences between physical and occupational therapy approaches

(Re)habilitation objective	Typical OT emphasis	Typical PT emphasis
Maintain or increase range of motion, muscle strength	Focus on upper body, primarily using purposeful activities that are selected according to their physical demands	Focus on lower body, primarily using active or passive exercise
Recommend need for assistive technology	Adapted toys, school materials, computers, self-care aids	Wheelchairs, ambulation aids, transfer equipment
Splinting and casting to 1) maintain or increase range of motion or 2) promote functional movement	Upper extremity	Lower extremity
Train in functional skills needed for daily living	Dressing, eating, toileting, personal hygiene	Ambulation, managing transfers and other mobility demands
Promote developmental progression of skills	Fine motor, adaptive, personal-social domains	Gross motor domain
Promote environmental accessibility	Adaptations to home and school environments including 1) organizing work/play areas for efficiency and 2) creating a sensory millieu that promotes attention and information processing	Reducing architectural barriers that limit full access and mobility including 1) ramps/lifts and 2) car seats or other transportation devices

Since then, interventions have focused on helping the child and family achieve confidence and independence with personally meaningful daily activities (Haley, Coster, & Binda-Sundberg, 1994). This requires therapy to be family centered, culturally relevant, and community based.

This shift in philosophy has led to a focus on the definition and measurement of function in childhood. In 1980, the World Health Organization (WHO) introduced a three-dimensional model for conceptualizing disability and functioning that has been widely recognized in the rehabilitation literature. In 1993, the National Center for Medical Rehabilitation Research (National Institutes of Health, 1993) expanded this model to include five dimensions. This newer model defines 1) *pathophysiology* as injury at the cellular level; 2) *impairment* as an abnormality of anatomical or physiological processes, such as muscle weakness or sensory loss; 3) *functional limitations* as limitations relating to the performance of daily activities, such as walking or self-care; 4) *disabilities* as functional limitations that interfere with participation in home, school, or community activities; and 5) *societal limitations* (disabilities, in the WHO model) as disabilities resulting from societal problems, such as architectural barriers or social misconceptions.

Many adaptations of this model have been proposed, including several that address the unique issues influencing the quality of life for children with disabilities (Braun & Granger, 1991; Coster & Haley, 1992; Heriza & Sweeney, 1994). Within this framework for defining disability, there are two major approaches to intervention: 1) *rehabilitation,* referring to interventions that are designed to restore functions lost through disease or injury or to help the child and family cope with the loss of function; and 2) *habilitation,* referring to strategies and interventions that help the child acquire new skills consistent with his or her potential and are particularly important for children with congenital delays or disabilities (Bramadatt & Melvin, 1987; Burkett, 1989). Both approaches are necessary for children whose disabilities occur during their formative years and may limit their ability to reach their full potential.

Guidelines for Referral

Referral to physical therapy is indicated whenever there is a known physical impairment, a reason to suspect a delay in gross motor development, or a qualitative impairment in postural or movement skills. Referral to occupational therapy is indicated whenever there is reason to suspect delay or qualitative impairment in the performance of daily tasks and routines, including self-care, play, social interaction, or the performance of school-related tasks (Committee on Children with Disabilities, 1996). Referral is recommended as soon as a problem is identified to help the family learn about the diagnosis, identify additional supportive services, and master child care practices that will promote development and prevent further complications. Depending on local regulations governing the practice of occupational and physical therapists, referral from a physician may be required prior to initiation of therapy.

(Re)habilitation Therapy in Early Intervention Programs

The role of occupational and physical therapists in early intervention programs covers a range of services, including screening for motor dysfunction, monitoring the development of children over time, suggesting specific neurodevelopmental management strategies to families, consulting with other members of the interdisciplinary team, and providing direct therapy. Specific goals may include teaching caregivers the appropriate techniques for handling and positioning. This permits the child to experience more flexibility in patterns of posture and movement and takes advantage of other developmental strengths. Generally, early intervention programs focus more on helping families adjust to their child's developmental delay or disability than on correcting the problems. Attention may be given to encouraging the development of a satisfying and nurturing relationship with the child as well as to learning practical methods for supporting the child's development (habilitation) in the natural environments of the home and community. Through the process of developing an individualized family service plan (IFSP), therapy goals are organized around the family's needs and priorities, taking into account the infant's unique abilities. Table 32.2 presents examples of how a family's goals for therapy might be expressed in an IFSP.

(Re)habilitation Therapy in the School

As the child enters school, he or she may be eligible for occupational or physical therapy services if they will allow the child to benefit from special education or gain access to a general education program. Therapists may fulfill multiple roles in support of the educational objectives for the student (Table 32.3).

A variety of service models may be used for implementing school-based therapy (American Occupational Therapy Association, 1989; Benson, 1993; Hanft & Place, in press; Rainforth, York, & Macdonald, 1992). *Direct service* implies that the therapist has frequent contact with

Table 32.2.   Examples of therapy goals for early intervention

Parent statement	IFSP goal(s)	Intervention	Criterion
"I want Karen to be able to get around on her own."	Karen will crawl using a reciprocal hand/knee pattern.	Provide neuro-developmental facilitation to promote proximal stability and weight shift in a quadruped position. Use strategically placed toys or other motivators directly in Karen's line of vision to encourage forward movement.	Karen will crawl reciprocally when placed in the correct position; she will move a distance of 3 feet at least one time during each scheduled PT session.
"We would like Rasheed to be able to play with his toys so he can be happier."	Rasheed will improve in his ability to visually direct and control his reach toward toys. Rasheed will use his hands to activate a Busy Box or simple cause-and-effect toy.	Provide corner seat with trunk harness to promote stability and scapular protraction during sitting. Provide resting hand splints to maintain range of motion. Provide several cause-and-effect toys that can be operated by having Rasheed activate a simple switch when strategically placed within his available reach.	When positioned in his corner seat, Rasheed will actively reach toward a jellybean switch and will apply sufficient force to activate a battery-operated toy in three of five trials.

Table 32.3.   Roles of therapists in school settings

- Promoting safe and efficient mobility
- Recommending classroom positioning to promote optimal postural control and function
- Modifying classroom materials and routines to improve attention and organization
- Treating specific perceptual and motor difficulties that interfere with academic achievement
- Providing assistance with self-care as related to such tasks as toileting or using the cafeteria
- Contributing to prevocational training

the student, either individually or in a group, typically at least once per week. It is often recommended for students with severe or newly acquired disabilities that limit school performance or for those who require consistent, hands-on therapy in order to meet educational objectives. *Monitoring* involves the development of an intervention plan that can be effectively carried out by the classroom teacher or other personnel. Infrequent direct contact by the therapist is required to establish the effectiveness of the intervention and to update and revise the plan based on the student's progress. *Consultation* refers to the sharing of specialized knowledge with other education team members to support the overall goals and objectives of the educational program. Consultation may be oriented toward the student (e.g., recommending an adaptation to sport equipment that allows a student to participate with peers in physical therapy); colleagues (e.g., providing in-service training to teachers regarding techniques for promoting independence in self-care skills); or the educational system (e.g., recommending environmental adaptations that allow all students with mobility limitations to have access to extracurricular activities). There is growing support for the provision of therapy in inclusive settings where interventions are carried out in the student's natural environment, in the presence of peers, and using the typical tasks and materials that are expected of other students (Case-Smith & Cable, 1996).

Unfortunately, children with disabilities who do not require special education (e.g., those with juvenile rheumatoid arthritis, spinal cord injuries) may be ineligible for physical or occupational therapy services under the Individuals with Disabilities Education Act (IDEA) of 1990, PL 101-476, even though therapy could support their progress in the educational setting. These children, however, may be eligible for special services and accommodations under other entitlements, including the Americans with Disabilities Act (ADA), PL 101-336; Section 504 of the Rehabilitation Act of 1973, PL 93-112; or state regulations governing education (Kalscheur, 1992). The practice of determining eligibility for occupational and physical therapy services varies among school systems as well as among individual schools within the same system. Furthermore, interpretation of the public laws that determine eligibility may change over time within a local school district. When children are not eligible for occupational and/or physical therapy services in school or are eligible for only limited services, families may seek supplemental therapy through hospital-based outpatient centers or private practices.

Assessment and Planning for Intervention

Initial assessment typically includes 1) an interview with the parent or other caregiver to determine any needs and concerns and 2) observation of the child at play or performing functional tasks. Therapists then clinically assess the child for muscle tone and strength, joint range of motion, sensory responses and perception, neurological maturation and organization, and social and behavior responses. Standardized tests of motor and adaptive development are also commonly administered. Depending on the specific diagnosis and the reason for referral, additional assessments may be appropriate.

The treatment plan will take into account results of these assessments as well as recommendations from all other people involved in the care of the child. The plan should address the model of intervention that will be used (e.g., individual, group, consultative); the optimal frequency of intervention; recommendations for special equipment or environmental adaptations; and the plan for parent or caregiver instruction. Goals should be developed for a specific time period with objective and measurable outcomes delineated. Periodically, the plan should be re-evaluated and revised as necessary

It is extremely important that the referring physician, the family, and all team members are in agreement with the plan. Also, because learning is enhanced by practice and repetition, parents, teachers, and all other caregivers need to understand how to reinforce the skills learned in therapy throughout the child's day. For example, opportunities for practice of a specific dressing skill, such as manipulating buttons, may exist during daily dressing routines at home as well as during school hours and play time.

SELECTED INTERVENTIONS

Neurodevelopmental Therapy

Neurodevelopmental therapy (NDT), based on the work of Drs. Karel and Berta Bobath, has been widely accepted and used by occupational and physical therapists in many countries, including the United States, since the 1960s (Bobath & Bobath, 1984). This treatment approach, based on a developmental model, emphasizes sensorimotor experience to facilitate the development of normal movement and postural responses and is most often used with young children diagnosed with cerebral palsy or other neurodevelopmental disorders.

NDT focuses on the use of therapeutic handling techniques that are designed to control abnormal patterns of movement while facilitating the development of more normal motor patterns. This allows the child to learn how to move through sensory feedback associated with active movement. Individualized handling techniques are selected according to the child's specific problems with muscle tone and control, cognitive abilities, and motivation to engage in tasks. As therapists incorporate recent information related to dynamic systems theory of motor control into their clinical practice, additional consideration is being given to the musculoskeletal system, cognition, environmental factors, motivation, task requirements, and practice effects—all of which are variables that can be manipulated to effect change in motor behavior (Campbell, 1994; Heriza, 1991). Caregivers are taught to incorporate these handling techniques into the child's daily routine, ensuring a functional approach to goal achievement as well as frequent practice of newly acquired skills (Figure 32.1) (Breslin, 1996; Darrah & Bartlett, 1995).

Other important outcomes of this approach include increased parental comfort with providing child care and improved learning as a result of allowing the child increased opportunities for spontaneous active movement and environmental exploration (Byarm, 1996). A number of research studies suggest that therapy incorporating a neurodevelopmental approach improves both the rate of motor development and the quality of motor control; however, some of these studies have been criticized for design flaws (Ottenbacher, Biocca, DeCremer, et al., 1986; Palisano, 1991; Stern & Gorga, 1988).

Figure 32.1.   This mother has learned that undressing her baby is easier when he is placed prone over her lap and his head is flexed. This position reduces excessive tone, allowing his limbs to move more freely.

Sensory Integration Therapy

Children with developmental disabilities including specific learning disabilities, attention-deficit/hyperactivity disorder, and pervasive developmental disorder (PDD) are commonly referred to therapists for evaluation and remediation of problems with motor coordination, self-care, handwriting, or the social isolation that may result from clumsiness and avoidance of playground activities or recreational sports.

Treatment approaches for this population are varied but commonly incorporate principles of sensory integration (SI) theory, based on the work of A. Jean Ayres (1979; Fisher, Murray, & Bundy, 1991). Ayres defined sensory integration as a normal developmental process involving the ability of the child's central nervous system to organize sensory feedback from the body and the environment in order to make successful adaptive responses. Problems with normal sensory integration are suggested when 1) the child exhibits difficulty with planning and execution of motor or behavior responses; 2) there is evidence of perceptual impairment, especially involving the tactile, proprioceptive, or visual systems; and 3) these problems are not attributable to overt brain damage or a specific visual or hearing impairment. SI therapy advocates the use of controlled sensory input to create a milieu that promotes the child's success in making adaptive responses to environmental challenges. Proponents of SI contend that therapy enhances neural organization leading to more mature learning and behavior patterns. Thus, rather than teaching specific functional skills, the goal of intervention is to enhance the brain's ability to learn. However, as with many other developmental interventions, there is limited scientific evidence to support its efficacy (Cermak & Henderson, 1989, 1990; Fallon, Mauer, & Neukirch, 1994; Ottenbacher, 1991). Sensory integration therapy requires frequent sessions (usually 2–3 times per week) and the use of a specially designed therapy area, making it difficult to provide within most school settings.

Many therapists recommend a holistic approach to intervention that combines SI therapy procedures with more traditional approaches to promoting skill development. For example, modification of classroom materials and routines to reduce motor challenges during school or homework assignments can help students with mild motor difficulties to focus their attention more effectively on the cognitive aspects of learning. Examples of such modification include providing a chair with armrests and a nonslip seat for the child who fidgets in his or her seat, a pencil grip for the child who has an immature grasp and fatigues during writing, or page separators for the child who is slow to locate a particular assignment in a workbook. Perceptual-motor interventions, usually involving the teaching and practice of specific motor skills, may help to improve the child's coordination for selected tasks, enhance self-esteem, and increase motivation for participation in physical education or recreational sports, although the effect on academic achievement has yet to be demonstrated (Schaffer, Law, Polatajko, et al., 1989). Group therapy organized around a common recreational interest may focus on preventing or minimizing the negative social consequences frequently associated with learning disabilities, including problems with self-esteem and social and behavioral interactions with peers (Tupper & Miesner, 1992; Williamson, 1993).

Splinting and Bracing

Orthotic management refers to the use of splints or braces to improve motor function. It may be used as an isolated intervention or as an adjunct to occupational and/or physical therapy. Splints may be either static (rigid) or dynamic (with moveable parts). They may be used to serve a variety of purposes, including 1) to support weak muscles, 2) to increase or maintain muscle length needed for mobility, 3) to control involuntary movement, 4) to immobilize a body part, or 5) to serve as a base of support for the attachment of toys or self-care devices (Blanchet & McGee, 1996).

Lower extremity orthotics, such as molded plastic ankle-foot orthoses (MAFOs), are worn inside the shoes. They are commonly used to enhance ambulatory function, for example, in children with spastic diplegia. Children with significant lower extremity weakness, such as those with meningomyelocele, may require more extensive orthoses that support the knees and/or hips to achieve ambulatory skills.

Static resting hand splints are often used to maintain muscle length and prevent the development of secondary musculoskeletal deformity in children with cerebral palsy. Their use during periods of inactivity, such as sleep, may promote increased flexibility and improved hand function when they are removed. Other static splints provide support to the hand in positions that improve function during purposeful activity. For example, a splint that supports the wrist in slight extension may make it easier for the child to oppose the thumb to the fingers, allowing easier grasp of objects. Dynamic hand splints may be designed to selectively increase muscle strength and/or control patterns of movement. Figure 32.2 presents some common examples of splints used by physical and occupational therapists.

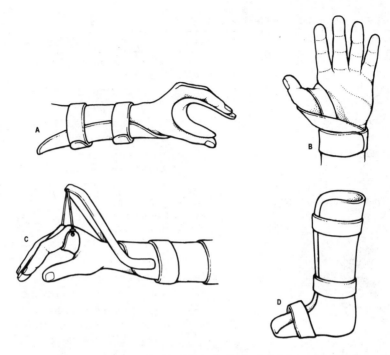

Figure 32.2. a) Resting hand splint: prevents deformity by maintaining a flaccid or spastic hand in a functional position to prevent deformity. b) Soft thumb loop: used for mild spasticity to allow better function. Decreases thumb flexion and adduction in a spastic hand through use of a reflex inhibiting pattern; allows use of hand for function. c) Dynamic wrist extension splint: provides assistance to weak wrist extension muscles. d) Molded ankle-foot orthosis: maintains ankle range of motion and prevents motion during gait. (From Kurtz, L.A., Dowrick, P.W., Levy, S.E., & Batshaw, M.L. [Eds.]. [1996]. *The Children's Seashore House handbook of developmental disabilities: Resources for interdisciplinary care* [p. 468]. Gaithersburg, MD: Aspen Publishers, Inc.; reprinted by permission.)

Assistive Technology

Approximately 2% of children require some type of nonmedical assistive technology (Millner, 1991). Assistive technology is a broad term used to describe a range of devices and services that help children with disabilities function more independently. This can allow them to be included in a full range of social experiences, thus improving their quality of life. Technology is recognized by therapists as an important component of the pediatric rehabilitation program. Assistive technology applications may be as simple as an enlarged spoon handle to compensate for a weak grasp, as commonplace as a wheelchair designed to promote mobility within the environment, or as futuristic as complex computerized systems for augmentative communication and environmental control. It may include products that are purchased commercially, modified, or custom-made according to the specific needs of the user. Table 32.4 presents some of the common applications of technology used for children.

Even very young children may benefit from early training in the use of technology. For example, infants as young as 6–7 months may be capable of understanding the cause-and-effect

Table 32.4.   Selected assistive technology devices

Functional application	Examples
Mobility	Wheelchairs (manual or power) Scooters Ambulation devices Myoelectric prostheses
Environmental control	Switch-operated lights or appliances Canine companions
Transportation safety	Adapted car seats Wheelchair restraints Hand controls for automobiles
Positioning/postural support	Sidelyers Corner seats Standing devices Cut-out tables to accommodate wheelchairs
Communication	Language boards Synthesized speech Alternative computer keyboards
Daily living skills	Velcro closures for clothing Automated feeding devices Hand-held shower head Long handled comb
Educational aids	Automatic page turners Calculators and spell-checkers Adapted pencil grips
Environmental accessibility	Ramps Grab bars Automatic door openers Adjusted-height counters and cabinets
Recreation	Hand-powered tricycle Switch-operated toys Sports wheelchairs
Vision aids	Magnifiers Large print or talking books Braille readers

relationships necessary to operate a single-switch computer program (Swinth, Anson, & Dietz, 1993). Children as young as 17 months can be taught to use powered mobility, allowing a much greater potential to explore and manipulate the environment (Neeley & Neeley, 1993). Early intervention programs attempt to teach young children how to access devices that promote their independence, because children who are able to enter school with these technologies in place may be able to achieve greater success in general education settings (Butler, 1988).

A number of pieces of federal legislation have improved access to assistive technology devices and services for children and have provided funding to support not only the purchase or lease of equipment but also a range of services to ensure success with their use. These include

1) evaluation of the child's technological needs, 2) maintenance and repair of equipment, 3) training in use of the devices, and 4) coordination of technology with other therapy services. PL 100-407, the Technology-Related Assistance for Individuals with Disabilities Act of 1988, created language to define assistive technology and provided funding for states to design technology-related assistance for all citizens with disabilities. Further provisions were defined under the ADA. IDEA requires schools to specifically address the special education student's assistive technology needs. If an evaluation indicates that a student requires assistive technology to benefit from special education, it must be provided as an integral part of the individualized education program (IEP). This means that schools hold the legal responsibility for evaluation, device selection and acquisition, and training in the use of educationally relevant assistive devices. It should be noted, however, that when assistive devices are recommended for purposes that are not related to educational objectives, it is often necessary to use creative strategies for funding equipment. Some examples of potential funding sources include Medical Assistance, private foundations or donors, and durable medical equipment riders on private insurance policies.

OUTCOMES MEASUREMENT

The importance of identifying valid, sensitive, and practical tools that can be used to measure and document the outcome of rehabilitative care cannot be overemphasized (Campbell, 1996). In the changing health care climate, rehabilitation professionals are under increasing pressure to identify creative alternatives for delivering high-quality care at lower cost. Outcomes measurement can be extremely useful in demonstrating the validity of various therapeutic regimens. Use of consultative versus direct service models, group versus individual therapy, cross-training of providers from different disciplines in selected aspects of intervention, and nonlicensed aides as therapy extenders are emerging practices that are under debate by the health care industry.

Accurate and appropriate measures of functional outcome are needed to compare the relative benefits of these various approaches to rehabilitation. The most commonly used tools for measurement of outcome focus on functional changes that may occur during the course of rehabilitation. Examples of pediatric functional assessment tools in common use include the Pediatric Evaluation of Disability Inventory (PEDI) (Coster & Haley, 1992) and the Uniform Data Set for Medical Rehabilitation for Children (WeeFIM) (Msall, DiGaudio, & Duffy, 1993).

Although progress has been made in the area of outcomes measurement, there remain many unresolved problems. Quality rehabilitation strives for more than the reduction of functional impairment. Ultimately, the goal of rehabilitative intervention is to prevent or ameliorate social disadvantages that may develop as consequences of the underlying impairment (Christiansen, 1993). Therefore, outcome measures need to demonstrate not only that gains made during therapy can be sustained over time and in the child's natural environment, but also that they result in an improved quality of life for the child and family (Mayhan, 1994; Smith & Illig, 1995). For example, children with cerebral palsy frequently receive physical and occupational therapy to improve mobility skills. One typical outcome measure, easy to obtain during therapy, is increased joint range of motion as measured by goniometry. However, one must question the real value of this therapy unless mobility gains can be easily maintained by parents or other caregivers at home; prevent the need for more invasive orthopedic or other medical intervention; reduce the costs for special education and related services; or promote access to social, educational, or recreational experiences that are desired by the child and family. Therapists must be increasingly prepared to demonstrate that recommended interventions are appropriate (i.e., address the needs as stated by the consumer), effective (i.e., achieve targeted outcomes), and efficient (i.e., at the lowest cost possible).

KIA: A SCHOOL-AGE CHILD WITH CEREBRAL PALSY AND ASSISTIVE TECHNOLOGY NEEDS

Kia was born at 30 weeks' gestation and was diagnosed with periventricular leukomalacia (see Chapter 7) shortly after birth. Physical therapy intervention began in the neonatal intensive care unit in the form of consultation to the unit staff regarding positioning. Also, in preparation for discharge home, the family began to learn handling and positioning techniques that would facilitate optimal postural control. By 6 months of age, Kia was actively engaged with her environment, playing with toys and interacting with people. The muscle tone in her legs, however, was noted to be increased relative to the tone in her arms, and she was unable to sit alone. A diagnosis of spastic diplegia was suspected. With intensive outpatient physical therapy, including a home management program, bilateral foot orthoses, and adaptive seating, Kia learned to assume and maintain a sitting position and crawl on her hands and knees. At 3 years of age, she began to walk independently with canes. Shortly thereafter, she was enrolled in an inclusive preschool program in which she began occupational therapy with an emphasis on learning dressing skills. At this time, a power scooter was recommended that provided more efficient mobility to explore an expanded environment. Because she had typical intellectual development and was not a candidate for special education, Kia was ineligible for therapy in school once she entered kindergarten. Her family was able to secure private therapy services, however, whenever they felt a need for further advice or consultation.

At age 6, Kia underwent orthopedic surgery to lengthen lower extremity muscles. A period of intensive physical therapy to improve her hip and knee control followed. Shortly thereafter, she became a community ambulator without the use of canes, although she continued to use a manual wheelchair for extended trips. In the third grade, an occupational therapist was consulted regarding her handwriting skills, and a computer was recommended to allow her to complete school assignments in a more efficient manner.

Kia has continued her schooling, attending general education classes with good grades, and has been an active participant in extracurricular programs through middle school. She is now ready to enter high school and is again considering a power scooter to improve efficiency in mobility within her expanded school setting as well as to allow her more freedom in the community with her peers. She continues to be monitored in a tertiary care center several times a year by both occupational and physical therapists in order to address current and/or potential problems and adjust her therapeutic management programs as needed.

GEORGE: A PRESCHOOL-AGE CHILD WITH PDD

Although George was a healthy baby whose early development seemed typical, he had some unusual habits including a fascination for letters and numbers, extreme tantrums, and unusual food preferences. At age 3, George's parents sought advice from a developmental pediatrician, who diagnosed the problem as pervasive developmental disorder (PDD) and recommended enrolling

George in an early intervention program. With intellectual functioning measuring in the low-average range, George progressed fairly well, although he continued to have limited play interests, delayed self-care skills, and frequent tantrums. At the age of 4½, he was referred to occupational therapy, where evaluation revealed evidence of sensory integrative dysfunction including severe tactile defensiveness and poor motor planning skills. Private occupational therapy combining sensory integrative and behavioral interventions was recommended and continued twice weekly for a period of 3 months, with active parent involvement. A typical session proceeded as follows:

1. George is assisted to remove his outer clothes, go to the toilet, and wash his hands, using behavioral intervention strategies to ensure his compliance.
2. Next, George is given a choice of two play activities that incorporate firm touch or proprioceptive input. Firm touch usually produces a calming effect and helps to reduce his tactile defensiveness and distractibility. For example, he may pretend to be a "hot dog" by wrapping himself in a foam mat (the "roll"), then have his mother apply make-believe mustard, relish, and onions, giving him a squeeze between each "condiment." He more willingly allows hand-over-hand instruction for subsequent tasks after this game.
3. George is next engaged in gross motor play selected to promote body awareness and motor planning, such as following a "map" that helps him to visualize the sequence of movements needed to maneuver an obstacle course.
4. Again using behavioral strategies, George is assisted in putting away his toys, washing his hands, and donning his coat, thus ending the session.

After 3 months of therapy, George was independent in most areas of self-care and showed a greater range of play interests. Although he continued to be tactilely defensive, his parents could anticipate potentially distressing situations and modify both the environment and their expectations accordingly to avoid tantrums. At age 5, George was enrolled as a special education student in an inclusive kindergarten class where consultative occupational therapy was included in his IEP. His therapist regularly visited his class, offering recommendations for improving school performance, such as using a classroom chair with arms and a nonslip seat to prevent squirming and substituting a glue stick for the typical classroom paste that George found irritating to touch.

SUMMARY

Pediatric occupational and physical therapy strive to minimize the effects of motor impairment, to promote full inclusion into the mainstream of society, and to enhance the overall quality of life for children with disabilities and their families. Although the two disciplines may overlap in certain knowledge and skills, there are important differences in their primary roles and methods of care. A holistic approach to (re)habilitation incorporates many different options for intervention selected according to therapeutic significance, as well as the family's unique needs and priorities. Examples of intervention methodology may include exercise, sensory stimulation, environmental adaptation, positioning, NDT, SI, behavior therapy, orthotics, or assistive technology. Some of these (splinting, exercise) are widely accepted, while others (NDT, SI) are in need of further research to support clinical efficacy.

REFERENCES

American Occupational Therapy Association. (1989). *Guidelines for occupational therapy services in school systems.* Rockville, MD: Author.

Americans with Disabilities Act (ADA) of 1990, PL 101-336, 42 U.S.C. § 12101 *et seq.*

Ayres, A.J. (1979). *Sensory integration and the child.* Los Angeles: Western Psychological Services.

Badell, A. (1992). Myelodysplasia. In G.E. Molnar (Ed.), *Pediatric rehabilitation* (pp. 222–253). Baltimore: Williams & Wilkins Co.

Behrman, M.M., Jones, J.K., & Wilds, M.L. (1989). Technology intervention for very young children with disabilities. *Infants and Young Children, 1*(4), 66–77.

Benson, S. (1993). Collaborative teaming: A model for occupational therapists working in inclusive schools. *Developmental Disabilities Special Interest Section Newsletter, 16*(4), 1–4. Rockville, MD: American Occupational Therapy Association.

Blanchet, D., & McGee, S.M. (1996). Principles of splint design and use. In L.A. Kurtz, P.W. Dowrick, S.E. Levy, & M.L. Batshaw (Eds.), *The Children's Seashore House handbook on developmental disabilities: Resources for interdisciplinary care* (pp. 465–480). Gaithersburg, MD: Aspen Publishers, Inc.

Bleakney, D.A., & Donohoe, M. (1994a). Arthrogryposis multiplex congenita. In S. Campbell (Ed.), *Physical therapy for children* (pp. 261–278). Philadelphia: W.B. Saunders.

Bleakney, D.A., & Donohoe, M. (1994b). Osteogenesis imperfecta. In S. Campbell (Ed.), *Physical therapy for children* (pp. 279–298). Philadelphia: W.B. Saunders.

Bly, L. (1991). A historical and current view of the basis of NDT. *Pediatric Physical Therapy, 3,* 131–135.

Bobath, K., & Bobath, B. (1984). Neuro-developmental treatment. In D. Scrutton (Ed.), *Management of the motor disorders of children with cerebral palsy: Clinics in developmental medicine* (No. 90, pp. 6–18). Philadelphia: J.B. Lippincott.

Bramadatt, I.J., & Melvin, C.L. (1987). Habilitation: Application of a concept. *Clinical Nurse Specialist, 1*(2), 76–79.

Braun, S.L., & Granger, C.V. (1991). A practical approach to functional assessment in pediatrics. *Occupational Therapy Practice, 2*(2), 46–51.

Breslin, D.M. (1996). Motor-learning theory and the neurodevelopmental treatment approach: A comparative analysis. *Occupational Therapy in Health Care, 10*(1), 25–40.

Burkett, K.W. (1989). Trends in pediatric rehabilitation. *Nursing Clinics of North America, 24,* 239–255.

Butler, C. (1988). High tech tots: Technology for mobility, manipulation, communication, and learning in early childhood. *Infants and Young Children, 1*(2), 66–73.

Butler, C. (1991). Augmentative mobility: Why do it? *Physical Medicine and Rehabilitation Clinics of North America, 2*(4), 801–815.

Butler, C., Okamoto, G.A., & McKay, T.M. (1983). Powered mobility for very young disabled children. *Developmental Medicine and Child Neurology, 25,* 472–474.

Byarm, L.E. (1996). Neurodevelopmental therapy. In L.A. Kurtz, P.W. Dowrick, S.E. Levy, & M.L. Batshaw (Eds.), *The Children's Seashore House handbook on developmental disabilities: Resources for interdisciplinary care* (pp. 249–259). Gaithersburg, MD: Aspen Publishers, Inc.

Campbell, S.K. (1994). The child's development of functional movement. In S. Campbell (Ed.), *Physical therapy for children* (pp. 3–37). Philadelphia: W.B. Sauders.

Campbell, S.K. (1996). Quantifying the effects of interventions for movement disorders resulting from cerebral palsy. *Journal of Child Neurology, 11*(1), S61–S70.

Case-Smith, J., & Cable, J. (1996). Perceptions of occupational therapists regarding service delivery models in school-based practice. *The Occupational Therapy Journal of Research, 16*(1), 23–44.

Cermak, S., & Henderson, A. (1989). The efficacy of sensory integration procedures: Part I. *Sensory Integration Quarterly, 17*(3), 1–5.

Cermak, S., & Henderson, A. (1990). The efficacy of sensory integration procedures: Part II. *Sensory Integration Quarterly, 18*(1), 1–5.

Christiansen, C. (1993). Continued challenges of functional assessment in rehabilitation: Recommended changes. *American Journal of Occupational Therapy, 47*(3), 258–259.

Committee on Children with Disabilities. (1996). The role of the pediatrician in prescribing therapy services for children with motor disabilities. *Pediatrics, 98,* 308–310.

Cook, A., & Hussey, S.M. (1995). *Assistive technologies: Principles and practice.* St. Louis: C.V. Mosby.

Coster, W.J., & Haley, S.M. (1992). Conceptualization and measurement of disablement in infants and young children. *Infants and Young Children, 4*(4), 11–22.

Craig, S.E., & Haggart, A.G. (1994). Including all children: The ADA's challenge to early intervention. *Infants and Young Children, 7*(2), 15–19.

Cusick, B. (1990). *Progressive casting and splinting in children with neuromotor dysfunction.* Tucson, AZ: Therapy Skill Builders.

Darrah, J., & Bartlett, D. (1995). Dynamic systems theory and management of children with cerebral palsy: Unresolved issues. *Infants and Young Children, 8*(1), 52–59.

David, K.S. (1994). Developmental coordination disorders. In S. Campbell (Ed.), *Physical therapy for children* (pp. 425–458). Philadelphia: W.B. Saunders.

DeGangi, G.A., & Royeen, C.B. (1994). Current practice among Neurodevelopmental Treatment Association Members. *American Journal of Occupational Therapy, 48*(9), 803–809.

Dunn, W., & DeGangi, G. (1992). Sensory integration and neurodevelopmental treatment for educational programming. In C.B. Royeen (Ed.), *AOTA self-study series: Classroom applications for school-based practice.* Rockville, MD: American Occupational Therapy Association, Inc.

Education for All Handicapped Children Act of 1975, PL 94-142, 20 U.S.C. § 1400 *et seq.*

Education of the Handicapped Act Amendments of 1986, PL 99-457, 20 U.S.C. § 1400 *et seq.*

Fallon, M.A., Mauer, D.M., & Neukirch, M. (1994). The effectiveness of sensory integration activities on language processing in preschoolers who are sensory and language impaired. *Infant–Toddler Intervention, 4*(3), 235–243.

Fisher, A.G., Murray, E.A., & Bundy, A.C. (1991). *Sensory integration: Theory and practice.* Philadelphia: F.A. Davis.

Gorga, D. (1989). Occupational therapy treatment practices with infants in early intervention. *American Journal of Occupational Therapy, 43*(11), 731–736.

Haley, S.M., Cioffi, M.I., Lewin, J.E., et al. (1990). Motor dysfunction in children and adolescents after traumatic brain injury. *Journal of Head Trauma Rehabilitation, 5,* 77–90.

Haley, S.M., Coster, W.J., & Binda-Sundberg, K. (1994). Measuring physical disablement: The contextual challenge. *Physical Therapy, 74*(5), 443–451.

Hanft, B. (1988). The changing environment of early intervention services: Implications for practice. *American Journal of Occupational Therapy, 42*(11), 26–33.

Hanft, B., & Place, P. (in press). *The consulting therapist: A guide for physical and occupational therapists in the schools.* Tucson, AZ: Therapy Skill Builders.

Harris, S.R., & Shea, A.M. (1991). Down syndrome. In S.K. Campbell (Ed.), *Pediatric neurologic physical therapy* (pp. 131–168). New York: Churchill-Livingstone.

Heriza, C.B. (1991). Motor development: Traditional and contemporary theories. In M.J. Lister (Ed.), *Contemporary control of motor problems: Proceedings of the Step II Conference* (pp. 99–126). Alexandria, VA: Foundations for Physical Therapy.

Heriza, C.B., & Sweeney, J.K. (1994). Pediatric physical therapy: Part I. Practice, scope, scientific basis, and theoretical foundation. *Infants and Young Children, 7*(2), 20–32.

Hinderer, K.A., Hinderer, S.R., & Shurtleff, D.B. (1994). Myelodysplasia. In S.K. Campbell (Ed.), *Physical therapy for children* (pp. 571–620). Philadelphia: W.B. Saunders.

Individuals with Disabilities Education Act (IDEA) of 1990, PL 101-476, 20 U.S.C. § 1400 *et seq.*

Kalscheur, J.A. (1992). Benefits of the Americans with Disabilities Act of 1990 for children and adolescents with disabilities. *American Journal of Occupational Therapy, 46*(5), 419–426.

Knuttson, L.M., & Clark, D.E. (1991). Orthotic devices for ambulation in children with cerebral palsy and myelomeningocele. *Physical Therapy, 71,* 947–960.

Kurtz, L.A., Dowrick, P.W., Levy, S.E., & Batshaw, M.L. (Eds.). (1996). *The Children's Seashore House handbook of developmental disabilities: Resources for interdisciplinary care.* Gaithersburg, MD: Aspen Publishers, Inc.

Kurtz, L.A., & Scull, S.A. (1993). Rehabilitation for developmental disabilities. *Pediatric Clinics of North America, 40*(3), 629–643.

Leach, J.C. (1994). Orthopedic conditions. In S.K. Campbell (Ed.), *Physical therapy for children* (pp. 353–382). Philadelphia: W.B. Saunders.

Mayhan, Y.D. (1994). The importance of outcomes measurement in managed care. *American Occupational Therapy Association, Administration and Management Special Interest Section Newsletter, 10*(4), 2–4.

McDonald, C.M., Jaffe, K.M., Mosca, V.S., et al. (1991). Ambulatory outcome of children with myelomeningocele: Effect of lower extremity muscle strength. *Developmental Medicine and Child Neurology, 33,* 482–490.

McEwen, I. (1994). Mental retardation. In S.K. Campbell (Ed.), *Physical therapy for children* (pp. 459–488). Philadelphia: W.B. Saunders.

McNary, H. (1947). The scope of occupational therapy. In H. Willard & C.S. Spackman (Eds.), *Occupational therapy.* Philadelphia: J.B. Lippincott.

Millner, B.N. (1991). Technology-dependent children in New York state. *Bulletin of the New York Academy of Medicine, 67,* 131–142.

Molnar, G.E. (1992). Cerebral palsy. In G.E. Molnar (Ed.), *Pediatric rehabilitation* (pp. 481–533). Baltimore: Williams & Wilkins Co.

Msall, M.E., DiGaudio, K.M., & Duffy, L.C. (1993). Use of functional assessment on children with developmental disabilities. *Physical Medicine and Rehabilitation Clinics of North America, 4*(3), 517–527.

National Information Center for Children and Youth with Disabilities. (1991). Related services for school-aged children with disabilities. *NICHCY News Digest, 1*(2).

National Institutes of Health. (1993). *Research plan for the National Center for Rehabilitation Research* (NIH Publication No. 93-3509). Bethesda, MD: Author.

Neeley, R.A., & Neeley, P.A. (1993). The relationship between powered mobility and early learning in young children with physical disabilities. *Infant–Toddler Intervention, 3*(2), 85–91.

O'Brien, S.P. (1993). Human occupation frame of reference. In P. Kramer & J. Hinojosa (Eds.), *Frames of reference for pediatric occupational therapy* (pp. 307–350). Baltimore: Williams & Wilkins Co.

Olney, S.J., & Wright, M.J. (1994). Cerebral palsy. In S.K. Campbell (Ed.), *Physical therapy for children* (pp. 489–524). Philadelphia: W.B. Saunders.

Ottenbacher, K. (1991). Research in sensory integration: Empirical perceptions and progress. In A.G. Fisher, E.A. Murray, & A.C. Bundy (Eds.), *Sensory integration: Theory and practice* (pp. 387–399). Philadelphia: F.A. Davis.

Ottenbacher, K.J., Biocca, Z., DeCremer, G., et al. (1986). Quantitative analysis of the effectiveness of pediatric therapy: Emphasis on the neurodevelopmental approach. *Physical Therapy, 66*(7), 1095–1101.

Palisano, R.J. (1991). Research on the effectiveness of neurodevelopmental treatment. *Pediatric Physical Therapy, 3*(3), 143–148.

Parette, H.P., Hourcade, J.J., & VanBiervliet, A. (1993). Selection of appropriate technology for children with disabilities. *Teaching Exceptional Children, 25*(3), 18–22.

Phillips, W.E., & Spotts, M.L. (1994). Medicolegal issues in the United States. In S.K. Campbell (Ed.), *Physical therapy for children* (pp. 895–912). Philadelphia: W.B. Saunders.

Rainforth, B., & York-Barr, J. (1997). *Collaborative teams for students with severe disabilities: Integrating therapy and educational services* (2nd ed.). Baltimore: Paul H. Brookes Publishing Co.

Rainforth, B., York, J., & Macdonald, C. (1992). *Collaborative teams for students with severe disabilities: Integrating therapy and educational services.* Baltimore: Paul H. Brookes Publishing Co.

Rehabilitation Act of 1973, PL 93-112, 29 U.S.C. § 701 *et seq.*

RESNA Technical Assistance Project. (1992). *Assistive technology and the Individualized Education Program,* Unpublished report. (Available from RESNA TA Project, 1101 Connecticut Avenue NW, Suite 700, Washington, DC 20036.)

Ryan, K.D., Pioski, C., & Emans, J.B. (1991). Myelodysplasia: The musculoskeletal problem: Habilitation from infancy to adulthood. *Physical Therapy, 71,* 935–946.

Schaffer, R., Law, M., Polatajko, H., et al. (1989). A study of children with learning disabilities and sensorimotor problems, or let's not throw the baby out with the bathwater. *Physical and Occupational Therapy in Pediatrics, 9*(3), 101–117.

Scherzer, A.L., & Tscharnuter, I. (1990). *Early diagnosis and therapy in cerebral palsy: A primer on infant developmental problems.* New York: Marcel Dekker.

Scull, S.A. (1994). Juvenile rheumatoid arthritis. In S.K. Campbell (Ed.), *Physical therapy for children* (pp. 207–226). Philadelphia: W.B. Saunders.

Smith, P.M., & Illig, S.B. (1995). Measuring post-discharge functional outcomes. *Far Horizons, 2*(1), 1–2.

Stern, F.M., & Gorga, D. (1988). Neurodevelopmental treatment (NDT): Therapeutic intervention and its efficacy. *Infants and Young Children, 1,* 22–32.

Stuberg, W.A. (1994). Muscular dystrophy and spinal muscular atrophy. In S.K. Campbell (Ed.), *Physical therapy for children* (pp. 295–324). Philadelphia: W.B. Saunders.

Swinth, Y., Anson, D., & Dietz, J. (1993). Single-switch computer access for infants and toddlers. *American Journal of Occupational Therapy, 47*(11), 1031–1038.

Tachdjian, M.O. (1990). Arthrogryposis multiplex congenita (multiple congenital contractures). In M.O. Tachdjian (Ed.), *Pediatric orthopedics* (pp. 2086–2114). Philadelphia: W.B. Saunders.

Technology-Related Assistance for Individuals with Disabilities Act of 1988, PL 100-407, 29 U.S.C. § 2201 *et seq.*

Tupper, L.C., & Miesner, K.E.K. (1992, March). The role of occupational therapy with the learning disabled child. *Sensory Integration Quarterly, 20*(1), 8–9.

Weiss, H., & Betts, H.B. (1967). Methods of rehabilitation in children with neuromuscular disorders. *Pediatric Clinics of North America, 14*(4), 1009–1016.

Williamson, G.G. (1993). Enhancing the social competence of children with learning disabilities. *Sensory Integration Special Interest Section Newsletter, 16*(1), 1–2.

Wilson, J.M. (1991). Cerebral palsy. In S.K. Campbell (Ed.), *Pediatric neurologic physical therapy* (pp. 301–360). New York: Churchill-Livingstone.

Wolf, L.S., & McLaughlin, J.F. (1992). Early motor development in infants with myelomeningocele. *Pediatric Physical Therapy, 4,* 12–17.

World Health Organization (WHO). (1980). *International classification of impairments, disabilities, and handicaps: A manual for classification relating to the consequences of disease.* Geneva, Switzerland: Author.

33 Ethical Choices

Questions of Care

Mark L. Batshaw
Mildred K. Cho

Upon completion of this chapter, the reader will:

- understand the basic ethical principles of autonomy, beneficence, and justice and how these principles are applied in making decisions for individuals with disabilities
- know how the concepts of informed consent and substitute decision making are applied to children with disabilities
- understand a number of ethical issues concerning people with disabilities, including withholding treatment, organ donation, human experimentation, sexual rights, genetic screening, prenatal diagnosis, and therapeutic abortion
- be conversant with the functions and activities of clinical ethics committees

Advances in reproductive, genetic, and life-support technology have raised a number of unique ethical questions in the care of children with disabilities: Are there instances in which medical care can ethically be withheld from a newborn infant with a disability; and, if so, who decides? Is it ethical to perform experimental research involving individuals with disabilities? Is it ethical to perform risky procedures on individuals who may not have the capacity to provide informed consent? Is it ethical to use infants who have ultimately fatal birth defects as organ donors? Should young adults with mental retardation have full "sexual rights"? Should screening and prenatal diagnosis be performed on women who are genetically at risk of having children with severe disabilities? Should fetuses found to have severe disabilities be aborted? In this chapter, these ethical questions are examined from various perspectives.

ETHICAL CHOICES IN HEALTH CARE

Ethical decisions result from our moral values and the consideration of certain basic principles that derive from these values. Dilemmas arise when these principles seem to be in conflict and the "right" thing to do is unclear (Beauchamp & Childress, 1994; Vevaina, Nora, & Bone, 1993;

Weil, 1989). In the delivery of American health care, three basic ethical principles are considered: autonomy (self-determination), beneficence (acting to benefit the individual), and justice (the fair distribution of treatment). Other principles that are derived from these include voluntary participation in medical treatment, informed consent, privacy, and confidentiality. Awareness of diversity in cultural values (including the nature of the parent–child relationship) and in the definitions of "typicality" and disease also play a role in ethical decision making. These issues, however, are usually placed in the context of a basic principle, such as deference to individual autonomy.

Ethical problems often arise in the medical treatment of children and individuals with severe disabilities because these individuals may not be able to make autonomous choices. They often cannot participate voluntarily in medical care or give informed consent. Instead, parents or guardians become the "substitute decision makers" who ideally make choices in the best interests of the child. In situations in which treatment decisions are made by "proxy," we try to ensure a higher benefit-to-risk ratio than for people who are making decisions on their own behalf. It is generally assumed that parents can make the best decisions about their children's care. Parental authority, however, is not absolute in the United States. Here, the state has affirmed society's strong interest in the well-being of its children, and the principle of beneficence is sometimes allowed to override parental wishes if the two principles appear to be in conflict.

WITHHOLDING TREATMENT

Some children with developmental disabilities are born with medical conditions that are life threatening in the newborn period. Decisions about how to treat these conditions may require weighing the risks and benefits of treatment. For example, children with Down syndrome are at increased risk for having a narrowing of the small intestine called duodenal atresia (see Chapter 17). This condition leads to vomiting and dehydration and, if not surgically repaired, results in death by starvation during the first weeks of life. Another example is open meningomyelocele (see Chapter 25). The exposed spinal cord that is part of this condition places affected infants at risk for developing meningitis, an infection of the spinal cord that carries a high mortality rate. For both of these disorders, the surgical correction of these problems could be considered routine. The damaged portion of the small intestine can be removed, and the child can then eat and drink. Likewise, the spinal opening can be closed, thereby preventing meningitis. But these children have remaining disabilities that last a lifetime. Should parents or others have the right to withhold treatment from these infants because of "quality of life" issues (American Academy of Pediatrics, Committee on Bioethics, 1994; Anspach, 1993; Weir, 1992)?

Based on the principle of autonomy, because the infant is not able to make the decision, the parents of the child may act as "surrogate decision makers." In order to give informed consent, they must receive information from the physician about the risks of the procedure, the possible benefits, and the long-term prognosis for their child. Yet, in giving information, physicians and other health care professionals may be influenced by their own personal or professional biases concerning a particular infant and his or her disability (Silverman, 1987). Studies have shown that physicians and nurses are often disinclined to treat infants with severe disabilities based on issues of quality of life, effect on the family, and cost of care. They are less optimistic about achieving a "satisfactory outcome" than are occupational and physical therapists, social workers, teachers, and parents (Lee, Penner, & Cox, 1991a,b). As a result of these biases, they may consciously or unconsciously accentuate certain risks, underestimate the quality of life of people with disabilities, and as a result unduly influence the parents' treatment decisions (Bach & Campagnolo, 1992; Gerhart, Koziol-Mclain, Lowenstein, et al., 1994). From the perspective of biomedical ethics, professionals need to be aware of their own biases and attempt to suppress them in providing information about the risks and benefits of a procedure.

Once the parents have received and processed the information, there are some who maintain that parents are still not in a position to give informed consent. They argue that parents faced with the birth of a child with severe disabilities are in such a state of shock and so overwhelmed by fear, guilt, and horror that they are not capable of making a reasonable decision. Others argue that even though parents have these feelings, they still retain their right to decide and their wishes should not be overridden (Strong, 1984). Generally, studies have found that parents' decisions in these situations are thoughtful and responsible, especially if they are given sufficient time to consider their choices (Strong, 1984). In most instances, delays of a few days will not adversely affect the infant's outcome, will lead to more informed decision making, and will help preserve the parents' right to make decisions about their child's care (Charney, Weller, Sutton, et al., 1985). Parents need to be reassured that they are "good parents" no matter what they decide to do.

Although parents' rights are paramount, there are some instances in which society has permitted health care providers to override the parents' autonomy in making treatment decisions about their children. One type of situation was defined by the "Indiana Baby Doe" cases in the early 1980s (Caplan, 1992; Fost, 1985). In 1982, an infant with Down syndrome had a **tracheoesophageal fistula** that precluded oral feeding because food or drink would go into the baby's lungs. Following the advice of their obstetrician, the baby's parents decided not to give permission for their child to have corrective surgery, and the infant was then denied food and water. An attempt was made by a consulting pediatrician to force treatment; however, the courts let the parents' decision stand and the infant died (Fost, 1982).

This case was followed by the "Baby Jane Doe" case in 1983, which involved a child who was born with meningomyelocele and hydrocephalus (Gallo, 1984). The child's prognosis, according to her doctors, was that she would develop mental retardation, a seizure disorder, and paraplegia. After consulting with physicians, nurses, religious counselors, and a social worker, her parents decided not to consent to surgery in which a ventricular-peritoneal shunt would be placed (Steinbock, 1984). At this point, a local lawyer heard of the case and filed a suit seeking the appointment of a guardian and additional treatment for the child. The judge authorized a court-appointed guardian's consent to surgery. The case was appealed, and the appellate court reversed the judge's order, saying that the parents' decision was in the best interests of the infant, and the court had no basis for intervention. The highest court in the state upheld this appellate decision. The parents subsequently changed their decision and permitted their child to receive a shunt. Following the surgery, they cared for their child at home.

As a result of the Indiana Baby Doe case in June of 1982, the federal government notified all hospitals that it was unlawful to withhold treatment from a baby born with a disability. Nine months later, the government issued another order requiring that signs be placed in public areas of nurseries and delivery rooms stating that discrimination against children with disabilities is prohibited and that federal funds could be withdrawn from hospitals violating this order. This rule resulted in an amendment to the Child Abuse and Neglect Prevention and Treatment Act of 1984, PL 98-457. The amendment stated that therapy should not be withheld unless

The infant is chronically and irreversibly comatose; the provision of such treatment would merely prolong dying, not be effective in ameliorating or correcting all of the infant's life-threatening conditions, or otherwise be futile in terms of the survival of the infant; or the provision of such treatment would be virtually futile in terms of the survival of the infant and the treatment itself under such circumstances would be inhumane. (U.S. Department of Health and Human Services, 1985, p. 1,111)

Using these guidelines, both of the Baby Does would have received corrective surgery. It is now generally accepted by the medical community that the benefit of life as a person with Down syndrome or meningomyelocele exceeds the risk of surgery and the burden of having these disorders. In other words, this legislation requires that when treatment of an ill infant has a reasonable chance of being successful and the infant is likely to survive and be able to interact with his or her environment, even with a serious disability, the best interests of that infant are served by treatment. It is only when treatment is likely to be futile that it need not be instituted (Loewy, 1994). These guidelines were intended to establish the boundaries of parental decision making and the health care provider's moral obligation to treat illness and preserve life. Ambiguity remains, however, because the guidelines require a determination of futility. In the 1994 case of "Baby K," a newborn infant with anencephaly, the mother was able to demand extraordinary medical treatment for her infant, including mechanical ventilation, even though the physicians considered these treatments futile (Annas, 1994).

It is interesting to note that violation of the Baby Doe rule carries fairly minor penalties. The maximum sanction is a loss of a limited amount of federal money. Neither criminal nor civil actions are authorized or threatened by the legislation. Despite this, evidence suggests that care of neonates with disabilities has been altered significantly by these rules (Lantos, 1987). One study done in the early 1970s found that, of 299 deaths in an intensive care nursery, 43 (14%) were related to the withholding of treatment (Duff & Campbell, 1973). In a survey of pediatricians taken 3 years after the Baby Doe regulations were instituted in 1985, the majority of respondents indicated that the regulations had significantly affected their care of infants with severe disabilities, making it much more likely for them to give maximal life-prolonging treatment (Kopelman, Irons, & Kopelman, 1988).

U.S. courts, including the Supreme Court, also have dealt with the boundaries of parental authority in the context of blood transfusions for Jehovah's Witnesses (Weinberger, Tierney, Greene, et al., 1982). Members of the Jehovah's Witness religion interpret passages in the Bible to mean that anyone receiving blood transfusions or blood products risks losing eternal life after a temporary life on earth. When children of Jehovah's Witnesses have been in need of blood transfusions and their parents have refused treatment on religious grounds, courts generally (but not always) have ruled that parents' religious rights may be overridden by the child's right to life and health.

Despite these court decisions and laws, a presidentially appointed commission acknowledged the importance of parents' involvement in decision making for their child. "In nearly all cases, parents are best suited to collaborate with practitioners in making decisions about an infant's care, and the range of choices practitioners offer should typically reflect the parents' preferences regarding treatment" (President's Commission for the Study of Ethical Problems in Medicine and Biomedical and Behavioral Research, 1983, p. 214). Indeed, the medical profession seems to be moving toward greater acceptance of parental authority; in the case of Jehovah's Witness individuals, physicians are more often trying to abide by individuals' religious beliefs by using medical alternatives to blood transfusions.

In the rare instances in which the courts have overruled the parents' decision to withhold therapy, a new issue arises—whether it remains the parents' responsibility to care for the child they did not want to have treated. One might argue that if the state decides to save a child's life, then it, and not the parents, should be responsible for the child's future care (Shaw, 1973). So far, this has not been the case; the children remain the parents' responsibility.

Advance Directives

Another example of withholding therapy is advance directives, which refers to a physician's order in an individual's medical chart to prospectively limit the amount of intervention that should occur in the event of a medical emergency (Cantor, 1993). Such an order might indicate that, in the event of a cardiopulmonary arrest, no resuscitative actions should be taken. Alternatively, it might limit, rather than exclude, intervention. For example, in the event of a cardiopulmonary arrest, resuscitation should be undertaken but the child should not be intubated. "Do not resuscitate" orders have been used in children with disabilities who are neurologically devastated and have no hope of improvement. In this case and according to the Baby Doe rules, normal care is provided, but extraordinary measures are not taken simply to prolong life. A "do not resuscitate" order is written by the attending physician after discussion with and consent of the parents for this advance directive. This order can be rescinded at any time during the hospitalization at the parents' request.

An even more difficult problem is whether to withdraw life support systems (American Academy of Pediatrics, Committee on Bioethics, 1996; Farrell & Fost, 1989). A critical case in the legal literature is that of Nancy Beth Cruzan, a 32-year-old woman who had been in a persistent vegetative state for almost 8 years following a motor vehicle accident (Meisel, 1990). Her parents wished to have her removed from technological assistance, which in her case consisted of gastrostomy tube feedings. Her parents believed that they were carrying out wishes she had expressed to them prior to the accident—that her life not be prolonged if she were unable to appreciate it. But the State of Missouri opposed the parents' request on the basis that there was no written directive by Ms. Cruzan to this effect. The Cruzan case was the first in which the Supreme Court addressed the "right to die" issue (*Cruzan v. Director, Missouri Department of Health*). The Court decided in favor of the State, noting that there needed to be "clear and convincing" evidence that a presently noncompetent person previously expressed specific wishes about medical care. The case subsequently went back to a Missouri county probate judge, who, after presentation of additional evidence, ruled that clear and convincing evidence did exist. The parents were permitted to discontinue nutrition and hydration, and Nancy Beth Cruzan died. These treatment issues remain thorny, especially for noncompetent individuals with mental retardation (Sprung, 1991). One change has been the presence of clinical ethics committees to advise in these and other ethically difficult matters.

Clinical Ethics Committees

A direct outcome of the Baby Doe rules has been the development of clinical ethics committees in most hospitals (Fletcher & Hoffman, 1993). These consist of multidisciplinary teams that meet to consider issues of medical treatment and advise physicians and other caregivers about how to approach ethical dilemmas (Thornton & Lilford, 1995). A typical committee consists of a physician, nurse, clergy member, community member, social worker, lawyer, and possibly a medical ethicist. Functions include advising parents about the potential benefit of a suggested treatment, mediating between parents and caregivers or among members of the caregiving team in situations in which there are irreconcilable differences of opinion, reviewing the ethical reasoning in decisions to withhold or withdraw life support systems, ensuring that the best interests of the child are being considered in treatment decisions, helping to formulate hospital policies that promote ethical practices, and educating hospital staff about ethical issues (Leikin, 1987; Levine-Ariff, 1989). These are consultative, not regulatory, committees. They do not have the authority to enforce rules. However, their presence has proved very helpful in leading to consensus and providing guidance in a number of ethically difficult hospital situations.

ORGAN DONATION

One of the first issues that confronted clinical ethics committees has been organ donation. There is a significant need for hearts, livers, and kidneys to be transplanted in infants who have been born with life-threatening malformations of these organs. Yet, few infant organ donors are available. One potential source of organs is infants with anencephaly, a uniformly fatal birth defect (see Chapter 25). Paradoxically, although these infants have a severe brain malformation, their other body organs are usually unaffected. They would seem to be ideal candidates as organ donors, and they were used as such in the past. Ethical problems exist, however, and since 1988 a moratorium has precluded the use of organs from anencephalic infants for the purpose of transplantation. There were a number of reasons for this decision (Caplan, 1995). First, in order to be useful for transplantation, organs must be "fresh." The only way to accomplish this in the anencephalic infant is to harvest the organ prior to "brain death," bringing up the issue of euthanasia. A second argument was that the life of a person should not be used solely as means to an end (i.e., organ donation). A third invoked the "slippery slope" argument that allowing an exception to the "brain death" rule for neonates with anencephaly might subsequently permit the application of the same principle to infants with other severe brain abnormalities, the terminally ill, or those in a permanently vegetative state (Ahmad, 1992). Despite these concerns, in 1995 the Council on Ethical and Judicial Affairs of the American Medical Association reversed its position and indicated that it was "ethically permissible to consider the anencephalic neonate as a potential organ donor" (p. 1,617). Such a furor ensued, however, that they suspended the new position. As a consequence of this decision, there are virtually no organ donors available for infants. Research is now focusing on the use of partial transplants of organs from adults, organs from nonhuman primates, and artificial organs (Shewmon, Capron, Peacock, et al., 1989).

Another ethical issue regarding transplantation is whether individuals with disabilities should have equal access to organ transplants (Avila, 1993; Bowling, 1996). Traditionally, organ transplantation was reserved for typically developing individuals. In the 1990s, however, access has increased for people with disabilities, although these individuals still remain at a disadvantage and prone to discrimination in organ transplantation. Quality of life and ability to comply with posttransplant drug regimens are among the many reasons given for assigning a low priority to individuals with disabilities. However, national attention has been drawn to the rights of such individuals to receive organs through the successful heart-lung transplant of Sandra Jensen, who has Down syndrome (Goldberg, 1996). A nondiscriminatory policy has been adopted by the International Society for Heart and Lung Transplantation, which will increase access for individuals with developmental disabilities.

The basic issue of rationing of care is likely to become more, rather than less, pervasive in this era of managed care and concern over health care costs. It will be important to be vigilant that individuals with disabilities are not discriminated against when these decisions are being made.

RESEARCH INVOLVING CHILDREN WITH DISABILITIES

Many of the guidelines for medical research were developed in response to research studies that took what would now be considered unethical advantage of the vulnerable nature of children, individuals with disabilities, and individuals in institutions (Dresser, 1996). One of the most egregious examples of such studies is from the 1950s and 1960s, when research was conducted on healthy children with mental retardation in a state institution in New York. Researchers infected the children with the hepatitis virus to study the efficacy of a new vaccine (Krugman, 1986). Some parents were not able to admit their child to the institution unless they permitted the researchers to enroll the child in the study (Levine, 1988). When this information became public, there was a great uproar. Subsequently, the National Commission for the Protection of Human Subjects formulated guidelines for research on children and other vulnerable individuals, which were codified as federal regulations (U.S. Department of Health and Human Services, 1983; U.S. Food and Drug Administration, 1981).

These regulations stipulate that, to be ethical, research must be scientifically sound, have a favorable ratio of risks to benefits, be performed with the informed consent of the participating individuals, and select individuals fairly so that no one group bears the brunt of the risks nor preferentially reaps the benefits of research (Baudouin, 1990; Levine, 1988; McNeill, 1993; Susman, Dorn, & Fletcher, 1992). Furthermore, because individuals with severe disabilities may be unable to give consent, researchers must maximize the chances of benefit from the research if risks are more than minimal (Gaylin, 1982). When there is no direct benefit to the participant, the research is acceptable only if the risk is no more than a minor increase over minimal and the research is likely to yield knowledge that is vital to the understanding and treatment of the individual's disability (Jonsen, 1978). (An example of a minimal risk procedure is performing standard psychoeducational testing [U.S. Department of Health and Human Services, Office of Protection from Research Risks, 1993].) Finally, if at all possible, research should be done first on animals, followed by adults and older children, before using young children or individuals with disabilities. When children or individuals with severe disabilities are used as research subjects, their participation should, if feasible, be voluntary (i.e., with their assent if mental age is at least 7 years and consent after age 13). If the intervention holds the promise of direct benefit to the individual and is available only in the context of the research study, then an exception can be made (National Commission for the Protection of Human Subjects of Biomedical and Behavioral Research, 1977). Other exceptions may be brought to the forefront in the near future with the testing of novel treatment approaches such as gene therapy (Fletcher, 1995; Vanderpool, 1996).

SEXUAL AND REPRODUCTIVE RIGHTS

What are the rights of people with mental retardation to have sexual relations, marry, and procreate? Sexual drive is presumed to be as strong in individuals with mental retardation as it is in the general population (Monat-Haller, 1992). It may be somewhat delayed in people with mental retardation requiring intermittent to limited supports, and it may be less evident in individuals with mental retardation requiring extensive to pervasive supports. Nevertheless, the attitude that previously ignored sexual drive and the right to sexual activity in individuals with mental retardation is now considered invalid and unacceptable.

In the past, this paternalistic attitude toward sex in individuals with mental retardation resulted in institutional policies of separating individuals by gender and punishing sexual "acting out" behavior. Segregation and punishment were generally ineffective, however, and are now considered ethically suspect because they deny individual autonomy to engage in activities that are pleasurable and not necessarily harmful to anyone. Obviously, there are appropriate and inappropriate times and places to engage in sexual behavior, and those guidelines can be learned. For example, people with mental retardation can be taught that masturbation is an acceptable but private expression of sexuality. Similarly, most individuals with mental retardation can learn to use contraception, to take precautions against sexually transmitted diseases (STDs), and to decline sexual opportunities.

Although in some states laws remain forbidding marriage and sexual relations among individuals with mental retardation, these have not been enforced. Furthermore, they may be unconstitutional. The rights to marry and bear children are protected under the Fourteenth Amendment to the Constitution. The right to procreate, however, is not absolute; it is accompanied by responsibility for the new human being that is created (Robertson, 1995). Therefore, decisions about marriage and procreation in individuals with disabilities may involve not only the couple but also the family and, possibly, professional guidance.

Sterilization may be considered for individuals with mental retardation requiring extensive supports who do not have the potential to fulfill the responsibility of parenthood. It is important, however, to recognize that sterilization does not solve a number of the most important issues of sexual relations. It can prevent pregnancy, but it does not prevent sexual exploitation or the contraction of STDs. These issues can be addressed only by socialization training and sex education. Consideration of sterilization is justified only if the individual would not be able to provide a minimum level of care and protection to a child, has no potential for support from family members or others, or if the pregnancy would pose a serious health risk to the woman (Robertson, 1995).

Society must take care to not unfairly single out individuals with mental retardation for sterilization. Such individuals might often be better able to care for their children than parents who have physically or sexually abused their children, who have prenatally exposed their children to drugs of abuse or human immunodeficiency virus, or who are severely physically ill, groups that are not subjected to sterilization. Furthermore, sterilization is not justified for the convenience of the parents, schools, institutions, or society (Cooke, 1991).

If a decision is made to consider sterilization (or any other medical treatment), the individual with mental retardation should be permitted to participate in the process of informed consent to whatever extent possible. This involves his or her understanding the alternatives, risks, and benefits of the procedures and being able to express a choice. Truly informed consent may require multiple interviews and simplification of information.

Informed consent is a particularly sensitive issue in the United States because of its eugenic policies of the 1920s and 1930s that paralleled and, in some cases, served as a model for the eugenic programs of Nazi Germany. These policies mandated compulsory, involuntary sterilization of "mental defectives" and the "feeble-minded" in order to "improve" the gene pool and public health. As a consequence of the 1927 U.S. Supreme Court decision *Buck v. Bell Superintendent,* which supported this practice, more than 60,000 individuals with mental retardation were sterilized (Smith & Polloway, 1993). Such sterilization policies were ethically indefensible in that they judged individuals with mental illness or mental retardation as being of less worth than other human beings and did not require voluntary participation or consent.

Guidelines of the American Academy of Pediatrics, Committee on Bioethics (1990) and the American College of Obstetricians and Gynecologists, Committee on Ethics (1988) concluded that sterilization of people with mental retardation is not often indicated but did not define what would comprise indications (Applebaum & La Puma, 1994). Areen (1989) developed nine criteria for involuntary sterilization that help define the boundaries of appropriateness. Of these nine, the three key clinical criteria are that 1) sterilization must be the only practicable means of contraception, 2) the proposed operation must be the least restrictive alternative available, and 3) the judge must examine the motivation for the request for sterilization.

GENETIC TESTING AND SCREENING PROGRAMS

Although the previous discussion focused on issues that affect the individual with developmental disabilities, there are related issues that affect the entire family. For example, tests for genetic conditions such as fragile X syndrome (see Chapter 18) can provide information not only about the person who is being tested, but also about that person's family (Modell, 1992). This is a potential ethical problem: People who did not want to know this information about themselves may have their autonomy violated as a consequence of another individual's test. Furthermore, genetic tests are often used to predict a future condition (e.g., Huntington disease, Alzheimer's disease, breast cancer), rather than to diagnose a current illness (Ball & Harper, 1992; Terrenoire, 1992). If the test results become part of a medical record, insurance companies can easily gain access to them and may use them as a basis for denying health care, disability, or life insurance coverage for the tested individual or other family members (Billings, Kohn, de Cuervas, et al., 1992; Wulfsberg, Hoffmann, & Cohen, 1994).

As new genetic screening tests become available, society will need to consider whether the benefit to the individual being tested outweighs the possible harm to the person and others in the family (American Society of Human Genetics, Board of Directors, and American College of Medical Genetics, Board of Directors, 1995). Some of these issues of risks and benefits are as follows: Is there a treatment for the condition being detected by the test? How accurate is the test? What are the consequences of false positives and false negatives? Will the parents or other family members be at risk of losing their health or life insurance as a consequence of a test result (Andrews, Fullarton, Holtzman, et al., 1994)?

Screening programs differ from genetic testing because they are performed on large populations that consist mostly of individuals who are at low risk of having the condition. The purpose of screening is usually to identify individuals at high risk for a condition before it becomes clinically apparent. This is beneficial if it permits early institution of therapy to prevent or lessen the impact of the disease. Common examples are blood pressure and cholesterol screening programs. If an individual is identified as having an abnormal screen, after further testing to confirm the risk, he or she may receive medications or be placed on a special diet to control the blood pressure or reduce the cholesterol level. This, in turn, may decrease the risk of stroke or heart attack. Most people agree that these screening programs are in the best interest of the individual and do not represent ethical dilemmas. But if the benefits are not substantial, screening programs can be at odds with the principles of voluntariness, privacy, confidentiality, and informed consent. For example, if these tests were required prior to being hired for a job, problems could arise if abnormal test results were used to prevent an individual from obtaining the job or health insurance (Ad Hoc Committee on Genetic Testing/Insurance Issues, 1995; Ostrer, Allen, Crandall, et al., 1993).

Newborn screening programs represent another ethical dilemma (Fryer, 1995). In the early 1960s, a newborn blood screening test was developed for phenylketonuria (see Chapter 19). Subsequent studies showed that affected children identified and treated in infancy with a special diet developed typically, while late identification was universally associated with mental retardation. States were so enthusiastic about the potential of preventing a source of mental retardation that most mandated screening of every newborn prior to discharge from the hospital. Yet, even considering its worthwhile nature, was it ethical to require this test? Some parents may object to the requirement on the grounds that it violates their right to give informed consent. In the mid-1970s, Maryland became the first state to repeal the law requiring this test, instead offering it on a voluntary basis. More than 95% of parents agreed to have the screening test performed (Culliton, 1976). The end result, therefore, was close to what had been previously legislated, while the rights of both the state and the individual were protected. Other states subsequently followed Maryland's lead.

In the 1990s, debate has surrounded the issue of newborn screening for cystic fibrosis (Wilfond & Nolan, 1993). In this case, it is not clear whether all newborns should be screened or if screening should include only those at risk because of family or medical history. The issue revolves around whether the test is worth the additional financial cost and the potential emotional distress associated with a high false positive rate (Beaudet, 1992). The problem is further complicated because treatment of cystic fibrosis is only palliative. There will probably be more enthusiasm about initiating this mass screening when a test is developed that has a lower false positive rate and/or when a curative treatment, such as gene therapy, becomes available.

PRENATAL DIAGNOSIS, THERAPEUTIC ABORTION, AND FETAL THERAPY

Closely linked to the question of genetic screening are the issues surrounding prenatal diagnosis and therapeutic abortion. Although it is true that prenatal diagnosis often leads to the therapeutic abortion of an affected fetus, in other situations, parents who would not consider aborting their fetus might use this information to prepare themselves and their families for the birth of a child with a disability and for the care of that child. It might also lead them to have the child delivered at a tertiary care hospital that has a newborn intensive care unit necessary for the early treatment of certain disabilities. In the future, it is hoped that prenatal diagnosis will lead to the additional option of fetal therapy for the disorder that is being tested.

In recognition of some of the concerns individuals have about prenatal diagnosis and the difficulties they face in deciding whether to have such diagnosis performed, the Hastings Center and the President's Commission for the Study of Ethical Problems in Medicine and Biomedical and Behavioral Research (Powledge & Fletcher, 1979) suggested that prenatal diagnostic programs should follow certain criteria. These are based on the principles of autonomy and informed consent and include the following: 1) a woman at risk should not be denied prenatal diagnosis simply because she has decided against having an abortion; 2) counseling must be noncoercive and respectful of the various opinions about abortion; 3) physicians must inform parents about possible postnatal treatment, if it exists; and 4) all results of the prenatal diagnosis should be shared with parents. In addition, these guidelines expressed opposition to the use of amniocentesis for sex selection alone but also opposed any restriction on this option, supporting a parent's right to choose (Fletcher, 1981).

When making a decision about prenatal diagnosis, a parent's views on abortion often take center stage (Fletcher, 1981). The ethics of abortion is one of the most difficult questions to resolve, as discussion is often complicated by religious, legal, and political arguments. The main ethical questions revolve around the issues of the "personhood" of the fetus and the conflict of autonomy of the woman versus autonomy of the fetus (Crosby, 1993). The question of personhood has important implications for the autonomy issue, because if a fetus is not legally considered to be a person, it cannot be assigned rights. The Supreme Court of the United States decided in the 1973 case of *Roe v. Wade* that, for the purposes of the Fourteenth Amendment to the Constitution, a fetus is not a person. On that basis, they ruled that the reproductive rights (autonomy) of the mother were not counterbalanced by any "personal" rights of the fetus and that abortion was legal.

Personhood also can be defined in terms of moral philosophy. One such criterion is based on the concept of "quality of life" and includes the "essential human traits" of consciousness, capacity to reason, self-motivated activity, capacity to communicate, and self-awareness (Warren, 1978). Here, too, the fetus (and certain individuals with mental retardation requiring pervasive supports) would not qualify as a person. An alternate personhood criterion that has been proposed is based on conception by human parents or the potential for becoming a human (Macklin, 1995). With this definition, the fetus would qualify as a person from the time of conception. A third position asserts that it is difficult to define a single point at which a fetus acquires personhood and that rights change with developmental stage (Cahill, 1992).

These moral philosophical approaches to "personhood" are difficult to apply to health care policy because they are so heavily value based. As an alternative, specific medical criteria have been proposed to define personhood. These included the onset of electroencephalographic activity (Brody, 1978) or the potential for viability outside the womb, which is designated as approximately at the 24th week of gestation (Peterfy, 1995). The viability criteria is implied in the *Roe v. Wade* decision. These criteria are also controversial.

Discussions about abortion often use the terms "rights," "privacy," "choice," or "control," which reflect the notion of autonomy of women. In the United States, the ability to control reproduction is granted to individuals as a right, to the extent that their actions do not interfere with the rights of others. If one believes that a fetus is accorded the same rights as the mother, abortion interferes with the rights of the fetus. If the fetus does not have rights, then there is no interference.

The concept of personhood is particularly relevant to fetuses diagnosed with malformations or genetic disorders. If personhood is based on a minimal standard of quality of life, then one is forced to make the difficult decision as to what constitutes this minimal standard (i.e., which conditions are serious enough to justify abortion?) (Veatch, 1977). A fear about the increasing numbers of prenatal diagnostic tests is that women will be pressured to undergo abortions of any damaged or potentially damaged fetus. Combined with this pressure may be society's unwillingness to continue to pay for the care of people with disabilities or to ration that care (Kolata, 1980).

The possibility of fetal therapy has added new dimensions to the prenatal diagnosis/therapeutic abortion debate (Fletcher, 1992). As treatment of the fetus for certain congenital disorders becomes more common (see Chapter 3), important questions will be raised about the rights of the mother and the rights of the fetus. Some court cases already have granted certain rights to the fetus, for example, forcing a mother to undergo treatment to protect the fetus (Bainbridge, 1983). If the fetus is assigned more rights in the future, one of the results may be an impact on the availability of, legality of, and access to abortion. The direction and pace of development of prenatal diagnosis and fetal therapy will depend on how the moral and legal status of the fetus evolves (Caplan, Annas, & Elias, 1996).

Even if it were granted that abortions, as a general concept, were acceptable, some people view prenatal diagnosis as nothing more than an attempt to "eliminate" individuals with disabilities. They point out that individuals, for example with Down syndrome, have much to offer both their families and society and that attempts to eliminate this group of individuals are little more than genocide. Their view is that if human variances that are reflected in disabilities are devalued, then the person with the disability also is devalued. On this basis, they oppose prenatal screening tests as well as prenatal diagnosis.

Others argue that if a family is given information about an identified genetic disorder, they have a wider range of choices about the intervention they wish to undertake. If this knowledge is technically available, families should not be deprived of it but rather taught how to use it in an effective and ethical manner. Obviously, if there was effective prenatal treatment so that the disorder could be prevented and the person preserved, this would speak to both sides of the issue.

GEORGE: A NEWBORN WITH TRISOMY 18

George was born at term but was noted to have multiple congenital anomalies while still in the delivery room. He was small for gestational age and had microcephaly, an unusual appearance with low-set ears, and clenched hands with overriding fingers. A tentative diagnosis of trisomy 18 was made, which was confirmed by chromosome analysis. George was also diagnosed as having a complex heart malformation that often accompanies trisomy 18. He was experiencing heart failure, and the cardiologists believed that the only hope for survival was a complicated, multistep, open-heart surgical procedure.

George's parents and doctors discussed the options. The life span of children with trisomy 18 is usually limited. Although this operation might prolong George's life, it would not alter the mental retardation and cerebral palsy that usually accompany this disorder. Both George's parents and doctors leaned toward not performing the operation, but they decided to seek the advice of the clinical ethics committee.

After considering George's case, the majority of the committee members concluded that it was ethical and consistent with federal guidelines to withhold cardiac surgery. They made this recommendation using the federal guidelines that surgery is not warranted in individuals in whom it would be "virtually futile in terms of the long-term survival of the infant" (U.S. Department of Health and Human Services, 1985, p. 14,879). However, there was also a minority opinion of the committee expressed that individuals with trisomy 18 are able to experience and enjoy life and have a right to the best medical care available throughout their life, especially when it was likely to prolong that life.

With the majority opinion of the ethics committee's confirming their initial judgment, George's parents and doctors decided to treat him conservatively with heart medications. These were unsuccessful in controlling the heart failure, and George died at 1 month of age.

EMILY: A YOUNG ADULT WITH DOWN SYNDROME

Emily is an active, friendly 20-year-old woman whose intellectual functioning requires limited supports. Emily wants to marry her boyfriend, Fred, who also has Down syndrome and is 25 years old. They met in a social group and have been dating for a year. Emily lives with her parents and commutes daily to her job at a McDonald's restaurant.

Emily's parents did not know what to do. They were worried she would become pregnant and have a child with Down syndrome (about a 50% risk). They were concerned that Emily and Fred would not be able to live independently, although they had always tried to practice social role valorization as much as possible. Emily had attended a general education public school in an inclusive setting and was always an active participant in family activities. They chastised themselves that it was they who had encouraged her participation in the social club where she met Fred.

They sought counseling from a social worker in a developmental disabilities center. Subsequently, discussions were held with Emily and Fred and, in the end, everyone agreed they were in love and were serious about the commitments of marriage. As part of the discussions, they were counseled about birth control, and Emily elected to take contraceptive pills. She is proud to say that she takes them each day after she brushes her teeth.

Emily and Fred have decided to live together until they are ready to marry. An apartment in a group home has been located, and they are very excited about starting their new life together.

SUMMARY

It is very difficult to make decisions on issues such as withholding treatment, organ donation, research on children with developmental disabilities, sterilization, genetic screening and treatment, prenatal diagnosis, and abortion. Yet, these issues can be analyzed to determine which ethical principles are in conflict. After identifying the relevant principles, we can then decide which takes precedence. Therefore, ethical issues must be discussed in an open and frank manner. All individuals should participate in the important decision-making process about health care, medical treatment, and research.

REFERENCES

Ad Hoc Committee on Genetic Testing/Insurance Issues. (1995). Genetic testing and insurance. *American Journal of Human Genetics, 56,* 327–331.

Ahmad, F. (1992). Anencephalic infants as organ donors: Beware the slippery slope. *Canadian Medical Association Journal, 146,* 236–244.

American Academy of Pediatrics, Committee on Bioethics. (1990). Sterilization of women who are mentally handicapped. *Pediatrics, 85,* 868–871.

American Academy of Pediatrics, Committee on Bioethics. (1994). Guidelines on forgoing life-sustaining medical treatment. *Pediatrics, 93,* 532–536.

American Academy of Pediatrics, Committee on Bioethics. (1996). Ethics and the care of critically ill infants and children. *Pediatrics, 98,* 149–152.

American College of Obstetricians and Gynecologists (ACOG), Committee on Ethics. (1988). *Sterilization of women who are mentally handicapped* [Committee Opinion No. 63]. Washington, DC: Author.

American Medical Association, Council on Ethical and Judicial Affairs. (1995). The use of anencephalic neonates as organ donors. *Council Report, 273,* 1614–1618.

American Society of Human Genetics, Board of Directors, and American College of Medical Genetics,

Board of Directors. (1995). Points to consider: Ethical, legal, and psychological implications of genetic testing in children and adolescents. *American Journal of Human Genetics, 57,* 1233–1241.

Andrews, L.B., Fullarton, J.E., Holtzman, N.A., et al. (Eds.). (1994). *Assessing genetic risks: Implications for health and social policy.* Washington, DC: National Academy Press.

Annas, G.J. (1994). Asking the courts to set the standard of emergency care: The case of Baby K. *New England Journal of Medicine, 330,* 1542–1545.

Anspach, R.R. (1993). *Deciding who lives: Fateful choices in the intensive-care nursery.* Berkeley: University of California Press.

Applebaum, G.M., & LaPuma, J. (1994). Sterilization and a mentally handicapped minor: Providing consent for one who cannot. *Cambridge Quarterly of Healthcare Ethics, 3,* 209–215.

Areen, J. (1989) Limiting procreation. In R.M. Veatch (Ed.), *Medical ethics* (pp. 106–107). Boston: Jones and Bartlett.

Avila, D. (1993). Medical treatment rights of older persons and persons with disabilities: 1991–1992 developments. *Issues in Law and Medicine, 8,* 429–466.

Bach, J.R., & Campagnolo, D.I. (1992). Psychosocial adjustment of post-poliomyelitis ventilator assisted individuals. *Archives of Physical Medicine and Rehabilitation, 73,* 934–939.

Bainbridge, J.S., Jr. (1983, May 29). More and more, courts grant fetuses legal rights. *The Baltimore Sun,* pp. K1, K3.

Ball, D.M., & Harper, P.S. (1992). Presymptomatic testing for late-onset genetic disorders: Lessons from Huntington's disease. *FASEB Journal, 6,* 2818–2819.

Baudouin, J.L. (1990). Biomedical experimentation on the mentally handicapped: Ethical and legal dilemmas. *Medicine and Law, 9,* 1052–1061.

Beauchamp, T.L., & Childress, J.F. (1994). *Principles of biomedical ethics* (4th ed.). New York: Oxford University Press.

Beaudet, A.L. (1992). Genetic testing for cystic fibrosis. *Pediatric Clinics of North America, 39,* 213–228.

Billings, P.R., Kohn, M.A., de Cuervas, M., et al. (1992). Discrimination as a consequence of genetic testing. *American Journal of Human Genetics, 50,* 476–482.

Bowling, A. (1996). Health care rationing. *British Medical Journal, 312,* 670–674.

Brody, B.A. (1978). On the humanity of the foetus. In T.L. Beauchamp & L. Walters (Eds.), *Contemporary issues in bioethics* (pp. 229–240). Encino, CA:. Dickenson Press.

Buck v. Bell Superintendent, 274 U.S. 200. (1927).

Cahill, L.S. (1992). Defining personhood: A dialogue. *Conscience, 13*(Spring), 19–28.

Cantor, N.L. (1993). *Advance directives and the pursuit of death with dignity.* Bloomington: Indiana University Press.

Caplan, A.L. (1992). Hard cases make bad law: The legacy of the Baby Doe controversy. In A.L. Caplan, R.H. Blank, & J.C. Merrick (Eds.), *Compelled compassion: Government intervention in the treatment of critically ill newborns* (pp. 105–122). Clifton, NJ: Humana Press.

Caplan, A.L. (1995). *Moral matters.* New York: John Wiley & Sons.

Caplan, A.L., Annas, G., & Elias, S. (1996). The politics of human-embryo research. *New England Journal of Medicine, 334*(20), 1329–1332.

Caplan, A.L., & Murray, T. (Eds.). (1985). *Which babies shall live? Humanistic dimensions of the care of imperiled newborns.* Clifton, NJ: Humana Press.

Charney, E.B., Weller, S.C., Sutton, L.N., et al. (1985). Management of the newborn with myelomeningocele: Time for a decision-making process. *Pediatrics, 75,* 58–64.

Cooke, R.E. (1991). Ethics and developmental disabilities. In A.J. Capute & P.J. Accardo (Eds.), *Developmental disabilities in infancy and childhood* (pp. 251–259). Baltimore: Paul H. Brookes Publishing Co.

Council on Ethical and Judicial Affairs of the American Medical Association. (1995). The use of anencephalic neonates as organ donors. *Journal of the American Medical Association, 273,* 1614–1618.

Crosby, J.F. (1993). The personhood of the human embryo. *Journal of Medicine and Philosophy, 18,* 399–417.

Cruzan v. Director, Missouri Department of Health, 100S Ct 2841 (1990).

Culliton, B.J. (1976). Genetic screening: States may be writing the wrong kinds of laws. *Science, 191,* 926–929.

Dresser, R. (1996). Mentally disabled research subjects: The enduring policy issues. *Journal of the American Medical Association, 276,* 67–72.

Duff, R.S., & Campbell, A.G.M. (1973). Moral and ethical dilemmas in the special care nursery. *New England Journal of Medicine, 289,* 890–894.

Farrell, P.M., & Fost, N.C. (1989). Long-term mechanical ventilation in pediatric respiratory failure: Medical and ethical considerations. *American Review of Respiratory Disease, 140,* S36–S40.

Fletcher, J.C. (1981). Ethical issues in genetic screening and antenatal diagnosis. *Clinical Obstetrics and Gynecology, 24,* 1151–1168.

Fletcher, J.C. (1992). Fetal therapy, ethics and public policies. *Fetal Diagnosis and Therapy, 7,* 158–168.

Fletcher, J.C. (1995). Gene therapy in mental retardation: Ethical considerations. *Mental Retardation and Developmental Disabilities Research Reviews, 1,* 7–13.

Fletcher, J.C., & Hoffman, D.E. (1993). Hospital ethics committees: Time to experiment with standards. *Annals of Internal Medicine, 120,* 335–338.

Fost, N.C. (1982). Putting hospitals on notice. *Hastings Center Report, 12,* 5–8.

Fost, N.C. (1985). Ethical issues in the care of handicapped, chronically ill, and dying children. *Pediatrics in Review, 6,* 291–296.

Fryer, A. (1995). Genetic testing of children. *Archives of Disease in Childhood, 73,* 97–99.

Gallo, A. (1984). The case of Baby Jane Doe: I. Spina bifida: The state of the art of medical management. *Hastings Center Report, 14,* 10–13.

Gaylin, W. (1982). The competence of children: No longer all or none. *Hastings Center Report, 12,* 33–38.

Gerhart, K.A., Koziol-Mclain, J., Lowenstein, S.R., et al. (1994). Quality of life following spinal cord injury: Knowledge and attitude of emergency care providers. *Annals of Emergency Medicine, 23,* 807–812.

Goldberg, C. (1996, March 3). Her survival proves doubters wrong. *New York Times,* p. A12.

Jonsen, A.R. (1978). Research involving children: Recommendations of the National Commission for the Protection of Human Subjects of Biomedical and Behavioral Research. *Pediatrics, 62,* 131–136.

Kolata, G.B. (1980). Mass screening for neural tube defects. *Hastings Center Report, 10,* 8–10.

Kopelman, L.M., Irons, T.G., & Kopelman, A.E. (1988). Neonatologists judge the "Baby Doe" regulations. *New England Journal of Medicine, 318,* 677–683.

Krugman, S. (1986). The Willowbrook hepatitis studies revisisted: Ethical aspects. *Reviews of Infectious Diseases, 8,* 157–162.

Lantos, J. (1987). Baby Doe five years later: Implications for child health. *New England Journal of Medicine, 317,* 444–447.

Lee, S.K., Penner, P.L., & Cox, M. (1991a). Comparison of the attitudes of health care professionals and parents toward active treatment of very low birth weight infants. *Pediatrics, 88,* 110–114.

Lee, S.K., Penner, P.L., & Cox, M. (1991b). Impact of very low birth weight infants on the family and its relationship to parental attitudes. *Pediatrics, 88,* 105–109.

Leikin, S. (1987). Children's Hospital ethics committees: A first estimate. *American Journal of Diseases of Children, 141,* 954–958.

Levine, R.J. (1988). *Ethics and regulation of clinical research* (2nd ed.). New Haven, CT: Yale University Press.

Levine-Ariff, J. (1989). Institutional ethics committees: A survey of children's hospitals. *Issues in Comprehensive Pediatric Nursing, 12,* 447–461.

Loewy, E.H. (1994). Limiting but not abandoning treatment in severely mentally impaired patients: A troubling issue for ethics consultants and ethics committees. *Cambridge Quarterly of Healthcare Ethics, 3,* 216–225.

Macklin, R. (1995). Abortion: Contemporary ethical and legal aspects. In T.W. Reich (Ed.), *Encylopedia of Bioethics* (2nd ed., pp. 1–8). New York: Simon & Schuster.

McNeill, P.M. (1993). *The ethics and politics of human experimentation.* New York: Cambridge University Press.

Meisel, A. (1990). Lessons from Cruzan. *Journal of Clinical Ethics, 1,* 245–250.

Modell, B. (1992). Ethical aspects of genetic screening. *Annals of Medicine, 24,* 549–555.

Monat-Haller, R.K. (1992). *Understanding and expressing sexuality: Responsible choices for individuals with developmental disabilities.* Baltimore: Paul H. Brookes Publishing Co.

National Commission for the Protection of Human Subjects of Biomedical and Behavioral Research. (1977). *Reports and recommendations: Research involving children* [DHEW Publ. No. OS 77–0004] (Vol 1, pp. 112–113). Washington DC: U.S. Government Printing Office.

Noonan, J.T., Jr. (1978). How to argue about abortion. In T.L. Beauchamp & L. Walters (Eds.), *Contemporary issues in bioethics* (pp. 210–217). Encino, CA: Dickenson Press.

Ostrer, H., Allen, W., Crandall, L.A., et al. (1993). Insurance and genetic testing: Where are we now? *American Journal of Human Genetics, 52,* 565–577.

Penslar, R.L. (Ed.). (1993). *Protecting human research subjects: Institutional review board guidebook.* Washington, DC: U.S. Department of Health and Human Services, Office of Protection from Research Risks.

Peterfy, A. (1995). Fetal viability as a threshold to personhood: A legal analysis. *Journal of Legal Medicine, 16,* 607–636.

Powledge, T.M., & Fletcher, J. (1979). Guidelines for the ethical, social, and legal issues in prenatal diagnosis: A report from the Genetics Research Group of the Hastings Center, Institute of Society, Ethics and the Life Sciences. *New England Journal of Medicine, 300,* 168–172.

President's Commission for the Study of Ethical Problems in Medicine and Biomedical and Behavioral Research. (1983). Seriously ill newborns. *Deciding to forego life-sustaining treatment* (pp. 197–229). Washington, DC: U.S. Government Printing Office.

Robertson, J.A. (1995). Norplant and irresponsible reproduction. *Hastings Center Report, 25,* S23–S26.

Roe v. Wade, 410 U.S. 113, 159 (1973).

Shaw, A. (1973). Dilemmas of "informed consent" in children. *New England Journal of Medicine, 289,* 885–890.

Shewmon, D.A. (1988). Anencephaly: Selected medical aspects. *Hastings Center Report, 18,* 11–19.

Shewmon, D.A., Capron, A.M., Peacock, W.J., et al. (1989). The use of anencephalic infants as organ sources: A critique. *Journal of the American Medical Association, 261,* 1773–1781.

Silverman, D. (1987). *Communication and medical practice: Social relations in the clinic.* Beverly Hills: Sage Publications.

Smith, D.J., & Polloway, E.A. (1993). Institutionalization, involuntary sterilization, and mental retardation: Profiles from the history of the practice. *Mental Retardation, 31,* 208–214.

Sprung, C.L. (1991). Changing attitudes and practices in foregoing life-sustaining treatments. *Journal of the American Medical Association, 263,* 2211–2215.

Steinbock, B. (1984). The case of Baby Jane Doe: II. Baby Jane Doe in the courts. *Hastings Center Report, 14,* 13–19.

Strong, C. (1984). The neonatologist's duty to patient and parents. *Hastings Center Report, 14,* 10–16.

Susman, E.J., Dorn, L.D., & Fletcher, J.C. (1992). Participation in biomedical research: The consent process as viewed by children, adolescents, young adults, and physicians. *Journal of Pediatrics, 121,* 547–552.

Terrenoire, G. (1992). Huntington's disease and the ethics of genetic prediction. *Journal of Medical Ethics, 18,* 79–85.

Thornton, J.G., & Lilford, R.J. (1995). Clinical ethics committee. *British Medical Journal, 311,* 667–669.

U.S. Department of Health and Human Services. (1983, March 8). *Additional protections for children involved as subjects in research* [45 CFR 46, Subpart D]. Washington, DC: Author.

U.S. Department of Health and Human Services. (1985, April 15). *Child abuse and neglect prevention and treatment program: Final rules* [45 CFR, Part 1340]. Federal Register, 50(72), 14,878–14,901.

U.S. Department of Health and Human Services, Office of Protection from Research Risks. (1993). *Protecting human research subjects.* Washington, DC: U.S. Government Printing Office.

U.S. Food and Drug Administration. (1981, January 27). *Protection of human subjects* [21 CFR 50]. Federal Register, 46(17).

Vanderpool, H.Y. (Ed.). (1996). *Research ethics with human subjects: Facing the 21st century.* Frederick, MD: University Publishing Group.

Veatch, R.M. (1977). *Case studies in medical ethics.* Cambridge, MA: Harvard University Press.

Vevaina, J.R., Nora, L.M., & Bone, R.C. (1993). Issues in biomedical ethics. *Disease-A-Month, 39,* 869–925.

Warren, M.A. (1978). On the moral and legal status of abortion. In T.L. Beauchamp & L. Walters (Eds.), *Contemporary issues in bioethics* (pp. 217–228). Encino, CA: Dickenson Press.

Weil, W.B., Jr. (1989). Ethical issues in pediatrics. *Current Problems in Pediatrics, 19,* 617–698.

Weinberger, M., Tierney, W.M., Greene, J.Y., et al. (1982). The development of physician norms in the United States. The treatment of Jehovah's Witness patients. *Social Science and Medicine, 16,* 1719–1723.

Weir, R.F. (1992). *Selective nontreatment of handicapped newborns: Moral dilemmas in neonatal medicine.* New York: Oxford University Press.

Wilfond, B.S., & Nolan, K. (1993). National policy development for the clinical application of genetic diagnostic technologies: Lessons from cystic fibrosis. *Journal of the American Medical Association, 270,* 2948–2954.

Wulfsberg, E.A., Hoffmann, D.E., & Cohen, M.M. (1994). Antitrypsin deficiency: Impact of genetic discovery on medicine and society. *Journal of the American Medical Association, 271,* 217–222.

34 Caring and Coping

The Family of a Child with Disabilities

Symme Wilson Trachtenberg
Mark L. Batshaw

> Upon completion of this chapter, the reader will:
>
> - understand the stages of family development during the life cycle
> - be aware of the initial and long-term emotional impact of a disability on the child and family
> - appreciate the importance of the family's culture and ethnicity
> - know how to empower families in care planning
> - be knowledgeable about strategies and resources to help families cope with a disability
> - recognize the influence of societal attitudes on the outcome of children with disabilities

The preceding chapters have focused on the medical, habilitative, and educational supports for various developmental disabilities. Equally important is the emotional impact of these disabilities on the child and family. How the family handles the day-to-day stresses, concerns, and needs of its members influences, to a great extent, the outcome of the child (Miller, 1994; Saddler, Hillman, & Benjamins, 1993; Snowdon, Cameron, & Dunham, 1994). Traditionally, professionals offered only those resources they believed were "appropriate" or "best" for the child and family and did not always adapt to the changing needs of the family. It is now recognized that to be effective in working with these families, professionals must 1) give sound therapeutic advice, 2) take into account the family's strengths and needs for empowerment, 3) be respectful of their cultural and religious backgrounds, and 4) respond to their specific requests for services. This chapter focuses on the issues that families face throughout the life of a child with a disability and the approaches professionals can take to help families cope.

THE LIFE CYCLE OF THE FAMILY

For the purposes of this chapter, the term *family* is used to refer to children and their parent(s) or family member(s) who are primary caregivers. Families today are structured in many different ways: traditional two-parent families, single-parent families, adoptive families, step-families, gay and lesbian families, and intergenerational families (Boyce, Miller, White, et al., 1995). The family unit, regardless of its composition, transmits traditions and values that keep its cultural and ethnic heritage alive. These traditions provide family members with stability, support, comfort, strength, guidance, and, often, strategies for coping with the difficulties of daily life (McCubbin, Thompson, Thompson, et al., 1993). These cultural differences should be respected and can be incorporated into service planning.

The life cycle of a mainstream Western family is analogous to the developmental stages of an individual. Carter and McGoldrick (1980) proposed a six-stage model of the family life cycle, which is useful for understanding the evolution of a family. Modifications must be made, however, when applying this model to nontraditional family units, to families that are having children later in their lives, and to families who have a child with disabilities (Gellerstedt & leRoux, 1995). In the first stage of the family life cycle, an unattached young adult separates from his or her family of origin, moves out of the house, and gets a job. Relationships with parents change from that of child–adult to adult–adult. In the second stage, this individual develops an intimate relationship with another independent person and they marry (or live together), joining together two families. The couple commits itself to the new nuclear family. In the third stage, the couple has children, and the relationship adjusts to make space, both emotionally and physically, for its new members. The relationships with the families of origin are adjusted to the new role of grandparents. In the fourth stage, the couple's children become adolescents and begin to separate and individuate. In the fifth stage, this next generation of children moves out, and the marital/couple relationship must readjust to once again having only two people in the home. At some point the parents also may have to deal with the ill health or dependency of their parents, reversing the original adult–child role. Finally, in the sixth stage of the life cycle model, the parents, in their older years, engage in a review of their lives and integrate their successes and failures.

For all families, the adjustments and realignments each member must make during transitions from one stage of the life cycle to the next are stressful. When a family has a child with a disability, the stress is amplified, especially if stages of the life cycle are not fully realized because the child never gains independence. In this case, on each occasion that a life cycle change should occur and does not, family members may feel the sorrow they experienced when the diagnosis was first made (Tunali & Power, 1992).

FAMILY REACTIONS AND ADAPTATIONS
TO HAVING A CHILD WITH A DISABILITY

When parents first learn that their child has a severe disability, their lives change immediately, and they must cope with many stresses. They must readjust their expectations for their child; they have to deal with financial issues and a host of healthcare professionals and systems; and they may face social isolation from family and friends. To cope effectively, there may need to be significant changes in family roles, relationships, and organization.

Individuals and families differ widely in their response to having a child with a disability, depending on past life experiences, religious and cultural backgrounds, and age of the child at diagnosis (Leyser, 1994; Miller, 1994). Other factors that may influence familial reactions include attitudes about individuals with disabilities; knowledge about health care practitioners; and receptiveness to accepting help from professionals, friends, and other family members (Hanline & Daley, 1992; Lynch & Hanson, 1992; McCubbin et al., 1993). For example, some individuals with a strong religious faith may believe that God has chosen them to care for a child with a disability; others may think it a curse for past life events. If the diagnosis has been delayed, parents may be relieved to finally receive answers and help for their child. They also may be angry with health care professionals, friends, or family members who previously reassured them that their child would "grow out of it." It is difficult to predict how a particular family member will react to the news that his or her child has a disability. Furthermore, what one family considers a mild disability may be a major disability to another.

The most common initial response of parents who are told that their child has a severe disability is some combination of shock, disbelief, guilt, and an overwhelming sense of loss (Bruce, Schultz, Smyrnios, et al., 1994). In addition, many parents initially deny their child's diagnosis and visit various professionals looking for a more optimistic diagnosis or prognosis.

After the initial period of shock and denial, some family members experience depression (Kobe & Hammer, 1994). This can result from emotional stress combined with the physical strain of following through on the many appointments, procedures, recommendations, and care required by the child (Dyson, 1993; Timko, Stovel, & Moos, 1992). Other factors contributing to depression may be spousal disagreement over acceptance of the diagnosis, assignment of blame, choice of treatment options, and/or responsibility in caring for the child. Symptoms of depression include extreme fatigue, restlessness or irritability, insomnia, eating disorder, or loss of sex drive. In this state, the parent(s) may not be able to ask for help, know what they need, or stay connected to significant support systems (Singer & Powers, 1993).

At a time when the parent(s) are most in need of support, family and friends may be unable to provide it. Grandparents may not accept the diagnosis or may assign blame to one of the parents, most commonly to the one unrelated to them. Friends may feel uncomfortable in the presence of the child with a severe disability or not know what to say in consolation; as a result, they often stay away. In addition, parents may be embarrassed by their child's disability or behavior and rarely venture from the house. All of these factors can lead to social isolation. Even if parents want to maintain their social contacts, their child's physical and medical needs may be so complex that simply going shopping becomes a major production and finding a skilled babysitter impossible.

By using cognitive approaches to problem solving, professionals can help families deal with isolation, depression, and discord, especially if these feelings are interfering with the parents' ability to care for their child. These cognitive therapies provide family members with an opportunity to examine feelings and develop solutions. Supportive therapy also allows parents to ventilate concerns and may help the family adapt to their new life circumstances. For most families, the depression lessens as members develop a routine of care, gain access to early intervention and respite care services, and begin seeing progress in their child's development (Turnbull et al., 1993). Support from friends, extended family, and other parents of children with disabilities also can be (re)established over time. Parenting networks, in which parents educate and support one another, are often very powerful and may be even more effective than professional information and support (see Appendix D).

As the child grows older, parental depression may reemerge if the family faces increasing behavior problems, new healthcare and physical needs, mounting financial concerns, or feelings of inadequacy in meeting the needs of other family members. Parents of children with the most severe developmental disabilities and/or medical fragility (who require prolonged technology assistance) are at greatest risk for caregiver burnout and decreased family functioning (Saddler et al., 1993; Snowdon et al., 1994; Timko et al., 1992; Trachtenberg & Trachtenberg, 1996; Walton, 1993). Ironically, these parents tend to have the most difficulty finding or accepting respite care or alternative placement for their child. As a result, they continue to experience chronic stress, which can lead to depression or physical illness and ultimately render them incapable of continuing to meet the demands of care. Even parents whose children have mild disabilities may experience recurrent episodes of sadness and feelings of despair, which, in some instances, become a condition called "chronic sorrow." It is perfectly natural for a parent to feel sorrow from time to time. Only when the feelings of sadness and grief become chronic and interfere with the parent's ability to function is psychological intervention indicated.

Depression may be accompanied or followed by anger, which may be directed at a person, an event, God, or life in general. If directed at a person, it may be the doctor, other professionals caring for the child, the other parent, one of the other children in the family, or even the child with the disability (Tunali & Power, 1992). Alternately, the anger may be self-directed; a parent may ask, "What did I do or not do that contributed to or caused the disability?" Regardless of where the anger is directed, it is important to recognize that such expressions are part of a coping strategy. Anger may well be an appropriate expression of frustration when parents feel their opinions are not being heard or respected. However, it may be inappropriately directed at a "safe" target (i.e., the spouse) rather than at the person for whom it is felt (i.e., the professional who communicated the diagnosis). Counseling and advocacy training can help parents channel their anger into productive interactions, so they can learn how to obtain the resources they need for their child and find ways to express their feelings more effectively (Padrone, 1994).

Eventually, most parents are able to accept and cope with their child's disability and recognize positive outcomes from the experience. This leads to improved family cohesion and hardiness, increased understanding and compassion among family members, and, for some, a more enriched and meaningful life (Cadman, Rosenbaum, Boyle, et al., 1991; Featherstone, 1981; Herman & Thompson, 1995; Leyser, 1994; Miller, 1994).

THE EFFECT OF THE DISABILITY ON
FAMILY MEMBERS, FRIENDS, AND THE CHILD

Effects on Parents

The problems engendered by having a child with a disability may include physical and time demands for in-home care that interferes with parents' jobs; requirements for medical, educational, and therapy appointments; financial burdens; added stress level; and specialized needs for recreational programs, legal services, and transportation (Herman & Thompson, 1995; Knoll, 1992; Leyser, 1994; Marcenko & Smith, 1992; Trachtenberg & Lewis, 1996). Parents or partners often react differently to these problems, perhaps as a result of their separate roles within the family unit or gender-specific issues.

In most families, women continue to carry the brunt of child care responsibilities, although men often are participating more than in the past. This responsibility carries both potential risks and benefits. A mother caring for a child who will remain dependent in daily living skills throughout life is at high risk for developing stress, depression, and burnout over time (Lambrenos, Weindling, Calam, et al., 1996). If she can efficiently and effectively master the child's care, however, she may feel a sense of accomplishment and competency that is positively reinforcing (Miller, Gordon, Daniele, et al., 1992; Saddler et al., 1993; Timko et al., 1992). Meanwhile, the traditional father who focuses on financial issues and long-term planning rather than taking part in the child's daily living activities may be avoiding having to deal with the reality of the child or the disability (Heaman, 1995; Timko et al., 1992). In contrast, he may find that by participating actively in the child's care, he not only provides relief for the mother but also experiences pleasure from an enhanced role in daily family life (Willoughby & Glidden, 1995).

Gender-specific differences also are found in communication styles (Tannen, 1990). Although men tend to talk in order to impart information, women talk to communicate feelings as well. This can lead to miscommunication. The husband may think his wife is complaining when she is sharing her feelings and experiences of the day. The wife may think her husband is insensitive when he imparts information without emotional content. This difference in communication styles is not unique to families of children with disabilities, but it is often accentuated in an environment of increased stress and inadequate financial and emotional resources.

Given these stresses, it has been found that strong marital relationships, good parenting and problem-solving skills, financial stability, and supportive social networks are advantageous for parents who have a child with a disability (Failla & Jones, 1991; Leyser, 1994; Simons, Lorenz, Wu, et al., 1993; Snowdon et al., 1994; Tunali & Power, 1992). For families who lack these supports, professionals need to be available to provide advice and support to ensure the child's optimal growth, development, and safety. Although some marriages are strengthened by the challenge, others deteriorate, especially if the relationship was not previously strong (Taanila, Kokkonen, & Jarvelin, 1996). Strong religious and community affiliation and effective behavioral interventions in the home are also associated with an increased likelihood of effective family functioning (Leyser, 1994; Leyser & Dekel, 1991). Related life experiences may also have, sometimes unpredictable, effects. For example, a parent who has dealt with a chronic illness or disability in another family member may feel more competent in handling this new disability. Or, a previous difficult caregiving experience may leave the parent "burned out" and unable to cope with this new responsibility.

Effects on Siblings

The siblings of a child with a disability have special needs and concerns that vary with gender, age, birth order, and temperament (Dallas, Stevenson, & McGurk, 1993a,b; Roeyers & Mycke, 1995). Coleby (1995) found that older male siblings had an increased appreciation for children with disabilities, while older female siblings showed increased behavior problems (perhaps because of being overburdened with child care responsibilities). The same study showed that near-age siblings had less contact with peers, and younger siblings showed increased anxiety (Coleby, 1995). Sibling concerns also appeared to reflect such situational variables as whether their own needs were being met, how the parents were handling the diagnosis emotionally, what the children were being told, and how much they understood.

In addition to recognizing age and gender differences, it is important to acknowledge that children, in general, have mixed feelings about their siblings with disabilities (Knott, Lewis, & Williams, 1995). They may be glad that they are able bodied yet also feel guilty that they do not have a disability. They may worry that they will "catch" the disability or fantasize that they actually caused it by having bad thoughts about their sibling. Adolescents may question whether they will pass a similar disability on to their future children. Furthermore, because of the extra care and time required by the child with a disability, the unaffected children may think that their parents love their brother or sister more than them. As a consequence, they may act out in order to get attention. Or they may withdraw, not wanting to ask for attention from their overly burdened parents (Klein & Schleifer, 1993). To avoid these problems, care must be taken to balance the parenting efforts so that the unaffected sibling(s) are not permanently forced into second place.

Despite these concerns, having a child with a disability in a family does not necessarily adversely affect the development of the unaffected siblings. In fact, there is some evidence that these children demonstrate increased maturity, a sense of responsibility, a tolerance for "being different," a feeling of closeness to the family, and enhanced self-confidence and independence. In one study, siblings ages 3–6 years showed more involvement in social play and nurturing activities than a control group (Lobato, Miller, Barbour, et al., 1991). Many siblings of individuals with disabilities ultimately enter helping professions (Lobato, 1990).

Siblings fare best psychologically when their parents' marriage is stable and supportive, when feelings are discussed openly, when the disability is explained completely, and when they are not overburdened with child care responsibilities (Lobato, 1990; Powell & Gallagher, 1993). Parents must remember that children take their lead. If the parents are upset, so too will be the children, even if they do not understand why. In contrast, parents who acknowledge their pain while being proud of the accomplishments of all their children show their ability to adapt to the increased emotional and physical demands of having a child with special needs. This sets the tone for the entire family. Parents should also avoid burdening siblings with caregiving responsibilities. It has been shown that mothers of children with disabilities are more likely to put child care demands on the siblings and reprimand them more (Lobato et al., 1991). Parents also must recognize that their other children often feel torn between protecting and caring for their brother or sister with a disability and being accepted by children outside the family who may tease them and their sibling. Siblings should be informed at an early age about their brother's or sister's disability, so their knowledge is based on fact, not misconception. This must be done in an age-appropriate fashion with the sibling feeling free to ask questions. These sessions will need to be repeated as the children grow older and require more information. By the time siblings have reached adolescence, the parents may be ready to share with them information about genetics, estate planning, guardianship arrangements, and wills.

Effects on Extended Family and Friends

Grandparents are also affected by the presence of a child with disabilities in the family. Typically, grandchildren are a source of joy, comfort, and satisfaction. When a grandchild is born with a disability, however, grandparents grieve for their own loss as well as for their child's loss. They may experience denial more strongly than do the parents of the child with the disability, and this can interfere with the family's adaptation to the disability. Yet, grandparents can be extremely helpful to the family as a strong source of emotional support. They also may provide respite care and financial assistance that may be crucial for maintaining the child with a severe disability at home (Sandler, Warren, & Raver, 1995). Counseling, support groups for grandparents, and/or information given via the parents can help them deal with the reality of the child's disability and lead them to become more involved in supporting the family.

Other extended family members and friends also can help or hinder the parents' ability to cope. Some family members may have their own issues that will interfere with their ability to be supportive. For example, parents' siblings may be concerned about their own risk for having a child with a genetically based condition, in addition to experiencing sadness or discomfort with the diagnosis. Professionals can suggest ways to discuss these issues with family and friends and should encourage parents to utilize support groups and community services agencies.

Effects on the Child with a Disability

School Age

Prior to school age, the child with a disability may not realize he or she is different from other children. By school age, most children with disabilities are aware of their abilities and disabilities and may need help in dealing with feelings of being different. If the child is given proper supports, he or she can learn to cope with the disability. First must come acceptance in the home. If the child is seen as being worthwhile by parents and siblings, the child's self-image is usually good. This acceptance includes being part of family activities (religious, recreational, and vacations); participating as much as possible in developmentally appropriate family responsibilities; and being permitted to discuss the disability openly.

Discussing and modeling how to handle different situations at home improves the child's ability to cope with social situations in the community as well. This is very important because acceptance outside of the home can be difficult to achieve. Classmates may tease the child with a disability and schoolwork may prove difficult, especially in an inclusive setting. This is particularly problematic if the teachers and school personnel have not been adequately informed and trained about the specific physical and cognitive needs of the child. Furthermore, if the child's communication or social skills are limited, this may interfere with interpersonal interactions. If the child is not accepted by others, he or she may develop a poor self-image and exhibit depression or behavior problems.

The transition to school can be eased by preparing the class for the child's entrance (Cutler, 1993). If possible, the child's parents should be included in this planning. They can help explain the child's disorder and the necessary adaptations to both the teacher and students. They also can share with the school staff their hopes and fears for their child's education and future. It should be noted that in the case of a recent disability (e.g., a traumatic brain injury [TBI]) as opposed to a congenital disorder (e.g., meningomyelocele), the parents may be less able to take such a proactive role because they may be coping with their own adjustment to the disability. Professionals from the treating hospital can assist in school reentry.

The child with disabilities gains self-confidence through participation in activities in which he or she can be successful. These can be either integrated or special activities. The philosophy of inclusion (or integration) is that children who are differently challenged are accepted in general activities with appropriate adaptations or assistance. This, however, should not preclude either participation in segregated programs such as the Special Olympics or development of friendships with children who have similar disabilities.

Some children with disabilities will need encouragement and assistance in socializing and developing friendships. Summer camps (be they integrated or segregated) that welcome children with special needs provide an avenue for children to develop important socialization skills and experience independence from parents. This not only encourages personal growth for the child, but for his or her parents and campmates as well. In camps with inclusion programs, the typically developing children learn to appreciate people with differences. This will prepare them for a future where they will live, work, and befriend people with disabilities (Davern & Schnorr, 1991).

Adolescence

Adolescence is a difficult time for all children, and for children with disabilities the problems are often magnified (Hill, 1993). As is true of other adolescents, these children may become preoccupied with comparing themselves with their peers (Wolman & Basco, 1994). Yet, the desire for sameness and peer approval in areas of physical and intellectual development may be unattainable because of the developmental disability (Stanton, Langley, & McGee, 1995). This will be less of an issue if the adolescent with a disability has a strong peer group or has already come to terms with being "different." If the adolescent has just acquired a disability (e.g., from TBI) or is having emotional or behavior difficulties, counseling may be helpful in working through his or her concerns.

Adolescents with disabilities should be acknowledged as having sexual interests. They should be given appropriate material about intimate relationships and "safe sex" and encouraged to discuss issues of sexuality with peers in a way and at a level they feel comfortable with and can understand. Although promiscuity is sometimes an issue, social isolation is a far more common problem during adolescence. This can result either from limitations imposed on the child by the disability or by attitudes and reactions of peers and family (Hill, 1993). For some developmental disabilities (e.g., pervasive developmental disorder), social skills impairments are an integral part of the disability. These adolescents may act in an odd manner in social interactions, often making peers feel uncomfortable in their presence. They may benefit from social skills training that entails modeling appropriate social interactions and learning to participate successfully in group activities. They also can learn to enjoy individual recreational activities, such as listening to music, watching movies, and participating in sports activities (e.g., swimming, horseback riding).

Adolescence is a critical time for predicting future independence; those individuals who remain dependent through adolescence tend not to move from this stage in later life (Powers, Singer, & Sowers, 1996). Adolescents who have the potential for independence but are having difficulties with issues of separation and individuation need assistance with these developmental tasks. Parents should be encouraged to give them the necessary freedom to become independent. At times, this requires taking certain reasonable risks and may require psychosocial intervention. If parents persist in managing their child's life and the disability, however, they are giving the adolescent the message that he or she is not competent to manage independently. This can have long-term adverse consequences.

Young Adulthood

The transition to adulthood is both important and difficult for parents and children with disabilities (see Chapter 35). The young adult's ability to cope and become as independent as possible depends on the degree of the disability and the effectiveness of the family in planning and managing this transition emotionally and financially (Hallum, 1995; Howe, Feinstein, Reiss, et al., 1993). The individual may be ready to move out of the family home and into an independent living arrangement. If he or she is affiliated with an agency focused on the needs of young adults with disabilities, such an arrangement can provide important socialization opportunities within the community, contributing to personal development, competency, maturity, and adaptive functioning (Whitman, 1995). However, it also can be a very difficult time, disrupting the established family structure. The family may need assistance in successfully supporting the young adult at this time.

THE ROLE OF THE PROFESSIONAL

Families of children with disabilities come into contact with a bevy of professionals (e.g., physicians, nurses, teachers, therapists, psychologists, social workers). Individually and as a group, they are responsible for explaining the results of the initial evaluation and testing, presenting various treatment options, and teaching intervention and advocacy strategies. Ideally, services should be in place shortly after the family first learns of the child's diagnosis. Often the initial contact the family has with professionals sets the tone for future interactions.

The overall approach of the professional toward the family should be one of empowerment (Kirkham, 1993; Singer, Powers, & Olson, 1996). This contrasts with the former paternalistic attitude with which professionals simply dispensed advice and made all the decisions for the family. Although empowering the parents removes control from the professionals, it promotes better decision making and mastery of care by the family. It also leads to a true partnership between parents and professionals (Singer & Powers, 1993). Families who develop a program consistent with their personal needs and cultural values are much more likely to follow through to their child's advantage (Brookins, 1993). Furthermore, it is their legal right to choose what help they do and do not want, as is clearly mandated for the individualized family service plans (IFSPs) for children in early intervention programs and for the individualized education programs (IEPs) in school-age children. In addition, professionals should also promote self-determination by encouraging individuals with disabilities to become actively involved in setting goals and making decisions.

As a consequence of this empowerment, families are more likely to challenge or reject the advice of professionals (Timko et al., 1992). If the family is resistant to suggestions, the professionals should try to understand the reasons. The resistance may relate to specific child-rearing and medical care practices advanced by ethnic and religious affiliations, specific cultural values, family authority figures and communication patterns, or decision-making practices (Trachtenberg & Hale Sills, 1996). Perhaps what has been suggested goes against their cultural or ethnic values or traditions, or perhaps the parents have found another professional whose views they prefer. Alternatively, compliance may be beyond their emotional, physical, or financial capacity. Professionals must, at times, be prepared to experience frustration and feelings of helplessness as a result of the parents' inability or unwillingness to follow through. If it is believed that their actions may be harmful to the child, collaboration with another colleague, perhaps a social worker or psychologist who can offer psychotherapy or provision of resources (e.g., respite care, behavioral counseling, training in stress management), may clarify the family's perspective. If no improvement occurs and the child is in danger of losing function or is not being cared for adequately, the professional must contact the local child welfare agency (or other authority) to rule out child abuse or neglect.

THE ROLE OF SOCIETY AND COMMUNITY

The family's social context plays an important role in determining the outcome of its members. Fortunately, in today's society there is greater appreciation for people with disabilities. There are more educational, vocational, housing services, and other entitlements available. Federal funding provides for a protection and advocacy system for people with disabilities.

Federal legislation also guarantees equal opportunities for all members of society. The Education of the Handicapped Act Amendments of 1986, PL 99-457, and its subsequent amendments, PL 102-119, provide early intervention programs for preschoolers with developmental disabilities; and the Individuals with Disabilities Education Act (IDEA) of 1990 (originally known as PL 94-142), PL 101-476, mandates free educational and rehabilitative services for school-age children (Diamond, Hestenes, & O'Connor, 1994; Parry, 1992). Reaching citizens of all ages with disabilities, the Americans with Disabilities Act (ADA) of 1990, PL 101-336, focuses on the establishment of rights regarding access to employment, transportation, telecommunications, and public accommodations. The effects of the ADA are increasingly visible. Most city sidewalks now have direct curb access so that wheelchairs can be used, and many buses are equipped with wheelchair lifts. Buildings have wheelchair access ramps, and theater and sporting events are able to accommodate individuals with disabilities. Public telephones have adjustable speaker volumes, and most offices have TTY capability. More, however, needs to be done.

As a result of these and other laws, people with disabilities and their families and friends are now empowered to obtain equal consideration. Parent advocates have paved the way for the current focus on family-centered care, with parents acting as true partners with healthcare professionals to enable the child to function at the highest possible level.

Although laws are important, they need to be accompanied by a change in the public's perception of individuals with disabilities. This too seems to be happening, perhaps as a consequence of "mainstreaming" that began in the mid-1970s. Young adults who have grown up in schools with children with disabilities are more sensitive to their needs and more cognizant of their abilities. Individuals with disabilities are seen in movies, on television, in commercials, and in magazine advertisements. Finally, there has been an increase in "volunteerism," with religious organizations, civic groups, and social-recreational groups championing the cause of individuals with disabilities (Schalock & Kiernan, 1990).

Although society has made itself more accessible to and supportive of individuals with disabilities, the future remains challenging. Supplemental Security Income, medical assistance, and food stamps all currently provide financial support for parents and eventually for children with disabilities when they turn 18. Many of these entitlement programs are being challenged, however, and may not exist in their current form in the future (see Chapter 36). For example, managed care plans may not cover all medications, rehabilitation therapies, and technologies that are presently funded by mandated programs (Waitzman, Romano, & Scheffler, 1994). New cost-effective care models must be developed that promote quality and outcome-oriented services that build on the strengths of the children, their families, and the professionals who serve them.

OLAY AND HIS FAMILY

Olay, now age 13, sustained severe brain damage as a result of complications of prematurity. When the neonatologist told Darnell and Nadina, Olay's parents, that their first child was likely to have cerebral palsy and mental retardation, they were crushed. They could not believe that the doctors and therapists could know so soon. They sought other opinions in the hope of being told that Olay would be all right. Within a few months, however, the consistent evaluations and their growing acknowledgment of Olay's delayed development led Nadina and Darnell to accept early intervention services. By this time, Olay had been conclusively diagnosed as having cerebral palsy and a significant developmental delay.

Fortunately, Darnell and Nadina had a strong and supportive relationship and viewed Olay's needs similarly. Although their extended family and the members of their church didn't always agree with their decisions, family members helped the young couple by providing financial assistance for some of Olay's needs that were not covered by mandated programs.

By the time Olay was 6 years old, Nadina had started to work part time. Before entering school, Olay was tested and found to be functioning cognitively at a 3-year-old level. He used a wheelchair because of his cerebral palsy. He was initially placed in a two-part program and spent his mornings in an inclusion program and his afternoons in a segregated program for children with similar disabilities. It became clear during the first year that he did better in the inclusion program, and his parents successfully advocated for his IEP to include his placement in the inclusion program with an aide for the entire day in the following year.

Olay is now entering adolescence and is less even-tempered than in the past. He now has two typically developing siblings who view Olay as their older brother; they don't consider him to be very different from themselves. In fact, he wants more independence. He is upset by an increasing distance from his classmates, who are including him less in their extracurricular activities. He and his parents are now considering whether inclusion is the right placement for high school. Nadina also is entering Olay in a social skills class, and he is participating in more segregated social and sports activities. If he shows increasing behavior or emotional problems, his parents know of a counselor they would like to work with him. Nadina and Darnell never expected it to be easy to raise Olay, and most of the time they remain ready for the challenge.

SUMMARY

As a family progresses through life, its members face many challenges and changes. These are magnified for the family of a child with a disability. The child, the parents, siblings, extended family members, step-family members, and friends are all affected and may undergo a period of grieving for their loss of a "normal child." Over time, the family's coping strategies generally improve. Parents learn to master the child's care and to advocate effectively for necessary medical, educational, and other services. The child learns to cope with the disability at school and in the community. The social worker, therapist, and physician working closely with the parents and child can play a critical role in promoting these adjustments and may be instrumental in determining the prognosis of the child and the outcome of the entire family.

REFERENCES

Americans with Disabilities Act (ADA) of 1990, PL 101-336, 42 U.S.C. § 12101 *et seq.*

Boyce, G.C., Miller, B.C., White, K.R., et al. (1995). Single parenting in families of children with disabilities. *Marriage and Family Review, 20*(3-4), 389–409.

Brookins, G.K. (1993). Culture, ethnicity, and bicultural competence: Implications for children with chronic illness and disability. *Pediatrics, 91,* 1056–1062.

Bruce, E.J., Schultz, C.L., Smyrnios, K.X., et al. (1994). Grieving related to development: A preliminary comparison of three age cohorts of parents of children with intellectual disability. *British Journal of Medical Psychology, 67,* 37–52.

Cadman, D., Rosenbaum, P., Boyle, M., et al. (1991). Children with chronic illness: Family and parent demographic characteristics and psychological adjustment. *Pediatrics, 87*(6), 884–889.

Carter, E.A., & McGoldrick, M. (Eds.). (1980). *The family life cycle: A framework for family therapy.* New York: Gardner Press.

Coleby, M. (1995). The school-aged siblings of children with disabilities. *Developmental Medicine and Child Neurology, 37,* 415–426.

Cutler, B.C. (1993). *You, your child, and "special" education: A guide to making the system work.* Baltimore: Paul H. Brookes Publishing Co.

Dallas, E., Stevenson, J., & McGurk, H. (1993a). Cerebral-palsied children's interaction with siblings: I. Influence of severity of disability, age, and birth order. *Journal of Child Psychology and Psychiatry and Allied Disciplines, 34,* 621–647.

Dallas, E., Stevenson, J., & McGurk, H. (1993b). Cerebral-palsied children's interaction with siblings: II. Interactional structure. *Journal of Child Psychology and Psychiatry and Allied Disciplines, 34,* 649–671.

Davern, L., & Schnorr, R. (1991). Public schools welcome students with disabilities as full members. *Children Today, 20*(2), 21–25.

Diamond, K.E., Hestenes, L.L., & O'Connor, C.E. (1994). Integrating young children with disabilities in preschool: Problems and promise. *Young Children, 49*(2), 68–75.

Dyson, L.L. (1993). Response to the presence of a child with disabilities: Parental stress and family functioning over time. *American Journal on Mental Retardation, 98,* 207–218.

Education of the Handicapped Act Amendments of 1986, PL 99-457, 20 U.S.C. § 1400 *et seq.*

Failla, S., & Jones, L.C. (1991). Families of children with developmental disabilities: An examination of family hardiness. *Research in Nursing and Health, 14*(1), 41–50.

Featherstone, H. (1981). *A difference in the family: Living with a disabled child.* New York: Penguin Press.

Gellerstedt, M.E., & leRoux, P. (1995). Beyond anticipatory guidance: Parenting and the family life cycle. *Pediatric Clinics of North America, 42,* 65–78.

Hallum, A. (1995). Disability and the transition to adulthood: Issues for the disabled child, the family, and the pediatrician. *Current Problems in Pediatrics, 25*(1), 12–50.

Hanline, M.F., & Daley, S.E. (1992). Family coping strategies and strengths in Hispanic, African-American, and Caucasian families of young children. *Topics in Early Childhood Special Education, 12*(3), 351–366.

Heaman, D.J. (1995). Perceived stressors and coping strategies of parents who have children with developmental disabilities: A comparison of mothers with fathers. *Journal of Pediatric Nursing, 10,* 311–320.

Herman, S.E., & Thompson, L. (1995). Families' perceptions of their resources for caring for children with developmental disabilities. *Mental Retardation, 33*(2), 73–83.

Hill, A.E., (1993). Problems in relation to independent living: A retrospective study of physically disabled school leavers. *Developmental Medicine and Child Neurology, 35*(12), 1111–1115.

Howe, G.W., Feinstein, C., Reiss, D., et al. (1993). Adolescent adjustment to chronic physical disorders: I. Comparing neurological and non-neurological conditions. *Journal of Child Psychology and Psychiatry and Allied Disciplines, 34*(7), 1153–1171.

Individuals with Disabilities Education Act (IDEA) of 1990 (IDEA), PL 101-476, 20 U.S.C. § 1400 *et seq.*

Kirkham, M.A. (1993). Two-year follow-up of skills training with mothers of children with disabilities. *American Journal on Mental Retardation, 97*(5), 509–520.

Klein, S.D., & Schleifer, M.J. (Eds.). (1993). *It isn't fair: Siblings of children with disabilities.* Westport, CT: Bergin and Garvey.

Knoll, J. (1992). Being a family: The experience of raising a child with a disability or chronic illness. *Monographs of the American Association on Mental Retardation, 18,* 9–56.

Knott, F., Lewis, C., & Williams, T. (1995). Sibling interaction of children with learning disabilities: A comparison of autism and Down's syndrome. *Journal of Child Psychology and Psychiatry and Allied Disciplines, 36,* 965–976.

Kobe, F.H., & Hammer, D. (1994). Parenting stress and depression in children with mental retardation and developmental disabilities. *Research in Developmental Disabilities, 15,* 209–221.

Lambrenos, K., Weindling, A.M., Calam, R., et al. (1996). The effect of a child's disability on mother's mental health. *Archives of Disease in Childhood, 74,* 115–120.

Leyser, Y. (1994). Stress and adaptation in orthodox Jewish families with a disabled child. *American Journal of Orthopsychiatry, 64*(3), 376–386.

Leyser, Y., & Dekel, G. (1991). Perceived stress and adjustment in religions Jewish families with a child who is disabled. *Journal of Psychology, 125,* 427–438.

Lobato, D.J. (1990). *Brothers, sisters and special needs: Information and activities for helping young siblings of children with chronic illnesses and developmental disabilities.* Baltimore: Paul H. Brookes Publishing Co.

Lobato, D.J., Miller, C.T., Barbour, L., et al. (1991). Preschool siblings of handicapped children: Interactions with mothers, brothers and sisters. *Research in Developmental Disabilities, 12*(4), 387–399.

Lynch, E.W., & Hanson, M.J. (Eds.). (1992). *Developing cross-cultural competence: A guide for working with young children and their families.* Baltimore: Paul H. Brookes Publishing Co.

Marcenko, M.O., & Smith, L.K. (1992). The impact of a family-centered case management approach. *Social Work in Health Care, 7*(1), 87–100.

McCubbin, H.I., Thompson, E.A., Thompson, M.S., et al. (1993). Culture, ethnicity and the family: Critical factors in childhood chronic illnesses and disabilities. *Pediatrics, 91*(5), 1063–1070.

Miller, A.C., Gordon, R.M., Daniele, R.J., et al. (1992). Stress, appraisal, and coping in mothers of disabled and non-disabled children. *Journal of Pediatric Psychology, 17*(5), 587–605.

Miller, N.B. (1994). *Nobody's perfect: Living and growing with children who have special needs.* Baltimore: Paul H. Brookes Publishing Co.

Padrone, F.J. (1994). Psychotherapeutic issues with family members of persons with physical disabilities. *American Journal of Psychotherapy, 48,* 195–207.

Parry, T.S. (1992). The effectiveness of early intervention: A critical review. *Journal of Paediatrics and Child Health, 28,* 343–346.

Powell, T.H., & Gallagher, P.A. (1993). *Brothers and sisters: A special part of exceptional families* (2nd ed.). Baltimore: Paul H. Brookes Publishing Co.

Powers, L.E., Singer, G.H.S., & Sowers, J-A. (Eds.). (1996). *On the road to autonomy: Promoting self-competence in children and youth with disabilities.* Baltimore: Paul H. Brookes Publishing Co.

Roeyers, H., & Mycke, K. (1995). Siblings of children with autism, mental retardation and with a normal development. *Child: Care, Health and Development, 21,* 305–319.

Saddler, A.L., Hillman, S.B., & Benjamins, D. (1993). The influence of disabling condition visibility on family functioning. *Journal of Pediatric Psychology, 18*(4), 425–439.

Sandler, A.G., Warren, S.H., & Raver, S.A. (1995). Grandparents as a source of support for parents of children with disabilities: A brief report. *Mental Retardation, 33,* 248–250.

Schalock, R., & Kiernan, W. (1990). *Habilitation planning for adults with disabilities.* New York: Springer-Verlag.

Simons, R.L., Lorenz, F.O., Wu, C.I., et al. (1993). Social network and marital support as mediators and moderators of the impact of stress and depression on parental behavior. *Developmental Psychology, 29*(2), 368–381.

Singer, G.H.S., & Powers, L.E. (Eds.). (1993). *Families, disability, and empowerment: Active coping skills and strategies for family interventions.* Baltimore: Paul H. Brookes Publishing Co.

Singer, G.H.S., Powers, L.E., & Olson, A.L. (Eds.). (1996). *Redefining family support: Innovations in public–private partnerships.* Baltimore: Paul H. Brookes Publishing Co.

Snowdon, A.W., Cameron, S., & Dunham, K. (1994) Relationships between stress, coping resources, and satisfaction with family functioning in families of children with disabilities. *Canadian Journal of Nursing Research, 26*(3), 63–76.

Stanton, W.R., Langley, J., & McGee, R. (1995). Disability in late adolescence: II. Follow-up of perceived limitation. *Disability and Rehabilitation, 17,* 70–75.

Taanila, A., Kokkonen, J., & Jarvelin, M-R. (1996). The long-term effects of children's early onset disability on marital relationships. *Developmental Medicine and Child Neurology, 38,* 576–577.

Tannen, D. (1990). *You just don't understand: Women and men in conversation.* New York: Ballantine Books.

Timko, C., Stovel, K.W., & Moos, R.H. (1992). Functioning among mothers and fathers of children with juvenile rheumatic disease: A longitudinal study. *Journal of Pediatric Psychology, 17*(6), 705–724.

Trachtenberg, S.W., & Hale Sills, N. (1996). Collaboration with parent and child. In L. Kurtz, P.W. Dowrick, S.E. Levy, & M.L. Batshaw (Eds.), *Children's Seashore House handbook of developmental disabilities: Resources for interdisciplinary care* (pp. 526–533). Gaithersburg, MD: Aspen Publishers.

Trachtenberg, S.W., & Lewis, D.F. (1996). Case management. In L. Kurtz, P.W. Dowrick, S.E. Levy, &

M.L. Batshaw (Eds.), *Children's Seashore House handbook of developmental disabilities: Resources for interdisciplinary care* (pp. 203–208). Gaithersburg, MD: Aspen Publishers, Inc.

Trachtenberg, S.W., & Trachtenberg, J.I. (1996). Prevention of burnout for parents and professionals. In L. Kurtz, P.W. Dowrick, S.E. Levy, & M.L. Batshaw (Eds.), *Children's Seashore House handbook of developmental disabilities: Resources for interdisciplinary care* (pp. 593–596). Gaithersburg, MD: Aspen Publishers, Inc.

Tunali, B., & Power, T.G. (1992). Creating satisfaction: A psychological perspective on stress and coping in families of handicapped children. *Journal of Child Psychology and Psychiatry, 34*(6), 945–957.

Turnbull, A.P., Patterson, J.M., Behr, S.K., Murphy, D.L., Marquis, J.G., & Blue-Banning, M.J. (1993). *Cognitive coping, families, and disability.* Baltimore: Paul H. Brookes Publishing Co.

Waitzman, N.J., Romano, P.S., & Scheffler, R.M. (1994). Estimates of the economic costs of birth defects. *Inquiry, 31,* 188–204.

Walton, W.T. (1993). Parents of disabled-children burnout too: Counselling parents of disabled-children on stress management. *International Journal for the Advancement of Counselling, 16*(2), 107–118.

Whitman, C. (1995). Heading toward normal: Deinstitutionalization for the mentally retarded client. *Marriage and Family Review, 21*(1–2), 51–64.

Willoughby, J.C., & Glidden, L.M. (1995). Fathers helping out: Shared child care and marital satisfaction of parents of children with disabilities. *American Journal on Mental Retardation, 99,* 399–406.

Wolman, C., & Basco, D.E. (1994). Factors influencing self-esteem and self-consciousness in adolescents with spina bifida. *Journal of Adolescent Health, 15,* 543–548.

35 Adulthood

What the Future Holds

Adadot Hayes
Lisa J. Bain
Mark L. Batshaw

Upon completion of this chapter, the reader will:

- understand the importance of beginning to plan for the transition to adulthood early in the life of a child with developmental disabilities

- be knowledgeable about the mandated programs available to assist in this transition

- be aware of the employment and residential options for adults with developmental disabilities

- recognize the need for addressing issues of leisure activities, sexuality, and socialization in individuals with disabilities

Individuals with developmental disabilities encounter the same transitions throughout their lives as typically developing people. Perhaps the most difficult of these is the transition to adulthood, a period of complex biological, social, and emotional change. This transition involves the evolution from dependence to independence, from residing at home to living in the community, from attending school to becoming employed, and from being part of one family to establishing a new nuclear family. Accompanying issues include education and employment, sexuality, social interactions, recreation, domestic life, and medical and physical care.

Planning for the transition to adulthood should start during childhood. Each disability has specific needs that must be addressed and accommodations that may be required. For example, individuals with mental retardation may need to focus on life skills training, while people with a physical disability may be more concerned with mobility issues. People with a pervasive developmental disorder may require more extensive social skills training than, for example, individuals with attention-deficit/hyperactivity disorder (ADHD) who may need help with developing attention skills for the workplace. Despite these differences, there are several universal transition issues for all individuals with disabilities. These similarities are the focus of this chapter. More specific interventions in making the transition to adulthood are described in the preceding chapters on individual developmental disabilities.

CHILDHOOD ACTIVITIES AS FOUNDATIONS FOR TRANSITION TO ADULTHOOD

Children with disabilities should be exposed to as many experiences and activities as possible during childhood that foster the independence and socialization skills needed for their transitions to adulthood. As the child matures and becomes more capable, parents should gradually increase that child's responsibilities while simultaneously granting him or her more independence (Hallum, 1995). Unfortunately, parents of children with disabilities often fail to recognize that as their children grow, they become capable of and desire increased independence, much like typically developing children. The failure of parents to acknowledge competence reinforces a sense of incompetence in these children. Anderson, Clark, and Spain (1982) reported that only 21% of children with disabilities are given responsibilities around the house as compared with 69% of typically developing children. Developmentally appropriate chores may range from cleaning one's room to making meals or developing a grocery list. Community activities also can be opportunities for learning appropriate behavior and demonstrating independence. The child should have specific requirements for behavior and discipline that are tailored to his or her developmental level. In addition to these "passive" experiences, children with disabilities need to learn to make "active" decisions. This may involve making schedules, keeping appointments, purchasing and preparing meals, maintaining personal hygiene and appearance, and using adaptive equipment (e.g., wheelchair, computer).

TRANSITION FROM DEPENDENCE TO INDEPENDENCE

Attaining independence is perhaps the essence of adulthood. For individuals with severe developmental disabilities, complete independence may not be a realistic goal. This does not mean, however, that significant aspects of independence are beyond the reach of these individuals. Evidence of independence includes the ability to complete activities of daily living (ADL) (e.g., dressing, eating) with minimal assistance; to separate emotionally or physically from parents; or to maintain employment. It is essential that every individual maximize his or her personal level of independence in order to build self-acceptance and self-esteem. Maximizing one's independence can give someone who feels helpless and insecure the confidence to assert him- or herself and develop a strong sense of autonomy.

Although children generally enter adolescence at approximately age 13, children with disabilities may have a lag between their chronological age and mental age that may delay the onset of this transitional period. During adolescence, most children test the limits of independence. Adolescent behavior may include slovenliness, opposition, defiance, and lack of communication. There also may be sadness or depression as the adolescent deals with social isolation or a poor self-image (see Chapter 34). It is interesting, however, to note that parents tend to rate their children's self-esteem lower than the children themselves do (King, Shultz, Steel, et al., 1993). Parents of children with disabilities should deal with these behaviors in the same way as parents of typically developing children. Children should be taught that independence is earned by mature and appropriate behavior. Parents may need to incorporate behavior management techniques (see Chapter 30) and open communication with their children in order to reinforce this message. Some parents choose to develop contracts that address both the child's quest for independence and the parents' need for security. If open communication is not occurring within the family, a professional counselor should be sought through the school or in the community. It is important for parents to remember that this stage is transitory; eventually they will develop a more stable, adult relationship with their child.

TRANSITION FROM HOME TO COMMUNITY LIVING

The transition to adulthood is usually the time when children move out of the family home to live independently in the community. This occurs less often and later in the case of a young adult with developmental disabilities. For some individuals, there may be no transition, and care at home continues indefinitely. Alternatively, the person may leave home for a community residence that affords less than complete independence. This may be a residential facility, a group home, or a supported apartment. For any of these venues to be successful, there must be planning and support for and from the family.

Home Care

Many families choose (or find they have no other option but) to continue to care for their child at home after he or she turns 18. There are advantages to this option: The individual with a severe disability can remain at the center of family life, participating in activities and receiving the love and affection of parents and siblings. In addition, the parents can continue to directly control the care and stimulation of their child and avoid feelings of guilt and abandonment that may accompany an out-of-home placement. However, there are also disadvantages to this option. Keeping young adults with developmental disabilities at home is often a physical and emotional burden for their parents. As a result of the increased size of the young adult with a severe cognitive or physical disability, lifting, transferring, bathing, dressing, and discipline can become physically very difficult for the aging parents. This is especially true for the mother who is usually the primary caregiver, but it may also affect fathers. For example, fathers may feel uncomfortable changing or bathing their adult daughters. Parents also may find it difficult to continue to be the primary source of intellectual and social stimulation for their child. In addition, prolonged care may affect parental lifestyle, especially if the young adult's needs are in direct conflict with the personal needs and desires of the parents. If the parents are retired and on a fixed income, they may have difficulty providing their child with the necessary financial support. Home care also may be to the detriment of the individual with a disability if it inhibits the development of his or her independent living skills. For example, if ADL skills are difficult for the individual to perform, the parents may unintentionally reinforce a sense of dependency by doing everything themselves in order to save time.

If individuals with disabilities continue to live at home as adults, families often require additional support services, including a van equipped for wheelchairs to permit community mobility, home renovations, electric beds, and a computer or other assistive technology. Provision of periodic respite care also is very important. Respite care not only relieves parents of the ongoing stresses of daily care on occasion but may also serve to promote independence in the individual with a disability. At times, respite care may serve as a transition to an out-of-home community placement. Respite care can take place in the home on a regular basis or in another setting. In addition, families may be able to obtain "wrap-around" services (e.g., nursing care, counseling, rehabilitation therapies) in the home and structured daytime activities and other support services through state agencies for adults with developmental disabilities (Molaison, Black, Sachs, et al., 1995).

Residential Facilities

At one time, most individuals with mental retardation requiring extensive support eventually were placed in residential institutions. As of 1997, new residential placements are fairly uncommon. Although there are a variety of potential residential placement options, not all are available in any given community. In fact, many residential services have long waiting lists and high costs. Furthermore, many states have moratoriums on admission to large state facilities, and a number of these facilities are closing. The clear emphasis is on community placement for these individuals. In rare instances, however, state institutions are still an acceptable option, particularly when there is a crisis situation or a severe medical or behavior problem.

Community-Based Programs

In keeping with the philosophy of **normalization,** the trend is toward community-based programs. Yet, because of the inadequate number of high-quality, integrated community support systems and residential programs, finding individuals with disabilities appropriate out-of-home placements is often a long and arduous procedure. Even when placements are available, parents may worry that the quality of the living environment and supervision cannot compare to that given in the family home (Hallum & Krumboltz, 1993). Parents need assurance that their child will live in a safe, healthy, clean, caring, and stimulating environment. They also need some assessment of the stability of that placement. The psychological cost of placement for parents is often high, as hired caregivers seldom provide the same level of care as parents. In addition, parents often have other issues to reconcile including conflict between parents on decisions for placement, concerns about distance from home, and general anxiety about their child's future.

Intermediate Care Facilities

Intermediate care facilities (ICFs) provide the most intensive group home setting for individuals who have significant health problems, multiple disabilities, or very limited skills for daily living. These are usually small facilities that house 8–20 individuals. In comparison with other community living arrangements, ICFs tend to be more restrictive and medically oriented (Conroy, 1996). Many states have "waiver programs" that provide funds for families to obtain services similar to those provided in ICFs or institutions but that are home based or in small community residences.

Community Homes

Community "homes" or alternate living units (ALUs) may be available for young adults with disabilities who require various levels of support. Family care homes enable a person to live with a family that is trained and licensed to care for individuals with developmental disabilities. Community residences provide a supervised group home setting for individuals who have the ability to care for themselves. Supportive residences offer an apartment-like environment for individuals who have average intelligence but severe physical disabilities (analogous to apartments for older adults). There are also adult foster care placements as well as boarding homes and programs for independent supervised living. Unfortunately, the growth of these programs has been impeded by community resistance, inadequate funding, and difficulty finding stable staff. Many programs have failed, giving participants only 1 month notice before closing and throwing families into upheaval. Yet, as the trend toward keeping individuals out of large institutions continues, it is hoped that there will be increasing funding and development of community-based services. There is also the need for family support services designed to help family members care for children or siblings with disabilities at home. These services include counseling, crisis intervention, respite care, service coordination, advocacy, and day programs.

Independent Living

For some individuals with severe physical disabilities, independent living may still be a possibility, provided there is adaptive equipment and/or a personal assistant. When successful, these placements permit individuals to live in an apartment or house in the general community and commute to a regular job. It is imperative, however, that the individual with a disability exhibit personal choice in selecting a personal assistant. The residence often requires adaptations such as ramps and widened doorways to accommodate a wheelchair. Adaptive equipment, such as environmental controls for lights, curtains, and electrical appliances, may enhance independence. Safety may be provided by speaker phones and "panic buttons." There often needs to be a modified minivan for transportation, possibly with adapted steering and brakes to permit independent operation. In most cases of severe physical disability, there will also need to be a personal assistant for a certain number of hours per day. The personal assistant helps with dressing, preparing meals, and washing/toileting. With these adaptations, more and more individuals with severe physical disabilities are able to live independently and be integrated into the community.

TRANSITION FROM SCHOOL TO WORK

Many individuals with developmental disabilities are unemployed and socially isolated (Wacker, Harper, Powell, et al., 1983). In the 1991 census, only 12% of adults with severe disabilities were in the paid work force, and 42% were classified as poor (U.S. Department of Education, 1992). It is hoped that the outlook will improve if planning and effort are made to teach the child the skills needed to be successful in the workplace during the elementary school years.

Educational Programs

Public School

Individuals with disabilities may continue their public education until age 21. This secondary education should be directed at each student's interests and abilities and should include basic job skills and work support behaviors in preparation for a fulfilling life and career in the community. In fact, the Individuals with Disabilities Education Act (IDEA) of 1990, PL 101-476, requires public schools to provide activities designed to facilitate the transition from school to postschool activities, including postsecondary education, employment, vocational training, adult services, independent living, and community participation. It also mandates that the individualized education program (IEP) of students ages 16 or older be supplemented with an individualized transition plan (ITP). While the IEP focuses on academic goals, the ITP is a guide to skills needed to make the transition into the community and work force. Some states, such as New Jersey, have lowered this to age 14. Provisions of the ITP require 1) the process to be outcome oriented, 2) students to be meaningfully involved in the process, 3) students' needs to be projected beyond 1 year, 4) schools to work with external agencies responsible for the provision of services or funding, and 5) schools to provide extensive community-based instruction. The ITP should further address these issues by delineating which agencies will be involved in providing necessary services, how these services will be coordinated, how the child's interests and skills will be incorporated into the plan, what kind of training the child will need, how he or she will obtain that training, and what other supportive services will be needed (Johnson, 1995).

Despite these mandates, not all school systems adequately plan and provide for the transition needs of students with disabilities. In some instances, this is because the educators believe that these requirements go well beyond the school's responsibilities or capabilities. Yet, even granting this possibility, because there is no multidisciplinary team designated to coordinate services for the individual with disabilities once he or she is out of school, it is essential that full advantage be taken of the public school system's services before the individual reaches the age of 21.

College

For those individuals whose cognitive skills allow them to attend college, increasing numbers of schools offer accommodations. Although some schools are better equipped to provide supports than others, most have an Office of Special Needs that oversees disability-related programs. The Bureau of Vocational Rehabilitation (VR) may be helpful in identifying appropriate programs; and there are catalogs that list specific programs for individuals with learning disabilities, ADHD, and sensory disabilities (e.g., *Lovejoy's College Guide for the Learning Disabled* [Straugh, 1988]). Certain schools, such as Boston University, have a special "track" for these students. They are included in general education classes but have tutorial help, untimed tests, and other accommodations to permit successful completion of the curriculum. For individuals with physical disabilities, the Americans with Disabilities Act (ADA) of 1990, PL 101-336, mandates wheelchair accessibility of most classrooms in colleges. For those with sensory impairments, the availability of frequency modulation (FM) amplification systems for individuals with hearing impairments and computerized scanning and projection for those with visual impairments has further permitted inclusion of individuals with these disabilities into many university settings. In addition, these individuals may benefit from the use of interpreters and note-takers, who may be provided by the college or another agency.

Vocational Training

Although college may be a realistic goal for individuals with at least average cognitive functioning, vocational training is an important goal for people who have mild to moderate cognitive impairments. In most parts of the United States, ITPs focus on vocational training. Some of the stipulations of an ITP may be provided through the Bureau of VR, an agency separate from school districts. This agency provides services to people with disabilities that help define suitable employment goals, give additional educational opportunities, and assist with obtaining employment. Services may include evaluation, counseling, placement, training, follow-up, and many other types of assistance. The goals of VR training include developing appropriate work and social skills, learning to use public transportation and manage finances, choosing leisure opportunities, and locating appropriate independent living environments. To be eligible, a person must have a condition, physical or cognitive, that results in a substantial disability to employment; there must also be a reasonable expectation that he or she will benefit from these services and eventually become employed.

Although few services are mandated for individuals with disabilities beyond age 21, there are several federal laws related to work and disability. Section 504 of the Rehabilitation Act of 1973, PL 93-112, prohibits discrimination by employers receiving federal funds and mandates equal opportunities and programs for individuals with disabilities. This Act also provides federal funds to agencies that develop programs for people with disabilities. In 1978, the Rehabilitation Act Amendments, PL 95-602, enhanced this initiative to guarantee access to programs for all individuals, even when gainful employment is not the expected outcome. More recently, the Rehabilitation Act Amendments of 1992, PL 102-569, articulated the role of VR counselors in working with young teenagers.

Work Options

Competitive Employment

Competitive employment implies placing an individual in a job in which he or she is expected to perform in a manner similar to other employees (and without a job coach). Abilities necessary for successful competitive employment include good social and communication skills, motivation, persistence, functional reading and writing (or computing), independent living skills, accessibility to reliable transportation, and independence in mobility. This is less likely to be a realistic goal for an individual with mental retardation but may well be achievable by individuals with average intelligence and significant physical or sensory disabilities.

Integrating individuals into general settings has many advantages, including higher wages and increased opportunities to interact with other adults. Unfortunately, it is still the exception rather than the rule that an individual with a severe disability will be offered competitive employment opportunities. Despite laws designed to encourage the employment of individuals with disabilities, competitive employment is impeded by society's bias that a person with a disability is not a capable person. This leads to prejudice, stereotyping, and discrimination that can create barriers beyond the physical or cognitive limitations of the individual. Parents sometimes pose an additional barrier to obtaining the required education and training for competitive employment if they underestimate their child's ability, wanting to "protect" the child from failure and disappointment. In doing this, they limit their child's potential for an independent life in the community.

Supported Employment

Since the mid-1980s, the Bureau of VR and state mental retardation/developmental disabilities (MR/DD) agencies have increasingly placed people with disabilities into community employment with needed supports including transportation, adaptations, prosthetic and orthotic devices, equipment, and job coaches—a concept called supported employment. Once appropriate job skills are learned, job coaches assist the client in making the transition to a job in the private sector and continue to work with the individual for as long as is necessary to ensure a smooth transition into the work force. For some individuals, this may entail little more than an occasional visit by the coach to the jobsite. Other individuals may require more long-term support. Supportive services are arranged by VR agencies. There are certain financial criteria, but they are less restrictive than those of many other programs. These programs have led to significant increases in the numbers of individuals in integrative employment.

Day Treatment Programs and Sheltered Workshops

Day treatment programs serve individuals with mental retardation requiring extensive support and focus on the development of independent ADL skills rather than job skills. Typically, these programs continue and expand upon the school systems' special education programs, usually adding instruction in recreation and leisure activities.

In contrast, sheltered workshops are usually appropriate for individuals with mental retardation requiring limited support and/or severe physical disabilities and focus on developing specific work skills. Sheltered workshops elicit contracts from businesses to provide goods or services. The work might include preparation of mass mailings or assembling items. Tasks vary, and individuals are paid by production, which usually does not affect eligibility for other forms of public assistance. However, the work is often repetitive and boring, and it takes place in a segregated setting. With the current focus on normalization, it is likely that most sheltered workshops will soon be eliminated and clients moved into supported employment. As of 1997, however, a significant number of individuals with developmental disabilities remain in these settings (McGaughey, Kiernan, McNally, et al., 1995).

TRANSITION FROM PEDIATRIC TO ADULT HEALTH CARE

The goals of transition to the adult health care system (medical, behavioral, and dental) are to provide uninterrupted, coordinated, developmentally appropriate, psychosocially sound, and comprehensive services. Ideally, the timing of this transition should coincide with mid-adolescence or young adulthood (ages 16–21); and it should involve not only the transfer of medical care from pediatrician to adult physician, but also the transfer of responsibility from parent to child. Although this may increase the anxiety for both, accepting responsibility for one's health care is one of the important tasks of gaining autonomy and independence as an adult. Health care then moves from being protective, parent oriented, and prescriptive to being independent, individual centered, and voluntary.

Unfortunately, the transition to adult health care services for individuals with disabilities is often by default rather than by design. Both families and physicians may be reluctant to make the transition, so future planning may not occur. Pediatricians develop strong bonds with patients and families, and the feelings tend to be mutual; families often do not want to "give up" their pediatrician. This is combined with the fact that many internists and family physicians have little training or interest in meeting the multidisciplinary needs of young adults with developmental disabilities. Consequently, adult health care services for individuals with chronic disabilities, whether hospital or community based, often are inadequate.

For effective transition in health care to occur, long-term planning is essential. This should start in childhood by including the child in decisions about his or her health care as soon as developmentally appropriate (around a 7-year-old cognitive level). At this time, the child should begin to "own" his or her disability by learning about it; being responsible for taking medication (under supervision); becoming independent in the use of appliances and other adaptive devices (e.g., self-catheterization in meningomyelocele); and communicating medical needs when problems develop. By adolescence, it may be appropriate for the doctor to meet alone with the child or at least to direct questions or explanations to the child rather than the parents. In this way, the child is treated as a competent person rather than as an object being examined and discussed.

Essentially, the physician and other health care professionals, the parents, and the child should form a health care team that logically progresses to an adult health care-delivery situation. Beginning in adolescence, the pediatrician can work together with the internist, gradually tapering off his or her services once the internist (or family physician) develops the skills and confidence needed to deal with the individual's developmental disabilities.

Health Care Insurance

In addition to identifying a health care provider, there also may be insurance issues and limitations (American Academy of Pediatrics, Committee on Children with Disabilities and Committee on Adolescence, 1996). If the individual remains a dependent of the parent, he or she can continue to be covered by a working parent's health insurance policy. The individual with disabilities may also qualify for Medicaid coverage through Supplemental Security Income (SSI; see Chapter 36). However, if the individual is no longer eligible for coverage as a dependent or as having a severe disability, finding individual health insurance coverage may be difficult. Contracts often contain a provision about preexisting medical conditions that may limit or even preclude insurance eligibility. Even if insurance is provided, coverage for therapies to improve mobility, communication, or physical functioning may be excluded or provide for only a limited number of visits. As a result, in seeking a job, the individual may be limited to those positions that carry good health insurance with no preexisting condition clause.

Mental Health Issues

Adults with mental retardation and other developmental disabilities are at a greater risk of developing psychiatric disorders than typically developing adults (see Chapter 20). Obtaining mental health care for these individuals, however, has proven problematic. Many mental health professionals have little training or interest in treating individuals with disabilities, especially those who are nonverbal or use alternate means of communication. Even if therapists are interested, there may be problems with reimbursement for long-term behavior health services in the managed care environment. This situation should improve with the 1996 passage of the Mental Health Parity Act, part of the Departments of Veterans Affairs and Housing and Urban Development and Independent Agencies Appropriations Act of 1997, PL 104-204, which mandates that insurers offer coverage for mental illness treatments that are equal to yearly or lifetime maximums set for physical illness treatments. Going into effect in January, 1998, this law should increase access to long-term mental health services for individuals with disabilities. Because many states have separate mental health and mental retardation programs, however, there may be a lack of coordinated care, and individuals may slip through the cracks. This is especially true in settings that favor deinstitutionalization, in which individuals with severe disabilities are placed in the community without first ensuring that all requisite services are in place. As a further complication, when individuals with developmental disabilities experience severe behavior or psychiatric problems, their community placement may be withdrawn.

Medical Complications in Young Adulthood

Most developmental disabilities are considered to be nonprogressive disorders. Yet, while the underlying condition may not change, its manifestations often vary over time or predispose the adult to new associated impairments. In cerebral palsy, for example, contractures may increase over time, making ambulation or seating more difficult. In adults with Down syndrome, the incidence of arthritis and cardiac problems in young adulthood is more common than in the typically developing population. Individuals with meningomyelocele (and many other disabilities) have a greater propensity toward obesity in adolescence, which may influence mobility and general health. The disability also may place the individual at increased risk for complications of common adult conditions; for example, women with cerebral palsy have more complications during labor and delivery (Winch, Bengston, McLaughlin, et al., 1993). Thus, health care professionals need to be alert to possible late-onset complications of developmental disabilities in order to begin prevention or early treatment measures.

RECREATION, LEISURE, AND SOCIALIZATION

Our lives are segmented into time spent in education, work, and leisure. Because a young adult with a severe disability completes schooling at age 21 and may have only partial or no employment, leisure time expands. If leisure time means "idle time," the hours will drag, the individual may become socially isolated, and life will have little meaning or purpose. Leisure time, however, can be a source of enjoyment and may contribute to skill development, participation in family activities, and meeting people in the community. Thus, preparation for participation in recreational and leisure activities should be one of the educational goals for children with disabilities during secondary school.

Leisure activities are as varied as personalities and interests. They can be passive, such as watching television or reading a book, or active, such as participating in sports, computer games, or community or religious events. Individuals with disabilities should have the training, experience, and opportunity to participate in a range of leisure activities. This is becoming easier with the establishment of both specialized recreational programs, such as the Special Olympics (for children with mental retardation), the Paraplegic Olympics (for children with average intelligence and physical disabilities), therapeutic horseback riding, wheelchair sports, and inclusion activities such as scouting, bowling, martial arts, hiking, playing board games or cards, and taking trips. Leisure activities also may include hobbies such as gardening, woodworking, model building, and dancing. If training to participate in leisure activities is begun in childhood, the activities chosen are likely to be maintained and expanded into adulthood. Persistence, flexibility, planning, and choices are the keys to success in developing an effective leisure and recreation program for an individual with a disability. Participation also is influenced by issues of mobility; the ability to drive or use public transportation leads to a greater range of possible activities.

Leisure activities are a time of socialization. This is particularly important for young adults with developmental disabilities who tend to become socially isolated. The potential for social isolation results from both internal and external forces. These individuals are more likely than their typically developing peers to be shy, introverted, and self-conscious. Alternatively, they may be inappropriately affectionate, garrulous, or aggressive. This combination, plus prejudice against individuals who are "different," results in individuals with disabilities being less sought after as friends and companions (Reinhard & Weibenborn, 1990). Social skills training using role-playing activities can be very helpful in improving these skills and making these individuals more attuned to the reactions of others to their behaviors. Assertiveness training also can help the person develop conversation skills, maintain eye contact, use appropriate body language, or recover from rejection. In addition, counseling can be effective in improving self-image.

ISSUES OF SEXUALITY

The onset of puberty, including the beginning of menstruation, is a period of emerging sexuality in children with disabilities, much as in typically developing adolescents. This is sometimes a sensitive subject for parents, who may have a hard time accepting that adolescents and young adults with developmental disabilities have sexual feelings. Parents also may worry that their child (especially their daughter) will be taken advantage of sexually, become pregnant, or be the victim of sexual abuse or sexually transmitted diseases (STDs). As a result of these concerns, parents may try to shield their child from heterosexual social contacts and knowledge about sex. It is important for professionals to counsel parents that, contrary to their beliefs, educating their child about sexuality is the most effective way of protecting him or her from abuse and the consequences of unprotected sexual activity.

All individuals should be recognized as sexual beings and be provided with appropriate education, support, and privacy. Considering the issue of sexual rights for young adults with disabilities requires integrating psychological, physical, societal, cultural, educational, economic, and spiritual factors. The Council on Child and Adolescent Health of the American Academy of Pediatrics (1996) has suggested that the goals of sexuality education should include 1) developing an appreciation of one's own body; 2) interacting with both genders in respectful and appropriate ways; 3) learning appropriate ways to express affection and love; 4) encouraging the development of meaningful interpersonal relationships; 5) learning to be assertive in protecting the privacy of one's own body; and 6) learning about conception, contraception, and protection from STDs.

Sexuality education can foster responsible decision-making skills and offer young people support and guidance in exploring and affirming their own value and rights as individuals. This education also should encourage adolescents to delay sexual behaviors until they are ready physically, cognitively, and emotionally for mature sexual relationships and their consequences. The course should teach about affection versus sex; intimacy; limit setting; resisting social, media, peer, and partner pressure; and the benefits of abstinence as well as information on pregnancy and prevention of STDs. Role-playing and videotapes can be very useful in this training.

PLANNING FOR THE TRANSITION

A smooth transition to adulthood in individuals with developmental disabilities involves three overlapping steps—planning, process, and evaluation. The planning phase is best accomplished in a noncrisis environment and should involve the child to whatever extent is feasible and all the team members working with him or her, including parents, health care professionals, educators, and social workers. Issues to be tackled include education/training, medical/rehabilitation needs, employment options, residence, social/recreational outlets, attendant care, and finances. In addressing these issues, the team should consider all reasonable options and foresee problems in their implementation. Effective planning may help the team to cope more effectively with future gaps in services and lack of funding. It also can mediate conflicting policies by different service providers and avoid fragmentation or duplication of services, role confusion, and communication problems. Once a plan has been developed, the process phase begins (i.e., implementation) in which chores are divided among the team members and meetings are held to keep track of the progress in achieving the goal of a successful and smooth transition. After the transition takes place, the reassessment phase begins. Here, the plan is periodically (usually yearly) reevaluated to determine its effectiveness and what modifications are needed. When this is done well, it becomes an effective life-care plan.

LIFE SPAN AND AGING

As a result of improved health and home care, the life span of individuals with severe developmental disabilities is increasing considerably. Most individuals are living into adulthood, and many have life spans similar to those of typically developing individuals. Although there is obviously a spectrum from the rapidly fatal anencephaly to the typical life span in learning disabilities and ADHD, even in populations in which there is known to be a severely diminished life span, such as trisomy 18, there is marked variability among those affected. (Although most children with trisomy 18 do not live beyond infancy, some affected children live into adolescence and young adulthood.)

Prediction of life span is influenced by improvements in technology and medical care. Most life-span studies reflect care that is decades old and thus may underestimate the potential life span of a child born today. For instance, before open-heart surgery was available to correct congenital heart disease, children with Down syndrome generally died before adulthood; in the 1990s, they are commonly surviving into their 60s. Furthermore, other previously fatal childhood illnesses that cause disabilities, such as muscular dystrophy and cystic fibrosis, are increasingly being treated as chronic diseases, with the life span of these children extending into the adult years.

Aging people with developmental disabilities, in fact, represent a new constituency within the developmental disabilities service system. Until the 1990s, this system had not included an aging network, but the Developmental Disabilities Assistance and Bill of Rights Act Amendments of 1987, PL 94-103, and the Older American Act Amendments of 1987, PL 98-459, called for integration of the two systems. At the same time, significant progress was made in reforming nursing home practices and reducing inappropriate placement of individuals with developmental disabilities into nursing homes. Many community aging programs have begun to develop specialized services for people with developmental disabilities.

Older individuals with developmental disabilities may have a number of medical problems that occur more frequently or at an earlier age than typically developing individuals. These include disturbances in feeding; incontinence; degenerating bone diseases; and central nervous system disorders (e.g., presenile dementia [Alzheimer disease] in Down syndrome) (Edgerton, Gaston, Kelly, et al., 1994). These problems present special challenges for service provision within this population.

For the most part, people both with and without developmental disabilities age in much the same way, although there may be differences in the way in which this process is manifested. Both groups have specialized needs that can be best met in community settings with individualized programs, including provisions for leisure opportunities (Browder & Cooper, 1994). In order to ensure the integration of these individuals at an older age, it is necessary to continue to modify the aging network services. Changes must occur to provide for such situations as retirement, larger group treatment settings, and a recognition that with increasing age maintenance rather than gaining of function may be the most appropriate goal for the individual.

COMPETENCY AS AN ADULT

By law, when an individual reaches the age of 18, he or she is presumed to be a competent adult. Legal guardians are appointed only if the person is proved incompetent. This requires demonstrating that the individual lacks the capacity to make and communicate responsible decisions and/or has behavior showing an inability to meet the daily need for medical care, nutrition, shelter, or safety (Johnson, 1995). Even if the person can manage his or her affairs and make, understand, and communicate decisions, help may be needed with various other issues including medical care, residential placement, and finances.

As a child with developmental disabilities approaches age 18, competence and consent should be discussed with a lawyer to determine whether establishing guardianship or some other protective service should be considered. A guardian is a decision maker for issues such as medical treatment, placement, and expenditure of funds. The guardian of a person with disabilities would see that appropriate services are provided to that individual, would coordinate these services, and would make certain that all necessary and available assistance is provided. The guardian might also make decisions about whether the individual is to live with another family, reside in a public or private institution, or live in some other residential placement. This individual has legally vested duties and prerogatives comparable with those of a parent and, in fact, usually is the parent. If the guardian is not the parent, he or she usually is not expected to take care of the individual in his or her own home or become financially responsible for the person. Guardianship can be private or public and involve either an individual or an organization. In some states, parents of children with disabilities have formed groups for the express purpose of employing social workers and other trained professionals to serve as guardians for their children. Another option is adoptive parenthood, which implies a more intimate and personal component in addition to the legal responsibilities of guardianship.

In addition to appointing a guardian to oversee the care of the person with disabilities, parents may decide to establish a guardianship of the property of the child. The same individual might serve as both the guardian of the child and of his or her property, but it is often advantageous to have separate people or institutions serve these functions; one may have more knowledge about the individual needs of the person, while the other may be highly sophisticated in financial matters.

Levels of competence also should be considered. This implies allowing the individual with disabilities to make certain decisions where appropriate. For instance, it may be appropriate for an individual with mental retardation requiring limited support to make choices about where he or she wants to live and whether or not to have a roommate, but it may not be appropriate for this individual to make decisions about selling inherited property. Issues regarding the individual's level of competence are best resolved by discussion with a lawyer.

A number of other legal issues of competency require consideration by adults with disabilities and their families. An adult with disabilities can make a will to the extent that he or she is legally competent. Although many states place limitations on the voting rights of people with mental disabilities, some states do not; the limitations that are in place have rarely been challenged. Situations involving criminal prosecutions are usually based on the issue of competence and understanding. When an adult with mental retardation is convicted of a crime, protection and special placement are often necessary, and these situations require special legal consultation.

ESTATE PLANNING

Estate planning always involves difficult choices and the process is even more complicated for families of an individual with a disability (Capowski, 1986). Parents who have already made decisions about who will care for their son or daughter after their deaths also worry about providing for them financially. It is important to retain an attorney with specialized knowledge in this area because of the effect that estate planning may have on other entitlements such as SSI and Medicaid. Because most of these programs have a financial means test dependent on income regardless of age, the parents' will should exclude the individual with a disability from inheriting substantial assets. A "special needs trust" can be established to provide for the individual's special needs while insulating the inheritance from government claims. For instance, if an individual with disabilities is living in his or her parents' home and the parents die, that person would usually be eligible for other community services. If the family has left many assets to this child in the form of property and money, however, these resources have to be utilized before the individual is eligible for public welfare programs. This may defeat the parents' original goal of making life easier for their child. A special needs trust controlled by someone other than the individual with disabilities might allow continued supplementary support of the individual who receives public welfare programs. For example, funds could be used for clothing, adaptive equipment, and other special items. If a special needs trust has not been set up prior to the parents' death, there is still an opportunity to transfer funds to the individual with disabilities without losing eligibility for public welfare programs. In 1993, the Payback Trust was established as part of the Omnibus Budget Reconciliation Act (OBRA) of 1993, PL 103-66. With this legislation, an individual with disabilities who receives funds (e.g., an inheritance) that would usually exclude him or her from participating in public welfare programs can transfer the funds to an irrevocable OBRA 1993 Payback Trust, so called because if there are any funds left in the trust when the beneficiary dies, the state is entitled to be paid back for the full amount of Medicaid monies paid on behalf of the beneficiary.

When the cost of administering a trust would be great in relationship to the assets in it, parents may decide to establish an "informal trust." For example, parents can arrange to have assets in their will pass to a sibling of the individual with a disability, with the understanding that the funds are to be used for the care of the sibling with disabilities.

Before the estate-planning process can begin, parents must consider the effect on other beneficiaries, such as siblings. There are several estate planning resources available to parents, such as the National Plan Alliance, a service component of the National Alliance for the Mentally Ill. These programs offer three key services: 1) developing a future care plan, 2) helping parents establish the necessary resources to fund the plan, and 3) identifying the people and/or programs responsible for carrying out the plan. In addition, the National Institute on Life Planning for People with Disabilities, a nonprofit organization affiliated with Sonoma State University in California, serves as a national clearinghouse for estate planning and conducts workshops on all aspects of life planning for parents and professionals.

Another important feature in the will is the appointment of an executor. This is different from a person who may be designated as a guardian and is responsible for carrying out the instructions of the will. Parents also should establish a power of attorney to designate a person who will carry out their wishes if they become unable to do so.

KELVIN

Kelvin is a 23-year-old man with spastic quadriplegia and mental retardation requiring extensive support, a consequence of complications of prematurity. He functions cognitively at around a 3-year-old level and uses a wheelchair. His mother, Martha, cared for him at home until this year when Kelvin entered a group home run by the United Cerebral Palsy Associations that is about 20 minutes from his mother's house. He lives there with three other young adults with similar disabilities, with whom he shares certain responsibilities in the home. He engages in many recreational and leisure activities, including therapeutic horseback riding, swimming, and bowling. Since he "graduated" from his special education program 2 years ago, Kelvin has attended an adult day program in which he works on enhancing his daily living skills and receives physical and speech therapy. He continues to come home for some weekends and for all holidays, and he remains an active participant in family functions with his two siblings, ages 16 and 18.

Kelvin's excellent living situation and program were the result of careful planning that started while he was in high school. Martha knew early on that Kelvin would eventually want to leave home and live with peers in the community. With the help of the school social worker, she got Kelvin on a waiting list for a number of group homes and, after 3 years, received a placement. His adult day program also was arranged through school contacts and represented a continuation of his special education program. In addition, Martha was able to arrange for a family practitioner to take over Kelvin's medical care from their pediatrician after he turned 18. Finally, Martha went to court to obtain guardianship of Kelvin, make a will, and establish a small trust fund. Kelvin is happy in his placement and his mother feels a level of comfort that he is in a stable and good environment. She now feels more confident about the future and content in the knowledge that she has established a good life-care plan for Kelvin.

SUMMARY

Improved care for children with severe disabilities has allowed most to live into adulthood. As individuals with developmental disabilities approach this period of transition, their medical and psychosocial needs change. Early and effective planning is essential for these individuals to reach their full potential and enjoy productive, healthy, and happy lives. Planning should start in the early teens with the active participation of the family and child together with teachers and health care providers. Consideration needs to be given to issues of socialization, sexuality, housing, employment, medical care, and financial planning. With adequate planning, the implementation of the transition plan is more likely to be smooth; however, all members of the team must continuously evaluate progress and be ready to modify services as needed.

REFERENCES

American Academy of Pediatrics, Committee on Children with Disabilities and Committee on Adolescence. (1996). Transition of care provided for adolescents with special health care needs. *Pediatrics, 98*(6), 1203–1205.

American Academy of Pediatrics, Council on Child and Adolescent Health. (1996). Sexuality education of children and adolescents with developmental disabilities. *Pediatrics, 97,* 275–278.

Americans with Disabilities Act (ADA) of 1990, PL 101-336, 42 U.S.C. § 12101 *et seq.*

Anderson, E.M., Clark, L., & Spain, B. (1982). *Disability in adolescence.* New York: Methuen & Company.

Browder, D.M., & Cooper, K.J.K. (1994). Inclusion of older adults with mental retardation in leisure opportunities. *Mental Retardation, 32,* 91–99.

Capowski, J. (1986). Public benefits, legal services, and estate planning. In M.L. Batshaw & Y.M. Perret (Eds.), *Children with disabilities: A medical primer* (2nd ed., pp. 381–396). Baltimore: Paul H. Brookes Publishing Co.

Conroy, J.W. (1996). The small ICF/MR program: Dimensions of quality and cost. *Mental Retardation, 34,* 13–26.

Developmental Disabilities Assistance and Bill of Rights Act Amendements of 1987, PL 94-103, 42 U.S.C. § 6000 *et seq.*

Edgerton, R.B., Gaston, M.A., Kelly, H., et al. (1994). Health care for aging people with mental retardation. *Mental Retardation, 32,* 146–150.

Epstein, R. (1996). More good news. *Exceptional Parent, X,* 71.

Epstein, R. (1996). Portability Act 1996. *Exceptional Parent, X,* 63–65.

Hallum, A. (1995). Disability and the transition to adulthood: Issues for the disabled child, the family, and the pediatrician. *Current Problems in Pediatrics, 25,* 12–50.

Hallum, A., & Krumboltz, J.D. (1993). Parents caring for young adults with severe physical disabilities: Psychological issues. *Developmental Medicine and Child Neurology, 35,* 24–32.

Individuals with Disabilities Education Act (IDEA) of 1990, PL 101-476, 20 U.S.C. § 1400 *et seq.*

Johnson, C.P. (1995). Transition into adulthood. *Pediatric Annals, 24,* 268–273.

Johnson, C.P. (1996). Transition in adolescents with disabilities. In A.J. Capute & P.J. Accardo (Eds.), *Developmental disabilities in infancy and childhood: Vol. 1. Neurodevelopmental diagnosis and treatment* (2nd ed., pp. 549–570). Baltimore: Paul H. Brookes Publishing Co.

King, G.A., Shultz, I.Z., Steel, E., et al. (1993). Self-evaluation and self-concept of adolescents with physical disabilities. *American Journal of Occupational Therapy, 47,* 132–140.

McGaughey, M.J., Kiernan, W.E., McNally, L.C., et al. (1995). A peaceful coexistence? State MR/DD agency trends in integrated employment and facility-based services. *Mental Retardation, 33,* 170–180.

Molaison, V.A., Black, M.M., Sachs, M.L., et al. (1995). Services for adult family members with mental retardation: Perceptions of accessibility and satisfaction. *Mental Retardation, 33,* 181–185.

Newacheck, P.W. (1989). Adolescents with special health needs: Prevalence, severity, and access to health services. *Pediatrics, 84,* 872–881.

Older American Act Amendments of 1987, PL 98-459, 20 U.S.C. § 1767 *et seq.*

Omnibus Budget Reconciliation Act of 1993, PL 103-66, 42 U.S.C. § 629 *et seq.*

Rehabilitation Act of 1973, PL 93-112, 29 U.S.C. § 701 *et seq.*

Rehabilitation Act Amendments of 1978, PL 95-602, 29 U.S.C. § 701 *et seq.*

Rehabilitation Act Amendments of 1992, PL 102-569, 29 U.S.C. § 701 *et seq.*

Reinhard, H.G., & Weibenborn. M. (1990). Isolation and the mastering of anxiety in physically handicapped children and adolescents. *Acta Paedopsychiatry, 53,* 298–304.

Straugh, C.T., II. (Ed.). (1988). *Lovejoy's college guide for the learning disabled* (2nd ed.). New York: Monarch Press.

U.S. Department of Education. (1992). People with work disability in the U.S. *Disability Statistical Abstract, 4.* San Francisco: University of California, Disability Statistics Program.

U.S. Departments of Veterans Affairs and Housing and Urban Development and Independent Agencies Appropriations Act of 1997, PL 104-204, 42 U.S.C. § 300 *et seq.*

Varnet, T. (1996). OBRA payback trusts. *Exceptional Parent, X,* 69–70.

Wacker, D.P., Harper, D.C., Powell, J.W., et al. (1983). Life outcomes and satisfaction ratings of multihandicapped adults. *Developmental Medicine and Child Neurology, 25,* 625–631.

Winch, R., Bengtson, L., McLaughlin, J., et al. (1993). Women with cerebral palsy: Obstetric experience and neonatal outcome. *Developmental Medicine and Child Neurology, 35,* 974–982.

36 Providing Health Care in the 21st Century

Angelo P. Giardino
Lowell Ives Arye

Upon completion of this chapter, the reader will:

- understand the definition of children with special health care needs
- recognize the differences between fee-for-service and prepaid health care delivery systems
- understand the basic concepts underlying managed care and its implications for children with special health care needs
- be aware of the different public benefits that children with special health care needs may utilize for a variety of services

Children with special health care needs may be broadly defined as the group of children who are at risk for or who have ongoing physical, developmental, behavior, or emotional disorders that require health care services beyond those needed by children without such conditions (Allen, 1995; Perrin, Newacheck, Pless, et al., 1993). This definition includes ongoing medical conditions such as hemophilia, diabetes, and asthma as well as developmental disabilities such as autism, mental retardation, sensory impairments, and cerebral palsy. It should be noted that some children will have both an ongoing medical condition and a developmental disability (e.g., a child with diabetes who develops visual impairment from diabetic retinopathy). Coordinating health care services for these children presents a challenge both to the child's family and to health care providers because of the complexity involved with coordinating different agencies, institutions, and professionals to work effectively together to fashion a comprehensive care plan (Perrin, 1990). This coordination is made even more complex as the child's needs may span a range of services, including some that are not traditionally seen as health related such as education and housing. Families and child advocates expend an enormous amount of time and energy attempting to align the available programs and services with the child's needs. This chapter examines the provision of health care services in an evolving health care environment for a subset of children with special health care needs, children with developmental disabilities. A particular emphasis is placed on the concepts of managed care and the financing issues involved in insurance coverage.

THE CHANGING HEALTH CARE ENVIRONMENT

The national systems of health care delivery and financing have undergone monumental changes since the 1960s (Kissick, 1994). Methods of financing clearly exert pressure on the health care delivery system's structure and function. As early as 1971, officials with the National Association of Children's Hospitals and Related Institutions (NACHRI) were voicing concerns about the impact that financing strategies would inevitably have on pediatric providers and ultimately on the children they served:

> The 70s threaten to be a difficult decade for children's hospitals because of increasing demands for services, rising costs, the shrinking value of the dollar, unreasonable ceilings on reimbursement in some states, an impending threat of restrictive limitations under a federal prospective reimbursement system, declining inpatient censuses, increased activity in preventive medicine and primary care, increased political interest in hospitals and greater pressure for community involvement. (Katz, 1993, p. 12)

This quotation continues to have relevance, and many of the issues identified in the early 1970s remain of concern to families and providers alike. The most significant change taking place in financing health care delivery in the 1990s is the movement from a fee-for-service model to managed care, with its focus on the integration of financing and delivery strategies.

For most of its history, the health care system in the United States has utilized a fee-for-service model, in which the health care provider receives a payment for each unit of service rendered (MacLeod, 1993). The typical fee has been based on a "usual and customary" charge for the service. This system is a **retrospective** payment system; payment is made after the service is provided. This approach has been criticized for encouraging health care professionals to provide too many services. Presently undergoing rapid change, this system continues to evolve toward a **prospective** or prepayment approach (Wagner, 1993). The notion of prepayment is a defining feature of managed care; in its purest form, the provider is paid a set fee based solely on the number of individuals to be served (capitation rate). No additional payment is made when services are provided. This approach is expected to result in the provision of only appropriate services, because providers are not compensated for "doing more." A criticism of managed care is that such a system may encourage providers to "do less" than is optimal for the individuals. This point is of particular concern to children with ongoing and disabling conditions because their care may be significantly more expensive than that of typically developing children (Neff & Anderson, 1995).

MANAGED CARE

Managed care includes five key elements: 1) prospective payment, 2) networks of selected providers, 3) credentialing of providers using explicit standards, 4) quality assurance and utilization review programs, and 5) incentives for use of network providers (Freund & Lewit, 1993). Using these techniques, managed care organizations (MCOs) in theory develop a more comprehensive range of health care services with incentives and oversight devices intended to maximize health benefits while limiting utilization and expenditures.

MCOs usually reimburse providers on a capitated basis providing a set payment each month for each individual covered, regardless of the amount of services that the individual uses (typically referred to as the "per-member-per-month" rate or the PMPM). If the individuals, on average, use fewer services than expected that month, the MCO realizes a financial gain; if the individuals, on average, use more services than expected, the MCO may face a financial loss. Thus, the MCOs seek to keep health care expenditures at or below monthly expectations in order to maximize their potential financial gain. Because the financial incentive structure discourages overuse of services, this prepaid approach to providing health care should lead to a system in which only appropriate services are delivered.

In theory, managed care programs have several advantages for children with disabilities and their families over the more traditional indemnity types of private insurance, including the following (Smith & Ashbaugh, 1995):

1. Increasing flexibility to design programs that will meet the children's special needs
2. Covering well-child care, routine immunizations, and other preventive care that may be excluded in traditional indemnity plans
3. Protecting families from excessive medical costs
4. Offering point-of-service (POS) plans that provide families with the benefits of managed care while retaining the choice of physician

Concerns have been raised, however, that managed care systems also can work to the disadvantage of children with disabilities (Smith & Ashbaugh, 1995). Many advocates and experts suggest that MCOs actually reduce the access children have to pediatric subspecialty and inpatient care. In one study of pediatric referrals in a managed care environment (not limited solely to children with special health care needs), 1,264 pediatricians were asked about their experiences with MCOs in making referrals to subspecialists (e.g., pediatric neurologist, child psychiatrist, pediatric gastroenterologist) (Cartland & Yudkowsky, 1992). More than 20% of these pediatricians reported that at least one referral to a subspecialist had been denied in the previous year, and more than 10% reported that a referral for inpatient care had been denied. Of those pediatricians who had service referral denied, 35% perceived that their patients' health was adversely affected by the denial (Cartland & Yudkowsky, 1992). This study is particularly troubling with regard to the potential impact on the health of children with developmental disabilities.

Health Maintenance Organizations

Health maintenance organizations (HMOs) are perhaps the best known kind of MCO. A number of HMO models exist, including the following:

1. **Staff model:** HMOs hire physicians directly and own the facilities in which their physicians work. The physicians in staff model HMOs are salaried by the HMO.
2. **Group model:** HMOs do not salary the physicians but contract exclusively with a multispecialty physician group practice that reimburses the physicians either via salaries or shares in the capitation payments. A variant of the group model is the network model in which the HMO contracts with several different multispecialty physician group practices.
3. **Individual practice association (IPA) model:** Physicians in the IPA contract with the HMO but do not necessarily interact with each other as would physicians in a staff or group model. The IPA physicians frequently operate their own practices and may chose to contract with many HMOs (Freund & Lewit, 1993).

Other Managed Care Plans

Two forms of managed care plans related to MCOs are preferred provider organizations (PPOs) and point-of-service (POS) plans. PPOs contract for services with physicians on a discounted fee-for-service basis. This plan uses the group's buying power to negotiate a discounted fee from physicians and other providers and then passes the discounts on to purchasers of the plan, provided that enrollees in the plan utilize services from physicians in the PPO network.

POS plans contract with providers in an HMO- or PPO-like arrangement and encourage enrollees to use these network providers. In the POS plan, however, unlike in an HMO or PPO, enrollees may obtain services outside of the network of participating providers and still receive some, although diminished, coverage from the plan. Typically, most services are nearly fully paid for by the plan if the individual uses an in-network provider. If the individual chooses to go outside the list of in-network providers, however, the additional costs associated with this choice are passed on to the individual directly. This additional cost is referred to as "out-of-pocket" expense because the enrollee pays for it directly. It may include higher copayments at the time of service and larger deductible amounts for which the enrollee is responsible. The POS plan offers consumers the comprehensive services and low out-of-pocket costs of an HMO while still allowing them to exercise choice in obtaining services much like a traditional indemnity plan (Hillman, 1995; Institute for Family Centered Care, 1996a; Sheils & Wolfe, 1992).

Families are increasingly turning to managed care plans for health care coverage. HMO membership rose from 29 million in 1987 to an estimated 50 million in 1994 (Weiss, 1995). In 1997, HMOs deliver health care to more than 25% of the entire U.S. population, essentially doubling their enrollment in less than 10 years (Mitka, 1995). Pediatricians increasingly are involved with managed care; at least 80% participated in some form of HMO, PPO, or IPA in 1994 (Emmons & Simon, 1994).

Managed care plans have little incentive to enroll children with developmental disabilities or ongoing medical conditions. As managed care becomes the dominant organizational form for health care services financing and delivery, however, the special health care needs of this population will become an area requiring special programming (Ireys, Grason, & Guyer, 1996). Child advocates are making careful arguments that, despite the variability in the special health care needs population, a capitated pricing system for children with special health care needs will need to reflect the higher costs that are inherent in caring for this population (Neff & Anderson, 1995).

PAYING FOR HEALTH CARE SERVICES FOR CHILDREN WITH DISABILITIES

Families of children with special health care needs utilize various public and private funding sources to finance the costs of health care, largely relying on health care insurance. Private insurance, often called commercial insurance, may be purchased by the parents' employers or by the parents themselves, if they have sufficient funds to do so. Publicly funded "insurance" for children essentially refers to programs funded via Medicaid. (Medicare coverage is uncommon in the pediatric age group.)

Private Insurance (Commercial Coverage)

There is a spectrum of private health insurance programs. These range from indemnity or major medical plans (e.g., traditional Blue Cross/Blue Shield coverage) (Table 36.1) that provide for

Table 36.1. Common attributes of nonmanaged care commercial insurance

	Individual insurance	Group insurance	Self-insurance
Description	Based on a contract between a purchaser and insurer in which the purchaser pays a fixed premium for the insurer's agreement to pay approved expenditures. Generally, premiums are set at a higher rate than other insurance.	Similar to individual insurance but premiums are kept relatively low for the payer by spreading the risk within a group, frequently an employee group. Average premiums for the entire group are set, taking into account the different ages, sex, and potential medical problems of the group.	Relatively larger employers may opt to construct their own plans that they fund themselves. They essentially function as their own insurers.
Advantages	Insurer can raise premiums each year to recoup the costs of business from the previous year.	The insurer minimizes risk of attracting a disproportionate share of high-risk individuals by mandating that all members of the group be included in the group insurance.	Advantageous to the employer because the Employment Retirement Income Security Act (ERISA) prohibits states from regulating self-insured plans and thus such plans are exempt from paying for state mandated benefits and avoid insurance premium taxes.
Disadvantages	Same as for group insurance.	Under small group or individual insurance plans, the insurer is more at risk for adverse selection. Private insurers use a process called medical underwriting, in which an assessment of the individual's or group's health risks is made to determine the premium rates, impose coverage limitations, or reject the insurance application.	The employer is responsible for all medical claims, even high claims (e.g., from low birth weight babies).
Example	The individual typically has a deductible (amount for which he or she is solely responsible) and a percentage for which he or she can expect reimbursement (e.g., if an individual has a plan that has a $100 deductible and an 80% reimbursement rate and incurs $1,000 of medical bills, he or she would submit the receipts, and the plan would first subtract $100 deductible from the $1,000; next, the $900 remaining would be reviewed, and the individual could expect to be reimbursed up to 80% [.8 × $900 = $720]).		

Adapted from Institute for Family Centered Care (1996a); Sheils & Wolfe (1992).

acute medical care to managed care plans that, in addition, offer a wide range of preventive and rehabilitative health care services. Table 36.2 lists the differences that might be expected in various types of health care insurance plans.

The principal form of health insurance for all Americans under age 65 is that provided by employers. There has been a decline in the number of workers who receive insurance through their work, however, from 66% in 1979 to 61% in 1993 (Schactman & Altman, 1995). Furthermore, the percentage of children with employer-based health insurance declined from 64% in 1987 to 57% in 1993. Most ominous is the growing number of children and families without any health insurance. In 1993, almost one in seven children, more than 9.4 million children across the United States, were uninsured. In 1994, 10 million children were without health care insurance (Children's Defense Fund, 1996b). In fact, 79% of the rising total number of uninsured people are children (Suh, 1995). In terms of coverage under indemnity plans for children with disabilities, a 1987 survey of 150 employers showed that a majority of the plans provided coverage for medical supplies, equipment, lab services, prescriptions, physical therapy, and speech therapy (Fox, Wicks, & Newacheck, 1993). Insurers, however, required that the therapies be used to restore loss of function associated with an illness or injury. These restrictions would limit coverage for children who require treatment to improve their age-appropriate function (e.g., mental retardation) or those who have congenital impairments (e.g., meningomyelocele). Many of the plans restricted the number of treatments to 90 per year and limited the financing of intervention services by annual or lifetime caps. Although lifetime caps seem high, on average $1 million, children with severe disabilities may reach this limit in just a few years. This forces the parents to use up most of their savings to pay for medical expenses prior to the child qualifying for Medicaid (often referred to as medical assistance or MA).

Table 36.2.   Effects of different health insurance plans on the delivery of medical care

Characteristic of medical care	Indemnity plan with utilization controls	Preferred provider organization	IPA	Staff/group model HMO	Point-of-service HMO
Ability to choose providers	0	−	−	−	−0
Preventive care	0	+	+	+	+
Illness-related visits to primary care physician	0	+	+?	+?	+?
Visits to specialists	0	+	?	−	+?
Use of diagnostic tests	−	−	−	−	−?
Rate of surgery	−	−	−	−	−
Admission to hospital	−	−	−	−	−
Use of emergency room	?	?	−	−	−

Adapted from Freund & Lewit (1993).

Note: Expected impact of plan on consumer use/physician practice (all else equal) as compared to traditional fee-for-service indemnity insurance plans or traditional fee-for-service Medicaid plans. (Key: 0 = No change. − = Tends to decrease. + = Tends to increase. ? = Direction unclear.)

Because premium costs in commercial insurance are based on the average of the insured group's expected medical expense, some employers, especially small ones, may limit coverage for employees whose health expenses exceed expectations. They also may eliminate health care coverage for dependents, placing children, especially those with disabilities, in a precarious position. It is interesting to note that the decline in employer-supported coverage of children is not due to a decrease in employment. Instead, it is the result of fewer employers offering or subsidizing health insurance plans that include coverage for dependents (Suh, 1995).

Publicly Funded Programs

The publicly funded Medicaid program for children serves as the societal safety net for children who are increasingly not being covered by private insurance. The growth in Medicaid, however, has not kept pace with the decline in private insurance coverage for children (Suh, 1995). Between 1990 and 1992, nearly one third of all children went for at least 1 month without any health insurance, and only a portion of these children subsequently acquired Medicaid coverage (Table 36.3). The proportion of children covered under Medicaid increased from less than 16% to more than 22% of the pediatric age group between 1988 and 1993 (Newacheck, Hughes, & Cisternas, 1995; Sheils & Wolfe, 1992). It is of note that although children (between birth and 21 years of age) comprise 57% of the Medicaid program population, they account for only 23% of the program expenditures (Flint, Yudkowsky, & Tang, 1995).

Federal and state government programs provide numerous avenues for children with disabilities and their families to gain access to a range of health care services. For example, Supplemental Security Income (SSI) and Parts B and H of the Individuals with Disabilities Education Act (IDEA) of 1990, PL 101-476, both provide a link to Medicaid. As many of these programs are administered by the states, however, there is considerable variation regarding who is eligible, the types of services covered, and the amount of care provided. A brief examination of these different programs is provided in Table 36.4. The most significant issue related to Medicaid coverage has been the shift toward enrollment in managed care plans. Three percent of the Medicaid population (approximately 750,000 people) were enrolled in managed care plans in 1993 compared with 23% (approximately 4.8 million people) in 1994 (Kaiser Commission on the Future of Medicaid, 1995). Although managed care programs hold the promise of expanding access to comprehensive medical services, they also carry the risk of becoming a vehicle of restricting children's access to essential services (Suh, 1995).

LOOKING TOWARD THE FUTURE

Coordinating health care services for children with disabilities remains a complicated and challenging task for family members, health care professionals, and child advocates. Because of the high cost of care and the existence of spending caps and benefit maximums, most children with

Table 36.3. Health insurance status of U.S. children and adolescents through age 21 in millions

	1990	1991	1992	1993
Private insurance	54.0 (68.1%)	53.0 (66.5%)	52.4 (65.2%)	49.9 (62.4%)
Medicaid	13.4 (16.9%)	15.1 (18.9%)	16.1 (20.1%)	17.8 (22.3%)
Uninsured	11.9 (15.0%)	11.7 (14.6%)	11.8 (14.7%)	12.2 (15.3%)

Source: Flint, Yudkowsky, & Tang (1995).

Table 36.4. Overview of federal assistance programs

Program	Description	Comments
Supplemental Security Income (SSI)	Provides cash benefits to low-income people who meet financial eligibility requirements and the Social Security Administration's (SSA) medical definition of disability. The SSA determines applicant's financial eligibility, contracts with, and funds state agencies, called Disability Determination Services (DDS), to decide the medical eligibility for benefits.	In 1991, the Supreme Court in *Sullivan v. Zebley* required SSA to develop a process to determine children's eligibility for disability benefits that was similar to that used for adults. This new Individual Functional Assessment (IFA) for children must show that the child's impairment limits his or her ability to function independently in an age-appropriate manner. "Specifically, the impairment must substantially reduce the child's ability to grow, develop, or mature physically, mentally, or emotionally to the extent it limits his or her ability to 1) attain age-appropriate developmental milestones; 2) attain age-appropriate daily activities at home, school, or work; or 3) acquire the skills needed to assume adult roles" (U.S. General Accounting Office, 1995).
	As of June 1995, 940,000 children received SSI benefits. The average monthly benefit amount including state supplementation was $420.	
	In 1995, approximately two thirds of all children receiving SSI benefits were eligible based on mental impairments and one third based on a physical disability (National Commission on Childhood Disability, 1995).	Welfare reform legislation passed in 1996 limits the use of the IFA. A smaller number of children with special health care needs will be determined eligible for SSI under the new law.
	Provides adults and children with disabilities a linkage to the Medicaid program. SSI recipients represent slightly over one quarter of the Medicaid population but account for over two thirds of all Medicaid expenditures (Hillman & Arye, 1995).	
Medicaid	Primary public health program for the poor.	Under the Early and Periodic Screening, Diagnosis, and Treatment (EPSDT) program children must receive screening and diagnostic services and any medically necessary treatments that may not be available under a state's Medicaid program but that are allowable under federal Medicaid law. This requirement makes EPSDT an important vehicle for children with disabilities.
	States are mandated by federal law to include categorically needy coverage groups: recipients of SSI and Aid to Families with Dependent Children (AFDC), low-income pregnant women and children, and people in institutional care. States also have the option to extend coverage to medically needy people. AFDC is to be converted to a new program, Temporary Assistance for Needy Families (TANF), under provisions of the welfare reform legislation contained in PL 104-193 (Children's Defense Fund, 1996b).	
During 1993, approximately 796,000 children with disabilities were enrolled in Medicaid throughout the United States. Approximately 665,000 of these children with disabilities also received SSI benefits.	Provides access to a range of ancillary therapies, home care, mental health, case management, and transportation to medical services. Most state Medicaid programs cover ongoing-maintenance	In an effort to control costs, and secondarily to ensure quality and access to health care, many states are moving toward managed care approaches. All but eight states currently have some type of managed care programs, covering nearly a quarter of Medicaid beneficiaries. In 1995, 18 states were enrolling people with disabilities in one or more risk-
In most states, Medicaid is the single largest and fastest growing item in the state's budget, accounting		

for more than 18% of states' total expenditures.

services, preventive services, and nursing home care, in addition to hospitalization and physician services.

States are mandated to cover a core set of benefits, including hospital, outpatient, physician services, basic home health services, and EPSDT program.

The states have an option to cover services by other health professionals, such as nurses, psychologists, social workers, case managers, and services provided in clinics.

Within federal guidelines, states have flexibility in determining reimbursement rates for particular services and providers.

based managed care plans mostly on a voluntary basis (Saucier, 1995).

In 1993, 50% of states with mandatory enrollment of Medicaid recipients exempted specific categories of children with special health care needs, thus allowing them to remain in the fee-for-service program (Ireys, Grason, & Guyer, 1996).

Title V

In 1992, 678,640 children received medical services via Children with Special Health Care Needs (CSHCN) programs (U.S. Department of Health and Human Services, 1990).

The Crippled Children Services program was authorized under Title V of the Social Security Act of 1935 and in 1985 it was renamed the CSHCN program. It currently exists under the Maternal and Child Health (MCH) Block Grant in Title V of the Social Security Act.

States are mandated to spend a minimum of 30% of their MCH Block Grant on CSHCN programs. States determine their own programmatic and financial eligibility requirements for defining children with special health needs who are eligible under the program and determine what services are provided.

Tremendous variability in eligibility and services exists throughout the United States. Most states provide screening and treatment of disabling conditions as well as ongoing support services, including case management and counseling.

Services are usually provided by physicians on a fee-for-service basis and through state health agencies (U.S. Department of Health and Human Services, 1990).

States are mandated to provide 1) rehabilitative services unavailable through Medicaid to children under 16 years of age who receive SSI and 2) community-based services for children with special health care needs.

CSHCN programs also address children with disabilities resulting from mental impairments.

continued

Table 36.4. *(continued)*

Program	Description	Comments
Individuals with Disabilities Education Act (IDEA) During the 1994 school year, more than 5.3 million children from birth to 21 years old received special education services. Approximately 7.7% of all children in school received special education services during the 1993–1994 academic year (Lewit & Baker, 1996).	States and localities fund the majority of special education services, but the federal government does provide funds through the Education for All Handicapped Children Act, initially known as PL 94-142 and renamed IDEA in 1990, which mandates states to provide children with specified disabilities a free appropriate public education. Part B of IDEA deals with the provision of related services for children age 3 and older deemed to need special education services. Part H of IDEA deals with the provision of services to infants and toddlers with disabilities (Perrin et al., 1993).

Services provided by Part B include classroom instruction, instruction in physical education, home instruction, and instruction in hospitals and institutions. Other related services are defined as transportation and corrective or other supportive services such as health-related services "including speech pathology, audiology, psychological services, physical and occupational therapy, early identification and assessment of disabilities, counseling services, school health services, social work services in schools, and medical services for evaluation and diagnostic purposes only" (U.S. Department of Health and Human Services, 1991).

Part H supports early intervention programs to infants and toddlers with disabilities and their families. This federal program funds states for planning early intervention services to promote the development of children from birth to age 3. States determine eligibility of services for infants and toddlers, develop needs assessments, and create a process for an individualized family services plan. This plan and the services provided through Part H begin the transition for the child into preschool programs provided under Part B. | State Medicaid programs can pay for related services provided through Parts B and H that are specified in the federal Medicaid law and determined to be medically necessary under the state Medicaid agency. Under Medicaid, the EPSDT program provides that children must receive not only screening and diagnostic services, but also any medically necessary treatments that are allowable under federal Medicaid law (U.S. Department of Health and Human Services, 1991). A provision in the Medicare Catastrophic Coverage Act of 1988 clarifies the linkage between Medicaid and Parts B and H by explaining that services covered under Medicaid will be reimbursed under Medicaid even if they are also educationally related and therefore reimbursable under the Education program (Fox, Wicks, McManus, Newacheck, 1992). |

Source: Flint, Yudkowsky, & Tang (1995).

782

special health care needs obtain some part of their health care services via publicly funded programs such as 1) SSI from the Social Security Administration, 2) Title V programs from Maternal and Child Health Bureau, and 3) Parts B and H services of IDEA through the Department of Education. This further complicates the task of fashioning care plans most likely to assist children in achieving their full developmental potential. Children and families must navigate through a number of different agencies, institutions, and providers, each with its own set of regulations and professional perspectives. In addition, publicly funded programs are coming under increased scrutiny as legislative and budgetary debates focus on cost. Thus, one can only assume that over time public resources for providing health care services for these children will become scarcer.

The health care environment is turning increasingly toward managed care as a financing strategy because of its goals of providing appropriate services while controlling costs. Despite this focus on reducing costs, the comprehensive approach of managed care toward service delivery has the potential of improving the health care of children with special health care needs. For managed care to become an ally of children with special needs, however, it must develop programs that recognize the services and supports needed by this special population (Committee on Child Financing, 1995; Institute for Family Centered Care, 1996b; Neff & Anderson, 1995; Newacheck, Stein, Walker, et al., 1996).

PROVIDING A MEDICAL HOME

Children with disabilities may have significant ongoing health care requirements and service coordination needs; thus, it is essential to provide a comprehensive, health promotion approach allowing for coordination of primary care with specialty care. In addressing this issue, the American Academy of Pediatrics (1992) calls for all children to have a "medical home" that receives appropriate compensation for the entire range of services required for heath care. A good medical home is defined as one that provides accessible, continuous, comprehensive, family-centered, coordinated, and compassionate health care in an atmosphere of mutual responsibility and trust among provider, child, and caregiver(s).

As health care systems have evolved and undergone reform, child care advocates have called for the establishment of pediatric standards of care for a medical home. These would define a comprehensive package of benefits and establish access parameters for services that would be binding for providers and insurers (Wehr & Jameson, 1994). The NACHRI recommends that all children receive health care through an integrated child health care network that is

1. Expert in meeting the full continuum of children's health care needs, including preventive, primary, acute, subspecialty, postacute, habilitative and rehabilitative, long-term, and mental health
2. Organized to work together to assume, on a capitated basis, the financial risks and responsibilities for managing the full continuum of care for a specific population of children
3. Accountable to the public for the health status (i.e., wellness) of the population of children covered, as well as for their use of services, according to agreed-upon measures of children's health status and pediatric care outcomes
4. Appropriate for the children's immediate needs as well as for their long-term physical, psychological, social, educational, and spiritual development as determined by experts in the care of children (NACHRI, Board of Trustees, 1994).

HEALTH CARE USE BY CHILDREN WITH DISABILITIES

Overall, children with special health care needs use at least twice as many health care services as the average child without special health care needs (Newacheck, 1989; Newacheck, Hughes, Stoddard, et al., 1994). Yet, while some children with special health care needs may utilize tremendous amounts of health care services, others may not utilize any more than a child without such a disability (Newacheck & Taylor, 1992). This extensive variation in costs and utilization rates for health care services among children with special health care needs leads to the observation that the majority of children with disabilities or ongoing conditions will not incur exorbitant medical expenditures in a given year (Ireys et al., 1996). The small number of catastrophically affected children, however, may incur extremely high medical care costs. For example, using 1990 hospital cost data, a premature infant weighing less than 1,000 grams cost more than 100 times more to care for than did a full-term infant (Blackman, Healy, & Ruppert, 1992).

PRINCIPLES TO GUIDE CARE MANAGEMENT

In responding to requests for guidance in the Medicaid managed care initiatives for people with developmental disabilities, the National Association of State Directors of Developmental Disabilities Services (NASDDDS) (1995) issued a comprehensive list of principles. These principles are valuable because they focus attention on what is best for the individual with special health care needs, not on what is most convenient for the plan designers. The NASDDDS (1995) maintains the position that any managed care approach being considered for implementation should have as its goal improved outcomes for people with developmental disabilities and their families as compared with the fee-for-service financing system.

Through their Medicaid programs, states continue to take a variety of approaches to meeting the service delivery requirements for children with special health care needs. The Medicaid Working Group provides insight into the complexity of the planning process and the pitfalls that are best avoided in fashioning a service delivery system for children with special health care needs, noting that diversity exists within this population. These differences span not only individual characteristics, but also a range of conditions, service needs, utilization patterns, and the aggregate cost of care both within and among diagnostic groups. They also point out the irrational nature of the fragmented system for meeting the full range of needs that individuals with disabilities may manifest. They advocate coordination among a variety of systems, including several nontraditional health care programs such as housing, income support, transportation, education, and employment services (Drainoni, Tobias, & Dreyfus, 1995). Figure 36.1 presents an outline that may help in organizing the available information concerning the child's projected needs. Families and service coordinators may find this helpful as they meet to formulate a care plan for the children with special health care needs.

DANIELLE

Danielle is a 10-year-old girl who was born 3 months prematurely. She had a difficult perinatal period with respiratory distress syndrome and an intracerebral hemorrhage. When discharged at 3 months of age, she was noted to have significant motor and cognitive delays and was enrolled in a home-based early intervention program funded through a collaboration between the county

Planning for Child and Family Needs **Parent–Professional Worksheet**	
Category	**Who/where/how**
Advocacy	
Attendant/nursing/respite care	
Service coordination	
Developmental needs	
Educational services	
Equipment	
Financial/health insurance	
Housing/placement	
Legal/guardianship	
Medical supervision	
General	
Specific	
Dental	
Vision	
Hearing	
Psychosocial needs	
Socialization/recreation	
Therapeutic modalities	
Physical therapy	
Occupational therapy	
Speech/language pathology	
Transportation	
Vocational planning	
Other	

Name: _____ Date completed: _____ By whom: _____

Figure 36.1. Sample parent–professional worksheet to aid in planning for a child and family's needs. (From Trachtenberg, S., & Lewis, D. [1996]. Interdisciplinary team process. In L. Kurtz, P. Dowrick, S.E. Levy, et al. (Eds.), *Handbook of developmental disabilities: Resources for interdisciplinary care* [p. 206]. Rockville, MD: Aspen Publishers, Inc., © 1996; reprinted by permission.)

mental health/mental retardation (MHMR) office and the Department of Education (Part H funding). Her parents' commercial insurance policy covered the majority of her hospital expenses; but once she was discharged, outpatient services were not covered. She was subsequently enrolled in a cerebral palsy clinic at the regional children's hospital that was funded through Title V Block Grants from the Maternal and Child Health Bureau. Through this program, her family applied for and received SSI and Medicaid coverage. Danielle has required several orthopedic operations that were paid for by Medicaid. Her parents now are concerned because their community is slated for inclusion in a mandatory Medicaid-managed care initiative. They fear that the multiple physician consultants and therapists who have worked with Danielle will not be included in any one "network," and, as a result, her care may become fragmented. They are working through these concerns with the guidance counselor at school where Danielle is enrolled in a special class that implements her individualized education program (IEP) and provides related services such as physical therapy and occupational therapy through Part B funding.

SUMMARY

Providing health care services to children with special health care needs will continue to be a challenge in the 21st century. Citizens must focus on designing a system of health care that meets the needs of the child and family in a coordinated, comprehensive, inclusive, culturally sensitive, and family-oriented manner (NACHRI, 1996). Because this group of children has the potential to use significant health care resources, they are vulnerable to cost-cutting initiatives. Therefore, health care providers and child advocates must cogently express the value of necessary services and supports to the child, family, and community at large. Managed care offers the potential to efficiently use resources and ultimately shift these from costly delivery models (e.g., heavy emphasis on inpatient care) to less costly, coordinated, prevention focused delivery models (e.g., the medical home concept with an emphasis on community-based service delivery). A great deal of attention will need to be given to the potential impact of any proposed systemwide change on children with disabilities to ensure that they are cared for in an appropriate manner.

REFERENCES

Allen, D. (1995). Different approaches to meeting special needs: Carve in, carve out and combinations. In *Serving people with disabilities in managed care: State experiences with program design and implementation.* Washington, DC: Medicaid Working Group.

American Academy of Pediatrics. (1992). Ad hoc task force on definition of the medical home. *Pediatrics, 90,* 774.

Blackman, J.A., Healy, A., & Ruppert, E.S. (1992). Participation by pediatricians in early intervention: Impetus from Public Law 99-457. *Pediatrics, 89*(1), 98–102.

Blancquaert, I.R., Zvagulis, I., Gray-Donald, K., et al. (1992). Referral patterns for children with chronic diseases. *Pediatrics, 90*(1), 71–74.

Boyle, C.A., Decoufle, P., & Yeargin-Allsopp, M. (1994). Prevalence and health impact of developmental disabilities in U.S. children. *Pediatrics, 93*(3), 399–403.

Cartland, D.C., & Yudkowsky, B.K. (1992). Barriers to pediatric referral in managed care systems. *Pediatrics, 89*(2), 183–188.

Centers for Disease Control. (1995). Disabilities among children less than 17 years: United States, 1991–1992. *Morbidity and Mortality Weekly Report, 44*(33), 609–613.

Children's Defense Fund. (1996a). Advocates help states plan seal reforms. *Children's Defense Fund Reports, 17,* 5–7.

Children's Defense Fund. (1996b). Children of working parents squeezed out of health care. *Children's Defense Fund Reports, 17,* 1–2, 14.

Committee on Child Financing. (1995). Guiding principles for managed care arrangements for the health care of infants, children, adolescents, and young adults. *Pediatrics, 95*(4), 613–615.

Committee on Children with Disabilities. (1993). Provision of related services for children with chronic disabilities. *Pediatrics, 92*(6), 879–881.

Council on Ethical and Judicial Affairs. (1995). Ethical issues in mangaged care. *Journal of the American Medical Association, 273*(4), 330–335.

Drainoni, M.L., Tobias, C., & Dreyfus, T. (1995). *Medicaid managed care for people with disabilities: Overview of the population.* Boston: Medicaid Working Group.

Education for All Handicapped Children Act of 1975, PL 94-142, 20 U.S.C. § 1400 *et seq.*

Emmons, D.W., & Simon, C. (1994). *Recent trends in managed care: Socioeconomic characteristics of medical practice.* Chicago: American Medical Association.

Flint, S.S., Yudkowsky, B.K., & Tang, S.S.(1995). Children's medicaid entitlement: What have you got to lose? *Pediatrics, 96*(5), 967–970.

Fox, H.B., Wicks, L.B., McManus, M.S., et al. (1992). Private and public health insurance for early intervention services. *Journal of Early Intervention, 6*(2), 109–122.

Fox, H.B., Wicks, L.B., & Newacheck, P.W. (1993). Health maintenance organizations and children with special needs. *American Journal of Diseases of Children, 147,* 546–552

Freund, D.A., & Lewit, E.M. (1993). Managed care for children and pregnant women: Promises and pitfalls. *The Future of Children, 3*(2), 92–122.

Hillman, A. (1995). The impact of physician financial incentives on high risk populations in managed care. *Journal of Acquired Immune Deficiency Syndrome, 8*(Suppl. 1), S23–S29.

Hillman, A., & Arye, L. (1995). States as payers: Managed care for Medicaid populations [Policy syntheses]. Philadelphia: University of Pennsylvania, Leonard Davis Institute of Health Economics.

Individuals with Disabilities Education Act (IDEA) of 1990, PL 101-476, 20 U.S.C. § 1400 *et seq.*

Institute for Family Centered Care. (1996a). Glossary of terms. *Advances in Family-Centered Care, 3*(1), 2.

Institute for Family Centered Care. (1996b). Primary care: Family-centered approaches for children with special health care needs. *Advances in Family-Centered Care, 3*(1), 10–14.

Ireys, H.T., Grason, H.A., & Guyer, B. (1996). Assuring quality of care for children with special needs in managed care organizations: Roles for pediatricians. *Pediatrics, 98*(2), 178–185.

Kaiser Commission on the Future of Medicaid. (1992). *Medicaid at the crossroads.* Menlo Park, CA: Henry J. Kaiser Foundation.

Kaiser Commission on the Future of Medicaid. (1995). *Medicaid and managed care: Lessons from the literature.* Menlo Park, CA: Henry J. Kaiser Foundation.

Katz, G. (1993). *The first 20 years: A history of the National Association of Children's Hospitals and Related Institutions.* Alexandria, VA: National Association of Childrens's Hospitals and Related Institutions.

Kissick, W.L. (1994). *Medicine's dilemmas: Infinite needs versus finite resources.* New Haven, CT: Yale University.

Klerman, L. (1992). Nonfinancial barriers to receipt of medical care. *The Future of Children, 2*(2), 171–185.

Lewit, E.M., & Baker, L.S. (1996). Children in special education: The future of children. *Special Education for Students with Disabilities, 6*(1), 139–151.

MacLeod, G.K. (1993). An overview of managed health care. In P.R. Kongstvedt (Ed.), *The managed health care handbook* (2nd ed., pp. 3–11). Gaithersburg, MD: Aspen Publications, Inc.

Mauldon, J., Leibowitz, A., Buchanan, J.L., et al. (1994). Rationing or rationalizing children's medical care: Comparision of a Medicaid HMO with fee-for-service care. *American Journal of Public Health, 84*(6), 899–904.

McManus, M., Flint, S., & Kelly, R. (1991). The adequacy of physician reimbursement for pediatric care under Medicaid. *Pediatrics, 87,* 909–920.

Mitka, M. (1995). HMOs see steady growth, some market shifts. *AMA News, 38,* 9.

National Association of Children's Hospitals and Related Institutions (NACHRI), Board of Trustees. (1994). *Health care reform should promote "integrated child health care networks."* Alexandria, VA: Author.

National Association of Children's Hospitals and Related Institutions, Board of Trustees. (1996). *Pediatric excellence in health delivery systems.* Alexandria, VA: Author.

National Association of State Directors of Developmental Disabilities Services. (1995). *Managed care and long term supports for people with developmental disabilities.* Alexandria, VA: National Association of State Directors of Developmental Disabilities Services, Inc.

National Commission on Childhood Disability. (1995). *Supplemental Security Income for children with disabilities* [Report to Congress].

Washington, DC: U.S. Government Printing Office.

Neff, J.M., & Anderson, G. (1995). Protecting children with chronic illness in a competitive marketplace. *Journal of the American Medical Association, 274*(23), 1866–1869.

Newacheck, P.W. (1989). Chronically ill children and their health care needs. *Caring, 8*(5), 4–10.

Newacheck, P.W., Hughes, D.C., & Cisternas, M. (1995). Children and health insurance: An overview of recent trends. *Health Affairs, 14*(1), 244–254.

Newacheck, P.W., Hughes, D.C., Stoddard, J.J., et al. (1994). Children with chronic illness and Medicaid managed care. *Pediatrics, 93,* 497–500.

Newacheck, P.W., & McManus, M.A. (1988). Financing health care for disabled children. *Pediatrics, 81*(3), 385—394.

Newacheck, P.W., Stein, R.E.K., Walker, D.K., et al. (1996). Monitoring and evaluating managed care for children. *Pediatrics, 98,* 952–958.

Newacheck, P.W., & Stoddard, J.J. (1994). Prevalence and impact of multiple childhood chronic illness. *Journal of Pediatrics, 124*(1), 40–48.

Newacheck, P.W., & Taylor, W. (1992). Childhood chronic illness: Prevalence, severity and impact. *American Journal of Public Health, 82,* 364–371.

Perrin, J.M. (1990). Children with special health needs: A United States perspective. *Pediatrics, 6*(2), 1120–1123.

Perrin, E.C., Newacheck, P., Pless, B., et al. (1993). Issues involved in the definition and classification of chronic health conditions. *Pediatrics, 91*(4), 787–793.

Saucier, P. (1995). *Summary of risk-based Medicaid managed care programs enrolling persons with disabilities, as of June 1, 1995.* Waltham, MA: Brandeis University, The Center for Vulnerable Populations.

Schactman, D., & Altman, S.H. (1995). *A study of the decline in employment based health insurance.* Waltham, MA: Brandeis University, Institute for Health Policy, Council on the Economic Impact of Health Care Reform.

Sheils, J.F., & Wolfe, P.R. (1992). The role of private health insurance in children's health care. *The Future of Children, 2*(2), 115–123.

Smith, G., & Ashbaugh, J. (1995). *Managed care and people with developmental disabilities: A guidebook.* Alexandria, VA: National Association of State Directors of Developmental Disabilities Services, Inc.

Stanton, W.R., McGee, R., & Silva, P. (1991). Indices of prenatal complications, family background, child rearing, and health as predictors of early cognitive and motor development. *Pediatrics, 88*(5), 954.

Suh, G. (1995). Health. In B. Finlay (Ed.), *The state of America's children: Yearbook 1995.* Washington, DC: Children's Defense Fund.

Trachtenberg, S.W., & Lewis, D.F. (1996). Case management. In L.A. Kurtz, P.W. Dowrick, S.E. Levy, et al. (Eds.), *Children's Seashore House handbook of developmental disabilities: Resources for interdisciplinary care.* Gaithersburg, MD: Aspen Publications, Inc.

U.S. Department of Health and Human Services, Assistant Secretary for Planning and Evaluation. (1990). *Federal programs for persons with disabilities* [Contract No. HHS-88-0047]. Washington, DC: Systemetrics under subcontract with Mathematica Policy Research.

U.S. Department of Health and Human Services, Assistant Secretary for Planning and Evaluation. (1991). *Medicaid coverage of health-related services for children receiving special education* [brochure]. Washington, DC: Lewin/ICF and Fox Health Policy Consultants.

U.S. General Accounting Office. (1995). *Social Security: New functional assessments for children raise eligibility* [GAO/HEHS-95-66]. Washington, DC: U.S. Government Printing Office.

Wagner, E.R. (1993). Types of managed care organizations. In P.R. Kongstvedt (Ed.), *The managed health care handbook* (2nd ed., pp. 12–21). Gaithersburg, MD: Aspen Publications, Inc.

Wehr, E., & Jameson, E.J. (1994). Critical health issues for children and youth. *The Future of Children, 4*(3), 115–133.

Weiss, B. (1995). Managed care: There's no stopping now. *Medical Economics, 14*(4), 6–16.

A Glossary

Mark L. Batshaw

Abduction   Moving part of the body away from one's midline.

Abruptio placenta   Premature detachment of a normally situated placenta.

Abscesses   Localized collections of pus in cavities caused by the disintegration of tissue, usually the consequence of bacterial infections.

Acetabulum   The cup-shaped cavity of the hip bone that holds the head of the femur in place creating a joint.

Acetaminophen   A medication used to control fever and pain. It has a different chemical structure than aspirin and fewer side effects.

Achondroplasia   Short-limbed dwarfism (*see* Autosomal dominant; *see* Syndromes and Inborn Errors of Metabolism, Appendix B).

Acid-base balance   In metabolism, the ratio of acidic to basic compounds necessary to keep pH of the blood neutral (about 7.42).

Acidotic   Having too much acid in the bloodstream. The normal pH is 7.42; acidosis is generally less than 7.30.

Acquired immunodeficiency syndrome (AIDS)   Severe immune deficiency disease caused by HIV (*see* Chapter 9).

Actin   Protein involved in muscle contraction.

Acute polyneuropathy   Ascending paralysis following a viral infection, also called Guillain-Barré syndrome.

ADA deficiency   Adenosine deaminase deficiency. An autosomal recessive disorder that causes a congenital severe combined immunodeficiency (*see* Syndromes and Inborn Errors of Metabolism, Appendix B).

Adduction   Moving a body part, usually a limb, toward the midline.

Adenoidal hypertrophy   Enlargement of the adenoids.

Adenoids   Lymphatic tissue located behind the nasal passages.

Adenoma sebaceum   Benign cutaneous growths, usually seen around the nose that resemble acne; occurs in individuals with tuberous sclerosis.

Adjustment disorders   A group of psychiatric disorders, usually of childhood, associated with difficulty adjusting to life changes.

Adrenalin   A potent stimulant of the autonomic nervous system. It increases blood pressure, heart rate, and stimulates other physiological changes needed for a "fight or flight" response.

Afebrile seizure   A seizure that is not precipitated by fever, usually implying an underlying seizure disorder.

Afferent   The neural signals sent from the peripheral nervous system to the central nervous system.

Agenesis of the corpus callosum   Absence of the band of white matter that normally connects the two hemispheres of the brain.

Agonist   1) A medication that enhances certain neural activity; 2) a muscle that works in concert with another muscle to produce movement.

Agyria   Absence of normal convolutions on the surface of the brain.

Akathisia   Involuntary motor restlessness, a complication of antipsychotic medication.

Alleles   Alternate forms of a gene that may exist at the same site on the chromosome.

Alopecia   Hair loss.

Alpha-fetoprotein (AFP)   Fetal protein found in amniotic fluid and serum of pregnant women. Its measurement is used to test for meningomyelocele and Down syndrome in the fetus.

Alveoli   Small air sacs in the lungs. Carbon dioxide and oxygen are exchanged through their walls.

Amaurosis   Blindness.

Amblyopia   Partial loss of sight resulting from disuse atrophy of neural circuitry during a critical period of development, most often associated with untreated strabismus in children.

Amino acids   The building blocks of protein needed for normal growth.

Amniocentesis   A prenatal diagnostic procedure performed in the second trimester in which amniotic fluid is removed by a needle inserted through the abdominal wall and into the uterine cavity.

Amniotic fluid   Fluid that surrounds and protects the developing fetus. This fluid is sampled through amniocentesis.

Anabolic   Growth producing.

Anaerobic   Without air.

Anaphase   The stage in cell division (mitosis and meiosis) when the chromosomes move from the center of the nucleus toward the poles of the cell.

Anaphylaxis   A life-threatening hypersensitivity response to a medication or food marked by breathing difficulty, hives, and shock.

Anemia   Disorder in which the blood has either too few red blood cells or too little hemoglobin.

Anencephaly   Birth defect in which either the entire brain or all but the most primitive regions of the brain are missing.

Anisometropia   A difference in the refractive power of the two eyes.

Anophthalmia   Congenital absence of the eyes.

Anorexia   A severe loss of appetite.

Antagonist   Opposite of agonist.

Antecedents   Those events or contextual factors that precede or coincide with a behavior.

Anterior   In front of or the front part of a structure.

Anterior fontanel   The membrane-covered area on the top of the head; also called the *soft spot*. It generally closes by 18 months of age.

Anterior horn cells   Cells in the spinal column that transmit impulses from the pyramidal tract to the peripheral nervous system.

Anthropometric   Measurements of the body and its parts.

Antibodies   Proteins formed in the bloodstream to fight infection.

Anticipation   In genetics, the concept that certain abnormalities (e.g., triplet repeat expansion) become more severe from one generation to the next.

Antidepressants   Medications used to control major depression.

Antihistamine   A drug that counteracts the effects of histamines, substances involved in allergic reactions.

Antipsychotic drugs   Medications used to treat psychosis, most commonly phenothiazines such as thioridazine (Mellaril).

Anxiety disorders   Psychiatric disorders characterized by feelings of anxiety. These include panic attacks, separation anxiety, obsessive-compulsive disorder, and posttraumatic stress disorder.

Aorta   The major artery of the body. It originates in the left ventricle of the heart and carries oxygenated blood to the rest of the body.

Apgar score   A scoring system used to assess neurological status in the newborn infant. Scores range from 0 to 10.

Apical   At the tip of a structure.

Apneic episodes   Episodic arrest of breathing.

Aqueous humor   The fluid in the eyeball that fills the space between the lens and the cornea.

Architectonic dysplasia   Developmental malformation affecting the neuronal architecture of the brain.

Arcuate fasciculus   A nerve tract that connects Wernicke's and Broca's areas of the brain. It is involved in the control of language.

Arthritis   An inflammatory disease of joints.

Articular   Referring to the surfaces of two bones at a joint space.

Articulation   The formulation of individual speech sounds.

Asphyxia   Interference with oxygenation of the blood that leads to loss of consciousness and possible brain damage.

Aspiration   Inhalation of a foreign body, usually a food particle, into the lung.

Aspiration pneumonia   Inflammation of the lung(s) caused by inhaling a foreign body, such as food, into the lungs.

Astigmatism   A condition of unequal curvature of the cornea leading to blurred vision.

Ataxic   Having an unbalanced gait caused by a disturbance of cerebellar control.

Ataxic cerebral palsy   A form of cerebral palsy in which the prominent feature is cerebellar ataxia.

Athetoid cerebral palsy   A form of dyskinetic cerebral palsy associated with athetosis.

Athetosis   Constant slow, writhing involuntary movements of the limbs.

Atonic   Absence of normal muscle tone.

Atresia   Congenital absence of a normal body opening.

Atria   The upper chambers of the heart.

Atrophy   A wasting away of a cell, tissue, or organ.

Audiometry   A hearing test using an audiometer.

Auditory brainstem response (ABR)   A test of central nervous system hearing pathways.

Aura   A sensation marking the onset of a seizure.

Auricle   The outer ear.

Autoimmune   Reaction in which one's immune system attacks other parts of the body.

Automatisms   Automatic fine motor movements (e.g., unbuttoning) that are part of a seizure.

Autonomic   The part of the nervous system that regulates certain automatic functions of the body—for example, heart rate, sweating, and bowel movement.

Autosomal dominant   Mendelian inheritance pattern in which a single copy of a gene leads to expression of the trait.

Autosomal recessive   Mendelian inheritance pattern in which two carrier parents have a 25% chance of passing the trait to each subsequent child.

Autosomes   The first 22 pairs of chromosomes. All chromosomes are autosomes except for the two sex chromosomes.

Avascular   An area of the body poorly supplied by blood vessels.

Aversive   A stimulus, often unpleasant, which decreases the likelihood of a particular response occurring.

Backward chaining   The instructor begins by teaching the last step in a sequence because this step is most likely to be associated with a potent positive reinforcer.

Bacteremia   Spread of a bacterial organism throughout the bloodstream.

Banding pattern   A series of dark and light bars that appear on chromosomes after they are stained. Each chromosome has a distinct banding pattern.

Barotrauma   Injury related to excess pressure, especially to the lungs or ears.

Basal   Near the base.

Baseline   The frequency, duration, and intensity of a behavior prior to intervention.

Beriberi   Disease caused by a deficiency of the vitamin thiamin and manifested as edema, heart problems, and a peripheral neuropathy.

Beta adrenergic blockers   Medications, including propranolol (Inderal), initially used to control high blood pressure that have subsequently been found to be useful in treating aggressive behavior, tremor and migraine headache.

Binocular vision   The focusing of both eyes on an object to provide a stereoscopic image.

Biotin   A B-complex vitamin needed to activate a number of important enzymatic reactions in the body.

Biotinidase deficiency   Inborn error of organic acid metabolism that results in the body's inability to recycle the vitamin biotin.

Bipolar disorder   A psychiatric disorder manifested by cycles of mania and depression.

Blastocyst   The embryonic group of cells that exists at the time of implantation.

Bolus   A small rounded mass of food made ready by tongue and jaw movement for swallowing.

Botulism   Poisoning by botulin toxin and manifested as muscle weakness or paralysis.

Brachialis   Arm muscle.

Brachycephaly   Tall head shape with flat occiput.

Bradycardia   Abnormal slowing of the heart rate, usually to fewer than 60 beats per minute.

Brainstem   The primitive portion of the brain that lies between the cerebrum and the spinal cord.

Braxton-Hicks   Usually painless, irregular contractions that occur intermittently throughout pregnancy.

Bronchopulmonary dysplasia (BPD)   A chronic lung disorder that occurs in a minority of premature infants who previously had respiratory distress syndrome. It is associated with "stiff" lungs that do not permit adequate exchange of oxygen and carbon dioxide and frequently leads to dependence on ventilator assistance for extended periods of time.

Bronchospasm   Acute constriction of the bronchial tube, most commonly associated with asthma.

Bruxism   Repetitive grinding of the teeth.

Bulk   Foodstuffs that increase the quantity of intestinal contents and stimulate regular bowel movements. Fruits, vegetables, and fiber provide bulk in the diet.

Butryrophenones   Drugs that inhibit the neurochemical dopamine in the brain and are used to control Tourette syndrome, psychosis, and self-injurious behavior. An example is haloperidol (Haldol).

Caffeine   A central nervous system stimulant found in coffee, tea, and cola.

Calcified   Hardened through the laying down of calcium salts.

Calculus   An abnormal collection of mineral salts on the tooth, predisposing it to decay.

Callus   A disorganized network of bone tissue formed around the edges of a fracture.

Camptodactyly   Flexion deformity of fingers or toes.

Cancellous   The lattice-like structure in long bones (e.g., the femur).

Catabolic   Pertaining to the breaking down of tissue.

Catalyze   Pertaining to a compound that stimulates a chemical reaction without being used up.

Cataracts   Clouding of the lenses of the eyes.

Catheter   A tube used to infuse or remove fluids.

Celiac disease   Congenital malabsorption syndrome that leads to failure to gain weight and passage of loose, foul-smelling stools. It is caused by intolerance of cereal products that contain gluten.

Central nervous system (CNS)   The portion of the nervous system that consists of the brain and spinal cord. It is primarily involved in voluntary movement and thought processes.

Central venous line   A catheter that is advanced through a peripheral vein to a position directly above the opening to the right atrium of the heart. It is used to infuse long-term medication or nutrition.

Centrioles   Tiny organelles that migrate to the opposite poles of a cell during cell division and align the spindles.

Centromere   The constricted area of the chromosome that usually marks the point of attachment of the sister chromatids to the spindle during cell division.

Cephalocaudal   From head to tail; refers to neurological development that proceeds from the head downward.

Cephalohematoma   A swelling of the head resulting from bleeding of scalp veins. Often found in newborn infants, it is usually not harmful.

Cerebral hemisphere   Either of the two halves of brain substance.

Cerebral palsy   A disorder of movement and posture due to a nonprogressive defect of the immature brain (*see* Chapter 24).

Cerumen   Ear wax.

Cervical   Pertaining to the neck.

Cervical cerclage   Surgical procedure done to prevent the pregnant cervix from opening prematurely.

CHARGE association   *See* Syndromes and Inborn Errors of Metabolism, Appendix B.

Choanal atresia   Congenital closure of the nasal passage.

Cholesteatoma   A complication of otitis media, in which skin cells from the ear canal migrate through the perforated eardrum into the middle ear, or mastoid region, forming a mass that must be removed surgically.

Choreoathetosis   Movement disorder involving frequent, involuntary spasms of the limbs.

Chorioamnionitis   Infection of the amniotic sac, which surrounds and contains the fetus and amniotic fluid.

Chorion   The outermost covering of the fetus.

Chorionic gonadotrophin   The hormone secreted by the embryo that prevents its expulsion from the uterus. A pregnancy test measures the presence of this hormone in the uterus.

Chorionic villus sampling   A prenatal diagnostic procedure done in the first trimester of pregnancy to obtain fetal cells for genetic analysis.

Chorioretinitis   An inflammation of the retina and choroid that produces severe visual loss.

Choroid   The middle layer of the eyeball between the sclera and the retina.

Choroid plexus   Cells that line the walls of the ventricles of the brain and produce cerebrospinal fluid.

Chromatid   Term given to chromosomes during cell division.

Chromatin   The unraveled structure of DNA that exists between periods of cell division.

Cilia   Hair-like projections attached to the surface of a cell. They beat rhythmically to move the cell.

Ciliary muscles   Small muscles that affect the shape of the lens of the eye, permitting accommodation.

Clonus   Alternate muscle contraction and relaxation in rapid succession.

Clubfoot   A congenital foot deformity.

Coarctation   A congenital narrowing of a segment of a blood vessel, most commonly the aorta.

Cochlea   The snail-shaped structure in the inner ear containing the organ of hearing.

Codons   Triplets of nucleotides that form the DNA code for specific amino acids.

Cognitive behavior therapy   A controversial behavior intervention designed to help individuals recovering from acquired brain injury to regain certain cognitive skills.

Coloboma   Congenital cleft in the retina, iris, or other ocular structure.

Compliance training   An important prerequisite to instructional training, the instructor orients the child to attend to the instructor and then issues a developmentally appropriate "do" request.

Computed tomography (CT)   An imaging technique in which X-ray "slices" of a structure are taken and synthesized by a computer, forming an image. It is most commonly used to visualize the brain. CT scans are less clear than MRI scans but are better at localizing certain tumors and areas of calcification.

Concave   Having a curved, indented surface.

Concussion   A clinical syndrome caused by a blow to the head, characterized by transient loss of consciousness.

Cone cells   Photoreceptor cells of the eye associated with color vision.

Congenital   Originating prior to birth.

Congenital myopathies   A group of inherited muscle disorders often associated with mitochondrial dysfunction.

Consanguinity   Intermarriage; relationship by blood.

Consequences   Those events or contextual factors that occur subsequent to a behavior and may or may not be causally related to it.

Contiguous gene syndrome   A genetic syndrome resulting from defects in a number of adjacent genes.

Contingent observation   The child is asked to "sit at the sidelines" while continuing to observe the ongoing activity from which he or she was withdrawn.

Contingent presentation   The application of a punisher following the occurrence of a behavior.

Contingent stimulation   Applying punishment following the occurrence of a misbehavior.

Contingent withdrawal   The removal of access to positive reinforcement following a misbehavior.

Continuous performance test   Test used to assess inattention and impulsivity. In the more popular versions, a child watches a series of numbers appear, one at time, on a screen and must press a button when a specific sequence of numbers occurs.

Contractures   Irreversible shortening of muscle fibers that causes decreased joint mobility.

Contusion (of brain)   Structural damage limited to the surface layer of the brain, caused by a blow to the head.

Convex   Having a curved, elevated surface, such as a dome.

Cornea   The transparent, dome-like covering of the iris.

Corpus callostomy   Surgical procedure in which the corpus callosum is cut to prevent the generalized spread of seizures from one hemisphere to another.

Corpus callosum   The bridge of white matter connecting the two cerebral hemispheres.

Cortical   Pertaining to the cortex or gray matter of the brain.

Cortical mapping   The placement of electrodes over the cortex during a neurosurgical operation. Stimulation of the electrodes results in motor or sensory activity that allows "mapping" of cortical control or body action.

Corticospinal   Referring to a nerve tract, leading from the cortex into the spinal column, involved in the control of voluntary motor movement. Damage to this tract leads to spasticity, commonly seen in cerebral palsy.

Craniofacial   Relating to the skull and bones of the face.

Craniosynostosis   Premature closure of cranial bones.

Creatine kinase (CK)   An enzyme released by damaged muscle cells. Its level is elevated in muscular dystrophy.

Cretinism (congenital hypothyroidism)   *See* Syndromes and Inborn Errors of Metabolism, Appendix B.

Cri-du-chat ("cat cry") syndrome   *See* Syndromes and Inborn Errors of Metabolism, Appendix B.

Cross over   The exchange of genetic material between two closely aligned chromosomes during the first meiotic division.

Cryo   Related to freezing.

Cryotherapy   The use of freezing temperatures to destroy tissue. A cryotherapy probe has been used to treat retinoblastoma and retinopathy of prematurity.

Cryptorchidism   Undescended testicles.

Cystic fibrosis   An autosomal recessively inherited disorder of the secretory glands leading to malabsorption and lung disease.

Cytomegalovirus (CMV)   A virus that may be asymptomatic or cause symptoms in adults that may resemble mononucleosis. However, in the fetus it can lead to severe malformations similar to congenital rubella.

Cytoplasm   The contents of the cell outside the nucleus.

Debridement   The surgical removal of dead tissue (e.g., after a burn or infection).

Deciduous   Baby teeth, which are shed.

Deletions   Loss of genetic material from a chromosome.

Delirium   An organically based psychosis characterized by impaired attention, disorganized thinking, altered and fluctuating levels of consciousness, and memory impairment. It may be caused by encephalitis, diabetes, or intoxication and is usually reversed by treating the underlying medical problem.

Delusions   False beliefs, often quite bizarre, that are symptoms of psychosis or drug intoxication.

Dementia   A progressive neurological disorder marked by loss of memory, decreased speech, impairment in abstract thinking and judgment, other disturbances of higher cortical function, and personality change. One example is Alzheimer's disease.

Dental caries   Tooth decay.

Dental lamina   A thickened band of tissue along the future dental arches in the human embryo.

Dental organ   The embryonic tooth bud.

Dental plaque   Patches of bacteria, bacterial by-products, and food particles on teeth predisposing them to decay.

Dental sealant   Plastic substance administered to teeth to increase their resistance to injury and decay.

Dentin   The principal substance of the tooth surrounding the tooth pulp and covered by the enamel.

Deoxyribonucleic acid (DNA)   The fundamental component of living tissue. It contains the genetic code.

Depolarization   Changing the electrical charge of a cell.

Depressed fracture   Fracture of bone, usually skull, that results in inward displacement of the bone at the point of impact. It requires surgical intervention to prevent damage to underlying tissue.

Deprivation   Denied access.

Descriptive and functional analysis   Observation period in behavior management that precedes treatment.

Detoxification   The conversion of a toxic compound to a nontoxic product.

Developmental apraxia   The inability of a child to perform age-appropriate fine motor skills despite the absence of motor or sensory impairments.

Developmental dislocation of the hip (DDH)   A congenital hip dislocation, usually evident at birth, occurring more commonly in girls.

Dialysis   A detoxification procedure, hemodialysis or peritoneal dialysis, used to treat kidney failure.

Diaphysis   The shaft of a long bone lying under the epiphysis.

Differential reinforcement   A behavior management technique in which a preferred alternate behavior is positively reinforced while a second less preferred behavior is ignored.

Diffuse axonal injury   Diffuse injury to nerve cell components, usually resulting from shearing forces. This is the type of traumatic brain injury commonly associated with motor vehicle accidents.

Diopters   Units of refractive power of a lens.

Diploid   Paired chromosomes in nondividing cells (i.e., 46 chromosomes in 23 pairs).

Dislocation   The displacement of a bone out of a joint space.

Distal   The part farthest away from the midline or trunk.

Diuretics   Medications used to reduce intercellular fluid buildup in the body (edema), especially in the lungs.

Dominant   In genetics, refers to a trait that only requires one copy of a gene to be expressed phenotypically. For example, brown eyes is a dominant trait, while blue eyes is a recessive trait.

Dual diagnosis   Mental retardation and psychiatric disorder.

Duchenne muscular dystrophy   *See* Chapter 15.

Ductus arteriosis   An arterial connection, open during fetal life, that diverts the blood flow from the pulmonary artery into the aorta, thereby bypassing the nonfunctional lungs.

Duodenal atresia   Congenital absence of a portion of the first section of the small intestine; often seen in individuals with Down syndrome.

Duodenum   First part of the small intestine.

Dynamic   Capable of active movement.

Dysarthria   Difficulty with speech due to impairment of oral motor structures or musculature.

Dyscalculia   Learning disability affecting arithmetic skills.

Dysgraphia   Learning disability in areas of processing and reporting information in written form.

Dyskinetic cerebral palsy   "Extrapyramidal" cerebral palsy often involving abnormalities of the basal ganglia and manifesting as rigidity, dystonia, or choreoathetosis.

Dyslexia   Learning disability affecting reading skills.

Dysostosis   An abnormal bony formation.

Dysphagia   Difficulty in swallowing function.

Dysphasia   Impairment of speech consisting of a lack of coordination and failure to arrange words in proper order; due to a central brain lesion.

Dysplasia   Abnormal tissue development.

Dyspraxia   Inability to perform coordinated movements despite normal function of the central and peripheral nervous system and muscles.

Dysthymia   A mild form of depression characterized by a mood disturbance that is present most of the time and is associated with feelings of low self-esteem, hopelessness, poor concentration, low energy, and changes in sleep and appetite. Often applied to depressed adolescents.

Dystocia   Structural abnormalities of the uterus that may cause premature or prolonged labor.

Dystonia   A disorder of the basal ganglia associated with altered muscle tone leading to contorted body positioning.

Dystonic cerebral palsy   A form of dyskinetic (extrapyramidal) cerebral palsy with prominent features of dystonia.

Echocardiography   An ultrasonic method of imaging the heart. It can be used to detect congenital heart defects.

Echodensities   Changes on ultrasound that reflect damage to brain tissue, seen in periventricular leukomalcia in premature infants.

Echolalia   Immediate repetition of a word or phrase said by others.

E. coli   Bacteria that can cause infections ranging from diarrhea and urinary tract infection to sepsis.

Ectodermal dysplasia   Abnormal skin development.

Ectopias   Congenital displacement of a body organ or tissue.

Ectrodactyly   Congenital absence of all or part of digits.

Edema   An abnormal accumulation of fluid in the tissues of the body.

Efferent   Impulse that goes to a nerve or muscle from the CNS.

Effusion   Fluid escaping from blood vessels or lymphatics that collects in body cavities (i.e., a pleural or lung effusion).

Electroencephalogram (EEG)   A recording of the electrical activity in the brain that is often used in the evaluation of seizures.

Electrolarynx   A vibrator/amplifier that permits the production of artificial speech sounds in an individual whose larynx is blocked by a tracheostomy tube or has been removed because of cancer.

Electrolyte   Mineral contained in the blood.

Ellis-van Creveld syndrome   *See* Syndromes and Inborn Errors of Metabolism, Appendix B.

Enamel   The calcified outer layer of the tooth.

Encephalitis   Inflammation of the brain, generally from a viral infection.

Encephalocele   Congenital cystic malformation of the brain associated with severe disabilities.

Encephalopathy   Disorder or disease of the brain.

Enchondral ossification   Formation of bone from cartilage.

Endocarditis   Inflammation of the inner lining of the heart.

Endorphins   The body's natural opiates, probably involved in the perception of pain and pleasure.

Enterovirus   Virus that can cause gastroenteritis (i.e., infection of stomach and small intestine).

Enzyme-multiplied immunoassay technique (EMIT)   A laboratory test performed on blood or urine to detect the recent use of cocaine or some other abused substances.

Epicanthal folds   Crescent-shaped fold of skin on either side of the nose, commonly associated with Down syndrome.

Epidemiological   Pertaining to the study of factors determining the frequency and distribution of diseases—for example, an outbreak of food poisoning.

Epidural anesthesia   Pain relief by infusing an anesthetic agent into the epidural space of the spine.

Epidural hematoma   Localized collection of clotted blood lying between the skull and the outer (dural) membrane of the brain, resulting from the hemorrhage of a blood vessel resting in the dura. This most commonly results from traumatic head injury.

Epiglottis   A lid-like structure that hangs over the entrance to the windpipe and prevents aspiration of food or liquid into the lungs during swallowing.

Epiphysis   The end plate of long bones; linear growth occurs here.

Epithelial   Pertaining to skin cells.

Equinus   Involuntary extension of the foot (like a horse). This position is often found in spastic cerebral palsy.

Esophageal transport   The rhythmic contraction of esophageal muscles to transport food from pharynx to stomach.

Esophagus   Tube through which food passes from the pharynx to the stomach.

Esotropia   A form of strabismus in which the eyes turn in; "cross eyed."

Estimated date of confinement (EDC)   Expected date of delivery.

Eustachian tube   Connection between oral cavity and middle ear, allowing equilibration of pressure and drainage of fluid.

Everted   Turned outward.

Excitotoxic receptors   Receptor in the brain for excitotoxins, chemicals that can cause neuronal cell death and have been implicated in hypoxic brain damage and AIDS encephalopathy.

Executive function   Brain processing involved in planning; it is thought to be deficient in individuals with learning disabilities.

Exotropia   A form of strabismus in which the eyes turn out; "wall-eyed."

Expressive language   Communication by spoken language, gesture, signing, or body language.

Extension   Movement of a limb part to bring it into a more straightened position.

Extinction   The consistent withholding of positive reinforcement contingent upon the occurrence of a nondangerous, nondestructive problem behavior.

Extinction burst   A transient increase in the frequency and intensity of the problem behavior before a subsequent reduction occurs.

Extract   A concentrated preparation.

Ex vivo   Outside of the body.

Fading   Process by which prompts are withdrawn gradually.

Failure to thrive   Inadequate growth of both weight and height in infancy or early childhood caused by malnutrition, chronic disease, or a congenital anomaly.

Febrile   Term referring to an individual who has an elevated body temperature. Normal temperature is 98.6°F (37°C). A child is considered febrile when the fever is above 100.4°F (38°C).

Femur   Long bone in the thigh connecting the hip to the knee.

Fetal alcohol syndrome (FAS)   *See* Chapter 8.

Flagellum   Whip-like projection of a cell that gives it mobility. The sperm is one example of a cell having a flagellum; plural: flagella.

Flexion   The act of bending.

Flexor   A muscle with the primary function of flexion at a joint.

Flora   Bacteria normally residing within the intestine, such as *E. coli*.

Fluency/rhythm   Aspects of speech production.

Focal   Localized.

Focal neurological signs   Those findings on neurological exams that are abnormal and indicative of a lesion in a particular part of the brain.

Forebrain   The front portion of the brain during fetal development; also called the prosencephalon.

Forward chaining   A behavior management technique in which the first skill in a sequence is taught first and the last skill is taught last.

Fovea centralis   The small pit in the center of the macula; the area of clearest vision, containing only cones.

Fragile X syndrome   *See* Chapter 18.

Frame shift   A type of gene mutation in which there is the insertion or deletion of a single nucleotide leading to the misreading of all subsequent codons.

Free radicals   Chemical compounds, the abnormal accumulation of which has been linked to cancer and neurotoxicity.

Frequency   Cycles per second, a measure of sound.

Full graduated guidance   Instructor keeps hands in contact with child's hands in teaching a task.

Fundal plication   An operation in which the top of the stomach is wrapped around the opening of the esophagus to prevent gastroesophageal reflux.

Fundus uteri   The upper portion of the uterus where the fallopian tubes attach.

Gastroenteritis   Stomach flu.

Gastroesophageal reflux   The backward flow of food into the esophagus after it has entered the stomach.

Gastroschisis   Congenital malformation of the abdominal wall resulting in the protrusion of abdominal contents.

Gastrostomy   An operation in which an artificial opening is made into the stomach through the wall of the abdomen.

Gene   A unit of genetic material (DNA) that encodes a single protein.

Genome   The complete set of hereditary factors (genes) in an organism.

Genomic imprinting   A condition manifested differently depending on whether the trait is inherited from the mother or father.

Genotype   The genetic composition of an individual.

Germ cells   The cells involved in reproduction (i.e., sperm, eggs).

Glaucoma   Increased pressure within the anterior chamber of the eye which can cause blindness.

Glossoptosis   Protruding tongue.

Glucose   A sugar, also called sucrose, contained in fruits and other carbohydrates.

Glycogen   The chief carbohydrate stored in the body, primarily in the liver and muscles.

Goiter   Enlargement of the thyroid gland.

Goniotomy   An operation to treat glaucoma that decreases pressure by providing an opening for the release of fluid from the anterior chamber of the eye.

Graduated guidance   A behavior management technique in which only the level of assistance (guidance) necessary for the child to complete the task is provided.

Graft versus host disease   A mechanism of the body's immune system that destroys foreign proteins. When it occurs in an immunosuppressed child who has received a bone marrow or organ transplant, it can be life threatening. Symptoms include diarrhea, skin breakdown, and shock.

Grammar   The characteristic system of inflections and syntax of language.

Grapheme   A unit, such as a letter, of a writing system.

Guided compliance   A behavior management technique involving the use of graduated guidance to teach functional tasks.

Guillain-Barré syndrome   An acute polyneuropathy (*see* Chapter 15).

Gynecomastia   Excessive breast growth in males.

Gyri   Convolutions of the surface of the brain; singular: gyrus.

Habilitation   The teaching of new skills to children with developmental disabilities. It is called *habilitation* rather than rehabilitation because these children did not possess these skills previously.

Hallerman-Streiff syndrome   *See* Syndromes and Inborn Errors of Metabolism, Appendix B.

Hallucinations   Sensory perceptions without a source in the external world. These most commonly occur as symptoms of psychosis, drug intoxication, or seizure.

Haploid   A single set of human chromosomes, 23, as in the sperm or egg.

Helix   The coiled structure of DNA.

Hemangioma   Congenital mass of blood vessels.

Hematocrit   Percentage of red blood cells in whole blood, normally about 35%–40%.

Hematopoietic   Relating to the formation of red blood cells.

Hemihypertrophy   Asymmetric hypertrophy of face or limbs.

Hemiplegia   Paralysis of one side of the body.

Hemoglobin   Blood protein capable of carrying oxygen to body tissues.

Hemosiderosis   Dangerous increase in tissue iron stores, which can lead to respiratory failure and death.

Hemostat   A small surgical clamp used to constrict a tube or blood vessel.

Herpes simplex virus   A virus leading to symptoms that range from cold sores to vaginal infections to encephalitis; also a cause of fetal malformations and sepsis in early infancy.

Heterotopia   Migration and development of normal neural tissue in an abnormal location in the brain.

Heterozygous   Carrying genes dissimilar for one trait.

Holoprosencephaly   A brain malformation in which there is a single ventricle and/or incomplete development of the cerebral lobes. Children with this disorder have mental retardation (*see* Syndromes and Inborn Errors of Metabolism, Appendix B).

Homeostasis   Equilibrium of fluid, chemical, and temperature regulation in the body.

Homocystinuria   *See* Syndromes and Inborn Errors of Metabolism, Appendix B.

Homozygous   Carrying identical genes for any given trait.

Hybrid   Offspring of parents of dissimilar species.

Hydrocephalus   A condition characterized by the abnormal accumulation of cerebrospinal fluid within the ventricles of the brain. In infants, this leads to enlargement of the head.

Hyperalimentation   Intravenous provision of high-quality nutrition (i.e., carbohydrates, protein, fat). This is also called *parenteral nutrition*. It is used in children with malabsorption, malnutrition, and short gut syndrome.

Hyperbilirubinemia   Excess accumulation of bilirubin in the blood.

Hyperglycemia   High blood sugar level, as seen in diabetes.

Hyperimmune serum   Blood that is especially rich in antibodies against a virus.

Hypermethylation   A chemical mechanism for shutting off gene function.

Hyperopia   Farsightedness.

Hyperparathyroidism   High level of blood parathyroid hormone which causes abnormalities in calcium and phosphorous metabolism.

Hypertelorism   Widely spaced eyes.

Hypertension   High blood pressure.

Hyperthyroidism   Condition resulting from excessive production of thyroid hormone.

Hypertrichosis   Excessive hair growth.

Hyperviscosity   Excessive thickening of the blood.

Hypocalcemia   Low blood calcium level.

Hypogenitalism   Small genitalia.

Hypoglycemia   Low blood-sugar level.

Hypogonadism   Decreased function of sex glands with resultant retarded growth and sexual development.

Hypoplasia   Defective formation of a tissue or body organ.

Hypospadias   Abnormal urethral opening in penis.

Hypothermia   Low body temperature.

Hypothyroidism   Condition resulting from deficient production of thyroid hormone.

Hypotonic   Having decreased muscle tone; noun: hypotonia.

Hypoxic   Reduced oxygen content in body tissues.

Hypsarrhythmia   Electroencephalographic (EEG) abnormality seen in infants with infantile spasms. It is marked by chaotic spike-wave activity.

Ictal   Pertaining to a seizure event.

Ileostomy   A surgically placed opening from the small intestine through the abdominal wall.

Ileum   Lower portion of the small intestine.

Immunoglobin G (IgG)   An antibody.

Impact   In reference to traumatic head injury, the forcible striking of the head against an object.

Impedance audiometry   Test to detect the presence of middle-ear fluid, commonly seen in otitis media. It also detects conductive hearing loss.

Imperforate   The lack of a normal opening in a body organ. The most common example in childhood is an absent or closed anus.

Imitation training   A behavior management technique in which the teacher demonstrates the desired behavior, asks the child to complete the action, and provides positive reinforcement when the task is completed.

Implantation   The attachment and imbedding of the fertilized egg into the mucus lining of the uterus.

Inborn error of metabolism   An inherited enzyme deficiency leading to the disruption of normal bodily metabolism, an example being phenylketonuria.

Individual practice association (IPA) model   In managed care, a physician group providing services to members.

Inertial   Pertaining to inertia; the tendency to keep moving in the same direction as the force that produced the movement.

Inferior   Below.

Influenza   An acute illness caused by a virus; attacks respiratory and gastrointestinal tracts.

Informed consent   The written consent of a child or guardian to undergo a procedure or treatment after its risks and benefits have been explained in easily understood language.

Instructional training   A behavior management technique in which the teacher describes the desired behavior, asks the child to perform it, and provides positive reinforcement upon completion of the task.

Insufflation   In this context, the "snorting" of cocaine into the nose.

Insult   An attack on a body organ causing damage to it. This may be physical, metabolic, immunological, or infectious.

Intensity   Strength.

Interictal pattern   The pattern seen on EEG readings during periods when seizures are not occurring.

Interphase   The period in the cell life cycle when it is not dividing.

Interval schedules   Provision or reinforcement after the passage of a certain amount of time relative to the child's performance of a behavior or task.

Intubation   The insertion of a tube through the nose or mouth into the trachea to permit mechanical ventilation.

In utero   Occurring during fetal development.

Inversions   The result of two breaks on a chromosome followed by the reinsertion of the missing fragment at its original site but in the inverted order.

Inverted   Reversed.

In vivo   Inside the body.

Ionic   Pertaining to mineral ions, a group of atoms carrying a charge of electricity.

Ionization   The separation of a substance in solution into its component atoms.

Iris   The circular, colored membrane behind the cornea, perforated by the pupil.

Ischemia   Decreased blood flow to an area of the body; leads to tissue death.

Islet cells   Cells in the pancreas that produce insulin and control blood sugar levels.

Isochromosome   A chromosome with two copies of one arm and no copy of the other.

Jejunum   Second portion of the small intestine.

Karyotyping   Photographing the chromosomal makeup of a cell. In a human, there are 23 pairs of chromosomes in a normal karyotype.

Kernicterus   *See* Syndromes and Inborn Errors of Metabolism, Appendix B.

Ketosis   The buildup of acid in the body, most often associated with starvation, inborn errors of metabolism, or diabetes.

Kwashiorkor   A form of protein malnutrition.

Kyphoscoliosis   A combination of humping and curvature of the spine.

Kyphosis   Humping deformity of the spine; "hunchback."

Lactase   Enzyme necessary to digest the milk sugar lactose.

Lactose   Milk sugar composed of glucose and galactose.

Lanugo   Fine body hair on babies.

Lateral   To the side.

Lateral ventricles   Cavities in the interior of the cerebral hemisphere containing cerebrospinal fluid. They are enlarged with hydrocephalus or with brain atrophy.

Lens   The biconvex, translucent body that rests in front of the vitreous humor of the eye and refracts light.

Lesch-Nyhan syndrome   *See* Syndromes and Inborn Errors of Metabolism, Appendix B.

Lesion   Injury or loss of function.

Ligaments   Fibrous tissue connecting bones.

Linear fracture   Break of a long bone in a straight line.

Lipoma   A benign, fatty tissue tumor.

Lissencephaly   A brain malformation in which few gyri are formed, usually associated with mental retardation.

Locus ceruleus   Area of the brain involved in attention.

Lumbar   Pertaining to the lower back.

Lumbar puncture   The tapping of the subarachnoid space to obtain cerebrospinal fluid from the lower back region. This procedure is used to diagnose meningitis and to measure chemicals in the spinal fluid. It is also called a *spinal tap*.

Lymphocyte   A type of white blood cell.

Lymphomas   Cancerous growths of lymphoid tissue.

Lyonization   The genetic concept that there is X chromosome inactivation in females.

Macrocephaly   Large head size.

Macro-orchidism   Large testicles.

Macrosomia   Large body size.

Macrostomia   Large mouth.

Macula   The area of the retina that contains the greatest concentration of cones and the fovea centralis.

Magnetic resonance imaging (MRI)   Imaging procedure that uses the magnetic resonance of atoms to provide clear images of interior parts of the body. It is particularly useful in diagnosing structural abnormalities of the brain.

Major depression   A prolonged period of depressed mood.

Malaria   An infectious, febrile illness caused by a protozoa; transmitted by mosquitos; tends to become chronic.

Malnutrition   Inadequate nutrition for normal growth and development to occur.

Malocclusion   The improper fitting together of the upper and lower teeth.

Mandible   Lower jaw bone.

Mania   A distinct period of abnormally and persistently elevated, expansive, or irritable mood. The mood disturbance is sufficiently severe to cause impairment in function.

Manic-depressive   Pertaining to a psychiatric disorder consisting of distinct periods of elevated and depressed moods. This is a type of psychosis and is associated with disorganization of personality and distortion of reality.

Maple sugar urine disease   *See* Syndromes and Inborn Errors of Metabolism, Appendix B.

Marasmus   A form of protein-calorie malnutrition.

Mastoiditis   Infection of the mastoid air cells that rest in the temporal bone behind the ear. This is an infrequent complication of a chronic middle-ear infection.

Maxilla   The bony region of the upper jaw.

Maxillary hypoplasia   Incomplete development of the upper jaw.

Meconium aspiration   Potentially severe illness due to a newborn infant inhaling meconium (i.e., feces) into lung passages with first respiratory efforts; can cause aspiration pneumonia and inadequate ventilation.

Median plane   The midline of the body.

Medium chain triglycerides (MCT)   Fatty food sources that can bypass normal uptake process and go directly to the liver.

Megavitamin therapies   *See* Orthomolecular therapy.

Meiosis   Reductive cell division occurring only in eggs and sperm in which the daughter cells receive half (23) the number of chromosomes of the parent cells (46).

Mendelian traits   Traits inherited according to the genetic principles put forward by Gregor Mendel: dominant and recessive traits.

Meningeal   Related to the meninges, the three membranes enveloping the brain and spinal cord.

Meningitis   Infection of the meninges.

Meningocele   Protrusion of the meninges through a defect in the skull or vertebral column.

Meningomyelocele   Protrusion of meninges and malformed spinal cord through a defect in the vertebral column.

Menses   The menstrual flow.

Messenger ribonucleic acid (mRNA)   RNA involved in the translation of genetic information.

Metachromatic leukodystrophy   A progressive white matter disorder caused by a lysosomal enzyme deficiency; *see* Syndromes and Inborn Errors of Metabolism, Appendix B.

Metaphase   The stage in cell division in which each chromosome doubles.

Metaphysis   The end of the shaft of long bones connected to the epiphysis.

Methylmalonic acidemia   An inborn error of organic acid metabolism (*see* Syndromes and Inborn Errors of Metabolism, Appendix B).

Microcephaly   Small head size.

Microdeletion   A microscopic deletion in a chromosome associated with a contiguous gene syndrome.

Micrognathia   Receding chin.

Microphthalmia   Small eye.

Microswitch   A switch, usually used to control a computer, environmental control system, or power wheelchair, that has been adapted so that less pressure than normal is required to activate it.

Microtia   Small ear.

Milligram   One thousandth of a gram.

Milliliter   One thousandth of a liter; equal to about 15 drops.

Missense mutation   Gene error resulting from the replacement of a single nucleic acid for another resulting in a misreading of the DNA code.

Mitochondrial myopathies   Congenital muscle disorders caused by a mutation in the mitochondrial DNA.

Mitosis   Cell division in which two daughter cells of identical chromosomal composition to the parent cell are formed; each contains 46 chromosomes.

Mixed cerebral palsy   A form of cerebral palsy with both spastic and dyskinetic components.

Molecular genetic techniques   Laboratory methods of locating genes on chromosomes.

Mononucleosis   A viral illness with symptoms of fever, malaise, sore throat, swollen lymph nodes, and an enlarged spleen.

Monosomy   Chromosome disorder in which one chromosome is absent; the most common example is Turner syndrome, XO.

Monosomy X   Turner syndrome.

Mood stabilizers   A category of medications used to control depression and other mood disorders, an example being lithium.

Morbidity   Medical complication of an illness, procedure, or operation.

Moro   Primitive reflex present in the newborn in which the infant throws the arms out in an "embrace" attitude.

Morphemes   The smallest linguistic units of meaning.

Morula   The group of cells formed by the first divisions of a fertilized egg.

Mosaicism   The presence of two genetically distinct types of cells in one individual—for example, a child with Down syndrome who has some cells containing 46 chromosomes and some cells containing 47 chromosomes.

Motor point block   The injection of a denaturing agent into the nerve supply of a spastic muscle.

Mucopolysaccharides   Product of metabolism that may accumulate in cells and cause a progressive neurological disorder. One example is Hurler disease.

Mucosal   Pertaining to the mucus membrane lining organs, such as the mouth, stomach, and vagina.

Multifactorial inheritance   Inheritance pattern in which both environment and heredity interact.

Multiple carboxylase deficiency   Inborn error of metabolism (organic acidemia) presenting in the newborn period; results in severe illness due to the inability to couple the vitamin biotin to certain enzymes that need it; fatal if untreated, but response to biotin supplementation is usually excellent.

Muscle spindles   Part of the reflex arc that controls muscle contraction.

Muscular dystrophy   *See* Chapter 15.

Mutation   A change in a gene that occurs by chance.

Myasthenia gravis   *See* Chapter 15.

Myelination   The production of a coating called *myelin* around an axon. This quickens neurotransmission.

Myopia   Nearsightedness.

Myosin   Protein necessary for muscle contraction.

Myotonia   Abnormal rigidity of muscles when voluntary movement is attempted.

Myringotomy   The surgical incision of the eardrum. It is usually accompanied by the placement of pressure equalizing tubes to drain fluid from the middle ear.

Nasal cannula   Plastic prongs placed in the nostrils to deliver oxygen.

Nasal pillows   A prop attached to an oxygen line to permit the flow of oxygen directly into the nose.

Nasogastric feeding-tube   A plastic feeding-tube placed in the nose and extended into the stomach.

Nasopharynx   Posterior portion of the oral cavity above the palate.

Necrosis   Death of tissue.

Necrotizing enterocolitis (NEC)   Severe inflammation of the small intestine and colon, more common among premature infants.

Negative reinforcement   Occurs when, as a result of an individual's behavior, an unpleasant event is avoided or escaped, resulting in an increase in this behavior in the future.

Nerve blocks   Direct injection of denaturing agents into motor nerves.

Neural fold   During embryonic life, the neural plate expands and rises to become the neural fold, later becoming the spinal column.

Neural network   A network involving many brain regions working in concert to store and use information obtained from the environment.

Neural plate   During embryonic life, part of the ectoderm forms an elongated, shoe-shaped body, the neural plate, a precursor to the spinal column.

Neural tube   The precursor of the spinal column.

Neural tube defects   *See* Chapter 25.

Neurodevelopmental therapy (NDT)   Therapy that includes an understanding and utilization of normal developmental stages in working with children; commonly used theory underlying physical and occupational therapy.

Neuroectoderm   Fetal skin cells that differentiate to form the retina and CNS.

Neurofibromatosis   *See* Syndromes and Inborn Errors of Metabolism, Appendix B.

Neuroleptic malignant syndrome   A rare toxic reaction to a phenothiazine medication (e.g., thioridazine [Mellaril]) in which there is a potentially life threatening high fever.

Neuroses   Psychiatric disorders associated with unresolved conflicts and characterized by anxiety, but without the disorganization of personality and distortion of reality that occur in psychosis. Examples of neuroses include panic disorder, conversion hysteria, obsessive-compulsive disorders, and phobias.

Neurotoxin   A chemical compound that can damage neurons.

Neurotransmitter   A chemical released at the synapse that permits transmission of an impulse from one nerve to another.

Neutropenia   Low white blood cell count.

Nondisjunction   Failure of a pair of chromosomes to separate during mitosis or meiosis, resulting in an unequal number of chromosomes in the daughter cells.

Nonsense mutation   Gene defect in which a single base pair substitution results in the premature termination of a message and the resultant production of an incomplete and inactive protein.

Normalization   The process of integrating individuals with developmental disabilities into the general community, as opposed to segregating them into special schools and residences.

Nuclear family   Parents and their children.

Nucleotide bases   The four nucleic acids that form DNA—adenine, guanine, cytosine, and thymine.

Nystagmus   Involuntary rapid movements of the eyes.

Obsessive-compulsive disorder (OCD)   A psychiatric disorder in which recurrent and persistent thoughts and ideas that cannot be suppressed are associated with repetitive behaviors, such as handwashing.

Ocular   Pertaining to the eye.

Oculomotor apraxia   Eye gaze difficulties.

Olfactory sensations   An aura preceding a seizure in which pungent odors not present in the environment are smelled.

Oligohydramnios   The presence of too little amniotic fluid. It may result in fetal deformities including club foot and atretic lungs.

Omphalocele   Congenital herniation of abdominal organs through the navel.

Operant model   The scientific basis of applied behavior analysis, in which certain antecedents can be shown to increase or decrease the subsequent occurrence of a behavior.

Ophthalmoplegia   Paralysis of eye gaze.

Opiate antagonists   A category of medications that block endorphin receptors of the brain. These drugs, such as naltrexone, have been used to treat self-injurious behavior.

Opisthotonus   Positioning of the body in which the back is arched, while head and feet touch the bed.

Opsin   Retinal pigment of rods, involved in perception of light and dark.

Ophthalmologist   Physician specializing in treatment of diseases of the eye.

Ophthalmoscope   An instrument containing a mirror and a series of magnifying lenses used to examine the interior of the eye.

Opticokinetic   Pertaining to movement of the eyes.

Oral preparatory   The step preceding swallowing in which food is formed into a bolus in the mouth.

Oral transport   The transport of a bolus of food to the back of the mouth so that it can then be swallowed.

Organ of Corti   A series of hair cells in the cochlea that form the beginning of the auditory nerve.

Organic acidemias   Inborn errors or organic acid metabolism (e.g., methylmalonic acidemia).

Orthodontist   Dentist who specializes in the correction of irregularities of the teeth or the improper alignment of the jaw.

Orthomolecular therapy   The use of at least 10 times the required amount of vitamins; also called *megavitamin therapy*.

Orthopedic   Relating to bones or joints.

Orthoses   Orthopedic devices, most commonly splints or braces, used to support, align, or correct deformities or to improve the function of limbs.

Orthotist   Professional trained in the fitting and construction of splints, braces, and artificial limbs.

Ossicles   The three small bones in the middle ear: the stapes, incus, and malleus.

Osteoarthritis   Degenerative joint disease.

Osteoblasts   Cell type that produces bony tissue.

Osteoclast   Cell type that absorbs and removes bone.

Osteogenesis imperfecta   *See* Syndromes and Inborn Errors of Metabolism, Appendix B.

Osteoid   Related to bone.

Osteopenia   The loss of bony tissue.

Osteopetrosis   A genetic disorder marked by deficient osteoclastic activity. A buildup of bone encroaches on the eye, brain, and other body organs, leading to early death. Treatment with bone marrow transplantation has been successful in some cases.

Ostomy   An artificial opening in the abdominal region for discharge of stool or urine.

Oxidative phosphorylation   A chemical reaction occurring in the mitochondrion resulting in energy production.

Oxygenation   The provision of sufficient oxygen for bodily needs.

Pachygyria   Abnormal convolutions on the surface of brain.

Palatal   Relating to the palate, the back portion of the roof of the mouth.

Panic   A psychiatric disorder in which the patient has episodes of sudden and irrational fears associated with hyperventilation and palpitations.

Parenteral   Providing nutrition or medication by vein rather than by oral route.

Parkinson disease   A progressive neurological disease usually occurring in older people; associated with tremor, slowed movements, and muscular rigidity.

Parvovirus   A group of extremely small DNA viruses. Intrauterine infection with this virus increases the risk of miscarriage but has not been shown to result in fetal malformations.

Partial graduated guidance   Instructor uses minimal physical contact but much praise in helping the child learn a desired task.

Patent ductus arteriosus (PDA)   The persistence of a fetal passage permitting blood to bypass the lungs.

Patterning   Controversial therapy program that involves repetition of movements in order to facilitate developmental progress.

Penicillamine   A drug used to bind and dispose of ingested heavy metals, particularly lead and copper.

Percutaneous umbilical blood sampling (PUBS)   A prenatal diagnostic procedure for obtaining fetal blood for genetic testing.

Percutaneously   Through the skin.

Periodontal diseases   Diseases of the gums and bony structures that surround the teeth.

Periosteum   Fibrous tissue covering and protecting all bones.

Peripheral nervous system   The parts of the nervous system that are outside the brain and spinal cord.

Peripheral venous line   Catheters that are placed in a superficial vein of the arm or leg to provide medication.

Peritoneal   Referring to the membrane surrounding the abdominal organs. In kidney failure, dialysis can be performed by perforating the peritoneum and "washing out" the abdominal cavity.

Periventricular-intraventricular   Around or within the ventricles of the brain.

Periventricular leukomalacia (PVL)   Injury to part of the brain near the ventricles; caused by lack of oxygen; occurs principally in premature infants.

Peroxisome   A cellular organelle involved in processing fatty acids.

Persistent fetal circulation   Failure of closure of the fetal circulatory bypasses, the foramen ovale and ductus arteriosus, after birth that interferes with oxygenation of the lungs. This can lead to respiratory failure and death and may require treatment with extracorporeal membrane oxygenation (ECMO).

Pervasive developmental disorder   *See* Chapter 21.

Pes cavus   High arched foot.

Phagocytes   Cells that ingest microorganisms or other foreign particles.

Phalanges   Bones of the fingers and toes.

Pharyngeal   *See* Pharynx.

Pharyngeal transfer   The transfer of a food bolus from the mouth to the pharynx on its way to being swallowed.

Pharynx   The back of the throat; adjective: pharyngeal.

Phenothiazines   Drugs that affect neurochemicals in the brain and are used to control behavior.

Phenotype   The physical appearance of a genetic trait.

Phenylketonuria (PKU)   *See* Chapter 19.

Philtrum   Groove between nose and mouth.

Phobias   Irrational fears.

Phocomelia   Congenitally foreshortened limbs.

Phoneme   The smallest unit of sound in speech.

Phonetic   The sounding out of words.

Phonology   The set of sounds in a language and the rules for using them.

Photoreceptors   Receptors for light stimuli, the rods and cones in the retina.

Physis   Growth plate of a developing long bone.

Pica   The hunger for nonfood items.

Pitch   The frequency of sounds, measured in cycles per second or Hertz (Hz). Low-pitched sound have a frequency less than 500 Hz and a bass quality. High-pitched sounds have a frequency above 2,000 Hz and a tenor quality.

Placenta   The organ of nutritional exchange between the mother and the embryo. It has both maternal and embryonic portions and is disc shaped and about 7 inches in diameter. The umbilical cord attaches in the center of the placenta. The placenta is also called the *afterbirth;* adjective: placental.

Placenta previa   Condition in which the placenta is implanted in the lower segment of the uterus extending over the cervical opening. This often leads to bleeding during labor.

Planned ignoring   A behavior management technique based on withholding positive reinforcement following an occurrence of a problem behavior.

Plasmapheresis   The removal of blood followed by filtering the plasma and reinfusing the blood products. This procedure is done to remove toxins and antibodies as in Guillain-Barré syndrome.

Plasticity   The ability of an organ or part of an organ to take over the function of another damaged organ.

***Pneumocystis carinii* pneumonia**   Lung infection often seen in immunocompromised individuals, such as those with AIDS.

Polar bodies   The nonviable eggs formed during meiosis.

Polarization   Separation of electrical charge between outside and inside the cells.

Polio   Viral infection of the spinal cord causing an asymmetrical ascending paralysis, now prevented by vaccination.

Polydactyly   Extra fingers or toes.

Polysomnogram   Procedure performed during sleep that involves monitoring EEG, EKG, and respiratory efforts.

Porencephalic cyst   Fluid-filled sac attached to the lateral ventricle of the brain; usually the consequence of liquefaction of brain tissue due to an *in utero* injury or infection.

Positive practice   Requires the child to demonstrate repeatedly a relevant prosocial alternative to a problem behavior.

Positive reinforcement   A method of increasing desired behaviors by rewarding them.

Positive reinforcers   Any tangible (e.g., food or toy) or action (e.g., hug) which is reinforcing to an individual and will lead to a subsequent increase in the behavior that preceded it.

Positron emission tomography (PET)   Imaging study utilizing radioactive labeled chemical compounds to study the metabolism of an organ, most commonly the brain.

Posterior   In the back, behind.

Posterior walkers   Walkers with supports and wheels placed behind, rather than in front of, the child.

Postictal   Immediately following a seizure episode.

Posttraumatic stress disorder (PTSD)   Psychiatric disorder in which a previously experienced stressful event is reexperienced psychologically many times, associated with anxiety and fear.

Postural reactions   Normal reflex-like protective responses of an infant to changes in position.

Prader-Willi syndrome   *See* Syndromes and Inborn Errors of Metabolism, Appendix B.

Pragmatics   Describes how language should be adapted to specific social situations, to convey emotion, and to emphasize meanings.

Preeclampsia   Illness of late pregnancy characterized by high blood pressure, swelling, and protein in the mother's urine.

Presbyopia   A decrease in the accommodation of the lens of the eye that occurs with aging.

Preterm birth   Birth prior to 36 weeks' gestation; prematurity.

Primary teeth   Baby teeth.

Prolonged pregnancy   A gestation lasting longer than 42 weeks.

Prompts   Cues (e.g., verbal, visual) that direct the child to participate in a targeted activity.

Prone   Face down.

Prophase   The initial stage in cell division when the chromosomes thicken and shorten to look like separate strands.

Prophylaxis   Preventive agent.

Proptosis   Appearance of protruding eyes.

Ptosis   Drooping of eyelid.

Prosocial   Socially acceptable.

Prospective   Treatment in anticipation of the development of a disorder.

Proximal   Nearest.

Pseudohypertrophy   Enlarged weak muscle, as found in muscular dystrophy.

Psychoeducational evaluation   Testing of intelligence, academic achievement, and other types of skills to determine the presence of a learning disability.

Psychosis   A psychiatric disorder characterized by hallucinations, delusions, loss of contact with reality, and unclear thinking; adjective: psychotic.

Psychotherapy   Providing treatment for an individual with an emotional disorder. There are varying types of psychotherapy ranging from supportive counseling to psychoanalysis. These services are usually provided by a psychologist, psychiatrist, or social worker.

Pulmonary   Pertaining to the lungs.

Pulmonary hypertension   Increased back pressure in the pulmonary artery leading to decreased oxygenation and right heart failure.

Pulp   The soft tissue under the dentin layer in teeth, containing blood vessels, lymphatics, connective tissue, and nerve fibers.

Punishment   In behavior management, a procedure or consequence that decreases the frequency of occurrence of a behavior.

Pupil   The aperture in the center of the iris.

Purine   A type of organic molecule found in RNA and DNA.

Pylorus   The valve separating the stomach from the first section of the small intestine, the duodenum.

Pyridostigmine   A medication used to treat myasthenia gravis.

Quadriparesis   Weakness of all four extremities.

Quickening   The first signs of life felt by the mother as a result of fetal movements in the fourth or fifth month of pregnancy.

Rachitic rosary   Bead-like processes along the ribs that are associated with rickets.

Rads   A measure of radioactivity.

Ratio schedules   The provision of reinforcement following a set number of correct responses.

Real time ultrasound   The use of sound waves to provide a moving (real time) image, used in fetal monitoring.

Rebound   A phenomenon in which behavior becomes worse than when not on medication as the medication wears off.

Receptive aphasia   Impairment of receptive language due to a disorder of the CNS.

Receptive language   The understanding of language.

Recessive   A trait that is expressed only if the child inherits two copies of the gene.

Refracted   Deflected.

Reinforcer   A response to a behavior that increases the likelihood of the behavior occurring again.

Resonance   Refers to the balance of airflow between the nose and the mouth.

Response cost   Loss of a positive reinforcer or the imposition of a penalty if and when the child demonstrates a targeted inappropriate behavior.

Restitution   The immediate restoration of any remediable damages caused by the child's misbehavior.

Retina   The photosensitive nerve layer of the eye.

Retinitis pigmentosa   *See* Syndromes and Inborn Errors of Metabolism, Appendix B.

Retinoscope   An instrument used to detect errors of refraction in the eye.

Retrospective   Looking backward.

Retrovirus   A DNA virus involved in gene transfer therapy. This is also the class of viruses in which HIV, the causative agent of AIDS, belongs.

Rh sensitization   Changes that occur when an Rh$^+$ baby's blood enters an Rh$^-$ mother's bloodstream. This predisposes subsequent Rh$^+$ babies to kernicterus. Sensitization is prevented by the use of the drug RhoGAM.

Ribonucleic acid   A molecule essential for protein synthesis within the cell.

Ribosome   Intracellular structure concerned with protein synthesis.

Rickets   Bone disease resulting from nutritional deficiency of vitamin D.

Rigid   Increased tone marked by stiffness; seen in dyskinetic cerebral palsy.

Ring chromosome   A ring-shaped chromosome formed when deletions occur at both tips of a normal chromosome with subsequent fusion of the tips forming a ring.

Robin sequence   Congenital facial anomaly consisting of a small recessed jaw, cleft palate, and posterior placement of the tongue.

Rods   Photoreceptor cells of the eye associated with low-light vision.

Rooting   A reflex in newborns that makes them turn their mouths toward the breast or bottle to feed.

Rootlets   Small branches of nerve roots.

Rubella   German measles.

Rumination   After swallowing, the regurgitation of food followed by rechewing.

Salicylates   Chemicals found in many food substances and in aspirin.

Sarcomeres   The contractile units of the myofibril.

Satiation   Having had enough or too much of something.

Saturated   In this context, a type of fatty acid in the diet that has been linked to heart disease less frequently than unsaturated fatty acids.

Schedule   The timing of reinforcement.

Schizophrenia   A psychiatric disorder with characteristic psychotic symptoms including prominent delusions, hallucinations, loose associations, catatonic behavior, and/or flat affect.

Sclera   The white, outer lining of the eyeball.

Scoliosis   Curvature of the spine.

Secondary   Occurring as a consequence of a primary disorder.

Seizure threshold   Tolerance levels of the brain for electrical activity. If level of tolerance is exceeded, a seizure occurs.

Semantics   The meaning of words.

Separation anxiety   Excessive concern about separation, usually of mother from child (e.g., school phobia).

Sepsis   Bacterial infection spread throughout the bloodstream; also called blood poisoning.

Sequential modification   If desired changes in behavior are not observed to occur across settings and behaviors, concrete steps are taken to introduce the effective intervention (e.g., positive reinforcement) to each of the behaviors or settings to which transfer of effects is inadequate.

Seropositivity   The presence in the blood of antibodies to a certain foreign protein indicating previous exposure. Testing for seropositivity has been used to detect exposure to viral protein, such as HIV.

Serotonin reuptake inhibitors   A groups of psychoactive drugs used to treat depression, an example being fluoxetine (Prozac).

Sex chromosomes   Those chromosomes that determine gender, the X and Y chromosomes.

Shadowing   Instructor keeps his or her hands within an inch of the child's hands as the child proceeds to complete the task.

Shaping   Reinforcing successive approximations to the goal behavior.

***Shigella* diarrhea**   An infection of the gastrointestinal tract due to a bacterium called *Shigella;* causes bloody diarrhea and can be associated with febrile seizures.

Siblings   Brothers and sisters.

Single photon emission computed tomography (SPECT)   An imaging technique that permits the study of the metabolism of a body organ, most commonly the brain.

Sister chromatid   Two identical strands of a duplicated chromosome.

Sleep apnea   Brief periods of arrested breathing during sleep, most commonly found in premature infants and in older children and adults with morbid obesity.

Sleep myoclonus   Sudden jerking movements of the body during sleep; may be confused with a seizure.

Soft neurological signs   A group of neurological findings that are normal in young children but when found in older children suggest immaturities in central nervous system development. Example includes difficulty performing sequential finger-thumb opposition or rapid alternating movements.

Somatic   Relating to the body.

Somatoform   Psychiatric disorder in which physical symptoms dominate (e.g., fibromyalgia).

Spastic   Increased muscle tone so that muscles are stiff and movements are difficult. Caused by damage to the pyramidal tract in the brain; noun: spasticity.

Spastic quadriplegia   A form of cerebral palsy in which all four limbs are affected. Increased muscle tone (i.e., spasticity) is caused by damage to the pyramidal tract in the brain.

Spasticity   Abnormally increased muscle tone.

Speaking valve   A valve that can be used in children who have tracheostomy tubes in place to permit vocalizations.

Spherical convex   The type of optical lens used to correct farsightedness. It can be incorporated into eyeglasses or contacts. The lens has a dome shape.

Spica cast   A cast that covers much of the lower body and is used following hip surgery.

Spina bifida   A developmental defect of the spine (*see* Chapter 25).

Spina bifida occulta   Generally benign congenital defect of the spinal column not associated with protrusion of the spinal cord or meninges.

Spinal muscular atrophy   Congenital neuromuscular disorder of childhood associated with progressive muscle weakness.

Spondyloepipheseal dysplasia   Congenital structural abnormality of vertebral column.

Spontaneous recovery   The reoccurrence of an undesirable behavior after it has been extinguished.

Sporadic   In this context, a disease that occurs by chance and carries little risk of reoccurrence.

Standardized rating scales   Questionnaires concerning specific behaviors that have been completed for large samples of children so that norms and normal degrees of variation are known.

Static   Unchanging.

Stereotypic movement disorder   Recurring purposeless but voluntary movements (e.g., hand flapping in children with autism).

Stereotypies   Stereotypic movement disorder.

Steroids   Medications used to treat severe inflammatory diseases and infantile spasms; also refers to certain natural hormones in the body.

Stimulant   Medication used to treat attention-deficit/hyperactivity disorder (e.g., methylphenidate [Ritalin]).

Strabismus   Deviation of one or both eyes during forward gaze.

Subarachnoid   Beneath the arachnoid membrane, or middle layer, of the meninges.

Subdural   Resting between the outer (dural) and middle (arachnoid) layers of the meninges.

Subdural hematomas   Localized collections of clotted blood lying in the space between the dural and arachnoid membranes that surround the brain. This results from bleeding of the cerebral blood vessels that rest between these two membranes.

Subluxation   Partial dislocation.

Substrate   A compound acted upon by an enzyme in a chemical reaction.

Suctioning   The advancing of a catheter through the nose or throat and into the trachea for the purposes of removing secretions by suction.

Sudden infant death syndrome (SIDS)   Diagnosis given to a previously well infant (often a former premature baby) who is found lifeless in bed without apparent cause; also called crib death (*see* Chapter 7).

Sulci   Furrow of the brain; singular: sulcus.

Superior   Above.

Supersensitivity psychosis   A rare toxic reaction to certain medications used in psychiatry leading to a psychotic reaction.

Supine   Lying on the back, face upward.

Surfactant   Substance that coats the alveoli in the lungs, keeping them open. A deficiency of it leads to respiratory distress syndrome in premature infants.

Sutures   In this context, the fibrous joint between certain bones (e.g., skull bones).

Synapses   The minute spaces separating one neuron from another. Neurochemicals breach this gap.

Synchronous   In the context of the CNS, the discharge of many neurons at the same time leading to a seizure.

Syndactyly   Webbed hands or feet.

Synophrys   Confluent eyebrow.

Syphilis   A venereal disease.

Systemic   Involving the whole body.

Tachycardia   Rapid heart rate.

Talipes equinovarus   Club foot.

Tangential speech   Conversation that is not on target with the subject being discussed. This is commonly seen in patients with psychosis.

Tangibles   Rewards given in positive reinforcement procedures (e.g, food, toys).

Tardive dyskinesia   A potentially severe movement disorder resulting from the long-term use of phenothiazines or other antipsychotic medication.

Target behavior   Behavior selected for assessment and management.

Telangiectasia   Abnormal cluster of small blood vessels.

Telophase   The final phase in cell division when the daughter chromosomes are at the opposite poles of the cell and new nuclear membranes form.

Tendons   Fibrous cords by which a muscle is attached.

Teratogens   Agents that cause malformations in a developing embryo.

Testosterone   Male sex hormone.

Tetraploidy   Condition in which the fetus has four copies of each chromosome or 92 chromosomes. This is incompatible with life.

Thrush   Monilial [fungal] yeast infection of the oral cavity in infants.

Tics   Brief repetitive movements or vocalizations that occur in a stereotyped manner and do not appear to be under voluntary control.

Time-out   A procedure whereby the possibility of positive reinforcement is withdrawn for a predetermined brief amount of time following the occurrence of a targeted problem behavior.

Time-out ribbons   A behavior management procedure in which a ribbon is worn by a child to indicate that he/she is in a "time-out" condition and should not be included in activities or given attention.

Tocolytic agents   Medications used to stop premature labor.

Tonic neck reflex   A primitive reflex found in infants.

Tonic-clonic   Spasmodic alteration of muscle contraction and relaxation.

Tonotopically   Arranged spatially by tone; the pattern found in the cochlea or inner ear.

Tooth bud   Embryonic tissue that is the precursor of the tooth.

Torsion dystonia   *See* Syndromes and Inborn Errors of Metabolism, Appendix B.

Torticollis   Wry neck.

Toxemia   Also called preeclampsia; the combination of high blood pressure, protein in the urine, and edema that may occur in the third trimester of pregnancy, especially in teenagers and women older than 35 years.

Toxoplasmosis   An infectious disease caused by a microorganism. It may be asymptomatic in adults but can lead to severe fetal malformations.

Trachea   Windpipe.

Tracheo-esophageal fistula   A congenital connection between the trachea and esophagus leading to aspiration of food and requiring surgical correction.

Tracheomalacia   Softening of the cartilage of the trachea.

Tracheostomy   The surgical creation of an opening into the trachea to permit insertion of a tube to facilitate mechanical ventilation.

Trachoma   A parasitic infection causing blindness in developing countries.

Transcription   The process in which an mRNA is formed from a DNA template.

Translation   The process in which an amino acid sequence is assembled according to the pattern specified by an mRNA.

Translocation   The transfer of a fragment of one chromosome to another chromosome.

Trauma   A wound or injury.

Triceps   A muscle in the arm.

Triplet repeat expansion   Abnormal number of copies of identical triplet nucleotides (as occurs in fragile X syndrome).

Triploidy   A condition in which a fetus has three copies of each chromosome, or 69 chromosomes; generally incompatible with life.

Trisomy   A condition is which there are three copies of one chromosome rather than two (e.g., trisomy 21, Down syndrome).

Tubers   Benign congenital tumors found in the brain of individuals with tuberous sclerosis.

Turner syndrome   *See* Syndromes and Inborn Errors of Metabolism, Appendix B.

Twinning   The production of twins.

Tympanometry   The measurement of flexibility of the tympanic membrane as an indicator of a middle-ear infection or fluid in the middle ear.

Undernutrition   Inadequate nutrition to sustain normal growth.

Unsaturated   In this context, a type of fatty acid in the diet that has been linked to heart disease in susceptible infants.

Urea   End product of protein metabolism.

Ureterostomy   Surgical procedure creating an outlet for the ureters through the abdominal wall.

Valgus   Bent outward.

Varicella   The virus that causes chickenpox and herpes.

Varus   Bent inward.

Vasoconstriction   The decrease in diameter of blood vessels.

Ventilator   A machine that provides a mixture of air and oxygen to an individual in respiratory failure. The oxygen content, pressure, volume, and frequency of respirators can be adjusted.

Ventricles   Small cavities, especially in the heart or brain.

Ventrico-peritoneal shunt   Tube connecting a cerebral ventricle with the abdominal cavity; used to treat hydrocephalus.

Vertebral arches   The bony structure of the spine.

Vertex presentation   Downward position of infant's head during vaginal delivery.

Vesicles   Small fluid-containing elevations in the upper layer of skin, as seen in chickenpox.

Vesicostomy   The surgical creation of an opening for the bladder to empty its contents through the abdominal wall.

Vestibular apparatus   Three ring-shaped bodies located in the labyrinth of the ear that are involved in maintenance of balance.

Villi   Tiny vascular projections coming from the embryo that become part of the placenta; singular: villus.

Vitreous humor   The gelatinous content of the eye located between the lens and retina.

Watershed infarct   Injury to brain due to lack of blood flow in the brain tissues between interfacing blood vessels.

Watershed zone   Tissue lying in between two major arteries and thus poorly supplied by blood.

X-linked recessive (trait)   A trait transmitted by a gene located on the X chromosome; also called sex-linked. It is passed on by a carrier mother to an affected son.

Syndromes and Inborn Errors of Metabolism

Gretchen Meyer

Children with certain developmental disabilities have a dysmorphic appearance. For example, children with Down syndrome share common facial features that experts recognize as a *pattern of malformation.* These children so resemble each other that they often look like siblings. When a combination of physical traits or malformations has one unifying cause, the condition is called a *syndrome* (Jones, 1996). A subgroup of these syndromes features specific metabolic patterns or abnormalities rather than physical malformations. These conditions are termed *inborn errors of metabolism.*

Many syndromes are the result of a defect in one or more genes or the presence of an added or deleted chromosome or part of a chromosome. These disorders may be inherited in families or may occur sporadically (for the first time in a family). In the 1990s, researchers have made great progress in mapping the human genome; thus, the genetic etiologies of many previously poorly defined syndromes have now been identified. As definitive genetic aberrations become detectable, the possibility of early detection and prenatal diagnosis increases. The future prospects for gene therapy also are raised.

This appendix lists a number of syndromes and inborn errors of metabolism that are often associated with developmental disabilities. Included are the principal characteristics, causes, patterns of inheritance, frequency of occurrence, common developmental abnormalities, and recent references that further define the syndrome. In addition, when the location of the abnormal gene or chromosome is known, it is listed. The first number or letter indicates the chromosome in which there is an abnormality (mutation); the second letter (p or q) represents the short or long arm of the chromosome, respectively; the number following the p or q is the actual abnormal site in the chromosome; for example, VCF syndrome is located on the long arm of chromosome 22 at position 11.2, designated #22q11.2. The pattern of inheritance is described as being *autosomal recessive (AR), autosomal dominant (AD), X-linked recessive (XLR), X-linked dominant (XLD), mitochondrial (M), multifactorial (MF),* or *sporadic (SP)* (i.e., noninherited). If treatment is available, it is included in the description. Unfortunately, in most syndromes, no specific treatment is available to correct the underlying defect. Treatment is more often available, however, for inborn errors of metabolism. This appendix is an attempt to list some of the more commonly recognized syndromes associated with developmental disabilities. It is not intended to be all inclusive. Medical terminology is defined in the glossary.

Aarskog syndrome   *Clinical features:* Short stature, widow's peak, broad nasal bridge with widely spaced eyes, shawl scrotum. *Associated complications:* Ptosis, ophthalmoplegia, strabismus, occasional cleft lip/palate. *Cause:* Mutation in chromosome #Xp11.21. *Inheritance:* XLR. *Prevalence:* Unknown.
   Reference: Teebi, A.S., Rucquoi, J.K., & Meyn, M.S. (1993). Aarskog syndrome: Report of a family with review and discussion of nosology. *American Journal of Medical Genetics, 46,* 501–509.

Achondroplasia   *Clinical features:* Disproportionate short stature, relatively large head, prominent forehead, depressed nasal bridge, short limbs, trident-shaped hand; intelligence is usually typical. *Associated complications:* Spinal cord compression, apnea, delays in motor milestones, occasional hearing loss. *Cause:* Defect in fibroblast growth factor caused by a mutation in chromosome #4p16.3. *Inheritance:* AD. *Prevalence:* 5/100,000–15/100,000 (see Chapter 15).

References: Brinkmann, B., Schlit, H., Zorowka, B., et al. (1993). Cognitive skills in achondroplasia. *American Journal of Medical Genetics, 47*(5), 800–804.

Committee on Genetics. (1995). Health supervision for children with achondroplasia. *Pediatrics, 95,* 443–451.

Adrenoleukodystrophy (X-linked ALD; for neonatal form *see* neonatal adrenoleukodystrophy)   *Clinical features:* Progressive neurological disorder of the brain white matter characterized by spasticity, ataxia, peripheral neuropathy, and speech disturbance. Primary adrenal insufficiency is a hallmark. The disease process commonly begins in late childhood. *Associated complications:* Gradual intellectual deterioration, seizures, endocrine abnormalities, conductive hearing loss, impaired color vision. *Cause:* Mutation in chromosome #Xq28. *Inheritance:* XLR. *Prevalence:* 1/10,000 males. *Treatment:* Dietary modifications, Lorenzo's oil, and bone marrow transplant have all been attempted with minimal success. The outcome of bone marrow transplant or Lorenzo's oil when treated before symptoms arise is yet to be determined.

References: DiGregorio, V.Y., & Schroeder, D.J. (1995). Lorenzo's oil therapy of adrenoleukodystrophy. *Annals of Pharmacotherapy, 29*(3), 312–313.

Moser, H.W. (1995). Adrenoleukodystrophy. *Current Opinion in Neurology, 8*(3), 221–226.

Aicardi syndrome   *Clinical features:* Infantile spasms, absence or hypoplasia of corpus callosum, abnormalities of eyes, vertebral or rib anomalies, mental retardation requiring extensive support. *Associated complications:* Poorly controlled seizures, visual impairment. *Cause:* Mutation in chromosome #Xp22. *Inheritance:* XLD; it is presumed to be a lethal mutation in males. *Prevalence:* Rare.

Reference: Manezes, A.V., MacGregor, D.L., & Buncic, J.R. (1994). Aicardi syndrome: Natural history and possible predictors of severity. *Pediatric Neurology, 11*(4), 313–318.

Alexander disease   *Clinical features:* Progressive neurological disorder characterized by macrocephaly, exaggerated startle response, optic atrophy, intellectual decline, seizures, and early death. *Associated complications:* Hydrocephalus, progressive spasticity, visual impairment. *Cause:* Unknown. *Inheritance:* AR. *Prevalence:* Rare.

Reference: Pridmore, C.L., Baraitser, M., Harding, B., et al. (1993). Alexander's disease: Clues to diagnosis. *Journal of Child Neurology, 8*(2), 134–144.

Anencephaly   *Clinical features:* Severe malformation of brain above the brainstem. *Associated complications:* Incompatible with prolonged survival. *Cause:* Defect in closure of the head portion of the embryonic neural tube. *Inheritance:* MF. *Prevalence:* 0.5/1,000–10/1,000 (see Chapter 25).

Reference: Medical Task Force on Anencephaly. (1990). The infant with anencephaly. *New England Journal of Medicine, 322,* 669–674.

Angelman syndrome   *Clinical features:* "Puppet-like" gait, large mouth, small head with brachycephaly, prominent jaw, ataxia, paroxysms of laughter, generalized depigmentation of hair. *Associated complications:* Seizures, mental retardation, paucity of speech. *Cause:* Deletion in chromosome #15q11-13 (maternal). *Inheritance:* Usually SP; occasionally inherited through uniparental disomy (two copies of one parent's chromosome and none from the other). *Prevalence:* Rare.

Reference: Saitoh, S., Harada, N., Jinno, Y., et al. (1994). Molecular and clinical study of 61 Angelman syndrome patients. *American Journal of Medical Genetics, 52,* 158–163.

Apert syndrome (Acrocephalosyndactyly, type I)   *Clinical features:* Premature fusion of the cranial sutures (craniosynostosis) with misshapen head, high forehead, and flat occiput, widely spaced eyes with downward slant, flat midface, and nasal bridge; severe syndactyly; limb anomalies; cleft palate in 30%. *Associated complications:* Hydrocephalus, varying degrees of mental retardation, hearing loss, tooth abnormalities, occasional heart and kidney anomalies. *Cause:* Mutation in FGFR2 gene (fibroblast growth factor receptor-2). *Inheritance:* Most are sporadic; occasional AD; recurrence risk for individual's offspring is 50%. *Prevalence:* 1.5/100,000. *Treatment:* Neurosurgical correction of sutures improves cosmesis and may reduce risk of mental retardation; plastic/orthopedic surgery for limb anomalies.

Reference: Cohen, M.M., Kreiborg, S., & Odont, D. (1993). An updated pediatric perspective on Apert syndrome. *American Journal of Diseases of Children, 147,* 989–993.

Arthrogryposis multiplex congenita   *Clinical features:* Nonprogressive joint contractures that begin prenatally; flexion contractures at the fingers, knees, and elbows with muscle weakness around involved joints. *Associated complications:* Occasional renal and ocular anomalies, cleft palate, defects of abdominal wall, scoliosis. *Cause:* Multiple; most frequently related to an underlying neuropathy, myopathy, or *in utero* crowding; may be associated with myopathies or maternal myasthenia gravis. *Inheritance:* Depends on cause. *Prevalence:* Unknown. *Treatment:* Casting of affected joints or surgery, if indicated.

Reference: Fedrizzi, E., Botteon, G., Inverno, M., et al. (1993). Neurogenic arthrogryposis multiplex congenta: Clinical and MRI findings. *Pediatric Neurology, 9*(5), 343–348.

Ataxia-telangiectasia   *Clinical features:* Slowly progressive ataxia, telangiectasias, immune defects, elevated alpha-fetoprotein in blood. *Associated complications:* Dystonia or choreoathetosis, increased risk of malignancy (often lymphoma), oculomotor apraxia, flexion-extension finger contractures, increased risk of sinus and pulmonary infections; intelligence is typical but may decline as disease progresses in severity. *Cause:* Mutation in chromosome #11q22-23. *Inheritance:* AR. *Prevalence:* 1/100,000–1/300,000.

References: Gatti, R.A. (1995). Ataxia-telangiectasia. *Dermatologic Clinics, 13*(1), 1–6.

Kastan, K. (1995). Clinical implications of basic research: Ataxia-telangiectasia: Broad implications for a rare disorder. *New England Journal of Medicine, 333,* 662–663.

Bardet-Beidl (Laurence-Moon-Bardet-Beidl) syndrome   *Clinical features:* Obesity, hypogenitalism, polydactyly, retinal anomalies. *Associated complications:* Abnormal liver functioning, cataracts, occasional cardiac and renal anomalies, delayed puberty, ataxia, spasticity, night blindness. *Cause:* Linked to three separate chromosomes: #11q13, #16q13-22, #3p11-13. *Inheritance:* AR. *Prevalence:* Rare.

Reference: Carmi, R., Elbedow, K., Stone, E.M., et al. (1995). Phenotypic differences among patients with Bardet-Beidl syndrome linked to three different chromosome loci. *American Journal of Medical Genetics, 59*(2), 199–203.

Batten disease (neuronal ceroid lipofuscinosis)   *Clinical features:* Typical development for first 2–4 years of life; gradual onset of ataxia, myoclonic or major motor seizures, and retinal degeneration; death in late childhood. *Associated complications:* Gradual intellectual decline, spasticity, psychosis, kyphoscoliosis, visual impairment. *Cause:* Mutation of chromosome #16p12.1. *Inheritance:* AR. *Prevalence:* 0.7/100,000.

Reference: Goebel, H.H. (1995). The neuronal ceroid-lipofuscinoses. *Journal of Child Neurology, 10*(6), 424–437.

Beckwith-Wiedemann syndrome   *Clinical features:* Omphalocele, large tongue, macrosomia, neonatal hypoglycemia. *Associated complications:* Advanced growth for the first 6 years with advanced bone age; occasional hemihypertrophy; renal or adrenal anomalies; increased risk of malignancy (liver, kidney, muscle); occasional mental retardation (may be due to hypoglycemia). *Cause:* Presumed failure to suppress gene for IGF2 (insulin-like growth factor-2) caused by a duplication of chromosome #11p15.5. *Inheritance:* SP; possible AD with variable penetrance. *Prevalence:* 0.07/1,000. *Treatment:* Early treatment of hypoglycemia is critical; surgical repair of omphalocele.

Reference: Elliot, M., & Maher, E.R. (1994). Beckwith-Wiedemann syndrome. *American Journal of Medical Genetics, 31,* 560–564.

Biotinidase deficiency   *See* Multiple carboxylase deficiency—late onset, juvenile form.

Borjeson-Forssman-Lehmann syndrome   *Clinical features:* Obesity, gynecomastia, long thick ears, protruding tongue, hypogonadism, cataracts or other eye anomalies, tapering fingers, varying degrees of mental retardation. *Associated complications:* Seizures, microcephaly. *Cause:* Mutation in chromosome #Xq26-27. *Inheritance:* XLR. *Prevalence:* Rare.

Reference: Turner, G., Gedeon, A., Mulley, J., et al. (1989). Borjeson-Forssman-Lehmann: Clinical manifestations and gene localization to Xq26-27. *American Journal of Medical Genetics, 34,* 463–469.

Brachmann de Lange   *See* de Lange syndrome.

Canavan disease (spongy degeneration of central nervous system)   *Clinical features:* Progressive neurological disease consisting of macrocephaly, hypotonia, hyperextension of legs with flexion of arms, visual impairment, and early death; symptoms begin at 3–6 months of age. *Associated complications:* Feeding difficulties with progressive swallowing problems, gastroesophageal reflux, mental retardation requiring extensive support. *Cause:* Deficiency in the enzyme aspartoacylase, caused by a mutation in chromosome #17pter-p13. *Inheritance:* AR. *Prevalence:* Rare; increased in Ashkenazic Jewish population. *Treatment:* Preclinical trials are currently under way using gene therapy.
Reference: Matalon, R., Michals, K., & Kaul, R. (1995). Canavan disease: From spongy degeneration to molecular analysis. *Journal of Pediatrics, 127*(4), 511–517.

Carpenter syndrome (Acrocephalosyndactyly II)   *Clinical features:* Craniosynostosis, flat nasal bridge, malformed and low-set ears, short digits, syndactyly and/or polydactyly, obesity, hypogenitalism/cryptorchidism. *Associated complications:* Occasional heart defects, hearing loss, mental retardation requiring intermittent support in 75%. *Cause:* Unknown. *Inheritance:* Presumed AR. *Prevalence:* Rare.
Reference: Tarauath, S., & Tonsgard, J.H. (1993). Cerebral malformations in Carpenter syndrome. *Pediatric Neurology, 9*(3), 230–234.

CHARGE association   *Clinical features:* **C**oloboma, **H**eart defect, **A**tresia choanae (congenital blockage of the nasal passages), **R**etarded growth and development, **G**enital anomalies, and **E**ar anomalies with or without hearing loss. *Associated complications:* Hypogenitalism, cryptorchidism, occasional cleft lip/palate, varying degrees of mental retardation, potentially severe visual and hearing impairments. *Cause:* Unknown. *Inheritance:* Usually SP. *Prevalence:* Unknown.
Reference: Edwards, B.M., Van Riper, L.A., & Kileny, P.R. (1995). Clinical manifestations of CHARGE association. *International Journal of Pediatric Otorhinolaryngology, 33,* 23–42.

Cohen syndrome   *Clinical features:* Obesity; microcephaly; short stature; long hands with tapering fingers; characteristic facial features including micrognathia, short philtrum, maxillary hypoplasia; varying degrees of mental retardation. *Associated complications:* Hypotonia, joint laxity, ocular abnormalities, occasional heart defect. *Cause:* Mutation in chromosome #8q22–22. *Inheritance:* AR. *Prevalence:* Unknown.
Reference: North, K.N., Fulton, A.B., & Whiteman, D.A. (1995). Identical twins with Cohen syndrome. *American Journal of Medical Genetics, 58*(1), 54–58.

Cornelia de Lange syndrome   *See* de Lange syndrome.

Cretinism   *See* (Congenital) Hypothyroidism.

Cri-du-chat (5p-) syndrome   *Clinical features:* Pre- and postnatal growth retardation, cat-like cry in infancy, widely spaced eyes with downward slant, microcephaly, single palmar crease, mental retardation requiring extensive support. *Associated complications:* Severe respiratory and feeding difficulties in infancy, hypotonia, inguinal hernias, occasional congenital heart defects. *Cause:* Partial deletion in chromosome #5p. *Inheritance:* Usually SP new mutation; in 10%–15% of cases, a parent carries a balanced translocation. *Prevalence:* 1/20,000–1/50,000.
Reference: Church, D.M., Bengtsson, U., Nielson, K.V., et al. (1995). Molecular definition of deletions of different segments of distal 5p that result in distinct phenotypic features. *American Journal of Medical Genetics, 56,* 1162–1172.

Crouzon syndrome (craniofacial dysostosis)   *Clinical features:* Craniosynostosis, shallow orbits with proptosis, hypertelorism, strabismus, parrot-beaked nose, short upper lip, maxillary hypoplasia, conductive hearing loss. *Associated complications:* Mental retardation, seizures, visual impairment, agenesis of corpus callosum, occasional cleft lip or palate, obstructive airway problems. *Cause:* Defect in FGR2 (fibroblast growth factor receptor-2), found on the long arm of chromosome #10q25-26. *Inheritance:* AD with variable expression; up to 25% may represent new mutations. *Prevalence:* Unknown.
Reference: Proudman, T.W., Moore, M.H., Abbott, A.H., et al. (1994). Noncraniofacial manifestations of Crouzon's disease. *Journal of Craniofacial Surgery, 5*(4), 218–222.

de Lange syndrome   *Clinical features:* Prenatal growth retardation, postnatal short stature, hypertrichosis, synophrys, anteverted nostrils, depressed nasal bridge, long philtrum, thin upper lip, microcephaly, low-set ears, limb anomalies, eye problems (myopia, ptosis, or nystagmus). *Associated complications:* Mental retardation requiring extensive support, occasional heart defect, gastrointestinal problems, autistic features, self-injurious behavior, occasional hearing loss. *Cause:* Mutation in #3q26.3 or #17q23. *Inheritance:* Usually SP; possibly AD in some families. *Prevalence:* 1/50,000.

References: Goodban, M.T. (1993). Survey of speech and language skills with prognostic indicators in 116 patients with Cornelia de Lange syndrome. *American Journal of Medical Genetics, 47,* 1059–1063.

Jackson, L., Kline, A.D., Barr, M.A., et al. (1993). de Lange syndrome: A clinical review of 310 individuals. *American Journal of Medical Genetics, 47,* 940–946.

Deletion #22q11.2 syndrome (DiGeorge syndrome, velocardiofacial syndrome [VCF])   *Clinical features:* Deletions of the long arm of chromosome #22 have varying presentations including DiGeorge syndrome, VCF, and isolated outflow tract defects of the heart. Characteristic facial appearance may include a small open mouth, short palpebral fissures, flat nasal bridge, and bulbous nasal tip; varying degrees of palatal abnormalities ranging from cleft to velopharyngeal insufficiency. Classic DiGeorge syndrome is associated with hypoplastic thymus, hypoparathyroidism, and congenital heart defect. *Associated complications:* Rare seizures, hypernasal speech, characteristic pattern of nonverbal learning disability; feeding problems in infancy. *Cause:* Deletion in chromosome #22q11.2. *Inheritance:* Usually SP; 10% familial; 50% recurrence in offspring. *Prevalence:* Unknown.

References: Driscoll, D.A., & Emanuel, B.S. (1996). DiGeorge and velocardiofacial syndromes: The 22Q11 deletion syndrome. *Mental Retardation and Dvevelopmental Disabilities Research Reviews, 2,* 130–138.

Goldberg, R., Motzkin, B., Marion, R., et al. (1993). VCF syndrome: A review of 120 patients. *American Journal of Medical Genetics, 45*(3), 313–319.

DiGeorge syndrome   *See* Deletion #22q11.2 syndrome.

Down syndrome   *Clinical features:* Hypotonia, flat facial profile, upwardly slanting eyes, small ears, small nose with low nasal bridge, single palmar crease, short stature, mental retardation, congenital heart disease. *Associated complications:* Atlanto-axial (cervical spine) instability; ligamentous laxity; strabismus; thyroid dysfunction; predisposition toward autoimmune disorders and leukemia; eye abnormalities including strabismus, nystagmus, cataracts, or glaucoma; hearing loss. Neurological abnormalities include risk of seizures, premature dementia, and behavioral disturbances. *Cause:* Extra chromosome #21 caused by trisomy, mosaicism, or translocation. *Inheritance:* SP; recurrence risk in the absence of translocation is 1%–2% and increases with maternal age. If translocation is present in parent, recurrence risk is higher. *Prevalence:* 1/100,000–1.5/100,000 (see Chapter 17).

Reference: Roizen, N.J. (1996). Down syndrome and associated medical disorders. *Mental Retardation and Developmental Disabilities Research Reviews, 2,* 85–89.

Dubowitz syndrome   *Clinical features:* Intrauterine growth retardation; postnatal short stature; eczema; sparse, coarse hair; microcephaly; cleft palate; dysmorphic facial features including high forehead, broad nasal bridge, ptosis, epicanthal folds. *Associated complications:* Mental retardation, behavioral disturbances, recurrent infections, increased frequency of malignancy, occasional hypospadias or cryptorchidism, hypoparathyroidism. *Cause:* Unknown. *Inheritance:* AR. *Prevalence:* Rare.

Reference: Hansen, K.E., Kirkpatrick, S.J., & Laxova, R. (1995). Dubowitz syndrome: Long term follow up of an original patient. *American Journal of Medical Genetics, 55,* 161–164.

Duchenne muscular dystrophy (DMD)   *See* Muscular dystrophy.

Ectrodactyly-ectodermal dysplasia (EEC)   *Clinical features:* Ectrodactyly (absence of fingers or toes), ectodermal dysplasia (abnormal shin development), cleft lip and palate, lacrimal (tear) duct abnormalities; intelligence is usually typical. *Associated complications:* Occasional renal (kidney) anomalies, hearing impairment. *Cause:* Mutation in #7q21-22. *Inheritance:* AD with variable penetrance and expressivity. *Prevalence:* Unknown.

Reference: Roelfsema, N.M., & Cobben, J.M. (1996). The EEC syndrome: A literature study. *Clinical Dysmorphology, 5,* 115–127.

Edwards syndrome   *See* Trisomy 18 syndrome.

Ehlers-Danlos syndrome   *Clinical features:* At least 10 distinct forms have been described. All include aspects of skin fragility, easy bruisibility, joint hyperextensibility, and hyperelastic skin. Types I and III are most commonly described and have a similar clinical presentation with the previously mentioned features; type IV is characterized by severe blood vessel involvement with risk of spontaneous arterial rupture; type VI is characterized by eye involvement including corneal fragility; type VIII includes periodontal disease; type IX may include bladder abnormalities. *Associated complications:* Occasional mental retardation, premature loss of teeth, mitral valve prolapse, intestinal hernias, premature delivery from premature rupture of membranes, abnormalities of thymus. *Cause:* Each form is associated with an abnormality in the formation of collagen. *Inheritance:* Types I, II, III, IV, VII, and VIII are AD with variable expression; types VI and X are AR; type V is XLR. *Prevalence:* Unknown.

Reference: Byers, P.H. (1994). Ehlers-Danlos syndrome: Recent advances and current understanding of the clinical and genetic heterogeneity. *Journal of Investigative Dermatology, 103*(Suppl. 5), 47S—52S.

Ellis-van-Creveld syndrome (Chondroectodermal dysplasia)   *Clinical features:* Short-limbed dwarfism (final height 43–60 inches), polydactyly, nail abnormalities, neonatal teeth, underdeveloped and premature loss of teeth, congenital heart defect in 50%; intelligence is usually typical. *Associated complications:* Severe cardiorespiratory problems in infancy, hydrocephalus, severe leg deformities. *Cause:* Mutation in chromosome #4p16. *Inheritance:* AR. *Prevalence:* Rare, increased in Pennsylvania Amish.

Reference: Avolio, A., Jr., Berman, A.T., & Israelite, C.L. (1994). Ellis-van Creveld syndrome (chondroectodermal dysplasia). *Orthopedics, 17*(8), 735–737.

Facio-auriculo-vertebral spectrum (Goldenhar syndrome)   *Clinical features:* Unilateral external ear deformity ranging from absence of ear to microtia, preauricular tags or pits, middle-ear anomaly with variable hearing loss, facial asymmetry with small size unilaterally, macrostomia, occasional cleft palate, microophthalmia or eyelid coloboma. *Associated complications:* Vertebral anomalies, occasional heart defect, occasional mental retardation. *Cause:* Unknown; disruption of blood flow *in utero* is postulated. *Inheritance:* Usually SP; genetically heterogeneous. *Prevalence:* Unknown.

References: Rollnick, B.R., Kaye, C.I., Nagatoshi, K., et al. (1987). Oculoauriculovertebral dysplasia and variants: Phenotypic characteristics of 294 patients. *American Journal of Medical Genetics, 26,* 361–375.

Sutphen, R., Galan-Gomez, E., Cortada, X., et al. (1995). Tracheoesophageal anomalies in oculauriculovertebral (Goldennar) spectrum. *Clinical Genetics, 48*(2), 66–71.

Fetal alcohol syndrome/fetal alcohol effects (FAS/FAE)   *See* Chapter 8.

Fetal hydantoin (Dilantin) syndrome   *See* Chapter 26.

Fragile X syndrome   *Clinical features:* Prominent jaw, macroorchidism, large ears, autistic behavior. Affected males (full mutation) often have mental retardation requiring limited to extensive support. Of females with a full mutation, 33% have average intelligence, 33% have average intelligence with significant learning disabilities, and 33% have mental retardation, occasional pervasive developmental disorder. *Associated complications:* Abnormalities of connective tissue with finger joint hypermobility or joint instability, mitral valve prolapse. *Cause:* Mutation in FMR1 gene on #Xq27-q28; molecular analysis reveals an increase in CGG trinucleotide repeats in the coding sequence of the FMR1 gene. Normal allele sizes vary from 6 to 54 CGG repeats. Phenotypically unaffected carriers have "premutations" with allele size ranging from 52 to 200. Allele sizes of greater than 200 CGG repeats generally indicate a "full mutation" with phenotypic expression of the syndrome. *Inheritance:* X-linked with genetic imprinting (full mutations are more often inherited from the mother) and anticipation (severity may increase with subsequent pregnancies or generations). *Prevalence:* 1/2,000 males; 1/4,000 females (see Chapter 18).

References: Fisch, G.S. (1993). What is associated with the fragile X syndrome? *American Journal of Medical Genetics, 48,* 112–121.

Laxova, R. (1994). The fragile X syndrome. *Advances in Pediatrics, 41,* 305–342.

Friedreich's ataxia   *Clinical features:* Slowly progressive neurological disorder characterized by cerebellar ataxia, dysarthria, nystagmus, pes cavus, kyphoscoliosis. In rare cases, progression is rapid. Onset is before adolescence; some features may be present at birth. *Associated complications:* Delayed motor milestones, cardiomyopathy, and/or congestive heart failure; increased risk of insulin-dependent diabetes mellitus; impaired color vision. *Cause:* Mutation in chromosome #9p13-q21.1. *Inheritance:* AR. *Prevalence:* 0.5/100,00–1/100,000. *Treatment:* Supportive care includes physical therapy, orthopedic surgery to correct progressive scoliosis, close cardiology follow-up. No drug treatment is available. Some groups have had minimal success with a diet restrictive in carbohydrates.
Reference: Shapiro, F., & Specht, L. (1993). The diagnosis and orthopaedic treatment of childhood spinal muscular atrophy, peripheral neuropathy, Friedreich ataxia, and arthrogryposis. *Journal of Bone and Joint Surgery, 75*(11), 1699–1714.

G (Opitz-Frias/BBB) syndrome (G and BBB refer to surnames of original patients described)   *Clinical features:* Hypertelorism, hypospadias, dysphagia, bifurcated (divided) nasal tip, widow's peak; occasional cleft lip/palate; mental retardation requiring intermittent to limited support in two thirds of affected individuals. *Associated complications:* Gastroesophageal reflux, esophageal dysmotility, hoarse cry, pulmonary aspiration, occasional congenital heart defect or agenesis of corpus callosum, platelet abnormalities, structural cerebellar anomalies including Dandy Walker formation. *Cause:* Mutation in #22q11.2 or Xp22. *Inheritance:* AD and XLR. *Prevalence:* Unknown.
References: Conlon, B.J., & O'Dwyer, X. (1995). The G syndrome/Opitz oculo-genital-laryngeal syndrome/Opitz BBB/G syndrome/Opitz-Frias syndrome. *Journal of Laryngology and Otology, 109*, 244–246.
Wilson, G.N., & Oliver, W.J. (1988). Further delineation of the G syndrome: A manageable genetic cause of infantile dysphagia. *American Journal of Medical Genetics, 25*(3), 157–163.

Galactosemia   *Clinical features:* Jaundice in the newborn period, failure to thrive with vomiting and diarrhea, cataracts, liver dysfunction. Varying degrees of intellectual impairment (severe if untreated). In 70% of treated children, IQ score is less than 90, but 50% have significant visual-perceptual impairments. Verbal dyspraxia is also seen in 62% of treated infants. *Associated complications:* Ovarian failure, hemolytic anemia, increased risk of sepsis (particularly *E. coli* in neonate), cerebellar ataxia, tremors, choreoathetosis. *Cause:* A deficiency of the enzyme galactose-1-phosphate uridyl transferase or less commonly, galactokinase (both are enzymes required for digestion of galactose, a natural sugar found in milk). This is due to a mutation in chromosome #9p13. *Inheritance:* AR. *Prevalence:* 1/50,000–1/70,000. *Treatment:* Galactose-free diet.
References: Nelson, C.D., Waggoner, D.D., Donnell, G.N., et al. (1991). Verbal dyspraxia in treated galactosemia. *Pediatrics, 88,* 346–350.
Schweitzer, S., Shin, Y., Jakobs, C., et al. (1993). Long-term outcome in 134 patients with galactosemia. *European Journal of Pediatrics, 152,* 36–43.

Gaucher disease   *Clinical features:* Three clinically distinct forms having in common an enlarged spleen, hematological abnormalities, bony lesions, abnormalities of skin pigmentation, and varying degrees of mental retardation. *Associated complications:* Seizures, myoclonic jerks, oculomotor abnormalities. *Cause:* Deficiency of the enzyme beta galactosidase. *Inheritance:* AR. *Prevalence:* Rare; increased in Ashkenazic Jewish population. *Treatment:* If available, bone marrow transplantation is treatment of choice. Enzyme replacement is now available but extremely costly. Gene therapy may be available in the future.
Reference: Frenkel, E.P. (1993). Gaucher disease: A heterogeneous clinical complex for which effective enzyme replacement has come of age. *American Journal of the Medical Sciences, 305*, 331–344.

Glutaric aciduria type I   *Clinical features:* A disorder of organic acid metabolism, it presents symptoms during the first year of life with hypotonia, dystonia, choreoathetosis, and seizures; macrocephaly is common. This disorder may mimic extrapyramidal cerebral palsy. *Associated complications:* Episodic acidosis, vomiting, coma, and hyperammonemia; these may be fatal. Mental retardation is usual although intellectual functioning may rarely remain intact. *Cause:* Deficiency of the enzyme glutaryl-CoA dehydrogenase caused by a mutation in chromosome #19p13.2. *Inheritance:* AR. *Prevalence:* Rare; 1/30,000 in Sweden.
References: Hoffman, G.F., Bohles, H.J., Burlina, A., et al. (1995). Early signs and course of disease of glutaryl-CoA dehydrogenase deficiency. *Journal of Inherited Metabolic Disease, 18*(2), 173–176.

Kyllerman, M., Skjeldal, O.H., Lundberg, M., et al. (1994). Dystonia and dyskinesia in glutaric aciduria type I: Clinical heterogeneity and therapeutic considerations. *Movement Disorders, 9,* 22–30.

Glutaric aciduria type II   *Clinical features:* An inborn error of metabolism that may present in infancy with severe metabolic acidosis, hypoglycemia, and cardiomyopathy. There is a characteristic odor of sweaty feet similar to that present in isovaleric aciduria. Dysmorphic facial features are seen in one half of cases (macrocephaly, large anterior fontanel, high forehead, flat nasal bridge, and malformed ears). This condition also can present later in life with episodic vomiting, acidosis, and hypoglycemia. *Associated complications:* Muscle weakness, liver disease, cataracts, respiratory distress, renal cysts. *Cause:* Defective dehydrogenation of isovaleryl CoA and butyryl CoA caused by a mutation in chromosome #15q23-25. *Inheritance:* AR. *Prevalence:* Rare.
Reference: Frerman, F.E., & Goodman, S.I. (1995). Glutaric acidemia type II. In C.R. Scriver, A.L. Beaudet, W.S. Sly, et al. (Eds.), *The metabolic and molecular bases of inherited disease* (pp. 1619–1623). New York: McGraw-Hill.

Glycogen storage diseases (glycogenoses)   *Clinical features:* More than 12 forms of glycogen storage diseases are currently known and there is a wide spectrum of clinical features among them. They have in common varying degrees of liver and muscle abnormalities and organs with large amounts of glycogen. Types I (Von Gierke disease), II (Pompe disease), III (Forbes disease), and VI (Hers disease) are the most common and represent almost 90% of cases. Common clinical features include hypoglycemia, short stature, enlarged spleen, and muscle weakness. *Associated complications:* Hypotonia, renal abnormalities, gouty arthritis, bleeding abnormalities, hypertension, respiratory distress. Type II disease characteristically has severe cardiac involvement. *Cause:* Various enzyme deficiencies involved in the utilization of glycogen. The following are the identified mutation loci for the various forms: I (#17q21), II (#17q25.2-q25.3), III (#1p21), IV (#3p12), V (#11q13), VI (#14q21-q22), VII (#1cen-q32), and VIII (#Xp22.2-p22.1). *Inheritance:* All except type VIII are inherited as AR; type VIII is XLR. *Prevalence:* Combined prevalence of 1/20,000–1/25,000. *Treatment:* No specific treatment is yet available for any of the glycogenoses. Increased protein intake and overnight tube feeding of starch to maintain normoglycemia have been shown to be useful for supportive care. Liver transplantation has been attempted in type IV, but long-term outcome is not yet known. The possible role of gene therapy in the future is hopeful.
Reference: Chen, Y.T., & Burchell, A. (1995). Glycogen storage diseases. In C.R. Scriver, A.L. Beaudet, W.S. Sly, et al. (Eds.), *The metabolic and molecular bases of inherited disease* (pp. 935–965). New York: McGraw-Hill.

Goldenhar syndrome   *See* Facio-auriculo-vertebral spectrum.

Hallermann-Streiff syndrome   *Clinical features:* Proportionate short stature; characteristic facial appearance including small eyes, narrow beaked nose, and small mouth; sparse thin hair; frontal bossing. *Associated complications:* Various eye abnormalities including nystagmus, strabismus, cataract, and/or decreased visual acuity; neonatal teeth and other dental abnormalities; narrow upper airway or tracheomalacia; snoring and daytime somnolence; occasional cardiac failure. *Cause:* Inherited. *Inheritance:* Most reported cases SP. *Prevalence:* Unknown.
Reference: Cohen, M.M., Jr. (1991). Hallermann-Streiff syndrome: A review. *American Journal of Medical Genetics, 41,* 488–499.

Holoprosencephaly   *Clinical features:* This classification encompasses a spectrum of midline defects of the brain and face. Many are severe and incompatible with life. Those who survive have varying degrees of disability ranging from normal brain development and single central incisor to mental retardation requiring extensive support and brain malformations. *Associated complications:* Seizures, endocrine abnormalities, micropenis, cleft of retinae. *Cause:* Genetically heterogeneous; sonic hedgehog gene; many cases have involved mutations of #13q, #18p11.3, #2p21, #3p24, or #7q36. *Inheritance:* Most are sporadic; AD and AR forms have been reported. *Prevalence:* 1/16,000.
Reference: Elias, D.L., Kawamoto, H.K., & Wilson, L.F. (1992). Holoprosencephaly and midline facial anomalies: Redefining classification and management. *Plastic and Reconstructive Surgery, 90,* 951–958.

Holt-Oram syndrome   *Clinical features:* Upper limb defect ranging from hypoplastic or absent thumbs to absent radius, ulna, or humerus, to complete phocomelia (absence of limbs). Congenital heart defect (ASD, VSD most common). *Associated complications:* Occasional abnormalities of chest muscles, and vertebral anomalies. *Cause:* Mutation in chromosome #12q21.3-q22. *Inheritance:* AD with variable expression; may increase in severity with each generation. *Prevalence:* Unknown.

References: Basson, C.T., Cowley, G.S., Solomon, S.D., et al. (1994). The clinical and genetic spectrum of Holt-Oram syndrome (heart-hand syndrome). *New England Journal of Medicine, 330,* 885–891.

Newbury-Ecob, R.A., Leanage, R., Raeburn, J.A., et al. (1996). Holt-Oram syndrome: A clinical genetic study. *American Journal of Medical Genetics, 33,* 300–307.

Homocystinuria   *Clinical features:* Downward dislocation of lens (usually evident between 3 and 10 years but may be detected as early as 18 months), slim tall habitus, hypopigmentation, sparse thin hair. Two forms have been described, differing in their responsiveness to pyridoxine. *Associated complications:* Mental retardation in one half to three fourths of untreated individuals; increased risk of myocardial infarction and stroke because of thrombosis; behavioral disorders, cataract, or glaucoma; scoliosis; osteoporosis. *Cause:* Inherited defect in the enzyme cystathionine beta-synthetase caused by a mutation in chromosome #21q22. *Inheritance:* AR. *Prevalence:* 1/200,000. *Treatment:* Folic acid supplementation, use of betaine hydrochloride, and dietary restriction of methionine have shown promise; pyridoxine is used in those individuals who have the pyridoxine-responsive form of the disease. Early treatment with pyridoxine in responsive cases may allow average intelligence.

Reference: Kraus, J.P. (1994). Molecular basis of phenotype expression in homocystinuria. *Journal of Inherited Metabolic Diseases, 17,* 383–390.

Hunter syndrome   *See* Mucopolysaccharidoses.

Huntington disease (Huntington chorea)   *Clinical features:* Progressive neurological disorder with choreiform movements, rigidity, and dementia. Usual age of onset is 35–40 years, but it can present in childhood or as late as 60–65 years. *Associated complications:* Joint contractures, swallowing dysfunction, depression or other psychiatric symptoms, seizures. *Cause:* Mutation in chromosome #4p16.3 leading to an increased number of CAG trinucleotide repeats (37–86). *Inheritance:* AD; paternally inherited disease has earlier on-set, greater severity, and more rapid progression than maternally inherited disease. *Prevalence:* 4/100,000–7/100,000.

References: Hayden, M.R., Bloch, M., & Wiggins, S. (1995). Psychological effects of predictive testing for Huntington's disease. *Advances in Neurology, 65,* 201–210.

Prudon, S.E., Mohr, E., Ilivitsky, V., et al. (1994). Huntington's disease: Pathogenesis, diagnosis and treatment. *Journal of Psychiatry and Neuroscience, 19*(5), 359–367.

Hurler syndrome   *See* Mucopolysaccharidoses.

Hypophosphatasia   *Clinical features:* A disorder of calcium and phosphate metabolism with a severe infantile form (which can be rapidly fatal) and a relatively mild childhood form. Short stature, bowed long bones, craniosynostosis, hypocalcemia, hypophosphatasia. *Associated complications:* Seizures, multiple fractures, premature loss of teeth. *Cause:* Abnormality in the gene that regulates tissue-nonspecific alkaline phosphatase caused by a mutation in chromosome #1p36. *Inheritance:* AR. *Prevalence:* 1/100,000.

Reference: Whyte, M.P. (1995). Hypophosphatasia. In C.R. Scriver, A.L. Beaudet, W.S. Sly, et al. (Eds.), *The metabolic and molecular bases of inherited disease* (pp. 4095–4111). New York: McGraw-Hill.

Incontinentia pigmenti   *Clinical features:* Swirling patterns of hyperpigmented skin lesions, tooth abnormalities, microcephaly, ocular abnormalities, thin wiry hair, mental retardation in approximately one third of cases. *Associated complications:* Spasticity, seizures, vertebral or rib anomalies, hydrocephalus. *Cause:* Mutation in chromosome #Xp11 or #Xq28. *Inheritance:* XLD with lethality in males. *Prevalence:* Rare.

Reference: Landy, S.J., & Donnai, D. (1993). Incontinentia pigmenti (Bloch-Sulzberger syndrome). *American Journal of Medical Genetics, 30,* 53–59.

Infantile Refsum disease   *Clinical features:* Failure to thrive, minor facial dysmorphism (flat facial profile and nasal bridge), retinal degeneration, hypotonia, liver enlargement and dysfunction. *Associated complications:*

Sensorineural hearing impairment, mental retardation, peripheral neuropathy, hypercholesterolemia. There is also a late onset form of this disease. *Cause:* Accumulation of phytanic acid due to defect in peroxisomal function. *Inheritance:* AR. *Prevalence:* Rare.

Reference: Moser, A.B., Rasmussen, M., Naidu, S., et al. (1995). Phenotype of patients with peroxisomal disorders subdivided into sixteen complementation groups. *Journal of Pediatrics, 127,* 13–22.

Isovaleric aciduria   *Clinical features:* A heterogeneous disorder of organic acid metabolism. An acute, often fatal neonatal form is characterized by recurrent acidosis and coma; a chronic form presents with recurrent attacks of ataxia, vomiting, lethargy, and ketoacidosis. Attacks are generally triggered by infection or increased protein load. Urine smell of "sweaty feet" is characteristic. *Associated complications:* Seizures, mental retardation if untreated, enlarged liver, vomiting, hematologic abnormalities. *Cause:* Deficiency of the enzyme isovaleric acid CoA dehydrogenase caused by a mutation in chromosome #15q14–q15. *Inheritance:* AR. *Prevalence:* Rare. *Treatment:* Treatment consisting of a low-protein diet with supplemental oral glycine and carnitine has resulted in a relatively good cognitive outcome.

Reference: Berry, G.T., Yudkoff, M., & Segal, S. (1988). Isovaleric acidemia: Medical and neurodevelopmental effects of long-term therapy. *Journal of Pediatrics, 113,* 58–64.

Joubert syndrome   *Clinical features:* Structural cerebellar abnormalities, abnormal eye movements, retinal dysplasia or coloboma, episodic hyperventilation. *Associated complications:* Hypoplasia of corpus callosum, meningoencephalocele, renal cysts, microcephaly, abnormalities of tongue, hypotonia, mental retardation. *Cause:* Inherited. *Inheritance:* AR. *Prevalence:* Rare.

Reference: Saraiva, J.M., & Baraitser, M. (1992). Joubert syndrome: A review. *American Journal of Medical Genetics, 43,* 726–731.

Kearns-Sayre syndrome   *See* Mitochondrial disorders.

Kernicterus   *Clinical features:* Mental retardation, choreoathetoid cerebral palsy, staining of secondary teeth, upward gaze paralysis, high-frequency hearing loss. *Associated complications:* Deafness, mental retardation requiring extensive support, cerebral palsy, hearing impairment. *Cause:* Excessive levels of bilirubin in infant's blood that pass to the central nervous system; underlying problem is usually Rh incompatibility. *Inheritance:* Depends on cause. *Prevalence:* Since the initiation of RhoGAM therapy and medical management of hyperbilirubinemia, extremely low; recurrence risk depends on cause and management.

Reference: Connolly, A.M., & Volpe, J.J. (1990). Clinical features of bilirubin encephalopathy. *Clinics in Perinatology, 17,* 371–379.

Klinefelter syndrome (XXY)   *Clinical features:* Male with tall slim stature, long limbs, relatively small penis and testes, gynecomastia in 40%. *Associated complications:* Intention tremor (20%–50%), low to average intelligence, infertility, behavioral disorders, increased prevalence of homosexuality, scoliosis, increased risk of diabetes mellitus as adult (8%). *Cause:* Chromosomal nondisjunction, resulting in 47, XXY constitution. *Inheritance:* SP. *Prevalence:* 1/500 liveborn males. *Treatment:* Hormone treatment is needed in adolescence for the development of secondary sex characteristics.

References: Money, J. (1993). Specific neuro-cognitive impairments associated with Turner (45, XO) and Klinefelter (XXY) syndromes: A review. *Social Biology, 40*(1-2), 147–151.

Sorensen, K. (1992). Physical and mental development of adolescent males with Klinefelter syndrome. *Hormone Research, 37*(Suppl. 3), 55–61.

Klippel-Feil syndrome   *Clinical features:* Cervical vertebral fusion, hemivertebrae. *Associated complications:* Torticollis as neonate, sacral agenesis, hearing loss, occasional congenital heart defect, laryngeal defect with severe voice impairment in rare cases. *Cause:* Mutation in chromosome #8p22.2. *Inheritance:* AD; most cases represent a new mutation. *Prevalence:* Unknown.

Reference: Pizzutillo, P.D., Woods, M., Nicholson, L., et al. (1994). Risk factors in Klippel-Feil syndrome. *Spine, 19*(18), 2110–2116.

Klippel-Trenauny-Weber syndrome   *Clinical features:* Asymmetric hypertrophy of limb, hemangiomata. *Associated complications:* Platelet deficiency. *Cause:* Unknown. *Inheritance:* SP versus AD with possible mosaic homozygosity. *Prevalence:* Unknown.

Reference: Samuel, M., & Spitz, L. (1995). Klippel-Trenauny-Weber syndrome: Clinical features, complications, and management in children. *British Journal of Surgery, 82,* 757–761.

Krabbe (globoid cell leukodystrophy)   *Clinical features:* In the classic form of this progressive neurological disorder, symptoms begin at 4–6 months of age with irritability, progressive stiffness, optic atrophy, mental deterioration, and retinal cherry red spots. There is also a late-onset form that progresses more slowly. *Associated complications:* Hypertonicity, opisthotonus, decerebrate posturing, visual and hearing impairment, episodic unexplained fevers, seizures. *Cause:* Deficiency of galactocerebroside beta-galactosidase resulting from a mutation in chromosome #14q24.3-q32.1. *Inheritance:* AR. *Prevalence:* 0.5/100,000–1/100,000, may be increased in Jewish and Sicilian populations.

Reference: Suzuki, K., Suzuki, Y., & Suzuki, K. (1995). Galactosylceramide lipidosis: Globoid-cell leukodystrophy (Krabbe disease). In C.R. Scriver, A.L. Beaudet, W.S. Sly, et al. (Eds.), *The metabolic and molecular bases of inherited disease* (pp. 2671–2685). New York: McGraw-Hill.

Leber congenital amaurosis   *See* Mitochondrial disorders.

Leigh syndrome   *See* Mitochondrial disorders.

Lesch-Nyhan syndrome   *Clinical features:* An inborn error of purine metabolism associated with elevated levels of uric acid in blood and urine. Affected males appear unaffected at birth but then have progressive development of dyskinetic movements and spasticity; severe self-injurious behavior characterized by biting of fingers, arms, and lips. *Associated complications:* Seizures in 50%, hematuria, renal stones, and ultimate renal failure. *Cause:* Defect in enzyme hypoxanthine guanine phosphoribosyltransferase (HGPRT) caused by mutation of #Xq26-q27.2. *Inheritance:* XLR. *Prevalence:* Rare. *Treatment:* Allopurinol is useful in preventing renal and joint deposition of uric acid. Numerous psychotropic agents have been used in management of self-injurious behavior without much success.

Reference: Rossiter, B.J.F., & Caskey, C.T. (1995). Hypoxanthine-guanine phosphoribosyltransferase deficiency: Lesch-Nyhan syndrome and gout. In C.R. Scriver, A.L. Beaudet, W.S. Sly, et al. (Eds.), *The metabolic and molecular bases of inherited disease* (pp. 1679–1697). New York: McGraw-Hill.

Lissencephaly syndromes (Miller-Diecker)   *Clinical features:* A heterogeneous group of disorders of which Miller-Diecker syndrome is the prototype. Features include agyria/pachygyria (absent or decreased cerebral convolutions); progressive spasticity; microcephaly; and characteristic facial features including short nose, broad nasal bridge, upturned nares, widely spaced eyes, prominent upper lip, malformed or malpositioned ears. *Associated complications:* Mental retardation, infantile spasms, late tooth eruption, failure to thrive, dysphagia, congenital heart defect, intestinal atresia, agenesis of corpus callosum; (90%). *Cause:* Incomplete development of the brain with resulting smooth surface, undermigration, and heterotopias; 90% of affected individuals have deletions in chromosome #17p13.3. *Inheritance:* AR. *Prevalence:* Rare.

Reference: Dobyns, W.B., & Truwit, C.L. (1995). Lissencephaly and other malformations of cortical development: 1995 update. *Neuropediatrics, 26*(3), 132–147.

Lowe syndrome (Oculo-cerebro-renal syndrome)   *Clinical features:* Bilateral cataracts at birth, hypotonia, absent deep tendon reflexes, renal tubular dysfunction. *Associated complications:* Failure to thrive, vitamin D resistant rickets, visual impairment, mental retardation in 75%, behavior problems, intention tremor, craniosynostosis, peripheral neuropathy. *Cause:* Mutation of #Xq26.1 causing a deficiency in the enzyme phosphatidylinositol-4,5-bisphosphate 5-phosphatase. *Inheritance:* XLR. *Prevalence:* Rare.

References: Charnas, L.R., Bernardini, I., Rader, D., et al. (1991). Clinical and laboratory findings in the oculo-cerebrorenal syndrome of Lowe, with special reference to growth and renal function. *New England Journal of Medicine, 324,* 1318–1325.

Kenworthy, L., Park, T., & Charnas, L.R. (1993). Cognitive and behavioral profile of the oculocerebrorenal syndrome of Lowe. *American Journal of Medical Genetics, 46,* 297–303.

Maple syrup urine disease (MSUD)   *Clinical features:* A disorder of branched-chain amino acid metabolism with four identified clinical variants (classic, intermittent, intermediate, and thiamine-responsive). The classic form comprises 75% of cases and is characterized by severe opisthotonus, hypertonia, hypoglycemia, and respiratory difficulties; it is most often fatal within 1 month. Untreated survivors have mental retardation requir-

ing extensive support and spasticity. The intermittent form presents with periods of ataxia, behavior disturbances, drowsiness, and seizures. Attacks are triggered by infections or other physiological stresses. Individuals with the intermediate form usually demonstrate mental retardation requiring intermittent to limited support. *Associated complications:* Acidosis, hypoglycemia, growth retardation, feeding problems. *Cause:*
Mutation in #19q13.1-q13.2. *Inheritance:* 1/220,000; increased prevalence in Mennonite population. *Prevalence:* AR. *Treatment:* Dietary restriction of branched-chain amino acids; if instituted early (within 2 weeks of
birth), the prognosis is good for typical intelligence. Thiamine is used in the thiamine-responsive form.
Reference: Chuang, D.T., & Shih, V.E. (1995). Disorders of branched-chain amino acid and ketoacid metabolism. In C.R. Scriver, A.L. Beaudet, W.S. Sly, et al. (Eds.), *Metabolic and molecular bases of inherited disease*
(pp. 1239–1277). New York: McGraw-Hill.

Marfan syndrome   *Clinical features:* Tall, thin body habitus; upward dislocation of ocular lens; high myopia;
spider-like limbs; hypermobile joints. Intelligence is usually average. *Associated complications:* Aortic
aneurysm (often detectable in infancy), congestive heart failure, cardiac valvular regurgitation; pneumothorax,
emphysema, sleep apnea; scoliosis. *Cause:* Mutation in the fibrillin gene located on chromosome #15q15-
q21.3. *Inheritance:* AD with wide clinical variability. *Prevalence:* 1/10,000.
Reference: Gray, J.R., & Davies, S.J. (1996). Marfan syndrome. *American Journal of Medical Genetics, 33,*
403–408.

Maroteaux-Lamy syndrome   *See* Mucopolysaccharidoses.

McCune-Albright syndrome (Polyostotic fibrous dysplasia)   *Clinical features:* Large café-au-lait spots with
irregular margins, fibrous dysplasia of bones, bowing of long bones, premature onset of puberty, advanced bone
age. *Associated complications:* Hearing or visual impairment, hyperthyroidism, hyperparathyroidism, abnormal adrenal function, increased risk of malignancy, occasional spinal cord anomalies. *Cause:* Mutation in the
GNAS1 gene (causing a defect in the enzyme adenyl cyclase) localized to #20q13. *Inheritance:* AD; theoretically lethal unless present in the mosaic form. *Prevalence:* Unknown.
Reference: Wilson, L.C., & Trembath, R.C. (1994). Albright's hereditary osteodystrophy. *American Journal of
Medical Genetics, 31*(10), 779–784.

MELAS syndrome   *See* Mitochondrial disorders.

Menkes (kinky hair) syndrome   *Clinical features:* An inborn error of copper metabolism presenting at age 1–2
months with "steely" hair, characteristic face with pudgy cheeks. *Associated complications:* Seizures, feeding
difficulties, mental retardation requiring extensive support, recurrent infections, visual loss, bony abnormalities
with tendency toward easy fracture. *Cause:* Copper deficiency from decreased absorption and/or missing enzymes. *Inheritance:* XLR. Localized to #Xq13. *Prevalence:* 1/298,000.
Reference: Bankier, A. (1995). Menkes disease. *American Journal of Medical Genetics, 32*(3), 213–215.

MERRF (Myoclonus Epilepsy with Ragged Red Fibers)   *See* Mitochondrial disorders.

Metachromatic leukodystrophy   *Clinical features:* A heterogeneous group of lysosomal storage disorders with
varying degrees of neurological impairment ranging from unsteady gait to severe rigidity and choreoathetosis.
Muscle weakness is a common feature. The infantile form has its onset by age 2 years and results in death by
age 5. The juvenile form generally begins between 4 and 10 years of age, is rarer, and progresses more slowly.
Associated complications: Seizures, abdominal distension, psychosis, mental deterioration. *Cause:* Deficiency
in enzyme arylsulfatase A caused by a mutation in chromosome #22q. *Inheritance:* AR. *Prevalence:* 1/40,000.
Treatment: Bone marrow transplantation may slow the progression of the illness.
Reference: Gieselmann, V., Zlotogora, J., Harris, A., et al. (1994). Molecular genetics of metachromatic
leukodystrophy. *Human Mutation, 4*(4), 233–242.

Methylmalonic acidemia   *Clinical features:* A disorder of organic acid metabolism that, in symptomatic
cases, is characterized by repeated episodes of vomiting, lethargy, and coma associated with acidosis. On
newborn screening analyses, some individuals with this metabolic abnormality may remain asymptomatic and
experience typical growth and development. *Associated complications:* Neutropenia, osteoporosis, infections,
feeding abnormalities, mental retardation. *Cause:* Deficiency of enzyme methylmalonyl CoA mutase, or defect in cobalamin metabolism; the genetic mutation has been localized to chromosome #6p21. *Inheritance:*

AR. *Prevalence:* 1/20,000. *Treatment:* Treatment consists of a low-protein diet and supplemental vitamin B_{12} in those who have a B_{12}-responsive form; supplementation with L-carnitine is also used.

Reference: van der Meer, S.B., Poggi, F., Spada, M., et al. (1994). Clinical outcome of long-term management of patients with vitamin B_{12}-unresponsive methylmalonic acidemia. *Journal of Pediatrics, 125,* 903–908.

Mitochondrial disorders (mitochondrial encephalopathies and myopathies)   *Clinical features:* This is a heterogeneous group of disorders linked by their common etiology: aberrant function of the mitochondria (cellular energy stations) or of mitochondrial metabolism. In addition, they share a unique pattern of inheritance that is non-Mendelian. Mitochondria are inherited exclusively from the mother. Five of these disorders are discussed here. **Kearns-Sayre** syndrome is characterized by short stature, ophthalmoplegia, visual impairment, cardiomyopathy, and hearing loss. **Leber congenital amaurosis** consists of optic atrophy and progressive pigmentary changes of the retina. Severe visual impairment is usually detected in infancy; one fourth of affected children have mental retardation. They are at risk for dystonia and other movement disorders; self-injurious behavior in the form of eye-gouging is common. **Leigh syndrome** is a rapidly progressive neurological disorder marked by lethargy, weakness, hypotonia, ataxia, blindness, and later, spasticity. Respiratory and cardiovascular compromise are common. Death occurs within infancy/early childhood in most cases. **MELAS** (Mitochondrial myopathy, Encephalopathy, Lactic Acidosis, and Stroke-like episodes) features migraine headaches, seizures, stroke-like episodes, dementia, encephalopathy, myopathy, progressive hearing loss, cortical blindness, and lactic acidosis. **MERRF** (Myoclonus Epilepsy with Ragged Red Fibers) presents with myoclonus epilepsy, ataxia, spasticity, myopathy, and sensorineural hearing loss. Characteristic ragged-red muscle fibers are seen on muscle pathology. *Inheritance:* Mitochondrial; MELAS and Kearns-Sayre have had reported cases of AD or AR inheritance. *Prevalence:* Unknown.

References: Barkovich, J., Good, W.V., Koch, T.K., et al. (1993) Mitochondrial disorders: Analysis of their clinical and imaging characteristics. *American Journal of Neuroradiology, 14,* 1119–1137.

Shoffner, J.M., & Wallace, D.C. (1995). Oxidative phosphorylation diseases. In C.R. Scriver, A.L. Beaudet, W.S. Sly, et al. (Eds.), *The metabolic and molecular bases of inherited disease* (pp. 1535–1609). New York: McGraw-Hill.

Moebius sequence (congenital facial diplegia)   *Clinical features:* Expressionless face, facial weakness, sixth and seventh nerve palsies, occasional twelfth nerve palsy, occasional abnormalities of fingers, often micrognathia. *Associated complications:* Feeding difficulties, oral motor dysfunction, articulation disorder, occasional tracheal or laryngeal anomalies. Mental retardation in 10%–50%. *Cause:* Mutations localized to chromosomes #13q12–13 and #1p34. *Inheritance:* Mostly SP; rare reports of AD with variable expressivity. *Prevalence:* Rare.

Reference: Kumar, D. (1990). Moebius syndrome. *American Journal of Medical Genetics, 27*(2), 122–126.

Morquio syndrome   *See* Mucopolysaccharidoses.

Mucopolysaccharidoses   *Clinical features:* A group of lysosomal storage disorders involving altered mucopolysaccharide metabolism. There are seven distinguishable forms, each with two or more subgroups. They are differentiated by their clinical features, enzymatic defects, genetic transmission, and urinary mucopolysaccharide (MPS) pattern. Hunter (MPS II), Hurler (MPS I), and Sanfilippo (MPS III) syndromes are discussed below. Others include Morquio (MPS IV), Scheie (MPS V), Maroteaux-Lamy (MPS VI), and Sly (MPS VII) syndromes.

Hunter syndrome (MPS II)   *Clinical features:* MPS type IIA is severe and type IIB is mild. Features include short stature, enlarged liver and spleen, coarsening of facial features with hypertrichosis beginning in early childhood. Mental retardation is mild or absent in type IIB; this subtype is compatible with survival to adulthood. Type IIA is highlighted by progressive mental deterioration first noted between 2 and 3 years of age; death occurs before age 15 in most cases. *Associated complications:* Sensorineural deafness, retinitis pigmentosa with visual loss, macrocephaly, stiffening of joints particularly the hands, cardiac valvular disease in 90%, hernia, respiratory insufficiency, chronic diarrhea in 65%, seizures in 66%. *Cause:* Deficiency of enzyme iduronidesulfate sulfatase caused by a mutation on #Xq28. *Inheritance:* XLR. *Prevalence:* 1/110,000–1/132,000. *Treatment:* Minimal success has been recorded with bone marrow transplantation; enzyme replacement and gene therapies are under investigation.

Hurler syndrome (MPS I)   *Clinical features:* Short stature, gradual coarsening of facial features in early childhood including hypertrichosis, macrocephaly, enlarged liver and spleen, prominent lips, corneal clouding, dysostosis, stiffening of joints. There is progressive mental deterioration and spasticity. *Associated complications:* Chronic ear infections, hearing loss, occasional hernia and cardiac valvular changes, visual impairment, arachnoid cysts, airway obstruction. *Cause:* Deficiency of enzyme alpha-L-iduronidase caused by a mutation of #22q11. *Inheritance:* AR. *Prevalence:* 1/144,000. *Treatment:* Bone marrow transplantation has shown some success in early cases; enzyme replacement and gene therapies are under investigation.

Sanfilippo syndrome (MPS III)   *Clinical features:* Four distinct types representing four different enzyme defects but similar clinical features; there is mild coarsening of facial features, absence of corneal clouding, mild enlargement of liver, joint stiffness, and progressive mental deterioration. Deterioration is most rapid in type IIIA; death occurs by 10–20 years in most cases. *Associated complications:* Severe behavioral disturbances by age 4–6 years, dysostosis, diarrhea in 50%, progressive spasticity and ataxia, bulbar palsy with advancing disease. *Cause:* Type IIIA: deficiency of enzyme heparan N-sulfatase caused by a mutation of #17q25.3; type IIIB: deficiency of enzyme alpha-N-acetylglucosaminidase caused by a mutation on #17q21; type IIIC: deficiency of enzyme acetyl-CoA:alpha-glucosamide-N-acetyltansferase caused by a mutation in chromosome #14; type IIID: deficiency of enzyme N-acetyl-alpha-glucosaminine-6-sulfatase caused by a mutation of #12q14. *Inheritance:* AR. *Prevalence:* 1/24,000. *Treatment:* Treatment is supportive only. Bone marrow transplantation has not been useful. Investigations into gene therapy are under way.

Reference: Neufeld, E.F., & Muenzer, J. (1995). The mucopolysaccharidoses. In C.R. Scriver, A.L. Beaudet, W.S. Sly, et al. (Eds.), *The metabolic and molecular bases of inherited disease* (pp. 2465–2494). New York: McGraw-Hill.

Multiple carboxylase deficiency—infantile or early form (holocarboxylase synthetase deficiency)   *Clinical features:* Disorder of organic acid metabolism characterized by seizures, lethargy, coma, skin rash, and acidosis. Often, the presenting feature is respiratory distress. *Associated complications:* Mental retardation, hearing impairment, optic atrophy with visual impairment, recurrent infections, vomiting. *Cause:* Deficiency of holocarboxylase synthetase. *Inheritance:* AR. *Prevalence:* Rare. *Treatment:* Oral biotin supplementation. Prenatal treatment with oral biotin has prevented development of disease in a few cases.

Reference: Wolf, B. (1995). Disorders of biotin metabolism. In C.R. Scriver, A.L. Beaudet, W.S. Sly, et al. (Eds.), *The metabolic and molecular bases of inherited disease* (pp. 3151–3177). New York: McGraw-Hill.

Multiple carboxylase deficiency—late onset, juvenile form (biotinidase deficiency)   *Clinical features:* A heterogeneous disorder characterized by varying degrees of mental retardation, hypotonia, seizures (often infantile spasms), alopecia, skin rash, and lactic acidosis. The onset of symptoms occurs usually between 2 weeks and 2 years. *Associated complications:* Hearing and visual impairment, respiratory difficulties and apnea, recurrent infections. *Cause:* A disorder of the biotin recycling enzyme biotinidase caused by a mutation in chromosome #3p25. *Inheritance:* AR. *Prevalence:* 1/166,000. *Treatment:* Supplementation with oral biotin; response is better if used early in the course of the disease.

References: Wolf, B. (1995). Disorders of biotin metabolism. In C.R. Scriver, A.L. Beaudet, W.S. Sly, et al. (Eds.), *The metabolic and molecular bases of inherited disease* (pp. 3151–3177). New York: McGraw-Hill.

Muscular dystrophy (Duchenne [DMD] and Becker types [BMD])   *Clinical features:* Progressive proximal muscular degeneration, pseudohypertrophy of calves, cardiomyopathy. Onset of symptoms in DMD occurs before 3 years. Affected boys are usually confined to a wheelchair by age 12. The onset in BMD is later, often occurring at 20–30 years of age. *Associated complications:* Varying degrees of intellectual impairment, congestive heart failure, scoliosis, flexion contractures, respiratory compromise, intestinal motility dysfunction. *Cause:* Mutation in the gene that encodes dystrophin localized to #Xp21.1. *Inheritance:* XLR. *Prevalence:* DMD 21.7/100,000; BMD 3.2/100,000 (see Chapter 15).

References: Boland, B.J., Silbert, P.L., Groover, R.V., et al. (1996). Skeletal, cardiac, and smooth muscle failure in Duchenne muscular dystrophy. *Pediatric Neurology, 14,* 7–12.

Bresolin, N., Castelli, E., Comi, P., et al. (1994). Cognitive impairment in Duchenne muscular dystrophy. *Neuromuscular Disorders, 4,* 359–369.

Myotonic dystrophy   *Clinical features:* Expressionless face, myotonia, myopathy, ptosis, frontal balding. The age of onset varies from childhood to adulthood. There is also a congenital form that is severe with neonatal hypotonia, motor delay, mental retardation (in 60%–70%), and facial diplegia. In congenital forms of the disease, classic myotonia does not begin until an average age of 10 years. *Associated complications:* Cataracts, cardiac conduction abnormalities, hypogonadism, feeding difficulties, and often severe respiratory problems. *Cause:* Mutation in chromosome #19q13 leading to an increased number of trinucleotide CTG repeats in the protein kinase gene. Severity varies with the number of CTG repeats; unaffected people have 5–30 repeat copies; mildly affected people 50–80; and severely affected individuals have 2,000 or more copies. *Inheritance:* AD with genetic anticipation (possible increased disease severity with subsequent pregnancies and generations). With rare exception, it is the mother who transmits the disease. *Prevalence:* 1/25,000; increased prevalence in certain areas of Quebec.
   Reference: Roig, M., Balliu, P.R., Navarro, C., et al. (1994). Presentation, clinical course, and outcome of the congenital form of myotonic dystrophy. *Pediatric Neurology, 11,* 208–213.

Nager acrofacial dysostosis   *Clinical features:* Micrognathia, downward slant of palpebral fissures, high nasal bridge, external ear defects, occasional cleft lip/palate, limb anomalies (hypoplastic thumb or radii—usually asymmetric). *Associated complications:* Scoliosis, severe conductive hearing loss, occasional heart or kidney defects, mental retardation present in 16%. *Cause:* Mutation in chromosome #9q32. *Inheritance:* SP in most cases. *Prevalence:* Rare.
   Reference: McDonald, J.T., & Gorski, J.L. (1993). Nager acrofacial dysostosis. *American Journal of Medical Genetics, 30*(9), 779–782.

Neonatal adrenoleukodystrophy   *Clinical features:* A peroxisomal disorder characterized by onset in early infancy of seizures, hypotonia, and adrenal insufficiency; mild dysmorphic facial features (high forehead, epicanthal folds, broad nasal bridge, and anteverted nostrils); death in early childhood is usual but there are known cases of affected individuals surviving until the second or third decade. *Associated complications:* Mental retardation, cataracts, visual impairment. *Cause:* Abnormality of peroxisomal function. The peroxisome is a recently described cellular organelle involved in processing fatty acids. *Inheritance:* AR. *Prevalence:* Rare.
   Reference: Moser, A.B., Rasmussen, M., Naidu, S., et al. (1995). Phenotype of patients with peroxisomal disorders subdivided into sixteen complementation groups. *Journal of Pediatrics, 127,* 13–22.

Neurofibromatosis type I (Von Recklinghausen disease)   *Clinical features:* Multiple café-au-lait spots, axillary and inguinal freckling, nerve tumors (fibromas) in body and on skin, Lisch nodules (white bumps on iris). *Associated complications:* Glaucoma, scoliosis, pseudoarthrosis, increased risk of numerous malignant and benign tumors, hypertension, attention-deficit/hyperactivity disorder (ADHD), increased risk of learning disabilities, macrocephaly or hydrocephalus, visual and hearing impairments. *Cause:* Mutation in chromosome #17q11.2. *Inheritance:* AD with variable expression. Approximately 50% represent new mutations. *Prevalence:* 1/3,500.
   Reference: Hofman, K.J., Harris, E.L., Bryan, R.N., et al. (1994). Neurofibromatosis type I: The cognitive phenotype. *Journal of Pediatrics, 124,* S1–S8.

Neurofibromatosis type II   *Clinical features:* Bilateral acoustic neuromas (benign tumor of auditory nerve), meningioma (benign tumor of meninges), schwannoma (tumors of dorsal roots of spinal cord), neuropathy. Café-au-lait spots are seen but number fewer than six in most cases. In contrast to type I, there are no Lisch nodules or skin fibromas. *Associated complications:* Deafness (average age of onset at 20 years), cataract or other ocular abnormalities. *Cause:* Mutation in chromosome #22q12.2. *Inheritance:* AD; up to 50% may represent new mutations. *Prevalence:* 1/40,000.
   Reference: Martuza, R.L., & Eldridge, R. (1988). Neurofibromatosis 2 (bilateral acoustic neurofibromatosis). *New England Journal of Medicine, 318,* 684–688.

Neuronal ceroid lipofuscinosis   *See* Batten disease.

Niemann-Pick disease (Types A and B)   *Clinical features:* Lysosomal storage disorder. Type A presents in infancy with failure to thrive, enlarged liver and spleen, and rapidly progressive neurological decline. Death occurs by age 2–3 years. Type B is variable but is compatible with survival to adulthood and may cause few or no neurological abnormalities. *Associated complications:* Mental retardation, ataxia, myoclonus, eye abnormalities, coronary artery disease, lung disease. *Cause:* Deficiency of enzyme sphingomyelinase caused by a mutation in chromosome #11p15.4. *Inheritance:*AR. *Prevalence:* Rare. *Treatment:* No specific therapy is currently available. However, research into gene therapy and enzyme replacement is underway.

Reference: Schuchman, E.H., & Desnick, R.J. (1995). Niemann-Pick disease types A and B: Acid sphingomyelinase deficiencies. In C.R. Scriver, A.L. Beaudet, W.S. Sly, et al. (Eds.), *The metabolic and molecular bases of inherited disease* (pp. 2601–2624). New York: McGraw-Hill.

Noonan syndrome   *Clinical features:* Short stature; characteristic facial features including triangular shape, deep philtrum, downslanting palpebral fissures, ptosis; low-set ears; low posterior hair line; short or webbed neck; congenital heart defects (usually pulmonary valve stenosis); shield chest. *Associated complications:* Sensorineural deafness, malocclusion of teeth, articulation difficulties, bleeding abnormalities. *Cause:* Unknown. *Inheritance:* Half of reported cases are SP; may be AD with variable expression. *Prevalence:* 1/1,000–1/2,500.

References: Noonan, J.A. (1994). Noonan syndrome: An update and review for the primary pediatrician. *Clinical Pediatrics, 33*(9), 548–555.

Wood, A., Massaran, A., Super, M., et al. (1995). Behavioral aspects and psychiatric findings in Noonan syndrome. *Archives of Diseases of Childhood, 72,* 153–155.

Opitz-Frias syndrome   *See* G (Opitz-Frias/BBB) syndrome.

Osteogenesis imperfecta   *Clinical features:* Four clinically distinct forms of this metabolic disease of bone have been described. Type I is characterized by bone fragility and blue sclera. Type II usually presents with severe bone deformity with death in the perinatal period. Type III is characterized by progressive bone deformity. Type IV is clinically similar to type I but has normal sclerae, milder bone deformity, variable short stature, and dental abnormalities. *Associated complications:* Increased prevalence of fractures (may be confused with physical abuse) that decreases after puberty; adolescent-onset hearing loss in 50% that can be progressive; scoliosis; mitral valve prolapse. *Cause:* Mutation in one of the genes regulating collagen formation. Types I, II, and III map to #17q21-22 (COLA1) and #7q21-22 (COLA2). *Inheritance:* Type I: AD; type II: AD (usually a new mutation), rare AR. *Prevalence:* 1/30,000 (see Chapter 15).

References: Binder, H., Conway, A., Hason, S., et al. (1993). Comprehensive rehabilitation of the child with osteogenesis imperfecta. *American Journal of Medical Genetics, 45*(2), 265–269.

Byers, P.H., & Steiner, R.D. (1992). Osteogenesis imperfecta. *Annual Review of Medicine, 43,* 269–282.

Pfeiffer syndrome (acrocephalosyndactyly type V)   *Clinical features:* Mild craniosynostosis with brachycephaly, flat midface, broad thumbs and toes, widely spaced eyes, and partial syndactyly (webbing of hands and feet). Intelligence is usually typical. *Associated complications:* Hydrocephalus, hearing impairment, seizures. *Cause:* Mutations in the gene that codes for fibroblast growth factor receptor on chromosome #8p11.2-11.1 and #10q25-26. *Inheritance:* AD with frequent prevalence of new mutation. *Prevalence:* Unknown.

Reference: Cohen, M.M., Jr. (1993). Pfeiffer syndrome update: Clinical subtypes, and guidelines for differential diagnosis. *American Journal of Medical Genetics, 45,* 300–307.

Phenylketonuria (PKU)   *Clinical features:* Inborn error of amino acid metabolism without acute clinical symptoms that results in mental retardation if untreated. Microcephaly, abnormal gait, and seizures also may develop in untreated individuals. Pale skin and blond hair are common features. *Associated complications:* Behavioral disturbances, cataracts, skin disorders, movement disorders. *Cause:* Classically caused by a deficiency of the enzyme phenylalanine hydroxylase; a mutation in chromosome #12q24.1. *Inheritance:* AR. *Prevalence:* 1/10,000 (regional variability). *Treatment:* Early identification is available by most newborn screening tests. A phenylalanine-restricted diet should be continued throughout childhood. Specialized formulas are available. The restricted diet should be resumed in women prior to conception to prevent fetal brain damage. Research into gene therapy is underway (see Chapter 19).

Reference: Potocnik, U., & Widhalm, K. (1994). Long-term follow-up of children with classical phenylketonuria after diet discontinuation: A review. *Journal of the American College of Nutrition, 13*(3), 232–236.

Pierre-Robin sequence *Clinical features:* Micrognathia, cleft palate, glossoptosis (downward displacement of tongue). *Associated complications:* Neonatal feeding problems, apnea or respiratory distress, upper airway obstruction. *Cause:* Impaired closure of the posterior palatal shelves early in embryogenesis. This defect can be an isolated finding or associated with trisomy 18 or other multiple defect syndromes. *Inheritance:* AR; rare X-linked form. *Prevalence:* Unknown.

References: Caouette-Laberge, L., Bayet, B., & Larocque, Y. (1994). The Pierre Robin sequence: Review of 125 cases and evolution of treatment modalities. *Plastic and Reconstructive Surgery, 93,* 934–942.

Shprintzen, R.J. (1992). The implications of the diagnosis of Pierre Robin sequence. *Cleft Palate-Craniofacial Journal, 29*(3), 205–209.

Prader Willi syndrome *Clinical features:* Short stature, failure to thrive in infancy followed by obesity and rapid weight gain after 2 years of age, almond-shaped eyes, viscous (thick) saliva, hypotonia (marked floppiness at birth particularly in neck region), hypogonadism with cryptorchidism, small hands and feet. *Associated complications:* Mental retardation, behavior problems, obstructive sleep apnea, neonatal temperature instability. *Cause:* Half have a deletion in chromosome #15q11-13 (paternal). *Inheritance:* Primarily SP; up to 15% may represent uniparental disomy (two copies of one parent's chromosome and none from the other). *Prevalence:* 1/25,000.

References: Curfs, L.M.G., Weigers, A.M., Sommers, J.R.M., et al. (1991). Strengths and weaknesses in the cognitive profile of youngsters with Prader-Willi syndrome. *Clinical Genetics, 40,* 430–434.

Donaldson, M.D., Chu, L.E., Cooke, A., et al. (1994). The Prader Willi syndrome. *Archives of Diseases of Childhood, 70*(1), 58–63.

Propionic acidemia *Clinical features:* A disorder of organic acid metabolism characterized by coma, hypotonia, hematological abnormalities, characteristic facies with puffy cheeks and exaggerated Cupid's bow upper lip. *Associated complications:* Impaired immunoglobin (antibody) production, mental retardation, seizures in 50%, tonal abnormalities. *Cause:* Deficiency of enzyme propionyl CoA carboxylase caused by a mutation of #13q32. *Inheritance:* AR. *Prevalence:* Rare. *Treatment:* Treatment consists of a diet low in valine, isoleucine, threonine, and methionine, with supplement of carnitine. A commercial formula is available.

Reference: North, K.N., Korson, M.S., Gopal, Y.R., et al. (1995). Neonatal-onset propionic acidemia: Neurologic and developmental profiles, and implications for management. *Journal of Pediatrics, 126,* 916–922.

Retinitis pigmentosa *Clinical features:* A group of diseases associated with retinal degeneration and progressive blindness; initial symptom is night blindness occurring in adolescence or adult life. *Associated complications:* Depends on severity of illness. *Cause:* Unknown. *Inheritance:* AR in 30%–40% of cases; AD and XLR also seen. *Prevalence:* 1/2,000–1/7,000; recurrence risk depends on cause.

Reference: Pagon, R.A. (1988). Retinitis pigmentosa. *Survey of Opthalmology, 33,* 137–177.

Rett syndrome *Clinical features:* Progressive encephalopathy after typical development for the first years of life, autistic features, loss of purposeful hand use with characteristic ringing of hands, ataxia, spastic paraparesis. *Associated complications:* Acquired microcephaly, seizures. *Cause:* Unknown. *Inheritance:* Not yet fully defined, but presumed XLD with lethality in males. *Prevalence:* 1/10,000–1/15,000 among females (see Chapter 21).

Reference: Hagberg, B. (1995). Rett syndrome: Clinical peculiarities and biological mysteries. *Acta Paediatrica, 84,* 971–976.

Riley-Day syndrome (Familial dysautonomia) *Clinical features:* Absent or sparse tears, absence of fungiform papillae on tongue, vasomotor instability, abnormal sweating, episodic vomiting, swallowing disorder, ataxia. *Associated complications:* Feeding difficulties, scoliosis, neuropathic joints, hypertension, aseptic necrosis of bones. *Cause:* Mutation of the gene which codes for beta nerve growth factor localized to chromosome #9q31-q33. *Inheritance:* AR. *Prevalence:* Rare; increased in Ashkenazic Jewish population (0.5/100,00–1/10,000).

Reference: Blumenfeld, A., Slaugenhaupt, S.A., Axelrod, F.B., et al. (1993). Localization of the gene for familial dysautonomia on chromosome 9 and definition of DNA markers for genetic diagnosis. *Nature Genetics, 4*(2), 160–164.

Robinow syndrome (fetal face syndrome) *Clinical features:* Slight to moderate short stature, short forearms, macrocephaly with frontal bossing, flat facial profile with apparent hypertelorism, small upturned nose, hypogenitalism, micrognathia. *Associated complications:* Vertebral or rib anomalies, dental malocclusion, inguinal hernia, enlarged liver and spleen. *Cause:* Inherited. *Inheritance:* Rare AD; AR form is most common, is clinically more severe, and is often accompanied by rib anomalies. *Prevalence:* Rare.

Reference: Robinow, M. (1993). The Robinow (fetal face) syndrome: A continuing puzzle. *Clinical Dysmorphology, 2*(3), 189–198.

Rubinstein-Taybi syndrome   *Clinical features:* Broad thumbs and toes, maxillary hypoplasia, slanted palpebral fissures, pouting upper lip, occasional agenesis of the corpus callosum. *Associated complications:* Apnea, constipation, cardiac defects, keloid scar formation, glaucoma, mental retardation. *Cause:* Interstitial deletions within #16p13.3 in the majority of cases. *Inheritance:* SP. *Prevalence:* 1/125,000.

Reference: Hennekam, R.C. (1993). Rubinstein-Taybi syndrome: A history in pictures. *Clinical Dysmorphology, 2*(1), 87–92.

Russell-Silver syndrome   *Clinical features:* Short stature of prenatal onset, skeletal asymmetry with hemihypertrophy (60%), triangular facies, beaked nose, thin upper lip, narrow high arched palate, blue sclerae, occasional café-au-lait spots, fifth finger clinodactyly. *Associated complications:* Delayed fontanel (soft spot) closure, hypocalcemia as neonate with sweating and tachypnea, increased risk of fasting hypoglycemia as toddler, precocious sexual development, vertebral anomalies. *Cause:* Mutation in chromosome #17q25. *Inheritance:* Not clear; new dominant mutation may be the cause of majority of cases; AR in rare cases. *Prevalence:* Unknown.

Reference: Patton, M.A. (1988). Russell Silver syndrome. *American Journal of Medical Genetics, 25*(8), 557–560.

Sanfilippo syndrome   *See* Mucopolysaccharidoses.

Scheie syndrome   *See* Mucopolysaccharidoses.

Sly syndrome   *See* Mucopolysaccharidoses.

Smith-Lemli-Opitz syndrome   *Clinical features*: Microcephaly, short nose with upturned nostrils, low serum cholesterol, syndactyly of second and third toes, underdevelopment of male genitalia. *Associated complications:* Hypotonia, mental retardation requiring limited to extensive support, seizures, feeding difficulties and vomiting, occasional heart defect. *Cause:* Defect in cholesterol metabolism caused by mutation in chromosome #7q34. *Inheritance:* AR. *Prevalence:* 1/20,000. *Treatment:* Dietary modifications including increased cholesterol ingestion.

References: Natowicz, M.R., & Evans, J.E. (1994). Abnormal bile acids in the Smith-Lemli-Opitz syndrome. *American Journal of Medical Genetics, 50*(4), 364–367.

Opitz, J.M. (1994). RSH/SLO ("Smith-Lemli-Opitz") syndrome: Historical, genetic, and developmental considerations. *American Journal of Medical Genetics, 50,* 344–346.

Smith-Magenis syndrome   *Clinical features:* Short stature, brachycephaly, cleft palate, congenital heart defect, high myopia, fingertip pads, midface hypoplasia, prominent chin, varying degrees of mental retardation. *Associated complications:* Genital or vertebral anomalies, scoliosis, hearing impairment, self-injurious behavior, other behavior problems. *Cause:* Deletion of #17p11.2. *Inheritance:* AD (most represent new mutations). *Prevalence:* 1/25,000.

Reference: Greenberg, F., Lewis, R.A., Potocki, L., et al. (1996). Multi-disciplinary clinical study of Smith-Magenis syndrome (deletion 17p11.2). *American Journal of Medical Genetics, 62,* 247–254.

Sotos syndrome   *Clinical features:* An overgrowth syndrome characterized by a distinctive head shape, macrocephaly, downslanting eyes, flat nasal bridge, physical overgrowth during first year of life, advanced bone age. *Associated complications:* Increased risk of abdominal tumors, hypotonia, marked speech delay, varying degrees of cognitive impairment. *Cause:* Mutation in chromosome #3p21. *Inheritance:* AD. *Prevalence:* Unknown.

Reference: Cole, T.R.P., & Hughes, H.E. (1994). Sotos syndrome: A study of the diagnostic criteria and natural history. *American Journal of Medical Genetics, 31,* 20–32.

Stickler syndrome (arthro-ophthalmopathy)   *Clinical features:* Flat facies, myopia, cleft of hard or soft palate, spondyloepiphyseal dysplasia. *Associated complications:* Hypotonia, hyperextensible joints, occasional scoliosis, risk of retinal detachment, cataracts, arthropathy in late childhood or adulthood, occasional hearing

loss or cognitive impairment. *Cause:* Mutation in type II procollagen gene (COLA2) that has been linked to #12q13-14 and #6p22-21. *Inheritance:* AD with variable expression. *Prevalence:* 1/20,000.
Reference: Lewkonia, R.M. (1992). The arthropathy of hereditary arthroophthalmopathy (Stickler syndrome). *Journal of Rheumatology, 19*(8), 1271–1275.

Sturge-Weber syndrome   *Clinical features:* Flat facial hemangiomata "port wine stains," seizures. *Associated complications:* Glaucoma, hemangiomata of meninges, occasional paresis; may be progressive in some cases with gradual visual or cognitive impairment. *Cause:* Unknown. *Inheritance:* Usually SP, AD in a few reported cases. *Prevalence:* 0.15/1,000.
Reference: Sujansky, E., & Conradi, S. (1995). Outcome of Sturge-Weber syndrome in 52 adults. *American Journal of Medical Genetics, 57,* 35–45.

TAR (thrombocytopenia-absent radius)   *Clinical features:* Radial (absent arm bone) aplasia with normal thumbs, thrombocytopenia (platelet deficiency). *Associated complications:* Knee joint abnormalities, neonatal foot swelling, occasional congenital heart or renal defect. *Cause:* Unknown. *Inheritance:* AR. *Prevalence:* Unknown.
Reference: MacDonald, M.R., Schaefer, G.B., Olney, A.H., et al. (1994). Hypoplasia of the cerebellar vermis and corpus callosum in thrombocytopenia with absent radius syndrome on MRI studies. *American Journal of Medical Genetics, 50,* 46–50.

Tay Sachs disease (GM2-gangliosidosis type I)   *Clinical features:* A progressive neurological disorder characterized by deafness, blindness, seizures. Development is typical for the first several months of life. Subsequently, there is increased startle response, hypotonia followed by hypertonia, cherry red spot in maculae; it is rapidly fatal. There is also an adult form of this disorder which presents with ataxia. *Associated complications:* Feeding abnormalities, aspiration. *Cause:* Deficiency of the enzyme hexosaminidase A caused by mutation of #15q23-q24. *Inheritance:* AR. *Prevalence:* 1/112,000; 1/3,800 in Ashkenazic Jewish population.
Reference: Gravel, R.A., Clarke, J.T.R., Kaback, M.M., et al. (1995). The GM2 gangliosidoses. In C.R. Scriver, A.L. Beaudet, W.S. Sly, et al. (Eds.), *The metabolic and molecular bases of inherited disease* (pp. 2839–2879). New York: McGraw-Hill.

Torsion dystonia (Dystonia musculorum deformans)   *Clinical features:* Progressive movement disorder characterized by involuntary posturing of the trunk and neck; intelligence is often superior. *Associated complications:* Contractures in affected limbs. *Cause:* Deletion of #9q32-q34. *Inheritance:* AD with variable penetrance. *Prevalence:* 1/20,000 in Ashkenazic Jewish population. *Treatment:* High dose trihexphenidyl (Artane) is helpful in early-onset disease, while L-dopa (Sinemet) is most beneficial in those with late-onset disease. Intrathecal baclofen (Lioresal) has also been useful.
References: Gasser, T., Fahn, S., & Breakefield, X.O. (1992). The autosomal dominant dystonias. *Brain Pathology, 2*(4), 297–308.
Zilber, N., Inzelberg, R., Kahana, E., et al. (1994). Natural course of idiopathic torsion dystonia among Jews. *Neuroepidemiology, 13,* 195–201.

Tourette syndrome   *Clinical features:* A genetic syndrome of vocal and motor tics with a fluctuating course. Onset is usually during childhood or early adolescence. *Associated complications:* ADHD, anxiety disorders, and learning disabilities.

Treacher-Collins syndrome (mandibulofacial dysostosis)   *Clinical features:* Characteristic facial appearance with malformation of external ear, flattened midface, absence of lower eyelashes, cleft palate, small chin. *Associated complications:* Conductive hearing loss, respiratory and feeding problems, apnea. Intelligence is average in 95% of cases. *Cause:* Mutation in TCOFI gene localized to chromosome #5q32-33. *Inheritance:* AD. *Prevalence:* Unknown. *Treatment:* Surgical repair of most malformations.
References: Dixon, M.J., Read, A.P., Donnai, D., et al. (1991). The gene for Treacher Collins syndrome maps to the long arm of chromosome 5. *American Journal of Human Genetics, 49,* 17–22.
Winter, R.M. (1996). What's in a face? *Nature Genetics, 12,* 124–129.

Trisomy 13 syndrome   *Clinical features:* Microphthalmia, cleft lip and palate, polydactyly, scalp defects, facial dysmorphic features, low-set ears, flexion deformity of fingers. *Associated complications:* Kidney and gastrointestinal tract anomalies, eye abnormalities, mental retardation requiring extensive support, visual impairment, cerebral palsy. *Cause:* Nondisjunction resulting in extra chromosome #13; rarely parental translocation. *Inheritance:* SP; may recur in families in presence of parental translocation. *Prevalence:* 1/8,000.

Reference: Baty, B.J., Blackburn, B.L., & Carey, J.C. (1994). Natural history of trisomy 18 and trisomy 13: I. Growth, physical assessment, medical histories, survival, and recurrence risk. *American Journal of Medical Genetics, 49,* 175–188.

Trisomy 18 syndrome (Edwards syndrome)   *Clinical features:* Intrauterine growth retardation, low-set ears, clenched hands with overriding fingers, congenital heart defects; 30% die within first month of life, 50% by second month, and only 10% survive their first year. *Associated complications:* Feeding problems, aspiration, mental retardation requiring extensive support. *Cause:* Nondisjunction resulting in extra chromosome #18. *Inheritance:* SP. *Prevalence:* 1/6,600.

Reference: Baty, B.J., Blackburn, B.L., & Carey, J.C. (1994). Natural history of trisomy 18 and trisomy 13: I. Growth, physical assessment, medical histories, survival, and recurrence risk. *American Journal of Medical Genetics, 49,* 175–188.

Trisomy 21   *See* Down syndrome, Chapter 17.

Tuberous sclerosis   *Clinical features:* Hypopigmented areas on skin, acne-like facial lesions (adenoma sebaceum), infantile spasms, calcium deposits in brain. *Associated complications:* Seizures, mental retardation requiring intermittent to limited support, tumors of the heart, increased risk of malignancy, abnormal tooth enamel, renal cysts, hypertension. *Cause:* Deletion on chromosome #16p13 or #9q34. *Inheritance:* AD with variable expressivity. *Prevalence:* 1/10,000–1/50,000.

Reference: Kwiatkowski, D.J., & Short, M.P. (1994). Tuberous sclerosis. *Archives of Dermatology, 130,* 348–354.

Turner syndrome (45, XO)   *Clinical features:* Female with short stature, broad chest with widely spaced nipples, short neck with extra skin fold at nape ("webbed" appearance). *Associated complications:* Abnormalities of ovaries resulting in infertility and delayed puberty, congenital heart defect (often coarctation of aorta), small ear canals, chronic otitis media in 90% with frequent hearing loss, occasional thyroid or renal disease. Intelligence usually average, but prevalence of learning disabilities is high. *Cause:* Missing X chromosome due to nondisjunction. *Inheritance:* SP. *Prevalence:* 1/5,000.

Reference: Saenger, P. (1996). Turner's syndrome. *New England Journal of Medicine, 335,* 1749–1754.

Usher syndrome   *Clinical features:* Sensorineural deafness, nystagmus, retinitis pigmentosa. *Associated complications:* Ataxia, psychosis, cataracts, occasional cognitive impairment. *Cause:* Linked to a mutation in chromosome #11q13, #14q, or #1q32. *Inheritance:* AR. *Prevalence:* 3/100,000–5/100,000.

Reference: Smith, R.J., Berlin, C.I., Hejtmancik, J.R., et al. (1994). Clinical diagnosis of the Usher syndromes: Usher Syndrome Consortium. *American Journal of Medical Genetics, 50*(1), 32–38.

VATER/VACTERL association   *Clinical features:* **V**ertebral defects, **A**nal atresia, **T**racheoesophageal fistula (connection between trachea and esophagus), **E**sophageal anomalies, **R**adial (arm) defects, **R**enal anomalies, and other **L**imb defects. *Associated complications:* Respiratory, cardiac, and renal abnormalities can be severe. Intelligence is usually average. *Cause:* Unknown. *Inheritance:* Usually SP; rare families with AR pattern. *Prevalence:* Unknown.

Reference: Lubinsky, M. (1986). VATER and other associations: Historical perspectives and modern interpretations. *American Journal of Medical Genetics, 45,* 313–319.

Velocardiofacial syndrome   *See* Deletion 22q11 syndrome.

Von Recklinghausen disease   *See* Neurofibromatosis type I.

Waardenburg syndrome (types I, II, III)   *Clinical features:* Widely spaced eyes (type I), irises of different colors (heterochromia), white forelock, nonprogressive sensorineural hearing loss, musculoskeletal abnormalities (type III). *Associated complications:* Impaired vestibular function, premature graying, vitiligo, occasional glaucoma. *Cause:* Type I and III: mutation in chromosome #2q35; type II: mutation in chromosome #3. *Inheritance:* AD. *Prevalence:* 1/20,000–1/40,000.

Reference: Lee, D., Lanza, J., & Har-El, G. (1996). Waardenburg syndrome. *Otolaryngology Head and Neck Surgery, 114*(1), 166–167.

Weaver syndrome   *Clinical features:* Micrognathia; distinctive chin with dimple; widely spaced eyes; macrocephaly; downslanting palpebral fissures; long philtrum; depressed nasal bridge; hoarse, low-pitched cry. *Associated complications:* Accelerated somatic growth with advanced bone age, hypertonia, camptodactyly (permanently flexed fingers), mental retardation. *Cause:* Unknown. *Inheritance:* All reported cases have been sporadic; question of possible AR. *Prevalence:* Unknown.

Reference: Cole, T.R.P., Dennis, N.R., & Hughes, H.E. (1992). Weaver syndrome. *American Journal of Medical Genetics, 29,* 332–337.

Williams syndrome   *Clinical features:* Characteristic "elfin" facies (full lips and cheeks, periorbital fullness); short stature; star-like pattern to iris; hoarse voice; cheerful, extroverted personality; congenital heart defect (often supravalvular aortic stenosis). *Associated complications:* Hypercalcemia, stenosis of blood vessels, renal anomalies, hypertension, joint contractures, mental retardation requiring intermittent to limited support (characteristic strength in verbal abilities). *Cause:* Deletion in chromosome #7q11 (elastin locus). *Inheritance:* AD. *Prevalence:* 1/10,000.

Reference: Brewer, C.M., Morrison, N., & Tolmie, J.L. (1996). Clinical and molecular cytogenic (FISH) diagnosis of Williams syndrome. *Archives of Diseases in Childhood, 74,* 59–61.

Wilson disease   *Clinical features:* Liver dysfunction, Kayser-Fleischer ring (eye finding), low serum ceruloplasmin. *Associated complications:* Movement disorders, dysphagia or oral motor dysfunction, behavioral disturbances. If untreated, death ensues in 1–3 years. *Cause:* Abnormality of copper metabolism leading to accumulation; this defect is caused by a mutation of chromosome #13q14.3. *Inheritance:* AR. *Prevalence:* 1/50,000.

References: Akil, M., & Brewer, G.J. (1995). Psychiatric and behavioral abnormalities in Wilson's disease. *Advances in Neurology, 65,* 171–178.

Monaco, A.P., & Chelly, J. (1995). Menkes and Wilson diseases. *Advances in Genetics, 33,* 233–253.

Wolf-Hirschhorn syndrome   *Clinical features:* Widely spaced eyes, broad characteristic beaked nose, microcephaly, marked intrauterine growth retardation, ear anomalies, mental retardation requiring extensive support. *Associated complications:* Hypotonia, seizures, occasional heart defect or cleft palate. *Cause:* Deletion in short arm of chromosome #4p16.3. *Inheritance:* SP; inherited if parent has a balanced translocation. *Prevalence:* 1/50,000.

Reference: Estabrooks, L.L., Lamb, A.N., Aylsworth, A.S., et al. (1994). Molecular characteristics of chromosome 4p deletions resulting in Wolf-Hirschhorn syndrome. *American Journal of Medical Genetics, 31*(2), 103–107.

XO   *See* Turner syndrome.

XXX (trisomy X; 47, XXX); XXXX (tetrasomy X); XXXXX (pentasomy X)   *Clinical features:* Females with XXX generally have above-average stature but otherwise normal physical appearance; 70% have significant learning disabilities. Tetrasomy X is associated with mild facial dysmorphism, behavior problems, and mental retardation requiring limited support. Pentasomy X presents with mental retardation requiring extensive support and multiple physical defects. *Associated complications:* Infertility, delayed pubertal development. *Cause:* Maternal nondisjunction during embryogenesis. *Inheritance:* SP. *Prevalence:* Unknown.

Reference: Linden, M.G., Bender, M.G., & Robinson, A. (1995). Sex chromosome tetrasomy and pentasomy. *Pediatrics, 96*(4, Part I), 672–682.

XXY   *See* Klinefelter syndrome.

XYY syndrome   *Clinical features:* Subtle findings including tall stature, severe acne, large teeth. *Associated complications:* Poor fine motor coordination, learning disabilities (characteristically language-based), varying degrees of behavioral disturbances including temper tantrums and aggression. *Cause:* Extra Y chromosome resulting from nondisjunction. *Inheritance:* SP. *Prevalence:* 1/1,000.

Reference: Fryns, J.P., Kleczkowska, A., Kubien, E., et al. (1995). XYY syndrome and other Y chromosome polysomies: Mental status and psychosocial functioning. *Genetic Counseling, 6*(3), 197–206.

Zellweger (cerebro-hepato-renal) syndrome   *Clinical features:* The most severe of the known peroxisomal disorders; affected infants have intrauterine growth retardation; characteristic facies (high forehead, upslanting palpebral fissures, hypoplastic supraorbital ridges, and epicanthal folds); hypotonia; eye abnormalities (cataracts, glaucoma, corneal clouding); and early onset of seizures. Death occurs by 1 year in most cases. *Associated complications:* Severe feeding difficulties with failure to thrive, liver disease, occasional cardiac disease, extremity contractures, renal cysts. *Cause:* Impaired peroxisome synthesis caused by mutation in chromosome #7q11.3. The peroxisome is a recently described cellular organelle involved in processing fatty acids. *Inheritance:* AR. *Prevalence:* 1/100,000. *Treatment:* No treatment is yet available. Trials are under way using oral cholic and deoxycholic acids; oral lipids are also being investigated.
References: Jones, K.L. (1996). *Smith's recognizable patterns of human malformation* (5th ed.). Philadelphia: W.B. Saunders.
Moser, A.B., Rasmussen, M., Naidu, S., et al. (1995). Phenotype of patients with peroxisomal disorders subdivided into sixteen complementation groups. *Journal of Pediatrics, 127,* 13–22.

C Commonly Used Medications

Mark L. Batshaw

This appendix contains information about commonly used medications but is not meant to be used to prescribe medication. The generic name of each drug is in CAPITALS; the trade name is in parentheses. The drug category, use, standard application, and side effects are listed.

ACTH (Corticotropin)

Category	Antiepileptic
Use(s)	Infantile spasms and Lennox-Gastaut seizures
Standard application	Intramuscular injection of 20–40 units per day; many regimens exist, but ACTH is generally used for weeks to months and then tapered off slowly
Side effects	Glucose in urine, high blood pressure, cataracts, brittle bones

ACYCLOVIR (Zovirax)

Category	Antiviral agent
Use(s)	Used primarily in children who are immunocompromised, to treat or protect against herpes simplex and varicella (chickenpox) infections
Standard application	Capsules, injectable suspension, ointment, depending on clinical situation
Side effects	Kidney impairment

ADDERALL (Adderall)

Category	Psychopharmacological agent
Use(s)	Attention-deficit/hyperactivity disorder (ADHD), obesity, narcolepsy
Standard application	Tablets: one to three doses daily; not recommended for children less than 3 years old; 3–5 year old children receive 2.5 milligrams per day initially, with an increase of 2.5 milligrams per week until optimal response; children older than 6 years receive 5 milligrams once per day or twice daily initially, with an increase of 5 milligrams per week until optimal response
Side effects	Insomnia, loss of appetite, emotional lability, addictive potential, arrhythmias

ALPRAZOLAM (Xanax)

Category	Psychopharmacological agent
Use(s)	Anxiety, aggression, panic attacks
Standard application	Tablets: titrate starting at minimal doses of .125 milligrams three times per day; safety and efficacy in children younger than 18 years is not known
Side effects	Drowsiness, insomnia, decreased salivation

AMITRIPTYLINE (Elavil)

Category	Psychopharmacological agent
Use(s)	ADHD, depression
Standard application	Tablets: 1–1.5 milligrams per kilograms per day, given in three doses; not recommended for children younger than 12 years
Side effects	Sedation, dry mouth, blurred vision, very rare sudden death from cardiac arrhythmia

AMOXICILLIN (Amoxil)

Category	Antibiotic
Use(s)	First-line drug for otitis media
Standard application	Tablets, capsules, chewables, liquid: 20–50 milligrams per kilograms per day, given three times daily
Side effects	Diarrhea, rash

AMOXICILLIN AND CLAVULANIC ACID (Augmentin)

Category	Antibiotic
Use(s)	Otitis media
Standard application	Tablets, chewables, liquid: 40 milligrams per kilograms per day, given three times daily
Side effects	Diarrhea (worse than amoxicillin alone), rash

BACLOFEN (Lioresal)

Category	Antispasticity
Use(s)	Spasticity of cerebral or spinal origin
Standard application	Tablets: 5 milligrams by mouth, two or three times daily initially; increase by 5 milligrams every 4–7 days to a maximum of 30–80 milligrams per day
Side effects	Drowsiness, muscle weakness; rare individuals experience nausea, dizziness, paresthesias; abrupt withdrawal can cause hallucinations and seizures

BUSPIRONE (Buspar)

Category	Psychopharmacological agent
Use(s)	ADHD, anxiety, aggression
Standard application	Tablets: safety and efficacy in children younger than 18 years is not known
Side effects	Chest pain, tinnitus, sore throat, nasal congestion

CALCIUM UNDECYLENATE (10%) (Caldesene powder)

Category	Skin
Use(s)	Diaper rash
Standard application	Ointment, powder: apply three or four times per day after bath or changing
Side effects	Irritation, allergic reaction

CARBAMAZEPINE (Tegretol)

Category	Antiepileptic
Use(s)	Generalized tonic-clonic, complex partial, simple partial seizures; also used to treat aggression
Standard application	Tablets, injectable suspension: 5–20 milligrams per kilograms per day; blood level should maintain at 4–14 micrograms per milliliter
Side effects	Ataxia, double vision, drowsiness, slurred speech, dizziness, tremor, headache, nausea, abnormalities in liver function, low white blood count

CHLORAL HYDRATE (Aquachloral [supplement], Noctec)

Category	Psychopharmacological agent
Use(s)	Sedation
Standard application	Capsules, suppositories, syrup: 5–15 milligrams per kilograms every 8 hours to a maximum dose of 2 grams
Side effects	Mucous membrane and gastrointestinal irritation, paradoxical excitement, hypotension

CHLORPROMAZINE (Thorazine)

Category	Psychopharmacological agent
Use(s)	Psychosis, anxiety, aggression, severe hyperactivity in mental retardation
Standard application	Tablets, suppositories, syrup, injectable suspension: oral dosage is 2.5–6 milligrams per kilograms per day to a maximum of 40 milligrams in children less than 5 years or 75 milligrams in children 5–12 years
Side effects	Drowsiness, tardive dyskinesia, electrocardiogram (ECG) changes, agranulocytosis, rash, hyperpigmentation of skin

CIMETIDINE (Tagamet)

Category	Gastrointestinal
Use(s)	Gastroesophageal reflux, gastric/duodenal ulcers; inhibits gastric acid secretion
Standard application	Liquid, tablets: 10–40 milligrams per kilograms per day, given four times daily
Side effects	Rarely diarrhea, headache, decreased white blood count, hepatotoxicity

CISAPRIDE (Propulsid)

Category	Gastrointestinal
Use(s)	Anti-reflux, increases gastric emptying
Standard application	Tablets, injectable suspension: 0.7–1.0 milligrams per kilograms per day, given three or four times daily
Side effects	Abdominal pain, diarrhea

CLARITHROMYCIN (Biaxin)

Category	Antibiotic
Use(s)	Wide-spectrum drug used against staph, strep, and mycoplasma ("walking pneumonia")
Standard application	Tablets, injectable suspension: 15 milligrams per kilograms per day, given twice daily for 10 days
Side effects	Stomach upset, but better tolerated than erythromycin

CLONAZEPAM (Klonopin)

Category	Antiepileptic
Use(s)	Lennox-Gastaut, absence, atonic, myoclonic, infantile spasms, and partial seizures
Standard application	Tablet: 0.01–0.2 milligrams per kilograms per day (usual maintenance dose is 0.5–2 milligrams per day, given twice daily)
Side effects	Sedation, hyperactivity, confusion, depression, especially if withdrawn quickly; tolerance to the drug can develop

CLONIDINE (Catapres)

Category	Psychopharmacological agent
Use(s)	Hypertension, ADHD

Standard application	Tablets: .005–.025 milligrams per kilograms per day, four times daily; increase every 5–7 days as needed; sustained release patch also available
Side effects	Dry mouth, sedation, low blood pressure, headache, nausea

CLOXACILLIN (Tegopen)

Category	Antibiotic
Use(s)	Useful against staph infections (e.g., impetigo)
Standard application	Capsules, liquid: 50–100 milligrams per kilograms per day, given four times daily
Side effects	Allergic reactions, diarrhea

COLLOIDAL OATMEAL (Aveeno)

Category	Skin
Use(s)	Emollient for dry skin, itching
Standard application	Oil, cleansing bar, cream, lotion: add to bath or apply as needed
Side effects	Allergic reaction

DANTROLENE SODIUM (Dantrium)

Category	Antispasticity
Use(s)	Spasticity of cerebral or spinal origin
Standard application	Capsules: 0.5 milligrams per killigram, twice daily, initially; increase by 0.5 milligrams per kilograms every 4–7 days, to a maximum of 3 milligrams per kilograms per dose, given from two to four times daily
Side effects	Weakness, drowsiness, lethargy, dizziness, paresthesias, nausea, diarrhea, rarely hepatotoxicity (liver function tests should be monitored); long-term side effects in children are not known

DESIPRAMINE (Norpramine)

Category	Psychopharmacological agent
Use(s)	Depression, anxiety, ADHD
Standard application	Tablet: not recommended in children younger than 12 years; 1–4.5 milligrams per kilograms per day, maximum 100 milligrams daily
Side effects	Hypotension, tinnitus, gastrointestinal discomfort, dry mouth, blurred vision, sudden death from cardiac arrhythmia has been reported

DEXTROAMPHETAMINE (Dexadrine)

Category	Psychopharmacological agent
Use(s)	ADHD, narcolepsy
Standard application	Tablets (5 milligrams): liquid: 0.1 milligrams per kilograms, twice daily initially; increase to 0.5–1.0 milligrams per kilograms per dose, from two to three times daily; sustained release capsules are available (5, 10, and 15 milligrams)
Side effects	Insomnia, restlessness, headache, abdominal cramps

DIAZEPAM (Valium)

Category	Antispasticity, antiepileptic, psychopharmacological agent
Use(s)	Sedation, aggression, anxiety, spasticity
Standard application	Capsules, tablets, liquid: 0.12–0.8 milligrams per kilograms by mouth per day, given three to four times daily
Side effects	Sedation, weakness, depression, ataxia, memory disturbance, difficulty handling secretions and chewing/swallowing foods, anxiety, hallucinations, agitation, insomnia,

respiratory and cardiac depression, urinary retention or incontinence, rash, and neutropenia; drug dependence can occur

DIPHENHYDRAMINE (Benadryl)

Category	Antihistamine
Use(s)	Sedation, antihistamine
Standard application	Capsules, tablets, liquid: 5 milligrams per kilograms per day given at 6- to 8-hour intervals, to a maximum of 300 milligrams per day
Side effects	Sedation, insomnia, dizziness, euphoria

DUODERM

Category	Skin
Use(s)	Skin ulcers/sores, burns (second degree), and minor abrasions
Standard application	Sterile occlusive dressing with hydroactive or gel formula
Side effects	Allergic reaction (to tape or gel formula)

ERYTHROMYCIN (2%) (T-stat)

Category	Skin
Use(s)	Acne
Standard application	Topical solution (apply to clean area twice daily)
Side effects	Dryness, peeling, and skin irritation

ERYTHROMYCIN (Various brands)

Category	Antibiotic
Use(s)	Used against staph, strep, and mycoplasma ("walking pneumonia"); used in combination with sulfisoxazole (Pediazole) for otitis media
Standard application	Tablets, capsules, liquid: 30–50 milligrams per kilograms per day, given four times daily
Side effects	Nausea, vomiting, interactions with other drugs

ETHOSUXIMIDE (Zarontin)

Category	Antiepileptic
Use(s)	Absence seizures
Standard application	Capsules, liquid: 15–40 milligrams per kilograms per day, given twice daily to a maximum of 1.5 grams per day; blood level: 40–80 micrograms per liter
Side effects	Sedation, unsteady gait (ataxia), rash, stomach distress, low white blood count

FAMOTIDINE (Pepcid)

Category	Gastrointestinal
Use(s)	Decreases stomach acidity, used for gastroesophageal reflux
Standard application	Tablets, liquid: 1 milligram per kilograms per day, given twice daily with meals
Side effects	Headache, dizziness

FELBAMATE (Felbatol)

Category	Antiepileptic
Use(s)	Lennox-Gastaut syndrome; also effective in generalized tonic-clonic, complex partial, and secondary generalized seizures
Standard application	Tablets, injectable suspension: 15–45 milligrams per kilograms per day
Side effects	Anorexia, vomiting, insomnia, headache, rash, risk of life-threatening hepatitis and aplastic anemia (FDA recommends CBC and liver function tests every 1–2 weeks)

FLUOXETINE (Prozac)

Category	Psychopharmacological agent
Use(s)	Depression, self-injurious behavior, Tourette syndrome
Standard application	Capsules, liquid: safety/efficacy in children has not been established; adults should initially receive 20 milligrams per day in morning, to a maximum of 80 milligrams per day
Side effects	Anxiety, agitation, sleep disruption, decreased appetite, seizures

GABAPENTIN (Neurontin)

Category	Antiepileptic
Use(s)	Adjunctive therapy in partial and secondarily generalized seizures
Standard application	Capsules: 20–30 milligrams per kilograms per day; safety and effectiveness in children younger than 12 years has not been established
Side effects	Sedation, dizziness, ataxia, fatigue

HALOPERIDOL (Haldol)

Category	Psychopharmacological agent
Use(s)	Self-injurious behavior, tics, severe agitation, psychosis
Standard application	Tablets, liquid: 0.01–0.03 milligrams per kilograms per day for agitation; 0.05–0.15 milligrams per kilograms per day, in two or three daily doses for psychosis; and 0.05–0.075 milligrams per kilograms per day, in two or three daily doses for Tourette syndrome
Side effects	Extrapyramidal symptoms, neuroleptic malignant syndrome, lowers seizure threshold in epilepsy

HYDROCORTISONE (Caldecort, Cort-Dome, Hytone)

Category	Skin
Use(s)	Eczema, dermatitis
Standard application	Cream, ointment: apply a thin film from two to four times daily
Side effects	Skin irritation, dryness, rash

HYDROCORTISONE, POLYMYXIN-B, NEOMYCIN (Cortisporin)

Category	Skin
Use(s)	Steroid-responsive skin conditions with secondary infection
Standard application	Cream, ointment: apply sparingly and massage into skin two or three times daily
Side effects	Local irritation, kidney/ear toxicity (if neomycin is absorbed in large amounts)

IMIPRAMINE (Tofranil, Janimine)

Category	Psychopharmacological agent
Use(s)	Depression, enuresis
Standard application	Tablets, capsules: 1.5 milligrams per kilograms per day, given in three daily doses to a maximum of 5 milligrams per kilograms per day; therapeutic blood level for depression is 150–225 nanograms per milliliter
Side effects	Dry mouth, drowsiness, constipation, ECG abnormalities, increased blood pressure

ISOTRETINOIN (Accutane)

Category	Skin
Use(s)	Severe acne in adolescents (or adults)

Standard application	Capsules: 0.5–2 milligrams per kilograms per day, given in two daily doses for 15–20 weeks
Side effects	Drying of mucous membranes, photosensitivity, teratogenic (do not use during pregnancy)

KETOGENIC DIET

Category	Antiepileptic
Use(s)	Infantile spasms, Lennox Gastault seizures, mixed-type seizure disorder
Standard application	Diet high in fats and low in carbohydrates; resulting ketosis can reduce seizure activity in about half the children treated; antiepileptic drugs may be reduced or eliminated
Side effects	Supplemental vitamins and minerals must be provided; height and weight gain is reduced, so diet is rarely used for more than 2 years

LAMOTRIGINE (Lamictal)

Category	Antiepileptic
Use(s)	Adjunctive therapy in partial and secondarily generalized seizures; may be effective in primary generalized seizures
Standard application	Tablets: 5–15 milligrams per kilograms per day (1–5 milligrams per kilograms per day if co-administered with valproate); safety and efficacy in children younger than 12 years has not been established
Side effects	Sedation, dizziness, potentially life-threatening Stevens-Johnson syndrome (allergic skin condition)

LANOLIN, PETROLATUM, VITAMINS A AND D, MINERAL OILS (A & D Ointment)

Category	Skin
Use(s)	Diaper rash
Standard application	Ointment: apply thin film at each diaper change
Side effects	Allergic reaction

LINDANE (Kwell)

Category	Skin
Use(s)	Scabicidal and lice
Standard application	Cream, lotion: apply thin layer and massage into body from neck down; wash off after 8–12 hours; shampoo: apply to dry hair, massage thoroughly into hair and leave on for 4 minutes, then form lather and rinse well
Side effects	None with prescribed use; risk of seizures with overuse in small children

MAGNESIUM HYDROXIDE AND ALUMINUM HYDROXIDE (Maalox)

Category	Gastrointestinal
Use(s)	Antacid for reflux, also helps treat constipation
Standard application	Liquid; 1–2 teaspoons with meals and at bedtime
Side effects	Minimal

METHYLPHENIDATE (Ritalin)

Category	Psychopharmacological agent
Use(s)	ADHD
Standard application	Tablets (5, 10, and 20 milligrams): 0.6 milligrams per kilograms per day, given twice daily initially; increase to 1–2 milligrams per kilograms per day, given two or three times daily, sustained release tablets (20 milligrams) are available

Side effects	Appetite suppression, insomnia, arrhythmias, hypo- or hypertension, abdominal pain

METHYLPREDNISOLONE (Solu-Medrol, Medrol)

Category	Respiratory
Use(s)	Reduction of airway inflammation during acute asthma attacks
Standard application	Injectable suspension: 1 milligram per killigram per dose; orally: 1 milligram per killigram per dose, twice daily for 3–5 days
Side effects	Side effects usually mild with short-term use

METOCLOPRAMIDE (Reglan)

Category	Gastrointestinal
Use(s)	Anti-reflux, increases gastric emptying
Standard application	Tablets, liquid: 0.1–0.5 milligrams per kilograms per day, given four times daily
Side effects	Acute dystonic reactions, drowsiness

MICONAZOLE (2%) (Monistat)

Category	Skin
Use(s)	Antifungal, candidal yeast infections
Standard application	Cream: apply twice daily for 2–4 weeks
Side effects	Skin irritation, peeling

MINERAL OIL (Alpha Keri)

Category	Skin
Use(s)	Emollient for dry skin
Standard application	Soap, oil, spray: add to bath or rub into wet skin as needed; rinse
Side effects	Allergic reaction

MINERAL OIL, PETROLATUM, LANOLIN (Nivea, Lubriderm)

Category	Skin
Use(s)	Emollient for dry skin
Standard application	Cream, moisturizing lotion, bath oil: apply as needed
Side effects	Allergic reaction

MUPIROCIN (2%) (Bactroban)

Category	Skin
Use(s)	Antibiotic for impetigo, skin ulcers, burns
Standard application	Ointment: apply sparingly three times per day, may cover with gauze
Side effects	Burning, itching, pain at site of application

NALTREXONE (Revia)

Category	Psychopharmacological agent
Use(s)	Opiate antagonist for treatment of self-injurious behavior
Standard application	Tablets, injectable suspension: 50 milligrams per day in adults; safety and efficacy in children younger than 18 years has not been established
Side effects	None in opioid-free individuals

NORTRIPTYLINE (Pamelor)

Category	Psychopharmacological agent
Use(s)	Depression

| Standard application | Capsules, syrup: 10 milligrams, three times per day and 20 milligrams at bedtime; not recommended for children under 12 years |
| Side effects | Dry mouth, drowsiness, constipation, ECG abnormalities, increased blood pressure, mania, sudden death from cardiac arrhythmia has been reported with overdose |

NYSTATIN (Mycostatin)

Category	Skin
Use(s)	Antifungal treatment of yeast and thrush infections of the mouth and gastrointestinal tract
Standard application	Cream, ointment, powder: apply twice daily; oral suspension: 0.5–1 milliliter to each side of mouth four times per day; liquid: up to 5 cubic centimeters, "swish and swallow"
Side effects	Diarrhea (oral form), redness, skin irritation, gastrointestinal upset

PEMOLINE (Cylert)

Category	Psychopharmacological agent
Use(s)	ADHD
Standard application	Tablets: 37.5 milligrams per day in morning initially; increase weekly to desired dose but do not exceed 112.5 milligrams per day; not recommended for children younger than 6 years
Side effects	Insomnia, anorexia, abdominal discomfort, potentially life-threatening hepatotoxicity

PENICILLIN (Pen Vee K)

Category	Antibiotic
Use(s)	Drug of choice for strep throat, which also can be treated by a single intramuscular injection of Bicillin
Standard application	Tablets, liquid: 25–50 milligrams per kilograms per day, given four times daily for 7 days
Side effects	Allergic reactions, diarrhea

PETROLATUM, MINERAL OIL AND WAX, ALCOHOL (Eucerin)

Category	Skin
Use(s)	Emollient for dry skin, itching
Standard application	Cream, lotion, facial lotion with sunscreen, cleansing bar: apply as needed
Side effects	Allergic reaction

PHENOBARBITAL (Luminal)

Category	Antiepileptic
Use(s)	Generalized tonic-clonic and simple partial and secondarily generalized seizures
Standard application	Tablets, capsules, liquid: 2–5 milligrams per kilograms per day for children; 1–2 milligrams per kilograms per day for adolescents; therapeutic blood level: 10–40 micrograms per milliliter
Side effects	Paradoxical hyperactivity, sedation, learning difficulties in older children, behavioral difficulties in 50% of children younger than 10 years, rash, irritability, unsteady gait

PHENYTOIN (Dilantin)

| Category | Antiepileptic |
| Use(s) | Generalized tonic-clonic and complex partial seizures |

| Standard application | Tablets, capsules, injectable, suspension: (maintenance dosage) 4–8 milligrams per kilograms per day; blood level: 10–20 micrograms per milliliter |
| Side effects | Swelling of gums, excessive hairiness, rash, coarsening of facial features, possible adverse effects on learning and behavior, risk of birth defects if taken during pregnancy, nystagmus and unsteady gait with toxic levels |

PRIMIDONE (Mysoline)

Category	Antiepileptic
Use(s)	Generalized tonic-clonic and complex partial seizures
Standard application	Tablets, suspension: 10–25 milligrams per kilograms per day for children; 125–250 milligrams three times per day for adolescents; therapeutic blood level of primidone is 5–12 micrograms per milliliter, also metabolized to phenobarbital (therapeutic blood level, 20–40 micrograms per milliliter)
Side effects	Drowsiness, dizziness, nausea, vomiting, and personality change (see also side effects of phenobarbital)

RANITIDINE (Zantac)

Category	Gastrointestinal
Use(s)	Decreases stomach acidity, used for gastroesophageal reflux
Standard application	Tablets, liquid: 2–4 milligrams per kilograms per day, given twice daily
Side effects	Headache, gastrointestinal upset, rare hepatotoxicity

SELENIUM SULFIDE (2.5%) (Selsun Blue)

Category	Skin
Use(s)	Scalp conditions (dandruff or seborrhea)
Standard application	Lotion, shampoo: apply to wet scalp, wait 3 minutes, rinse, repeat; use twice a week for 2 weeks, then as needed
Side effects	Irritation, dry or oily scalp

SERTRALINE (Zoloft)

Category	Psychopharmacological agent
Use(s)	Depression
Standard application	50 milligrams per day initially to a maximum dose of 200 milligrams per day in adults; safety and efficacy not established in children
Side effects	Anxiety, agitation, sleep disruption, decreased appetite, seizures

SULFISOXAZOLE (Gantrisin)

Category	Antibiotic
Use(s)	Otitis media prophylaxis
Standard application	Tablets, liquid: 50–75 milligrams per kilograms per day, given from four to six times daily
Side effects	Bone marrow suppression, allergic reactions

THEOPHYLLINE (Theo-Dur, Slo-Bid, Uniphyl, Aerolate)

Category	Respiratory
Use(s)	A bronchodilator that may be used in conjunction with other treatments for acute or chronic asthma
Standard application	Oral theophylline: children ages 6 weeks–6 months: 10 milligrams per kilograms per day; children ages 6 months–1 year: 12–18 milligrams per kilograms per day;

children ages 1–9 years: 20–24 milligrams per kilograms per day; children ages 9–12 years: 20 milligrams per kilograms per day; children ages 12–16 years: 18 milligrams per kilograms per day; maximum adult dose: 900 milligrams per day

Side effects   Nausea, vomiting, and stomach pain (especially common at high blood levels)

THIORIDAZINE (Mellaril)

Category	Psychopharmacological agent
Use(s)	Self-injurious behavior, psychosis
Standard application	Not recommended for children younger than 2 years; children ages 2–12 years: 0.5–3 milligrams per kilograms per day; children older than 12 years with mild disorders: 10 milligrams two or three times daily; children older than 12 years with severe disorders: 25 milligrams two or three times daily
Side effects	Drowsiness, extrapyramidal reactions, ECG abnormalities, arrhythmias, pigmentary retinopathy, autonomic symptoms

THIOTHIXENE (Navane)

Category	Psychopharmacological agent
Use(s)	Self-injurious behavior, psychosis
Standard application	Tablets, syrup, injectable suspension: 2 milligrams, three times daily, increase to 15 milligrams per day if needed; not recommended for children younger than 12 years
Side effects	Tardive dyskinesia, neuroleptic malignant syndrome, tachycardia, hypotension, drowsiness, agranulocytosis/blood dyscrasia

TOLNAFTATE (Tinactin)

Category	Skin
Use(s)	Antifungal, ringworm
Standard application	Nontoxic

TRIAMCINOLONE (Kenalog, Aristocort [skin]; Azmacort [respiratory])

Category	Skin; respiratory
Use(s)	Eczema, dermatitis; inhibition of airway inflammation in patients with chronic asthma symptoms
Standard application	Powder, cream, ointment, lotion: apply a thin film from two to four times daily; inhaler: 100 micrograms per spray; children ages 6–12 years: 1–2 puffs three or four times daily; adults: 2 puffs three or four times daily
Side effects	Skin irritation, rash, dryness, cough, hoarseness, dry mouth, increased wheezing; rinse mouth after use to prevent thrush

TRIMETHOPRIM (TMP) AND SULFAMETHOXAZOLE (Bactrim, Septra)

Category	Antibiotic
Use(s)	Convenient dosing for otitis media and for urinary tract infections
Standard application	Tablets, liquid: 8–10 milligrams per kilograms per day, given twice daily
Side effects	Bone marrow suppression, allergic reactions, photosensitivity

VALPROIC ACID (Depakene, Depakote)

Category	Antiepileptic
Use(s)	Myoclonic, simple absence, generalized tonic-clonic seizures, Lennox-Gastaut, infantile spasms; also used to treat aggression and mood disorders
Standard application	Capsules; syrup, sprinkle: 15–60 milligrams per kilograms per day; therapeutic blood level: 50–100 micrograms per milliliter

Side effects   Hair loss, weight loss or gain, abdominal distress, static tremor, low platelet count; risk of birth defects if taken during pregnancy; major adverse reaction is potentially fatal liver necrosis (risk is 1:800 in children with developmental disabilities less than 2 years of age on more than one antiepileptic drug)

ZINC OXIDE, COD LIVER OIL, LANOLIN, PETROLATUM (Caldesene ointment)

Category   Skin
Use(s)   Diaper rash
Standard application   Ointment: apply three or four times per day after diaper change or bath
Side effects   Allergic reaction

Table 1. Medications according to trade name

Trade name	Generic name
A&D Ointment	Lanolin, petrolatum, vitamins A and D, mineral oils
Accutane	Isotretinoin
Adderall	Adderall
Aerolate	Theophylline
Alpha Keri	Mineral oil
Amoxil	Amoxicillin
Aquachloral (supplement)	Chloral hydrate
Aristocort (skin)	Triamcinolone
Augmentin	Amoxicillin and clavulanic acid
Aveeno	Colloidal oatmeal
Azmacort (respiratory)	Triamcinolone
Bactrim	Trimethoprim (TMP) and sulfamethoxazole
Bactroban	Mupirocin (2%)
Benadryl	Diphenhydramine
Biaxin	Clarithromycin
Buspar	Buspirone
Caldecort	Hydrocortisone
Caldesene ointment	Zinc oxide, cod liver oil, lanolin, petrolatum
Caldesene powder	Calcium undecylenate (10%)
Catapres	Clonidine
Cort-Dome	Hydrocortisone
Corticotropin	ACTH
Cortisporin	Hydrocortisone, polymyxin-B, and neomycin
Cylert	Pemoline
Dantrium	Dantrolene sodium
Depakene	Valproic acid
Depakote	Valproic acid
Dexadrine	Dextroamphetamine
Dilantin	Phenytoin
Elavil	Amitriptyline
Eucerin	Petrolatum, mineral oil and wax, alcohol
Felbatol	Felbamate
Gantrisin	Sulfisoxazole
Haldol	Haloperidol
Hytone	Hydrocortisone
Janimine	Imipramine
Kenalog	Triamcinolone
Klonopin	Clonazepam
Kwell	Lindane
Lamictal	Lamotrigine
Lioresal	Baclofen
Lubriderm	Mineral oil, petrolatum, lanolin
Luminal	Phenobarbital
Maalox	Magnesium hydrochloride and aluminum hydrochloride
Medrol	Methylprednisolone

(continued)

Table 1.   (*continued*)

Trade name	Generic name
Mellaril	Thioridazine
Monistat	Miconazole (2%)
Mycostatin	Nystatin
Mysoline	Primidone
Navane	Thiothixene
Neurontin	Gabaentin
Nivea	Mineral oil, petrolatum, lanolin
Noctec	Choral hydrate
Norpramine	Desipramine
Pamelor	Nortriptyline
Pen Vee K	Penicillin
Pepcid	Famotidine
Propulsid	Cisapride
Prozac	Fluoxetine
Reglan	Metroclopramide
Revia	Naltrexone
Ritalin	Methylphenidate
Selsun Blue	Selenium sulfide (2.5%)
Septra	Trimethorprim (TMP) and sulfamethoxazole
Slo-bid	Theophylline
Solu-medrol	Methylprednisolone
T-Stat	Erythromycin (2%)
Tagamet	Cimetidine
Tegopen	Cloxacillin
Tegretol	Carbamazepine
Theo-dur	Theophylline
Thorazine	Chlorpromazine
Tinactin	Tolnaftate
Tofranil	Imipramine
Uniphyl	Theophylline
Valium	Diazepam
Xanax	Alprazolam
Zantac	Ranitidine
Zarontin	Ethosuximide
Zoloft	Sertraline
Zovirax	Acyclovir

Adapted from Kurtz, Dowrick, Levy, et al. (1996).

Table 2. Medications according to use

Antiepileptic drugs	Antispasticity medications	Gastrointestinal medications	Antibiotics	Psychotropic medications	Skin medications
ACTH (Corticotropin)	Alprazolam (Xanax)	Cimetidine (Tagamet)	Acyclovir (Zovirax)	**CNS stimulants**	Calcium undecytenate (10%) (Caldesene Powder)
Carbamazepine (Tegretol)	Baclofen, oral (Lioresal)	Cisapride (Propulsid)	Amoxicillin (Amoxil)	Adderall	Colloidal oatmeal (Aveeno)
Clonazepam (Klonopin)	Clonazepam (Klonopin)	Famotidine (Pepcid)	Amoxicillin and clavulanic acid (Augmentin)	Clonidine (Catapres)	Erythromycin 2% (T-stat)
Ethosuximide (Zarontin)	Dantrolene sodium (Dantrium)	Magnesium hydroxide and aluminum hydroxide (Maalox)	Clarithromycin (Biaxin)	Dextroamphetamine (Dexadine)	Hydrocortisone (Caldecort, Cort-Dome, Hytone)
Felbamate (Felbatol)	Diazepam (Valium)	Metoclopramide (Reglan)	Cloxacillin (Tegopen)	Methylphenidate (Ritalin)	Hydrocortisone, Polymyxin B, & Neomycin (Cortisporin)
Gabapentin (Neurontin)		Ranitidine (Zantac)	Erythromycin (Various brands)	Nortriptyline (Pamelor)	Lanolin (A&D Ointment)
Lamotrigine (Lamictal)			Nystatin (Mycostatin)	Pemoline (Cylert)	Lindane (Kwell)
Phenobarbital (Luminal)			Penicillin (Pen Vee K)	Zoloft (Sertraline)	Miconazole 2%
Phenytoin (Dilantin)			Sulfisoxazole (Gantrisin)	**Antidepressants**	Monistat
Primidone (Mysoline)			Trimethroprim and Sulfamethoxazole (Bactim, Septra)	Amitriptyline (Elavil)	Mineral oil (Lubriderm, Nivea)
Valproic acid (Depakene, Depakote)				Desipramine (Norpramine)	Mineral oil (Alpha Keri)
				Fluoxetine (Prozac)	Mupirocin, 2% (Bactroban)
				Imipramine (Janimine, Tofranil)	Nystatin (Mycostatin)
				Antipsychotic	Petrolatum (Eucerin)
				Chlorpromazine (Thorazine)	
				Haloperidol (Haldol)	

(continued)

Table 2. (continued)

Antiepileptic drugs	Antispasticity medications	Gastrointestinal medications	Antibiotics	Psychotropic medications	Skin medications
				Thiothixene (Navane)	Isotretinoin (Accutane)
				Thioridazine (Mellaril)	Tolnaftate (Tinactin)
				Endorphin	Triamcinolone (Kenalog, Aristocort)
				Naltrexone (Revia)	Zinc oxide (Caldesene ointment)

Adapted from Kurtz, Dowrick, Levy, et al. (1996).

Resources
for Children
with Disabilities

Margaret Rose

NATIONAL ORGANIZATIONS

Listed below are a number of national organizations that provide services in the area of developmental disabilities. A brief description of the purpose of the organization follows each listing. This section is a representative sample and is not intended to be all-inclusive. We have tried to make addresses and telephone numbers as current as possible. We apologize if readers find any of these have changed.

ACCESSIBILITY

Indoor Sports Club, Inc.

1145 Highland Street, Napoleon, OH 43545 (419-592-5756). Educates the public to promote and support opportunities that provide accessibility, rehabilitation, and employment for people with disabilities.

National Center on Accessibility

Bradford Woods/Indiana University, 5040 State Road 67 N, Martinsville, IN 46151 (317-349-9240 [voice or TDD]; 800-424-1877). Works with departments of parks, recreation, and tourism throughout the United States to improve accessibility. Runs 800 hotline to provide technical assistance. Sponsors several training sessions each year throughout the United States to educate employers on making their workplaces accessible.

The Center for Universal Design and Accessible Housing

North Carolina State University School of Design, Box 8613, Raleigh, NC 27695-8613 (919-515-3082; 800-647-6777; FAX: 919-515-3023; e-mail address: cahd@ncsu.edu; Internet Web site: http://www2.ncsu.edu/ncsu/design/cud). Provides publications and information to parents and professionals concerning accessible housing design and financing issues; makes referrals to local organizations.

U.S. Architectural and Transportation Barriers Compliance Board

1331 F Street NW, Suite 1000, Washington, DC 20004-1111 (202-272-5434, 800-872-2253; FAX: 202-272-5447; e-mail address: info@access-board.gov). An organization created by Section 504 of the Rehabilitation Act of 1973, PL 93-112, to enforce the Architectural Barriers Act of 1968, PL 90-480. Offers free publications and answers to technical questions about accessibility.

ACQUIRED IMMUNODEFICIENCY SYNDROME (AIDS)

CDC National AIDS Clearinghouse

Centers for Disease Control, Post Office Box 6003, Rockville, MD 20849-6003 (800-458-5231; TTY/TDD: 800-243-7012; FAX: 301-738-6616). A national reference, referral, and publications distribution service for human immunodeficiency virus (HIV) and AIDS information; also offers CDC NAC ONLINE, an electronic bulletin board.

CDC National AIDS Hotline

Centers for Disease Control (800-458-5231 [English & Spanish]; TTY/TDD: 800-243-7012). A weekday hotline, 9 A.M.-7 P.M., that provides confidential information on transmission and prevention, testing, local referrals, and educational materials to the public.

White House Office of National AIDS Policy

808 17th Street, NW, Washington, DC 20006 (202-632-1090; FAX: 202-632-1096). Provides broad direction for federal AIDS policy and fosters interdepartmental communication on HIV and AIDS. Works closely with the AIDS community in the United States and around the world.

ALCOHOL AND OTHER DRUGS OF ABUSE

Clean Water International

Clean Water International, 9077 161st Street, W, Lakeville, MN 55044 (e-mail address: Clean Water International; Internet Web site: http://www.shadeslanding.com/clean-water). Nonprofit group dedicated to protecting the environment in which the human fetus grows and preventing fetal alcohol syndrome (FAS).

Cocaine Babies: Florida's Substance-Exposed Youth

Available from Florida Department of Education, Prevention Center, Suite 332, 325 West Gaines Street, Tallahassee, FL 32399 (904-488-6304). A 119-page compilation, distributed nationwide, on prenatal drug exposure with reprints of research papers, case studies, sources for help, and the Slavin teaching strategies (which form the basis for the widely disseminated Success for All program that teaches children to become joyful, creative self-aware problem solvers).

CSAP National Women's Resource Center for the
Prevention of Perinatal Abuse of Alcohol and Other Drugs

9300 Lee Highway, Fairfax, VA 22031 (703-218-5600; 800-354-8824; e-mail address: nwrc@smtp.nafare.com; Internet Web site: http://www.nwrc.org). Addresses priority issues for women at risk for substance abuse and/or mental illness. Local teams create a national network.

Family Empowerment Network (FEN)

610 Langdon Street, Room 521, Madison, WI 53703 (800-462-5254; 608-262-6590; FAX: 608-265-2329; e-mail address: mbchambe@facstaff.wisc.edu). National, nonprofit organization that exists to empower families affected by FAS and other drug-related birth defects through education and support; also publishes newsletter *FenPen*.

National Organization on Fetal Alcohol Syndrome

1819 H Street, SW, Suite 750, Washington, DC 20006 (202-785-4585; FAX: 202-466-6456; e-mail address: nofas@erols.com; Internet Web site: http//www.nofas.org). Nonprofit organization founded in 1990 dedicated to eliminating birth defects caused by alcohol consumption during pregnancy and improving the quality of life for those individuals and families affected. NOFAS, which applies a multicultural approach in its prevention and healing strategies, is the only national organization focusing solely on FAS.

ATTENTION-DEFICIT/HYPERACTIVITY DISORDER (ADHD)

CHADD National

499 NW 70th Avenue, Suite 101, Plantation, FL 33317 (305-587-3700; FAX: 305-587-4599; Internet Web site: http://www.chadd.org). Support group for parents of children with attention-deficit disorders. Provides continuing education for both parents and professionals, serves as a community resource for information, and advocates for appropriate educational programs.

AUTISM

Autism Research Institute

4182 Adams Avenue, San Diego, CA 92116. Information and referral for parents, teachers, physicians, and students working with children with autism and similar developmental disabilities. Publishes quarterly newsletter, *Autism Research Review International.*

Autism Society of America

7910 Woodmont Ave, Suite 650, Bethesda, MD 20814-3015 (800-3-AUTISM, 301-657-0881; FAX: 301-657-0869, 800-329-0899; Internet Web site: http://www.autism-society.org/). Provides information about autism including options, approaches, methods, and systems available to parents of children with autism, family members, and the professionals who work with them. Advocates for rights and needs of individuals with autism and their families.

National Autism Hotline/Autism Services Center

605 9th Street, Prichard Building, Post Office Box 507, Huntington, WV 25710-0507 (304-525-8014; FAX: 304-525-8026). Provides direct-care services locally (e.g., group homes, supervised apartments, intensively staffed one-to-one settings for individuals with challenging behaviors) and information, advocacy, training, consultation, and seminars for individuals with autism and other developmental disabilities.

CAREER COUNSELING

ERIC Clearinghouse on Disabilities and Gifted Education

1920 Association Drive, Reston, VA 22091-1589 (800-328-0272; TDD: 703-264-9449; e-mail address: ericec@cec.sped.org; Internet Web site: http://www.cec.sped.org/ericec.htm). Provides educational information on assessment, intervention, and enrichment for gifted children and children with developmental disabilities.

Job Accommodation Network (JAN)

West Virginia University, 918 Chestnut Ridge Road, Suite 1, Post Office Box 6080, Morgantown, WV 26506-6080 (United States: 800-526-7234; 800-ADA-WORK; Canada: 800-526-2262; FAX: 304-293-5407; e-mail address: jan@jan.icdi.wvu.edu; Internet Web site: http://janweb.icdi.wvu.edu). Information and resources to make workplaces accessible to those with disabilities.

CEREBRAL PALSY

American Academy for Cerebral Palsy and Developmental Medicine

6300 North River Road, Suite 727, Rosemont, IL 60018 (708-698-1635; FAX: 708-823-0536). Multidisciplinary scientific society that fosters professional education, research, and interest in the problems associated with cerebral palsy.

United Cerebral Palsy Associations

1660 L Street, NW, Suite 700, Washington, DC 20036 (800-872-5827; Voice: 202-776-0406; TDD: 202-973-7197; FAX: 202-776-0414; Internet Web site: http://www.ucpa.org). Direct services to children and adults with cerebral palsy that include medical diagnosis, evaluation and treatment, special education, career development, counseling, social and recreational programs, and adapted housing.

CHILDREN'S SPECIALIZED HOSPITALS

While the majority of children with disabilities can receive services on an outpatient basis, short-term inpatient treatment is sometimes necessary. Some of the prominent hospitals offering pediatric rehabilitation facilities with both inpatient and outpatient units and programs include the following:

District of Columbia

Hospital for Sick Children, 1731 Bunker Hill Road, NE, Washington, DC 20017 (202-832-4400).

Illinois

LaRabida Children's Hospital and Research Center, East 65th Street at Lake Michigan, Chicago, IL 60649 (312-363-6700).

Maryland

Kennedy-Krieger Institute, 707 North Broadway, Baltimore, MD 21205 (410-550-9000).

Minnesota

Gillette Children's Hospital, 200 East University Avenue, St. Paul, MN 55101 (612-229-3838).

New Jersey

Children's Specialized Hospital, 150 New Providence Road, Mountainside, NJ 07092 (908-233-3720).

New York

Blythedale Children's Hospital, Bradhurst Avenue, Valhalla, NY 10595 (914-592-7555).

Ohio

Health Hill Hospital for Children, 2801 Martin Luther King Jr. Drive, Cleveland, OH 44104 (216-721-5400).

Pennsylvania

Children's Seashore House, 3405 Civic Center Boulevard, Philadelphia, PA 19104 (215-895-3600).

Texas

Texas Scottish Rite Hospital for Children, 2222 Welborn, Post Office Box 19567, Dallas, TX 75219 (214-559-5000).

CHRONIC ILLNESS

Candlelighters Childhood Cancer Foundation

7910 Woodmont Avenue, Suite 460, Bethesda, MD 20814 (301-657-8401; 800-366-2223; FAX: 301-718-2686). Provides support, information, and advocacy to families of children with cancer, adults who had childhood cancer, and professionals who work with them. Publishes newsletters, reports, and other publications. Provides network of support groups.

Families of Children Under Stress (FOCUS)

P.O. Box 941445, Atlanta, GA 31141 (770-270-5072). Publishes bimonthly newsletter for families of chronically or terminally ill children.

CLEFT LIP AND PALATE

AboutFace USA

Post Office Box 93, Limekiln, PA 19535 (800-225-FACE [3223]; FAX: 610-689-4479; e-mail address: abtface@aol.com). Provides information, emotional support, public education programs, and community awareness to individuals with facial differences and their families (also available AboutFace International, 99 Crowns Lane, 4th floor, Toronto, Ontario M5R 3P4, Canada [800-665-FACE (3223); FAX: 416-944-2488; e-mail address: aface@io.org]).

COMPUTERS

Center for Accessible Technology

2547 8th Street, 12-A, Berkeley, CA 94710 (510-841-3224; e-mail address: cforat@aol.com; Internet Web site: http://www.el.net/cat). A resource and demonstration center open to people with disabilities and their families as well as professionals and others interested in adaptive technology. Programs include seminars for parents and professionals, play groups for children, and adult assessment services. Small membership fee.

CYSTIC FIBROSIS

Cystic Fibrosis Foundation

6931 Arlington Road, Bethesda, MD 20814 (301-951-4422; 800-FIGHT CF [800-344-4823]; FAX: 301-951-6378; Internet Web site: http://www.cff.org). Provides referral for diagnostic services and medical care; offers professional and public information and supports research and professional training.

DOWN SYNDROME

Association for Children with Down Syndrome

2616 Martin Avenue, Bellmore, NY 11710 (516-221-4700; FAX: 516-221-5867). Information and referral services, including free publication list.

National Down Syndrome Congress (NDSC)

1605 Chantilly Drive, Suite 250, Atlanta, GA 30324 (800-232-6372; 404-633-1555; FAX: 404-633-2817; e-mail address: ndsc@charitiesusa.com; Internet Web site: http://www.carol.net/ndsc/). Provides information and referral materials and publishes a newsletter.

National Down Syndrome Society

666 Broadway, Suite 800, New York, NY 10012 (800-221-4602; 212-460-9330; FAX: 212-979-2873; Internet Web site: http://www.ndss.org). Provides information and publishes a newsletter and clinical care booklets.

EDUCATION

American Educational Research Association (AERA)

1230 17th Street, NW, Washington, DC 20036-3078 (202-223-9485; FAX: 202-775-1824). International professional organization with the goal of advancing educational research and its practical education. Members are educators, counselors, evaluators, graduate students, behavioral scientists, and directors or administrators of research, testing, or evaluation.

Association for Supervision and Curriculum Development (ASCD)

1250 North Pitt Street, Alexandria, VA 22314 (703-549-9110). Professional membership organization for educators with interest in instruction, curriculum, and supervision. Publishes journal, *Educational Leadership*.

Association on Higher Education and Disability (AHEAD)

Post Office Box 21192, Columbus, OH 43221 (Voice/TDD: 614-488-4972; FAX: 614-488-1174; e-mail address: ahead@postbox.acs.ohio-state.edu; Internet Web site: http://www.ahead.org). Professional organization committed to full participation in higher education for people with disabilities.

Council for Exceptional Children (CEC)

1920 Association Drive, Reston, VA 22091 (703-620-3660; FAX: 703-264-9494; e-mail address: cec@cec.sped.org; Internet Web site: http://www.cec.sped.org). Provides information to teachers, administrators, and others concerned with the education of gifted children and children with disabilities. Maintains a library and database on literature in special education; provides information and assistance on legislation.

National Association of Private Schools for Exceptional Children (NAPSEC)

1522 K Street, NW, Suite 1032, Washington, DC 20005 (202-408-3338; FAX: 202-408-3340; e-mail address: napsec@aol.com; Internet Web site: http://www.spedschools.com/napsec.html). A nonprofit association that represents more than 200 schools nationally and more than 600 at the state level through its Council of Affiliated State Associations, which provides special education and therapeutic services for both publicly and privately placed children. NAPSEC provides a free referral service to parents and professionals seeking an appropriate placement for a child with a disability and publishes a directory of member schools.

National Information Center for Educational Media (NICEM)

Post Office Box 8640, Albuquerque, NM 87198-8640 (800-926-8328, 505-265-3591; FAX: 505-256-1080; e-mail address: nicem@nicem.com; Internet Web site: http://www.nicem.com). Provides database of educational audio-visual materials, including video, motion pictures, filmstrips, audiotapes, and slides.

EPILEPSY

Epilepsy Foundation of America

4351 Garden City Drive, Suite 406, Landover, MD 20785-2267 (800-332-1000; TDD: 800-332-2070; 301-459-3700; FAX: 301-577-4941; e-mail address: postmaster@efa.org; Internet Web site: http://www.efa.org). Provides programs of information and education, advocacy, support of research, and the delivery of needed services to people with epilepsy and their families.

EQUIPMENT

ABLEDATA

8455 Colesville Road, Suite 935, Silver Spring, MD 20910 (800-227-0216; 301-588-9285; Internet Web site: http://www. abledata.com). National database of information on assistive technology and rehabilitation equipment.

Independent Living Aids, Inc.

27 East Mall, Plainview, NY 11803 (516-752-8080; FAX: 516-752-3135). Provides, at a cost, aids that make daily tasks easier for those with physical disabilities; also carries clocks, calculators, magnifying lamps, and easy-to-see low vision and talking watches for those with visual problems. Will send free catalog.

PAM Assistance Centre

1023 South U.S. Route 27, St. Johns, MI 48879 (800-274-7426; FAX: 517-224-0957). Provides free information on low-tech devices and equipment available for individuals with disabilities.

RESNA (Association for Advancement of Rehabilitation Technology)

1101 Connecticut Avenue, NW, Suite 700, Washington, DC 20036 (202-857-1199). Multidisciplinary organization of professionals interested in the identification, development, and delivery of technology to people with disabilities. Offers numerous publications.

FEDERAL

National Information Center for Children and Youth with Disabilities (NICHCY)

Post Office Box 1492, Washington, DC 20013 (Voice/TDD: 800-695-0285; 202-884-8200; FAX: 202-884-8441; e-mail address: nichcy@aed.org; Internet Web site: http://www.aed.org/nichcy). Provides information to assist parents, educators, caregivers, advocates, and others in helping children and youth with disabilities become participating members of the community. Services include personal responses to specific questions, referrals to other organizations or sources of help, prepared information packets, and publications on current issues.

Office of Special Education and Rehabilitative Services (OSERS)

Communication and Information Services, U.S. Department of Education, 330 C Street, SW, Room 3132, Washington, DC 20202-2524 (202-205-8241; FAX: 202-401-2608). Responds to inquiries and researches and documents information operations serving the field of disabilities. Specializes in providing information in the areas of federal funding for programs serving people with disabilities, federal legislation affecting individuals with disabilities, and federal programs benefiting people with disabilities.

President's Committee on Employment of People with Disabilities

1331 F Street, NW, Washington, DC 20004-1107 (202-376-6200; TDD: 202-376-6205; FAX: 202-376-6219). One of the oldest presidential committees in the United States. Promotes acceptance of people with physical and mental disabilities in the world of work, both the public and the private sectors. Promotes the elimination of barriers, both physical and attitudinal, to the employment of people with disabilities.

FRAGILE X SYNDROME

National Fragile X Foundation

1441 York Street, Suite 303, Denver, CO 80206 (800-688-8765; 303-333-6155; FAX: 303-333-4369; e-mail address: natfragx@ix.netcom.com; Internet Web site: http://www.fragilex.org). Promotes education concerning diagnosis, treatment, and research in fragile X syndrome and provides referral to local resource centers. Sponsors a biannual conference. Offers extensive audiovisual and teaching aids.

GAUCHER DISEASE

National Gaucher Foundation

11140 Rockville Pike, Suite 350, Rockville, MD 20852 (800-925-8885; 301-816-1515; e-mail address: sadamsngf@aol.com; Internet Web site: http:q.continuum.net/wrosen.gaucher.html). Publishes quarterly newsletter, operates support groups and chapters, provides referrals to organizations for appropriate services, and funds research on Gaucher disease.

GENERAL

ACCENT on Information

Post Office Box 700, Bloomington, IL 61702 (309-378-2961; FAX: 309-378-4420; e-mail address: acntivng@aol.com). Computerized retrieval system that has information on a variety of topics, including employment, aids for independent living, laws and legislation, special education, home management, housing and architectural barriers, and special facilities. Publishes *ACCENT on Living* magazine and *ACCENT Special Publications,* a series of books with answers, how-to tips, instructions, and ideas on specific topics.

American Academy of Pediatrics

141 Northwest Point Boulevard, Post Office Box 927, Elk Grove Village, IL 60009-0927 (847-228-5005; FAX: 847-228-5097; e-mail address: kidsdocs@aap.org; Internet Web site: http://www.aap.org). Professional membership association for board-certified pediatricians that offers professional continuing education, health education materials, and other programs.

American Association for the Advancement of Science, Project on Science, Technology, and Disability

1200 New York Avenue, NW, Washington, DC 20005 (Voice/TDD: 202-326-6672; FAX: 202-371-9849; e-mail address: vstern@aaas.org). Primarily an information center that seeks to increase the number of people with disabilities entering and advancing in science, mathematics, and engineering fields. Links people with disabilities, their families, professors, teachers, and counselors to scientists, mathematicians, and engineers with disabilities who can share coping strategies. Addresses accessibility, technology, and education issues in the sciences.

American Association of University Affiliated Programs for Persons with Developmental Disabilities

8630 Fenton Street, Suite 410, Silver Spring, MD 20910 (301-588-8252; FAX: 301-588-2842). Represents the professional interests of the national network of 51 University Affiliated Facilities (UAFs) that serve people with developmental disabilities.

Avenues

Post Office Box 5192, Sonora, CA 95370 (209-928-3688; e-mail address: avenues@sonnet.com; Internet Web site: http://www.sonnet.com/avenues). Publishes a semiannual newsletter that provides lists of parents, physicians, and experienced medical centers that are concerned with people with disabilities.

Barnes & Noble/B. Dalton Bookseller

(see local yellow pages under "bookstores, retail") Provides a "Children with Special Needs" collection of useful books for families with children with disabilities in the "Family and Child Care" section of their stores.

Center on Human Policy

Syracuse University, 805 South Crouse Avenue, Syracuse, NY 13244-2280 (315- 443-3851; FAX: 315-443-4338; e-mail address: thechp@sued.syr.edu; Internet Web site: http://soeweb.syr.edu/thechp/). Involved in a range of local, state, national, and international activities including policy studies, research, information and referral.

Coalition on Sexuality, Inc.

122 East 23rd Street, New York, NY 10010-4516 (212-243-3900 [answering service; staff member will return call]). Committed to assisting people with disabilities to achieve full integration into society with confidence in their sexuality. Offers seminars and workshops on sexuality and disability; advocates for individuals with disabilities.

FEDCAP Rehabilitation Services, Inc.

211 West 14th Street, New York, NY 10011 (212-727-4200; TDD: 212-727-4384; FAX: 212-727-4374). Services include vocational training and job placement for adults with severe disabilities and/or other disadvantages.

March of Dimes National Birth Defects Foundation

1275 Mamaroneck Avenue, White Plains, NY 10605 (914- 428-7100; FAX: 914-428-8203; e-mail address: resourcecenter@modimes.org; Internet Web site: http://www.modimes.org). Awards grants to institutions and organizations for development of genetic services, perinatal care in high-risk pregnancies, prevention of premature delivery, parent support groups, and other community programs. Campaign for Healthier Babies distributes information about birth defects and related newborn health problems. Spanish-language materials are available.

National Association of Developmental Disabilities Councils

1234 Massachusetts Avenue, NW, Suite 103, Washington, DC 20005 (202-347-1234; FAX: 202-347-4023; e-mail address: naddc@igc.apc.org; Internet Web site: http://www.igc.apc.org/naddc). Organization of Developmental Disability Councils that exist in each state to provide information on and advocate for resources and services for people with developmental disabilities and their families.

National Center for Education in Maternal and Child Health

2000 15th Street North, Suite 701, Arlington, VA 22201-2617 (703-524-7802; FAX: 703-524-9335; e-mail address: ncemch01@gumedlib.dml.georgetown.edu; Internet Web site: www.ncemch.georgetown.edu). Disseminates publications and fact sheets to the public and professionals in the field; develops and maintains database of topics, agencies, and organizations related to maternal and child health.

National Council on Independent Living

2111 Wilson Boulevard, Suite 405, Arlington, VA 22201 (703-525-3406; TTY: 703-525-3407; FAX: 703-525-3409; e-mail address: ncil@tsbbs02.tnet.com). A national membership association of nonprofit corporations that advances the full integration and participation of people with disabilities in society and the development of centers for independent living. Provides members with technical assistance and training, a quarterly newsletter, and sponsors a national conference.

National Easter Seal Society

230 West Monroe Street, Suite 1800, Chicago, IL 60606 (312-726-6200; TDD: 312-726-4258; 800-221-6827). Nonprofit, community-based health agency dedicated to increasing the independence of people with disabilities. Offers a range of quality services, research, and programs. Serves more than a million people each year through a nationwide network of 170 affiliates.

National Organization on Disability

910 16th Street, NW, Suite 600, Washington, DC 20006 (202-293-5960; FAX: 202-293-7999; TDD: 202-293-5968; Internet Web site: www.nod.org). Promotes the acceptance and understanding of the needs of citizens with disabilities through a national network of communities and organizations; facilitates exchange of information regarding resources available to persons with disabilities.

National Organization for Rare Disorders, Inc. (NORD)

100 Route 37, Post Office Box 8923, New Fairfield, CT 06812-8923 (800-999-NORD; 203-746-6518; FAX: 203-746-6481; TDD: 203-746-6972; e-mail address: orphan@nord-rdb.com; Internet Web site: http://www.nord-rdb.com/orphan). Clearinghouse for information about rare disorders (e.g., inborn errors of metabolism); encourages and promotes research; represents people with rare diseases who are not otherwise represented; educates the public and the medical profession about these diseases.

Society for Developmental and Behavioral Pediatrics

19 Station Lane, Philadelphia, PA 19118 (215-248-9168; FAX: 215-248-1981; e-mail address: nmspota@aol.com). Interdisciplinary organization that promotes research and teaching in developmental and behavioral pediatrics. Sponsors the *Journal of Developmental and Behavioral Pediatrics* and conducts annual scientific meetings.

Society for Developmental Pediatrics

Post Office Box 23836, Baltimore, MD 21203 (410-550-9446; 410-550-9420). Provides list of pediatricians who specialize in evaluation and treatment of children with disabilities. Sponsors the scientific journal *Mental Retardation and Developmental Disabilities Research Reviews.*

GENETICS

Genetics Society of America and American Society of Human Genetics

15501-B Monona Drive, Derwood, MD 20855 (301-571-1825; Internet Web site: www./faseb.orggenetics/gsa/gsa.int.htm). Professional organization that aims to bring together genetic investigators and provide a forum for sharing research findings. Publishes journal, *The American Journal of Human Genetics*, and other resources.

National Tay-Sachs and Allied Diseases Association

2001 Beacon Street, Suite 204, Brookline, MA, 02146 (617-277-4463; FAX: 617-277-0134; e-mail address: ntsadboston@worldnet.att.net). Promotes genetic screening programs nationally; has updated listing of Tay-Sachs prevention centers in a number of countries; provides educational literature to general public and professionals; and peer group support for parents.

HEARING, SPEECH, AND LANGUAGE

ADARA (formerly American Deafness and Rehabilitation Association)

Post Office Box 251554, Little Rock, AR 72225 (Voice/TTY: 501-868-8850; FAX: 501-868-8812). Serves deaf professionals and people interested in deafness. Publishes a journal and newsletter by subscription; offers memberships.

Alexander Graham Bell Association for the Deaf

3417 Volta Place, NW, Washington, DC 20007 (Voice/TTY: 202-337-5220; FAX: 202-337-8314; e-mail address: agbell2@aol.com; Internet Web site: http://www.agbell.org). Umbrella organization for International Organization for the Education of the Hearing Impaired (IOEHI), Parents' Section (PS), and Oral Hearing Impaired Section. Provides general information and information on resources. Encourages improved communication, better public understanding, and detection of early hearing loss. Works for better educational opportunities; provides scholarships and training for teachers.

American Society for Deaf Children

2848 Arden Way, Suite 210, Sacramento, CA 95825 (V/TTY: 800-942-2732, 916-482-0210; FAX: 916-482-0121; e-mail address: asdc1@aol.com). Provides information and support to parents and families with children who are deaf or who have hearing impairment.

American Speech-Language-Hearing Association (ASHA)

10801 Rockville Pike, Rockville, MD 20852 (Voice/TDD: 301-897-5700; 800-638-8255; FAX: 301-897-7348). Professional and scientific organization; certifying body for professionals providing speech, language, and hearing therapy; conducts research in communication disorders; publishes several journals; provides consumer information and professional referral.

Captioned Films/Videos

1447 East Main Street, Spartanburg, SC 29307 (800-237-6213; TTY: 800-237-6819; FAX: 800-538-5636; e-mail address: nadcfv@aol.com). Government-sponsored distribution of open-captioned materials to eligible institutions, individuals, and families. Application sent upon request.

Deafness Research Foundation

15 West 39th Street, New York, NY 10018-3806 (212-768-1181; FAX: 212-768-1782; e-mail address: drf1@village.ios.com). Solicits funds for the support of research into the causes, treatment, and prevention of deafness and other hearing disorders.

Deafpride

Gallaudet University, 800 Florida Avenue, NE, Washington, DC 20002 (Voice/TTY: 202-675-6700; FAX: 202-547-0547). Information gathering and distribution and advocacy programs for the rights of deaf people. Also offers community-based services for the deaf involving AIDS awareness, substance abuse issues, maternal and child health issues, and sign language classes.

Hearing Aid Helpline

20361 Middlebelt Road, Livonia, MI 48152 (U.S. and Canada: 800-521-5247; FAX: 810-478-4520). Information on how to proceed when hearing loss is suspected; free consumer kit, facts about hearing aids, and a variety of literature on hearing-related subjects is available.

National Center for Stuttering, Inc.

200 East 33rd Street, New York, NY 10016 (800-221-2483; 212-532-1460; e-mail address: executive-director@stuttering.com; Internet Web site: http://www.stuttering.com). Provides free information for parents of young children just starting to show symptoms of stuttering; runs training programs for speech professionals in current therapeutic approaches; provides treatment for people over 7 years of age who stutter.

National Information Center on Deafness

Gallaudet University, 800 Florida Avenue, NE, Washington, DC 20002-3695 (202-651-5051; TDD: 202-651-5052; FAX: 202-651-5054; e-mail address: nicd@gallux-gallaudet.edu; Internet Web site: http://www.gallaudet.edu/~nicd). Provides information related to deafness; has a multitude of resources and experts available for individuals with hearing impairment, their families, and professionals. Collects information about resources around the country.

Self Help for Hard of Hearing People (SHHH)

7910 Woodmont Avenue, Suite 1200, Bethesda, MD 20814 (301-657-2248; TTY: 301-657-2249; FAX: 301-913-9413; e-mail address: 71162.634@compuserve.com; Internet Web site: http://ourworld.compuserve.com/homepages/shhh). Educational organization that provides assistance to those who are committed to participating fully in society. Publishes journal, newsletter, and other materials; provides advocacy and outreach programs and extensive network of local chapters and self-help groups; and hosts an annual convention.

Signing Exact English (SEE) Center for the Advancement of Deaf Children

Post Office Box 1181, Los Alamitos, CA 90720 (Voice/TTY: 310-430-1467; FAX: 310-795-6614). Information and referral services for parents of newly diagnosed children.

LEARNING DISABILITIES

Dyslexia Research Institute

4745 Centerville Road, Tallahassee, FL 32308 (904-893-2216; FAX: 904-893-2440). Provides training, workshops, and seminars for professionals. Literature sent on request.

Learning Disabilities Association of America

4156 Library Road, Pittsburgh, PA 15234 (412-341-1515; FAX: 412-344-0224; e-mail address: /danat/@ usaor.net; Internet Web site: http://www./danat/.org). Encourages research and the development of early detection programs, disseminates information, serves as an advocate, and works to improve education for individuals with learning disabilities.

National Center for Learning Disabilities (NCLD)

381 Park Avenue, South, Suite 1420, New York, NY 10016 (212-545-7510; 212-687-7211; FAX: 212-545-9665). Promotes public awareness of learning disabilities; provides computerized information and referral services to consumers and professionals on learning disabilities. Publishes *Their World,* an annual magazine for parents and professionals.

The Orton Dyslexia Society

8600 LaSalle Road, Chester Building Suite 382, Baltimore, MD 21286-2044 (800-222-3123; FAX: 410-321-5069; 410-296-0232; e-mail address: info@ods.org; Internet Web site: http://ods.org). Devoted to the study and treatment of dyslexia; provides information and referrals, sponsors conferences, seminars and support groups; has two regular publications and 45 branches in the United States and abroad.

LEGAL

American Bar Association Center on Children and the Law

740 15th Street, NW, 9th floor, Washington, DC 20061 (202-662-1720; FAX: 202-662-1032). Offers information and advocacy to professionals and parents of children and adolescents with disabilities.

American Civil Liberties Union (ACLU)

132 West 43rd Street, New York, NY 10036 (212-944-9800; 212-302-7035; FAX: 212-921-7916). Nationwide test-case litigation program designed to protect and expand the statutory and constitutional rights of children, in particular those in foster care.

Children's Defense Fund

25 E Street, NW, Washington, DC 20001 (800-233-1200; 202-628-8787; FAX: 202-662-3510; e-mail address: mlallen@childrensdefense.org; Internet Web site: http://www.tmm.com/cdf/index.html). Provides information about legislation in health care, child welfare, and special education. Publishes a guide for parents and advocates for the rights of the Education for All Handicapped Children Act of 1975, PL 94-142.

Disabilities Rights Education and Defense Fund (DREDF)

2212 Sixth Street, Berkeley, CA 94710 (Voice/TDD: 510-644-2555; FAX: 510-841-8645; e-mail address: dlipton@dredf.org; Internet Web site: DREDFCA@aol.com). Law and policy center to protect the rights of people with disabilities. Referral and information regarding rights of people with disabilities is offered. This organization educates legislators and policymakers about issues affecting the rights of people with disabilities and also educates the public about the Americans with Disabilities Act of 1990, PL 101-336.

Judge David L. Bazelon Center for Mental Health Law

1101 15th Street, NW, Suite 1212, Washington, DC 20017 (202-467-5730; TDD: 202-467-4342; FAX: 202-223-0409; e-mail address: hn1660@handsnet.org; Internet Web site: http://www.bazelon.org). Legal advocacy program that works to define, establish, and protect the rights of children and adults with mental disabilities, using test-case litigation, federal policy advocacy, and training and technical assistance for legal services lawyers and other advocates nationwide.

MENTAL RETARDATION

American Association on Mental Retardation (AAMR)

444 North Capitol Street, NW, Suite 846, Washington, DC 20001 (202-387-1968; FAX: 202-387-2193; e-mail address: aamr@access.digex.net; Internet Web site: http://www.aamr.org). Professional organization that promotes cooperation among those involved in services, training, and research in mental retardation. Encourages research, dissemination of information, development of appropriate community-based services, and the promotion of preventive measures designed to further reduce the incidence of mental retardation.

President's Committee on Mental Retardation

Room 352G, 200 Independence Avenue, SW, Washington, DC 20201 (202-619-0634; FAX: 202-205-9519). Advises the president and secretary of Health and Human Services on all matters pertaining to mental retardation; publishes annual reports and information on the rights of people with mental retardation.

The Arc (formerly Association for Retarded Citizens of the United States)

500 East Border Street, 3rd floor, Arlington, TX 76010 (817-261-6003; TDD: 817-277-0553; FAX: 817-277-3491; e-mail address: thearc@metronet.com; Internet Web site: http://thearc.org/welcome.html). National advocacy organization working on behalf of individuals with mental retardation and their families; has 1,100 state and local chapters.

MUSCULAR DYSTROPHY

Muscular Dystrophy Association

3300 East Sunrise Drive, Tucson, AZ 85718 (520-529-2000; FAX: 520-529-5300; e-mail address: 74431.2513@compuserv.com; Internet Web site: http://www.mdausa.org). Voluntary health care agency that fosters research and provides direct services to individuals with muscular dystrophy; concerned with conquering muscular dystrophy and other neuromuscular diseases.

NEUROFIBROMATOSIS

The National Neurofibromatosis Foundation, Inc.

95 Pine Street, 16th floor, New York, NY 10005 (800-323-7938; 212-344-6633; FAX: 212-747-0004; e-mail address: NNFF@aol.com; Internet Web site: http://www.nf.org). Supplies information to laypeople and professionals; offers genetic counseling and support groups throughout the United States.

OCCUPATIONAL THERAPY

American Occupational Therapy Association, Inc.

4720 Montgomery Lane, Post Office Box 31220, Bethesda, MD 20824 (301-652-2682; FAX: 301-652-7711). Professional organization of occupational therapists; provides services including accreditation of educational programs, professional publications, public education, and continuing education for practitioners.

PARENTS AND FAMILIES

Beach Center on Families and Disability

3111 Haworth Hall, University of Kansas, Lawrence, KS 66045 (913-864-7600). Research and training center that disseminates information about families with members who have developmental disabilities. Publishes newsletter and offers many other publications.

The Compassionate Friends

Post Office Box 3696, Oak Brook, IL 60522-3696 (630-990-0010; FAX: 630-990-0246; e-mail address: TZHT72A@prodigy.com; Internet Web site: http://pages.prodigy.com/CA/1ycq97a/1ycq97tcf.html). National and worldwide organization that supports and aids parents in the positive resolution of the grief experienced upon the death of their child; fosters the physical and emotional health of bereaved parents and siblings.

Exceptional Parent

Post Office Box 3000, Department EP, Denville, NJ 07834 (800-247-8080). This magazine, published since 1971, provides straightforward, practical information for families and professionals involved in the care of children and young adults with disabilities; many articles are written by parents.

Federation for Children with Special Needs

95 Berkeley Street, Suite 104, Boston, MA 02116 (Voice/TTY: 617-482-2915; in MA Voice/TTY: 800-331-0688; FAX: 617-695-2939; e-mail address: kidinfo@fcsn.org; Internet Web site: http://www.fcsn.org). Offers parent-to-parent training and information; projects include Technical Assistance for Parent Programs (TAPP), Collaboration Among Parents and Health Professionals (CAPP), Parents Engaged in Educational Reform (PEER), and National Early Childhood Technical Assistance System (NEC*TAS).

National Parent Network on Disabilities (NPND)

1600 Prince Street, Suite 115, Alexandria, VA 22314 (703-684-NPND [6763]; Voice/TDD: 703-684-6763; FAX: 703-836-1232; e-mail address: npnd@cs.com). Coalition of parent organizations and parents that works to influence policy issues concerning the needs of people with disabilities and their families.

PACER Center, Inc. (Parent Advocacy Coalition for Educational Rights)

4826 Chicago Avenue, S, Minneapolis, MN 55417-1098 (Voice/TDD: 612-827-2966; FAX: 612-827-3065; 800-848-4912). Provides education and training to help parents understand the special education laws and to obtain appropriate school programs for their children. Workshops and program topics include early intervention, emotional disabilities, and health/medical services. Also provides disability awareness puppet program for schools, child abuse prevention program services, newsletters, booklets, extensive written materials, videos.

Parent Educational Advocacy Training Center

10340 Democracy Lane, Fairfax, VA 22030 (Voice/TTY: 703-691-7826; FAX: 703-691-8148). Professionally staffed organization that helps parents to become effective advocates for their children with school personnel and the educational system.

Parent to Parent

c/o Betsy Santelli, Beach Center on Families and Disability, University of Kansas, Institute for Life Span Studies, 3111 Haworth Hall, Lawrence, KS 66045 (913-864-7606). State and local chapters that provide one-to-one, parent-to-parent support by matching trained parents to newly referred parents on the basis of their children's disabilities and/or family issues they are encountering or have encountered.

Team Advocates for Special Kids (TASK)

100 West Cerritos Avenue, Anaheim CA 92805 (714-533-TASK; FAX: 714-533-2533; e-mail address: taskca@aol.com). Provides services to enable children with disabilities to reach their maximum potential. Offers training, education, support, information, resources, and community awareness programs to families of children with disabilities and the professionals who serve them. A member of the Alliance for Technology Access (ATN), TASK's Tech Center conducts one-to-one guided exploration of technology to determine appropriate adapted hardware and software for persons with disabilities. Conducts an advocacy training course and other workshops; publishes a bimonthly newsletter.

PHYSICAL THERAPY

American Physical Therapy Association

1111 North Fairfax Street, Alexandria, VA 22314 (information services: 800-999-2782, ext. 3210; FAX: 703-684-7343; Internet Web site: www.apta.org). Professional membership association of physical therapists, physical therapist assistants, and physical therapy students. Operates clearinghouse for questions on physical therapy and disabilities. Publishes bibliographies on a range of topics.

RECREATION AND SPORTS

American Alliance for Health, Physical Education, Recreation and Dance (AAHPERD)

1900 Association Drive, Reston, VA 22091 (703-476-3400). National organization supporting and assisting individuals involved in physical education, recreation, dance, and health, leisure, fitness, and education. An alliance of six national associations, AAHPERD offers numerous publications.

American Association for Active Lifestyles and Fitness

1900 Association Drive, Reston, VA 20191 (703-476-3400; FAX: 703-476-9527; e-mail address: aaalf@aahperd.org; Internet Web site: http://www.aahperd.org/aalf.html). Association of professionals in physical education, sports and athletics, health and safety education, recreation and leisure, and dance. Supports and disseminates research, promotes better public understanding of these professions, and supports and provides opportunities for professional growth to members.

Boy Scouts of America, Scouting for the Handicapped Division

1325 Walnut Hill Lane, Post Office Box 152079, Irving, TX 75015 (214-580-2000; FAX: 214-580-2502). Provides educational, recreational, and therapeutic resource programs through the Boy Scouts of America.

Disabled Sports USA (DS/USA)

451 Hungerford Drive, Suite 100, Rockville, MD 20850 (301-217-0960; TDD: 301-217-0693; FAX: 301-217-0968; e-mail address: dsusa@dsusa.org; Internet Web site: http://www.dsusa.org/~dsusa/dsusa.html). DS/USA offers summer programs and competitions, fitness programs, "fitness is for everyone" videotapes, and winter ski programs. Local chapters offer activities including: camping, hiking, biking, horseback riding, 10-K runs, water skiing, white water rafting, rope courses, mountain climbing, sailing, yachting, canoeing, kayaking, aerobic fit-

ness, and snow skiing. Provides year-round sports and recreational opportunities to people with orthopedic, spinal cord, neuromuscular, and visual impairments through a national network of local chapters.

Girl Scouts of the U.S.A.

420 5th Avenue, New York, NY 10018 (212-852-8000; FAX: 212-852-6515; http://www.gsusa.org). Open to all girls ages 5-17 (or kindergarten-grade 12). Runs camping programs, sports and recreational activities, and service programs. Incorporates children with disabilities into general Girl Scout troop activities.

Special Olympics International

1325 G Street, NW, Suite 500, Washington, DC 20005-3104 (202-628-3630; FAX: 202-824-0200; e-mail address: specialolympics@msn.com; Internet Web site: http://www.specialolympics.org). Largest organization to provide year-round sports training and athletic competition for children and adults with mental retardation; sanctioned by the U.S. Olympic Committee. Local, state, and national games are held throughout the United States and in over 140 countries.

Very Special Arts

1300 Connecticut Avenue, NW, Washington, DC 20036 (202-628-0800; FAX: 202-737-0725). Nonprofit gallery that represents artists with disabilities.

Wheelchair Sports, USA

3595 East Fountain Blvd., Suite L1, Colorado Springs, CO 80910-1740 (719-574-1150; FAX: 719-574-9840; e-mail address: wsusa@aol.com). Governing body of various sports of wheelchair athletics including swimming, archery, weightlifting, track and field, table tennis, and air weapons. Publishes a newsletter.

REHABILITATION

National Institute on Disability and Rehabilitation Research (NIDRR)

Office of Special Education and Rehabilitative Services, U.S. Department of Education, 200 Independence Avenue, SW, Washington, DC 20202 (Internet Web site: http://www.ed.gov/offices/OSERS/NIDRR/nidrr.htm/).

National Rehabilitation Information Center (NARIC)

8455 Colesville Road, Suite 935, Silver Spring, MD 20910 (800-346-2742; 301-588-9285; TYY: 301-495-5626; FAX: 301-587-1967). Rehabilitation information service and research library; provides quick-reference and referral, bibliographic searches, and photocopies of documents. Publishes several directories and resource guides.

RETT SYNDROME

International Rett Syndrome Association

9121 Piscataway Road, Suite 2B, Clinton, MD 20735 (800-818-RETT; 301-856-3334; FAX: 301-856-3336; e-mail address: irsa@paltech.com; Internet Web site: http://www2.paltech.com/irsa/irsa.h). Provides information and referral, support to families, and acts as a liaison with professionals. Also facilitates research on Rett syndrome.

SCOLIOSIS

National Scoliosis Foundation, Inc.

5 Cabot Place, Stoughton, MA 02072 (617-341-6333; FAX: 617-341-8333; e-mail address: scoliosis@aol.com). Nonprofit organization with state chapters dedicated to informing the public about scoliosis, promoting early detection and treatment of scoliosis. Publishes newsletter called *Spinal Connection.*

Scoliosis Research Society

6300 North River Road, Suite 727, Rosemont, IL 60018-4226 (847-698-1627; FAX: 847-823-0536). Sponsors and promotes research on the etiology and treatment of scoliosis and spinal disorders.

SEVERE/MULTIPLE DISABILITIES

Helen Keller National Center for Deaf-Blind Youths and Adults

111 Middle Neck Road, Sands Point, NY 11050 (516-944-8900; TDD: 516-944-8637). Has specialists at its New York training center as well as representatives in 10 regional offices who can assist with locating assistive/adaptive devices. Also offers technical assistance to local agencies that are serving deaf-blind individuals.

The Association for Persons with Severe Handicaps (TASH)

29 West Susquehanna Avenue, Suite 210, Baltimore, MD 21204 (410-828-8274; TDD: 410-828-1306; FAX: 410-828-6706; e-mail address: info@tash.org; Internet Web site: http://www.tash.org). Advocates inclusive education and community opportunities for people with disabilities, disseminates research findings and practical applications for education and community living, encourages sharing of experience and expertise. Publishes a newsletter and journal.

SIBLINGS

Sibling Information Network

The A.J. Pappanikou Center, 249 Glenbrook Road, U-64, Storrs, CT 06269-2064 (860-486-4985; e-mail address: speadm01.uconnvm.uconn.edu). Assists individuals and professionals interested in serving the needs of families of individuals with disabilities; disseminates bibliographic material and directories; places people in touch with each other; publishes a newsletter written for and by siblings and parents.

The Sibling Support Project

Children's Hospital and Medical Center, Post Office Box 5371, CL-09, Seattle, WA 98105-0371 (206-368-4911; FAX: 206-368-4816; e-mail address: dmeyer@chmc.org; Internet Web site: http://www.chmc.org/department/sibsupp). National program dedicated to the interests of brothers and sisters of people with special health and developmental needs. The Project's primary goal is to increase the availability of peer support and education programs for such siblings.

SICKLE CELL DISEASE

Howard University Center for Sickle Cell Disease

2121 Georgia Avenue, NW, Washington, DC 20059 (202-806-7930; FAX: 202-806-4517). Screening and counseling for sickle cell disease; provides services to both adults and children, including medical treatment and psychosocial intervention.

Sickle Cell Association of America

200 Corporate Point, Suite 495, Culver City, CA 90230-7633 (310-216-6363; 800-421-8453; FAX: 310-215-3722). Provides education, screening, genetic counseling, technical assistance, tutorial services, vocational rehabilitation, and research support in the United States and Canada.

SPINA BIFIDA

Spina Bifida Association of America

4590 MacArthur Blvd., NW, Suite 250, Washington, DC 20007-4226 (800-621-3141; 202-944-3285; FAX: 202-944-3295; e-mail address: spinabifida@aol.com; Internet Web site: http://www.infohiway.com/spinabifida). Provides information and referral for new parents and literature on spina bifida; supports a public awareness program; advocates for individuals with spina bifida and their families; supports research; conducts conferences for parents and professionals.

SYNDROMES

There are many support organizations and networks for children with various syndromes and their families. A representative sample is listed here (for a more complete listing, contact NORD [800-999-NORD]).

Arnold-Chiari Family Network

c/o Kevin and Maureen Walsh, 67 Spring Street, Weymouth, MA 02188 (617-337-2368). Informal family support network for those with Chiari I and Chiari II malformations. Literature and occasional newsletter provided upon request.

Cornelia de Lange Syndrome Foundation, Inc.

60 Dyer Avenue, Collinsville, CT 06022 (860-693-0159; FAX: 860-693-6819; Internet Web site: http://cdlsoutreach.org). Supports parents and children affected by Cornelia de Lange syndrome, encourages research, and disseminates information to increase public awareness through a newsletter and informational pamphlet.

The 5p-Society (Cri du chat syndrome)

11609 Oakmount, Overland Park, KS 66210 (913-469-8900; FAX: 913-469-5246; e-mail address: fivepminus@aol.com). Family support and information group for parents, grandparents, and guardians. Publishes a newsletter and sponsors an annual meeting.

Guillain-Barré Syndrome Foundation, International

Post Office Box 262, Wynnewood, PA 19096 (610-667-0131; FAX: 610-667-7036; e-mail address: gbint@ix.netcom.com; Internet Web site: http://www.webmast.com/gbs/). Provides emotional support to individuals with Guillain-Barré syndrome and their families; fosters research; educates the public about the disorder; develops nationwide support groups; and directs people with this syndrome to resources, meetings, newsletters, and symposia.

Little People of America, Inc.

Post Office Box 9897, Washington, DC 20016 (888-LPA-2001). Nationwide, voluntary organization dedicated to helping people of short stature. Provides fellowship, moral support, and information to "little people," those individuals with dwarfism. An 888 helpline provides information on organizations, products and services, and local doctors to callers.

Osteogenesis Imperfecta Foundation, Inc.

804 West Diamond Avenue, Suite 210, Gaithersburg, MD 20878 (800-981-2663; FAX: 301-947-0456; e-mail address: Bonelink@aol.com; Internet Web site: http://users.aol.com/bonelink). Supports research on osteogenesis imperfecta and provides information to those with this disorder, their families, and other interested people.

Prader-Willi Syndrome Association

2510 South Brentwood Boulevard, Suite 220, St. Louis, MO 63144 (800-926-4797; FAX: 314-962-7869; e-mail address: pwsausa@aol.com; Internet Web site: http://www.alhenet.net/~pwsausa/index.html). National organization that serves as a clearinghouse for information on Prader-Willi syndrome; shares information with parents, professionals, and other interested people.

Support Organization for Trisomy 18, 13, and Related Disorders (SOFT)

2982 South Union Street, Rochester, NY 14624 (800-716-7638; 716-594-4621; e-mail address: barbsoft @aol.com; Internet Web site: http://www.trisomy.org). Chapters in most states provide support and family packages with a newsletter and appropriate literature underscoring the common problems for children with trisomy 13 and trisomy 18. Holds yearly conference for families and professionals.

Tourette Syndrome Association

42-40 Bell Boulevard, Bayside, NY 11361 (212-224-2999; FAX: 718-279-9596; e-mail address: Tourette@ix. netcom.com; Internet Web site: http://neuro.www2.mgh.harvard.edu/tsa/tsamain/nclk). Offers information, referral, advocacy, education, research, and self-help groups to those affected by Tourette syndrome.

Treacher Collins Foundation

Post Office Box 683, Norwich, VT 05055 (800-823-2055; 802-649-3050). Resource and referral for families, individuals, and professionals who are interested in developing and sharing knowledge and experience about Treacher Collins syndrome and related disorders. Newsletter is published, and print and video resources are available by loan.

TRAUMATIC BRAIN INJURY

Brain Injury Association (formerly National Head Injury Foundation)

1776 Massachusetts Avenue, NW, Suite 100, Washington, DC 20036-1904 (Helpline: 800-444-6443; 202-296-6443; FAX: 202-296-8850). Provides information to educate the public, politicians, businesses, and schools about brain injury, including effects, causes, and prevention.

TUBEROUS SCLEROSIS

National Tuberous Sclerosis Association

8181 Professional Place, Suite 110, Landover, MD 20785 (800-225-NTSA; 301-459-9888; FAX: 301-459-0394; e-mail address: ntsa@aol.com; Internet Web site: http://www.title14.com/ntsa/index.html). Offers public information about manifestations of the disease to newly diagnosed individuals, their families, and interested professionals. Referrals are made to support groups located in most states. Funds research through membership fees and donations.

UREA CYCLE DISORDERS

National Urea Cycle Disorders Foundation

Post Office Box 32, Sayreville, NJ 08872 (800-275-2285; Internet Web site: http://www.execpc.com/ fenders/nucdf.html). Provides information and support for families. Supports and stimulates medical research and increased awareness by the public and the legislators of issues related to urea cycle disorders.

VISION

American Foundation for the Blind, Inc.

11 Penn Plaza, Suite 300, New York, NY 10011 (212-502-7600; FAX: 212-501-7774; e-mail address: newyork@afb.org; Internet Web site: http://www.afb.org). Works in cooperation with other agencies, organizations, and schools to offer services to blind people and those with visual impairments; provides consultation, public education, referrals, and information; produces and distributes talking books; publishes and sells materials for the blindness field.

American Printing House for the Blind (APH)

Post Office Box 6085, Louisville, KY 40206-0085 (502-895-2405; FAX: 502-895-1509; e-mail address: info@aph.org; Internet Web site: http://www.aph.org). Nonprofit publishing house for people with visual impairments; books in braille, large type, recordings, and computer disk are available. A range of aids, tools, and supplies for education and daily living is also available. Free catalog.

National Association for Visually Handicapped

22 West 21st Street, 6th Floor, New York, NY 10010 (212-889-3141; FAX: 212-727-2931; e-mail address: staff@navh.org; Internet Web site: http://www.navh.org). Provides informational literature, guidance and counseling in the use of visual aids, emotional support, and referral services for parents of partially sighted children and those who work with them. Publishes free large-print newsletter.

National Braille Association, Inc.

3 Townline Circle, Rochester, NY 14623-2513 (716-427-8260; FAX: 716-427-0263; e-mail address: 74051.1105@compuserve.com). Produces and distributes braille reading materials for people with visual impairment. Collection consists of college-level textbooks, materials of general interest, standard technical tables, and music.

National Federation of the Blind

1800 Johnson Street, Baltimore, MD 21230 (410-659-9314; FAX: 410-685-5653; Internet Web site: http://www.nfb.org). Strives for complete integration of blind people into society on a basis of equality. Offers advocacy services for the blind in such areas as discrimination in housing and insurance. Operates a job referral and listing system to help blind individuals find competitive employment. Runs an aids and appliances department to assist blind people in independent living. Has a scholarship program for blind college students and a loan program for blind people who are going into business for themselves. Publishes monthly and quarterly publications.

National Library Service for the Blind and Physically Handicapped

1291 Taylor Street, NW, Washington, DC 20542 (202-707-5100; TDD: 202-707-0744; FAX: 202-707-0712; e-mail address: NLS@loc.gov; Internet Web site: http://www.loc.gov/nls). Administers a national library service that provides braille and recorded books and magazines on free loan to anyone who cannot read standard print because of visual or physical disabilities.

Prevent Blindness America

500 East Remington Road, Schaumburg, IL 60173 (800-331-2020; FAX: 708-843-8458; e-mail address: 74777.100@compuserv.com; Internet Web site: http://www.prevent-blindness.org). Committed to the reduction of needless blindness. Provides information to the public, people who are blind, and professionals working with them.

PROTECTION AND ADVOCACY AGENCIES
Listed below are the protection and advocacy agencies mandated by law to serve and protect the rights of people with disabilities.

Alabama
Alabama Disabilities Advocacy Program, The University of Alabama, Post Office Drawer 870395, Tuscaloosa, AL 35487-0395 (800-826-1675; 205-348-4928; TDD: 205-348-1675; FAX: 205-348-3909).

Alaska
Disability Law Center of Alaska, 615 East 82nd Avenue, Suite 101, Anchorage, AK 99518 (800-478-1234; 907-344-1002).

American Samoa
Client Assistance and P and A Program, Post Office Box 3937, Pago Pago, AS 96799 (684-633-2441).

Arizona
Arizona Center for Disability Law, 3208 East Fort Lowell, Suite 106, Tucson, AZ 85716 (602-327-9547).

Arkansas
Advocacy Services, Inc., Evergreen Place, Suite 201, 1100 North University, Little Rock, AR 72201 (800-482-1174; 501-296-1775).

California
Client Assistance Program, 830 K Street Mall, Room 220, Sacramento, CA 95814 (916-322-5066).
Protection and Advocacy, Inc., 100 Howe Avenue, Suite 185N, Sacramento, CA 95825 (800-776-5746; 916-488-9950).

Colorado
The Legal Center, 455 Sherman Street, Suite 130, Denver, CO 80203 (303-722-0300; FAX: 303-722-0720).

Connecticut
Office of Protection and Advocacy for Persons with Disabilities, 60 Weston Street, Hartford, CT 06120-1551 (203-297-4300; TDD: 203-566-2102; statewide toll free: 800-842-7303; FAX: 203-566-8714).

Delaware
Disabilities Law Program, 913 Washington Street, Wilmington, DE 19801 (302-575-0660).

District of Columbia
I.P.A.C.H.I., 4455 Connecticut Avenue, NW, Suite B100, Washington, DC 20008 (202-966-8081; TDD: 202-966-2500).

Florida
Advocacy for Persons with Disabilities, 2671 Executive Center, Circle W, Suite 100, Tallahassee, FL 32301-5024 (904-488-9071; 800-342-0823; TDD: 800-346-4127; FAX: 904-488-8640).

Georgia
Georgia Advocacy Office, Inc., 999 Peachtree Street, NE, Suite 870, Atlanta, GA 30309 (404-885-1234; 800-282-4538; FAX: 494-607-8286).

Guam

The Advocacy Office, Post Office Box 8830, Tamuning, Guam 96931 (671-672-8985; TDD: 671-472-8989).

Hawaii

Protection and Advocacy Agency, 1580 Makaloa Street, Suite 1060, Honolulu, HI 96814 (808-949-2922).

Idaho

Co-Ad, Inc., 4477 Emerald Street, Suite B-100, Boise, ID 83706 (208-336-5353; FAX: 208-336-5396).

Illinois

Equip for Equality, 11 East Adams, Suite 1200, Chicago, IL 60603 (312-341-0022; FAX: 312-341-0295).

Indiana

Indiana Advocacy Services, 850 North Meridian Street, Suite 2-C, Indianapolis, IN 46204 (317-232-1150; 800-622-4845).

Iowa

Iowa P and A Service, Inc., 3015 Merle Hay Road, Suite 6, Des Moines, IA 50310 (515-278-2502; FAX: 215-278-0539).

Kansas

Kansas Advocacy and Protection Service, 2601 Anderson Avenue, Suite 200, Manhattan, KS 66502-2876 (913-776-1541; 800-432-8276).

Kentucky

Office of Public Advocacy, Division for Protection and Advocacy, 100 Fair Oaks Lane, 3rd floor, Frankfort, KY 40601 (502-564-2967; 800-372-2988; FAX: 502-564-7890).

Louisiana

Advocacy Center for the Elderly and Disabled, 210 O'Keefe, Suite 700, New Orleans, LA 70112 (504-522-2337; 800-662-7705; FAX: 504-522-5507).

Maine

Maine Advocacy Services, 32 Winthrop Street, Post Office Box 2007, Augusta, ME 04338 (800-452-1948; 207-626-2774; FAX: 207-287-8001).

Maryland

Maryland Disability Law Center, 2510 St. Paul Street, Baltimore, MD 21218 (800-233-7201; 410-235-4700; TDD: 410-235-4227).

Massachusetts

Disability Law Center, Inc., 11 Beacon Street, Suite 925, Boston, MA 02108 (617-723-8455; FAX: 617-723-9125).

Michigan

Michigan Protection and Advocacy Service, 106 Allegan, Suite 210, Lansing, MI 48933 (517-487-1755; FAX: 517-487-0827).

Minnesota

Minnesota Disability Law Center, 430 First Avenue, N, Suite 300, Minneapolis, MN 55401-1780 (612-332-1441; 612-332-4668).

Mississippi

Mississippi Protection and Advocacy System for Developmental Disabilities, Inc., 5330 Executive Pl., Suite A, Jackson, MS 39206 (601-981-8207; 800-772-4057; FAX: 601-981-8313).

Missouri

Missouri Protection and Advocacy Services, Inc., 925 South Country Club Drive, Unit B-1, Jefferson City, MO 64109 (314-893-3333; FAX: 314-893-4231).

Montana

Montana Advocacy Program, Inc., 316 North Park, Room 211, Post Office Box 1680, Helena, MT 59624 (800-245-4743; 406-444-3889; FAX: 406-444-0261).

Nebraska

Nebraska Advocacy Services, 522 Lincoln Center Building, 215 Centennial Mall, S, Lincoln, NE 68508 (402-474-3183; FAX: 402-559-5737).

Nevada

Disability Advocacy and Law Center, Inc., Financial Plaza, 1135 Terminal Way, Suite 105, Reno, NV 89502 (702-688-1233; TDD: 702-622-0243; statewide toll free: 800-992-5715).

New Hampshire

Disabilities Rights Center, Inc., Post Office Box 3660, 18 Low Avenue, Concord, NH 03302-3660 (603-228-0432; FAX: 603-225-2007).

New Jersey

Protection and Advocacy, Inc., 210 South Broad Street, Trenton, NJ 08608 (609-292-9742; 800-792-8600; FAX: 609-777-0187).

New Mexico

Protection and Advocacy System, Inc., 1720 Louisiana Boulevard, NE, Suite 204, Albuquerque, NM 87110 (505-256-3100; 800-432-4682).

New York

New York State Commission on Quality of Care for the Mentally Disabled, 99 Washington Avenue, Suite 1002, Albany, NY 12210 (518-473-4057; TDD: 800-624-4143; FAX: 518-473-6296).

North Carolina

Governor's Advocacy Council for Persons with Disabilities, 2113 Cameron Street, Suite 218, Raleigh, NC 27605 (919-733-9250; FAX: 919-733-9173).

North Dakota

Protection and Advocacy Project, 400 East Broadway, Suite 515, Bismarck, ND 58501 (701-224-2972; 800-472-2670; TDD: 800-366-6888).

North Mariana Islands

Catholic Social Services, Box 745, Saipan, CM 96950 (670-234-6981).

Ohio

Ohio Legal Rights Service, 8 E. Long Street, 6th floor, Columbus, OH 43215 (614-466-7264; 800-282-9181).

Oklahoma

Disability Law Center, Inc., 4150 South 100th East Avenue, 210 Cherokee Bldg., Tulsa, OK 74145 (918-664-5883).

Oregon

Oregon Advocacy Center, 620 SW 5th Avenue, 5th floor, Portland, OR 97204-1428 (800-452-1692; 503-243-2081; TDD: 800-556-5351).

Pennsylvania

Pennsylvania Protection and Advocacy, Inc., 116 Pine Street, Harrisburg, PA 17101 (717-236-8110; toll free: 800-692-7443).

Puerto Rico

Ombudsman for the Disabled, Post Office Box 4234, San Juan, PR 00902-4234 (800-981-4125; 809-721-4229; TDD: 809-705-4014).

Rhode Island

Rhode Island Protection and Advocacy System (RIPAS), Inc., 155 Broadway Street, 3rd floor, Providence, RI 02903 (401-831-3150; 800-733-5332; FAX: 401-274-5568).

South Carolina

South Carolina P and A System for the Handicapped, Inc., 3710 Landmark Drive, Suite 208, Columbia, SC 29204 (800-922-5225; 803-282-0639).

South Dakota

South Dakota Advocacy Services, Inc., 221 South Central Avenue, Pierre, SD 57501 (605-224-8294; statewide toll free: 800-658-4782; FAX: 605-677-6274).

Tennessee

Protection and Advocacy, Inc., Post Office Box 121257, Nashville, TN 37212 (615-298-1080; statewide toll free: 800-342-1660; FAX: 615-298-2046).

Texas

Advocacy, Inc., 7800 Shoal Creek Blvd., Suite 171-E, Austin, TX 78757 (512-454-4816; statewide toll free: 800-252-9108).

Utah

Legal Center for People with Disabilities, 455 East 400 South, Suite 201, Salt Lake City, UT 84111 (801-363-1347; 800-662-9080; FAX: 801-363-1437).

Vermont

Vermont Developmental Disabilities Law Project, 12 North Street, Burlington, VT 05401 (802-863-2881).

Virgin Islands

Advocacy Agency, 7A Whim Street, Suite 2, Fredericksted, VI 00840 (809-772-1200; TDD: 809-772-4641).

Virginia

Department of Rights of Virginians with Disabilities, James Monroe Building, 101 North 14th Street, 17th floor, Richmond, VA 23219 (804-225-2042; 800-552-3962).

Washington

Washington P and A System, 1401 East Jefferson, Suite 506, Seattle, WA 98122 (206-324-1521).

West Virginia

West Virginia Advocates, Inc., Litton Building, 4th floor, 1207 Quarrier Street, Charleston, WV 25301 (304-346-0847; statewide toll free: 800-950-5250).

Wisconsin

Wisconsin Coalition for Advocacy, Inc., 16 North Carroll Street, Suite 400, Madison, WI 53703 (608-267-0214).

Wyoming

Wyoming Protection and Advocacy System, Inc., 2424 Pioneer Avenue, Suite 100, Cheyenne, WY 82001 (307-638-7668; 800-624-7648; TDD: 800-624-7648).

UNIVERSITY AFFILIATED PROGRAMS

Listed below are the university affiliated programs that provide diagnostic and treatment services to children with disabilities and their families (entries alphabetized by state).

Alabama

University Affiliated Program, Civitan International Research Center, University of Alabama-Birmingham, 1719 Sixth Avenue, S, Birmingham, AL 35294-0021 (205-934-8900).

Alaska

University of Alaska, Center for Human Development, University Affiliated Program, 2330 Nichols Street, Anchorage, AK 99508 (907-272-8270).

Arizona

Institute for Human Development, Northern Arizona University, Post Office Box 5630, Flagstaff, AZ 86011 (520-523-4791; e-mail address: Rwc@nauvax.ucc.nau.edu).

Arkansas

University Affiliated Program of Arkansas, 501 Woodlane Road, Suite 210, Little Rock, AR 72201 (501-682-9900; e-mail address: aruap@exchange.uams.edu).

California

University of California-Los Angeles, University Affiliated Program, 300 UCLA Medical Plaza, Suite 3302, Los Angeles, CA 90095-6967 (310-825-8902; 310-825-8902; e-mail address: cbetz@npih.medsch.ucla.edu).

Colorado

J.F. Kennedy Center for Developmental Disabilities, University of Colorado Health Sciences Center, Campus Box C234, 4200 East Ninth Avenue, Denver, CO 80262 (303-270-7724).

Connecticut

A.J. Pappanikou Center on Special Education and Rehabilitation, A University Affiliated Program, 249 Glenbrook Road, Box U-64, Storrs, CT 96269-2064 (860-486-5035).

Delaware

University of Delaware University Affiliated Program for Families and Developmental Disabilities, 101 Alison Hall, University of Delaware, Newark, DE 19716 (302-831-6974; e-mail address: Donald.Peters@MVS. udel.edu).

District of Columbia

Georgetown University Child Development Center, 3307 M Street, NW, Suite 401, Washington, DC 20007 (202-687-8635; e-mail address: guide@medlib.georgetown.edu).

Florida

Mailman Center for Child Development, University of Miami School of Medicine, Post Office Box 016820, D-820, Miami, FL 33101 (305-243-6810; e-mail address: Turbano@peds.med.miami.edu).

Georgia

University Affiliated Program for Persons with Developmental Disabilities, The University of Georgia, Dawson Hall, Athens, GA 30602-3622 (706-542-3457).

Hawaii

University Affiliated Program for Developmental Disabilities, University of Hawaii at Manoa, 1776 University Avenue, UA4-6, Honolulu, HI 96822 (808-956-5009).

Idaho

Idaho Center on Developmental Disabilities (ICDD), University of Idaho, 129 West Third, Moscow, ID 83844-4401 (208-885-3559; e-mail address: icdd@uidaho.edu).

Illinois

Institute on Disability and Human Development, College of Associated Health Professions, The University of Illinois at Chicago, 1640 West Roosevelt Road, Chicago, IL 60608-6904 (312-413-1647).

Indiana

The University Affiliated Program of Indiana, Institute for Study of Developmental Disabilities, Indiana University, 2853 East Tenth Street, Bloomington, IN 47408-2601 (812-855-6508; e-mail address: Uap@isdd.isdd.indiana.edu). Riley Child Development Center, Indiana University Medical Center, 702 Barnhill Dr., Indianapolis, IN 46202-5225 (317-274-8167; e-mail address: sviehweg@indyuap.iupui.edu).

Iowa

Iowa University Affiliated Program, University Hospital School, The University of Iowa, Iowa City, IA 52242-1011 (319-353-6390; e-mail address: Disability-resources@uiowa.edu).

Kansas

Institute for Life Span Studies, University of Kansas, 1052 Robert Dole Human Development Center, University of Kansas, Lawrence, KS 66045 (913-864-4295; e-mail address: Schroede@kuhub.cc.ukans.edu).

Kentucky

Human Development Institute, University of Kentucky, 126 Mineral Industries Building, Lexington, KY 40506-0051 (606-257-1714).

Louisiana

Human Development Center, Louisiana's University Affiliated Program, Louisiana State University Medical Center, Building 138, 1100 Florida Avenue, New Orleans, LA 70119-2799 (504-942-8200; e-mail address: sschwa@1sumc.edu).

Maine

Center for Community Inclusion, UAP, 5717 Corbett Hall, University of Maine, Orono, ME 04469-5717 (207-581-1084; e-mail address: Anne_levasseur.cci@admin.umead.maine.edu).

Maryland

Kennedy Krieger Institute, The Center for Leadership in Disabilities, Maryland's University Affiliated Program, 2911 East Biddle Street, Baltimore, MD 21213 (410-550-9700).

Massachusetts

Institute for Community Inclusion University Affiliated Program, Children's Hospital, 300 Longwood Avenue, Boston, MA 02115 (617-355-6506; e-mail address: ici@a1.tch.harvard.edu).
Eunice Shriver Center University Affiliated Program, 200 Trapelo Road, Waltham, MA 02254 (617-642-0238).

Michigan

Developmental Disabilities Institute, Wayne State University, 326 Justice Bldg., 6001 Cass Avenue, Detroit, MI 48202 (313-577-2654; e-mail address: Eelder@cms.cc.wayne.edu).

Minnesota

Institute on Community Integration, 102 Pattee Hall, 150 Pillsbury Drive, SE, Minneapolis, MN 55455 (612-624-6300; e-mail address: Ici@mail.ici.coled.umn.edu).

Mississippi

Institute for Disability Studies, Mississippi University Affiliated Program, University of Southern Mississippi, Box 5163, Hattiesburg, MS 39406-5163 (601-266-5163; e-mail address: Uap@bull.cc.usm.edu).

Missouri

University Affiliated Program, University of Missouri-Kansas City, Institute for Human Development, 2220 Holmes Street, 3rd floor, Kansas City, MO 64108 (816-235-1770).

Montana

University Affiliated Rural Institute on Disabilities, 52 Corbin Hall, University of Montana, Missoula, MT 59812 (406-243-5467; e-mail address: Muarid@sclway.umt.edu).

Nebraska

Meyer Rehabilitation Institute, University of Nebraska Medical Center, 600 South 44th Street, Omaha, NE 68198-5450 (402-559-6430; e-mail address: Mleibowi@unmc.edu).

Nevada

University Affiliated Program, Research and Educational Planning Center, MS285, College of Education, University of Nevada, Reno, NV 89557 (702-784-4921; e-mail address: Rock@unr.edu).

New Hampshire

University Affiliated Program, Institute on Disability, University of New Hampshire, 7 Leavitt Lane, Suite 101, Durham, NH 03824-3595 (603-862-4320; e-mail address: IOD@unh.edu).

New Jersey

The University Affiliated Program of New Jersey, New Jersey's University of the Health Sciences, Robert Wood Johnson Medical School, Brookwood II, 45 Knightsbridge Road, Post Office Box 6810, Piscataway, NJ 08855-6810 (908-235-4447).

New Mexico

University of New Mexico University Affiliated Program, Health Sciences Center, Albuquerque, NM 87131 (505-272-3000; e-mail address: Nmuap@unm.edu).

New York

Rose F. Kennedy Center, Albert Einstein College of Medicine, Yeshiva University, 1410 Pelham Parkway S, Bronx, NY 10461 (718-430-8523; email address: birenbau@aecom.yu.edu).
Developmental Disabilities Center, St. Lukes-Roosevelt Hospital Center, 1000 Tenth Avenue, New York, NY 10019 (212-523-6248/6280).
Strong Center for Developmental Disabilities, University of Rochester Medical Center, 601 Elmwood Avenue, Rochester, NY 14642 (716-275-2986; e-mail address: Pwd1@mvs.cc.rochester.edu).
Westchester Institute for Human Development, 325 Cedarwood Hall, Valhalla, NY 10595 (914-285-8204; e-mail address: Ansley_Bacon@NYMC.EDU).

North Carolina

Clinical Center for the Study of Development and Learning, University of North Carolina-Chapel Hill, CB# 7255, BSRC, Chapel Hill, NC 27599-7255 (919-966-5171).

North Dakota

The North Dakota Center for Disabilities, Minot State University, 500 University Avenue W., Minot, ND 58707 (701-858-3580; e-mail address: NDCDMAIL@Farside.cc.misu.nodak.edu).

Ohio

University Affiliated Cincinnati Center for Developmental Disorders, Pavilion Building, 3333 Burnet Avenue, Cincinnati, OH 45229-3039 (513-559-4688).
The Nisonger Center, The Ohio State University, 1581 Dodd Drive, Columbus, OH 43210-1296 (614-292-8365).

Oklahoma

University Affiliated Program of Oklahoma, University of Oklahoma, Health Sciences Center, Post Office Box 26901, ROB 342, Oklahoma City, OK 73190-3042 (405-271-4500; e-mail address: Valerie-Williams @uokhsc.edu).

Oregon

Center on Human Development, University of Oregon–Eugene, Clinical Services Bldg., Eugene, OR 97403-1265 (503-346-3591).
Child Development and Rehabilitation Center, Oregon Health Sciences University, Post Office Box 574, Portland, OR 97207 (503-494-8364).

Pennsylvania

Pennsylvania Institute on Disabilities, Temple University, 423 Ritter Annex, 13th Street and Cecil B. Moore Avenue, Philadelphia, PA 19122 (215-204-1356; e-mail address: Dianeb@astro.ocis.temple.edu.).

Children's Seashore House, University of Pennsylvania School of Medicine, 3405 Civic Ctr. Blvd., Philadelphia, PA 19104 (215-895-3208; e-mail address: dowrick@mail.med.upenn.edu).

University Community Leaders and Individuals with Disabilities (UCLID) Center at the University of Pittsburgh, 3705 Fifth Avenue, Pittsburgh, PA 15213-2583 (412-692-6300; e-mail address: Feldman@chp-link.chp.edu).

Puerto Rico

Institute on Developmental Disabilities, University Affiliated Program, Graduate School of Public Health, Medical Sciences Campus, University of Puerto Rico, Box 365067, San Juan, PR 00936-5067 (809-754-4377; e-mail address: Mamiranda@rcmaca.upr.clu.edu).

Rhode Island

University Affiliated Program, Institute for Developmental Disabilities at Rhode Island College, 600 Mt. Pleasant Avenue, Providence, RI 02908 (401-456-8072).

South Carolina

University Affiliated Program of South Carolina–Columbia, Center for Developmental Disabilities, Benson Building, 1st floor, Columbia, SC 29208 (803-935-5231; e-mail address: Richardf@cdd.sc.edu).

South Dakota

University Affiliated Program, Department of Pediatrics, University of South Dakota, School of Medicine, 1400 West 22nd Street, Sioux Falls, SD 57105 (605-357-1439; e-mail address: Ljlarson@charlie.usd.edu).

Tennessee

Boling Center for Developmental Disabilities, University of Tennessee, Memphis, 711 Jefferson Avenue, Memphis, TN 38105 (901-488-6511; e-mail address: W.wilson@utmem1.utmem.edu).

Texas

University Affiliated Program, University of Texas at Austin, SZB 306/35300, Austin, TX 78712-1290 (214-471-7621).

Utah

Center for Persons with Disabilities/A University Affiliated Program, Utah State University, Logan, UT 84322-6800 (801-797-1981).

Vermont

The University Affiliated Program of Vermont, 499C Waterman Building, University of Vermont, Burlington, VT 05405-0160 (802-656-4031; e-mail address: Uapvt@moose.uvm.edu).

Virginia

Institute for Developmental Disabilities, Virginia Commonwealth University, PO Box 843020, Richmond, VA 23284-3020 (804-828-3876).

Washington

Center on Human Development and Disability, University of Washington, Box 357920, Seattle, WA 98195-7920 (206-543-2832; e-mail address: Chdd@u.washington.edu).

West Virginia

University Affiliated Center for Developmental Disabilities (UIACCD), West Virginia University, 955 Hartman Run Road, Morgantown, WV 26505-8334 (304-293-4692).

Wisconsin

Waisman Center University Affiliated Program, University of Wisconsin, 1500 Highland Avenue, Madison, WI 53705-2280 (608-263-1656; e-mail address: Dolan@Waisman.Wisc.Edu).

Wyoming

Institute for Disabilities, 152 A&S Building, Box 4298, University Station, University of Wyoming, Laramie, WY 82071-4298 (307-766-2761; e-mail address: WIND.uw@uyo.edu).

REFERENCES

American Association of University Affiliated Programs (AAUAP). (1996). *AAUAP 1996 Resource Guide.* Silver Spring, MD: Author.
Annual Directory of National Organizations 1991-1992. (1991). *Exceptional Parent, 21,* D1-D40.
1997 Resource Guide. (1997). *Exceptional Parent, 27.*

Index

Page numbers followed by "*f*" indicate figures; those followed by "*t*" indicate tables.

AAMR, *see* American Academy on Mental Retardation
Aarskog syndrome, 811
ABC, *see* Autism Behavior Checklist
Abdominal wall defects, prenatal diagnosis of, 38
Abduction, 316, 789
Abortion
  ethical debate over, 736–737
  therapeutic, ethics of, 736–738
ABR, *see* Auditory brainstem response
Abruptio placenta, 77*f*, 78, 789
ABS, *see* American Association on Mental Deficiency
    Adaptive Behavior Scale
Abscesses, in pediatric HIV infection, 170
Absence epilepsy, 305, 557
Abstract thinking, frontal lobe in, 303–304
Academic achievement tests, 481
Academic impairments, with traumatic brain injury, 608
ACCENT on Information, 851
Accessibility, assistive technology for, 718*t*
Accommodation, visual, 217, 219*f*
Accutane, *see* Isotretinoin
Acetabular dysplasia, 320
Acetabulum, 789
  dislocation, 320
  subluxation, 320
Acetaminophen (Tylenol), 789
  with pertussis vaccine, 567
  safety, in pregnancy, 62
Acetazolamide (Diamox), for shunt failure, 537
Acetylcholine, 300, 327
Acetylcholinesterase (ACH), in neural tube defects
    diagnosis, 533
ACH, *see* Acetylcholinesterase
Achilles tendon, lenghtening of, 515, 516*f*
Achondroplasia, 319, 319*f*, 789, 811–812
  dental problems with, 646
  genetics of, 26–27
  risk of, father's age and, 21*f*
Acoustic reflex measurements, 256
Acquired immunodeficiency syndrome (AIDS), 163–181,
    789
  learning problems with, 479
  natural history of, in children, 167*f*, 167–171
  resources on, 846
Acrocephalosyndactyly type I, *see* Apert syndrome
Acrocephalosyndactyly type II, *see* Carpenter syndrome
Acrocephalosyndactyly type V, *see* Pfeiffer syndrome
Acrodermatitis enteropathica, 192*t*
ACTH, *see* Adrenocorticotropic hormone
Actin, 323, 789
Activities of daily living (ADL), 758

Acute inflammatory demyelinating polyneuropathy, and
    Guillain-Barré syndrome, 328
Acute maternal illnesses, and pregnancy outcome, 74–75
Acute necrotizing ulcerative gingivitis (ANUG), 649
Acute primary herpetic gingivostomatitis (APHG), 649
Acute subdural hematomas, 599–600, 600*f*
Acyclovir (Zovirax), 64–65, 106, 174, 833
ADA, *see* Americans with Disabilities Act of 1990
ADA deficiency, *see* Adenosine deaminase deficiency
Adaptive functioning, tests of, 353
Adaptive impairments, 346–347
Adaptive skills, and cognitive skills, 347
ADARA, 853
Adderall, 833
Adduction, 316, 789
Adductor tenotomy, 515, 517*f*
Adenine (A), 18, 19*f*
Adenoid(s), 789
  enlargement of, 281
  removal of, 262
Adenosine deaminase (ADA) deficiency, treatment of,
    396*t*, 400*f*, 400–401
ADHD, *see* Attention-deficit/hyperactivity disorder
ADI, *see* Autism Diagnostic Interview
Adjustment disorders, 410, 789
  with mental retardation, 410
ADL, *see* Activities of daily living
A & D ointment, *see* Lanolin; Petrolatum; Vitamins A
    and D; Mineral oils
Adolescents, effects of disability on, 750
Adrenocorticotropic hormone (ACTH) (Corticotropin),
    833
  for infantile spasms, 564
  for Landau-Kleffner syndrome, 440
  for seizure disorders, 580
Adrenoleukodystrophy, X-linked, 812
Adult, child with disability as, competency of, 769
Adulthood
  of children with disabilities, medical complications in,
    765–766
  independence in, 758–759
  transition to
    for a child with a disability, 750–751, 757–772
    childhood activities as foundations for, 758
    planning for, 767–768
Advance directives, 731
AED, *see* Antiepileptic drugs
Aerolate, *see* Theophylline
Afebrile seizures, 553, 789
Affective disorders, 407–409
  with mental retardation, 407

AFP, *see* Alpha-fetoprotein
AGA, *see* Appropriate in size for gestational age
Aggression
　pharmacological management of, 438–439
　treatment of, 418–419
Aging, of children with disabilities, 768
Aicardi syndrome, 566, 812
　epilepsy and, 563
　eye abnormality with, 215*t*
　seizures and, 555
AIDS, *see* Acquired immunodeficiency syndrome
Air conduction, 256, 257*f*–258*f*
Airways, 692*f*; *see also* Respiratory system
Akathisia, 418
Alcohol, 841
　abuse, resources on, 846
　exposure to, and predisposition to ADHD, 451, 452*t*
　injection of, for spasticity, 513
　intake
　　definition of, 147
　　and fetal effects, 147–148
　　during pregnancy, prenatal intervention programs
　　　for, 157
　maternal use of, and neural tube defects, 532
　prenatal exposure to, effects on growth and develop-
　　ment, 158, 158*t*
　teratogenic potential of, 147
Alcohol dehydrogenase, 148
Alcohol-related birth defects (ARBD), 144
　characteristics of, 144–146
　comprehensive intervention approach for, 148
　outcome of, 148
　prevalence of, 146–147
　risk of, 146–147
Alcohol-related neurodevelopmental disorder (ARND),
　　144
Alexander disease, 812
Alleles, 23, 790
Allen Kindergarten Chart, 228*f*
Allergy(ies)
　and behavior problems, 462
　to latex, with meningomyelocele, 546
Alopecia areata, with Down syndrome, 368
Alpha adrenergic agonists
　for attention-deficit/hyperactivity disorder, 456, 457*t*,
　　459–461
　for sleep disorders, 440
　for tic disorders, 461, 570
Alpha Keri, *see* Mineral oil
Alpha-1-antitrypsin deficiency, newborn screening for,
　　394
Alphabetic Phonics, 483
Alpha-fetoprotein (AFP), 37, 790
　and neural tube defects diagnosis, 532–533
Alprazolam (Xanax), 833
Alternate living units (ALU), 760–761
ALU, *see* Alternate living units
Aluminum, excess, effect on fetal development, 185*t*
Alveoli, 94, 790
　in normal newborn, 121, 122*f*

in premature infant with respiratory distress syndrome,
　　121, 122*f*
Amblyopia, 214–215, 224, 790
　prevention of, 226
　treatment of, 215
American Academy of Pediatrics
　Committee on Bioethics, 735
　Council on Adolescent Health, 767
American Academy on Mental Retardation (AAMR),
　　definition of mental retardation, 346–347
American Association on Mental Deficiency Adaptive
　　Behavior Scale (ABS), 353–355
American Psychiatric Association
　definition of mental retardation, 346–347
　diagnostic criteria for attention-deficit/hyperactivity
　　disorder, 453, 454*t*
American Sign Language (ASL), 268
Americans with Disabilities Act (ADA) of 1990,
　　PL 101-336, 521, 654–655, 719, 752, 762
Amino acids, 19, 20*f*, 189, 790
　essential, 189
Aminoglycosides, ototoxicity, 251–252
Amitriptyline hydrochloride (Elavil), 834
Ammonia, neurotoxic effect, 392
Amniocentesis, 37–39, 41–43, 43*f*, 86
　indications for, 36*t*
　risks with, 42
Amniotic fluid, 57, 790
　assessment of, 86
　insufficient, 66, 66*f*
Amniotic sac, 55
Amoxicillin (Amoxil), 834
Amoxicillin and clavulanic acid (Augmentin), 834
Amoxil, *see* Amoxicillin
Amplification, for child with hearing loss, 263–265
Amygdala, in simple partial seizures, 561*f*
Amyloid, 363
Amyotrophic lateral sclerosis, 303
Anaerobic metabolism, 108
Anafranil, *see* Clomipramine
Anaphase, 5, 6*f*, 790
Anaphylaxis, and latex allergy, 546
Anemia, 790
　iron deficiency
　　in children, 191–194
　　during pregnancy, 73–74
　in pediatric HIV infection, 171
　in pregnancy, 73
　of prematurity, 128
　and simulation of ADHD, 452, 452*t*
Anencephaly, 111, 298, 529–530, 790, 812
　development of, 531
　ethical issues concerning, 730
　and organ donation, 732
　prenatal diagnosis of, 37, 39
　prevalence of, 530
Angelman syndrome, 30, 812
Anger, of family of child with disability, 746
Aniridia, type I, 59
Anisometropia, 226, 790

Anodontia, 646
Anophthalmia, 213, 790
Anorexiant medications, 202
Antacid, potential nutrient reactions, 204*t*
Antecedents, to behavior problems, definition of, 659
Anterior, 316
Anterior chamber of eye, 212, 212*f*
   disorders of, 216
   functions of, 216
Anterior fontanel, 790
Anterior horn cells, 327–328, 790
   damage to, 327
   decreased numbers of, 328
Anterior protective (propping) response, 506–507
Anthropometric data, 196
Antibiotics, ototoxicity, 251–252
Antibodies, in immune defense, 104
Anti-cancer drugs, teratogenic effects, 61
Anticipation, 30, 790
   genetic, 379
Anticonstipation drugs, potential nutrient reactions, 204*t*
Anticonvulsants, for febrile convulsions, 568
Antidepressants, 790
   for attention-deficit/hyperactivity disorder, 456, 457*t*, 459
   for individuals with mental retardation, 417
   see also Tricyclic antidepressants
Antiepileptic drugs (AED), 439, 553
   and carnitine loss, 191
   compliance with, 580–581
   dental problems with use of, 649, 653–654
   maternal exposure to, and neural tube defects, 532
   new, 579–580
   pathological fractures with, 322
   potential nutrient reactions, 204*t*
   psychiatric symptoms with, 413
   for seizure disorders, 575–580, 577*f*
   and simulation of ADHD, 452, 452*t*
   stopping of treatment, 581, 582*f*–583*f*
   teratogenic effects of, 61
Antipsychotic drugs
   for individuals with mental retardation, 418
   side effects, 418
Antireflux drugs, potential nutrient reactions, 204*t*
Antiretroviral therapy, 172–173
   long-term effects, 173
ANUG, *see* Acute necrotizing ulcerative gingivitis
Anus, imperforate, with Down syndrome, 367
Anxiety disorders, 790
   with attention-deficit/hyperactivity disorder, 450, 461
   with mental retardation, 409
   and simulation of ADHD, 452
Apert syndrome, 812
Apgar score, 93–94, 95*t*, 790
   and neurodevelopment, 94
   predictive value of, 94
APHG, *see* Acute primary herpetic gingivostomatitis
Apnea
   and bradycardia, 125–126
   in premature infants, 125

Apnea of prematurity, 125–126
Apneic episodes, in premature infants, 125
Appendico-vesicostomy, 544
Appendix, in digestive process, 627*f*
Appetite, promotion of, 637
Appropriate in size for gestational age (AGA), 116, 116*f*
Aquachloral (supplement), *see* Chloral hydrate
Aqueous humor, 212, 216, 790
Arachnoid mater, of spinal cord, 307*f*
ARBD, *see* Alcohol-related birth defects
Architectonic dysplasia, 475, 790
Arginase, 394*f*
Argininosuccinate lyase, 394*f*
Argininosuccinate synthesis, 394*f*
Aristocort, *see* Triamcinolone
Arm circumference, 196
ARND, *see* Alcohol-related neurodevelopmental disorder
Artane, *see* Trihexyphenidyl
Arterial hematoma, 597–598
Arthritis, 322–323, 324*f*, 790
Arthrogryposis multiplex congenita, 813
Arthro-ophthalmopathy, *see* Stickler syndrome
Articular surface, 316
Articulation, of speech, 276
Articulation skills
   development of, 281
   disorders of, 281
Artificial sweeteners, and hyperactivity, 463
Ash leaf spots, 565
ASL, *see* American Sign Language
Asperger disorder, 426, 430
   biological basis of, 432
   hyperactivity with, 438
Asperger syndrome, 426
   inclusion versus specialized educational setting for children with, 437
Asphyxia, 791
   and cerebral palsy, 500*t*
   and hypoglycemia, 108
   intrauterine, 98–99
   neonatal, 98–99
   and status epilepticus, 571
Aspiration, 628–629, 630*f*, 791
   evaluation of, 632
Aspirin, teratogenicity, 62
Assistive learning devices, 263–265
Assistive technology, 520–521
   nonmedical, 717–719, 718*t*
Asthma
   and feeding problems, 627
   medications for, and simulation of ADHD, 452
Astigmatism, 217*f*, 225, 791
Asymmetrical tonic neck reflex (ATNR), 504–505, 505*f*, 506
Ataxia, 305, 316, 791
   with traumatic brain injury, 604
   walking and, 519
Ataxia-telangiectasia, 813
Ataxic cerebral palsy, 502*f*, 503, 791

Athetoid cerebral palsy, 501, 502*f*, 503, 791
Athetosis, 316, 503, 791
Ativan, *see* Lorazepam
Atlantoaxial subluxation
   with Down syndrome, 366, 367*f*
   evaluation for, 371–372
ATNR, *see* Asymetrical tonic neck reflex
Atopic dermatitis, with Down syndrome, 368
Atrial septal defect, with Down syndrome, 364
Atrophy, 308, 791
Attention-deficit/hyperactivity disorder (ADHD), 304,
    449–470
   in adolescents, 450, 465
   in adults, 450, 465
   with autistic disorder, 429
   behavior management and, 455–456
   causes of, 450–453
   with cerebral palsy, 510
   characteristics of, 449–450
   combined type, 460
   counseling and, 455–456
   dental problems with, 654
   diagnosis of, 453
   diagnostic criteria for, 453, 454*t*
   educational interventions, 454–455
   EEG biofeedback training and, 463
   elimination diets for, 462–463
   and internalizing disorders, treatment of, 461
   and learning disabilities, 476
   management of, 453–463
   with mental retardation, 349–350, 410
     treatment of, 460
   mineral supplementation for, 461–462
   nonconventional treatments for, 461–463
   with other disorders of learning, behavior, or emotion,
    450
   prevalence of, 449
   primarily hyperactive-impulsive type, 460
   primarily inattentive type, 460
   sensory integration therapy for, 715–716
   subtypes, treatment of, 460
   and tic disorders, treatment of, 461
   treatment, environmental modifications, 455
   with Tourette syndrome, 570
   treatment of
     with medication, 456–461, 457*t*
     for stimulant nonresponders, 459–460
     with stimulants, 456–458
       outcome of, 459
   vitamin supplementation for, 461–462
Audiological assessment, 255
Audiometry, behavioral observation, in infants, 254
Auditory brainstem response (ABR), 108, 127, 246*f*, 791
   audiometry, in infants, 255
   with Down syndrome, 371
Auditory cortex, 244, 278
   function of, assessing, 256–259
Auditory impairments, with cerebral palsy, 510*t*
Auditory integration training, for pervasive
    developmental disorders, 440–441

Auditory nerve, 242, 243*f*, 244, 244*f*–246*f*
Auditory pathway(s), 246*f*
   in language comprehension, 278
Auditory structures, embryological development of,
    244–247
Auditory system
   central, 242
   peripheral, 242
Augmentin, *see* Amoxicillin and clavulanic acid
Aura(s), before seizures, 561
Aural/oral educational methods, 263, 268
Auricle, 242, 791
Autism, 284, 425–447
   associated impairments, 429–430
   behavioral abnormalities in, 428–429
   versus childhood schizophrenia, 433
   communication impairments with, 426–428
   definition of, 425
   versus developmental language disorders, 433
   early identification of, 434
   historical perspective on, 425–426
   impaired reciprocal social interactions in, 428
   inclusion versus specialized educational setting for
    children with, 437
   versus mental retardation, 433
   versus neurodegenerative disorders, 433
   versus other childhood developmental disorders, 433
   pharmacological management, 438–440
   versus psychiatric disorders, 433
   recurrence risk of, 432
   resources on, 846–847
   versus sensory impairments, 433
   see also Autistic disorders; Pervasive developmental
    disorders
Autism Behavior Checklist (ABC), 434
Autism Diagnostic Interview (ADI), 434
Autism Research Institute, 846
Autistic disorders, 426–430
   biological basis of, 432
   diagnostic criteria, 427*t*
   see also Autism; Pervasive developmental disorders
Autoimmune response, 328
Automatic movement reactions, 805
   with cerebral palsy, 506–507, 508*f*
Automatisms, with seizures, 557
Autonomic movement reactions, 508*f*
Autonomic nervous system, 293, 308, 309*f*
   function of, 308
Autonomy, 728
   and abortion, 737
Autosomal dominant disorders, 26–27
   characteristics of, 28*t*
   inheritance of, 26–27, 27*f*
Autosomal recessive disorders, 23–26
   characteristics of, 28*t*
   inheritance of, 23–25, 25*f*
Autosomes, 4, 791
   nondisjunction of, 8–10
Aveeno, *see* Colloidal oatmeal
Axon(s), 298–299, 300*f*

myelination, 301
Azmacort, *see* Triamcinolone
AZT, *see* Zidovudine

B cells, in immune defense, 104
Babbling
    of infants, 252–253, 277
    in sign language, 277
Baby Does, 729–731
Backward chaining, 668, 791
Baclofen (Lioresal), 834
    for cerebral palsy, 512–513
    for spasticity, 604
Bacteremia, 205, 791
Bacterial infections
    neonatal, 105
    in pediatric HIV infection, 170
    and pregnancy outcome, 75
Bactrim, *see* Trimethoprim-sulfamethoxazole
Bactroban, *see* Mupirocin (2%)
BAER, *see* Brainstem auditory evoked response
        audiometry
BAL, 203
Banding pattern, 5, 791
Barbiturates, withdrawal, in infant, 109
Bardet-Beidl syndrome, *see* Laurence-Moon-Bardet-
        Beidl syndrome
Barium swallow, with videofluoroscopy, 633
Barotrauma, 122, 791
Basal ganglia, 294, 305
Baseline, 456, 791
Basilar membrane, 243, 244f
Batten disease, 813
    retinal dysfunction in, 230
Bayley Scales of Infant Development (BSID), 342,
        351–352, 352t
Beckwith-Wiedemann syndrome, 813
Behavior
    consequences of, 676–677
    see also Self-injurious behavior
Behavior analysis
    functional, 414
    principles and procedures of, 659–665, 660f
Behavior disorders
    with cerebral palsy, 508, 510
    and learning disabilities, 477
    with mental retardation, 411–412
        control of, 354
    origin of, 658
    with traumatic brain injury, 608
Behavior management, 657–686
    attention-deficit/hyperactivity disorder and, 455–456
    building of momentum in, 667
    case-centered consultation, 680
    differential diagnosis in, 675–678, 676t
    with dual diagnosis, 416
    follow-up assessment/care, 676t, 682–683
    functional context for, 668
    generalization in, 676t

generalization programming in, 680–682
    goal of, 659
    intervention in, 676t, 678–680
        fading of, 676t, 680–682
    operant model, 416
    steps in, 676t
    strategy of, 416
    treatment planning, 676t, 678–680
Behavior modification, sequential modification in, 681
Behavior problem(s), 571
    antecedents to, 659
    in children on mechanical ventilation, 703
    in children with disabilities, 658, 658t
    consequences to, 659
    functional equivalence and, 678–679
    in infant exposed to cocaine, 152–153
Behavior Problem Checklist, 675
Behavior therapy, *see* Behavior management
Behavior traps, 681
Behavioral momentum, 667
Behind-the-ear (BTE) hearing aid(s), 264, 265f
Benadryl, *see* Diphenhydramine
Bender Visual Motor Gestalt Test, 478, 479f, 481, 482t
Beneficence, 728
Benzodiazepines, for seizure disorders, 579
Benztropine (Cogentin), for aggression, 438
Beriberi, 193t, 791
Beta adrenergic blockers, for individuals with mental
        retardation, 418
Beta-carotene, safety, in pregnancy, 62
Bethanechol, *see* Urecholine
Biaxin, *see* Chlarithromycin
Biceps muscle, 324, 325f
Bilingual-bicultural approach, for deaf child, 268
Bill of Rights Act Amendments of 1987, PL 94-103, 768
Binocular vision, 224, 791
    development of, 213
Biofeedback, for bowel control, 544
Biomedical ethics, *see* Ethics
Biophysical profile, 83–84
    scoring, 84, 84t
Biotin, 791
Biotinidase deficiency, 791, 824
    newborn screening for, 393
Bipolar disorder, 408–409, 791
    treatment of, 418
Birth
    physiological changes at, 94–97
    preterm, 71, 805
Birth defects
    Mendelian, recurrence risk, 36
    non-Mendelian, recurrence risk, 36
    population screening tests for, 37
    and problems with labor and delivery, 80
    rubella and, 63–64
    see also Alcohol-related birth defects
Birth weight
    maternal nicotine intake and, 149
    and neurodevelopmental outcome, 131
Bisacodyl (Dulcolax), for bowel control, 544

Bladder augmentation procedure, 544
Bladder function
  control of, 308
  meningomyelocele and, 537*f*, 542–544
Blastocyst, 55, 791
Blepharitis, with Down syndrome, 364
Blind spot, 222
Blindisms, 232–233
  behavior modification of, 233–234
Blindness, 231–235
  with cataracts, 218
  causes of, 231–232
  in children with multiple developmental disabilities
    incidence of, 235
    intervention for, 235
  color, *see* Color blindness
  with cortical visual impairment, 224
  definition of, 231
  detection of, 232
  with glaucoma, 216
  incidence of, 231
  mind, 428
  night, 220
Blissymbols, 288
Body hearing aids, 264
Body splint, 511
Bone, 316–322
  deformities of, 66, 319–321
  development, 316–319
  remodeling, 318–319
  structure, 316–319
Bone conduction, 256, 257*f*–258*f*
Bone conduction hearing aids, 264
Bone marrow, 318, 318*f*
  transplantation, 398
  in utero transplantation, 48
Bony structures, of mouth, 625, 626*f*
Borjeson-Forssman-Lehmann, 813
Botox, *see* Botulinum-A toxin
Botulin toxin, injectable, for spasticity, 513
Botulinum-A toxin (Botox), for spasticity, 604–605
Botulism, 513, 792
Bowed legs, 66
Bowel function
  control of, 308
  meningomyelocele and, 537*f*, 542–544
BPD, *see* Bronchopulmonary dysplasia
BPP, *see* Biophysical profile
Braces, for cerebral palsy, 511
Brachial plexus, injury, 79–80
Brachialis muscle, 324, 792
Brachmann de Lange, *see* de Lange syndrome
Bracing, 716–717
Bradycardia, 120, 792
  in premature infants, 125
Braille, 235
Brain
  with attention-deficit/hyperactivity disorder, 451
  development of
    anomalies, 111

during fetal life, 294, 295*f*
  stages of, 296–301, 297*t*
imaging, 311–312
in language comprehension, 278–280
mature, 301
organization, 299–300
in speech production, 279–280
typical, 539*f*
ventricular system of, 308, 310*f*
Brain damage, 597
  minimal, *see* Attention-deficit/hyperactivity disorder
Brain imaging techniques
  for cerebral palsy, 501
  for seizures, 574–575
Brain infections, and predisposition to ADHD, 451, 452*t*
Brain injury(ies), *see also* Traumatic brain injury
  detection of, 600–601
  severity of, 601–602
  treatment for, 602–604
  types of, 597
Brain malformations, and cerebral palsy, 500*t*
Brainstem, 294, 295*f*, 302*f*, 305, 306*f*, 792
  malformations of, with meningomyelocele, 534*t*
Brain tumors
  and status epilepticus, 571
  with tuberous sclerosis, 566
Brainstem auditory evoked response audiometry (BAER),
    in infants, 255
Breast milk, 184, 189, 197
  caloric supplements, 197
Breath-holding spells, 569
Breech delivery, 66*f*, 80
  of second twin, 81, 81*f*–82*f*
Broca's area, 279–280
  in language function, 280
Bronchi, 692*f*
Bronchopulmonary dysplasia (BPD), 121–122, 792
  caloric intake requirements, 696
  developmental delays in, 703
  medical technology assistance for, 689
Brow presentation, 80
Brushfield spots, 364
Bruxism, with cerebral palsy, 653
BSID, *see* Bayley Scales of Infant Development
BTE, *see* Behind-the-ear hearing aid(s)
Bubble baby syndrome, *see* Severe combined immuno-
    deficiency
Buck v. Bell, 734–735
Bupropion (Wellbutrin), for attention-deficit/hyperactivity
    disorder, 457*t*, 460
Bureau of Vocational Rehabilitation (VR), 762
  and job placement, 763
Buspar, *see* Buspirone
Buspirone (Buspar), 834
  for aggression, 439

Café-au-lait spots, 565
Calcium
  deficiency, 192*t*

dental problems with, 646
in newborn, 109
excess, 192*t*
food sources, 192*t*
functions of, 192*t*
Calcium undecylenate (10%) (Caldenase powder), 834
Calculus, 792
Calculus buildup, on teeth, 651
Caldecort, *see* Hydrocortisone
Caldenase powder, *see* Calcium undecylenate (10%)
Caldesene ointment, *see* Zinc oxide; Cod liver oil;
    Lanolin; Petrolatum
California Verbal Learning Test–Children's Version, 481*t*
Callus formation, 322, 323*f*
Caloric requirements, of children with selected disorders,
    197*t*
Campylobacter jejuni, and Guillain-Barré syndrome,
    328
Canavan disease, 813–814
Cancellous bone, 316–318, 318*f*
Cancer, medical technology assistance for, 688*t*, 690
Canes, for cerebral palsy, 520
Captioned Films/Videos, 854
Car seats, for cerebral palsy, 520
Carbamazepine (Tegretol), 354, 834
    for aggression, 439
    and carnitine loss, 191
    for individuals with mental retardation, 418
    and neural tube defects, 532
    potential nutrient reactions, 204*t*
    for rage reactions, 571
    for seizure disorders, 439, 575–576, 577*f*, 578
    for simple partial seizures, 560
    teratogenic effects, 61
Carbamyl phosphate synthetase, 394*f*
Carbidoa-levodopa (Sinemet), for cerebral palsy, 512
Carbohydrates
    complex, 190
    requirements for, 190
Carbon dioxide, 691
Cardiopulmonary resuscitation (CPR), 126, 696
Cardiorespiratory monitor, 126, 696
Career counseling, 486
Carnitine, 191
    deficiency, 191
    supplemental, 191
Carpenter syndrome, 814
Carrier detection, 37, 46–48
CARS, *see* Childhood Autism Rating Scale
Cartilage, 318, 318*f*
Casts, 511
Cataplexy, 569
Catapres, *see* Clonidine
Cataract(s), 217–219, 220*f*, 792
    congenital, 218
    with Down syndrome, 365, 369
    extraction, 218
Cat cry syndrome, *see* Cri-du-chat syndrome
Catheter, 692, 792
Cavities, *see* Dental caries

CDC National AIDS Clearinghouse, 846
CDC National AIDS Hotline, 846
CDD, *see* Childhood disintegrative disorder
Cell, 3–4
    nuclei, 3–4, 4*f*
Cell division, 4–7
    errors in, 7–15
    nonreductive, 4
    reductive, 4
Central auditory processing deficit, 284
Central nervous system (CNS), 293, 792
    development of, 294*f*, 294–301
        genetics versus environment and, 295–296
    embryology, 56*f*
    infections, and cerebral palsy, 500*t*
    mature, 301–306
Central rhythm generator (CRG), 623
Centriole(s), 6*f*, 792
Centromere, 5, 792
Cephalocaudal development, 55
Cephalohematoma, 101, 101*f*, 792
Cerebellum, 294, 295*f*, 302*f*, 305
    malformations of, with meningomyelocele, 534*t*
Cerebral cortex, 301
    dysplasia of, with meningomyelocele, 534*t*
Cerebral hemisphere(s), 294, 295*f*, 301–304, 302*f*, 792
Cerebral palsy, 499–528, 792
    assistive technology for, 520–521
    associated impairments in, 508–510, 510*t*
    ataxic, 502*f*, 503, 791
    athetoid, 501, 502*f*, 503, 791
    automatic movement reactions with, 506–507, 508*f*
    behavior disorders with, 508, 510
    behavioral symptoms of, 503
    bony deformities with, 321
    brain regions affected by, 502, 502*f*
    bruxism with, 653
    caloric requirements in, 197*t*
    causes of, 499, 500*t*, 500–502
    dental problems with, 653
    dyskinetic, *see* Dyskinetic cerebral palsy
    dystonic, 501, 502*f*, 503, 795
    early diagnosis of, 503–510
    early intervention services, 516–517
    emotional disorders with, 508, 510
    and epilepsy, 555
    equipment for, 519–520
    feeding abnormalities with, 508–510
    functional mobility with, 519–520
    growth abnormalities with, 508–510
    habilitation, 510
    after hypoxia-ischemia, 100
    incidence of, 131
    interdisciplinary care, 510
    medical complications in, during young adulthood, 766
    medical technology assistance for, 688*t*, 689
    medication for, 512–513
    with mental retardation, 349–350
    mixed, 503, 801
        associated impairments in, 510*t*

Cerebral palsy—*continued*
  musculoskeletal complications of, management of, 511–516
  neurodevelopmental therapy for, 517
  neurosurgery for, 513–515
  orthopedic surgery for, 515–516
  pathological fractures with, 322
  patterning for, 518–519
  permanence of, 131
  physical activity and sports with, 520
  positioning in, 511–512
  prevalence of, 500, 501*f*
  primitive reflexes with, 504–506
  prognosis for, 523–524, 524*t*
  pyramidal, 503
  resources on, 847
  in school setting, 521
  spastic, *see* Spastic cerebral palsy
  strabismus with, 224–225
  types of, 502–503
  and walking, 507–508
Cerebro-hepato-renal syndrome, *see* Zellweger syndrome
Cerebrospinal fluid, 308–311
  flow, 309, 310*f*
Cerumen, 242, 792
Cesarean delivery, 87–88
CHADD, *see* Children and Adults with Attention Deficit Disorder
CHARGE association, 245, 814
  eye abnormality with, 215*t*
  findings in, 250*t*
  and hearing loss, 250*t*
  inheritance pattern, 250*t*
CHAT, *see* Checklist for Autism in Toddlers
Checklist for Autism in Toddlers (CHAT), 434, 435*f*
Cheilitis, with Down syndrome, 368
Chelation therapy, 203
Chemotherapeutic agents
  ototoxicity, 252
  teratogenic effects, 61
Chest physiotherapy and suctioning, 692–693
Chest X rays
  of normal newborn, 120, 120*f*
  of premature infant with respiratory distress syndrome, 120, 120*f*
Chiari malformation, 539*f*
  with meningomyelocele, 534–537, 539*f*
Chickenpox, *see* Varicella
Child abuse, drug abuse and, 153
Child Abuse and Neglect Prevention and Treatment Act of 1984, PL 98-457, 729–730
Child Behavior Checklist, 675
Childbirth, 71–91
Childhood Autism Rating Scale (CARS), 434
Childhood developmental disorder(s), prevalence of, 432
Childhood disintegrative disorder (CDD) (Heller syndrome), 426, 431
Childhood-onset metachromatic leukodystrophy, and simulation of ADHD, 452
Childhood viral illnesses, in pediatric HIV infection, 170

Children and Adults with Attention Deficit Disorder (CHADD), 456
Children with disabilities
  adolescents, effects of disability on, 750
  adulthood of
    competency in, 769
    medical complications in, 765–766
  aging of, 768
  effects of disability on, 749–751
  effects of medical technology assistance on, 698–699
  life span of, 768
  and organ transplantation, 732
  research involving, 733
  at school age, effects of disability on, 749–750
  transition to adulthood, 757–772
  young adulthood, effects of disability on, 750–751
Children with special health care needs
  definition of, 773
  health care use by, 784
Chlarithromycin (Biaxin)
Chloral hydrate (Noctec), 835
  for sleep disorders, 440
Chlorhexidine (Peridex), for Vincent disease, 649
Chlorhexidine gluconate, 651
Chlorpromazine (Thorazine), 835
  for attention-deficit/hyperactivity disorder, 457*t*
Choking, 629
Cholesteatoma, 261, 792
Chondroectodermal dysplasia, *see* Ellis van-Creveld syndrome
Chorea, 503
Choreoathetosis, 305, 392, 509, 793
Chorioamnionitis, 86, 793
Chorion, 39
  chromosomal mosaicism, 41
Chorionic gonadotropin, 55, 793
Chorionic villus sampling, 37, 39–41, 793
  difficulty with, 41
  indications for, 36*t*
  risks with, 41
  transabdominal, 40–41
  transcervical, 40, 42*f*
Chorioretinitis, 213, 793
Choroid, 212*f*, 219, 793
Choroid plexus, 309, 310*f*, 793
Chromatid(s), 6*f*, 793
Chromatin, 5, 793
Chromosomal abnormality(ies), 7–8, 58, 811
  and cerebral palsy, 500*t*
  frequency of, 14
  prenatal diagnosis of, 42–43
  and problems with labor and delivery, 80
  risk of, maternal age and, 35–36, 36*f*
Chromosomal disorders
  dental problems with, 646
  and neural tube defects, 532
  prevalence of, 24*t*
Chromosome(s), 3–4, 4*f*
  breakage, 14–15
  loss, 11–12

Chromosome #21, critical region for Down syndrome phenotype, 363, 363*f*
Chronic illness
  maternal, 73–74
    and risk of malformations, 65
  simulating learning disability, 478–480
Chronic sorrow, 746
CIC, *see* Clean intermittent catheterization
Cilia, of fallopian tube, 54
Ciliary muscles, 216–217, 793
Cimetidine (Tagamet), 835
  for gastroesophageal reflux, 634–635
Circulating fetal cell diagnosis, 46
Circulation
  adult, 96*f*, 98*f*
  fetal, 96*f*, 98*f*
  postnatal, 96*f*, 96–97
Circulatory system, changes at birth, 96
Cisipride (Propulsid), 835
  for gastroesophageal reflux, 634
CK, *see* Creatine kinase
Clarithromycin, 835
Clean intermittent catheterization (CIC), 543–544
Cleft lip/palate, 57, 281–282
  dental problems with, 646
  fetal surgery for, 49
  findings in, 250*t*
  and hearing loss, 249, 250*t*
  inheritance pattern, 250*t*
  prevalence of, 24*t*
Clinical ethics committees, 731–732
Clinical Evaluation of Language Fundamentals, 286, 287*t*, 481
  Preschool, 287*t*
Clomipramine (Anafranil)
  for individuals with mental retardation, 417
  for stereotypies, 439
Clonazepam (Klonopin), 835
  for seizure disorders, 579
Clonic seizures
  focal, 110
  multifocal, 110
  in newborn, 110
Clonidine (Catapres), 836
  for attention-deficit/hyperactivity disorder, 457*t*, 461
  for hyperactivity, 438
  for sleep disorders, 440
  for tic disorders, 457*t*, 461, 570
Clonus, 793
Clorazepate (Tranxene), for seizure disorders, 579
Cloxacillin (Tegopen), 836
Clozapine (Clozaril), for aggression, 439
Clozaril, *see* Clozapine
Club foot, 66, 66*f*, 320, 809
  causes of, 320
  idiopathic, 320
  incidence of, 320
  with meningomyelocele, 542
  neurogenic, 320
  prevalence of, 24*t*

treatment for, 320
CMV, *see* Cytomegalovirus
CNS, *see* Central nervous system
Coalition on Sexuality, Inc., 851–852
Coarctation, of aorta, 11
Cocaethylene, 150
Cocaine
  abuse, prevalence of, 149–150
  action of, 150
  addiction, 150–151
  and alcohol, 150
  effects of, on family, 153–154
  exposure to, and predisposition to ADHD, 451, 452*t*
  fetal effects of, 151–152
  fetal exposure to, 149–154
    prognosis in, 154
  hydrochloride salt, 150
  infant exposed to
    behavior problems in, 152–153
    growth and motor development of, 152
  intrauterine exposure to, long-term effects of, 109
  mechanism of action of, 150, 151*f*
  metabolism of, 150
  neonatal withdrawal symptoms, 152
  and other drugs of abuse, 150
  overdose of, 150
  and perinatal outcomes, 152, 152*t*
  prenatal exposure to, effects on growth and development, 158, 158*t*
  teratogenic effect, 152
  toxic symptoms, in newborn infants, 152
Cochlea, 243, 243*f*–245*f*, 793
  tonotopic organization of, 243–244, 267
Cochlear implant, 266*f*, 266–267
Cod liver oil, 844
Codons, 19, 793
Cogentin, *see* Benztropine
Cognitive functioning, assessment of, 480, 481*t*
Cognitive impairments
  with meningomyelocele, 540–541
  with traumatic brain injury, 606–607, 607*f*
Cognitive therapy
  for family of child with disability, 745
  operant model, 416
Cohen syndrome, 814
Colace, *see* Dioctyl sodium
Cold sores, in pediatric HIV infection, 170
College, 762
Colloidal oatmeal (Aveeno), 836
Colobomas, 213, 231, 793
Colon, in digestive process, 627*f*
Color blindness, 219–220, 221*f*
  red-green, 28
Color vision, 219, 221*f*
Colostomy, 697–698
Coma
  ammonia-induced, 392
  medical management of, 602–603
  nutritional treatment during, 605
  recovery from, 603–604

Coma—*continued*
  rehabilitation after, 604
  severity of, and brain injury, 601–602
Commercial coverage insurance, 776–779
Common stimuli, programming for, 682
Communication
  alternative modes of, 288
  assistive technology for, 718*t*
  for child with hearing impairment, 267–268
  gender-specific differences in, 747
Communication boards, 288, 289*f*
Communication impairments
  early identification of, 285
  with mental retardation, 349–350
  prognosis for, 289–290
  with traumatic brain injury, 606
Communication skills, screening of, 285
Community, role of, for children with disabilities, 752
Community homes, 760–761
Community-based care programs, 760–761
Complement system, in immune defense, 105
Complex partial seizures, 304
Compliance training, 666–667, 793
Compound presentation, 80
Computed tomography (CT), 311, 793
  for cerebral palsy, 501
  of concussion, 598
  of diffuse axonal injury, 599*f*
  for hydrocephalus, 534
  for seizures, 574
Computers
  as assistive technology, 520–521
  for children with severe visual impairments, 235
  resources on, 848
Concrete operations, stage of, 341
Concussions, 598, 793
Conditioned orienting response audiometry (COR), 256
Conditioned play audiometry, 256
Conduct disorder, 411
  with attention-deficit/hyperactivity disorder, 450
Conduct problems, 411
  with mental retardation, 411
Cone cells, 219, 221*f*, 793
  abnormalities in, 219
Congenital abnormalities
  causes, 58
  definition of, 58
  and neonatal death, 72
  in newborn, 111
Congenital facial diplegia, *see* Moebius sequence
Congenital heart disease
  dental problems with, 646
  with Down syndrome, 364
Congenital myopathies, 327, 793
Congenital nephrosis, prenatal diagnosis of, 37
Congenital rubella syndrome, 63–64
Congestive heart failure, with Down syndrome, 364
Conjunctiva, 212*f*, 213
Conjunctivitis, 213
Consanguinity, 26, 26*f*

Consequences, 793
  of behavior, 676–677
  to behavior problems, 659
Constipation, 627, 631–632
  management of, 204*t*, 635–636
Consultation, in (re)habilitation, 713
Contact lenses, 218, 226
Content area literacy, 485
Contiguous gene syndromes, 14, 363, 793
Contingent observation, 673, 793
Contingent stimulation, punishment by, 664, 670
Contingent withdrawal, punishment by, 664, 670–671
Continuous positive airway pressure (CPAP), 121, 201, 693
Continuous reinforcement, for positive reinforcement, 662
Contraction stress test, 83–85
Contractures, with cerebral palsy, 511
Contrast sensitivity, 227
Convulsion, *see* Tonic-clonic seizures
Copper, deficiency, 191
COR, *see* Conditioned orienting response audiometry
Cordocentesis, *see* Percutaneous umbilical blood sampling
Cornea, 212, 212*f*
  disorders of, 216
  functions of, 216
Cornelia de Lange syndrome, *see* de Lange syndrome
Corpus callosotomy, 301
  for seizure disorders, 584–585
Corpus callosum, 301
Cort-Dome, *see* Hydrocortisone
Cortical, definition of, 794
Cortical blindness, 304
  with traumatic brain injury, 605
Cortical bone, 316, 318*f*
Cortical visual impairment (CVI), 222–223, 231
Corticospinal tract, 303
Corticosteroids
  potential nutrient reactions, 204*t*
  for seizure disorders, 580
Corticotropin, *see* Adrenocorticotropic hormone
Cortisporin, *see* Hydrocortisone; Polymyxin-B; Neomycin Coughing, 629
Counseling
  for attention-deficit/hyperactivity disorder, 455–456
  for learning disabilities, 485–486
Cow's milk, 189
CPAP, *see* Continuous positive airway pressure
CPR, *see* Cardiopulmonary resuscitation
CR, *see* Cardiorespiratory monitor
Crack cocaine, 150
Cranial nerves, 305, 306*f*
Craniofacial dysotosis, *see* Crouzon syndrome
Creatine kinase (CK), in muscular dystrophy, 325
Cretinism, *see* Hypothyroidism
CRG, *see* Central rhythm generator
Cri-du-chat syndrome, 13, 13*f*, 814
Crossing over, 5, 8*f*
Crouzon syndrome, 814

dental problems with, 646
Crowding effect, 227
Crutches, for cerebral palsy, 520
Cruzan v. Director, Missouri Department of Health, 731
CT, *see* Computed tomography
Cued speech, 268
Cuspids, 645*f*
    emergence of, 646*t*
    shedding of, 646*t*
CVI, *see* Cortical visual impairment
Cyclophosphamide, teratogenic effects, 61
Cyclops, 298
Cyclosporin (Sandimmune), dental problems with use of,
    649
Cylert, *see* Pemoline
Cystic fibrosis, 22
    carrier detection, 46
    and feeding problems, 627
    gene therapy for, 401
    genetic screening for, 48
    life span with, 768
    newborn screening for, 394
    screening test for, ethics of, 736
Cystic fibrosis transmembrane conductive regulator gene,
    defect in, 22
Cystometrogram, 543
    congenital infection, 74
    and hearing loss, 249
    infection
        in newborns, 106
        in pregnant women, 106
    intrauterine infection, 64
    in pediatric HIV infection, 170
Cytoplasm, 3–4, 4*f*
Cytosine (C), 18, 19*f*

DAI, *see* Diffuse axonal injuries
Daily living skills, assistive technology for, 718*t*
Dantrium, *see* Dantrolene
Dantrolene (Dantrium), 836
    for cerebral palsy, 512–513
    for spasticity, 604
Daughter cells, 5, 6*f*
ddC, 173
DDH, *see* Developmental dislocation of the hip
ddI, *see* Dideoxyinosine
Deafness
    definition of, 247
    hereditary, 249
Debridement, 545
Decadron, *see* Dexamethasone
Decibels, 242
Deconditioning, 416
Decubitus ulcers, with meningomyelocele, 545
Deep tendon reflex (DTR)
    with cerebral palsy, 503–504, 514
    motor (efferent) component, 514
    sensory (afferent) component, 514
Deflazacort, for muscular dystrophy, 326

Deformations, 66, 66*f*
    definition of, 66
Déjà vu, 304
de Lange syndrome, 814–815
    and risk of pervasive developmental disorder, 432
Delayed visual maturity (DVM), 224
Deletion #22q11.2 syndrome (DiGeorge syndrome, Velo-
    cardiofacial syndrome), 13–14, 282, 815
Deletions, 12–14, 794
    visible, 13
Delirium, 409
Delivery
    breech, *see* Breech delivery
    cesarean, 87–88
    complications with, and cerebral palsy, 500*t*
    of placenta, 71
    premature, after fetal surgery, 49
    preterm, 79
        and neonatal death, 72
        problems wtih, birth defects and, 80
Deltoid muscle, 325*f*
Dendrites, 298–299, 300*f*
Dendritic spines, 296*f*
Dental care, 643–652
    for children with developmental disabilities, 653–655
Dental caries (cavities), 647*f*, 647–649, 648*f*, 794
    with Down syndrome, 366–367
    in pediatric HIV infection, 170
Dental examination, 651
Dental lamina, 643
Dental organ, 643
Dental plaque, 647
Dental problems
    conditions associated with, 646, 653–655
    pharamcological therapy and, 649, 653–654
Dental sealants, 651
Dental trauma, 650
    with cerebral palsy, 653
Dentin, 644, 644*f*
    decay of, 648*f*
Denver Developmental Screening Test, 343, 503
Deoxyribonucleic acid (DNA), 3, 18, 19*f*
    mitochondrial, 31, 31*f*, 327
Depakene, *see* Valproic acid
Depakote, *see* Valproic acid
Departments of Veterans Affairs and Housing and Urban
    Developmkent and Independent Agencies Appro-
    priations Act of 1997, PL 104-204, 765
Dependence, transition to independence, 758–759
Depression
    with attention-deficit/hyperactivity disorder, 450, 461
    in family of child with disability, 745–746
    major, 407–408, 800
        in children with mental retardation, 408*t*
    pharmacological management, 439; *see also*
        Antidepressants
    and simulation of ADHD, 452
Deprivation, and positive reinforcement, 661
DES, *see* Diethylstilbestrol
Descriptive analysis, 677–678

Desipramine (Norpramin), 836
  for attention-deficit/hyperactivity disorder, 457t, 459, 461
Desipramine (Norpramin)—*continued*
  for depression, 439
  for mental retardation, 417
  side effects, 459
  for tic disorders, 461
Development, early, 335–340, 337t–338t
Developmental apraxia, 282, 794
Developmental delay(s), 341–343
  with blindness, 232
  early identification of, 342–343
  early intervention services for, 343–344
Developmental disability(ies)
  for children on mechanical ventilation, 703
  dental care for children with, 653–655
  simulating learning disability, 478–480
Developmental dislocation of the hip (DDH), 320, 321f
Developmental milestones, early, 336
Developmental scales, non-visually based, 233
Developmental testing, correction for prematurity in, 131–132
Dexamethasone (Decadron)
  in prevention of respiratory distress syndrome, 121
  for protection against intraventricular hemorrhage, 125
  for shunt failure, 537
Dexedrine, *see* Dextroamphetamine
Dextroamphetamine (Dexedrine), 836
  abuse of, 458
  for attention-deficit/hyperactivity disorder, 457t
  for individuals with mental retardation, 417
Diabetes
  with Down syndrome, 366, 372
  learning problems with, 479
  maternal, and neural tube defects, 532
  pregnancy in, 73
  and risk of malformations, 65
Diagnostic and Statistical Manual of Mental Disorders, Fourth Edition (DSM-IV), 405, 407
Dialysis, 698
Diamox, *see* Acetazolamide
Diaphysis, 316, 318f
Diazepam (Valium), 836–837
  for cerebral palsy, 512
  for febrile convulsions, 568
  for seizure disorders, 579
  for spasticity, 604
  teratogenic effects, 61
Dideoxycytidine, 173
Dideoxyinosine (ddI, Videx), 172
Diencephalon, 302f, 306f
Diet
  assessment, 196
  healthy, 187
  ketogenic, *see* Ketogenic diet
  macrobiotic, 194–195
  megavitamin, 195
  natural or organic food, 195
  nontraditional alternatives, 194–195
  orthomolecular, 195
  phenylalanine-restricted, 395
  special, facilitating acceptance of, 202, 202t
  vegetarian, 194–195
  for weight reduction, 201
Diethylstilbestrol (DES), teratogenic effects of, 62
Differential reinforcement, 665–666, 794
  of appropriate behavior (DRA), 665t
  of communicative skill (DRC), 665t
  of incompatible behavior (DRI), 665t
  of low rate behavior (DRL), 665t
  of other behavior (DRO), 665t
Diffuse axonal injuries (DAI), 599, 795
  neuroimaging of, 599f
Diffuse hypodense areas, 99–100, 100f
DiGeorge syndrome, *see* Deletion #22q11.2 syndrome
Dilantin, *see* Phenytoin
Dioctyl sodium (Colace), for bowel control, 544
Diphenhydramine (Benadryl), 837
  safety, in pregnancy, 62
Diploid number, 4, 55
Diplopia, with traumatic brain injury, 605
Direct service, in (re)habilitation, 713
Disabilities, definition of, 711
Disapproval, statements of, in behavioral management, 670
Discrepancy model, for determination of learning disabilities, 472
Dislocation, 316, 795
Distal, 316
Ditropan, *see* Oxybutynin chloride
Diuretics, 795
  ototoxicity, 252
  potential nutrient reactions, 204t
DMD, *see* Duchenne muscular dystrophy
DNA, *see* Deoxyribonucleic acid
DNR, *see* Do not resuscitate
Do not resuscitate (DNR), 731
Dominant trait, 18
Dopamine, 300
  and attention-deficit/hyperactivity disorder, 451
  and self-injurious behavior, 412
Doppler stethoscope, 57
Doppler ultrasound
  blood flow analysis, 85–86
  with placental insufficiency, 85–86
Double helix, 18
Down syndrome, 10f, 12–13, 300, 348, 361–375, 815
  alternative therapies and, 372
  and Alzheimer's disease, 363, 369
  caloric requirements in, 197t
  chromosomal abnormalities in, 361–362
  congenital heart disease with, 364
  dendritic spines in, 296f, 299
  dental problems with, 366–367, 646, 654
  developmental brain abnormalities in, 363
  early identification of, 364
  early intervention for, 372
  endocrine abnormalities with, 366
  ethical issues concerning, 728–730

etiology, 363
evaluation of children with, 369, 371f–372f
findings in, 250t
gastrointestinal malformations with, 367
genetics of, 8, 11f
and hearing loss, 250t
hematological disorders with, 368
and infantile spasms, 563
inheritance pattern of, 250t
language impairments in, 285
and life expectancy, 373, 768
medical complications in, 364–368, 365t
    during young adulthood, 765–766
and mental retardation, 296, 349–350, 369
and mosaicism, 361–362
neurodevelopmental and behavioral impairments with,
    368–369
neuroimaging in, 345–346, 369
neuropsychological testing results in, 345
and obesity, 187
orthopedic problems with, 366
partial, 13
physical characteristics of, 362f
population screening for, 37
prenatal diagnosis of, 38f, 46, 362, 364
prevalence of, 24t, 362
prognosis for, 372–373
psychiatric disorders with, 369
and quality of life, 373
resources on, 848–849
risk of, maternal age and, 35–36, 36f
screening for, 38–39
seizure disorders with, 368
sensory impairments with, 364–365
skin conditions with, 368
and supported employment, 373
and translocation, 361–362
ultrasound findings in, 39, 41t
DPT immunization, and febrile seizures, 567
DRA, see Differential reinforcement of appropriate
    behavior
DRC, see Differential reinforcement of communicative skill
DRI, see Differential reinforcement of incompatible
    behavior
DRL, see Differential reinforcement of low rate behavior
DRO, see Differential reinforcement of other behavior
Drug abuse, see Substance abuse
Drug dependence, pregnant woman with, intervention for,
    156
Drug–nutrient interactions, 203–204, 204t
Drug reactions, psychiatric symptoms with, 413
d4T, 173
DTR, see Deep tendon reflexes
Dual diagnosis, 405–424
    definition of, 405
    historical perspective on, 406
    pharmacological management, 417
Dubowitz syndrome, 815
Duchenne muscular dystrophy (DMD), 28, 324–327
    interdisciplinary treatment, 325–326

medical technology assistance for, 689
    muscle biopsy from child with, 326f
    prevalence of, 24t
    prognosis for, 326
    and respiratory pump failure, 691
    see also Muscular dystrophy
Ductus arteriosus, 96–97
    closure of, 97
    patent (open), 96f, 125
    premature closure of, 62
Ductus venosus, 96–97, 98f
Dulcolax, see Bisacodyl
Dumping syndrome, 631
    with Down syndrome, 367
Duodenal stenosis, with Down syndrome, 367
Duodenum, 696
    in digestive process, 626, 627f
Duoderm, 837
Dura mater, of spinal cord, 307f
DVM, see Delayed visual maturity
Dwarfism, short-limbed, 319
Dynamic wrist extension splint, 717, 717f
Dysarthria, 282
    with traumatic brain injury, 606
Dyscalculia, 473, 485
Dysgraphia, 484
Dyskinetic cerebral palsy, 305, 502f, 502–503
    associated impairments in, 510t
    caloric intake requirements, 696
    and epilepsy, 555
    and hearing loss, 509
Dyslexia, 473
Dysphasia, with traumatic brain injury, 606
Dysplasia
    acetabular, 320
    architectonic, 475, 790
    bronchopulmonary, see Bronchopulmonary dysplasia
    of cerebral cortex, with meningomyelocele, 534t
    chondroectodermal, see Ellis van-Creveld syndrome
    ectodermal, 795
        dental problems with, 646
    ectrodactyly-ectodermal, 815
    polyostotic fibrous, see McCune-Albright syndrome
    spondyloepipheseal, 808
Dyspraxia, 282
Dysthymia, 407
Dystocia, 79
Dystonia musculorum deformans, see Torsion dystonia
Dystonic cerebral palsy, 501, 502f, 503
Dystrophin, 324

Ear
    embryological development, 56f, 244–247, 247f
    external, 242, 243f
    inner, 243, 243f
    in language comprehension, 278
    middle, see Middle ear
    structure, 243f
    trauma, and hearing loss, 251

Ear canal, 242, 243*f*
Eardrum, 242, 243*f*
Early intervention programs, 133
    for developmental disabilities, 343–344
    (re)habilitation therapy in, 711–712, 712*t*
Echodensities, 123
Echolalia, in autism, 426–428
Eclampsia, 73, 76
ECMO, *see* Extracorporeal membrane oxygenation
Ectoderm, 55
Ectodermal dysplasia, dental problems with, 646
Ectopias, 475
Ectrodactyly-ectodermal dysplasia (EEC), 815
EDC, *see* Estimated date of confinement
Education
    for child with hearing impairment, 267–268
    programs, 761–763
    resources on, 849
Education for All Handicapped Children Act of 1975,
        PL 94-142, 355, 487, 521, 608
Education of the Handicapped Act Amendments of 1986,
        PL 99-457, 344, 752
    Part H of, 263
Educational aids, assistive technology for, 718*t*
Edwards syndrome, *see* Trisomy 18
EEC, *see* Ectrodactyly-ectodermal dysplasia
EEG, *see* Electroencephalography
Effusion, in middle-ear disease, 251
Egg(s), 4, 53
    meiosis of, 7
    mutation rate, age and, 21
Ehlers-Danlos syndrome, 815–816
Elavil, *see* Amitriptyline hydrochloride
Electroencephalography (EEG)
    of absence seizures, 559*f*
    biofeedback training, and attention-deficit/
        hyperactivity disorder, 463
    of complex partial seizures, 562*f*
    for epilepsy, 572–574
    of infantile spasms, 564*f*
    normal, 573*f*
    for seizures, 553, 554*f*
    of tonic-clonic seizures, 558*f*
    video monitoring, 574
Electrolarynx, 703
Electrolyte(s), 191
Electrolyte disturbances, and status epilepticus, 571
Electrolyte replacement, formula for, 200*t*
Electroretinogram (ERG), 230
Elimination diet(s), 194
    for attention-deficit/hyperactivity disorder, 462–463
Ellis-van Creveld syndrome (Chondroectodermal
        dysplasia), 816
    dental problems with, 646
Embryo biopsy, 46, 47*f*
Embryogenesis, 55–57, 56*f*
EMIT, *see* Enzyme-multiplied immunoassay technique
Emotional disorders
    with cerebral palsy, 508, 510
    and learning disabilities, 477

Employment
    competitive, 763
    supported, 763
Enamel, 644, 644*f*
    decay of, 648*f*
Encephalitis, learning problems with, 480
Encephalocele, 529–530
    prevalence of, 530
Encephalopathy, 796
    in HIV-infected infants, 171
Enchondral ossification, 318
Endocardial cushion defect, with Down syndrome, 364
Endocrine abnormalities, maternal and fetal effects, 73
Endoderm, 55
Endodontic therapy, 650
Endolymphatic duct, 245
Endoscopy, 632–633
Enemas, 635–636
    for bowel control, 544
Enhancer, mutations, 22
Enteral feeding, 198
    tubes for, 636*f*
Enterovirus, 796
    and risk of miscarriage, 63
Environmental accessibility, assistive technology for, 718*t*
Environmental control, assistive technology for, 718*t*
Enzyme deficiency, 26, 389, 390*f*
EOAE, *see* Evoked otoacoustic emissions testing
Epicanthal folds, 796
    with fragile X syndrome, 380, 380*t*
Epidural hematoma(s), 597–598, 598*f*, 796
Epilepsy
    absence, 305, 557
    benign rolandic, 560, 563
    complex partial, 563
    definition of, 553
    diagnosis of, 572–575
    intractable, treatment of, 566
    learning problems with, 479
    with pervasive developmental disorders, 439
    pharmacological management of, *see* Antiepileptic
        drugs
    photosensitive, 574
    psychosocial issues with, 586–587
    surgical treatment of, 582–585
    see also Seizure(s); Seizures disorders
Epileptic syndromes, 563–566
Epileptic-like disorders, 566–571
Epiphysis, 318, 318*f*
Epivir, 173
Equinus, 316
Erb's palsy, 79–80
ERG, *see* Electroretinogram
Erythema infectiosum, 75
Erythrocytosis, with Down syndrome, 368
Erythromycin, 837
Erythromycin (2%) (T-Stat), 837
    infection, in newborn, 105
Esophageal atresia, with Down syndrome, 367
Esophagitis

evaluation of, 632–633
  in pediatric HIV infection, 170
Esophagus, in digestive process, 625–626, 627*f*
Esotropia, 224, 225*f*
Essential fatty acids, 189
  deficiency, effect on fetal development, 185*t*
Estate planning, 770
Estimated date of confinement (EDC), 71
Estrogen, teratogenic effects, 62
Ethics, 727–742
Ethosuximide (Zarontin), 837
  for absence seizures, 559
  for seizure disorders, 579
Ethylene diaminetetraacetic acid, 203
Eucerin, *see* Petrolatum; Mineral oil; Alcohol
Eugenics, 734–735
Eustachian tube, 243, 243*f*
Eversion, 316, 317*f*
Evoked otoacoustic emissions testing (EOAE), in infants,
    254–255
Exchange transfusion(s), 129
  for hyperbilirubinemia, 107–108
Exclusionary time-out, 671–672
  advantages of, 672
  disadvantages of, 672
Executive function(s), 341, 796
  abnormalities, 382
  assessment of, 481, 481*t*
  impairments in, and learning disabilities, 476
Exotropia, 224, 225*f*
  treatment, 226
Expressive language
  disorders, with cerebral palsy, 509
  impairments, with traumatic brain injury, 606
Expressive One Word Picture Vocabulary Test–Revised,
    287*t*
Extended family, effect of child with disability on,
    748–749
Extension, 316, 796
External ear, 242, 243*f*
Extinction, 660*f*, 662–663, 796
  difficulty of, 663
  reappearance of problem behavior with, 663
  worsening of behavior with, 663
Extracorporeal membrane oxygenation (ECMO), 97
Eyberg Child Behavior Inventory, 675
Eye
  abnormalities, genetic syndromes associated with,
    215*t*
  development of, 213, 214*f*
  diseases of, 216–225
  embryology, 56*f*
  structure of, 211–213, 212*f*
Eye charts, 227, 228*f*
Eye muscles, 224–225, 225*f*
Eye pressing, 232
Eyeglasses, 226
Eyelashes, 213
Eyelid, 212*f*

Face presentation, 80
Facilitated communication, for pervasive developmental
    disorders, 440
Facio-auriculo-vertebral spectrum (Goldenhar syndrome),
    816
Fading, of prompts, in graduated guidance, 669–670
FAE, *see* Fetal alcohol effects
Failure to thrive, 186, 632, 796
  nonorganic, 186
  organic, 186
Fainting, 570
Familial dysautonomia, *see* Riley-Day syndrome
Family(ies), *see also* Parents
  of a child with a disability, 743–756
    reactions and adaptations of, 744–746
  definition of, 744
  difficulties, with traumatic brain injury, 609
  effects of medical technology assistance on, 698–699
  extended, effect of child with disability on, 748–749
  life cycle of, 744
  relationships with professionals, 751
  resources for, 856–857
Famotidine (Pepcid), 837
  for gastroesophageal reflux, 635
  potential nutrient reactions, 204*t*
Farsightedness, 217*f*, 225–226
  and esotropia, 224
FAS, *see* Fetal alcohol syndrome
Fastin, *see* Phentermine
Fats
  dietary, 189–190
    requirements for, 189–190
  polyunsaturated, 189
  saturated, 189
Fatty acid, deficiency, 189
Febrile convulsions, 567–568
  ages of occurrence, 557*t*
  prevalence of, 567
  and status epilepticus, 571
Federal assistance programs, 780*t*–782*t*
Feeding, 621–641
  adaptive devices for, 637
  alternative methods of, 636*f*, 638, 638*f*
  enteral, 198
    tubes for, 636*f*
  influence of development on, 628
  influence of medical conditions on, 625–627
  medical technology assistance for, 689–690, 696–697
  positioning during, 636
  problems with
    in children with disabilities, 628–632
    effect on teeth, 652
    evaluation of, 632–633
    management of, 634–638
  process of, 621–627, 627*f*
  promoting appetite for, 637
  tube, 198, 696–697
    in very low birth weight infants, 689
  work involved in, 637
Feeding abnormalities, with cerebral palsy, 508–510

Feeding disorders, with traumatic brain injury, 605
Feeding problems, 627
    with mental retardation, 349–350
Feeding tubes, 638, 697*f*
    enteral, 636*f*
Feingold Association, 462
Feingold diet, 195, 462–463
Felbamate (Felbatol), 580, 837–838
    for Lennox-Gastaut syndrome, 565
    for seizure disorders, 576
Felbatol, *see* Felbamate
Femur, 316, 797
Fencer's response, *see* Asymetrical tonic neck reflex
Fenfluramine (Pondimin), 202
    for stereotypies, 439
Fernald approach to reading, 484
Fertilization, 53–55, 54*f*
Fetal alcohol effects (FAE), 144–145
    outcome of, 148
    prevalence of, 146
Fetal alcohol syndrome, 144
    behavior and/or emotional disturbances with, 145
    cardiac anomalies with, 144
    criteria for diagnosis of, 144, 145*t*
    facial appearance with, 146*f*
    incidence of, 157
    and mental retardation, 349–350
    outcome of, 148
    prevalence of, 146
Fetal circulation, 96*f*
Fetal development, 56*f*, 57
Fetal face syndrome, *see* Robinow sequence
Fetal heart rate, 57
    late decelerations, 85
    monitoring, with uterine contractions, 86–87
    normal baseline, 83
    periodic decelerations, 86
Fetal lung maturity, assessment, 86
Fetal movements
    monitoring, 83
    quiet-active cycle, 83
Fetal period, 56*f*
Fetal/placental functioning, problems in, and cerebral
        palsy, 500*t*
Fetal surgery, 48–49, 49*f*
    endoscopic techniques, 49
    premature delivery after, 49
Fetal surveillance, antenatal, 82–87
Fetal therapy, 48–49
    ethics of, 737–738
Fetopelvic disproportion, 79
Fiber, dietary, 190
Fiber supplement (Metamucil), for bowel control, 544
Fifth disease, 75
Fight or flight response, 308, 309*f*
Fine motor development, 336–339, 337*t*–338*t*
FISH, *see* Fluorescent in situ hybridization
Flagellum, 55
Flexion, 316
Fluency/rhythm, of speech, 276

Fluorescent in situ hybridization (FISH), 46
Fluoride deficiency, 191
Fluoride treatments, 651–652, 652*t*
Fluorosis, 646
Fluoxetine (Prozac), 354, 838
    for attention-deficit/hyperactivity disorder, 460
    for individuals with mental retardation, 417
    for stereotypies, 439
FM system, *see* Frequency modulation amplification
        system
FMR1 (fragile X mental retardation) gene, 377, 382–383
FMRP (FMR1 protein), 377, 382–383
Focal infarct(s), 99, 100*f*
Focal resection, for seizure disorders, 583–584
Folate, *see* Folic acid
Folic acid (Folate)
    deficiency, 193*t*
        effect on fetal development, 185*t*
        and neural tube defects, 530
        during pregnancy, 74
    excess, 193*t*
    food sources, 193*t*
    for fragile X syndrome, 384
    functions, 193*t*
    supplementation
        for neural tube defects, 532
        in pregnancy, 74
Food guide pyramid, 187, 188*f*
Food labeling information, 187–188
Food pocketing, 629
Food-borne pathogens, 205
Foramen ovale, 96, 96*f*, 97
    closure of, 97
Forebrain, 57, 294, 295*f*, 298, 797
Formal operations, stage of, 341
Forward chaining, 668, 797
Foster care, and cocaine-exposed infants, 153–154
Fovea centralis, 212*f*, 213, 216, 219
Fracture(s), 323*f*
    disorders causing, 321–322
    healing, 321, 323*f*
    pathological, 321
    of skull, 597
Fragile X chromosome, 377, 378*f*
    carrier females, 379, 381
    genetics of, 378–379
    prevalence of, 378
    transmitting males, 379
Fragile X mental retardation gene, 377, 382–383
Fragile X syndrome, 22, 28, 296, 299, 377–388, 816
    behavioral characteristics of, 380–381, 381*t*, 413
    cognitive characteristics of, 380–381, 381*t*
    diagnosis of, 383, 436
    discovery of, 377
    DNA testing for, 383
    in females, 381–382
    and gene therapy, 383
    intervention strategies for, 383–384
    learning disabilities with, 474
    in males, 380

and mental retardation, 349–350, 377–378
    mouse model of, 382–383
    outcome, 384
    physical characteristics of
        in males, 378*f*, 380, 380*t*
        origins of, 382–383
    and predisposition to ADHD, 451, 452*t*
    prenatal diagnosis of, 43
    prevalence of, 24*t*
    and risk of pervasive developmental disorder, 432
Frame shift, 22, 22*f*, 797
FRAXA site, 379
FRAXE site, 379
Free radicals, 797
Frenulum, 281
Frequency modulation (FM) amplification system, 263, 762
Friedrich's ataxia, 816–817
Friends, effect of child with disability on, 748–749
Frontal lobe, 301, 302*f*, 303–304
    in simple partial seizures, 561*f*
Functional analysis, 677–678, 794
Functional context, for behavior management, 668
Functional equivalence, 678–679
Functional limitations, definition of, 711
Fundal plication, for gastroesophageal reflux, 635, 635*f*
Fundus uteri, 797
Fungal infections, treatment of, for pervasive developmental disorders, 441
Furosemide (Lasix), for shunt failure, 537
    potential nutrient reactions, 204*t*

GABA, *see* Gamma aminobutyric acid
Gabapentin (Neurontin), 580, 838
    for seizure disorders, 576
Gag reflex, hyperactive, with cerebral palsy, 509
Gagging, 629
Gait
    analysis, 515–516
    disturbances, 507
Galactosemia, 817
    eye abnormality with, 215*t*
    newborn screening for, 393
    treatment, 396*t*
Gallbladder, in digestive process, 627*f*
Gamma aminobutyric acid (GABA), 300
    and self-injurious behavior, 412
Ganciclovir, 106, 174
Gantrisin, *see* Sulfisoxazole
Gastroenteritis, 797
    and febrile seizures, 567
Gastroesophageal duodenoscopy, 632–633
Gastroesophageal reflux (GER), 126–127, 571, 630, 631*f*
    evaluation of, 632, 633*f*
    and feeding problems, 627
    management of, 634–635
    with mechanical ventilation, 704
    medical technology assistance for, 689

Gastrointestinal malformations, with Down syndrome, 367
Gastro-jejunostomy (G-J) tube, 696
    for gastroesophageal reflux, 635, 636*f*
    prenatal diagnosis of, 37
Gastrostomy (GT) feeding tube, 636*f*, 638
Gates-MacGintie Reading Test, 482*t*
Gaucher disease, 817
    clinical manifestations of, 392
    treatment of, 396*t*, 398
GCS, *see* Glasgow Coma Scale
Gene(s), 4, 18–23
    foundations of, 18
    size of, 18
Gene therapy
    ex vivo, 399–401, 400*f*
    in vivo, 399, 401
    for muscular dystrophy, 326–327
    using viral vectors, 399
Gene transfer, in mouse embryo, 399, 399*f*
Generalization programming, in behavior management, 680–682
Genetic abnormalities, 58–59
Genetic code, 18
Genetic counseling, 35, 38
Genetic disorders, 17
    carrier detection for, 46–48
    incidence of, 22–23
    prevalence of, 24*t*
Genetic screening, ethics of, 735–736
Genetic syndromes
    with behavioral phenotypes, 413
    and cerebral palsy, 500*t*
    and learning disabilities, 474
Genetic testing, ethics of, 735–736
Genitalia, embryology, 56*f*
Genome, human, 18
Genomic imprinting, 30, 797
Genotype, 18
Gentamicin, ototoxicity, 251–252
GER, *see* Gastroesophageal reflux
Germ cells, 4
German measles, *see* Rubella
Gingivitis, 649
    acute necrotizing ulcerative, 649
    with Down syndrome, 366
G-J tube, *see* Gastro-jejunostomy tube
Glasgow Coma Scale (GCS), 601*t*, 601–602
Glasses
    for children, 226
    tinted, for pervasive developmental disorders, 441
Glaucoma, 216, 218*f*
    congenital, 216
Glial tumors, with tuberous sclerosis, 565
Globoid cell leukodystrophy, *see* Krabbe disease
Glutamate, 300
Glutaric acidemia type I, 393
Glutaric aciduria type I, 817
Glutaric aciduria type II, 817–818
Gluten avoidance, for pervasive developmental disorders, 441

Glycogen, 797
Glycogen storage disease (Glycogenoses), 818
    treatment, 396*t*
Glycogenoses, *see* Glycogen storage disease
GM2-gangliosidosis type I, *see* Tay Sachs disease
Goldenhar syndrome, *see* Facio-auriculo-vertebral
        spectrum
Goldman-Fristoe Test of Articulation–Revised, 287*t*
Golgi body(ies), 4*f*, 19
Goniometry, 719
Goodenough-Harris Drawing Test, 481, 482*t*
Gordon Diagnostic System, 481*t*
Graduated guidance, 667–670
    adjusting amount of, 669
    full, 669
    partial, 669
    positive reinforcement with, 669–670
    shadowing in, 669
Grammar, 276
Grand mal seizure, *see* Tonic-clonic seizures
Grandparents, effect of child with disability on, 748–749
Grating visual acuity, 229, 230*f*
Gray matter, 301
    of spinal cord, 307*f*
Gray Oral Reading Test–Revised, 482*t*
Gross motor development, 336, 337*t*–338*t*
Ground glass appearance, 120
Group insurance, 777*t*
Growth, typical, during childhood, 183–184
Growth abnormalities, with cerebral palsy, 508–510
Growth charts, specialized, 196
Growth failure, postnatal, 186
Growth hormone, treatment with, 128
    for achondroplasia, 319
    for Down syndrome, 366
Growth plate, 318, 318*f*
Growth retardation, prenatal, 184–185
G (Opitz-Frias/BBB) syndrome, 817
G-tube, 638, 638*f*, 696, 697*f*
Guanfacine (Tenex)
    for attention-deficit/hyperactivity disorder, 457*t*, 461
    for hyperactivity, 438
    for tic disorders, 461
Guanine (G), 18, 19*f*
Guardianship, of person with disability, 769
Guided compliance, 667–670
Guillain-Barré syndrome, 328
    autoimmune response in, 328
    medical technology assistance for, 689
    predisposing infections, 328

Habilitation, 711
Hair cells, in organ of Corti, 243–244, 245*f*
Haldol, *see* Haloperidol
Hallermann-Streiff syndrome, 818
    dental problems with, 646
Hallucinations, 798
    with simple partial seizures, 560
Haloperidol (Haldol), 354, 838

for aggression, 438
for attention-deficit/hyperactivity disorder, 457*t*
for individuals with mental retardation, 418
for tics, 570
Haploid number, 4, 9*f*
Hazardous ingestions, 202–205
Head circumference
    increase, in childhood, 183–184
    measurements of, 196, 210
    predictive value, for neurodevelopmental impairments,
        131
Head injuries, incidence of, 595
Health care
    changing environment of, 774
    for children disabilities, financing of, 776–779
    ethical issues in, 727–742
    financing of, 774
        prepayment, 774
        prospective payment system, 774
        retrospective payment system, 774
    future of, 779–783
    management of, 784, 785*f*
    transition from pediatric to adult, 764–766
    in 21st century, 773–788
Health care insurance, *see* Insurance
Health maintenance organization (HMO), 775
    group model, 775, 778*t*
    individual practice association model, 775
    point-of-service model, 778*t*
    staff model, 775, 778*t*
Hearing, 241–274
    milestones, 252–253
    system for, 242–244
Hearing aid(s), 263–265
    behind-the-ear (BTE), 264, 265*f*
    binaural fittings, 265
    body, 264
    bone conduction, 264
    components, 264
    in-the-ear (ITE), 264
Hearing impairment(s)
    amplification for, 263–265
    with cerebral palsy, 508–509
    definition of, 247
    early intervention for, 263
    family/parent response to, 268–269
    signs of, 253
    supportive therapy for, 268–269
    with traumatic brain injury, 605–606
Hearing loss, 127, 247–253
    acquired, 248
    bilateral, 248
    causes of, 248–252
        genetic, 248, 250*t*
        pre-, peri-, and postnatal factors, 249
    with cleft palate, 249
    and communication, 267–268
    conductive, 248
        diagnosis of, 256, 258*f*
    definition of, 247

degrees of, 259–261
with Down syndrome, 365, 371
and education, 267–268
effect of, on speech and language, 247–248
identification of, 252–253
incidence of, 248
mixed, 248
moderate, 259–261
with prematurity, 249
profound, 259–261
prognosis for, 270
risk factors for, 254
screening for, 253–259
    in infants under 6 months of age, 254–255
    Joint Committee on Infant Hearing Position
        Statement on, 254
    National Institutes of Health consensus statement
        on, 254
sensorineural, 248
    diagnosis of, 256, 258*f*
    surgical interventions for, 266–267
severe, 259–261
slight to moderate, 259–261
treatment of, 262–269
types of, 248
unilateral, 248
Hearing tests
    for children with developmental ages from 6 months to
        2½ years, 255–256
    for children with developmental ages greater than 2½
        years, 256
Heart defects, prenatal diagnosis of, 39
Heart, embryology, 56*f*
Heart disease
    in pediatric HIV infection, 170
    see also Congenital heart disease
Height
    increase, in infant/child, 183
    measurements of, 196, 209
Heller syndrome, *see* Childhood disintegrative disorder
Hematocrit, in anemia of pregnancy, 73
Hematomas
    acute subdural, 599–600, 600*f*
    epidural, 597–598, 598*f*
Hemispherectomy, 566
    focal resection for, 585
Hemodialysis, 698
Hemoglobin, in anemia of pregnancy, 73
Hemoglobinopathies, during pregnancy, 74
Hemophilia, 28
Hemorrhage
    intracranial, 101–102
    intraventricular, *see* Intraventricular hemorrhage
    periventricular, 124–125
    subarachnoid, 101, 101*f*, 102
    subdural, 101*f*, 101–102
Hemorrhagic disease of newborn, 193*t*
Hemosiderosis, 585
Hepatitis B, and heroin abuse, 154–155
Heredity, 17–33

Hernias, inguinal, with fragile X syndrome, 383
Heroin, 154
    abuse, 154–155
    fetal effects, 155
    fetal exposure, long-term effects of, 155
    infant withdrawal, 109
    intrauterine exposure to, long-term effects of, 109
    neonatal withdrawal, 155
    prenatal exposure to, effects on growth and
        development, 158, 158*t*
Herpes simplex virus, 798
    dental problems with, 649
    disseminated infection, 106
    disseminated neonatal infection, 65
    fetal infection, 64–65
    and hearing loss, 249
    maternal infection, 74
    neonatal infection, 74
    newborn infection, 64–65, 106
    perinatal infection, 64–65
Herpes skin infections, in pediatric HIV infection, 170
Hertz (Hz), 241
Heterozygous, combinations of alleles, 23–24
Hexosaminidase A, 23
High probability requests, 667
High-risk pregnancies, perinatal mortality in, 72
Hindbrain, 294, 295*f*
Hip deformities, with meningomyelocele, 542
Hip dislocation, 515, 517*f*–518*f*
    developmental, 320, 321*f*
Hip-knee-ankle-foot orthosis (HKAFO), 541*f*
Hippocampus, in simple partial seizures, 561*f*
Hirschsprung disease, with Down syndrome, 367
HIV, *see* Human immunodeficiency virus
HKAFO, *see* Hip-knee-ankle-foot orthosis
HMO, *see* Health maintenance organization
Holocarboxylase synthetase deficiency, *see* Multiple
        carboxylase deficiency, infantile or early form
Holoprosencephaly, 111, 298
    isolated, gene for, 298
Holt-Oram syndrome, 818–819
Home care, 759–760
    choices for, 759–761
    medical technology assistance in, criteria for, 701*t*,
        701–702
Homeobox (Hox) genes, abnormalities in, 58–59
Homework, and learning disabilities, 488
Homocystinuria, 819
    eye abnormality with, 215*t*
    newborn screening for, 393
    treatment, 396*t*
Homozygous, combinations of alleles, 23–24
Honomonous hemianopsia, 509
Hospital(s), with pediatric rehabilitation facilities,
        847–848
Hospitalization, prolonged, effects of, 698
Human B$_{19}$ parvovirus, and pregnancy outcome, 75
Human immunodeficiency virus
    destruction of T4 cells by, 164, 165*f*
    and fetal malformations, 63

Human immunodeficiency virus—*continued*
  and heroin abuse, 154–155
  infection, in infants, 106
  seropositivity, 164
  vaccine, 173–174
Human immunodeficiency virus (HIV) infection, 163–181
  biological basis of, 163–164, 165*f*
  child with
    developmental assistance for, 174–175
    early intervention services for, 174–175
    hyperimmune globulin for, 174
    immunization against common childhood illnesses, 174
    risks for vaccine-preventable illnesses, 174
    in school setting, 169
  and cocaine abuse, 151, 153
  confidentiality regarding, 169
  dental problems with, 654–655
  diagnosis, in infants and young children, 172
  epidemiology of
    in adults, 164–166
    in children, 166
  medical technology assistance for, 688*t*, 690
  neurodevelopmental effects of, 171–172
  and other sexually transmitted diseases, 166
  pediatric
    interdisciplinary management of, 172–176
    medical management of, 172–174
    natural history of, 167*f*, 167–171
    prognostic factors in, 169
    psychosocial aspects of, 175–176
    survival with, 169, 170*f*
  prevalence of, 164
  prevention, 176
  rates, among women and children, 164
  transmission of
    in adults, 166
    in infants and children, 166–168
    risk of, in home and school, 168–169
    vertical, 75, 167–168
    therapeutic intervention for, 168
Hunter syndrome, *see* Mucopolysaccharidoses
Huntington chorea, *see* Huntington disease
Huntington disease (Huntington chorea), 22, 819
  anticipation in, 30, 30*f*
Hurler disease, clinical manifestations, 392
Hurler syndrome
  eye abnormality with, 215*t*
  and mental retardation, 349
Hydrocephalus, 58, 102, 309, 310*f*, 539*f*, 798
  causes of, 311
  ethical issues concerning, 729
  management of, 311
  with meningomyelocele, 534–537, 539*f*
  and mobility, 536*t*
  prenatal diagnosis of, 39
  shunts for, 540*f*
  strabismus with, 225
  with tuberous sclerosis, 565
Hydrocortisone (caldecort, Cort-Dome, Hytone), 838

Hydrops fetalis, 75
Hyperactive child syndrome, *see* Attention-deficit/hyperactivity disorder
Hyperactive gag reflex, with cerebral palsy, 509
Hyperactivity, pharmacological management of, 438
Hyperalimentation, during coma, 605
Hyperbilirubinemia, 106–108, 129, 798
  in premature neonates, 127–128
Hyperglycemia, in fetuses of diabetic mothers, 73
Hyperlexia, 429–430
Hypermethylation, 382
Hypermetropia, 217*f*
Hyperopia, 225
Hypertelorism, 213, 798
Hypertension
  chronic, and pregnancy, 73
  and pregnancy outcome, 65
Hyperthermia, maternal, and neural tube defects, 532
Hyperthyroidism, treatment, fetal effect, 65
Hyperventilation
  and absence seizures, 557–559
  and seizures, 574
Hyperviscosity, 185, 799
Hypocalcemia, in premature infants, 128
Hypodontia, 646
Hypogenitalism, 799
Hypoglycemia, 799
  in infants of diabetic mothers, 73, 108
  in newborns, 108–109
  in premature infants, 128
Hypophosphatasia, 819
Hypoplasia, 646
Hypoplastic left heart syndrome, 111
Hypospadias, 62
Hypothermia, in premature infants, 128
Hypothyroidism (Cretinism), 65
  congenital, 65, 301, 389
    with Down syndrome, 366, 371
    newborn screening for, 393
    and risk of pervasive developmental disorder, 432
    treatment, 396*t*
  and obesity, 187
  psychiatric symptoms in, 412–413
  subclinical, with Down syndrome, 366
  treatment, fetal effect, 65
Hypotonia
  with cerebral palsy, 509
  with Down syndrome, 368
Hypoxia, 691
Hypoxic, definition of, 799
Hypoxic-ischemic brain injury, types of, 100*f*
Hypoxic-ischemic encephalopathy, 98–100, 109, 300
Hypsarrhythmia, 564*f*, 572
Hytone, *see* Hydrocortisone
Hz, *see* Hertz

Ichthyosis, with Down syndrome, 368
IDEA, *see* Individuals with Disabilities Education Act of 1990, PL 101-476

IEP, *see* Individualized education program
IFSP, *see* Individualized family service plan
Ileostomy, 543, 697–698
Ileum, in digestive process, 626, 627*f*
Illicit drugs, use of, 75, *see also* Substance abuse
Imipramine (Janimine, Tofranil), 838
    for attention-deficit/hyperactivity disorder, 457*t*, 459
    for depression, 439
    for individuals with mental retardation, 417
    for sleep disorders, 440
    for urinary continence, 544
Imitation training, 666
Immune system, 103–105
Immune therapy, for pervasive developmental disorders,
    440–441
Immunization, and febrile seizures, 567
Immunoglobin G, maternal, and toxoplasmosis, 63
Immunoglobulins, in immune defense, 104
Impairment, definition of, 711
Imperforate anus, with Down syndrome, 367
Implantation, 54*f*, 55
Imprinting, genomic, 379
Inborn errors of metabolism, 37, 109, 221, 299–301, 389,
    390*f*, 811–831
    associated disabilities, 392–393
    brain damage in, causes of, 392
    clinical manifestations of, 391–392
    definition of, 811
    dental problems with, 646
    diagnosis of, 391, 393
    and feeding problems, 627
    newborn screening for, 393–394
    nutritional management in, 202
    outcomes in, 401, 402*f*
    and predisposition to ADHD, 451, 452*t*
    prenatal diagnosis of, 43
    presenting in acute metabolic crises, 390–391, 391*t*
    with progressive neurological deterioration, 390–391,
        391*t*
    seizures and, 555
    silent, 390–391, 391*t*
    and status epilepticus, 571
    treatment of, 394–401, 395*f*
        by enzyme replacement, 395*f*, 396*t*, 398
        by gene therapy, 395*f*, 396*t*, 399–401
        by limiting intake of potentially toxic substrate,
          395*f*, 395–397, 396*t*
        by organ transplantation, 395*f*, 396*t*, 398
        by providing vitamin-cofactor to activate residual
          enzyme activity, 395*f*, 396*t*, 397–398
        by stimulating an alternative metabolic pathway,
          395*f*, 396*t*, 397
        by supplying the deficient product, 395*f*, 396*t*,
          397
    types of, 390–391
Incisors, 645*f*
    emergence of, 646*t*
    shedding of, 646*t*
Inclusion
    for children with disabilities, 749–750

and learning disabilities, 487–488
Inclusive classrooms, and cerebral palsy, 521
Incontinentia pigmenti, 819
    dental problems with, 646
Incus, 242–243, 243*f*
Indemnity plan, with utilization controls, 778*t*
Independence, transition from dependence, 758–759
Independent living, 761
Inderal, *see* Propranolol
Indiana Baby Doe, 729
Individual insurance, 777*t*
Individual practice association (IPA), 775, 778*t*
Individualized education program (IEP), 344, 751, 761
    and learning disabilities, 487
Individualized family service plan (IFSP), 343–344, 712,
    712*t*, 751
Individualized reading, 484
Individualized transition plan (ITP), 761–762
Individuals with Disabilities Education Act (IDEA)
    Amendments of 1991, PL 102-119, 344
Individuals with Disabilities Education Act (IDEA) of
    1990, PL 101-476, 268, 344, 437, 455, 487, 608,
    713, 719, 752, 761, 779, 782*t*
    definition of learning disability, 471
        problems with, 472
Indomethacin
    for patent ductus arteriosus, 125
    for periventricular-intraventricular hemorrhage, 102
    for protection against intraventricular hemorrhage, 125
Infant developmental tests, 352
Infant formula(s), 184, 189, 197, 199*t*
    for tube-feeding, 198
Infantile myoclonic epilepsy, *see* Infantile spasms
Infantile phytanic acid storage disease, retinal dysfunc-
    tion in, 230
Infantile Refsum disease, 819
Infantile spasms, 560, 563–565
    ages of occurrence, 557*t*
    cryptogenic, 563
    with Down syndrome, 368
    electroencephalography of, 564*f*, 572
    symptomatic, 563
    treatment of, 576, 580–582
Infant mortality
    causes of, 99*f*
    definition of, 72
    rates of, 72, 72*t*
Infections
    congenital, 63
    and hearing loss, 249–251
    intrauterine, 62–65
    neonatal, 102–106
    in premature infants, 127
Inferior, 316
Influenza, and risk of miscarriage, 63
Influenza A/B vaccine, for children with HIV infection,
    174
Informal trust, 770
Informed consent, 734, 799
Inguinal hernias, with fragile X syndrome, 383

Inheritance
  autosomal dominant, 811
  autosomal recessive, 811
  mitochondrial, 811
  multifactorial, 811
  sporadic, 811
  X-linked dominant, 811
  X-linked recessive, 811
Inner ear, 243, 243f
Instructional training, 666
Insulin, overproduction, in infant of mother with diabetes, 108
Insurance, 765
  effects on delivery of care, 778t
  group, 777t
  individual, 777t
  and medical technology assistance, 699–701, 700f
  private, 776–779
  publicly funded programs, 779, 780t–782t
  self, 777t
  status of, for U.S. children and adolescents, 779t
Intellectual development, Piaget's theory of, 340–341
Intelligence, 345
  bimodal distribution of, 346f
Intelligence test(s), 351–353
  for children, 352–353
Interictal pattern, 799
Intermediate care facilities, 760
Internalizing disorders, and attention-deficit/hyperactivity disorder, treatment of, 461
International League Against Epilepsy (ILAE), 555
International Society for Heart and Lung Transplantation, 732
Interphase, 5, 6f
Interval schedules, for positive reinforcement, 662
In-the-ear (ITE) hearing aid(s), 264
Intracerebral insults, in premature infants, 122–125
Intracranial hemorrhage, 101–102
Intraocular lens implant, 218–219
Intraocular pressure, elevated, 216
Intrauterine growth retardation, 73, 76, 128, 184–185
  disproportionate, 185
  and maternal nicotine intake, 149
  proportional, 185
Intrauterine infections
  blindness caused by, 231
  and cerebral palsy, 500t
  and hearing loss, 509
Intravenous immunoglobulin (IVIG), 172–173
Intravenous therapy, 698
Intraventricular hemorrhage
  on CT scan, 102, 104f
  and hydrocephalus, 311
  on ultrasound, 102, 103f
Intubation, 121, 799
Inversion(s), 14, 316, 317f, 799
Iodine, deficiency, 191
  effect on fetal development, 185t
Ionic currents, seizures and, 554

Ionization, 800
IPA, see Individual practice association
IQ scores, 344–346, 346f
  with Down syndrome, 369
  with fragile X syndrome, 380
IQ tests, 480
Iris, 211–212, 212f
Iron
  deficiency, 191–194, 192t
    effect on fetal development, 185t
    with lead poisoning, 203
  excess, 192t
  food sources, 192t
  functions of, 192t
  supplementation
    for children, 194
    in pregnancy, 74
Iron deficiency anemia
  in children, 191–194
  during pregnancy, 73–74
Ischemia, cerebral, 124
Islets of ability, with autism, 429
Isochromosome, 12, 14, 15f
Isotretinoin (Accutane), 839
  and neural tube defects, 532
  teratogenicity, 62
Isovaleric acidemia, treatment, 396t
Isovaleric aciduria, 819–820
ITE, see In-the-ear hearing aid(s)
ITP, see Individualized transition plan
IVIG, see Intravenous immunoglobulin

Jacksonian march, 560
Janimine, see Imipramine
Jargon, development, 339
Jaundice
  causes of, 106
  neonatal, 106–108
  physiological, 107
  in premature neonates, 127–128
Jaw, growth of, 625, 626f
Jehovah's Witnesses, and medical ethics, 730
Jejunostomy, 638, 696
Jejunum, 696, 800
  in digestive process, 626, 627f
Joint(s), 322–323, 324f
  ball-and-socket, 322, 324f
  completely mobile, 322
  hinge, 322, 324f
  immobile, 322
  mobile, 322
  pivot, 322, 324f
Joint cavity, 322
Joint deformities, with cerebral palsy, 515
Joubert syndrome, 820
J-tube, 638, 696
Justice, 728
Juvenile metachromatic leukodystrophy, treatment of, 398

K-ABC, *see* Kauffman Assessment Battery for Children
Kanamycin, ototoxicity, 251–252
Kangaroo pump, 638, 638*f*
Karyotype
    with Down syndrome, 11*f*
    female, 7*f*
    in prenatal diagnosis, 42–43
Karyotyping, 5
Kauffman Assessment Battery for Children (K-ABC),
    352, 480–481
Kaufman Test of Educational Achievement (KTEA),
    482*t*
Kearns-Sayre syndrome, *see* Mitochondrial disorders
Kenalog, *see* Triamcinolone
Kernicterus, 107–108, 128, 820
    and cerebral palsy, 501
Ketogenic diet, 839
    for Lennox-Gastaut syndrome, 565
    for seizure disorders, 566, 581–582
Ketosis, 581, 800
Key Math–Revised, 482*t*
Kidney dialysis, 698
Kidney disease
    learning problems with, 479
    in pediatric HIV infection, 171
Kidney failure, medical technology assistance for, 688*t*,
    690
Kinky hair syndrome, 822
Klinefelter syndrome (47, XYY), 10–11, 820
    learning disabilities with, 474
    and predisposition to ADHD, 451
    prenatal diagnosis of, 46
    prevalence of, 24*t*
Klippel-Feil syndrome, 820
Klippel-Trenauny-Weber syndrome, 820
Klonopin, *see* Clonazepam
Klumpke's palsy, 79–80
Krabbe disease (Globoid cell leukodystrophy),
    820–821
KTEA, *see* Kaufman Test of Educational Achievement
Kwashiorkor, 800
Kwell, *see* Lindane
Kyphectomy, with meningomyelocele, 542
Kyphoscoliosis, with meningomyelocele, 542
Kyphosis, with meningomyelocele, 542, 543*f*

Labor
    active phase of, 79
    complications with, and cerebral palsy, 500*t*
    first stage of, 71
        abnormalities of, 79
    latent phase of, 79
    preterm, 79
    second stage of, 71
        abnormalities of, 79
    third stage of, 71
Labyrinth, 243, 243*f*
Lactase, 800
Lactobacillus acidophilus, and dental caries, 647

Lacto-ovovegetarian, 194
Lacto-vegetarian, 194
Lactose, 190, 800
    intolerance, 630–631
Lamictal, *see* Lamotrigine
Lamotrigine (Lamictal), 565, 580, 839
    for seizure disorders, 576
Lamuvidine, 173
Landau-Kleffner syndrome (LKS), 284
    unproved treatment for, 440
Language, 275–292
    biological basis of, 278–280
    brain basis of, 278–280
    components of, 276
    definition of, 275
    domains of, 276
    grammar of, 276
    phonology of, 276
    pragmatics of, 276
    semantics of, 276
    and speech, 275–276
Language development, 276–277, 337*t*–338*t*
    delayed, with blindness, 232
    and hearing loss, 253, 260
Language disorder(s)
    acquired, 284
    causes of, 283–285
    congenital, 284
    expressive, 283
        versus receptive, 283
    with general impairments, 283
    mixed receptive-expressive, 283
    receptive, 283
Language experience reading instruction, 484
Language functioning, assessment of, 481, 482*t*
Language impairments
    expressive, with traumatic brain injury, 606
    receptive, with traumatic brain injury, 606
Language skills, development, 339
Lanolin, 839–840, 844
Lanugo, 117, 800
Larynx, growth of, 625, 626*f*
Lasix, *see* Furosemide
Lateral, 316
Latex allergy
    and dental care, 654
    with meningomyelocele, 546
Laughing gas, *see* Nitrous oxide
Laurence-Moon-Bardet-Beidl syndrome (Bardet-Beidl
        syndrome), 813
    findings in, 250*t*
    and hearing loss, 250*t*
    inheritance pattern, 250*t*
    retinal dysfunction in, 230
Laxative(s), 635
    with senna (Senokot), for bowel control, 544
LBW, *see* Low birth weight
Lead
    chelation therapy, 203
    exposure to, and predisposition to ADHD, 451, 452*t*

Lead—*continued*
  intoxication, and simulation of ADHD, 452, 452*t*
  toxicity, 202–203
Learning disabilities, 471–497
  assessment of, 480–482
  with attention-deficit/hyperactivity disorder, 450
  with cerebral palsy, 509
  comorbid conditions, 476–477
  definition of, 471–472
  determination of, 472
  early identification of, 477–478
  genetics of, 474
  homework and, 488
  inclusion and, 487–488
  individualized education programs for, 487
  instructional interventions, 483–485
  intervention strategies for, 482–487
  interventions for, periodic reevaluations of, 488
  and medication, 486
  nontraditional treatment approaches, 486–487
  outcome, 490
  prevalence of, 473–474
  resources on, 855
  school problems simulating, 478
  and simulation of attention-deficit/hyperactivity
      disorder, 452
  subtypes of, 473
Leber congenital amaurosis, *see* Mitochondrial disorders
Leber optic neuropathy, prevalence of, 24*t*
Legal resources, 855–856
Leigh syndrome, *see* Mitochondrial disorders
Leisure, for children with disabilities, 766
Lennox-Gastaut syndrome, 560, 563, 565
  ages of occurrence, 557*t*
  tonic clonic, 581–582
  treatment of, 580
Lens, 212, 212*f*
  functions of, 216–217
Lesch-Nyhan syndrome, 300, 392, 406, 821
  behavior problems with, 658
  behavioral characteristics of, 413
  dental problems with, 646
Lesion(s), 306
Leukemia
  with Down syndrome, 368, 372
  pathological fractures with, 322
Leuprolide (Lupron), for precocious puberty, 545
Life span, of children with disabilities, 768
Life support, withdrawal of, 731
Ligaments, 323, 324*f*
Limb(s), embryology, 56*f*
Limb abnormalities, prenatal diagnosis of, 39
Limb buds, 57
Limbic seizure, *see* Seizures, complex partial
Lindamood Auditory Conceptualization Test, 478
Lindane (Kwell), 839
Lioresal, *see* Baclofen
Lip, cleft, *see* Cleft lip/palate
Lipids, dietary, 189–190
Lipoma, 546

Lissencephaly, 301, 821
  epilepsy and, 563
  seizures and, 555
Literature-based reading instruction, 484
Lithium
  for aggression, 439
  for depression, 439
  for individuals with mental retardation, 418
  for rage reactions, 571
  for self-injurious behavior, 439
Liver
  in digestive process, 627*f*
  transplantation, 398
Liver disease, learning problems with, 479
Liver failure, dental problems with, 646
LKS, *see* Landau-Kleffner syndrome
Local anesthetic agents, for spasticity, 513
Locus ceruleus, 800
Lorazepam (Ativan), for seizure disorders, 579
Lorenzo's oil, 812
Lovaas therapy, 437
Low birth weight (LBW), 58
  and cerebral palsy, 500
  definition of, 115
  with fetal alcohol syndrome, 144
  incidence of, 116–117
  and neonatal death, 72
  and predisposition to ADHD, 451, 452*t*
Low birth weight (LBW) infants
  individualized developmental care for, 130
  medical care of, 129–130
  neurodevelopmental outcomes for, 130*t*, 130–132
  prevention, 129
  survival, 130–132
Low vision, definition of, 231
Lowe syndrome, 821
  eye abnormality with, 215*t*
L/S ratio, 86, 87*f*
Lubriderm, *see* Lanolin, Mineral oil, Petrolatum
Luminal, *see* Phenobarbital
Lung disease, in pediatric HIV infection, 171
Lungs, 692*f*
Lupron, *see* Leuprolide
Lupus erythematosus, and pregnancy outcome, 65
Lymphoid interstitial pneumonia, in pediatric HIV
    infection, 171
Lymphoma(s), in pediatric HIV infection, 170
Lyonization, 29
Lysosomal storage disorder(s)
  clinical manifestations, 392
  diagnosis of, 393
  treatment of, 398

Maalox, *see* Magnesium hydroxide and aluminum
    hydroxide
MacArthur Communicative Development Inventories,
    286
Macrobiotic diet, 194–195
Macrocephaly, 800

Macro-orchidism, 800
  with fragile X syndrome, 380, 380t, 383–384
Macrosomia, 800
Macrostomia, 800
Macula, 212f, 213, 216, 219, 797, 800
MAFO, see Molded ankle-foot orthosis
Magnesium
  and autism, 440
  deficiency, 192t
    in newborns, 109
  excess, 192t
  food sources, 192t
  functions of, 192t
Magnesium hydroxide and aluminum hydroxide
    (Maalox), 839
Magnesium sulfate, intravenous, 76
Magnetic resonance imaging (MRI), 800
  for attention-deficit/hyperactivity disorder, 451
  of brain, 108, 302f
    in pervasive developmental disorder, 432–433
  for cerebral palsy, 501
  of diffuse axonal injury, 599f
  functional, 312, 312f
  for hydrocephalus, 534
  for seizures, 574
  and specific reading disability, 475
Magneto-electroencephalography, for seizures, 574–575
Major depression, 407–408
  symptoms of, in children with mental retardation,
    408t
Major motor seizure, see Tonic-clonic seizures
Malaria, and risk of miscarriage, 63
Malformations, 58–65
Malleus, 242, 243f
Malnutrition, 184–187
  definition of, 184
  dental problems with, 646
  and neurodevelopmental impairments, 186
  neurodevelopmental outcomes, and onset of early
    supplementary feedings, 187
  nutritional rehabilitation for, 186–187
  nutritional replenishment in, 198–201
  in pregnancy, 58
  for very low birth weight infants, 129
Malocclusion, 650
  with cerebral palsy, 653
Managed care, 774–776
Managed care organizations (MCO), 774–776
Managed care plans, 776
Mandible, 57
  teeth in, 643, 645f
Mandibulofacial dysostosis, see Treacher-Collins
    syndrome
Mania, 408–409
  symptoms of, in children with mental retardation,
    408t
Manic-depressive disorder, and simulation of ADHD,
    452
Maple syrup urine disease (MSUD), 109, 821
  newborn screening for, 393

treatment, 396t
Marasmus, 801
Marfan syndrome, 822
  eye abnormality with, 215t
Marijuana, 156
  adverse effects, 156
  prenatal exposure to, effects on growth and
    development, 158, 158t
  use, during pregnancy, 156
Maroteaux-Lamy syndrome, see Mucopolysaccharidoses
Mastoiditis, 261
  treatment, 261
Masturbation, 571
Maternal age, 117
  and Down syndrome, 362
  as indicator for prenatal testing, 35
Maternal factors, and perinatal outcome, 73–80
Maternal nutrition, fetal effects, 58
Maternal serum alpha-fetoprotein (MSAFP), 37–38, 38f
  in neural tube defects diagnosis, 533
Maternal serum testing, 37–39
Mathematics
  instructional interventions for, 485
  standardized tests of, 482t
Maxilla, teeth in, 643, 645f
McCune-Albright syndrome (Polyostotic fibrous), 822
MCO, see Managed care organizations
MCT, see Medium chain triglycerides
MDI, see Mental Development Index score
Measles
  dental problems with, 646
  and hearing loss, 251
  immunization, and febrile seizures, 567
  in pediatric HIV infection, 170
Measles, mumps, rubella (MMR) vaccine, for children
    with HIV infection, 174
Mechanical ventilation, 693–695, 695f
  components in care of child receiving, 694t
  liberation from, 702
  long-term, developmental and behavioral complica-
    tions associated with, 703–704
Meconium aspiration, 122
Median, 316
Medicaid, 778–779, 779t–781t
Medicaid Working Group, 784
Medical home, 783
Medical technology assistance, 687–708
  categories of, 691t
  definition of, 687–688
  disorders associated with, 688t, 688–690
  effects on child and family, 698–699
  for feeding, 696–697
  funding of, 699–701, 700f
  in home care, criteria for, 701t, 701–702
  incidence of, 687–688
  nutritional assistive devices, 696–697
  outcome of, 702
  respiratory, 690–695
  surveillance devices, 695–696
  types of, 689t, 690–698

Medication(s), 833–845
    for attention-deficit/hyperactivity disorder, 456–461, 457t
    for cerebral palsy, 512–513
    learinig disabilities and, 486
    multiple, for pervasive developmental disorders, 440
    for psychiatric disorders, 417
    and simulation of ADHD, 452
    see also specific medication
Medium chain triglycerides (MCT), 801
Medrol, see Methylprednisolone
Medulla, 305, 306f
Megavitamin diet, 195
Megavitamin therapy, 194, 398
    for pervasive developmental disorders, 440
Meiosis, 3–7, 9f, 801
    errors in, 8–15
    nondisjunction in, 8, 10f
    I, 5
    II, 7
MELAS, 31
    prevalence of, 24t
Mellaril, see Thioridazine
Memory, in language function, 280
Memory for Words versus Memory for Sentences Test, 478
Memory impairments, and learning disabilities, 476
Mendelian disorders, 23–29
    autosomal dominant, 26–27
    autosomal recessive, 23–26
Mendelian genetics, 17–18
    revising, 30
Mendelian traits, 18, 23, 801
Meningeal sac, 529
Meninges, 306
    of spinal cord, 307f
Meningitis
    bacterial, and hearing loss, 251
    and cerebral palsy, 500t
    and hydrocephalus, 311
    learning problems with, 480
    in pediatric HIV infection, 170
    and status epilepticus, 571
Meningocele, 529, 530f, 801
Meningomyelocele, 17, 40f, 298, 529, 530f–531f, 535f, 801
    bladder dysfunction with, 542–544
    bladder function in, 537f
    bowel dysfunction with, 542, 544
    bowel function in, 537f
    caloric requirements in, 197t
    Chiari malformation with, 534–537, 539f
    cognitive impairments with, 540–541
    dental problems with, 654
    development of, 531
    educational programs for, 546
    ethical issues concerning, 728–730
    hydrocephalus with, 311, 534–537, 539f
    latex allergy with, 546
    loss of sensation with, 533–534, 535f, 536t, 537f–538f

mobility and, 538–540
    multidisciplinary management of, 547
    musculoskeletal deformities with, 542
    neurological impairments with, 533–537, 534t, 546
    and obesity, 187
    paralysis with, 533–534, 535f, 536t, 537f–538f
    pathological fractures with, 322
    population screening for, 37
    prenatal diagnosis of, 37, 39, 40f
    prevalence of, 530
    prognosis for, 548
    psychosocial issues with, 547
    seizure disorders with, 541
    sexual dysfunction with, 545
    skin sores with, 545
    spinal curvatures and humps with, 542, 543f
    stature abnormalities with, 545
    symptoms, 529
    treatment of, in newborn, 533
    visual impairments with, 541
    weight abnormalities with, 545
    see also Neural tube defects
Menkes (kinky hair) syndrome, 822
Menses, 53, 801
Mental Development Index (MDI) score, 342, 352
Mental health, 765
Mental Health Parity Act, 765
Mental retardation, 335–355
    adaptive impairments and, 346–347
    age of onset, 346
    associated problems, 349t, 349–350
        medication for, 354
        psychiatric symptoms in, 412–413
        treatment, 355
    and attention-deficit/hyperactivity disorder, treatment of, 460
    with autistic disorder, 429
    behavior disorders with, control of, 354
    biological origins of, 350–351
    causes of, 348, 350–351
    with cerebral palsy, 508, 510t
    with chromosomal abnormalities, 350, 350t, 351
    definition of, 344–347
    degrees of, 347–348
    dental problems with, 654
    diagnostic criteria for, 345t
    with Down syndrome, 296, 349–350, 369
    DSM-IV definition of, 347, 353
    early identification of, 342–343
    educational services for, 353–354
    and epilepsy, 555
    extensive, 347
    and family counseling, 355
    with fetal alcohol syndrome, 145–146
    intermittent, 347
    intervention approaches for, 353–355
    and IQ score, 345, 347
    leisure and recreational needs with, 354
    and life expectancy, 355–356, 356f
    limited, 347

medical diagnostic testing with, 351
mild, 347
moderate, 347
and periodic reevaluation, 355
pervasive, 347
and pervasive developmental disorder, 432
prevalence of, 348–349
profound, 347
prognosis for, 355–356
and psychiatric disorders, 405–424
    behavior therapy for, 416
    diagnosis of, 407
    evaluation for, 414
    psychotherapy for, 415
    rehabilitation therapy for, 415
    social skills training for, 416
    special education programs for, 415
    treatment, 415
psychological testing with, 351–353
recurrence risk in families, 348–349
requiring extensive support
    causes of, 350–351
    prevalence of, 348
requiring intermittent support
    causes of, 350–351
    prevalence of, 348
seizures with, 576
severe, 347
sex distribution, 348
and simulation of ADHD, 452
and social activities, 354
Mental retardation/developmental disabilities (MR/DD)
    agencies, and job placement, 763
Mercury, excess, effect on fetal development, 185t
MERRF (Myoclonus Epilepsy with Ragged Red Fibers),
    see Mitochondrial disorders
Mesencephalon, 294, 295f
Mesoderm, 55
Messenger ribonucleic acid (mRNA), 18–19, 19f–20f,
    801
Mestinon, see Pyridostigmine
Metabolic disorders, and simulation of ADHD, 452
Metabolism
    anaerobic, 108
    of cocaine, 150
    inborn errors of, see Inborn errors of metabolism
Metachromatic leukodystrophy, 801, 822
    clinical manifestations, 392
    treatment, 396t
Metamucil, see Fiber supplement
Metaphase, 5, 6f, 801
Metaphysis, 316, 318f, 801
Methadone, 154
    fetal effects, 155
    fetal exposure, long-term effects of, 155
    intrauterine exposure to, long-term effects of, 109
    neonatal withdrawal, 155
    withdrawal, in infant, 109
5–10-Methylenetetrahydrofolate reductase gene,
    abnormalities in, 531

Methylmalonic acidemia, 801, 822
    treatment of, 396t, 398
    vitamin B$_{12}$-responsive, fetal therapy, 48
Methylphenidate (Ritalin), 354, 839–840
    abuse of, 458
    for attention-deficit/hyperactivity disorder, 457, 457t
    for hyperactivity, 438
    for individuals with mental retardation, 417
    side effects of, 457
    and tics, 570
Methylprednisolone (Medrol, Solu-Medrol), 840
Metoclopramide (Reglan), 840
    for gastroesophageal reflux, 634
    potential nutrient reactions, 204t
Metropolitan Readiness Test, 478
Miconazole (Monistat), 840
Microcephaly, 131, 146f, 185, 298, 801
    with fetal alcohol syndrome, 144
    prenatal diagnosis of, 39
Microdeletion(s), 13–14, 801
Micropremies, definition of, 115
Microwave safety, in pregnancy, 60
Midbrain, 294, 295f, 305, 306f
Middle ear, 242, 243f
    function, assessing, 256
Middle-ear disease(s)
    complications of, 261
    and hearing loss, 251
    surgical management of, 261–262
    treatment of, 261–262
Middle-ear infection(s)
    with cleft palate, 249
    and febrile seizures, 567
    follow-up for, 261
    with fragile X syndrome, 383
    and hearing loss, 251
    in pediatric HIV infection, 170
    treatment, 261
Migraine headaches, 570
Milk
    breast, 184, 189, 197
    cow's, 189
Milk of magnesia, potential nutrient reactions, 204t
Milk scan, 632, 633f
Miller-Diecker syndrome, 821
Milligram, 801
Milliliter, 801
Mind blindness, 428
Mineral(s), 191–192
    deficiency, 191
    requirements for, 191
Mineral oil(s), 839–841
    potential nutrient reactions, 204t
Mineral supplementation, for attention-deficit/
    hyperactivity disorder, 461–462
Minimal brain damage, see Attention-deficit/hyperactivity
    disorder
Minimal cerebral dysfunction, see Attention-deficit/
    hyperactivity disorder
Minor-motor seizures, with quadriplegia, 509

Missense mutation, 21–22, 22*f*, 801
Mitochondria, 31, 327
Mitochondrial disorders, 31, 327, 801, 822–823
    prevalence of, 24*t*
Mitochondrial encephalomyelopathy, lactic acidosis, and
        stroke-like episodes, *see* MELAS
Mitochondrial encephalopathy, prevalence of, 24*t*
Mitochondrial inheritance, 31, 32*f*
    prevalence of, 24*t*
Mitochondrial myopathies, *see* Mitochondrial disorders
Mitosis, 3–5, 6*f*, 801
    errors in, 7–15
Mitral valve prolapse, with fragile X syndrome, 380,
        380*t*, 383–384
Mixed cerebral palsy, 503, 801
    associated impairments in, 510*t*
MMR vaccine, *see* Measles, mumps, rubella vaccine
Mobility
    assistive technology for, 718*t*
    and cerebral palsy, 519–520
    with meningomyelocele, 538–540
Moebius sequence, 823
Molars, 645, 645*f*
    emergence of, 646*t*
    shedding of, 646*t*
Molded ankle-foot orthosis (MAFO), 511, 716, 717*f*, 718*t*
Molecular genetic techniques, 801
Momentum, building of, for behavior management, 667
Monistat, *see* Miconazole
Monitoring, in (re)habilitation, 713
Mononucleosis, 802
    and risk of miscarriage, 63
Monosomies, frequency of, 14
Monosomy, 8, 10*f*, 802
Monosomy X, 11, 802
Mood disorders, 407–409
    with attention-deficit/hyperactivity disorder, 450
Mood stabilizers, for individuals with mental retardation,
        418
Moro reflex, 504
Morphine, 154
Morquio syndrome, *see* Mucopolysaccharidoses
Morula, 55
Mosaicism, 10, 12
Motor impairments, with traumatic brain injury, 604–605
Motor point block, for spasticity, 513
Motor skills
    delayed, with blindness, 232
    development of, 508*f*
Motor strip, 302*f*, 303, 303*f*
    in simple partial seizures, 561*f*
Movement, terminology for, 316, 317*f*
Movement disorders, 305
MR/DD, *see* Mental retardation/developmental disabili-
        ties agencies
MRI, *see* Magnetic resonance imaging
mRNA, *see* Messenger ribonucleic acid
MSAFP, *see* Maternal serum alpha-fetoprotein
MSUD, *see* Maple syrup urine disease
Mucopolysaccharides, 802

Mucopolysaccharidoses (Hunter syndrome), 823
    dental problems with, 646
    I (Hurler syndrome), 823
    II (Hunter syndrome), 823
    III (San Filippo syndrome), 823–824
    IV (Morquio), 823
    V (Scheie), 823
    VI (Maroteaux-Lamy), 823
    VII (Sly), 823
Mucosal secretions, of vagina and cervix, 54
Mucous secretions, in immune defense, 104
Multifactorial disorders, 17
Multifactorial inheritance, 32, 802
    prevalence of, 24*t*
Multifetal pregnancy, complications associated with, 81
Multiple carboxylase deficiency, 802
    fetal therapy for, 48
    infantile or early form, 824
    late onset, juvenile form, 824, *see also* Biotinidase
        deficiency
    treatment of, 396*t*, 397–398
Multiple medications, for pervasive developmental
        disorders, 440
Multiple Sleep Latency Test, 569
Mumps, and hearing loss, 251
Munching, 625
Mupirocin (2%) (Bactroban), 840
Muscle(s), 323–327, 325*f*
    agonist, 324
    antagonist, 323, 325*f*
    functions of, 323
Muscle biopsy
    with congenital myopathies, 327
    in muscular dystrophy, 325, 326*f*
    normal, 326*f*
Muscle movement, 324
    voluntary, 303
Muscle spindles, 514, 802
Muscle tone, 308
    with cerebral palsy, 503–504
Muscular dystrophy, 17, 324–327, 824
    diagnosis of, 325
    gene therapy for, 401
    life span with, 768
    and obesity, 187
    prenatal diagnosis of, 43
    see also Duchenne muscular dystrophy
Musculoskeletal deformities, with meningomyelocele,
        542
Musculoskeletal system, 315–327
Mutation(s), 18, 21–23, 802
    harmful, 23
    helpful, 23
    single gene, 21–22, 22*f*
    via insertion of deletion of one or more bases, 22
Myasthenia gravis, 329
Myelin, 301
Myelination, 301, 802
    in brain development, 297*t*
Myelomeningocele, *see* Meningomyelocele

Myoblast transplantation, for muscular dystrophy, 326–327
Myoclonic seizures, in newborn, 110
Myoclonus Epilepsy with Ragged Red Fibers, *see* Mitochondrial disorders
Myopia, 217*f*, 220–221, 225–226, 802
    with fragile X syndrome, 383
Myosin, 323, 802
Myotonic dystrophy, 824–825
Myringotomy, 261–262, 262*f*, 802
Mysoline, *see* Primidone

NA, *see* Nucleus ambiguous
NACHRI, *see* National Association of Children's Hospitals and Related Institutions
Nager acrofacial dysostosis, 825
Naltrexone (Revia, Trexan), 840
    for individuals with mental retardation, 418
    for self-injurious behavior, 439
Narcolepsy, 569
Nasal cannula, 692, 802
Nasogastric feeding tube, 696, 802
Nasojejunal feeding tube, 696
National Alliance for the Mentally Ill, 770
National Association of Children's Hospitals and Related Institutions (NACHRI), 774
    recommendations for child health care, 783
National Association of State Directors of Developmental Disabilities Services (NASDDDS), 784
National Commission for the Protection of Human Subjects, 733
National Institute on Life Planning for People with Disabilities, 770
National Joint Committee on Learning Disabilities, definition of learning disability, 472
National Plan Alliance, 770
Natural selection, 22–23
Navane, *see* Thiothixene
NDT, *see* Neurodevelopmental therapy
Near-infrared spectroscopy, 124
Nearsightedness, 217*f*, 220–221, 225
NEC, *see* Necrotizing enterocolitis
Necrotizing enterocolitis (NEC), 126, 802
Negative reinforcement, 660*f*, 663–664, 802
    versus punishment, 663
    worsening of behavior with, 664
Nelson-Denny Reading Test, 482*t*
Neomycin, ototoxicity, 251–252
Neonatal adrenoleukodystrophy, 825
Neonatal deaths, prevalence of, 72
Neonatal seizures, 568
Nerve blocks, for spasticity, 513
Neural fold, 294, 294*f*, 802
Neural network, 279, 802
Neural plate, 294, 294*f*, 802
Neural tube, 55, 294, 294*f*, 802
    formation of, 296–298
    typical formation of, 531*f*

Neural tube defects (NTD), 38*f*, 58, 298, 529–552
    associated impairments and medical conditions, 538–546
    educational programs for, 546
    origin of, 531*f*, 531–532
    prenatal diagnosis of, 532–533
    prevalence of, 24*t*, 530
    prevention of, using folic acid supplementation, 532
    screening for, 37–38
    see also Meningomyelocele
Neurocutaneous syndromes, 565–566
    and risk of pervasive developmental disorder, 432
    and status epilepticus, 571
Neurodegenerative disorders, and simulation of ADHD, 452
Neurodevelopment, 335–340
    atypical, 341–342
    early identification of, 342–343
Neurodevelopmental therapy (NDT), 714–715, 715*f*, 802
    for cerebral palsy, 517
Neurofibromatosis
    and mental retardation, 349
    prenatal diagnosis of, 43
    prevalence of, 24*t*
    and risk of pervasive developmental disorder, 432
    type I, 825
        learning disabilities with, 474
        and predisposition to ADHD, 451, 452*t*
    type II, 825
Neuroimaging, 311
    in Down syndrome, 345–346, 369
    with fragile X syndrome, 382
    in Williams syndrome, 345
Neuroimaging techniques
    for attention-deficit/hyperactivity disorder, 451
    for hydrocephalus, 534
Neuroleptic malignant syndrome, 418
Neuroleptics
    for attention-deficit/hyperactivity disorder with mental retardation, 460
    for attention-deficit/hyperactivity disorder, 456, 457*t*
    for self-injurious behavior, 439
Neurological deterioration, with meningomyelocele, 546
Neuromuscular disorders, medical technology assistance for, 688*t*, 689
Neuromuscular junction, 327, 329–330
    disease of, 329
Neuromuscular system, 327–330
Neuron, 294
    component elements, 296*f*
Neuron(s)
    development of, during fetal life and first year of life, 109–110, 110*f*
    heterotopias, 299
    synchronous discharge of, seizures and, 554
Neuronal ceroid lipofuscinosis, *see* Batten disease
Neuronal heterotopias, 284
Neuronal migration, 298–299, 299*f*
    in brain development, 297*t*

Neuronal proliferation, 298
  in brain development, 297*t*
Neurontin, *see* Gabapentin
Neuropathy, with fragile X syndrome, 382
Neurosurgery, for cerebral palsy, 513–515
Neurotoxin(s), in metabolic disorders, 392
Neurotransmitter(s), 300, 300*f*, 329, 803
  abnormalities in, 300
  and self-injurious behavior, 412
Neurulation, 296–298, 297*t*
Newborn(s)
  and alcohol withdrawal syndrome, 145–146
  assessment of, scoring system for, 117, 118*f*
  causes of illness and death in, 97–111
  drug withdrawal in, 109
  immune defense in, 103–105
  medical disorders in, 99*t*
  weight chart, by gestational age, 116*f*
Newborn intensive care unit (NICU), 129
Newborn screening programs, 736
NG-tube, 638
Niacin
  deficiency/excess, 193*t*
  food sources, 193*t*
  functions, 193*t*
Nicotine
  fetal effects, 148–149
  prenatal exposure to, effects on growth and
    development, 158, 158*t*
NICU, *see* Newborn intensive care unit
Niemann-Pick disease
  type A, 825
  type B, 825
Nifedipine (Procardia), dental problems with use of, 649
Night blindness, 220
Night terrors, 569
Night vision, 219, 221*f*
  impairment of, 220
Nitrazepam, for seizure disorders, 579
Nitrous oxide (laughing gas), 651
Nivea, *see* Lanolin, Mineral oil, Petrolatum
Noctec, *see* Chloral hydrate
Noise levels, hearing loss with, 251
Nondisjunction, 7, 803
  of autosomes, 8–10
  of sex chromosomes, 10–11
Nonexclusionary time-out, 671–674
Nonketotic hyperglycemia, 300, 392
Nonmedical assistive technology, 717–719
Nonsense mutation, 21–22, 22*f*, 803
Nonsteroidal anti-inflammatory drugs, ototoxicity, 252
Nonstress test (NST), 83
Noonan syndrome, 825–826
Norepinephrine, 300
  and attention-deficit/hyperactivity disorder, 451
Norpramin, *see* Desipramine
Nortriptyline (Pamelor), 841
  for attention-deficit/hyperactivity disorder, 457*t*, 459,
    461
  for depression, 439

  for tic disorders, 461
NST, *see* Nonstress test
NTD, *see* Neural tube defects
NTS, *see* Nucleus tractus solitarius
Nucleotide(s), 19*f*, 803
Nucleotide bases, 18, 19*f*
Nucleus ambiguous (NA), 623
Nucleus tractus solitarius (NTS), 623
Nursing caries syndrome, 649
Nutrients, 187–194
Nutrition, 183–210
  effect on teeth, 652, 653*t*
  infant, 184
  liquid oral, 197
  in newborn, 97
  parenteral, 198, 798
  solid oral, 197
Nutrition Labeling and Education Act Amendments of
    1993, 187–188
Nutritional assessment, 195–196
Nutritional assistive devices, 696–697
Nutritional problems, interventions for, 196–202
Nutritional treatment, of specific disorders, 198–202
Nystagmus, 305, 803
  with cerebral palsy, 508–509
  with Down syndrome, 364
  with fragile X syndrome, 383
  with traumatic brain injury, 605

Obesity, 187
  with Down syndrome, 366
  morbid, treatment, 201–202
  weight reduction in, 201–202
OBRA, *see* Omnibus Budget Reconciliation Act of
    1993
Obsessive-compulsive disorder (OCD), 409
  symptoms of, in children with mental retardation, 408*t*
Obstetric complications, and perinatal mortality, 76–80
Occipital lobe, 301, 302*f*, 304
  in simple partial seizures, 561*f*
Occupational therapy, 709–725
  assessment in, 714
  in early intervention programs, 711–712, 712*t*
  frames of reference guiding, 710*t*, 710–714
  guidelines for referral, 711
  intervention planning in, 714
  outcome, 719–720
  resource on, 856
  in school, 712–714, 713*t*
OCD, *see* Obsessive-compulsive disorder
Ocular, definition of, 803
Ocular disorders, in children with disabilities, 215–216
Oculo-cerebro-renal syndrome, *see* Lowe syndrome
Office of Special Education and Rehabilitative Services,
    850
OI, *see* Osteogenesis imperfecta
OKN, *see* Optokinetic nystagmus
Older Americans Act Amendments of 1987, PL 98-459,
    768

Olfactory sensations, with simple partial seizures, 560
Oligodontia, 646
Oligohydramnios, 86, 803
Omeprazole, potential nutrient reactions, 204*t*
Omnibus Budget Reconciliation Act (OBRA) of 1993,
    PL 103-66, 700, 770
Omphalocele, prenatal diagnosis of, 37
Onychomycosis, with Down syndrome, 368
Oocytes, 7, 53
Ophthalmic abnormalities, with Down syndrome, 365
Ophthalmic disorders
    with Down syndrome, 369
    with fragile X syndrome, 383
Ophthalmic evaluation
    through acuity charts and observation, 227
    through higher technology, 227–231
Opiate(s), 154–155
Opiate antagonists, for individuals with mental
    retardation, 418
Opioids, and self-injurious behavior, 412
Opisthotonos, 503, 534
Opitz-Frias/BBB syndrome, 817
Opportunistic infection(s), 164
    in pediatric HIV infection, 170
Oppositional defiant disorders, with attention-deficit/
    hyperactivity disorder, 450
Optacon, 235
Optic chiasm, 222, 223*f*, 306*f*
Optic disc, 212*f*, 222
Optic nerve(s), 212, 212*f*, 213, 222, 223*f*
    hypoplasia and, 231
Optic tract, 306*f*
Opticokinetic, definition of, 803
Optokinetic nystagmus (OKN), 229
Optometric approaches, to learning disabilities, 486–487
Oral diseases, 647–649
Oralism, 263, 268
Oral-motor dysfunction, 628
    with mechanical ventilation, 704
Oral-motor function, 637
Oral-motor structures, 625, 626*f*
Orbit, 212
Oregon Project, 233
ORG 2766, for autism, 440
Organ donation, 732–733
Organ of Corti, 243–244, 244*f*, 803
Organ transplantation, children with disabilities and, 732
Organic acidemia(s), 109, 803
    treatment of, 396*t*, 397–398
Organic food diet, 195
Organization, in brain development, 297*t*
Orientation, 234
Ornithine transcarbamoylase (OTC) deficiency, 393, 394*f*
    gene therapy for, 401
    treatment of, 396*t*, 398
Orofacial digital syndrome, dental problems with, 646
Orthomolecular diets, 195
Orthomolecular psychiatry, 195, 461
Orthomolecular therapy, 803; *see also* Megavitamin
    therapy

Orthopedic abnormalities, with fragile X syndrome, 383
Orthopedic surgery, for cerebral palsy, 515–516
Orthotic management, 716–717
Orthotics, for cerebral palsy, 511
Orton Dyslexia Society, Research Committee, definition
    of specific reading disability, 475
Orton-Gillilngham approach to reading, 483–484
Oscillating eye movements, with cerebral palsy, 508–509
Ossicles, 243, 803
Osteoblasts, 318–319, 803
Osteoclast cells, 319, 803
Osteogenesis imperfecta (OI), 826
    bony deformities with, 321
    dental problems with, 646
    eye abnormality with, 215*t*
    musculoskeletal problems with, 321–322
    and problems with labor and delivery, 80
Osteoid, 319
Osteomyelitis, in pediatric HIV infection, 170
Osteopenia, 321
Osteopetrosis, 320, 803
    eye abnormality with, 215*t*
Osteosarcoma, pathologic fractures with, 322
Ostomy, 697–698, 804
OTC deficiency, *see* Ornithine transcarbamoylase
    deficiency
Otitis media
    acute, 251
    complications of, 261
    diagnosis, 251
    follow-up, 261
    and hearing loss, 251
    and language delays, 284
    recurrent or chronic, 251
    treatment, 261
Ototoxic agents, 251–252
Oval window, 243*f*
Overcorrection, 674
    positive practice in, 674
    restitution in, 674
Oxidative phosphorylation, 31, 804
Oxybutynin chloride (Ditropan), for urinary continence,
    544
Oxygen, 691
    supplementation, 691–692
Oxygen free radicals, and retinopathy of prematurity,
    127
Oxytocin, infusion, 79

Paired box genes, abnormalities in, 59
Palatal arches, 57
    incomplete fusion of, 282, 282*f*
Palatal dysfunction, 281
Palate
    cleft, *see* Cleft lip/palate
    embryology, 56*f*
    growth of, 625, 626*f*
Pamelor, *see* Nortriptyline
Pancreas, in digestive process, 626, 627*f*

Panic, symptoms, 409
Parachute response, 507–508
Paralysis, with meningomyelocele, 533–534, 535*f*, 536*t*, 537*f*–538*f*, 539
Paraplegic Olympics, 766
Parapodium, 539, 541*f*
Parasomnias, 569
Parent(s)
    education of, concerning behavioral problems, 679–680
    effect of child with disability on, 746–747
    resources for, 856–857
    see also Family(ies)
Parenteral nutrition, 198, 798
Parenting networks, for family of child with disability, 745–746
Parietal lobe, 301, 302*f*, 304
Paroxetine (Paxil)
    for attention-deficit/hyperactivity disorder, 460
    for individuals with mental retardation, 417
Partial graduated guidance, 804
Parvovirus, and risk of miscarriage, 63
Patent ductus arteriosus (PDA), 125, 804
Pathogens, food-borne, 205
Pathophysiology, definition of, 711
Patterning, for cerebral palsy, 518–519
PAVI, 233
Pavlik harness, 320
PAX gene(s), 298
    abnormalities in, 59, 531
Paxil, *see* Paroxetine
Payback Trust, 770
PCP, prenatal exposure to, effects on growth and development, 158, 158*t*
PDA, *see* Patent ductus arteriosus
PDD, *see* Pervasive developmental disorder
PDD-NOS, *see* Pervasive developmental disorder-not otherwise specified
PDI, *see* Psychomotor Development Index
Peabody Individual Achievement Test–Revised (PIAT–R), 482*t*
PECS, *see* Picture Exchange Communications System
PEDI, *see* Pediatric Evaluation of Disability Inventory
Pediatric Evaluation of Disability Inventory (PEDI), 719
Pediatric Examination of Educational Readiness, 478
Pediatric formulas, 200*t*
PEEP, *see* Positive end-expiratory pressure
Pee Vee K, *see* Penicillin
PEG procedure, 696
Pemoline (Cylert), 458, 841
    for attention-deficit/hyperactivity disorder, 457*t*
Penicillamine, 804
Penicillin (Pen Vee K), 841
    safety, in pregnancy, 62
    for Vincent disease, 649
Penile implants, 545
Pentasomy X, *see* XXXXX
Pepcid, *see* Famotidine
Peptide bond, 20*f*
Peracetam, for pervasive developmental disorders, 441

Percutaneous, 696
Percutaneous umbilical blood sampling (PUBS), 37, 43–45, 45*f*, 804
Peridex, *see* Chlorhexidine
Perilymph, 245*f*
Perinatal insults, and predisposition to ADHD, 452*t*
Perinatal mortality, 72
    fetal factors in, 80–82
    maternal factors in, 73–80
Periodontal disease(s), 649, 804
    with Down syndrome, 366, 371
Periodontitis, in pediatric HIV infection, 170
Periosteum, 318, 318*f*, 804
Peripheral nerve, 307*f*, 328–329
Peripheral nervous system, 293, 307–308, 804
    motor (efferent) fibers, 307
    sensory (afferent) fibers, 307
Peritoneal dialysis, 698
Periventricular hemorrhage, 124–125
Periventricular hemorrhagic infarction, 124–125
Periventricular leukomalacia (PVL), 100, 123*f*, 123–124, 131, 301, 501
    on ultrasound, 123
Periventricular-intraventricular hemorrhage, 101–102
    with periventricular leukomalacia, 102
    prognosis after, 102
    treatment for, 102
Per-member-per-month (PMPM) rate, 775
Persistent pulmonary hypertension of the newborn (PPHN), 97
Personhood, definitions of, 737
Pertussis immunization, and febrile seizures, 567
Pervasive developmental disorder-not otherwise specified (PDD-NOS), 426, 430
    biological basis of, 432
    hyperactivity with, 438
Pervasive developmental disorder (PDD), 410, 426–431
    aggression with, 438–439
    behavioral interventions for, 436
    biological basis of, 432
    definition of, 425
    dental problems with, 654
    depression with, 439
    diagnosis of, 434–436
    early intervention for, 436–437
    educational programs for, 436–437
    family support for, 440
    with fragile X syndrome, 381
    individualized educational programming for, 437
    male-to-female ratio for, 432
    mental disorders associated with, 432
    with mental retardation, 410
    neurochemistry of, 432
    neuroimaging in, 432–433
    pharmacological management, 438–440
    prevalence of, 432
    prognosis for, 442–443
    rigid behaviors in, 439
    seizure disorders with, 439
    self-injury with, 439 .

sensory integration therapy for, 715–716
and simulation of ADHD, 452
sleep disorders with, 439–440
speech-language therapy for, 437–438
stereotypies in, 439
treatment of, 436–441
unproven therapies for, 440–441
see also Asperger disorder; Autism; Autistic disorders;
    Childhood disintegrative disorder; Rett syndrome
PET, *see* Positron emission tomography
Petit mal seizures, *see* Seizures, absence
Petrolatum, 839–841, 844
Pfeiffer syndrome, 826
Phalanges, 316
Pharmacotherapy, *see* Medication(s)
Pharyngeal arches, 57
Phencyclidine, 155
Phenobarbital (Luminal), 841
    and carnitine loss, 191
    dental problems with use of, 649, 654
    for febrile convulsions, 568
    pathological fractures with, 322
    potential nutrient reactions, 204*t*
    for protection against intraventricular hemorrhage, 125
    for seizure disorders, 439, 575–576, 578
    teratogenic effects, 61
Phenol, injection of, for spasticity, 513
Phenotype, 18
Phentermine (Fastin), 202
Phenylalanine, teratogenic effect on fetal brain, 396–397
Phenylalanine hydroxylase, deficiency, 389, 390*f*
Phenylalanine-restricted diet, 395
Phenylketonuria (PKU), 18, 300, 348, 389, 390*f*, 826
    and infantile spasms, 563
    newborn screening for, 393
    prenatal diagnosis, 44*f*
    prevalence of, 24*t*
    and risk of pervasive developmental disorder, 432
    screening test for, ethics of, 736
    treatment of, 395–396, 396*t*
        results of, 397*t*
    women of childbearing age with, management of,
        396–397
Phenytoin (Dilantin), 842
    and carnitine loss, 191
    dental problems with use of, 649, 653–654
    effect on cerebellar function, 305
    pathological fractures with, 322
    potential nutrient reactions, 204*t*
    for seizure disorders, 439, 567–577
    teratogenic effects, 61
Phobias, 409
Phocomelia, 60
Phoneme(s), 474
Phonics, 483
Phonology, 276
Phosphatidylglycerol, in amniotic fluid, 86
Phosphorus
    deficiency, 192*t*
        dental problems with, 646

excess, 192*t*
    food sources, 192*t*
    functions, 192*t*
Photoreceptors, 219, 805
    disorders of, 219–220
Photosensitive epilepsy, 574
Phototherapy, 107, 129
pH probe, 632–633, 634*f*
Physical exercise, and cerebral palsy, 520
Physical therapy, 709–725
    assessment in, 714
    in early intervention programs, 711–712, 712*t*
    frames of reference guiding, 710*t*, 710–714
    guidelines for referral, 711
    intervention planning in, 714
    outcomes, 719–720
    in school, 712–714, 713*t*
Physiological abnormalities, in premature infants, 127–128
Physis, 318, 318*f*
Pia mater, of spinal cord, 307*f*
PIAT–R, *see* Peabody Individual Achievement
    Test–Revised
Pica, 203, 412, 805
    in mental retardation, 412
    with mental retardation, 406
    treatment for, 412
Picture Exchange Communications System (PECS), 288
Pierre-Robin sequence, 826
Piracetam, 372
PKU, *see* Phenylketonuria
PL 93-112, *see* Rehabilitation Act of 1973; Rehabilitation
    Act of 1973, section 504 of
PL 94-103, *see* Bill of Rights Act Amendments of 1987
PL 94-142, *see* Education for All Handicapped Children
    Act of 1975
PL 95-602, *see* Rehabilitation Act Amendments
PL 98-457, *see* Child Abuse and Neglect Prevention and
    Treatment Act of 1984
PL 98-459, *see* Older Americans Act Amendments of
    1987
PL 99-457, *see* Education of the Handicapped Act
    Amendments of 1986
PL 100-407, *see* Technology-Related Assistance for
    Individuals with Disabilities Act of 1988
PL 101-336, *see* Americans with Disabilities Act (ADA)
    of 1990; Individuals with Disabilities Education
    Act (IDEA) of 1990
PL 101-476, 752, *see* Individuals with Disabilities
    Education Act (IDEA) of 1990
PL 102-119, *see* Individuals with Disabilities Education
    Act Amendments of 1991
PL 102-569, *see* Rehabilitation Act Amendments of 1992
PL 103-66, *see* Omnibus Budget Reconciliation Act of
    1993
PL 104-204, *see* Departments of Veterans Affairs and
    Housing and Urban Development and Indepen-
    dent Agencies Appropriations Act of 1997
Placenta, 55, 57, 805
    delivery of, 71
    normal, 77*f*

Placenta accreta, 78
Placenta previa, 76–78, 77*f*, 805
  ultrasound of, 76, 77*f*
Planned ignoring, *see* Extinction
Plaque, dental, 647
Plasmapheresis, 328–329, 805
  for myasthenia gravis, 329
Platelets, abnormalities, with Down syndrome, 368
Play skills, delayed, with blindness, 233
PMPM, *see* Per-member-per-month rate
Pneumatic otoscopy, 251
Pneumococcal vaccine, for children with HIV infection,
    174
Pneumocystis carinii
  in pediatric HIV infection, 170
  pneumonia, 805
  prophylactic antibiotics for, 173
Pneumonia, in pediatric HIV infection, 170
Pocketing, of food, 629
Point economies, in behavioral management, 673
Point mutation, 21
Point-of-service model, 778*t*
Point-of-service (POS) plans, 775–776
Polar body(ies), 7
  biopsy, 46
Polio, 327, 805
  medical technology assistance for, 689
  vaccine, 327
    for children with HIV infection, 174
  virus, 306
Polydrug use, 143
Polymerase chain reaction, in diagnosis of HIV infection,
    172
Polyneuropathy
  acute, 789
  acute inflammatory demyelinating, and Guillain-Barré
    syndrome, 328
Polyostotic fibrous dysplasia, *see* McCune-Albright
    syndrome
Polypeptide, formation of, 18, 20*f*
Polysaccharides, 190
Polysomnogram, 371
Pondimin, *see* Fenfluramine
Pons, 305, 306*f*
Population screening, 37–39
Porencephalic cyst, 102
POS, *see* Point-of-service plans
Positioning
  assistive technology for, 718*t*
  for cerebral palsy, 511–512
  during feeding, 636
  for gastroesophageal reflux, 634
Positive airway pressure, 693
Positive end-expiratory pressure (PEEP), 121, 693
Positive reinforcement, 659–662, 805
  age-appropriateness of, 661
  in behavioral management of attention-deficit/
    hyperactivity disorder, 455–456
  examples of, 661*t*
  factors influencing effectiveness of, 661–662

with graduated guidance, 669–670
  positive side effects of, 659
  problems with, 662
  schedule of, 662
  timing of, 661–662
  variation in, 660
Positive support reflex (PSR), 504–505, 507*f*
Positron emission tomography (PET), 311, 805
  for attention-deficit/hyperactivity disorder, 451
  for cerebral palsy, 501–502
  in pervasive developmental disorder, 433
  for seizures, 574, 575*f*
  and specific reading disability, 475
Posterior, 316
Posttraumatic stress disorder (PTSD), 410
  with mental retardation, 410–411
Postural reactions, *see* Automatic movement reactions
Postural support, assistive technology for, 718*t*
Potassium
  deficiency/excess, 192*t*
  food sources, 192*t*
  functions of, 192*t*
Potter syndrome, 66, 111
Power of attorney, 770
PPHN, *see* Persistent pulmonary hypertension of the new-
    born
PPO, *see* Preferred provider organizations
Prader-Willi syndrome, 30, 826–827
  behavior problems with, 658
  behavioral characteristics of, 413
  caloric requirements in, 197*t*
  obesity in, 187
    treatment, 202
Pragmatics, 276, 805
Precocious puberty, with meningomyelocele, 545
Prednisone
  for Landau-Kleffner syndrome, 440
  for muscular dystrophy, 326
  potential nutrient reactions, 204*t*
  for seizure disorders, 580
Preeclampsia/eclampsia, 73, 76, 805
Preferential looking techniques, 229, 230*f*
Preferred provider organizations (PPO), 776, 778*t*
Prefrontal leukotomy, 303
Pregnancy
  alcohol intake during, prenatal intervention programs
    for, 157
  anemia in, 73
  duration of, 71, 805
  high-risk, perinatal mortality in, 72
  hypertension in, 65
  malnutrition in, 58
  marijuana use during, 156
  multifetal, complications associated with, 81
  outcomes, 73–75
  pharmacological safety in, 62
  radiation safety in, 59–60
  smoking during, 148–149
  substance abuse during, 143
  ultrasound during, 39, 40*f*

Preimplantation diagnosis, 45–46, 47*f*
Premature infant(s)
  caloric requirements of, 197*t*
  definition of, 115
  early intervention programs for, 133
  hearing loss in, 249
  home care for, 132–133
  physical and developmental characteristics of,
    117–119, 119*f*
  risk for cognitive impairments, 131
  support system for family of, 133
  usual hospital stay for, 132–133
Premature rupture of membranes (PROM), 78, 86
Prematurity, 58, 299
  causes of, 117, 117*t*
  and cerebral palsy, 500, 500*t*
  complications of, 120–128
  extreme, definition of, 115
  medical technology assistance for, 688*t*, 689–690
  and predisposition to ADHD, 451
  risk factors for, 117
Premolars, 645*f*
Prenatal diagnosis, 35, 37
  criteria for, 736–737
  ethics of, 736–738
Preoccupations, in children with autism, 429
Preoperational stage, 340–341
Presbyopia, 217, 805
Preschool Language Scale–Third Edition, 286, 287*t*
Presentation, abnormal, 80
President's Commission for the Study of Ethical
    Problems in Medicine and Biomedical and
    Behavioral Research, 736
Pressure-equalization tube, insertion in ear, 261–262, 262*f*
Preterm birth, 71, 805
Preterm delivery, 79
  and neonatal death, 72
Preterm infants, sleeping position for, 126
Preterm labor, 79
Primary teeth, 643–645, 645*f*
Primidone (Mysoline), 842
  potential nutrient reactions, 204*t*
  for seizure disorders, 575–576, 578
  teratogenic effects, 61
Primitive reflexes, 508*f*
  with cerebral palsy, 504–506
Private insurance, 776–779
Procardia, *see* Nifedipine
Professionals, role of, for children with disabilities, 751
Progestins, teratogenic effects, 62
Programming for common stimuli, 682
Progressive neurological disorders, and simulation of
    ADHD, 452*t*
Project Read, 483
Prolonged feeding time, 629
Prolonged pregnancy, 71, 805
PROM, *see* Premature rupture of membranes
Promoter, mutations, 22
Prompting
  in graduated guidance, 667–668

types of, 668*t*
Prompts, 805
Prone, 317*f*
Prone wedges, for cerebral palsy, 512, 512*f*
Prophase, 5, 6*f*, 806
Propionic acidemia, 827
Propranolol (Inderal)
  for aggression, 439
  for rage reactions, 571
  for self-injurious behavior, 439
Propulsid, *see* Cisipride
Propylthiouracil, 65
Prosencephalic development, 297*t*, 298
Prosencephalon, 294, 295*f*
Prosocial behavior, 659
Prosody, 276
Protease inhibitors, 173
Protection and advocacy agencies, 863–868
Protein
  complete, 189
  deficiency, 189
  food sources, 188–189
  incomplete, 189
  production of, 18–19, 19*f*
  requirements for, 188–189
  secretion, 19
Protein-calorie malnutrition, effect on fetal development,
    185*t*
Proximal, 316
Prozac, *see* Fluoxetine
Pseudoephedrine (Sudafed), for urinary continence, 544
Pseudohypertrophy, of calf muscles, 324
PSR, *see* Positive support reflex
Psychiatric disorders, 382
  causes of, 406–407
  with mental retardation, 349–350
  prevalence of, 406–407
  and simulation of ADHD, 452, 452*t*
Psychobehavioral impairments, with traumatic brain
    injury, 608
Psycholinguistic tests, 256–259
Psychometric tests, used in diagnosing mental
    retardation, 351–352, 352*t*
Psychomotor Development Index (PDI), 352
Psychomotor seizure, *see* Seizures, complex partial
Psychosis, 409–410
Psychosocial problems
  with seizure disorders, 586–587
  simulating learning disability, 478–480
Psychosocial-deprivation dwarfism, 186
Psychotherapy, with dual diagnosis, 415
Ptosis, 806
  with Down syndrome, 365
  with fragile X syndrome, 383
PTSD, *see* Posttraumatic stress disorder
Puberty, 767
Public schools, 761–762
PUBS, *see* Percutaneous umbilical blood sampling
Pulmonary hypertension, 121, 806
Pulp, 644, 644*f*, 806

decay of, 648*f*
Pulse oximetry, 692, 695–696
Punishment, 660*f*, 664–665, 670–675, 806
  cautions concerning, 675
  by contingent stimulation, 664, 670
  by contingent withdrawal, 664, 670–671
  controversy concerning, 664
  effectiveness of, 675
    factors influencing, 675
  formats of, 664
  versus negative reinforcement, 663
  purposes of, 664–665
  and reinforcement, 665
Pupil, 211, 212*f*, 806
Purine, 806
PVL, *see* Periventricular leukomalacia
Pyloric stenosis, 32
  with Down syndrome, 367
  prevalence of, 24*t*
Pylorus, 696
Pyramidal cerebral palsy, 503
Pyramidal tract, 306*f*
Pyridostigmine (Mestinon), 330, 806
Pyridoxine, *see* Vitamin B6

Quadriplegia, 131
Quality of life, ethical issues concerning, 728
Quickening, 57

Radiation
  dose to uterus, for common radiological procedures of
    concern in obstetrics, 60*t*
  fetal effects, 59–60
  safety, in pregnancy, 59–60
  teratogenic effects, 59–60
Rage reactions, 571
Ranitidine (Zantac), 842
  for gastroesophageal reflux, 635
  potential nutrient reactions, 204*t*
Rapid Automatized Naming Test, 478
Ratio schedules, for positive reinforcement, 662
RDA, *see* Recommended Dietary Allowances
Reactive airway disease, *see* Asthma
Reading
  instructional interventions for, 483–484
  standardized tests of, 482*t*
  disability, subtypes of, 473
Rebound, 458
Receptive aphasia, 304
Receptive language disorders
  with cerebral palsy, 509
  with traumatic brain injury, 606
Recessive trait, 18
Recipe for Reading, 483
Reciprocal gait orthosis (RGO), 539
Recommended Dietary Allowances (RDA), 190
Recreation
  assistive technology for, 718*t*

for children with disabilities, 749–750, 766
Rectum, in digestive process, 627, 627*f*
Reflexes, primitive
  with cerebral palsy, 504–506
  in premature infants, 119
Refractive errors, 217*f*
  in children, 225–226
  with Down syndrome, 364
Reglan, *see* Metoclopramide
Rehabilitation
  definition of, 711
  see also Occupational therapy; Physical therapy
Rehabilitation Act of 1973, PL 93-112
  Section 504, 268, 455, 713, 763
Rehabilitation Act Amendments of 1992, PL 102-569, 763
Rehabilitation interventions, 709–725
Rehabilitation therapy, with dual diagnosis, 415
Reinforcement
  withdrawal of, 682
  see also Differential reinforcement; Negative
    reinforcement; Positive reinforcement
Reinforcer, 806
Religious beliefs, and medical ethics, 730
Renal disease, and feeding problems, 627
Renal transplant recipients, pregnancy in, 65
Replantation, of teeth, 650
Reproductive rights, 733–735
Research, involving children with disabilities, 733
Residential facilities, 760
RESNA (Association for Advancement of Rehabilitation
    Technology), 850
Resonance, 806
  disorders of, 281
  of speech, 276
Respiratory distress syndrome, 96, 120–121
  chest X ray in, 120, 120*f*
  risk for, 86, 87*f*
Respiratory failure, 691
Respiratory pump, 693*f*
  failure of, 691
Respiratory system, 692*f*–693*f*
  changes at birth, 94–96
Respiratory technology assistance, 690–695
Response cost, 672–673, 806
Resting hand splint, 716–717, 717*f*
Retina, 57, 212, 212*f*, 806
  disorders of, 221, 230
  functions of, 219–221
Retinitis pigmentosa, 220, 827
  retinal dysfunction in, 230
Retinoblastoma, 221
Retinopathy of prematurity (ROP), 127, 216, 220–221,
    222*f*
  prevention, 221
  treatment, 221
Retinoscopy, 226
Retrograde ejaculations, with meningomyelocele, 545
Retrovirus, 163, 806
Rett syndrome, 426, 430–431, 827
  behavioral characteristics of, 413

behavior problems with, 658
clinical stages in, 431*t*
diagnosis of, 436
genetics of, 432
prevalence of, 432
Revia, *see* Naltrexone
Reynell Zinkin Scales, 233
RGO, *see* Reciprocal gait orthosis
Rheumatoid arthritis, and pregnancy outcome, 65
Rh Immunoglobulin (RhoGAM), 107
Rh incompatibility, 107
RhoGAM, *see* Rh Immunoglobulin
Rhombencephalon, 294, 295*f*
Riboflavin
deficiency/excess, 193*t*
food sources, 193*t*
functions, 193*t*
Ribosome(s), 4*f*, 18–19, 20*f*, 807
Rickets, 192*t*–193*t*, 807
bony deformities with, 321
pathological fractures with, 322
Right to die, 731
Rigid behaviors, pharmacological management, 439
Riley-Day syndrome, 827
Ring chromosome(s), 14, 14*f*, 807
Risperdal, *see* Risperidone
Risperidone (Risperdal), for aggression, 439
Ritalin, *see* Methylphenidate
Rituals, with autism, 429
Robin sequence, 807
Robinow syndrome (Fetal face syndrome), 827
Rods, 219, 221*f*, 807
abnormalities in, 219
Roe v. Wade, 737
Root canal therapy, 650
ROP, *see* Retinopathy of prematurity
Roseola, and febrile seizures, 567
Round window, 245*f*
Rubella (German measles), 807
birth defects caused by, 63–64
blindness caused by, 231
congenital, 63–64
extended, 64
and hearing loss, 249, 509
prenatal diagnosis of, 64
vaccine, 64
Rubeola immunization, and febrile seizures, 567
Rubinstein-Taybi syndrome, 827
Russell-Silver syndrome, 827–828

Salicylates, 807
Salvin Special Education Center in Los Angeles, 157
Sandimmune, *see* Cyclosporin
Sanfilippo syndrome, *see* Mucopolysaccharidoses
Sarcomeres, 323, 807
Satiation, and positive reinforcement, 662
Scala media, 243, 244*f*
Scala tympani, 244*f*
Scala vestibuli, 244*f*

Scalp, injuries to, 597
SCANS (Secretary's Commission on Achieving
    Necessary Skills) reports, 486
Schedule, 807
Scheie syndrome, *see* Mucopolysaccharidoses
Schizophrenia, 409, 807
with mental retardation, 409–410
symptoms of, in children with mental retardation, 408*t*
Schlemm's canal, 216, 218*f*
School
cerebral palsy in, 521
experience of, for children with disabilities, 749–750
(re)habilitation therapy in, 712–714, 713*t*
transition to work, 761–764
Scissoring, 507, 509*f*, 517*f*
Sclera, 211, 212*f*, 219, 807
Scoliosis, 516, 519*f*, 807
medical technology assistance for, 689
with meningomyelocele, 542, 543*f*
resources on, 859
Scotopic sensitivity, and learning disabilities, 487
Scurvy, 193*t*
SDR, *see* Selective dorsal rhizotomy
Seborrheic dermatitis, with Down syndrome, 368
Seckel syndrome, dental problems with, 646
Secretary's Commission on Achieving Necessary Skills
    reports, 486
Seizure(s)
absence, 555, 556*t*, 557–559
ages of occurrence, 557*t*
electroencephalography of, 559*f*, 572
after brain injury, 603
atonic, 555, 559–560
atypical absence, 555, 559–560, 581–582
with autistic disorder, 429
with cerebral palsy, 508
clonic, *see* Clonic seizures
complex partial, 555, 556*t*, 561–563, 568
ages of occurrence, 557*t*
aura preceding, 560
electroencephalography of, 562*f*
conditions that mimic, 568–571
definition of, 554–555
febrile convulsions, ages of occurrence, 557*t*
first aid for, 585
focal motor, 560
focal onset, 555
generalized, 555–560, 561*f*
infantile spasms, ages of occurrence, 557*t*
intractable, surgery for, 304
with mental retardation, 429–430
myoclonic, 555, 559–560
neonatal, 109–111
prognosis after, 111
treatment, 111
occurrence of, 555
partial, 555, 560–563
treatment of, 577
postictal period, 556
primary generalized, 556

Seizure(s)—*continued*
    secondary generalized, 556
    simple partial, 555, 560–561
        ages of occurrence, 557*t*
        spread of, 560, 561*f*
    tonic-clonic, *see* Tonic-clonic seizure(s)
    types of, 555–563
Seizure disorders, 553–593
    with cerebral palsy, 509, 510*t*
    corpus callostomy for, 584–585
    dental problems with, 653–654
    in educational setting, 586
    focal resection for, 583–584
    with fragile X syndrome, 383–384
    with meningomyelocele, 541
    with mental retardation, 349–350
    mixed, 555
    multidisciplinary intervention, 586–587
    pharmacological management of, 439
    prognosis for, 588
    psychosocial issues with, 586–587
    and simulation of ADHD, 452, 452*t*
    surgical treatment of, 582–585
    treatment of, 575–585
Seizure medications, and simulation of ADHD, 452
Selective dorsal rhizotomy (SDR), 514, 514*f*
    for spasticity, 604
Selenium, deficiency, 191
Selenium sulfide (2.5%) (Selsun blue), 842
Self-injurious behavior (SIB), 392, 411–412, 571
    with autism, 429
    cause of, 412
    with cerebral palsy, 510
    with mental retardation, 406, 412
    treatment, 418–419
Self-injury, pharmacologic management of, 439
Self-insurance, 777*t*
Self-limited disorders, 566–571
Self-stimulatory behavior, 571
Selsun blue, *see* Selenium sulfide (2.5%)
Semantics, 276, 807
Senokot, *see* Laxative with senna
Sensation, loss of, with meningomyelocele, 533–534,
        535*f*, 536*t*, 537*f*–538*f*
Sensorimotor stage, 340
Sensorineural hearing loss, with traumatic brain injury,
        605–606
Sensory impairments
    with mental retardation, 349–350
    and simulation of ADHD, 452*t*
    with traumatic brain injury, 605–606
Sensory integration (SI) therapy, 715–716
Sensory integration training, for learning disabilities, 487
Separation anxiety, 409, 807
Sepsis, 807
    and cerebral palsy, 500*t*
    in low birth weight infants, 130
    neonatal, 102–106
    in pediatric HIV infection, 170
    in premature infants, 127

Septra, *see* Trimethoprim and sulfamethoxazole
Sequential modification, in behavior modification, 681
Serotonin, 300
    and self-injurious behavior, 412
Serotonin reuptake inhibitors, 807
    for attention-deficit/hyperactivity disorder, 460
    for individuals with mental retardation, 417
    for self-injurious behavior, 439
    for stereotypies, 439
Sertraline (Zoloft), 842
    for attention-deficit/hyperactivity disorder, 460
    for individuals with mental retardation, 417
Severe combined immunodeficiency
    fetal therapy, 48
    treatment of, 400–401
Severe/multiple disabilities, resources on, 859
Severe visual impairment(s)
    detection of, 232
    development of child with, 232–234
    educating child with, 234–235
    prognosis for, 235
    stimulating the infant and young child with, 234
    see also Blindness
Sex chromosome(s), 4, 807
    abnormalities, and predisposition to ADHD, 451, 452*t*
    nondisjunction of, 10–11
Sex hormones, teratogenic effects, 62
Sex-linked disorders, 28–29
    inheritance of, 28–29, 29*f*
Sexual dysfunction, with meningomyelocele, 545
Sexual rights, 733–735
Sexuality, issues of, for children with disabilities, 767
Sexually transmitted diseases (STD), 767
SGA infants, *see* Small for gestational age infants
Shadowing, in graduated guidance, 669
Shaping, in behavioral management, 667–670
Sheltered workshops, 764
Shigella
    diarrhea, 807
    and febrile seizures, 567
Short gut syndrome, 126
Short stature, with Down syndrome, 366
Short-limbed dwarfism, *see* Achondroplasia
Shoulder dystocia, 79
Shunts
    failure of, 535
        recognition of, 537
        treatment of, 537
    for hydrocephalus, 535–537
SI therapy, *see* Sensory integration therapy
SIB, *see* Self-injurious behavior
Sibling(s), 807
    effect of child with disability on, 747–748
    variability among, 5
Sickle cell anemia, 21–23
    carrier detection, 46
    newborn screening for, 394
    during pregnancy, 74
    resources on, 860
Sidelyers, for cerebral palsy, 512, 512*f*

Sidelyers, for cerebral palsy, 512, 512*f*
Side-lying position, 126
SIDS, *see* Sudden infant death syndrome
Sign language, 263, 268, 288
  and cochlear implant, 267
  for individuals with significant hearing losses,
    260–261
Silver nitrate drops, 232
Sinemet, *see* Carbidoa-levodopa
Single photon emission computed tomography (SPECT),
    311, 807
  for cerebral palsy, 501–502
  for seizures, 574
Single-gene defects, 58–59
Single-gene disorders, 17
  prevalence of, 24*t*
Sinusitis, in pediatric HIV infection, 170
Sister chromatid(s), 5, 807
Skinfold thickness, measurements of, 196
Skin, in immune defense, 103
Skin sores/rashes
  with meningomyelocele, 545
  viruses associated with, and febrile seizures, 567
Skull
  fractures, 597
  injuries to, 597
Sleep apnea, 201, 807
  with Down syndrome, 365, 371
Sleep disorders, 569
  pharmacological management of, 439–440
Sleep disturbances
  with autism, 429
  seizures, 572–574
Sleep myoclonus, 571, 807
SLI, *see* Specific language impairment
Slo-Bid, *see* Theophylline
Sly syndrome, *see* Mucopolysaccharidoses
Small for gestational age (SGA) infants, 116, 116*f*,
    128–129
  and cerebral palsy, 501
  complications of, 128
  definition of, 115
  developmental disabilities in, 128–129
  growth and development, 128
  origin of, 128
Small intestine, 630–631
Smith-Lemli-Opitz syndrome, 828
Smith-Magenis syndrome, 828
Smoking, during pregnancy, 148–149
Social imagination and understanding, impaired, with
    autism, 428
Social isolation, of children with disabilities, 699
Social recognition, impaired, with autism, 428
Social skills
  development, 339–340
  impairments
    with autism, 428
    with blindness, 233
    and learning disabilities, 477
    with traumatic brain injury, 609

  training, 485
  with dual diagnosis, 416
Social smiling, 277
Social-adaptive development, 337*t*–338*t*, 339–340
Socialization, for children with disabilities, 766
Societal limitations, definition of, 711
Society, role of, for children with disabilities, 752
Sodium
  deficiency/excess, 192*t*
  food sources, 192*t*
  functions, 192*t*
Sodium phenylbutyrate, 397
Soft thumb loop, 716–717, 717*f*
Solu-Medrol, *see* Methylprednisolone
Somatic nervous system, 293, 308
Sonic hedgehog gene, 298
Sotos syndrome, 828
Sound
  frequency of, 241, 242*f*
  intensity, 242
  pitch, 241, 242*f*
Spastic cerebral palsy, 303, 323, 502, 502*f*
  and epilepsy, 555
  medical technology assistance for, 689
  seizure disorders with, 509
Spastic diplegia, 124, 131, 501–502, 502*f*
  associated impairments in, 510*t*
  intellectual functioning with, 508
Spastic hemiplegia, 124, 502, 502*f*, 509
  associated impairments in, 510*t*
  and hemispherectomy, 585
  intellectual functioning with, 508
  walking and, 519
Spastic quadriplegia, 502, 502*f*, 808
  associated impairments in, 510*t*
  walking and, 519
Spasticity, 303, 316, 808
  with traumatic brain injury, 604–605
Special education, and cerebral palsy, 521
Special needs trust, 770
Special Olympics, 766, 858
Specific language impairment, 283–284
  genetic contribution to, 284–285
Specific learning disabilities, sensory integration therapy
    for, 715–716
Specific reading disability, 473
  causes of, 474–475
  with cerebral palsy, 509
  definition of, 475
  determination of, 472
  neuroanatomy of, 475
SPECT, *see* Single photon emission computed tomography
Speech
  acoustics of, 278, 278*f*
  in autism, 426–428
  brain basis of, 278–280
  definition of, 275
  domains of, 276
  dysfluencies, 281–282
  fluency/rhythm of, 276, 797

and hearing loss, 253, 260
Speech—*continued*
    hearing of, for individual with hearing loss, 242
    hypernasal, 281
        with cleft lip and palate, 282
    hyponasal, 281
    and language, 275–276
    production, 279–280
    unimodal, 268
Speech disorders, 280–282
    prevalence of, 281
Speech perception, motor theory of, 279–280
Speech sounds, of infants, 252–253
Speech-language disorders
    with cerebral palsy, 508–509
    with traumatic brain injury, 606
Speech-language evaluation, 285–286
    bilingual, 286
    indications for, 285–286, 286*t*
    instruments, 286, 287*t*
Speech-language pathologist, referral to, 285
Speech-language therapy, 287
    for children on mechanical ventilation, 703
    for child with hearing impairment, 267–268
Sperm, 4, 53–54
    meiosis of, 7
    mutation rate, and age, 21
Spermatocytes, 7
Spherical convex lens, 808
Sphincter, in digestive process, 625–627, 627*f*
Spica cast, 808
Spina bifida, 529, 530*f*–531*f*, 808
    and epilepsy, 555
    occulta, 529, 808
Spinal column, 307*f*
Spinal cord, 302*f*, 306, 307*f*
    anterior horn cell, 303, 307*f*
    damage to, 306
    mature, 301
Spinal cord injury
    medical technology assistance for, 688*t*, 688–689
    and respiratory pump failure, 691
Spinal curvature, *see* Scoliosis
Spinal deformities, with meningomyelocele, 542, 5543*f*
Spinal humps, with meningomyelocele, 542, 543*f*
Spinal muscular atrophy, 808
    medical technology assistance for, 689
    and respiratory pump failure, 691
Spinal muscular dystrophies, 327–328
Spindle, 5–6, 6*f*
Spironalactone, potential nutrient reactions, 204*t*
Splinter skills, with autism, 429
Splinting, 716–717
Splints, for cerebral palsy, 511, 712*t*
Spondyloepipheseal dysplasia, 808
Spongy degeneration of central nervous system,
        see Canavan disease
Spontaneous recovery, 808
Sports, resources on, 858–859
Squint, *see* Strabismus

SSI, *see* Supplemental Security Income
Standard Diagnostic Reading Test, 482*t*
Standers, for cerebral palsy, 512, 512*f*
Stanford-Binet Intelligence Scale, 342, 352*t*, 352–353
Stapes, 243, 243*f*, 245*f*
Statements of disapproval, in behavioral management, 670
Stature abnormalities
    with Down syndrome, 366
    with meningomyelocele, 545
Status epilepticus, 571–572
Status marmoratus, 100
Stavudine, 173
STD, *see* Sexually transmitted diseases
Stereotypic movement disorder, 412, 808
    with mental retardation, 406
Stereotypies, 425, 808
    pharmacological management, 439
Sterilization, ethics of, 734
Steroids, in prevention of respiratory distress syndrome,
        121
Stickler syndrome, 828
Stillbirths
    prevalence of, 72
    risk factors for, 80
Stimulant medications, 808
    for attention-deficit/hyperactivity disorder, 456–458,
        457*t*
        long-term treatment, 458
        outcome of, 459
    as drugs of abuse, 458
    for individuals with mental retardation, 417
Stomach, in digestive process, 626, 627*f*
Stool softeners, 635
Stop codons, 19
STORCH, 62–63
Strabismus, 213, 224–225, 225*f*, 808
    with cerebral palsy, 509
    with Down syndrome, 364, 369
    with fragile X syndrome, 383
    with meningomyelocele, 541
    treatment, 226
Streptococcus infection, Group B
    maternal, 75
    neonatal, 75
    in newborns, 105
Streptococcus mutans, and dental caries, 647
Stroke(s)
    and language function, 280
    with traumatic brain injury, 605
Strollers, for cerebral palsy, 520, 521*f*
Sturge-Weber syndrome, 565–566, 828
Stuttering, 276, 281
Subarachnoid hemorrhage, 101, 101*f*, 102
Subdural hematoma(s), 101, 808
    acute, 599–600, 600*f*
Subdural hemorrhage, 101*f*, 101–102
Subependymal giant cell astrocytomas, with tuberous
        sclerosis, 566
Subluxation, 316, 808
Subscapular skinfold thickness, 196

Substance abuse, 143–162
    and child abuse, 153
    and confounding maternal factors, 143–144
    and intervention strategies for infants of drug-
        dependent mothers, 156–157
    maternal, neonatal effects, 109
    with mental retardation, 411
    during pregnancy, prevalence of, 143
    prevention strategies, 157
    resources on, 846
Substrate, 389, 808
Subtle seizures, in newborn, 110
Succimer, 203
Sucking, 623–625
Suckling, 623
Sucrose, 190
Sudafed, *see* Pseudoephedrine
Sudden infant death syndrome (SIDS), 126, 690
    and crack infants, 152
Sugar(s)
    and hyperactivity, 463
    simple, 190
Suicide, 610
Sulci, 301
Sulfisoxazole, 842
Sullivan v. Zebley, 700–701
Superior, 316
Supersensitivity psychosis, 418
Supine, 317*f*
Supine sleeping position, 126
Supplemental Security Income (SSI), 700–701, 765, 779,
    780*t*
Supportive therapy, for family of child with disability,
    745–746
Suppositories, 635
    for bowel control, 544
Surfactant, 86, 87*f*, 96, 120, 808
    production, stimulation, 121
    replacement therapy, 121
Surveillance devices, in medical technology assistance,
    695–696
Sutures, 809
    of skull, 322
Swallowing, 621–622, 622*f*
    esophageal transport phase, 622, 622*f*
    influence of development of, 623–625
    neurological control of, 623, 624*f*
    oral preparatory phase, 621, 622*f*
    oral transport phase, 621, 622*f*
    pharyngeal transport phase, 621, 622*f*
Synapse(s), 296*f*, 300*f*, 809
    definition of, 295
    formation of, 295, 299
Synaptic cleft, 299–300, 300*f*
Synaptic transmission, 300
Synchronous, definition of, 809
Syncope, *see* Fainting
Syndrome(s), 811–831
    and simulation of ADHD, 452
Syphilis, 809

congenital, 63
    fetal infection, 63
    and hearing loss, 249
    and heroin abuse, 154–155
Syringomas, with Down syndrome, 368
Systemic lupus erythematosus, pregnancy in, 73

Tagamet, *see* Cimetidine
Talipes equinovarus, *see* Club foot
Tangential speech, 382
TAR (thrombocytopenia-absent radius), 828
Tardive dyskinesia, 418
Target behavior(s), 659, 678, 809
    observations of, 677–678
Tay-Sachs disease (GM2-gangliosidosis type I), 23–25,
    221, 433, 829
    carrier detection, 46
    clinical manifestations, 392
    eye abnormality with, 215*t*
    and infantile spasms, 563
    prevalence of, 24*t*
    screening for, 46
TBI, *see* Traumatic brain injury
3TC, 173
T cells, in immune defense, 104
TEACCH (Treatment and Education of Autistic and
        related Communications Handicapped Children),
    437
Teaching, in functional context, 668
Team Advocates for Special Kids, 857
Tear duct obstruction, with Down syndrome, 365
Tear gland, 212*f*
Technological assistance, *see* Assistive technology,
        nonmedical; Medical technology assistance
Technology-Related Assistance for Individuals with
        Disabilities Act of 1988, PL 100-407, 719
Teeth
    brushing of, 651–652
    development of, problems affecting, 646
    and diet, 652
    embryology, 56*f*
    emergence of, 643–646, 644*f*
        timetable for, 646*t*
    flossing of, 652
    fluoride treatments for, 652, 652*t*
    formation of, 643–646, 644*f*
    parts of, 644, 644*f*
    primary, 643–645, 645*f*, 805
    secondary (permanent), 643–645, 645*f*
Tegopen, *see* Cloxacillin
Tegretol, *see* Carbamazepine
Telophase, 5, 6*f*, 809
Temperature regulation, in newborn, 97
Temporal lobe, 301, 302*f*, 304
    seizure, *see* Seizures, complex partial
Tendons, 323, 809
Tenex, *see* Guanfacine
Tension-fatigue syndrome, 462
Teratogens, 56*f*, 58–62, 809

and cerebral palsy, 500*t*
Teratogens—*continued*
  definition of, 59
  susceptibility to, 59
Test of Awareness of Language Segments, 478
Test of Phonological Awareness, 478
Test of Variables of Attention, 481*t*
Test of Written Spelling–Second Edition, 482*t*
Testosterone, 10, 809
Tethered spinal cord, 546
Tetracycline
  dental problems with, 646
  teratogenicity, 62
Tetraploids, frequency of, 14
Tetraploidy, 8, 809
Tetrasomy X, *see* XXXX
Thalamus, 294, 305
Thalassemia(s), 22
  carrier detection, 46
  during pregnancy, 74
Thalidomide, teratogenic effects, 60
Thematics, 484
Theo-Dur, *see* Theophylline
Theophylline (Aerolate, Slo-Bid, Theo-Dur, Uniphyl),
    842–843
Therapeutic abortion, ethics of, 736–738
Thiamin
  deficiency, 193*t*
    effect on fetal development, 185*t*
  excess, 193*t*
  food sources, 193*t*
  functions, 193*t*
Thioridazine (Mellaril), 843
  for attention-deficit/hyperactivity disorder, 457*t*
  for individuals with mental retardation, 418
Thiothixene (Novane), 843
Thorazine, *see* Chlorpromazine
Thrombocytopenia-absent radius, 828
Thrush, 809
Thymectomy, 330
Thymine (T), 18, 19*f*
Thyroid disease
  and simulation of ADHD, 452, 452*t*
  treatment, fetal effect, 65
Thyroid function test, in Down syndrome, 371
Thyroid hormone
  antenatal treatment with, 121
  deficiency, 392
  treatment, for premature infants, 128
Tiagabine, 580
Tic disorders, 569–570, 809
  and attention-deficit/hyperactivity disorder, treatment
    of, 461
  and stimulants, 458
Time-in, 670
Time-out, 670, 671*t*, 671–672, 809
  exclusionary, 671–672
  nonexclusionary, 671–674
Time-out ribbon, 673–674
Timing, of positive reinforcement, 661

Tinactin, *see* Tolnaftate
Title V, 781*t*
TLR, *see* Tonic labyrinthine reflex
Tobramycin, ototoxicity, 251–252
Toe walking, 507, 509*f*
Tofranil, *see* Imipramine
Token economies, in behavioral management, 673
Tolnaftate (Tinactin), 843
Tongue thrust, with cerebral palsy, 509
Tonic bite reflex, with cerebral palsy, 509
Tonic labyrinthine reflex (TLR), 504–506, 506*f*
Tonic neck reflex, 504, 809
Tonic seizure, in newborn, 110–111
Tonic-clonic seizure(s), 555–556, 581–582
  ages of occurrence, 557*t*
  aura preceding, 560
  electroencephalography of, 558*f*
  electroencephalography of, 572
  with hemiplegia, 509
  treatment of, 575, 577
Tooth bud, 643, 809
Tooth decay, 647–649, 648*f*
Topiramate, 580
Torsion dystonia, 829
Torticollis (Wry neck), 809
Total body cerebral palsy, 503
Total communication, 263, 268
Total parenteral nutrition (TPN), 698
  in very low birth weight infants, 689
Tourette syndrome, 570, 829
  behavior problems with, 658
  and predisposition to ADHD, 451, 452*t*
  treatment of, 461
Toxemia, 809
Toxins, and cerebral palsy, 500*t*
Toxoplasmosis, 63, 809
  blindness caused by, 231
  fetal, 63
  and hearing loss, 249
  neonatal screening for, 63
TPN, *see* Total parenteral nutrition
Trace minerals, 191
  deficiency, 191
Trachea, 692*f*, 694, 809
Tracheo-esophageal fistula, 363, 809
  with Down syndrome, 367
Tracheostomy, 693–695, 695*f*, 696, 809
  ethical issues concerning, 729
Tracheostomy tube, 692
Trachoma, 809
Transcription, 18, 19*f*, 809
Transfer ribonucleic acid, 19, 20*f*
Translation, 18, 20*f*, 809
Translocation(s), 12–14, 13*f*, 19*f*, 809
Transplantation, children with disabilities and, 732
Transportation safety, assistive technology for, 718*t*
Tranxene, *see* Clorazepate
Traumatic brain injury (TBI), 284, 406, 595–617, *see also*
    Brain injury(ies)
  academic impairments with, 608

acute medical management, 602–603
causes of, 596, 596*f*
and cerebral palsy, 500*t*
cognitive impairments with, 606–607, 607*f*
communication impairments with, 606
definition of, 595
family difficulties with, 609
feeding disorders with, 605
functional impairments with, 604–609
learning problems with, 480
motor impairments with, 604–605
prevention of, 609–610
prognosis for, 612–613
psychobehavioral impairments with, 608
psychosocial issues with, 609
recovery from, 603–604
rehabilitation after, 604
sensory impairments with, 605–606
social difficulties with, 609
and status epilepticus, 571
treatment for, 602–604
Traumatic noise levels, hearing loss with, 251
Treacher-Collins syndrome (Mandibulofacial dysostosis), 829
findings in, 250*t*
and hearing loss, 250*t*
inheritance pattern, 250*t*
Treatment, withholding, 728–731
Treatment and Education of Autistic and related Communications Handicapped Children, 437
Tremors, with traumatic brain injury, 604
Trexan, *see* Naltrexone
Triamcinolone (Azmacort, Kenalog), 843
Triceps muscle, 324, 325*f*, 809
Triceps skinfold measurement, 196
Tricyclic antidepressants
for attention-deficit/hyperactivity disorder, 457*t*, 459, 461
for depression, 439
side effects, 459
for sleep disorders, 439–440
for stereotypies, 439
for tic disorders, 461
Tridione, *see* Trimethadione
Triglycerides, 189
Trihexyphenidyl (Artane), for cerebral palsy, 512
Trimethadione (Tridione), teratogenic effects, 61
Trimethoprim-sulfamethoxazole (Bactrim, Septra), 843
for prophylaxis against PCP, 173
Triplet repeat(s), 379
Triplet repeat expansion, 22, 382, 810
in Huntington disease kindred, 30, 30*f*
Triploids, frequency of, 14
Triploidy, 810
Trisomies, frequency of, 14
Trisomy, 8, 810
Trisomy 13, 10, 829
eye abnormality with, 215*t*
findings in, 250*t*
and hearing loss, 250*t*

inheritance pattern, 250*t*
and neural tube defects, 532
prenatal diagnosis of, 46
prevalence of, 24*t*
ultrasound findings in, 39, 41*t*
Trisomy 16, 15
Trisomy 18, 10, 829
eye abnormality with, 215*t*
findings in, 250*t*
and hearing loss, 250*t*
inheritance pattern, 250*t*
life span with, 768
and neural tube defects, 532
population screening for, 37
prenatal diagnosis of, 46
prevalence of, 24*t*
screening for, 38–39
ultrasound findings in, 39, 41*t*
Trisomy 21, *see* Down syndrome
Trisomy X, *see* XXX
tRNA, *see* Transfer ribonucleic acid
Trust funds, 770
T-Stat, *see* Erythromycin (2%)
Tube feeding, 198, 696–697
in very low birth weight infants, 689
Tuberous sclerosis, 299, 565–566, 829–830
epilepsy and, 563
eye abnormality with, 215*t*
and infantile spasms, 563
and risk of pervasive developmental disorder, 432
and simulation of ADHD, 452
Tubers, in brain, 565
Turner syndrome (45,x), 11–12, 12*f*, 14, 830
learning disabilities with, 474
and predisposition to ADHD, 451
prenatal diagnosis of, 46
prevalence of, 24*t*
Twins
complications associated with, 81
concordance for speech-language disorders, 284
fraternal, 55
identical, 55
Tylenol, *see* Acetaminophen
Tympanic membrane, 242, 243*f*
Tympanometry, 251, 256, 259*f*, 810
Tyrosinemia, treatment of, 396*t*, 398

UCPA, *see* United Cerebral Palsy Associations
Ultrasonography, 37
for cerebral palsy, 501
real time, during pregnancy, 39, 40*f*
safety, in pregnancy, 60
Umbilical circulation, 97, 98*f*
Umbilical cord, 81–82
compression, 85*f*
Uncus, in simple partial seizures, 561*f*
Undernutrition, 810
definition of, 184
early signs of, 186

Undernutrition—*continued*
  postnatal, 301
  risk factors for, 186
Uniform Data Set for Medical Rehabilitation for Children
    (WeeFIM), 719
Unimodal speech, 268
Uniphyl, *see* Theophylline
United Cerebral Palsy Associations (UCPA), 510
Universal precautions, 168–169
Upper respiratory illnesses, and febrile seizures, 567
Uracil, 19*f*
Urea cycle, 393, 394*f*
  inborn errors of, 109
Urea cycle disorders, 300, 393
  and feeding problems, 627
  treatment of, 396*t*, 397
Urecholine (Bethanechol), for gastroesophageal reflux,
    634
Ureterostomy, 698, 810
Urinary dysfunction, with meningomyelocele, 542–544
Usher syndrome, 830
  findings in, 250*t*
  and hearing loss, 250*t*
  inheritance pattern, 250*t*
  retinal dysfunction in, 230
Uteroplacental insufficiency, 84–85, 85*f*

VABS, *see* Vineland Adaptive Behavior Scales
Vaccines, for children with HIV infection, 174
Vacuum devices, 545
Valgus, 316, 810
Valium, *see* Diazepam
Valproate, *see* Valproic acid
Valproic acid (Depakene, Depakote, Valproate), 843–844
  for aggression, 439
  and carnitine loss, 191
  for individuals with mental retardation, 418
  for Lennox-Gastaut syndrome, 565
  and neural tube defects, 532
  potential nutrient reactions, 204*t*
  for rage reactions, 571
  for seizure disorders, 439, 575–576, 579
  teratogenic effects, 61
Vancomycin, ototoxicity, 251–252
Varicella, 810
  dental problems with, 646
  fetal malformations with, 63
  and hearing loss, 251
  in pediatric HIV infection, 170
  pneumonia, 75
  and pregnancy outcome, 75
  vaccine, 75
    for children with HIV infection, 174
Varicella embryopathy, 63
Varicella-zoster immune globulin (VZIG), 75
Varus, 316, 810
Varus osteotomy, 515, 518*f*
VATER/VACTERL association, 830
VCF sydrome, *see* Velocardiofacial syndrome

Vegan, 194
Vegetarian diet, 194–195
Velocardiofacial syndrome (VCF), *see* Deletion #22q11.2
    syndrome
Venous angiomas, 566
Venous hematoma, 597–598
Ventilation, *see* Mechanical ventilation
Ventrico-peritoneal (V-P) shunt, 810
Ventricular septal defect, with Down syndrome, 364
Ventriculo-peritoneal shunt, 125, 311, 535, 540*f*
VEP, *see* Visual evoked potential
VersaBraille, 235
Vertebrae, 307*f*
Vertebral arches, 529, 810
Vertebral columns, divisions of, 535*f*
Vertex presentation, 80, 810
Very low birth weight (VLBW) infants, 115
  medical care of, 129
  tube feeding for, 689
Vesicostomy, 544, 698
Vestibular apparatus, 243, 243*f*
Vidarabine, 64
Video electroencephalography monitoring, 574
Videx, *see* Dideoxyinosine
Vigabatrin, 565, 580
Vincent infection, 649
Vineland Adaptive Behavior Scales (VABS), 342, 353
Viral infections
  in newborn, 103, 105–106
  and pregnancy outcome, 74–75
Viral vector, 48
Vision, 211–239
  assistive technology for, 718*t*
Vision impairments, with traumatic brain injury, 605
Vision tests, 226–231
Visual acuity, 227–229
  adult levels, 213
  at birth, 213
Visual communication, for individuals with significant
    hearing losses, 260–261
Visual cortex, 222–224, 223*f*
Visual evoked potential (VEP), 230–231
Visual impairment(s)
  with cerebral palsy, 508–509, 510*t*
  common sites of, 231
  definition of, 231
  incidence of, 231
  with meningomyelocele, 541
  with mental retardation, 349–350
  severe, *see* Severe visual impairment(s)
Visual pathway, 222, 223*f*
Visual reinforcement audiometry (VRA), 255–256
Visual skills
  assessment of, 481, 482*t*
  development of, 213–216
  impairments in, 478
Visual system, electrophysical testing of, 230–231
Visual-receptive area, 304
Vitamin A, 839
  deficiency, 192*t*, 220, 232

deficiency, 192*t*, 220, 232
  dental problems with, 646
excess, 192*t*
  effect on fetal development, 185*t*
food sources, 192*t*
functions, 192*t*
teratogenicity, 62
Vitamin B₆
  and autism, 440
  deficiency/excess, 193*t*
  food sources, 193*t*
  functions, 193*t*
Vitamin B₁₂
  deficiency/excess, 193*t*
  food sources, 193*t*
  functions, 193*t*
Vitamin C
  deficiency, 193*t*
    dental problems with, 646
  excess, 193*t*
  food sources, 193*t*
  functions, 193*t*
Vitamin D, 839
  deficiency, 193*t*
    dental problems with, 646
  excess, 193*t*
  food sources, 193*t*
  functions, 193*t*
Vitamin E
  deficiency/excess, 193*t*
  food sources, 193*t*
  functions, 193*t*
  for periventricular-intraventricular hemorrhage, 102
  for protection against intraventricular hemorrhage, 125
  and retinopathy of prematurity, 127
Vitamin K
  deficiency/excess, 193*t*
  food sources, 193*t*
  functions, 193*t*
  for protection against intraventricular hemorrhage, 125
Vitamin supplementation, 190–191
  for attention-deficit/hyperactivity disorder, 461–462
Vitiligo, with Down syndrome, 368
Vitreous humor, 212, 212*f*, 810
VLBW, *see* Very low birth weight
Vocal tics, 570
Vocational training, 762–763
  and learning disabilities, 486
Voice, of speech, 276
Voice disorders, 281
Voluntary movement, 303, 305
Volunteerism, 752
Vomiting
  with mechanical ventilation, 704
  as result of gastroesophageal reflux, 630
Von Recklinghausen disease, *see* Neurofibromatosis type I
V-P shunt, *see* Ventriculo-peritoneal shunt
VR, *see* Bureau of Vocational Rehabilitation
VRA, *see* Visual reinforcement audiometry
VZIG, *see* Varicella-zoster immune globulin

Waardenburg syndrome, 245, 830
  findings in, 250*t*
  and hearing loss, 250*t*
  inheritance pattern, 250*t*
  type I, 59
Walkers, for cerebral palsy, 520
Walking, and cerebral palsy, 507–508, 519
Water, requirements for, 188
Watershed infarct(s), 99, 100*f*, 810
Watershed zone, 124, 810
Weak suck, with cerebral palsy, 509
Weaver syndrome, 830
Wechsler Individual Achievement Test (WIAT), 482*t*
Wechsler Intelligence Scale(s), 352
Wechsler Intelligence Scale for Children–III (WISC–III),
    352*t*, 353, 480–481, 481*t*
  Digit Span subtest of, 476, 478
Wechsler Preschool and Primary Scale of
    Intelligence–Revised, 352*t*, 353
WeeFIM, *see* Uniform Data Set for Medical Rehabilita-
    tion for Children
Weight
  gain, in infant/child, 183
  measurements of, 196, 209
  reduction, in treatment of obesity, 201–202
Weight abnormalities, with meningomyelocele, 545
Wellbutrin, *see* Bupropion
Werdnig-Hoffman disease, 303, 328
Wernicke's area, 279
  in language function, 280
West syndrome, *see* Infantile spasms
Wheelchair(s), 539
  for cerebral palsy, 519–520, 521*f*
White matter, 301
  of spinal cord, 307*f*
Whole language, 484
Whooping cough immunization, and febrile seizures, 567
WIAT, *see* Wechsler Individual Achievement Test
Wide Range Achievement Test, 478
Williams syndrome, 192*t*, 830
  and affective disorder, 413
  behavioral characteristics of, 413
  dental problems with, 646
  language impairments in, 285
  neuropsychological testing results in, 345
Wilson disease, 831
  treatment, 396*t*
Wilson Reading System, 483
WISC–III, *see* Wechsler Intelligence Scale for Children–III
Wisconsin Card Sorting Test, 481*t*
Wisdom teeth, 645
Withholding treatment, 728–731
Wolf-Hirschhorn syndrome, 831
Woodcock-Johnson Psycho-Educational Battery–Revised
    Tests of Cognitive Ability, 481, 481*t*–482*t*
Woodcock-Johnson Scales of Independent Behavior, 353
Work
  options for, 763–764
  transition from school, 761–764
Writing, instructional interventions for, 484–485

Written espression, standardized tests of, 482*t*
Wry neck, *see* Torticollis

45,X, *see* Turner syndrome
Xanax, *see* Alprazolam
X chromosome(s), 4, 55
    extra, 11
Xerosis, with Down syndrome, 368
X-linked disorders, 28–29
    characteristics of, 28*t*
X-linked recessive trait, 810
45,XO, *see* Turner syndrome
XO syndrome, *see* Turner syndrome
XXX, 831
47,XXX, 11, *see* XXX
XXXX, 831
XXXXX, 831
48,XXXXY, 11
48,XXXY, 11
47,XXY, *see* Klinefelter syndrome
48,XXYY, 11
XYY syndrome, 831, *see also* Klinefelter syndrome

Y chromosome, 4, 55

Zalcitabine, 173
Zantac, *see* Ranitidine
Zarontin, *see* Ethosuximide
Zellweger syndrome (Cerebro-hepato-renal syndrome),
    393, 831
    eye abnormality with, 215*t*
Zerit, 173
Zidovudine (AZT), 75, 172–173
    for HIV-infection prevention, 168
    side effect of, 172
Zinc
    deficiency, 191, 192*t*
        effect on fetal development, 185*t*
    excess, 192*t*
    food sources, 192*t*
    functions, 192*t*
Zinc oxide, 844
Zoloft, *see* Sertraline
Zonula fibers, 212*f*
Zovirax, *see* Acyclovir